Shakespeare
From Page to Stage

An Anthology of the
Most Popular Plays and Sonnets

Michael Flachmann

California State University, Bakersfield

PEARSON
Prentice
Hall

Upper Saddle River, New Jersey 07458

Library of Congress Cataloging-in-Publication Data

Shakespeare, William, 1564–1616.
[Plays. Selections]
Shakespeare: from page to stage / [compiled by] Michael Flachmann.
 p. cm.
Includes bibliographical references and index.
ISBN 0–13–020754–3 (alk. paper)
I. Flachmann, Michael. II. Title.
PR2759.F57 2007
822.3′3—dc22

2005029477

Editorial Director: Leah Jewell
Acquisitions Editor: Vivian Garcia
Editorial Assistant: Christina Volpe
Production Liaison: Joanne Hakim
Director of Marketing: Brandy Dawson
Assistant Marketing Manager: Andrea Messineo
Marketing Assistant: Kara Pottle
Manufacturing Buyer: Christina Amato
Cover Art Director: Jayne Conte
Cover Design: Bruce Kenselaar
Cover Images: Eric J. Stein as Mustardseed in the Utah Shakespearean Festival's 1999 production of William Shakespeare's "A Midsummer Nights' Dream." Photo by Karl Hugh. © Utah Shakespearean Festival; Kieran Connolly as Petruchio and Leslie Brott as Kate in the Utah Shakespearean Festival's 2004 production of "The Taming of the Shrew." Photo by Karl Hugh. © Utah Shakespearean Festival; David Toney as Othello and Susan Shunk as Desdemona in the Utah Shakespearean Festival's 2002 production of William Shakespeare's "Othello." Photo by Karl Hugh. © Utah Shakespearean Festival; Don Burroughs as King Henry V in the Utah Shakespearean Festival's 1997 production of William Shakespeare's "Henry V." Photo by Karl Hugh. © Utah Shakespearean Festival; William Metzo as King Lear and Caroline Shaffer as Cordelia in the Utah Shakespearean Festival's 1999 production of William Shakespeare's "King Lear." Photo by Karl Hugh. © Utah Shakespearean Festival; Pat Sibley, Afton Quast, and Misty Cotton as the witches in the Utah Shakespearean Festival's 2004 production of William Shakespeare's "Macbeth." Photo by Karl Hugh. © Utah Shakespearean Festival.
Director, Image Resource Center: Melinda Reo
Manager, Rights and Permissions: Zina Arabia
Manager, Visual Research: Beth Brenzel
Manager, Cover Visual Research & Permissions: Karen Sanatar
Photo Coordinator: Joanne Dippel
Composition/Full-Service Project Management: Bruce Hobart/Pine Tree Composition, Inc.
Printer/Binder: The Courier Companies

Credits and acknowledgments borrowed from other sources and reproduced, with permission, in this textbook appear on appropriate page within text.

Pearson Education LTD., London
Pearson Education Singapore, Pte. Ltd
Pearson Education, Canada, Ltd
Pearson Education—Japan
Pearson Education Australia PTY, Limited

Pearson Education North Asia Ltd
Pearson Educación de Mexico, S.A. de C.V.
Pearson Education Malaysia, Pte. Ltd
Pearson Education, Upper Saddle River, New Jersey

10 9 8 7 6 5 4 3 2 1
ISBN 0-13-020754-3

Contents

Preface

An Inspiring Journey

Congratulations! You are about to begin one of the greatest adventures of your life. The book you hold in your hand will be your guide as you study the work of William Shakespeare, who wrote the most wonderful dramatic literature ever produced in the history of the world. Not only will you meet such exciting characters as Hamlet, Portia, Bottom, Prospero, Hotspur, and Beatrice within these pages, but you will also enjoy timeless stories of love, adventure, ghosts, revenge, shipwrecks, murder, betrayal, and many other classic narratives that have intrigued readers and theatregoers for centuries. In addition, through your study of the plays, you will learn a great deal about Shakespeare's life and times, the beauty and power of language, the enchanting world of theatre, the craft of acting, and the wide range of literary terms and approaches available to help interpret these brilliant theatrical documents. Most important, if you truly welcome these plays into your mind and heart, you should also discover some significant insights about yourself and the ways in which you respond to the complex and ever-changing environment around you. Since each of Shakespeare's characters lives inside you, all you have to do is study yourself in order to understand and appreciate his dramatic universe. Although you may have read or seen productions of some of these plays before, this book will help you understand them even more clearly by providing the most useful, appropriate, up-to-date, and innovative resources available to assist you in appreciating eleven of Shakespeare's most accessible and best-loved plays. The following pages of this preface detail the wide array of educational opportunities this book provides as you embark on your journey of discovery about the world of Shakespeare and the manner in which his magnificent plays enchant us and fulfill our spirits.

Script Theory

The basic philosophical premise behind this book is that Shakespeare's plays are not only radiant literary documents but also exciting dramatic <u>scripts</u> intended for performance before live audiences. This dual emphasis on the literary and theatrical nature of the <u>genre</u> is apparent in the book's title, *Shakespeare: From Page to Stage,* and in all the instructional material surrounding the plays themselves. The first and most important resource available to you, therefore, is this innovative blended approach to the study of Shakespeare, which combines the exhilaration of live theatre with time-honored elements of literary analysis to help bring the plays alive for a new generation of students. The relationship between a "script" and a "play" is similar to the correspondence between a recipe and a meal, a musical score and the orchestral performance that follows, and a set of blueprints and the eventual high-rise office building it begets, in which the printed document wants desperately to become its more exciting and fully realized counterpart. <u>Scripts</u> want to become plays in the same way that a recipe in a book yearns to become a steaming hot plate of *coq au vin*. While no one in his right mind would tear a recipe out of a cookbook, cram it in his mouth, and eat it, the process of treating plays solely as literature implies that reading a play is just as satisfying and fulfilling as watching it on stage, which severely distorts the <u>genre</u> and does scant justice to the expansive cre- ativity of these wonderful <u>scripts</u>. In fact, if you hold this book to your ear and use a little imagination, you can almost hear it whispering "find me some great actors, stitch together a few costumes, add a little music, hire a good lighting designer, select a theatre, attract an audience, and *put me on stage!*"

Shakespeare was a playwright in the same sense that a cartwright made carts and a boatwright made boats. He "built" his plays from the ground up, starting with an idea usually taken from earlier <u>source</u> material and then turning that idea into the rough draft of a <u>script</u>. Next he got together with his theatrical company and decided who would play which roles, what <u>cos- tumes</u> the actors would wear, where everyone would enter, exit, and stand on stage, and all the other magical elements of live theatre. At the same time, he was no doubt constantly revising his manuscripts based on the various talents and limitations of his leading actors, the social and political climate of the time, and his innate sense of what would "sell" to his audience of London theatregoers. Only when all the important elements of the theatrical process were in perfect alignment—including the final <u>script</u>, the actors, the stage, and the audience—could a "play" take place. The writing of a <u>script</u>, there- fore, is only one step in the magnificent and enduring dance of theatre. Al- though Shakespeare's plays have great literary value and can profitably be studied within the artificial confines of an English classroom, to isolate them totally from the theatrical world that brings them meaning and purpose steals from the <u>genre</u> much of the energy and power that make the plays truly fas- cinating for today's students. As a result, the entire focus of this book is on the way Shakespeare combines the literary merit of his <u>scripts</u> with the theatrical vitality of his plays in order to dazzle readers and viewers alike. To do any- thing less would rob students of the essential genius of the playwright's work.

Page Layout

The second important resource awaiting you in this book is apparent on each page of the text, with the <u>script</u> on the left-hand side of every page and the notes on the right-hand side. Unlike many other anthologies of this kind, which require students to look up to the <u>script</u> then down to the bottom of the page for notes, the textual explanations in this edition are conveniently placed on the same latitude as the words and phrases they explain, which means that consulting the side notes will interfere as little as possible with reading the <u>script</u> of the plays. At the bottoms of each page are "Discovering Shakespeare" questions, which focus attention on language, themes, imagery, cultural/historical contexts, staging possibilities, and other important topics as a means of guiding you through the most intriguing moments in each play. These questions are numbered so you can refer easily to them in class, and your instructor can assign them for in-class discussion or out-of-class homework. The best and most efficient way to use these questions is to postpone reading them until the end of each <u>scene</u> or act so they do not disrupt the flow of reading the play. Notice also that the act and <u>scene</u> numbers are given at the top of each page in Arabic (for example, 1.3) rather than Roman numerals and that the speech prefixes (e.g., Egeus) are spelled out entirely instead of abbreviated, as is the case in many similar editions. Finally, line numbers appear at the right-hand side of each page in five-line increments so specific references in the plays can be quickly and easily identified.

Instructional Material

Additional resources include **newly written introductions** preceding each of the plays that feature a brief history of publication dates and <u>source</u> materials, a summary of principal literary <u>themes</u>, and a review of prominent theatrical productions throughout the years. Following each play is a thorough list of **Research and Discussion Topics,** a **Filmography** describing and rating each of the major cinematic productions of the script, and an **Annotated Bibliography** (including Library of Congress call numbers for each entry). **Two photographs from modern theatrical productions** accompany each play, offering vibrant evidence of the many innovative interpretations available to today's audiences. Another distinctive feature this anthology boasts is **a special Website, www.prenhall.com/flachmann,** where information about Shakespeare's world is displayed in vivid color rather than being buried awkwardly within the introduction of the book. On this site you will find many exciting resources to enrich your study of the plays, including material on Shakespeare's biography, a typical day in London during the year 1600, performance reviews, artists' renderings of the original Globe Theatre, and a thorough catalog of Shakespearean sites on the Web, which contains search engines and Internet sources for Shakespeare's life and times, Elizabethan pronunciation, costume design, resources for individual plays, and a selection of Shakespearean sites that are "just for fun." Also on this Website, in a special section available only to instructors, are answers to the "Discovering Shakespeare" questions and over three hundred classroom-tested suggestions for teaching these wonderful plays to today's students. Perhaps the best feature of this Website is that you can consult it at any time, even when your're in the midst of reading one of the scripts.

Three final important pedagogical resources may be found in the appendices to the anthology. The first is a selection of **twenty-five of the best known and most interesting Shakespearean sonnets,** accompanied by thorough footnotes. The second is **an appendix titled "Reading Shakespeare Aloud"** that includes useful tips on reading lines from the plays in the classroom and on the stage, with special attention paid to vocal delivery, breath control, punctuation marks, and articulation of specific words and phrases. Last and perhaps most helpful is a **"Glossary" of literary and theatrical terms** used in the anthology, each of which is indicated in the text proper by underlining (e.g., "As is the case in all Shakespearean tragedies, however, the protagonist's demise is counterbalanced by the spiritual and psychological insights he gains prior to his death."

Time to Begin

So, buckle your seatbelt and prepare for a thrilling ride through the plays of William Shakespeare. The characters and stories await you; the anthology's extensive instructional material will give you all the assistance you need; and the joy, knowledge, and satisfaction you gain from the journey will help sustain you for the rest of your life.

Acknowledgments

Because for the past thirty years I've had parallel careers in the worlds of academia and professional theatre, I have many people to thank for my devotion to Shakespeare. In my undergraduate and graduate work at the University of the South, the University of Virginia, and the University of Chicago, I am most indebted to David Bevington, William Ringler, Fredson Bowers, Charles Harrison, and Hugh Caldwell; from Oxford University, Roma Gill and Paige Newmark; from my research at the Huntington Library, Stanley Stewart, James Riddell, and Virginia Renner; from Southern Illinois University, Jack Ades; from California State University Bakersfield, Victor Lasseter, Lorna Clymer, Jeff Mason, Anita DuPratt, and Mandy Reese; and from other campuses in the CSU and elsewhere, David Fox-Brenton, Jane Carducci, Lois Feuer, Kay Stanton, Ed Rocklin, Renee Pigeon, Melissa Aaron, William Babula, S. S. Moorty, Michael Bahr, Todd Lidh, Homer Swander, Lillian Wilds, Joseph Stoddard, Diana Major Spencer, Curtis Bostick, and Matthew Nickerson.

From my involvement in professional theatre, I am especially grateful to my long-time colleagues at the Utah Shakespearean Festival, including Fred Adams, Doug Cook, Cameron Harvey, R. Scott Phillips, J. R. Sullivan, Kathleen Conlin, Mitzi McKay, Lise Mills, Bruce Lee, Phil Hermansen, Donna Law, and Becky Stucker; to the many superb directors whom I've assisted as dramaturg, especially Libby Appel, Robert Cohen, Eli Simon, Howard Jensen, Russell Treyz, Jim O'Connor, Des McAnuff, Henry Woronicz, Liz Huddle, Paul Barnes, Jim Edmondson, Kent Thompson, Michael Addison, Leslie Reidel, Scott Glasser, Pat Patton, Bruce Sevy, Peter Kjenass, Ina Marlowe, Kate Buckley, John Neville-Andrews, Timothy Douglas, Fontaine Syer, Eberle Thomas, Malcolm Morrison, Mark Rucker, Kevin Dressler, Richard Risso, Jules Aaron, Randy Messick, Hank Webb, Robert Kempf, Nagle Jackson, and Jared Sakren; and to the many creative designers, vocal coaches, and stage managers I've worked with in the past, including Jeff Lieder, Carey Lawless, Rosemary Ingham, Janet Swenson, Bill Black, Donna Ruzika, Bill Forrester, David Kay Mickelsen, Robin McFarquhar, Joe Payne, Terence Alexander, Karen Wegner, Stephanie Baker, Mindy Johnson, Janice Benning, George Maxwell, Roy Fitzell, Randy Kovitz, Christine Frezza, Linda Pisano, Amanda French, Philip

Thompson, Erica Tobolski, Grant Hilgenkamp, Ben Hohman, Lonnie Alcaraz, Linda Essig, John Iacovelli, David Boushey, Jan Gist, Liz Terry, Dudley Knight, Susan Branch, Judith Shahn, Charles O'Connor, Brian Baker, Daniel Robinson, and Dean Mogle.

My special thanks to the hundreds of great actors from whom I've learned so much about Shakespeare over the years, among them Amanda Plummer, Caitlin Clarke, John Vickery, Brian Bedford, Monica Bell, Mimi Carr, Rex Rabold, Ray Porter, Robert Beltran, Patrick Page, Scott Cunningham, LeWan Alexander, David Ivers, Richard Kinter, Chris Mixon, Corliss Preston, Ray Chapman, Fredi Olster, Kathleen McCall, Angela Iannone, Hassan El-Amin, Leslie Brott, Peter Sham, Ben Livingston, Donald Sage Mackay, Robert Gerard Anderson, Laurie Birmingham, Andy Patterson, Mikel Mac-Donald, Erik Stein, Libby George, Michael Sharon, Danforth Comins, Mick Hilgers, Carole Healey, Charles Metten, Elisabeth Adwin, Fredi Olster, Russ Benton, Jeannie Naughton, Maren Maclean, William Metzo, Jonathan Gillard Daly, Eric J. Stein, Paul Hurley, Tiffany Scott, Michael Harding, Victoria Adams, Kurt Ziskie, Brian Vaughn, Marco Barricelli, Phil Hubbard, Gary Armagnac, Sheridan Crist, David Janoviak, Tyler Layton, George Judy, Melinda Pfundstein, John Tillotson, Richard Elmore, Caroline Shaffer, Barry Kraft, A. Bryan Humphrey, Joe Cronin, Guy Molnar, William Leach, Melanie van Betten, Jason Heil, Kirsten Potter, Scott Coopwood, Dan Frezza, Mary Dolson, Susan Shunk, Aimee DeShayes, Megan L. Noble, Sara Kathryn Bakker, James Knight, Shelby Davenport, Carrie Baker, David Toney, Craig Spidle, Christine Williams, Jonathan Brathwaite, Kieran Connolly, Anne Newhall, Kelly Lamont, Michael David Edwards, Chris Hatch, Baron Kelly, Harold Gould, Robert Martini, Don Burroughs, Carol Johnson, Todd Denning, and Martin Kildare.

I am also indebted to three decades of first-rate students who have helped me investigate Shakespeare's plays, not only in the lower division, upper division, and graduate classes at my university, but also in my summer educational programs at the Utah Shakespearean Festival and elsewhere, in which the following participants have played especially prominent roles: Charley and JoAnn Lawson, Dan and Carol Aseltine, Father Bill O'Neill, Eve Kaplan, Beth Smick, David and Betty Rogers, Eleanor Packwood, Etta Walton, Ted and Barbara Spendlove, Joan Silberschlag, Julie Welch, Hilda and Crimson Aguilar, Don and Eden Thompson, Margery Widroe, Joyce Chelberg, Dick and Joan Burritt, An and Arnold Chamberlin, Don and Paula Lindsay, Dick and Marti Sharp, Gary Graupman, the Mears family, and Tom, Aleta, Billy, Jimmy, and Andy Gunn.

The heart of any Shakespeare anthology, of course, resides in the scripts of the plays and the accompanying notes, which we have kindly received permission to reprint from the brilliantly edited Pelican Shakespeare Series (Penguin Books). My most sincere thanks to the General Editors, Stephen Orgel and A. R. Braunmuller, and to the editors of each individual volume for granting us rights to the plays and sonnets.

Of the many people at Prentice Hall Publishers who have helped with this book, I am particularly grateful to Yolanda De Rooy, President of Humanities and Social Sciences; Leah Jewell, Editorial Director; my original editor, Carrie Brandon, who had faith in the project from the beginning; my current editor, Vivian Garcia, who has been immensely supportive in shaping the manuscript and preparing it for publication; Karen Schultz, Assistant Editor; Brandy Dawson, Director of Marketing; Bruce Hobart, Project Manager; Claire Carrier, Paginator; Joanne Hakim, Production Liaison; Tally Morgan, Copy Editor; and Melissa Casciano, Editorial Assistant. For clerical assistance with the book, I am thankful to Therese Paetschow, Marianne DeSilva, Brooke King, Rakel Fisher, Dustin Crawford, Jacklyn Orgel, and Amber Preisendorfer, and for help with production photos and cover design, Phil Hermansen.

I especially wish to thank four admirable colleagues and close friends who have assisted with important sections of the manuscript. First of all, my gratitude to Ace Pilkington, an expert in the field of Shakespearean cinema, who—with the assistance of Olga Pilkington, Stephanie Chidester, and Nicole Wilkes—contributed the very useful and informative Filmography sections of the book. I'm equally proud to have the work of world-renowned speech and voice teacher Susan Sweeney represented in Appendix A, Reading Shakespeare Aloud, which should be a great help to students as they grapple with the challenge of bringing these plays to life in the classroom. Likewise, Elise Ann Earthman has created an excellent website for our book, which will help thousands of students appreciate and understand the world in which Shakespeare lived and worked. Finally, I am indebted to my dear friend Cheryl Smith, who has read every word of the manuscript and offered many valuable suggestions for its improvement.

The following reviewers provided a great deal of useful advice: Roger Apfelbaum, Seton Hall University; Carmela B. Arnold, Glendale Community College; John Gregg, San Diego Mesa College; Miguel Powers, Fullerton College; James P. Saeger, Vassar College; Andrew Lamers, Bakersfield College; Melinda Barth, El Camino College; Scott Douglass, Chattanooga State Technical Community College; Robert W. Kopfstein, Saddleback College; Lynne Collins, American River College; Janet M. Anderson, Clackamas Community College; Henry P. Galmish, Green River Community College; Jeannette Webber, Santa Barbara City College; Lolly Smith, Everett Community College; David L. Anderson, Butler County Community College; Jonathan Burton, West Virginia University; Vern Lindquist, Sullivan Community College; Lynne Lerych, Grays Harbor College; James Glickman, Community College Rhode Island; James Haney, Middlesex Community College; Verne Underwood, Rogue Community College; Marian Anders, Pierce College; Tina Margolis, Westchester Community College; Mark A. Weinstein, University of Nevada, Las Vegas; Ian F. Moulton, Arizona State University; Gary Mitchner, Sinclair Community College; and Barbara J. Baines, North Carolina State University.

My last and greatest debt is to my wife, Kim Flachmann, whose love of literature, theatre, and the teaching profession have continually inspired me during our thirty-six-year marriage. I proudly dedicate this book to her and to our two children, Christopher and Laura.

Michael Flachmann
California State University, Bakersfield

The Taming of the Shrew

The Taming of the Shrew *at the Oregon Shakespeare Festival in Ashland, Oregon, with Jonathan Adams as Petruchio and Robynn Rodriguez as Katherina (2000). Photograph by David Cooper.*

Shakespeare's *The Taming of the Shrew* is a difficult play to read and perform in modern times because of its focus on the subjugation of a high-spirited woman to the demands of a husband who "tames" her. Surprisingly, however, a close study of the <u>script</u> offers fascinating insights into the society that produced it and into our own contemporary battle between the sexes. An early <u>comedy</u> (1592–1594) not printed till the 1623 <u>First Folio</u>, it is indebted to two primary <u>sources</u>: the Lucentio-Bianca <u>sub-plot</u> is taken from Ariosto's *I Suppositi* (originally written in 1509 and translated by George Gascoigne as *Supposes* in 1566), while the Kate-Petruchio main <u>plot</u> descends from a wide range of anti-feminist stories and <u>ballads</u> like the anonymous *A Merry Jest of a Shrewd and Curst Wife Lapped in Morrel's Skin for Her Good Behavior* (1550), Vives' *The Office and Duty of an Husband* (1553), and Erasmus' *A Merry Dialogue Declaring the Properties of Shrewd Shrews and Honest Wives* (1557). The Sly framing episode comes from an old tale which appeared first in *The Arabian Nights* and resurfaced in many later Renaissance texts.

Despite its misogynistic subject matter, the play is traditionally considered a "comedy" because the plot moves from bad fortune to good through two typical comic patterns. The first, a movement from society to wilderness to improved society, chronicles the change in locale from Padua to Petruchio's country house back to Padua again. The second, the shift from union to wandering to reunion, alternates from Kate's role as the "older sister" in her household to her adventures with Petruchio and back to the reunion with her family at the end of the play. The sub-plot, with all its "supposes" and disguises, helps us see more clearly the various "poses" of the main plot, in which Kate is forced into her shrewish behavior by an insensitive father, a simpering sister, and a collection of uncouth suitors. Even the Induction, which features Christopher Sly's transformation into a lord, reminds us of the power of perception and persuasion over an individual's behavior.

Within these comic patterns, Shakespeare investigates the relationship between men and women through a number of intriguing themes and images featuring game playing, psychic metamorphosis, the balancing of humors, self-discovery through love, and the always popular distinction between illusion and reality. Typical of Shakespeare's early plays, the metaphor of inversion is also prominent: A drunk turns into a lord, servants become masters, tutors change to wooers, the sun converts into the moon, and the old man appears as a "young budding virgin." In this ever-changing context of dramatic inversions, Katherine's transformation from shrew to dutiful wife seems oddly appropriate: Ironically, of the three newlywed couples at the play's conclusion, Petruchio and Kate have the happiest marriage of all. Recent scholarship focusing on such topics as culture, power, romance, the subjection of women, sexual identity, and the failure of rhetorical persuasion has opened the play to many new critical approaches, all confirming the depth and complexity of this fascinating comedy.

Understandably, the script has had a long and tortured stage history as producers and directors have tried diligently to make the play more politically correct. Early sixteenth-century productions at the Globe and Blackfriars were followed by a sequel written by John Fletcher and first performed in 1633 entitled *The Woman's Prize, or The Tamer Tamed,* in which Kate dies, and Petruchio is tamed by his domineering second wife. In 1667, John Lacy's prose adaptation of Shakespeare's play titled *The Taming of a Shrew* was first performed, then later published as *Sauny the Scott: or The Taming of the Shrew: A Comedy,* in which the Sly Induction is omitted entirely and Grumio (Sauny) speaks in an impenetrable Scottish dialect. These early revisions of Shakespeare's play were soon followed by James Wordale's "ballad-farce" entitled *A Cure for a Scold* (1735) and David Garrick's *Catharine and Petruchio* (1756), which maintained much of Shakespeare's original dialogue and was popular for over one hundred years.

Not until the mid-nineteenth century was Shakespeare's script restored to the London stage by J. R. Planche in 1844, followed by successive productions featuring Samuel Phelps as Sly in 1856, Augustin Daly's New York adaptation in 1887, and Martin Harvey's 1913 version, all of which tried various methods of solving Sly's early disappearance in the play and Kate's distasteful monologue in 5.2. More recent modernized versions include a theatrical adaptation by Charles Marowitz, a cinematic release starring Richard Burton and Elizabeth Taylor, and the 1948 Cole Porter musical *Kiss Me Kate,* all of which have intensified debate over the play since updating the relationship between Kate and Petruchio makes her final "submission" speech even more difficult to stomach for most contemporary viewers.

In the final analysis, *The Taming of the Shrew* is a very sophisticated theatrical Rorschach test in which readers and audience members will see dramatic inkblots that either delight or irritate them according to their own sensibilities. Several recent critics have made sense of the play as an elaborate display of behavioral modification techniques, while others have argued that love between two persons is a kind of mutual "taming" in which both partners agree to subdue their wilder aspects for the good of the marriage. However audiences interpret *The Taming of the Shrew,* most people would agree that Shakespeare's play asks some very provocative questions about the nature of men and women and their relative "roles," "poses," and "supposes" in a mutually satisfying relationship. People are still people, no matter which era they inhabit, and our desire to control them transcends continents and centuries. The Battle of the Sexes still rages after all these years. How do you feel about Shakespeare's strategy to win this romantic war?

The Taming of the Shrew *at the Utah Shakespearean Festival in Cedar City, Utah, with Michelle Six as Bianca and David Janoviak as Lucentio (1998). Photograph by Steve Yates.*

The Taming of the Shrew

NAMES OF THE ACTORS

In the Induction:

A LORD, *later posing as a servant*
CHRISTOPHER SLY
BARTHOLOMEW, *page to the Lord, posing as Sly's wife*
A COMPANY OF STROLLING PLAYERS
HUNTSMEN AND SERVANTS TO THE LORD
HOSTESS OF A TAVERN

In the play proper:

BAPTISTA MINOLA, *father to Kate and Bianca*
VINCENTIO, *father to Lucentio*
GREMIO, *a pantaloon, a suitor to Bianca*
LUCENTIO, *in love with Bianca, later posing as Cambio*
HORTENSIO, *suitor to Bianca, later posing as Litio*
PETRUCHIO, *suitor to Kate*
A PEDANT, *later posing as Vincentio*
TRANIO, *servant to Lucentio, later posing as Lucentio*
BIONDELLO, *page to Lucentio*
GRUMIO, *servant to Petruchio*
CURTIS, *servant to Petruchio*
A TAILOR
A HABERDASHER
KATHERINE (KATE), *the shrew*
BIANCA
A WIDOW
SERVANTS *to Baptista, Petruchio, Lucentio*

SCENE: *Warwickshire; Padua; near Verona*

INDUCTION

Induction° 1 *Enter Beggar (Christophero Sly) and Hostess.*

SLY   I'll feeze° you, in faith.
HOSTESS   A pair of stocks,° you rogue!
SLY   You're a baggage, the Slys are no rogues. Look in the chronicles: we came in with Richard Conqueror.° Therefore *pocas palabras*,° let the world slide.° Sessa!°

Induction, scene 1: A country inn

feeze: fix
A . . . stocks: (she threatens to have him put in the stocks)
Richard Conqueror: (Sly's error for William the Conqueror)
pocas palabras: few words (Spanish); **let . . . slide:** (proverbial: "forget it"); **Sessa:** shut up, stop it (perhaps from French *cessez*)

5

4

HOSTESS   You will not pay for the glasses you have burst?°
SLY   No, not a denier.° Go by, Saint Jeronimy,° go to thy
cold bed and warm thee.
HOSTESS   I know my remedy: I must go fetch the head-
borough.°   [Exit.]
SLY   Third or fourth or fifth borough, I'll answer him by
law. I'll not budge an inch, boy:° let him come, and
kindly.
    Falls asleep.
    Wind° horns. Enter a Lord from hunting, with his train.

LORD
Huntsman, I charge thee, tender° well my hounds.
Breathe° Merriman, the poor cur is embossed,°
And couple° Clowder with the deep-mouthed° brach.°
Saw'st thou not, boy, how Silver made it good
At the hedge corner in the coldest fault?°
I would not lose the dog for twenty pound.

FIRST HUNTSMAN
Why Bellman is as good as he, my lord.
He cried upon it at the merest loss°
And twice today picked out the dullest scent.
Trust me, I take him for the better dog.

LORD
Thou art a fool. If Echo were as fleet,°
I would esteem him worth a dozen such.
But sup them well and look unto them all.
Tomorrow I intend to hunt again.

FIRST HUNTSMAN
I will, my lord.

LORD
What's here? One dead or drunk? See, doth he breathe?

SECOND HUNTSMAN
He breathes, my lord. Were he not warmed with ale
This were a bed but cold to sleep so soundly.

LORD
O monstrous beast, how like a swine he lies!
Grim death, how foul and loathsome is thine image!
Sirs, I will practice° on this drunken man.
What think you, if he were conveyed to bed,
Wrapped in sweet° clothes, rings put upon his fingers,
A most delicious banquet by his bed,
And brave° attendants near him when he wakes,
Would not the beggar then forget himself?

FIRST HUNTSMAN
Believe me, lord, I think he cannot choose.

SECOND HUNTSMAN
It would seem strange unto him when he waked.

---

burst: broken
denier: French copper coin of little value; **Go . . . Jeronimy:** i.e., forget it (Sly misquotes a famous line from Kyd's *The Spanish Tragedy*, "Hieronymo beware, go by, go by," 3. 12.30, mistaking the hero of the play for Saint Jerome)
headborough: constable (the alternative term was "thirdborough," hence Sly's reply)
boy: (an interjection, not addressed to anyone)

Wind: sound

tender: care for
Breathe: rest; **embossed:** exhausted
couple: leash together; **deep-mouthed:** with a deep bark; **brach:** bitch
in . . . fault: even though the scent was cold

cried . . . loss: barked to show that he had picked up the scent after it had been utterly lost

fleet: swift

practice: play a trick

sweet: perfumed

brave: finely dressed

(line numbers: 10, 15, 20, 25, 30, 35, 40)

DISCOVERING SHAKESPEARE

(1) Staging [Induction 1.13]: Exactly where and when does Sly fall asleep on stage? What information do we know about him by the time he falls asleep? When does he wake up?

(2) Teaser [Induction 1.31]: Which other Shakespearean plays have an induction or prologue? What is the difference between an induction and a dumb show? (*Hint:* See *Hamlet,* act 3, scene 2.)

LORD
Even as a flatt'ring dream or worthless fancy.
Then take him up and manage well the jest.
Carry him gently to my fairest chamber   45
And hang it round with all my wanton pictures.
Balm his foul head in warm distillèd waters
And burn sweet wood to make the lodging sweet.
Procure me music ready when he wakes
To make a dulcet and a heavenly sound.
And if he chance to speak be ready straight,°   **straight:** immediately   50
And with a low submissive reverence
Say, "What is it your honor will command?"
Let one attend him with a silver basin
Full of rose water and bestrewed with flowers,
Another bear the ewer, the third a diaper,°   **diaper:** linen towel   55
And say, "Will't please your lordship cool your hands?"
Some one be ready with a costly suit
And ask him what apparel he will wear,
Another tell him of his hounds and horse
And that his lady mourns at his disease.   60
Persuade him that he hath been lunatic,
And when he says he is,° say that he dreams,   **is:** i.e., must be lunatic
For he is nothing but a mighty lord.
This do, and do it kindly,° gentle sirs.   **kindly:** naturally
It will be pastime passing° excellent,   **passing:** surpassingly   65
If it be husbanded° with modesty.°   **husbanded:** managed; **modesty:** moderation
FIRST HUNTSMAN
My lord, I warrant you we will play our part,
As° he shall think, by our true diligence,   **As:** so that
He is no less than what we say he is.
LORD   70
Take him up gently, and to bed with him,
And each one to his office when he wakes.
                    [Sly is carried out.] Sound trumpets.
Sirrah,° go see what trumpet 'tis that sounds.   **Sirrah:** (usual form of address to an inferior)
                              [Exit Servingman.]
Belike° some noble gentleman that means,   **Belike:** probably
Traveling some journey, to repose him here.
  Enter Servingman.   75
How now, who is it?
SERVINGMAN
An't° please your honor, players   **An't:** if it
That offer service to your lordship.
  Enter Players.
LORD
Bid them come near. – Now, fellows, you are welcome.
PLAYERS
We thank your honor.
LORD   80
Do you intend to stay with me tonight?

DISCOVERING SHAKESPEARE

(3) Characterization [Induction 1.51]: Explain how the Lord plans to trick Christopher Sly. How are Sly and the Lord different? How are they similar?

A PLAYER
So please your lordship to accept our duty.°   **duty:** service
LORD
With all my heart. This fellow I remember
Since once he played a farmer's eldest son.
'Twas where you wooed the gentlewoman so well.
I have forgot your name, but sure that part   85
Was aptly fitted and naturally performed.
A PLAYER
I think 'twas Soto that your honor means.
LORD
'Tis very true, thou didst it excellent.
Well, you are come to me in happy° time,   **happy:** opportune
The rather for I have some sport in hand   90
Wherein your cunning° can assist me much.   **cunning:** skill
There is a lord will hear you play tonight;
But I am doubtful of your modesties,°   **modesties:** discretion
Lest, overeyeing of° his odd behavior –   **overeyeing of:** witnessing
For yet his honor never heard a play –   95
You break into some merry passion°   **merry passion:** laughing fit
And so offend him; for I tell you, sirs,
If you should smile he grows impatient.
A PLAYER
Fear not, my lord, we can contain ourselves
Were he the veriest antic° in the world.   **veriest antic:** greatest buffoon   100
LORD
Go, sirrah, take them to the buttery°   **buttery:** larder
And give them friendly welcome every one.
Let them want nothing that my house affords.
                  Exit one with the Players.
Sirrah, go you to Barthol'mew° my page   **Barthol'mew:** (pronounced "Bartlemy")
And see him dressed in all suits° like a lady.   **suits:** respects   105
That done, conduct him to the drunkard's chamber
And call him madam; do him obeisance.
Tell him from me – as he will win my love –
He bear himself with honorable action
Such as he hath observed in noble ladies   110
Unto their lords, by them accomplishèd.°   **accomplishèd:** performed
Such duty to the drunkard let him do
With soft low tongue and lowly courtesy,°   **lowly courtesy:** humble curtsy
And say, "What is't your honor will command
Wherein your lady and your humble wife   115
May show her duty and make known her love?"

DISCOVERING SHAKESPEARE

(4) History [Induction 1.82]: Name another Shakespearean play in which traveling players visit a nobleman. How common was this practice in England around the year 1600? Do some research on traveling theatrical companies, and find out how many actors were usually involved; what sort of scenery, <u>costumes</u>, and <u>props</u> they carried with them; how they moved from town to town; and how much money they made.

(5) Acting [Induction 1.104]: The Lord's instructions to Bartholomew on how to impersonate Sly's "wife" could easily have echoed those given by Shakespeare to the boy actors playing the roles of women in his plays. How many boy actors would have been needed to perform a production of *The Taming of the Shrew*? Construct a <u>doubling chart</u> that shows the number of male and female roles vs. the number of actors necessary to stage this play.

And then with kind embracements, tempting kisses,
And with declining head into his bosom,
Bid him shed tears, as being overjoyed
To see her noble lord restored to health   120
Who for this seven years hath esteemed him°   **esteemed him:** considered himself
No better than a poor and loathsome beggar.
And if the boy have not a woman's gift
To rain a shower of commanded tears,
An onion will do well for such a shift,°   **shift:** purpose   125
Which in a napkin° being close° conveyed   **napkin:** handker-chief; **close:** secretly
Shall in despite enforce a watery eye.
See this dispatched with all the haste thou canst:
Anon° I'll give thee more instructions.   **Anon:** shortly
                                    Exit a Servingman.
I know the boy will well usurp° the grace,   **usurp:** assume   130
Voice, gait, and action of a gentlewoman.
I long to hear him call the drunkard husband,
And how my men will stay themselves from laughter
When they do homage to this simple peasant.
I'll in to counsel them; haply my presence   135
May well abate their overmerry spleen°   **spleen:** mood
Which otherwise would grow into extremes.   *[Exeunt.]*

❧ **Induction 2°** *Enter aloft° the Drunkard [Sly] with Attendants,*
some with apparel, basin and ewer, and other appurtenances; and Lord [as
a Servant].

Induction, scene 2: The lord's manor house
aloft: i.e., in the tiring-house gallery over the stage
(Capell, 1768, supplied a stage direction calling for a
bed and other stage properties, but l. 35 makes clear
that a bed was not used in the original staging)

SLY   For God's sake, a pot of small° ale.   **small:** weak (hence cheap)
FIRST SERVINGMAN
   Will't please your lordship drink a cup of sack?°   **sack:** sherry (a gentleman's drink)
SECOND SERVINGMAN
   Will't please your honor taste of these conserves?°   **conserves:** candied fruit
THIRD SERVINGMAN
   What raiment will your honor wear today?
SLY   I am Christophero Sly, call not me honor nor lord-   5
   ship. I ne'er drank sack in my life, and if you give me
   any conserves, give me conserves of beef.° Ne'er ask me   **conserves of beef:** salt beef
   what raiment I'll wear, for I have no more doublets°   **doublets:** coats
   than backs, no more stockings than legs, nor no more
   shoes than feet; nay, sometime more feet than shoes, or   10
   such shoes as my toes look through the overleather.
LORD
   Heaven cease this idle humor° in your honor!   **humor:** obsession
   O that a mighty man of such descent,
   Of such possessions and so high esteem,
   Should be infusèd with so foul a spirit!   15

DISCOVERING SHAKESPEARE

(6) Acting [Induction 1.125]: Compare and contrast the Lord's advice to his page in this scene (Induction 1.104–129)
to Hamlet's famous instructions to the players at the beginning of act 3, scene 2 in *Hamlet*.
(7) Verse [Induction 2.5–23]: Why does Sly speak in prose, while the Lord and his servants speak in verse at the beginning of the second Induction? What does this metrical distinction tell us about the social status of these characters?

SLY   What, would you make me mad? Am not I Christopher Sly, old Sly's son of Burton-heath,° by birth a peddler, by education a cardmaker,° by transmutation a
bearherd,° and now by present profession a tinker?° Ask
Marian Hacket, the fat alewife of Wincot,° if she know
me not. If she say I am not fourteen pence on the score°
for sheer° ale, score me up for the lyingest knave in
Christendom. What, I am not bestraught:° here's –

THIRD SERVINGMAN
O this it is that makes your lady mourn.

SECOND SERVINGMAN
O this it is that makes your servants droop.

LORD
Hence comes it that your kindred shuns your house,
As beaten hence by your strange lunacy.
O noble lord, bethink thee of thy birth,
Call home thy ancient° thoughts from banishment
And banish hence these abject lowly dreams.
Look how thy servants do attend on thee,
Each in his office ready at thy beck.
Wilt thou have music? Hark, Apollo° plays,
   Music.
And twenty cagèd nightingales do sing.
Or wilt thou sleep? We'll have thee to a couch
Softer and sweeter than the lustful bed
On purpose trimmed up for Semiramis.°
Say thou wilt walk, we will bestrew° the ground.
Or wilt thou ride? Thy horses shall be trapped,°
Their harness studded all with gold and pearl.
Dost thou love hawking? Thou hast hawks will soar
Above the morning lark. Or wilt thou hunt?
Thy hounds shall make the welkin° answer them
And fetch shrill echoes from the hollow earth.

FIRST SERVINGMAN
Say thou wilt course,° thy greyhounds are as swift
As breathèd° stags, ay, fleeter than the roe.°

SECOND SERVINGMAN
Dost thou love pictures? We will fetch thee straight
Adonis° painted by a running brook
And Cytherea° all in sedges° hid,
Which seem to move and wanton° with her breath
Even as the waving sedges play with wind.

LORD
We'll show thee Io° as she was a maid
And how she was beguilèd and surprised,
As lively° painted as the deed was done.

THIRD SERVINGMAN
Or Daphne° roaming through a thorny wood,

Burton-heath: Barton-on-the-Heath (a village near Stratford)
cardmaker: (a card was a comb used in preparing wool for spinning)
bearherd: keeper of a tame bear; **tinker:** itinerant pot mender (proverbially a hard drinker)
Wincot: a hamlet four miles southwest of Stratford (Hackets were living in the parish in 1591)
on the score: chalked up as owing
sheer: unmixed; *score me up for* write me down as
bestraught: distraught, mad

ancient: former

Apollo: god of music

Semiramis: notoriously lustful queen of Assyria
bestrew: spread carpets on
trapped: adorned

welkin: sky

course: hunt hares
breathèd: in good wind; **roe:** small deer

Adonis: (loved by Venus and killed by a wild boar while hunting; cf. Shakespeare's *Venus and Adonis*)
Cytherea: Venus (associated with the island of Cythera); **sedges:** water rushes
wanton: sway seductively

Io: (loved by Jupiter in the shape of a cloud and changed by him into a heifer to deceive the jealous Juno)
lively: energetically

Daphne: (wooed by Apollo and changed into a laurel tree to escape his pursuit)

DISCOVERING SHAKESPEARE

(8) Mythology [Induction 2.34–58]: What is the purpose of all the mythological references in lines 34–58? What "pictures" is the Second Servingman talking about in line 47? How many of these erotic <u>images</u> came from Ovid's *Metamorphoses*?

Scratching her legs that one shall swear she bleeds,
And at that sight shall sad Apollo weep,
So workmanly the blood and tears are drawn.

LORD
Thou art a lord and nothing but a lord.
Thou hast a lady far more beautiful   60
Than any woman in this waning° age.   **waning:** degenerate

FIRST SERVINGMAN
And till the tears that she hath shed for thee
Like envious° floods o'errun her lovely face   **envious:** hateful
She was the fairest creature in the world,
And yet° she is inferior to none.   **yet:** even now   65

SLY
Am I a lord, and have I such a lady?
Or do I dream? Or have I dreamed till now?
I do not sleep: I see, I hear, I speak,
I smell sweet savors and I feel soft things.
Upon my life, I am a lord indeed,   70
And not a tinker nor Christopher Sly.
Well, bring our lady hither to our sight,
And once again, a pot o' th' smallest° ale.   **smallest:** weakest

SECOND SERVINGMAN
Will't please your mightiness to wash your hands?
O how we joy to see your wit° restored.   **wit:** reason   75
O that once more you knew but what you are!
These fifteen years you have been in a dream,
Or when you waked, so waked as if you slept.

SLY
These fifteen years? By my fay,° a goodly nap.   **fay:** faith
But did I never speak of all that time?   80

FIRST SERVINGMAN
O yes, my lord, but very idle words,
For though you lay here in this goodly chamber,
Yet would you say ye were beaten out of door   **house:** inn
And rail upon the hostess of the house,°
And say you would present her at the leet°   **present . . . leet:** accuse her before the court
Because she brought stone jugs and no sealed quarts.° held by the lord of the manor (which had
Sometimes you would call out for Cicely Hacket.°   authority to punish such minor crimes as selling   85
                                                       short weights and measures)

SLY   **brought . . . quarts:** i.e., brought the liquor in
Ay, the woman's maid of the house.   open stoneware pottery jugs, in which the
                                                       quantity was uncertain and variable, rather than in
THIRD SERVINGMAN   sealed, officially certified, quart bottles
Why, sir, you know no house nor no such maid,
Nor no such men as you have reckoned up,°   **Cicely Hacket:** (presumably related to the
As Stephen Sly, and old John Naps of Greet,°   alewife Marian Hacket of 1. 20, and working as a   90
And Peter Turph, and Henry Pimpernell,   maid at her inn)
And twenty more such names and men as these,
Which never were nor no man ever saw.   **reckoned up:** named

                                                     Greet: a Gloucestershire village near Stratford

---

DISCOVERING SHAKESPEARE

(9) History [Induction 2.71]: What was a "tinker" (Induction 2.71)? Name another Shakespearean script in which a "tinker" plays a role. What were the exact duties of tinkers? How much were they paid daily? How respected was the profession?

(10) Verse [Induction 2.79]: When did Sly start speaking <u>verse</u> in this scene? Why does he do so? When does he return to his normal habit of speaking <u>prose</u>? Why?

SLY
    Now Lord be thankèd for my good amends!°   **amends:** recovery   95
ALL   Amen.
        Enter [the Page as a] Lady, with Attendants.
SLY   I thank thee, thou shalt not lose by it.
PAGE   How fares my noble lord?
SLY   Marry,° I fare well, for here is cheer° enough. Where is   **Marry:** (a mild interjection, originally an oath
    my wife?   invoking the Virgin Mary); **cheer:** entertainment   100
PAGE
    Here, noble lord, what is thy will with her?
SLY
    Are you my wife and will not call me husband?
    My men should call me lord; I am your goodman.°   **goodman:** husband (but the term is appropriate
PAGE   to a peasant, not a lord)
    My husband and my lord, my lord and husband,
    I am your wife in all obedience.   105
SLY   I know it well. What must I call her?
LORD   Madam.
SLY   Al'ce madam or Joan madam?
LORD
    Madam and nothing else, so lords call ladies.
SLY
    Madam wife, they say that I have dreamed   110
    And slept above some fifteen year or more.
PAGE
    Ay, and the time seems thirty unto me,
    Being all this time abandoned° from your bed.   **abandoned:** banished
SLY
    'Tis much. Servants, leave me and her alone.
                            [Exeunt Lord and Servants.]
    Madam, undress you and come now to bed.   115
PAGE
    Thrice-noble lord, let me entreat of you
    To pardon me yet for a night or two,
    Or if not so, until the sun be set.
    For your physicians have expressly charged,
    In peril to incur your former malady,   120
    That I should yet absent me from your bed.
    I hope this reason stands for my excuse.
SLY   Ay, it stands so° that I may hardly tarry so long – but   **it stands so:** (1) as it happens, (2) since I have an
    I would be loath to fall into my dreams again. I will   erection
    therefore tarry in despite of the flesh and the blood.   125
        Enter a Messenger.°   **Messenger:** (presumably the lord reenters as the
MESSENGER   messenger)
    Your honor's players, hearing your amendment,
    Are come to play a pleasant comedy,
    For so your doctors hold it very meet,

DISCOVERING SHAKESPEARE

(11) Staging [Induction 2.101]: How does Sly respond when he is told that the page, now dressed as a woman, is his wife? Which do you think would be more humorous: an ugly wife or a beautiful wife? Why?

(12) Language [Induction 2.123]: What bawdy <u>pun</u> is available in Sly's "Ay, it stands so that I may hardly tarry so long" (Induction 2.123)?

Seeing too much sadness hath congealed your blood
And melancholy is the nurse of frenzy.°   **frenzy:** madness   130
Therefore they thought it good you hear a play
And frame your mind to mirth and merriment,
Which bars a thousand harms and lengthens life.

SLY   Marry, I will, let them play it. Is not a commonty° a   **commonty:** (Sly's mistake for "comedy")
Christmas gambol or a tumbling trick?   135

PAGE
No, my good lord, it is more pleasing stuff.

SLY   What, household stuff?

PAGE   It is a kind of history.°   **history:** story

SLY   Well, we'll see't. Come, madam, wife, sit by my side
and let the world slip: we shall ne'er be younger.   140
[They sit over the stage.]

❧ **1.1**°   *Flourish. Enter [below] Lucentio and his man° Tranio.*°   **1.1:** A street in Padua
    man: servant; **Tranio:** (name from the *Mostellaria* of Plautus connoting "clarifier, revealer")

LUCENTIO
Tranio, since for the great desire I had
To see fair Padua,° nursery of arts,   **Padua:** (famous for its university)
I am arrived in fruitful Lombardy,°   **Lombardy:** northern Italy
The pleasant garden of great Italy,
And by my father's love and leave am armed   5
With his good will and thy good company,
My trusty servant, well approved° in all,   **approved:** i.e., proved dependable
Here let us breathe and haply institute
A course of learning and ingenious° studies.   **ingenious:** intellectual
Pisa, renownèd for grave citizens,   10
Gave me my being and my father first,°   **first:** i.e., before me
A merchant of great traffic through the world,
Vincentio, come of the Bentivolii.
Vincentio's son, brought up in Florence,
It shall become to serve all hopes conceived,°   **serve . . . conceived:** i.e., fulfill his father's hopes for him   15
To deck his fortune with his virtuous deeds.
And therefore, Tranio, for the time I study
Virtue, and that part of philosophy
Will I apply° that treats of happiness   **apply:** pursue
By virtue specially to be achieved.   20
Tell me thy mind, for I have Pisa left
And am to Padua come, as he that leaves
A shallow plash° to plunge him in the deep   **plash:** pool
And with satiety seeks to quench his thirst.

TRANIO
Mi perdonato,° gentle master mine.   **Mi perdonato:** pardon me (Italian)   25
I am in all affected° as yourself,   **affected:** inclined
Glad that you thus continue your resolve
To suck the sweets of sweet philosophy.

DISCOVERING SHAKESPEARE

(13) Staging [1.1.1]: Where will Sly and his "wife" sit so they can see the production of *The Taming of the Shrew*, yet not interfere with the audience's view of the play or distract from the action on stage?

(14) Language [1.1.25]: Shakespeare has his characters use an occasional Italian expression to add some local flavor to the action (see, for example, Tranio's "Me pardonato" in 1.1.25). How many Italian phrases does Shakespeare use in this first scene? When does he stop using them? Why?

Only, good master, while we do admire
This virtue and this moral discipline,
Let's be no stoics nor no stocks,° I pray,
Or so devote to Aristotle's checks°
As Ovid be an outcast quite abjured.°
Balk logic° with acquaintance that you have
And practice rhetoric in your common talk.
Music and poesy use to quicken° you.
The mathematics and the metaphysics,
Fall to them as you find your stomach° serves you.
No profit grows where is no pleasure ta'en.
In brief, sir, study what you most affect.°

LUCENTIO
Gramercies,° Tranio, well dost thou advise.
If Biondello now were come ashore,°
We could at once put us in readiness
And take a lodging fit to entertain
Such friends as time in Padua shall beget.
But stay awhile, what company is this?

TRANIO
Master, some show to welcome us to town.
Enter Baptista with his two daughters
Kate and Bianca, Gremio a pantaloon,°
[and] Hortensio suitor to Bianca.
Lucentio [and] Tranio stand by.

BAPTISTA
Gentlemen, importune me no further,
For how I firmly am resolved you know.
That is, not to bestow my youngest daughter
Before I have a husband for the elder.
If either of you both love Katherina,
Because I know you well and love you well,
Leave shall you have to court her at your pleasure.

GREMIO
To cart her° rather, she's too rough for me.
There, there, Horrensio, will you any wife?

KATE
I pray you, sir, is it your will
To make a stale° of me amongst these mates?°

HORTENSIO
"Mates," maid, how mean you that? No mates for you
Unless you were of gentler, milder mold.°

KATE
I' faith, sir, you shall never need to fear:
Iwis° it° is not halfway to her° heart.
But if it were, doubt not her care should be
To comb your noddle with a three-legged stool
And paint° your face and use you like a fool.

30

stocks: posts (i.e., incapable of feeling; punning on *stoics*)
checks: restraints
As . . . abjured: i.e., that we would have to give up everything that Ovid, the Roman love poet, represents (cf. 3.1.28–29; 4.2.8)   35
Balk logic: bandy logical arguments
quicken: enliven
stomach: appetite

affect: like   40

Gramercies: many thanks
come ashore: (like Mantua and Bergamo later, Padua is not, in fact, a seaport, though one could reach it from Venice by river and canal)

45

pantaloon: foolish old man (a stock character in the commedia dell'arte)

50

cart her: i.e., have her driven through the streets in a cart, like a prostitute undergoing punishment   55

stale: (1) laughingstock, (2) prostitute (suggested by *cart*); **mates:** (1) boors, (2) potential husbands (and the conjunction quibbles on "stalemate")
mold: character   60

Iwis: indeed; **it:** i.e., marriage; **her:** i.e., Kate's

paint: redden (by drawing blood)   65

DISCOVERING SHAKESPEARE

(15) Geography [1.1.42]: When Lucentio refers to Biondello coming "ashore" (42), he implies that Padua is a seaport. Was this true in 1600? If not, was Shakespeare confused (compare his Italian geography in *Two Gentlemen of Verona*), or did other water trade routes exist via river systems and canals through which travelers could "come ashore" in Padua?

HORTENSIO
From all such devils, good Lord deliver us.
GREMIO
And me too, good Lord.
TRANIO [Aside]
Hush, master, here's some good pastime toward.°
That wench is stark mad or wonderful froward.°

toward: in prospect
wonderful froward: extremely obstinate

LUCENTIO
But in the other's silence do I see   70
Maid's mild behavior and sobriety.
Peace, Tranio!
TRANIO
Well said, master; mum, and gaze your fill.
BAPTISTA
Gentlemen, that I may soon make good
What I have said – Bianca, get you in,   75
And let it not displease thee, good Bianca,
For I will love thee ne'er the less, my girl.
KATE
A pretty peat!° it is best
Put finger in the eye, an she knew why.°

peat: spoiled darling
it . . . why: if she knew what she was doing, she
would have been better off to put on a show of
weeping

BIANCA
Sister, content you in my discontent.   80
Sir, to your pleasure humbly I subscribe.
My books and instruments shall be my company,
On them to look and practice by myself.
LUCENTIO [Aside]
Hark, Tranio, thou mayst hear Minerva° speak.

Minerva: goddess of wisdom and of the arts

HORTENSIO
Signor Baptista, will you be so strange?°   85
Sorry am I that our good will effects
Bianca's grief.

strange: unnatural

GREMIO   Why, will you mew° her up,
Signor Baptista, for this fiend of hell
And make her bear the penance of her tongue?

mew: coop (term for caging a falcon)

BAPTISTA
Gentlemen, content ye, I am resolved.   90
Go in, Bianca.   [Exit Bianca.]
And for° I know she taketh most delight

for: since

In music, instruments, and poetry,
Schoolmasters will I keep within my house,
Fit to instruct her youth. If you, Hortensio,   95
Or Signor Gremio, you, know any such,
Prefer° them hither, for to cunning° men

Prefer: recommend; **cunning:** well-trained

I will be very kind, and liberal
To mine own children in good bringing-up.

DISCOVERING SHAKESPEARE
(16) Characterization [1.1.70]: Write brief descriptions of the following characters: Lucentio, Tranio, Baptista, and Kate. Which of the four interests you most? Why?
(17) Metaphor [1.1.87]: When Gremio asks Baptista why he is going to "mew" (1.1.87) Bianca up, what animal reference is the elderly suitor making? Contrast this use of the word with a similar example in 3.4.11 of *Romeo and Juliet*. In what respect are Juliet and Bianca both birds of prey?

And so, farewell. Katherina, you may stay,
For I have more to commune° with Bianca. *Exit.* 100

KATE Why, and I trust I may go too, may I not? What, shall I be appointed hours, as though, belike,° I knew not what to take and what to leave? Ha! *Exit.*

GREMIO You may go to the devil's dam.° Your gifts are so good, here's none will hold° you. Their° love is not so great, Hortensio, but we may blow our nails together° and fast it fairly out. Our cake's dough° on both sides. Farewell — yet for the love I bear my sweet Bianca, if I can by any means light on a fit man to teach her that wherein she delights, I will wish° him to her father.

HORTENSIO So will I, Signor Gremio. But a word, I pray. Though the nature of our quarrel yet never brooked parley,° know now, upon advice° it toucheth us both, that we may yet again have access to our fair mistress and be happy rivals in Bianca's love, to labor and effect one thing specially.

GREMIO What's that, I pray?

HORTENSIO Marry, sir, to get a husband for her sister.

GREMIO A husband? A devil.

HORTENSIO I say, a husband.

GREMIO I say, a devil. Think'st thou, Hortensio, though her father be very rich, any man is so very a° fool to be married to hell?

HORTENSIO Tush, Gremio, though it pass your patience and mine to endure her loud alarums,° why, man, there be good fellows in the world, an° a man could light on them, would take her with all her faults, and money enough.

GREMIO I cannot tell, but I had as lief take her dowry with this condition, to be whipped at the high cross° every morning.

HORTENSIO Faith, as you say, there's small choice in rotten apples. But come, since this bar° in law makes us friends, it shall be so far forth friendly maintained, till by helping Baptista's eldest daughter to a husband we set his youngest free for a husband, and then have to't° afresh. Sweet Bianca! Happy man be his dole.° He that runs fastest gets the ring.° How say you, Signor Gremio?

GREMIO I am agreed, and would I had given him the best horse in Padua to begin his wooing that would thoroughly woo her, wed her, and bed her, and rid the house of her. Come on.

Exeunt ambo.° Manent° Tranio and Lucentio.

TRANIO
I pray, sir, tell me, is it possible
That love should of a sudden take such hold? 145

---

commune: discuss

belike: presumably

dam: mother 105
hold: endure; **Their:** i.e., women's
blow . . . together: i.e., be patient
Our cake's dough: i.e., our expectations are disappointed (proverbial)

110

wish: recommend

brooked parley: permitted discussion;
advice: reflection 115

120

so very a: such a complete

125

alarums: calls to arms
an: if

130

high cross: market cross (i.e., the center of town)

bar: obstacle

135

have to't: let us set to it
Happy . . . dole: happiness be his lot (i.e., his who wins her; proverbial)
ring: prize (playing on "wedding ring") 140

ambo: both (Gremio and Hortensio); **Manent:** remain

DISCOVERING SHAKESPEARE

(18) Characterization [1.1.120]: Gremio is described in a 1.1.47 stage direction and in Lucentio's speech in 3.1.36 as a "pantaloon" or aged stock comic character of the Italian *commedia dell'arte*. Compare the speech by Jaques in 2.7.158–163 of *As You Like It*. Which of Jaques' "seven ages" would represent the "pantaloon"? How could Jaques' speech help an actor playing Gremio to develop his character in a production of *The Taming of the Shrew*?

LUCENTIO

  O Tranio, till I found it to be true
  I never thought it possible or likely.
  But see, while idly I stood looking on,
  I found the effect of love-in-idleness°   **love-in-idleness:** the pansy (supposed to have magical power in love) 150
  And now in plainness do confess to thee,
  That art to me as secret and as dear
  As Anna° to the Queen of Carthage was,   **Anna:** Dido's sister and confidante
  Tranio, I burn, I pine, I perish, Tranio,
  If I achieve° not this young modest girl.   **achieve:** win
  Counsel me, Tranio, for I know thou canst.   155
  Assist me, Tranio, for I know thou wilt.

TRANIO

  Master, it is no time to chide you now.
  Affection is not rated° from the heart.   **rated:** driven out by scolding
  If love have touched you, nought remains but so,
  "Redime te captum, quam queas minimo."°   **Redime . . . minimo:** redeem yourself from 160 captivity as cheaply as you can (from the *Eunuchus* of Terence but quoted from Lily's *Latin Grammar*)

LUCENTIO

  Gramercies, lad. Go forward, this contents;
  The rest will comfort, for thy counsel's sound.

TRANIO

  Master, you looked so longly° on the maid,   **longly:** longingly
  Perhaps you marked not what's the pith of all.

LUCENTIO

  O yes, I saw sweet beauty in her face,   165
  Such as the daughter of Agenor° had,   **daughter of Agenor:** Europa (loved by Jupiter, who in the shape of a bull abducted her)
  That made great Jove to humble him to her hand
  When with his knees he kissed the Cretan strand.

TRANIO

  Saw you no more? Marked you not how her sister
  Began to scold and raise up such a storm   170
  That mortal ears might hardly endure the din?

LUCENTIO

  Tranio, I saw her coral° lips to move,   **coral, perfume:** (hackneyed comparisons of the Petrarchan sonnet tradition; cf. Shakespeare's Sonnet 130)
  And with her breath she did perfume° the air.
  Sacred and sweet was all I saw in her.

TRANIO

  Nay, then, 'tis time to stir him from his trance.   175
  I pray, awake, sir. If you love the maid
  Bend thoughts and wits to achieve her. Thus it stands:
  Her elder sister is so curst° and shrewd°   **curst:** bad-tempered; **shrewd:** shrewish
  That till the father rid his hands of her,
  Master, your love must live a maid at home,   180
  And therefore has he closely mewed° her up,   **mewed:** cooped
  Because° she will not be annoyed with suitors.   **Because:** so that

---

DISCOVERING SHAKESPEARE

(19) Teaser [1.1.149]: In which other Shakespearean <u>script</u> does the flower "love in idleness" (1.1.149) play a prominent role? [*Hint:* See a Shakespeare Concordance.] What effect of the flower has Lucentio experienced?

(20) Language [1.1.160]: Why does Tranio speak Latin in 1.1.160? How would you translate these words, and what do they mean in the context of this play?

(21) <u>Metaphor</u> [1.1.172–173]: Compare and contrast Lucentio's comments about Bianca's "coral lips" (172) and her breath with which "she did perfume the air" (173) to Shakespeare's Sonnet 130 ("My mistress' eyes are nothing like the sun"). What do Lucentio's <u>metaphors</u> imply about the depth and quality of his love for Bianca? How does Shakespeare use the same exaggerated flattery in Sonnet 130 for <u>ironic</u> effect?

LUCENTIO
Ah, Tranio, what a cruel father's he.
But art thou not advised° he took some care   **advised:** aware
To get her cunning schoolmasters to instruct her?   185
TRANIO
Ay, marry, am I, sir, and now 'tis plotted.°   **'tis plotted:** I have a plan
LUCENTIO
I have it, Tranio.
TRANIO   Master, for my hand,°   **for . . . hand:** I'll wager
Both out inventions° meet and jump° in one.   **inventions:** plans; **jump:** agree
LUCENTIO
Tell me thine first.
TRANIO   You will be schoolmaster
And undertake the teaching of the maid.   190
That's your device.
LUCENTIO   It is. May it be done?
TRANIO
Not possible, for who shall bear your part
And be in Padua here Vincentio's son,
Keep house and ply his book, welcome his friends,
Visit his countrymen and banquet them?   195
LUCENTIO
Basta,° content thee, for I have it full.°   **Basta:** enough; **have it full:** see it clearly
We have not yet been seen in any house
Nor can we be distinguished by our faces
For man or master. Then it follows thus.
Thou shalt be master, Tranio, in my stead,   200
Keep house and port° and servants as I should.   **port:** style of living
I will some other be, some Florentine,
Some Neapolitan or meaner° man of Pisa.   **meaner:** i.e., of lower than my true rank
'Tis hatched and shall be so. Tranio, at once
Uncase° thee, take my colored hat and cloak.   **Uncase:** uncloak   205
When Biondello comes he waits on thee,
But I will charm him first to keep his tongue.
TRANIO
So had you need.
    [They exchange cloaks and hats.]
In brief, sir, sith° it your pleasure is   **sith:** since
And I am tied to be obedient –   210
For so your father charged me at our parting,
"Be serviceable to my son," quoth he,
Although I think 'twas in another sense –
I am content to be Lucentio
Because so well I love Lucentio.   215
LUCENTIO
Tranio, be so, because Lucentio loves,
And let me be a slave, t' achieve that maid

DISCOVERING SHAKESPEARE

(22) Themes [1.1.201]: When Lucentio suggests that he and Tranio trade places, the theme of disguises in the play seems to echo one of Shakespeare's plot <u>sources</u>, George Gascoigne's *Supposes* (1566). What other disguises or "supposes" occur in this play? Come back to this question as you read through the <u>script</u> and record every instance of disguise you can find. Why do you think this play uses disguise so heavily?

Whose sudden sight hath thralled° my wounded eye.
Enter Biondello.
Here comes the rogue. – Sirrah,° where have you been?

thralled: enslaved

Sirrah: (usual form of address to an inferior)

BIONDELLO
Where have I been? Nay, how now, where are you? 220
Master, has my fellow Tranio stol'n your clothes,
Or you stol'n his, or both? Pray, what's the news?

LUCENTIO
Sirrah, come hither. 'Tis no time to jest,
And therefore frame your manners to the time.
Your fellow Tranio, here, to save my life, 225
Puts my apparel and my count'nance° on,
And I for my escape have put on his,
For in a quarrel since I came ashore
I killed a man and fear I was descried.
Wait you on him, I charge you, as becomes, 230
While I make way from hence to save my life.
You understand me?

count'nance: appearance, deportment

BIONDELLO   I, sir? Ne'er a whit.

LUCENTIO
And not a jot of Tranio in your mouth.
Tranio is changed into Lucentio.

BIONDELLO
The better for him, would I were so too. 235

TRANIO
So could I, faith, boy, to have the next wish after,
That Lucentio indeed had Baptista's youngest daughter.
But, sirrah, not for my sake but your master's, I advise
You use your manners discreetly in all kind of companies.
When I am alone, why then I am Tranio. 240
But in all places else, your master Lucentio,

LUCENTIO
Tranio, let's go.
One thing more rests,° that thyself execute° –
To make one among these wooers. If thou ask me why,
Sufficeth my reasons are both good and weighty. 245

rests: remains; **execute:** arrange

Exeunt.

The Presenters° above speak.

FIRST SERVINGMAN   My lord, you nod, you do not mind°
the play.

Presenters: choral characters of an induction who "present" the play proper
mind: pay attention to

SLY   Yes, by Saint Anne, do I. A good matter, surely.
Comes there any more of it?

PAGE   My lord, 'tis but begun. 250

SLY   'Tis a very excellent piece of work, madam lady –
would 'twere done.
They sit and mark.°

They sit and mark: (the presenters are not heard from again; see the Introduction); **mark:** watch

---

DISCOVERING SHAKESPEARE

(23) Characterization [1.1.220]: What kind of character is Biondello? How old do you think he is? How is he dressed? And what is the difference in occupation and status between him and Tranio?

❧ **1.2°**   *Enter [below] Petruchio° and his man Grumio.°*

PETRUCHIO
    Verona, for awhile I take my leave
    To see my friends in Padua, but of all
    My best belovèd and approvèd friend
    Hortensio; and I trow° this is his house.
    Here, sirrah Grumio, knock, I say.
GRUMIO   Knock, sir? Whom should I knock? Is there
    any man has rebused° your worship?
PETRUCHIO   Villain, I say, knock me° here soundly.
GRUMIO   Knock you here, sir? Why, sir, what am I, sir,
    that I should knock you here, sir?
PETRUCHIO
    Villain, I say, knock me at this gate,°
    And rap me well or I'll knock your knave's pate.
GRUMIO
    My master is grown quarrelsome. I should knock you first,
    And then I know after who comes by the worst.
PETRUCHIO
    Will it not be?
    Faith, sirrah, an you'll not knock, I'll ring° it.
    I'll try how you can sol, fa,° and sing it.
        He wrings him by the ears.
GRUMIO
    Help, masters,° help! My master is mad.
PETRUCHIO
    Now, knock when I bid you, sirrah villain.
        Enter Hortensio.
HORTENSIO   How now, what's the matter? My old friend
    Grumio, and my good friend Petruchio! How do you
    all at Verona?
PETRUCHIO
    Signor Hortensio, come you to part the fray?
    Con tutto il cuore bentrovato,° may I say.
HORTENSIO
    Alla nostra casa benvenuto,
    Molto honorato signor mio Petruchio.°
    Rise, Grumio, rise, we will compound° this quarrel.
GRUMIO   Nay, 'tis no matter, sir, what he 'leges° in Latin.
    If this be not a lawful cause for me to leave his service!
    Look you, sir; he bid me knock him and rap him
    soundly, sir. Well, was it fit for a servant to use his mas-
    ter so, being perhaps, for aught I see, two and thirty,
    a pip out?°

1.2: A street in Padua; **Petruchio:** (Shakespeare's phonetic spelling of Petruccio, diminutive of Pietro; pronounced "Petrutchio," not "Petruckio"); **Grumio:** (the name, like Tranio, is that of a slave in Plautus's *Mostellaria*)

trow: believe

5

rebused: (Grumio's mistake for "abused")
me: i.e., for me (but Grumio, perhaps deliberately, misunderstands)

10

gate: door

15

ring: (playing on "wring")
sol, fa: sing the scale

Help, masters: (to the audience)

20

Con . . . trovato: with all my heart well met (Italian)
Alla . . . Petruchio: welcome to our house, my   25
very honorable Signor Petruchio (Italian)
compound: settle
'leges: alleges

30

two . . . out: very drunk; (a slang expression derived from the card game one-and-thirty, hence a little more drunk than drunk; a *pip* is the mark identifying the suit on a playing card, such as a heart or spade)

DISCOVERING SHAKESPEARE

(24) Characterization [1.2.1]: How would you characterize the relationship between Petruchio and Grumio? The stage direction at the top of act 1, scene 2 describes Grumio as Petruchio's "man." What does this mean in terms of costuming, props, blocking, and language use?

(25) Verse [1.2.1–19]: Scan lines 1–19 in act 1, scene 2, in order to determine who is speaking verse and who is speaking prose. How does the alternation between verse and prose help us understand the action of the scene?

Whom would to God I had well knocked at first,
Then had not Grumio come by the worst.   35

PETRUCHIO
A senseless villain. Good Hortensio,
I bade the rascal knock upon your gate
And could not get him for my heart to do it.

GRUMIO   Knock at the gate? O heavens! Spake you not
these words plain, "Sirrah, knock me here, rap me here,   40
knock me well, and knock me soundly"? And come you
now with "knocking at the gate"?

PETRUCHIO
Sirrah, be gone, or talk not, I advise you.

HORTENSIO
Petruchio, patience, I am Grumio's pledge.
Why, this'° a heavy chance° 'twixt him and you,   **this':** this is; **heavy chance:** sad event   45
Your ancient, trusty, pleasant servant Grumio.
And tell me now, sweet friend, what happy gale
Blows you to Padua here from old Verona?

PETRUCHIO
Such wind as scatters young men through the world
To seek their fortunes farther than at home,   50
Where small experience grows. But in a few,°   **in a few:** i.e., words
Signor Hortensio, thus it stands with me.
Antonio my father is deceased,
And I have thrust myself into this maze,
Happily° to wive and thrive as best I may.   **Happily:** (1) cheerfully, (2) by chance   55
Crowns in my purse I have and goods at home,
And so am come abroad to see the world.

HORTENSIO
Petruchio, shall I then come roundly° to thee   **come roundly:** speak plainly
And wish thee to a shrewd° ill-favored° wife?   **shrewd:** shrewish; **ill-favored:** ill-natured
Thou'dst thank me but a little for my counsel.
And yet I'll promise thee she shall be rich,   60
And very rich – but thou'rt too much my friend
And I'll not wish thee to her.

PETRUCHIO
Signor Hortensio, 'twixt such friends as we
Few words suffice. And therefore if thou know   65
One rich enough to be Petruchio's wife –
As wealth is burden° of my wooing dance –   **burden:** bass or undersong
Be she as foul° as was Florentius'° love,   **foul:** ugly; **Florentius:** (A knight who married
an old hag in return for the answer to a riddle—
"What do women most desire?"—that would save
his life; the answer is to rule their husbands. She
then turned into a beautiful maiden; cf. Gower's
Confessio Amantis, Book I, or Chaucer's Wife of
Bath's Tale.)

DISCOVERING SHAKESPEARE

(26) Language [1.2.36–42]: What verbal confusion do Petruchio and Grumio have over the word "knock" (1.2.36–42)? What does this brief interchange tell us about the dramatic appetite of Shakespeare's audience?

(27) Plot [1.2.50]: How wealthy is Petruchio? How much of a fortune hunter is he (1.2.50)? See, for example, his admission to Hortensio that he is looking for "one rich enough to be Petruchio's wife" (1.2.66). How would his wealth (or lack thereof) affect the relationship between himself and Katherine? How could such theatrical elements as costuming, props, music, and set design signal to the audience his social and financial status?

As old as Sibyl,° and as curst and shrewd
As Socrates' Xanthippe,° or a worse,
She moves me not, or not removes, at least,
Affection's edge in me, were she as rough
As are the swelling Adriatic seas.
I come to wive it wealthily in Padua –
If wealthily, then happily in Padua.

GRUMIO   Nay, look you, sir, he tells you flatly what his mind is. Why, give him gold enough and marry him to a puppet or an aglet-baby° or an old trot° with ne'er a tooth in her head, though she have as many diseases as two and fifty horses. Why, nothing comes amiss, so money comes withal.°

HORTENSIO
Petruchio, since we are stepped thus far in,
I will continue that° I broached in jest.
I can, Petruchio, help thee to a wife
With wealth enough, and young and beauteous,
Brought up as best becomes a gentlewoman.
Her only fault – and that is faults enough –
Is that she is intolerable curst,
And shrewd and froward,° so beyond all measure,
That were my state far worser than it is
I would not wed her for a mine of gold.

PETRUCHIO
Hortensio, peace. Thou know'st not gold's effect.
Tell me her father's name, and 'tis enough,
For I will board° her though she chide as loud
As thunder when the clouds in autumn crack.

HORTENSIO
Her father is Baptista Minola,
An affable and courteous gentleman.
Her name is Katherina Minola,
Renowned in Padua for her scolding tongue.

PETRUCHIO
I know her father though I know not her,
And he knew my deceasèd father well.
I will not sleep, Hortensio, till I see her,
And therefore let me be thus bold with you,
To give you over° at this first encounter
Unless you will accompany me thither.

GRUMIO   I pray you, sir, let him go while the humor° lasts. A° my word, an she knew him as well as I do, she would think scolding would do little good upon him. She may perhaps call him half a score knaves or so – why, that's nothing, an he begin once, he'll rail in his

Sibyl: the Cumaean Sibyl (a phrophetess to whom Apollo granted as many years of life as she could hold grains of sand in her hand)   70
Xanthippe: (the philosopher's wife, reputedly a shrew)

75

aglet-baby: tiny doll figure (aglet indicating either a spangle or the metal "point" of a lace);
trot: hag   80
withal: at the same time

that: that which   85

froward: obstinate   90

board: (as in attacking a ship)   95

100

give you over: leave you   105

humor: whim
A: on, by   110

DISCOVERING SHAKESPEARE

(28) Metaphor [1.2.72–73]: Many of Petruchio's metaphors here and elsewhere in the play are taken from warfare and seafaring (such as his reference to "the swelling Adriatic seas" in 1.2.73). Find three other similar metaphors and explain what his choice of these comparisons implies about Petruchio as a person. [*Hint:* See especially his long speech in 1.2.197–208.]

(29) Language [1.2.89]: Look up in the *Oxford English Dictionary* all the meanings of the words "shrew" and "shrewd" available to Shakespeare in the year 1600. Which definitions seem most appropriate to this play?

rope tricks.° I'll tell you what, sir, an she stand° him but a little, he will throw a figure° in her face and so disfigure her with it that she shall have no more eyes to see withal than a cat. You know him not, sir.

rope tricks: (Grumio's mistake for "rhetoric" — i.e., abusive language, with a glance at tricks punishable by hanging); **stand:** withstand
figure: rhetorical figure (i.e., a telling expression)

HORTENSIO
Tarry, Petruchio, I must go with thee,   115
For in Baptista's keep° my treasure is.
He hath the jewel of my life in hold,°
His youngest daughter, beautiful Bianca,
And her withholds from me and other more,
Suitors to her and rivals in my love,   120
Supposing it a thing impossible,
For those defects I have before rehearsed,
That ever Katherina will be wooed.
Therefore this order° hath Baptista ta'en,
That none shall have access unto Bianca   125
Till Katherine the curst have got a husband.

keep: (1) keeping, (2) fortified tower
hold: confinement

order: measure

GRUMIO
Katherine the curst!
A title for a maid of all titles the worst.

HORTENSIO
Now shall my friend Petruchio do me grace°
And offer me, disguised in sober robes,   130
To old Baptista as a schoolmaster
Well seen° in music, to instruct Bianca,
That so I may, by this device, at last
Have leave and leisure to make love to her
And unsuspected court her by herself.   135
    Enter Gremio [with a paper] and Lucentio disguised [as a schoolmaster].

grace: a favor

seen: versed

GRUMIO   Here's no knavery! See, to beguile the old folks, how the young folks lay their heads together! Master, master, look about you. Who goes there, ha?

HORTENSIO
Peace, Grumio, it is the rival of my love.
Petruchio, stand by awhile.   140

GRUMIO
A proper stripling,° and an amorous!
    [They stand aside.]

proper stripling: handsome youth (ironically, of the "pantaloon" Gremio)

GREMIO
O very well, I have perused the note.°
Hark you, sir, I'll have them very fairly bound,
All books of love, see that at any hand,°
And see you read° no other lectures° to her.   145
You understand me. Over and beside
Signor Baptista's liberality,
I'll mend° it with a largess.° Take your paper° too,

note: i.e., a list of books for Bianca

at any hand: in any case
read: teach; **lectures:** lessons

mend: increase; **largess:** gift of money; **paper:** i.e., the *note*

DISCOVERING SHAKESPEARE

(30) Rhetoric [1.2.112]: When Grumio brags that Petruchio "will throw a figure" in Katherine's face (1.2.112), what does he mean? Name at least three "rhetorical figures" used in Shakespeare's time.

(31) Teaser [1.2.144]: Find out the titles of at least three "books of love" (1.2.144) that would have been popular during the Renaissance. What "books of love" are popular these days?

And let me have them° very well perfumed,
For she is sweeter than perfume itself
To whom they go. What will you read to her?

them: i.e., the books

150

LUCENTIO
Whate'er I read to her, I'll plead for you,
As for my patron, stand you so assured,
As firmly as yourself were still in place,°
Yea and perhaps with more successful words
Than you – unless you were a scholar, sir.

in place: present

155

GREMIO
O this learning, what a thing it is!

GRUMIO *[Aside]*
O this woodcock,° what an ass it is!

woodcock: (bird easily caught, hence proverbially stupid)

PETRUCHIO
Peace, sirrah.

HORTENSIO
Grumio, mum! *[Advancing]* God save you, Signor
Gremio.

160

GREMIO
And you are well met, Signor Hortensio.
Trow° you whither I am going? To Baptista Minola.
I promised to inquire carefully
About a schoolmaster for the fair Bianca,
And by good fortune I have lighted well
On this young man, for learning and behavior
Fit for her turn,° well read in poetry
And other books, good ones, I warrant ye.

Trow: know

165

turn: need

HORTENSIO
'Tis well, and I have met a gentleman
Hath promised me to help me to another,
A fine musician to instruct our mistress.°
So shall I no whit be behind in duty
To fair Bianca, so beloved of me.

170

mistress: beloved

GREMIO
Beloved of me, and that my deeds shall prove.

GRUMIO *[Aside]*
And that his bags° shall prove.

bags: moneybags

175

HORTENSIO
Gremio, 'tis now no time to vent° our love.
Listen to me, and if you speak me fair
I'll tell you news indifferent° good for either.
Here is a gentleman whom by chance I met,
Upon agreement° from us to his liking,
Will undertake° to woo curst Katherine,
Yea and to marry her if her dowry please.

vent: utter

indifferent: equally

agreement: terms (they will pay his expenses of wooing, l. 213)
Will undertake: i.e., who, upon agreement, will undertake

180

GREMIO
So said, so done, is well.
Hortensio, have you told him all her faults?

DISCOVERING SHAKESPEARE

(32) History [1.2.182]: What was a dowry (1.2.182)? How many other references to Katherine's "dowry" can you find in this script? Why would a dowry have been important to Petruchio? (*Hint:* See also 2.1.121–128.)

PETRUCHIO
  I know she is an irksome brawling scold.   185
  If that be all, masters, I hear no harm.
GREMIO
  No, sayst me so, friend? What countryman?
PETRUCHIO
  Born in Verona, old Antonio's son.
  My father dead, my fortune lives for me,
  And I do hope good days and long to see.   190
GREMIO
  O sir, such a life, with such a wife, were strange.
  But if you have a stomach,° to't a° God's name,   **stomach:** appetite; **a:** in
  You shall have me assisting you in all.
  But will you woo this wildcat?
PETRUCHIO   Will I live?°   **Will I live?:** i.e., certainly   195
GRUMIO *[Aside]*
  Will he woo her? Ay, or he'll hang her.
PETRUCHIO
  Why came I hither but to that intent?
  Think you a little din can daunt mine ears?
  Have I not in my time heard lions roar?
  Have I not heard the sea, puffed up with winds,
  Rage like an angry boar chafed with sweat?   200
  Have I not heard great ordnance in the field
  And heaven's artillery thunder in the skies?
  Have I not in a pitchèd battle heard
  Loud 'larums,° neighing steeds, and trumpets' clang?   **'larums:** calls to arms
  And do you tell me of a woman's tongue,   205
  That gives not half so great a blow to th'ear
  As will a chestnut in a farmer's fire?
  Tush, tush, fear° boys with bugs.°   **fear:** frighten; **bugs:** bogeymen
GRUMIO *[Aside]*   For he fears none.
GREMIO
  Hortensio, hark.
  This gentleman is happily arrived,   210
  My mind presumes, for his own good and ours.
HORTENSIO
  I promised we would be contributors,
  And bear his charge° of wooing whatsoe'er.   **charge:** expenses
GREMIO
  And so we will, provided that he win her.
GRUMIO *[Aside]*
  I would I were as sure of a good dinner.   215
    Enter Tranio brave° [as Lucentio], and Biondello.   **brave:** finely dressed
TRANIO
  Gentlemen, God save you. If I may be bold,

DISCOVERING SHAKESPEARE

(33) Language [1.2.191–196]: Lines 191–196 in act 1, scene 2 make considerable use of <u>alliteration</u>. Underline in your <u>script</u> all the words beginning with the letter "W." Do you think <u>alliteration</u> is more often used for serious or for comic effect? Why? What effect does it have in this particular passage?

(34) Characterization [1.2.216]: When Tranio enters in this scene (line 216), how have his clothing and mannerisms changed from 1.1 when we saw him last? Why are these changes important to his new role in the play?

Tell me, I beseech you, which is the readiest way
To the house of Signor Baptista Minola?
BIONDELLO   He that has the two fair daughters, is't he
you mean?
TRANIO   Even he, Biondello.
GREMIO
Hark you, sir; you mean not her to woo?
TRANIO
Perhaps him and her, sir, what have you to do?°
PETRUCHIO
Not her that chides, sir, at any hand, I pray.
TRANIO
I love no chiders, sir – Biondello, let's away.
LUCENTIO   *[Aside]*
Well begun, Tranio.
HORTENSIO   Sir, a word ere you go.
Are you a suitor to the maid you talk of, yea or no?
TRANIO
An if I be, sir, is it any offense?
GREMIO
No, if without more words you will get you hence.
TRANIO
Why, sir, I pray, are not the streets as free
For me as for you?
GREMIO   But so is not she.
TRANIO
For what reason, I beseech you?
GREMIO   For this reason, if you'll
know,
That she's the choice love of Signor Gremio.
HORTENSIO
That she's the chosen of Signor Hortensio.
TRANIO
Softly, my masters. If you be gentlemen,
Do me this right, hear me with patience.
Baptista is a noble gentleman,
To whom my father is not all unknown,
And were his daughter fairer than she is
She may more suitors have, and me for one.
Fair Leda's daughter° had a thousand wooers,
Then well one more° may fair Bianca have.
And so she shall: Lucentio shall make one,
Though Paris° came° in hope to speed° alone.
GREMIO
What, this gentleman will outtalk us all.
LUCENTIO
Sir, give him head. I know he'll prove a jade.°
PETRUCHIO
Hortensio, to what end are all these words?
HORTENSIO
Sir, let me be so bold as to ask you,
Did you yet ever see Baptista's daughter?
TRANIO
No, sir, but I do hear that he hath two,

what . . . do: what business is it of yours	220
	225
	230
	235
	240
Leda's daughter: Helen of Troy (Leda was made love to by Jupiter in the shape of a swan)	
one more: i.e., than she now has	
Paris: Helen's lover (who took her away from her husband, Menelaus); **came:** were to come; **speed:** succeed	245
jade: worthless horse (easily tired)	
	250

The one as famous for a scolding tongue
As is the other for beauteous modesty.

PETRUCHIO
Sir, sir, the first's for me, let her go by.

GREMIO
Yea, leave that labor to great Hercules,
And let it be more than Alcides'° twelve.°

       Alcides: Hercules (so called from his grandfather   255
Alcaeus); **twelve:** (Hercules was required to
perform twelve labors, or impossible tasks)

PETRUCHIO
Sir, understand you this of me, in sooth.°
The youngest daughter, whom you hearken for,°
Her father keeps from all access of suitors
And will not promise her to any man
Until the elder sister first be wed.
The younger then is free, and not before.

       sooth: truth
       hearken for: ask after

       260

TRANIO
If it be so, sir, that you are the man
Must stead° us all, and me amongst the rest,
And if you break the ice and do this feat,
Achieve° the elder, set the younger free
For our access, whose hap° shall be to have her
Will not so graceless be to be ingrate.

       stead: help

       Achieve: win   265
       whose hap: he whose luck

HORTENSIO
Sir, you say well, and well you do conceive,°
And since you do profess to be a suitor,
You must, as we do, gratify° this gentleman,
To whom we all rest generally beholding.°

       well you . . . conceive: you understand the
matter well
       gratify: reward   270
       beholding: beholden, indebted

TRANIO
Sir, I shall not be slack, in sign whereof,
Please ye we may contrive° this afternoon
And quaff carouses° to our mistress' health,
And do as adversaries° do in law,
Strive mightily but eat and drink as friends.

       contrive: pass the time
       quaff carouses: drink toasts
       adversaries: lawyers (not their clients)   275

GRUMIO, BIONDELLO
O excellent motion! Fellows, let's be gone.

HORTENSIO
The motion's good indeed, and be it so.
Petruchio, I shall be your *benvenuto.*°   *Exeunt.*   **benvenuto:** welcome (Italian)

  2.1°   *Enter Kate and Bianca [with her hands tied].*   **2.1:** Baptista's house

BIANCA
Good sister, wrong me not, nor wrong yourself,
To make a bondmaid and a slave of me –
That I disdain. But for these other gawds,°
Unbind my hands, I'll pull them off myself,
Yea, all my raiment, to my petticoat,
Or what you will command me will I do,
So well I know my duty to my elders.

       gawds: ornaments

       5

DISCOVERING SHAKESPEARE

(35) Mythology [1.2.254–255]: Who was Hercules (also called Alcides), and what were his twelve "labors" (1.2.255)?
(36) Staging [2.1.1]: Most productions begin act 2, scene 1 with Bianca tied up in some fashion. If you were directing the scene, how would she be bound?

KATE
    Of all thy suitors, here I charge thee, tell
    Whom thou lov'st best. See thou dissemble not.
BIANCA
    Believe me, sister, of all the men alive   10
    I never yet beheld that special face
    Which I could fancy more than any other.
KATE
    Minion,° thou liest. Is't not Hortensio?   **Minion:** minx
BIANCA
    If you affect° him, sister, here I swear   **affect:** love
    I'll plead for you myself but you shall have him.   15
KATE
    O then, belike,° you fancy riches more.   **belike:** probably
    You will have Gremio to keep you fair.°   **fair:** in finery
BIANCA
    Is it for him you do envy° me so?   **envy:** hate
    Nay, then you jest, and now I well perceive
    You have but jested with me all this while.   20
    I prithee, sister Kate, untie my hands.
KATE
    If that be jest then all the rest was so.
    Strikes her.
    Enter Baptista.
BAPTISTA
    Why, how now, dame, whence grows this insolence?
    Bianca, stand aside. Poor girl, she weeps.
    Go ply thy needle, meddle not with her.   25
    For shame, thou hilding° of a devilish spirit,   **hilding:** vicious beast
    Why dost thou wrong her that did ne'er wrong thee?
    When did she cross thee with a bitter word?
KATE
    Her silence flouts me and I'll be revenged.
    Flies after Bianca.
BAPTISTA
    What, in my sight? Bianca, get thee in.   *Exit [Bianca.]*   30
KATE
    Will you not suffer me? Nay, now I see
    She is your treasure, she must have a husband;
    I must dance barefoot on her wedding day,°   **dance . . . day:** (proverbially the fate of an
    And for your love to her lead apes in hell.°   unmarried elder sister)
    Talk not to me, I will go sit and weep   **lead . . . hell:** (proverbial fate of old maids)   35
    Till I can find occasion of revenge.   *[Exit.]*
BAPTISTA
    Was ever gentleman thus grieved as I?
    But who comes here?
    Enter Gremio, [with] Lucentio [as a schoolmaster] in
    the habit° of a mean° man, Petruchio with [Hortensio as   **habit:** garments; **mean:** lower-class;
    a music master, and] Tranio [as Lucentio] with his boy°   **boy:** page
    [Biondello] bearing a lute and books.

DISCOVERING SHAKESPEARE

(37) Staging [2.1.20]: How threatening is this scene initially? When does Bianca begin to cry? Why does she do so at that particular moment?

GREMIO   Good morrow, neighbor Baptista.

BAPTISTA   Good morrow, neighbor Gremio. God save   40
you, gentlemen.

PETRUCHIO
And you, good sir. Pray, have you not a daughter
Called Katherina, fair and virtuous?

BAPTISTA
I have a daughter, sir, called Katherina.

GREMIO
You are too blunt, go to it orderly.°   **orderly:** politely   45

PETRUCHIO
You wrong me, Signor Gremio, give me leave.
I am a gentleman of Verona, sir,
That, hearing of her beauty and her wit,
Her affability and bashful modesty,
Her wondrous qualities and mild behavior,   50
Am bold to show myself a forward guest
Within your house, to make mine eye the witness
Of that report which I so oft have heard.
And for an entrance° to my entertainment°   **entrance:** entrance fee; **entertainment:**
I do present you with a man of mine,   welcome (as a suitor)   55
    [Presenting Hortensio]
Cunning in music and the mathematics,
To instruct her fully in those sciences,
Whereof I know she is not ignorant.
Accept of him or else you do me wrong.
His name is Litio,° born in Mantua.   **Litio:** (or Lizio, an old Italian word for garlic;   60
                                                     pronounced "Leet-sio")

BAPTISTA
You're welcome, sir, and he for your good sake.
But for my daughter Katherine, this I know,
She is not for your turn,° the more my grief.   **turn:** purpose

PETRUCHIO
I see you do not mean to part with her,
Or else you like not of my company.   65

BAPTISTA
Mistake me not, I speak but as I find.
Whence are you, sir? What may I call your name?

PETRUCHIO
Petruchio is my name, Antonio's son,
A man well known throughout all Italy.

BAPTISTA
I know him° well, you are welcome for his sake.   **know him:** i.e., know who he is   70

DISCOVERING SHAKESPEARE

(38) Costuming [2.1.39]: In this scene, three characters enter in disguise: Lucentio as Cambio the schoolmaster, Hortensio as Litio the musician, and Tranio as Lucentio the suitor. Describe each character's disguise, paying specific attention to any elements that might bring forth audience laughter (e.g., fake noses, goofy-looking glasses, outrageous mustaches, etc.).

(39) Staging [2.1.46–60]: During Petruchio's long speech praising Kate's many "virtues" in 2.1.46–60, how do the other characters react?

(40) Characterization [2.1.71]: Assuming that Gremio is played as a very old man, what kinds of sight gags could the actor use to exaggerate his physical infirmities? (*Hint:* Consider, for example, a huge "ear trumpet," incredibly thick spectacles, and/or difficulty moving around the stage.) Try some of these gags out in class; then decide which would be most effective.

GREMIO Saving° your tale, Petruchio, I pray, let us, that are poor petitioners, speak too. Backare,° you are marvelous forward.

PETRUCHIO
O pardon me, Signor Gremio, I would fain° be doing.

GREMIO I doubt it not, sir, but you will curse your wooing. Neighbor, this is a gift very grateful, I am sure of it. To express the like kindness, myself, that have been more kindly beholding to you than any, freely give unto you this young scholar, *[Presenting Lucentio]* that hath been long studying at Rheims;° as cunning in Greek, Latin, and other languages as the other in music and mathematics. His name is Cambio,° pray accept his service.

BAPTISTA A thousand thanks, Signor Gremio. Welcome, good Cambio. *[To Tranio]* But, gentle sir, methinks you walk like a stranger. May I be so bold to know the cause of your coming?

TRANIO
Pardon me, sir, the boldness is mine own,
That, being a stranger in this city here,
Do make myself a suitor to your daughter,
Unto Bianca, fair and virtuous.
Nor is your firm resolve unknown to me
In the preferment of the eldest sister.
This liberty is all that I request,
That, upon knowledge of my parentage,
I may have welcome 'mongst the rest that woo,
And free access and favor as the rest.
And toward the education of your daughters
I here bestow a simple instrument,
And this small packet of Greek and Latin books.
If you accept them, then their worth is great.

BAPTISTA
Lucentio° is your name, of whence, I pray?

TRANIO
Of Pisa, sir, son to Vincentio.

BAPTISTA
A mighty man of Pisa by report,
I know him° well. You are very welcome, sir.
[To Hortensio]
Take you the lute, *[To Lucentio]* and you the set of books.
You shall go see your pupils presently.°
Holla, within!
Enter a Servant.

Saving: with no disrespect to
Backare: back off (pronounced "back-AR-ay"; mock Latin)

fain: gladly

75

Rheims: (here pronounced "reams")   80

Cambio: (the word means "exchange" in Italian)

85

90

95

100

Lucentio: (Tranio has not mentioned the name yet: does he offer Baptista some identification? Does Baptista find his name in one of the books?)

know him: i.e., know who he is   105

presently: immediately

DISCOVERING SHAKESPEARE

(41) Teaser [2.1.83]: In Gremio's speech to Baptista in 2.1.75–83, we learn that Lucentio has taken on the identity of "Cambio," which is appropriate, since the word means "exchange" in Italian. As Bianca explains to her father when all the "supposed" identities have been revealed at the end of the play, "Cambio is changed into Lucentio" (5.1.113). Examine the following other names in the play, and show how each helps predict the character's behavior or personality: Sly, Baptista, Bianca, Petruchio, Grumio, and Gremio.

(42) Geography [2.1.104]: How far is Pisa from Padua? How long do you think it would have taken someone to travel from one city to the other by horseback?

Sirrah, lead these gentlemen
To my daughters, and tell them both   110
These are their tutors; bid them use them well.
                            [Exit Servant with Hortensio,
                                 Lucentio, and Biondello.]
We will go walk a little in the orchard°   **orchard:** garden
And then to dinner.° You are passing° welcome,   **dinner:** (the main meal, served at midday);
And so I pray you all to think yourselves.   **passing:** exceedingly

PETRUCHIO
Signor Baptista, my business asketh haste,   115
And every day I cannot come to woo.
You knew my father well, and in him me,
Left solely heir to all his lands and goods,
Which I have bettered rather than decreased.
Then tell me, if I get your daughter's love   120
What dowry shall I have with her to wife?

BAPTISTA
After my death the one half of my lands,
And in possession° twenty thousand crowns.   **possession:** i.e., immediate possession

PETRUCHIO
And for that dowry, I'll assure her of
Her widowhood,° be it that she survive me,   **widowhood:** income if widowed   125
In all my lands and leases whatsoever.
Let specialties° be therefore drawn between us,   **specialties:** contracts
That covenants may be kept on either hand.

BAPTISTA
Ay, when the special thing is well obtained,
That is, her love, for that is all in all.   130

PETRUCHIO
Why, that is nothing, for I tell you, father,
I am as peremptory° as she proud-minded,   **peremptory:** determined
And where two raging fires meet together
They do consume the thing that feeds their fury.
Though little fire grows great with little wind,   135
Yet extreme gusts will blow out fire and all.
So I to her, and so she yields to me,
For I am rough and woo not like a babe.

BAPTISTA
Well mayst thou woo, and happy be thy speed,°   **speed:** fortune
But be thou armed for some unhappy words.   140

PETRUCHIO
Ay, to the proof,° as mountains are for winds,   **to the proof:** in tested armor
That shakes not though they blow perpetually.
    Enter Hortensio [as Litio] with his head broke.°   **broke:** i.e., with the skin broken, bleeding

BAPTISTA
How now, my friend, why dost thou look so pale?

HORTENSIO
For fear, I promise you, if I look pale.

BAPTISTA
What, will my daughter prove a good musician?   145

DISCOVERING SHAKESPEARE

(43) **Metaphor** **[2.1.131–138]:** Explain the metaphor about "two raging fires" (2.1.133) which Petruchio uses to assure Baptista that his suit to Kate will be successful.

HORTENSIO
  I think she'll sooner prove a soldier.
  Iron may hold with her° but never lutes.°
BAPTISTA
  Why, then thou canst not break° her to the lute?
HORTENSIO
  Why, no, for she hath broke the lute to me.
  I did but tell her she mistook her frets°
  And bowed° her hand to teach her fingering,
  When, with a most impatient devilish spirit,
  "Frets, call you these?" quoth she, "I'll fume with them."
  And with that word she struck me on the head,
  And through the instrument my pate made way,
  And there I stood amazèd for a while
  As on a pillory, looking through the lute,
  While she did call me rascal, fiddler,
  And twangling Jack,° with twenty such vile terms,
  As had she studied to misuse me so.
PETRUCHIO
  Now, by the world, it is a lusty° wench.
  I love her ten times more than e'er I did.
  O how I long to have some chat with her!
BAPTISTA   *[To Hortensio]*
  Well, go with me, and be not so discomfited.
  Proceed in practice with my younger daughter.
  She's apt° to learn and thankful for good turns.
  Signor Petruchio, will you go with us
  Or shall I send my daughter Kate to you?
PETRUCHIO
  I pray you do. I will attend° her here,
        Exit [Baptista with Gremio, Tranio,
        and Hortensio]. Manet Petruchio.
  And woo her with some spirit when she comes.
  Say that she rail, why then I'll tell her plain
  She sings as sweetly as a nightingale.
  Say that she frown, I'll say she looks as clear
  As morning roses newly washed with dew.
  Say she be mute and will not speak a word,
  Then I'll commend her volubility
  And say she uttereth piercing eloquence.
  If she do bid me pack I'll give her thanks
  As though she bid me stay by her a week.
  If she deny° to wed I'll crave the day
  When I shall ask the banns,° and when be marrièd.
  Enter Kate.

hold with her: (1) suit her, (2) withstand her;
lutes: (playing on "cement made of clay")

break: tame

frets: rings of gut, placed on the fingerboard to   150
regulate the fingering (Kate quibbled on "fret and
fume," be indignant)

bowed: bent

  155

Jack: knave

  160

lusty: lively

  165

apt: willing

attend: wait for

  170

  175

deny: refuse 180
ask the banns: announce in church the intent
to marry

DISCOVERING SHAKESPEARE

(44) <u>Props</u> **[2.1.148]:** How many different lutes would a <u>prop</u> master have to provide for a production of this play? What other <u>props</u> would be necessary in act 2, scene 1 and act 3, scene 1?

(45) <u>Soliloquy</u> **[2.1.169–182]:** Read Petruchio's <u>soliloquy</u> in 2.1.169–182 carefully; then explain how you were affected by it. Does a <u>soliloquy</u> at this point in the play make the audience more or less sympathetic to Petruchio? Why doesn't Shakespeare allow Kate a similar <u>soliloquy</u> this early in the play? Does she have any <u>soliloquies</u> at all? To what extent does her lack of <u>soliloquies</u> hinder us in understanding and identifying with her character? Does a long <u>monologue</u> (see, for example, 5.2.142–185) have the same effect as a <u>soliloquy</u>? Why or why not?

But here she comes, and now, Petruchio, speak.
Good morrow, Kate, for that's your name, I hear.

KATE
Well have you heard, but something hard° of hearing.
They call me Katherine that do talk of me.

hard: (playing on *heard,* pronounced similarly)

185

PETRUCHIO
You lie, in faith, for you are called plain Kate,
And bonny° Kate, and sometimes Kate the curst.
But Kate, the prettiest Kate in Christendom,
Kate of Kate Hall, my superdainty Kate,
For dainties° are all cates,° and therefore, Kate,
Take this of me, Kate of my consolation:
Hearing thy mildness praised in every town,
Thy virtues spoke of, and thy beauty sounded,°
Yet not so deeply as to thee belongs,
Myself am moved to woo thee for my wife.

bonny: strapping

dainties: delicacies; **cates:** choice foods (playing, of course, on "Kates")

190

sounded: proclaimed (with a play, in *deeply,* on "plumbed")

195

KATE
Moved? In good time:° let him that moved you hither
Remove you hence. I knew you at the first,
You were a movable.°

In good time: indeed

movable: piece of furniture

PETRUCHIO   Why, what's a movable?

KATE   A joint stool.°

PETRUCHIO   Thou hast hit it: come sit on me.

joint stool: stool made by a joiner ("I took you for a joint stool" was a standard joke, meaning "you're not worth noticing")

200

KATE
Asses are made to bear, and so are you.

PETRUCHIO
Women are made to bear,° and so are you.

KATE
No such jade° as you, if me you mean.

bear: (1) bear children, (2) bear the weight of men in lovemaking

jade: worthless horse

PETRUCHIO
Alas, good Kate, I will not burden thee,
For knowing° thee to be but young and light.°

205

For knowing: because I know; **light:** (1) weak, (2) inconsequential, (3) flirtatious

KATE
Too light for such a swain° as you to catch,
And yet as heavy as my weight should be.°

swain: peasant lover

heavy . . . be: (the image is from coinage: not counterfeit or cut down)

PETRUCHIO
Should be? should – buzz!°

KATE   Well ta'en, and like a buzzard.°

PETRUCHIO
O slow-winged turtle!° Shall a buzzard take thee?

buzz: (exclamation meaning "nonsense," playing on *be[e]*); **buzzard:** untrainable type of hawk, hence fool

turtle: turtledove

210

KATE
Ay, for a turtle, as he takes a buzzard.°

PETRUCHIO
Come, come, you wasp, i' faith you are too angry.

KATE
If I be waspish best beware my sting.

buzzard: (the term was applied to large moths and beetles, insects that the dove doesn't like: the line means "you're a fool if you think I'm a turtledove")

PETRUCHIO
My remedy is then to pluck it out.

DISCOVERING SHAKESPEARE

(46) Blocking [2.1.201]: In this classic confrontation between Kate and Petruchio, blocking is suggested in the dialogue at several different moments (see, for example, "Come sit on me" in 2.1.201). Read through the dialogue between the two characters, and underline each reference to physical action.

KATE
Ay, if the fool could find it where it lies.   215
PETRUCHIO
Who knows not where a wasp does wear his sting?
In his tail.
KATE   In his tongue.
PETRUCHIO   Whose tongue?
KATE
Yours, if you talk of tales, and so farewell.   220
PETRUCHIO
What, with my tongue in your tail?
Nay, come again, good Kate, I am a gentleman.
KATE   That I'll try.
    She strikes him.
PETRUCHIO
I swear I'll cuff you if you strike again.
KATE
So may you lose your arms.°   **arms:** coat of arms   225
If you strike me you are no gentleman,
And if no gentleman, why then no arms.
PETRUCHIO
A herald, Kate? O put me in thy books.°   **in thy books:** in your heraldic registers (playing
                                                                    on "in your good graces")
KATE
What is your crest,° a coxcomb?°   **crest:** armorial device; **coxcomb:** cap of a
                                                                    court fool (playing on *crest,* comb; Petruchio then
PETRUCHIO   quibbles on "cock's comb")   230
A combless° cock, so Kate will be my hen.   **combless:** gentle (with "comb" or crest cut down)
KATE
No cock of mine, you crow too like a craven.°   **craven:** cock that will not fight
PETRUCHIO
Nay, come, Kate, come, you must not look so sour.
KATE
It is my fashion when I see a crab.°   **crab:** crab apple (notoriously sour)
PETRUCHIO
Why, here's no crab, and therefore look not sour.
KATE
There is, there is.   235
PETRUCHIO
Then show it me.
KATE   Had I a glass° I would.   **glass:** looking glass
PETRUCHIO   What, you mean my face?
KATE   Well aimed° of such a young° one.   **aimed of:** guessed for; **young:** inexperienced
PETRUCHIO
Now, by Saint George, I am too young for you.
KATE
Yet you are withered.   240
PETRUCHIO   'Tis with cares.
KATE   I care not.
PETRUCHIO
Nay, hear you, Kate, in sooth° you scape not so.   **sooth:** truth

---

DISCOVERING SHAKESPEARE

(47) __Blocking__ **[2.1.221]:** Suggest three different _blocking_ possibilities for Petruchio's "What, with my tongue in your tail?" (2.1.221).

KATE
  I chafe you if I tarry; let me go.
PETRUCHIO
  No, not a whit. I find you passing gentle.
  'Twas told me you were rough and coy° and sullen,   **coy:** haughty
  And now I find report a very liar,   245
  For thou art pleasant, gamesome, passing courteous,
  But slow in speech, yet sweet as springtime flowers.
  Thou canst not frown, thou canst not look askance,°   **askance:** scornfully
  Nor bite the lip as angry wenches will,
  Nor hast thou pleasure to be cross in talk.   250
  But thou with mildness entertain'st thy wooers,
  With gentle conference, soft and affable.
  Why does the world report that Kate doth limp?
  O sland'rous world! Kate like a hazel twig
  Is straight and slender, and as brown in hue   255
  As hazelnuts and sweeter than the kernels.
  O let me see thee walk. Thou dost not halt.°   **halt:** limp
KATE
  Go, fool, and whom thou keep'st° command.   **whom thou keep'st:** i.e., your servants
PETRUCHIO
  Did ever Dian° so become a grove   **Dian:** Diana (goddess of virginity and of the hunt)
  As Kate this chamber with her princely gait?   260
  O be thou Dian and let her be Kate.
  And then let Kate be chaste and Dian sportful.°   **sportful:** amorous
KATE
  Where did you study all this goodly speech?
PETRUCHIO
  It is extempore, from my mother wit.°   **mother wit:** native intelligence
KATE
  A witty mother, witless else her son.°   **witless . . . son:** otherwise her son would be   265
                                                                                                     witless (his only wit being inherited from her)
PETRUCHIO   Am I not wise?
KATE   Yes, keep you warm.°   **keep you warm:** i.e., take care of yourself (to
PETRUCHIO   have the wit or wisdom to keep warm being
  Marry, so I mean, sweet Katherine, in thy bed.   proverbial)
  And therefore, setting all this chat aside,
  Thus in plain terms. Your father hath consented   270
  That you shall be my wife, your dowry 'greed upon,
  And will you, nill you,° I will marry you.   **will you, nill you:** whether you will or not
  Now, Kate, I am a husband for your turn,°   **for your turn:** to suit you
  For by this light, whereby I see thy beauty –
  Thy beauty that doth make me like thee well –   275
  Thou must be married to no man but me,
    Enter Baptista, Gremio, [and] Tranio [as Lucentio].
  For I am he am born to tame you, Kate,
  And bring you from a wild Kate° to a Kate   **wild Kate:** (punning on "wildcat")

DISCOVERING SHAKESPEARE

(48) Blocking [2.1.253]: Create three possible reasons through the blocking in this scene to explain why Petruchio says, "Why does the world report that Kate doth limp?" (2.1.253).
(49) Characterization [2.1.270–271]: What is Kate's reaction when Petruchio says "your father hath consented / That you shall be my wife" (2.1.270–271)? Why doesn't she have any lines here? What do you think she would have said if Shakespeare had allowed her to respond immediately to Petruchio's statement?

Conformable as other household Kates.
Here comes your father. Never make denial, 280
I must and will have Katherine to my wife.

BAPTISTA
Now, Signor Petruchio, how speed° you with my daughter? **speed:** succeed

PETRUCHIO
How but well, sir? How but well?
It were impossible I should speed amiss.

BAPTISTA
Why, how now, daughter Katherine? In your dumps? 285

KATE
Call you me daughter? Now, I promise° you **promise:** assure
You have showed a tender fatherly regard
To wish me wed to one half lunatic,
A madcap ruffian and a swearing Jack,
That thinks with oaths to face° the matter out. **face:** brazen 290

PETRUCHIO
Father, 'tis thus. Yourself and all the world
That talked of her have talked amiss of her.
If she be curst it is for policy,° **policy:** cunning
For she's not froward but modest as the dove.
She is not hot° but temperate as the morn. **hot:** of angry disposition 295
For patience she will prove a second Grissel,° **Grissel:** Griselda (the epitome of wifely patience
And Roman Lucrece° for her chastity. and obedience; cf. Boccaccio's *Decameron*, X, 10,
And, to conclude, we have 'greed so well together or Chaucer's *Clerk's Tale*)
That upon Sunday is the wedding day. **Lucrece:** (she killed herself after being raped by
Sextus Tarquinius, hence became the epitome of
wifely chastity and honor; cf. Shakespeare's *The
Rape of Lucrece*)

KATE
I'll see thee hanged on Sunday first. 300

GREMIO
Hark, Petruchio, she says she'll see thee hanged first.

TRANIO
Is this your speeding?° Nay, then good night our part!° **speeding:** success; **good . . . part:** good-bye to
our hopes (of marrying Bianca)

PETRUCHIO
Be patient, gentlemen, I choose her for myself.
If she and I be pleased, what's that to you?
'Tis bargained 'twixt us twain, being alone, 305
That she shall still be curst in company.
I tell you, 'tis incredible to believe
How much she loves me. O the kindest Kate!
She hung about my neck, and kiss on kiss
She vied° so fast, protesting oath on oath, **vied:** raised the bid (cardplaying term) 310
That in a twink she won me to her love.
O you are novices. 'Tis a world° to see **world:** i.e., worth a world
How tame, when men and women are alone,
A meacock° wretch can make the curstest shrew. **meacock:** cowardly
Give me thy hand, Kate, I will unto Venice 315
To buy apparel 'gainst° the wedding day. **'gainst:** in anticipation of
Provide the feast, father, and bid the guests.
I will be sure my Katherine shall be fine.° **fine:** finely dressed

---

DISCOVERING SHAKESPEARE

(50) Metaphor [2.1.290]: What does Kate mean when she says that Petruchio is trying to "face the matter out" (2.1.290)? How does this metaphor work? (*Hint:* Look up the word "face" in the *Oxford English Dictionary*.)

BAPTISTA

I know not what to say – but give me your hands.
God send you joy! Petruchio, 'tis a match.   320

GREMIO, TRANIO

Amen, say we, we will be witnesses.

PETRUCHIO

Father, and wife, and gentlemen, adieu.
I will to Venice. Sunday comes apace.
We will have rings and things and fine array,
And kiss me, Kate, *[Sings.]* "We will be married a Sun-   325
      day."

                 Exeunt Petruchio and Kate [severally°].   **severally:** at different doors

GREMIO

Was ever match° clapped up° so suddenly?   **match:** contract (with a play on "mating");
                                         clapped up: shaken hands on, agreed to

BAPTISTA

Faith, gentlemen, now I play a merchant's part
And venture madly on a desperate mart.°   **mart:** bargain

TRANIO

'Twas a commodity lay fretting° by you.   **fretting:** (of a stored commodity that decays, as
'Twill bring you gain or perish on the seas.   wool "fretted" by moths; with a play on "chafing")   330

BAPTISTA

The gain I seek is quiet in the match.

GREMIO

No doubt but he hath got a quiet catch.
But now, Baptista, to your younger daughter.
Now is the day we long have lookèd for.
I am your neighbor and was suitor first.   335

TRANIO

And I am one that love Bianca more
Than words can witness or your thoughts can guess.

GREMIO

Youngling, thou canst not love so dear as I.

TRANIO

Graybeard, thy love doth freeze.

GREMIO
                             But thine doth fry.
Skipper,° stand back, 'tis age that nourisheth.   **Skipper:** flighty youth   340

TRANIO

But youth in ladies' eyes that flourisheth.

BAPTISTA

Content you, gentlemen, I will compound° this strife.   **compound:** settle
'Tis deeds must win the prize, and he of both°   **he of both:** whichever of the two (of you)
That can assure° my daughter greatest dower°   **assure:** guarantee; **dower:** portion of the
Shall have Bianca's love.   husband's estate left to the widow   345
Say, Signor Gremio, what can you assure her?

DISCOVERING SHAKESPEARE

(51) Characterization [2.1.320]: Why doesn't Kate say anything when her father announces "'tis a match" (2.1.320)? What stage action might explain her silence? What could she be doing in terms of blocking or gestures at this moment? How would the scene change if Petruchio has his hand over Kate's mouth, thereby preventing her from speaking?

(52) Rhyme [2.1.327–328]: Baptista's rhyme on the words "part" and "mart" at the ends of lines 327–328 signals a shift in the plot at this point in the play (or what some directors call a "beat change"). What new direction does the plot take here? What other rhymes help illustrate the new mood of this portion of the scene?

(53) Paraphrase [2.1.343]: Paraphrase Baptista's statement that "deeds must win the prize" (2.1.343). How does each of the suitors react to this news?

GREMIO

First, as you know, my house within the city
Is richly furnishèd with plate and gold,
Basins and ewers to lave° her dainty hands;
My hangings all of Tyrian° tapestry;
In ivory coffers I have stuffed my crowns;°
In cypress chests my arras counterpoints,°
Costly apparel, tents, and canopies,°
Fine linen, Turkey cushions bossed° with pearl,
Valance° of Venice gold in needlework,
Pewter and brass, and all things that belongs
To house or housekeeping. Then at my farm
I have a hundred milk kine to the pail,°
Six score fat oxen standing in my stalls,
And all things answerable to this portion.°
Myself am struck° in years, I must confess,
And if I die tomorrow this is hers,
If whilst I live she will be only mine.

TRANIO

That "only" came well in. Sir, list to me.
I am my father's heir and only son.
If I may have your daughter to my wife
I'll leave her houses three or four as good,
Within rich Pisa walls, as any one
Old Signor Gremio has in Padua,
Besides two thousand ducats° by the year
Of° fruitful land, all which shall be her jointure.°
What, have I pinched you, Signor Gremio?

GREMIO

Two thousand ducats by the year of land!
  [Aside]
My land amounts not to so much in all. —
That she shall have, besides an argosy°
That now is lying in Marseilles'° road.°
What, have I choked you with an argosy?

TRANIO

Gremio, 'tis known my father hath no less
Than three great argosies, besides two galliasses°
And twelve tight° galleys. These I will assure her
And twice as much whate'er thou off'rest next.

GREMIO

Nay, I have offered all, I have no more,
And she can have no more than all I have.
If you like me, she shall have me and mine.

TRANIO

Why, then the maid is mine from all world
By your firm promise. Gremio is outvied.°

---

lave: wash
Tyrian: purple · 350
crowns: money
arras counter-points: quilted tapestry counterpanes
tents, canopies: (types of bed hangings)
bossed: embroidered · 355
Valance: drapery for the bed canopy

milk kine . . . pail: dairy cows

all . . . portion: all my possessions are equally · 360
valuable
struck: advanced

· 365

ducats: gold coins · 370
Of: i.e., the income from; **jointure:** settlement

argosy: large merchant ship · 375
Marseilles': (pronounced "Marsellus");
road: harbor

galliasses: large galleys
tight: sound, well caulked · 380

· 385
outvied: outbid

DISCOVERING SHAKESPEARE

(54) Language [2.1.370–375]: What is the difference between Tranio's boast that his land provides "two thousand ducats by the year" (2.1.370) and Gremio's confession in an <u>aside</u> that "My land amounts not to so much in all" (2.1.374)? Why does Gremio make this statement in an <u>aside</u>? How would the scene be different if Baptista and Tranio were able to hear the line?

BAPTISTA
    I must confess your offer is the best,
    And let your father make her the assurance,°   **assurance:** guarantee
    She is your own, else you must pardon me.
    If you should die before him, where's her dower?   390
TRANIO
    That's but a cavil. He is old, I young.
GREMIO
    And may not young men die as well as old?
BAPTISTA
    Well, gentlemen, I am thus resolved.
    On Sunday next, you know,
    My daughter Katherine is to be married.   395
    Now on the Sunday following shall Bianca
    Be bride to you, if you make this assurance.
    If not, to Signor Gremio.
    And so I take my leave and thank you both.   *Exit.*
GREMIO
    Adieu, good neighbor. Now I fear thee not.   400
    Sirrah° young gamester, your father were° a fool   **Sirrah:** (contemptuous to a person of equal rank);
    To give thee all and in his waning age   **were:** would be
    Set foot under thy table.° Tut, a toy!°   **Set . . . table:** i.e., become your dependent;
    An old Italian fox is not so kind, my boy.   *Exit.*   **a toy:** nonsense
TRANIO
    A vengeance on your crafty withered hide!   405
    Yet I have faced it with a card of ten.°   **faced . . . ten:** bluffed successfully with a ten-spot
    'Tis in my head to do my master good.
    I see no reason but supposed Lucentio
    Must get a father, called supposed Vincentio;
    And that's a wonder. Fathers commonly   410
    Do get° their children, but in this case of wooing   **get:** beget
    A child shall get a sire if I fail not of my cunning.   *Exit.*

❧ **3.1°**   *Enter Lucentio [as Cambio], Hortensio*   **3.1:** Baptista's house
    [as Litio], and Bianca.

LUCENTIO
    Fiddler, forbear, you grow too forward, sir.
    Have you so soon forgot the entertainment
    Her sister Katherine welcomed you withal?
HORTENSIO
    But, wrangling pedant, this is
    The patroness° of heavenly harmony.   **patroness:** goddess   5
    Then give me leave to have prerogative,°   **prerogative:** precedence
    And when in music we have spent an hour
    Your lecture° shall have leisure for as much.   **lecture:** lesson

---

DISCOVERING SHAKESPEARE

(55) Characterization [2.1.387]: How do Tranio and Gremio each respond to Baptista's decision that Tranio's offer "is the best" (2.1.387)? What does Tranio mean in <u>soliloquy</u> when he confesses to the audience that he has "faced it with a card of ten" (2.1.406)?

(56) <u>Verse</u> [2.1.408–412]: In lines 408–412, the play's regular <u>iambic</u> <u>pentameter</u> <u>verse</u> form breaks down into more irregular <u>meter</u>. Why does the <u>verse</u> change at this particular moment in the scene? What is the relationship between the shift in <u>verse</u> form and the problem that Tranio must solve?

LUCENTIO
Preposterous ass, that never read so far
To know the cause why music was ordained! 10
Was it not to refresh the mind of man
After his studies or his usual pain?°   **pain:** toil
Then give me leave to read° philosophy,   **read:** teach
And while I pause, serve in your harmony.

HORTENSIO
Sirrah, I will not bear these braves° of thine.   **braves:** insults   15

BIANCA
Why, gentlemen, you do me double wrong
To strive for that which resteth in my choice.
I am no breeching scholar° in the schools.   **breeching scholar:** schoolboy liable to whipping
I'll not be tied to hours nor 'pointed times,
But learn my lessons as I please myself.   20
And, to cut off all strife, here sit we down.
Take you your instrument, play you the whiles;°   **the whiles:** meanwhile
His lecture will be done ere you have tuned.

HORTENSIO
You'll leave his lecture when I am in tune?

LUCENTIO
That will be never. Tune your instrument.   25

BIANCA   Where left we last?

LUCENTIO   Here, madam:
    [Reads.]
      "Hic ibat Simois, hic est Sigeia tellus,
      Hic steterat Priami regia celsa senis."°   **Hic . . . senis:** here flowed the Simois, here lies the Sigeian plain, here stood the lofty palace of old Priam (Ovid, *Epistolae Heroidum,* I, a letter from Penelope to Ulysses)   30

BIANCA   Conster° them.   **Conster:** construe (translate)

LUCENTIO   "Hic ibat," as I told you before; "Simois," I am Lucentio; "hic est," son unto Vincentio of Pisa; "Sigeia tellus," disguised thus to get your love; "Hic steterat," and that Lucentio that comes a-wooing; "Priami," is my man Tranio; "regia," bearing my port;°   **bearing my port:** behaving as I would   35
"celsa senis," that we might beguile the old pantaloon.°   **pantaloon:** foolish old man

HORTENSIO   Madam, my instrument's in tune.

BIANCA   Let's hear. *[He plays.]* O fie, the treble jars.°   **jars:** is discordant

LUCENTIO   Spit in the hole,° man, and tune again.   **Spit in the hole:** (to make the peg hold)

BIANCA   Now let me see if I can conster it.   40
"Hic ibat Simois," I know you not; "hic est Sigeia tellus," I trust you not; "Hic steterat Priami," take heed he hear us not; "regia," presume not; "celsa senis," despair not.

HORTENSIO
Madam, 'tis now in tune.

LUCENTIO   All but the bass.   45

DISCOVERING SHAKESPEARE

(57) Teaser [3.1.28–29]: Lucentio's Latin lesson is taken from Ovid's *Heroides* (lines 33–34). Why is the reference to Ovid appropriate in this wooing scene? What else did the author write that might have been more familiar to a Renaissance audience?

(58) Language [3.1.39]: What does Lucentio mean when he tells Hortensio to "Spit in the hole" (3.1.39)? What comic action might follow this line?

HORTENSIO
The bass is right, 'tis the base knave that jars.
[Aside]
How fiery and forward our pedant° is!
Now, for my life, the knave doth court my love.
Pedascule,° I'll watch you better yet.

pedant: schoolmaster or tutor

Pedascule: (Latin coinage from *pedant,* contemptuously diminutive; four syllables)

50

BIANCA
In time I may believe, yet I mistrust.

LUCENTIO
Mistrust it not, for sure Aeacides°
Was Ajax,° called so from his grandfather.

Aeacides: descendant of Aeacus (Lucentio explains a reference in the line of Ovid's epistle that follows immediately after the two lines already quoted)
Ajax: one of the Greek heroes at Troy

BIANCA
I must believe my master, else I promise you,
I should be arguing still upon that doubt.
But let it rest. Now, Litio, to you.
Good master, take it not unkindly, pray,
That I have been thus pleasant with you both.

55

HORTENSIO
You may go walk and give me leave a while.
My lessons make no music in three parts.°

in three parts: for three voices

LUCENTIO
Are you so formal,° sir? *[Aside]* Well, I must wait
And watch withal,° for but° I be deceived,
Our fine musician groweth amorous.

formal: precise   60
withal: at the same time; **but:** unless

HORTENSIO
Madam, before you touch the instrument
To learn the order of my fingering,
I must begin with rudiments of art,
To teach you gamut° in a briefer sort,
More pleasant, pithy, and effectual
Than hath been taught by any of my trade.
And there it is in writing, fairly drawn.

65

gamut: the scale

BIANCA
Why, I am past my gamut long ago.

70

HORTENSIO
Yet read the gamut of Hortensio.

BIANCA   *[Reads.°]*
    "*Gamut* I am, the ground° of all accord,°
    A re, to plead Hortensio's passion;
    B mi, Bianca, take him for thy lord,
    C fa ut, that loves with all affection;
    D sol re, one clef, two notes have I;
    E la mi,° show pity or I die."
Call you this gamut? Tut, I like it not.
Old fashions please me best; I am not so nice°
To change true rules for odd inventions.
    Enter a Messenger.

Reads: (she sings each line on the appropriate note)

ground: (*gamut* is also the lowest note, or ground, of the scale; also called *ut,* as in l. 75, or, in modern terminology, "do"); **accord:** harmony

75

ut, re, mi: (repeated because a second scale starts at C)

nice: capricious

80

MESSENGER
Mistress, your father prays you leave your books
And help to dress your sister's chamber up.
You know tomorrow is the wedding day.

DISCOVERING SHAKESPEARE

(59) Language [3.1.72–77]: What do the various sounds signify in Hortensio's "gamut"? (See, for example, "*C fa ut*" in line 75.)

BIANCA
Farewell, sweet masters both, I must be gone.
[Exeunt Bianca and Messenger.]

LUCENTIO
Faith, mistress, then I have no cause to stay. *[Exit.]* 85

HORTENSIO
But I have cause to pry into this pedant.
Methinks he looks as though he were in love.
Yet if thy thoughts, Bianca, be so humble
To cast thy wand'ring eyes on every stale,°   **stale:** decoy, bait
Seize thee that list.° If once I find thee ranging,°   **Seize . . . list:** let him take you that pleases; 90
Hortensio will be quit° with thee by changing.° *Exit.*   **ranging:** straying
    be quit: get even; **changing:** i.e., to another love

❧ **3.2**°   *Enter Baptista, Gremio, Tranio [as Lucentio],*   **3.2:** Before Baptista's house
    Kate, Bianca, [Lucentio as Cambio,] and others
    (Attendants).

BAPTISTA *[To Tranio]*
Signor Lucentio, this is the 'pointed day
That Katherine and Petruchio should be married,
And yet we hear not of our son-in-law.
What will be said? What mockery will it be
To want° the bridegroom when the priest attends   **want:** lack 5
To speak the ceremonial rites of marriage?
What says Lucentio to this shame of ours?

KATE
No shame but mine. I must, forsooth,° be forced   **forsooth:** indeed
To give my hand opposed against my heart
Unto a mad-brain rudesby,° full of spleen,°   **rudesby:** boor; **spleen:** capriciousness 10
Who wooed in haste and means to wed at leisure.
I told you, I, he was a frantic fool,
Hiding his bitter jests in blunt behavior.
And to be noted for° a merry man,   **noted for:** known as
He'll woo a thousand, 'point the day of marriage,
Make friends, invite, and proclaim the banns, 15
Yet never means to wed where he hath wooed.
Now must the world point at poor Katherine
And say, "Lo, there is mad Petruchio's wife,
If it would please him come and marry her." 20

TRANIO
Patience, good Katherine, and Baptista too.
Upon my life, Petruchio means but well,
Whatever fortune stays him from his word.
Though he be blunt, I know him passing wise;
Though he be merry, yet withal° he's honest.   **withal:** at the same time 25

DISCOVERING SHAKESPEARE

(60) Costumes [3.2.1]: Create a costume design for each of the major characters at the beginning of act 3, scene 2. How much off-stage time will each actor have to change into his or her new costume for this scene? Why do Petruchio and Grumio need more time to change than the other characters?

(61) Characterization [3.2.24–25]: Tranio, in his disguise as a suitor to Bianca, assures everyone that Petruchio is "wise" and "honest" (24–25). Do you agree with this description of Petruchio? Why or why not?

KATE
　Would Katherine had never seen him though!

Exit weeping.

BAPTISTA
　Go, girl, I cannot blame thee now to weep,
　For such an injury would vex a very saint,
　Much more a shrew of thy impatient humor.° | **humor:** disposition

　Enter Biondello.

BIONDELLO　Master, master, old° news! And such news as | **old:** great, rare (Baptista misunderstands)　30
you never heard of!

BAPTISTA　Is it new and old too? How may that be?

BIONDELLO　Why, is it not news to hear of Petruchio's
coming?

BAPTISTA　Is he come?

BIONDELLO　Why, no, sir.

BAPTISTA　What then?

BIONDELLO　He is coming.

BAPTISTA　When will he be here?

BIONDELLO　When he stands where I am and sees you
there.

TRANIO　But say, what to° thine old news? | **to:** about

BIONDELLO　Why, Petruchio is coming, in a new hat and
an old jerkin;° a pair of old breeches thrice turned; a pair
of boots that have been candle cases,° one buckled, another laced; an old rusty sword ta'en out of the town ar-
mory, with a broken hilt and chapeless;° with two
broken points;° his horse hipped° — with an old mothy
saddle and stirrups of no kindred — besides, possessed°
with the glanders° and like to mose in the chine;° troubled with the lampas,° infected with the fashions,° full of
windgalls,° sped with spavins,° rayed with the yellows,°
past cure of the fives,° stark° spoiled with the staggers,°
begnawn with the bots,° swayed in the back, and
shoulder-shotten;° near-legged before,° and with a half-
checked bit° and a headstall° of sheep's leather° which,
being restrained° to keep him from stumbling, hath
been often burst and new-repaired with knots; one
girth six times pieced,° and a woman's crupper° of velure°
which hath two letters° for her name fairly set down in
studs, and here and there pieced° with packthread.

BAPTISTA　Who comes with him?

BIONDELLO　O sir, his lackey, for all the world ca-
parisoned like the horse: with a linen stock° on one leg
and a kersey boothose° on the other, gartered with a red
and blue list;° an old hat and the humor of forty fancies°
pricked° in't for a feather — a monster, a very monster in
apparel, and not like a Christian footboy° or a gentleman's lackey.

jerkin: jacket
candle cases: (worn-out boots were sometimes hung on the wall to hold candle ends and the like)
chapeless: without the metal plate on the scabbard covering the sword point　35
points: laces holding up his breeches; **hipped:** lamed in the hip
possessed: afflicted
glanders: horse disease affecting the nose and mouth; **mose . . . chine:** grow weak in the back (chine is the spine, but mose has not been satisfactorily explained)　40
lampas: infected mouth; **fashions:** (or "farcins") equine ulcerations
windgalls: leg tumors; **sped . . . spavins:** destroyed by inflammations of the joints; **rayed . . . yellows:** streaked with jaundice　45
fives: (or "avives") swelling of the glands behind the ears; **stark:** utterly; **staggers:** equine palsy
begnawn . . . bots: eaten up by intestinal worms
shoulder-shotten: weak in the shoulder; **near-legged before:** knock-kneed in front　50
half-checked bit: bit that is only halfway effective; **headstall:** part of the bridle going around the head; **sheep's leather:** (inferior to pigskin)
restrained: drawn back　55
pieced: patched; **crupper:** strap that passes under the horse's tail to keep the saddle in place; **velure:** velvet (the crupper would normally be of leather; a velvet one would be largely useless for serious riding)
two letters: (the initials of the woman whose velvet crupper Petruchio is using)　60
pieced: tied together
stock: stocking
kersey boothose: coarse woolen overstocking
list: strip of cloth; **humor . . . fancies:** (not satisfactorily explained: presumably a wildly fanciful decoration)　65
pricked: pinned
footboy: page

DISCOVERING SHAKESPEARE

(62) Verse [3.2.43]: Why is Biondello's description of Petruchio and his horse in prose rather than in verse? Select any three lines, and try to rewrite them in verse. Have you improved the speech? Why or why not?

(63) Renaissance History [3.2.68]: According to Biondello, how many different equine diseases does Petruchio's horse suffer from? Pick any three of them, and look them up in a modern scientific dictionary. Then find a late sixteenth-century definition of all three in the *Oxford English Dictionary*. How have the meanings of these diseases changed over the years?

TRANIO
'Tis some odd humor° pricks° him to this fashion,   **humor:** whim; **pricks:** drives   70
Yet oftentimes he goes but mean-appareled.
BAPTISTA   I am glad he's come, howsoe'er he comes.
BIONDELLO   Why, sir, he comes not.
BAPTISTA   Didst thou not say he comes?
BIONDELLO   Who? That Petruchio came?   75
BAPTISTA   Ay, that Petruchio came.
BIONDELLO   No, sir, I say his horse comes, with him on
his back.
BAPTISTA   Why, that's all one.°   **all one:** the same thing
BIONDELLO   *[Sings.]*
    Nay, by Saint Jamy,   80
    I hold° you a penny,   **hold:** bet
    A horse and a man
    Is more than one
    And yet not many.
 Enter Petruchio and Grumio.
PETRUCHIO
Come, where be these gallants? Who's at home?   85
BAPTISTA
You are welcome, sir.
PETRUCHIO   And yet I come not well.
BAPTISTA   And yet you halt° not.   **halt:** limp (Baptista quibbles on *come* in the sense
TRANIO   Not so well appareled as I wish you were.   of "walk")
PETRUCHIO
Were it° better, I should rush in' thus.   **it:** i.e., my apparel
But where is Kate? Where is my lovely bride?   90
How does my father? Gentles, methinks you frown.
And wherefore gaze this goodly company
As if they saw some wondrous monument,
Some comet or unusual prodigy?°   **prodigy:** unnatural phenomenon
BAPTISTA
Why, sir, you know this is your wedding day.   95
First were we sad, fearing you would not come,
Now sadder that you come so unprovided.°   **unprovided:** improperly equipped
Fie, doff this habit,° shame to your estate,°   **habit:** clothing; **estate:** social position
An eyesore to our solemn festival.
TRANIO
And tell us what occasion of import   100
Hath all so long detained you from your wife
And sent you hither so unlike yourself?
PETRUCHIO
Tedious it were to tell and harsh to hear.
Sufficeth I am come to keep my word,
Though in some part enforcèd to digress,°   **digress:** deviate (from his intention to dress well;   105
Which at more leisure I will so excuse   see 2.1.316)
As you shall well be satisfied with all.
But where is Kate? I stay too long from her.
The morning wears,° 'tis time we were at church.   **wears:** is passing

---

DISCOVERING SHAKESPEARE

(64) <u>Verse</u> [3.2.85–88]: What comic effect is achieved by the mixture of <u>prose</u> and <u>verse</u> lines immediately after Petruchio's entrance in act 3, scene 2 (lines 85–88)? Which of the lines are in <u>verse</u>, and which are in <u>prose</u>? Why do you think Petruchio shifts into <u>verse</u> at line 89?

TRANIO
See not your bride in these unreverent robes.   110
Go to my chamber; put on clothes of mine.
PETRUCHIO
Not I, believe me. Thus I'll visit her.
BAPTISTA
But thus, I trust, you will not marry her?
PETRUCHIO
Good sooth,° even thus. Therefore ha' done with words.   **Good sooth:** indeed
To me she's married, not unto my clothes.   115
Could I repair what she will wear° in me   **wear:** wear out
As I can change these poor accoutrements,
'Twere well for Kate and better for myself.
But what a fool am I to chat with you
When I should bid good morrow to my bride   120
And seal the title° with a lovely° kiss.   **seal the title:** confirm my rights;
                          Exit [with Grumio].   **lovely:** loving
TRANIO
He hath some meaning in his mad attire.
We will persuade him, be it possible,
To put on better ere he go to church.
BAPTISTA
I'll after him and see the event° of this.   **event:** outcome   125
                Exit [with Bianca, Gremio, and Attendants].
TRANIO
But sir, to love concerneth us to add   **to love . . . liking:** i.e., to woo Bianca successfully
Her father's liking,° which to bring to pass,   we need her father's approval in addition (the speech
As I before imparted to your worship,   appears to begin in the middle of the conversation)
I am to get a man – whate'er he be
It skills° not much, we'll fit him to our turn° –   **skills:** matters; **turn:** purpose   130
And he shall be Vincentio of Pisa,
And make assurance° here in Padua   **make assurance:** give guarantees
Of greater sums than I have promisèd.
So shall you quietly enjoy your hope
And marry sweet Bianca with consent.   135
LUCENTIO
Were it not that my fellow schoolmaster
Doth watch Bianca's steps so narrowly,°   **narrowly:** closely
'Twere good, methinks, to steal our marriage,°   **steal . . . marriage:** elope
Which once performed, let all the world say no,
I'll keep mine own despite of all the world.   140
TRANIO
That by degrees we mean to look into
And watch our vantage° in this business.   **watch our vantage:** look out for our
We'll overreach the graybeard, Gremio,   opportunity
The narrow-prying father, Minola,
The quaint° musician, amorous Litio –   **quaint:** crafty   145

DISCOVERING SHAKESPEARE

(65) Verse [3.2.115–118]: Read Petruchio's speech to Baptista in lines 114–121; then write a prose paraphrase of these lines on a separate piece of paper. What is gained or lost in changing the speech from verse to prose?

(66) Plot [3.2.129]: Why does Tranio have to "get a man" to play the role of Vincentio of Pisa (3.2.129–131)? How will this device help further the plot of the play?

All for my master's sake, Lucentio.
   Enter Gremio.
Signor Gremio, come you from the church?
GREMIO
  As willingly as e'er I came from school.
TRANIO
  And is the bride and bridegroom coming home?
GREMIO
  A bridegroom, say you? 'Tis a groom° indeed,   **groom:** (quibbling on "servant," "boor")   150
  A grumbling groom, and that the girl shall find.
TRANIO
  Curster than she? Why, 'tis impossible.
GREMIO
  Why, he's a devil, a devil, a very fiend.
TRANIO
  Why, she's a devil, a devil, the devil's dam.°   **dam:** mother
GREMIO
  Tut, she's a lamb, a dove, a fool to° him.   **a fool to:** an innocent compared with   155
  I'll tell you, Sir Lucentio. When the priest
  Did ask if Katherine should be his wife,
  "Ay, by gogs wouns,°" quoth he, and swore so loud   **by gogs wouns:** by God's (Christ's) wounds
  That, all amazed, the priest let fall the book,
  And as he stooped again to take it up   160
  This mad-brained bridegroom took° him such a cuff   **took:** gave
  That down fell priest and book, and book and priest.
  "Now, take° them up," quoth he, "if any list."°   **take:** pick; **if any list:** if anyone pleases
TRANIO
  What said the wench when he rose again?
GREMIO
  Trembled and shook, for why° he stamped and swore,   **for why:** because   165
  As if the vicar meant to cozen° him.   **cozen:** cheat (with an invalid ceremony)
  But after many ceremonies done
  He calls for wine. "A health!" quoth he, as if
  He had been aboard, carousing to his mates
  After a storm; quaffed off the muscadel°   **muscadel:** (or muscatel) a sweet wine (Petruchio   170
  And threw the sops° all in the sexton's face,   should be offering it to the guests, not drinking it
  Having no other reason   himself)
  But that his beard grew thin and hungerly°   **sops:** cakes dipped in the wine
  And seemed to ask him° sops as he was drinking.   **hungerly:** sparsely
  This done, he took the bride about the neck   **ask him:** ask him for
  And kissed her lips with such a clamorous smack   175
  That at the parting all the church did echo.
  I, seeing this, came thence for very shame,
  And after me, I know, the rout° is coming.   **rout:** mob
  Such a mad marriage never was before.
  Hark, hark, I hear the minstrels play.   180
   Music plays.

DISCOVERING SHAKESPEARE

(67) Teaser [3.2.155]: Why does Shakespeare have Gremio report what happened at Petruchio and Kate's wedding? Why doesn't the playwright simply show the wedding on stage? (*Hint:* Can you think of any Renaissance plays that include an on-stage wedding?)

(68) Music [3.2.181]: When Gremio says "Hark, hark, I hear the minstrels play" (3.2.181), most productions add some off-stage music. Where else is music called for in the <u>script</u>? Would you add music at any other moments in the play? Why?

Enter Petruchio, Kate, Bianca, Hortensio [as Litio],
Baptista [, and Grumio, with Attendants].

PETRUCHIO
Gentlemen and friends, I thank you for your pains.
I know you think to dine with me today
And have prepared great store of wedding cheer,°   **cheer:** entertainment
But so it is, my haste doth call me hence   185
And therefore here I mean to take my leave.

BAPTISTA
Is't possible you will away tonight?

PETRUCHIO
I must away today, before night come.
Make° it no wonder. If you knew my business   **Make:** consider
You would entreat me rather go than stay.   190
And, honest company, I thank you all,
That have beheld me give away myself
To this most patient, sweet, and virtuous wife.
Dine with my father, drink a health to me,
For I must hence; and farewell to you all.   195

TRANIO
Let us entreat you stay till after dinner.

PETRUCHIO
It may not be.

GREMIO   Let me entreat you.

PETRUCHIO
It cannot be.

KATE   Let me entreat you.   200

PETRUCHIO
I am content.

KATE   Are you content to stay?

PETRUCHIO
I am content you shall entreat me stay,
But yet not stay, entreat me how you can.

KATE
Now if you love me, stay.

PETRUCHIO   Grumio, my horse!°   **horse:** horses (old plural)

GRUMIO   Ay, sir, they be ready; the oats have eaten the   **the oats . . . horses:** (Grumio gets it backwards)   205
horses.°

KATE
Nay then,
Do what thou canst, I will not go today,
No, nor tomorrow nor till I please myself.
The door is open, sir, there lies your way;   210
You may be jogging whiles your boots are green.°   **You may . . . green:** (proverbial for getting an early start); **green:** i.e., fresh
For me, I'll not be gone till I please myself.
'Tis like you'll prove a jolly° surly groom,   **jolly:** arrogant
That take it on you° at the first so roundly.°   **take it on you:** assert yourself; **roundly:** unceremoniously

PETRUCHIO
O Kate, content thee; prithee, be not angry.   215

DISCOVERING SHAKESPEARE

(69) Language [3.2.205–206]: Scholars are uncertain why Grumio tells Petruchio that "the oats have eaten the horses" (3.2.205–206). What do you think he means? <u>Paraphrase</u> these words on a separate sheet of paper.

KATE
    I will be angry. What hast thou to do?°   **What . . . do:** what business is it of yours
    Father, be quiet, he shall stay my leisure.
GREMIO
    Ay, marry, sir, now it begins to work.
KATE
    Gentlemen, forward to the bridal dinner.
    I see a woman may be made a fool   220
    If she had not a spirit to resist.
PETRUCHIO
    They shall go forward, Kate, at thy command.
    Obey the bride, you that attend on her,
    Go to the feast, revel and domineer,°   **domineer:** carouse
    Carouse full measure to her maidenhead,   225
    Be mad and merry or go hang yourselves.
    But for my bonny Kate, she must with me.
    Nay, look not big,° nor stamp, nor stare, nor fret;   **big:** threatening
    I will be master of what is mine own.
    She is my goods, my chattels; she is my house,   230
    My household stuff, my field, my barn,
    My horse, my ox, my ass,° my anything;   **my house . . . ass:** (echoing the Tenth
    And here she stands, touch her whoever dare.   Commandment, "Thou shalt not covet thy
    I'll bring mine action° on the proudest he   neighbor's house, . . . nor his ox, nor his ass . . .")
    That stops my way in Padua. Grumio,   **action:** lawsuit
    Draw forth thy weapon, we are beset with thieves.   235
    Rescue thy mistress, if thou be a man.
    Fear not, sweet wench; they shall not touch thee, Kate.
    I'll buckler° thee against a million.   **buckler:** shield
                     Exeunt Petruchio, Kate [, and Grumio].
BAPTISTA
    Nay, let them go, a couple of quiet ones.   240
GREMIO
    Went they not quickly, I should die with laughing.
TRANIO
    Of all mad matches never was the like.
LUCENTIO
    Mistress, what's your opinion of your sister?
BIANCA
    That being mad herself, she's madly mated.
GREMIO
    I warrant him, Petruchio is Kated.   245
BAPTISTA
    Neighbors and friends, though bride and bridegroom
        wants°   **wants:** are missing
    For to supply the places at the table,
    You know there wants no junkets° at the feast.   **junkets:** delicacies
    Lucentio, you supply the bridegroom's place,
    And let Bianca take her sister's room.°   **room:** place   250

DISCOVERING SHAKESPEARE

(70) Renaissance History [3.2.229–233]: How much power and control did men have over their wives during the English Renaissance? Is Petruchio correct in boasting that he has absolute authority over Kate and that she is little more than a "possession," like his horse or his ox? To what extent do you think Petruchio believes his own words here? Compare his language in this speech to the tenth commandment in the Bible.

TRANIO
Shall sweet Bianca practice how to bride it?
BAPTISTA
She shall, Lucentio. Come, gentlemen, let's go. *Exeunt.*

❧ **4.1**° *Enter Grumio.*

4.1: Petruchio's country house

GRUMIO Fie, fie, on all tired jades,° on all mad masters, and all foul ways!° Was ever man so beaten? Was ever man so rayed?° Was ever man so weary? I am sent before to make a fire, and they are coming after to warm them. Now were not I a little pot and soon hot,° my very lips might freeze to my teeth, my tongue to the roof of my mouth, my heart in my belly, ere I should come by a fire to thaw me. But I with blowing the fire shall warm myself, for considering the weather, a taller° man than I will take cold. Holla, ho! Curtis.
  Enter Curtis (a Servant).

jades: worthless horses
ways: roads
rayed: dirtied

a little . . . hot: (proverbial for a small person easily angered) 5

taller: better

10

CURTIS Who is that° calls so coldly?

is that: is it who

GRUMIO A piece of ice. If thou doubt it, thou mayst slide from my shoulder to my heel with no greater a run but my head and my neck. A fire, good Curtis.

CURTIS Is my master and his wife coming, Grumio?

15

GRUMIO O ay, Curtis, ay, and therefore fire, fire; cast on no water.°

fire . . . water: (alluding to the popular round "Scotland's Burning": "Fire, fire! Cast on water!")

CURTIS Is she so hot a shrew as she's reported?

GRUMIO She was, good Curtis, before this frost. But thou know'st winter tames man, woman, and beast, for it hath tamed my old master and my new mistress and myself, fellow Curtis.

20

CURTIS Away, you three-inch° fool! I am no beast.°

three-inch: i.e., very short; **I am no beast:** (Grumio having called himself a *beast* and Curtis his *fellow*)

GRUMIO Am I but three inches? Why, thy horn° is a foot, and so long am I at the least. But wilt thou make a fire or shall I complain on thee to our mistress, whose hand – she being now at hand – thou shalt soon feel, to thy cold comfort, for being slow in thy hot office?°

horn: i.e., of a cuckold 25

hot office: task of providing heat

CURTIS I prithee, good Grumio, tell me, how goes the world?

30

GRUMIO A cold world, Curtis, in every office but thine, and therefore fire. Do thy duty, and have thy duty,° for my master and mistress are almost frozen to death.

have thy duty: have thy due, reward (proverbial)

CURTIS There's fire ready, and therefore, good Grumio, the news.

35

GRUMIO Why, *[Sings.]* "Jack boy, ho boy," and as much news as thou wilt.

CURTIS Come, you are so full of cony-catching.°

cony-catching: trickery (a cony being a rabbit; with a play on *Jack boy, ho boy*, a "catch" or round)

DISCOVERING SHAKESPEARE

(71) Costumes [4.1.1]: How is Grumio dressed at the beginning of act 4, scene 1? How can his clothes indicate his social status, the weather, and the relative luxury (or lack thereof) of Petruchio's country house?

(72) Language [4.1.23]: Does the language in the first thirty lines of this scene give us any clue concerning Grumio's size? Is he particularly tall or short? Which lines hint at his stature? Do any of the lines carry an additional bawdy meaning? If so, which ones?

GRUMIO   Why therefore fire, for I have caught extreme cold. Where's the cook? Is supper ready, the house trimmed, rushes strewed,° cobwebs swept, the servingmen in their new fustian° and white stockings, and every officer his wedding garment on? Be the jacks° fair within, the jills° fair without, the carpets° laid, and everything in order?

CURTIS   All ready, and therefore, I pray thee, news.

GRUMIO   First, know my horse is tired, my master and mistress fall'n out.

CURTIS   How?

GRUMIO   Out of their saddles into the dirt – and thereby hangs a tale.

CURTIS   Let's ha't, good Grumio.

GRUMIO   Lend thine ear.

CURTIS   Here.

GRUMIO   There.

[Strikes him.]

CURTIS   This is to feel a tale, not to hear a tale.

GRUMIO   And therefore 'tis called a sensible° tale, and this cuff was but to knock at your ear and beseech listening. Now I begin. Imprimis,° we came down a foul hill, my master riding behind my mistress –

CURTIS   Both of° one horse?

GRUMIO   What's that to thee?

CURTIS   Why, a horse.

GRUMIO   Tell thou the tale – but hadst thou not crossed° me thou shouldst have heard how her horse fell, and she under her horse; thou shouldst have heard in how miry a place; how she was bemoiled,° how he left her with the horse upon her, how he beat me because her horse stumbled, how she waded through the dirt to pluck him off me; how he swore, how she prayed, that never prayed before; how I cried, how the horses ran away, how her bridle was burst; how I lost my crupper – with many things of worthy memory, which now shall die in oblivion, and thou return unexperienced° to thy grave.

CURTIS   By this reck'ning he is more shrew than she.

GRUMIO   Ay, and that thou and the proudest of you all shall find when he comes home. But what° talk I of this? Call forth Nathaniel, Joseph, Nicholas, Philip, Walter, Sugarsop, and the rest. Let their heads be sleekly combed, their blue coats° brushed, and their garters of an indifferent° knit. Let them curtsy with their left legs°

rushes strewed: i.e., on the floor (the normal floor covering)

fustian: coarse cotton cloth

jacks: leather drinking vessels (playing on "fellows," servingmen)

jills: metal measuring cups (playing on "girls," maidservants); **carpets:** table covers

sensible: (playing on "capable of being felt")

Imprimis: first

of: on

crossed: interrupted

bemoiled: bemired

unexperienced: (hence ignorant)

what: why

blue coats: (dark blue was the usual color of a servant's dress)

indifferent: (either not different, matching, or any knit whatever); **curtsy . . . legs:** (like kissing their hands, absurdly elaborate forms of welcome)

40
45
50
55
60
65
70
75
80

DISCOVERING SHAKESPEARE

(73) Renaissance History [4.1.41]: What were "rushes" (4.1.41) used for in a typical Renaissance house or tavern?

(74) Costumes [4.1.59]: Read Grumio's description of what happened to Kate and Petruchio during their journey to his country house (4.1.59–75); then design costumes for each that would reflect their misfortunes. Write your descriptions of the two costumes on a separate sheet of paper.

(75) Plot [4.1.76]: What does Curtis mean when he claims that "he is more shrew than she" (4.1.76)? To what extent do you think Petruchio's behavior in this scene is part of his plan to "tame" Kate?

and not presume to touch a hair of my master's horse-
tail till they kiss their hands. Are they all ready?

CURTIS They are. 85

GRUMIO Call them forth.

CURTIS Do you hear, ho! You must meet my master to
countenance° my mistress.

> **countenance:** do honor to (Grumio then quibbles on countenance as *face*)

GRUMIO Why, she hath a face of her own.

CURTIS Who knows not that? 90

GRUMIO Thou, it seems, that calls for company to countenance her.

CURTIS I call them forth to credit° her.

> **credit:** pay respect to (Grumio then quibbles on the financial sense)

Enter four or five Servingmen.

GRUMIO Why, she comes to borrow nothing of them.

NATHANIEL Welcome home, Grumio! 95

PHILIP How now, Grumio?

JOSEPH What, Grumio!

NICHOLAS Fellow Grumio!

NATHANIEL How now, old lad!

GRUMIO Welcome, you; how now, you; what, you; fellow, you; and thus much for greeting. Now, my spruce
companions, is all ready and all things neat? 100

NATHANIEL All things is ready. How near is our master?

GRUMIO E'en at hand, alighted by this.° And therefore be
not – Cock's passion,° silence, I hear my master.

> **this:** this time
> **Cock's passion:** God's (Christ's) passion (on the Cross)

105

Enter Petruchio and Kate.

PETRUCHIO
Where be these knaves? What, no man at door
To hold my stirrup nor to take my horse?
Where is Nathaniel, Gregory, Philip?

ALL SERVINGMEN Here, here, sir; here, sir.

PETRUCHIO
Here, sir; here, sir; here, sir; here, sir! 110
You loggerheaded° and unpolished grooms!
What, no attendance? No regard? No duty?
Where is the foolish knave I sent before.

> **loggerheaded:** blockheaded

GRUMIO
Here, sir, as foolish as I was before.

PETRUCHIO
You peasant swain,° you whoreson° malt-horse drudge!° 115
Did I not bid thee meet me in the park°
And bring along these rascal knaves with thee?

> **swain:** lout; **whoreson:** contemptible;
> **malt-horse drudge:** brewer's horse (which ploddingly turns a grain mill)
> **park:** deer park

GRUMIO
Nathaniel's coat, sir, was not fully made,
And Gabriel's pumps were all unpinked° i' th' heel.
There was no link° to color Peter's hat, 120
And Walter's dagger was not come from sheathing.
There were none fine° but Adam, Rafe, and Gregory;

> **unpinked:** without their ornamental patterns
> **link:** torch (the smoke was used to blacken hats)
> **fine:** well turned out

DISCOVERING SHAKESPEARE

(76) Characterization [4.1.106]: Describe the different moods of Kate and Petruchio when they enter his country house in 4.1.106. Is either of them happy? Why or why not?

The rest were ragged, old, and beggarly.
Yet, as they are, here are they come to meet you.

PETRUCHIO
Go, rascals, go, and fetch my supper in.   125

Exeunt Servants.

[Sings.]
          "Where is the life that late I led?
          Where are those° – ?"
Sit down, Kate,

[They sit at table.]
And welcome. Food, food, food, food!

Enter Servants with supper.
Why, when, I say? – Nay, good sweet Kate, be merry.   130
Off with my boots, you rogues! You villains, when?

[Sings.]
          "It was the friar of orders gray,
          As he forth walkèd on his way" –
Out, you rogue! You pluck my foot awry.

[Strikes him.]
Take that, and mend° the plucking off the other.   135
Be merry, Kate. Some water here, what ho!

Enter one with water.
Where's my spaniel Troilus? Sirrah, get you hence
And bid my cousin Ferdinand come hither –

[Exit Servant.]
One, Kate, that you must kiss and be acquainted with.
Where are my slippers? Shall I have some water?   140
Come, Kate, and wash, and welcome heartily.
You whoreson villain, will you let it fall?

[Strikes him.]

KATE
Patience, I pray you, 'twas a fault unwilling.

PETRUCHIO
A whoreson, beetle-headed,° flap-eared knave!
Come, Kate, sit down; I know you have a stomach.°   145
Will you give thanks,° sweet Kate, or else shall I?
What's this, mutton?

FIRST SERVANT°   Ay.

PETRUCHIO   Who brought it?

PETER   I.   150

PETRUCHIO
'Tis burnt, and so is all the meat.
What dogs are these! Where is the rascal cook?
How durst you, villains, bring it from the dresser,°
And serve it thus to me that love it not?

[He throws it at them.]
There, take it to you, trenchers,° cups, and all.   155
You heedless joltheads and unmannered slaves!
What, do you grumble? I'll be with you° straight.

[Exeunt Servants.]

Where are those: (the ballad continues, "Where are those pleasant days?")

mend: do better at

beetle-headed: blockheaded, stupid (the "head" of a "beetle," or mallet, being a heavy block of wood)

stomach: appetite (playing on "temper")

give thanks: i.e., say grace

FIRST SERVANT: (Curtis or Peter)

dresser: sideboard

trenchers: wooden plates

with you: even with you

DISCOVERING SHAKESPEARE

(77) Plot [4.1.134]: What are Petruchio's principal complaints about his servants in 4.1.106–168? How does Kate react to his anger?

KATE
I pray you, husband, be not so disquiet.
The meat was well if you were so contented.

PETRUCHIO
I tell thee, Kate, 'twas burnt and dried away, 160
And I expressly am forbid to touch it,
For it engenders choler,° planteth anger,
And better 'twere that both of us did fast,
Since of ourselves, ourselves are choleric,
Than feed it° with such overroasted flesh. 165
Be patient. Tomorrow't shall be mended,
And for this night we'll fast in company.
Come, I will bring thee to thy bridal chamber.   *Exeunt.*
       Enter Servants severally.°

NATHANIEL   Peter, didst ever see the like?

PETER   He kills her in her own humor.° 170
       Enter Curtis.

GRUMIO   Where is he?

CURTIS   In her chamber, making a sermon of continency
to her,
And rails and swears and rates,° that° she, poor soul,
Knows not which way to stand, to look, to speak, 175
And sits as one new-risen from a dream.
Away, away, for he is coming hither.   *[Exeunt.]*
       Enter Petruchio.

PETRUCHIO
Thus have I politicly° begun my reign,
And 'tis my hope to end successfully.
My falcon now is sharp° and passing empty, 180
And till she stoop° she must not be full-gorged,
For then she never looks upon her lure.°
Another way I have to man° my haggard,°
To make her come and know her keeper's call:
That is, to watch° her as we watch these kites° 185
That bate and beat° and will not be obedient.
She ate no meat today, nor none shall eat.
Last night she slept not, nor tonight she shall not.
As with the meat, some undeservèd fault
I'll find about the making of the bed, 190
And here I'll fling the pillow, there the bolster,°
This way the coverlet, another way the sheets.
Ay, and amid this hurly I intend°
That all is done in reverent care of her.
And in conclusion she shall watch all night, 195
And if she chance to nod I'll rail and brawl
And with the clamor keep her still awake.

choler: that "humor" (hot and dry) which produces anger (roast meat was to be avoided by persons of such disposition)

it: i.e., their choler

severally: at different doors

kills . . . humor: subdues her by acting like her

rates: berates; **that:** so that

politicly: cunningly

sharp: starved
stoop: fly to and seize the lure (playing on "bow to authority")
lure: decoy bird used to recall a hawk
man: tame (hawking term, with a quibble); **haggard:** wild female hawk
watch: keep awake (as in taming a wild hawk); **kites:** inferior hawks
bate and beat: flutter and flap the wings

bolster: long narrow cushion supporting the pillow

intend: pretend

DISCOVERING SHAKESPEARE

(78) Renaissance History [4.1.162]: What was "choler" (4.1.162), and how would fasting help diminish its symptoms? Which foods were assumed to increase choler? (*Hint:* See especially 4.3.19 and Robert Burton's *Anatomy of Melancholy*.)

(79) Soliloquy [4.1.183]: Once again, Shakespeare gives Petruchio a soliloquy without allowing Kate to have one. Note especially Petruchio's direct address to the audience in the following lines: "He that knows better how to tame a shrew, / Now let him speak; 'tis charity to show" (4.1.200–201). With which of the major characters do you most identify at this point in the play? Why? Write your answer on a separate sheet of paper.

This is a way to kill a wife with kindness,°
And thus I'll curb her mad and headstrong humor.°
He that knows better how to tame a shrew,°
Now let him speak: 'tis charity to show.   *Exit.*

kill . . . kindness: (ironically, referring to the proverb for spoiling a wife through overindulgence)
humor: disposition   200
shrew: (pronounced "shrow"; a rhyme with *show*)

❧ **4.2**°   *Enter Tranio [as Lucentio] and Hortensio*
[as Litio].

4.2: Before Baptista's house

TRANIO
Is't possible, friend Litio, that Mistress Bianca
Doth fancy any other but Lucentio?
I tell you, sir, she bears me fair in hand.°

bears . . . hand: encourages me

HORTENSIO
Sir, to satisfy you in what I have said,
Stand by and mark the manner of his teaching.
[They stand aside.]
Enter Bianca [and Lucentio as Cambio].

5

LUCENTIO
Now mistress, profit you in what you read?°

read: study

BIANCA
What, master, read° you? First resolve° me that.

read: (quibbling on "teach"); **resolve:** answer

LUCENTIO
I read that I profess,° *The Art to Love.*°

that I profess: what I'm an expert on; **The Art to Love:** Ovid's *Ars amatoria*

BIANCA
And may you prove, sir, master of your art.°

master . . . art: (quibbling on the "M.A. degree")

LUCENTIO
While you, sweet dear, prove mistress of my heart.
[They stand aside.]

10

HORTENSIO   *[Advancing with Tranio]*
Quick proceeders,° marry!° Now tell me, I pray,
You that durst swear that your mistress Bianca
Loved none in the world so well as Lucentio –

proceeders: degree candidates; **marry:** indeed (originally an oath on the name of the Virgin Mary)

TRANIO
O despiteful° love, unconstant womankind!
I tell thee, Litio, this is wonderful.°

despiteful: spiteful
wonderful: amazing   15

HORTENSIO
Mistake no more: I am not Litio,
Nor a musician, as I seem to be,
But one that scorn to live in this disguise,
For such a one as leaves a gentleman
And makes a god of such a cullion.°
Know, sir, that I am called Hortensio.

cullion: scoundrel (the schoolmaster)   20

TRANIO
Signor Hortensio, I have often heard
Of your entire affection to Bianca,
And since mine eyes are witness of her lightness°
I will, with you, if you be so contented,
Forswear Bianca and her love forever.

lightness: inconstancy

25

DISCOVERING SHAKESPEARE

(80) Themes [4.2.1]: Give some thought to the different levels of reality in act 4, scene 2: Bianca and Lucentio are being observed by Tranio and Hortensio, who are in turn being watched by Sly, with the entire group of actors under the gaze of the audience. How does this "layering of reality" help mirror some of Shakespeare's major themes in the play?

HORTENSIO
  See how they kiss and court. Signor Lucentio,
  Here is my hand and here I firmly vow
  Never to woo her more, but do forswear her,
  As one unworthy all the former favors
  That I have fondly° flattered her withal.   30

fondly: foolishly

TRANIO
  And here I take the like unfeignèd oath,
  Never to marry with her though she would entreat.
  Fie on her, see how beastly° she doth court him.

beastly: lasciviously

HORTENSIO
  Would all the world but he had quite forsworn.°   35
  For me, that I may surely keep mine oath,
  I will be married to a wealthy widow
  Ere three days pass, which hath as long loved me
  As I have loved this proud disdainful haggard.°
  And so farewell, Signor Lucentio.   40
  Kindness in women, not their beauteous looks,
  Shall win my love – and so I take my leave,
  In resolution as I swore before.   *[Exit.]*

Would . . . forsworn: i.e., would that he were my only competition

haggard: wild hawk

TRANIO
  Mistress Bianca, bless you with such grace
  As 'longeth to a lover's blessed case.   45
  Nay, I have ta'en you napping, gentle love,
  And have forsworn you with Hortensio.

BIANCA *[Advancing.]*
  Tranio,° you jest. But have you both forsworn me?

Tranio: (Lucentio has revealed Tranio's identity to Bianca in 3.1.35)

TRANIO
  Mistress, we have.

LUCENTIO   Then we are rid of Litio.

TRANIO
  I' faith, he'll have a lusty° widow now,   50
  That shall be wooed and wedded in a day.

lusty: (1) merry, (2) lustful

BIANCA
  God give him joy.

TRANIO
  Ay, and he'll tame her.

BIANCA   He says so, Tranio.

TRANIO
  Faith, he is gone unto the taming school.

BIANCA
  The taming school? What, is there such a place?   55

TRANIO
  Ay, mistress, and Petruchio is the master,
  That teacheth tricks eleven and twenty long°
  To tame a shrew and charm her chattering tongue.
    Enter Biondello.

eleven . . . long: i.e., a great many (referring to the card game of one-and-thirty)

DISCOVERING SHAKESPEARE

(81) Staging [4.2.27]: If you were directing a production of this play, how would you stage the beginning 43 lines of 4.2, in which Tranio and Hortensio secretly watch the behavior of Bianca and Lucentio? Where would you put all the characters on stage?

(82) Plot [4.2.50]: Why do you think Shakespeare introduces a "wealthy widow" (4.2.37) at this point in the play? What does Hortensio's sudden interest in the widow tell us about his character? About Renaissance society in general?

BIONDELLO
  O master, master, I have watched so long
  That I am dog-weary, but at last I spied
  An ancient angel° coming down the hill
  Will serve the turn.°
TRANIO   What is he, Biondello?
BIONDELLO
  Master, a mercatante° or a pedant,°
  I know not what; but formal in apparel,
  In gait and countenance° surely like a father.
LUCENTIO
  And what of him, Tranio?
TRANIO
  If he be credulous and trust my tale°
  I'll make him glad to seem Vincentio,
  And give assurance to Baptista Minola
  As if he were the right Vincentio.
  Take in your love and then let me alone.
                 [Exeunt Lucentio and Bianca.]
   Enter a Pedant.
PEDANT
  God save you, sir.
TRANIO   And you, sir. You are welcome.
  Travel you far on,° or are you at the farthest?°
PEDANT
  Sir, at the farthest for a week or two,
  But then up farther and as far as Rome,
  And so to Tripoli,° if God lend me life.
TRANIO
  What countryman, I pray?
PEDANT   Of Mantua.
TRANIO
  Of Mantua, sir? Marry, God forbid!
  And come to Padua, careless of your life?
PEDANT
  My life, sir? How, I pray? For that goes hard.°
TRANIO
  'Tis death for anyone in Mantua
  To come to Padua. Know you not the cause?
  Your ships are stayed° at Venice, and the duke –
  For private quarrel 'twixt your duke and him –
  Hath published and proclaimed it openly.
  'Tis marvel, but that° you are newly come,
  You might have heard it else proclaimed about.
PEDANT
  Alas, sir, it is worse for me than so,
  For I have bills for money by exchange°
  From Florence and must here deliver them.
TRANIO
  Well, sir, to do you courtesy,°

angel: fellow of the good old stamp (an "angel" being a gold coin)

the turn: our purposes

mercatante: merchant; **pedant:** schoolmaster

countenance: appearance

trust my tale: believe what I tell him

far on: farther; **at the farthest:** i.e., at your destination

up . . . Tripoli: (Padua is "up" from Mantua, but Rome is very far south; Tripoli is either the North African city and state or the city in Syria)

goes hard: is serious

stayed: impounded

but that: except for the fact that

bills . . . exchange: (bills of exchange were money orders due on a certain date)

courtesy: a good turn

60

65

70

75

80

85

90

DISCOVERING SHAKESPEARE

(83) Plot [4.2.77]: What made-up story does Tranio use to encourage the Pedant to play the part of his "father"?

This will I do and thus I will advise you –
First, tell me, have you ever been at Pisa?

PEDANT
Ay, sir, in Pisa have I often been,
Pisa, renownèd for grave citizens.   95

TRANIO
Among them, know you one Vincentio?

PEDANT
I know him not but I have heard of him,
A merchant of incomparable wealth.

TRANIO
He is my father, sir, and sooth to say,
In count'nance somewhat doth resemble you.   100

BIONDELLO   *[Aside]* As much as an apple doth an oyster,
and all one.°   **all one:** no matter

TRANIO
To save your life in this extremity
This favor will I do you for his sake,
And think it not the worst of all your fortunes   105
That you are like to Sir Vincentio.
His name and credit° shall you undertake,°   **credit:** reputation; **undertake:** assume
And in my house you shall be friendly lodged.
Look that you take upon you° as you should.   **take upon you:** play your part
You understand me, sir. So shall you stay   110
Till you have done your business in the city.
If this be courtesy, sir, accept of it.

PEDANT
O sir, I do, and will repute° you ever   **repute:** consider
The patron of my life and liberty.

TRANIO
Then go with me to make the matter good.   115
This, by the way,° I let you understand.   **by the way:** along the way, as we go
My father is here looked for every day
To pass° assurance° of a dower in marriage   **pass:** convey (legal term);
'Twixt me and one Baptista's daughter here.   **assurance:** a guarantee
In all these circumstances I'll instruct you.   120
Go with me to clothe you as becomes you.   *Exeunt.*

❧ **4.3**°   *Enter Kate and Grumio.*   **4.3:** Petruchio's house

GRUMIO
No, no, forsooth, I dare not for my life.

KATE
The more my wrong,° the more his spite appears.   **my wrong:** i.e., the wrong done me
What, did he marry me to famish me?
Beggars that come unto my father's door,
Upon entreaty have a present° alms;   **a present:** immediate   5

DISCOVERING SHAKESPEARE

(84) <u>Asides</u> **[4.2.101]:** How does the playwright use <u>asides</u> (4.2.101), here and elsewhere in the <u>script</u>, to help manipulate audience response? Which characters have most of the <u>asides</u>? Why?

(85) <u>Blocking</u> **[4.3.1]:** Where are Grumio and Kate at the beginning of this scene, and what are they doing? What does Grumio mean when he says "I dare not for my life" (4.3.1)? Exactly what is he afraid to do?

If not, elsewhere they meet with charity.
But I, who never knew how to entreat
Nor never needed that I should entreat,
Am starved for meat,° giddy for lack of sleep,   **meat:** food
With oaths kept waking and with brawling fed.   10
And that which spites me more than all these wants,
He does it under name of perfect love,
As who° should say, if I should sleep or eat   **As who:** as though one
'Twere deadly sickness or else present death.
I prithee go and get me some repast,   15
I care not what, so it be wholesome food.

GRUMIO
What say you to a neat's foot?°   **a neat's foot:** an ox's or a calf's foot

KATE
'Tis passing good, I prithee let me have it.

GRUMIO
I fear it is too choleric° a meat.   **choleric:** engendering anger
How say you to a fat tripe finely broiled?   20

KATE
I like it well, good Grumio, fetch it me.

GRUMIO
I cannot tell; I fear 'tis choleric.
What say you to a piece of beef and mustard?

KATE
A dish that I do love to feed upon.

GRUMIO
Ay, but the mustard is too hot a little.   25

KATE
Why then, the beef, and let the mustard rest.

GRUMIO
Nay then, I will not; you shall have the mustard
Or else you get no beef of Grumio.

KATE
Then both or one, or anything thou wilt.

GRUMIO
Why then, the mustard without the beef.   30

KATE
Go, get thee gone, thou false deluding slave,
   Beats him.
That feed'st me with the very° name of meat.   **very:** i.e., mere
Sorrow on thee and all the pack of you
That triumph thus upon my misery.
Go, get thee gone, I say.   35
   Enter Petruchio and Hortensio with meat.

PETRUCHIO
How fares my Kate? What, sweeting,° all amort?°   **sweeting:** sweetheart; **all amort:** spiritless, dejected

HORTENSIO
Mistress, what cheer?

KATE   Faith, as cold as can be.

DISCOVERING SHAKESPEARE

(86) Renaissance History [4.3.19]: Do you think Grumio is honestly trying to improve Kate's health, or is he simply attempting to harass her? Why do you feel this way?

PETRUCHIO
  Pluck up thy spirits, look cheerfully upon me.
  Here, love, thou seest how diligent I am
  To dress° thy meat myself and bring it thee.   **dress:** prepare   40
  I am sure, sweet Kate, this kindness merits thanks.
  What, not a word? Nay then, thou lov'st it not,
  And all my pains is sorted to no proof.°   **is . . . proof:** have resulted in nothing
  Here, take away this dish.
KATE   I pray you, let it stand.
PETRUCHIO
  The poorest service is repaid with thanks,   45
  And so shall mine before you touch the meat.
KATE
  I thank you, sir.
HORTENSIO
  Signor Petruchio, fie, you are to blame.
  Come, Mistress Kate, I'll bear you company.
    [They sit at table.]
PETRUCHIO *[Aside]*
  Eat it up all, Hortensio, if thou lov'st me.   50
  Much good of it unto thy gentle heart.
  Kate, eat apace.° And now, my honey love,   **apace:** quickly
  Will we return unto thy father's house
  And revel it as bravely° as the best,   **bravely:** finely dressed
  With silken coats and caps and golden rings,   55
  With ruffs and cuffs and farthingales° and things;   **farthingales:** hooped petticoats
  With scarfs and fans and double change of bravery,°   **bravery:** finery
  With amber bracelets, beads, and all this knavery.
  What, hast thou dined? The tailor stays thy leisure,
  To deck thy body with his ruffling° treasure.   **ruffling:** ornamented with ruffles   60
    Enter Tailor [with a gown].
  Come, tailor, let us see these ornaments.
    Enter Haberdasher [with a cap].
  Lay forth the gown. – What news with you, sir?
HABERDASHER
  Here is the cap your worship did bespeak.°   **bespeak:** order
PETRUCHIO
  Why, this was molded on a porringer:°   **porringer:** porridge bowl
  A velvet dish. Fie, fie, 'tis lewd° and filthy.   **lewd:** vile   65
  Why, 'tis a cockle° or a walnut shell,   **cockle:** cockleshell
  A knack,° a toy, a trick,° a baby's cap.   **knack:** trinket; **trick:** trifle
  Away with it. Come, let me have a bigger.
KATE
  I'll have no bigger, this doth fit the time,°   **fit the time:** accord with present fashion
  And gentlewomen wear such caps as these.   70
PETRUCHIO
  When you are gentle you shall have one too,
  And not till then.

DISCOVERING SHAKESPEARE

(87) Staging [4.3.50]: Petruchio tells Hortensio to devour all the food (4.3.50), yet he also encourages Kate to "eat apace" (52). If you were directing a production of the play, how would you stage this scene? Would you allow Kate to eat any food at all? Why or why not?

HORTENSIO   That will not be in haste.

KATE
Why, sir, I trust I may have leave to speak,
And speak I will. I am no child, no babe.
Your betters have endured me say° my mind,   **say:** speak   75
And if you cannot, best you stop your ears.
My tongue will tell the anger of my heart
Or else my heart, concealing it, will break,
And rather than it shall, I will be free
Even to the uttermost, as I please, in words.   80

PETRUCHIO
Why, thou sayst true. It is a paltry cap,
A custard coffin,° a bauble, a silken pie.°   **custard coffin:** crust of a custard pie;
I love thee well in that thou lik'st it not.   **silken pie:** pie of silk

KATE
Love me or love me not, I like the cap,
And I will have it or I will have none.   85

                   [Exit Haberdasher.]

PETRUCHIO
Thy gown? Why, ay – come, tailor, let us see't.
O mercy, God, what masquing stuff° is here?   **masquing stuff:** clothing fit for masquerades
What's this, a sleeve? 'Tis like a demicannon.°   **demicannon:** large cannon
What, up and down carved like an apple tart?°   **carved . . . tart:** (the sleeve has slashes, like the
Here's snip and nip and cut and slish and slash,   slits in a piecrust, to show the fabric beneath)   90
Like to a censer° in a barber's shop.   **censer:** incense burner (with perforated cover)
Why, what a devil's name, tailor, call'st thou this?

HORTENSIO   *[Aside]*
I see she's like to have neither cap nor gown.

TAILOR
You bid me make it orderly and well,
According to the fashion and the time.   95

PETRUCHIO
Marry, I did. But if you be remembered,
I did not bid you mar it to the time.
Go, hop me over every kennel home,°   **hop . . . home:** you can hop home over every
For you shall hop without my custom, sir.   gutter for all I care
I'll none of it. Hence, make your best of it.   100

KATE
I never saw a better-fashioned gown,
More quaint,° more pleasing, nor more commendable.   **quaint:** elegant
Belike° you mean to make a puppet° of me.   **Belike:** it seems; **puppet:** (contemptuous term
                                           for a woman)

PETRUCHIO
Why, true, he means to make a puppet of thee.

TAILOR
She says your worship means to make a puppet of her.   105

DISCOVERING SHAKESPEARE

(88) <u>**Verse**</u> **[4.3.73]:** <u>Scan</u> Kate's speech from lines 73–80, paying particular attention to any unusual metrical patterns. Why do you think the play's normal <u>iambic pentameter</u> becomes so choppy and irregular in these lines? How does the agitated rhythm of the speech enable the actress to find and display Kate's predominant mood in this portion of the scene?
(89) **Language [4.3.104]:** Where else does Petruchio deliberately misunderstand Kate? How does this tactic help in his attempt to "tame" her?

PETRUCHIO
    O monstrous arrogance!
    Thou liest, thou thread, thou thimble,
    Thou yard, three-quarters, half-yard, quarter, nail!°
    Thou flea, thou nit,° thou winter cricket thou!
    Braved° in mine own house with° a skein of thread?
    Away, thou rag, thou quantity,° thou remnant,
    Or I shall so bemete° thee with thy yard°
    As thou shalt think on° prating whilst thou liv'st.
    I tell thee, I, that thou hast marred her gown.
TAILOR
    Your worship is deceived. The gown is made
    Just as my master had direction.
    Grumio gave order how it should be done.
GRUMIO   I gave him no order, I gave him the stuff.°
TAILOR
    But how did you desire it should be made?
GRUMIO   Marry, sir, with needle and thread.
TAILOR
    But did you not request to have it cut?
GRUMIO   Thou hast faced° many things.
TAILOR   I have.
GRUMIO   Face not me. Thou hast braved° many men:
brave not me. I will neither be faced nor braved. I say
unto thee, I bid thy master cut out the gown but I did
not bid him cut it to pieces. Ergo,° thou liest.
TAILOR   Why, here is the note of the fashion to testify.°
PETRUCHIO   Read it.
GRUMIO   The note lies in's throat° if he say I said so.
TAILOR   *[Reads.]* "Imprimis,° a loose-bodied gown –"
GRUMIO   Master, if ever I said loose-bodied gown,° sew
me in the skirts of it and beat me to death with a bot-
tom° of brown thread. I said, a gown.
PETRUCHIO   Proceed.
TAILOR   "With a small compassed° cape –"
GRUMIO   I confess the cape.
TAILOR   "With a trunk° sleeve –"
GRUMIO   I confess two sleeves.
TAILOR   "The sleeves curiously° cut."
PETRUCHIO   Ay, there's the villainy.
GRUMIO   Error i' th' bill, sir, error i' th' bill. I com-
manded the sleeves should be cut out and sewed up
again, and that I'll prove upon thee,° though thy little
finger be armed in a thimble.
TAILOR   This is true that I say. An I had thee in place
where° thou shouldst know it.

---

nail: two and a quarter inches (a measure of length for cloth)
nit: louse egg   110
Braved: defied; **with:** by
quantity: fragment
bemete: punish; **yard:** yardstick
think on: think before

115

stuff: cloth

faced: (1) trimmed, (2) faced down

braved: (1) dressed finely, (2) defied
125

Ergo: therefore (Latin)
to testify: as evidence

lies . . . throat: (1) is a low (musical) note, (2) is 130
an outrageous lie
Imprimis: first; **loose-bodied gown:** (Loose gowns were fashionable; all editors claim that the point is that prostitutes wore them, but they wore them because fashionable ladies wore them. The point is that there is nothing wrong with the dress.) 135
bottom: skein
compassed: flared
trunk: very full
curiously: elaborately 140

prove upon thee: maintain by defeating you in combat 145

An . . . where: if only I had you in the right place

110
120

DISCOVERING SHAKESPEARE

(90) Verse [4.3.118]: Why are lines 118–160 mostly in prose? How does this abrupt shift from verse to prose help suggest how the scene should be staged?

(91) Blocking [4.3.140]: Most productions of the play feature a mock battle between Grumio and the Tailor at some point in this scene. Where do you think such a fight would be most effective? What weapons would the combatants use? How does this comic battle mirror the play's larger symbolic confrontation between Kate and Petruchio?

GRUMIO   I am for thee straight. Take thou the bill,° give
   me thy meteyard,° and spare not me.

bill: (punning on the weapon: a bill was a halberd)
meteyard: yardstick

HORTENSIO   God-a-mercy, Grumio, then he shall have
   no odds.°

he . . . odds: he won't have a chance   150

PETRUCHIO   Well, sir, in brief, the gown is not for me.

GRUMIO   You are i' th' right, sir, 'tis for my mistress.

PETRUCHIO   Go, take it up unto thy master's use.°

take . . . use: i.e., return it to your master for whatever use he can make of it   155

GRUMIO   Villain, not for thy life. Take up my mistress'
   gown° for thy master's use!

Take . . . gown: i.e., lift up her skirts

PETRUCHIO   Why, sir, what's your conceit° in that?

conceit: meaning

GRUMIO
   O sir, the conceit is deeper than you think for.
   Take up my mistress' gown to his master's use!
   O fie, fie, fie!

160

PETRUCHIO   *[Aside]*
   Hortensio, say thou wilt see the tailor paid.
      [To Tailor]
   Go take it hence, be gone and say no more.

HORTENSIO
   Tailor, I'll pay thee for thy gown tomorrow.
   Take no unkindness of his hasty words.
   Away, I say. Commend me to thy master.   *Exit Tailor.*

165

PETRUCHIO
   Well, come, my Kate; we will unto your father's,
   Even in these honest mean habiliments.°
   Our purses shall be proud, our garments poor,
   For 'tis the mind that makes the body rich;
   And as the sun breaks through the darkest clouds
   So honor peereth° in the meanest habit.°
   What, is the jay more precious than the lark
   Because his feathers are more beautiful?
   Or is the adder better than the eel
   Because his painted skin contents the eye?
   O no, good Kate; neither art thou the worse
   For this poor furniture° and mean array.
   If thou account'st it shame, lay it° on me.
   And therefore frolic; we will hence° forthwith°
   To feast and sport us at thy father's house.
      [To Grumio]
   Go call my men, and let us straight to him;
   And bring our horses unto Long Lane end.
   There will we mount, and thither walk on foot.
   Let's see, I think 'tis now some seven o'clock,
   And well we may come there by dinnertime.°

honest . . . habiliments: respectable, plain clothes

170

peereth in: appears through; **habit:** clothing

175

furniture: clothing
lay it: blame it
hence: i.e., go hence; **forthwith:** immediately

180

dinnertime: about noon   185

KATE
   I dare assure you, sir, 'tis almost two,
   And 'twill be suppertime ere you come there.

PETRUCHIO
   It shall be seven ere I go to horse.
   Look what° I speak or do or think to do,

Look what: whatever

DISCOVERING SHAKESPEARE

(92) Metaphor [4.3.166]: How many <u>similes</u> and <u>metaphors</u> does Petruchio use in his <u>monologue</u> in lines 166–180? What principal point is he trying to make through the use of all these comparisons?

You are still crossing it. Sirs, let's alone.   190
I will not go today, and ere I do,
It shall be what o'clock I say it is.
HORTENSIO
Why, so this gallant will command the sun.   *[Exeunt.]*

❧ **4.4°**   *Enter Tranio [as Lucentio] and the Pedant booted° and*   **4.4:** Before Baptistas house
dressed like Vincentio.   **booted:** (as from traveling)

TRANIO
Sir, this is the house. Please it you that I call?
PEDANT
Ay, what else? And but° I be deceived,   **but:** unless
Signor Baptista may remember me,°   **may remember me:** (the pedant is rehearsing
Near twenty years ago, in Genoa,   his part)
Where we were lodgers at the Pegasus.°   **Pegasus:** (name of an inn, after the winged horse   5
                                                                                of classical myth)
TRANIO
'Tis well, and hold your own in any case
With such austerity° as longeth to° a father.   **austerity:** dignity; **longeth to:** befits
      Enter Biondello.
PEDANT
I warrant you. But sir, here comes your boy;
'Twere good he were schooled.°   **schooled:** taught how to play his part
TRANIO
Fear you not him. Sirrah Biondello,   10
Now do your duty throughly,° I advise you.   **throughly:** thoroughly
Imagine 'twere the right Vincentio.
BIONDELLO
Tut, fear not me.
TRANIO
But hast thou done thy errand to Baptista?
BIONDELLO
I told him that your father was at Venice,   15
And that you looked for° him this day in Padua.   **looked for:** expected
TRANIO
Thou'rt a tall° fellow. Hold thee that to drink.°   **tall:** fine; **Hold . . . drink:** have a drink on me
      [Gives money.]
Here comes Baptista. Set your countenance,° sir.   **Set . . . countenance:** i.e., look dignified;
      Enter Baptista and Lucentio [as Cambio]. Pedant bareheaded.°   **bareheaded:** (the pedant doffs his hat to
Signor Baptista, you are happily met.   Baptista)
      [To Pedant]
Sir, this is the gentleman I told you of.   20
I pray you, stand° good father to me now,   **stand:** prove to be a
Give me Bianca for my patrimony.
PEDANT
Soft, son.
Sir, by your leave. Having come to Padua

DISCOVERING SHAKESPEARE

(93) Paraphrase [4.4.6]: Paraphrase the following lines by Tranio: "'Tis well, and hold your own in any case/With such
austerity as longeth to a father" (4.4.6–7).
(94) Diction [4.4.23]: In his first speech to Baptista (4.4.23–37), how does the Pedant elevate his diction in order to
sound like Tranio's father? Which words seem particularly "fatherly" to you?

To gather in some debts, my son Lucentio   25
Made me acquainted with a weighty cause
Of love between your daughter and himself.
And – for the good report I hear of you,
And for the love he beareth to your daughter,
And she to him – to stay° him not too long,   **stay:** delay   30
I am content, in a good father's care,
To have him matched. And if you please to like°   **like:** approve (the match)
No worse than I, upon some agreement
Me shall you find ready and willing
With one consent° to have her so bestowed.   **With . . . consent:** i.e., with the same consent as   35
For curious° I cannot be with you,   yours
Signor Baptista, of whom I hear so well.   **curious:** overparticular, fussy

BAPTISTA
Sir, pardon me in what I have to say.
Your plainness and your shortness please me well.
Right true it is, your son Lucentio here   40
Doth love my daughter, and she loveth him –
Or both dissemble deeply their affections.
And therefore if you say no more than this,
That like a father you will deal with him
And pass° my daughter a sufficient dower,   **pass:** settle on   45
The match is made and all is done:
Your son shall have my daughter with consent.

TRANIO
I thank you, sir. Where then do you know best
We be affied° and such assurance ta'en   **affied:** formally betrothed
As shall with either part's agreement stand?° **such . . . stand:** such guarantees be given as shall   50
                                               formalize our agreement

BAPTISTA
Not in my house, Lucentio, for you know
Pitchers have ears, and I have many servants.
Besides, old Gremio is hearkening still,°   **hearkening still:** always eavesdropping
And happily° we might be interrupted.   **happily:** perhaps

TRANIO
Then at my lodging, an it like you.°   **an . . . you:** if you please   55
There doth my father lie,° and there this night   **lie:** lodge
We'll pass° the business privately and well. **pass:** transact
Send for your daughter by your servant here.
My boy shall fetch the scrivener° presently. **scrivener:** notary (a scribe empowered to draw
The worst is this, that at so slender warning up legal agreements)   60
You are like to have a thin and slender pittance.° **pittance:** meal

BAPTISTA
It likes me° well. Cambio, hie you home   **likes me:** pleases me
And bid Bianca make her ready straight.
And if you will, tell what hath happenèd:
Lucentio's father is arrived in Padua,   65
And how she's like to be Lucentio's wife.

                              [Exit Lucentio.]

BIONDELLO
I pray the gods she may with all my heart.   *Exit.*

DISCOVERING SHAKESPEARE

(95) Plot [4.4.57]: Why does Tranio want Baptista and the Pedant to sign the marriage contract "privately" (4.4.57) in the Pedant's lodging?

TRANIO
    Dally not with the gods, but get thee gone.
    Signor Baptista, shall I lead the way?
    Welcome, one mess° is like to be your cheer.°   **mess:** dish; **cheer:** entertainment   70
    Come, sir, we will better it in Pisa.
BAPTISTA   I follow you.   *Exeunt.*
    Enter [severally] Lucentio [as Cambio] and Biondello.
BIONDELLO   Cambio!
LUCENTIO   What sayst thou, Biondello?   75
BIONDELLO   You saw my master wink and laugh upon you?
LUCENTIO   Biondello, what of that?
BIONDELLO   Faith, nothing, but he's left me here behind
    to expound the meaning or moral° of his signs and to-   **moral:** deep significance
    kens.   80
LUCENTIO   I pray thee, moralize° them.   **moralize:** explain
BIONDELLO   Then thus. Baptista is safe,° talking with the   **safe:** i.e., safely dealt with
    deceiving father of a deceitful son.
LUCENTIO   And what of him?
BIONDELLO   His daughter is to be brought by you to the   85
    supper.
LUCENTIO   And then?
BIONDELLO   The old priest at Saint Luke's church is at
    your command at all hours.
LUCENTIO   And what of all this?   90
BIONDELLO   I cannot tell, except they are busied about a   **assurance:** agreement (the betrothal);
    counterfeit assurance.° Take you assurance° of her, "cum   **Take . . . assurance:** insure yourself (by
    privilegio ad imprimendum solum."° To th' church with   marrying her)
    the priest, clerk, and some sufficient honest witnesses.   **cum . . . solum:** with exclusive right to print
    If this be not that you look for, I have no more to say.   (Latin; the publisher's copyright formula,   95
    But bid Bianca farewell forever and a day.   analogized to the husband's exclusive right to
LUCENTIO   Hear'st thou, Biondello –   "imprint himself on" his wife)
BIONDELLO   I cannot tarry. I knew a wench married in an
    afternoon as she went to the garden for parsley to stuff a
    rabbit, and so may you, sir, and so adieu, sir. My master   100
    hath appointed me to go to Saint Luke's, to bid the
    priest be ready against you come° with your appendix.°   **against . . . come:** in anticipation of your coming;
                                           Exit   **appendix:** appendage (i.e., bride)

LUCENTIO
    I may and will, if she be so contented.
    She will be pleased, then wherefore should I doubt?
    Hap what hap may,° I'll roundly go about her.°   **Hap . . . may:** whatever comes of it;   105
    It shall go hard° if Cambio go° without her.   *Exit.*   **I'll . . . her:** I'll go find her immediately
                                                 go hard: be hard to bear; **go:** return

   4.5°   *Enter Petruchio, Kate, Hortensio [, and Grumio,*   **4.5:** A country road
    with Attendants].

PETRUCHIO
    Come on, a° God's name, once more toward our father's.   **a:** in
    Good Lord, how bright and goodly shines the moon!

DISCOVERING SHAKESPEARE

(96) <u>Plot</u> **[4.4.82]:** On a separate sheet of paper, <u>paraphrase</u> Biondello's instructions to Lucentio in 4.4.82–96. Exactly
what is the plan that Tranio has devised to get Lucentio and Bianca to the church?
(97) <u>Staging</u> **[4.5.1]:** If you were directing the beginning of act 4, scene 5, how many characters would you have on
stage, how would they be dressed, and what items would they be carrying?

KATE
  The moon? The sun. It is not moonlight now.
PETRUCHIO
  I say it is the moon that shines so bright.
KATE
  I know it is the sun that shines so bright.   5
PETRUCHIO
  Now by my mother's son, and that's myself,
  It shall be moon or star or what I list,°   **list:** please
  Or° e'er I journey to your father's house.   **Or:** ere, before
    [To Servants]
  Go on and fetch our horses back again.
  Evermore crossed and crossed, nothing but crossed.   10
HORTENSIO   *[Aside to Kate]*
  Say as he says or we shall never go.
KATE
  Forward, I pray, since we have come so far,
  And be it moon or sun or what you please.
  An if you please to call it a rush candle,°   **rush candle:** rush dipped in grease to serve as
  Henceforth I vow it shall be so for me.   candle   15
PETRUCHIO
  I say it is the moon.
PETRUCHIO
  Nay, then you lie. It is the blessèd sun.
KATE
  Then God be blessed, it is the blessèd sun,
  But sun it is not when you say it is not,
  And the moon changes even as your mind.   20
  What you will have it named, even that it is,
  And so it shall be still° for Katherine.   **still:** always
HORTENSIO
  Petruchio, go thy ways, the field is won.
PETRUCHIO
  Well, forward, forward! Thus the bowl° should run,   **bowl:** ball in game of bowls
  And not unluckily° against the bias.°   **unluckily:** unsuccessfully; **against the bias:**   25
  But soft, what company is coming here?   contrary to the intended course (the bias being a
    Enter Vincentio.   weight in the side of the bowl that enables the
    [To Vincentio]   bowler to roll it in a curve)
  Good morrow, gentle mistress, where away?
  Tell me, sweet Kate, and tell me truly too,
  Hast thou beheld a fresher gentlewoman?
  Such war of white and red within her cheeks!   30
  What stars do spangle heaven with such beauty
  As those two eyes become that heavenly face?
  Fair lovely maid, once more good day to thee.
  Sweet Kate, embrace her for her beauty's sake.
HORTENSIO   *[Aside]*
  A° will make the man mad, to make a woman of him.   **A:** he   35

DISCOVERING SHAKESPEARE

(98) <u>Metaphor</u> [4.5.24]: How would a knowledge of the sport of British lawn bowling help us understand Petruchio's <u>metaphor</u> about a bowl running "against the bias" (4.5.25)? Exactly what is Petruchio comparing to the straight path of a well-thrown bowling ball?

KATE
 Young budding virgin, fair and fresh and sweet,
 Whither away, or where is thy abode?
 Happy the parents of so fair a child,
 Happier the man whom favorable stars
 Allots thee for his lovely bedfellow.   40
PETRUCHIO
 Why, how now, Kate, I hope thou art not mad.
 This is a man, old, wrinkled, faded, withered,
 And not a maiden, as thou sayst he is.
KATE
 Pardon, old father,° my mistaking eyes   **father:** (respectful term of address to an old man)
 That have been so bedazzled with the sun   45
 That everything I look on seemeth green.°   **green:** young
 Now I perceive thou art a reverend father.
 Pardon, I pray thee, for my mad mistaking.
PETRUCHIO
 Do, good old grandsire, and withal make known
 Which way thou travelest. If along with us,   50
 We shall be joyful of thy company.
VINCENTIO
 Fair sir, and you my merry mistress,
 That with your strange encounter° much amazed me,   **encounter:** greeting
 My name is called Vincentio, my dwelling Pisa,
 And bound I am to Padua, there to visit   55
 A son of mine, which long I have not seen.
PETRUCHIO
 What is his name?
VINCENTIO   Lucentio, gentle sir.
PETRUCHIO
 Happily met, the happier for thy son.
 And now by law, as well as reverend age,
 I may entitle thee my loving father.   60
 The sister to my wife, this gentlewoman,
 Thy son by this° hath married.° Wonder not   **this:** this time; **Thy . . . married:** (since
 Nor be not grieved. She is of good esteem,°   Petruchio has been out of town, he should not
 Her dowry wealthy, and of worthy birth;   know this information, and in any case, Lucentio
 Beside, so qualified° as may beseem   and Bianca are not married yet; moreover,
 The spouse of any noble gentleman.   Hortensio has heard the suitor he knows as   65
 Let me embrace with old Vincentio,   Lucentio forswear her);
 And wander we° to see thy honest son,   **esteem:** reputation
 Who will of thy arrival be full joyous.   **so qualified:** having such qualities
VINCENTIO   **wander we:** let's go out of our way
 But is this true, or is it else your pleasure,   70
 Like pleasant° travelers, to break a jest   **pleasant:** merry
 Upon° the company you overtake?   **break . . . Upon:** play a joke on
HORTENSIO
 I do assure thee, father, so it is.

DISCOVERING SHAKESPEARE

(99) Teaser [4.5.45]: In most modern productions, the actress playing Katherine pauses between the words "the" and "sun" in the phrase "so bedazzled with the . . . sun" (4.5.45), which is accompanied by a quizzical glance at Petruchio, who nods in agreement. Why is this moment funny?

PETRUCHIO
　　Come, go along, and see the truth hereof,
　　For our first merriment hath made thee jealous.°   **jealous:** suspicious   75
　　　　　　　　　　　　　Exeunt [all but Hortensio].

HORTENSIO
　　Well, Petruchio, this has put me in heart.
　　Have to my widow, and if she be froward,°   **froward:** stubborn
　　Then hast thou taught Hortensio to be untoward.°   **untoward:** perverse, difficult (and thereby how
　　　　　　　　　　　　　　　　　Exit.   to tame her)

❦ **5.1**° *Enter Biondello, Lucentio [as Cambio], and Bianca. Gremio*   **5.1:** Before Lucentio's house
　　is out before° *[and stands aside].*   **out before:** onstage before the others (whom he
　　　　　　　　　　　　　　　　　 does not "see")

BIONDELLO   Softly and swiftly, sir, for the priest is ready.
LUCENTIO   I fly, Biondello – but they may chance to
　　need thee at home; therefore leave us.
　　　　　　　　　　　　　　　Exit [with Bianca].
BIONDELLO   Nay, faith, I'll see the church a your back,°   **a your back:** at your back (i.e., I'll see you
　　and then come back to my master as soon as I can.   enter it)   5
　　　　　　　　　　　　　　　　　[Exit.]

GREMIO
　　I marvel Cambio comes not all this while.
　　　Enter Petruchio, Kate, Vincentio, [and] Grumio, with
　　　Attendants.
PETRUCHIO
　　Sir, here's the door, this is Lucentio's house.
　　My father's bears° more toward the marketplace.   **bears:** lies
　　Thither must I, and here I leave you, sir.
VINCENTIO
　　You shall not choose but drink before you go.   10
　　I think I shall command your welcome here,
　　And by all likelihood some cheer is toward.
　　　Knock.
GREMIO   *[Advancing]* They're busy within; you were best
　　knock louder.
　　　Pedant [as Vincentio] looks out of the window.°   **looks . . . window:** i.e., appears in the gallery
PEDANT   What's° he that knocks as he would beat down   over the stage—are Sly, the lord, and his retinue   15
　　the gate?   still there?
VINCENTIO   Is Signor Lucentio within, sir?   **What's:** who's
PEDANT   He's within, sir, but not to be spoken withal.°   **withal:** with
VINCENTIO   What if a man bring him a hundred pound
　　or two, to make merry withal?   20
PEDANT   Keep your hundred pounds to yourself. He
　　shall need none so long as I live.
PETRUCHIO   Nay, I told you your son was well beloved in
　　Padua. Do you hear, sir? To leave frivolous circum-

DISCOVERING SHAKESPEARE

(100) <u>Rhyme</u> [4.5.77–78]: How does the final <u>slant rhyme</u> in this scene between the words "froward" and "untoward"
(4.5.77–78) <u>foreshadow</u> the awkward marital relationship between Hortensio and his widow? Will she be "froward"? Will
their marriage be "untoward"?

stances, I pray you tell Signor Lucentio that his father is   25
come from Pisa and is here at the door to speak with
him.

PEDANT   Thou liest. His father is come from Pisa and is
here looking out at the window.

VINCENTIO   Art thou his father?   30

PEDANT   Ay sir, so his mother says, if I may believe her.

PETRUCHIO   *[To Vincentio]* Why how now, gentleman!   **flat:** downright
Why this is flat° knavery, to take upon you another
man's name.

PEDANT   Lay hands on the villain. I believe a means to   35
cozen° somebody in this city under my countenance.°   **cozen:** cheat; **under my countenance:** by
    Enter Biondello.   posing as me

BIONDELLO   I have seen them in the church together.   **good shipping:** fair sailing
God send 'em good shipping!° But who is here? Mine   **undone:** ruined
old master, Vincentio! Now we are undone° and
brought to nothing.   40

VINCENTIO   Come hither, crackhemp.°   **crackhemp:** fellow ripe for hanging

BIONDELLO   I hope I may choose,° sir.   **choose:** do as I choose

VINCENTIO   Come hither, you rogue. What, have you
forgot me?

BIONDELLO   Forgot you? No sir. I could not forget you,   45
for I never saw you before in all my life.

VINCENTIO   What, you notorious villain, didst thou
never see thy master's father, Vincentio?

BIONDELLO   What, my worshipful old master? Yes,
marry, sir, see where he looks out of the window.   50

VINCENTIO   Is't so indeed?
    He beats Biondello.

BIONDELLO   Help, help, help! Here's a madman will
murder me.   *[Exit.]*

PEDANT   Help, son! Help, Signor Baptista!   *[Exit above.]*

PETRUCHIO   Prithee, Kate, let's stand aside and see the   55
end of this controversy.
    [They stand aside.]
    Enter [below] Pedant [as Vincentio] with Servants,
    Baptista, [and] Tranio [as Lucentio].

TRANIO   Sir, what° are you that offer to beat my servant?   **what:** who

VINCENTIO   What am I, sir? Nay, what are you, sir? O immortal gods! O fine villain! A silken doublet, a velvet
hose, a scarlet cloak, and a copatain° hat! O I am undone,   **copatain:** high-crowned   60
I am undone! While I play the good husband° at home,   **good husband:** careful manager
my son and my servants spend all at the university.

TRANIO   How now, what's the matter?

BAPTISTA   What, is the man lunatic?

TRANIO   Sir, you seem a sober ancient gentleman by your   65
habit,° but your words show you a madman. Why sir,   **habit:** bearing

---

DISCOVERING SHAKESPEARE

(101) Repetition [5.1.25–29]: In the brief exchange between Petruchio, Vincentio, and the Pedant in 5.1.25–29, Shakespeare uses repetition for comic effect. Find three other examples of this comic technique in the play. Why do you think such repetition is humorous?

(102) Staging [5.1.51]: Why does Vincentio beat Biondello in 5.1.51? Which other characters are beaten or physically abused in the play? To what extent does the physical mistreatment of Biondello remind you of the psychological and social abuse Kate has suffered? Which type of punishment is most likely to bring about behavioral change? Why?

what 'cerns° it you if I wear pearl and gold? I thank my
good father, I am able to maintain it.

VINCENTIO   Thy father! O villain, he is a sailmaker in
Bergamo.°

BAPTISTA   You mistake, sir, you mistake, sir. Pray, what
do you think is his name?

VINCENTIO   His name? As if I knew not his name! I have
brought him up ever since he was three years old, and
his name is Tranio.

PEDANT   Away, away, mad ass! His name is Lucentio. He
is mine only son, and heir to the lands of me, Signor
Vincentio.

VINCENTIO   Lucentio? O he hath murdered his master!
Lay hold on him, I charge you in the duke's name. O
my son, my son! Tell me, thou villain, where is my son
Lucentio?

TRANIO   *[To a Servant]* Call forth an officer.
   [Enter an Officer.]
Carry this mad knave to the jail. Father Baptista, I
charge you see that he be forthcoming.°

VINCENTIO   Carry me to the jail!

GREMIO   Stay, officer, he shall not go to prison.

BAPTISTA   Talk not, Signor Gremio. I say he shall go to prison.

GREMIO   Take heed, Signor Baptista, lest you be cony-
catched° in this business. I dare swear this is the right
Vincentio.

PEDANT   Swear, if thou dar'st.

GREMIO   Nay, I dare not swear it.

TRANIO   Then thou wert best° say that I am not Lucentio.

GREMIO   Yes, I know thee to be Signor Lucentio.

BAPTISTA   Away with the dotard, to the jail with him!
   Enter Biondello, Lucentio, and Bianca.

VINCENTIO   Thus strangers may be halèd° and abused. O
monstrous villain!

BIONDELLO   O we are spoiled, yonder he is. Deny him,
forswear him, or else we are all undone.
   Exeunt Biondello, Tranio, and Pedant
   as fast as may be.

LUCENTIO   Pardon, sweet father.
   Kneel.

VINCENTIO   Lives my sweet son?

BIANCA   Pardon, dear father.

BAPTISTA
How hast thou offended? Where is Lucentio?

'cerns: concerns

Bergamo: (like Mantua and Padua, not a
seaport)   70

                                                                 75

                                                                 80

forthcoming: i.e., to stand trial   85

cony-catched: duped   90

wert best: might as well   95

halèd: hauled about, molested

                                                                 100

                                                                 105

DISCOVERING SHAKESPEARE

(103) Geography [5.1.69–70]: Although Vincentio claims that Tranio's father is "a sail-maker in Bergamo" (5.1.69–70),
Shakespeare's audience would undoubtedly have known that Bergamo was not a sea-port. Whose mistake do you think this
is: Vincentio's or Shakespeare's? Or is the reference a mistake at all?

(104) Teaser [5.1.90–91]: Find out everything you can about the phrase "cony-catched" (5.1.90–91) by looking up the
word in the *Oxford English Dictionary* and reading Robert Greene's "Cony Catching" pamphlets.

(105) Staging [5.1.102]: In 5.1.102–107, who kneels to whom? How would you stage this portion of the scene? Read
this brief section out loud, paying particular attention to the <u>shared lines</u> between the characters.

LUCENTIO
Here's Lucentio, right son to the right Vincentio,
That have by marriage made thy daughter mine
While counterfeit supposes° bleared thine eyne.°

GREMIO
Here's packing,° with a witness,° to deceive us all!

VINCENTIO
Where is that damnèd villain Tranio,
That faced and braved° me in this matter so?

BAPTISTA
Why, tell me, is not this my Cambio?

BIANCA
Cambio is changed into Lucentio.

LUCENTIO
Love wrought these miracles. Bianca's love
Made me exchange my state with Tranio
While he did bear my countenance° in the town,
And happily I have arrived at the last
Unto the wished haven of my bliss.
What Tranio did, myself enforced him to;
Then pardon him, sweet father, for my sake.

VINCENTIO   I'll slit the villain's nose that would have sent
me to the jail.

BAPTISTA   *[To Lucentio]* But do you hear, sir? Have you
married my daughter without asking my good will?

VINCENTIO   Fear not, Baptista, we will content you, go
to.° But I will in, to be revenged for this villainy.   *Exit.*

BAPTISTA   And I, to sound the depth of this knavery.
                                                        Exit.

LUCENTIO   Look not pale, Bianca, thy father will not
frown.   *Exeunt [Lucentio and Bianca].*

GREMIO
My cake is dough,° but I'll in among the rest,
Out of hope of all but my share of the feast.   *[Exit.]*

KATE   *[Advancing]* Husband, let's follow, to see the end
of this ado.

PETRUCHIO   First kiss me, Kate, and we will.

KATE   What, in the midst of the street?

PETRUCHIO   What, art thou ashamed of me?

KATE   No sir, God forbid, but ashamed to kiss.

PETRUCHIO
Why, then let's home again.
    [To Grumio]   Come, sirrah, let's away.

KATE
Nay, I will give thee a kiss. Now pray thee, love, stay.

PETRUCHIO
Is not this well? Come, my sweet Kate.
Better once° than never, for never's too late.°   *Exeunt.*

---

counterfeit supposes: false assumptions (with an allusion to Gascoigne's play *Supposes*); **eyne:** eyes

packing: plotting; **with a witness:** with a vengeance   110

faced and braved: outfaced and defied

bear my countenance: pose as me   115

                                            120

                                            125

go to: (expression of impatience)

My cake is dough: i.e., my hopes are dashed   130
(proverbial)

                                            135

                                            140

Better . . . late: i.e., better late than never
(proverbial); **once:** at one time or another

DISCOVERING SHAKESPEARE

(106) Paraphrase [5.1.130]: Paraphrase Gremio's "My cake is dough" (5.1.130). Is he happy or unhappy here? Why?

❧ **5.2°**   *Enter Baptista, Vincentio, Gremio, the Pedant,*
Lucentio, and Bianca; Tranio, Biondello, [and]
Grumio; [Petruchio, Kate, Hortensio,] and Widow;
the Servingmen with Tranio bringing in° a banquet.°

5.2: Lucentio's house

bringing in: i.e., carrying onstage;
banquet: dessert (sweets, fruit, and wine)

LUCENTIO
At last, though long,° our jarring notes agree,
And time it is, when raging war is done,
To smile at scapes and perils overblown.
My fair Bianca, bid my father welcome
While I with selfsame kindness welcome thine.   5
Brother Petruchio, sister Katherina,
And thou, Hortensio, with thy loving widow,
Feast with the best and welcome to my house.
My banquet is to close our stomachs up
After our great good cheer.° Pray you, sit down,   10
For now we sit to chat as well as eat.
    [They sit at table.]

long: after a long time

After . . . cheer: (Lucentio's banquet apparently
follows a bridal feast given by Baptista)

PETRUCHIO
Nothing but sit and sit, and eat and eat!
BAPTISTA
Padua affords this kindness, son Petruchio.
PETRUCHIO
Padua affords nothing but what is kind.
HORTENSIO
For both our sakes I would that word were true.   15
PETRUCHIO
Now, for my life, Hortensio fears° his widow.
WIDOW
Then never trust me if I be afeard.°

fears: is afraid of (the widow quibbles on
"frightens")

afeard: frightened (Petruchio quibbles on
"suspicious")

PETRUCHIO
You are very sensible, and yet you miss my sense:
I mean Hortensio is afeard of you.
WIDOW
He that is giddy thinks the world turns round.   20
PETRUCHIO
Roundly° replied.
KATE   Mistress, how mean you that?
WIDOW
Thus I conceive by° him.

Roundly: straightforwardly

conceive by: am inspired by (Petruchio quibbles
on "become pregnant by")

PETRUCHIO
Conceive by me? How likes Hortensio that?
HORTENSIO
My widow says, thus she conceives° her tale.
PETRUCHIO
Very well mended. Kiss him for that, good widow.   25

conceives: devises

DISCOVERING SHAKESPEARE

(107) <u>Metaphor</u> **[5.2.1]:** When Lucentio says "At last, though long, our jarring notes agree" (5.2.1), to which specific situation, scene, and character might he be referring? In a broader, more <u>metaphorical</u> sense, how many different "jarring notes" can you catalog in the entire play?

(108) <u>Paraphrase</u> **[5.2.20]:** Write a <u>paraphrase</u> in modern English of the Widow's line "He that is giddy thinks the world turns round" (5.2.20). Whom is she making fun of here?

KATE
"He that is giddy thinks the world turns round" –
I pray you, tell me what you meant by that.
WIDOW
Your husband, being troubled with a shrew,°
Measures° my husband's sorrow by his woe –
And now you know my meaning.

shrew, woe: (a rhyme, as at 4.1.200-1)
Measures: judges

30

KATE
A very mean° meaning.
WIDOW   Right, I mean you.
KATE
And I am mean indeed, respecting° you.

mean: contemptible (the widow quibbles on "have in mind," and Kate then quibbles on "moderate"— i.e., in shrewishness)
respecting: compared with

PETRUCHIO
To her, Kate!
HORTENSIO
To her, widow!
PETRUCHIO
A hundred marks, my Kate does put her down.°

put her down: defeat her (Hortensio quibbles on "have sex with her")

35

HORTENSIO
That's my office.
PETRUCHIO
Spoke like an officer – ha' to° thee, lad.
    Drinks to Hortensio.

ha' to: here's to

BAPTISTA
How likes Gremio these quick-witted folks?
GREMIO
Believe me, sir, they butt together well.
BIANCA
Head and butt! An hasty-witted body°
Would say your head and butt were head and horn.°

hasty-witted body: quick-witted person
Would . . . horn: (presumably the usual joke about cuckoldry, but it is not clear why this should be aimed at the unmarried Gremio)

40

VINCENTIO
Ay, mistress bride, hath that awakened you?
BIANCA
Ay, but not frighted me; therefore I'll sleep again.
PETRUCHIO
Nay, that you shall not; since you have begun,
Have at you for° a bitter jest or two.

Have . . . for: get ready for

45

BIANCA
Am I your bird? I mean to shift my bush,
And then pursue me as you draw your bow.
You are welcome all.°
    Exit Bianca [with Kate and Widow].

You . . . all: (Bianca, as the hostess, leads the ladies out)

PETRUCHIO
She hath prevented° me. Here, Signor° Tranio,
This bird you aimed at, though you hit her not.
Therefore a health to all that shot and missed.

prevented: forestalled; **Signor:** (Petruchio ironically addresses Tranio as a gentleman)

50

TRANIO
O sir, Lucentio slipped° me, like his greyhound,
Which runs himself and catches for his master.

slipped: unleashed

DISCOVERING SHAKESPEARE

(109) Teaser [5.2.35]: How much money would "A hundred marks" (5.2.35) be worth in contemporary American dollars?

PETRUCHIO
  A good swift simile but something currish.
TRANIO
  'Tis well, sir, that you hunted for yourself;   55
  'Tis thought your deer does hold you at a bay.
BAPTISTA
  O ho, Petruchio! Tranio hits you now.
LUCENTIO
  I thank thee for that gird,° good Tranio.   **gird:** taunt
HORTENSIO
  Confess, confess, hath he not hit you here?
PETRUCHIO
  A° has a little galled° me, I confess,   **A:** he; **galled:** annoyed   60
  And as the jest did glance away from me,
  'Tis ten to one it maimed you two outright.
BAPTISTA
  Now, in good sadness,° son Petruchio,   **sadness:** seriousness
  I think thou hast the veriest° shrew of all.   **veriest:** most perfect
PETRUCHIO
  Well, I say no. And therefore, for assurance,°   **assurance:** proof   65
  Let's each one send unto his wife,
  And he whose wife is most obedient,
  To come at first when he doth send for her,
  Shall win the wager which we will propose.
HORTENSIO
  Content. What's the wager?   70
LUCENTIO   Twenty crowns.
PETRUCHIO
  Twenty crowns?
  I'll venture so much of° my hawk or hound,   **of:** on
  But twenty times so much upon my wife.
LUCENTIO
  A hundred then.
HORTENSIO   Content.
PETRUCHIO   A match,° 'tis done.   **match:** bet
HORTENSIO
  Who shall begin?   75
LUCENTIO
  That will I.
  Go, Biondello, bid your mistress come to me.
BIONDELLO I go.   *Exit.*
BAPTISTA
  Son, I'll be your half,° Bianca comes.   **be your half:** take half your bet that
LUCENTIO
  I'll have no halves; I'll bear it all myself.   80
    Enter Biondello.
  How now, what news?
BIONDELLO
  Sir, my mistress sends you word
  That she is busy and she cannot come.

DISCOVERING SHAKESPEARE

(110) Metaphor [5.2.60–62]: Explain Petruchio's fencing metaphor in 5.2.60–62. Specifically, what has "galled" him; which jest did "glance away"; and which two characters have been "maimed . . . outright" by it?

PETRUCHIO
How? "She's busy and she cannot come"?
Is that an answer?   85
GREMIO   Ay, and a kind one too.
Pray God, sir, your wife send you not a worse.
PETRUCHIO   I hope better.
HORTENSIO   Sirrah Biondello, go and entreat my wife to
come to me forthwith.°   *Exit Biondello.*   **forthwith:** immediately
PETRUCHIO   O ho, "entreat her"! Nay, then she must   90
needs come.
HORTENSIO   I am afraid, sir, do what you can, yours will
not be entreated. *(Enter Biondello.)* Now where's my
wife?
BIONDELLO
She says you have some goodly jest in hand.   95
She will not come. She bids you come to her.
PETRUCHIO
Worse and worse, "she will not come"!
O vile, intolerable, not to be endured!
Sirrah Grumio, go to your mistress,
Say I command her come to me.   *Exit [Grumio].*   100
HORTENSIO   I know her answer.
PETRUCHIO   What?
HORTENSIO   She will not.
PETRUCHIO
The fouler fortune mine, and there an end.
  Enter Kate [with Grumio].
BAPTISTA
Now, by my halidom,° here comes Katherina!   **by my halidom:** bless my soul (originally an   105
KATE   oath by a sacred relic)
What is your will, sir, that you send for me?
PETRUCHIO
Where is your sister and Hortensio's wife?
KATE
They sit conferring by the parlor fire.
PETRUCHIO
Go fetch them hither. If they deny to come,
Swinge me them° soundly forth unto their husbands.   **Swinge me them:** whip them for me   110
Away, I say, and bring them hither straight.
                              [Exit Kate.]
LUCENTIO
Here is a wonder, if you talk of a wonder.
HORTENSIO
And so it is. I wonder what it bodes.
PETRUCHIO
Marry, peace it bodes, and love, and quiet life,

DISCOVERING SHAKESPEARE
(111) Language [5.2.85]: In 5.2.77–100, Lucentio, Hortensio, and Petruchio all ask their wives to come to them in different ways. Lucentio tells Biondello to "bid your mistress come to me"; Hortensio "entreats" his wife to join him; and Petruchio "commands" Kate to enter. How do these three distinct words—"bid," "entreat," and "command"—bring forth different responses from the women?

An awful° rule and right° supremacy,   **awful:** awe-inspiring; **right:** proper   115
And, to be short, what not° that's sweet and happy.   **what not:** everything

BAPTISTA
Now fair befall thee, good Petruchio.
The wager thou hast won, and I will add
Unto their losses twenty thousand crowns,
Another dowry to another daughter,   120
For she is changed as she had never been.

PETRUCHIO
Nay, I will win my wager better yet
And show more sign of her obedience,
Her new-built virtue and obedience.
   Enter Kate, Bianca, and Widow.
See where she comes and brings your froward wives   125
As prisoners to her womanly persuasion.
Katherine, that cap of yours becomes you not.
Off with the bauble, throw it under foot.
   [She obeys.]

WIDOW
Lord, let me never have a cause to sigh
Till I be brought to such a silly pass.°   **pass:** predicament   130

BIANCA
Fie, what a foolish duty call you this?

LUCENTIO
I would your duty were as foolish too.
The wisdom of your duty, fair Bianca,
Hath cost me a hundred crowns since suppertime.

BIANCA
The more fool you for laying° on my duty.   **laying:** betting   135

PETRUCHIO
Katherine, I charge thee, tell these headstrong women
What duty they do owe their lords and husbands.

WIDOW
Come, come, you're mocking; we will have no telling.

PETRUCHIO
Come on, I say, and first begin with her.

WIDOW
She shall not.   140

PETRUCHIO
I say she shall — and first begin with her.

KATE
Fie, fie, unknit that threat'ning unkind° brow   **unkind:** (1) unfriendly, (2) unnatural
And dart not scornful glances from those eyes
To wound thy lord, thy king, thy governor.°   **governor:** ruler
It blots thy beauty as frosts do bite the meads,   145
Confounds thy fame° as whirlwinds shake fair buds,   **Confounds thy fame:** spoils your good name
And in no sense is meet or amiable.

DISCOVERING SHAKESPEARE

(112) <u>Foreshadowing</u> [5.2.114–115]: To what extent do you agree with Petruchio that Kate's apparent submissiveness predicts "love, and quiet life, / An awful rule and right supremacy" (5.2.114–115) in their marriage?

(113) Characterization [5.2.139]: Why does Petruchio tell Kate to begin her lecture on "duty" with the Widow (5.2.139)? Why does she need special instruction?

A woman moved° is like a fountain troubled,
Muddy, ill-seeming, thick, bereft of beauty,
And while it is so, none so dry or thirsty   150
Will deign to sip or touch one drop of it.
Thy husband is thy lord, thy life, thy keeper,
Thy head,° thy sovereign; one that cares for thee
And for thy maintenance; commits his body
To painful labor both by sea and land,   155
To watch the night in storms, the day in cold,
Whilst thou liest warm at home, secure and safe;
And craves no other tribute at thy hands
But love, fair looks, and true obedience –
Too little payment for so great a debt.   160
Such duty as the subject owes the prince,°
Even such a woman oweth to her husband;
And when she is froward, peevish,° sullen, sour,
And not obedient to his honest will,
What is she but a foul contending rebel   165
And graceless traitor to her loving lord?
I am ashamed that women are so simple°
To offer war where they should kneel for peace,
Or seek for rule, supremacy, and sway,
When they are bound to serve, love, and obey.   170
Why are our bodies soft and weak and smooth,
Unapt to° toil and trouble in the world,
But that our soft conditions° and our hearts
Should well agree with our external parts?
Come, come, you froward and unable° worms,   175
My mind hath been as big° as one of yours,
My heart as great, my reason haply more,
To bandy° word for word and frown for frown.
But now I see our lances are but straws,
Our strength as weak, our weakness past compare,   180
That seeming to be most which we indeed least are.
Then vail your stomachs,° for it is no boot,°
And place your hands below your husband's foot,
In token of which duty, if he please,
My hand is ready, may it° do him ease.   185
PETRUCHIO
  Why, there's a wench! Come on and kiss me, Kate!
LUCENTIO
  Well, go thy ways, old lad, for thou shalt ha't.
VINCENTIO
  'Tis a good hearing° when children are toward.°
LUCENTIO
  But a harsh hearing when women are froward.

Glosses:

moved: angry

head: (1) ruler, (2) principle of reason

prince: monarch

peevish: obstinate

simple: foolish

Unapt to: unsuited for
conditions: qualities

unable: feeble
big: haughty

bandy: exchange (as in hitting a tennis ball back and forth)

vail your stomachs: curb your willfulness;
no boot: no use

may it: if it may

a good hearing: i.e., good news;
toward: docile

DISCOVERING SHAKESPEARE

(114) Metaphor [5.2.156]: How many different metaphors and similes does Kate use in her long speech in 5.2.142–185? Why does she use so much figurative language?

(115) Teaser [5.2.186]: Who wrote a musical entitled *Kiss Me Kate?* How is the plot different from Shakespeare's play?

PETRUCHIO

    Come, Kate, we'll to bed.   190

    We three are married, but you two are sped.°   **sped:** done for (through having disobedient

    [To Lucentio]   wives)

    'Twas I won the wager, though you hit the white,°   **white:** bull's-eye (playing on "Bianca," white)

    And being a winner, God give you good night.

                       Exit Petruchio [with Kate].

HORTENSIO

    Now, go thy ways, thou hast tamed a curst shrew.°   **shrew, so:** (a rhyme)

LUCENTIO

    'Tis a wonder, by your leave, she will be tamed so.   195

                       [Exeunt.]

DISCOVERING SHAKESPEARE

(116) <u>Rhyme</u> **[5.2.190]:** To what extent does the <u>perfect rhyme</u> at the conclusion of the play in lines 190–193 (bed/sped, white/night) suggest a happy ending? Which characters end the play most harmoniously? Which will be most unhappy? Why do you think this is true?

ଈ

Research and Discussion Topics

INDUCTION 1

  1. What was an <u>Induction</u>?

  2. What were stocks (Induction 1.2)? How many different types of stocks were there in Renaissance England? In what other ways were people punished?

  3. Who was Richard the Conqueror (Induction 1.4)?

  4. What was a "headborough" (Induction 1.9–10)?

  5. Research the following hunting terms in Induction I: embossed, brach, coldest fault, merest loss, and dullest scent (14–22).

  6. What was a buttery (101)?

  7. What was "spleen" (136)?

INDUCTION 2

  1. Where were Burton Heath (Induction 2.17) and Wincot (2.20)?

  2. What was a cardmaker (Induction 2.18)?

  3. Who was Apollo (Induction 2.33)?

  4. Who were the following: Semiramis (Induction 2.37), Adonis (48), Cytherea (49), lo (52), and Daphne (55)?

  5. What was a "leet" (Induction 2.85)?

ACT I

  1. Find a map of Italy, and locate Padua (1.1.2), Lombardy (1.1.3), Pisa (1.1.10), Verona (1.2.1), Mantua (2.1.60), Genoa (4.4.4), and Bergamo (5.1.70).

  2. Who were Aristotle (1.1.32) and Ovid (1.1.33)?

3. What was the *commedia dell'arte*?

4. Who was Minerva (1.1.84)?

5. What was a "high cross" (1.1.131)?

6. Who were Anna and the Queen of Carthage (1.1.152)?

7. Who were Agenor (1.1.166) and Jove (1.1.167)? What was the Cretan strand (1.1.168)?

8. Who was Saint Anne (1.1.248)?

9. Who are Sibyl and Socrates' Xanthippe (1.2.69–70)?

10. Where is the Adriatic Sea (1.2.73)?

11. Who were Leda (1.2.241) and Paris (1.2.244)?

ACT II

1. Research the proverbial tradition that "old maids" would "lead apes in hell" (2.1.34).

2. Where was Rheims (2.1.80)?

3. Research all the puns Petruchio makes on the word "kate" in 2.1.186–195.

4. What was a movable (2.1.198)?

5. What was the difference between a "turtledove" and a "buzzard" (2.1.211)?

6. Do some research on coats of arms (2.1.227).

7. Who was Dian (2.1.259)?

8. Find out as much as you can about Elizabethan marriage conventions. Was a father's consent always necessary (2.1.270)?

9. Who were Grissel (2.1.296) and Lucrece (2.1.297)?

10. Distinguish among an argosy (2.1.379), a galliass (2.1.379), and a galley (2.1.380).

ACT III

1. How much information can you discover about "the cause why music was ordained" (3.1.10)?

2. Who were Aeacides (3.1.51) and Ajax (3.1.52)?

3. What was a gamut (3.1.70)?

4. Research contemporary laws prohibiting the on-stage representation of any religious ceremonies, including marriages (see especially 3.2.156–181).

5. How would Elizabethan men and women have dressed for their weddings?

ACT IV

1. What were rushes (4.1.41) and fustian (4.1.42)?

2. How were shoes "pinked" (4.1.119)?

3. Explain the theory of Humors (see especially 4.1.160–170 and 4.3.17–30). What did the word "choleric" mean (4.1.164)?

4. Explain the following terms from falconry: falcon (4.1.180), full-gorged (181), lure (182), haggard (183), keeper's call (184), kites (185), bate (186), and beat (186).

5. What was *The Art to Love* (4.2.8) or Ovid's *Ars Amatoria?*

6. What was a custard-coffin (4.3.82)?

7. What was Pegasus (4.4.5)?

ACT V

1. What were conditions like in Renaissance jails (5.1.84)?

2. Research George Gascoigne's *Supposes,* the source for Shakespeare's sub-plot in the play (see 5.1.108).

3. What was a greyhound?

Filmography

1982
A CBC Production
Rating:

Directed by: Norman Campbell

Sharry Flett as Kate
Len Cariou as Petruchio
Barney O'Sullivan as Baptista
Lynne Griffin as Bianca
Peter Hutt as Lucentio
Desmond Ellis as Christopher Sly

By including the Induction and emphasizing the play-within-the-play aspect of *Shrew,* the Stratford Festival has done what a stage production can do best. It is both theatrical and playful. Christopher Sly appears throughout, finally (equipped with lines from the bad quarto *The Taming of a Shrew*) going home to tame his own wife. The violence was minimized, giving more attention to the combat of wits and the high spirits of Kate and Petruchio. Sharry Flett and Len Cariou bring enormous energy and sheer fun to their parts. For this production, the end result of Petruchio's behavior modification was not a broken or even subdued Kate, but a Kate who has seen through the layers of role playing to reality. When she realizes what Petruchio is up to, her enlightenment consists of a small "oh," then a larger one, followed by quiet laughter.

1980
BBC Television Shakespeare
Rating:

Directed by: Jonathan Miller

Simon Chandler as Lucentio
Anthony Pedley as Tranio
John Franklyn-Robbins as Baptista
Frank Thornton as Gremio
Sarah Badel as Katherine
Jonathan Cecil as Hortensio
Susan Penhaligon as Bianca
John Cleese as Petruchio

Jonathan Miller ends the BBC *Taming of the Shrew* with a Puritan hymn, and Kate's speech of submission is delivered in all seriousness. Miller believes that Shakespeare was a man of his time and that this play is about Kate's sacrificing personal liberty to the good order of society. Nevertheless, the BBC has important strengths even for those who find this interpretation wrongheaded. The words are the thing, and violence between Kate and Petruchio is limited to Kate's striking Petruchio and his grasping her arm and later twisting it to prevent her leaving the room. He does not even carry her off stage after the wedding. Although Sarah Badel's Katherine is less fiery and beautiful than is traditional for the part, John Cleese's Petruchio makes his concern for her especially clear. Petruchio's confiding his strategy to the audience is given full weight both before his first meeting with Katherine and in his own home. Cleese's clever glances out at the television audience make it plain that his own shrewishness is mere performance and that his goal is not to subjugate Katherine but rather to educate her by showing in his own person a mirror of her behavior.

1967
A Royal Films International/F.A.I. Production
Rating:

Directed by: Franco Zeffirelli

Elizabeth Taylor as Katherina
Richard Burton as Petruchio
Michael Hordern as Baptista
Natasha Pyne as Bianca
Michael York as Lucentio

Zeffirelli's *Taming of the Shrew* is a good film, but bad Shakespeare. With the help of inserted, cut, and rearranged lines, Petruchio becomes a money-hungry pauper who is concerned for Kate's safety only until he gets her dowry. After that, he would as soon be rid of her. Taylor and Burton's over-the-top performances and manic energy are entertaining, and the subtext that their personal relationship adds is occasionally poignant (especially when Taylor delivers Kate's speech of submission at the end of the play "straight" before running away), but they seem too old and coarse to play young lovers. The rest of the cast is effective, with Michael York an especially believable Lucentio. Zeffirelli has created a plausible Italian Renaissance background, and he has his usual moments of cinematic beauty. In one of Zeffirelli's more interesting innovations, Petruchio's wooing of Katherine becomes a chase scene through Baptista's house and over the rooftop with opportunities for swinging on ropes, smashing wooden structures, and repeatedly falling into a large pile of wool. Unfortunately, Shakespeare's words suffer to make room, since this production uses only thirty percent of the text.

1999
10 Things I Hate About You
A Mad Chance/Jaret Entertainment Production

Rating:

Directed by: Gil Junger
Heath Ledger as Patrick Verona (Petruchio)
Julia Stiles as Katarina Stratford (Katherine)
Joseph Gordon-Levitt as Cameron James (Lucentio)
Larisa Oleynik as Bianca Stratford (Bianca)
David Krumholtz as Michael Eckman (Tranio)
Andrew Keegan as Joey Donner (Hortensio)
Larry Miller as Walter Stratford (Baptista)

The Taming of the Shrew has been adapted often, sometimes by cutting and changing the play itself and sometimes by retelling the story completely. The first Shakespearean "talkie," a 1929 movie starring Mary Pickford and Douglas Fairbanks, keeps many of the lines but adds whips, silent film techniques, and some unintended humor. Also in this category is a 1950 "live" television production (now available on videotape) starring Charlton Heston that runs a mere sixty minutes. The brilliantly filmed 1953 *Kiss Me Kate,* which tells the story of a musical production of *Shrew,* has some lines from the play, plus the great advantage of Katherine Grayson and Howard Keel in the main roles. The Bruce Willis and Cybil Shepherd television series, *Moonlighting,* did a version with its own rhyming dialogue and a scattering of lines from *Shrew* and other Shakespeare plays. The original *Star Trek* presented the story as science fiction with Kate and Petruchio coming from warring planets and Captain Kirk taking over the job of taming in an episode titled "Elaan of Troyius." The most recent big-screen adaptation, *10 Things I Hate About You,* moves the story to a twentieth century high school in Seattle. Only a couple of Shakespeare's lines survive; however, the film does some interesting subtextual exploration, speculating about what happened to Katherine and Bianca's missing mother. Julia Stiles is an intelligent, feisty, and striking (in both senses) Katherine. Larisa Oleynik, also well cast, does not overshadow Stiles, but manages to be both appealing and spoiled. Joseph Gordon-Levitt (Lucentio) has a certain klutzy charm as a very young lover, and Heath Ledger brings strength, compassion, and mischief to this version of Petruchio.

1983
Bard Productions, Ltd.
Rating:

Directed by: John Allison

Karen Austin as Katherina
Franklyn Seales as Petruchio
Bruce Davison as Tranio

Larry Drake as Baptista
Jeremy Lawrence as Grumio
Kay E. Kuter as Gremio
Nathan Adler as Biondello
Charles Berendt as Hortensio
David Chemel as Lucentio
Bill Erwin as Vincentio
Kathryn Johnson as Bianca

The Bard *Shrew* reduces the play to a Punch and Judy Show with Kate and Petruchio doing more roughhousing than wooing. Kate punches Petruchio in the jaw and knocks him to the ground. He grabs her from behind, and she flips him over her back. Kate bites Petruchio's hand, and later, he bites her toe. There is much struggling on the floor and bending of knees into awkward positions. Nothing in the production moves very far beyond farce. Everyone on stage sighs whenever Bianca is mentioned, and the entire cast leans whenever anyone says "Pisa." Lucentio makes an unsuccessful attempt to quote a Shakespearean sonnet, and Petruchio and Hortensio act as though they are afraid of being struck by lightning when the former mentions thunderclouds and the latter mentions Katherina Minola. The costumes and the acting are equally garish.

Annotated Bibliography

Andersen-Thom, Martha. "Shrew-Taming and Other Rituals of Aggression: Baiting and Bonding on the Stage and in the Wild." *Women's Studies* 9:2 (1982): 121–143. journal HQ 1101.W77.

    Andersen-Thom divides her essay into five parts, discussing in turn Kate's last speech, the survival of the male contingent upon "gratification of appetite and acquisition of territory," male–male versus male–female roles, the trip to Verona, and Shakespeare's comic vision. The author also uses many examples from the 1978 Ashland Shakespeare Festival's production.

Bloom, Harold, ed. *Modern Critical Interpretations: William Shakespeare's "The Taming of the Shrew."* New York: Chelsea House Publishers, 1988. PR 2832.W54.

    This collection of essays focuses on such topics as "dream and structure," "patriarchy and play," metamorphoses in the play, "bourgeoisie in love," and comic form. Principal contributors include Marjorie B. Garber, Richard A. Burt, Ruth Nero, Joel Fineman, and Coppelia Kahn.

Boose, Lynda E. "Scolding Brides and Bridling Scolds: Taming the Woman's Unruly Member." *Shakespeare Quarterly* 42:2 (Summer 1991): 179–213. journal PR 2885.S63.

    Boose discusses first male superiority in the play and the techniques many productions have used to "soften the edges"; then she examines bridles that were at one time used to curb women's tongues (accompanied by illustrations).

Burns, Margie. "The Ending of *The Shrew.*" *Shakespeare Studies* XVIII. Ed. J. Leeds Barroll. New York: Burt Franklin & Co., Inc., 1986. 41–64. journal PR 2885.S64.

> Bums argues that the "missing" ending in *The Taming of the Shrew* is actually not as problematic as audiences would believe. In this essay, she demonstrates how Christopher Sly's absence at the conclusion and how Kate's final metamorphosis actually unite the play.

Cole, David W. "Shakespeare's *The Taming of the Shrew.*" *Explicator* 58:4 (Summer 2000): 184–185. journal PR 1.E9.

> Cole proves in this article that Petruchio is not the honest person Tranio claims him to be in 3.2. Although Petruchio states that his alliances are with Hortensio, Petruchio must have known about Tranio and Lucentio's scheme to woo Bianca.

Dusinberre, Juliet. "*The Taming of the Shrew.* Women, Acting, and Power." *Studies in the Literary Imagination* 26.1 (1993): 67–84. journal PR 1.S84.

> In this essay, Dusinberre shows that when Christopher Sly calls the Hostess "boy," he is inviting the audience to envision the characters as actors playing roles in the comedy. This argument takes on additional importance when Dusinberre illustrates how the play assumes an entirely different meaning when audiences realize that the female parts were initially written for cross-dressing boys.

Hodgdon, Barbara. "Katherina Bound; or, Play(K)ating the Strictures of Everyday Life." *PMLA: Publications of the Modern Language Association of America* 107:3 (May 1992): 538–553. journal PB 6.M6.

> This essay is part of a book-length study that assesses the extent to which theatrical, cinematic, and televised reproductions of Shakespeare's plays focus our attention on cultural issues, especially those concerning gender relations and the construction of subjectivity.

Huston, Dennis J. " 'To Make a Puppet': Play and Play-Making in *The Taming of the Shrew.*" *Shakespeare Studies* IX (1976): 73–87. journal PR 2885. S64.

> Huston begins his article with a discussion of how Old and New Comedy play roles in *The Taming of the Shrew.* He then compares how Petruchio uses Kate as a puppet to the manner in which Shakespeare treats his audience. Huston states that the audience plays a role in this play and that Shakespeare pulls the strings to elicit the responses he wants.

Jaster, Margaret R. "Controlling Clothes, Manipulating Mates: Petruchio's Griselda." *Shakespeare Studies* XXIX (2001): 93–109. journal PR 2885 S64.

> This article discusses the significance of Petruchio's dressing and undressing of Katharina in *The Taming of the Shrew* as it relates to the social and legal mores of the period. Jaster also explores the connection between this motif and the story of Griselda in Boccacio's *Decameron* and Chaucer's *Canterbury Tales.*

Jayne, Sears. "The Dreaming of *The Shrew.*" *Shakespeare Quarterly* 17 (1966): 41–56. journal PR 2885.S63.

> Jayne considers several different ways to cope with Sly's disappearance at the conclusion of the play. She then introduces a new solution to the

problem by proposing that the play-within-a-play should be seen as though it were Christopher Sly's dream.

Kahn, Coppelia. "*The Taming of the Shrew.* Shakespeare's Mirror of Marriage." *Modern Language Studies* 5:1 (1975): 88–102. journal PB 6.M6.

> In this article, Kahn evaluates the gender roles in the play, focusing principally on the relationship between Kate and Petruchio. Kahn demonstrates how each character fits within an established gender role and ultimately shows how Petruchio's manhood is contingent upon Kate's submission.

Maguire, Laurie E. "Cultural Control in *The Taming of the Shrew.*" *Renaissance Drama XXVI: Explorations in Renaissance Drama.* Mary Beth Rose, ed. Evanston: Northwestern University Press and the Newberry Library Center for Renaissance Studies, 1995. 83–104. journal PN 1785.R4.

> In this essay, Maguire investigates three types of cultural control in the play: hunting, music, and marriage. Maguire argues that through cultural control, audiences can observe how man's progress is "grounded in manipulation" and thereby experience the risky playfulness of the play.

Mikesell, Margaret Lael. "'Love Wrought These Miracles': Marriage and Genre in *The Taming of the Shrew.*" *Renaissance Drama XX: Essays on Dramatic Traditions: Challenges and Transmissions.* Mary Beth Rose, ed. Evanston: Northwestern University Press and The Newberry Library Center for Renaissance Studies, 1989. 141–167. journal PN 1785.R4.

> Mikesell looks at the New Comedy plot of Bianca and the folk tale and the ballad plot of Kate to explain how Shakespeare molded these two narratives and changed them from his sources. Mikesell also examines how Shakespeare's emendations altered the meanings in the plots.

Moisan, Thomas. "'What's that to you?' or, Facing Facts: Anti-Paternalist Chords and Social Discord in *The Taming of the Shrew.*" *Renaissance Drama XXVI: Explorations in Renaissance Drama.* Mary Beth Rose, ed. Evanston: Northwestern University Press and The Newberry Library Center for Renaissance Studies, 1995. 105–129. journal PN 1785.R4.

> Moisan investigates how *The Taming of the Shrew* mimics the ambivalent voices of its society. He believes the play contains anti-paternalistic references that bring "to the surface dissonances in the structure of familial relations" which go unsettled in the end.

Newman, Karen. "Renaissance Family Politics and Shakespeare's *The Taming of the Shrew.*" *English Literary Renaissance* 16.1 (Winter 1986): 86–100. journal PR 1.E43.

> Newman provides readers with a historical incident in Wetherden in 1604 which could be the basis for the Induction scene. Newman then explores family politics in the Renaissance and gives a history of the play. She concludes her essay by showing how the play is culturally rather than "naturally" constructed.

Seronsky, Cecil C. "'Supposes' as the Unifying Theme in *The Taming of the Shrew.*" *Shakespeare Quarterly* 14 (1963): 15–30. journal PR 2885.S63.

> Seronsky begins his article by providing brief outlines of *The Taming of the Shrew, The Taming of a Shrew,* and *The Supposes.* He then demonstrates how

Shakespeare used ideas from *The Supposes* to create a unity between the shrew plot, sub-plot, and the induction.

Shapiro, Michael. "Framing the Taming: Metatheatrical Awareness of Female Impersonation in *The Taming of the Shrew.*" *The Yearbook of English Studies.* Ed. Andrew Gurr. Volume 23. London: The Modern Humanities Research Association, 1993. 143–166. journal PR 2885.63.

Shapiro explores the idea that *The Taming of the Shrew* has metatheatrical components beyond the Induction. He believes that before audiences can study the ending of the play or the play's female characters as "being both theatrically and culturally constructed," they must first examine the fact that all females in Shakespeare's troupe were cross-dressing males, which must have created a theatrical awareness for the female roles.

Shurgot, Michael W. "From Fiction to Reality: Character and Stagecraft in *The Taming of the Shrew.*" *Theatre Journal* 33:3 (October 1981): 327–340. journal PN 3171.E38.

In this essay, Shurgot quotes John Dover Wilson's words about *The Taming of the Shrew:* "Although it reads rather ill in the library, it goes rather well on the stage." Within this context, Shurgot demonstrates why this play must be seen on stage and why it is often misinterpreted on the page.

Smith, Amy L. "Performing Marriage with a Difference: Wooing, Wedding and Bedding in *The Taming of the Shrew.*" *Comparative Drama* 36:3–4 (Fall/Winter 2002): 289–320. PN 1601.C66.

Smith reexamines the theme of marriage with regard to early modern patriarchies within *The Taming of the Shrew,* arguing that Katharina's final speech is neither one of submission nor acceptance of the contemporary marital standard. Instead, the author asserts that Katharina and Petruchio, as well as other married figures in the play, illustrate a constant state of negotiation in regards to marital power which Smith observes in the wooings, weddings, and banquets depicted in the play.

West, Michael. "The Folk Background of Petruchio's Wooing Dance: Male Supremacy in *The Taming of the Shrew.*" *Shakespeare Studies VII.* Ed. J. Leeds Barroll. Columbia: University of South Carolina Press, 1974. 65–73. journal PR 2885.S64.

In this article, West explores various folklore traditions evident in *The Taming of the Shrew.* He further connects these folk traditions to the manner in which audiences perceive a positive, loving relationship between Petruchio and Kate.

A Midsummer Night's Dream

A Midsummer Night's Dream *at the Shakespeare Theatre in Washington, D.C., with (in the foreground) Erik Sorensen as Demetrius, Tricia Paoluccio as Hermia, Gregory Wooddell as Lysander, and Anna Cody as Helena and (in the background) Andrew Long as Oberon and Blair Singer as Puck (2000). Photograph by T. Charles Erickson.*

A Midsummer Night's Dream is an enchanting <u>comedy</u> guaranteed to bring pleasure to readers and theater-goers alike through its unique combination of love, humor, broad physical action, Greek mythology, fairy lore, and magical spells. One of Shakespeare's earlier plays (1595), it presents the adventures of four separate groups of characters: (1) Theseus, Duke of Athens, and his Amazon Warrior Queen, Hippolyta; (2) two sets of young lovers—Hermia and Lysander, Helena and Demetrius; (3) six good-natured, bumbling working men nicknamed the "rude mechanicals"; and (4) the fairy world, including Oberon and Titania, King and Queen of the fairies, and their mischievous servant, Puck. Typical of most Shakespearean comedies, each of these character groups is confronted with a problem that must be solved during the progress of the play. As a result, the action moves from "society" to "wilderness" to "improved society" as the various characters journey from the legalistic, male-dominated world of Athens to the regenerative forest and back again to Athens, which is a better place at the end of the play because of the magical events that take place in the woods.

Like several other Shakespearean comedies, *A Midsummer Night's Dream* is structured around a holiday experience. In this case, the principal holiday is Midsummer Eve, which took place around June 22 and conjured up, much like Halloween, images of fairies, goblins, and witchcraft that had been traditional for centuries in English society. Shakespeare also seamlessly blends in aspects of May Day, celebrated on May 1 each year in tribute to fertility cycles in the agricultural calendar, during which young lovers got up early in the morning and traveled to the woods to commune with nature. Just as Shakespeare's characters go on holiday by taking this comic, ritual journey to the woods, so too do we as spectators take a holiday by allowing his brilliant comedy to program our dreams through the magical progress of the play. If psychologist C. G. Jung was correct in suggesting that our minds instinctively solve problems during sleep that we are unable to work out during the day, Shakespeare's play serves as a theatrical dream that helps us understand ourselves more clearly. As C. L. Barber argues in *Shakespeare's Festive Comedies,* we find "release" from our everyday trials and tribulations through the dramatic experience, which allows us the "clarification" to see our lives more accurately because of the brief but meaningful vacation we have taken in the theater.

As in all his plays, Shakespeare borrowed plot elements from several well-known earlier sources. For the Theseus–Hippolyta episodes, he was probably indebted to Chaucer's *The Knight's Tale,* Thomas North's translation of *Plutarch's Life of Theseus,* and Ovid's *Metamorphoses.* For the fairy scenes, he used oral tradition and folklore, plus Chaucer's *The Merchant's Tale,* the French romance *Huon of Bordeaux,* Edmund Spenser's *The Faerie Queene,* Reginald Scott's *The Discovery of Witchcraft,* and other contemporary sources. For the story about a mortal given an ass's head, he may have borrowed from Apuleius' *The Golden Ass,* Anthony Munday's *John a Kent and John a Cumber,* and the familiar fable in which Apollo punishes the prideful King Midas with a set of ass's ears. The Pyramus and Thisbe story was undoubtedly based upon Ovid, though scholars are still debating whether Shakespeare created the comic narrative first for *A Midsummer Night's Dream* or its tragic version in *Romeo and Juliet,* which was written and produced during approximately the same time span (1594–1596).

As might be expected, the plot of *A Midsummer Night's Dream* is a vehicle intended to carry a number of deeper themes and images that reappear throughout the script and make the dramatic experience more meaningful and profound. Chief among these are the many oxymorons typical of the playwright's early work, including sun/moon, woods/city, love/law, fairy/mortal, merry/tragical, and tedious/brief. Additional important themes include the value of dreaming in life, the opposition between parents and children, the forest as a distorted mirror image of the Athenian world, the conflict between magic and love, the difference between royalty and working-class characters, the great variety of language use in the play, and the metatheatrical concept of the play as a dream experience being performed for its sleeping audience. Recent scholarship has investigated festive rites (especially St. Valentine's Day), the transformation of power, production promptbooks, erotic desire, astrology, bestiality, and Elizabethan marriage customs in an attempt to broaden the variety of critical approaches to this fascinating play.

Though little is known of the <u>script's</u> earliest performances, it has survived an exciting series of stage transformations. In 1692, for example, it was made into a spectacular opera entitled *The Fairy Queen,* with music by Henry Purcell. Later operatic versions in which Shakespeare's text was heavily cut included David Garrick's *The Fairies* in 1755, Frederic Reynolds' Covent Garden production in 1816 (which used for the first time the famous Mendelssohn overture), and Madame Lucia Vestris' spectacular London rendition in 1840 which featured fourteen songs, ballerina fairies dressed in white lacy costumes, and Puck entering the stage on a huge mushroom. This tradition of treating the play as an operatic ballet continued into the twentieth century with the now-famous Max Reinhardt film adaptation starring Olivia de Havilland, James Cagney, and Mickey Rooney. More recent productions include the elaborate Harley Granville-Barker version at the Savoy Theatre in 1914 (which restored most of the original text), Peter Hall's in 1959, and Benjamin Britten's opera in 1960. Perhaps the most influential modern production of the play, however, was staged by Peter Brook at the Royal Shakespeare Theatre in 1970 using a three-sided "white box" set within which the actors juggled, tumbled, and flew through space as if they were circus performers. This production also achieved fame as the first in which the roles of Theseus/Oberon and Hippolyta/Titania were doubled, thereby emphasizing the important parallels between the two contrasting worlds of the play.

As each age has attempted to make this play its own through unique signature theatrical approaches, so too will you and your classmates take ownership of the <u>script</u> by reading, discussing, and staging it while you delve into its darker mysteries. In the same way the four lovers are transformed by their pilgrimage into Shakespeare's magical forest, you, too, can be changed by making the play part of your life's journey. All you have to do is dream.

A Midsummer Night's Dream at the Oregon Shakespeare Festival in Ashland, Oregon, with David Kelly as Bottom and B. W. Gonzalez as Titania (1998). Photograph by T. Charles Erickson.

A Midsummer's Night's Dream

NAMES OF THE ACTORS

THESEUS, *Duke of Athens*
HIPPOLYTA, *Queen of the Amazons, betrothed to Theseus*
EGEUS, *father of Hermia*
LYSANDER ⎫
DEMETRIUS ⎭ *suitors to Hermia*
HERMIA, *in love with Lysander*
HELENA, *in love with Demetrius*
PHILOSTRATE, *Master of the Revels in the court*

PETER QUINCE, *a carpenter*
NICK BOTTOM, *a weaver*
FRANCIS FLUTE, *a bellows mender*
TOM SNOUT, *a tinker*
SNUG, *a joiner*
ROBIN STARVELING, *a tailor*

OBERON, *King of the Fairies*
TITANIA, *Queen of the Fairies*
PUCK, *or* ROBIN GOODFELLOW
PEASEBLOSSOM ⎫
COBWEB ⎪
MOTH ⎬ *fairies*
MUSTARDSEED ⎭

OTHER FAIRIES *attending Oberon and Titania*
ATTENDANTS *on Theseus and Hippolyta*

SCENE: *Athens, and a wood nearby*

❧ **1.1°** *Enter Theseus, Hippolyta, [Philostrate,] with others.*　　**1.1:** The duke's palace at Athens

THESEUS
　Now, fair Hippolyta, our nuptial hour
　Draws on apace. Four happy days bring in
　Another moon; but O, methinks, how slow
　This old moon wanes! She lingers° my desires,　　**lingers:** frustrates by delaying

---

DISCOVERING SHAKESPEARE

(1) Characterization [1.1.1]: Try to determine what kind of character Theseus is based upon his speech habits. For example, what type of man would say "our nuptial hour/Draws on apace" instead of "We will be married very soon"? Similarly, what kind of character is Hippolyta? Are her lines more <u>end-stopped</u> than Theseus'? If so, is this significant in any way? What does her beautiful <u>metaphor</u> about how the days "will quickly steep themselves in night" tell us about her personality? Her imagination? Write your descriptions of Theseus and Hippolyta on a separate sheet of paper.

Like to a stepdame or a dowager   5
Long withering out a young man's revenue.°

Like to a stepdame . . . revenue: (Theseus compares himself to a young man impatiently awaiting a diminished inheritance from a long-lived stepmother or widow)

HIPPOLYTA

Four days will quickly steep themselves in night,
Four nights will quickly dream away the time,
And then the moon, like to a silver bow   10
New-bent in heaven, shall behold the night
Of our solemnities.

THESEUS   Go, Philostrate,
Stir up the Athenian youth to merriments,
Awake the pert and nimble spirit of mirth,
Turn melancholy forth to funerals:
The pale companion° is not for our pomp.°   15

[Exit Philostrate.]

companion: fellow; **pomp:** i.e., splendid marriage ceremony

Hippolyta, I wooed thee with my sword,°
And won thy love doing thee injuries,
But I will wed thee in another key,
With pomp, with triumph,° and with reveling.

Enter Egeus and his daughter Hermia, and Lysander and Demetrius.

Hippolyta . . . sword: (one version of the Theseus myth records that he captured Hippolyta in his war against the Amazons)

triumph: victorious procession

EGEUS

Happy be Theseus, our renownèd duke.   20

THESEUS

Thanks, good Egeus.° What's the news with thee?

Egeus: (pronounced "E-jée-us")

EGEUS

Full of vexation come I, with complaint
Against my child, my daughter Hermia.
Stand forth, Demetrius. My noble lord,
This man hath my consent to marry her.   25
Stand forth, Lysander. And, my gracious duke,
This hath bewitched the bosom of my child.
Thou, thou, Lysander, thou hast given her rhymes
And interchanged love tokens with my child;
Thou hast by moonlight at her window sung   30
With feigning voice verses of feigning° love,
And stol'n the impression of her fantasy°
With bracelets of thy hair, rings, gauds,° conceits,°
Knacks,° trifles, nosegays, sweetmeats – messengers
Of strong prevailment in unhardened youth.   35
With cunning hast thou filched my daughter's heart,
Turned her obedience (which is due to me)
To stubborn harshness.° And, my gracious duke,
Be it so she will not here before your grace
Consent to marry with Demetrius,   40
I beg the ancient privilege of Athens:
As she is mine, I may dispose of her,
Which shall be either to this gentleman

feigning: (1) longing ("faining"), (2) soft, (3) deceitful

stol'n . . . fantasy: secretly imprinted your image on her imagination (fancy)

gauds: trinkets; **conceits:** fanciful gifts or notions

Knacks: knickknacks

harshness: i.e., hardness of heart

DISCOVERING SHAKESPEARE

(2) Pacing [1.1.22]: Do single syllables slow a line down or speed it up? That is, would Shakespeare's word choices encourage an actor to say the following lines slowly or rapidly: "but O, methinks, how slow/This old moon wanes" or "Full of vexation come I, with complaint/Against my child"? Pick several different sections from the first scene of the play and count all the single-syllable words for each line. Which lines carry the most single syllables? Why?

Or to her death, according to our law
Immediately° provided in that case.
THESEUS
What say you, Hermia? Be advised, fair maid.
To you your father should be as a god,
One that composed your beauties, yea, and one
To whom you are but as a form in wax,
By him imprinted, and within his power
To leave the figure or disfigure it.°
Demetrius is a worthy° gentleman.
HERMIA
So is Lysander.
THESEUS   In himself he is;
But in this kind,° wanting your father's voice,°
The other must be held the worthier.
HERMIA
I would my father looked but with my eyes.
THESEUS
Rather your eyes must with his judgment look.
HERMIA
I do entreat your grace to pardon me.
I know not by what power I am made bold,
Nor how it may concern my modesty
In such a presence here to plead my thoughts,
But I beseech your grace that I may know
The worst that may befall me in this case
If I refuse to wed Demetrius.
THESEUS
Either to die the death, or to abjure
For ever the society of men.
Therefore, fair Hermia, question your desires,
Know of your youth, examine well your blood,°
Whether, if you yield not to your father's choice,
You can endure the livery° of a nun,
For aye° to be in shady cloister mewed,°
To live a barren sister all your life,
Chanting faint hymns to the cold fruitless moon.°
Thrice blessèd they that master so their blood°
To undergo such maiden pilgrimage;
But earthlier happy is the rose distilled°
Than that which, withering on the virgin thorn,
Grows, lives, and dies in single blessedness.
HERMIA
So will I grow, so live, so die, my lord,
Ere I will yield my virgin patent° up
Unto his lordship whose unwishèd yoke
My soul consents not to give sovereignty.

Immediately: directly, without question   45

50

To leave . . . it: to leave the image as it is or to destroy it
worthy: noble

in this kind: in this respect (as a suitor);
wanting . . . voice: lacking your father's   55
approval

60

65

blood: passions

livery: habit   70
aye: ever; **mewed:** caged

Chanting . . . moon: i.e., Hermia would become a priestess of Diana, virgin goddess of the moon
Thrice blessèd . . . pilgrimage: (perhaps a compliment to Elizabeth, the Virgin Queen, thus softening the critique of virginity)   75
distilled: i.e., made into perfume

virgin patent: privilege of virginity   80

DISCOVERING SHAKESPEARE

(3) History [1.1.60]: How much power do you think parents had over their children during the Renaissance? What choices does Hermia have if she doesn't obey her father?

(4) Gender [1.1.66–73]: What other patterns or motifs can you find in the play that involve female submission to male authority figures? What do these motifs imply about the treatment of women during the Renaissance?

THESEUS
  Take time to pause, and by the next new moon –
  The sealing day betwixt my love and me
  For everlasting bond of fellowship –   85
  Upon that day either prepare to die
  For disobedience to your father's will,
  Or else to wed Demetrius, as he would,
  Or on Diana's altar to protest°   **protest:** vow
  For aye austerity and single life.   90
DEMETRIUS
  Relent, sweet Hermia, and, Lysander, yield
  Thy crazèd° title to my certain right.   **crazèd:** cracked, faulty
LYSANDER
  You have her father's love, Demetrius,
  Let me have Hermia's: do you marry him.
EGEUS
  Scornful Lysander, true, he hath my love,   95
  And what is mine my love shall render him,
  And she is mine, and all my right of her
  I do estate unto° Demetrius.   **estate unto:** bestow upon, will to (consistent with Egeus's description of Hermia as his property)
LYSANDER
  I am, my lord, as well derived° as he,   **well derived:** well born
  As well possessed;° my love is more than his;   **well possessed:** wealthy   100
  My fortunes every way as fairly ranked
  (If not with vantage°) as Demetrius';   **with vantage:** even better
  And (which is more than all these boasts can be)
  I am beloved of beauteous Hermia.
  Why should not I then prosecute my right?   105
  Demetrius – I'll avouch it to his head –°   **to his head:** to his face
  Made love to Nedar's daughter, Helena,
  And won her soul, and she (sweet lady) dotes,
  Devoutly dotes, dotes in idolatry,
  Upon this spotted° and inconstant man.   **spotted:** i.e., morally stained, untruthful   110
THESEUS
  I must confess that I have heard so much,
  And with Demetrius thought to have spoke thereof;
  But, being overfull of self-affairs,
  My mind did lose it. But, Demetrius, come,
  And come, Egeus. You shall go with me;   115
  I have some private schooling° for you both.   **schooling:** advice
  For you, fair Hermia, look you arm yourself°   **look . . . yourself:** see that you prepare
  To fit your fancies° to your father's will;   **fancies:** affection (throughout the play "fancy" means both "imagination" and "love")
  Or else the law of Athens yields you up
  (Which by no means we may extenuate°)   **extenuate:** mitigate, alter   120
  To death, or to a vow of single life.
  Come, my Hippolyta. What cheer, my love?
  Demetrius and Egeus, go along:
  I must employ you in some business
  Against° our nuptial and confer with you   **Against:** in advance of, concerning   125
  Of something nearly° that concerns yourselves.   **nearly:** closely (may modify *confer* or *concerns*)

DISCOVERING SHAKESPEARE

(5) Language [1.1.100]: How does Lysander's use of language help us understand his personality? (*Hint:* Look for all his legal images and for his habit of rephrasing ideas that have already been expressed. Do you think he would make a good lawyer?) How would you characterize Demetrius based upon his linguistic choices?

EGEUS
    With duty and desire we follow you.

Exeunt [all but Lysander and Hermia].

LYSANDER
    How now, my love? Why is your cheek so pale?
    How chance the roses there do fade so fast?

HERMIA
    Belike° for want of rain, which I could well
    Beteem° them from the tempest of my eyes.

LYSANDER
    Ay me, for aught that I could ever read,
    Could ever hear by tale or history,
    The course of true love never did run smooth:
    But either it was different in blood –

HERMIA
    O cross! too high to be enthralled to low.

LYSANDER
    Or else misgraffèd° in respect of years –

HERMIA
    O spite! too old to be engaged to young.

LYSANDER
    Or merit stood upon the choice of friends° –

HERMIA
    O hell! to choose love by another's eyes.

LYSANDER
    Or if there were a sympathy in choice,
    War, death, or sickness did lay siege to it,
    Making it momentany° as a sound,
    Swift as a shadow, short as any dream,
    Brief as the lightning in the collied° night,
    That, in a spleen,° unfolds both heaven and earth,
    And ere a man hath power to say "Behold!"
    The jaws of darkness do devour it up:
    So quick° bright things come to confusion.°

HERMIA
    If then true lovers have been ever crossed,
    It stands as an edict in destiny.°
    Then let us teach our trial patience,°
    Because it is a customary cross,°
    As due to love as thoughts, and dreams, and sighs,
    Wishes, and tears, poor Fancy's followers.°

LYSANDER
    A good persuasion. Therefore hear me, Hermia.
    I have a widow aunt, a dowager,
    Of great revenue,° and she hath no child.
    From Athens is her house remote seven leagues,°
    And she respects me as her only son.
    There, gentle Hermia, may I marry thee,
    And to that place the sharp Athenian law

Belike: perhaps   130
Beteem: allow, afford

135

misgraffèd: ill-grafted, mismatched

friends: relatives

140

momentany: (common sixteenth-century form of "momentary," from Latin *momentaneus*)
collied: murky (literally, blackened with coal dust)   145
in a spleen: (1) on impulse, hence in a flash, (2) in a fit of fierce temper (the spleen was considered the seat of violent outbursts)
quick: (1) quickly (adv.), (2) vital (adj.);
confusion: ruin
150

stands . . . destiny: can't be changed
teach . . . patience: learn patience in this trial
cross: obstacle, vexation

poor Fancy's followers: sad courtiers to the   155
monarch Love

revenue: (here pronounced "revènue")
seven leagues: "a long distance"

160

DISCOVERING SHAKESPEARE

(6) Verse [1.1.136]: The interchange between Hermia and Lysander in lines 136–140 is called <u>stichomythia</u>, which means alternating single lines of <u>dialogue</u>. Pair up with another student and <u>rehearse</u> the delivery of these lines. How rapidly do they have to be spoken in order to be humorous?

Cannot pursue us. If thou lovest me then,
Steal forth thy father's house tomorrow night,
And in the wood, a league without the town 165
(Where I did meet thee once with Helena
To do observance to a morn of May),°
There will I stay for thee.

observance . . . May: i.e., outdoor festivities associated with but not limited to May Day

HERMIA   My good Lysander,
I swear to thee by Cupid's strongest bow,
By his best arrow, with the golden head,° 170
By the simplicity° of Venus' doves,°
By that which knitteth souls and prospers° loves,
And by that fire which burned the Carthage queen
When the false Troyan under sail was seen,°
By all the vows that ever men have broke
(In number more than ever women spoke),
In that same place thou hast appointed me
Tomorrow truly will I meet with thee.

best . . . head: (Cupid's sharp golden arrow engenders love; his blunt leaden one causes dislike) 170
simplicity: innocence, sincerity; **Venus' doves:** (doves drew her chariot)
prospers: nurtures, causes to flourish
fire . . . seen: (Dido, Queen of Carthage, committed suicide on a funeral pyre when the Trojan Aeneas abandoned her to sail for Italy) 175

LYSANDER
Keep promise, love. Look, here comes Helena.
     Enter Helena.

HERMIA
God speed fair° Helena. Whither away?

fair: beautiful (and implicitly blonde or light-complexioned, the Elizabethan standard of female beauty) 180

HELENA
Call you me fair? That "fair" again unsay.
Demetrius loves your fair.° O happy fair!
Your eyes are lodestars,° and your tongue's sweet air°
More tuneable than lark to shepherd's ear
When wheat is green, when hawthorn buds appear.
Sickness is catching. O, were favor° so,
Yours would I catch, fair Hermia; ere I go
My ear should catch your voice, my eye your eye,
My tongue should catch your tongue's sweet melody.
Were the world mine, Demetrius being bated,°
The rest I'll give to be to you translated.°
O, teach me how you look, and with what art°
You sway the motion° of Demetrius' heart.

your fair: i.e., your beautiful coloring (Hermia is dark; see 2.2.114)
lodestars: guiding lights, like the polestar; **air:** music 185
favor: appearance, especially good looks

bated: excepted 190
translated: transformed
art: i.e., craft or magic (see 1.1.27, 36)
motion: tendency, affection

HERMIA
I frown upon him, yet he loves me still.

HELENA
O that your frowns would teach my smiles such skill! 195

HERMIA
I give him curses, yet he gives me love.

HELENA
O that my prayers could such affection move!

DISCOVERING SHAKESPEARE

(7) Syntax [1.1.168–178]: How many "by" clauses does Hermia have in this speech? What is she trying to prove to Lysander, and how does repetition help make her point?

(8) Verse [1.1.180–193]: Hermia's question and Helena's thirteen-line answer combine to make a fourteen-line sonnet. What rhyme scheme does Shakespeare use in these lines? How does his reliance on rhyme here and in the following lines help to portray Helena's frustration? In lines 194–201, when Helena "tops" each of Hermia's lines by completing the rhyme, which of the women seems more anxious? Why is this true?

HERMIA
The more I hate, the more he follows me.
HELENA
The more I love, the more he hateth me.
HERMIA
His folly, Helena, is no fault° of mine.   **fault:** (in early modern slang, *fault* was a term for   200
                                            the vagina or for fornication; those secondary
HELENA   meanings may pertain here and at 3.2.243)
None but your beauty. Would that fault were mine!
HERMIA
Take comfort. He no more shall see my face;
Lysander and myself will fly this place.
Before the time I did Lysander see,
Seemed Athens as a paradise to me.   205
O, then, what graces in my love do dwell
That he hath turned a heaven unto a hell!
LYSANDER
Helen, to you our minds we will unfold.
Tomorrow night, when Phoebe° doth behold   **Phoebe:** the moon, or Diana
Her silver visage in the wat'ry glass,   210
Decking with liquid pearl the bladed grass
(A time that lovers' flights doth still° conceal),   **still:** always
Through Athens' gates have we devised to steal.
HERMIA
And in the wood where often you and I
Upon faint° primrose beds were wont° to lie,   **faint:** pale-colored; **wont:** accustomed   215
Emptying our bosoms of their counsel° sweet,   **counsel:** secret plans, confidences
There my Lysander and myself shall meet,
And thence from Athens turn away our eyes
To seek new friends and stranger companies.°   **stranger companies:** the company of strangers
Farewell, sweet playfellow. Pray thou for us;   220
And good luck grant thee thy Demetrius.
Keep word,° Lysander. We must starve our sight   **Keep word:** i.e., don't break your promise
From lovers' food till morrow deep midnight.
LYSANDER
I will, my Hermia.   *Exit Hermia.*
              Helena, adieu.
As you on him, Demetrius dote on you.   *Exit Lysander.*   225
HELENA
How happy some o'er other some° can be!   **other some:** other people
Through Athens I am thought as fair as she.
But what of that? Demetrius thinks not so;
He will not know what all but he do know.
And as he errs, doting on Hermia's eyes,   230
So I, admiring of his qualities.°   **admiring of his qualities:** marveling at his
Things base and vile, holding no quantity,°   attractions, or "parts"
Love can transpose to form and dignity.   **holding no quantity:** without proportion,
Love looks not with the eyes, but with the mind,   therefore shapeless and unappealing
And therefore is winged Cupid painted blind.   235

DISCOVERING SHAKESPEARE

(9) Arc [1.1.226]: How does Helena's personality change when she begins her soliloquy in 1.1.226? A good way to describe a soliloquy is that it is "living thought." That is, Helena is clearly trying to figure something out during this long, solitary speech. What problem is she trying to grapple with, and how does she solve it?

Nor hath Love's mind of any judgment taste:°
Wings, and no eyes, figure° unheedy haste.
And therefore is Love said to be a child,
Because in choice he is so oft beguiled.
As waggish° boys in game themselves forswear,
So the boy Love is perjured everywhere.
For ere Demetrius looked on Hermia's eyne,°
He hailed down oaths that he was only mine;
And when this hail some heat from Hermia felt,
So he dissolved, and show'rs of oaths did melt.
I will go tell him of fair Hermia's flight.
Then to the wood will he tomorrow night
Pursue her; and for this intelligence°
If I have thanks, it is a dear expense.°
But herein mean I to enrich my pain,
To have his sight° thither and back again.   *Exit.*

Nor hath . . . taste: i.e., in matters of the heart, the imagination (*Love's mind*) has no trace of reason (*judgment*)
figure: symbolize

waggish: playful, teasing   240

eyne: eyes (archaic plural)

                                                     245

intelligence: secret information
a dear expense: a costly but worthwhile effort
                                                     250
his sight: the sight of him

❧ **1.2**° *Enter Quince*° *the Carpenter, and Snug*° *the Joiner, and Bottom*° *the Weaver, and Flute*° *the Bellows Mender, and Snout*° *the Tinker, and Starveling*° *the Tailor.*

QUINCE   Is all our company here?
BOTTOM   You were best to call them generally,° man by man, according to the scrip.°
QUINCE   Here is the scroll of every man's name which is thought fit, through all Athens, to play in our interlude° before the duke and the duchess on his wedding day at night.
BOTTOM   First, good Peter Quince, say what the play treats on,° then read the names of the actors, and so grow to a point.
QUINCE   Marry,° our play is "The most lamentable comedy and most cruel death of Pyramus and Thisby."
BOTTOM   A very good piece of work, I assure you, and a merry. Now, good Peter Quince, call forth your actors by the scroll. Masters, spread yourselves.
QUINCE   Answer as I call you. Nick Bottom the weaver.
BOTTOM   Ready. Name what part I am for, and proceed.
QUINCE   You, Nick Bottom, are set down for Pyramus.
BOTTOM   What is Pyramus? a lover, or a tyrant?°
QUINCE   A lover that kills himself, most gallant, for love.
BOTTOM   That will ask some tears in the true performing of it. If I do it, let the audience look to their eyes. I

1.2: Peter Quince's house (?) (The names of the actors refer specifically to their professions.
Quince: probably refers to "quoins" or "quines," wedge-shaped pieces of wood used by carpenters.
Snug: implies the tightness of joints required in cabinetry.
Bottom: is named for the reel on which the weaver's thread is wound.
Flute: perhaps repairs the leather bellows that   5
supply air to a flute organ.
Snout: refers to the spout of the kettle that a tinker mends.
Starveling: is named for the proverbial skinniness of tailors.)
generally: i.e., individually (here, as elsewhere,   10
Bottom says the opposite of what he means)
scrip: list, script
interlude: brief play, comedy
treats on: deals with, represents
Marry: (a mild interjection diluted from an oath,   15
"By the Virgin Mary")

lover . . . tyrant: (familiar leading roles in
Elizabethan plays)   20

DISCOVERING SHAKESPEARE

(10) Teaser [1.1.240]: Who claimed earlier that Helena "dotes in idolatry" on Demetrius? Identify specific lines in her soliloquy that sound as if she is doting on him.
(11) History [1.2.1]: What do you suppose the following jobs were like during the Renaissance: weaver, bellows-mender, tinker, joiner? Were these "white collar" or "blue collar" occupations? Can you find any information about how much money such workers were paid each day and what their job conditions were?
(12) Characterization [1.2.16]: What indications can you find in this scene of a power struggle between Bottom and Quince? To what lines would you refer in order to support your argument? Which other power struggles have appeared in the play so far? Compare and contrast the <u>objectives</u> of each of the characters in 1.2. What does each want?

will move storms; I will condole° in some measure. To the rest. Yet my chief humor° is for a tyrant. I could play Ercles° rarely, or a part to tear a cat in, to make all split.°

> "The raging rocks
> And shivering shocks
> Shall break the locks
>   Of prison gates,
> And Phibbus' car°
> Shall shine from far
> And make and mar
>   The foolish Fates."

This was lofty. Now name the rest of the players. This is Ercles' vein, a tyrant's vein. A lover is more condoling.°

QUINCE Francis Flute the bellows mender.

FLUTE Here, Peter Quince.

QUINCE Flute, you must take Thisby on you.

FLUTE What is Thisby? a wandering knight?°

QUINCE It is the lady that Pyramus must love.

FLUTE Nay, faith,° let not me play a woman. I have a beard coming.°

QUINCE That's all one.° You shall play it in a mask, and you may speak as small as you will.

BOTTOM An° I may hide my face, let me play Thisby too. I'll speak in a monstrous little voice: "Thisne, Thisne!" "Ah, Pyramus, my lover dear, thy Thisby dear, and lady dear!"

QUINCE No, no, you must play Pyramus; and Flute, you Thisby.

BOTTOM Well, proceed.

QUINCE Robin Starveling the tailor.

STARVELING Here, Peter Quince.

QUINCE Robin Starveling, you must play Thisby's mother. Tom Snout the tinker.

SNOUT Here, Peter Quince.

QUINCE You, Pyramus' father; myself, Thisby's father;° Snug the joiner, you the lion's part. And I hope here is a play fitted.°

SNUG Have you the lion's part written? Pray you, if it be, give it me, for I am slow of study.

QUINCE You may do it extempore,° for it is nothing but roaring.

BOTTOM Let me play the lion too. I will roar that° I will do any man's heart good to hear me. I will roar that I will make the duke say, "Let him roar again; let him roar again."

condole: lament
humor: (1) temperament, (2) mood
Ercles: Hercules (a familiar ranting part, as in versions of Seneca's *Hercules Furens*); **to tear . . . all split:** (clichés for heroic, emotional parts) 25

Phibbus' car: the chariot of Phoebus Apollo, the sun god (the mock-heroic style glances at English translations of Seneca) 30

condoling: pathetic, lamenting 35

wandering knight: knight-errant (another typical role) 40
faith: in faith, by my faith (another mild oath)
I have . . . coming: i.e., I'm no longer a boy and so can't play a woman
That's all one: it makes no difference
An: if 45

50

55

Thisby's mother, Pyramus' father, Thisby's father: (these characters do not appear in the version performed in Act 5; they do appear in Shakespeare's source story)
fitted: cast 60

extempore: extemporaneously, off the top of your head

that: so that

65

DISCOVERING SHAKESPEARE

(13) Teaser [1.2.23–24]: What do the words "To the rest" mean? And how does the meaning of those words in context help us realize the extent of the power struggle in the scene?

(14) Verse [1.2.30]: The first scene of the play is in verse, while the second is in prose (with a brief verse insert from lines 26–33). How is the audience affected by this alternation between poetry and prose?

(15) Voice [1.2.45–48]: What could the actor playing Bottom do with his voice in lines 45–48 to bring Thisby's character to life? Which words would be spoken in Bottom's low voice and which in Thisby's higher, more feminine pitch?

QUINCE   An you should do it too terribly, you would fright the duchess and the ladies, that they would shriek; and that were enough to hang us all.   70

ALL   That would hang us, every mother's son.

BOTTOM   I grant you, friends, if you should fright the ladies out of their wits, they would have no more discretion° but to hang us; but I will aggravate° my voice so that I will roar you° as gently as any sucking dove; I will roar you an 'twere° any nightingale.

QUINCE   You can play no part but Pyramus; for Pyramus is a sweet-faced man, a proper° man as one shall see in a summer's day, a most lovely gentlemanlike man. Therefore you must needs play Pyramus.

BOTTOM   Well, I will undertake it. What beard were I best to play it in?

QUINCE   Why, what you will.

BOTTOM   I will discharge it in either your straw-color beard,° your orange-tawny° beard, your purple-in-grain° beard, or your French-crown-color° beard, your perfit° yellow.

QUINCE   Some of your French crowns° have no hair at all, and then you will play barefaced. But masters, here are your parts;° and I am to° entreat you, request you, and desire you to con° them by tomorrow night, and meet me in the palace wood, a mile without the town, by moonlight. There will we rehearse, for if we meet in the city, we shall be dogged with company, and our devices° known. In the meantime I will draw a bill° of properties, such as our play wants. I pray you fail me not.

BOTTOM   We will meet, and there we may rehearse most obscenely° and courageously. Take pains, be perfit.° Adieu.

QUINCE   At the Duke's Oak we meet.

BOTTOM   Enough. Hold, or cut bowstrings.°   *Exeunt.*

no more discretion: no choice
aggravate: (again Bottom means the opposite — i.e., minimize, soften)   75
roar you: (a colloquialism suggesting "roar for you"; compare *your straw-color beard* in ll. 84–85)
an 'twere: as if it were
proper: good-looking   80

your . . . beard: (*your* is used colloquially to introduce items in a list, a linguistic practice that survives today)   85
orange-tawny: reddish or brownish orange; **purple-in-grain:** i.e., dyed deep red
French-crown-color: golden color of a French coin; **perfit:** perfect
French crowns: bald heads (syphilis, "the French   90
disease," caused hair loss)
parts: (technical term for each actor's personal script or part, containing only the lines and cues of his role); **am to:** have to
con: learn by heart   95
devices: schemes, purposes
bill: list
obscenely: (error, perhaps a mixture of "obscurely" and "seemly," for "privately"; perhaps Bottom's invention for "offstage," ob-scene); **be perfit:** i.e., know your lines perfectly   100
Hold . . . bowstrings: (from archery, probably "do as you should or get out")
2.1: The wood outside Athens

❧ **2.1°** *Enter a Fairy at one door, and Robin Goodfellow [Puck] at another.*

PUCK
How now, spirit, whither wander you?

FAIRY
            Over hill, over dale,
               Thorough° bush, thorough brier,
            Over park, over pale,°
               Thorough flood,° thorough fire;
            I do wander everywhere,
            Swifter than the moon's° sphere;
            And I serve the Fairy Queen,

Thorough: (common two-syllable form of "through")
pale: enclosed area (virtually synonymous with   5
park)
flood: water
moon's: (as with "thorough," pronounced with two syllables, from the old possessive "moones")

DISCOVERING SHAKESPEARE

(16) Staging [2.1.1]: In this scene, we meet an entirely new set of characters: the fairies. Most scholars divide the characters in the play into the following categories: *the young lovers* (Hermia, Lysander, Helena, and Demetrius), *the mature lovers* (Theseus and Hippolyta), *the fairies* (Oberon, Titania, Puck, and the other fairies), and *the Rude Mechanicals* (Bottom, Quince, Flute, Snout, Snug, and Starveling). Try to distinguish between these different groups by (1) the way they talk, (2) their physical mannerisms, and (3) their views about love.

To dew her orbs° upon the green.
The cowslips tall her pensioners° be.
In their gold coats spots you see:
Those be rubies, fairy favors;
In those freckles live their savors.°
I must go seek some dewdrops here,
And hang a pearl in every cowslip's ear.
Farewell, thou lob° of spirits; I'll be gone.
Our queen and all her elves come here anon.

PUCK
The king doth keep his revels here tonight.
Take heed the queen come not within his sight.
For Oberon is passing fell and wrath,°
Because that she, as her attendant, hath
A lovely boy, stolen from an Indian king;
She never had so sweet a changeling.°
And jealous Oberon would have the child
Knight of his train, to trace° the forests wild.
But she perforce° withholds the lovèd boy,
Crowns him with flowers,° and makes him all her joy.
And now they never meet in grove or green,
By fountain° clear or spangled starlight sheen,°
But they do square,° that all their elves, for fear,
Creep into acorn cups and hide them there.

FAIRY
Either I mistake your shape and making quite,
Or else you are that shrewd° and knavish sprite
Called Robin Goodfellow.° Are not you he
That frights the maidens of the villagery,°
Skim milk, and sometimes labor in the quern,°
And bootless° make the breathless housewife° churn,
And sometime make the drink to bear no barm,°
Mislead night wanderers, laughing at their harm?
Those that Hobgoblin° call you, and sweet Puck,°
You do their work, and they shall have good luck.
Are not you he?

PUCK   Thou speakest aright;
I am that merry wanderer of the night.
I jest to Oberon, and make him smile
When I a fat and bean-fed horse beguile,
Neighing in likeness of a filly foal;
And sometime lurk I in a gossip's° bowl
In very likeness of a roasted crab,°
And when she drinks, against her lips I bob
And on her withered dewlap° pour the ale.
The wisest aunt,° telling the saddest° tale,
Sometime for three-foot stool mistaketh me:

orbs: circles (here, fairy rings)
pensioners: attendants (members of Queen Elizabeth's bodyguard, who wore splendid uniforms, were called "pensioners") — 10

savors: scent

— 15

lob: lout or rustic (suggesting an adult spirit, as opposed to the child-fairy)

passing fell and wrath: surpassingly fierce and angry — 20

changeling: (pronounced as three syllables: here, the child stolen by fairies; usually, the ugly child left to the human parents)
trace: travel — 25
perforce: by force
flowers: (pronounced as a monosyllable throughout)
fountain: spring; **spangled starlight sheen:** shining starlight — 30
square: quarrel, square off

shrewd: mischievous (literally, evil or cursed)
Robin Goodfellow: (the proper name of this impish spirit, whose generic name is *Puck*; see note to l. 40) — 35
villagery: village folk
quern: hand grinder, for pepper, malt, etc.
bootless: in vain (because the liquid won't harden into butter); **housewife:** (in Elizabethan times spelled "huswife" and pronounced "huss-if") — 40
barm: head on the ale
Hobgoblin: Robin the goblin ("Hob" being a rural form of Robert or Robin); **Puck:** (from Anglo-Saxon "puca")

— 45

gossip: old woman
crab: crab apple

dewlap: folds of skin around the throat — 50
aunt: old lady; **saddest:** most serious

DISCOVERING SHAKESPEARE

(17) Characterization [2.1.35]: What sort of character is Puck? What kinds of pranks, according to the First Fairy, does he play on mortals? What is his relationship like with Oberon? What historical <u>source</u> can you discover for his behavior? How do you suppose people during Shakespeare's time felt about fairies?

(18) Staging [2.1.42–58]: Stage Puck's speech from lines 42–58 by adding appropriate sounds, gestures, and other stage actions to help dramatize the events he describes.

Then slip I from her bum, down topples she,
And "tailor"° cries, and falls into a cough,
And then the whole quire° hold their hips and laugh,
And waxen° in their mirth, and neeze,° and swear
A merrier hour was never wasted there.
But room, fairy:° here comes Oberon.

FAIRY
And here my mistress. Would that he were gone!
Enter [Oberon,] the King of Fairies, at one door,
with his train; and the Queen [Titania], at another,
with hers.

OBERON
Ill met by moonlight, proud Titania.

TITANIA
What, jealous Oberon? Fairies, skip hence.
I have forsworn his bed and company.

OBERON
Tarry, rash wanton.° Am not I thy lord?

TITANIA
Then I must be thy lady; but I know
When thou hast stolen away from fairyland,
And in the shape of Corin sat all day,
Playing on pipes of corn,° and versing love
To amorous Phillida.° Why art thou here,
Come from the farthest steep° of India,
But that, forsooth, the bouncing° Amazon,
Your buskined° mistress and your warrior love,
To Theseus must be wedded, and you come
To give their bed joy and prosperity?

OBERON
How canst thou thus, for shame, Titania,
Glance at my credit with Hippolyta,°
Knowing I know thy love to Theseus?
Didst thou not lead him through the glimmering night
From Perigenia, whom he ravishèd?
And make him with fair Aegles break his faith,
With Ariadne, and Antiopa?°

TITANIA
These are the forgeries of jealousy,
And never, since the middle summer's spring,°
Met we on hill, in dale, forest, or mead,
By pavèd fountain° or by rushy brook,
Or in the beachèd margent° of the sea,
To dance our ringlets° to the whistling wind,
But with thy brawls thou hast disturbed our sport.
Therefore the winds, piping to us in vain,
As in revenge, have sucked up from the sea
Contagious fogs which, falling in the land,
Hath every pelting° river made so proud
That they have overborne their continents.°

tailor: (proverbial shout for a fall, perhaps because tailors sat cross-legged on the floor to sew) [55]

quire: company, gathering

waxen: increase; **neeze:** sneeze

But room, fairy: i.e., out of the way (Pope emends to "But make room")

[60]

rash wanton: willful creature (*wanton* means "indiscriminate," implying its sexual sense of "lewd")

[65]

pipes of corn: flutes made of oat straw (*corn* is any kind of grain)

Corin, Phillida: (conventional names for a shepherd and shepherdess in pastoral poetry) [70]

steep: slope of a mountain (Q1 reads "steppe," perhaps the modern "step")

bouncing: big, strapping (perhaps also "boasting")

buskined: wearing buskins, leather leggings

Glance at my credit with Hippolyta: [75]
mention my standing with Hippolyta

Perigenia, Aegles, Ariadne, Antiopa: (a partial list of Theseus's mistresses from Sir Thomas North's translation of Plutarch: *Perigenia* was the daughter of Sinnis, slain by Theseus, who then seduced her [Plutarch calls her "Perigouna"]; *Ariadne,* daughter of King Minos, helped him thread the labyrinth and defeat the Minotaur; after escaping with her, Theseus abandoned Ariadne for *Aegles; Antiopa* is sometimes identified with Hippolyta, although here she is obviously another mistress) [80] [85]

middle summer's spring: beginning of midsummer (i.e., around June 21)

pavèd fountain: spring with pebbly bottom

beachèd margent: shore, margin

ringlets: dances in a ring [90]

pelting: paltry

continents: containing banks

DISCOVERING SHAKESPEARE

(19) Characterization [2.1.90]: Why are Oberon and Titania quarreling, and how is the disagreement between them affecting the weather?

The ox hath therefore stretched his yoke in vain,
The plowman lost his sweat, and the green corn
Hath rotted ere his youth attained a beard;°
The fold stands empty in the drownèd field,
And crows are fatted with the murrion° flock;
The nine-men's morris° is filled up with mud,
And the quaint mazes° in the wanton green°
For lack of tread are undistinguishable.
The human mortals want their winter cheer;°
No night is now with hymn or carol° blessed.
Therefore° the moon, the governess of floods,°
Pale in her anger, washes all the air,
That° rheumatic diseases° do abound.
And thorough this distemperature° we see
The seasons alter: hoary-headed frosts
Fall in the fresh lap of the crimson rose,
And on old Hiems' thin and icy crown°
An odorous chaplet° of sweet summer buds
Is, as in mockery, set. The spring, the summer,
The childing° autumn, angry winter change
Their wonted liveries;° and the mazèd° world,
By their increase,° now knows not which is which.
And this same progeny of evils comes
From our debate, from our dissension;
We are their parents and original.

OBERON
Do you amend it then; it lies in you.
Why should Titania cross her Oberon?
I do but beg a little changeling boy
To be my henchman.°

TITANIA   Set your heart at rest.
The fairyland° buys not the child of me.
His mother was a vot'ress° of my order,
And in the spicèd Indian air, by night,
Full often hath she gossiped by my side,
And sat with me on Neptune's yellow sands,
Marking th' embarkèd traders on the flood;°
When we have laughed to see the sails conceive
And grow big-bellied with the wanton° wind,
Which she, with pretty and with swimming gait
Following (her womb then rich with my young squire),
Would imitate, and sail upon the land
To fetch me trifles, and return again,
As from a voyage, rich with merchandise.
But she, being mortal, of that boy did die,
And for her sake do I rear up her boy,

---

corn/Hath rotted ere his youth attained a 95
beard: grain has rotted before reaching maturity, with the obvious visual image,

beard: of silks

murrion: afflicted with murrain, a disease of sheep and cattle

nine-men's morris: board game, which, when 100
played outdoors, employed a pattern cut in turf

quaint mazes: tricky paths laid out for races;
wanton green: uncontrolled growth

winter cheer: (Theobald's emendation of Q1's problematic "winter here"; whichever reading is 105
chosen, the sense—confirmed in the next line—is that the country folk must suffer the pains of winter without the pleasures)

hymn or carol: i.e., of the Christmas season

Therefore: (as in ll. 88 and 93, "Because the fairies are quarreling"); **floods:** tides 110

That: so that; **rheumatic diseases:** (1) colds and flu (diseases of "rheum," or mucus), (2) rheumatism (*rheumatic* is pronounced with stress on the first syllable, roughly like "lunatic")

distemperature: disorder in nature 115

Hiems' . . . crown: the god of winter's head

chaplet: garland for the head

childing: pregnant, bounteous

wonted liveries: normal garments;
mazèd: amazed, bewildered

increase: produce, crops 120

henchman: page

The fairyland: i.e., all of fairyland
vot'ress: votaress, woman who had taken a vow to serve a deity

125

Marking . . . flood: watching the trading ships on the tide

wanton: playful, amorous

130

135

DISCOVERING SHAKESPEARE

(20) Teaser [2.1.115]: Some scholars believe that the references to unseasonably cold weather in this scene help readers and viewers determine the year in which Shakespeare wrote his play. How could these references lead to such a conclusion?

(21) Themes [2.1.122]: Shakespeare joins together many opposite images or oxymorons throughout the play, including day/night, woods/city, sun/moon, dreaming/waking, illusion/reality, love/law, and many others. Begin making a list of all the oxymorons you find in the script. How does Shakespeare's fusion of these opposing images help bring meaning to his play?

And for her sake I will not part with him.
OBERON
How long within this wood intend you stay?
TITANIA
Perchance till after Theseus' wedding day.
If you will patiently dance in our round°   **round:** round dance (cf. *ringlets*, 2.1.86)   140
And see our moonlight revels, go with us.
If not, shun me, and I will spare° your haunts.   **shun, spare:** (here synonymous)
OBERON
Give me that boy, and I will go with thee.
TITANIA
Not for thy fairy kingdom. Fairies, away!
We shall chide° downright if I longer stay.   **chide:** brawl   145
                    Exeunt [Titania and her train].
OBERON
Well, go thy way. Thou shalt not from this grove
Till I torment thee for this injury.°   **injury:** insult
My gentle Puck, come hither. Thou rememb'rest
Since° once I sat upon a promontory°   **Since:** when; **promontory:** a point of high
And heard a mermaid,° on a dolphin's back,   land jutting into the sea   150
Uttering such dulcet° and harmonious breath°   **mermaid:** (equivalent to "siren" in early modern
That the rude sea grew civil° at her song,   usage)
And certain stars shot madly from their spheres   **dulcet:** sweet; **breath:** voice, song
To hear the sea-maid's music?   **civil:** mannerly, gentle
PUCK   I remember.
OBERON
That very time I saw (but thou couldst not)   155
Flying between the cold moon and the earth
Cupid, all armed. A certain aim he took
At a fair vestal,° thronèd by the west,°   **vestal:** virgin priestess (probably an allusion to
And loosed his love shaft° smartly from his bow,   Elizabeth, the Virgin Queen, here figured as a
As° it should pierce a hundred thousand hearts.   votaress of Diana, chaste goddess of the moon);
But I might see° young Cupid's fiery shaft   **by the west:** i.e., in England   160
Quenched in the chaste beams of the wat'ry moon,°   **love shaft:** Cupid's arrow
And the imperial vot'ress passèd on,   **As:** as if
In maiden meditation, fancy-free.°   **I might see:** I could see
Yet marked I where the bolt° of Cupid fell.   **wat'ry moon:** (see 2.1.103)   165
It fell upon a little western flower,   **fancy-free:** safe from thoughts of love
Before milk-white, now purple with love's wound,   **bolt:** arrow
And maidens call it love-in-idleness.°   **love-in-idleness:** (another name for the pansy,
Fetch me that flower; the herb I showed thee once.   from French *pensée*, "meditation")
The juice of it, on sleeping eyelids laid,   170
Will make or man or° woman madly dote   **or . . . or:** either . . . or
Upon the next live creature that it sees.
Fetch me this herb, and be thou here again
Ere the leviathan° can swim a league.   **leviathan:** biblical sea monster, usually thought
PUCK   of as the whale
I'll put a girdle round about the earth   175
In forty minutes.   *[Exit.]*

DISCOVERING SHAKESPEARE

(22) History [2.1.166]: The "little western flower" that Oberon refers to was a pansy (also called "love-in-idleness").
How many other flowers can you identify in the play? Why do you think the author has included so many references to
flowers in the script? Are the flowers mentioned mostly in the city or in the woods? Why?

OBERON   Having once this juice,
    I'll watch Titania when she is asleep
    And drop the liquor° of it in her eyes.   **liquor:** liquid essence
    The next thing then she, waking, looks upon
    (Be it on lion, bear, or wolf, or bull,   180
    On meddling monkey, or on busy° ape)   **busy:** meddlesome (as in "busybody")
    She shall pursue it with the soul of love.
    And ere I take this charm from off her sight
    (As I can take it with another herb)
    I'll make her render up her page to me.   185
    But who comes here? I am invisible,
    And I will overhear their conference.
        Enter Demetrius, Helena following him.
DEMETRIUS
    I love thee not; therefore pursue me not.
    Where is Lysander and fair Hermia?
    The one I'll slay, the other slayeth me.   190
    Thou told'st me they were stol'n unto this wood,
    And here am I, and wood° within this wood   **and wood:** and mad (from a Germanic root for
    Because I cannot meet my Hermia.   "raging" or "frantic")
    Hence, get thee gone, and follow me no more!
HELENA
    You draw me, you hardhearted adamant!°   **adamant:** lodestone, magnet (the hardest stone,   195
    But yet you draw not iron, for my heart   often confused with the diamond)
    Is true as steel.° Leave you° your power to draw,   **But . . . steel:** i.e., your magnetism attracts the
    And I shall have no power to follow you.   finest metal, steel, rather than iron (the passage is
DEMETRIUS   full of puns on hardness, attraction, magnetism,
    Do I entice you? Do I speak you fair?   and the violence associated with swords);
    Or rather do I not in plainest truth   **Leave you:** give up
    Tell you I do not nor I cannot love you?   200
HELENA
    And even for that do I love you the more.
    I am your spaniel, and Demetrius,
    The more you beat me, I will fawn on you.
    Use me but as your spaniel – spurn me, strike me,   205
    Neglect me, lose me; only give me leave,
    Unworthy as I am, to follow you.
    What worser place can I beg in your love –
    And yet a place of high respect with me –
    Than to be usèd as you use your dog?   210
DEMETRIUS
    Tempt not too much the hatred of my spirit,
    For I am sick when I do look on thee.
HELENA
    And I am sick when I look not on you.

DISCOVERING SHAKESPEARE

(23) Staging [2.1.186]: When Oberon says "I am invisible," do you think his line should be punctuated by any particular sound or lighting effect? Why or why not?

(24) Comic Pattern [2.1.195]: One important quality of a comedy is that it moves from bad fortune to good fortune or from problem to solution. Name one major problem that each of the character groups has, and then explain how you think each of these problems will be solved by the end of the play.

DEMETRIUS

  You do impeach° your modesty too much
  To leave the city and commit yourself
  Into the hands of one that loves you not,
  To trust the opportunity of night
  And the ill counsel of a desert° place
  With the rich worth of your virginity.

impeach: call in question, imperil　　215

desert: deserted, wild

HELENA

  Your virtue is my privilege.° For that°
  It is not night when I do see your face,
  Therefore I think I am not in the night,
  Nor doth this wood lack worlds of company,
  For you, in my respect,° are all the world.
  Then how can it be said I am alone
  When all the world is here to look on me?

Your . . . privilege: your excellence gives me　　220
license; **For that:** because

respect: estimation

  225

DEMETRIUS

  I'll run from thee and hide me in the brakes°
  And leave thee to the mercy of wild beasts.

brakes: thickets

HELENA

  The wildest hath not such a heart as you.
  Run when you will. The story shall be changed:
  Apollo flies and Daphne holds the chase,°
  The dove pursues the griffin,° the mild hind°
  Makes speed to catch the tiger – bootless speed,
  When cowardice pursues, and valor flies.

  230

The story . . . chase: i.e., we will reverse the
story of Daphne (who fled Apollo's advances and
was transformed into a laurel tree)
griffin: mythical winged creature with the head
of an eagle and the body of a lion; **hind:** doe

DEMETRIUS

  I will not stay thy questions.° Let me go!
  Or if thou follow me, do not believe
  But I shall do thee mischief in the wood.

stay thy questions: wait for or endure further　　235
conversation

HELENA

  Ay, in the temple, in the town, the field
  You do me mischief. Fie, Demetrius.
  Your wrongs do set a scandal on my sex.°
  We cannot fight for love, as men may do;
  We should be wooed, and were not made to woo.
                       [Exit Demetrius.]
  I'll follow thee, and make a heaven of hell
  To die upon the hand I love so well.　　　　*[Exit.]*

set a scandal on my sex: cause me to disgrace　　240
my gender

OBERON

  Fare thee well, nymph. Ere he do leave this grove,
  Thou shalt fly him, and he shall seek thy love.
   Enter Puck.
  Hast thou the flower there? Welcome, wanderer.

  245

DISCOVERING SHAKESPEARE

(25) Comic Pattern [2.1.214]: Another more specific attribute of a <u>comedy</u> is that its characters generally travel from society to wilderness to improved society. As you continue to read the play, give some thought to the manner in which the young lovers move from the restrictive society of Athens to the forest and then back into improved society again at the play's conclusion. How do you think their progress through Shakespeare's magical woods will change their lives?

(26) History [2.1.227]: The lovers' flight into the woods would have reminded many Renaissance viewers of the popular May Day custom of celebrating the rebirth of spring each year by getting up early in the morning, making a ritual journey to the forest, and erecting festively decorated maypoles. Similarly, the author invokes images of another important sixteenth-century holiday, Midsummer Eve, in his title and in his depiction of the fairy world. How much can you find out about these two Renaissance holidays, and how does Shakespeare use each of them to help bring meaning to his play?

PUCK
    Ay, there it is.
OBERON   I pray thee give it me.
    I know a bank where the wild thyme blows,°
    Where oxlips° and the nodding violet grows,
    Quite overcanopied° with luscious woodbine,°
    With sweet musk roses,° and with eglantine.°
    There sleeps Titania sometime of° the night,
    Lulled in these flowers with dances and delight;
    And there the snake throws her enameled skin,
    Weed° wide enough to wrap a fairy in.
    And with the juice of this I'll streak her eyes
    And make her full of hateful fantasies.°
    Take thou some of it and seek through this grove.
    A sweet Athenian lady is in love
    With a disdainful youth. Anoint his eyes;
    But do it when the next thing he espies
    May be the lady. Thou shalt know the man
    By the Athenian garments he hath on.
    Effect it with some care, that he may prove
    More fond on° her than she upon her love;
    And look thou meet me ere the first cock crow.
PUCK
    Fear not, my lord; your servant shall do so.   *Exeunt.*

❧ **2.2°** *Enter Titania, Queen of Fairies, with her train.*

TITANIA
    Come, now a roundel° and a fairy song;
    Then, for the third part of a minute, hence:
    Some to kill cankers° in the musk-rose buds,
    Some war with reremice° for their leathern wings,
    To make my small elves coats, and some keep back
    The clamorous owl, that nightly hoots and wonders
    At our quaint° spirits. Sing me now asleep.
    Then to your offices,° and let me rest.
        Fairies sing.
[FIRST FAIRY]
        You spotted snakes with double° tongue,
            Thorny hedgehogs, be not seen;
        Newts° and blindworms,° do no wrong,
            Come not near our Fairy Queen.
        [Chorus]
            Philomele,° with melody
            Sing in our sweet lullaby,

blows: blooms
oxlips: (species of primrose similar to a cowslip) 250
overcanopied: (modifies *bank*); **woodbine:** honeysuckle (but also applied to different vines; cf. 4.1.41)
musk roses: large, fragrant roses; **eglantine:** sweetbrier, a wild rose
sometime of: at some time during 255
Weed: garment

fantasies: fancies, affections

260

265

fond on: mad about, in love with

2.2: Another part of the wood

roundel: (1) round dance (cf. *ringlets, round,* 2.1.86, 140), (2) song with a refrain
cankers: worms, caterpillars
reremice: bats

5

quaint: fine, elegant
offices: tasks

double: forked

10

Newts: poisonous water lizards; **blindworms:** small snakes

Philomele: Ovid's Philomela, raped by her brother-in-law and turned into a nightingale (*Metamorphoses,* VI)

DISCOVERING SHAKESPEARE

(27) Verse [2.1.249]: Scan lines 249–258 by assigning either a stress mark (′) or an unstress mark (u) to each syllable. For example, the word "hateful" would be scanned as a stressed syllable followed by an unstressed syllable; unimportant words like "a" and "the" would normally be unstressed, while verbs and nouns are usually stressed. How many stresses do most of these lines contain? How is this pattern different from the verse form of the young lovers or Theseus and Hippolyta? (See the Glossary for further information about scansion and versification.)

Lulla, lulla, lullaby; lulla, lulla, lullaby;   15
    Never harm
    Nor spell nor charm
Come our lovely lady nigh.
So good night, with lullaby.

FIRST FAIRY
Weaving spiders, come not here: 20
    Hence, you long-legged spinners, hence!
Beetles black, approach not near;
    Worm nor snail, do no offense.
   [Chorus]
    Philomele, with melody, etc.
   [She sleeps.]

SECOND FAIRY
Hence, away! Now all is well.   25
    One aloof stand sentinel.   *[Exeunt Fairies.]*

*Enter Oberon [and squeezes the flower onto Titania's
eyelids].*

OBERON
What thou seest when thou dost wake,
Do it for thy true love take;
Love and languish for his sake.
Be it ounce° or cat or bear,   **ounce:** lynx   30
Pard,° or boar with bristled hair,   **Pard:** leopard
In thy eye that° shall appear   **that:** that which
When thou wak'st, it is thy dear.
Wake when some vile thing is near.   *[Exit.]*

Enter Lysander and Hermia.

LYSANDER
Fair love, you faint with wand'ring in the wood;   35
And to speak troth,° I have forgot our way. **to speak troth:** to tell the truth, frankly
We'll rest us, Hermia, if you think it good,
And tarry for the comfort of the day.

HERMIA
Be it so, Lysander. Find you out a bed,
For I upon this bank will rest my head.   40

LYSANDER
One turf shall serve as pillow for us both,
One heart, one bed, two bosoms, and one troth.° **troth:** faithful love

HERMIA
Nay, good Lysander. For my sake, my dear,
Lie further off yet; do not lie so near.

LYSANDER
O, take the sense, sweet, of my innocence.°   **take . . . innocence:** recognize the innocence of   45
                                                my intentions

DISCOVERING SHAKESPEARE

(28) Rhyme (2.2.27): What is the <u>rhyme scheme</u> of Oberon's charm (2.2.27–34)? What <u>rhyming</u> pattern do other charms in the play follow? (See, for example, Puck's charm later in the same scene in lines 78–83.) What do you think the flower should look like (color, size, shape)? What type of music or forest sounds should accompany the charm? And how should Titania respond physically while the charm is being applied to her eyes?

(29) Objectives (2.2.35): Actors and directors often talk about dramatic <u>objectives</u>—that is, what the characters want and what they are willing to do to obtain their goals. What primary <u>objectives</u> do Hermia and Lysander have in this scene? Whose <u>objectives</u> are achieved and whose are not? How would this scene (and the entire play) be different if both characters had shared Lysander's <u>objective</u> at the beginning of the scene?

Love takes the meaning in love's conference.°
I mean that my heart unto yours is knit,
So that but one heart we can make of it:
Two bosoms interchainèd with an oath,
So then two bosoms and a single troth.
Then by your side no bed room me deny,
For lying so, Hermia, I do not lie.

HERMIA
Lysander riddles very prettily.
Now much beshrew° my manners and my pride
If Hermia meant to say Lysander lied.
But, gentle friend, for love and courtesy°
Lie further off, in human modesty.°
Such separation as may well be said
Becomes a virtuous bachelor and a maid,
So far be distant;° and good night, sweet friend.
Thy love ne'er alter till thy sweet life end.

LYSANDER
Amen, amen, to that fair prayer say I,
And then end life when I end loyalty.
Here is my bed. Sleep give thee all his rest!

HERMIA
With half that wish° the wisher's eyes be pressed!°
[They sleep.]
Enter Puck.

PUCK
Through the forest have I gone,
But Athenian found I none
On whose eyes I might approve°
This flower's force in stirring love.
Night and silence! Who is here?
Weeds of Athens he doth wear.
This is he (my master said)
Despisèd the Athenian maid;
And here the maiden, sleeping sound
On the dank and dirty ground.
Pretty soul, she durst not lie
Near this lack-love, this kill-courtesy.°
Churl,° upon thy eyes I throw
All the power this charm doth owe:°
[He squeezes the flower onto Lysander's eyelids.]
When thou wak'st, let love forbid
Sleep his seat on thy eyelid.°
So awake when I am gone,
For I must now to Oberon. 　　　　　　　　　　　*Exit.*

Enter Demetrius and Helena, running.

HELENA
Stay, though thou kill me, sweet Demetrius.

DEMETRIUS
I charge thee, hence, and do not haunt me thus.

HELENA
O, wilt thou darkling° leave me? Do not so.

DEMETRIUS
Stay, on thy peril!° I alone will go. 　　　　　*[Exit.]*

Love . . . conference: when lovers talk, love should interpret the meaning appropriately

50

beshrew: curse (in a mild sense)

55

courtesy: good manners
human modesty: (Q1 and F print "humane modesty," and the adjective may carry the sense of "thoughtful")

So far be distant: be just that distant (as propriety requires)　60

With . . . wish: may you have half of *all* sleep's rest; **pressed:** closed in sleep　65

approve: test, put to proof

70

75

this lack-love, this kill-courtesy: this hardhearted, insensitive man
Churl: rude, unmannerly person (literally, "peasant")
owe: own, possess　80

let love forbid/Sleep his seat on thy eyelid: let love make you sleepless (prevent *Sleep* from taking *his* seat)

85

darkling: in the dark

Stay, on thy peril!: don't follow me, or else

HELENA

O, I am out of breath in this fond° chase.
The more my prayer, the lesser is my grace.°
Happy is Hermia, wheresoe'er she lies,
For she hath blessèd and attractive eyes.   90
How came her eyes so bright? Not with salt tears.
If so, my eyes are oft'ner washed than hers.
No, no! I am as ugly as a bear,
For beasts that meet me run away for fear.   95
Therefore no marvel though Demetrius
Do, as a monster,° fly my presence thus.
What wicked and dissembling glass° of mine
Made me compare° with Hermia's sphery eyne?°   100
But who is here? Lysander, on the ground?
Dead, or asleep? I see no blood, no wound.
Lysander, if you live, good sir, awake.

LYSANDER   *[Starts up.]*

And run through fire I will for thy sweet sake.
Transparent° Helena, nature shows art,°   105
That through thy bosom makes me see thy heart.
Where is Demetrius? O, how fit a word
Is that vile name to perish on my sword!

HELENA

Do not say so, Lysander, say not so.
What though he love your Hermia? Lord! what
  though?°
Yet Hermia still loves you. Then be content.   110

LYSANDER

Content with Hermia? No! I do repent
The tedious minutes I with her have spent.
Not Hermia, but Helena I love.
Who will not change a raven for a dove?°
The will° of man is by his reason swayed,   115
And reason says you are the worthier maid.
Things growing are not ripe until their season:
So I, being young, till now ripe not° to reason.
And touching now the point of human skill,°
Reason becomes the marshal to my will   120
And leads me to your eyes, where I o'erlook°
Love's stories, written in Love's richest book.

HELENA

Wherefore was I to this keen mockery born?
When at your hands did I deserve this scorn?
Is't not enough, is't not enough, young man,   125
That I did never, no, nor never can,
Deserve a sweet look from Demetrius' eye,

fond: foolish
grace: blessing, favorable answer

as a monster: i.e., as he would from a monster
glass: mirror
compare: (perhaps "compare myself with," but more probably "compete with, attempt to rival");
sphery eyne: eyes as bright as stars in their spheres

Transparent: brilliant (but also the modern sense of "able to be seen through"); **nature shows art:** i.e., nature displays her ingenuity and craftsmanship (in allowing me to see your heart)

What though: so what if

raven for a dove: (perhaps referring to Hermia's dark hair and complexion, 3.2.257)
will: desire (possibly with specific sexual sense: *will* could also mean "penis")
ripe not: have not yet ripened
touching . . . skill: i.e., reason reaching the height of its development
o'erlook: survey, read

DISCOVERING SHAKESPEARE

(30) Rhyme (2.2.102–103): Notice that Lysander awakens into a rhyme ("awake" and "sake"), thereby completing Helena's couplet. Which of the four character groups in this play makes the most use of rhyme? Why do you think this is so? Which group uses rhyme the least? What can the use of rhyme tell us about the creativity, education level, and age of the characters who employ it most often?

(31) Teaser (2.2.114): Does Lysander's "Who will not change a raven for a dove?" (2.2.120) offer any advice to directors and designers concerning which of these women is dark haired and which is blonde? Which character is taller? Quote a line that supports your opinion.

But you must flout my insufficiency?
Good troth, you do me wrong! good sooth,° you do,
In such disdainful manner me to woo.
But fare you well. Perforce I must confess
I thought you lord of more true gentleness.°
O, that a lady, of one man refused,
Should of another therefore be abused!   *Exit.*

LYSANDER
She sees not Hermia. Hermia, sleep thou there,   135
And never mayst thou come Lysander near.
For, as a surfeit° of the sweetest things
The deepest loathing to the stomach brings,
Or as the heresies that men do leave°
Are hated most of those they did deceive,   140
So thou, my surfeit and my heresy,
Of all be hated, but the most of me!
And, all my powers, address° your love and might
To honor Helen and to be her knight.°   *Exit.*

HERMIA   *[Awakes.]*
Help me, Lysander, help me! Do thy best   145
To pluck this crawling serpent from my breast.
Ay me, for pity. What a dream was here!
Lysander, look how I do quake with fear.
Methought a serpent eat° my heart away,
And you sat smiling at his cruel prey.°   150
Lysander! What, removed? Lysander! lord!
What, out of hearing gone? No sound, no word?
Alack, where are you? Speak, an if° you hear.
Speak, of all loves!° I swoon almost with fear.
No? Then I well perceive you are not nigh.   155
Either death, or you, I'll find immediately.   *Exit.*

❧ **3.1**° *Enter the Clowns [Quince, Snug, Bottom, Flute, Snout, and Starveling].*

BOTTOM   Are we all met?

QUINCE   Pat, pat; and here's a marvelous convenient place for our rehearsal. This green plot shall be our stage, this hawthorn brake° our tiring house,° and we will do it in action as we will do it before the duke.

BOTTOM   Peter Quince?

QUINCE   What sayest thou, bully° Bottom?

Good troth, good sooth: (emphatic phrases—"indeed")   130

gentleness: gentility, courtesy

surfeit: excess

leave: give up, renounce

address: direct
knight: true love, amorous servant

eat: ate (pronounced "ĕt")
prey: act of preying   150

an if: if
of all loves: by all true love

3.1 Enter the Clowns: (although the folio begins a new act, the continuous text in Q1 shows that there is no break and that the stage is not entirely cleared: Titania remains asleep, apart from the rehearsing mechanicals)

brake: thicket or hedge; **tiring house:** dressing room ("attiring house")   5

bully: (here a term of affection meaning "gallant," "fine fellow")

DISCOVERING SHAKESPEARE

(32) Alliteration (2.2.145): Notice that Hermia's dream about the serpent eating her heart away is set up by several alliterative hissing sounds in Lysander's pervious speech: sleep, surfeit, sweetest, stomach, heresy, powers, and address. Find at least two other prominent uses of alliteration and consonance in Shakespeare's play.

(33) Imagery (2.2.150): How do the images of the eating serpent and the smiling lover combine to create Hermia's nightmare in 2.2.145–150?

(34) Psychology [2.2.156]: A contemporary audience watching this scene might conclude that a sexually repressed young woman having a dream about a snake offers clear proof of Sigmund Freud's theories about the suggestive power of phallic symbols. How do you feel about the appropriateness of using modern psychoanalytic theory to help interpret a late sixteenth-century play? Since Shakespeare had never heard of Freud, how valid is it for scholars to employ his theories to help decipher plays like *A Midsummer Night's Dream?*

BOTTOM   There are things in this comedy of Pyramus and Thisby that will never please. First, Pyramus must draw a sword to kill himself, which the ladies cannot abide. How answer you that?

SNOUT   By'r lakin,° a parlous° fear.

STARVELING   I believe we must leave the killing out, when all is done.

BOTTOM   Not a whit. I have a device to make all well. Write me° a prologue, and let the prologue seem to say, we will do no harm with our swords, and that Pyramus is not killed indeed; and for the more better assurance, tell them that I Pyramus am not Pyramus, but Bottom the weaver. This will put them out of fear.

QUINCE   Well, we will have such a prologue, and it shall be written in eight and six.°

BOTTOM   No, make it two more; let it be written in eight and eight.

SNOUT   Will not the ladies be afeard of the lion?°

STARVELING   I fear it, I promise you.

BOTTOM   Masters, you ought to consider with yourselves, to bring in (God shield us) a lion among ladies is a most dreadful thing. For there is not a more fearful wildfowl than your lion living, and we ought to look to't.

SNOUT   Therefore another prologue must tell he is not a lion.

BOTTOM   Nay, you must name his name, and half his face must be seen through the lion's neck, and he himself must speak through, saying thus, or to the same defect: "Ladies," or "Fair ladies, – I would wish you" or "I would request you" or "I would entreat you – not to fear, not to tremble. My life for yours! If you think I come hither as a lion, it were pity of my life.° No! I am no such thing. I am a man as other men are." And there, indeed, let him name his name and tell them plainly he is Snug the joiner.

QUINCE   Well, it shall be so. But there is two hard things: that is, to bring the moonlight into a chamber; for you know, Pyramus and Thisby meet by moonlight.

SNOUT   Doth the moon shine that night we play our play?

BOTTOM   A calendar, a calendar! Look in the almanac. Find out moonshine, find out moonshine.

QUINCE   Yes, it doth shine that night.

10

By'r lakin: (a diluted oath from "by our Lady" —i.e., the Virgin Mary); **parlous:** perilous, serious

15

Write me: i.e., write (a colloquialism, like *roar you,* 1.2.75)

20

eight and six: i.e., common ballad meter (alternating lines of eight and six syllables, or four and three stresses)

Will not . . . the lion?: (at the baptismal   25 celebration of Prince Henry of Scotland, August 30, 1594, a plan to have a chariot pulled by a lion was discarded as too dangerous and unpredictable)

30

35

it were . . . life: i.e., I wouldn't for the life of me   40 want you to think that

45

50

DISCOVERING SHAKESPEARE

(35) Characterization (3.1.12): One of Snout's primary character traits is that he is a "doubter." In 3.1.12, for example, he expresses fear about the swordplay; then later he worries about the ladies being afraid of the lion (25) and about whether he and his fellow actors can bring a wall into the Great Chamber (61). Find one or two words to characterize each of the other rude mechanicals. Then see if you can discover one action verb to capture the essence of each of these working-class characters. If, for example, Snout's action verb is "to worry," what would Bottom's be? Quince's? Flute's? Snug's? Starveling's?

(36) Verse (3.1.22): By the phrase "eight and six" (3.1.22), Quince means what we now call ballad measure: poetic lines of eight syllables alternating with lines of six syllables. Write a four-line poem in eight and six. Then try to write one in eight and eight.

BOTTOM   Why, then may you leave a casement of the great chamber window, where we play, open, and the moon may shine in at the casement.

QUINCE   Ay. Or else one must come in with a bush of thorns° and a lantern, and say he comes to disfigure,° or to present,° the person of Moonshine. Then there is another thing. We must have a wall in the great chamber; for Pyramus and Thisby, says the story, did talk through the chink of a wall.

bush of thorns: bundle of sticks from a thornbush (the man in the moon was traditionally supposed to have such a bundle and a dog; one legend held that he had been banished to the moon for stealing wood)

disfigure: (blunder for "figure"—i.e., represent)

present: play, represent (in theatrical parlance)

SNOUT   You can never bring in a wall. What say you, Bottom?

BOTTOM   Some man or other must present Wall; and let him have some plaster, or some loam, or some roughcast° about him, to signify wall; and let him hold his fingers thus, and through that cranny shall Pyramus and Thisby whisper.

roughcast: mixture like plaster for covering walls or buildings

QUINCE   If that may be, then all is well. Come, sit down every mother's son, and rehearse your parts. Pyramus, you begin. When you have spoken your speech, enter into that brake; and so every one according to his cue.

Enter Robin [Puck].

PUCK
What hempen homespuns° have we swagg'ring here,
So near the cradle of the Fairy Queen?
What, a play toward?° I'll be an auditor;
An actor too perhaps, if I see cause.

hempen homespuns: bumpkins dressed in coarse peasant garb

toward: on the way

QUINCE   Speak, Pyramus. Thisby, stand forth.

BOTTOM   *[As Pyramus]*
Thisby, the flowers of° odious savors sweet —

of: (perhaps Bottom's pronunciation of "have")

QUINCE   Odorous, odorous.

BOTTOM   *[As Pyramus]*
— odors savors sweet;
   So hath thy breath, my dearest Thisby dear.
But hark, a voice! Stay thou but here awhile,
   And by and by° I will to thee appear.   *Exit.*

by and by: shortly, soon

PUCK
A stranger Pyramus than e'er played here!   *[Exit.]*

FLUTE   Must I speak now?

QUINCE   Ay, marry, must you. For you must understand he goes but to see a noise that he heard, and is to come again.

FLUTE   *[As Thisby]*
Most radiant Pyramus, most lily-white of hue,
   Of color like the red rose on triumphant brier,
Most bristly juvenile,° and eke° most lovely Jew,°
   As true as truest horse, that yet would never tire,
I'll meet thee, Pyramus, at Ninny's tomb.

bristly juvenile: bearded youth (an absurd characteristic of the play-within-the-play); **eke:** also (already archaic in the 1590s); **Jew:** (a poetic joke; Quince's—the playwright's—desperate rhyme for *hue*)

55
60
65
70
75
80
85
90

DISCOVERING SHAKESPEARE

(37) Teaser (3.1.55–57): In popular Renaissance legends associated with the Man in the Moon, why does this mythological character have the following: a lantern, a bush of thorns, and a dog? Has there ever been a "woman in the moon"? Which rude mechanical is chosen to play Moonshine?

QUINCE   "Ninus' tomb,"° man. Why, you must not speak
    that yet. That you answer to Pyramus. You speak all
    your part at once, cues and all. Pyramus, enter. Your
    cue is past; it is "never tire."

FLUTE   O – [As Thisby]
    As true as truest horse, that yet would never tire.

[Enter Puck, and Bottom with the ass head.°]

BOTTOM   *[As Pyramus]*
    If I were fair,° Thisby, I were only° thine.

QUINCE   O monstrous! O strange! We are haunted. Pray,
    masters! Fly, masters! Help!

[Exeunt all the Clowns but Bottom.]

PUCK
    I'll follow you; I'll lead you about a round,°
        Through bog, through bush, through brake, through
        brier.
    Sometime a horse I'll be, sometime a hound,
        A hog, a headless bear, sometime a fire;°
    And neigh, and bark, and grunt, and roar, and burn,
    Like horse, hound, hog, bear, fire, at every turn.   *Exit.*

BOTTOM   Why do they run away? This is a knavery of
    them to make me afeard.

Enter Snout.

SNOUT   O Bottom, thou art changed. What do I see on
    thee?

BOTTOM   What do you see? You see an ass head of your
    own, do you?   *[Exit Snout.]*

Enter Quince.

QUINCE   Bless thee, Bottom, bless thee! Thou art trans-
    lated.°   *Exit.*

BOTTOM   I see their knavery. This is to make an ass of
    me, to fright me, if they could. But I will not stir from
    this place, do what they can. I will walk up and down
    here, and I will sing, that they shall hear I am not afraid.

[Sings.]
        The ouzel° cock so black of hue,
            With orange-tawny° bill,
        The throstle° with his note so true,
            The wren with little quill° –

TITANIA   *[Arising]*
    What angel wakes me from my flowery bed?

Ninus' tomb: (In Ovid the lovers meet secretly at the tomb of Ninus, mythical founder of Nineveh. Legend holds that his wife, Semiramis, built the walls of Babylon, home of Pyramus and Thisby.)   95

Enter Puck, and Bottom with the ass head: (this stage direction, adapted from the folio, indicates theatrical practice of the time—i.e., "*the* ass head" prepared for the production)
fair: good-looking; **were only:** would be only   100

about a round: round about

fire: will-o'-the-wisp   105

translated: transformed (literally "gone over to the other side")   115

ouzel: the English blackbird
orange-tawny: reddish-brown   120
throstle: song thrush, the mavis
quill: song pipe made of a reed (a metonymy for the bird's song)

DISCOVERING SHAKESPEARE

(38) Staging (3.1.93): Flute is <u>rehearsing</u> from what we call an <u>acting side</u>: a written <u>script</u> containing his own speeches preceded by the <u>cue</u> lines before them. What amateur mistake does he make in reading his lines in 3.1.88–92? Why would Renaissance actors have been issued acting <u>sides</u> instead of complete <u>scripts</u> of the plays they were <u>rehearsing</u>?

(39) Staging (3.1.115): Most actors playing Bottom would use words like "knavery" (3.1.115) and "nay" (127) to make ass-like neighing sounds. What other words in this scene can you find that would allow Bottom to bray a bit?

(40) <u>Source Material</u> (3.1.123): One of Shakespeare' primary <u>sources</u> for the Bottom–Titania episodes is a Latin fable by Apuleius entitled *The Golden Ass*, in which a young man magically transformed into a donkey makes love with beautiful women. Name some contemporary "beauty and the beast" myths that might be more familiar to modern audiences of this play.

BOTTOM *[Sings.]*
> The finch, the sparrow, and the lark,
> The plainsong° cuckoo gray,
> Whose note full many a man doth mark,°
> And dares not answer nay.°
> For, indeed, who would set his wit° to so foolish a bird?
> Who would give a bird the lie, though he cry "cuckoo"
> never so?

plainsong: with a simple and repetitive song (like the traditional plainsong chant) 125
mark: notice
And dares not answer nay: i.e., the listener can't deny the cuckoo's implication of cuckoldry (perhaps with a homonym for the ass's "neigh")
would set his wit: would bother to respond 130

TITANIA
> I pray thee, gentle mortal, sing again.
> Mine ear is much enamored of thy note;
> So is mine eye enthrallèd to thy shape;
> And thy fair virtue's force° perforce doth move me,
> On the first view, to say, to swear, I love thee.

thy . . . force: your manly strength 135

BOTTOM Methinks, mistress, you should have little reason for that. And yet, to say the truth, reason and love keep little company together nowadays. The more the pity that some honest neighbors° will not make them friends. Nay, I can gleek,° upon occasion.

honest neighbors: (Bottom personifies "reason" and "love" as people who don't get along and need friends to reconcile them) 140
gleek: wisecrack

TITANIA
> Thou art as wise as thou art beautiful.

BOTTOM Not so, neither; but if I had wit enough to get out of this wood, I have enough to serve mine own turn.

TITANIA
> Out of this wood do not desire to go.
> Thou shalt remain here, whether thou wilt or no.
> I am a spirit of no common rate,°
> The summer still° doth tend upon° my state,
> And I do love thee. Therefore go with me.
> I'll give thee fairies to attend on thee,
> And they shall fetch thee jewels from the deep,
> And sing while thou on pressèd flowers dost sleep;
> And I will purge thy mortal grossness so
> That thou shalt like an airy spirit go.
> Peaseblossom, Cobweb, Moth,° and Mustardseed!

145

rate: rank
still: always, continually; **doth tend upon:** serves

150

Enter four Fairies [Peaseblossom, Cobweb, Moth, and Mustardseed].

PEASEBLOSSOM Ready.
COBWEB
> And I.
MOTH And I.
MUSTARDSEED And I.
ALL Where shall we go?

Moth: i.e., probably Mote, a speck (both words were spelled "moth" and pronounced "mote") 155

TITANIA
> Be kind and courteous to this gentleman.
> Hop in his walks and gambol in his eyes;

DISCOVERING SHAKESPEARE

(41) Verse (3.1.136 ff.): After Bottom wakes Titania with his braying, she speaks in <u>verse</u>, while he speaks in <u>prose</u>. Why is each method of speech appropriate for these two characters? How would this scene have been different if both had spoken in <u>verse</u> or both in <u>prose</u>?

(42) Renaissance Fairy Lore [3.1.156]: How should Titania's four fairies be costumed? To what extent should their names (Peaseblossom, Cobweb, Moth, and Mustardseed) help dictate their characterization, costuming, speech habits, gestures, and other physical attributes?

Feed him with apricocks° and dewberries,°
With purple grapes, green figs, and mulberries.
The honey bags steal from the humblebees,°
And for night tapers crop their waxen thighs,
And light them at the fiery glowworm's eyes,
To have my love to bed and to arise;
And pluck the wings from painted butterflies
To fan the moonbeams from his sleeping eyes.
Nod to him, elves, and do him courtesies.

PEASEBLOSSOM   Hail, mortal!

COBWEB   Hail!

MOTH   Hail!

MUSTARDSEED   Hail!

BOTTOM   I cry your worships mercy, heartily. I beseech
your worship's name.

COBWEB   Cobweb.

BOTTOM   I shall desire you of more acquaintance, good
Master Cobweb. If I cut my finger, I shall make bold
with you.° Your name, honest gentleman?

PEASEBLOSSOM   Peaseblossom.

BOTTOM   I pray you, commend me to Mistress Squash,°
your mother, and to Master Peasecod,° your father.
Good Master Peaseblossom, I shall desire you of more
acquaintance too. Your name, I beseech you, sir?

MUSTARDSEED   Mustardseed.

BOTTOM   Good Master Mustardseed, I know your pa-
tience° well. That same cowardly, giantlike ox beef hath
devoured many a gentleman of your house. I promise
you your kindred hath made my eyes water ere now. I
desire you of more acquaintance, good Master Mustardseed.

TITANIA
Come wait upon him; lead him to my bower.
   The moon, methinks, looks with a wat'ry eye,
And when she weeps,° weeps every little flower,
   Lamenting some enforcèd° chastity.
Tie up my lover's tongue, bring him silently.
                    Exit [Titania with Bottom and Fairies].

❧ **3.2°** *Enter [Oberon,] King of Fairies.*

OBERON
I wonder if Titania be awaked;
Then, what it was that next came in her eye,
Which she must dote on in extremity.
   [Enter Puck.]
Here comes my messenger. How now, mad spirit?
What night rule° now about this haunted grove?

apricocks: apricots (early form); **dewberries:** (probably blackberries, although some early writers consider the dewberry another form of gooseberry)
humblebees: bumblebees

If . . . you: (cobweb was used to stanch blood)

Squash: an unripe peapod (i.e., not the familiar gourd)
Peasecod: a ripe peapod

your patience: what you have had to endure

she weeps: i.e., causes dew
enforcèd: (1) violated by force, (2) involuntary

3.2: The wood

night rule: disorder, revels

160

165

170

175

180

185

190

195

5

DISCOVERING SHAKESPEARE

(43) Set Design [3.1.192]: Titania's reference to the moon has led many set designers to include a large, luminous moon in their scenic design. If you were designing a production of this play, would you have a moon on stage visible to the audience? Why or why not? If so, would it be a full moon or a crescent (the "silver bow/New bent in heaven" described by Hippolyta in 1.1.9–10)?

PUCK

My mistress with a monster is in love.
Near to her close° and consecrated bower,
While she was in her dull° and sleeping hour,
A crew of patches,° rude mechanicals°
That work for bread upon Athenian stalls,
Were met together to rehearse a play
Intended for great Theseus' nuptial day.
The shallowest thickskin° of that barren sort,°
Who Pyramus presented° in their sport,
Forsook his scene° and entered in a brake.
When I did him at this advantage take,
An ass's nole° I fixèd on his head.
Anon his Thisby must be answerèd,
And forth my mimic° comes. When they him spy,
As wild geese that the creeping fowler° eye,
Or russet-pated choughs,° many in sort,°
Rising and cawing at the gun's report,
Sever themselves and madly sweep the sky,
So at his sight away his fellows fly,
And at our stamp° here o'er and o'er one falls;
He "murder" cries and help from Athens calls.
Their sense thus weak, lost with their fears thus strong,
Made senseless things begin to do them wrong,°
For briers and thorns at their apparel snatch:
Some, sleeves — some, hats; from yielders all things
    catch.°
I led them on in this distracted fear
And left sweet Pyramus translated° there,
When in that moment (so it came to pass)
Titania waked, and straightway loved an ass.

OBERON

This falls out better than I could devise.
But hast thou yet latched° the Athenian's eyes
With the love juice, as I did bid thee do?

PUCK

I took him sleeping — that is finished too —
And the Athenian woman by his side,
That,° when he waked, of force she must be eyed.°
    Enter Demetrius and Hermia.

OBERON

Stand close. This is the same Athenian.

PUCK

This is the woman, but not this the man.

DEMETRIUS

O, why rebuke you him that loves you so?
Lay breath so bitter on your bitter foe.

HERMIA

Now I but chide, but I should use thee worse,
For thou, I fear, hast given me cause to curse.
If thou hast slain Lysander in his sleep,

close: private
dull: drowsy
patches: clowns, bumpkins; **rude mechanicals:** rough, manual laborers   10

thickskin: dull person; **barren sort:** witless group
presented: acted   15
scene: stage
nole: head (from "noddle"; cf. "noodle")

mimic: burlesque actor or mime
fowler: bird hunter   20
russet-pated choughs: gray-headed jackdaws (russet was gray or reddish-brown homespun cloth); **in sort:** in a flock

at our stamp: (a disputed passage: the mythical   25
Robin Goodfellow was known to stamp fiercely, but some editors follow Dr. Johnson's conjecture, "at a stump")
Made senseless . . . wrong: they thought themselves attacked by inanimate objects
                                                  30
from yielders all things catch: everything grabs at (or steals from) the fearful
translated: transformed (as elsewhere)

                                                  35
latched: moistened (from verbal form of "leak"; but perhaps "secured")

That: so that; **of force she must be eyed:** she   40
will certainly be noticed

                                                  45

DISCOVERING SHAKESPEARE

(44) Verse (3.2.12): <u>Scan</u> the line "Intended for great Theseus' nuptial day." Assuming that the director wishes to maintain the pattern of ten-syllable <u>verse</u> lines, how should the actor playing Puck pronounce the words "Theseus' " and "nuptial"?

Being o'er shoes° in blood, plunge in the deep,
And kill me too.
The sun was not so true unto the day
As he to me. Would he have stolen away
From sleeping Hermia? I'll believe as soon
This whole earth may be bored, and that the moon
May through the center creep, and so displease
Her brother's noontide with th' antipodes.°
It cannot be but thou hast murdered him.
So should a murderer look – so dead,° so grim.

DEMETRIUS
So should the murdered look, and so should I,
Pierced through the heart with your stern cruelty.
Yet you, the murderer, look as bright, as clear,
As yonder Venus in her glimmering sphere.°

HERMIA
What's this to° my Lysander? Where is he?
Ah, good Demetrius, wilt thou give him me?

DEMETRIUS
I had rather give his carcass to my hounds.

HERMIA
Out, dog! out, cur! Thou driv'st me past the bounds
Of maiden's patience. Hast thou slain him then?
Henceforth be never numbered among men.
O, once tell true: tell true, even for my sake.
Durst thou have looked upon him, being awake?
And hast thou killed him sleeping? O brave touch!°
Could not a worm, an adder, do so much?
An adder did it; for with doubler tongue
Than thine, thou serpent, never adder stung.

DEMETRIUS
You spend your passion on a misprised mood.°
I am not guilty of Lysander's blood,
Nor is he dead, for aught that I can tell.

HERMIA
I pray thee, tell me then that he is well.

DEMETRIUS
An if° I could, what should I get therefor?

HERMIA
A privilege never to see me more;
And from thy hated presence part I so.
See me no more, whether he be dead or no.   *Exit.*

DEMETRIUS
There is no following her in this fierce vein.
Here therefore for a while I will remain.
So sorrow's heaviness doth heavier grow

Being o'er shoes: i.e., having waded thus far, being already guilty

50

I'll believe as soon . . . antipodes: i.e., it's
impossible: I could as easily believe that the solid
(*whole*) earth could be bored through, and that the
moon (a metonymy for "night") could pass
through the opening, disrupting the sunshine (*Her
brother's noontide*) and annoying those on the
opposite side (*th' antipodes*)

55

dead: deadly   60

sphere: orbit in which the planet moved (a
technical term from Ptolemaic astronomy)

What's this to: what does this have to do with

65

brave touch: noble stroke (ironic)   70

on a misprised mood: in mistaken anger

75

An if: if

80

DISCOVERING SHAKESPEARE

(45) History (3.2.65): In this scene, the sweet and docile Hermia turns suddenly angry at Demetrius, who she thinks
may have murdered Lysander. To what extent do you believe the lovers' journey from the patriarchal and restrictive society
of Athens into the magical forest has allowed them to behave in a more natural and instinctive fashion?

(46) Gender [3.2.79]: Are women more or less repressed by society today than they were during the Renaissance? How
much differently would we all behave if we were not subject to the laws and social pressures that surround us?

For debt that bankrout° sleep doth sorrow owe;°
Which now in some slight measure it will pay,
If for his tender here I make some stay.°
    Lie down [and sleep].°

OBERON
What hast thou done? Thou hast mistaken quite
And laid the love juice on some true love's sight.
Of thy misprision° must perforce ensue
Some true love turned, and not a false turned true.

PUCK
Then fate o'errules, that, one man holding troth,
A million fail, confounding oath on oath.°

OBERON
About the wood, go swifter than the wind,
And Helena of Athens look thou find.
All fancy-sick° she is, and pale of cheer°
With sighs of love, that costs the fresh blood dear.°
By some illusion see thou bring her here.
I'll charm his eyes against she do appear.°

PUCK
I go, I go, look how I go,
Swifter than arrow from the Tartar's bow.°   *[Exit.]*

OBERON
    Flower of this purple dye,
    Hit with Cupid's archery,
    Sink in apple of his eye!°
[He squeezes the flower onto Demetrius's eyelids.]
    When his love he doth espy,
    Let her shine as gloriously
    As the Venus of the sky.
    When thou wak'st, if she be by,
    Beg of her for remedy.°
    Enter Puck.

PUCK
    Captain of our fairy band,
    Helena is here at hand,
    And the youth, mistook by me,
    Pleading for a lover's fee.°
    Shall we their fond pageant° see?
    Lord, what fools these mortals be!

OBERON
    Stand aside. The noise they make
    Will cause Demetrius to awake.

---

bankrout: bankrupt (an early form, retained in this edition for its sound; the word establishes the legal discourse running through the end of the speech)   85

sorrow's heaviness . . . sorrow owe: (Demetrius says that his sorrow has become even more intense for lack of sleep: "heavy" means both "sad" and "drowsy")

If for . . . stay: (sleep has made an offer—*tender* —that will begin to repay his debt, and Demetrius will stop here—*make some stay*—to accept it); **Lie down [and sleep]:** (an imperative form of stage direction common in Elizabethan plays)   90

misprision: error, misunderstanding

Then . . . on oath: then fate must have taken over, since for every man who is faithful (*holding troth*), a million are breaking (*confounding*) their promises   95

fancy-sick: lovesick; **cheer:** face, look

that . . . dear: (each sigh was thought to extract a drop of blood from the heart)

against she do appear: in anticipation of her arrival

   100

Tartar's bow: famously strong Oriental bow

apple of his eye: pupil

   105

dye . . . remedy: (all these "y" sounds were probably pronounced similarly, making eight rhymes on the same sound)

   110

lover's fee: payment (e.g., kisses)
fond pageant: foolish performance

   115

DISCOVERING SHAKESPEARE

(47) Paraphrase (3.2.84): Translate the following lines into modern English: "So sorrow's heaviness doth heavier grow / For debt that bankrout sleep doth sorrow owe" (3.2.84–85). Does your paraphrase contain more or fewer words than the original lines? Shakespeare, like all great poets, is able to "compress" thought into a minimal number of perfectly chosen words. Do the prose speeches of the rude mechanicals illustrate this same concept of compression of speech, or does prose work differently than poetry in this regard?

(48) Characterization (3.2.112): Do you think Puck actually made a mistake in anointing Lysander's eyes with the love potion earlier (2.2.80–84), or was this "error" part of Puck's power struggle with Oberon? What other moments in the play exhibit conflict between these two powerful spirits?

PUCK

> Then will two at once woo one:
> That must needs be sport alone.°
> And those things do best please me
> That befall prepost'rously.°

[They withdraw.]
Enter Lysander and Helena.

LYSANDER

> Why should you think that I should woo in scorn?
> Scorn and derision never come in tears.
> Look, when I vow, I weep; and vows so born,
> In their nativity all truth appears.
> How can these things in me seem scorn to you,
> Bearing the badge of faith° to prove them true?

HELENA

> You do advance° your cunning more and more.
> When truth kills truth,° O devilish-holy fray!°
> These vows are Hermia's. Will you give her o'er?
> Weigh oath with oath, and you will nothing weigh.
> Your vows to her and me, put in two scales,
> Will even weigh; and both as light as tales.°

LYSANDER

> I had no judgment when to her I swore.

HELENA

> Nor none, in my mind, now you give her o'er.

LYSANDER

> Demetrius loves her; and he loves not you.°

DEMETRIUS *[Awakes.]*

> O Helen, goddess, nymph, perfect, divine!
> To what, my love, shall I compare thine eyne?
> Crystal is muddy. O, how ripe in show
> Thy lips, those kissing cherries, tempting grow!
> That pure congealèd white, high Taurus'° snow,
> Fanned with° the eastern wind, turns to a crow
> When thou hold'st up thy hand. O, let me kiss
> This princess of pure white,° this seal of bliss.

HELENA

> O spite! O hell! I see you all are bent
> To set against me for your merriment.
> If you were civil° and knew courtesy,
> You would not do me thus much injury.°
> Can you not hate me, as I know you do,
> But you must join in souls to mock me too?
> If you were men, as men you are in show,
> You would not use a gentle° lady so,
> To vow, and swear, and superpraise my parts,°
> When I am sure you hate me with your hearts.
> You both are rivals, and love Hermia,
> And now both rivals to mock Helena.
> A trim° exploit, a manly enterprise,
> To conjure tears up in a poor maid's eyes
> With your derision! None of noble sort
> Would so offend a virgin and extort°
> A poor soul's patience, all to make you sport.

alone: unmatched

prepost'rously: back to front, ass-backward

badge of faith: (servants wore badges; for Lysander, the tears *prove* his allegiance to Helena)
advance: display
truth kills truth: one vow cancels another;
devilish-holy fray: paradoxically, a holy war

tales: falsehoods, fictions

you: (Some editors, noticing the break in rhymed couplets, posit a missing line here; others regard the broken rhyme scheme as deliberate.)

Taurus': the Taurus Mountains in Turkey
Fanned with: (1) blown gently by, (2) winnowed by
This . . . white: i.e., Helena's hand, outclassing all others in whiteness

civil: civilized
injury: insult

gentle: (1) wellborn, (2) mild-mannered
superpraise my parts: i.e., exaggerate my attractions

trim: fine (ironic)

extort: twist, torture

120

125

130

135

140

145

150

155

160

LYSANDER
    You are unkind, Demetrius. Be not so!
    For you love Hermia: this you know I know.
    And here, with all good will, with all my heart,
    In Hermia's love I yield you up my part;   165
    And yours of Helena to me bequeath,
    Whom I do love, and will do till my death.

HELENA
    Never did mockers waste more idle° breath.   **idle:** pointless

DEMETRIUS
    Lysander, keep thy Hermia: I will none.
    If e'er I loved her, all that love is gone.   170
    My heart to her but as guestwise sojourned,°   **My . . . sojourned:** i.e., my heart visited Hermia
    And now to Helen is it home returned,   only temporarily
    There to remain.

LYSANDER   Helen, it is not so.

DEMETRIUS
    Disparage not the faith thou dost not know,
    Lest, to thy peril, thou aby it dear.°   **thou aby it dear:** you have to pay (*aby*) a high   175
    Look where thy love comes. Yonder is thy dear.   price
    Enter Hermia.

HERMIA
    Dark night, that from the eye his° function takes,°   **his:** its (common neuter possessive in
    The ear more quick of apprehension makes.   Shakespeare's English); **takes:** takes away
    Wherein it doth impair the seeing sense,
    It pays the hearing double recompense.   180
    Thou art not by mine eye, Lysander, found;
    Mine ear, I thank it, brought me to thy sound.
    But why unkindly didst thou leave me so?

LYSANDER
    Why should he stay whom love doth press to go?

HERMIA
    What love could press Lysander from my side?   185

LYSANDER
    Lysander's love, that would not let him bide:
    Fair Helena, who more engilds the night
    Than all yon fiery oes° and eyes of light.   **oes:** round spangles (i.e., stars—with puns on
    Why seek'st thou me? Could not this make thee know,   "ohs" and "ays" in *oes* and *eyes*)
    The hate I bare° thee made me leave thee so?   **bare:** (original past tense of "bear"; Shakespeare   190
    uses both "bare" and the modern "bore")

DISCOVERING SHAKESPEARE

(49) <u>Rhyme</u> (3.2.166–167): The words "bequeath" and "death" at the ends of lines 166–167 provide what scholars call a <u>slant rhyme</u>—a slightly off-key sound between two words that almost <u>rhyme</u>. Why would Shakespeare put a <u>slant rhyme</u> here in the midst of so many <u>perfect rhymes</u> like "heart" and "part," "know" and "so," and "takes" and "makes"? (*Clue:* How sincere is Lysander in his expression of love for Helena?)

(50) <u>Rhyme</u> [3.2.175–176]: Can you find any other examples of <u>slant rhyme</u> in this scene? If so, do these rhymes function in the same way as "bequeath" and "death"?

(51) Staging (3.2.177): In line 177, Hermia refers to "Dark night," then explains later that her ear and not her eye brought her to Lysander (181–182). How dark should the stage be in order to indicate nighttime in the forest, yet also allow the audience enough light to see the action? How else can night be suggested on stage? (Remember that Shakespeare's plays were presented during the Renaissance in daylight at the open-roofed Globe Theatre in London, so he had to "tell" his audience the time of day rather than "show" them in the way modern lighting designers do.) Which scenes in this play take place during the night? Which happen during the day?

HERMIA
  You speak not as you think. It cannot be.
HELENA
  Lo, she is one of this confederacy.
  Now I perceive they have conjoined all three
  To fashion this false sport in spite of me.°
  Injurious° Hermia, most ungrateful maid,
  Have you conspired, have you with these contrived
  To bait° me with this foul derision?
  Is all the counsel° that we two have shared,
  The sister's vows, the hours that we have spent
  When we have chid° the hasty-footed time
  For parting us – O, is all forgot?
  All schooldays' friendship, childhood innocence?
  We, Hermia, like two artificial° gods,
  Have with our needles° created both one flower,
  Both on one sampler, sitting on one cushion,
  Both warbling of one song, both in one key;
  As if our hands, our sides, voices, and minds
  Had been incorporate.° So we grew together,
  Like to a double cherry, seeming parted,
  But yet an union in partition,
  Two lovely berries molded on one stem.
  So, with two seeming bodies, but one heart;
  Two of the first, like coats in heraldry,
  Due but to one, and crownèd with one crest.°
  And will you rent° our ancient love asunder,
  To join with men in scorning your poor friend?
  It is not friendly, 'tis not maidenly.
  Our sex, as well as I, may chide you for it,
  Though I alone do feel the injury.
HERMIA
  I am amazèd at your passionate words.
  I scorn you not. It seems that you scorn me.
HELENA
  Have you not set Lysander, as in scorn,
  To follow me and praise my eyes and face?
  And made your other love, Demetrius
  (Who even° but now did spurn me with his foot),
  To call me goddess, nymph, divine, and rare,
  Precious, celestial? Wherefore speaks he this
  To her he hates? And wherefore doth Lysander
  Deny your love, so rich within his soul,
  And tender° me, forsooth, affection,
  But by your setting on,° by your consent?
  What though I be not so in grace° as you,
  So hung upon with love, so fortunate,
  But miserable most, to love unloved?
  This you should pity rather than despise.
HERMIA
  I understand not what you mean by this.
HELENA
  Ay, do. Persever,° counterfeit sad looks,
  Make mouths upon me when I turn my back,
  Wink each at other, hold the sweet jest up.

in spite of me: to spite me
Injurious: insulting   195

bait: torment (literally, to set on dogs to bite, as in bearbaiting)
counsel: secrets
chid: criticized (past tense of "chide")   200

artificial: creating, skillful in artifice
needles: (pronounced "neeles," and often so spelled)   205

incorporate: in one body

    210

Two . . . crest: (a complex metaphor, in which the two girls are represented by the identical sections of a heraldic shield: *the first* is a technical term for the first color or quarter of a shield, and Helena imagines a shield with a repeated coat of arms surmounted by a single crest, analogous to the *double cherry* on *one stem* in ll. 209–11)   215
rent: tear

    220

even: (pronounced "e'en")   225

tender: offer   230
setting on: prompting
grace: favor

    235

Ay, do. Persever: i.e., great, keep it up (Pronounced "persèver." The early texts read "I doe," suggesting a response to Hermia's claim not to understand.)

This sport, well carried, shall be chronicled. 240
If you have any pity, grace, or manners,
You would not make me such an argument.°   **argument:** theme or butt of a joke
But fare ye well. 'Tis partly my own fault,
Which death or absence soon shall remedy.

LYSANDER

Stay, gentle Helena, hear my excuse, 245
My love, my life, my soul, fair Helena!

HELENA

O excellent!

HERMIA   Sweet, do not scorn her so.

DEMETRIUS

If she cannot entreat, I can compel.°   **If . . . compel:** i.e., if Helena can't succeed by
    pleading, I can force you to stop (scorning her)

LYSANDER

Thou canst compel no more than she entreat.
Thy threats have no more strength than her weak 250
  prayers.
Helen, I love thee; by my life, I do!
I swear by that which I will lose for thee
To prove him false that says I love thee not.

DEMETRIUS

I say I love thee more than he can do.

LYSANDER

If thou say so, withdraw and prove it too. 255

DEMETRIUS

Quick, come!

HERMIA   Lysander, whereto tends all this?

LYSANDER

Away, you Ethiope!°   **Ethiope:** (a dig at Hermia's dark coloring; the
    quarrel is degenerating into ethnic slurs, as in

DEMETRIUS   No, no, sir, yield.°   *tawny Tartar,* l. 263); **No, no, sir, yield:** (Gary
Seem to break loose, take on as you would follow,   Taylor's convincing solution to a notorious crux.
But yet come not. You are a tame man, go!   Q1 reads "No, no: heele [he'll?]"; F prints "No,
    no, Sir.")

LYSANDER   *[To Hermia]*

Hang off, thou cat, thou burr! Vile thing, let loose, 260
Or I will shake thee from me like a serpent.

HERMIA

Why are you grown so rude? What change is this,
Sweet love?

LYSANDER   Thy love? Out, tawny Tartar, out!
Out,° loathèd med'cine! O hated potion,° hence!   **Out:** Away! get out!

HERMIA   **med'cine, potion:** (common synonyms for
Do you not jest?   "poison") 265

HELENA   Yes, sooth!° and so do you.   **sooth:** in truth

LYSANDER

Demetrius, I will keep my word with thee.

DEMETRIUS

I would I had your bond,° for I perceive   **your bond:** your promise (with pun on "chain"
A weak bond° holds you. I'll not trust your word.   in the following line)
    weak bond: i.e., Hermia's arms

DISCOVERING SHAKESPEARE

(52) Rhetorical Build (3.2.237–240): Helena's lines 237–240 are a good example of a <u>build</u>, in which she gives five sequential examples of how she thinks the other characters are conspiring against her, then sums up her feelings in a final burst of emotion: "This sport, well carried, shall be chronicled." Find at least three other examples of such a <u>build</u> in the play; then act them out in a voice that becomes gradually stronger and more confident.

LYSANDER
What, should I hurt her, strike her, kill her dead?
Although I hate her, I'll not harm her so.   270

HERMIA
What, can you do me greater harm than hate?
Hate me? Wherefore? O me, what news, my love?°   **what news, my love:** i.e., what's the trouble
Am not I Hermia? Are not you Lysander?
I am as fair now as I was erewhile.
Since night you loved me, yet since night you left me.   275
Why then you left me – O, the gods forbid! –
In earnest, shall I say?

LYSANDER   Ay, by my life!
And never did desire to see thee more.
Therefore be out of hope, of question, of doubt;
Be certain. Nothing truer. 'Tis no jest   280
That I do hate thee and love Helena.

HERMIA *[To Helena]*
O me! You juggler,° you canker blossom,°   **juggler:** cheater, trickster (pronounced with
You thief of love! What, have you come by night   three syllables); **canker blossom:** worm that
And stol'n my love's heart from him?   destroys (cankers) a blossom

HELENA   Fine, i' faith.
Have you no modesty, no maiden shame,   285
No touch of bashfulness? What, will you tear
Impatient answers from my gentle tongue?
Fie, fie, you counterfeit, you puppet° you!   **puppet:** (1) counterfeit human, doll, (2)
                                                     miniature person

HERMIA
Puppet? Why, so! Ay, that way goes the game.°   **that . . . game:** i.e., now I get it
Now I perceive that she hath made compare   290
Between our statures; she hath urged her height,
And with her personage, her tall personage,°   **personage:** personal appearance, figure
Her height, forsooth, she hath prevailed with him.
And are you grown so high in his esteem
Because I am so dwarfish and so low?°   **low:** short   295
How low am I, thou painted maypole?° Speak!   **painted maypole:** i.e., tall and skinny, with the
How low am I? I am not yet so low   implication that Helena's light complexion is
But that my nails can reach unto thine eyes.   cosmetically enhanced

HELENA
I pray you, though you mock me, gentlemen,
Let her not hurt me. I was never curst.°   **curst:** shrewish, quarrelsome   300
I have no gift at all in shrewishness.
I am a right° maid for my cowardice.   **right:** regular, real
Let her not strike me. You perhaps may think,

DISCOVERING SHAKESPEARE

(53) Acting [3.2.269]: Most good actors, when faced with a series like "should I hurt her, strike her, kill her dead" (269), will try to imagine a different image for each item in the series. Try saying the line with a separate vision in your mind for each of the three perils threatened by Lysander: "hurt her, strike her, kill her dead" (3.2.269). How is this different from simply saying the words without any emotional or imaginative energy?

(54) Imagery (3.2.296): When Hermia calls Helena a "painted maypole" (3.2.296), she packs three insults into one image: Helena is too tall, too skinny, and uses too much make-up. Shakespeare also alludes here to the Mayday celebration which lies at the heart of the play's holiday atmosphere. Find at least two other insults in this scene that have the same depth of meaning.

Because she is something lower than myself,
That I can match her.°   **match her:** i.e., in a fight   305

HERMIA   Lower? Hark again!

HELENA
Good Hermia, do not be so bitter with me.
I evermore did love you, Hermia,
Did ever keep your counsels, never wronged you,
Save that, in love unto Demetrius,
I told him of your stealth unto this wood.   310
He followed you; for love I followed him.
But he hath chid me hence, and threatened me
To strike me, spurn me, nay, to kill me too.
And now, so° you will let me quiet go,   **so:** if only
To Athens will I bear my folly back   315
And follow you no further. Let me go.
You see how simple and how fond° I am.   **fond:** foolish

HERMIA
Why, get you gone. Who is't that hinders you?

HELENA
A foolish heart, that I leave here behind.

HERMIA
What, with Lysander?   320

HELENA   With Demetrius.

LYSANDER
Be not afraid. She shall not harm thee, Helena.

DEMETRIUS
No, sir, she shall not, though you take her part.

HELENA
O, when she is angry, she is keen and shrewd.°   **keen and shrewd:** sharp and shrewish
She was a vixen when she went to school,
And though she be but little, she is fierce.   325

HERMIA
"Little" again? nothing but "low" and "little"?
Why will you suffer her to flout me° thus?   **suffer her to flout me:** allow her to mock me
Let me come to her.

LYSANDER   Get you gone, you dwarf!
You minimus,° of hind'ring knotgrass° made!   **minimus:** tiny thing; **knotgrass:** low-growing
You bead, you acorn!   plant that hinders the plow and was thought to   330
                                                         stunt growth

DEMETRIUS   You are too officious
In her behalf that scorns your services.
Let her alone. Speak not of Helena;
Take not her part. For if thou dost intend
Never so little show of love to her,
Thou shalt aby it.   335

LYSANDER   Now she holds me not.
Now follow, if thou dar'st, to try whose right,
Of thine or mine, is most in Helena.

DEMETRIUS
Follow? Nay, I'll go with thee, cheek by jowl.
                    [Exeunt Lysander and Demetrius.]

HERMIA
You, mistress, all this coil is long of you.°   **coil is long of you:** uproar is your fault
Nay, go not back.   340

HELENA   I will not trust you, I,
Nor longer stay in your curst° company.   **curst:** contentious

Your hands than mine are quicker for a fray;
My legs are longer, though, to run away.

HERMIA
I am amazed,° and know not what to say.

amazed: bewildered (as in a maze)

Exeunt [Helena and Hermia].

OBERON   *[Coming forward]*
This is thy negligence. Still thou mistak'st,   345
Or else committ'st thy knaveries willfully.

PUCK
Believe me, king of shadows, I mistook.
Did not you tell me I should know the man
By the Athenian garments he had on?
And so far blameless proves my enterprise   350
That I have 'nointed an Athenian's eyes;
And so far am I glad it so did sort°   **so did sort:** happened this way
As this their jangling I esteem a sport.

OBERON
Thou seest these lovers seek a place to fight.
Hie therefore, Robin, overcast the night.   355
The starry welkin° cover thou anon   **welkin:** sky
With drooping fog as black as Acheron,°   **Acheron:** Hades (from the name of one of its rivers)
And lead these testy rivals so astray
As one come not within another's way.
Like to Lysander sometime frame thy tongue,   360
Then stir Demetrius up with bitter wrong,°   **wrong:** insults
And sometime rail thou like Demetrius.
And from each other look thou lead them thus
Till o'er their brows death-counterfeiting sleep
With leaden legs and batty° wings doth creep.   **batty:** batlike   365
Then crush this herb° into Lysander's eye,   **this herb:** the antidote to the love-in-idleness applied earlier
Whose liquor° hath this virtuous° property,   **liquor:** essence; **virtuous:** powerful
To take from thence all error with his might°   **his might:** its power
And make his eyeballs roll with wonted° sight.   **wonted:** accustomed, normal   370
When they next wake, all this derision°   **derision:** ridiculous behavior (pronounced with four syllables)
Shall seem a dream and fruitless° vision,   **fruitless:** inconsequential, worthless
And back to Athens shall the lovers wend
With league whose date° till death shall never end.   **league whose date:** agreement whose term or duration
Whiles I in this affair do thee employ,
I'll to my queen and beg her Indian boy;   375
And then I will her charmèd eye release
From monster's view, and all things shall be peace.

DISCOVERING SHAKESPEARE

(55) Metatheater (3.2.345): What have Puck and Oberon been doing during this long scene between the lovers? Where should they be located on stage so the audience can see them, but the lovers can not? Try to find other scenes in the play in which one or more characters spy on the actions of others. A useful word for this concept is metatheater, because Shakespeare often uses such a "layering" device in his plays to make his audience aware that they are, indeed, an "audience" watching characters on stage who are watching other characters.

(56) Staging [3.2.366]: Oberon produces here another "herb" (366) which is apparently the antidote to the "love-in-idleness" flower discussed in 2.1.168. What would this new flower look like, and how would it affect the sleeping lovers later in this scene?

PUCK

My fairy lord, this must be done with haste,
For night's swift dragons° cut the clouds full fast,
And yonder shines Aurora's harbinger,°
At whose approach ghosts, wand'ring here and there,
Troop home to churchyards. Damnèd spirits all,
That in crossways and floods have burial,°
Already to their wormy beds are gone;
For fear lest day should look their shames upon,
They willfully themselves exile from light,
And must for aye° consort with black-browed night.

OBERON

But we are spirits of another sort.
I with the Morning's love° have oft made sport,
And, like a forester,° the groves may tread
Even till the eastern gate, all fiery red,
Opening on Neptune, with fair blessèd beams
Turns into yellow gold his salt green streams.
But notwithstanding, haste; make no delay.
We may effect this business yet ere day.   *[Exit.]*

PUCK

      Up and down, up and down,
      I will lead them up and down.
      I am feared in field and town.
      Goblin,° lead them up and down.
Here comes one.
   Enter Lysander.

LYSANDER

Where art thou, proud Demetrius? Speak thou now.

PUCK

Here, villain, drawn° and ready. Where art thou?

LYSANDER

I will be with thee straight.

PUCK   Follow me then
To plainer° ground.   *[Exit Lysander.]°*
   Enter Demetrius.

DEMETRIUS   Lysander, speak again!
Thou runaway, thou coward, art thou fled?
Speak! In some bush? Where dost thou hide thy head?

PUCK

Thou coward, art thou bragging to the stars,
Telling the bushes that thou look'st for wars,
And wilt not come? Come, recreant!° come, thou child!
I'll whip thee with a rod. He is defiled
That draws a sword on thee.

DEMETRIUS   Yea, art thou there?

PUCK

Follow my voice. We'll try no manhood here.   *Exeunt.*
  [Enter Lysander.]

---

night's swift dragons: the mythical creatures thought to pull the chariot of the goddess of night   380
Aurora's harbinger: the morning star, sign of dawn
Damnèd spirits . . . burial: the ghosts of suicides, buried at crossroads (as was the custom) or drowned and therefore unrecovered   385

for aye: forever

the Morning's love: the hunter Cephalus, lover of Aurora (Ovid, *Metamorphoses,* VII; Bottom as   390 Pyramus mistakenly refers to him at 5.1.197 as *Shafalus*)
forester: keeper of a royal park

  395

Goblin: (Puck presumably addresses himself)

  400

drawn: i.e., with sword drawn

plainer: smoother, more open
Exit Lysander: (Neither Q1 nor F indicates comings and goings for Lysander and Demetrius, as the action seems to imply, so most modern editors supply them. F includes a marginal s.d.—   405 "shifting places"—which may indicate that Lysander and Demetrius remain onstage and grope in the "darkness.")

recreant: traitor, coward (literally, "promise breaker")   410

DISCOVERING SHAKESPEARE

(57) Mythology [3.2.378–395]: How many different types of spirits do Puck and Oberon discuss in lines 378–395? Which do you think are most powerful?

LYSANDER

   He goes before me and still dares me on;
   When I come where he calls, then he is gone.
   The villain is much lighter-heeled than I.   415
   I followed fast, but faster he did fly,
   That° fallen am I in dark uneven way,   **That:** so that
   And here will rest me.
     [Lies down.]   Come, thou gentle day.
   For if but once thou show me thy gray light,
   I'll find Demetrius and revenge this spite.   420
     [Sleeps.]
     [Enter] Robin [Puck] and Demetrius.

PUCK

   Ho, ho, ho! Coward, why com'st thou not?

DEMETRIUS

   Abide° me, if thou dar'st; for well I wot°   **Abide:** wait for; **wot:** know
   Thou runn'st before me, shifting every place,
   And dar'st not stand nor look me in the face.
   Where art thou now?   425

PUCK   Come hither. I am here.

DEMETRIUS

   Nay then, thou mock'st me. Thou shalt buy this dear°   **buy this dear:** pay dearly for this (probably a
   If ever I thy face by daylight see.   form of *aby;* cf. 3.2.175)
   Now go thy way. Faintness constraineth me
   To measure out my length° on this cold bed.   **measure out my length:** i.e., lie down
   By day's approach look to be visited.   430
     [Lies down and sleeps.]
     Enter Helena.

HELENA

   O weary night, O long and tedious night,
     Abate thy hours.° Shine comforts from the east,   **Abate thy hours:** shorten your time
   That I may back to Athens by daylight
     From these that my poor company detest;°   **my poor company detest:** hate being with me
   And sleep, that sometimes shuts up sorrow's eye,   435
   Steal me awhile from mine own company.
     Sleep.

PUCK

             Yet but three? Come one more.
             Two of both kinds makes up four.
             Here she comes, curst° and sad.   **curst:** out of sorts
             Cupid is a knavish lad   440
             Thus to make poor females mad.
     [Enter Hermia.]

HERMIA

   Never so weary, never so in woe,
     Bedabbled with the dew, and torn with briers,
   I can no further crawl, no further go,°   **go:** walk
     My legs can keep no pace with my desires.   445
   Here will I rest me till the break of day.

DISCOVERING SHAKESPEARE

(58) Staging [3.2.418–447]: How does Puck put each of the lovers to sleep on the ground? Would his charms be accompanied by any physical gestures or lighting/sound effects?

Heavens shield Lysander, if they mean a fray!
[Lies down and sleeps.]

PUCK
<blockquote>
On the ground
Sleep sound.
I'll apply
To your eye,
Gentle lover, remedy.
</blockquote>

450

[Squeezes the herb onto Lysander's eyelids.]

<blockquote>
When thou wak'st,
Thou tak'st
True delight
In the sight
Of thy former lady's eye;
</blockquote>

455

And the country proverb known,
That every man should take his own,
In your waking shall be shown:

460

<blockquote>
Jack shall have Jill,°
Nought shall go ill,
</blockquote>

The man shall have his mare again, and all shall be well.°
[Exit.]

Jack, Jill: (generic names for "boy" and "girl")

The man . . . well: (a proverb suggesting a happy ending); **s.d.** (F adds the s.d. "They sleepe all the Act," which may indicate that the four lovers remain asleep on the stage [1] as the action continues, [2] during an interval between Acts Three and Four, or [3] during the interval and through the ensuing action—suggested by F's "Sleepers lye still" at 4.1.100.)

4.1 *Enter [Titania,] Queen of Fairies, and [Bottom the] Clown and Fairies [Peaseblossom, Cobweb, Moth, Mustardseed, and others]; and the King [Oberon] behind them.*

TITANIA
Come, sit thee down upon this flowery bed,
  While I thy amiable° cheeks do coy,°
And stick musk roses in thy sleek smooth head,
  And kiss thy fair large ears, my gentle joy.

amiable: lovable
coy: caress

BOTTOM Where's Peaseblossom?

5

PEASEBLOSSOM Ready.

BOTTOM Scratch my head, Peaseblossom. Where's Monsieur Cobweb?

COBWEB Ready.

BOTTOM Monsieur Cobweb, good monsieur, get you your weapons in your hand, and kill me a red-hipped humblebee on the top of a thistle; and, good monsieur, bring me the honey bag. Do not fret yourself too much in the action, monsieur; and, good monsieur, have a care the honey bag break not. I would be loath to have you overflowen° with a honey bag, signor. Where's Monsieur Mustardseed?

10

overflowen: flooded

15

MUSTARDSEED Ready.

BOTTOM Give me your neaf,° Monsieur Mustardseed. Pray you, leave your curtsy,° good monsieur.

MUSTARDSEED What's your will?

neaf: fist (i.e., shake my hand)
leave your curtsy: don't be so formal, you can stop bowing now (a *curtsy* was any gesture of respect)

20

DISCOVERING SHAKESPEARE

(59) Teaser (4.1.16): The term "honey-bag" was slang for what common household item during the Renaissance?

BOTTOM   Nothing, good monsieur, but to help Cavalery
Peaseblossom° to scratch. I must to the barber's, monsieur; for methinks I am marvelous hairy about the
face, and I am such a tender ass, if my hair do but tickle
me, I must scratch.

TITANIA
What, wilt thou hear some music, my sweet love?

BOTTOM   I have a reasonable good ear in music. Let's
have the tongs and the bones.°

[Music: Tongs, rural music.]

TITANIA
Or say, sweet love, what thou desirest to eat.

BOTTOM   Truly, a peck of provender. I could munch
your good dry oats. Methinks I have a great desire to a
bottle° of hay. Good hay, sweet hay, hath no fellow.

TITANIA
I have a venturous fairy that shall seek
The squirrel's hoard, and fetch thee [ ] new nuts.°

BOTTOM   I had rather have a handful or two of dried
peas. But I pray you, let none of your people stir me. I
have an exposition° of sleep come upon me.

TITANIA
Sleep thou, and I will wind thee in my arms.
Fairies, be gone, and be always away.°   *[Exeunt Fairies.]*
So doth the woodbine the sweet honeysuckle
Gently entwist;° the female ivy so
Enrings the barky fingers of the elm.
O, how I love thee! how I dote on thee!

[They sleep.]
Enter Robin Goodfellow [Puck].

OBERON   *[Advances.]*
Welcome, good Robin. Seest thou this sweet sight?
Her dotage now I do begin to pity,
For, meeting her of late behind the wood,
Seeking sweet favors° for this hateful fool,
I did upbraid her and fall out with her.
For she his hairy temples then had rounded
With coronet of fresh and fragrant flowers;
And that same dew which sometime° on the buds
Was wont to° swell, like round and orient° pearls,
Stood now within the pretty flowerets' eyes
Like tears that did their own disgrace bewail.
When I had at my pleasure taunted her,
And she in mild terms begged my patience,
I then did ask of her her changeling child;
Which straight she gave me, and her fairy sent

Cavalery Peaseblossom: (Bottom's error for *cavaliere*, an Italian title for a gallant. The early texts read "Cavalery Cobweb," the alliteration of which suggests that Shakespeare made an error: Cobweb has been sent on a mission, and Peaseblossom is the scratcher, l. 7. But Bottom himself may be confused, and may in fact say "Cavalery Cobweb.") 25

the tongs and the bones: (crude instruments: the tongs were struck like a triangle, while the bones were clappers held between the fingers)

30

bottle: small bundle

thee [ ] new nuts: (the defective meter indicates that the early texts omitted something from the line; editors have suggested "fetch thee thence" and "fetch thee off") 35

exposition: (Bottom's error for "disposition," inclination to)

be always away: i.e., get out and stay out 40

So . . . entwist: (the bindweed, or *woodbine*, twists to the right, the *honeysuckle* to the left, creating an inseparable tangle, as the syntax implies)

45

favors: love gifts

50

sometime: formerly; **Was wont to:** used to;
orient: lustrous (the rarest pearls were from the East)

55

DISCOVERING SHAKESPEARE

(60) Staging (4.1.22): Why does Bottom refer to Peaseblossom as "Cavalery" (4.1.22)?

(61) Language (4.1.32–33): Bottom fuses both aspects of his personality—human and ass—when he asks for a "bottle of hay" (4.1.32–33). Find at least three other examples of Bottom's tendency to bring together aspects of both worlds in his language. (*Hint:* Several can be found in his role as Pyramus in the play-within-the-play in the last act.)

(62) Staging [4.1.59]: Should the audience actually see Titania return the changeling child (59)? If you were directing a production of this play, would you use a young actor to play the part of the child? If so, how old would he/she be? How often would the child appear in the play? Could the play be staged without an actor in this role?

To bear him to my bower in fairyland.   60
And now I have the boy, I will undo
This hateful imperfection of her eyes.
And, gentle Puck, take this transformèd scalp
From off the head of this Athenian swain;°   **swain:** young man (the word had lower-class
That, he awaking when the other° do,   associations)   65
May all to Athens back again repair,   **other:** others (common plural)
And think no more of this night's accidents
But as the fierce vexation of a dream.
But first I will release the Fairy Queen.
[He squeezes the herb onto her eyelids.]   70
       Be as thou wast wont to be;
       See as thou wast wont to see.
       Dian's bud° o'er Cupid's flower   **Dian's bud:** (perhaps *Agnus castus* or another
       Hath such force and blessèd power.   plant associated with Diana and chastity;
Now, my Titania, wake you, my sweet queen.   dramatically, it is the herbal antidote, mentioned at
TITANIA   2.1.184, to *Cupid's flower,* the love-in-idleness, or
My Oberon, what visions have I seen!   pansy)
Methought I was enamored of an ass.   75
OBERON
There lies your love.
TITANIA   How came these things to pass?
O, how mine eyes do loathe his visage now!
OBERON
Silence awhile. Robin, take off this head.
Titania, music call, and strike more dead   80
Than common sleep of all these five° the sense.   **these five:** Bottom and the lovers
TITANIA
Music, ho, music! such as charmeth sleep.
 [Soft music.]
PUCK   *[Removes the ass head.]*
Now, when thou wak'st, with thine own fool's eyes
  peep.
OBERON
Sound, music!
 [Louder music.]
         Come, my queen, take hands with me.
And rock the ground° whereon these sleepers be.   **rock the ground:** (gently, as with a cradle; not   85
 [Dance.]   in the modern sense)
Now thou and I are new in amity,
And will tomorrow midnight solemnly°   **solemnly:** with ceremony (cf. *solemnities,* 1.1.11)
Dance in Duke Theseus' house triumphantly°   **triumphantly:** in celebration
And bless it to all fair prosperity.
There shall the pairs of faithful lovers be   90
Wedded, with Theseus, all in jollity.

DISCOVERING SHAKESPEARE

(63) Music (4.1.80): Music and sleep, the two great restorative powers in Shakespeare, join together here to help mend all the amorous relationships in the play. What type of music would Titania call for? Should it be played by on-stage musicians or be piped in through the theater's sound system? Why is Titania, rather than Oberon, the one who presides over music in the play?

(64) Music [4.1.85]: At what other moments does Shakespeare add music to his <u>script</u>? If you were directing a production of this play, where else would you add music (for example, between scenes, as <u>motifs</u> for certain characters, or to add suspense and excitement to on-stage action)?

PUCK

> Fairy King, attend and mark:
> I do hear the morning lark.

OBERON

> Then, my queen, in silence sad°
> Trip we after night's° shade.
> We the globe can compass soon,
> Swifter than the wand'ring moon.

TITANIA

> Come, my lord, and in our flight
> Tell me how it came this night
> That I sleeping here was found
> With these mortals on the ground.　　　*Exeunt.*
> 　*Wind horn. Enter Theseus and all his train [with*
> 　*Hippolyta and Egeus].*

THESEUS

> Go, one of you, find out the forester,
> For now our observation° is performed;
> And since we have the vaward of the day,°
> My love shall hear the music of my hounds.
> Uncouple° in the western valley; let them go.
> Dispatch, I say, and find the forester.　　*[Exit Attendant.]*
> We will, fair queen, up to the mountain's top
> And mark the musical confusion
> Of hounds and echo in conjunction.

HIPPOLYTA

> I was with Hercules and Cadmus° once
> When in a wood of Crete they bayed° the bear
> With hounds of Sparta.° Never did I hear
> Such gallant chiding;° for, besides the groves,
> The skies, the fountains, every region near
> Seemed all one mutual cry. I never heard
> So musical a discord, such sweet thunder.

THESEUS

> My hounds are bred out of the Spartan kind:
> So flewed, so sanded,° and their heads are hung
> With ears that sweep away the morning dew;
> Crook-kneed, and dewlapped like Thessalian bulls;°
> Slow in pursuit, but matched in mouth like bells,
> Each under each.° A cry° more tuneable°
> Was never holloed to nor cheered with horn
> In Crete, in Sparta, nor in Thessaly.
> Judge when you hear. But soft!° What nymphs° are these?

EGEUS

> My lord, this is my daughter here asleep,
> And this, Lysander, this Demetrius is,
> This Helena, old Nedar's Helena.
> I wonder of their being here together.

sad: serious
night's: (pronounced with two syllables: "nightes," the old possessive form)　　95

100

observation: observance (i.e., of the rite of May: 1.1.167; 4.1.132)
vaward . . . day: vanguard of the day, morning　　105
Uncouple: unleash (the pairs of *hounds*)

110

Cadmus: the legendary founder of Thebes
bayed: brought to bay, cornered
hounds of Sparta: (a breed of dog famous in the ancient world)
chiding: barking　　115

So flewed, so sanded: i.e., resembling the Spartan dogs, with hanging chaps (*flewed*) and a sandy color　　120
dewlapped like Thessalian bulls: i.e., with large hanging flaps of skin beneath the throat
matched . . . each: i.e., with harmonious voices differently pitched, from high to low
cry: noise of the pack, hence the pack itself;　　125
tuneable: in tune, musical
soft: wait; **nymphs:** woodland creatures, usually female

130

DISCOVERING SHAKESPEARE

(65) <u>Sources</u> (4.1.111): One possible reason why Theseus and Hippolyta are still arguing at the conclusion of the play is that their marriage in Shakespeare's <u>source</u> did not end happily. What can you discover about their mythological life together?

THESEUS
No doubt they rose up early to observe
The rite of May, and, hearing our intent,
Came here in grace of our solemnity.°

in grace . . . solemnity: to honor our celebration

But speak, Egeus. Is not this the day
That Hermia should give answer of her choice?

135

EGEUS
It is, my lord.

THESEUS
Go, bid the huntsmen wake them with their horns.
                              [Exit an Attendant.]
    Shout within: they all start up. Wind horns.
Good morrow, friends. Saint Valentine is past:
Begin these wood birds but to couple° now?°

couple: pair off

LYSANDER
Pardon, my lord.
    [They kneel.]

Saint Valentine . . . now: (according to legend, birds mate on Saint Valentine's Day)

140

THESEUS   I pray you all, stand up.
I know you two are rival enemies.
How comes this gentle concord in the world,
That hatred is so far from jealousy°
To sleep by hate and fear no enmity?

jealousy: suspicion

LYSANDER
My lord, I shall reply amazèdly,°
Half sleep, half waking; but as yet, I swear,

amazèdly: confusedly

145

I cannot truly say how I came here.
But, as I think – for truly would I speak –
And now I do bethink me, so it is,
I came with Hermia hither. Our intent

150

Was to be gone from Athens, where° we might,
Without° the peril of the Athenian law –

where: wherever
Without: outside

EGEUS
Enough, enough, my lord! you have enough.
I beg the law, the law, upon his head.
They would have stol'n away, they would, Demetrius,

155

Thereby to have defeated° you and me –
You of your wife, and me of my consent,
Of my consent that she should be your wife.

defeated: (1) cheated, (2) deprived

DEMETRIUS
My lord, fair Helen told me of their stealth,
Of this their purpose hither, to this wood,

160

And I in fury hither followed them,
Fair Helena in fancy° following me.
But, my good lord, I wot° not by what power –
But by some power it is – my love to Hermia,
Melted as the snow, seems to me now

in fancy: in love
wot: know

165

As the remembrance of an idle gaud°
Which in my childhood I did dote upon,
And all the faith, the virtue° of my heart,

idle gaud: worthless trinket

virtue: power

DISCOVERING SHAKESPEARE

(66) Staging (4.1.159): Despite Demetrius' wonderful declaration of love for Helena in lines 159–175, we must remember that he apparently remains under the influence of Puck's love potion. Does it bother you that his love for her is still substance-induced? How long do you think this spell will last?

The object and the pleasure of mine eye,
Is only Helena. To her, my lord,   170
Was I betrothed ere I saw Hermia,
But, like a sickness,° did I loathe this food;   **like a sickness:** i.e., as in sickness
But, as in health, come to my natural taste,
Now I do wish it, love it, long for it,
And will for evermore be true to it.   175
THESEUS
Fair lovers, you are fortunately met.
Of this discourse we more will hear anon.
Egeus, I will overbear your will,
For in the temple, by and by,° with us,   **by and by:** shortly
These couples shall eternally be knit;   180
And, for° the morning now is something worn,   **for:** because
Our purposed hunting shall be set aside.
Away, with us to Athens! Three and three,
We'll hold a feast in great solemnity.
Come, Hippolyta.   185
          [Exeunt Theseus, Hippolyta, Egeus, and Lords.]
DEMETRIUS
These things seem small and undistinguishable,
Like far-off mountains turnèd into clouds.
HERMIA
Methinks I see these things with parted eye,°   **with parted eye:** i.e., with the eyes not in focus
When everything seems double.
HELENA   So methinks;
And I have found Demetrius like a jewel,   190
Mine own,° and not mine own.   **And I . . . own:** i.e., like a gem found by
DEMETRIUS   Are you sure   accident, and therefore not really mine
That we are awake? It seems to me
That yet we sleep, we dream. Do not you think
The duke was here and bid us follow him?
HERMIA
Yea, and my father.   195
HELENA   And Hippolyta.
LYSANDER
And he did bid us follow to the temple.
DEMETRIUS
Why then, we are awake. Let's follow him,
And by the way let us recount our dreams.   *[Exeunt.]*
BOTTOM   *[Wakes.]* When my cue comes, call me, and I
  will answer. My next is "Most fair Pyramus." Hey-ho.   200
  Peter Quince? Flute the bellows mender? Snout the tin-
  ker? Starveling? God's my life!° Stolen hence, and left   **God's my life:** (a common oath, perhaps
  me asleep? I have had a most rare vision. I have had a   contracted from "God save my life")
  dream, past the wit of man to say what dream it was.
  Man is but an ass if he go about to expound this dream.   205
  Methought I was – there is no man can tell what.

DISCOVERING SHAKESPEARE

(67) Staging [4.1.178]: How should Egeus respond when Theseus decides to "overbear" his will (178) and allow Hermia to marry Lysander?

Methought I was, and methought I had – But man is but a patched fool° if he will offer to say what methought I had. The eye of man hath not heard, the ear of man hath not seen, man's hand is not able to taste, his tongue to conceive, nor his heart to report° what my dream was. I will get Peter Quince to write a ballet° of this dream. It shall be called "Bottom's Dream," because it hath no bottom;° and I will sing it in the latter end of our play, before the duke. Peradventure,° to make it the more gracious, I shall sing it at her death.°   [Exit.]

❧ 4.2° *Enter Quince, Flute [with Snout and Starveling].*

QUINCE   Have you sent to Bottom's house? Is he come home yet?

STARVELING   He cannot be heard of. Out of doubt he is transported.°

FLUTE   If he come not, then the play is marred; it goes not forward, doth it?

QUINCE   It is not possible. You have not a man in all Athens able to discharge Pyramus but he.

FLUTE   No, he hath simply the best wit° of any handicraft man in Athens.

QUINCE   Yea, and the best person° too, and he is a very paramour for a sweet voice.

FLUTE   You must say "paragon." A paramour is (God bless us!) a thing of naught.°
Enter Snug the Joiner.

SNUG   Masters, the duke is coming from the temple, and there is two or three lords and ladies more married. If our sport had gone forward, we had all been made men.°

FLUTE   O sweet bully° Bottom! Thus hath he lost sixpence a day° during his life. He could not have scaped sixpence a day. An° the duke had not given him sixpence a day for playing Pyramus, I'll be hanged! He would have deserved it. Sixpence a day in Pyramus, or nothing!
Enter Bottom.

BOTTOM   Where are these lads? Where are these hearts?°

a patched fool: i.e., a fool in motley

210

The eye . . . report: (Bottom's garbled version of I Corinthians 2:9–10: "But we preach as it is written, things which eye hath not seen, and ear hath not heard, neither have entered into man's mind, which things God hath prepared for them that love him. But God hath opened them unto us by his spirit, for the spirit searcheth all things, yea, the bottom of God's secrets." Some believe the last phrase to be the source of Bottom's name.)
ballet: ballad
because it hath no bottom: i.e., (1) because its meaning is unclear (he "can't get to the bottom of it"), (2) because it is like a tangled skein of wool with no base or *bottom* (a metaphor from weaving)
Peradventure: perhaps
her death: (probably Thisby's)
4.2: Quince's house (?)
transported: carried off by spirits (see *translated*, 3.1.113–14)

215

5

wit: brains

10

person: figure, appearance

a thing of naught: (1) a wicked thing (stronger than the modern "naughty"), (2) worth nothing

15

If our sport . . . made men: i.e., if we had been able to perform our play, our fortunes would have been *made*
bully: jolly
sixpence a day: i.e., a pension from the duke
An: if

20

hearts: good fellows

25

DISCOVERING SHAKESPEARE

(68) Rhetoric (4.1.207–210): Since dream interpretation is a relatively modern invention, we should not be surprised that Bottom makes little attempt to figure out the meaning of his night in the woods with Titania. What rhetorical device in lines 207–210 of this speech does Shakespeare use to indicate that Bottom is still intoxicated with love for his Fairy Queen?

(69) Teaser (4.2.19–24): Flute's obsession with the loss of "sixpence a day" (4.2.19–24) implies that Bottom could have gained a lot of money by performing the play well. In 1594, sixpence was approximately the cost of a seat in the theatre, the price of a printed copy of the play, and a day's wages for common laborers like the rude mechanicals. If the Duke had granted Bottom a pension of sixpence per day, how much money in British pounds would he have earned each year for the rest of his life?

QUINCE Bottom! O most courageous° day! O most happy° hour!

BOTTOM Masters, I am to° discourse wonders, but ask me not what. For if I tell you, I am not true Athenian. I will tell you everything, right as it fell out.

QUINCE Let us hear, sweet Bottom.

BOTTOM Not a word of° me. All that I will tell you is, that the duke hath dined. Get your apparel together, good strings to your beards,° new ribbands° to your pumps; meet presently° at the palace; every man look o'er his part; for the short and the long is, our play is preferred.° In any case, let Thisby have clean linen; and let not him that plays the lion pare his nails, for they shall hang out for the lion's claws. And, most dear actors, eat no onions nor garlic, for we are to utter sweet breath; and I do not doubt but to hear them say it is a sweet comedy. No more words. Away, go, away!

[Exeunt.]

courageous: brave, splendid (?) (perhaps auspicious, lucky)
happy: fortunate
am to: have to

30

word of: word out of

strings to your beards: i.e., to hold them on;
ribbands: (common spelling of "ribbons")   35
presently: right away
preferred: recommended, chosen

40

❧ **5.1**° *Enter Theseus, Hippolyta, and Philostrate [with Lords and Attendants].*

5.1: The duke's palace

HIPPOLYTA
'Tis strange, my Theseus, that° these lovers speak of.

THESEUS
More strange than true. I never may believe
These antique° fables nor these fairy toys.°
Lovers and madmen have such seething brains,
Such shaping fantasies,° that apprehend
More than cool reason ever comprehends.
The lunatic, the lover, and the poet
Are of imagination all compact.°
One sees more devils than vast hell can hold:
That is the madman. The lover, all as frantic,
Sees Helen's beauty in a brow of Egypt.°
The poet's eye, in a fine frenzy rolling,
Doth glance from heaven to earth, from earth to heaven,
And as imagination bodies forth°
The forms of things unknown, the poet's pen
Turns them to shapes, and gives to airy nothing
A local habitation and a name.
Such tricks hath strong imagination
That, if it would but apprehend some joy,°
It comprehends some bringer of that joy;
Or in the night, imagining some fear,
How easy is a bush supposed a bear!

that: that which, what

antique: (1) mad or bizarre, "antic," (2) ancient, old; **fairy toys:** i.e., foolish, supernatural stories (*toys* are "trifles")
shaping fantasies: creative imaginations, powers of fantasy   5

of imagination all compact: composed entirely of imagination—i.e., without reason

10

Sees Helen's beauty . . . of Egypt: i.e., imagines that he sees female perfection (the Greek Helen was the ancient model of beauty) in the face of a gypsy

bodies forth: gives reality to, embodies

15

if . . . joy: i.e., if it wants to feel pleasure, it invents some imaginary source of that feeling   20

DISCOVERING SHAKESPEARE

(70) Characterization [5.1.1–27]: In this brilliant analysis of the art of writing dramatic poetry, Theseus and Hippolyta respond to the lovers' story very differently. Find two other examples in act five that illustrate their continuing disagreements with each other.

HIPPOLYTA
But all the story of the night told over,
And all their minds transfigured so together,°
More witnesseth than fancy's images°
And grows to something of great constancy;°
But howsoever,° strange and admirable.°
    Enter Lovers: Lysander, Demetrius, Hermia, and
    Helena.
THESEUS
Here come the lovers, full of joy and mirth.
Joy, gentle friends, joy and fresh days of love
Accompany your hearts!
LYSANDER   More than to us
Wait in your royal walks, your board, your bed!
THESEUS
Come now, what masques,° what dances shall we have,
To wear away this long age of three hours
Between our aftersupper° and bedtime?
Where is our usual manager of mirth?°
What revels are in hand? Is there no play
To ease the anguish of a torturing hour?
Call Philostrate.°
PHILOSTRATE   Here, mighty Theseus.
THESEUS
Say, what abridgment° have you for this evening?
What masque? what music? How shall we beguile
The lazy time, if not with some delight?
PHILOSTRATE
There is a brief° how many sports are ripe.°
Make choice of which your highness will see first.
    [Gives a paper.]
THESEUS
"The battle with the Centaurs,° to be sung
By an Athenian eunuch to the harp."
We'll none of that. That have I told my love
In glory of my kinsman Hercules.
"The riot of the tipsy Bacchanals,
Tearing the Thracian singer in their rage."°
That is an old device,° and it was played
When I from Thebes came last a conqueror.
"The thrice three Muses mourning for the death
Of Learning, late deceased in beggary."°
That is some satire keen and critical,
Not sorting with° a nuptial ceremony.
"A tedious brief scene of young Pyramus
And his love Thisby; very tragical mirth."
Merry and tragical? tedious and brief?

transfigured so together: so entirely changed all at once   25

More . . . images: speaks of more than mere figments of the imagination

constancy: certainty (because of the consistency of the evidence)

howsoever: in any case; **admirable:** provoking wonder

30

masques: courtly skits or pageants involving costumed, sometimes masked, dancers

aftersupper: light course finishing the evening meal   35

manager of mirth: supervisor of entertainments

Philostrate: (Philostrate describes the possible diversions only in the QQ texts; in F his part is assigned to Egeus)

abridgment: pastime (i.e., a diversion to "bridge" the hours between supper and bed)   40

brief: list, memorandum; **sports are ripe:** entertainments are prepared

The battle . . . Centaurs: (a famous ancient episode in which the Centaurs attempted to steal the bride of Pirithous, Theseus's friend, during a wedding festival; in this version, as Theseus's response indicates, Hercules was a participant in the defense)   45

The riot . . . rage: (Ovid's story of Orpheus, dismembered by the Bacchantes; *Metamorphoses,* XI)   50

device: show

The thrice . . . beggary: (apparently a poetic lament over the decline of learning and poetry; cf. Spenser's "The Teares of the Muses," 1591)   55

sorting with: appropriate to

DISCOVERING SHAKESPEARE

(71) **Themes (5.1.58):** After reading that the rude mechanicals' play will be "merry and tragical," "tedious and brief" (5.1.58), Theseus is intrigued by these <u>oxymorons</u> and wonders, "How shall we find the concord of this discord? (60)" What other important opposites has Shakespeare brought together in his play? (*Hint:* Begin with sun/moon, woods/city, love/law, and then search for others.)

That is hot ice and wondrous strange snow.°
How shall we find the concord of this discord?

strange snow: (perhaps a textual error; *hot ice* earlier in the line would seem to call for a similarly oxymoronic phrase, such as "scorching snow" or "sable snow") 60

PHILOSTRATE
A play there is, my lord, some ten words long,
Which is as brief as I have known a play;
But by ten words, my lord, it is too long,
Which makes it tedious. For in all the play
There is not one word apt, one player fitted. 65
And tragical, my noble lord, it is,
For Pyramus therein doth kill himself.
Which when I saw rehearsed, I must confess,
Made mine eyes water, but more merry tears
The passion° of loud laughter never shed.

passion: eruption (of powerful feeling) 70

THESEUS
What are they that do play it?

PHILOSTRATE
Hardhanded men that work in Athens here,
Which never labored in their minds till now;
And now have toiled their unbreathed° memories
With this same play, against° your nuptial.

unbreathed: unused, unexercised
against: in preparation for 75

THESEUS
And we will hear it.

PHILOSTRATE   No, my noble lord,
It is not for you. I have heard it over,
And it is nothing, nothing in the world;
Unless you can find sport in their intents,°
Extremely stretched and conned with cruel pain,
To do you service.

intents: (refers both to their overtaxed intentions—*Extremely stretched*—and to their intended roles, which have been difficult to learn, *conned with cruel pain*) 80

THESEUS   I will hear that play,
For never anything can be amiss
When simpleness° and duty tender it.
Go bring them in; and take your places, ladies.
                              [Exit Philostrate.]

simpleness: i.e., innocent good will

HIPPOLYTA
I love not to see wretchedness o'ercharged,°
And duty in his service perishing.

o'ercharged: required to do too much 85

THESEUS
Why, gentle sweet, you shall see no such thing.

HIPPOLYTA
He says they can do nothing in this kind.°

in this kind: of this sort

THESEUS
The kinder we, to give them thanks for nothing. 90
Our sport shall be to take what they mistake,
And what poor duty cannot do, noble respect°
Takes it in might, not merit.°
Where I have come, great clerks° have purposèd
To greet me with premeditated welcomes;
Where I have seen them shiver and look pale, 95
Make periods in the midst of sentences,

noble respect: aristocratic sensitivity
Takes . . . merit: i.e., takes the intention for the actual performance
great clerks: important scholars

DISCOVERING SHAKESPEARE

(72) Staging (5.1.84): How would you arrange the actors on stage so the audience has a clear view of the three newly married couples watching the play-within-the-play?

Throttle their practiced accent° in their fears,

And, in conclusion, dumbly have broke off,

Not paying me a welcome. Trust me, sweet,

Out of this silence yet I picked a welcome,

And in the modesty of fearful duty

I read as much as from the rattling tongue

Of saucy° and audacious eloquence.

Love, therefore, and tongue-tied simplicity

In least° speak most, to my capacity.°

   [Enter Philostrate.]

PHILOSTRATE

So please your grace the Prologue is addressed.°

THESEUS

Let him approach.

   [Flourish trumpets.] Enter the Prologue [Quince].°

PROLOGUE

If we offend, it is with our good will.°

   That you should think, we come not to offend

But with good will. To show our simple skill,

   That is the true beginning of our end.

Consider then, we come but in despite.

   We do not come, as minding to content you,

Our true intent is. All for your delight,

   We are not here. That you should here repent you,

The actors are at hand: and, by their show,

You shall know all, that you are like to know.

THESEUS   This fellow doth not stand upon points.°

LYSANDER   He hath rid his prologue like a rough° colt; he knows not the stop.° A good moral, my lord: it is not enough to speak, but to speak true.

HIPPOLYTA   Indeed he hath played on this prologue like a child on a recorder° – a sound, but not in government.°

THESEUS   His speech was like a tangled chain; nothing impaired, but all disordered. Who is next?

   Enter Pyramus and Thisby, and Wall and Moonshine and Lion.

PROLOGUE

Gentles, perchance you wonder at this show,

   But wonder on, till truth make all things plain.

This man is Pyramus, if you would know;

   This beauteous lady Thisby is certain.°

This man, with lime and roughcast, doth present

   Wall, that vile Wall which did these lovers sunder;

---

practiced accent: rehearsed manner

100

saucy: impudent

In least: in speaking least; **to my capacity:** to my way of thinking 105

addressed: ready

s.d.: (F specifies the trumpet flourish and identifies Quince as the speaker of the prologue)

will: (the indiscriminate punctuation—noted by Theseus in l. 118—was a standard comic routine and source of laughter) 110

115

doth not stand upon points: i.e., doesn't worry about (1) punctuation, (2) subtleties

rough: unbroken 120

he . . . stop: i.e., the speech is running away with the speaker; **stop:** plays on (1) the checking of a horse in full gallop, (2) a period

recorder: flutelike instrument; **in government:** under control

125

certain: (the accent on the second syllable, as required by the rhyme, was already archaic in the 1590s) 130

DISCOVERING SHAKESPEARE

(73) Verse (5.1.108–117): This speech is funny because Quince, confused by the punctuation, often says exactly the opposite of what he intends to say (e.g., "All for your delight, / We are not here" [114–115]). Try to repunctuate this speech so it makes sense. What theatrical device would explain why Quince delivers his prologue "like a rough colt" (119)? (For example, perhaps he is excessively nervous or he breaks his glasses or the script falls into a puddle of water.) How would you solve this problem on stage?

(74) Stage History (5.1.126): The technique of having a narrator explain the action while the actors mime their parts is called a dumb show. Another good example of the same convention in Shakespeare may be found in 3.2 of *Hamlet,* where *The Murder of Gonzago* is enacted in pantomime prior to the actual performance of the play. Why do you think dumb shows were traditional during the Renaissance, and why does Shakespeare include one here?

And through Wall's chink, poor souls, they are content
    To whisper. At the which let no man wonder.
This man, with lantern, dog, and bush of thorn,°

lantern . . . thorn: (see 3.1.55–56)
135

    Presenteth Moonshine. For, if you will know,
By moonshine did these lovers think no scorn
    To meet at Ninus' tomb, there, there to woo.
This grisly beast (which Lion hight° by name)

hight: is called (already archaic in the 1590s)

The trusty Thisby, coming first by night,
140
Did scare away, or rather did affright;
And as she fled, her mantle she did fall,°

fall: let fall

    Which Lion vile with bloody mouth did stain.
Anon comes Pyramus, sweet youth and tall,°

tall: brave, handsome (as well as referring to height)

    And finds his trusty Thisby's mantle slain;
145
Whereat, with blade, with bloody blameful blade,
    He bravely broached his boiling bloody breast.°

bravely broached . . . breast: (here and below Shakespeare mocks the extravagant alliteration of old-fashioned plays)

And Thisby, tarrying in mulberry shade,
    His dagger drew, and died. For all the rest,
Let Lion, Moonshine, Wall, and lovers twain
At large° discourse while here they do remain.

at large: at length
150

THESEUS   I wonder if the lion be to speak.
DEMETRIUS   No wonder, my lord. One lion may, when
    many asses do.   *Exit [Prologue, with Pyramus,] Lion, Thisby,*
                                and Moonshine.

WALL
    In this same interlude° it doth befall
    That I, one Snout by name, present° a wall;

interlude: (old-fashioned term for a play)
present: play the role of, represent
155

    And such a wall, as I would have you think,
    That had in it a crannied hole or chink,°

chink: (a slang term for "vagina" or "anus," and part of a network of obscene jokes running through the mechanicals' play)

    Through which the lovers, Pyramus and Thisby,
    Did whisper often, very secretly.
160
    This loam, this roughcast, and this stone doth show
    That I am that same wall: the truth is so.
    And this the cranny is, right and sinister,°

sinister: left (the cranny is horizontal, right and left)

    Through which the fearful lovers are to whisper.
THESEUS   Would you desire lime and hair to speak bet-
    ter?
165
DEMETRIUS   It is the wittiest partition° that ever I heard

partition: (1) wall, (2) section of an oration

    discourse, my lord.
    [Enter Pyramus.]
THESEUS   Pyramus draws near the wall. Silence!
PYRAMUS
    O grim-looked night, O night with hue so black,
    O night, which ever art when day is not!
170
    O night, O night, alack, alack, alack,
    I fear my Thisby's promise is forgot.
    And thou, O wall, O sweet, O lovely wall,
    That stand'st between her father's ground and mine,
    Thou wall, O wall, O sweet and lovely wall,
175
    Show me thy chink, to blink through with mine eyne.
    [Wall holds up his fingers.]

DISCOVERING SHAKESPEARE
(75) Costumes [5.1.154]: If you were designing costumes for a production of this play, how would you create a "wall" for Snout to bring on stage?

Thanks, courteous wall. Jove shield thee well for this.
    But what see I? No Thisby do I see.
O wicked wall, through whom I see no bliss,
    Cursed be thy stones° for thus deceiving me!

THESEUS   The wall, methinks, being sensible,° should curse again.

PYRAMUS   No, in truth, sir, he should not. "Deceiving me" is Thisby's cue. She is to enter now, and I am to spy her through the wall. You shall see it will fall pat as I told you. Yonder she comes.
    Enter Thisby.

THISBY
    O wall, full often hast thou heard my moans
        For parting my fair Pyramus and me.
    My cherry lips have often kissed thy stones,
        Thy stones with lime and hair knit up in thee.

PYRAMUS
    I see a voice. Now will I to the chink,
        To spy an° I can hear my Thisby's face.
    Thisby!

THISBY
    My love! thou art my love, I think.

PYRAMUS
    Think what thou wilt, I am thy lover's grace;°
    And, like Limander, am I trusty still.

THISBY
    And I, like Helen, till the Fates me kill.

PYRAMUS
    Not Shafalus to Procrus° was so true.

THISBY
    As Shafalus to Procrus, I to you.

PYRAMUS
    O, kiss me through the hole of this vile wall!

THISBY
    I kiss the wall's hole, not your lips at all.

PYRAMUS
    Wilt thou at Ninny's tomb meet me straightway?

THISBY
    'Tide life, 'tide death;° I come without delay.
                  [Exeunt Pyramus and Thisby.]

WALL
    Thus have I, Wall, my part dischargèd so;
    And, being done, thus Wall away doth go.   *[Exit.]*

THESEUS   Now is the mural° down between the two neighbors.

DEMETRIUS   No remedy, my lord, when walls are so willful to hear without warning.°

HIPPOLYTA   This is the silliest stuff that ever I heard.

THESEUS   The best in this kind are but shadows,° and the worst are no worse, if imagination amend them.

---

stones: the components of the wall (but with a pun on "testicles," one of a string of obscene jokes: cf. *hair* at l. 190 and *hole* at l. 199)
sensible: capable of perception

an: if

thy lover's grace: i.e., thy gracious lover

Limander . . . Procrus: (there is much intentional confusion here, with mixed-up stories and inappropriate examples: *Limander* is Bottom's error for Leander, from Marlowe's poem "Hero and Leander"; *Helen* is not the lover of Limander/Leander, and she is hardly *trusty*; *Shafalus* and *Procrus* are slips for Cephalus and Procris, another pair of tragic lovers)

'Tide . . . death: come (betide) life, come death

mural: wall (a famous textual problem: Q1 reads "Now is the moon used"; F reads "Now is the morall down"; the emendation here was first proposed by Alexander Pope)
to hear without warning: i.e., without alerting the lovers' families (a joke on walls having ears)
best . . . shadows: best of this sort—i.e., the best actors—aren't real anyway (*shadows* was a conventional term for "players")

180

185

190

195

200

205

210

DISCOVERING SHAKESPEARE

(76) <u>Rhyme</u> Scheme (5.1.190): What is the <u>meter</u> and <u>rhyme</u> scheme of *Pyramus and Thisby,* and how does this <u>poetic</u> pattern contribute to the humor of the rude mechanicals' play?

HIPPOLYTA   It must be your imagination then, and not theirs.

THESEUS   If we imagine no worse of them than they of themselves, they may pass for excellent men. Here come two noble beasts in, a man and a lion.   215

Enter Lion and Moonshine.

LION

You, ladies, you whose gentle hearts do fear
   The smallest monstrous mouse that creeps on floor,
May now perchance both quake and tremble here,
   When lion rough in wildest rage doth roar.   220
Then know that I, as Snug the joiner, am
A lion fell,° nor else no lion's dam;°
For if I should as lion come in strife
Into this place, 'twere pity on my life.°

THESEUS   A very gentle° beast, and of a good conscience.

DEMETRIUS   The very best at a beast,° my lord, that e'er I saw.

LYSANDER   This lion is a very fox for his valor.°

THESEUS   True, and a goose for his discretion.

DEMETRIUS   Not so, my lord, for his valor cannot carry his discretion, and the fox carries the goose.

THESEUS   His discretion, I am sure, cannot carry his valor, for the goose carries not the fox. It is well. Leave it to his discretion, and let us listen to the moon.

MOON

This lanthorn° doth the hornèd moon present –

DEMETRIUS   He should have worn the horns on his head.°

THESEUS   He is no crescent,° and his horns are invisible within the circumference.

MOON

This lanthorn doth the hornèd moon present.
Myself the man i' th' moon do seem to be.

THESEUS   This is the greatest error of all the rest. The man should be put into the lanthorn. How is it else the man i' th' moon?

DEMETRIUS   He dares not come there, for the candle;° for you see it is already in snuff.°

HIPPOLYTA   I am aweary of this moon. Would he would change!

THESEUS   It appears, by his small light of discretion, that he is in the wane; but yet, in courtesy, in all reason, we must stay the time.

LYSANDER   Proceed, Moon.

MOON   All that I have to say is to tell you that the lanthorn is the moon; I, the man i' th' moon; this thornbush, my thornbush; and this dog, my dog.

DEMETRIUS   Why, all these should be in the lanthorn, for all these are in the moon. But silence: here comes Thisby.   255

Enter Thisby.

---

lion fell: (1) fierce lion, (2) lion's skin

I . . . dam: (Snug scrupulously distinguishes between an actual lion and his impersonation of a lion, in light of the concerns expressed during the rehearsal)   225

'twere pity on my life: i.e., I'd sooner die than frighten you into thinking I am really a lion

gentle: courteous, well-mannered

best at a beast: (a pun based on similar pronunciation: the wordplay introduces a series of   230 jests among the spectators—involving *discretion, horns,* and *snuff*—amounting to a kind of verbal one-upmanship)

This lion . . . valor: (alluding to the proverb "Discretion is the better part of valor"; the lion was known for courage, the fox for cunning [*discretion*], and the *goose* [l. 229] for stupidity)   235

lanthorn: lantern (pronounced "lant-horn" or "lantern")

on his head: (*horns* on the forehead were the sign of a cuckold, a betrayed husband)

no crescent: not waxing or growing (Starveling is probably thin)   240

for the candle: for fear of the burning candle

in snuff: (1) in need of snuffing, (2) in a huff, fit   245 of anger (Starveling may have become impatient with the interruptions of the spectators)

     250

DISCOVERING SHAKESPEARE

(77) Costumes [5.1.217]: How should Snug be costumed as the lion? What type of hair and make-up design would you suggest?

THISBY
    This is old Ninny's tomb. Where is my love?

LION   O!   *[The Lion roars. Thisby runs off].*

DEMETRIUS   Well roared, Lion.   260

THESEUS   Well run, Thisby.

HIPPOLYTA   Well shone, Moon. Truly, the moon shines
    with a good grace.
                      [The Lion tears Thisby's mantle, and exits.]

THESEUS   Well moused,° Lion.   **Well moused:** i.e., the lion with the mantle in

DEMETRIUS   And then came Pyramus.   his mouth is like a cat with a mouse   265

LYSANDER   And so the lion vanished.
    Enter Pyramus.

PYRAMUS
    Sweet moon, I thank thee for thy sunny beams;
      I thank thee, moon, for shining now so bright;
    For, by thy gracious, golden, glittering gleams,
      I trust to take of truest Thisby sight.   270
              But stay: O spite!°   **spite:** bad fortune
              But mark, poor knight,
          What dreadful dole° is here?   **dole:** cause of sadness
              Eyes, do you see?
              How can it be?   275
           O dainty duck, O dear!
              Thy mantle good,
              What, stained with blood?
          Approach, ye Furies fell!°   **Furies fell:** fierce agents of fate (invoked in
            O Fates, come, come,   imitation of Senecan tragedy)   280
            Cut thread and thrum,°   **thrum:** the end of the weaver's thread left
         Quail,° crush, conclude, and quell!° attached to the loom after the web was cut away
                              (Bottom's shorthand for "finish the job")

THESEUS   This passion, and the death of a dear friend,   **Quail:** overpower; **quell:** kill
    would go near to make a man look sad.°

HIPPOLYTA   Beshrew my heart° but I pity the man.   **This passion . . . sad:** i.e., this breast-beating by 285
                                  itself isn't emotionally touching

PYRAMUS   **Beshrew my heart:** (a mild curse or oath—
    O, wherefore, Nature, didst thou lions frame?   "Damned if I don't feel pity")
      Since lion vile hath here deflowered° my dear;   **deflowered:** attacked
    Which is – no, no! – which was the fairest dame
      That lived, that loved, that liked, that looked with cheer.
              Come, tears, confound,   290
             Out, sword, and wound
            The pap° of Pyramus: **pap:** breast
              Ay, that left pap
             Where heart doth hop.

    [Stabs himself.]
             Thus die I, thus, thus, thus.   295
             Now am I dead,
             Now am I fled,

DISCOVERING SHAKESPEARE

(78) Staging (5.1.258 sd.): The folio stage direction in 5.1.258 reads "The Lion worries the mantle." What does the word "worries" mean in this context? Should Thisby's mantle be bloodstained? If so, how will Lion get blood on it? What other blood effects would you use in *Pyramus and Thisby*? Why are many directors and designers reluctant to use blood on stage?

(79) Teaser (5.1.281): How do the words "thread and thrum" relate to (1) Bottom's profession and (2) the Fates (281)?

My soul is in the sky.
　　Tongue, lose thy light,
　　Moon, take thy flight. *[Exit Moonshine.]*　　　　　　　　　　300
　　Now die, die, die, die, die.
[Dies.]
DEMETRIUS　　No die, but an ace,° for him! for he is but one.°

ace: the one-spot on a die (with a pun on *ass* in l. 306); **one:** (pun on "unique" and "one man")

LYSANDER　　Less than an ace, man; for he is dead, he is
　　nothing.
THESEUS　　With the help of a surgeon he might yet recover,　　　　305
　　and prove an ass.
HIPPOLYTA　　How chance Moonshine is gone before
　　Thisby comes back and finds her lover?
　　[Enter Thisby.]
THESEUS　　She will find him by starlight. Here she comes,
　　and her passion° ends the play.

passion: emotional speech　　　　310

HIPPOLYTA　　Methinks she should not use a long one for
　　such a Pyramus. I hope she will be brief.
DEMETRIUS　　A mote will turn the balance, which Pyramus,
　　which Thisby, is the better: he for a man, God
　　warrant° us; she for a woman, God bless us!

warrant: protect, save　　　　315

LYSANDER　　She hath spied him already with those sweet
　　eyes.
DEMETRIUS　　And thus she means,° videlicet:°

means: (1) moans, laments (an Anglo-Saxon form), (2) lodges a complaint; **videlicet:** to wit, as you see

THISBY
　　　　　Asleep, my love?
　　　　　What, dead, my dove?　　　　320
　　　O Pyramus, arise!
　　　　　Speak, speak. Quite dumb?
　　　　　Dead, dead? A tomb
　　　Must cover thy sweet eyes.
　　　　　These lily lips,　　　　325
　　　　　This cherry nose,
　　　These yellow cowslip cheeks,
　　　　　Are gone, are gone.
　　　　　Lovers, make moan.
　　　His eyes were green as leeks.　　　　330
　　　　　O Sisters Three,°
　　　　　Come, come to me,

Sisters Three: the Fates

　　　With hands as pale as milk;
　　　　　Lay them in gore,
　　　　　Since you have shore°　　　　335
　　　With shears his thread of silk.

shore: (archaic form of "shorn"—for comic effect)

　　　　　Tongue, not a word.
　　　　　Come, trusty sword,
　　　Come, blade, my breast imbrue!°

imbrue: (1) stain with blood, (2) plunge into

[Stabs herself.]
　　　　　And farewell, friends.　　　　340
　　　　　Thus Thisby ends.
　　　　　Adieu, adieu, adieu.
[Dies.]
[Enter Lion, Moonshine, and Wall.]
THESEUS　　Moonshine and Lion are left to bury the dead.
DEMETRIUS　　Ay, and Wall too.
LION°　　No, I assure you; the wall is down that parted their

lion: (F assigns this speech to Bottom)　　　　345

fathers. Will it please you to see the epilogue, or to hear a Bergomask dance° between two of our company?

THESEUS No epilogue, I pray you; for your play needs no excuse. Never excuse, for when the players are all dead, there need none to be blamed. Marry, if he that writ it had played Pyramus and hanged himself in Thisby's garter,° it would have been a fine tragedy; and so it is truly, and very notably discharged. But, come, your Bergomask. Let your epilogue alone.

    [A dance.]

The iron tongue of midnight hath told° twelve.
Lovers, to bed; 'tis almost fairy time.
I fear we shall outsleep the coming morn
As much as we this night have overwatched.°
This palpable gross play hath well beguiled
The heavy gait° of night. Sweet friends, to bed.
A fortnight hold we this solemnity
In nightly revels and new jollity.   *Exeunt.*

    Enter Puck [with a broom].

PUCK
            Now the hungry lion roars,
                And the wolf behowls the moon,
            Whilst the heavy plowman snores,
                All with weary task fordone.°
            Now the wasted brands° do glow,
                Whilst the screech owl, screeching loud,
            Puts the wretch that lies in woe
                In remembrance of a shroud.
            Now it is the time of night
                That the graves, all gaping wide,
            Every one° lets forth his° sprite,°
                In the churchway paths to glide.
            And we fairies, that do run
                By the triple Hecate's team°
            From the presence of the sun,
                Following darkness like a dream,
            Now are frolic.° Not a mouse
            Shall disturb this hallowed house.
            I am sent, with broom, before,
            To sweep the dust behind the door.°

    Enter King and Queen of Fairies, with all their train.

OBERON
            Through the house give glimmering light,
                By the dead and drowsy fire;
            Every elf and fairy sprite

Bergomask dance: rustic dance (originally Italian, from Bergamo; plays in the public theaters—comedies and tragedies—were often followed by jigs or rousing dances)   350

hanged . . . garter: (condescending description of suicide; from a proverbial phrase, "To hang himself in his own garters")

told: counted (including the sense of "tolled")   355

overwatched: stayed up too late

heavy gait: plodding pace   360

fordone: undone, exhausted
brands: coals   365

Every one: each grave (l. 372); **his:** its;
sprite: spirit, ghost   375

triple Hecate's team: i.e., the dragons pulling the chariot of the goddess known in the underworld as Hecate, on earth as Diana, and in the sky as Cynthia or Luna or Phoebe
frolic: merry, frolicsome   380

behind the door: from behind the door (in folklore Puck was traditionally represented with broom and candle, signifying his role as housekeeper)

385

DISCOVERING SHAKESPEARE

(80) Stage History (5.1.347): What was a Bergomask dance (V.i.347), and why is it an appropriate conclusion to the rude mechanicals' play?

(81) Staging (5.1.383): How would you stage this final blessing by Oberon, Titania, and the fairies? Some productions have each fairy enter holding a candle, others set the entire speech to music, and still others have all the actors move into the audience to involve the entire theater in this special moment. What would you do to make this last section of the play exciting and meaningful?

Hop as light as bird from brier;
And this ditty, after me,
Sing, and dance it trippingly.

TITANIA

First rehearse your song by rote,
To each word a warbling note.   390
Hand in hand with fairy grace
Will we sing and bless this place.

[Song and dance.]°   **Song and dance:** (the song may be lost, or *Song*
                         may refer to Oberon's verses that follow; headed
                         "The Song" in F)

OBERON

Now until the break of day
Through this house each fairy stray.
To the best bridebed will we,   395
Which by us shall blessèd be,
And the issue there create
Ever shall be fortunate.
So shall all the couples three
Ever true in loving be,   400
And the blots of Nature's hand
Shall not in their issue stand.
Never mole, harelip, nor scar,
Nor mark prodigious° such as are   **mark prodigious:** ominous birthmark
Despisèd in nativity   405
Shall upon their children be.
With this field dew consecrate°   **field dew consecrate:** (the field dew, blessed,
Every fairy take his gait,   serves as a kind of fairy holy water)
And each several chamber bless
Through this palace with sweet peace.   410
And the owner of it blest
Ever shall in safety rest.
Trip away, make no stay,
Meet me all by break of day.

Exeunt [all but Puck].

PUCK

If we shadows° have offended,   **shadows:** (1) spirits, (2) actors (an Elizabethan   415
Think but this, and all is mended –   term)
That you have but slumbered here
While these visions did appear.
And this weak and idle° theme,   **idle:** foolish
No more yielding but° a dream,   **No more yielding but:** yielding no more than   420
Gentles, do not reprehend.°   **reprehend:** complain, blame us
If you pardon, we will mend.
And, as I am an honest Puck,
If we have unearnèd luck
Now to scape° the serpent's tongue,° **scape:** escape; **serpent's tongue:** i.e., hissing 425
We will make amends ere long;
Else the Puck a liar call.
So, good night unto you all.
Give me your hands,° if we be friends, **Give . . . hands:** i.e., applaud for us
And Robin shall restore amends.   *[Exit.]*   430

DISCOVERING SHAKESPEARE

(82) Epilogue (5.1.415): Why does Shakespeare include this final epilogue by Puck asking us to imagine that we "have but slumber'd here / While these visions did appear" (5.1.417–418)? How does Puck's speech help us interpret the entire play? Why do you suppose the author chose this particular character to have the last word?

Research and Discussion Topics

ACT I

1. Who were Theseus and Hippolyta? Were they ever married? Did their love end happily or unhappily?

2. Who were the Amazons? Find out as much as you can about these mythological figures.

3. At what time of the month were Greek weddings performed (*hint*: see Theseus' reference to "another moon" in 1.1.3)?

4. Who or what was a "philostrate"?

5. What can you discover about parental authority and Athenian law? Would Hermia's father have been able to have her executed if she refused to marry Demetrius?

6. How do you feel about the way Hermia's father is treating her? Do you think modern fathers have as much power over their daughters as Egeus has in this play? Why or why not?

7. What can you find out about nunneries during the Renaissance (see 1.1.65–78)?

8. Who was Phoebe (1.1.209)?

9. In 1.2, what kind of written <u>script</u> or "roll" would Quince have given his actors to help them memorize their parts?

10. What do you guess Bottom means by "a part to tear a cat in" (1.2.25)?

ACT II

1. Do you think most Elizabethans believed in fairies? What information can you discover about fairy lore during the Renaissance to support your answer?

2. How big do you believe Shakespeare's fairies are? What clues can you find in the script that support your conclusion?

3. Who were Puck and Robin Goodfellow? Oberon and Titania?

4. What is a "changeling boy" (2.1.120)?

5. Who were Apollo and Daphne (2.1.231)?

6. What is a "roundel" (2.2.1)? Can you demonstrate one in class?

7. What were "reremice" (2.2.4) and "blindworms" (2.2.11)?

8. Examine the <u>symbolism</u> of Hermia's dream (2.2.145–150). How accurate is it in describing what Lysander has done to her?

ACT III

1. What was a "tiring-house" (3.1.4), and what did it have to do with the acting profession?

2. What was a <u>prologue</u> (3.1.16), and why did playwrights include them in their <u>scripts</u>?

3. What were "loam" and "roughcast" (3.1.64–65), and how were they used in making a wall during the Renaissance?

4. What does Quince mean when he tells Flute, "You speak all your part at once, cues and all" (3.1.94–95)?

5. Helena uses the word "puppet" (3.2.288) to ridicule Hermia, who is rather short. What other words or phrases can you find that describe Hermia's lack of height?

6. Who or what was "Aurora's harbinger" (3.2.380)?

7. According to Puck, what were ghosts required to do immediately before daybreak (see 3.2.378–387)?

ACT IV

1. Who was Hercules (4.1.111)?

2. Who was Cadmus (4.1.111)?

3. In 4.1.138, what is the relationship between birds and St. Valentine's Day?

4. Examine Bottom's dream in 4.1.199–217. What other dreams occur in the play? What do you think *A Midsummer Night's Dream* is trying to tell us about the relationship between dreaming and reality?

5. When Bottom explains to his fellow actors that their play is "preferred" (4.2.37), what specific advice does he give them about apparel, beards, pumps, clean linen, nails, and bad breath?

ACT V

1. Create plot outlines for one or more of the play titles rejected by Theseus in 5.1.44–55.

2. Discuss the many similarities between "Pyramus and Thisby" and Shakespeare's *Romeo and Juliet*. Which do you believe was written first? Why?

3. Chart the changes in rhyme scheme and verse form throughout the final act. Why does each of these changes occur?

4. Who were the three fates (the "sisters three" in 5.1.331)?

5. What was a "Bergomask" (5.1.347)?

6. Why does Puck refer to the "triple Hecate's team" in 5.1.376? Who was Hecate and why is she associated with the number three?

7. What is the "serpent's tongue" in 5.1.425? Why would the actors want to escape it?

Filmography

1935 (b/w)
Warner Brothers
Rating:

Directed by Max Reinhardt and William Dieterle

Victor Jory as Oberon
Anita Louise as Titania
Ian Hunter as Theseus
Verree Teasdale as Hippolyta
Mickey Rooney as Puck
Olivia de Havilland as Hermia
Jean Muir as Helena
Dick Powell as Lysander
Ross Alexander as Demetrius
James Cagney as Bottom

Hollywood and Shakespeare have not always made for a happy marriage. In this case, they probably stayed together for the sake of the children. This film is not so much by Shakespeare as descended from him. Mendelssohn and Korngold are also recent ancestors, and the true power in this *Dream* is not in the deliberately American and unintentionally uneven acting (or singing rather), but in the cloud-capped, gauze-colored visuals. Oberon and his henchmen become black bat figures, while Titania and her fairies are the whitest of Hollywood's angels. Spectacles have their own magic, and this one has reappeared in later films, most obviously the 1981 BBC version.

1964 (b/w)
Rediffusion Network Television
Rating:

Directed by Joan Kemp-Welch

Peter Wyngarde as Oberon
Anna Massey as Titania
Tony Tanner as Puck
Patrick Allen as Theseus
Eira Heath as Hippolyta
Maureen Beck as Hermia
Jill Bennett as Helena
John Fraser as Lysander
Clifford Elkin as Demetrius
Benny Hill as Bottom

This black and white version of *Midsummer* is unexpectedly magical, delicately balancing the poetry and the comedy. This fairy kingdom—ruled by a Titania and Oberon who are powerful, impulsive, not entirely kindly beings—seems genuinely otherworldly despite the inclusion of Mendelssohn's music and ballet dancers. Though Patrick Allen's Theseus occasionally rants and rages, the play is well acted, with engaging young lovers and amiable, thickheaded mechanicals. In his scenes with Titania, Benny Hill's Bottom is charmingly bashful. However, the mechanicals are so much in earnest during the performance of Pyramus and Thisby that Theseus and the young lovers seem cruel in their responses.

1968
Royal Shakespeare Company
Rating:

Directed by Peter Hall

Ian Richardson as Oberon
Judi Dench as Titania
Ian Holm as Puck
Derek Godfrey as Theseus
Barbara Jefford as Hippolyta

Helen Mirren as Hermia
Diana Rigg as Helena
David Warner as Lysander
Michael Jayston as Demetrius
Paul Rogers as Bottom

Forget the green body stockings for the fairies, the sixties costumes on the young lovers, and the experimental camera techniques with everybody. No other *Midsummer* has treated the text more carefully or been acted more powerfully. The film cuts from scene to scene at the ends of lines or in <u>caesuras</u>. Oberon is lighthearted but darkly menacing, Titania is both sensual and ethereal, and Puck has a child's sense of mischief plus an adult's understanding of folly. The mechanicals (especially Bottom) are as funny as they have ever been on film, while the young lovers have charm, humor, and love-induced stupidity in equal portions.

1981
BBC
Rating:

Directed by Elijah Moshinsky

Peter McEnery as Oberon
Helen Mirren as Titania
Phil Daniels as Puck
Nigel Davenport as Theseus
Estelle Kohler as Hippolyta
Pippa Guard as Hermia
Cherith Mellor as Helena
Robert Lindsay as Lysander
Nicky Henson as Demetrius
Brian Glover as Bottom

The strengths of this tribute to the Reinhardt-Dieterle film are compelling original music, an effectively magical if brooding atmosphere, and an angelically fiery Titania. Its weaknesses include an Oberon who is at once too dangerous and too dull (an odd combination even for this play of opposites); distinctly unfunny mechanicals, who, like everyone else in the film, are forced into poses inspired by Dutch painters; a Helena who is played ugly in spite of all the lines to the contrary; and a Puck who seems a nearly mindless animal, as far from humor as he is from humanness.

1982
New York Shakespeare Festival
Rating:

Directed by James Lapine and Emile Ardolino

William Hurt as Oberon
Michele Shay as Titania

Marcel Rosenblatt as Puck
James Hurdle as Theseus
Diane Venora as Hippolyta
Deborah Rush as Hermia
Christine Baranski as Helena
Kevin Conroy as Lysander
Rick Lieberman as Demetrius
Jeffrey De Munn as Bottom

The performances in this film of a New York Shakespeare Festival stage production are hit and miss. Though Titania and the mechanicals are credible, William Hurt's delivery of Oberon's lines contains all the emotion of an accountant mumbling numbers; Marcel Rosenblatt's Puck has a braying laugh better suited to a jackass than a sprite; and the young lovers frequently substitute shouting and gesturing for acting. In the middle of the play-within-the-play, Bottom's acting improves in the after-glow of Titania's affection; alas, those thirty seconds are the best acted of the entire production.

1999
Fox Searchlight Pictures
Rating:

Directed by Michael Hoffmann

Rupert Everett as Oberon
Michelle Pfeiffer as Titania
Stanley Tucci as Puck
David Strathaim as Theseus
Sophie Marceau as Hippolyta
Anna Friel as Hermia
Calista Flockhart as Helena
Dominic West as Lysander
Christian Bale as Demetrius
Kevin Kline as Bottom

The cast glitters (sometimes literally), the special effects twinkle, and the Italian locations shine. However, well over half Shakespeare's lines have been cut and replaced with Italian opera, a wife for Bottom who speaks Italian, an interminable amount of bicycling, and even a bout of mud wrestling. Kevin Kline as Bottom is too pathetic to be funny, Rupert Everett's Oberon is too quiet to be in control, and Stanley Tucci's Puck seems a bit old for the pranks he plays. Michelle Pfeiffer, though, is a radiant Titania in spite of her heavy makeup, and Calista Flockhart an extremely effective Helena with only occasional touches of Ally McBeal.

Annotated Bibliography

Barber, C. L. *Shakespeare's Festive Comedy: A Study of Dramatic Form and Its Relation to Social Custom.* Princeton: Princeton University Press, 1959. 3–15, 119–62. PR 2981.B3.

In the introductory chapter, Barber analyzes the principal comedic elements (including the importance of holidays and the pattern of "release" to "clarification") that help define a "festive comedy." Such subsequent chapters as "Holiday Custom and Entertainment," "The Lord of Misrule," and "Misrule as Comedy; Comedy as Misrule" further examine the "festive" elements in Shakespeare's comedies. Chapter six deals exclusively with *A Midsummer Night's Dream.*

Brown, John Russell. "Love's Truth and the Judgment of *A Midsummer Night's Dream* and *Much Ado About Nothing.*" In *Shakespeare and His Comedies,* by John Russell Brown. London: Methuen and Company Limited, 1968. 82–123. PR 2981.B7.

Brown persuasively explains how love in various Shakespearean comedies exposes truth. In his section on *A Midsummer Night's Dream,* the author compares how the lovers' quest for the realization of beauty leads them to their own individual truths.

Calderwood, James. "*A Midsummer Night's Dream:* Anamorphism and Theseus' Dream." *Shakespeare Quarterly* 42.4 (Winter 1991): 409–430. journal PR 2885.S63.

This engaging essay discusses several interesting ways in which an audience can view *A Midsummer Night's Dream,* including the doubling of Titania and Oberon with Hippolyta and Theseus and the parallel between Egeus and Aegeus (Theseus' father in mythology) as the father figure Theseus defies in the end.

Conlan, J.P. "Puck's Dread Broom." *English Language Notes* 40:4 (June 2003): 33–41. PE 1.E53.

This fascinating essay links Puck's act of sweeping the stage at the end of the play to the contemporary issue of public health and hygiene during the plague years. Conlan shows how the play connects the theater, the church, and the government to the subject of domestic health.

Dutton, Richard, ed. *A Midsummer Night's Dream.* New York: St. Martin's Press, 1996. PR 2827.M53.

This interesting collection of ten essays discusses various intriguing topics in *A Midsummer Night's Dream,* ranging from psychoanalysis to gender equity and historicism. Prominent authors include David Bevington, Shirley Nelson Gamer, Norman Holland, and Annabel Patterson.

Garber, Marjorie B. "Spirits of Another Sort: *A Midsummer Night's Dream.*" In *Dream in Shakespeare: From Metaphor to Metamorphosis* by Marjorie B. Garber. New Haven: Yale University Press, 1974. 59–87. PR 3069.D67.G3.

Garber compares and contrasts characters, themes, and situations in many of Shakespeare's comedies in order to prove that dreams are often a "reliable source of vision and heightened insight, consistently truer than the reality they seek to interpret."

Halio, Jay. "The Staging of *A Midsummer Night's Dream,* 1595–1895." In *Shakespeare's Universe: Renaissance Ideas and Conventions,* edited by John M. Mucciolo. Hants: Scolar Press, 1996. 155–172. PR 2894.S55.

This informative essay explores various influential productions of *A Midsummer Night's Dream* from 1595 to 1895. Halio presents numerous adaptations of Shakespeare's script, showing transformations the play underwent before again being produced in its original state.

Holland, Norman N. "Hermia's Dream." In *Representing Shakespeare: New Psychoanalytic Essays,* by Murray M. Schwartz and Coppelia Kahn. Baltimore: John Hopkins University Press, 1980. 1–20. PR 2976.R4.

> In an essay that takes several psychological approaches to explain Hermia's dream in the forest, Holland investigates the characters and symbols of the dream, as well as the dream as it relates to the play as a whole.

Howard, Skiles. "Hands, Feet, and Bottoms: Decentering the Cosmic Dance in *A Midsummer Night's Dream*." *Shakespeare Quarterly* 44.3 (Fall 1993): 325–342. journal PR 2885.S63.

> Both the function and meaning of dance in Elizabethan society and *A Midsummer Night's Dream* are addressed in this interesting article in which Howard discusses many different forms of dance, including courtly, cosmic, country, popular, and bergomask.

Kott, Jan. "The Bottom Translation." In *Assays: Critical Approaches to Medieval and Renaissance Texts.* Volume 1. Pittsburgh: University of Pittsburgh Press, 1981. 117–149. journal PN 671.A87.

> Kott introduces "Puck as Cupid" and "Bottom as Bacchus" themes in this fascinating article that traces numerous classical ideas throughout *A Midsummer Night's Dream.* Kott compares the play with such classics as Apuleius' *The Golden Ass,* Ovid's *Metamorphoses,* Erasmus' *The Praise of Folly,* and St. Paul in *Corinthians.*

Kott, Jan. "Titania and the Ass's Head." In *Shakespeare: Our Contemporary,* by Ian Kott. Translated by Boleslaw Taborski. Garden City: Doubleday and Company, 1964. 207–228. PR 2979.P58.K63.

> In this well researched essay, Kott examines the character of Puck and comments on dreams, eroticism, and love in the play. He compares the bestial relationship between Titania and Bottom to paintings by Goya in order to draw some interesting conclusions.

Lamb, Mary E. "Taken by the Fairies: Fairy Practices and the Production of Popular Culture in *A Midsummer Night's Dream*." *Shakespeare Quarterly* 51:3 (Fall 2000): 277–312. journal PR 2885.S63.

> Lamb's article investigates two distinct questions in the play: (1) the historical and social role fairies played in the popular culture of the working class and (2) how *A Midsummer Night's Dream* betrays the elite's desire to break with the notions of popular culture as well as the impossibility of such a separation.

Montrose, Louis Adrian. "*A Midsummer Night's Dream* and the Shaping Fantasies of Elizabethan Culture: Gender, Power, and Form." In *Rewriting the Renaissance: The Discourse of Sexual Difference in Early Modern Europe,* by Margaret W. Ferguson, Maureen Quilligan, and Nancy J. Vickers. Chicago: University of Chicago Press, 1986. 65–87. HQ 1075.5.E85.R48.

> Focusing upon an age when a woman ruled England, Montrose exposes the difficulties men had with female authority, discusses the Amazon legends in the Renaissance, and shows how the mystique of Queen Elizabeth helped shape an entire culture.

Phialas, Peter G. "*A Midsummer Night's Dream.*" In *Shakespeare's Romantic Comedies: The Development of Their Form and Meaning,* by Peter G. Phialas. Chapel Hill: University of North Carolina Press, 1966. 102–133. PR 2981.P5.

This engaging essay examines the date the play was written and evaluates the probable sources Shakespeare used. Phialas discusses a variety of elements in *A Midsummer Night's Dream,* including characters, plot, comedic patterns, the play within the play, and the juxtaposition between the "ideal" and the "real."

Richmond, Hugh. "Bottom as Romeo." In *Shakespeare's Sexual Comedy: A Mirror for Lovers,* by Hugh Richmond. Indianapolis: Bobbs-Merrill, 1971. 102–122. PR 2981.R5.

In this essay, Richmond analyzes love, sex, characterization, and relationships in *A Midsummer Night's Dream* by comparing the play with the "sexual conduct" of Romeo in *Romeo and Juliet.*

Summers, Joseph H. "Dreams of Love and Power: *A Midsummer Night's Dream.*" In *Dreams of Love and Power: On Shakespeare's Plays,* by Joseph H. Summers. Oxford: Clarendon Press, 1984. 1–22. PR 2976.S777.

In this highly entertaining essay, Summers explores the themes of love and power in *A Midsummer Night's Dream* and details how the play follows the traditional structure of a romantic comedy.

Swander, Homer. "Editors vs. Text: The Scripted Geography of *A Midsummer Night's Dream.*" *Studies in Philology* (Winter 1990): 83–108. journal P25.S8.

Swander cleverly explains the various contextual contradictions concerning Titania's "bower" between the Quarto, Folio, later editions, and various productions; he also examines the character of Bottom and his transformation from man to ass to enlightened man, Titania's rape of Bottom, and Puck's decision to transform Bottom into an ass.

Williams, Gary Jay. *Our Moonlight Revels: "A Midsummer Night's Dream" in the Theatre.* Iowa City: University of Iowa Press, 1997. PR 2827.W59.

Williams traces the chronology of several *A Midsummer Night's Dream* performances in this thoroughly researched book, explaining how each performance was affected by its cultural surroundings and how each one may have influenced those that followed.

Young, David P. *Something of Great Constancy: The Art of "A Midsummer Night's Dream."* New Haven: Yale University Press, 1966. PR 2827.Y6.

Young conducts an in-depth study of the play in this illuminating book, establishing "the importance of *A Midsummer Night's Dream* in the development of Shakespeare's art." The author argues that many themes within each scene blend to accomplish a "constancy" or unity within the play as a whole. Young focuses particularly on the non-dramatic and dramatic backgrounds, style, structure, and Bottom's dream.

The Merchant of Venice

The Merchant of Venice *at the Oregon Shakespearean Festival in Ashland, Oregon, with Lisa Ivary as Portia and Richard Elmore as Shylock (1991). Photograph by Christopher Briscoe.*

One of Shakespeare's most complex and fascinating plays, *The Merchant of Venice* may have been written as early as 1596, soon after the trial and execution in 1594 of Roderigo Lopez, a Portuguese Jewish physician who had been convicted of plotting to poison Queen Elizabeth. Additional contemporary anti-Semitic influences included Christopher Marlowe's well-known drama *The Jew of Malta,* with its bloodthirsty stereotypical villain, and an earlier play entitled *The Jew,* now lost, that may have blended many of the <u>plot</u> elements in Shakespeare's <u>script</u>. The author's primary <u>source</u> was undoubtedly a <u>prose</u> <u>romance</u> found in Giovanni Fiorentino's *Il Pecorone* ("The Dunce"), which includes the relationship between a younger man and his older, wealthy male friend; a beautiful young woman who must be won by a love strategy; the indebtedness to a Jewish money-lender; the climactic courtroom appearance of the woman dressed as a lawyer; and a concluding episode featuring the gift of a wedding ring. The casket episodes may have come from such earlier <u>sources</u> as the *Mahabharata,* the *Cursor Mundi,* and the *Gesta Romanorum,* although their psychological connotations, descending ultimately from ancient myth and legend, confer great <u>symbolic</u> significance upon Shakespeare's play.

The precise <u>genre</u> of the <u>script</u> is difficult to determine, since Shakespeare has skillfully wrapped Shylock's <u>tragic</u> fate within a <u>comic</u> envelope of romance, prosperity, and happiness. The unhappy Jew's ill-fated "pound of flesh," his daughter's elopement with a Christian suitor, and his forced religious conversion at the conclusion of the play contrast sharply with the love intrigues, camaraderie, and lust for wealth of his hypocritical tormentors. As a result, the play confounds viewers and readers alike through the absence of any truly sympathetic characters with whom we can identify. While most of us sincerely empathize with the struggles of the romantic young couples, we are simultaneously revolted by the ethnic abuse heaped upon Shylock by these so-called "Christian" characters. The result is a deeply ambivalent play that has challenged and frustrated audiences for over four hundred years with its somewhat awkward mixture of dramatic <u>genres.</u>

Out of this fusion of opposites come most of the play's major <u>themes,</u> such as the geographical division between the two primary locales of the play: Venice is mercantile, discordant, ruled by men, and filled with hate, while Belmont is magical, musical, ruled by women, and characterized by love. The <u>script's</u> comic pattern, therefore, moves from society (Venice), to wilderness (Belmont), and back to society (Venice) again, just as it shifts from the union of the two friends Bassanio and Antonio, to their separation, and then to their eventual reunion prior to the conclusion of the play. Additional important <u>themes</u> include the relationship between prosperity and happiness, the <u>ironic</u> difference between Christian "mercy" and pagan "retribution," the extent to which Shylock is a sympathetic character, the great number of economic <u>images</u>, the characters' religious bigotry, and the ever-present Shakespearean <u>theme</u> of appearance vs. reality. Viewed from a feminist perspective, Portia and Nerissa must prove themselves as men before being truly accepted as women; they may, therefore, be seen as archetypes of "modern" women through their achievement of power and social status in the play. Further, we might ask who the "merchant" of Shakespeare's title is. Antonio certainly lays most claim to the distinction, although most of the other characters in the play are somehow involved in the buying and selling of merchandise. Recent scholarship has added a number of important topics to the debate over the play, including the role of women, cross-dressing, promise vs. obligation, politics, ethical standards, multiculturalism, and the intriguing number of performances in Israel.

Not surprisingly, the play's <u>stage</u> history has had a long and intriguing tradition. Early productions seem to have exploited Shylock as a stock villain, focusing upon his stereotypical hooked nose, red beard, and comic defeat by his Christian persecutors—a theatrical approach tolerated because few Jews lived in England during the sixteenth and early seventeenth centuries. Officially banished from the country in 1290 by King Edward I, they returned later in small numbers and under severe economic and social restrictions. Despised as "non-believers," Jews were forbidden to engage in most common occupations except for usury (the lending of money at high interest rates), which suffered under religious prohibition, but was nevertheless necessary for the expanding mercantile economy represented by Antonio and his fellow merchants.

Seldom performed during the Renaissance, the play was adapted and revived by George Granville in 1701 in a production entitled *The Jew of Venice,* which included a lengthy <u>masque</u>, a drastically abbreviated script, and the loss of nearly all its comic characters. Charles Macklin returned Shakespeare's original play to popularity in 1741 by restoring its comedy and acting the role of Shylock himself. Edmund Kean's production in 1814 made Shylock more of a <u>tragic</u> character and set the stage for a variety of later sympathetic portrayals by William Charles Macready, Charles Kean, Henry Irving, Edwin Booth, and director Theodore Komisarjevsky. More recent post-Holocaust interpretations by Jonathan Miller, John Barton, Patrick Stewart, and David Suchet at the Royal Shakespeare Company have helped define the <u>script's</u> rich and varied stage history, as have Tyrone Guthrie's fascinating 1959 modern-dress Israeli production, Dustin Hoffman's 1980's New York version, and contrasting twentieth-century productions at the Oregon Shakespearean Festival directed by Angus Bowmer and Libby Appel.

Whatever your own response to *The Merchant of Venice* is, be assured that you will respond! Through this intriguing <u>script</u>, Shakespeare forces us to confront the latent racism in our own hearts and minds. Just as a little bit of Portia, Bassanio, and Antonio lurk within us, so too does the character of Shylock reside deep within our psyches. Our response to the play, therefore, is in large part a reaction to the hopes, fears, dreams, and prejudices that define us as unique and flawed human beings. Shakespeare's play sets up a mirror to our very souls and invites us to seek within ourselves the "touches of sweet harmony" (5.1.57) that can help lead us to better and more fulfilling lives.

The Merchant of Venice *at the Alabama Shakespeare Festival in Montgomery, Alabama, with Laura McCord as Nerissa, John G. Preston as Gratiano, Monica Bell as Portia, and Brian G. Kurlander as Bassanio (1997). Photograph by Phil Scarsbrook.*

The Merchant of Venice

NAMES OF THE ACTORS

THE DUKE OF VENICE
THE PRINCE OF MOROCCO ⎱ *Portia's suitors*
THE PRINCE OF ARAGON ⎰
ANTONIO, *a merchant of Venice*
BASSANIO, *his friend, suitor to Portia*
GRATIANO ⎫
SALARINO ⎬ *friends to Antonio and Bassanio*
SOLANIO ⎭
LORENZO
SHYLOCK, *a financier*
TUBAL, *his friend*
LANCELOT GOBBO, *a clown, servant to Shylock*
OLD GOBBO, *father to Lancelot*
LEONARDO, *servant to Bassanio*
BALTHASAR ⎱ *servants to Portia*
STEPHANO ⎰
SALERIO, *a messenger*
PORTIA, *an heiress*
NERISSA, *her waiting gentlewoman*
JESSICA, *Shylock's daughter*
MAGNIFICOES OF VENICE, COURT OFFICERS, JAILER,
   SERVANTS, AND OTHER ATTENDANTS

SCENE: *Venice and Belmont*

1.1° *Enter Antonio, Salarino, and Solanio.*

1.1: A street in Venice

ANTONIO
  In sooth° I know not why I am so sad.°
  It wearies me, you say it wearies you;
  But how I caught it, found it, or came by it,
  What stuff 'tis made of, whereof it is born,
  I am to learn;°
  And such a want-wit° sadness makes of me
  That I have much ado to know myself.
SALARINO
  Your mind is tossing on the ocean,

In sooth: truly (Antonio answers a question asked before the dialogue and play begin); **sad:** serious, thoughtful

am to learn: have yet to learn
want-wit: (1) dullard, (2) forgetful person

5

DISCOVERING SHAKESPEARE

(1) Motivation [1.1.1]: Why do you think Antonio is sad in this first scene? And what principal motive do Salarino and Solanio have for trying to cheer him up? Return to this question periodically as you read the <u>dialogue</u>, and remember your initial impressions about Antonio's sadness and the motive of the two "Salads" (a well-known theatrical nickname for Salarino and Solanio).

There where your argosies° with portly° sail –
Like signors and rich burghers on the flood,
Or as it were, the pageants° of the sea –
Do overpeer° the petty traffickers
That curtsy° to them, do them reverence,
As they fly by them with their woven wings.

SOLANIO
Believe me, sir, had I such venture forth,
The better part of my affections would
Be with my hopes abroad. I should be still
Plucking the grass to know where sits the wind,
Peering in maps for ports and piers and roads;°
And every object that might make me fear
Misfortune to my ventures, out of doubt
Would make me sad.

SALARINO   My wind cooling my broth
Would blow me to an ague° when I thought
What harm a wind too great might do at sea.
I should not see the sandy hourglass run
But I should think of shallows and of flats,
And see my wealthy *Andrew*° docked in sand,
Vailing° her high top° lower than her ribs
To kiss her burial. Should I go to church
And see the holy edifice of stone
And not bethink me straight of dangerous rocks,
Which touching but my gentle vessel's side
Would scatter all her spices° on the stream,
Enrobe the roaring waters with my silks,
And in a word, but even now worth this,
And now worth nothing? Shall I have the thought
To think on this, and shall I lack the thought
That such a thing bechanced° would make me sad?
But tell not me: I know Antonio
Is sad to think upon his merchandise.

ANTONIO
Believe me, no. I thank my fortune for it
My ventures are not in one bottom° trusted,
Nor to one place; nor is my whole estate
Upon the fortune of this present year.°
Therefore my merchandise makes me not sad.

SOLANIO
Why then you are in love.

ANTONIO   Fie, fie!

SOLANIO
Not in love neither? Then let us say you are sad
Because you are not merry; and 'twere as easy
For you to laugh and leap, and say you are merry

argosies: large merchant ships; **portly:** (1) stately, (2) swelling (billowing)   10

pageants: i.e., like "floats" in a procession
overpeer: tower above
curtsy: bow, dip (i.e., while moving on the waves)

15

roads: anchorages

20

ague: fit of trembling

25

Andrew: (name of ship)
Vailing: bowing; **high top:** topmast

30

spices: (a common cargo from Asia to Venice)

35

bechanced: having happened

40

bottom: ship

nor is . . . year: nor is all my wealth risked at this one time   45

DISCOVERING SHAKESPEARE

(2) Metaphor [1.1.25]: List all the common, everyday occurrences that would remind Salarino of the peril to his ships if he, like Antonio, had risked all his fortune at sea.

(3) Characterization [1.1.46]: When Solanio asks if Antonio is sad because he is in love, Antonio replies "Fie, fie." What could this response indicate about his attitude toward women?

Because you are not sad. Now by two-headed Janus,°
Nature hath framed strange fellows in her time:
Some that will evermore peep through their eyes.
And laugh like parrots at a bagpiper,
And other of such vinegar aspect
That they'll not show their teeth in way of smile
Though Nestor° swear the jest be laughable.
　Enter Bassanio, Lorenzo, and Gratiano.
Here comes Bassanio your most noble kinsman,
Gratiano, and Lorenzo. Fare ye well;
We leave you now with better company.

SALARINO
I would have stayed till I had made you merry,
If worthier friends had not prevented° me.

ANTONIO
Your worth is very dear in my regard.
I take it your own business calls on you,
And you embrace th' occasion to depart.

SALARINO
Good morrow, my good lords.

BASSANIO
Good signors both, when shall we laugh? Say, when?
You grow exceeding strange.° Must it be so?

SALARINO
We'll make our leisures to attend on° yours.
　　　　　　　　Exeunt Salarino and Solanio.

LORENZO
My Lord Bassanio, since you have found Antonio,
We two will leave you; but at dinnertime
I pray you have in mind where we must meet.

BASSANIO
I will not fail you.

GRATIANO
You look not well, Signor Antonio.
You have too much respect upon° the world;
They lose it that do buy it with much care.
Believe me, you are marvelously changed.

ANTONIO
I hold the world but as the world, Gratiano:
A stage where every man must play a part,
And mine a sad one.

GRATIANO　　　　　　Let me play the fool!
With mirth and laughter let old wrinkles come,
And let my liver° rather heat with wine
Than my heart cool with mortifying° groans.
Why should a man whose blood is warm within
Sit like his grandsire cut in alabaster?°
Sleep when he wakes? and creep into the jaundice°
By being peevish? I tell thee what, Antonio,
I love thee, and 'tis my love that speaks:
There are a sort° of men whose visages

Janus: Roman god with two faces, one facing the past, the other the future (Shakespeare also thinks [see ll. 52–55] of the classical masks of comedy and tragedy, one smiling, one sad, or *vinegar*)

Nestor: old and solemn character in the *Iliad*

prevented: forestalled

strange: like strangers

attend on: wait on (i.e., fit)

respect upon: concern for

liver: (to Elizabethans, the seat of the emotions)
mortifying: (1) deadening, (2) penitential

alabaster: stone used for funerary monuments
jaundice: (jaundice was associated with grief, as cause or consequence)

sort: kind, type

DISCOVERING SHAKESPEARE
(4) Characterization [1.1.73]: What kind of a person is Gratiano? Describe him on a separate piece of paper.

Do cream and mantle like a standing pond,°
And do a willful stillness entertain°
With purpose to be dressed in an opinion°
Of wisdom, gravity, profound conceit,°
As who should say, "I am Sir Oracle,°
And when I ope my lips, let no dog bark!"
O my Antonio, I do know of these
That therefore only are reputed wise
For saying nothing, when I am very sure
If they should speak would almost damn those ears,
Which hearing them would call their brothers fools.°
I'll tell thee more of this another time.
But fish not with this melancholy bait
For this fool gudgeon,° this opinion.°
Come, good Lorenzo. Fare ye well awhile;
I'll end my exhortation after dinner.

LORENZO
Well, we will leave you then till dinnertime.
I must be one of these same dumb wise men,
For Gratiano never lets me speak.

GRATIANO
Well, keep me company but two years more,
Thou shalt not know the sound of thine own tongue.

ANTONIO
Fare you well; I'll grow a talker for this gear.°

GRATIANO
Thanks i' faith; for silence is only commendable
In a neat's° tongue dried and a maid not vendible.°

                        Exeunt [Gratiano and Lorenzo].

ANTONIO   Is that anything now?

BASSANIO   Gratiano speaks an infinite deal of nothing, more than any man in all Venice. His reasons are as two grains of wheat hid in two bushels of chaff: you shall seek all day ere you find them, and when you have them they are not worth the search.

ANTONIO
Well, tell me now what lady is the same
To whom you swore a secret pilgrimage,
That you today promised to tell me of.

BASSANIO
'Tis not unknown to you, Antonio,
How much I have disabled° mine estate
By something showing a more swelling port°
Than my faint means would grant continuance.°
Nor do I now make moan° to be abridged°

---

cream . . . pond: cover themselves (*mantle*) in scum (*cream*) like a stagnant pool   90

entertain: take on, assume

opinion: reputation (so also in l. 102)

conceit: thought

Sir Oracle: (the mock title ridicules pretended gravity)   95

If they . . . fools: (See Matthew 5:22: ". . . but whosoever shall say, Thou fool, shall be in danger   100 of hellfire.")

gudgeon: (proverbially, an easily caught fish); **opinion:** (compared to a fish not worth catching with cheap bait)

 105

for this gear: because of what you have just said   110 (Antonio implies that by talking he will escape Gratiano's accusation)

neat: ox (the long, thin, and withered tongue is analogous to an impotent old man's penis); **vendible:** marketable (i.e., marriageable)

 115

 120

disabled: impaired, reduced

something . . . port: somewhat exhibiting a more lavish appearance (i.e., putting up a good   125 "front")

grant continuance: allow to continue

make moan: complain; **abridged:** cut down, reduced

DISCOVERING SHAKESPEARE

(5) Relationships [1.1.105]: Describe the relationship between Gratiano and Lorenzo. Which of the two is more talkative? Which one would most likely be a friend of yours? Why?

(6) Language [1.1.122–130]: On a separate piece of paper, <u>paraphrase</u> the first eight and one-half lines of Bassanio's request for money from Antonio. Underline all the difficult language in Bassanio's lines; then explain why you think he uses so many complex and multi-syllable words.

From such a noble rate;° but my chief care
Is to come fairly off from the great debts
Wherein my time, something too prodigal,
Hath left me gaged.° To you, Antonio,
I owe the most in money and in love,
And from your love I have a warranty°
To unburden all my plots and purposes
How to get clear of all the debts I owe.

ANTONIO
I pray you, good Bassanio, let me know it,
And if it stand as you yourself still do,
Within the eye of honor,° be assured
My purse, my person,° my extremest means
Lie all unlocked to your occasions.

BASSANIO
In my schooldays, when I had lost one shaft°
I shot his fellow of the selfsame° flight
The selfsame way, with more advisèd watch
To find the other forth; and by adventuring both
I oft found both. I urge this childhood proof
Because what follows is pure innocence.°
I owe you much, and like a willful youth
That which I owe is lost; but if you please
To shoot another arrow that self way
Which you did shoot the first, I do not doubt,
As I will watch the aim, or to find both
Or bring your latter hazard back again°
And thankfully rest debtor for the first.

ANTONIO
You know me well, and herein spend but time
To wind about my love with circumstance;°
And out of doubt you do me now more wrong
In making question of my uttermost°
Than if you had made waste of all I have.
Then do but say to me what I should do
That in your knowledge may by me be done,
And I am prest° unto it: therefore speak.

BASSANIO
In Belmont is a lady richly left;°
And she is fair, and fairer than that word,
Of wondrous virtues. Sometimes from her eyes
I did receive fair speechless messages.
Her name is Portia, nothing undervalued
To° Cato's daughter, Brutus' Portia;°

noble rate: high scale

gaged: pledged for, owing   130

from . . . warranty: i.e., my confidence in your love authorizes me

if . . . honor: if your plan is as honorable as you have always been
person: reputation (as collateral, but an unwittingly literal remark)

shaft: arrow   140
selfsame: same size and kind

innocence: childlike sincerity, with perhaps a touch of folly   145

or . . . again: either to discover both arrows (i.e., loans) or return your second arrow

spend . . . circumstance: i.e., needlessly persuade me with elaborate talk   155
making . . . uttermost: questioning that I will do all I can

prest: ready   160

richly left: rich by inheritance

nothing undervalued/To: of no less worth than   165
Cato's . . . Portia: historically wife to Brutus, the conspirator against Julius Caesar, and daughter to the honest Cato Uticensis, a tribune

135

150

DISCOVERING SHAKESPEARE

(7) Metaphor [1.1.140–152]: Rephrase Bassanio's archery metaphor in more modern language, using a different sport or analogy to describe his plan for repaying the money Antonio has loaned him.
(8) Social History [1.1.160]: Antonio's expression that he is willing to be "prest unto" (160) assisting Bassanio implies a common torture technique during the Renaissance by which victims were pressed to death under heavy weights. How many other torture metaphors can you find in the play? (*Hint:* See especially 1.1.181, where Antonio agrees that his credit may be "racked" to help his friend, and the beginning of 3.2, immediately before Bassanio's casket choice.) Why are so many early torture metaphors associated with Antonio?

Nor is the wide world ignorant of her worth,
For the four winds blow in from every coast
Renownèd suitors, and her sunny° locks
Hang on her temples like a golden fleece,
Which makes her seat° of Belmont Colchos' strand,°
And many Jasons come in quest of her.°
O my Antonio, had I but the means
To hold a rival place with one of them,
I have a mind presages me such thrift°
That I should questionless be fortunate!

ANTONIO
Thou know'st that all my fortunes are at sea;
Neither have I money, nor commodity°
To raise a present sum. Therefore go forth.
Try what my credit can in Venice do;
That shall be racked° even to the uttermost
To furnish thee to Belmont to fair Portia.
Go presently° inquire, and so will I,
Where money is; and I no question make
To have it of my trust or for my sake.°   *Exeunt.*

❧ **1.2**° *Enter Portia with her waiting woman, Nerissa.*

PORTIA   By my troth,° Nerissa, my little body is aweary° of
this great world.

NERISSA   You would be, sweet madam, if your miseries
were in the same abundance as your good fortunes are;
and yet for aught I see, they are as sick that surfeit with
too much as they that starve with nothing. It is no
mean° happiness, therefore, to be seated in the mean;°
superfluity comes sooner by° white hairs, but compe-
tency° lives longer.

PORTIA   Good sentences,° and well pronounced.

NERISSA   They would be better if well followed.

PORTIA   If to do were as easy as to know what were good
to do, chapels had been churches, and poor men's cot-
tages princes' palaces. It is a good divine° that follows his
own instructions; I can easier teach twenty what were
good to be done than to be one of the twenty to follow
mine own teaching. The brain may devise laws for the
blood, but a hot temper° leaps o'er a cold decree;° such a
hare is madness the youth to skip o'er the meshes° of
good counsel° the cripple. But this reasoning is not in
the fashion° to choose me a husband. O me, the word
"choose"! I may neither choose who I would nor refuse
who I dislike, so is the will of a living daughter curbed

sunny: i.e., blond (highly valued by Elizabethan canons of beauty)   170

seat: principal residence; **strand:** shore

golden . . . of her: (reference to Jason's mythical quest for the Golden Fleece)

thrift: (1) profit, (2) thriving   175

commodity: goods

180

racked: stretched, as on the rack

presently: immediately (as throughout the play)

of my trust . . . sake: on the basis of my credit or as a personal favor (cf. *My purse, my person* in l. 138)   185

1.2: Belmont

troth: faith;
aweary: (Portia's weariness matches Antonio's sadness in 1.1)

5

mean: small; **seated . . . mean:** with neither too much nor too little (*mean* is a middle way)
comes sooner by: gets sooner
competency: modest means   10
sentences: maxims, proverbs

divine: preacher

15

temper: temperament
brain . . . decree: (this contrast between hot emotion and cold reason reflects Portia's conflict between desire and her father's will: see ll. 20–25)   20
meshes: net for catching hares
good counsel: wisdom
not . . . fashion: not the way

DISCOVERING SHAKESPEARE

(9) Characterization [1.2.1]: Like Antonio, Portia begins the play in sadness. Why do you think Shakespeare has two successive scenes in this play introduce sad characters? How is this dramatic choice related to the play's comic structure?

(10) Characterization [1.2.23]: What kind of person do you think Portia's father was? Try to compose, using legal language, the will he wrote involving the three caskets of gold, silver, and lead. How does Portia feel about the restrictions imposed by her father's will?

by the will of a dead father.° Is it not hard, Nerissa, that I cannot choose one, nor refuse none?°

NERISSA Your father was ever virtuous, and holy men at their death have good inspirations. Therefore the lottery that he hath devised in these three chests of gold, silver, and lead – whereof who chooses his meaning chooses you – will no doubt never be chosen by any rightly but one who you shall rightly° love. But what warmth is there in your affection towards any of these princely suitors that are already come?

PORTIA I pray thee overname them,° and as thou namest them I will describe them, and according to my description level at my affection.°

NERISSA First, there is the Neapolitan prince.

PORTIA Ay, that's a colt° indeed, for he doth nothing but talk of his horse, and he makes it a great appropriation° to his own good parts° that he can shoe him himself. I am much afeard° my lady his mother played false with a smith.

NERISSA Then is there the County° Palatine.

PORTIA He doth nothing but frown – as who should say, "An° you will not have me, choose!"° He hears merry tales and smiles not; I fear he will prove the weeping philosopher when he grows old, being so full of unmannerly sadness in his youth. I had rather be married to a death's-head with a bone in his mouth than to either of these. God defend me from these two!

NERISSA How say you by the French lord, Monsieur Le Bon?

PORTIA God made him, and therefore let him pass for a man. In truth, I know it is a sin to be a mocker, but he – why he hath a horse better than the Neapolitan's, a better bad habit of frowning than the Count Palatine: he is every man in no man.° If a throstle° sing, he falls straight a-capering; he will fence with his own shadow. If I should marry him, I should marry twenty husbands. If he would despise me, I would forgive him; for if he love me to madness, I shall never requite him.

NERISSA What say you then to Falconbridge, the young baron of England?

PORTIA You know I say nothing to him, for he understands not me, nor I him. He hath neither Latin, French, nor Italian, and you will come into the court and swear that I have a poor pennyworth in the English. He is a proper° man's picture, but alas who can converse with a dumb show?° How oddly he is suited!° I think he bought his doublet° in Italy, his round hose° in France, his bonnet in Germany, and his behavior everywhere.

---

will of a dead father: dead father's bequest (with pun on *will* as determination) 25
refuse none: refuse any chance at the *lottery* (ll. 27–28)

30
rightly . . . rightly: correctly . . . truly

overname them: list their names (these lines are a compendium of Elizabethan stereotypes for foreigners) 35
level . . . affection: try to decide, or to guess, how I feel toward them
colt: raw adolescent
appropriation: addition 40
parts: abilities
afeard: afraid

County: count

An: if; **choose:** have it your way (i.e., choose whom you will) 45

50

every . . . man: everyone in no one; **throstle:** thrush

60

65

proper: handsome
dumb show: pantomime; **suited:** dressed (ll. 69–71 ridicule English aping of other nations' fashions and customs) 70

doublet: coat; **hose:** breeches

DISCOVERING SHAKESPEARE

(11) Social History [1.2.38]: Make a list of Portia's suitors including the principal character flaws exhibited by each of them. To what extent do these national stereotypes still exist?

(12) Nationalism [1.2.62]: Judging from Portia's description of "Falconbridge, the young Baron of England" (62–63), how do you think Shakespeare felt about the defects of his own countrymen?

NERISSA   What think you of the Scottish lord, his neighbor?

PORTIA   That he hath a neighborly charity in him, for he borrowed a box of the ear of the Englishman and swore he would pay him again when he was able. I think the Frenchman became his surety° and sealed under° for another.

NERISSA   How like you the young German, the Duke of Saxony's nephew?

PORTIA   Very vilely in the morning when he is sober, and most vilely in the afternoon when he is drunk. When he is best he is a little worse than a man, and when he is worst he is little better than a beast. And° the worst fall that ever fell, I hope I shall make shift° to go without him.

NERISSA   If he should offer to choose, and choose the right casket, you should refuse to perform your father's will if you should refuse to accept him.

PORTIA   Therefore, for fear of the worst, I pray thee set a deep glass of Rhenish wine on the contrary° casket, for if the devil be within and that temptation without, I know he will choose it. I will do anything, Nerissa, ere I will be married to a sponge.

NERISSA   You need not fear, lady, the having any of these lords. They have acquainted me with their determinations, which is indeed to return to their home and to trouble you with no more suit, unless you may be won by some other sort° than your father's imposition, depending on the caskets.

PORTIA   If I live to be as old as Sibylla,° I will die as chaste as Diana° unless I be obtained by the manner of my father's will. I am glad this parcel of wooers are so reasonable, for there is not one among them but I dote on his very absence; and I pray God grant them a fair departure.

NERISSA   Do you not remember, lady, in your father's time, a Venetian, a scholar and a soldier, that came hither in the company of the Marquis of Montferrat?

PORTIA   Yes, yes, it was Bassanio — as I think, so was he called.

NERISSA   True, madam. He, of all the men that ever my foolish eyes looked upon, was the best deserving a fair lady.

PORTIA   I remember him well, and I remember him worthy of thy praise.

Enter a Servingman.

How now, what news?

SERVINGMAN   The four strangers seek for you, madam, to take their leave, and there is a forerunner come from

75

became his surety: (a reference to the historical Franco-Scottish alliance against England); **sealed under:** put his seal under the Scot's, as a further guarantor (a comic parallel to the Antonio-Bassanio relation)

80

And: if
make shift: manage

85

90

contrary: other, or "wrong"

95

sort: way

100

Sibylla: prophetess to whom Apollo promised as many years of life as there were grains in her handful of sand
Diana: goddess of chastity

105

110

115

DISCOVERING SHAKESPEARE

(13) Ethical Behavior [1.2.90]: How seriously do you take Portia's joke that she might consider cheating in order to avoid a distasteful husband?

(14) Plot [1.2.118]: If these suitors are all leaving, why does Shakespeare have Portia and Nerissa discuss them?

a fifth, the Prince of Morocco, who brings word the
prince his master will be here tonight.

PORTIA If I could bid the fifth welcome with so good
heart as I can bid the other four farewell, I should be
glad of his approach. If he have the condition of a saint
and the complexion of a devil, I had rather he should
shrive me than wive me.° Come, Nerissa. Sirrah,° go before. Whiles we shut the gate upon one wooer, another
knocks at the door.   *Exeunt.*

❧ **1.3**° *Enter Bassanio with Shylock the Jew.*

SHYLOCK   Three thousand ducats° – well.
BASSANIO   Ay, sir, for three months.
SHYLOCK   For three months – well.
BASSANIO   For the which, as I told you, Antonio shall be
bound.°
SHYLOCK   Antonio shall become bound—well.
BASSANIO   May you stead° me? Will you pleasure me?
Shall I know your answer?
SHYLOCK   Three thousand ducats for three months, and
Antonio bound.
BASSANIO   Your answer to that.
SHYLOCK   Antonio is a good° man.
BASSANIO   Have you heard any imputation to the con-
trary?
SHYLOCK   Ho no, no, no, no! My meaning in saying he
is a good man is to have you understand me that he is
sufficient.° Yet his means are in supposition.° He hath an
argosy bound to Tripolis, another to the Indies; I un-
derstand, moreover, upon the Rialto,° he hath a third at
Mexico, a fourth for England, and other ventures he
hath squandered° abroad. But ships are but boards,
sailors but men; there be land rats and water rats, water
thieves and land thieves – I mean pirates; and then
there is the peril of waters, winds, and rocks. The man
is, notwithstanding, sufficient. Three thousand ducats –
I think I may take his bond.
BASSANIO   Be assured you may.
SHYLOCK   I will be assured I may; and that I may be assured, I will bethink me. May I speak with Antonio?
BASSANIO   If it please you to dine with us.
SHYLOCK   Yes, to smell pork, to eat of the habitation°
which your prophet the Nazarite conjured the devil
into!° I will buy with you, sell with you, talk with you,
walk with you, and so following; but I will not eat with
you, drink with you, nor pray with you. What news on
the Rialto?° Who is he comes here?
Enter Antonio.

If . . . wive me: i.e., if his inner nature (*condition*) is
saintly and his outer appearance (*complexion*)
devilish, I'd want him to hear my confession (*shrive
me*) rather than marry me (but note the implicit
racism, since Elizabethans often regarded Moroccans
as "black," supposedly the devil's skin color)
Sirrah: (form of address to servants)

1.3: Venice

ducats: gold coins (3,000 ducats was a very large
sum; later a diamond is valued at 2,000 ducats: see
3.1.77-78)

bound: responsible, as a surety

stead: accommodate

good: reliable in business dealings

sufficient: good as a guarantor; **in supposition:**
uncertain
Rialto: area of the Venetian Exchange (i.e., "stock
exchange" or "bourse")
squandered: scattered (but with a hint of foolish
financial speculation)

habitation: body

Nazarite . . . into: (reference to Jesus' [*the
Nazarite*] casting of evil spirits into a herd of
swine; see Luke 8:26-33, Mark 5:1-13, Matthew
8:28-32)
What . . . Rialto: (Shylock changes the subject)

DISCOVERING SHAKESPEARE

(15) Costuming [1.3.1]: If you were designing a production of this play set during the Italian Renaissance, how would you
dress Shylock? How would his costume be different than those of Antonio and Bassanio? What else would you do in terms of
make-up and hair design, mannerisms, and speech habits to distinguish between the Jewish moneylender and the Christians?

BASSANIO
 This is Signor Antonio.

SHYLOCK *[Aside]*
 How like a fawning publican° he looks.
 I hate him for° he is a Christian;
 But more, for that in low simplicity
 He lends out money gratis and brings down
 The rate of usance° here with us in Venice.
 If I can catch him once upon the hip,°
 I will feed fat the ancient grudge I bear him.
 He hates our sacred nation, and he rails,
 Even there where merchants most do congregate,
 On me, my bargains, and my well-won thrift,
 Which he calls interest. Cursèd be my tribe
 If I forgive him.

BASSANIO   Shylock, do you hear?

SHYLOCK
 I am debating of my present store,°
 And by the near guess of my memory
 I cannot instantly raise up the gross°
 Of full three thousand ducats. What of that?
 Tubal, a wealthy Hebrew of my tribe,
 Will furnish me. But soft, how many months
 Do you desire?   *[To Antonio]*
 Rest you fair, good signor!
 Your worship was the last man in our mouths.

ANTONIO
 Shylock, albeit I neither lend nor borrow
 By taking nor by giving of excess,°
 Yet to supply the ripe° wants of my friend
 I'll break a custom.   *[To Bassanio]*
 Is he yet possessed
 How much ye would?°

SHYLOCK   Ay, ay, three thousand ducats.

ANTONIO
 And for three months.

SHYLOCK
 I had forgot – three months, you told me so.
 Well then, your bond. And let me see – but hear you,°
 Methoughts° you said you neither lend nor borrow
 Upon advantage.

ANTONIO   I do never use it.

SHYLOCK
 When Jacob° grazed his uncle Laban's sheep –
 This Jacob from our holy Abram was,
 As his wise mother wrought in his behalf,
 The third possessor;° ay, he was the third –

publican: tax collector (see Luke 18:9–14, where the humble *publican* is contrasted with the arrogant Pharisee—the allusion works against Shylock's hostility)   40

for: because

usance: interest

catch . . . hip: i.e., get him in a weak position (figure of speech from wrestling)

45

store: wealth   50

gross: full amount

55

excess: interest

ripe: immediate   60

possessed . . . would: informed of how much you want

65

but hear you: (equivalent to "wait a minute")   65

Methoughts: it seemed to me

Jacob: (see Genesis 27 and 30:25–43)

70

third possessor: i.e., of the birthright descending from his grandfather Abraham

---

DISCOVERING SHAKESPEARE

(16) <u>Aside</u> **[1.3.38]:** What is the difference between an "<u>aside</u>" and a "<u>soliloquy</u>"? What do you think Antonio and Bassanio are doing during Shylock's <u>aside</u> in 1.3.38–49? What could they be talking about? Do you think they hear Shylock's comments? Why or why not? Why do you think Shakespeare allows Shylock to betray his true feelings about Antonio so early in the script?

(17) **Teaser [1.3.53]:** How much would three thousand ducats be worth in today's money?

ANTONIO

    And what of him? Did he take interest?

SHYLOCK

    No, not take interest – not as you would say

    Directly interest. Mark what Jacob did:

    When Laban and himself were compromised°

    That all the eanlings° which were streaked and pied°

    Should fall as Jacob's hire,° the ewes being rank°

    In end of autumn turnèd to the rams;

    And when the work of generation was

    Between these woolly breeders in the act,

    The skillful shepherd peeled me° certain wands,°

    And in the doing of the deed of kind°

    He stuck them up before the fulsome° ewes,

    Who then conceiving, did in eaning° time

    Fall parti-colored° lambs, and those were Jacob's.

    This was a way to thrive, and he was blest;

    And thrift° is blessing if men steal it not.

ANTONIO

    This was a venture, sir, that Jacob served for,

    A thing not in his power to bring to pass,°

    But swayed and fashioned by the hand of heaven.

    Was this inserted to make interest good?°

    Or is your gold and silver ewes and rams?°

SHYLOCK

    I cannot tell; I make it breed as fast.

    But note me, signor –

ANTONIO   Mark you this, Bassanio,

    The devil can cite Scripture for his purpose.

    An evil soul producing holy witness

    Is like a villain with a smiling cheek,

    A goodly apple rotten at the heart.

    O what a goodly outside falsehood hath!

SHYLOCK

    Three thousand ducats – 'tis a good round sum.

    Three months from twelve – then let me see, the rate –

ANTONIO

    Well, Shylock, shall we be beholding° to you?

SHYLOCK

    Signor Antonio, many a time and oft

    In the Rialto you have rated° me

    About my moneys and my usances.

    Still have I borne it with a patient shrug,

    For suff'rance° is the badge° of all our tribe.

compromised: agreed   75

eanlings: lambs; **pied:** spotted

hire: share, recompense; **rank:** in heat

          80

peeled me: peeled (*me* is Shylock's colloquial way of asserting the story's importance to him); **wands:** branches, shoots

kind: nature

fulsome: lustful (?)   85

eaning: lambing

peeled . . . parti-colored: (Jacob's success depends on the now outmoded theory of prenatal influence: here the variegated *wands* induce variegated *lambs*)

thrift: (ety-mologically derived from *thrive*)

venture . . . pass: i.e., a commercial venture of   90 some uncertainty

inserted . . . it good: brought in to justify charging interest

gold . . . rams: (a main Elizabethan argument against usury was that it blasphemously caused inanimate metal to multiply as living creatures did at God's command; see Genesis 8:17 and 9:1)

          95

          100

beholding: in debt

rated: railed at, reviled

          105

suff'rance: forbearance, endurance; **badge:** distinctive mark (the word can specifically mean a metal or cloth emblem worn to indicate one's master's family or, in Renaissance Venice, one's Judaism)

DISCOVERING SHAKESPEARE

(18) Language [1.3.74–87]: In Shylock's long "Laban speech" (74–87), underline each of the words that seems unusual or exotic to you. Then <u>scan</u> the lines to determine their predominant <u>meter</u> and <u>verse form</u>. Based upon this analysis of <u>syntax</u>, <u>meter</u>, and <u>verse</u>, how would you characterize Shylock's speech habits?

(19) <u>Themes</u> [1.3.95]: One of Shakespeare's predominant <u>themes</u>—in this play, as well as others—is the opposition between appearance and reality. What other instances of this <u>theme</u> can you find in *The Merchant of Venice* in addition to Antonio's speech in 1.3.94–99?

You call me misbeliever, cutthroat dog,
And spit upon my Jewish gaberdine,°   **gaberdine:** cloak
And all for use of that which is mine own.   110
Well then, it now appears you need my help.
Go to° then. You come to me and you say,   **Go to:** (exclamation of impatience, like "Come, come!")
"Shylock, we would have moneys" – you say so,
You that did void your rheum° upon my beard   **rheum:** spittle
And foot me as you spurn a stranger cur   115
Over your threshold: moneys is your suit.
What should I say to you? Should I not say,
"Hath a dog money? Is it possible
A cur can lend three thousand ducats?" Or
Shall I bend low, and in a bondman's key,   120
With bated breath and whisp'ring humbleness,
Say this:
"Fair sir, you spit on me on Wednesday last,
You spurned me such a day, another time
You called me dog; and for these courtesies   125
I'll lend you thus much moneys."

ANTONIO
I am as like to call thee so again,
To spit on thee again, to spurn thee too.
If thou wilt lend this money, lend it not
As to thy friends, for when did friendship take   130
A breed for barren metal of his friend?°   **A . . . friend:** (see note to l.92, above)
But lend it rather to thine enemy,
Who if he break,° thou mayst with better face   **break:** goes bankrupt
Exact the penalty.

SHYLOCK   Why look you, how you storm!
I would be friends with you and have your love,   135
Forget the shames that you have stained me with,
Supply your present wants, and take no doit°   **doit:** coin of very small value
Of usance for my moneys, and you'll not hear me.
This is kind I offer.°   **kind I offer:** i.e., a kindly offer (with a suggestion of "natural" dealing; Antonio has called usury unnatural)

BASSANIO
This were kindness.   140

SHYLOCK
This kindness will I show:
Go with me to a notary; seal me there
Your single° bond, and – in a merry sport° –   **single:** without other security; **in . . . sport:** i.e., as a jesting penalty (but flesh is *kind,* "natural," which Shylock said he offered)
If you repay me not on such a day,
In such a place, such sum or sums as are   145
Expressed in the condition, let the forfeit
Be nominated° for an equal° pound   **nominated:** named, prescribed; **equal:** exact
Of your fair flesh, to be cut off and taken
In what part of your body pleaseth me.

ANTONIO
Content, in faith. I'll seal to such a bond,   150
And say there is much kindness in the Jew.

DISCOVERING SHAKESPEARE

(20) Staging [1.3.143]: How literally do you take Shylock's reference to the "merry sport" (143) proposed in his bond, particularly in light of his <u>aside</u> in lines 38–49? How should Shylock's speech be delivered in order to calm Antonio's suspicion? Do you believe at this point in the script that Shylock intends to kill Antonio? Why or why not?

BASSANIO
You shall not seal to such a bond for me!
I'll rather dwell in my necessity.°

dwell . . . necessity: i.e., remain in need

ANTONIO
Why fear not, man; I will not forfeit it.
Within these two months – that's a month before   155
This bond expires – I do expect return
Of thrice three times the value of this bond.

SHYLOCK
O father Abram, what these Christians are,
Whose own hard dealings teaches them suspect
The thoughts of others! Pray you tell me this: 160
If he should break his day,° what should I gain

break his day: fail to pay on the due date

By the exaction of the forfeiture?
A pound of man's flesh taken from a man
Is not so estimable, profitable neither,
As flesh of muttons, beefs, or goats. I say   165
To buy his favor I extend this friendship.
If he will take it, so; if not, adieu.
And for my love I pray you wrong me not.

ANTONIO
Yes, Shylock, I will seal unto this bond.°

Yes . . . bond: (Antonio does not respond to Shylock's preceding line)

SHYLOCK
Then meet me forthwith at the notary's;   170
Give him direction for this merry bond,
And I will go and purse° the ducats straight,

purse: procure, gather

See to my house, left in the fearful° guard

fearful: (1) timorous, (2) to be feared (hence suspected)

Of an unthrifty° knave, and presently

unthrifty: careless, extravagant   175

I'll be with you.   *Exit.*

ANTONIO   Hie thee, gentle° Jew.

gentle: (with pun on "gentile")

The Hebrew will turn Christian; he grows kind.

BASSANIO
I like not fair terms and a villain's mind.

ANTONIO
Come on. In this there can be no dismay;
My ships come home a month before the day.   *Exeunt.*

🍃 **2.1**° [*Flourish*° *of cornets.*] *Enter* [*the Prince of*] *Morocco, a tawny*° *Moor all in white, and three or four followers accordingly,*° *with Portia, Nerissa, and their train.*

2.1: Portia's house, Belmont
Flourish: distinctive melody introducing important persons; **tawny:** (often used by Elizabethans to describe the skin color of North Africans); **accordingly:** i.e., the followers are made up and dressed as Morocco is

MOROCCO
Mislike me not for my complexion,
The shadowed livery of the burnished sun,°

shadowed . . . sun: darkened official garb of the sun's retainers (i.e., dark skin)

DISCOVERING SHAKESPEARE

(21) Verse [1.3. 175–179]: Notice that Shakespeare ends this scene with three rhymes: you/Jew, kind/mind, and dismay/day. Can you find other scenes in the play that end in rhyming couplets? What effect would this theatrical custom have on the audience?

(22) Characterization [2.1.1]: How would you describe Morocco? Is he a noble warrior, a comic braggart, or something in between? How would he be dressed? How would he act? Does he swing his scimitar around, frightening the ladies, or does he behave in a more dignified fashion? Since he is the first suitor we actually see with Portia, how will his characterization affect the audience's perception of the final two suitors, Aragon and Bassanio?

To whom I am a neighbor and near bred.
Bring me the fairest creature northward born,
Where Phoebus'° fire scarce thaws the icicles,

Phoebus: the sun   5

And let us make incision° for your love

make incision: cut to draw blood

To prove whose blood is reddest, his or mine.
I tell thee, lady, this aspect° of mine

aspect: countenance

Hath feared° the valiant. By my love I swear

feared: frightened
                                                          10

The best-regarded virgins of our clime
Have loved it too. I would not change this hue,
Except to steal your thoughts,° my gentle queen.

steal your thoughts: i.e., win your favor

PORTIA
In terms° of choice I am not solely led

terms: matters

By nice° direction of a maiden's eyes.

nice: fastidious

Besides, the lott'ry of my destiny
                                                          15

Bars me the right of voluntary choosing.
But if my father had not scanted° me,

scanted: restricted

And hedged me by his wit to yield myself
His wife who wins me by that means I told you,
Yourself, renownèd prince, then stood as fair
                                                          20

As any comer I have looked on yet
For my affection.
MOROCCO   Even for that I thank you.
Therefore I pray you lead me to the caskets
To try my fortune. By this scimitar,
That slew the Sophy° and a Persian prince

Sophy: Shah of Persia   25

That won three fields of Sultan Solyman,°

Solyman: a Turkish ruler

I would o'erstare° the sternest eyes that look,

o'erstare: outstare

Outbrave the heart most daring on the earth,
Pluck the young sucking cubs from the she-bear,
Yea, mock the lion when a° roars for prey,

a: he   30

To win thee, lady. But alas the while,
If Hercules and Lichas° play at dice

Lichas: servant of Hercules (Lichas unwittingly gave Hercules a poisoned shirt, which drove him to madness and death)

Which is the better man, the greater throw
May turn by fortune from the weaker hand.
So is Alcides° beaten by his rogue,

Alcides: Hercules   35

And so may I, blind Fortune leading me,
Miss that which one unworthier may attain,
And die with grieving.
PORTIA   You must take your chance,
And either not attempt to choose at all
Or swear before you choose, if you choose wrong
                                                          40

Never to speak to lady afterward
In way of marriage. Therefore be advised.°

be advised: consider, reflect

MOROCCO
Nor will not.° Come, bring me unto my chance.

Nor will not: i.e., I agree to the conditions just imposed

DISCOVERING SHAKESPEARE

(23) Source Material [2.1.38–42]: In Shakespeare's principal source for the plot of *The Merchant of Venice,* Ser Giovanni Fiorentino's *Il Pecorone* ("The Dunce"), the hero will win the hand of the Lady of Belmont if he is able to make love with her. Unknown to him, she laces his wine with sleeping potion, which means that he falls asleep, fails to seduce her, and thereby forfeits a huge sum of money. In Shakespeare's play, of course, the hero must select the correct casket or promise to remain celibate forever if he fails. In what important ways does this change from Shakespeare's source affect the plot of his play?

PORTIA
First, forward to the temple;° after dinner
Your hazard shall be made.

MOROCCO   Good fortune then,
To make me blest or cursèd'st among men!

[Flourish of cornets.] Exeunt.

❧ **2.2**° *Enter [Lancelot Gobbo] the Clown, alone.*

LANCELOT   Certainly my conscience will serve me to run from this Jew my master. The fiend is at mine elbow and tempts me, saying to me, "Gobbo, Lancelot Gobbo, good Lancelot," or "good Gobbo," or "good Lancelot Gobbo – use your legs, take the start, run away." My conscience says, "No. Take heed, honest Lancelot; take heed, honest Gobbo," or as aforesaid, "honest Lancelot Gobbo; do not run, scorn running with thy heels."° Well, the most courageous fiend bids me pack.° "Fia!"° says the fiend; "away!" says the fiend. "For the heavens,° rouse up a brave mind," says the fiend, "and run." Well, my conscience hanging about the neck of my heart says very wisely to me, "My honest friend Lancelot, being an honest man's son," or rather "an honest woman's son," for indeed my father did something smack, something grow to; he had a kind of taste:° Well, my conscience says, "Lancelot, budge not." "Budge," says the fiend. "Budge not," says my conscience. "Conscience," say I, "you counsel well." "Fiend," say I, "you counsel well." To be ruled by my conscience, I should stay with the Jew my master who, God bless the mark, is a kind of devil; and to run away from the Jew, I should be ruled by the fiend, who, saving your reverence,° is the devil himself. Certainly the Jew is the very devil incarnation;° and in my conscience, my conscience is but a kind of hard conscience to offer to counsel me to stay with the Jew. The fiend gives the more friendly counsel. I will run, fiend; my heels are at your commandment; I will run.

Enter Old Gobbo with a basket.

GOBBO   Master young man, you, I pray you, which is the way to Master Jew's?

LANCELOT   *[Aside]* O heavens, this is my true-begotten father who, being more than sand-blind,° high-gravel-blind,° knows me not. I will try confusions° with him.

GOBBO   Master young gentleman, I pray you which is the way to Master Jew's?

2.2: A street in Venice

scorn . . . heels: reject, despise (with pun on "kick at")
pack: be off; **Fia** away (Italian *via*)
For the heavens: for heaven's sake

smack . . . grow to . . . taste: kiss noisily . . . have an erection . . . leaning, enjoyment (i.e., Gobbo's father was promiscuous, not *honest*)

God . . . mark, saving . . . reverence: (conventional phrases of apology for what one is about to say)
incarnation: i.e., incarnate (Gobbo's error comes close to identifying devil and Christ)

sand-blind: half blind
high-gravel-blind: blinder than *sand-blind*
try confusions: (wordplay on "try conclusions" —to experiment)

(line numbers: 45, 5, 10, 15, 20, 25, 30, 35)

---

to the temple: i.e., to swear the oath

DISCOVERING SHAKESPEARE

(24) Costuming [2.2.1]: If you were designing <u>costumes</u> for a Renaissance period production of this play, how would you dress Lancelot as a "Clown"? How would his <u>costume</u> change if you were doing a modern production? Why?

LANCELOT   Turn up on your right hand at the next turning, but at the next turning of all, on your left; marry,°
at the very next turning turn of no hand, but turn
down indirectly to the Jew's house.

GOBBO   Be° God's sonties,° 'twill be a hard way to hit! Can
you tell me whether one Lancelot that dwells with him,
dwell with him or no?

LANCELOT   Talk you of young Master° Lancelot?   *[Aside]*
Mark me now; now will I raise the waters.° – Talk you
of young Master Lancelot?

GOBBO   No master, sir, but a poor man's son. His father,
though I say't, is an honest exceeding poor man and,
God be thanked, well to live.°

LANCELOT   Well, let his father be what a will, we talk of
young Master Lancelot.

GOBBO   Your worship's friend, and Lancelot, sir.

LANCELOT   But I pray you, ergo old man, ergo° I beseech
you, talk you of young Master Lancelot?

GOBBO   Of Lancelot, an't please your mastership.

LANCELOT   Ergo, Master Lancelot. Talk not of Master
Lancelot, father, for the young gentleman, according to
fates and destinies and such odd sayings, the Sisters
Three° and such branches of learning, is indeed deceased,
or as you would say in plain terms, gone to heaven.

GOBBO   Marry, God forbid! The boy was the very staff of
my age, my very prop.

LANCELOT   Do I look like a cudgel or a hovel-post,° a staff
or a prop? Do you know me, father?

GOBBO   Alack the day, I know you not, young gentleman, but I pray you tell me, is my boy, God rest his
soul, alive or dead?

LANCELOT   Do you not know me, father?

GOBBO   Alack, sir, I am sand-blind! I know you not.

LANCELOT   Nay, indeed if you had your eyes you might
fail of the knowing me; it is a wise father that knows his
own child.° Well, old man, I will tell you news of your
son. *[Kneels.]* Give me your blessing. Truth will come
to light; murder cannot be hid long, a man's son may,
but in the end truth will out.

GOBBO   Pray you, sir, stand up. I am sure you are not
Lancelot my boy.

LANCELOT   Pray you let's have no more fooling about it,
but give me your blessing. I am Lancelot – your boy
that was, your son that is, your child that shall be.

GOBBO   I cannot think you are my son.

LANCELOT   I know not what I shall think of that, but I
am Lancelot, the Jew's man, and I am sure Margery
your wife is my mother.

marry: to be sure (an interjection)

40

Be: by; **sonties:** saints (?), sanctities (?)

Master: (title applied to young gentlemen)
raise the waters: i.e., start something (raise
tears?)   45

well to live: well-to-do   50

ergo: therefore (Latin)

55

Sisters Three: the three Fates

60

hovel-post: timber supporting a shack

65

70

wise . . . child: (proverb that recalls old Gobbo's
dishonest reputation, ll. 14–17)

75

80

DISCOVERING SHAKESPEARE

(25) Staging [2.2.37]: Why does Lancelot try to confuse his father here? Do you approve of the way he is treating his father? Why or why not? How could this scene be staged in such a way that Lancelot's behavior is funny rather than cruel?

(26) Teaser [2.2.69]: Look up the meaning of the term "sand-blind" (2.2.69) in the *Oxford English Dictionary*. What is its
origin? How could a more detailed knowledge of the term help the actors playing Lancelot and Gobbo stage this scene?

GOBBO   Her name is Margery indeed! I'll be sworn, if
thou be Lancelot thou art mine own flesh and blood.
Lord worshiped might he be, what a beard° hast thou
got! Thou hast got more hair on thy chin than Dobbin
my fill horse° has on his tail.

LANCELOT   *[Rises.]* It should seem then that Dobbin's tail
grows backward. I am sure he had more hair of his tail
than I have of my face when I last saw him.

GOBBO   Lord, how art thou changed! How dost thou
and thy master agree? I have brought him a present.
How 'gree you now?

LANCELOT   Well, well; but for mine own part, as I have
set up my rest° to run away, so I will not rest till I have
run some ground. My master's a very° Jew. Give him a
present? Give him a halter!° I am famished in his service;
you may tell° every finger I have with my ribs. Father, I
am glad you are come. Give me your present to one
Master Bassanio, who indeed gives rare new liveries.° If I
serve not him, I will run as far as God has any ground.
O rare fortune, here comes the man! To him, father, for
I am a Jew if I serve the Jew any longer.

*Enter Bassanio, with [Leonardo and] a follower or
two.*

BASSANIO   You may do so, but let it be so hasted that
supper be ready at the farthest by five of the clock. See
these letters delivered, put the liveries to making, and
desire Gratiano to come anon° to my lodging.

[Exit one of his men.]

LANCELOT   To him, father!

GOBBO   God bless your worship!

BASSANIO   Gramercy.° Wouldst thou aught with me?

GOBBO   Here's my son, sir, a poor boy —

LANCELOT   Not a poor boy, sir, but the rich Jew's man
that would, sir, as my father shall specify —

GOBBO   He hath a great infection,° sir, as one would say,
to serve —

LANCELOT   Indeed, the short and the long is, I serve the
Jew, and have a desire, as my father shall specify —

GOBBO   His master and he, saving your worship's reverence, are scarce cater-cousins.°

LANCELOT   To be brief, the very truth is that the Jew having done me wrong doth cause me, as my father, being
I hope an old man, shall frutify° unto you —

beard: (apparently Gobbo has placed his hand on
the back of Lancelot's head)

fill horse: cart horse

set . . . rest: i.e., determined

very: complete, entire (an intensive)

halter: hangman's noose

tell: count

liveries: costumes for servants

anon: presently, at once

Gramercy: many thanks

infection: i.e., "affection"

cater-cousins: close friends

frutify: i.e., "fructify"

85

90

95

100

105

110

115

120

DISCOVERING SHAKESPEARE

(27) Renaissance Ethics [2.2.88]: What principal differences do you see between the behavior of "working class" characters like Lancelot and his father, Old Gobbo, vs. such "aristocratic" characters as Bassanio, Gratiano, and Lorenzo? Which
group of characters has the highest ethical and moral values? Why do you think so?

(28) Language [2.2.116]: When Old Gobbo tells Bassanio that Lancelot has a "great infection" (2.2.116) to serve him,
what word does he probably mean instead of "infection"? This literary device of choosing the wrong word is called a malapropism, a term derived from Mrs. Malaprop in Sheridan's *The Rivals*. What other examples of malapropism can you find
in this play? To what extent does each of these words carry some hint of truth with it? For example, how will Lancelot "infect" Bassanio by serving him?

GOBBO I have here a dish of doves that I would bestow upon your worship, and my suit is — [125]

LANCELOT In very brief, the suit is impertinent° to myself, as your worship shall know by this honest old man, and though I say it, though old man, yet poor man, my father — [130]

impertinent: i.e., "pertinent"

BASSANIO One speak for both. What would you?

LANCELOT Serve you, sir.

GOBBO That is the very defect° of the matter, sir.

defect: i.e., "effect"

BASSANIO
I know thee well; thou hast obtained thy suit. [135]
Shylock thy master spoke with me this day,
And hath preferred° thee, if it be preferment
To leave a rich Jew's service to become
The follower of so poor a gentleman.

preferred: recommended for advancement

LANCELOT The old proverb is very well parted between my master Shylock and you, sir. You have the grace of God, sir, and he hath enough.° [140]

proverb . . . enough: (play on the proverb "He who has the grace of God has enough")

BASSANIO
Thou speak'st it well. Go, father, with thy son;
Take leave of thy old master and inquire
My lodging out. *[To a follower]* Give him a livery
More guarded° than his fellows'. See it done. [145]

guarded: decorated with braid

LANCELOT Father, in. I cannot get a service; no! I have ne'er a tongue in my head; well! *[Looks at his palm.]* If any man in Italy have a fairer table° which doth offer to swear upon a book — I shall have good fortune! Go to, here's a simple line of life. Here's a small trifle of wives! Alas, fifteen wives is nothing; eleven widows and nine maids is a simple coming-in° for one man. And then to scape drowning thrice, and to be in peril of my life with the edge of a feather-bed!° Here are simple scapes.° Well, if Fortune be a woman, she's a good wench for this gear.° Father, come. I'll take my leave of the Jew in the twinkling.   *Exit Clown [Lancelot, with Old Gobbo].* [150] [155]

table: palm of hand (Lancelot now "reads" the lines of his palm)

simple coming-in: just a start (with wordplay on "coming in" women)

peril . . . feather-bed: i.e., endangered by an angry cuckolded spouse (?) (*feather-bed* seems to mean [someone else's] marriage bed); **scape, scapes:** escape, escapes

this gear: these matters

BASSANIO
I pray thee, good Leonardo, think on this:
These things being bought and orderly bestowed,
Return in haste, for I do feast tonight [160]
My best esteemed acquaintance. Hie thee, go.

LEONARDO
My best endeavors shall be done herein.
     Enter Gratiano.

GRATIANO
Where's your master?

LEONARDO   Yonder, sir, he walks.   *[Exit.]*

DISCOVERING SHAKESPEARE

(29) <u>Verse</u> [2.2.142–165]: Have one student read Bassanio's lines beginning with "Thou speak'st it well" (2.2.142) and another read Lancelot's following speech. How does this alternation between <u>verse</u> and <u>prose</u> affect the audience? Why does Bassanio speak in <u>verse</u>, while Lancelot's speech is in <u>prose</u>? Later in the scene, in lines 163–165, how should the <u>shared verse</u> lines be delivered by the actors? How is the rhythm of the scene affected when one character finishes another character's <u>verse</u> line?

GRATIANO
　Signor Bassanio!
BASSANIO　　　　Gratiano?
GRATIANO
　I have suit to you.　　　　　　　　　　　　　　　　　　　165
BASSANIO　　　　　You have obtained it.
GRATIANO　　You must not deny me. I must go with you
　to Belmont.
BASSANIO
　Why then you must. But hear thee, Gratiano:
　Thou art too wild, too rude, and bold of voice –
　Parts° that become thee happily enough　　　**Parts:** qualities　　170
　And in such eyes as ours appear not faults;
　But where thou art not known, why there they show
　Something too liberal.° Pray thee take pain　　**liberal:** free
　To allay with some cold drops of modesty°　　**modesty:** expected behavior
　Thy skipping spirit, lest through thy wild behavior　　　　　　175
　I be misconstered° in the place I go to,　　**misconstered:** misunderstood
　And lose my hopes.
GRATIANO　　　　　Signor Bassanio, hear me:
　If I do not put on a sober habit,°　　**habit:** (1) garb, (2) demeanor
　Talk with respect, and swear but now and then,
　Wear prayer books in my pocket, look demurely,　　　　　　180
　Nay more, while grace is saying hood° mine eyes　　**hood:** cover
　Thus with my hat, and sigh and say "amen,"
　Use all the observance of civility°　　**civility:** polite behavior
　Like one well studied in a sad ostent°　　**sad ostent:** solemn appearance
　To please his grandam, never trust me more.　　　　　　185
BASSANIO
　Well, we shall see your bearing.
GRATIANO
　Nay, but I bar tonight. You shall not gauge° me　　**gauge:** measure, judge
　By what we do tonight.
BASSANIO　　　　　No, that were pity.
　I would entreat you rather to put on
　Your boldest suit of mirth, for we have friends　　　　　　190
　That purpose merriment. But fare you well;
　I have some business.
GRATIANO
　And I must to Lorenzo and the rest,
　But we will visit you at suppertime.　　　　　*Exeunt.*

❧ **2.3**° *Enter Jessica and [Lancelot] the Clown.*　　**2.3:** Shylock's house

JESSICA
　I am sorry thou wilt leave my father so;
　Our house is hell, and thou a merry devil
　Didst rob it of some taste of tediousness.

DISCOVERING SHAKESPEARE

(30) Chronology [2.2.193–194]: In the last two lines of this scene, Gratiano promises to meet Bassanio at "suppertime" (194). What other references to time can you find in the <u>script</u>? Can you make any conclusions from these references concerning how many days are covered by the action of the play? How far do you think Venice was from Belmont? How would Bassanio and Gratiano have traveled to Belmont, and how long would the trip have taken them?

But fare thee well; there is a ducat for thee.
And, Lancelot, soon at supper shalt thou see   5
Lorenzo, who is thy new master's guest.
Give him this letter; do it secretly.
And so farewell; I would not have my father
See me in talk with thee.

LANCELOT   Adieu! Tears exhibit° my tongue. Most beautiful pagan, most sweet Jew! If a Christian do not play
the knave and get° thee,° I am much deceived. But adieu!
These foolish drops do something drown my manly
spirit. Adieu!

> **exhibit:** i.e., inhibit (but also: "tears say what my   10
> tongue cannot")
> **get:** beget
> **If . . . thee:** (cf. ll. 17–18)

JESSICA
Farewell, good Lancelot.   *[Exit Lancelot.]*   15
Alack, what heinous sin° is it in me
To be ashamed to be my father's child.
But though I am a daughter to his blood,
I am not to his manners. O Lorenzo,
If thou keep promise, I shall end this strife,   20
Become a Christian and thy loving wife!   *Exit.*

> **sin:** i.e., Jessica breaks the Fourth Commandment

2.4° *Enter Gratiano, Lorenzo, Salarino, and Solanio.*

> **2.4:** A public place

LORENZO
Nay, we will slink away° in suppertime,
Disguise us at my lodging, and return
All in an hour.

> **slink away:** get away unnoticed

GRATIANO
We have not made good preparation.

SALARINO
We have not spoke us yet of torchbearers.°

> **spoke . . . torchbearers:** ordered torchbearers   5

SOLANIO
'Tis vile, unless it may be quaintly ordered,°
And better in my mind not undertook.

> **quaintly ordered:** nicely, or elaborately,
> arranged

LORENZO
'Tis now but four of clock. We have two hours
To furnish us.
    Enter Lancelot [with a letter].
            Friend Lancelot, what's the news?

LANCELOT   An it shall please you to break up° this, it shall
seem to signify.

> **break up:** break open   10

LORENZO
I know the hand. In faith, 'tis a fair hand,
And whiter than the paper it writ on
Is the fair hand that writ.

GRATIANO   Love news, in faith!

LANCELOT   By your leave, sir.   15

LORENZO   Whither goest thou?

LANCELOT   Marry, sir, to bid my old master the Jew to
sup tonight with my new master the Christian.

DISCOVERING SHAKESPEARE

(31) <u>Rhyme</u> **[2.3.20–21]:** In the last <u>couplet</u> of Jessica's <u>soliloquy</u> at the end of 2.3, how do the rhyming words "strife"
and "wife" <u>foreshadow</u> her predicament at the conclusion of the play?

LORENZO
    Hold here, take this.   *[Gives money.]*
    Tell gentle Jessica
    I will not fail her. Speak it privately.   20
                                  Exit Clown [Lancelot].
    Go, gentlemen:
    Will you prepare you for this masque tonight?
    I am provided of a torchbearer.
SALARINO
    Ay, marry, I'll be gone about it straight.°   **straight:** right away
SOLANIO
    And so will I.   25
LORENZO   Meet me and Gratiano
    At Gratiano's lodging some hour hence.
SALARINO
    'Tis good we do so.   *Exit [with Solanio].*
GRATIANO
    Was not that letter from fair Jessica?
LORENZO
    I must needs tell thee all. She hath directed
    How I shall take her from her father's house,   30
    What gold and jewels she is furnished with,
    What page's suit she hath in readiness.
    If e'er the Jew her father come to heaven,
    It will be for his gentle° daughter's sake;   **gentle:** (with pun on "gentile")
    And never dare misfortune° cross her foot,   **never dare misfortune:** may misfortune never   35
    Unless she° do it under this excuse,   dare
    That she° is issue° to a faithless° Jew.   **she:** i.e., misfortune
    Come, go with me; peruse this as thou goest.   **she:** i.e., Jessica; **issue:** offspring; **faithless:** i.e.,
    Fair Jessica shall be my torchbearer.   not Christian, but Lorenzo's actions are also
                                Exit [with Gratiano].   *faithless*

❧ **2.5**° *Enter [Shylock the] Jew and [Lancelot,] his man*   **2.5:** Shylock's house
that was the Clown.

SHYLOCK
    Well, thou shalt see, thy eyes shall be thy judge,
    The difference of° old Shylock and Bassanio –   **of:** between
    What, Jessica! – Thou shalt not gormandize
    As thou hast done with me – What, Jessica! –
    And sleep, and snore, and rend apparel out –°   **rend apparel out:** wear out clothing through   5
    Why, Jessica, I say!   tearing
LANCELOT   Why, Jessica!
SHYLOCK
    Who bids thee call? I do not bid thee call.
LANCELOT   Your worship was wont to tell me I could do
    nothing without bidding.
    Enter Jessica.
                                                                               10

DISCOVERING SHAKESPEARE

(32) <u>Verse</u> [2.4.21]: In 2.4.21, four syllables carry the weight of an entire line. How could an accomplished actor make use of this disruption in Shakespeare's regular verse pattern of <u>iambic pentameter</u> lines? In line 21, what kind of stage business (<u>blocking</u>, gestures, facial expressions) could the actor playing Lorenzo use to fill up the space of six absent syllables?

JESSICA Call you? What is your will?

SHYLOCK

I am bid forth to supper, Jessica.
There are my keys. But wherefore° should I go?

wherefore: why

I am not bid for love, they flatter me;
But yet I'll go in hate to feed upon

15

The prodigal Christian. Jessica my girl,
Look to my house. I am right loath to go.
There is some ill a-brewing towards my rest,
For I did dream of money bags° tonight.°

money bags: (Elizabethan dream interpretation worked by contraries, so to dream of money was a prediction of its loss); **tonight:** last night

20

LANCELOT I beseech you, sir, go. My young master doth expect your reproach.°

reproach: i.e., "approach," but the error is also wordplay, as Shylock makes clear

SHYLOCK So do I his.

LANCELOT And they have conspired together. I will not say you shall see a masque, but if you do, then it was not for nothing that my nose fell a-bleeding on Black Monday° last at six o'clock i' th' morning, falling out that year on Ash Wednesday was four year in th' afternoon.°

Black Monday: Easter Monday

25

falling . . . afternoon: (Lancelot departs into a gibberish of omens and fortunetelling)

SHYLOCK

What, are there masques? Hear you me, Jessica:
Lock up my doors; and when you hear the drum
And the vile squealing of the wry-necked fife,°

wry-necked fife: i.e., played with a musician's head awry (?)

30

Clamber not you up to the casements then,
Nor thrust your head into the public street
To gaze on Christian fools with varnished faces;°

varnished faces: painted masks

But stop my house's ears — I mean my casements;
Let not the sound of shallow foppery° enter

foppery: frivolity

35

My sober house. By Jacob's staff° I swear

By . . . staff: (an appropriate oath because Jacob set out from his homeland with only a staff and returned twenty years later a wealthy man: see Genesis 32:10)

I have no mind of feasting forth tonight;
But I will go. Go you before me, sirrah.
Say I will come.

LANCELOT   I will go before, sir.
Mistress, look out at window for all this:
          There will come a Christian by
          Will be worth a Jewès eye.°   *[Exit.]*

40

Jewès eye: object of great value (the disyllabic form of "Jew-es" is needed for the meter)

SHYLOCK

What says that fool of Hagar's offspring?° Ha?

JESSICA

His words were "Farewell, mistress," nothing else.

Hagar's offspring: i.e., a gentile and an outcast (Hagar, Abraham's Egyptian bondwoman, bore Ishmael, and both became gentile outcasts: see Genesis 16 and 21:9)

SHYLOCK

The patch° is kind enough, but a huge feeder,
Snail-slow in profit,° and he sleeps by day

patch: fool

profit: productive work

45

More than the wildcat. Drones hive not with me,
Therefore I part with him, and part with him
To one that I would have him help to waste
His borrowed purse. Well, Jessica, go in.

50

Perhaps I will return immediately.
Do as I bid you; shut doors after you.

DISCOVERING SHAKESPEARE

(33) Metaphor [2.5.14]: Examine Shylock's desire to "feed upon" Antonio. How literally does he mean this phrase? Find other "feeding" metaphors, and explain why Shakespeare uses so many of them in this play.

Fast° bind, fast find:
A proverb never stale in thrifty mind.   *Exit.*

Fast: secure

JESSICA
Farewell; and if my fortune be not crost,
I have a father, you a daughter, lost.   *Exit.*

55

❧ **2.6**° *Enter the Masquers, Gratiano and Salarino.*

2.6: Shylock's house

GRATIANO
This is the penthouse° under which Lorenzo
Desired us to make stand.°

penthouse: projecting upper story of a building
make stand: wait

SALARINO   His hour is almost past.
GRATIANO
And it is marvel he outdwells his hour,
For lovers ever run before the clock.
SALARINO
O ten times faster Venus' pigeons° fly
To seal love's bonds new made than they are wont
To keep obligèd° faith unforfeited!°

Venus' pigeons: doves that draw her chariot   5

obligèd: bound by marriage or marriage contract; **unforfeited:** unbroken

GRATIANO
That ever holds. Who riseth from a feast
With that keen appetite that he sits down?
Where is the horse that doth untread again
His tedious measures with the unbated fire
That he did pace them first? All things that are
Are with more spirit chasèd than enjoyed.
How like a younger° or a prodigal
The scarfèd° bark puts from her native bay,
Hugged and embracèd by the strumpet wind!
How like the prodigal doth she return,°
With overweathered ribs and ragged sails,
Lean, rent, and beggared by the strumpet wind!
    Enter Lorenzo.

10

younger: i.e., younger son
scarfèd: decked with flags or streamers   15

How . . . return: (see Luke 15:11–32 for the parable of the Prodigal Son, which is alluded to here)

SALARINO
Here comes Lorenzo; more of this hereafter.

20

LORENZO
Sweet friends, your patience for my long abode.°
Not I but my affairs have made you wait.
When you shall please to play the thieves for° wives,
I'll watch° as long for you then. Approach;
Here dwells my father° Jew. Ho! Who's within?
    [Enter] Jessica above [in a page's clothes].

abode: delay

play the thieves for: steal
watch: wait
father: i.e., father-in-law to be   25

JESSICA
Who are you? Tell me for more certainty,
Albeit I'll swear that I do know your tongue.
LORENZO
Lorenzo, and thy love.
JESSICA
Lorenzo certain, and my love indeed,

DISCOVERING SHAKESPEARE

(34) Proverbs [2.5.53–54]: How often does Shylock resort to <u>proverbs</u> to support his arguments in the play? How many other examples, in addition to "Fast bind, fast find" (2.5.53), can you discover to illustrate his reliance on <u>proverbial</u> wisdom? What does his use of <u>proverbs</u> tell us about his character? About his relationship with others around him?

For who love I so much? And now who knows   30
But you, Lorenzo, whether I am yours?
LORENZO
Heaven and thy thoughts are witness that thou art.
JESSICA
Here, catch this casket; it is worth the pains.
I am glad 'tis night, you do not look on me,
For I am much ashamed of my exchange.°   **exchange:** change of clothes (but also "theft" and   35
But love is blind, and lovers cannot see   "elopement")
The pretty follies that themselves commit;
For if they could, Cupid himself would blush
To see me thus transformèd to a boy.
LORENZO
Descend, for you must be my torchbearer.   40
JESSICA
What, must I hold a candle to my shames?
They in themselves, good sooth, are too too light.°   **light:** frivolous, immodest (with pun on moral
Why, 'tis an office of discovery,° love,   "lightness")
And I should be obscured.   **'tis . . . discovery:** i.e., to bear a torch is to
LORENZO   So are you, sweet,   reveal
Even in the lovely garnish° of a boy.   **garnish:** dress, trimmings   45
But come at once,
For the close° night doth play the runaway,°   **close:** secret; **doth . . . runaway:** i.e., is passing
And we are stayed for° at Bassanio's feast.   rapidly
JESSICA   **stayed for:** awaited
I will make fast the doors, and gild° myself   **gild:** cover in gold leaf (i.e., make more valuable,
With some more ducats, and be with you straight.   but also "brighten")   50
                      [Exit above.]
GRATIANO
Now by my hood,° a gentle° and no Jew!   **by . . . hood:** (meaningless emphatic phrase);
LORENZO   **gentle:** gentile
Beshrew me° but I love her heartily!
For she is wise, if I can judge of her,   **Beshrew me:** evil come to me (a weak oath)
And fair she is, if that mine eyes be true,
And true she is, as she hath proved herself;
And therefore, like herself, wise, fair, and true,   55
Shall she be placèd in my constant soul.
    Enter Jessica [below].
What, art thou come? On, gentlemen, away!
Our masquing mates by this time for us stay.
             Exit [with Jessica and Salarino].
    Enter Antonio.
ANTONIO   Who's there?   60
GRATIANO   Signor Antonio?
ANTONIO
Fie, fie, Gratiano! Where are all the rest?
'Tis nine o'clock; our friends all stay for you.

DISCOVERING SHAKESPEARE

(35) Language [2.6.33]: When Jessica tells Lorenzo to "catch this casket" (2.6.33), what linguistic echo does Shakespeare create? Who else in this play chooses the correct "casket"? Why do you think Shakespeare used the same word for such different objects? What does the word "casket" mean to a modern audience?

(36) Audience Sympathy [2.6.59]: With whom do you identify most in this play: Lorenzo/Jessica or Shylock? Why? What dramatic signals does Shakespeare send to help us make our decision?

No masque tonight. The wind is come about;
Bassanio presently° will go aboard.   **presently:** immediately   65
I have sent twenty out to seek for you.
GRATIANO
I am glad on't. I desire no more delight
Than to be under sail and gone tonight.   *Exeunt.*

🍃 **2.7**° *[Flourish of cornets.] Enter Portia with Morocco*   **2.7:** Portia's house, Belmont
and both their trains.

PORTIA
Go, draw aside the curtains and discover°   **discover:** reveal
The several° caskets to this noble prince.   **several:** various
Now make your choice.
MOROCCO
This first, of gold, who this inscription bears,
"Who chooseth me shall gain what many men desire."   5
The second, silver, which this promise carries,
"Who chooseth me shall get as much as he deserves."
This third, dull lead, with warning all as blunt,°   **blunt:** i.e., the casket is plain, *dull* as *lead*
"Who chooseth me must give and hazard all he hath."
How shall I know if I do choose the right?   10
PORTIA
The one of them contains my picture, prince.
If you choose that, then I am yours withal.
MOROCCO
Some god direct my judgment! Let me see:
I will survey th' inscriptions back again.
What says this leaden casket?   15
"Who chooseth me must give and hazard all he hath."
Must give – for what? for lead! Hazard for lead?
This casket threatens; men that hazard all
Do it in hope of fair advantages.
A golden mind stoops not to shows of dross;   20
I'll then nor give nor° hazard aught for lead.   **nor . . . nor:** neither . . . nor
What says the silver with her virgin hue?
"Who chooseth me shall get as much as he deserves."
As much as he deserves? Pause there, Morocco,
And weigh thy value with an even hand:°   **with . . . hand:** impartially   25
If thou be'st rated by thy estimation,°   **estimation:** reputation
Thou dost deserve enough; and yet enough
May not extend so far as to the lady;
And yet to be afeard of my deserving
Were but a weak disabling° of myself.   **disabling:** underrating   30
As much as I deserve? Why that's the lady.
I do in birth deserve her, and in fortunes,
In graces, and in qualities of breeding;

DISCOVERING SHAKESPEARE
(37) Plot [2.7.10]: Why do you suppose Shakespeare broke Morocco's visit into two different scenes (2.1 and 2.7)? What do you imagine Portia and Morocco have been doing between the two scenes? In some modern productions, 2.1 and 2.7 are performed back to back, as one long scene. Do you think combining the two scenes would be effective? Why or why not?

But more than these, in love I do deserve.
What if I strayed no farther, but chose here? 35
Let's see once more this saying graved in gold:
"Who chooseth me shall gain what many men desire."
Why that's the lady! All the world desires her;
From the four corners of the earth they come
To kiss this shrine, this mortal breathing° saint. 40
The Hyrcanian deserts° and the vasty wilds
Of wide Arabia are as throughfares now
For princes to come view fair Portia.
The watery kingdom,° whose ambitious head
Spits in the face of heaven, is no bar 45
To stop the foreign spirits,° but they come
As o'er a brook to see fair Portia.
One of these three contains her heavenly picture.
Is't like that lead contains her? 'Twere damnation
To think so base a thought; it° were too gross 50
To rib° her cerecloth° in the obscure° grave.
Or shall I think in silver she's immured,
Being ten times undervalued to tried° gold?
O sinful thought! Never so rich a gem
Was set in worse than gold. They have in England 55
A coin that bears the figure of an angel°
Stamped in gold; but that's insculped upon:°
But here an angel in a golden bed
Lies all within. Deliver me the key.
Here do I choose, and thrive I as I may! 60

PORTIA
There, take it, prince; and if my form lie there,
Then I am yours.

[He opens the golden casket.]

MOROCCO   O hell! What have we here?
A carrion death,° within whose empty eye
There is a written scroll! I'll read the writing.
          "All that glisters° is not gold; 65
          Often have you heard that told.
          Many a man his life hath sold
          But my outside° to behold.
          Gilded tombs do worms infold.
          Had you been as wise as bold, 70
          Young in limbs, in judgment old,
          Your answer had not been inscrolled.°
          Fare you well, your suit is cold."
Cold indeed, and labor lost.
Then farewell heat,° and welcome frost! 75
Portia, adieu. I have too grieved a heart

mortal breathing: living 40
Hyrcanian deserts: i.e., wilderness area southeast of the Caspian Sea, noted for fierce tigers since classical times

watery kingdom: i.e., Neptune's realm, the seas

foreign spirits: i.e., spirited (courageous) foreigners (Portia's other suitors)

it: i.e., lead
rib: cover, enclose; **cerecloth:** waxed cloth used in wrapping for burial; **obscure:** (accent on first syllable)
tried: tested, assayed

coin . . . angel: i.e., the "angel," a coin with Saint Michael's image
insculped upon: engraved on the surface

death: death's-head, skull

glisters: glitters

my outside: i.e., my shining surface

inscrolled: thus inscribed

heat: i.e., of love, now *labor lost* (l. 74)

DISCOVERING SHAKESPEARE

(38) Language [2.7.37]: The inscription on the golden casket reads "Who chooseth me shall gain what many men desire." To what extent are all three inscriptions <u>ironic</u>? What riddle does each contain?

(39) <u>Themes</u> [2.7.65]: The scroll in the golden casket contains the well-known phrase "All that glisters is not gold" (2.7.65), which clearly reminds us of the appearance vs. reality <u>theme</u> running through the script. Identify at least five other appearance vs. reality references in the play, and determine how each of these references is unique.

To take a tedious leave. Thus losers part.

Exit [with his train. Flourish of cornets].

PORTIA
A gentle riddance. Draw the curtains, go.
Let all of his complexion° choose me so.   *Exeunt.*

complexion: (1) skin's appearance (see 2.1.1), (2) temperament, personality (hence, a person who would choose the gold casket)

❧ **2.8**° *Enter Salarino and Solanio.*

2.8: A street in Venice

SALARINO
Why, man, I saw Bassanio under sail;
With him is Gratiano gone along,
And in their ship I am sure Lorenzo is not.
SOLANIO
The villain Jew with outcries raised° the duke,
Who went with him to search Bassanio's ship.

raised: aroused

5

SALARINO
He came too late – the ship was under sail,
But there the duke was given to understand
That in a gondola were seen together
Lorenzo and his amorous Jessica.
Besides, Antonio certified° the duke
They were not with Bassanio in his ship.

certified: authoritatively attested (to)

10

SOLANIO
I never heard a passion so confused,
So strange, outrageous, and so variable
As the dog Jew did utter in the streets:
"My daughter! O my ducats! O my daughter!
Fled with a Christian! O my Christian ducats!
Justice! The law! My ducats and my daughter!
A sealèd bag, two sealèd bags of ducats,
Of double ducats, stolen from me by my daughter!
And jewels – two stones, two rich and precious stones,°
Stolen by my daughter! Justice! Find the girl!
She hath the stones upon her, and the ducats!"

15

stones: jewels (but also slang for "testicles," a bawdy joke about emasculation—as the boys and their cries, ll. 23-24, make clear)

20

SALARINO
Why, all the boys in Venice follow him,
Crying his stones, his daughter, and his ducats.
SOLANIO
Let good Antonio look he keep his day,°
Or he shall pay for this.

keep his day: repay his debt on the day agreed

25

SALARINO   Marry, well remembered.
I reasoned° with a Frenchman yesterday,
Who told me, in the narrow seas that part

reasoned: talked

DISCOVERING SHAKESPEARE

(40) Teaser [2.7.79]: How do you interpret Portia's comment after Morocco exits ("Let all of his complexion choose me so")? Is this a racist remark, or could the word "complexion" have meant something other than skin color during the Renaissance? Consult the *Oxford English Dictionary* to determine the range of meanings of the word available to Shakespeare's audience around the year 1600.

(41) Language [2.8.20–24]: Examine Solanio and Salarino's comments in 2.8.20–24 in light of the fact that the word "stones" was often interpreted as "testicles" during the Renaissance. How might this interpretation change the <u>stage business</u> during this section of 2.8? Can you find any other plays by Shakespeare that use this same bawdy pun? (*Hint:* See the play-within-the-play at the end of *A Midsummer Night's Dream.*)

The French and English there miscarrièd
A vessel of our country richly fraught.° | **fraught:** loaded | 30
I thought upon Antonio when he told me,
And wished in silence that it were not his.

SOLANIO
You were best to tell Antonio what you hear.
Yet do not suddenly, for it may grieve him.

SALARINO
A kinder gentleman treads not the earth. | | 35
I saw Bassanio and Antonio part:
Bassanio told him he would make some speed
Of his return; he answered, "Do not so.
Slubber° not business for my sake, Bassanio, | **Slubber:** perform hastily, botch
But stay the very riping of the time; | | 40
And for the Jew's bond which he hath of me,
Let it not enter in your mind of love.° | **mind of love:** thoughts of wooing
Be merry, and employ your chiefest thoughts
To courtship and such fair ostents° of love | **ostents:** shows
As shall conveniently become you there." | | 45
And even there, his eye being big with tears,
Turning his face, he put his hand behind him,
And with affection wondrous sensible° | **wondrous sensible:** wonderfully strong in feeling
He wrung Bassanio's hand; and so they parted.

SOLANIO
I think he only loves the world for him.
I pray thee let us go and find him out | | 50
And quicken his embracèd heaviness° | **quicken . . . heaviness:** enliven the sadness he has embraced
With some delight or other.

SALARINO   Do we so.   *Exeunt.*

❧ **2.9**° *Enter Nerissa and a Servitor.* | **2.9:** Portia's house, Belmont

NERISSA
Quick, quick, I pray thee, draw° the curtain° straight.° | **draw:** pull; **curtain:** i.e., the one hiding the caskets; **straight:** at once
The Prince of Aragon hath ta'en his oath,
And comes to his election° presently.° | **election:** choice; **presently:** immediately
    [Flourish of cornets.] Enter Aragon, his train, and
    Portia.

PORTIA
Behold, there stand the caskets, noble prince.
If you choose that wherein I am contained, | | 5
Straight shall our nuptial rites be solemnized;
But if you fail, without more speech, my lord,
You must be gone from hence immediately.

ARAGON
I am enjoined by oath to observe three things:
First, never to unfold to any one | | 10
Which casket 'twas I chose; next, if I fail
Of the right casket, never in my life

DISCOVERING SHAKESPEARE

(42) Plot [2.8.50]: How reliable are Solanio and Salarino in their descriptions of Antonio and Shylock? How much do we as spectators trust their comments?

To woo a maid in way of marriage;
Lastly, if I do fail in fortune of my choice,
Immediately to leave you and be gone. 15

PORTIA
To these injunctions every one doth swear
That comes to hazard for my worthless self.

ARAGON
And so have I addressed me.° Fortune° now
To my heart's hope! Gold, silver, and base lead.

addressed me: prepared myself (i.e., by thus swearing); **Fortune:** good luck

20
"Who chooseth me must give and hazard all he hath."
You shall look fairer ere I give or hazard.°

You . . . hazard: (addressed to the leaden casket)

What says the golden chest? Ha, let me see:
"Who chooseth me shall gain what many men desire."
What many men desire – that "many" may be meant
By° the fool multitude that choose by show,

meant/By: intended to mean, to suggest 25
fond: foolish

Not learning more than the fond° eye doth teach,
Which pries not to th' interior, but like the martlet°

martlet: a bird (Aragon may make a mistaken analogy here, since the martlet was often used as an image of prudence)

Builds in° the weather on the outward wall,
Even in the force and road of casualty.°

in: exposed to 30
force . . . casualty: power and path of mishap

I will not choose what many men desire,
Because I will not jump with° common spirits

jump with: go along with

And rank me with the barbarous multitudes.
Why then, to thee, thou silver treasure house:
Tell me once more what title thou dost bear.

"Who chooseth me shall get as much as he deserves." 35

And well said too, for who shall go about
To cozen° fortune, and be honorable

cozen: cheat

Without the stamp of merit? Let none presume
To wear an undeservèd dignity.
O that estates, degrees,° and offices

estates, degrees: social ranks 40

Were not derived corruptly, and that clear honor
Were purchased by the merit of the wearer!
How many then should cover that stand bare,°

cover . . . bare: wear hats who now stand bareheaded (i.e., retain the dignity of wearing their hats rather than removing them in deference)

How many be commanded that command;
How much low peasantry would then be gleaned°
From the true seed of honor, and how much honor°

45
gleaned: culled
honor: noble rank

Picked from the chaff and ruin of the times
To be new varnished.° Well, but to my choice.

new varnished: refurbished

"Who chooseth me shall get as much as he deserves."
I will assume desert. Give me a key for this, 50
And instantly unlock my fortunes here.
[He opens the silver casket.]

PORTIA
Too long a pause for that which you find there.

ARAGON
What's here? The portrait of a blinking idiot
Presenting me a schedule!° I will read it.

schedule: scroll

How much unlike art thou to Portia! 55
How much unlike my hopes and my deservings!

DISCOVERING SHAKESPEARE

(43) Characterization [2.9.20]: What clues does Shakespeare give us about the personality and behavior of Aragon? How old do you think he is? How is he <u>costumed</u>? How many people are in his "train"? To what extent do you think Shakespeare is guilty of the same racial and geographic stereotyping exhibited by Portia in 1.2 and elsewhere in the script?

"Who chooseth me shall have as much as he deserves."
Did I deserve no more than a fool's head?
Is that my prize? Are my deserts no better?

PORTIA
To offend and judge are distinct offices,
And of opposèd natures.°

ARAGON   What is here?
"The fire seven times tried this;°
Seven times tried that judgment is
That did never choose amiss.
Some there be that shadows° kiss;
Such have but a shadow's bliss.
There be fools alive iwis,°
Silvered o'er, and so was this.
Take what wife you will to bed,
I will ever be your head.
So be gone, you are sped."°
Still more fool I shall appear
By the time I linger here.
With one fool's head I came to woo,
But I go away with two.
Sweet, adieu. I'll keep my oath,
Patiently to bear my wroath.°   *[Exit with his train.]*

PORTIA
Thus hath the candle singed the moth.
O these deliberate° fools! When they do choose,
They have the wisdom by their wit to lose.

NERISSA
The ancient saying is no heresy:
Hanging and wiving goes by destiny.

PORTIA
Come draw the curtain, Nerissa.
Enter Messenger.

MESSENGER
Where is my lady?

PORTIA   Here. What would my lord?

MESSENGER
Madam, there is alighted at your gate
A young Venetian, one that comes before
To signify th' approaching of his lord,
From whom he bringeth sensible regreets,°
To wit, besides commends and courteous breath,
Gifts of rich value. Yet I have not seen
So likely an ambassador of love.
A day in April never came so sweet
To show how costly° summer was at hand,
As this forespurrer° comes before his lord.

To offend . . . natures: i.e., those who are subject to judgment may not be their own judges

this: i.e., the silver

shadows: illusive images

iwis: certainly

sped: done for

wroath: (the quarto's word is ambiguous: it could mean "wrath" or "ruth")

deliberate: reasoning, deliberating

sensible regreets: tangible greetings (i.e., more than words)

costly: rich, bountiful
forespurrer: forerunner

DISCOVERING SHAKESPEARE

(44) Themes [2.9.60–61]: As you read the rest of the play, pay particular attention to Portia's treatment of Shylock in the trial scene in 4.1. Then return to this quote and consider how Portia treats all the characters in this play. In what ways does she both "offend" and "judge" Morocco, Aragon, Shylock, and Jessica?

(45) Pronunciation [2.9.77–78]: How could the actress playing Portia pronounce the word "moth" (2.9.78) in order to parody or ridicule Aragon's last word in the scene?

PORTIA

No more, I pray thee. I am half afeard　　　　　　　　　　　95
Thou wilt say anon he is some kin to thee,
Thou spend'st such highday° wit in praising him.
Come, come, Nerissa, for I long to see
Quick Cupid's post° that comes so mannerly.

highday: holiday (i.e., suitable for a special occasion)

post: messenger

NERISSA

Bassanio, Lord Love,° if thy will it be!　　　*Exeunt.*

Lord Love: god of love (i.e., Cupid)　　　100

&。　**3.1**° *[Enter] Solanio and Salarino.*

3.1: A street in Venice

SOLANIO　　Now what news on the Rialto?

SALARINO　　Why, yet it lives° there unchecked° that Antonio hath a ship of rich lading wrecked on the narrow
seas – the Goodwins° I think they call the place, a very
dangerous flat, and fatal, where the carcasses of many a
tall ship lie buried as they say, if my gossip Report° be an
honest woman of her word.

lives: i.e., circulates; **unchecked:** uncontradicted

Goodwins: Goodwin Sands (dangerous shoal off the southeastern English coast)　　　5

gossip Report: (a humorous comparison of *Report*—rumor—to a neighborly or friendly source of information, a *gossip*)

SOLANIO　　I would she were as lying a gossip in that as
ever knapped° ginger or made her neighbors believe she
wept for the death of a third husband. But it is true,
without any slips of prolixity° or crossing the plain highway of talk,° that the good Antonio, the honest Antonio – O that I had a title good enough to keep his
name company! –

knapped: nibbled

10

slips of prolixity: lapses into wordiness
crossing . . . talk: i.e., deviation from plain speech

SALARINO　　Come, the full stop!°

full stop: period, end of statement (Salarino is tired of his friend's verbosity)　　　15

SOLANIO　　Ha, what sayest thou? Why the end is, he hath
lost a ship.

SALARINO　　I would it might prove the end of his losses.

SOLANIO　　Let me say "amen" betimes lest the devil cross°
my prayer, for here he comes in the likeness of a Jew.
Enter Shylock.
How now, Shylock? What news among the merchants?

cross: thwart

20

SHYLOCK　　You knew, none so well, none so well as you,
of my daughter's flight.

SALARINO　　That's certain. I for my part knew the tailor
that made the wings° she flew withal.

wings: i.e., the page's suit (with pun on *flight*)　　　25

SOLANIO　　And Shylock for his own part knew the bird
was fledge,° and then it is the complexion° of them all to
leave the dam.°

fledge: ready to fly; **complexion:** disposition
dam: mother (i.e., parent)

SHYLOCK　　She is damned for it.

SALARINO　　That's certain, if the devil may be her judge.

30

SHYLOCK　　My own flesh and blood to rebel!

SOLANIO　　Out upon it, old carrion!° Rebels it at these
years?°

carrion: dead, putrefied flesh (cf. 2.7.63)
Rebels . . . years: i.e., do you have fleshly desires at your age

DISCOVERING SHAKESPEARE

(46) Rhyme [2.9.96–100]: Examine the rhyme scheme at the conclusion of 2.9, and determine whether it predicts a happy or an unhappy ending to the play. Why do you think your opinion is accurate?

(47) Staging [3.1.20]: Many modern productions of the play locate their intermission or act break between 2.9 and 3.1. Do you think this would be an effective place for an intermission? Why or why not? What special qualities would a director look for in choosing an act break?

SHYLOCK   I say my daughter is my flesh and my blood.

SALARINO   There is more difference between thy flesh and hers than between jet° and ivory, more between your bloods than there is between red wine and Rhenish. But tell us, do you hear whether Antonio have had any loss at sea or no?   35

jet: a black stone

SHYLOCK   There I have another bad match!° A bankrupt, a prodigal, who dare scarce show his head on the Rialto, a beggar that was used to come so smug upon the mart!° Let him look to his bond. He was wont to call me usurer. Let him look to his bond. He was wont to lend money for a Christian courtesy. Let him look to his bond.   40   45

match: bargain

mart: exchange

SALARINO   Why, I am sure if he forfeit thou wilt not take his flesh. What's that good for?

SHYLOCK   To bait fish withal. If it will feed nothing else, it will feed my revenge. He hath disgraced me and hindered me half a million, laughed at my losses, mocked at my gains, scorned my nation, thwarted my bargains, cooled my friends, heated mine enemies — and what's his reason? I am a Jew. Hath not a Jew eyes? Hath not a Jew hands, organs, dimensions,° senses, affections, passions? — fed with the same food, hurt with the same weapons, subject to the same diseases, healed by the same means, warmed and cooled by the same winter and summer as a Christian is? If you prick us, do we not bleed? If you tickle us, do we not laugh? If you poison us, do we not die? And if you wrong us, shall we not revenge? If we are like you in the rest, we will resemble you in that. If a Jew wrong a Christian, what is his humility?° Revenge. If a Christian wrong a Jew, what should his° sufferance be by Christian example? Why revenge! The villainy you teach me I will execute, and it shall go hard but I will better the instruction.   50   55   60   65

dimensions: parts of the body

what is his humility: i.e., how does the Christian express *humility* (Shylock is deeply ironic)
his: i.e., the Jew's

Enter a Man from Antonio.

MAN   Gentlemen, my master Antonio is at his house and desires to speak with you both.

SALARINO   We have been up and down to seek him.   70

Enter Tubal.

SOLANIO   Here comes another of the tribe. A third cannot be matched,° unless the devil himself turn Jew.

Exeunt [Solanio, Salarino, and Man].

cannot be matched: cannot be found to match them

SHYLOCK   How now, Tubal! What news from Genoa? Hast thou found my daughter?

TUBAL   I often came where I did hear of her, but cannot find her.   75

DISCOVERING SHAKESPEARE

(48) <u>Verse</u> **[3.1.49–67]:** Surprisingly, Shylock's famous "Hath not a Jew eyes" speech (3.1.49–67) is entirely in <u>prose</u>, rather than <u>verse</u>. Why do you think Shakespeare wrote it this way? Try to rewrite a few lines of the speech in <u>iambic pentameter</u>; then determine what the speech gains or loses in its transition from <u>prose</u> to <u>verse</u>. What does the <u>prose</u> format tell us about Shylock's emotional state during this scene?

SHYLOCK   Why there, there, there, there! A diamond gone cost me two thousand ducats in Frankfurt! The curse° never fell upon our nation till now; I never felt it till now. Two thousand ducats in that, and other precious, precious jewels. I would my daughter were dead at my foot, and the jewels in her ear! Would she were hearsed at my foot, and the ducats in her coffin. No news of them, why so? And I know not what's spent in the search. Why thou loss upon loss! The thief gone with so much, and so much to find the thief, and no satisfaction, no revenge, nor no ill luck stirring but what lights o' my shoulders, no sighs but o' my breathing, no tears but o' my shedding.

TUBAL   Yes, other men have ill luck too. Antonio, as I heard in Genoa –

SHYLOCK   What, what, what? Ill luck, ill luck?

TUBAL   Hath an argosy cast away coming from Tripolis.

SHYLOCK   I thank God, I thank God! Is it true, is it true?

TUBAL   I spoke with some of the sailors that escaped the wreck.

SHYLOCK   I thank thee, good Tubal. Good news, good news! Ha, ha! Heard in Genoa?

TUBAL   Your daughter spent in Genoa, as I heard, one night fourscore ducats.

SHYLOCK   Thou stick'st a dagger in me. I shall never see my gold again. Fourscore ducats at a sitting, fourscore ducats!

TUBAL   There came divers° of Antonio's creditors in my company to Venice that swear he cannot choose but break.°

SHYLOCK   I am very glad of it. I'll plague him; I'll torture him. I am glad of it.

TUBAL   One of them showed me a ring that he had of your daughter for a monkey.

SHYLOCK   Out upon her! Thou torturest me, Tubal. It was my turquoise; I had it of Leah° when I was a bachelor. I would not have given it for a wilderness of monkeys.

TUBAL   But Antonio is certainly undone.

SHYLOCK   Nay, that's true, that's very true. Go, Tubal, fee° me an officer;° bespeak° him a fortnight before. I will have the heart of him if he forfeit, for were he out of Venice I can make what merchandise I will.° Go, Tubal, and meet me at our synagogue, go, good Tubal, at our synagogue, Tubal.   *Exeunt.*

curse: (probably the prophecy of Jerusalem's destruction; see Matthew 23:38)   80

85

90

95

100

divers: several

105

break: go bankrupt

110

Leah: (Shylock's wife)

115

fee: hire
officer: arresting officer; **bespeak:** engage

make . . . will: drive what bargains I wish

120

DISCOVERING SHAKESPEARE

(49) Characterization [3.1.81–83]: When Shylock says "I would my daughter were dead at my foot, and the jewels in her ear" (3.1.81–82), which do you think he cares more about: his daughter or his lost wealth? What other evidence can you find in the <u>script</u> to support your opinion?

❧ **3.2°** *Enter Bassanio, Portia, Gratiano, [Nerissa,] and all their trains.*

3.2: Portia's house, Belmont

PORTIA
    I pray you tarry; pause a day or two
    Before you hazard, for in choosing wrong
    I lose your company. Therefore forbear awhile.
    There's something tells me, but it is not love,
    I would not lose you; and you know yourself   5
    Hate counsels not in such a quality.°

quality: way

    But lest you should not understand me well –
    And yet a maiden hath no tongue but thought –
    I would detain you here some month or two
    Before you venture for me. I could teach you   10
    How to choose right, but then I am forsworn.°

forsworn: false to my oath

    So will I never be. So may you miss me.
    But if you do, you'll make me wish a sin –
    That I had been forsworn. Beshrew your eyes!
    They have o'erlooked° me and divided me;   15

o'erlooked: bewitched

    One half of me is yours, the other half yours –
    Mine own I would say; but if mine then yours,
    And so all yours! O these naughty° times

naughty: evil

    Puts bars between the owners and their rights!
    And so, though yours, not yours. Prove it so,°   20

Prove it so: if it prove so

    Let fortune go to hell for it, not I.
    I speak too long, but 'tis to peize° the time,

peize: retard (the image is from adding weights to a clock)

    To eke° it and to draw it out in length,

eke: increase

    To stay you from election.
BASSANIO   Let me choose,
    For as I am, I live upon the rack.   25
PORTIA
    Upon the rack, Bassanio? Then confess
    What treason° there is mingled with your love.

upon the rack . . . treason: (refers to confessions of treason obtained by torture on the rack)

BASSANIO
    None but that ugly treason of mistrust
    Which makes me fear th' enjoying of my love.
    There may as well be amity and life   30
    'Tween snow and fire, as treason and my love.
PORTIA
    Ay, but I fear you speak upon the rack,
    Where men enforcèd do speak anything.
BASSANIO
    Promise me life and I'll confess the truth.
PORTIA
    Well then, confess and live.   35

DISCOVERING SHAKESPEARE

(50) Themes [3.2.1–2]: To what extent do the words "tarry" and "hazard" in Portia's first two lines in act 3, scene 2 represent two of the major themes of the play? Which characters want to slow down or "tarry" the action? Which want to speed it up and risk all their resources on a single "hazard" or roll of the dice? Which of these characters is the protagonist of the play? Which is the antagonist?

(51) Metaphor [3.2.24–25]: Bassanio begins a torture metaphor with his "Let me choose,/For as I am, I live upon the rack" (3.2.24–25). Underline in your script all the other references to torture in this scene. Where does the metaphor end? Why does it stop at that particular point?

BASSANIO   Confess and love
Had been the very sum of my confession!
O happy torment, when my torturer
Doth teach me answers for deliverance.
But let me to my fortune and the caskets.

PORTIA
Away then! I am locked in one of them;   40
If you do love me, you will find me out.
Nerissa and the rest, stand all aloof.
Let music sound while he doth make his choice;
Then if he lose he makes a swanlike end,°   **swanlike end:** (the ordinarily mute swan was
Fading in music. That the comparison   thought to sing just before death)   45
May stand more proper, my eye shall be the stream
And watery deathbed for him. He may win;
And what is music then? Then music is
Even as the flourish° when true subjects bow   **flourish:** sounding of trumpets
To a new-crownèd monarch. Such it is   50
As are those dulcet sounds in break of day
That creep into the dreaming bridegroom's ear
And summon him to marriage. Now he goes,
With no less presence but with much more love
Than young Alcides when he did redeem   55
The virgin tribute paid by howling Troy
To the sea monster.° I stand for sacrifice.°   **Alcides . . . monster:** (Alcides, or Hercules,
The rest aloof are the Dardanian° wives,   rescued the daughter of the Trojan king from
With blearèd° visages come forth to view   sacrifice to a sea monster); **stand for sacrifice:**
The issue° of th' exploit. Go, Hercules!   represent the sacrificial victim   60
Live thou,° I live. With much, much more dismay   **Dardanian:** Trojan
I view the fight than thou that mak'st the fray.   **blearèd:** tear-stained
                                                    issue: outcome
                                                    Live thou: if you live
                                                    fancy: fond love, infatuation
          A song the whilst Bassanio comments on the caskets to himself.
                    Tell me where is fancy° bred,
                    Or in the heart, or in the head?
                    How begot, how nourishèd?   65
                       Reply, reply.
                    It is engendered in the eye,
                     With gazing fed, and fancy dies
                    In the cradle where it lies.
                       Let us all ring fancy's knell.   70
                       I'll begin it – Ding, dong, bell.
ALL   Ding, dong, bell.

BASSANIO
So may the outward shows be least themselves;°   **be least themselves:** i.e., belie the inner quality
The world is still deceived with ornament.
In law, what plea so tainted and corrupt   75
But being seasoned with a gracious voice,
Obscures the show of evil? In religion,
What damnèd error but some sober brow

DISCOVERING SHAKESPEARE

(52) <u>Blocking</u> [3.2.50]: What is Bassanio doing during Portia's long speech in lines 40–62? How could his stage actions move the plot along despite the fact that he has no verbal response during this speech?

(53) Music [3.2.70]: How would you stage the music in this scene? Would a musician come on stage to sing the song? Would the music be played off stage? Or should Portia or Nerissa sing the song? How do the lyrics help Bassanio make his eventual choice?

Will bless it and approve it with a text,
Hiding the grossness with fair ornament? 80
There is no vice so simple° but assumes
Some mark of virtue on his outward parts.
How many cowards whose hearts are all as false
As stairs of sand, wear yet upon their chins 85
The beards of Hercules and frowning Mars,
Who inward searched, have livers white as milk!°
And these assume but valor's excrement°
To render them redoubted.° Look on beauty,
And you shall see 'tis purchased by the weight,° 90
Which therein works a miracle in nature,
Making them lightest° that wear most of it.
So are those crispèd° snaky golden locks,
Which maketh such wanton gambols with the wind
Upon supposèd fairness,° often known 95
To be the dowry of a second head,
The skull that bred them in the sepulcher.°
Thus ornament is but the guilèd° shore
To a most dangerous sea, the beauteous scarf
Veiling an Indian° beauty; in a word, 100
The seeming truth which cunning times put on
To entrap the wisest. Therefore then, thou gaudy gold,
Hard food for Midas,° I will none of thee,
Nor none of thee, thou pale and common drudge°
'Tween man and man. But thou, thou meager lead 105
Which rather threaten'st than dost promise aught,
Thy paleness moves me more than eloquence;
And here choose I. Joy be the consequence!

PORTIA *[Aside]*
How all the other passions fleet to air:
As° doubtful thoughts, and rash-embraced despair, 110
And shudd'ring fear, and green-eyed jealousy.
O love, be moderate, allay thy ecstasy,
In measure rain thy joy, scant° this excess!
I feel too much thy blessing. Make it less
For fear I surfeit.

BASSANIO *[Opening the leaden casket]*
What find I here?
Fair Portia's counterfeit!° What demigod 115
Hath come so near creation?° Move these eyes?
Or whether,° riding on the balls of mine,
Seem they in motion? Here are severed lips
Parted with sugar breath; so sweet a bar
Should sunder such sweet friends.° Here in her hairs 120
The painter plays the spider, and hath woven
A golden mesh t' entrap the hearts of men
Faster° than gnats in cobwebs. But her eyes —

simple: unadulterated (but also implying "simple-minded," "foolish")

livers . . . milk: (cowards were supposed to have white livers)
excrement: outer growth (as hair)
redoubted: feared
weight: (e.g., of cosmetics)
lightest: least heavy (with pun on "light" in the sense of "light woman")
crispèd: curled
Upon supposèd fairness: on the head of a supposed beauty
dowry . . . sepulcher: i.e., hair taken from a person now dead and buried
guilèd: beguiling
Indian: i.e., dark-skinned, not fair

Midas: (all that Midas touched, including food, turned to gold)
common drudge: everyone's servant (i.e., silver)

As: such as

scant: lessen

counterfeit: image, portrait
What demigod . . . creation: i.e., only a demigod could have painted such a lifelike picture
Or whether: or

sweet friends: i.e., the two lips

Faster: more securely

DISCOVERING SHAKESPEARE

(54) <u>Doubling</u> [3.2.110]: In director Eli Simon's 1992 production of *The Merchant of Venice* at the Utah Shakespearean Festival, the actor playing Bassanio impersonated both Morocco and Aragon (that is, he came on stage in disguise, unknown to Portia, and played the parts of her two earlier suitors). How would this bold directorial choice have influenced audience response at the moment when Bassanio chooses the correct casket in this scene?

How could he see to do them? Having made one,
Methinks it should have power to steal both his   125
And leave itself unfurnished.° Yet look, how far

    unfurnished: without a companion eye

The substance of my praise doth wrong this shadow°

    shadow: picture

In underprizing it, so far this shadow

    substance: i.e., the real Portia

Doth limp behind the substance.° Here's the scroll,
The continent° and summary of my fortune.   130

    continent: container

    [He reads.]

        "You that choose not by the view
        Chance as fair,° and choose as true.

    Chance as fair: hazard as fortunately

        Since this fortune falls to you,
        Be content and seek no new.
        If you be well pleased with this   135
        And hold your fortune for your bliss,
        Turn you where your lady is,
        And claim her with a loving kiss."°

    kiss: (the quarto does not specify when or how often Portia and Bassanio kiss)

A gentle scroll. Fair lady, by your leave,
I come by note,° to give and to receive.   140

    come by note: come according to the scroll

Like one of two contending in a prize
That thinks he hath done well in people's eyes,
Hearing applause and universal shout,
Giddy in spirit, still gazing in a doubt
Whether those peals of praise be his° or no –   145

    his: addressed to him

So, thrice-fair lady, stand I even so,
As doubtful whether what I see be true,
Until confirmed, signed, ratified by you.
PORTIA
You see me, Lord Bassanio, where I stand,
Such as I am. Though for myself alone   150
I would not be ambitious in my wish
To wish myself much better, yet for you
I would be trebled twenty times myself,
A thousand times more fair, ten thousand times
More rich, that° only to stand high in your account,°   155

    that: so that; **account:** estimation

I might in virtues, beauties, livings,° friends,

    livings: possessions

Exceed account. But the full sum of me
Is sum of something° – which to term in gross°

    something: i.e., at least something; **term in gross:** state in full

Is an unlessoned girl, unschooled, unpracticed;
Happy in this, she is not yet so old   160
But she may learn; happier than this,
She is not bred so dull but she can learn;
Happiest of all, is that her gentle spirit
Commits itself to yours to be directed,
As from° her lord, her governor, her king.   165

    from: by

Myself and what is mine to you and yours
Is now converted.° But now° I was the lord

    converted: transferred; **But now:** a moment ago

Of this fair mansion, master of my servants,
Queen o'er myself; and even now, but now,
This house, these servants, and this same myself   170

DISCOVERING SHAKESPEARE

(55) Rhyme [3.2.135]: Do you think Portia's father was a good poet? Why or why not?
(56) Teaser [3.2.165]: Compare and contrast Portia's speech in 3.2.149–174 with Kate's speech in 5.2.136–179 at the conclusion of *The Taming of the Shrew.* Which speech seems more submissive to you? Why?

Are yours, my lord's. I give them with this ring,
Which when you part from, lose, or give away,
Let it presage the ruin of your love
And be my vantage to exclaim on you.°

    vantage . . . you: opportunity to denounce you

BASSANIO
Madam, you have bereft me of all words.   175
Only my blood speaks to you in my veins,
And there is such confusion in my powers°

    powers: faculties

As, after some oration fairly spoke
By a belovèd prince, there doth appear
Among the buzzing pleasèd multitude,   180
Where every something° being blent together

    something: i.e., individual remark or comment

Turns to a wild of nothing, save of joy
Expressed and not expressed. But when this ring
Parts from this finger, then parts life from hence;
O then be bold to say Bassanio's dead!   185
NERISSA
My lord and lady, it is now our time,
That° have stood by and seen our wishes prosper,

    That: who

To cry "good joy." Good joy, my lord and lady!
GRATIANO
My Lord Bassanio, and my gentle lady,
I wish you all the joy that you can wish –   190
For I am sure you can wish none from me;
And when your honors mean to solemnize
The bargain of your faith, I do beseech you
Even at that time I may be married too.
BASSANIO
With all my heart, so° thou canst get a wife.   195

    so: if

GRATIANO
I thank your lordship, you have got me one.
My eyes, my lord, can look as swift as yours:
You saw the mistress, I beheld the maid.
You loved, I loved; for intermission°

    intermission: pausing

No more pertains to me, my lord, than you.   200
Your fortune stood upon the caskets there,
And so did mine too as the matter falls.
For wooing here until I sweat again,°

    again: repeatedly

And swearing till my very roof° was dry

    roof: (of the mouth)

With oaths of love, at last – if promise last° –

    if promise last: i.e., if Nerissa's promise is still good   205

I got a promise of this fair one here
To have her love, provided that your fortune
Achieved her mistress.
PORTIA   Is this true, Nerissa?
NERISSA
Madam, it is, so you stand pleased withal.°

    so . . . withal: if it pleases you

DISCOVERING SHAKESPEARE

(57) Characterization [3.2.190]: When Gratiano explains that he and Nerissa have also fallen in love, Shakespeare's comic pattern begins to unfold. At this point in the play, which of the major characters are paired up with a mate? Which characters are still alone? Come back to this question at the end of the play, and determine which characters are together and which are not. What does the fate of the "single" characters at the end of the <u>script</u> tell us about Shakespeare's comic vision in this play?

BASSANIO
And do you, Gratiano, mean good faith? 210

GRATIANO
Yes, faith, my lord.

BASSANIO
Our feast shall be much honored in your marriage.

GRATIANO   We'll play with them the first boy for a thou-
sand ducats.°   **play . . . ducats:** wager a thousand ducats, the couple having the first boy to be the winner

NERISSA   What, and stake down?°   **stake down:** bets made with cash down 215

GRATIANO   No, we shall ne'er win at that sport, and stake
down.°   **stake down:** (Gratiano quibbles on the meaning "limp penis")
But who comes here? Lorenzo and his infidel!°   **infidel:** i.e., Jessica
What, and my old Venetian friend Salerio!
*Enter Lorenzo, Jessica, and Salerio, a messenger from
Venice.*

BASSANIO
Lorenzo and Salerio, welcome hither, 220
If that the youth of my new interest° here   **interest:** position in the household
Have power to bid you welcome. By your leave,
I bid my very friends and countrymen,
Sweet Portia, welcome.

PORTIA   So do I, my lord.
They are entirely welcome. 225

LORENZO
I thank your honor. For my part, my lord,
My purpose was not to have seen you here,
But meeting with Salerio by the way,
He did entreat me past all saying nay
To come with him along. 230

SALERIO   I did, my lord,
And I have reason for it. Signor Antonio
Commends him° to you.   **Commends him:** sends his greetings
[Gives Bassanio a letter.]

BASSANIO   Ere I ope his letter,
I pray you tell me how my good friend doth.

SALERIO
Not sick, my lord, unless it be in mind,
Nor well unless in mind. His letters there 235
Will show you his estate.°   **estate:** condition
Opens the letter.

GRATIANO
Nerissa, cheer yond stranger, bid her welcome.
Your hand, Salerio. What's the news from Venice?
How doth that royal merchant,° good Antonio?   **royal merchant:** i.e., a "king" among merchants
I know he will be glad of our success; 240
We are the Jasons, we have won the fleece.°   **Jasons . . . fleece:** (see 1.1.170–72)

DISCOVERING SHAKESPEARE

(58) <u>Puns</u> **[3.2.215]:** What bawdy pun is Gratiano making in his repetition of Nerissa's reference to "stake down" (3.2.215)?

(59) **Historical References [3.2.241]:** What does Gratiano mean when he compares himself and Bassanio to "the Jasons" (3.2.241)? What does this reference suggest about Gratiano's social standing and education? About the literacy level of Shakespeare's audience?

SALERIO
I would you had won the fleece that he hath lost!

PORTIA
There are some shrewd° contents in yond same paper   **shrewd:** cursed, bitter
That steals the color from Bassanio's cheek:
Some dear friend dead, else nothing in the world   245
Could turn so much the constitution
Of any constant man. What, worse and worse?
With leave, Bassanio, I am half yourself,
And I must freely have the half of anything
That this same paper brings you.   250

BASSANIO   O sweet Portia,
Here are a few of the unpleasant'st words
That ever blotted paper. Gentle lady,
When I did first impart my love to you,
I freely told you all the wealth I had
Ran in my veins – I was a gentleman –   255
And then I told you true; and yet, dear lady,
Rating myself at nothing, you shall see
How much I was a braggart. When I told you
My state° was nothing, I should then have told you   **state:** estate, property
That I was worse than nothing; for indeed   260
I have engaged myself° to a dear friend,   **engaged myself:** become indebted
Engaged my friend to his mere° enemy   **mere:** unqualified, sheer
To feed my means. Here is a letter, lady,
The paper as the body of my friend,
And every word in it a gaping wound   265
Issuing lifeblood. But is it true, Salerio?
Hath all his ventures failed? What, not one hit?
From Tripolis, from Mexico, and England,
From Lisbon, Barbary, and India,
And not one vessel scape the dreadful touch   270
Of merchant°-marring rocks?   **merchant:** merchant ship

SALERIO   Not one, my lord.
Besides, it should appear that if he had
The present money to discharge° the Jew,   **discharge:** pay off
He° would not take it. Never did I know   **He:** i.e., the Jew
A creature that did bear the shape of man   275
So keen and greedy to confound° a man.   **confound:** ruin
He plies the duke at morning and at night,
And doth impeach the freedom of the state°   **freedom . . . state:** freedom of commerce, of
If they deny him justice. Twenty merchants,   contract, in Venice
The duke himself, and the magnificoes°   **magnificoes:** Venetian magnates   280
Of greatest port° have all persuaded° with him,   **port:** eminence; **persuaded:** argued
But none can drive him from the envious° plea   **envious:** malicious
Of forfeiture, of justice, and his bond.

JESSICA
When I was with him, I have heard him swear

DISCOVERING SHAKESPEARE

(60) Metaphor [3.2.263–266]: Examine Bassanio's metaphor in which he compares the letter from Antonio with the body of his dear friend, with "every word in it a gaping wound / Issuing lifeblood" (3.2.263–266). How does this comparison help foreshadow Antonio's peril later in the play? What other metaphors are used in this scene to indicate future danger to Antonio?

To Tubal and to Chus, his countrymen,   285
That he would rather have Antonio's flesh
Than twenty times the value of the sum
That he did owe him; and I know, my lord,
If law, authority, and power deny not,
It will go hard with poor Antonio.   290

PORTIA
Is it your dear friend that is thus in trouble?

BASSANIO
The dearest friend to me, the kindest man,
The best-conditioned° and unwearied spirit   **best-conditioned:** best-natured
In doing courtesies, and one in whom
The ancient Roman honor more appears   295
Than any that draws breath in Italy.

PORTIA
What sum owes he the Jew?

BASSANIO
For me, three thousand ducats.

PORTIA   What, no more?
Pay him six thousand, and deface° the bond.   **deface:** cancel
Double six thousand and then treble that,   300
Before a friend of this description
Shall lose a hair through Bassanio's fault.
First go with me to church and call me wife,
And then away to Venice to your friend!
For never shall you lie by Portia's side   305
With an unquiet soul. You shall have gold
To pay the petty debt twenty times over;
When it is paid, bring your true friend along.
My maid Nerissa and myself meantime
Will live as maids and widows. Come away,   310
For you shall hence° upon your wedding day.   **hence:** go hence
Bid your friends welcome, show a merry cheer;°   **cheer:** countenance
Since you are dear bought, I will love you dear.
But let me hear the letter of your friend.

BASSANIO   *[Reads.]* "Sweet Bassanio, my ships have all   315
miscarried, my creditors grow cruel, my estate is very
low, my bond to the Jew is forfeit. And since in paying
it, it is impossible I should live, all debts are cleared between you and I if I might but see you at my death.
Notwithstanding, use your pleasure. If your love do not   320
persuade you to come, let not my letter."

PORTIA
O love! Dispatch all business and be gone.

BASSANIO
Since I have your good leave to go away,

DISCOVERING SHAKESPEARE

(61) Language [3.2.299–314]: How many of the sentences in Portia's speech in 3.2.299–314 are <u>imperatives</u>? That is, how many "orders" does she give to other people in this speech? What do all these <u>imperatives</u> tell us about Portia's character? About her ability to take charge in a crisis?

(62) <u>Puns</u> [3.2.313]: What <u>pun</u> does Portia make on the word "dear" in 3.2.313? In what other ways are love and money mixed together in this play? Find at least three other examples of the relationship between love and money.

I will make haste, but till I come again
No bed shall e'er be guilty of my stay,   325
Nor rest be interposer 'twixt us twain.   *Exeunt.*

❧ **3.3°** *Enter [Shylock] the Jew and [Solanio and]*   **3.3:** A street in Venice
Antonio and the Jailer.

SHYLOCK
Jailer, look to him. Tell not me of mercy.
This is the fool that lent out money gratis.
Jailer, look to him.
ANTONIO   Hear me yet, good Shylock.
SHYLOCK
I'll have my bond, speak not against my bond,
I have sworn an oath that I will have my bond.   5
Thou call'dst me dog before thou hadst a cause,
But since I am a dog,° beware my fangs.   **since . . . dog:** i.e., now that I am acting like an
The duke shall grant me justice. I do wonder,   animal (some actors take this line literally and bark
Thou naughty° jailer, that thou art so fond°   and snarl here)
To come abroad with him at his request.   **naughty:** wicked, corrupt; **fond:** foolish   10
ANTONIO
I pray thee hear me speak.
SHYLOCK
I'll have my bond. I will not hear thee speak,
I'll have my bond, and therefore speak no more.
I'll not be made a soft and dull-eyed° fool,   **dull-eyed:** easily deceived
To shake the head, relent, and sigh, and yield   15
To Christian intercessors. Follow not.
I'll have no speaking; I will have my bond.   *Exit.*
SOLANIO
It is the most impenetrable cur
That ever kept° with men.   **kept:** dwelled, associated
ANTONIO   Let him alone;
I'll follow him no more with bootless° prayers.   **bootless:** fruitless   20
He seeks my life. His reason well I know:
I oft delivered° from his forfeitures   **delivered:** saved
Many that have at times made moan to me.
Therefore he hates me.
SOLANIO   I am sure the duke
Will never grant this forfeiture to hold.   25
ANTONIO
The duke cannot deny the course of law;
For the commodity° that strangers° have   **commodity:** benefit (i.e., trading rights or
With us in Venice, if it be denied,   privileges); **strangers:** non-Venetians, including
Will much impeach the justice of the state,   Jews

DISCOVERING SHAKESPEARE

(63) <u>Plot</u> [3.3.1]: Act 3, scene 3 begins, like most Shakespearean scenes, <u>in medias res</u> ("in the middle of things"). Write a brief description of what has happened prior to Shylock's first line in the scene. What have the characters been doing? What have they been saying to each other?

(64) <u>Paraphrase</u> [3.3.27–31]: <u>Paraphrase</u> lines 3.3.27–31, attempting to use no more words than Shakespeare did in Antonio's speech. Why is the process of <u>paraphrasing</u> Shakespeare so difficult? Do you think dramatic <u>poetry</u> elicits more or less meaning from language than ordinary, everyday speech? Why?

Since that the trade and profit of the city   30
Consisteth of all nations. Therefore go.
These griefs and losses have so bated° me   **bated:** reduced
That I shall hardly spare a pound of flesh
Tomorrow to my bloody creditor.
Well, jailer, on. Pray God Bassanio come   35
To see me pay his debt, and then I care not!   *Exeunt.*

❧ **3.4°** *Enter Portia, Nerissa, Lorenzo, Jessica, and*   **3.4:** Portia's house, Belmont
[Balthasar,] a man of Portia's.

LORENZO
Madam, although I speak it in your presence,
You have a noble and a true conceit°   **conceit:** conception, understanding
Of godlike amity,° which appears most strongly   **amity:** friendship (i.e., that of Antonio and
In bearing thus the absence of your lord.   Bassanio)
But if you knew to whom you show this honor,   5
How true a gentleman you send relief,
How dear a lover of my lord your husband,
I know you would be prouder of the work
Than customary bounty can enforce you.°   **Than . . . you:** than ordinary kindness can make
PORTIA   you
I never did repent for doing good,   10
Nor shall not now; for in companions
That do converse and waste° the time together,   **waste:** spend
Whose souls do bear an equal yoke of love,
There must be needs a like proportion
Of lineaments, of manners, and of spirit;   15
Which makes me think that this Antonio,
Being the bosom lover of my lord,
Must needs be like my lord. If it be so,
How little is the cost I have bestowed
In purchasing the semblance of my soul°   **purchasing . . . soul:** i.e., redeeming Antonio,   20
From out the state of hellish cruelty.   the likeness of Bassanio, *my soul*
This comes too near the praising of myself;
Therefore no more of it. Hear other things:
Lorenzo, I commit into your hands
The husbandry° and manage of my house   **husbandry:** care   25
Until my lord's return. For mine own part,
I have toward heaven breathed a secret vow
To live in prayer and contemplation,
Only attended by Nerissa here,
Until her husband and my lord's return.   30
There is a monastery two miles off,
And there we will abide. I do desire you
Not to deny this imposition,°   **imposition:** duty, charge

DISCOVERING SHAKESPEARE

(65) Morality [3.4.10]: Read the rest of the play; then write down how much "good" (3.4.10) you think Portia has done in her treatment of Shylock in the court. Which of the characters in this play exhibit the highest moral and ethical behavior? Which the lowest? Which characters are most like you? Why?

(66) Plot [3.4.31]: Why do you think Portia and Nerissa plan on going to a monastery? What do they really intend to do? Write your guess on a separate sheet of paper; then return to this question after you have read the rest of the play. How close was your guess to the actual events of the plot?

The which my love and some necessity
Now lays upon you.   35
LORENZO   Madam, with all my heart;
I shall obey you in all fair commands.
PORTIA
My people do already know my mind
And will acknowledge° you and Jessica   **acknowledge:** obey
In place of Lord Bassanio and myself.
So fare you well till we shall meet again.   40
LORENZO
Fair thoughts and happy hours attend on you!
JESSICA
I wish your ladyship all heart's content.
PORTIA
I thank you for your wish, and am well pleased
To wish it back on you. Fare you well, Jessica.
                    Exeunt [Jessica and Lorenzo].
Now, Balthasar,   45
As I have ever found thee honest-true,
So let me find thee still. Take this same letter,
And use thou all th' endeavor of a man
In speed to Padua. See thou render this
Into my cousin's hands, Doctor Bellario;   50
And look,° what notes and garments he doth give thee.   **look:** (an injunction: "pay attention to")
Bring them, I pray thee, with imagined speed°   **imagined speed:** swiftness of thought (?) all
Unto the traject,° to the common ferry   imaginable speed (?)
Which trades to Venice. Waste no time in words   **traject:** (from Italian *traghetto,* a ferry)
But get thee gone. I shall be there before thee.   55
BALTHASAR
Madam, I go with all convenient° speed.   *[Exit.]*   **convenient:** appropriate
PORTIA
Come on, Nerissa; I have work in hand
That you yet know not of. We'll see our husbands
Before they think of us.
NERISSA   Shall they see us?
PORTIA
They shall, Nerissa, but in such a habit°   **habit:** costume   60
That they shall think we are accomplishèd°   **accomplishèd:** equipped, completed
With that we lack.° I'll hold thee any wager,   **that we lack:** i.e., male genitals
When we are both accoutered° like young men,   **accoutered:** dressed
I'll prove the prettier fellow of the two,
And wear my dagger with the braver grace,   65
And speak between the change of man and boy°   **change . . . boy:** i.e., puberty (when the voice
With a reed° voice, and turn two mincing steps   breaks)
Into a manly stride, and speak of frays   **reed:** reedy, piping
Like a fine bragging youth, and tell quaint° lies,   **quaint:** clever, contrived
How honorable ladies sought my love,   70
Which I denying, they fell sick and died –
I could not do withal.° Then I'll repent,   **I . . . withal:** I could not help it
And wish, for all that, that I had not killed them.

DISCOVERING SHAKESPEARE

(67) Gender [3.4.60–78]: What kinds of on-stage <u>blocking</u> and gestures could Portia exhibit to help illustrate what she is saying in these lines? How different do you think stereotypical male behavior was in the Renaissance than it is today?

And twenty of these puny lies I'll tell,
That men shall swear I have discontinued school
Above° a twelvemonth. I have within my mind
A thousand raw° tricks of these bragging jacks,°
Which I will practice.

NERISSA   Why, shall we turn to° men?

PORTIA
Fie, what a question's that,
If thou wert near a lewd interpreter!
But come, I'll tell thee all my whole device
When I am in my coach, which stays for us
At the park gate; and therefore haste away,
For we must measure twenty miles today.   *Exeunt.*

Above: more than (i.e., at least)   75
raw: immature; **jacks:** knaves

turn to: turn into (with bawdy pun)

  80

❦ **3.5**° *Enter [Lancelot the] Clown and Jessica.*

3.5: Portia's house

LANCELOT   Yes truly; for look you, the sins of the father are to be laid upon the children. Therefore, I promise you I fear you.° I was always plain° with you, and so now I speak my agitation° of the matter. Therefore be o' good cheer, for truly I think you are damned. There is but one hope in it that can do you any good, and that is but a kind of bastard hope neither.°

fear you: am afraid for you; **plain:** frank
agitation: (playing on "cogitation")

  5

neither: (simply emphasizes the statement)

JESSICA   And what hope is that, I pray thee?

LANCELOT   Marry, you may partly hope that your father got you not – that you are not the Jew's daughter.

  10

JESSICA   That were a kind of bastard hope indeed! So the sins of my mother should be visited upon me.

LANCELOT   Truly then, I fear you are damned both by father and mother. Thus when I shun Scylla your father, I fall into° Charybdis your mother. Well, you are gone° both ways.

fall into: (with bawdy wordplay, "enter sexually"); **gone:** done for   15

JESSICA   I shall be saved by my husband. He hath made me a Christian.

LANCELOT   Truly, the more to blame he! We were Christians enow before,° e'en as many as could well live one by another. This making of Christians will raise the price of hogs; if we grow all to be pork eaters, we shall not shortly have a rasher° on the coals for money.
     Enter Lorenzo.

enow before: i.e., numerous enough before Jessica became a Christian   20

rasher: thin slice (of bacon)

JESSICA   I'll tell my husband, Lancelot, what you say. Here he comes.

LORENZO   I shall grow jealous of you shortly, Lancelot, if you thus get my wife into corners.

  25

JESSICA   Nay, you need not fear us, Lorenzo. Lancelot and I are out.° He tells me flatly there's no mercy for me in heaven because I am a Jew's daughter; and he says you

are out: have quarreled

  30

DISCOVERING SHAKESPEARE

(68) Puns [3.4.80]: Find and explain Portia's two bawdy puns in this scene. What additional dimension does this sexual awareness add to her character?

(69) Language [3.5.19–23]: Rephrase in your own words Lancelot's joke about the relationship between the price of hogs and the conversion of Jews.

are no good member of the commonwealth, for in converting Jews to Christians you raise the price of pork.

LORENZO *[To Lancelot]* I shall answer° that better to the
commonwealth than you can the getting up of the
Negro's belly. The Moor° is with child by you, Lancelot.

answer: justify

Moor: (the play's only mention of this character)   35

LANCELOT It is much that the Moor should be more
than reason;° but if she be less than an honest° woman,
she is indeed more than I took her for.

more than reason: larger than is reasonable
(with pun on *Moor*); **honest:** chaste

LORENZO How every fool can play upon the word! I
think the best grace° of wit will shortly turn into silence,
and discourse grow commendable in none only but
parrots. Go in, sirrah; bid them prepare for dinner.

best grace: highest quality   40

LANCELOT That is done, sir. They have all stomachs.°

stomachs: appetites

LORENZO Goodly Lord, what a wit-snapper are you!
Then bid them prepare dinner.

45

LANCELOT That is done too, sir. Only "cover"° is the word.

cover: i.e., lay the table

LORENZO Will you cover then, sir?

LANCELOT Not so, sir, neither! I know my duty.°

Not so . . . duty: (to Lancelot *cover* now means
to put on his cap; cf. 2.9.43)

LORENZO Yet more quarreling with occasion!° Wilt thou
show the whole wealth of thy wit in an instant? I pray
thee understand a plain man in his plain meaning: go
to thy fellows, bid them cover the table, serve in the
meat, and we will come in to dinner.

quarreling with occasion: i.e., quibbling   50

LANCELOT For the table,° sir, it shall be served in; for the
meat, sir, it shall be covered;° for your coming in to dinner, sir, why let it be as humors and conceits° shall govern.   *Exit Clown [Lancelot].*

table: (Lancelot quibbles with the word so that it
now means the food itself)   55
covered: served in a covered dish
humors and conceits: whims and ideas

LORENZO
O dear discretion,° how his words are suited!°
The fool hath planted in his memory
An army of good words; and I do know
A many° fools that stand in better place,°
Garnished like him,° that for a tricksy word
Defy the matter.° How cheer'st thou,° Jessica?
And now, good sweet, say thy opinion.
How dost thou like the Lord Bassanio's wife?

dear discretion: precious (or precise) discrimination;
suited: used to suit the occasion

60

A many: many; **stand . . . place:** have higher
social rank
Garnished like him: i.e., resembling him
Defy the matter: i.e., refuse to talk sense; **How
cheer'st thou:** what cheer   65

JESSICA
Past all expressing. It is very meet
The Lord Bassanio live an upright life
For having such a blessing in his lady;
He finds the joys of heaven here on earth,
And if on earth he do not merit it,
In reason he should never come to heaven.
Why, if two gods should play some heavenly match
And on the wager lay° two earthly women,
And Portia one, there must be something else°
Pawned° with the other, for the poor rude world
Hath not her fellow.

70

lay: bet
else: more
Pawned: staked   75

DISCOVERING SHAKESPEARE

(70) Verse [3.5.58]: Following Lancelot's exit after line 57, why does the scene shift from <u>prose</u> to <u>verse</u>? Do Jessica and
Lorenzo always speak to each other in <u>verse</u>? If so, why?

LORENZO   Even such a husband
   Hast thou of me as she is for a wife.
JESSICA
   Nay, but ask my opinion too of that.
LORENZO
   I will anon. First let us go to dinner.
JESSICA
   Nay, let me praise you while I have a stomach.°   **stomach:** inclination, appetite   80
LORENZO
   No, pray thee, let it serve for table talk;
   Then howsome'er° thou speak'st, 'mong other things   **howsome'er:** however
   I shall digest it.
JESSICA   Well, I'll set you forth.°   **set you forth:** serve you up, as at a feast (i.e.,
                              Exit [with Lorenzo].   praise you ironically)

❧ **4.1°** *Enter the Duke, the Magnificoes, Antonio,*   **4.1:** A room in the doge's palace (often imagined
Bassanio, [Salerio,] and Gratiano [with others].   as a court of justice)

DUKE   What, is Antonio here?
ANTONIO   Ready, so please your grace.
DUKE
   I am sorry for thee. Thou art come to answer
   A stony adversary, an inhuman wretch,
   Uncapable of° pity, void and empty   **Uncapable of:** without the capacity for   5
   From° any dram of mercy.   **From:** of
ANTONIO   I have heard
   Your grace hath ta'en great pains to qualify°   **qualify:** moderate, temper
   His rigorous course; but since he stands obdurate,
   And that no lawful means can carry me
   Out of his envy's° reach, I do oppose   **envy:** malice   10
   My patience to his fury, and am armed°   **armed:** prepared
   To suffer with a quietness of spirit
   The very tyranny and rage of his.
DUKE
   Go one, and call the Jew into the court.
SALERIO
   He is ready at the door; he comes, my lord.   15
     Enter Shylock.
DUKE
   Make room, and let him stand before our° face.   **our:** my (the "royal" plural)
   Shylock, the world thinks, and I think so too,
   That thou but leadest this fashion° of thy malice   **fashion:** pretense
   To the last hour of act;° and then 'tis thought   **last . . . act:** very edge of doing
   Thou'lt show thy mercy and remorse° more strange   **remorse:** pity   20
   Than is thy strange° apparent cruelty;   **strange . . . strange:** remarkable, unusual . . .
   And where thou now exacts the penalty,   extraordinary (or "alien"?)
   Which is a pound of this poor merchant's flesh,
   Thou wilt not only loose° the forfeiture,   **loose:** let go
   But touched with human gentleness and love,   25

DISCOVERING SHAKESPEARE

(71) Racism [4.1.14]: Count how many times Shylock is referred to as "the Jew" and how many times his actual name is used. What does this imbalance tell us about the characters in the play? About Shakespeare's society?

Forgive a moiety° of the principal,
Glancing an eye of pity on his losses,
That have of late so huddled on his back,
Enow° to press a royal merchant° down
And pluck commiseration of his state
From brassy bosoms and rough hearts of flint,
From stubborn Turks and Tartars never trained
To offices° of tender courtesy.
We all expect a gentle answer, Jew.

SHYLOCK
I have possessed° your grace of what I purpose,
And by our holy Sabaoth° have I sworn
To have the due and forfeit of my bond.
If you deny it, let the danger light
Upon your charter and your city's freedom!°
You'll ask me why I rather choose to have
A weight of carrion flesh than to receive
Three thousand ducats. I'll not answer that,
But say it is my humor. Is it answered?
What if my house be troubled with a rat,
And I be pleased to give ten thousand ducats
To have it baned?° What, are you answered yet?
Some men there are love not a gaping pig,°
Some that are mad if they behold a cat,
And others, when the bagpipe sings i' th' nose,
Cannot contain their urine; for affection,°
Master of passion, sways it to the mood
Of what it likes or loathes. Now for your answer:
As there is no firm reason to be rendered
Why he cannot abide a gaping pig,
Why he a harmless necessary cat,
Why he° a woolen bagpipe,° but of force°
Must yield to such inevitable shame
As to offend, himself being offended;
So can I give no reason, nor I will not,
More than a lodged° hate and a certain loathing
I bear Antonio, that I follow thus
A losing° suit against him. Are you answered?

BASSANIO
This is no answer, thou unfeeling man,
To excuse the current of thy cruelty!

SHYLOCK
I am not bound to please thee with my answers.

BASSANIO
Do all men kill the things they do not love?

SHYLOCK
Hates any man the thing he would not kill?

BASSANIO
Every offense° is not a hate at first.

moiety: portion

Enow: enough; **royal merchant:** (see 3.2.239)

30

offices: duties

possessed: informed   35
Sabaoth: armies, hosts (Hebrew; Q2 and F read "Sabbath")

freedom: (see 3.2.278)

40

45

baned: poisoned
gaping pig: i.e., served roasted with its mouth propped open

affection: feeling, impulse   50

55

he . . . he . . . he: i.e., one man . . . another . . . a third; **woolen bagpipe:** i.e., with flannel-covered bag; **of force:** perforce, of necessity

lodged: deep-seated   60

losing: unprofitable

65

offense: injury, grievance

DISCOVERING SHAKESPEARE

(72) Puns [4.1.34]: What pun is implied on the word "gentle" in the Duke's "We all expect a gentle answer, Jew" (4.1.34)?

(73) Verse [4.1.65–69]: Lines 65–69 in 4.1 are a good example of stichomythia (alternating lines of verse). Although the rhetorical device is generally used in comic situations, it has a different effect here. What is its purpose in this scene?

SHYLOCK

    What, wouldst thou have a serpent sting thee twice?

ANTONIO

    I pray you think° you question° with the Jew.   **think:** keep in mind; **question:** argue   70

    You may as well go stand upon the beach

    And bid the main flood° bate° his usual height;   **main flood:** sea at flood tide; **bate:** reduce

    You may as well use question with the wolf

    Why he hath made the ewe bleat for the lamb;

    You may as well forbid the mountain pines   75

    To wag° their high tops and to make no noise   **wag:** sway, bend

    When they are fretten° with the gusts of heaven;   **fretten:** fretted, vexed

    You may as well do anything most hard

    As seek to soften that – than which what's harder? –

    His Jewish heart. Therefore I do beseech you   80

    Make no more offers, use no farther means,

    But with all brief and plain conveniency°   **conveniency:** propriety

    Let me have judgment, and the Jew his will.

BASSANIO

    For thy three thousand ducats here is six.

SHYLOCK

    If every ducat in six thousand ducats   85

    Were in six parts, and every part a ducat,

    I would not draw° them. I would have my bond.   **draw:** take

DUKE

    How shalt thou hope for mercy, rendering none?

SHYLOCK

    What judgment shall I dread, doing no wrong?

    You have among you many a purchased slave,   90

    Which like your asses and your dogs and mules

    You use in abject and in slavish parts,°   **parts:** duties, functions

    Because you bought them. Shall I say to you,

    "Let them be free! Marry them to your heirs!

    Why sweat they under burdens? Let their beds   95

    Be made as soft as yours, and let their palates

    Be seasoned with such viands"? You will answer,

    "The slaves are ours." So do I answer you.

    The pound of flesh which I demand of him

    Is dearly bought, 'tis mine, and I will have it.   100

    If you deny me, fie upon your law!

    There is no force in the decrees of Venice.

    I stand for judgment. Answer: shall I have it?

DUKE

    Upon° my power I may dismiss this court   **Upon:** in accordance with

    Unless Bellario, a learned doctor   105

    Whom I have sent for to determine this,°   **determine this:** resolve this issue

    Come here today.

SALERIO   My lord, here stays without°   **stays without:** waits outside

    A messenger with letters from the doctor,

    New come from Padua.

DUKE

    Bring us the letters. Call the messenger.   110

DISCOVERING SHAKESPEARE

(74) Historical References [4.1.90]: How does Shylock's mention of Venetian "slaves" in 4.1.90 bring a new aspect to the <u>theme</u> of racism in the play? How "Christian" are these characters if they owned slaves?

BASSANIO
Good cheer, Antonio! What, man, courage yet!
The Jew shall have my flesh, blood, bones, and all,
Ere thou shalt lose for me one drop of blood.

ANTONIO
I am a tainted wether° of the flock,
Meetest for death;° the weakest kind of fruit
Drops earliest to the ground, and so let me.
You cannot better be employed, Bassanio,
Than to live still, and write mine epitaph.
   Enter Nerissa [dressed as a lawyer's clerk].

DUKE
Came you from Padua, from Bellario?

NERISSA
From both, my lord. Bellario greets your grace.
   [Presents a letter.]

BASSANIO
Why dost thou whet thy knife so earnestly?

SHYLOCK
To cut the forfeiture from that bankrupt there.

GRATIANO
Not on thy sole,° but on thy soul, harsh Jew,
Thou mak'st thy knife keen; but no metal can –
No, not the hangman's° ax – bear half the keenness
Of thy sharp envy. Can no prayers pierce thee?

SHYLOCK
No, none that thou hast wit enough to make.

GRATIANO
O be thou damned, inexecrable dog,°
And for thy life° let justice be accused!
Thou almost mak'st me waver in my faith,
To hold opinion with Pythagoras°
That souls of animals infuse themselves
Into the trunks of men. Thy currish spirit
Governed a wolf who, hanged for human slaughter,
Even from the gallows did his fell° soul fleet,°
And whilst thou layest in thy unhallowed dam°
Infused itself in thee; for thy desires
Are wolvish, bloody, starved, and ravenous.

SHYLOCK
Till thou canst rail the seal from off my bond,
Thou but offend'st thy lungs to speak so loud.
Repair thy wit, good youth, or it will fall
To cureless ruin. I stand here for law.

DUKE
This letter from Bellario doth commend
A young and learned doctor to our court.
Where is he?

NERISSA   He attendeth here hard by
To know your answer whether you'll admit him.

wether: castrated ram
Meetest for death: most fit for slaughter   115

120

sole: (many productions have Shylock sharpen his knife on his shoe here)
hangman's: executioner's   125

inexecrable dog: dog that cannot be execrated (cursed) enough
for thy life: i.e., because you are allowed to live   130
Pythagoras: Greek philosopher who thought souls migrated at death into another living creature

fell: cruel; **fleet:** pass   135
dam: mother (typically a word applied to animals, not humans)

140

145

DISCOVERING SHAKESPEARE

(75) Imagery [4.1.113]: How does Bassanio's reference to "one drop of blood" (4.1.113) help <u>foreshadow</u> Portia's legal maneuvering later in the scene? Write out your answer after you have read the entire scene.

DUKE
With all my heart. Some three or four of you
Go give him courteous conduct to this place.
Meantime the court shall hear Bellario's letter.
    [Reads.]
"Your grace shall understand that at the receipt of your
letter I am very sick; but in the instant that your messenger came, in loving visitation was with me a young
doctor of Rome. His name is Balthasar. I acquainted
him with the cause in controversy between the Jew and
Antonio the merchant. We turned o'er many books together. He is furnished with my opinion which, bettered with his own learning, the greatness whereof I
cannot enough commend, comes with him° at my importunity to fill up your grace's request in my stead. I
beseech you let his lack of years be no impediment to
let him lack° a reverend estimation, for I never knew so
young a body with so old a head. I leave him to your
gracious acceptance, whose trial° shall better publish his
commendation."°
    Enter Portia [dressed as a Doctor of Laws] for
    Balthasar.
You hear the learn'd Bellario, what he writes;
And here, I take it, is the doctor come.
Give me your hand. Come you from old Bellario?

PORTIA
I did, my lord.

DUKE   You are welcome; take your place.
Are you acquainted with the difference
That holds this present question in the court?°

PORTIA
I am informèd throughly° of the cause.°
Which is the merchant here and which the Jew?°

DUKE
Antonio and old Shylock, both stand forth.

PORTIA
Is your name Shylock?

SHYLOCK   Shylock is my name.

PORTIA
Of a strange nature is the suit you follow,
Yet in such rule° that the Venetian law
Cannot impugn° you as you do proceed.
    [To Antonio]
You stand within his danger,° do you not?

ANTONIO
Ay, so he says.

PORTIA   Do you confess the bond?

150

155

comes with him: i.e., brings my opinion

160

to let him lack: i.e., which will cause him to lack

trial: i.e., actual performance

"Your grace . . . commendation.": (no reader is designated in the early texts, and it is possible that the letter is read by the duke or by Nerissa, the "clerk")

165

with . . . court: i.e., with the case being tried   170

throughly: thoroughly (the quarto's obsolete *throughly* is important rhythmically); **cause:** case
Which . . . Jew: (In performance a key moment —does Portia not distinguish Shylock from Antonio, or are they undistinguishable, or is she pretending she cannot distinguish plaintiff and defendant?)

175

in such rule: so within the rules
impugn: oppose, regard as illegal

danger: power, control

DISCOVERING SHAKESPEARE
(76) Characterization [4.1.150–164]: Why does Portia want this description of Balthasar read before she enters the courtroom? What specific qualities of the young lawyer are praised in Bellario's letter?
(77) Language [4.1.172]: Why does Portia ask "Which is the merchant here and which the Jew" (4.1.172)? Couldn't she distinguish between the two men based upon their clothes, their relative positions on stage, and the number of friends around them? And why does she identify one man by his occupation and the other by his religion?

ANTONIO
I do.   180
PORTIA   Then must the Jew be merciful.
SHYLOCK
On what compulsion must I? Tell me that.
PORTIA
The quality of mercy is not strained;°   **strained:** constrained, forced
It droppeth as the gentle rain from heaven
Upon the place beneath. It is twice blest;
It blesseth him that gives and him that takes.   185
'Tis mightiest in the mightiest; it becomes
The thronèd monarch better than his crown.
His scepter shows the force of temporal power,
The attribute to awe and majesty,
Wherein doth sit the dread and fear of kings;   190
But mercy is above this sceptered sway.
It is enthronèd in the hearts of kings,
It is an attribute to God himself,
And earthly power doth then show likest God's
When mercy seasons justice. Therefore, Jew,   195
Though justice be thy plea, consider this:
That in the course of justice° none of us   **in . . . justice:** i.e., if justice should actually run
Should see salvation. We do pray for mercy,   its course
And that same prayer doth teach us all to render
The deeds of mercy. I have spoke thus much   200
To mitigate° the justice of thy plea,°   **mitigate:** temper, moderate; **justice . . . plea:**
Which if thou follow, this strict court of Venice   your appeal to strict justice
Must needs give sentence 'gainst the merchant there.
SHYLOCK
My deeds upon my head! I crave the law,
The penalty and forfeit of my bond.   205
PORTIA
Is he not able to discharge the money?
BASSANIO
Yes, here I tender it for him in the court,
Yea, thrice the sum. If that will not suffice,
I will be bound to pay it ten times o'er
On forfeit of my hands, my head, my heart.   210
If this will not suffice, it must appear
That malice bears down° truth. And I beseech you,   **bears down:** overwhelms
Wrest once the law° to your authority: **Wrest . . . law:** i.e., for once, subject the law
To do a great right, do a little wrong,
And curb this cruel devil of his will.   215
PORTIA
It must not be. There is no power in Venice
Can alter a decree establishèd.
'Twill be recorded for a precedent,

DISCOVERING SHAKESPEARE

(78) <u>Paraphrase</u> [4.1.182–203]: <u>Paraphrase</u> Portia's brilliant "mercy" speech on a separate sheet of paper; then write a brief paragraph explaining which quality you think is more important in the law: mercy or justice.

(79) <u>Asides</u> [4.1.203–240]: Which of the following lines might be played as <u>asides</u> between Portia and Shylock? What could a production gain by creating a special rapport between the two characters at this point in the play?

And many an error° by the same example
Will rush into the state: it cannot be.

error: exception to establish legal precedent

220

SHYLOCK
A Daniel come to judgment! Yea, a Daniel!°
O wise young judge, how I do honor thee!

Daniel: the shrewd young man and judge who exposed the elders in their false charges against Susannah (see the apocryphal Book of Susannah)

PORTIA
I pray you let me look upon the bond.

SHYLOCK
Here 'tis, most reverend doctor, here it is.

PORTIA
Shylock, there's thrice thy money offered thee.

225

SHYLOCK
An oath, an oath! I have an oath in heaven!
Shall I lay perjury upon my soul?
No, not for Venice!

PORTIA   Why, this bond is forfeit,
And lawfully by this the Jew may claim
A pound of flesh, to be by him cut off

230

Nearest the merchant's heart. Be merciful.
Take thrice thy money; bid me tear the bond.

SHYLOCK
When it is paid, according to the tenor.°
It doth appear you are a worthy judge;
You know the law, your exposition

tenor: substance of its terms

235

Hath been most sound. I charge you by the law,
Whereof you are a well-deserving pillar,
Proceed to judgment. By my soul I swear
There is no power in the tongue of man
To alter me. I stay° here on my bond.

stay: stand

240

ANTONIO
Most heartily I do beseech the court
To give the judgment.

PORTIA   Why then, thus it is:
You must prepare your bosom for his knife –

SHYLOCK
O noble judge! O excellent young man!

PORTIA
For the intent and purpose of the law

245

Hath full relation to° the penalty,
Which here appeareth due upon the bond.

Hath full relation to: is completely in accord with

SHYLOCK
'Tis very true. O wise and upright judge,
How much more elder art thou than thy looks!

PORTIA
Therefore lay bare your bosom.

250

SHYLOCK   Ay, his breast,
So says the bond, doth it not, noble judge?
"Nearest his heart": those are the very words.

DISCOVERING SHAKESPEARE

(80) Biblical References [4.1.221]: Why does Shylock mention Daniel in 4.1.221? To which Biblical story is he alluding? How does Gratiano echo his remarks later in the scene?

(81) Language [4.1.252]: Write out your best estimate of the legal language of the bond, including the words "Nearest his heart" (4.1.252).

PORTIA
  It is so. Are there balance° here to weigh   **balance:** scales
  The flesh?
SHYLOCK   I have them ready.
PORTIA
  Have by some surgeon, Shylock, on your charge,°   **charge:** expense   255
  To stop his wounds, lest he do bleed to death.
SHYLOCK
  Is it so nominated in the bond?
PORTIA
  It is not so expressed, but what of that?
  'Twere good you do so much for charity.
SHYLOCK
  I cannot find it; 'tis not in the bond.   260
PORTIA
  You, merchant, have you anything to say?
ANTONIO
  But little. I am armed and well prepared.
  Give me your hand, Bassanio; fare you well.
  Grieve not that I am fall'n to this for you,
  For herein Fortune shows herself more kind   265
  Than is her custom: it is still her use
  To let the wretched man outlive his wealth
  To view with hollow eye and wrinkled brow
  An age of poverty; from which ling'ring penance
  Of such misery doth she cut me off.   270
  Commend me to your honorable wife.
  Tell her the process° of Antonio's end,   **process:** course (with pun on "legal
  Say how I loved you, speak me fair° in death,   proceeding"?)
  And when the tale is told, bid her be judge   **speak me fair:** speak well of me
  Whether Bassanio had not once a love.   275
  Repent but you° that you shall lose your friend,   **Repent . . . you:** i.e., if only you regret (*repents*
  And he repents not that he pays your debt;   in the next line also means "regrets")
  For if the Jew do cut but deep enough,
  I'll pay it instantly with all my heart.
BASSANIO
  Antonio, I am married to a wife   280
  Which is as dear to me as life itself;
  But life itself, my wife, and all the world
  Are not with me esteemed above thy life.
  I would lose all, ay, sacrifice them all
  Here to this devil, to deliver you.   285
PORTIA
  Your wife would give you little thanks for that
  If she were by to hear you make the offer.
GRATIANO
  I have a wife who I protest I love.
  I would she were in heaven, so she could
  Entreat some power to change this currish Jew.   290

DISCOVERING SHAKESPEARE

(82) Blocking [4.1.280–296]: How close on stage are Portia and Nerissa to Bassanio and Gratiano when the two men offer to trade their marital happiness for Antonio's life? Why would Shakespeare include these comic asides within the heart of such a serious scene?

NERISSA
'Tis well you offer it behind her back;
The wish would make else an unquiet house.
SHYLOCK
These be the Christian husbands! I have a daughter;
Would any of the stock of Barabbas°
Had been her husband, rather than a Christian!
We trifle time. I pray thee pursue sentence.
PORTIA
A pound of that same merchant's flesh is thine.
The court awards it, and the law doth give it –
SHYLOCK
Most rightful judge!
PORTIA
And you must cut this flesh from off his breast.
The law allows it, and the court awards it.
SHYLOCK
Most learnèd judge! A sentence: come, prepare!
PORTIA
Tarry a little, there is something else.
This bond doth give thee here no jot of blood;
The words expressly are "a pound of flesh."
Take then thy bond, take thou thy pound of flesh;
But in the cutting it if thou dost shed
One drop of Christian blood, thy lands and goods
Are by the laws of Venice confiscate
Unto the state of Venice.
GRATIANO
O upright judge! Mark, Jew – O learnèd judge!
SHYLOCK
Is that the law?
PORTIA   Thyself shalt see the act;
For, as thou urgest justice, be assured
Thou shalt have justice more than thou desirest.
GRATIANO
O learnèd judge! Mark, Jew. A learnèd judge!
SHYLOCK
I take this offer then. Pay the bond thrice
And let the Christian go.
BASSANIO   Here is the money.
PORTIA
Soft!°
The Jew shall have all justice. Soft, no haste;
He shall have nothing but the penalty.
GRATIANO
O Jew! An upright judge, a learnèd judge!
PORTIA
Therefore prepare thee to cut off the flesh.
Shed thou no blood, nor cut thou less nor more

Barabbas: a murderer set free by Pontius Pilate when Jesus was condemned; also the central character's name ("Barabas") in Christopher Marlowe's play *The Jew of Malta* (Shylock prefers Jessica to have married a Jewish murderer rather than a Christian thief)

295

300

305

310

315

Soft: wait

320

DISCOVERING SHAKESPEARE

(83) **Language [4.1.303]:** Where else in the script have we heard the word "tarry." In what sense is this word anti-climactic at this moment in the play? Why doesn't Portia shout "Stop!" or "Wait!"? What do you think is happening on stage between Shylock and Antonio when Portia says "Tarry a little" (4.1.303)?

But just° a pound of flesh. If thou tak'st more   **just:** exactly
Or less than a just pound, be it but so much   325
As makes it light or heavy in the substance
Or the division° of the twentieth part   **substance . . . division:** quantity or a fraction
Of one poor scruple° – nay, if the scale do turn   **scruple:** one gram in apothecaries' weight (hence
But in the estimation of a hair° –   a very small amount)
Thou diest, and all thy goods are confiscate.   **estimation of a hair:** a hair's breadth   330

GRATIANO
A second Daniel; a Daniel, Jew!
Now, infidel, I have you on the hip!°   **on the hip:** (cf. 1.3.43)

PORTIA
Why doth the Jew pause? Take thy forfeiture.

SHYLOCK
Give me my principal, and let me go.

BASSANIO
I have it ready for thee; here it is.   335

PORTIA
He hath refused it in the open court.
He shall have merely justice and his bond.

GRATIANO
A Daniel still say I, a second Daniel!
I thank thee, Jew, for teaching me that word.

SHYLOCK
Shall I not have barely° my principal?   **barely:** even   340

PORTIA
Thou shalt have nothing but the forfeiture,
To be so taken at thy peril, Jew.

SHYLOCK
Why, then the devil give him good of it!
I'll stay no longer question.°   **stay . . . question:** press my case no further

PORTIA   Tarry, Jew!
The law hath yet another hold on you.   345
It is enacted in the laws of Venice,
If it be proved against an alien
That by direct or indirect attempts
He seek the life of any citizen,
The party 'gainst the which he doth contrive   350
Shall seize one half his goods; the other half
Comes to the privy coffer of the state;°   **privy . . . state:** personal funds of the sovereign
And the offender's life lies in° the mercy   **lies in:** lies at
Of the duke only, 'gainst all other voice.
In which predicament I say thou stand'st,   355
For it appears by manifest proceeding
That indirectly, and directly too,
Thou hast contrived against the very life
Of the defendant, and thou hast incurred
The danger formerly by me rehearsed.°   **danger . . . rehearsed:** penalty I have cited   360
Down therefore, and beg mercy of the duke.

DISCOVERING SHAKESPEARE

(84) Metaphor [4.1.332]: What does Gratiano mean when he tells Shylock, "I have you on the hip" (4.1.332)? (*Hint:* See 1.3.43.)

(85) Plot [4.1.345–361]: What is Portia's decision about Shylock's monetary penalty? In Antonio's next speech (4.1.378–388), what adjustments does he suggest in the legal distribution of Shylock's wealth?

GRATIANO
Beg that thou mayst have leave to hang thyself!
And yet, thy wealth being forfeit to the state,
Thou hast not left the value of a cord;
Therefore thou must be hanged at the state's charge.°

charge: expense 365

DUKE
That thou shalt see the difference of our spirit,
I pardon thee thy life before thou ask it.
For° half thy wealth, it is Antonio's;

For: as for

The other half comes to the general state,
Which humbleness may drive unto a fine.°

Which . . . fine: which humility on your part 370
may reduce to a fine

PORTIA
Ay, for the state, not for Antonio.°

Ay . . . Antonio: (Portia specifies that a fine
might replace the state's, not Antonio's, half of
Shylock's fortune)

SHYLOCK
Nay, take my life and all! Pardon not that!
You take my house° when you do take the prop

house: (1) dwelling, (2) family, lineage

That doth sustain my house; you take my life
When you do take the means whereby I live.

375

PORTIA
What mercy can you render him, Antonio?
GRATIANO
A halter° gratis, nothing else, for God's sake!

halter: hangman's noose

ANTONIO
So please my lord the duke and all the court
To quit° the fine for one half of his goods,
I am content; so he will let me have

quit: remit (Antonio is proposing that Venice
neither confiscate half of Shylock's wealth not fine 380
him)

The other half in use,° to render it
Upon his death unto the gentleman

in use: in trust (but the earlier meaning, "lend at
interest," is probably present; see 1.3.110)

That lately stole his daughter.
Two things provided more: that for this favor
He presently° become a Christian;

presently: immediately 385

The other, that he do record a gift
Here in the court of all he dies possessed
Unto his son Lorenzo and his daughter.

DUKE
He shall do this, or else I do recant°

recant: withdraw

The pardon that I late pronouncèd here.

390

PORTIA
Art thou contented,° Jew? What dost thou say?

contented: i.e., willing to accept these terms

SHYLOCK
I am content.
PORTIA   Clerk, draw a deed of gift.
SHYLOCK
I pray you give me leave to go from hence;
I am not well. Send the deed after me,
And I will sign it.

395

DUKE   Get thee gone, but do it.
GRATIANO
In christening shalt thou have two godfathers.

DISCOVERING SHAKESPEARE

(86) Staging [4.1.385]: When Antonio demands that Shylock "presently become a Christian" (4.1.385), what stage action could accompany his words?

Had I been judge, thou shouldst have had ten more° —
To bring thee to the gallows, not to the font.

Exit [Shylock].

DUKE
Sir, I entreat you home with me to dinner.

PORTIA
I humbly do desire your grace of pardon.   400
I must away this night toward Padua,
And it is meet I presently set forth.

DUKE
I am sorry that your leisure serves you not.°
Antonio, gratify° this gentleman,
For in my mind you are much bound to him.   405

Exit Duke and his train.

BASSANIO
Most worthy gentleman, I and my friend
Have by your wisdom been this day acquitted
Of grievous penalties, in lieu whereof,°
Three thousand ducats due unto the Jew
We freely cope° your courteous pains withal.   410

ANTONIO
And stand indebted, over and above,
In love and service to you evermore.

PORTIA
He is well paid that is well satisfied,
And I delivering you am satisfied,
And therein do account myself well paid;   415
My mind was never yet more mercenary.
I pray you know me when we meet again.
I wish you well, and so I take my leave.

BASSANIO
Dear sir, of force I must attempt you° further.
Take some remembrance of us as a tribute,
Not as fee. Grant me two things, I pray you —   420
Not to deny me, and to pardon me.

PORTIA
You press me far, and therefore I will yield.
Give me your gloves; I'll wear them for your sake.
And for your love I'll take this ring from you.   425
Do not draw back your hand; I'll take no more,
And you in love shall not deny me this.

BASSANIO
This ring, good sir, alas, it is a trifle!
I will not shame myself to give you this.

PORTIA
I will have nothing else but only this,   430
And now methinks I have a mind to it.

BASSANIO
There's more depends on this than on the value.°
The dearest ring in Venice will I give you,

---

ten more: i.e., to make a jury of twelve

your leisure . . . not: i.e., you do not have leisure
gratify: reward

in lieu whereof: in return for which

cope: repay

attempt you: try to persuade you

more . . . value: more than the ring's value is involved in this

---

DISCOVERING SHAKESPEARE

(87) Characterization [4.1.425]: Why do you think Portia tests Bassanio by asking for his ring (4.1.425)? What do we learn about her character from this demand?

And find it out by proclamation.
Only for this,° I pray you pardon me.°

for this: as for this ring; **pardon me** i.e., release   435
me from my obligation

PORTIA

I see, sir, you are liberal in offers.
You taught me first to beg, and now methinks
You teach me how a beggar should be answered.

BASSANIO

Good sir, this ring was given me by my wife,
And when she put it on she made me vow   440
That I should neither sell nor give nor lose it.

PORTIA

That scuse° serves many men to save their gifts.

scuse: (an alternate form of "excuse")

And if your wife be not a mad woman,
And know how well I have deserved this ring,
She would not hold out enemy for ever   445
For giving it to me. Well, peace be with you.

Exeunt [Portia and Nerissa].

ANTONIO

My Lord Bassanio, let him have the ring.
Let his deservings, and my love withal,
Be valued 'gainst your wife's commandement.

BASSANIO

Go, Gratiano, run and overtake him;   450
Give him the ring and bring him if thou canst
Unto Antonio's house. Away, make haste.

Exit Gratiano.

Come, you and I will thither presently,
And in the morning early will we both
Fly toward Belmont. Come, Antonio.   *Exeunt.*   455

❧ **4.2**° *Enter [Portia and] Nerissa [disguised as before].*

4.2: A street in Venice

PORTIA

Inquire the Jew's house out, give him this deed,°

deed: deed of gift (see 5.1.292–93)

And let him sign it. We'll away tonight
And be a day before our husbands home.
This deed will be well welcome to Lorenzo.

Enter Gratiano.

GRATIANO

Fair sir, you are well o'erta'en.°

o'erta'en: overtaken   5

My lord Bassanio upon more advice°

advice: consideration

Hath sent you here this ring, and doth entreat
Your company at dinner.

PORTIA   That cannot be.
His ring I do accept most thankfully,
And so I pray you tell him. Furthermore,   10
I pray you show my youth old Shylock's house.

GRATIANO

That will I do.

DISCOVERING SHAKESPEARE

(88) Plot [4.2.1]: Write out your version of this "deed of gift" (4.2.1). Why will Lorenzo be pleased with it?

NERISSA   Sir, I would speak with you.
      [Aside to Portia]
      I'll see if I can get my husband's ring,
      Which I did make him swear to keep for ever.
PORTIA   *[Aside to Nerissa]*
      Thou mayst, I warrant. We shall have old° swearing   **old:** i.e., plenty of, continuous   15
      That they did give the rings away to men;
      But we'll outface them, and outswear them too. –
      Away, make haste! Thou know'st where I will tarry.
NERISSA
      Come, good sir, will you show me to this house?
                                    [Exeunt.]

❧ **5.1**° *Enter Lorenzo and Jessica.*   **5.1:** The grounds of Portia's house

LORENZO
      The moon shines bright. In such a night as this,
      When the sweet wind did gently kiss the trees
      And they did make no noise, in such a night
      Troilus° methinks mounted the Troyan walls,   **Troilus:** Trojan whose beloved, eventually false,
      And sighed his soul toward the Grecian tents   Cressida was sent unwillingly to the Greek camp   5
      Where Cressid lay that night.
JESSICA   In such a night
      Did Thisby° fearfully o'ertrip the dew,   **Thisby:** beloved of Pyramus; she fled from the
      And saw the lion's shadow ere° himself,   lovers' meeting place when a lion approached
      And ran dismayed away.   **ere:** before
LORENZO   In such a night
      Stood Dido° with a willow° in her hand   **Dido:** queen of Carthage loved, then deserted, by   10
      Upon the wild sea banks, and waft° her love   Aeneas; **willow:** willow branch (symbol of
      To come again to Carthage.   forsaken love)
JESSICA   In such a night   **waft:** beckoned
      Medea° gathered the enchanted herbs
      That did renew old Aeson.°   **Medea:** enchantress in the legend of Jason and
LORENZO   In such a night   the Golden Fleece
      Did Jessica steal° from the wealthy Jew   **Troilus . . . Aeson:** (these legendary stories of
      And with an unthrift love° did run from Venice   doomed lovers derive their details from Ovid and   15
      As far as Belmont.   Chaucer)
JESSICA   In such a night   **Aeson:** Jason's father
      Did young Lorenzo swear he loved her well,   **steal:** slip away (but the other meaning, "rob," is
      Stealing her soul° with many vows of faith,   likely present)
      And ne'er a true one.   **unthrift love:** unthrifty love (?) unthrifty lover—
LORENZO   In such a night   i.e., Lorenzo (?)
      Did pretty Jessica, like a little shrew,   **Stealing her soul:** (Jessica may be joking   20
      Slander her love, and he forgave it her.   playfully, but she has also converted to Christianity
JESSICA   for Lorenzo's sake)
      I would outnight you, did nobody come:
      But hark, I hear the footing of a man.
      Enter [Stephano,] a messenger.
LORENZO
      Who comes so fast in silence of the night?   25

DISCOVERING SHAKESPEARE
(89) Teaser [5.1.7]: Why is Jessica's reference to Thisby (5.1.7) so interesting and significant in this play?

MESSENGER   A friend.

LORENZO
A friend? What friend? Your name I pray you, friend.

MESSENGER
Stephano is my name, and I bring word
My mistress will before the break of day   30
Be here at Belmont. She doth stray about
By holy crosses° where she kneels and prays   **holy crosses:** wayside shrines marked with
For happy wedlock hours.   crosses

LORENZO   Who comes with her?

MESSENGER
None but a holy hermit and her maid.
I pray you, is my master yet returned?

LORENZO
He is not, nor we have not heard from him.   35
But go we in, I pray thee, Jessica,
And ceremoniously let us prepare
Some welcome for the mistress of the house.
    Enter [Lancelot the] Clown.

LANCELOT   Sola, sola! Wo ha! Ho sola, sola!°   **Sola:** (sound imitating a post horn; see ll.46–47)

LORENZO   Who calls?   40

LANCELOT   Sola! Did you see Master Lorenzo? Master
Lorenzo! Sola, sola!

LORENZO   Leave holloaing, man! Here.

LANCELOT   Sola! Where, where?

LORENZO   Here!   45

LANCELOT   Tell him there's a post come from my master,
with his horn full of good news. My master will be here   (Lancelot might exit here: he has no further
ere morning, sweet soul.°   *[Exit.]*   dialogue)

LORENZO
Let's in, and there expect their coming.
And yet no matter: why should we go in?   50
My friend Stephano, signify,° I pray you,   **signify:** announce
Within the house, your mistress is at hand,
And bring your music forth into the air.
                            [Exit Stephano.]
How sweet the moonlight sleeps upon this bank!
Here will we sit and let the sounds of music   55
Creep in our ears; soft stillness and the night
Become° the touches of sweet harmony.   **Become:** befit; touches notes, strains
Sit, Jessica. Look how the floor of heaven
Is thick inlaid with patens° of bright gold.   **patens:** metal plates or tiling
There's not the smallest orb which thou behold'st   60
But in his motion like an angel sings,°   **motion . . . sings:** (reference to the music of the
Still quiring° to the young-eyed cherubins;   spheres)
Such harmony is in immortal souls,   **quiring:** choiring, singing
But whilst this muddy vesture° of decay   **muddy vesture:** clay (i.e., flesh)
Doth grossly close it in, we cannot hear it.   65
    [Enter Musicians.]

DISCOVERING SHAKESPEARE

(90) Staging [5.1.39–44]: Why does Lancelot continue calling for Lorenzo? What is happening on stage that prohibits him from seeing his master?

(91) Paraphrase [5.1.58–65]: Paraphrase Lorenzo's great speech concerning celestial and earthly harmony (5.1.58–65). Why does he explain this religious concept to Jessica?

Come ho, and wake Diana° with a hymn.   **Diana:** the virgin moon goddess
With sweetest touches pierce your mistress' ear
And draw her home with music.
 Play music.
JESSICA
 I am never merry° when I hear sweet music.   **merry:** lighthearted
LORENZO
 The reason is, your spirits are attentive.   70
 For do but note a wild and wanton herd
 Or race of youthful and unhandled colts°   **unhandled colts:** unbroken young stallions
 Fetching mad bounds, bellowing and neighing loud,
 Which is the hot condition of their blood;
 If they but hear perchance a trumpet sound,   75
 Or any air of music touch their ears,
 You shall perceive them make a mutual stand,°   **make . . . stand:** all stand still together
 Their savage eyes turned to a modest gaze
 By the sweet power of music. Therefore the poet°   **poet:** Ovid, in *Metamorphoses*, 10
 Did feign° that Orpheus° drew° trees, stones, and floods;   **feign:** imagine; **Orpheus:** legendary musician;   80
 Since nought so stockish,° hard, and full of rage   **drew:** attracted, bent to his musical spell
 But music for the time doth change his nature.   **stockish:** blockish, dull
 The man that hath no music in himself,
 Nor is not moved with concord of sweet sounds,
 Is fit for treasons, stratagems, and spoils;°   **spoils:** plundering   85
 The motions of his spirit are dull as night,
 And his affections dark as Erebus.°   **Erebus:** classical place of darkness in the region
 Let no such man be trusted. Mark the music.   of hell
 Enter Portia and Nerissa.
PORTIA
 That light we see is burning in my hall;
 How far that little candle throws his beams!   90
 So shines a good deed in a naughty° world.   **naughty:** wicked (see Matthew 5:14–16)
NERISSA
 When the moon shone we did not see the candle.
PORTIA
 So doth the greater glory dim the less.
 A substitute° shines brightly as a king   **substitute:** deputy (of the king)
 Until a king be by, and then his state   95
 Empties itself, as doth an inland brook
 Into the main of waters. Music, hark!
NERISSA
 It is your music,° madam, of the house.   **music:** group of musicians
PORTIA
 Nothing is good, I see, without respect;°   **without respect:** without reference to
 Methinks it sounds much sweeter than by day.   accompanying things   100
NERISSA
 Silence bestows that virtue on it, madam.
PORTIA
 The crow doth sing as sweetly as the lark
 When neither is attended;° and I think   **attended:** noticed (?), expected (?)
 The nightingale, if she should sing by day

DISCOVERING SHAKESPEARE

(92) Morality [5.1.90–91]: What "good deed" (5.1.91) is Portia describing here? How "good" do you think her deed really was?

When every goose is cackling, would be thought   105
No better a musician than the wren.
How many things by season seasoned are
To their right praise and true perfection.°   **by season . . . perfection:** i.e., are made perfect
Peace! How the moon sleeps with Endymion,°   by coming at the right time
And would not be awaked.   **Endymion:** shepherd loved by the moon   110
    [Music ceases.]   goddess (the line is apparently an elaborate way of
LORENZO   That is the voice,   saying the moon has passed behind a cloud: see
Or I am much deceived, of Portia.   l. 92)
PORTIA
He knows me as the blind man knows the cuckoo –
By the bad voice.
LORENZO   Dear lady, welcome home.
PORTIA
We have been praying for our husbands' welfare,
Which speed° we hope the better for our words.   **speed:** prosper   115
Are they returned?
LORENZO   Madam, they are not yet,
But there is come a messenger before
To signify their coming.
PORTIA   Go in, Nerissa.
Give order to my servants that they take
No note at all of our being absent hence –   120
Nor you, Lorenzo, Jessica nor you.
    [A tucket° sounds.]   **tucket:** short flourish of trumpets
LORENZO
Your husband is at hand; I hear his trumpet.
We are no telltales, madam; fear you not.
PORTIA
This night methinks is but the daylight sick;
It looks a little paler. 'Tis a day   125
Such as the day is when the sun is hid.
   Enter Bassanio, Antonio, Gratiano, and
   their followers.
BASSANIO
We should hold day with the antipodes°   **hold . . . antipodes:** i.e., share daylight with the
If you would walk in absence of the sun.   other side of the earth
PORTIA
Let me give light, but let me not be light,°   **be light:** i.e., be unfaithful
For a light wife doth make a heavy° husband,   **heavy:** sad   130
And never be Bassanio so for me.
But God sort° all! You are welcome home, my lord.   **sort:** dispose
BASSANIO
I thank you, madam. Give welcome to my friend.
This is the man, this is Antonio,
To whom I am so infinitely bound.   135
PORTIA
You should in all sense° be much bound to him,   **in all sense:** in every meaning of the word
For, as I hear, he was much bound for you.

DISCOVERING SHAKESPEARE

(93) Sound Effects [5.1.121]: What was a "tucket" (5.1.121)? What other music or sound effects would be useful in 5.1?
(94) Puns [5.1.136–137]: Exactly what pun is Portia making in 5.1.136–137 when she mentions Antonio being "bound for" Bassanio? How do these lines help suggest on-stage action in 4.1?

ANTONIO
No more than I am well acquitted of.°

acquitted of: released from

PORTIA
Sir, you are very welcome to our house.
It must appear in other ways than words:
Therefore I scant this breathing courtesy.°

scant . . . courtesy: cut short this courtesy of breath—i.e., of words

GRATIANO   *[To Nerissa]*
By yonder moon I swear you do me wrong!
In faith, I gave it to the judge's clerk.
Would he were gelt° that had it, for my part,°
Since you do take it, love, so much at heart.

gelt: gelded; **for my part:** so far as I am concerned

PORTIA
A quarrel ho, already! What's the matter?

GRATIANO
About a hoop of gold, a paltry ring
That she did give me, whose posy° was
For all the world like cutler's poetry°
Upon a knife – "Love me, and leave me not."

posy: inscription (commonly in verse)
cutler's poetry: banal verse or stale mottoes carved in a knife handle

NERISSA
What° talk you of the posy or the value?
You swore to me when I did give it you
That you would wear it till your hour of death,
And that it should lie with you in your grave.
Though not for me, yet for° your vehement oaths,
You should have been respective° and have kept it.
Gave it a judge's clerk! No, God's my judge,
The clerk will ne'er wear hair on's face that had it!

What: why

Though . . . yet for: even if not for my sake, still because of
respective: concerned (for the way you received it)

GRATIANO
He will, an if° he live to be a man.

an if: if

NERISSA
Ay, if a woman live to be a man.

GRATIANO
Now by this hand, I gave it to a youth,
A kind of boy, a little scrubbèd° boy
No higher than thyself, the judge's clerk,
A prating boy that begged it as a fee.
I could not for my heart deny it him.

scrubbèd: scrubby, short

PORTIA
You were to blame – I must be plain with you –
To part so slightly with your wife's first gift,
A thing stuck on with oaths upon your finger
And so riveted with faith unto your flesh.
I gave my love a ring, and made him swear
Never to part with it, and here he stands.
I dare be sworn for him he would not leave° it
Nor pluck it from his finger for the wealth
That the world masters. Now in faith, Gratiano,
You give your wife too unkind a cause of grief.
An 'twere to me, I should be mad° at it.

leave: part with

mad: (1) furious, (2) distracted

BASSANIO   *[Aside]*

DISCOVERING SHAKESPEARE

(95) Blocking [5.1.166]: What is Bassanio doing as he listens to Portia's speech from lines 166–176? When he freely admits his fault in lines 186–188, does he show us a new and different side to his character?

140

145

150

155

160

165

170

175

Why, I were best to cut my left hand off
And swear I lost the ring defending it.

GRATIANO
My lord Bassanio gave his ring away
Unto the judge that begged it, and indeed   180
Deserved it too; and then the boy his clerk
That took some pains in writing, he begged mine;
And neither man nor master would take aught
But the two rings.

PORTIA   What ring gave you, my lord?
Not that, I hope, which you received of me.   185

BASSANIO
If I could add a lie unto a fault,°   **fault:** misdeed
I would deny it; but you see my finger
Hath not the ring upon it — it is gone.

PORTIA
Even so void is your false heart of truth.
By heaven, I will ne'er come in your bed   190
Until I see the ring!

NERISSA   Nor I in yours
Till I again see mine!

BASSANIO   Sweet Portia,
If you did know to whom I gave the ring,
If you did know for whom I gave the ring,
And would conceive for what I gave the ring,   195
And how unwillingly I left the ring
When nought would be accepted but the ring,
You would abate the strength of your displeasure.

PORTIA
If you had known the virtue° of the ring,   **virtue:** power
Or half her worthiness that gave the ring,   200
Or your own honor to contain° the ring,   **honor to contain:** solemn duty to keep
You would not then have parted with the ring.
What man is there so much unreasonable,
If you had pleased to have defended it°   **defended it:** i.e., resisted giving it away
With any terms of zeal, wanted the modesty   205
To urge° the thing held as a ceremony?°   **urge:** demand as a gift; **ceremony:** token, keepsake
Nerissa teaches me what to believe:
I'll die for't but some woman had° the ring!   **but . . . had:** if some woman didn't get

BASSANIO
No, by my honor, madam! By my soul
No woman had it, but a civil doctor,°   **civil doctor:** doctor of civil law   210
Which did refuse three thousand ducats of me
And begged the ring, the which I did deny him,
And suffered° him to go displeased away —   **suffered:** allowed
Even he that had held up the very life
Of my dear friend. What should I say, sweet lady?   215
I was enforced to send it after him.
I was beset with° shame and courtesy.   **beset with:** attacked (or surrounded by)

DISCOVERING SHAKESPEARE

(96) Language [5.1.192–202]: Bassanio's speech from lines 192–198 and Portia's response in lines 199–202 provide a wonderful example of <u>parody</u>. Read the two speeches with a partner, focusing on ways in which Portia could mimic Bassanio's speech rhythms and mode of delivery.

My honor would not let ingratitude
So much besmear it. Pardon me, good lady!
For by these blessèd candles of the night, 220
Had you been there I think you would have begged
The ring of me to give the worthy doctor.

PORTIA
Let not that doctor e'er come near my house.
Since he hath got the jewel that I loved
And that which you did swear to keep for me, 225
I will become as liberal as you;
I'll not deny him anything I have,
No, not my body nor my husband's bed.
Know° him I shall, I am well sure of it. **Know:** (1) recognize, (2) have sexual intercourse
Lie not a night from home; watch me like Argus.° with (see 4.1.417) 230
If you do not, if I be left alone, **Argus:** mythological figure with a hundred eyes
Now by mine honor which is yet mine own,
I'll have that doctor for my bedfellow.

NERISSA
And I his clerk. Therefore be well advised° **well advised:** very careful
How you do leave me to mine own protection. 235

GRATIANO
Well, do you so. Let not me take° him then, **take:** catch
For if I do, I'll mar the young clerk's pen.° **pen:** i.e., penis

ANTONIO
I am th' unhappy subject of these quarrels.

PORTIA
Sir, grieve not you; you are welcome notwithstanding.

BASSANIO
Portia, forgive me this enforcèd° wrong, **enforcèd:** unavoidable 240
And in the hearing of these many friends
I swear to thee, even by thine own fair eyes,
Wherein I see myself –

PORTIA   Mark you but that!
In both my eyes he doubly sees himself,
In each eye one. Swear by your double° self, **double:** (1) twofold, (2) deceitful 245
And there's an oath of credit.° **oath of credit:** oath that can be believed (said
BASSANIO   Nay, but hear me. ironically)
Pardon this fault, and by my soul I swear
I never more will break an oath with thee.

ANTONIO
I once did lend my body for his wealth,
Which but for him that had your husband's ring 250
Had quite miscarried. I dare be bound again,
My soul upon the forfeit, that your lord
Will never more break faith advisedly.° **advisedly:** intentionally

PORTIA
Then you shall be his surety. Give him this,
And bid him keep it better than the other. 255

DISCOVERING SHAKESPEARE

(97) Mythology [5.1.230]: What type of mythological monster was Argus (5.1.230)? In what way is Portia's behavior here "monstrous"? What other references to eyes and sight can you find in the script? Why are they significant in this particular play?

ANTONIO
Here, Lord Bassanio. Swear to keep this ring.
BASSANIO
By heaven, it is the same I gave the doctor!
PORTIA
I had it of him.° Pardon me, Bassanio,   **of him:** from him
For by this ring the doctor lay with me.
NERISSA
And pardon me, my gentle Gratiano,   260
For that same scrubbèd boy, the doctor's clerk,
In lieu of° this last night did lie with me.   **In lieu of:** in return for
GRATIANO
Why, this is like the mending of highways
In summer, where the ways are fair enough.
What, are we cuckolds° ere we have deserved it?   **cuckolds:** deceived husbands   265
PORTIA
Speak not so grossly. You are all amazed.°   **amazed:** lost in a maze, befuddled
Here is a letter; read it at your leisure.
It comes from Padua from Bellario.
There you shall find that Portia was the doctor,
Nerissa there her clerk. Lorenzo here   270
Shall witness I set forth as soon as you,
And even but now returned; I have not yet
Entered my house. Antonio, you are welcome,
And I have better news in store for you
Than you expect. Unseal this letter soon;   275
There you shall find three of your argosies
Are richly come to harbor suddenly.
You shall not know by what strange accident
I chancèd on this letter.
ANTONIO   I am dumb.°   **dumb:** silenced
BASSANIO
Were you the doctor, and I knew you not?   280
GRATIANO
Were you the clerk that is to make me cuckold?
NERISSA
Ay, but the clerk that never means to do it,
Unless he live until he be a man.
BASSANIO
Sweet doctor, you shall be my bedfellow.
When I am absent, then lie with my wife.   285
ANTONIO
Sweet lady, you have given me life and living,°   **living:** material means to live
For here I read for certain that my ships
Are safely come to road.°   **road:** anchorage
PORTIA   How now, Lorenzo?
My clerk hath some good comforts too for you.

DISCOVERING SHAKESPEARE

(98) Staging [5.1.257]: When does Bassanio realize that the ring Antonio gives him in this scene is the same one he had given to Portia? How would you stage his discovery of this fact?

(99) Teaser [5.1.270]: Why does Shakespeare have Portia explain the <u>plot</u> in lines 266–279 when the audience already knows what has happened? Compare this speech with Friar Lawrence's much longer <u>monologue</u> at the end of *Romeo and Juliet* (5.3.229–269) in which he begins by saying "I will be brief" and then spends forty-one lines relating what has occurred between the two lovers.

NERISSA
  Ay, and I'll give them him without a fee.   290
  There do I give to you and Jessica
  From the rich Jew, a special deed of gift,
  After his death, of all he dies possessed of.
LORENZO
  Fair ladies, you drop manna° in the way   **manna:** i.e., food from heaven (see Exodus
  Of starvèd people.   16:15)   295
PORTIA   It is almost morning,
  And yet I am sure you are not satisfied
  Of these events at full.° Let us go in,   **satisfied . . . full:** fully satisfied with the
  And charge us there upon inter'gatories,°   explanation of these events
  And we will answer all things faithfully.   **charge . . . inter'gatories:** require ourselves
GRATIANO   there to answer interrogatories (legally framed
  Let it be so. The first inter'gatory   questions answerable under oath)
  That my Nerissa shall be sworn on is,   300
  Whether till the next night she had rather stay,°   **stay:** wait
  Or go to bed now, being two hours to day.
  But were the day come, I should wish it dark
  Till I were couching with the doctor's clerk.°   **clerk:** (pronounced "clark")   305
  Well, while I live I'll fear no other thing
  So sore as keeping safe Nerissa's ring.°   *Exeunt.*   **ring:** (with the bawdy meaning "vulva")

DISCOVERING SHAKESPEARE

(100) Plot [5.1.306–307]: Why do you think Shakespeare ended his play with Gratiano as the last speaker, and why is Gratiano's final comment a sexual pun?

❧

Research and Discussion Topics
ACT I

1. Antonio is a business entrepreneur who spends large amounts of money buying merchandise intended for resale abroad. Find out everything you can about this practice during the Renaissance.

2. What were the major perils for trading vessels like those employed by Antonio? Try to find drawings of such ships and information about their use during the Renaissance.

3. Antonio's admission that he sees the world as a stage "where every man must play a part" (1.1.77–79) is an example of a literary <u>trope</u> called the *theatrum mundi* ("all the world's a stage"). Find examples of this <u>trope</u> in other plays by Shakespeare.

4. Do some research on "Cato's daughter, Brutus' Portia" (1.1.166), and Jason and the "golden fleece" (1.1.170–172) in order to clarify what specific use Shakespeare was making of these references.

5. Investigate the uses and abuses of "credit" (1.1.180) during the Renaissance. What was the general attitude toward borrowing money? What was "usury"? What other Shakespearean plays deal with the concept of "interest"? (*Hint:* See *Timon of Athens.*)

6. Research the concept of sadness (often called "melancholy") during Shakespeare's time. Would you say that Antonio and Portia are "depressed" in the first two scenes of the

play? See Robert Burton's *Anatomy of Melancholy* (1621) for a thorough description of this condition in the Renaissance.

7. Who were Sibylla and Diana, and why does Shakespeare have Portia mention their names (1.2.101–102)?

8. Research the exorcism referred to by Shylock in *Matthew* 8: 28–34 and its impact upon Jewish dietary habits (1.3.31–33).

9. Read the Jacob and Laban story in Genesis 27 to help explain Shylock's biblical defense of interest. How convincing is his analogy?

10. What is "Jewish gaberdine" (1.3.109)? What specific clothing restrictions were Jews forced to abide by in England at this time? In Italy? How many Jews were living in England and Europe around the year 1600?

11. Who or what were "notaries" (1.3.142)? What did they do?

ACT II

1. Find the country of Morocco on a map of Renaissance Europe, and determine how far from Venice it was.

2. Who was Phoebus (2.1.5)? Who was Solyman (2.1.26)?

3. Who were Hercules and Lichas (2.1.32)?

4. What was a "gobbo," and how could a translation of the name help influence the actions of Lancelot and his father?

5. Research the various degrees of blindness during the Renaissance, and examine Lancelot's misuse of the terms in 2.2.33–34.

6. What were "liveries" (2.2.108)?

7. How much was a "ducat" (2.3.4) worth in Renaissance Italy?

8. What was a "masque" (2.4.22), and why did it require "torchbearers" (2.2.23)?

9. When Shylock says he dreamed of "money-bags" (2.5.18), does he interpret this as a good or bad omen? Why?

10. Where were the "Hyrcanian deserts" (2.7.41)?

11. Where was the country of Aragon (2.9.2)?

12. Who wrote *The Jew of Malta,* and what was its relationship to Shakespeare's *The Merchant of Venice?*

13. Who was Dr. Roderigo Lopez?

ACT III

1. Where were "the Goodwins," and why were they dangerous to ships (3.1.4)?

2. What was the Rialto (3.1.41–42)? What sort of business was transacted there?

3. How far from Venice is Genoa (3.1.72)? How long would it have taken Jessica and Lorenzo to travel there? Where was Tripolis (3.1.93) in relation to Venice?

4. Who is Leah (3.1.112)? What Biblical parallels does the name suggest?

5. Who was Alcides (3.2.55), and why does Portia mention his name at this point in the scene?

6. Who was Midas (3.2.102), and why does Bassanio mention his name?

7. Why has the Jailer let Antonio out of prison in 3.3? What interesting facts can you discover about Renaissance jails?

8. How long would it have taken travelers to ride twenty miles in a coach during the Renaissance (3.4.84)?

9. Who is the Moor (3.5.36)? And how does Lancelot's impregnation of her impact the other racial themes in the play?

ACT IV

1. Was there a duke (or doge) of Venice at this time during the Renaissance? How historically accurate is Shakespeare's mention of the duke?

2. Who were Turks and Tartars (4.1.32)?

3. What types of slaves were owned in Venice at this time (4.1.90)?

4. What kind of knife would Shylock have been sharpening in this scene (4.1.121 ff.)? Find some pictures of Renaissance knives, especially those of Hebrew origin.

5. What sort of legal "books" (4.1.155) could Bellario and Balthasar have consulted together? Discover the titles of some prominent Italian and English law books available in the year 1600.

6. Find as many Biblical quotations as you can that deal with the concept of "mercy" (4.1.182 ff).

7. Would a human heart weigh more or less than "a pound of flesh" (4.1.272–279)?

8. Who was Daniel (lines 221 and 331)? Why do both Shylock and Gratiano refer to him?

9. Why does Gratiano offer Shylock a "halter" (4.1.377)? What other forms of execution were popular during the Renaissance?

10. What was "a deed of gift" (4.1.392)? Can you find an example of one in any Renaissance sources?

ACT V

1. Find out all you can about the following pairs of lovers: Troilus and Cressida (5.1.1–6), Pyramus and Thisby (5.1.6–9), Dido and Aeneas (5.1.9–12), and Aeson and Medea (5.1.12–14).

2. What were "patens" (5.1.59)? Who were the "cherubins" (5.1.62)? Who was Diana, and why does Lorenzo refer to her at this point in the play (5.1.66)? Who was Orpheus (5.1.80)?

3. Who was Endymion (5.1.109)? Why is Portia reminded of him at this moment?

4. Which bird reputedly had the sweetest voice: the nightingale (5.1.104), the wren (106), or the cuckoo (112)?

5. What were the "Antipodes" (5.1.127)?

6. What was "cutler's poetry" (5.1.149)?

7. What does the word "doctor" mean in this context (5.1.222)? When did physicians begin to refer to themselves as "doctors"? Which professions awarded the first "doctorates"?

8. Who was Argus (5.1.230)?

9. What was a "cuckold" (5.1.265)? What was "manna" (5.1.294), and how does Lorenzo's reference to it here tie in with the play's earlier religious themes?

10. What was an "inter'gatory" (5.1.298)? Why is Portia's use of this legal term significant at the play's conclusion?

11. Judging from Gratiano's rhyme in lines 304–305, how was the word "clerk" pronounced in Renaissance England?

Filmography

1980
BBC
Rating:

Directed by Jack Gold

John Franklyn-Robbins as Antonio
John Nettles as Bassanio
Warren Mitchell as Shylock
Gemma Jones as Portia
Susan Jameson as Nerissa
Kenneth Cranham as Gratiano
Richard Morrant as Lorenzo
Leslee Udwin as Jessica
Enn Reitel as Lancelot

The BBC *Merchant of Venice* might almost be described as neutral ground in the interpretive struggle over the play. Most of the text (including Shylock's <u>asides</u>) and all of the characters are in place. Jessica and Lorenzo are authentic young lovers, both romantic and sexual, who hold each other as they lie under the stars. Shylock is a villainous plotter who still deserves our sympathy. The Venetian Christians are good and bad by turns and sometimes both together. Portia and Nerissa can seem kind or cruel, merciful or vengeful. The entire cast is professional, with Warren Mitchell's Shylock especially powerful, and Enn Reitel's Lancelot very likeable. However, charm can seem in short supply in this production, and Gemma Jones's Portia frequently appears unattractive.

1973
ATV Network LTD.
Rating:

Directed by: John Sichel

Anthony Nicholls as Antonio
Jeremy Brett as Bassanio
Laurence Olivier as Shylock
Joan Plowright as Portia
Anna Carteret as Nerissa
Michael Jayston as Gratiano

Malcolm Reid as Lorenzo
Louise Purnell as Jessica
Denis Lawson as Lancelot

If *The Merchant of Venice* were a <u>tragedy</u> and Shylock its <u>protagonist</u>, this would be a perfect production. Since it is a comedy, and Shylock is the villain, there are problems. This British National Theatre version cuts Shylock's <u>asides</u>, Jessica's scene in male attire, Old Gobbo, and much of Lancelot Gobbo. Set in Edwardian England, it adds voice-overs (an off-screen scream after Shylock leaves the court and a Jewish requiem—the "Kaddish"—at the end of the play) and photographs of his beloved wife and daughter to make Shylock seem more sympathetic. As part of this process, Jessica and Lorenzo become unsympathetic characters who do not appear to be in love with each other. The romantic, "in-such-a-night" scene (5.1) is played with the two standing as far apart as possible, with the cold, presumably fortune-hunting Lorenzo smoking a pipe. The production ends with a guilt-stricken Jessica alone. The cast, though a bit old for the parts, is uniformly and undeniably charming, and Olivier ranges from excellent to superb. This reinterpretation of the play is by no means unusual or unjustifiable in a post-Holocaust world, and it makes an effective film.

2004
Distributed by Sony Pictures Classics
Rating:

(R—Restricted)
Directed by Michael Radford

Al Pacino as Shylock
Jeremy Irons as Antonio
Joseph Fiennes as Bassanio
Lynn Collins as Portia

This film had a shadow cast—the company that might have been—including Dustin Hoffman as Shylock (but Pacino was already cast when he expressed interest), Ian McKellan as Antonio (whose schedule got too complicated), and Cate Blanchett as Portia (who left because she was pregnant). Regardless, the movie is intelligent and meticulous, though it has lost too many lines and too much humor. At the same time, it adds scenes not present in the script about the mistreatment of the Jews. Both Fiennes and Collins look their parts better than they speak their lines. Still, any Shakespeare film featuring Al Pacino and Jeremy Irons is an important cinematic event. Irons is a human, humane, and unsettling Antonio, who is at once warm and cynical, sympathetic and secret. No one does charm with a touch of chill as well. Pacino's Shylock brings to the role an unprecedented authority. For the first time on film, we believe Shylock just might win his case. His hatred becomes more dangerous because it presents a real threat to the Christian community. If the rest of the cast seems pale by comparison, their talent is less to blame than the size of their competition.

Annotated Bibliography

Barton, John. *Exploring a Character*. Playing Shakespeare: The Royal Shakespeare Company. Princeton: Films for the Humanities, 1984. PR 3091.B37.

> In interviews with actors David Suchet and Patrick Stewart, both of whom have played the role of Shylock, Barton emphasizes Shakespeare's ability to create characters who defy simple classification. For instance, Barton draws upon each actor's interpretation of Shylock's Jewishness: Stewart sees him as a merchant who just happens to be a Jew, and Suchet sees him as a Jewish merchant. Barton also discusses varying interpretations of the play as pure comedy or a tragic-comic combination.

Benston, Alice. "Portia, the Law, and the Tripartite Structure of *The Merchant of Venice*." *Shakespeare Quarterly* 30 (1979): 367–385. journal PR 2885.S63.

> Contending that *The Merchant of Venice* is composed of three trials (Bassanio's selection of the third casket, Antonio's trial, and the ring scene), Benston suggests that Portia, by being somehow involved in all three, unifies the incidents to inform the play's overriding theme of justice. Benston argues that Portia upholds the law (of both her father and Venice) and exposes Shylock as avaricious and unlawful. However, she also suggests that Portia redeems the merchant in the third trial by asking Antonio to release Bassanio from previous commitments.

Bulman, James C. *"The Merchant of Venice": Shakespeare in Performance*. Manchester: Manchester University Press, 1991. PR 2825.B78.

> Analyzing a broad variety of *Merchant of Venice* productions, Bulman illuminates the play's range of possible interpretations as well as the specific plot requirements that may influence each production. In particular, he considers productions by Henry Irving, Theodore Komisarjevsky, Jonathan Miller, and Bill Alexander, noting in the process how each director deals with the disparate elements of the casket/bond plots and Portia's pure/impure motives. Bulman also devotes a significant portion of his analysis to representations of Shylock and how class differences can be highlighted or diminished depending upon each production's emphasis.

Dessen, Alan C. "The Elizabethan Stage Jew and Christian Example: Gerontus, Barabas, and Shylock." *Modern Language Quarterly* 35 (1974): 231–245. journal PB 1.M642.

> Contending that Elizabethan theater often used a "stage Jew" to expose Christian hypocrisy, Dessen suggests that Shylock's principal function is to indict the Christian religion. Highlighting Shylock's attack on Christianity in act 3, scene 1, as well as the play's reference to Christians owning slaves, Dessen proposes that Shakespeare recognized the complexities and contradictions inherent in all religions. Far from condemning Christianity in its entirety, the playwright juxtaposes the generosity of the Duke and Antonio with the sinful actions of less humane Christian characters.

Freud, Sigmund. "The Theme of the Three Caskets." *The Standard Edition of the Complete Psychological Works of Sigmund Freud* 12. Trans. James Strachey et al. London: Hogarth, 1973. 289–302. BF 173.F6253.

> Using his famous dream analysis approach to studying the intricacies of human motivation, Freud advances a psychoanalytic reading of *King Lear*

and *The Merchant of Venice* to suggest that Bassanio's admiration of the leaden casket can only be explained by subconscious motives. The psychologist argues that the casket represents a woman and that the third casket in particular represents a sister figure. Thus, by psychoanalytic displacement, Bassanio desires his sister. As with much of Freud's work, this essay serves as the foundation of later psychological readings of *The Merchant of Venice*.

Grebanier, Bernard. *The Truth About Shylock.* New York: Random House, 1962. PR 2825.G67.

Warning against sentimental readings of *The Merchant of Venice*, Grebanier contends that Shylock is an anti-Semitic Elizabethan representation of Jews as money-hungry, loveless, and irreligious, and he should therefore be viewed as an inaccurate representation of Jewishness. The critic believes that while Shylock is minimized in his one-dimensional devotion to money, the play's other characters (like Antonio, Bassanio, and Portia) are more admirable and three-dimensional. Interestingly, however, Grebanier considers the trial scene to be devoid of irony; it is, he believes, an expression of the victory of truth mixed with mercy.

Gross, John. *Shylock: A Legend and Its Legacy.* New York: Simon and Schuster, 1992. PR 2825.G76.

Offering a comprehensive study of Shylock, Gross divides his book into three historical stages. In the first, he examines the textual and religious elements that went into Shylock's creation; in the second, Gross discusses the primary British and American theatrical interpretations of Shylock up to 1939; and in the third, the author examines Shylock's impact upon world cultures, particularly non-English-speaking cultures. In this final section, Gross pays particular attention to Marxist, psychoanalytical, and cultural approaches to the text.

Holderness, Graham. *William Shakespeare: "The Merchant of Venice."* Penguin Critical Studies. Harmondsworth: Penguin, 1993. PR 2825.H63.

In this comprehensive study of *The Merchant of Venice*, Holderness uses several critical approaches to study the play. Offering perspectives ranging from historicist to poststructuralist, he includes several contradictory essays to indicate the range of interpretations of the play. Holderness also appends a short bibliography for further study, as well as explanatory notes for readers unfamiliar with the broad array of critical approaches mentioned in the book.

Lyon, John. *The Merchant of Venice.* Twayne's New Critical Introductions to Shakespeare. Boston: Twayne, 1988. PR 2825.L96.

Reviewing past critical reception of *The Merchant of Venice*, Lyon evaluates the validity of many past interpretations of the play. In particular, he believes that new theoretical approaches have not contributed very much to the existing body of *Merchant* scholarship. To rebuff such faulty analyses, Lyon encourages readers to arrive at their own conclusions about the play. The book concludes with close readings of each act of the play.

Novy, Marianne L. *Love's Argument: Gender Relations in Shakespeare.* Chapel Hill: Univ. of North Carolina Press, 1984. Chap. 4, 63–82. PR 3069.L6.N6.

Arguing that Shylock and Portia share a commonality in their marginalized status in patriarchal, Christian Venice, Novy suggests that *The Merchant of Venice* is dominated by issues of gender, competition, and mercantilism. She indicates that these issues were prominent in the social, religious, and historical atmosphere of Renaissance England and that Shakespeare attempted to expose these conflicts in dramatic form. Indeed, Novy argues that Shakespeare creates Portia as an aggressor to European patriarchal oppression of femininity, since she combines aspects of both sexual and self-denying women.

O'Rourke, James. "Racism and Homophobia." *ELH* 70:2 (Summer 2003): 375–398. journal PR 1.E5.

O'Rourke attempts to illustrate a connection between Italians and Jews, both thought predisposed to evil, in the Renaissance English imagination. The author claims that his goal, unlike most criticism that lends to an antisemitic analysis of *The Merchant of Venice,* is to demonstrate that Shakespeare was actually writing an anti-racist play by offering playgoers an illuminating juxtaposition of the two cultures.

Penuel, Suzanne. "Castrating the Creditor in *The Merchant of Venice.*" *Studies in English Literature* 44:2 (Spring 2004): 255–275. journal PR 1.S82.

This article connects the creditor–debtor binary present in *The Merchant of Venice* to a parent–child binary (specifically the father). Penuel claims that the tension in the relationships between debtors and creditors is not solely monetary but also reflects displaced filial resentment. The author uses evidence from the text, cultural examples from England (including Shakespeare's own life), and the relationship between Christianity and Judaism.

Stewart, Patrick. "Shylock in *The Merchant of Venice.*" In *Players of Shakespeare: Essays in Shakespearean Performance by Twelve Players with the Royal Shakespeare Company.* Ed. Philip Brockbank. Cambridge: Cambridge University Press, 1985. 11–28. PR 3112.P55.

A classically trained Shakespearean actor now perhaps better known in America as Captain Jean Luc Picard in television's *Star Trek* series, Stewart discusses his performance of Shylock in a recent Royal Shakespeare Company production of *The Merchant of Venice.* The actor notes that he made efforts to avoid stereotypical views of the Jewish character while still allowing Shylock to be vicious, isolated, and nearly mechanical in his lack of human love and feeling. Stewart clearly states, however, that Shylock must use extreme measures to survive in a society that views him as an outcast.

Much Ado About Nothing

Much Ado About Nothing *at the Oregon Shakespearean Festival in Ashland, Oregon, with Richard Farrell as Verges and Sandy McCallum as Dogberry (1999). Photograph by Andree Lanthier.*

The title of *Much Ado About Nothing* (1598) is certainly <u>ironic,</u> since the play deals with such serious topics as a young woman falsely accused of infidelity; her apparent death; and a fiery romance between two independent, strong-willed, high-spirited individuals who are convinced, against their own sexual appetites, that they love each other. As a result, *Much Ado About Something* might be a more accurate description of the <u>comic</u> action of the play. Shakespeare's understated title is interesting in another respect, too. Since the word "nothing" was pronounced like "noting" in Elizabethan English, the play features numerous <u>puns</u> on overhearing, slander, musical notation, and sexuality, all of which help structure the <u>plot</u> and enliven the <u>script.</u> As anyone who has ever been the object of gossip—sexual or otherwise—can attest, it is the "notings" that prompt all the "ado."

Written about the same time as *The Merchant of Venice* (1597), *As You Like It* (1598), and *Twelfth Night* (1600), *Much Ado* exhibits Shakespeare's "mature" comic style, which includes sophisticated <u>verse</u> patterns, wonderfully realistic <u>prose,</u> extended wit combat, and a complex double <u>plot</u> joining together two pairs of lovers: Beatrice and Benedick, the reluctant suitors, and Claudio and his fiancee, Hero, who dies from slander and is then reborn into a happy marriage at the conclusion of the play. Shakespeare's <u>comedy</u> also involves the diabolical plotting of Don John the Bastard, surely a precursor of such later villains as Iago in *Othello* and Edmund in *King Lear,* the hilarious <u>malapropisms</u> of Constable Dogberry and the bumbling Watch; and enough royalty, parents, servants, and other characters to create a believable world in the idyllic Italian village of Messina.

Shakespeare's principal <u>source</u> for the Hero-Claudio plot was undoubtedly the twenty-second story from Matteo Bandello's Italian *Novelle* (1554), which was translated into French by Francois de Belleforest in his *Histoires Tragiques* (1569). The story of the maiden falsely accused surfaces frequently in Greek and Roman romances, however, and is repeated in such Renaissance <u>sources</u> as Edmund Spenser's *The Faerie Queen* (1590) and Ludovico Ariosto's *Orlando Furioso* (originally written in Italian in 1516 and translated into English by Sir John Harrington in 1591). Bandello's version supplies Shakespeare with the central <u>plot,</u> the location of Messina, and such chief characters as Lionato and King Piero of Aragon. No original has been found for Dogberry or the Beatrice-Benedick wooing episodes, although the playwright had shown his fascination with amorous wit combat earlier in *The Taming of the Shrew* (1593) and *Love's Labor's Lost* (1596).

The double <u>plot</u> of *Much Ado* supports a number of important <u>themes</u> and <u>images</u> in addition to the wit combat and the <u>puns</u> on "noting" mentioned above. For example, the <u>motif</u> of death and rebirth—prominent in such later romances as *Cymbeline, Pericles,* and *The Winter's Tale*—is apparent in Hero's miraculous resurrection from the grave, as are the dual views of love, idealized and realistic, represented respectively by the relationships between Hero–Claudio and Beatrice–Benedick. The movement from "real" war at the outset of the play to "amorous" war reminds us of the classical concept of the *miles amores* or "soldier of love"—an <u>oxymoron</u> suggesting that military men, like Claudio in *Much Ado* and Cleopatra's Antony, are out of their depth in affairs of the heart. The popular Renaissance <u>theme</u> of appearance vs. reality is certainly present in the play, especially in such devices as disguise, role playing, and the use of masks. Not surprisingly, the function of language is also crucial. This is a comic universe where people speak beautifully; even Dogberry's <u>malapropisms</u> serve as a <u>parody</u> of the linguistic expertise swirling around him. In addition, the <u>plot</u> relies heavily on dramatic <u>irony,</u> which means that only the audience knows the complete truth at any given moment in the play. Recent scholarship has rekindled interest in such areas as feminist perspectives, role playing, identity, marriage contracts, guilt, male bonding, and courtship rituals during the Renaissance.

The production history of *Much Ado* has been an unqualified success. Described on the title page of the 1600 First <u>Quarto</u> as having been "sundrie times publikely acted," the play was consistently popular through the Restoration and eighteenth century. During the nineteenth century, <u>sets</u> and <u>costumes</u> became increasingly elaborate, while productions featured such notable performers as Sarah Siddons, David Garrick, Anne Brunton, and

Charles Kemble in the coveted roles of Beatrice and Benedick. Creative twentieth-century productions have included John Gielgud's renowned 1949 Renaissance interpretation in Stratford, England; a spirited 1957 "Tex-Mex" rendition in Connecticut (with Alfred Drake and Katharine Hepburn serenaded by mariachi music); Franco Zeffirelli's 1965 Sicilian "Mafia" production at the National Theatre in England; J. J. Antoon's 1972 "Teddy Roosevelt" setting in New York's Central Park (in which the Watch became Keystone Kops); and John Barton's 1976 Stratford production staged in late nineteenth-century India (featuring Judi Dench and Donald Sinden).

Whether it is set in London, Sicily, New Delhi, or Laredo, *Much Ado About Nothing* is sure to please audiences with its unique blend of witty word play, low comedy, moral dilemmas, and genuine romantic love. Readers and viewers of all ages can find someone to identify with in the script's broad range of comic characters. Beneath the apparent humor, however, Shakespeare's play asks some fascinating questions about the raging war between the sexes, the ever-changing roles of men and women in society, and the home-spun virtues of honest, working-class characters. If we look closely at the surface of the play, we can easily see our own reflections on stage before us—which turns the title of the comedy into *Much Ado About Us.*

Much Ado About Nothing *at the Folger Theatre in Washington, D.C., with Rhea Seehorn as Hero and Holly Twyford as Beatrice (foreground) and Rick Foucheux as Leonato, Chuck Young as the Friar, and Cam Magee as Innogen (1998). Photograph by K. W. Cobb.*

Much Ado About Nothing

❦⧉⧉

NAMES OF THE ACTORS

DON PEDRO, *Prince of Aragon*

BENEDICK, *of Padua* ⎱ *lords attending on Don*
CLAUDIO, *of Florence* ⎰ *Pedro*

BALTHASAR, *a singer, attending on Don Pedro*

A BOY, *serving Benedick*

DON JOHN, *the bastard brother of Don Pedro*

BORACHIO ⎱ *followers of Don John*
CONRAD ⎰

LEONATO, *Governor of Messina*

HERO, *his daughter*

BEATRICE, *his niece*

ANTONIO, *an old man, Leonato's brother*

MARGARET ⎱ *waiting gentlewomen, attending on Hero*
URSULA ⎰

FRIAR FRANCIS

DOGBERRY, *the constable in charge of the watch*

VERGES, *the headborough*

A SEXTON

WATCHMEN *(including George Seacoal)*

ATTENDANTS, MESSENGERS, MUSICIANS

SCENE: *Messina*

❦

❦ **1.1°** *Enter Leonato, Governor of Messina, Hero his daughter, and Beatrice his niece, with a Messenger.*

LEONATO   I learn in this letter that Don Pedro of Aragon comes this night to Messina.

MESSENGER   He is very near by this. He was not three leagues off when I left him.

LEONATO   How many gentlemen have you lost in this action?°

MESSENGER   But few of any sort,° and none of name.°

LEONATO   A victory is twice itself when the achiever brings home full numbers. I find here that Don Pedro hath bestowed much honor on a young Florentine called Claudio.

1.1: Messina **s.d.** (Q includes here, and at the opening of 2.1, an entry for "Innogen," Leonato's wife; editors have assumed from the fact that she never speaks and her absence from her daughter's wedding that she was an early thought of Shakespeare's, subsequently incompletely dropped. But she could be played onstage, even in the shadowy form Q offers.)

5

action: battle

sort: rank; **name:** importance

10

DISCOVERING SHAKESPEARE

(1) <u>Themes</u> [1.1.1]: References to letters in a Shakespearean play (see 1.1.1 and 1.1.19) often forecast communication problems elsewhere in the script. Compare, for example, *Romeo and Juliet* (see especially 5.2) and *King Lear* (1.2). After reading these early references to letters in *Much Ado About Nothing,* put a * by each communication problem the characters experience later in the play.

MESSENGER Much deserved on his part, and equally remembered° by Don Pedro. He hath borne himself beyond the promise of his age, doing in the figure of a lamb the feats of a lion. He hath indeed better bettered expectation than you must expect of me to tell you how.

LEONATO He hath an uncle here in Messina will be very much glad of it.

MESSENGER I have already delivered him letters, and there appears much joy in him, even so much that joy could not show itself modest° enough without a badge of bitterness.°

LEONATO Did he break out into tears?

MESSENGER In great measure.

LEONATO A kind° overflow of kindness. There are no faces truer than those that are so washed. How much better is it to weep at joy than to joy at weeping!

BEATRICE I pray you, is Signor Montanto° returned from the wars or no?

MESSENGER I know none of that name, lady. There was none such in the army of any sort.

LEONATO What is he that you ask for, niece?

HERO My cousin means Signor Benedick° of Padua.

MESSENGER O, he's returned, and as pleasant as ever he was.

BEATRICE He set up his bills° here in Messina and challenged Cupid at the flight,° and my uncle's fool,° reading the challenge, subscribed° for Cupid and challenged him at the bird bolt.° I pray you, how many hath he killed and eaten in these wars? But how many hath he killed? For indeed I promised to eat all of his killing.

LEONATO Faith, niece, you tax° Signor Benedick too much, but he'll be meet° with you, I doubt it not.

MESSENGER He hath done good service, lady, in these wars.

BEATRICE You had musty victual,° and he hath holp° to eat it. He is a very valiant trencherman,° he hath an excellent stomach.°

MESSENGER And a good soldier too, lady.

BEATRICE And a good soldier to a lady, but what is he to° a lord?

MESSENGER A lord to a lord, a man to a man, stuffed° with all honorable virtues.

BEATRICE It is so indeed. He is no less than a stuffed man;° but for the stuffing — well, we are all mortal.

---

remembered: rewarded

15

20

modest: moderate
badge of bitterness: i.e., tears

kind: natural   25

Montanto: montanto, an upward thrust in fencing (suggesting a social climber and someone who "mounts" sexually)   30

Benedick: (from Latin *benedictus,* blessed)

35

set up his bills: posted advertisements
at the flight: to an archery duel; **my uncle's fool:** (possibly Beatrice herself)
subscribed: signed (as Cupid's representative)
bird bolt: small blunt arrow allowed to boys as harmless, but also Cupid's arrow   40
tax: criticize
meet: even

45

musty victual: stale provisions; **holp:** helped
trencherman: eater
stomach: appetite

to: in comparison with   50

stuffed: supplied

stuffed man: figure stuffed to look like a man   55

DISCOVERING SHAKESPEARE

(2) Teaser [1.1.28]: In describing Benedick, Beatrice uses the fictitious name "Signor Montanto" (1.1.28)–a term taken from fencing that refers to an upward thrust of the blade (with side glances, no doubt, at social climbing and sexual promiscuity). What do the following other names in the play suggest to you: Beatrice, Benedick, Hero, Leonato, Dogberry, and Verges?

(3) Characterization [1.1.50]: Based solely upon her initial conversation with Leonato and the Messenger, how would you characterize Beatrice's personality? As you read further into the play, come back to this question and revise your impression if your opinion of Beatrice changes substantially from your early analysis of her.

LEONATO   You must not, sir, mistake my niece. There is a kind of merry war betwixt Signor Benedick and her. They never meet but there's a skirmish of wit between them.

BEATRICE   Alas, he gets nothing by that! In our last conflict four of his five wits° went halting° off, and now is the whole man governed with one, so that if he have wit enough to keep himself warm, let him bear° it for a difference° between himself and his horse, for it is all the wealth that he hath left to be known a reasonable° creature. Who is his companion now? He hath every month a new sworn brother.

five wits: mental faculties; **halting:** limping

bear: show (in his coat of arms)
difference: distinguishing mark (heraldic term)
reasonable: capable of reasoning

MESSENGER   Is't possible?

BEATRICE   Very easily possible. He wears his faith° but as the fashion of his hat: it ever changes with the next block.°

faith: truth to his oath

block: hat block – i.e., style

MESSENGER   I see, lady, the gentleman is not in your books.°

books: favor

BEATRICE   No. An° he were, I would burn my study. But I pray you, who is his companion? Is there no young squarer° now that will make a voyage with him to the devil?

An: if

squarer: quarreler

MESSENGER   He is most in the company of the right noble Claudio.

BEATRICE   O Lord, he° will hang upon him like a disease! He is sooner caught than the pestilence,° and the taker° runs presently° mad. God help the noble Claudio! If he have caught the Benedick, it will cost him a thousand pound ere a° be cured.

he: i.e., Benedick
pestilence: plague; **taker:** infected person
presently: immediately

a: he

MESSENGER   I will hold° friends with you, lady.

hold: remain

BEATRICE   Do, good friend.

LEONATO   You will never run mad,° niece.

run mad: i.e., "catch the Benedick"

BEATRICE   No, not till a hot January.

MESSENGER   Don Pedro is approached.

Enter Don Pedro, Claudio, Benedick, Balthasar, and [Don] John the Bastard.

PEDRO   Good Signor Leonato, are you come to meet your trouble?° The fashion of the world is to avoid cost, and you encounter° it.

your trouble: the trouble of entertaining a noble guest
encounter: go to meet

LEONATO   Never came trouble to my house in the likeness of your grace, for trouble being gone, comfort should remain, but when you depart from me, sorrow abides and happiness takes his leave.

PEDRO   You embrace your charge° too willingly. I think this is your daughter.

charge: expense, but also responsibility

LEONATO   Her mother hath many times told me so.

BENEDICK   Were you in doubt, sir, that you asked her?

60

65

70

75

80

85

90

95

100

DISCOVERING SHAKESPEARE

(4) Simile [1.1.80]: In her discussion with the Messenger, Beatrice claims that Benedick will hang on Claudio "like a disease" (1.1.80). Examine this simile in the next four lines of her speech, and explain what other comparisons she uses to help illustrate her point.

(5) Social History [1.1.93]: Immediately after Don Pedro's entrance in 1.1.90, Leonato is obsessively courteous to him (see especially 1.1.93–96). What is the difference in rank between the two characters? Make a list of the principal characters in the play, ranking them from the highest social category down to the lowest.

LEONATO Signor Benedick, no, for then were you a child.

PEDRO You have it full,° Benedick. We may guess by this what you are, being a man. Truly the lady fathers herself.° Be happy, lady, for you are like an honorable father.

BENEDICK If Signor Leonato be her father, she would not have his head° on her shoulders for all Messina, as like him as she is.

BEATRICE I wonder that you will still be talking, Signor Benedick. Nobody marks° you.

BENEDICK What, my dear Lady Disdain! Are you yet living?

BEATRICE Is it possible disdain should die while she hath such meet° food to feed it as Signor Benedick? Courtesy itself must convert° to disdain if you come in her presence.

BENEDICK Then is courtesy a turncoat. But it is certain I am loved of all ladies, only you excepted, and I would I could find in my heart that I had not a hard heart, for truly I love none.

BEATRICE A dear° happiness to women! They would else have been troubled with a pernicious suitor. I thank God and my cold blood, I am of your humor for that.° I had rather hear my dog bark at a crow than a man swear he loves me.

BENEDICK God keep your ladyship still in that mind! So some gentleman or other shall scape a predestinate° scratched face.

BEATRICE Scratching could not make it worse an 'twere such a face as yours were.

BENEDICK Well, you are a rare° parrot teacher.°

BEATRICE A bird of my tongue° is better than a beast of yours.°

BENEDICK I would my horse had the speed of your tongue, and so good a continuer.° But keep your way, a God's name! I have done.

BEATRICE You always end with a jade's trick.° I know you of old.

PEDRO That is the sum of all,° Leonato. Signor Claudio and Signor Benedick, my dear friend Leonato hath invited you all. I tell him we shall stay here at the least a month, and he heartily prays some occasion may detain us longer. I dare swear he is no hypocrite, but prays from his heart.

LEONATO If you swear, my lord, you shall not be forsworn.° *[To Don John]* Let me bid you welcome, my lord. Being° reconciled to the prince your brother, I owe you all duty.

---

have it full: are fully answered

fathers herself: resembles and so indicates her father   105

his head: (with its white hair and beard)

110

marks: notices

meet: suitable   115
convert: change

120

dear: great

humor for that: opinion on that point

125

predestinate: predestined, inevitable

130

rare: exceptional; **parrot teacher:** one who teaches a parrot by repeating monotonously
A bird of my tongue: a bird that speaks
a beast of yours: a dumb beast   135
continuer: one having endurance

a jade's trick: stopping suddenly (in this race of wit) like a recalcitrant horse

sum of all: whole account (of the recent   140
campaign? Don Pedro and Leonato have been talking apart)

145

forsworn: proved a liar
Being: since you are

DISCOVERING SHAKESPEARE

(6) Language [1.1.132]: What does Benedick mean when he calls Beatrice "a rare parrot-teacher" (1.1.132)?

JOHN   I thank you. I am not of many words, but I thank you.   150

LEONATO   *[To Don Pedro]* Please it your grace lead on?

PEDRO   Your hand, Leonato. We will go together.°
Exeunt. Manent° Benedick *and* Claudio.

> **go together:** (the prince refuses to take precedence of his host); **s.d. Manent:** remain

CLAUDIO   Benedick, didst thou note the daughter of Signor Leonato?   155

BENEDICK   I noted° her not, but I looked on her.

> **noted:** noticed especially

CLAUDIO   Is she not a modest young lady?

BENEDICK   Do you question me as an honest man should do, for my simple true judgment? or would you have me speak after my custom, as being a professed tyrant to° their sex?   160

> **tyrant to:** railer against, detractor of

CLAUDIO   No, I pray thee speak in sober judgment.

BENEDICK   Why, i' faith, methinks she's too low° for a high praise, too brown for a fair praise, and too little for a great praise. Only this commendation I can afford her, that were she other than she is, she were unhandsome, and being no other but as she is, I do not like her.   165

> **low:** short

CLAUDIO   Thou thinkest I am in sport. I pray thee tell me truly how thou lik'st her.   170

BENEDICK   Would you buy her, that you inquire after her?

CLAUDIO   Can the world buy such a jewel?

BENEDICK   Yea, and a case° to put it into. But speak you this with a sad brow?° or do you play the flouting jack,° to tell us Cupid is a good hare finder and Vulcan a rare carpenter?° Come, in what key shall a man take you to go° in the song?   175

> **case:** (1) jewel case, (2) clothing, (3) vagina ("it" would then mean "penis")
> **sad brow:** serious mind; **flouting jack:** mocking fellow
> **hare finder . . . carpenter:** (Cupid was blind and therefore hopeless at spotting hares in the field; Vulcan, a blacksmith)
> **go:** join

CLAUDIO   In mine eye she is the sweetest lady that ever I looked on.   180

BENEDICK   I can see yet without spectacles, and I see no such matter. There's her cousin, an she were not possessed with a fury, exceeds her as much in beauty as the first of May doth the last of December. But I hope you have no intent to turn husband, have you?   185

CLAUDIO   I would scarce trust myself, though I had sworn the contrary, if Hero would be my wife.

BENEDICK   Is't come to this? In faith, hath not the world one man but he will wear his cap with suspicion?° Shall I never see a bachelor of threescore again? Go to,° i' faith, an thou wilt needs thrust thy neck into a yoke, wear the print of it and sigh away Sundays.° Look! Don Pedro is returned to seek you.   190

> **with suspicion:** for fear he has grown horns (i.e., been made a cuckold by an unfaithful wife)
> **Go to:** go on
> **sigh away Sundays:** i.e., become a good "Sunday citizen," a responsible and sober married man

Enter Don Pedro.

PEDRO   What secret hath held you here, that you followed not to Leonato's?   195

DISCOVERING SHAKESPEARE

(7) Characterization [1.1.150]: Don John the Bastard is the principal <u>antagonist</u> of the play. What early indications can you find in this scene that forecast his villainy?

(8) <u>Paraphrase</u> [1.1.174]: <u>Paraphrase</u> Benedick's speech to Claudio in 1.1.174–178 in modern English, taking special care to translate such terms as "flouting Jack," "Cupid," "Vulcan," and "rare carpenter" into contemporary <u>idiom</u>. How does Benedick, the confirmed bachelor, feel about the fact that his best friend has fallen in love with Hero?

BENEDICK   I would your grace would constrain° me to tell.

PEDRO   I charge thee on thy allegiance.°

BENEDICK   You hear, Count Claudio. I can be secret as a dumb man, I would have you think so, but, on my allegiance – mark you this – on my allegiance! He is in love. With who? Now that is your grace's part.° Mark how short his answer is: with Hero, Leonato's short daughter.

CLAUDIO   If this were so, so were it uttered.°

BENEDICK   Like the old tale,° my lord: "It is not so, nor 'twas not so, but indeed, God forbid it should be so!"

CLAUDIO   If my passion change not shortly, God forbid it should be otherwise.

PEDRO   Amen, if you love her, for the lady is very well worthy.

CLAUDIO   You speak this to fetch me in,° my lord.

PEDRO   By my troth, I speak my thought.

CLAUDIO   And, in faith, my lord, I spoke mine.

BENEDICK   And, by my two faiths and troths,° my lord, I spoke mine.

CLAUDIO   That I love her, I feel.

PEDRO   That she is worthy, I know.

BENEDICK   That I neither feel how she should be loved, nor know how she should be worthy, is the opinion that fire cannot melt out of me.° I will die in it at the stake.

PEDRO   Thou wast ever an obstinate heretic in the despite° of beauty.

CLAUDIO   And never could maintain his part but in the force of his will.°

BENEDICK   That a woman conceived me, I thank her; that she brought me up, I likewise give her most humble thanks; but that I will have a recheat° winded in my forehead, or hang my bugle in an invisible baldrick,° all women shall pardon me. Because I will not do them the wrong to mistrust any, I will do myself the right to trust none; and the fine° is (for the which I may go the finer),° I will live a bachelor.

PEDRO   I shall see thee, ere I die, look pale with love.

BENEDICK   With anger, with sickness, or with hunger, my lord, not with love. Prove that ever I lose more blood with love° than I will get again with drinking, pick out mine eyes with a ballad-maker's pen° and hang me up at the door of a brothel house for the sign° of blind Cupid.

PEDRO   Well, if ever thou dost fall from this faith, thou wilt prove a notable argument.°

constrain: force

allegiance: loyalty to me as your prince

200

part: speech, in the theatrical sense

so were it uttered: so would he tell it   205
old tale: (a version of the Bluebeard story in which the heroine's report of her discoveries is punctuated by these words of protest from the murderer)

210

fetch me in: trick me

two faiths and troths: one to each (but also   215
double-dealing is implied).

220

fire . . . me: i.e., he will die at the stake for his opinion

in the despite: in showing scorn

225

maintain . . . will: win the argument except by stubborn refusal to give in (punning on "maintain his erection" and "will" as "sexual desire")

recheat: series of notes on a horn sounded to call the hounds together (with the usual reference   230
to the cuckold's horns)

hang . . . baldrick: hang my horn on an invisible shoulder belt (i.e., be unaware of my cuckoldry)

fine: finis, conclusion

finer: more richly dressed (because spared the   235
expense of a wife)

lose . . . love: (lover's sighs were supposed to consume blood)

pick out . . . pen: i.e., let me be blinded by   240
weeping over love laments

sign: printed sign hung outside a shop, inn, or brothel

notable argument: famous example

DISCOVERING SHAKESPEARE

(9) Staging [1.1.196]: How does Claudio respond in 1.1.196–197 when Benedick begs Don Pedro to force him to reveal Claudio's love for Hero?

(10) Language [1.1.232]: Find as many "cuckold" references as you can in 1.1.227–256. Then look up these terms in the *Oxford English Dictionary,* and explain what each of them means.

BENEDICK If I do, hang me in a bottle° like a cat and shoot at me; and he that hits me, let him be clapped on the shoulder and called Adam.°

PEDRO Well, as time shall try.
"In time the savage bull doth bear the yoke."°

BENEDICK The savage bull may, but if ever the sensible° Benedick bear it, pluck off the bull's horns and set them in my forehead, and let me be vilely painted, and in such great letters as they write "Here is good horse to hire," let them signify under my sign "Here you may see Benedick the married man."

CLAUDIO If this should ever happen, thou wouldst be horn-mad.°

PEDRO Nay, if Cupid have not spent all his quiver in Venice,° thou wilt quake° for this shortly.

BENEDICK I look for an earthquake too then.

PEDRO Well, you will temporize with the hours.° In the meantime, good Signor Benedick, repair to Leonato's, commend me to him and tell him I will not fail him at supper, for indeed he hath made great preparation.

BENEDICK I have almost matter° enough in me for such an embassage, and so I commit you —

CLAUDIO To the tuition° of God. From my house — if I had it —

PEDRO The sixth of July. Your loving friend, Benedick.

BENEDICK Nay, mock not, mock not. The body of your discourse is sometime guarded° with fragments, and the guards are but slightly basted° on neither. Ere you flout old ends° any further, examine your conscience. And so I leave you.   *Exit.*

CLAUDIO
My liege, your highness now may do me good.°

PEDRO
My love is thine to teach. Teach it but how,
And thou shalt see how apt° it is to learn
Any hard lesson that may do thee good.

CLAUDIO
Hath Leonato any son, my lord?

PEDRO
No child but Hero; she's his only heir.
Dost thou affect° her, Claudio?

CLAUDIO   O my lord,
When you went onward on this ended action,°
I looked upon her with a soldier's eye,
That liked, but had a rougher task in hand
Than to drive liking to the name of love.
But now I am returned and that° war thoughts

---

bottle: basket or cage (cats were shot as targets)   245

Adam: i.e., Adam Bell, a famous archer

"In time . . . yoke": (proverbial)
sensible: sensitive
250

255

horn-mad: raving mad, also mad with jealousy

Venice: (famous for prostitutes); **quake:** i.e., with fear (with pun on "quiver")

temporize with the hours: weaken with time   260
("hours" may pun on "whores," pronounced similarly)

matter: sense
265

tuition: protection (Claudio is imitating the formal close of a letter)

guarded: trimmed   270
basted: lightly sewed
flout old ends: mock tag ends of wisdom (or cloth)

do me good: do me a favor

275
apt: ready

affect: love, aim at   280

ended action: war just ended

that: because   285

═══════════════════════════════

DISCOVERING SHAKESPEARE

(11) Social Customs [1.1.244]: Why does Benedick ask to be hung in a wicker "bottle like a cat" and shot at with a bow and arrow (1.1.244)? What crime must he commit to be treated so horribly?

(12) Metaphor [1.1.269]: Explain Benedick's metaphor in which he accuses Don Pedro and Claudio of allowing the "body" of their discourse to be "guarded with fragments" (1.1.269–272).

(13) Verse [1.1.285]: At what point in this scene does the language of the play turn from prose to verse? Why does it do so?

Have left their places vacant, in their rooms
Come thronging soft and delicate desires,
All prompting° me how fair young Hero is,
Saying I liked her ere I went to wars.

prompting: reminding

PEDRO

Thou wilt be like a lover presently
And tire the hearer with a book of words.°
If thou dost love fair Hero, cherish it,
And I will break with° her and with her father,
And thou shalt have her. Was't not to this end
That thou began'st to twist° so fine a story?

290

book of words: volume of pretty speeches

break with: broach the subject to

twist: (cf. "spin a yarn")

295

CLAUDIO

How sweetly you do minister to love,
That know love's grief by his complexion!°
But lest my liking might too sudden seem,
I would have salved° it with a longer treatise.°

complexion: appearance (referring to the lover's pallor)

salved: smoothed over; **treatise:** discourse

PEDRO

What need the bridge much broader than the flood?
The fairest grant is the necessity.°
Look, what will serve is fit. 'Tis once,° thou lovest,
And I will fit thee with the remedy.
I know we shall have reveling tonight.
I will assume thy part in some disguise
And tell fair Hero I am Claudio,
And in her bosom° I'll unclasp my heart
And take her hearing prisoner with the force
And strong encounter of my amorous tale.
Then after to her father will I break,
And the conclusion is, she shall be thine.
In practice let us put it presently.°   *Exeunt.*

300

The . . . necessity: the best gift is whatever is needed

once: once for all

305

in her bosom: in private to her

310

presently: immediately

🔖 **1.2°** *Enter Leonato and an old man [Antonio], brother to Leonato [meeting].*

LEONATO   How now, brother? Where is my cousin° your son? Hath he provided this music?

ANTONIO   He is very busy about it. But, brother, I can tell you strange news that you yet dreamt not of.

LEONATO   Are they good?

ANTONIO   As the event stamps° them; but they have a good cover, they show well outward. The prince and Count Claudio, walking in a thick-pleached alley° in mine orchard,° were thus much overheard by a man of mine: the prince discovered° to Claudio that he loved my niece your daughter and meant to acknowledge it this night in a dance, and, if he found her accordant,° he meant to take the present time by the top° and instantly break with you of it.

LEONATO   Hath the fellow any wit that told you this?

1.2: The house of Leonato s.d. *old man* (editors assume that the unnamed old brother of this scene, Leonato's brother Antonio [named at 5.1.91], and the Antonio of 2.1.107 are all the same person, growing in identity as Shakespeare wrote the play)

cousin: kinsman (this nephew is never referred to again and by 5.1.279 has ceased to exist; Shakespeare seems to have slimmed down the household, for a cousin of Hero ought to have challenged Claudio later in the play)

5

event stamps: outcome determines (the figure is of a printed newsbook)

thick-pleached alley: walk lined by trees with interwoven branches

orchard: garden (Shakespeare seems, perhaps carelessly, to have imagined that the conversation at the end of 1.1 was repeated in the orchard)

10

discovered: disclosed

accordant: agreeable

take . . . top: seize the moment

15

DISCOVERING SHAKESPEARE

(14) **Plot** **[1.1.305]:** Why does Don Pedro decide to disguise himself as Claudio? How will this action help further the plot of the play?

ANTONIO   A good sharp fellow. I will send for him, and question him yourself.

LEONATO   No, no. We will hold it as a dream till it appear° itself, but I will acquaint my daughter withal, that she may be the better prepared for an answer, if peradventure° this be true. Go you and tell her of it. *[Enter various people.]*°

Cousins, you know what you have to do. – O, I cry you mercy,° friend. Go you with me, and I will use your skill. – Good cousin, have a care this busy time.

Exeunt.

appear: show

20

peradventure: perhaps

s.d. (some of Leonato's kinsmen, servants, and, perhaps, a musician or two, whose "skill" [l. 24] Leonato will make use of, might be among those bustling across the stage here)

cry you mercy: beg your pardon

❧ **1.3** *Enter [Don] John the Bastard and Conrad, his companion.*

CONRAD   What the goodyear,° my lord! Why are you thus out of measure° sad?

JOHN   There is no measure in the occasion that breeds,° therefore the sadness is without limit.

CONRAD   You should hear reason.

JOHN   And when I have heard it, what blessing brings it?

CONRAD   If not a present remedy, at least a patient sufferance.°

JOHN   I wonder that thou (being, as thou sayst thou art, born under Saturn)° goest about to apply a moral° medicine to a mortifying mischief.° I cannot hide what I am: I must be sad when I have cause, and smile at no man's jests; eat when I have stomach,° and wait for no man's leisure; sleep when I am drowsy, and tend on no man's business; laugh when I am merry, and claw° no man in his humor.

CONRAD   Yea, but you must not make the full show of this till you may do it without controlment.° You have of late stood out° against your brother, and he hath ta'en you newly into his grace,° where it is impossible you should take true root but by the fair weather that you make yourself. It is needful that you frame° the season for your own harvest.

JOHN   I had rather be a canker° in a hedge than a rose in his grace, and it better fits my blood° to be disdained of all than to fashion a carriage° to rob love° from any. In this, though I cannot be said to be a flattering honest man, it must not be denied but I am a plain-dealing villain. I am trusted with a muzzle° and enfranchised with a clog,° therefore I have decreed not to sing in my cage. If I had my mouth, I would bite; if I had my liberty, I would do my liking. In the meantime let me be that I am, and seek not to alter me.

What the goodyear: (mild expostulation, "what the heck")

out of measure: immoderately

breeds: causes it

5

sufferance: endurance

born under Saturn: saturnine, ill-disposed;   10
moral: philosophical
mortifying mischief: deadly disease
stomach: appetite

claw: flatter   15

controlment: restraint
stood out: rebelled
grace: favor   20

frame: create

canker: wild dog rose (despised as a weed)
blood: humor, temper   25
fashion a carriage: assume a manner; **rob love:** gain love undeserved

with a muzzle: but muzzled (i.e., not fully trusted)   30
enfranchised with a clog: freed, but with a ball and chain

DISCOVERING SHAKESPEARE

(15) Staging [1.2.18]: How does Leonato feel about Antonio's revelation that Don Pedro loves Hero? How should the actor playing Leonato react to the news? Should he be happy? Sad? Cautious? Why would you argue for this particular response?

(16) Characterization [1.3.14]: In this scene, we learn more about the motives for Don John's villainy. What three principal reasons does he give for his "discontent" (1.3.34)?

CONRAD   Can you make no use of your discontent?

JOHN   I make all use of it, for I use it only. Who comes here? *Enter Borachio.* What news, Borachio?°

BORACHIO   I came yonder from a great supper. The prince your brother is royally entertained by Leonato, and I can give you intelligence° of an intended marriage.

JOHN   Will it serve for any model to build mischief on? What is he for a fool° that betroths himself to unquietness?

BORACHIO   Marry,° it is your brother's right hand.

JOHN   Who? the most exquisite Claudio?

BORACHIO   Even he.

JOHN   A proper squire!° And who? and who? which way looks he?

BORACHIO   Marry, one Hero, the daughter and heir of Leonato.

JOHN   A very forward March chick!° How came you to this?

BORACHIO   Being entertained for° a perfumer, as I was smoking° a musty room, comes me the prince and Claudio, hand in hand in sad° conference. I whipped me behind the arras° and there heard it agreed upon that the prince should woo Hero for himself, and having obtained her, give her to Count Claudio.

JOHN   Come, come, let us thither. This may prove food to my displeasure. That young start-up hath all the glory of my overthrow. If I can cross him any way, I bless myself every way. You are both sure,° and will assist me?

CONRAD   To the death, my lord.

JOHN   Let us to the great supper. Their cheer is the greater that I am subdued. Would the cook were o' my mind!° Shall we go prove° what's to be done?

BORACHIO   We'll wait upon your lordship.   *[Exeunt.]*

🐝 **2.1**° *Enter Leonato, his brother [Antonio], Hero his daughter, and Beatrice his niece [also Margaret and Ursula].*

LEONATO   Was not Count John here at supper?

ANTONIO   I saw him not.

BEATRICE   How tartly° that gentleman looks! I never can see him but I am heartburned° an hour after.

HERO   He is of a very melancholy disposition.

BEATRICE   He were° an excellent man that were made just in the midway between him and Benedick. The one is too like an image° and says nothing, and the other too like my lady's eldest son,° evermore tattling.

Borachio: (from Spanish for "wine bottle," hence "drunkard") 35

intelligence: news

What is he for a fool: what fool is he 40

Marry: why, to be sure (originally an oath on the name of the Virgin Mary)

proper squire: fine fellow (contemptuous) 45

forward March chick: precocious youngster 50

entertained for: hired as
smoking: sweetening the smell with the smoke of burning herbs
sad: serious (this is yet another account of the conversation at the end of 1.1, which was, supposedly, repeated in the orchard, according to 1.2.9–10) 55
arras: tapestry wall hanging

sure: trustworthy 60

o' my mind: i.e., disposed to poison them; 65
prove: try

2.1: s.d. (Q adds Leonato's wife [see n. to 1.1 s.d.] and an unnamed, mute kinsman; Q gives no entry in the scene for Margaret and Ursula, who are more likely to enter with the rest of Leonato's household than with the maskers)

tartly: sour
am heartburned: have indigestion 5

He were: that man would be

image: statue
my lady's eldest son: a spoiled child who talks too much

DISCOVERING SHAKESPEARE

(17) Teaser [1.3.36]: How does the name "Borachio" (1.3.36) help predict the character's behavior?

(18) Plot [1.3.56]: At this moment in the play, who do Claudio, Don Pedro, Benedick, and Don John each think is in love with Hero? Which characters know the real truth?

LEONATO   Then half Signor Benedick's tongue in Count   10
John's mouth, and half Count John's melancholy in
Signor Benedick's face –

BEATRICE   With a good leg and a good foot,° uncle, and
money enough in his purse,° such a man would win any
woman in the world – if a could get her good will.°

> **foot:** (often a euphemism for "penis")
> **purse:** (punning on "scrotum")
> **good will:** (1) agreement, (2) sexual desire,   15
> (3) genitalia

LEONATO   By my troth, niece, thou wilt never get thee a
husband if thou be so shrewd° of thy tongue.

ANTONIO   In faith, she's too curst.°

BEATRICE   Too° curst is more than curst. I shall lessen
God's sending that way,° for it is said, "God sends a
curst cow short horns,"° but to a cow too curst he sends
none.

> **shrewd:** satirical
> **curst:** shrewish, ill-tempered
> **Too:** (punning on "two")
> **that way:** in that respect   20
> **short horns:** (punning on "small penises")

LEONATO   So, by being too curst, God will send you no
horns.

BEATRICE   Just,° if he send me no husband,° for the which
blessing I am at him upon my knees every morning and
evening. Lord, I could not endure a husband with a
beard on his face. I had rather lie in the woolen!°

> **Just:** exactly; **no husband:** (because she will   25
> not have sex and hence will not cuckold him)
>
> **in the woolen:** between blankets without sheets

LEONATO   You may light on° a husband that hath no
beard.

> **light on:** find
>
> 30

BEATRICE   What should I do with him? dress him in my
apparel and make him my waiting gentlewoman? He
that hath a beard is more than a youth, and he that
hath no beard is less than a man; and he that is more
than a youth is not for me, and he that is less than a
man, I am not for him. Therefore I will even take sixpence in earnest° of the bearherd° and lead his apes° into
hell.

> 35
>
> **in earnest:** as deposit; **bearherd:** (who often
> also kept trained apes); **lead his apes:** (the
> proverbial punishment of women who die virgins)

LEONATO   Well then, go you into hell?

BEATRICE   No, but to the gate, and there will the devil   40
meet me like an old cuckold with horns on his head,
and say, "Get you to heaven, Beatrice, get you to
heaven. Here's no place for you maids." So deliver I up
my apes, and away to Saint Peter. For the heavens,° he
shows me where the bachelors° sit, and there live we as
merry as the day is long.

> **For the heavens:** i.e., (1) as my share of heavens,
> (2) in front of ("'fore"), (3) as an exclamation   45
> **bachelors:** unmarried men and women

ANTONIO   [To Hero] Well, niece, I trust you will be ruled
by your father.

BEATRICE   Yes, faith. It is my cousin's duty to make
curtsy° and say, "Father, as it please you." But yet for all
that, cousin, let him be a handsome fellow, or else make
another curtsy, and say, "Father, as it please me."

> **make curtsy:** curtsy, show respect   50

LEONATO   Well, niece, I hope to see you one day fitted
with a husband.

DISCOVERING SHAKESPEARE

(19) Parable [2.1.19]: Rephrase in modern English Beatrice's little story about why "God sends a curst cow short horns" (2.1.19–22). What is the "moral" of her story? Do you agree with this moral? Why or why not?

(20) Proverbs [2.1.37–38]: Consult M. P. Tilley's *A Dictionary of the Proverbs in England in the Sixteenth and Seventeenth Centuries* to discover the background of the commonplace adage that older, unmarried women would lead apes into hell. See also 1.2.34 in *The Taming of the Shrew*. Which play did Shakespeare write first: *Much Ado About Nothing* or *The Taming of the Shrew*? Why do you think so?

BEATRICE   Not till God make men of some other metal° than earth. Would it not grieve a woman to be overmastered with a piece of valiant dust? to make an account of her life to a clod of wayward marl?° No, uncle, I'll none. Adam's sons are my brethren, and truly I hold it a sin to match in my kindred.°

metal: material 55

marl: clay, earth

match . . . kindred: i.e., wed a brother 60

LEONATO   *[To Hero]* Daughter, remember what I told you. If the prince do solicit you in that kind,° you know your answer.

solicit . . . kind: propose

BEATRICE   The fault will be in the music, cousin, if you be not wooed in good time. If the prince be too important,° tell him there is measure° in everything, and so dance out the answer. For, hear me, Hero: wooing, wedding, and repenting is as a Scotch jig, a measure, and a cinquepace.° The first suit° is hot and hasty like a Scotch jig (and full as fantastical); the wedding, mannerly modest, as a measure, full of state° and ancientry;° and then comes Repentance and with his bad legs falls into the cinquepace faster and faster, till he sink into his grave.

65

important: importunate
measure: moderation (but also a stately dance)

cinquepace: lively dance (pronounced "sink-a-pace," hence the pun at l. 73); **suit:** courtship 70
state: dignity; **ancientry:** traditional formality

LEONATO   Cousin, you apprehend passing shrewdly.°

apprehend passing shrewdly: perceive with unusual sharpness 75

BEATRICE   I have a good eye, uncle, I can see a church by daylight.

LEONATO   The revelers are entering, brother. Make good room.

Enter° [masked] Prince [Don] Pedro, Claudio, and Benedick, and Balthasar; [also, unmasked,] Don John [and Borachio and Musicians, including a Drummer. The dance begins].

s.d.: (F adds "Maskers with a drum" to Q's s.d.; at some point after l. 79 Antonio needs to put on a mask)

PEDRO   *[To Hero]* Lady, will you walk a bout° with your friend?°

a bout: a turn 80
friend: a lover of either sex

HERO   So you walk softly and look sweetly and say nothing, I am yours for the walk; and especially when I walk away.

PEDRO   With me in your company?

85

HERO   I may say so when I please.

PEDRO   And when please you to say so?

HERO   When I like your favor,° for God defend° the lute should be like the case!°

favor: face; **defend:** forbid, prevent
lute . . . case: i.e., your face should be like your mask 90

PEDRO   My visor° is Philemon's° roof; within the house is Jove.

visor: mask; **Philemon:** an old peasant who entertained Jove and Mercury in his humble cottage

HERO   Why then, your visor should be thatched.°

thatched: i.e., whiskered

PEDRO   Speak low if you speak love.

[They dance aside.]

BALTHASAR   *[To Margaret]* Well, I would you did like me.

MARGARET   So would not I for your own sake, for I have many ill qualities.°

95

qualities: traits of character

DISCOVERING SHAKESPEARE

(21) <u>Paraphrase</u> [2.1.56]: Rephrase in modern English the following question by Beatrice: "Would it not grieve a woman to be overmastered with a piece of valiant dust, to make an account of her life to a clod of wayward marl?" (2.1.56–58). Do you agree with her? Why or why not?

(22) Renaissance Dance [2.1.68]: Research the following dances; then demonstrate each of them in class: the Scotch jig, the measure, and the cinquepace (2.1.68–69).

BALTHASAR   Which is one?

MARGARET   I say my prayers aloud.

BALTHASAR   I love you the better. The hearers may cry
amen.   100

MARGARET   God match me with a good dancer!

BALTHASAR   Amen.

MARGARET   And God keep him out of my sight when
the dance is done! Answer, clerk.°

> **clerk:** (the parish clerk read the responses in church services)   105

BALTHASAR   No more words. The clerk is answered.
[They dance aside.]

URSULA   *[To Antonio]* I know you well enough. You are
Signor Antonio.

ANTONIO   At a word, I am not.

URSULA   I know you by the waggling° of your head.

> **waggling:** shaking (with old age?)   110

ANTONIO   To tell you true, I counterfeit him.

URSULA   You could never do him so ill-well° unless you
were the very man. Here's his dry hand° up and down.°
You are he, you are he!

> **do him so ill-well:** imitate his ills so well
> **dry hand:** (a sign of age); **up and down:** exactly

ANTONIO   At a word, I am not.

URSULA   Come, come, do you think I do not know you
by your excellent wit? Can virtue hide itself? Go to,
mum, you are he. Graces° will appear, and there's an end.
[They dance aside.]   115

> **Graces:** good qualities

BEATRICE   *[To Benedick]* Will you not tell me who told
you so?

BENEDICK   No, you shall pardon me.   120

BEATRICE   Nor will you not tell me who you are?

BENEDICK   Not now.

BEATRICE   That I was disdainful, and that I had my good
wit out of the *Hundred Merry Tales.*° Well, this was
Signor Benedick that said so.

> **Hundred Merry Tales:** a popular book of crude comic stories, first published in 1526   125

BENEDICK   What's he?

BEATRICE   I am sure you know him well enough.

BENEDICK   Not I, believe me.

BEATRICE   Did he never make you laugh?

BENEDICK   I pray you, what is he?   130

BEATRICE   Why, he is the prince's jester, a very dull fool.
Only his gift° is in devising impossible° slanders. None
but libertines° delight in him, and the commendation is
not in his wit, but in his villainy,° for he both pleases
men and angers them, and then they laugh at him and
beat him. I am sure he is in the fleet.° I would he had
boarded° me.

> **Only his gift:** his only gift; **impossible:** incredible
> **libertines:** freethinkers, loose livers
> **villainy:** rudeness   135
> **fleet:** company of maskers (with play on "sea fleet")
> **boarded:** assaulted (nautical term)

BENEDICK   When I know the gentleman, I'll tell him
what you say.

BEATRICE   Do, do. He'll but break a comparison° or two
on me; which peradventure, not marked or not laughed

> **break a comparison:** tilt with words   140

DISCOVERING SHAKESPEARE

(23) Teaser [2.1.109]: When Ursula claims to recognize Antonio by the "waggling" of his head (2.1.109) and his "dry hand" (2.1.112), which specific diseases might Antonio have had that would produce these symptoms? Which Shakespearean plays feature characters who exhibit signs of epilepsy and Alzheimer's disease?

(24) Staging [2.1.134]: When does Beatrice begin to see through Benedick's disguise? What proof can you offer to support your contention?

at, strikes him into melancholy, and then there's a
partridge wing° saved, for the fool will eat no supper
that night. *[Music.]* We must follow the leaders.°

partridge wing: (considered a great delicacy)
leaders: (in the dance)

145

BENEDICK   In every good thing.

BEATRICE   Nay, if they lead to any ill, I will leave them at
the next turning.

Dance. Exeunt [all but Don John,
Borachio, and Claudio].

JOHN   *[To Borachio]* Sure my brother is amorous on Hero
and hath withdrawn her father to break with him about
it. The ladies follow her and but one visor remains.

150

BORACHIO   And that is Claudio. I know him by his
bearing.

JOHN   *[To Claudio]* Are not you Signor Benedick?

CLAUDIO   You know me well. I am he.

JOHN   Signor, you are very near my brother in his love.
He is enamored on Hero. I pray you dissuade him from
her; she is no equal for his birth. You may do the part of
an honest man in it.

155

CLAUDIO   How know you he loves her?

JOHN   I heard him swear his affection.

160

BORACHIO   So did I too, and he swore he would marry
her tonight.

JOHN   Come, let us to the banquet.°

banquet: light dessert after "supper," 2.1.1

Exeunt. Manet Claudio.

CLAUDIO
Thus answer I in name of Benedick
But hear these ill news with the ears of Claudio.

165

'Tis certain so. The prince woos for himself.
Friendship is constant in all other things
Save in the office° and affairs of love.

office: business, employment

Therefore all° hearts in love use their own tongues.

all: let all

Let every eye negotiate for itself

170

And trust no agent, for beauty is a witch
Against whose charms faith melteth into blood.°

blood: passion

This is an accident of hourly proof,°

accident . . . proof: common occurrence

Which I mistrusted° not. Farewell therefore Hero!

mistrusted: suspected

Enter Benedick.

BENEDICK   Count Claudio?

175

CLAUDIO   Yea, the same.

BENEDICK   Come, will you go with me?

CLAUDIO   Whither?

BENEDICK   Even to the next willow, about your own
business, county.° What fashion will you wear the

county: count

180

garland° of? about your neck,° like an usurer's chain? or

garland: i.e., of willow, symbol of forsaken love;
about your neck: i.e., as a symbol of wealth

under your arm,° like a lieutenant's scarf? You must wear
it one way, for the prince hath got your Hero.

under your arm: across your chest

CLAUDIO   I wish him joy of her.

DISCOVERING SHAKESPEARE

(25) Staging [2.1.153]: Does Don John really think that the disguised Claudio is Benedick? Why do you believe this is
true?

(26) Plot [2.1.176]: Why is Claudio hurt and angry here? What does he think has happened? What has actually occurred?

BENEDICK   Why, that's spoken like an honest drover.° So they sell bullocks. But did you think the prince would have served you thus?

drover: cattle trader   185

CLAUDIO   I pray you leave me.

BENEDICK   Ho! now you strike like the blind man!° 'Twas the boy that stole your meat, and you'll beat the post.°

the blind man: (unidentified allusion to a proverb or familiar story)   190
post: (1) pillar, (2) messenger

CLAUDIO   If it will not be,° I'll leave you.   *Exit.*

If . . . be: if you will not go

BENEDICK   Alas, poor hurt fowl, now will he creep into sedges.° But, that my Lady Beatrice should know me, and not know me! The prince's fool! Ha! it may be I go under that title because I am merry. Yea, but so I am apt to do myself wrong. I am not so reputed. It is the base (though bitter)° disposition of Beatrice that puts the world into her person° and so gives me out.° Well, I'll be revenged as I may.
    Enter the Prince [Don Pedro].°

sedges: reeds

195

bitter: biting
puts . . . person: attributes to the world her own personal feelings
gives me out: reports me
s.d. (Q's s.d. here is almost certainly wrong in giving entrances for Don John, Borachio, and Conrad; F gives an entry for Don Pedro alone, but Hero and Leonato could enter here [as in Q] and stand apart, rather than entering at, say, 247 with Claudio and Beatrice, where F marks their entry—this would make Benedick's "this young lady," at l. 205, a direct reference—or they could enter at l. 284)   200

205

PEDRO   Now, signor, where's the count? Did you see him?

BENEDICK   Troth, my lord, I have played the part of Lady Fame.° I found him here as melancholy as a lodge in a warren.° I told him, and I think I told him true, that your grace had got the good will of this young lady, and I offered him my company to a willow tree, either to make him a garland, as being forsaken, or to bind him up a rod, as being worthy to be whipped.

Lady Fame: bearer of tidings
lodge . . . warren: gamekeeper's hut in a game reserve (symbol of isolation)

PEDRO   To be whipped? What's his fault?

BENEDICK   The flat° transgression of a schoolboy who, being overjoyed with finding a bird's nest, shows it his companion, and he steals it.

flat: plain   210

PEDRO   Wilt thou make a trust a transgression? The transgression is in the stealer.

BENEDICK   Yet it had not been amiss the rod had been made, and the garland too, for the garland he might have worn himself, and the rod he might have bestowed on you, who, as I take it, have stolen his bird's nest.

215

PEDRO   I will but teach them to sing and restore them to the owner.

220

BENEDICK   If their singing answer your saying,° by my faith you say honestly.

If . . . saying: if it turns out as you say

PEDRO   The Lady Beatrice hath a quarrel to you. The gentleman that danced with her told her she is much wronged° by you.

225

wronged: slandered

BENEDICK   O, she misused° me past the endurance of a block! An oak but with one green leaf on it would have answered her; my very visor began to assume life and scold with her. She told me, not thinking I had been myself, that I was the prince's jester, that I was duller than a great thaw,° huddling jest upon jest with such

misused: abused

230

thaw: (when roads are impassable and one must stay at home)

DISCOVERING SHAKESPEARE

(27) History [2.1.202–203]: Who was Lady Fame, and what was her relationship to gossip?
(28) Paraphrase [2.1.222–223]: Paraphrase into modern English the following speech by Benedick: "If their singing answer your saying, by my faith you say honestly" (2.1.222–223).

impossible conveyance° upon me that I stood like a man at a mark,° with a whole army shooting at me. She speaks poniards,° and every word stabs. If her breath were as terrible as her terminations,° there were no living near her; she would infect° to the North Star. I would not marry her though she were endowed with all that Adam had left him before he transgressed. She would have made Hercules have turned spit,° yea, and have cleft his club to make the fire too. Come, talk not of her. You shall find her the infernal Ate° in good apparel. I would to God some scholar would conjure her,° for certainly, while she is here, a man may live as quiet in hell as in a sanctuary, and people sin upon purpose, because they would go thither. So indeed all disquiet, horror, and perturbation follows° her.

Enter Claudio and Beatrice [Leonato and Hero].

PEDRO　Look, here she comes.

BENEDICK　Will your grace command me any service to the world's end? I will go on the slightest errand now to the Antipodes that you can devise to send me on, I will fetch you a toothpicker° now from the furthest inch of Asia, bring you the length of Prester John's° foot, fetch you a hair off the Great Cham's° beard, do you any embassage to the Pygmies,° rather than hold three words' conference with this harpy.° You have no employment for me?

PEDRO　None, but to desire your good company.

BENEDICK　O God, sir, here's a dish I love not! I cannot endure my Lady Tongue.　*Exit.*

PEDRO　Come, lady, come, you have lost the heart of Signor Benedick.

BEATRICE　Indeed, my lord, he lent it me awhile, and I gave him use° for it – a double heart for his single one. Marry, once before he won it of me with false dice;° therefore your grace may well say I have lost it.

PEDRO　You have put him down,° lady; you have put him down.

BEATRICE　So I would not he should do me, my lord, lest I should prove the mother of fools. I have brought Count Claudio, whom you sent me to seek.

PEDRO　Why, how now, count? Wherefore are you sad?

CLAUDIO　Not sad, my lord.

---

impossible conveyance: incredible dexterity
at a mark: beside a target
poniards: daggers　235
terminations: terms (i.e., name-calling)
infect: emit foul odors (supposed to carry infection)

Hercules . . . spit: (The Amazon Omphale　240 enslaved Hercules and set him to spinning dressed as a woman. Turning a spit was an even more humble chore, assigned to a boy or even a dog.)
Ate: goddess of discord
conjure her: (scholars were supposed to have the power to call up or dismiss evil spirits)　245

follows: attends on

250

toothpicker: toothpick
Prester John: a mythical Christian monarch of Ethiopia
Cham: Khan of Tartary, ruler of the Mongols　255
Pygmies: a legendary race of dwarfs said to dwell in Ethiopia or in the Far East
harpy: a mythical predatory creature, with a woman's face and body and a bird's wings and claws

260

use: interest
double heart . . . dice: (she gave him her heart　265 but he deceived her)

put him down: humiliated him (Beatrice at 269 punningly takes it as "having sex with him")

270

DISCOVERING SHAKESPEARE

(29) Staging [2.1.238]: If you were directing a production of this play, exactly when would you have Beatrice enter this scene? (*Hint:* Remember that she could appear to the audience long before Don Pedro actually sees her in 2.1.260.) How much of Benedick's speeches in 2.1.227–257 would she hear? How would she react to them?

(30) Geography [2.1.249]: Find a globe of the world, and locate on it the following places mentioned in Benedick's speech in 2.1.249–257: the Antipodes, Asia, Ethiopia (Prester John's kingdom), China (ruled by the Great Cham or Kubla Khan), and the Far East (thought, incorrectly, to be home to the pigmies). For more details on these and other exotic locations, see Sir John Mandeville's *Voyages and Travels* (1583).

(31) Plot [2.1.266]: Beatrice's confession to Don Pedro that Benedick had "lent" her his heart for a while and won her heart "with false dice" (2.1.263–266) implies that the two had enjoyed a relationship prior to the beginning of the play, but that he had ended it. Do you agree with this "prior history"? In the space below, explain what you think happened between Beatrice and Benedick before the action of the play.

PEDRO   How then? Sick?

CLAUDIO   Neither, my lord. 275

BEATRICE   The count is neither sad, nor sick, nor merry, nor well; but civil count – civil° as an orange, and something of that jealous complexion.°

PEDRO   I' faith, lady, I think your blazon° to be true, though I'll be sworn, if he be so, his conceit° is false. Here, Claudio, I have wooed in thy name, and fair Hero is won. I have broke with her father, and his good will obtained. Name the day of marriage, and God give thee joy!

LEONATO   Count, take of me my daughter, and with her my fortunes. His grace hath made the match, and all grace° say amen to it!

BEATRICE   Speak, count, 'tis your cue.

CLAUDIO   Silence is the perfectest herald of joy. I were but little happy if I could say how much. *[To Hero]* Lady, as you are mine, I am yours. I give away myself for you and dote upon the exchange.

BEATRICE   *[To Hero]* Speak, cousin, or, if you cannot, stop his mouth with a kiss and let not him speak neither.

PEDRO   In faith, lady, you have a merry heart.

BEATRICE   Yea, my lord, I thank it. Poor fool,° it keeps on the windy° side of care. My cousin tells him in his ear that he is in her heart.

CLAUDIO   And so she doth, cousin.

BEATRICE   Good Lord, for alliance!° Thus goes everyone to the world° but I, and I am sunburned.° I may sit in a corner and cry "Heigh-ho for a husband!"°

PEDRO   Lady Beatrice, I will get° you one.

BEATRICE   I would rather have one of your father's getting.° Hath your grace ne'er a brother like you? Your father got excellent husbands, if a maid could come by them.

PEDRO   Will you have me, lady?

BEATRICE   No, my lord, unless I might have another for working days: your grace is too costly to wear every day. But I beseech your grace pardon me. I was born to speak all mirth and no matter.°

PEDRO   Your silence most offends me, and to be merry best becomes you, for out o' question you were born in a merry hour.

BEATRICE   No, sure, my lord, my mother cried, but then there was a star danced, and under that was I born. *[To Hero and Claudio]* Cousins, God give you joy!

LEONATO   Niece, will you look to those things I told you of?°

---

civil: grave, sober (with a pun on "oranges of Seville")

of . . . complexion: i.e., yellow (symbolic of jealousy) 280

blazon: description (heraldic term)

conceit: conception, idea (with the additional suggestion here, after *blazon,* of the fanciful device painted on a knight's shield)

285

all grace: i.e., God, the source of all grace

290

295

fool: innocent creature

windy: windward, safe

for alliance: (Claudio has just called her *cousin* in 300 anticipation of becoming her cousin by marriage)

goes . . . world: everybody gets married

sunburned: i.e., suntanned and therefore unattractive

"Heigh-ho for a husband": (from an old 305 song)

get: procure

getting: begetting

310

matter: substance

315

things I told you of: (Does Leonato invent 320 those tasks to cover an awkward moment?)

DISCOVERING SHAKESPEARE

(32) Staging [2.1.295]: Stage 2.1.288–302 in class, paying particular attention to the moment when Claudio and Hero kiss and when she whispers in his ear.

(33) Characterization [2.1.308]: How serious do you think Don Pedro is when he asks Beatrice if she would be interested in marrying him? How graceful is her reply? How do you think Don Pedro would respond to her refusal?

BEATRICE   I cry you mercy, uncle. *[To Don Pedro]* By your grace's pardon.°   *Exit Beatrice.*

By your grace's pardon: excuse me

PEDRO   By my troth, a pleasant-spirited lady.

LEONATO   There's little of the melancholy element in her, my lord. She is never sad but when she sleeps, and not ever sad then, for I have heard my daughter say she hath often dreamt of unhappiness and waked herself with laughing.

325

PEDRO   She cannot endure to hear tell of a husband.

330

LEONATO   O, by no means! She mocks all her wooers out of suit.°

mocks . . . suit: makes fun of them until they do not dare to woo her

PEDRO   She were an excellent wife for Benedick.

LEONATO   O Lord, my lord, if they were but a week married, they would talk themselves mad.

PEDRO   County Claudio, when mean you to go to church?

335

CLAUDIO   Tomorrow, my lord. Time goes on crutches till Love have all his rites.

LEONATO   Not till Monday, my dear son, which is hence a just sevennight, and a time too brief too, to have all things answer my mind.°

340

answer my mind: as I wish them

PEDRO   Come, you shake the head at so long a breathing, but I warrant thee, Claudio, the time shall not go dully by us. I will in the interim undertake one of Hercules' labors, which is, to bring Signor Benedick and the Lady Beatrice into a mountain of affection th' one with th' other. I would fain° have it a match, and I doubt not but to fashion it if you three will but minister such assistance as I shall give you direction.

345

fain: gladly

LEONATO   My lord, I am for you, though it cost me ten nights' watchings.°

350

watchings: staying awake

CLAUDIO   And I, my lord.

PEDRO   And you too, gentle Hero?

HERO   I will do any modest office, my lord, to help my cousin to a good husband.

355

PEDRO   And Benedick is not the unhopefulest husband that I know. Thus far can I praise him: he is of a noble strain,° of approved valor, and confirmed honesty. I will teach you how to humor your cousin, that she shall fall in love with Benedick; and I, *[To Leonato and Claudio]* with your two helps, will so practice on Benedick that, in despite° of his quick wit and his queasy° stomach, he shall fall in love with Beatrice. If we can do this, Cupid is no longer an archer; his glory shall be ours, for we are the only love gods. Go in with me, and I will tell you my drift.°   *Exit [with the others].*

strain: family

360

in despite: in spite
queasy: delicate

365

drift: plan

DISCOVERING SHAKESPEARE

(34) History [2.1.324]: When Leonato explains that "There's little of the melancholy element" in Beatrice (2.1.324), he is commenting on the mixture of the four humors in her personality (black bile, blood, phlegm, and choler). Which of the characters in this play exhibit symptoms of melancholy? (*Hint:* Cf. 2.1.5 in *Much Ado* and Robert Burton's *Anatomy of Melancholy,* 1621). Compare also the descriptions of Kate and Petruchio in *The Taming of the Shrew* as choleric personalities (see especially 4.1.158–166 and 4.3.19–30 in *Shrew*).

(35) Mythology [2.1.344]: What were the twelve labors imposed on Hercules by Hera? What new labor does Don Pedro propose here?

❧ **2.2** *Enter [Don] John and Borachio.*

JOHN It is so. The Count Claudio shall marry the daughter of Leonato.

BORACHIO Yea, my lord, but I can cross it.

JOHN Any bar, any cross, any impediment will be medicinable° to me. I am sick in displeasure to him, and whatsoever comes athwart his affection ranges evenly with mine.° How canst thou cross this marriage?

BORACHIO Not honestly, my lord, but so covertly° that no dishonesty shall appear in me.

JOHN Show me briefly how.

BORACHIO I think I told your lordship, a year since, how much I am in the favor of Margaret, the waiting gentle-woman to Hero.

JOHN I remember.

BORACHIO I can, at any unseasonable instant of the night, appoint her to look out at her lady's chamber window.

JOHN What life is in that to be the death of this marriage?

BORACHIO The poison of that lies in you to temper.° Go you to the prince your brother, spare not to tell him that he hath wronged his honor in marrying the renowned Claudio (whose estimation° do you mightily hold up) to a contaminated stale,° such a one as Hero.

JOHN What proof shall I make of that?

BORACHIO Proof enough to misuse the prince, to vex Claudio, to undo Hero, and kill Leonato. Look you for any other issue?

JOHN Only to despite° them I will endeavor anything.

BORACHIO Go then, find me a meet hour° to draw Don Pedro and the Count Claudio alone, tell them that you know that Hero loves me, intend° a kind of zeal both to the prince and Claudio, as, in love of your brother's honor, who hath made this match, and his friend's reputation, who is thus like to be cozened° with the semblance° of a maid, that you have discovered thus. They will scarcely believe this without trial. Offer them instances,° which shall bear no less likelihood than to see me at her chamber window, hear me call Margaret Hero, hear Margaret term me Claudio; and bring them to see this the very night before the intended wedding (for in the meantime I will so fashion the matter that Hero shall be absent) and there shall appear such seeming truth of Hero's disloyalty that jealousy° shall be called assurance° and all the preparation overthrown.

medicinable: curative 5

whatsoever . . . mine: whatever vexes his love suits me
covertly: secretly

10

15

temper: compound, mix 20

estimation: reputation
stale: prostitute

25

despite: spite
meet hour: suitable time 30

intend: pretend

cozened: deceived, cheated 35
semblance: outward appearance

instances: proofs

40

jealousy: suspicion
assurance: proof 45

DISCOVERING SHAKESPEARE

(36) Staging [2.2.1]: Where does this brief scene between Don John and Borachio take place? What time of day is it? Try to determine how many days pass during the entire play.

(37) <u>Plot</u> [2.1.31]: In your own words, explain Borachio's plan to discredit Hero. How much money does Don John promise to pay him for carrying out this deception? How much do you think this would be worth in modern dollars?

JOHN   Grow this to what adverse issue it can, I will put it in practice. Be cunning in the working this, and thy fee is a thousand ducats.°

ducats: gold coins

BORACHIO   Be you constant in the accusation, and my cunning shall not shame me.

JOHN   I will presently° go learn their day of marriage.

Exit [with Borachio].

50

presently: immediately

❧ **2.3** *Enter Benedick alone.*

BENEDICK   Boy!

[Enter Boy.]

BOY   Signor?

BENEDICK   In my chamber window lies a book. Bring it hither to me in the orchard.

BOY   I am here already, sir.

5

BENEDICK   I know that, but I would have thee hence and here again. *Exit [Boy].* I do much wonder that one man, seeing how much another man is a fool when he dedicates his behaviors to love, will, after he hath laughed at such shallow follies in others, become the argument° of his own scorn by falling in love; and such a man is Claudio. I have known when there was no music with him but the drum and the fife, and now had he rather hear the tabor and the pipe.° I have known when he would have walked ten mile afoot to see a good armor,° and now will he lie ten nights awake carving° the fashion of a new doublet.° He was wont to speak plain and to the purpose, like an honest man and a soldier, and now is he turned orthography;° his words are a very fantastical banquet – just so many strange dishes. May I be so converted° and see with these eyes?° I cannot tell. I think not. I will not be sworn but love may transform me to an oyster; but I'll take my oath on it, till he have made an oyster of me he shall never make me such a fool. One woman is fair, yet I am well; another is wise, yet I am well; another virtuous, yet I am well. But till all graces be in one woman, one woman shall not come in my grace. Rich she shall be, that's certain; wise, or I'll none; virtuous, or I'll never cheapen° her; fair, or I'll never look on her; mild, or come not near me; noble, or not I for an angel;° of good discourse, an excellent musician, and her hair shall be of what color it please God. Ha, the prince and Monsieur Love! I will hide me in the arbor.   *[He hides.]*

Enter Prince [Don Pedro], Leonato, Claudio.

10

argument: subject

drum . . . pipe: (drum and fife were used for military music, tabor and pipe for festivities)   15
armor: suit of armor
carving: designing
doublet: jacket
orthography: fashionable and overelaborate in his choice and pronunciation of words   20
converted: changed; **these eyes:** the eyes of a lover

25

cheapen: bargain for

30

noble . . . angel: (play on the names of gold coins; the noble was worth about a third less than the angel)

DISCOVERING SHAKESPEARE

(38) Verse [2.3.7]: Notice that Claudio's earliest soliloquy is in verse (2.1.164 ff.), while Benedick's is in prose (2.3.7 ff.). Why do these two men "think" differently on stage? Does it have anything to do with the fact that one man is in love, and the other isn't? What other factors might influence the form of these soliloquies?

PEDRO
  Come, shall we hear this music?   35
CLAUDIO
  Yea, my good lord. How still the evening is,
  As hushed on purpose to grace harmony!
PEDRO
  See you where Benedick hath hid himself?
CLAUDIO
  O, very well, my lord. The music ended,
  We'll fit the kid fox with a pennyworth.°

  Enter Balthasar with music.°

fit . . . pennyworth: give the sly young fellow   40
all he bargained for ("kid fox" is often emended to
"hid fox," a children's hiding game); **s.d. with
music:** (either "with musicians" or "with a
musical instrument")

PEDRO
  Come, Balthasar, we'll hear that song again.
BALTHASAR
  O, good my lord, tax not so bad a voice
  To slander music any more than once.
PEDRO
  It is the witness° still of excellency

witness: evidence

  To put a strange face on° his own perfection.

put . . . on: pretend not to know   45

  I pray thee sing, and let me woo no more.
BALTHASAR
  Because you talk of wooing, I will sing,
  Since many a wooer doth commence his suit
  To her he thinks not worthy, yet he woos,
  Yet will he swear he loves.   50
PEDRO   Nay, pray thee come,
  Or if thou wilt hold longer argument,°

argument: talk

  Do it in notes.
BALTHASAR   Note this before my notes:
  There's not a note of mine that's worth the noting.
PEDRO
  Why, these are very crotchets° that he speaks!

crotchets: notes of half the value of a minim,
quibbles

  Note notes, forsooth, and nothing!°   55

nothing: (pronounced the same as *noting* above,
and so punned on)

  [Music.]
BENEDICK   *[Aside]* Now divine air! Now is his soul rav-

hale: draw

  ished! Is it not strange that sheep's guts should hale°
  souls out of men's bodies? Well, a horn° for my money,

horn: (for hunting or military calls)

  when all's done.
BALTHASAR

                    The Song.
          Sigh no more, ladies, sigh no more.   60
            Men were deceivers ever,
        One foot in sea, and one on shore,
            To one thing constant never.
              Then sigh not so,
              But let them go,
          And be you blithe and bonny,°   65

bonny: carefree

DISCOVERING SHAKESPEARE

(39) <u>Verse</u> [2.3.36]: Why does the scene shift into <u>verse</u> at this point? Which characters speak predominantly in <u>verse</u> in the play and which in <u>prose</u>? Why is this the case?

(40) History [2.3.57]: As Benedick implies, "sheeps' guts" (2.3.57) were used to make strings for musical instruments. What other materials were employed to construct guitars, lutes, and other stringed instruments? Why does Benedick prefer horns (58)?

> Converting all your sounds of woe
> Into Hey nonny, nonny.
>
> Sing no more ditties, sing no moe,
> Of dumps° so dull and heavy.
> The fraud of men was ever so,
> Since summer first was leafy.
> Then sigh not so, etc.

dumps: sad songs, usually love songs   70

PEDRO   By my troth, a good song.

BALTHASAR   And an ill singer, my lord.   75

PEDRO   Ha, no, no, faith! Thou sing'st well enough for a shift.°

for a shift: at a pinch

BENEDICK   *[Aside]* An he had been a dog that should have howled thus, they would have hanged him, and I pray God his bad voice bode no mischief. I had as lief° have heard the night raven,° come what plague could have come after it.

lief: willingly   80
night raven: (portent of disaster)

PEDRO   Yea, marry. Dost thou hear, Balthasar? I pray thee get us some excellent music, for tomorrow night we would have it at the Lady Hero's chamber window.   85

BALTHASAR   The best I can, my lord.

PEDRO   Do so. Farewell. *Exit Balthasar [with music].* Come hither, Leonato. What was it you told me of today? that your niece Beatrice was in love with Signor Benedick?   90

CLAUDIO   O, ay! — *[Aside to Pedro]* Stalk on, stalk on; the fowl sits.° — I did never think that lady would have loved any man.

the fowl sits: (the victim's ready)

LEONATO   No, nor I neither, but most wonderful that she should so dote on Signor Benedick, whom she hath in all outward behaviors seemed ever to abhor.   95

BENEDICK   *[Aside]* Is't possible? Sits the wind in that corner?

LEONATO   By my troth, my lord, I cannot tell what to think of it, but that she loves him with an enraged° affection, it is past the infinite° of thought.

enraged: frenzied   100
infinite: furthest reach

PEDRO   May be she doth but counterfeit.

CLAUDIO   Faith, like enough.

LEONATO   O God, counterfeit? There was never counterfeit of passion came so near the life of passion as she discovers° it.   105

discovers: reveals

PEDRO   Why, what effects of passion shows she?

CLAUDIO   *[Aside]* Bait the hook well! This fish will bite.

LEONATO   What effects, my lord? She will sit you — you heard my daughter tell you how.   110

CLAUDIO   She did indeed.

DISCOVERING SHAKESPEARE

(41) Symbols [2.3.81]: Benedick mentions a "night-raven" as a bad omen in 2.3.81. What other birds and beasts predicted disaster during the Renaissance? (*Hint:* See *Julius Caesar,* 2.2.13–26, and *Macbeth,* 2.2.1–8.)

(42) Staging [2.3.109]: Most productions have Leonato forget the agreed upon "script" at this point (2.3.109–110), which means that Claudio and Don Pedro must come to his rescue and make up examples of Beatrice's affection for Benedick. Which of the following lines do you think are invented on the spot by Claudio and Don Pedro?

PEDRO   How, how, I pray you? You amaze me. I would have thought her spirit had been invincible against all assaults of affection.

LEONATO   I would have sworn it had, my lord – especially against Benedick. 115

BENEDICK   *[Aside]* I should think this a gull° but that the white-bearded fellow speaks it. Knavery cannot, sure, hide himself in such reverence.

gull: hoax, trick

CLAUDIO   *[Aside]* He hath ta'en th' infection. Hold° it up. 120

Hold: keep

PEDRO   Hath she made her affection known to Benedick?

LEONATO   No, and swears she never will. That's her torment.

CLAUDIO   'Tis true indeed. So your daughter says. "Shall I," says she, "that have so oft encountered him with scorn, write to him that I love him?" 125

LEONATO   This says she now when she is beginning to write to him, for she'll be up twenty times a night, and there will she sit in her smock° till she have writ a sheet of paper. My daughter tells us all.

smock: garment that served as both slip and nightdress 130

CLAUDIO   Now you talk of a sheet of paper, I remember a pretty jest your daughter told us of.

LEONATO   O, when she had writ it, and was reading it over, she found "Benedick" and "Beatrice" between the sheet?°

between the sheet: in the folded sheet of paper, with pun on "bedsheets" 135

CLAUDIO   That.

LEONATO   O, she tore the letter into a thousand halfpence,° railed at herself that she should be so immodest to write to one that she knew would flout° her. "I measure him," says she, "by my own spirit, for I should flout him if he writ to me. Yea, though I love him, I should."

halfpence: i.e., small pieces
flout: mock 140

CLAUDIO   Then down upon her knees she falls, weeps, sobs, beats her heart, tears her hair, prays, curses – "O sweet Benedick! God give me patience!" 145

LEONATO   She doth indeed; my daughter says so. And the ecstasy° hath so much overborne her that my daughter is sometime afeard she will do a desperate outrage to herself. It is very true.

ecstasy: excess of passion

PEDRO   It were good that Benedick knew of it by some other, if she will not discover it. 150

CLAUDIO   To what end? He would make but a sport of it and torment the poor lady worse.

PEDRO   An he should, it were an alms° to hang him! She's an excellent sweet lady, and (out of all suspicion) she is virtuous.

an alms: a good deed 155

CLAUDIO   And she is exceeding wise.

PEDRO   In everything but in loving Benedick.

LEONATO   O, my lord, wisdom and blood° combating in so tender a body, we have ten proofs to one that blood

blood: nature, natural feeling, passion 160

DISCOVERING SHAKESPEARE

(43) Teaser [2.3.137]: In what other early Shakespearean comedy is a letter torn to pieces? Which of these two plays did Shakespeare write first?

(44) Metaphor [2.3.159]: What does Leonato mean when he says, "O my lord, wisdom and blood combating in so tender a body, we have ten proofs to one that blood hath the victory" (2.3.159–162)?

hath the victory. I am sorry for her, as I have just cause, being her uncle and her guardian.

PEDRO   I would she had bestowed this dotage° on me. I would have doffed° all other respects° and made her half myself. I pray you tell Benedick of it and hear what a will say.

dotage: doting affection
doffed: put aside; **respects:** considerations

165

LEONATO   Were it good, think you?

CLAUDIO   Hero thinks surely she will die, for she says she will die if he love her not, and she will die ere she make her love known, and she will die, if he woo her, rather than she will bate° one breath of her accustomed crossness.

170

bate: abate, give up

PEDRO   She doth well. If she should make tender° of her love, 'tis very possible he'll scorn it, for the man (as you know all) hath a contemptible° spirit.

tender: offer

contemptible: contemptuous   175

CLAUDIO   He is a very proper° man.

proper: handsome

PEDRO   He hath indeed a good outward happiness.°

outward happiness: attractive exterior

CLAUDIO   Before God, and in my mind, very wise.

PEDRO   He doth indeed show some sparks that are like wit.°

wit: intelligence   180

CLAUDIO   And I take him to be valiant.

PEDRO   As Hector,° I assure you, and in the managing of quarrels you may say he is wise, for either he avoids them with great discretion, or undertakes them with a most Christianlike fear.

Hector: the most valiant Trojan

185

LEONATO   If he do fear God, a must necessarily keep peace. If he break the peace, he ought to enter into a quarrel with fear and trembling.

PEDRO   And so will he do, for the man doth fear God, howsoever it seems not in him by° some large jests he will make. Well, I am sorry for your niece. Shall we go seek Benedick and tell him of her love?

by: to judge by   190

CLAUDIO   Never tell him, my lord. Let her wear it out with good counsel.°

counsel: reflection

195

LEONATO   Nay, that's impossible; she may wear her heart out first.

PEDRO   Well, we will hear further of it by your daughter. Let it cool the while. I love Benedick well, and I could wish he would modestly examine himself to see how much he is unworthy so good a lady.

200

LEONATO   My lord, will you walk? Dinner is ready.

CLAUDIO   [Aside] If he do not dote on her upon this, I will never trust my expectation.

PEDRO   [Aside] Let there be the same net spread for her, and that must your daughter and her gentlewomen carry.° The sport will be, when they hold one an opinion of another's dotage,° and no such matter. That's the scene that I would see, which will be merely a dumb show.° Let us send her to call him in to dinner.

carry: manage   205

they . . . dotage: each thinks the other is in love
dumb show: pantomime (because they can no longer carry on their usual banter)

[Exeunt Don Pedro, Claudio, and Leonato.]

DISCOVERING SHAKESPEARE

(45) Mythology [2.3.182]: Who was Hector (2.3.182), and why was he "valiant"?

(46) Teaser [2.3.208]: What was a "dumb show" (2.3.208)? In which Shakespearean plays are dumb shows actually presented on stage?

BENEDICK *[Advancing]* This can be no trick. The conference was sadly borne;° they have the truth of this from Hero; they seem to pity the lady. It seems her affections have their full bent.° Love me? Why, it must be requited. I hear how I am censured. They say I will bear myself proudly if I perceive the love come from her. They say too that she will rather die than give any sign of affection. I did never think to marry. I must not seem proud. Happy are they that hear their detractions° and can put them to mending. They say the lady is fair — 'tis a truth, I can bear them witness; and virtuous — 'tis so, I cannot reprove° it; and wise, but for loving me — by my troth, it is no addition to her wit, nor no great argument of her folly, for I will be horribly in love with her. I may chance have some odd quirks° and remnants of wit broken on me because I have railed so long against marriage. But doth not the appetite alter? A man loves the meat in his youth that he cannot endure in his age. Shall quips and sentences° and these paper bullets° of the brain awe° a man from the career of his humor?° No, the world must be peopled. When I said I would die a bachelor, I did not think I should live till I were married. Here comes Beatrice. *Enter Beatrice.* By this day, she's a fair lady! I do spy some marks of love in her.

BEATRICE Against my will I am sent to bid you come in to dinner.

BENEDICK Fair Beatrice, I thank you for your pains.

BEATRICE I took no more pains for those thanks than you take pains to thank me. If it had been painful, I would not have come.

BENEDICK You take pleasure then in the message?

BEATRICE Yea, just so much as you may take upon a knife's point, and choke a daw withal.° You have no stomach,° signor? Fare you well. *Exit.*

BENEDICK Ha! "Against my will I am sent to bid you come in to dinner." There's a double meaning in that. "I took no more pains for those thanks than you took pains to thank me." That's as much as to say, "Any pains that I take for you is as easy as thanks." If I do not take pity of her, I am a villain; if I do not love her, I am a Jew.° I will go get her picture. *Exit.*

❧ **3.1°** *Enter Hero and two Gentlewomen, Margaret and Ursula.*

HERO

Good Margaret, run thee to the parlor.
There shalt thou find my cousin Beatrice

Glosses (right column):

210

sadly borne: seriously carried on

affections . . . bent: emotions are like a bow fully bent

215

their detractions: themselves criticized

220

reprove: disprove

quirks: quips, quibbles

225

sentences: maxims, wise sayings; **paper bullets:** words; **awe:** frighten
career of his humor: action he fancies   230

235

240

daw withal: jackdaw with
stomach: appetite

245

Jew: (Elizabethan stereotype of lack of Christian charity)   250

3.1: Leonato's garden

DISCOVERING SHAKESPEARE

(47) Language [2.3.229–230]: What does Benedick mean when he says "The world must be peopled" (2.3.229–230)?

(48) History [2.3.249–250]: When Benedick says "If I do not love her, I am a Jew" (2.3.249–250), most scholars take that remark to imply that he would not see himself as a "faithful" lover. If you were directing a production of this play, would you retain this racist reference and thereby risk offending some of your audience members, or would you cut or somehow edit the line? Why would you do so?

Proposing° with the prince and Claudio.   **Proposing:** conversing
Whisper her ear and tell her I and Ursley
Walk in the orchard, and our whole discourse   5
Is all of her. Say that thou overheard'st us,
And bid her steal into the pleachèd° bower,   **pleachèd:** hidden by thickly interwoven branches
Where honeysuckles, ripened° by the sun,   **ripened:** brought to full development
Forbid the sun to enter – like favorites,
Made proud by princes, that advance their pride   10
Against that power that bred it. There will she hide her
To listen our propose.° This is thy office.   **propose:** conversation
Bear thee well in it and leave us alone.°   **leave us alone:** leave the rest to us

MARGARET
I'll make her come, I warrant you, presently.°   *[Exit.]*   **presently:** immediately

HERO
Now, Ursula, when Beatrice doth come,   15
As we do trace° this alley up and down,   **trace:** walk along
Our talk must only be of Benedick.
When I do name him, let it be thy part
To praise him more than ever man did merit.
My talk to thee must be how Benedick   20
Is sick in love with Beatrice. Of this matter
Is little Cupid's crafty arrow made,
That only wounds by hearsay.
    Enter Beatrice [and hides].   Now begin,
For look where Beatrice like a lapwing° runs   **lapwing:** kind of plover
Close by the ground, to hear our conference.   25

URSULA
The pleasant'st angling is to see the fish
Cut with her golden oars° the silver stream   **oars:** i.e., fins
And greedily devour the treacherous bait.
So angle we for Beatrice, who even now
Is couchèd° in the woodbine° coverture.°   **couchèd:** hidden; **woodbine:** honeysuckle;   30
Fear you not my part of the dialogue.   **coverture:** arbor

HERO
Then go we near her, that her ear lose nothing
Of the false sweet bait that we lay for it.
    [They move to where Beatrice is hiding.]
No, truly, Ursula, she is too disdainful.
I know her spirits are as coy° and wild   **coy:** disdainful   35
As haggards° of the rock.   **haggards:** untamed mature female hawks

URSULA   But are you sure
That Benedick loves Beatrice so entirely?

HERO
So says the prince, and my new-trothèd lord.

URSULA
And did they bid you tell her of it, madam?

HERO
They did entreat me to acquaint her of it,   40
But I persuaded them, if they loved Benedick,

DISCOVERING SHAKESPEARE

(49) <u>Paraphrase</u> [3.1.21]: <u>Paraphrase</u> in modern English the following statement by Hero: "Of this matter / Is little Cupid's crafty arrow made, / That only wounds by hearsay" (3.1.21–23).

To wish him wrestle with affection
And never to let Beatrice know of it.
URSULA
Why did you so? Doth not the gentleman
Deserve as full° as fortunate a bed   **as full:** fully   45
As ever Beatrice shall couch upon?
HERO
O god of love! I know he doth deserve
As much as may be yielded to a man.
But nature never framed a woman's heart
Of prouder stuff than that of Beatrice.   50
Disdain and scorn ride sparkling in her eyes,
Misprizing° what they look on, and her wit   **Misprizing:** undervaluing, mistaking
Values itself so highly that to her
All matter else seems weak. She cannot love,
Nor take no shape nor project° of affection,   **project:** idea, notion   55
She is so self-endeared.
URSULA   Sure I think so,
And therefore certainly it were not good
She knew his love, lest she'll make sport at it.
HERO
Why, you speak truth. I never yet saw man,
How wise, how noble, young, how rarely featured,   60
But she would spell him backward.° If fair-faced,   **spell him backward:** turn him inside out
She would swear the gentleman should be her sister;
If black,° why, nature, drawing of an antic,°   **black:** dark-complexioned; **antic:** grotesque
Made a foul blot; if tall, a lance ill-headed;   figure, buffoon
If low, an agate° very vilely cut;   **agate:** figure carved on an agate and so very   65
If speaking, why, a vane° blown with° all winds;   small
If silent, why, a block movèd with none.   **vane:** weather vane; **with:** by
So turns she every man the wrong side out
And never gives to truth and virtue that
Which simpleness° and merit purchaseth.   **simpleness:** plain sincerity   70
URSULA
Sure, sure, such carping° is not commendable.   **carping:** faultfinding
HERO
No, not to be so odd, and from° all fashions,   **from:** contrary to
As Beatrice is, cannot be commendable.
But who dare tell her so? If I should speak,
She would mock me into air, O, she would laugh me   75
Out of myself, press me to death° with wit!   **press me to death:** (The usual penalty in
Therefore let Benedick, like covered fire,   England for refusing to plead guilty or not guilty.
Consume away in sighs,° waste inwardly.   Weights were piled on the victim's body until he
It were a better death than die with mocks,   either pleaded or died.)
Which is as bad as die with tickling.   **Consume . . . sighs:** (since each sigh was held
                                                     to cost the heart a drop of blood)   80

DISCOVERING SHAKESPEARE

(50) Staging [3.1.47]: Why is the gulling of Beatrice in <u>verse</u>, while the earlier scene tricking Benedick (2.3) was in <u>prose</u>? How could each dramatic medium provide different staging possibilities?

(51) Metaphor [3.1.61]: What does Hero mean when she tells Ursula that Beatrice would "spell" a man "backward" (3.1.61)? (*Hint:* See 3.1.68.)

(52) Metaphor [3.1.76]: Hero's fear that Beatrice would "press me to death with wit" (3.1.76) alludes to the torture method of placing heavy weights on a person's body till he either confessed his crime or died (see also 5.1.268). What other forms of torture were common during the English Renaissance? Do you feel these punishments were more or less barbaric than our own?

URSULA
  Yet tell her of it. Hear what she will say.

HERO
  No, rather I will go to Benedick
  And counsel him to fight against his passion.
  And truly, I'll devise some honest slanders°   **honest slanders:** adverse criticisms, but not of
  To stain my cousin with. One doth not know   such a nature as to impugn her honesty (i.e., her   85
  How much an ill word may empoison liking.   chastity)

URSULA
  O, do not do your cousin such a wrong!
  She cannot be so much without true judgment
  (Having so swift and excellent a wit
  As she is prized° to have) as to refuse   **prized:** esteemed   90
  So rare a gentleman as Signor Benedick.

HERO
  He is the only man of Italy,
  Always excepted my dear Claudio.

URSULA
  I pray you be not angry with me, madam,   95
  Speaking my fancy: Signor Benedick,
  For shape, for bearing,° argument,° and valor,   **bearing:** deportment; **argument:** discourse
  Goes foremost in report through Italy.

HERO
  Indeed he hath an excellent good name.

URSULA
  His excellence did earn it ere he had it.
  When are you married, madam?   100

HERO
  Why, every day tomorrow!° Come, go in.   **every day tomorrow:** tomorrow and forever
  I'll show thee some attires, and have thy counsel   after
  Which is the best to furnish° me tomorrow.   **furnish:** dress

URSULA [Aside]
  She's limed,° I warrant you! We have caught her, madam.   **limed:** caught with birdlime

HERO [Aside]
  If it prove so, then loving goes by haps.°   **haps:** chance   105
  Some Cupid kills with arrows, some with traps.
                        [Exeunt Hero and Ursula.]

BEATRICE [Coming forward]
  What fire is in mine ears?° Can this be true?   **What . . . ears:** how my ears burn
     Stand I condemned for pride and scorn so much?
  Contempt, farewell! and maiden pride, adieu!
     No glory lives behind the back of such.°   **No . . . such:** the proud and contemptuous are   110
  And, Benedick, love on, I will requite thee,   never praised except to their faces
     Taming my wild heart to thy loving hand.°   **Taming . . . hand:** (the hawk figure again)
  If thou dost love, my kindness shall incite thee
     To bind our loves up in a holy band,
  For others say thou dost deserve, and I   115
  Believe it better than reportingly.°   *Exit.*   **better than reportingly:** not merely as hearsay

---

DISCOVERING SHAKESPEARE

(53) Rhyme [3.1.105]: Hero's rhyming couplet in 3.1.105–106 introduces the rhyme in Beatrice's following speech (lines 107–116). What is the rhyme scheme of her speech? Why do you think it ends with the slant rhyme between "I" and "reportingly" (lines 115–116)? Is this the first time Beatrice speaks in verse in the play? If so, why?

🙚 **3.2** *Enter Prince [Don Pedro], Claudio, Benedick, and Leonato.*

PEDRO   I do but stay till your marriage be consummate, and then go I toward Aragon.

CLAUDIO   I'll bring you thither, my lord, if you'll vouch-safe° me.

PEDRO   Nay, that would be as great a soil in the new gloss of your marriage as to show a child his new coat and forbid him to wear it. I will only be bold with° Benedick for his company, for, from the crown of his head to the sole of his foot, he is all mirth. He hath twice or thrice cut Cupid's bowstring, and the little hangman° dare not shoot at him. He hath a heart as sound as a bell, and his tongue is the clapper, for what his heart thinks, his tongue speaks.

BENEDICK   Gallants, I am not as I have been.

LEONATO   So say I. Methinks you are sadder.°

CLAUDIO   I hope he be in love.

PEDRO   Hang him, truant!° There's no true drop of blood in him to be truly touched with love. If he be sad, he wants money.

BENEDICK   I have the toothache.°

PEDRO   Draw° it.

BENEDICK   Hang it!

CLAUDIO   You must hang it first and draw it afterwards.

PEDRO   What? sigh for the toothache?

LEONATO   Where is but a humor° or a worm.°

BENEDICK   Well, everyone can master a grief° but he that has it.

CLAUDIO   Yet say I he is in love.

PEDRO   There is no appearance of fancy in him, unless it be a fancy° that he hath to strange disguises,° as to be a Dutchman today, a Frenchman tomorrow, or in the shape of two countries at once, as a German from the waist downward, all slops,° and a Spaniard from the hip upward, no doublet.° Unless he have a fancy to this fool-ery, as it appears he hath, he is no fool for fancy,° as you would have it appear he is.

CLAUDIO   If he be not in love with some woman, there is no believing old signs. A brushes his hat o' mornings. What should that bode?

PEDRO   Hath any man seen him at the barber's?

CLAUDIO   No, but the barber's man hath been seen with him, and the old ornament of his cheek hath already stuffed tennis balls.°

vouchsafe: permit

5

be bold with: ask

hangman: executioner, rogue   10

sadder: more serious   15

truant: (from love)

toothache: (supposed to be common among   20
lovers)
Draw: extract (but with punning reference
below to the hanging, drawing, and quartering of
traitors)

humor: one of the four bodily fluids, in this case   25
rheum; **worm:** (supposed to cause toothache)
grief: physical as well as mental pain

fancy . . . fancy: love . . . whim   30
strange disguises: (the Englishman's dress was a
perennial joke)
slops: loose breeches
no doublet: (wearing a short Spanish cloak over
his doublet)
   35
fool for fancy: i.e., lover

   40

ornament . . . balls: i.e., his beard has been
shaved (tennis balls were stuffed with curled hair)

DISCOVERING SHAKESPEARE

(54) Costumes [3.2.1]: Describe Benedick's clothing before he falls in love. How is he different in this scene in terms of dress, mannerisms, and attitude?

(55) Staging [3.2.24]: In most productions of the play, Benedick begins this scene with a handkerchief or bandage covering part of his face, which signifies that he has a toothache (and also hides the fact that he has recently shaved off his beard). At what point in the scene do you think Claudio and Don Pedro discover that Benedick is now clean-shaven? Why has he shaved off his beard?

(56) Teaser [3.2.43]: What were Renaissance "tennis balls" (3.2.43) made of? When and where did the game first de-velop, and how was it different from the game we play today?

LEONATO   Indeed he looks younger than he did, by the loss of a beard. 45

PEDRO   Nay, a rubs himself with civet.° Can you smell him out° by that?

    civet: (a popular perfume)
    smell him out: (1) smell him, (2) work out his secret

CLAUDIO   That's as much as to say, the sweet youth's in love.

PEDRO   The greatest note of it is his melancholy. 50

CLAUDIO   And when was he wont to wash his face?°

    wash his face: apply cosmetics

PEDRO   Yea, or to paint himself? for the which I hear what they say of him.

CLAUDIO   Nay, but his jesting spirit, which is now crept into a lute string, and now governed by stops.° 55

    stops: fingerings, or positions, marked for the fingers on the fingerboard of a lute, the lover's instrument

PEDRO   Indeed that tells a heavy tale for him. Conclude, conclude, he is in love.

CLAUDIO   Nay, but I know who loves him.

PEDRO   That would I know too. I warrant, one that knows him not. 60

CLAUDIO   Yes, and his ill conditions,° and in despite of all, dies for him.°

    ill conditions: bad qualities
    dies . . . him: (punning on "die" as "have an orgasm")

PEDRO   She shall be buried with her face upwards.°

    face upwards: (because she will have "died," had an orgasm, when on her back under Benedick during intercourse)

BENEDICK   Yet is this no charm° for the toothache. Old° signor, walk aside with me. I have studied eight or nine wise words to speak to you, which these hobbyhorses° must not hear.   *[Exeunt Benedick and Leonato.]* 65

    charm: i.e., cure; **Old:** (a term of respect)
    hobbyhorses: buffoons (originally an antic figure in a morris dance)

PEDRO   For my life,° to break with him about Beatrice!

    For my life: upon my life

CLAUDIO   'Tis even so. Hero and Margaret have by this played their parts with Beatrice, and then the two bears will not bite one another when they meet. 70

    Enter John the Bastard.

JOHN   My lord and brother, God save you.

PEDRO   Good den,° brother.

    Good den: good evening

JOHN   If your leisure served, I would speak with you.

PEDRO   In private? 75

JOHN   If it please you. Yet Count Claudio may hear, for what I would speak of concerns him.

PEDRO   What's the matter?

JOHN   *[To Claudio]* Means your lordship to be married tomorrow? 80

PEDRO   You know he does.

JOHN   I know not that, when he knows what I know.

CLAUDIO   If there be any impediment, I pray you discover° it.

    discover: disclose

JOHN   You may think I love you not. Let that appear hereafter, and aim better at me° by that I now will manifest. For my brother, I think he holds you well and in dearness of heart° hath holp° to effect your ensuing marriage — surely suit ill spent and labor ill bestowed! 85

    aim . . . me: judge better of me

    dearness of heart: friendship; **holp:** helped

DISCOVERING SHAKESPEARE

(57) History [3.2.63]: Don Pedro's prediction that Beatrice will be "buried with her face upward" (3.2.63) is not only a sexual pun, but also a commentary on Renaissance burial practices. How were corpses buried at that time? When did coffins come into vogue?

(58) Language [3.2.85]: What linguistic clues can you find in Don John's speech in 3.2.85–89 that suggest he is lying to Claudio and Don Pedro?

PEDRO   Why, what's the matter?   90

JOHN   I came hither to tell you, and, circumstances shortened° (for she has been too long a-talking of),° the lady is disloyal.°

CLAUDIO   Who? Hero?

JOHN   Even she – Leonato's Hero, your Hero, every man's Hero.

CLAUDIO   Disloyal?

JOHN   The word is too good to paint out° her wickedness. I could say she were worse; think you of a worse title, and I will fit her to it. Wonder not till further warrant.° Go but with me tonight, you shall see her chamber window entered, even the night before her wedding day. If you love her then, tomorrow wed her. But it would better fit your honor to change your mind.

CLAUDIO   May this be so?

PEDRO   I will not think it.

JOHN   If you dare not trust that you see, confess not that° you know. If you will follow me, I will show you enough; and when you have seen more and heard more, proceed accordingly.

CLAUDIO   If I see anything tonight why I should not marry her tomorrow, in the congregation° where I should wed there will I shame her.

PEDRO   And, as I wooed for thee to obtain her, I will join with thee to disgrace her.

JOHN   I will disparage her no farther till you are my witnesses. Bear it coldly° but till midnight, and let the issue show itself.

PEDRO   O day untowardly° turned!

CLAUDIO   O mischief strangely thwarting!

JOHN   O plague° right well prevented!°

So will you say when you have seen the sequel.

                                            [Exeunt.]

3.3° *Enter Dogberry and his compartner [Verges],° with the Watch.°*

DOGBERRY   Are you good men and true?

VERGES   Yea, or else it were pity but they should suffer salvation,° body and soul.

DOGBERRY   Nay, that were a punishment too good for them if they should have any allegiance° in them, being chosen for the prince's watch.°

VERGES   Well, give them their charge,° neighbor Dogberry.

DOGBERRY   First, who think you the most desertless° man to be constable?°

---

circumstances shortened: circumstantial details omitted
a-talking of: talked of
disloyal: unfaithful   95

paint out: portray

till further warrant: till further assured by proof   100

that: what

congregation: company   115

coldly: coolly

untowardly: unfavorably, unluckily   120

plague: misfortune; **prevented:** forestalled

3.3: A street in Messina s.d. *Dogberry* (from the shrub dogwood); **Verges:** (probably from "verge," a staff of office); **Watch:** (Exactly how many watchmen there are [at least three] and who speaks which lines are unclear; the speech prefix is often simply *Watch,* suggesting Shakespeare might have left it to the actors to decide who spoke which lines. I have kept to Q's speech prefixes except at 88, 96, and 106, which I have assigned to the Second Watchman, George Seacoal, who is the leader of the watch.)   5
salvation: (his mistake for "damnation")
allegiance: (for "treachery")
watch: men chosen to police the streets at night
charge: orders   10
desertless: (for "deserving")
constable: deputy leader of the watch (Dogberry is the *right master constable,* 3.3.164)

DISCOVERING SHAKESPEARE

(59) Paraphrase [3.2.103–104]: Paraphrase in modern English the following line by Don John: "But it would better fit your honor to change your mind" (3.2.103–104).

FIRST WATCHMAN   Hugh Oatcake, sir, or George Seacoal, for they can write and read.

DOGBERRY   Come hither, neighbor Seacoal. God hath blessed you with a good name. To be a well-favored° man is the gift of fortune, but to write and read comes by nature.

well-favored: handsome

15

SECOND WATCHMAN [GEORGE SEACOAL]   Both which, master constable –

DOGBERRY   You have. I knew it would be your answer. Well, for your favor,° sir, why, give God thanks and make no boast of it, and for your writing and reading, let that appear when there is no need of such vanity. You are thought here to be the most senseless° and fit man for the constable of the watch. Therefore bear you the lantern. This is your charge: you shall comprehend° all vagrom° men; you are to bid any man stand, in the prince's name.

favor: appearance

20

senseless: (for "sensible")

comprehend: (for "apprehend")

25

vagrom: vagrant

SECOND WATCHMAN   How if a will not stand?

DOGBERRY   Why then, take no note of him, but let him go, and presently call the rest of the watch together and thank God you are rid of a knave.

30

VERGES   If he will not stand when he is bidden, he is none of the prince's subjects.

DOGBERRY   True, and they are to meddle with none but the prince's subjects. You shall also make no noise in the streets, for, for the watch to babble and to talk is most tolerable,° and not to be endured.

35

tolerable: (for "intolerable")

A WATCHMAN   We will rather sleep than talk. We know what belongs to° a watch.

belongs to: is the duty of

DOGBERRY   Why, you speak like an ancient° and most quiet watchman, for I cannot see how sleeping should offend. Only have a care that your bills° be not stolen. Well, you are to call at all the alehouses and bid those that are drunk get them to bed.

ancient: elderly, staid

40

bills: halberds (long poles with combination ax and spear heads carried chiefly as a badge of office)

A WATCHMAN   How if they will not?

45

DOGBERRY   Why then, let them alone till they are sober. If they make you not then the better answer, you may say they are not the men you took them for.

A WATCHMAN   Well, sir.

DOGBERRY   If you meet a thief, you may suspect him, by virtue of your office, to be no true° man, and for such kind of men, the less you meddle or make° with them, why, the more is° for your honesty.

50

true: honest

meddle or make: associate

the more is: the better it is

A WATCHMAN   If we know him to be a thief, shall we not lay hands on him?

55

DISCOVERING SHAKESPEARE

(60) Names [3.3.11]: How would the names "Hugh Oatcake" and "George Seacoal" (3.3.11) help a casting director select actors to play these two members of the watch? How would the two men probably be dressed in a Renaissance period production of the play? In 3.5.54–55, Dogberry refers to a "Francis" Seacoal. Do you think this is Shakespeare's mistake or Dogberry's? Why do you feel this way?

(61) <u>Props</u> [3.3.40]: What sort of "bills" (3.3.42) did the members of the watch carry? What other <u>props</u> might be used by Dogberry, Verges, and the watch in this scene?

DOGBERRY   Truly, by your office you may, but I think they that touch pitch will be defiled.° The most peaceable way for you, if you do take a thief, is to let him show himself what he is, and steal out of your company.

VERGES   You have been always called a merciful man, partner.

DOGBERRY   Truly, I would not hang a dog by my will, much more° a man who hath any honesty in him.

VERGES   If you hear a child cry in the night, you must call to the nurse and bid her still it.

A WATCHMAN   How if the nurse be asleep and will not hear us?

DOGBERRY   Why then, depart in peace and let the child wake her with crying, for the ewe that will not hear her lamb when it baas will never answer a calf° when he bleats.

VERGES   'Tis very true.

DOGBERRY   This is the end of the charge: you, constable, are to present° the prince's own person. If you meet the prince in the night, you may stay him.

VERGES   Nay, by'r Lady,° that I think a cannot.

DOGBERRY   Five shillings to one on't with any man that knows the statutes,° he may stay him! Marry, not without the prince be willing; for indeed the watch ought to offend no man, and it is an offense° to stay a man against his will.

VERGES   By'r Lady, I think it be so.

DOGBERRY   Ha, ah, ha!° Well, masters, good night. An there be any matter of weight chances, call up me. Keep your fellows' counsels and your own, and good night. *[To Verges]* Come, neighbor.

SECOND WATCHMAN   Well, masters, we hear our charge. Let us go sit here upon the church bench till two, and then all to bed.

DOGBERRY   One word more, honest neighbors. I pray you watch about Signor Leonato's door, for the wedding being there tomorrow, there is a great coil° tonight. Adieu. Be vigitant,° I beseech you.

Exeunt [Dogberry and Verges].

Enter Borachio and Conrad.

BORACHIO   What, Conrad!

SECOND WATCHMAN   *[Aside]* Peace! stir not!

BORACHIO   Conrad, I say!

CONRAD   Here, man. I am at thy elbow.

BORACHIO   Mass,° and my elbow itched! I thought there would a scab° follow.

they . . . defiled: (paraphrased from Ecclesiasticus 13:1)

more: (for "less")

calf: (Dogberry's comparison has led him to call the watchman a calf, or dolt)

present: represent

by'r Lady: by Our Lady (a mild oath)

statutes: acts of Parliament (but the principle actually belongs to common law)

offense: (in the legal sense)

Ha, ah, ha: (a laugh of triumph)

coil: bustle
vigitant: (for "vigilant")

Mass: (a mild interjection; originally, by the mass)
scab: i.e., an itching scab, with play on slang term for a scurvy fellow

60

65

70

75

80

85

90

95

100

DISCOVERING SHAKESPEARE

(62) Plot [3.3.66]: Later in the scene, Shakespeare allows the inept, bumbling members of the watch to discover the conspiracy against Hero. How does this wonderful plot device help us appreciate the playwright's fondness for working-class characters?

(63) Staging [3.3.96]: If you were directing a production of this play, how would you stage this scene in which the watch is spying on Borachio and Conrad, with both groups of characters in full view of the audience? What use, if any, would you make of the upper stage, the inner below, and/or the voms?

CONRAD   I will owe thee an answer° for that, and now forward with thy tale.

BORACHIO   Stand thee close then under this penthouse,° for it drizzles rain, and I will, like a true drunkard,° utter all to thee.

SECOND WATCHMAN   *[Aside]* Some treason, masters. Yet stand close.

BORACHIO   Therefore know I have earned of Don John a thousand ducats.

CONRAD   Is it possible that any villainy should be so dear?°

BORACHIO   Thou shouldst rather ask if it were possible any villainy should be so rich, for when rich villains have need of poor ones, poor ones may make what price they will.

CONRAD   I wonder at it.

BORACHIO   That shows thou art unconfirmed.° Thou knowest that the fashion of a doublet, or a hat, or a cloak, is nothing to a man.

CONRAD   Yes, it is apparel.

BORACHIO   I mean the fashion.

CONRAD   Yes, the fashion is the fashion.

BORACHIO   Tush! I may as well say the fool's the fool. But seest thou not what a deformed thief° this fashion is?

A WATCHMAN   *[Aside]* I know that Deformed. A has been a vile thief this seven year; a goes up and down° like a gentleman. I remember his name.

BORACHIO   Didst thou not hear somebody?

CONRAD   No, 'twas the vane° on the house.

BORACHIO   Seest thou not, I say, what a deformed thief this fashion is? how giddily a turns about all the hot-bloods between fourteen and five-and-thirty? sometimes fashioning them like Pharaoh's soldiers in the reechy° painting, sometime like god Bel's priests° in the old church window, sometime like the shaven Hercules° in the smirched worm-eaten tapestry, where his codpiece° seems as massy as his club?

CONRAD   All this I see, and I see that the fashion wears out more apparel than the man. But art not thou thyself giddy with the fashion too, that thou hast shifted out of thy tale into telling me of the fashion?

BORACHIO   Not so neither. But know that I have tonight wooed Margaret, the Lady Hero's gentlewoman, by the name of Hero. She leans me out at her mistress' chamber window, bids me a thousand times good night – I tell this tale vilely. I should first tell thee how the prince,

owe thee an answer: answer that later

penthouse: overhanging roof
true drunkard: (punning on his name, since *borrachón* is Spanish for "drunkard," and there was a proverb, "The drunkard tells all")

105

110

dear: expensive

115

unconfirmed: inexperienced

120

deformed thief: deforming rascal

125

goes up and down: walks about

vane: weather vane

130

reechy: grimy, smoky; **Bel's priests:** the priests of Baal (in the Apocryphal book of the Bible Bel and the Dragon)

135

shaven Hercules: (probably a confusion with Samson, whose hair was cut by Delilah)
codpiece: front part of breeches, often stuffed and ornamented

140

145

DISCOVERING SHAKESPEARE

(64) History [3.3.121]: Borachio is probably drinking some kind of liquor as he tells his story to Conrad. What type of container is he drinking from: a bottle, a mug, a goblet, or a flask? What varieties of alcoholic beverages were most popular during the English Renaissance? Which of these are still popular today?

(65) Plot [3.3.141]: Do you think Margaret knew she was helping to slander Hero? Explain your reasons on a separate piece of paper. Then read ahead to 5.1.291–292, and revise your answer if necessary.

Claudio, and my master, planted and placed and pos-
sessed° by my master Don John, saw afar off in the orchard this amiable encounter.°

possessed: deluded
amiable encounter: lovers' meeting   150

CONRAD   And thought they Margaret was Hero?

BORACHIO   Two of them did, the prince and Claudio,
but the devil my master knew she was Margaret, and
partly by his oaths, which first possessed them, partly   155
by the dark night, which did deceive them, but chiefly
by my villainy, which did confirm any slander that Don
John had made, away went Claudio enraged, swore he
would meet her, as he was appointed, next morning at
the temple, and there, before the whole congregation,   160
shame her with what he saw o'ernight and send her
home again without a husband.

FIRST WATCHMAN   We charge you in the prince's name,
stand!

SECOND WATCHMAN   Call up the right master constable.
We have here recovered° the most dangerous piece of   165
lechery° that ever was known in the commonwealth.

recovered: (for "discovered")
lechery: (for "treachery")

FIRST WATCHMAN   And one Deformed is one of them. I
know him; a wears a lock.°

lock: lovelock (a wisp of hair worn beside the
left ear, often down to the shoulder)

CONRAD   Masters, masters —

SECOND WATCHMAN   You'll be made bring Deformed   170
forth, I warrant you.

CONRAD   Masters —

A WATCHMAN   Never speak, we charge you. Let us obey
you° to go with us.

Let us obey you: (for "we command you")

BORACHIO   We are like to prove a goodly commodity,°
being taken up° of these men's bills.°

commodity: merchandise   175
taken up: (1) arrested, (2) obtained on credit
from a usurer; **bills:** (1) halberds, (2) bonds of
goods

CONRAD   A commodity in question,° I warrant you.
Come, we'll obey you.   *Exeunt.*

in question: (1) subject to examination, (2) of
doubtful quality

&ea; **3.4°** *Enter Hero, and Margaret and Ursula.*

3.4: The house of Leonato

HERO   Good Ursula, wake my cousin Beatrice and desire
her to rise.

URSULA   I will, lady.

HERO   And bid her come hither.

URSULA   Well.   *[Exit.]*   5

MARGARET   Troth, I think your other rebato° were better.

rebato: stiff, flaring collar or ruff, usually of
starched or wired lace

HERO   No, pray thee, good Meg, I'll wear this.

MARGARET   By my troth 's not so good, and I warrant
your cousin will say so.

HERO   My cousin's a fool, and thou art another. I'll wear   10
none but this.

MARGARET   I like the new tire° within° excellently, if the
hair were a thought browner; and your gown's a most
rare fashion, i' faith. I saw the Duchess of Milan's gown
that they praise so.   15

tire: headdress with wig and elaborate ornaments
attached; **within:** in the next room

DISCOVERING SHAKESPEARE

(66) History [3.3.168]: What was a "lovelock" (3.3.168) and a "rebato" (3.4.6)? Find a picture of each to share with your
class.

HERO   O, that exceeds, they say.

MARGARET   By my troth, 's but a nightgown° in respect of yours – cloth a gold and cuts,° and laced with silver,° set with pearls, down sleeves,° side sleeves,° and skirts, round underborne° with a bluish tinsel. But for a fine, quaint,° graceful, and excellent fashion, yours is worth ten on't.

HERO   God give me joy to wear it! for my heart is exceeding heavy.

MARGARET   'Twill be heavier soon by the weight of a man.

HERO   Fie upon thee! art not ashamed?

MARGARET   Of what, lady? of speaking honorably? Is not marriage honorable in° a beggar? Is not your lord honorable without marriage? I think you would have me say, "saving your reverence,° a husband." An bad thinking do not wrest° true speaking, I'll offend nobody. Is there any harm in "the heavier for a husband"? None, I think, an it be the right husband and the right wife. Otherwise 'tis light,° and not heavy. Ask my Lady Beatrice else.° Here she comes.

Enter Beatrice.

HERO   Good morrow, coz.°

BEATRICE   Good morrow, sweet Hero.

HERO   Why, how now? Do you speak in the sick tune?

BEATRICE   I am out of all other tune, methinks.

MARGARET   Clap's into° "Light a love."° That goes without a burden.° Do you sing it, and I'll dance it.

BEATRICE   Ye light a love with your heels!° then, if your husband have stables enough, you'll see he shall lack no barns.°

MARGARET   O illegitimate construction! I scorn that with my heels.

BEATRICE   'Tis almost five o'clock, cousin, 'tis time you were ready. By my troth, I am exceeding ill. Heigh-ho!

MARGARET   For a hawk, a horse, or a husband?°

BEATRICE   For the letter that begins them all, H.°

MARGARET   Well, an you be not turned Turk,° there's no more sailing by the star.°

BEATRICE   What means the fool, trow?°

MARGARET   Nothing I, but God send everyone their heart's desire!

HERO   These gloves the count sent me, they are an excellent perfume.°

BEATRICE   I am stuffed,° cousin, I cannot smell.

MARGARET   A maid, and stuffed!° There's goodly catching of cold.

---

nightgown: dressing gown
cuts: slashes or notches to show the underbody;
laced with silver: with silver threads applied, usually in a diagonal pattern — 20
down sleeves: close-fitting long sleeves; **side sleeves:** second, purely ornamental, sleeves hanging open from the armhole
round underborne: held out, stiffened from underneath
quaint: elegant — 25

in: even in

30

saving your reverence: (conventional apology for mentioning a delicate subject)
wrest: twist, misunderstand

light: (pun on "wanton") — 35
else: if it be otherwise

coz: cousin

40

Clap's into: let us begin briskly; **"Light a love":** (an old tune)
burden: refrain (with a punning reference to *heavier for a husband*)
light . . . heels: i.e., grow wanton — 45
barns: (punning on "bairns," children)

husband: (treating Beatrice's sigh as a hunting cry) — 50
H: (with a play on "ache," then pronounced "aitch")
turned Turk: i.e., turned renegade, changed your vow
star: North Star — 55
trow: I wonder

perfume: (gloves were often perfumed)
I am stuffed: i.e., my nose is stopped with a cold — 60
stuffed: pregnant

DISCOVERING SHAKESPEARE

(67) Language [3.4.25]: Explain Margaret's sexual <u>puns</u> on the following words and phrases: "heavier soon by the weight of a man" (3.4.25–26), "burden" (42), "barns" (45), and "stuffed" (60).

(68) Music [3.4.41]: "Light o' Love" (3.4.41) was a popular song mentioned in *The Two Gentlemen of Verona* and *The Two Noble Kinsmen*. Make up your own lyrics to a four-<u>stanza</u> song in <u>iambic pentameter</u> <u>rhyming</u> ABAB CDCD EFEF GHGH.

BEATRICE   O, God help me, God help me! How long have you professed apprehension?°

MARGARET   Ever since you left it. Doth not my wit become me rarely?°

BEATRICE   It is not seen enough. You should wear it in your cap.° By my troth, I am sick.

MARGARET   Get you some of this distilled *Carduus benedictus*° and lay it to your heart. It is the only thing for a qualm.°

HERO   There thou prick'st° her with a thistle.

BEATRICE   *Benedictus?* why *benedictus?* You have some moral° in this *benedictus.*

MARGARET   Moral? No, by my troth, I have no moral meaning. I meant plain holy thistle. You may think perchance that I think you are in love. Nay, by'r Lady, I am not such a fool to think what I list, nor I list° not to think what I can, nor indeed I cannot think, if I would think my heart out of thinking, that you are in love, or that you will be in love, or that you can be in love. Yet Benedick was such another, and now is he become a man.° He swore he would never marry, and yet now in despite of his heart he eats his meat without grudging° — and how you may be converted I know not, but methinks you look with your eyes as other women do.

BEATRICE   What pace is this that thy tongue keeps?

MARGARET   Not a false gallop.°

Enter Ursula.

URSULA   Madam, withdraw. The prince, the count, Signor Benedick, Don John, and all the gallants of the town are come to fetch you to church.

HERO   Help to dress me, good coz, good Meg, good Ursula.   *[Exeunt.]*

❧ **3.5** *Enter Leonato and the Constable [Dogberry] and the Headborough° [Verges].*

LEONATO   What would you with me, honest neighbor?

DOGBERRY   Marry, sir, I would have some confidence° with you that decerns° you nearly.

LEONATO   Brief, I pray you, for you see it is a busy time with me.

DOGBERRY   Marry, this it is, sir.

VERGES   Yes, in truth it is, sir.

LEONATO   What is it, my good friends?

DOGBERRY   Goodman Verges, sir, speaks a little off the matter — an old man, sir, and his wits are not so blunt°

---

professed apprehension: pretended to wit

rarely: excellently   65

in your cap: (like a feather, where it would show)

Carduus benedictus: holy thistle (regarded as a universal remedy, with pun on "Benedick")   70

qualm: sudden faintness or nausea

prick'st: (with pun on "penis")

moral: figurative meaning

75

list: like, please

80

a man: i.e., a normal man

eats . . . grudging: has a normal appetite

85

false gallop: canter, but the emphasis is on "false"

90

s.d. Headborough: petty or local constable

confidence: (for "conference")
decerns: (for "concerns")

5

blunt: (for "sharp")   10

DISCOVERING SHAKESPEARE

(69) History [3.4.68]: Although Margaret is <u>punning</u> on Benedick's name, the herb *carduus benedictus* (3.4.68–69), or "holy thistle," was used for a variety of medicinal purposes. Research the drug in order to discover its primary uses during the Renaissance.

(70) Staging [3.5.1]: Why is Leonato in a hurry, and how could his haste, combined with Dogberry's "tediousness," help make this scene humorous?

as, God help, I would desire they were, but, in faith,
honest as the skin between his brows.°

VERGES Yes, I thank God I am as honest as any man living that is an old man and no honester than I.

DOGBERRY Comparisons are odorous.° *Palabras,*° neighbor Verges.

LEONATO Neighbors, you are tedious.

DOGBERRY It pleases your worship to say so, but we are
the poor duke's° officers; but truly, for mine own part, if
I were as tedious as a king, I could find in my heart to
bestow it all of your worship.

LEONATO All thy tediousness on me, ah?

DOGBERRY Yea, an 'twere a thousand pound more than
'tis, for I hear as good exclamation° on your worship as
of any man in the city, and though I be but a poor man,
I am glad to hear it.

VERGES And so am I.

LEONATO I would fain know what you have to say.

VERGES Marry, sir, our watch tonight, excepting° your
worship's presence, ha' ta'en a couple of as arrant knaves
as any in Messina.

DOGBERRY A good old man, sir, he will be talking. As
they say,° "When the age is in, the wit is out." God help
us, it is a world to see! Well said, i' faith, neighbor
Verges. Well, God's a good man. An two men ride of a
horse, one must ride behind. An honest soul, i' faith,
sir, by my troth he is, as ever broke bread, but God is to
be worshiped, all men are not alike, alas, good neighbor!

LEONATO Indeed, neighbor, he comes too short of you.

DOGBERRY Gifts that God gives.

LEONATO I must leave you.

DOGBERRY One word, sir. Our watch, sir, have indeed
comprehended° two aspicious° persons, and we would
have them this morning examined before your worship.

LEONATO Take their examination yourself and bring it
me. I am now in great haste, as it may appear unto you.

DOGBERRY It shall be suffigance.°

LEONATO Drink some wine ere you go. Fare you well.
[Enter a Messenger.]

MESSENGER My lord, they stay for you to give your
daughter to her husband.

LEONATO I'll wait upon them. I am ready.
[Exeunt Leonato and Messenger.]

DOGBERRY Go, good partner, go get you to Francis Seacoal.° Bid him bring his pen and inkhorn to the jail. We
are now to examination° these men.

VERGES And we must do it wisely.

---

honest . . . brows: (proverbial)

odorous: (for "odious"); **Palabras:** (from 15
Spanish *pocas palabras,* few words)

poor duke's: (for "duke's poor") 20

exclamation: (for "acclamation") 25

excepting: (for "respecting") 30

As they say: etc. (what follows is a string of "old
ends," or stock phrases) 35

40

comprehended: (for "apprehended");
aspicious: (for "suspicious") 45

suffigance: (for "sufficient") 50

Francis Seacoal: (the sexton or town clerk of 55
4.2, not the same as George Seacoal, constable of
the watch, in 3.3, who could read and write)
examination: (for "examine")

DISCOVERING SHAKESPEARE

(71) Staging [3.5.27]: How old do you think Verges is in this play? If he is quite elderly, what kinds of funny "old man"
sight gags could make him a particularly comical character?

(72) History [3.5.55]: What was an "inkhorn" (3.5.55)? What materials were pens made of during the Renaissance?

DOGBERRY We will spare for no wit, I warrant you. Here's that shall drive some of them to a noncome.° Only get the learned writer to set down our excommunication,° and meet me at the jail.　　　*[Exeunt.]*

noncome: (abbreviation of *non compos mentis,* but he probably means "nonplus")　　60
excommunication: (for "examination")

❧ **4.1**° *Enter Prince [Don Pedro], [John the] Bastard, Leonato, Friar [Francis], Claudio, Benedick, Hero, and Beatrice.*

4.1: A church **s.d.** (editors often add entries for servants and wedding guests)

LEONATO Come, Friar Francis, be brief. Only to the plain form° of marriage, and you shall recount their particular duties° afterwards.

plain form: simple prescribed formula
particular duties: the usual preliminary sermon on the duties of husband and wife

FRIAR You come hither, my lord, to marry this lady?
CLAUDIO No.
LEONATO To be married to her. Friar, you come to marry her.　　5
FRIAR Lady, you come hither to be married to this count?
HERO I do.　　10
FRIAR If either of you know any inward impediment° why you should not be conjoined, I charge you on your souls to utter it.

inward impediment: secret, or mental, reservation

CLAUDIO Know you any, Hero?
HERO None, my lord.　　15
FRIAR Know you any, count?
LEONATO I dare make his answer – none.
CLAUDIO O, what men dare do! what men may do! what men daily do, not knowing what they do!　　20
BENEDICK How now? interjections? Why then, some be of laughing, as, ah, ha, he!°

some . . . ah, ha, he: (he is quoting Lily's *Latin Grammar,* a standard textbook of the day, which says of interjections, "Some are of Laughing: as, Ha, ha, he.")

CLAUDIO
Stand thee by,° friar. Father, by your leave,°
Will you with free and unconstrainèd soul
Give me this maid your daughter?

Stand thee by: stand aside; **by your leave:** if I may call you so

LEONATO
As freely, son, as God did give her me.　　25
CLAUDIO
And what have I to give you back whose worth
May counterpoise° this rich and precious gift?

counterpoise: balance

PEDRO
Nothing, unless you render her again.
CLAUDIO
Sweet° prince, you learn° me noble thankfulness.
There, Leonato, take her back again.　　30
Give not this rotten orange to your friend.
She's but the sign° and semblance of her honor.
Behold how like a maid she blushes here!
O, what authority° and show of truth
Can cunning sin cover itself withal!°　　35

Sweet: dear; **learn:** teach

sign: appearance

authority: assurance
withal: with

DISCOVERING SHAKESPEARE

(73) <u>Verse</u> [4.1.24]: Notice that this scene begins in <u>prose</u>, then shifts into <u>verse</u>. When and why do the characters start using <u>verse</u>?

Comes not that blood° as modest evidence   **blood:** blush
To witness° simple virtue? Would you not swear,   **witness:** bear witness to
All you that see her, that she were a maid,
By these exterior shows? But she is none:
She knows the heat of a luxurious° bed;   **luxurious:** lustful   40
Her blush is guiltiness, not modesty.

LEONATO
What do you mean, my lord?

CLAUDIO   Not to be married,
Not to knit my soul to an approvèd° wanton.   **approvèd:** proved

LEONATO
Dear my lord, if you, in your own proof,°   **proof:** experience
Have vanquished the resistance of her youth   45
And made defeat of her virginity –

CLAUDIO
I know what you would say. If I have known her,
You will say she did embrace me as a husband,
And so extenuate the forehand sin.°   **extenuate . . . sin:** excuse the sin of anticipating
No, Leonato,   the marriage state   50
I never tempted her with word too large,°   **large:** broad, immodest
But, as a brother to his sister, showed
Bashful sincerity and comely love.

HERO
And seemed I ever otherwise to you?

CLAUDIO
Out° on thee seeming! I will write against it.   **Out:** shame   55
You seem to me as Dian° in her orb,°   **Dian:** Diana, goddess of chastity; **orb:** sphere,
As chaste as is the bud ere it be blown,°   the moon
But you are more intemperate° in your blood   **blown:** in blossom
Than Venus, or those pampered animals   **intemperate:** ungoverned
That rage in savage sensuality.   60

HERO
Is my lord well that he doth speak so wide?°   **wide:** far from the truth

LEONATO
Sweet prince, why speak not you?

PEDRO   What should I speak?
I stand dishonored that have gone about°   **gone about:** undertaken
To link my dear friend to a common stale.°   **stale:** prostitute

LEONATO
Are these things spoken, or do I but dream?   65

JOHN
Sir, they are spoken, and these things are true.

BENEDICK
This looks not like a nuptial.

HERO   "True"! O God!

CLAUDIO
Leonato, stand I here?

DISCOVERING SHAKESPEARE

(74) History [4.1.49]: What does Claudio mean by "extenuate the forehand sin" (4.1.49)? Do some research on courtship customs during the Renaissance.

(75) Staging [4.1.67]: In Kenneth Branagh's 1993 film version of *Much Ado,* the director cut Benedick's "This looks not like a nuptial" (4.1.67). How do you think this cut would affect the staging of the scene? If you were directing a production of the play, would you omit the line or leave it in? Why?

Is this the prince? Is this the prince's brother?
Is this face Hero's? Are our eyes our own? 70
LEONATO
All this is so; but what of this, my lord?
CLAUDIO
Let me but move one question to your daughter,
And by that fatherly and kindly° power   **kindly:** natural
That you have in her, bid her answer truly.
LEONATO
I charge thee do so, as thou art my child. 75
HERO
O, God defend me! How am I beset!
What kind of catechizing call you this?
CLAUDIO
To make you answer truly to your name.
HERO
Is it not Hero? Who can blot that name
With any just reproach? 80
CLAUDIO   Marry, that can Hero!
Hero itself° can blot out Hero's virtue.   **Hero itself:** i.e., the name by which he had
What man was he talked with you yesternight,   heard Borachio call Margaret
Out at your window betwixt twelve and one?
Now, if you are a maid, answer to° this.   **answer to:** explain
HERO
I talked with no man at that hour, my lord. 85
PEDRO
Why, then are you no maiden. Leonato,
I am sorry you must hear. Upon mine honor
Myself, my brother, and this grievèd° count   **grievèd:** aggrieved, wronged
Did see her, hear her, at that hour last night
Talk with a ruffian at her chamber window, 90
Who hath indeed, most like a liberal° villain,   **liberal:** licentious
Confessed the vile encounters they have had
A thousand times in secret.
JOHN
Fie, fie! they are not to be named, my lord –
Not to be spoke of; 95
There is not chastity enough in language
Without offense to utter them. Thus, pretty lady,
I am sorry for thy much misgovernment.°   **much misgovernment:** great misconduct
CLAUDIO
O Hero! what a Hero hadst thou been
If half thy outward graces had been placed 100
About thy thoughts and counsels of thy heart!
But fare thee well, most foul, most fair! Farewell,
Thou pure impiety and impious purity!
For thee I'll lock up all the gates of love,
And on my eyelids shall conjecture° hang,   **conjecture:** doubt, suspicion 105
To turn all beauty into thoughts of harm,
And never shall it more be gracious.

DISCOVERING SHAKESPEARE

(76) Language [4.1.103]: Compare the <u>oxymorons</u> in Claudio's "Thou pure impiety and impious purity" (4.1.103) with similar contrasting phrases in 3.2.73–85 of *Romeo and Juliet*. Paraphrase Claudio's <u>oxymoron</u> into modern English.

LEONATO
  Hath no man's dagger here a point for me?
    [Hero swoons.]
BEATRICE
  Why, how now, cousin? Wherefore sink you down?
JOHN
  Come let us go. These things, come thus to light,   110
  Smother her spirits° up.   **spirits:** vital powers
                [Exeunt Don Pedro, Don John, and Claudio.]
BENEDICK
  How doth the lady?
BEATRICE   Dead, I think. Help, uncle!
  Hero! why, Hero! Uncle! Signor Benedick! Friar!
LEONATO
  O Fate, take not away thy heavy hand!
  Death is the fairest cover for her shame   115
  That may be wished for.
BEATRICE   How now, cousin Hero?
FRIAR   Have comfort, lady.
LEONATO   Dost thou look up?°   **look up:** (a sign of innocence)
FRIAR   Yea, wherefore should she not?
LEONATO
  Wherefore? Why, doth not every earthly thing   120
  Cry shame upon her? Could she here deny
  The story that is printed in her blood?°   **printed in her blood:** written in her blushes
  Do not live, Hero, do not ope thine eyes,
  For, did I think thou wouldst not quickly die,
  Thought I thy spirits were stronger than thy shames,   125
  Myself would on the rearward of reproaches°   **on . . . reproaches:** after reproaching you
  Strike at thy life. Grieved I, I had but one?
  Chid I for that at frugal nature's frame?°   **frame:** plan, design
  O, one too much by thee! Why had I one?
  Why ever wast thou lovely in my eyes?   130
  Why had I not with charitable hand
  Took up a beggar's issue at my gates,
  Who smirchèd thus and mired with infamy,
  I might have said, "No part of it is mine;
  This shame derives itself from unknown loins"?   135
  But mine, and mine I loved, and mine I praised,
  And mine that I was proud on – mine so much
  That I myself was to myself not mine,°   **I myself . . . mine:** I lost or forgot myself
  Valuing of her – why she, O, she is fall'n
  Into a pit of ink, that the wide sea   140
  Hath drops too few to wash her clean again,
  And salt too little which may season give°   **season give:** provide a preservative
  To her foul tainted flesh!
BENEDICK   Sir, sir, be patient.
  For my part, I am so attired in wonder,
  I know not what to say.   145

DISCOVERING SHAKESPEARE

(77) Staging [4.1.125]: What kind of stage action or <u>blocking</u> could break up Leonato's long and anguished speech about Hero's "shame"? Give the speech in class, while everyone else suggests blocking to accompany it.

BEATRICE
  O, on my soul, my cousin is belied!
BENEDICK
  Lady, were you her bedfellow last night?
BEATRICE
  No, truly not, although, until last night,
  I have this twelvemonth been her bedfellow.
LEONATO
  Confirmed, confirmed! O, that is stronger made   150
  Which was before barred up with ribs of iron!
  Would the two princes lie? and Claudio lie,
  Who loved her so that, speaking of her foulness,
  Washed it with tears? Hence from her! let her die.
FRIAR
  Hear me a little;   155
  For I have only been silent so long,
  And given way unto this course of fortune,°   **course of fortune:** turn of events
  By noting of the lady. I have marked
  A thousand blushing apparitions°   **blushing apparitions:** blushes (personified)
  To start into her face, a thousand innocent shames   160
  In angel whiteness beat away those blushes,
  And in her eye there hath appeared a fire
  To burn the errors° that these princes hold   **errors:** (personified as heretics)
  Against her maiden truth. Call me a fool,
  Trust not my reading nor my observations,   165
  Which with experimental seal° doth warrant   **experimental seal:** seal of experience
  The tenor of my book,° trust not my age,   **warrant . . . book:** confirm the tone of my
  My reverence, calling, nor divinity,   philosophy
  If this sweet lady lie not guiltless here
  Under some biting error.   170
LEONATO   Friar, it cannot be.
  Thou seest that all the grace that she hath left
  Is that she will not add to her damnation
  A sin of perjury: she not denies it.
  Why seek'st thou then to cover with excuse
  That which appears in proper nakedness?   175
FRIAR
  Lady, what man is he you are accused of?
HERO
  They know that do accuse me; I know none.
  If I know more of any man alive
  Than that which maiden modesty doth warrant,
  Let all my sins lack mercy! O my father,   180
  Prove you that any man with me conversed

DISCOVERING SHAKESPEARE

(78) Staging [4.1.153]: When Leonato claims that Claudio, speaking of Hero's "foulness," "Washed it with tears" (4.1.153–154), he seems to imply that Claudio shed tears while denouncing her. Can you find any indication earlier in this scene that Claudio actually cried during the accusation scene (4.1.22–111)? If he did so on stage, how would this affect the audience's reaction toward him?

(79) Paraphrase [4.1.166]: Paraphrase in modern English the following phrase by the Friar: "Which with experimental seal doth warrant/ The tenor of my book" (4.1.166–167). Why do you think the Friar speaks in such elevated, artificial language here?

At hours unmeet,° or that I yesternight
Maintained° the change° of words with any creature,
Refuse° me, hate me, torture me to death!

FRIAR
There is some strange misprision° in the princes.

BENEDICK
Two of them have the very bent° of honor;
And if their wisdoms be misled in this,
The practice° of it lives in John the Bastard,
Whose spirits toil in frame of° villainies.

LEONATO
I know not. If they speak but truth of her,
These hands shall tear her. If they wrong her honor,
The proudest of them shall well hear of it.
Time hath not yet so dried this blood of mine,
Nor age so eat up my invention,°
Nor fortune made such havoc of my means,
Nor my bad life reft me so much of friends,
But they shall find awaked in such a kind°
Both strength of limb and policy of mind,°
Ability in means, and choice of friends,
To quit me of° them throughly.°

FRIAR   Pause awhile
And let my counsel sway you in this case.
Your daughter here the princess° (left for dead),
Let her awhile be secretly kept in,°
And publish it that she is dead indeed,
Maintain a mourning ostentation,°
And on your family's old monument
Hang mournful epitaphs, and do all rites
That appertain unto a burial.

LEONATO
What shall become of this? What will this do?

FRIAR
Marry, this well carried° shall on her behalf
Change slander to remorse. That is some good.
But not for that dream I on this strange course,
But on this travail° look for greater birth.
She dying, as it must be so maintained,
Upon the instant that she was accused,
Shall be lamented, pitied, and excused
Of every hearer; for it so falls out
That what we have we prize not to the worth°
Whiles we enjoy it, but being lacked and lost,
Why, then we rack° the value, then we find
The virtue that possession would not show us

unmeet: improper
Maintained: carried on; **change:** exchange
Refuse: disown

misprision: mistake   185

bent: shape, form

practice: plotting
in frame of: in framing

                                                            190

invention: power to make plans

                                                            195

kind: manner
policy of mind: mental power

quit me of: settle accounts with; **throughly:**   200
thoroughly

princess: (So in quarto and folio texts, although
Hero is not, in this version of the story, a princess.
Perhaps a courtesy title, or perhaps an author's
inconsistency; often emended to "princes left for
dead.")   205
in: at home
mourning ostentation: formal show of
mourning

carried: managed   210

on this travail: as a result of this effort

                                                            215

to the worth: for what it is worth

rack: stretch as on a torture rack   220

DISCOVERING SHAKESPEARE

(80) Verse [4.1.182]: Scan the verse in Hero's speech in 4.1.177–184, paying particular attention to the number of single syllable words that slow down the delivery of the lines. How could a slower verse rhythm help exhibit Hero's state of mind at this point in the play?

(81) History [4.1.205]: What does the Friar mean by "a mourning ostentation" (4.1.205)? Contrast the Friar in this play with Friar Laurence in *Romeo and Juliet*. Each of them meddles in worldly affairs; each pretends that a young woman is dead when she is actually alive; and each speaks in lofty, "religious" diction. How are the two characters different?

Whiles it was ours. So will it fare with Claudio.
When he shall hear she died upon his words,
Th' idea of her life° shall sweetly creep
Into his study of imagination,°
And every lovely organ of her life°
Shall come appareled in more precious habit,°
More moving, delicate, and full of life,
Into the eye and prospect of his soul
Than when she lived indeed. Then shall he mourn
(If ever love had interest in his liver)°
And wish he had not so accusèd her —
No, though he thought his accusation true.
Let this be so, and doubt not but success°
Will fashion the event° in better shape
Than I can lay it down in likelihood.
But if all aim but this be leveled false,°
The supposition of the lady's death
Will quench the wonder of her infamy.
And if it sort° not well, you may conceal her,
As best befits her wounded reputation,
In some reclusive° and religious life,
Out of all eyes, tongues, minds, and injuries.

BENEDICK
Signor Leonato, let the friar advise you,
And though you know my inwardness° and love
Is very much unto the prince and Claudio,
Yet, by mine honor, I will deal in this
As secretly and justly as your soul
Should with your body.

LEONATO   Being that I flow° in grief,
The smallest twine may lead me.

FRIAR
'Tis well consented. Presently away,
For to strange sores strangely they strain the cure.°
Come, lady, die to live. This wedding day
Perhaps is but prolonged.° Have patience and endure.

Exit [with all but Beatrice and Benedick].

BENEDICK   Lady Beatrice, have you wept all this while?
BEATRICE   Yea, and I will weep a while longer.
BENEDICK   I will not desire that.
BEATRICE   You have no reason. I do it freely.
BENEDICK   Surely I do believe your fair cousin is
wronged.
BEATRICE   Ah, how much might the man deserve of me
that would right her!
BENEDICK   Is there any way to show such friendship?
BEATRICE   A very even° way, but no such friend.
BENEDICK   May a man do it?

---

idea . . . life: i.e., memory of her
his . . . imagination: the thoughts of his musing hours   225
organ of her life: part of her when she was alive
habit: apparel

230

liver: (the presumed physiological seat of love, in contrast to the heart, the romantic seat)

success: what succeeds or follows (i.e., the course of time)   235
event: outcome
be leveled false: be directed falsely (and so miss the mark)

sort: turn out   240

reclusive: cloistered

inwardness: intimacy   245

flow: am afloat (and hence easily pulled)   250

strain the cure: i.e., use desperate remedies

prolonged: deferred

255

260

even: direct

265

DISCOVERING SHAKESPEARE

(82) Imagery [4.1.225]: Read the Friar's speech in 4.1.210–243, underlining or writing down all the images he uses to persuade Leonato that they should feign Hero's death.

(83) Metaphor [4.1.252]: Paraphrase the Friar's "For to strange sores strangely they strain the cure" (4.1.252). Try to put the same sentiment into a regular line of iambic pentameter. Why do you think the Friar's language is so contorted here?

BEATRICE   It is a man's office, but not yours.

BENEDICK   I do love nothing in the world so well as you. Is not that strange?

BEATRICE   As strange as the thing I know not. It were as possible for me to say I loved nothing so well as you. But believe me not – and yet I lie not. I confess nothing, nor I deny nothing. I am sorry for my cousin.   270

BENEDICK   By my sword, Beatrice, thou lovest me.

BEATRICE   Do not swear and eat it.°

swear and eat it: i.e., eat the words of this oath, go back on it   275

BENEDICK   I will swear by it that you love me, and I will make him eat it that says I love not you.

BEATRICE   Will you not eat your word?

BENEDICK   With no sauce that can be devised to it. I protest° I love thee.

protest: solemnly affirm

BEATRICE   Why then, God forgive me!   280

BENEDICK   What offense, sweet Beatrice?

BEATRICE   You have stayed° me in a happy hour. I was about to protest I loved you.

stayed: stopped

BENEDICK   And do it with all thy heart.

BEATRICE   I love you with so much of my heart that none is left to protest.   285

BENEDICK   Come, bid me do anything for thee.

BEATRICE   Kill Claudio.

BENEDICK   Ha! not for the wide world!

BEATRICE   You kill me to deny it. Farewell.   290

BENEDICK   Tarry, sweet Beatrice.

BEATRICE   I am gone, though I am here. There is no love in you. Nay, I pray you let me go.

BENEDICK   Beatrice –

BEATRICE   In faith, I will go.   295

BENEDICK   We'll be friends first.

BEATRICE   You dare easier be friends with me than fight with mine enemy.

BENEDICK   Is Claudio thine enemy?

BEATRICE   Is a not approved° in the height° a villain, that hath slandered, scorned, dishonored my kinswoman? O that I were a man! What? bear her in hand° until they come to take hands,° and then with public accusation, uncovered° slander, unmitigated rancor – O God, that I were a man! I would eat his heart in the marketplace.

approved: proved; **height:** highest degree   300

bear her in hand: lead her on, delude her
take hands: marry
uncovered: undisguised

    305

BENEDICK   Hear me, Beatrice –

BEATRICE   Talk with a man out at a window! – a proper saying!

BENEDICK   Nay, but Beatrice –

    310

DISCOVERING SHAKESPEARE

(84) <u>Verse</u> [4.1.270]: Why do Beatrice and Benedick shift into <u>prose</u> in this section of the scene?

(85) <u>Plot</u> [4.1.288]: Beatrice's "Kill Claudio" (4.1.288) comes as an abrupt surprise in the midst of an amorous scene between the two lovers. How do you feel about the intrusion of this "love test" into a tender moment between the two? Why does Beatrice wait till after Benedick declares his love for her to ask him to kill Claudio?

(86) <u>Metaphor</u> [4.1.305]: Compare and contrast Beatrice's "I would eat his heart in the marketplace" (4.1.305) to her earlier comic promise to eat all the enemy soldiers that Benedick has killed (1.1.41)? Which declaration is most <u>metaphoric</u>? Which is most literal? Why? In what way has Beatrice changed between these two statements?

BEATRICE Sweet Hero! she is wronged, she is slandered, she is undone.°

undone: ruined

BENEDICK Beat –

BEATRICE Princes and counties!° Surely a princely testimony, a goodly count, Count° Comfit,° a sweet gallant surely! O that I were a man for his sake! or that I had any friend would be a man for my sake! But manhood is melted into curtsies, valor into compliment, and men are only turned into tongue, and trim ones too. He is now as valiant as Hercules that only tells a lie, and swears it. I cannot be a man with wishing, therefore I will die a woman with grieving.

counties: counts
Count: legal indictment and account (with a pun on Claudio's title); **Comfit:** sugar candy 315

320

BENEDICK Tarry, good Beatrice. By this hand, I love thee.

BEATRICE Use it for my love some other way than swearing by it.

325

BENEDICK Think you in your soul the Count Claudio hath wronged Hero?

BEATRICE Yea, as sure as I have a thought or a soul.

BENEDICK Enough, I am engaged. I will challenge him. I will kiss your hand, and so I leave you. By this hand, Claudio shall render me a dear account. As you hear of me, so think of me. Go comfort your cousin. I must say she is dead – and so farewell. *[Exeunt.]*

330

❧ **4.2**° *Enter the Constables [Dogberry and Verges] and the Town Clerk [Sexton] in gowns, Borachio [, Conrad, and Watch].*

4.2: (the speech prefixes in Q show that Will Kemp and Richard Cowley played, or were imagined by Shakespeare as playing, Dogberry and Verges)

DOGBERRY Is our whole dissembly° appeared?

dissembly: (for "assembly")

VERGES O, a stool and a cushion for the sexton.

SEXTON Which be the malefactors?

DOGBERRY Marry, that am I and my partner.

VERGES Nay, that's certain. We have the exhibition° to examine.

exhibition: (for "commission") 5

SEXTON But which are the offenders that are to be examined? Let them come before master constable.

DOGBERRY Yea, marry, let them come before me. What is your name, friend?

10

BORACHIO Borachio.

DOGBERRY Pray write down Borachio. Yours, sirrah?°

CONRAD I am a gentleman, sir, and my name is Conrad.

sirrah: sir (a derogatory form, resented by Conrad)

DOGBERRY Write down Master Gentleman Conrad. Masters, do you serve God?

15

BOTH Yea, sir, we hope.

DOGBERRY Write down that they hope they serve God; and write God first, for God defend° but God should go

defend: forbid

DISCOVERING SHAKESPEARE

(87) History [4.1.329]: When Benedick says he is "engaged" (4.1.329), what exactly does he mean? What additional connotations of the word were available to Shakespeare's audience?

(88) Social Customs [4.2.13]: What does Conrad mean when he brags to the watch that he is a "gentleman" (4.2.13)? How would this distinction help the actor playing the role find mannerisms and affectations that would bring his character to life?

before such villains! Masters, it is proved already that you are little better than false knaves, and it will go near to be thought so shortly. How answer you for yourselves? 20

CONRAD Marry, sir, we say we are none.

DOGBERRY A marvelous witty fellow, I assure you, but I will go about with° him. *[To Borachio]* Come you hither, sirrah. A word in your ear. Sir, I say to you, it is thought you are false knaves.

> **go about with:** undertake, deal with 25

BORACHIO Sir, I say to you we are none.

DOGBERRY Well, stand aside. 'Fore God, they are both in a tale.° Have you writ down that they are none?

> **they . . . tale:** both tell the same story 30

SEXTON Master constable, you go not the way to examine. You must call forth the watch that are their accusers.

DOGBERRY Yea, marry, that's the eftest° way. Let the watch come forth. Masters, I charge you in the prince's name accuse these men.

> **eftest:** easiest, quickest 35

FIRST WATCHMAN This man said, sir, that Don John the prince's brother was a villain.

DOGBERRY Write down Prince John a villain. Why, this is flat perjury, to call a prince's brother villain. 40

BORACHIO Master constable —

DOGBERRY Pray thee, fellow, peace. I do not like thy look, I promise thee.

SEXTON What heard you him say else?

SECOND WATCHMAN Marry, that he had received a thousand ducats of Don John for accusing the Lady Hero wrongfully. 45

DOGBERRY Flat burglary as ever was committed.

VERGES Yea, by mass, that it is.

SEXTON What else, fellow? 50

FIRST WATCHMAN And that Count Claudio did mean, upon his words, to disgrace Hero before the whole assembly, and not marry her.

DOGBERRY O villain! Thou wilt be condemned into everlasting redemption° for this.

> **redemption:** (for "damnation") 55

SEXTON What else?

WATCHMEN This is all.

SEXTON And this is more, masters, than you can deny. Prince John is this morning secretly stolen away. Hero was in this manner accused, in this very manner refused, and upon the grief of this suddenly died. Master constable, let these men be bound and brought to Leonato's. I will go before and show him their examination.   *[Exit.]* 60

DOGBERRY Come, let them be opinioned.°

> **opinioned:** (for "pinioned") 65

VERGES Let them be in the hands —

CONRAD Off, coxcomb!°

> **coxcomb:** fool (derived from the comb of red flannel worn on the head of a professional court jester)

DISCOVERING SHAKESPEARE

(89) Language [4.2.40]: Find and explain all of Dogberry's <u>malapropisms</u> in this scene.

DOGBERRY   God's my life, where's the sexton? Let him
write down the prince's officer coxcomb. Come, bind
them. – Thou naughty° varlet!°

naughty: wicked; **varlet:** scoundrel   70

CONRAD   Away! you are an ass, you are an ass.

DOGBERRY   Dost thou not suspect° my place? Dost thou
not suspect my years? O that he were here to write me
down an ass! But, masters, remember that I am an ass.
Though it be not written down, yet forget not that I
am an ass. No, thou villain, thou art full of piety,° as
shall be proved upon thee by good witness. I am a wise
fellow; and which is more, an officer; and which is
more, a householder; and which is more, as pretty a
piece of flesh as any is in Messina, and one that knows
the law, go to! and a rich fellow enough, go to! and a
fellow that hath had losses;° and one that hath two
gowns and everything handsome about him. Bring him
away. O that I had been writ down an ass!

suspect: (for "respect")

piety: (for "impiety")   75

had losses: (implying that he had had possessions
to lose)   80

Exit [with the others].

❧ **5.1** *Enter Leonato and his brother [Antonio].*

ANTONIO
If you go on thus, you will kill yourself,
And 'tis not wisdom thus to second° grief
Against yourself.

second: support, assist

LEONATO   I pray thee cease thy counsel,
Which falls into mine ears as profitless
As water in a sieve. Give not me counsel,
Nor let no comforter delight mine ear
But such a one whose wrongs do suit with° mine.
Bring me a father that so loved his child,
Whose joy of her is overwhelmed° like mine,
And bid him speak of patience.
Measure his woe the length and breadth of mine,
And let it answer every strain for strain,°
As thus for thus, and such a grief for such,
In every lineament, branch, shape, and form.
If such a one will smile and stroke his beard,°
Bid sorrow wag,° cry "hem" when he should groan,
Patch grief with proverbs, make misfortune drunk
With candlewasters° – bring him yet to me,
And I of him will gather patience.
But there is no such man, for, brother, men
Can counsel and speak comfort to that grief
Which they themselves not feel, but, tasting it,
Their counsel turns to passion, which before
Would give preceptial medicine° to rage,
Fetter strong madness in a silken thread,

suit with: match   5

overwhelmed: drowned, as with tears   10

strain: trait

stroke his beard: (a gesture of complacency)   15
wag: go away

candlewasters: i.e., moral philosophers or
carousers   20

preceptial medicine: remedy in the form of
precepts   25

DISCOVERING SHAKESPEARE

(90) History [4.2.68]: What was a "sexton" (4.2.68), and what were his principal duties?
(91) Social Customs [4.2.79]: Dogberry refers to himself with pride as "a householder" (4.2.79). What percentage of
people during the Renaissance actually owned property? Why does he want Conrad to know that he has "two gowns"
(4.2.82–83)?

Charm ache with air° and agony with words.　　Charm . . . air: allay pain with talk
No, no! 'Tis all men's office to speak patience
To those that wring° under the load of sorrow,　　wring: writhe
But no man's virtue nor sufficiency
To be so moral when he shall endure　　　　　　　　　　　　　　　　　30
The like himself. Therefore give me no counsel.
My griefs cry louder than advertisement.°　　advertisement: advice

ANTONIO
Therein do men from children nothing differ.

LEONATO
I pray thee peace. I will be flesh and blood;
For there was never yet philosopher　　　　　　　　　　　　　　　　　35
That could endure the toothache patiently,
However they have writ° the style of gods　　writ: written in
And made a pish° at chance° and sufferance.°　　made a pish: scoffed; chance: mischance;
　　　　　　　　　　　　　　　　　　　　　　　　sufferance: suffering

ANTONIO
Yet bend not all the harm upon yourself.
Make those that do offend you suffer too.　　　　　　　　　　　　　　40

LEONATO
There thou speak'st reason. Nay, I will do so.
My soul doth tell me Hero is belied,
And that shall Claudio know, so shall the prince,
And all of them that thus dishonor her.
　　Enter Prince [Don Pedro] and Claudio.

ANTONIO
Here comes the prince and Claudio hastily.　　　　　　　　　　　　　　45

PEDRO
Good den, good den.°　　　　　　　　　　　　Good den: good evening

CLAUDIO　　　　　　　　Good day to both of you.

LEONATO
Hear you, my lords –

PEDRO　　　　　　　　　We have some haste, Leonato.

LEONATO
Some haste, my lord! well, fare you well, my lord.
Are you so hasty now? Well, all is one.°　　all is one: it does not matter

PEDRO
Nay, do not quarrel with us, good old man.　　　　　　　　　　　　　50

ANTONIO
If he could right himself with quarreling,
Some of us° would lie low.　　　　　　　　　Some of us: i.e., Don Pedro and Claudio

CLAUDIO　　　　　　　　Who wrongs him?

LEONATO
Marry, thou dost wrong me, thou dissembler, thou!°　　thou: (distinguished from the more respectful
Nay, never lay thy hand upon thy sword;　　　　"you" with which he addresses the prince)
I fear thee not.　　　　　　　　　　　　　　　　　　　　　　　　55

CLAUDIO　　　　Marry, beshrew° my hand　　beshrew: (mild curse)
If it should give your age such cause of fear.
In faith, my hand meant nothing to my sword.

DISCOVERING SHAKESPEARE

(92) <u>Verse</u> [5.1.46]: In 5.1.46–47, Don Pedro, Claudio, and Leonato share two <u>verse</u> lines, with each character speaking at least half a line. What effect does this sharing of lines have on the delivery of the <u>verse</u>? Does it speed up or slow down the action of the scene? Why?

LEONATO
  Tush, tush, man! never fleer° and jest at me.   **fleer:** jeer
  I speak not like a dotard nor a fool,
  As under privilege of age to brag   60
  What I have done being young, or what would do,
  Were I not old. Know, Claudio, to thy head,
  Thou hast so wronged mine innocent child and me
  That I am forced to lay my reverence by°   **lay . . . by:** renounce the respect due to old age
  And, with gray hairs and bruise° of many days,   **bruise:** wear and tear   65
  Do challenge thee to trial of a man.°   **trial of a man:** manly trial (i.e., a duel)
  I say thou hast belied mine innocent child.
  Thy slander hath gone through and through her heart,
  And she lies buried with her ancestors –
  O, in a tomb where never scandal slept,   70
  Save this of hers, framed° by thy villainy!   **framed:** made
CLAUDIO
  My villainy?
LEONATO   Thine, Claudio, thine I say.
PEDRO
  You say not right, old man.
LEONATO   My lord, my lord,
  I'll prove it on his body if he dare,
  Despite his nice fence° and his active practice,   **nice fence:** clever sword-play   75
  His May of youth and bloom of lustihood.°   **lustihood:** vigor, strength
CLAUDIO
  Away! I will not have to do with you.
LEONATO
  Canst thou so doff° me? Thou hast killed my child.   **doff:** put aside
  If thou kill'st me, boy, thou shalt kill a man.
ANTONIO
  He shall kill two of us, and men indeed.   80
  But that's no matter, let him kill one first.
  Win me and wear me!° Let him answer me.   **Win . . . wear me:** (a proverb, serving as a form
  Come, follow me, boy. Come, sir boy, come follow   of challenge)
    me.
  Sir boy, I'll whip you from your foining° fence!   **foining:** thrusting
  Nay, as I am a gentleman, I will.   85
LEONATO
  Brother –
ANTONIO
  Content° yourself. God knows I loved my niece,   **Content:** calm
  And she is dead, slandered to death by villains,
  That dare as well answer a man indeed
  As I dare take a serpent by the tongue.   90
  Boys, apes, braggarts, jacks,° milksops!   **jacks:** knaves
LEONATO   Brother Antony –
ANTONIO
  Hold you content. What, man! I know them, yea,
  And what they weigh, even to the utmost scruple,°   **scruple:** smallest measure of weight

---

DISCOVERING SHAKESPEARE

(93) Language [5.1.75]: During the quarrel between the two groups of men in 5.1.46–109, several "ageist" comments are made by each group (see especially the references to "old man," "your age," "dotard," "boy," etc.). Who begins these insults, and how do the terms escalate the argument?

Scambling,° outfacing,° fashionmonging° boys,
That lie and cog° and flout,° deprave° and slander,
Go anticly° and show an outward hideousness,°
And speak off half a dozen dangerous words,
How they might hurt their enemies, if they durst;
And this is all.

LEONATO
But, brother Antony –

ANTONIO   Come, 'tis no matter.
Do not you meddle, let me deal in this.

PEDRO
Gentlemen both, we will not wake your patience.°
My heart is sorry for your daughter's death,
But, on my honor, she was charged with nothing
But what was true, and very full of proof.°

LEONATO
My lord, my lord –

PEDRO
I will not hear you.

LEONATO
No? Come, brother, away! – I will be heard.

ANTONIO
And shall, or some of us will smart for it. *Exeunt Leonato
and Antonio.*°
    Enter Benedick.

PEDRO   See, see! Here comes the man we went to seek.
CLAUDIO   Now, signor, what news?
BENEDICK   Good day, my lord.
PEDRO   Welcome, signor. You are almost come° to part al-
most a fray.
CLAUDIO   We had liked to have had our two noses
snapped off with two old men without teeth.
PEDRO   Leonato and his brother. What think'st thou?
Had we fought, I doubt° we should have been too
young for them.
BENEDICK   In a false quarrel there is no true valor. I came
to seek you both.
CLAUDIO   We have been up and down to seek thee; for
we are high-proof° melancholy, and would fain have it
beaten away. Wilt thou use thy wit?
BENEDICK   It is in my scabbard. Shall I draw it?
PEDRO   Dost thou wear thy wit by thy side?
CLAUDIO   Never any did so, though very many have
been beside their wit.° I will bid thee draw,° as we do the
minstrels – draw to pleasure us.
PEDRO   As I am an honest man, he looks pale. Art thou
sick, or angry?

Scambling: quarrelsome; **outfacing:**
impudent; **fashionmonging:** fashionmongering   95

cog: cheat; **flout:** jeer at; **deprave:** defame

anticly: fantastically dressed; **hideousness:**
frightening aspect

100

wake your patience: cause you to need
patience

full of proof: fully proved   105

s.d. ambo: both (Leonato and Antonio)

110

almost come: come almost in time

115

doubt: suspect

120

high-proof: in a high degree

125

beside their wit: out of their minds; **draw:**
(used of a sword, and of a minstrel's bow)

130

DISCOVERING SHAKESPEARE

(94) Verse [5.1.110]: After the iambic pentameter quarrel between the two groups of men, when Benedick comes in at 5.1.110 the scene shifts to prose. Why do you think the first section of the scene is in verse, while the second is in prose?
(95) Staging [5.1.126]: When do Claudio and Don Pedro discover that Benedick is angry? Can you find any clues early in the scene between the three men (5.1.110–188) that Benedick is furious with Claudio?

CLAUDIO What, courage, man! What though care killed a cat, thou hast mettle° enough in thee to kill care.

BENEDICK Sir, I shall meet your wit in the career° an you charge it° against me. I pray you choose another subject.

CLAUDIO Nay then, give him another staff; this last was broke cross.°

PEDRO By this light, he changes more and more. I think he be angry indeed.

CLAUDIO If he be, he knows how to turn his girdle.°

BENEDICK Shall I speak a word in your ear?

CLAUDIO God bless me from a challenge!

BENEDICK *[Aside to Claudio]* You are a villain. I jest not; I will make it good how you dare, with what you dare, and when you dare. Do me right,° or I will protest° your cowardice. You have killed a sweet lady, and her death shall fall heavy on you. Let me hear from you.

CLAUDIO Well, I will meet you, so I may have good cheer.

PEDRO What, a feast? a feast?

CLAUDIO I' faith, I thank him, he hath bid° me to a calf's° head and a capon,° the which if I do not carve most curiously,° say my knife's naught.° Shall I not find a woodcock° too?

BENEDICK Sir, your wit ambles well; it goes easily.

PEDRO I'll tell thee how Beatrice praised° thy wit the other day. I said thou hadst a fine° wit: "True," said she, "a fine little one." "No," said I, "a great wit." "Right," says she, "a great gross one." "Nay," said I, "a good wit." "Just," said she, "it hurts nobody." "Nay," said I, "the gentleman is wise." "Certain," said she, "a wise gentleman."° "Nay," said I, "he hath the tongues."° "That I believe," said she, "for he swore a thing to me on Monday night which he forswore° on Tuesday morning. There's a double tongue; there's two tongues." Thus did she an hour together transshape° thy particular virtues. Yet at last she concluded with a sigh, thou wast the properest° man in Italy.

CLAUDIO For the which she wept heartily and said she cared not.

PEDRO Yea, that she did; but yet, for all that, an if she did not hate him deadly, she would love him dearly. The old man's daughter told us all.

CLAUDIO All, all! And moreover, God saw him° when he was hid in the garden.

PEDRO But when shall we set the savage bull's horns° on the sensible Benedick's head?

mettle: vivacity
in the career: while running at full speed
an you charge it: if you charge with it (as with a lance in a tilt)   135
broke cross: broken across (as by an unskillful tilter)

turn his girdle: prepare for a bout   140

Do me right: accept my challenge; **protest:** report abroad   145

150

bid: invited; **calf's:** i.e., fool's
capon: a castrated cock
curiously: expertly
naught: good for nothing
woodcock: bird famous for its stupidity   155
praised: appraised
fine: excellent, also small

160

wise gentleman: wiseacre
hath the tongues: can speak several languages
forswore: denied

165

transshape: transform
properest: handsomest

170

God saw him: (alluding to Genesis 3:8, but also to the hoaxing of Benedick)   175
the savage bull's horns: (see 1.1.248 ff.)

DISCOVERING SHAKESPEARE

(96) History [5.1.148]: What were the rules for challenging someone to a duel during the Renaissance? (*Hint:* For an interesting contrast to this scene, see Touchstone's catalog of "the degrees of the lie" in *As You Like It,* 5.4.48–97.)

(97) Paraphrase [5.1.172]: Paraphrase into modern English the following sentence by Don Pedro: "But yet for all that, an if she did not hate him deadly, she would love him dearly" (5.1.171–172). How does this line present a stereotypical view of women?

CLAUDIO Yea, and text° underneath, "Here dwells Benedick, the married man"?

BENEDICK Fare you well, boy; you know my mind. I will leave you now to your gossiplike humor. You break jests as braggarts do their blades, which God be thanked hurt not. *[To the Prince]* My lord, for your many courtesies I thank you. I must discontinue your company. Your brother the bastard is fled from Messina. You have among you killed a sweet and innocent lady. For my Lord Lackbeard there, he and I shall meet, and till then peace be with him.   *[Exit.]*

PEDRO He is in earnest.

CLAUDIO In most profound earnest, and, I'll warrant you, for the love of Beatrice.

PEDRO And hath challenged thee?

CLAUDIO Most sincerely.

PEDRO What a pretty thing man is when he goes in his doublet and hose° and leaves off his wit!

Enter Constables [Dogberry and Verges, with the Watch, leading] Conrad and Borachio.

CLAUDIO He is then a giant to an ape, but then is an ape a doctor to such a man.°

PEDRO But, soft you, let me be! Pluck up, my heart, and be sad!° Did he not say my brother was fled?

DOGBERRY Come you, sir. If justice cannot tame you, she shall ne'er weigh more reasons in her balance.° Nay, an you be a cursing hypocrite once, you must be looked to.

PEDRO How now, two of my brother's men bound? Borachio one.

CLAUDIO Hearken after their offense, my lord.

PEDRO Officers, what offense have these men done?

DOGBERRY Marry, sir, they have committed false report; moreover, they have spoken untruths; secondarily, they are slanders; sixth and lastly, they have belied a lady; thirdly, they have verified° unjust things; and to conclude, they are lying knaves.

PEDRO First, I ask thee what they have done; thirdly, I ask thee what's their offense; sixth and lastly, why they are committed;° and to conclude, what you lay to their charge?

CLAUDIO Rightly reasoned, and in his own division,° and by my troth there's one meaning well suited.°

PEDRO Who have you offended, masters, that you are thus bound to your answer?° This learned constable is too cunning to be understood. What's your offense?

BORACHIO Sweet prince, let me go no farther to mine answer.° Do you hear me, and let this count kill me. I

Side glosses:

text: in capital letters — 180

— 185

— 190

in . . . hose: i.e., fully dressed — 195

a giant . . . man: much bigger than an ape, but the ape is much wiser than he

Pluck . . . sad: pull up a moment, my mind, and be serious — 200

balance: scales (symbol of justice)

— 205

— 210

verified: sworn to

committed: arrested and held for trial — 215

division: scheme of argument

well suited: provided with several different suits, or modes of speech

bound to your answer: bound over, indicted — 220

answer: trial

DISCOVERING SHAKESPEARE

(98) Plot [5.1.199]: Why is Don John's departure from Messina significant (cf. 5.1.184–185, 5.1.199, and 5.1.241)?

(99) Parody [5.1.216]: In 5.1.213–216, Don Pedro parodies Dogberry's illogical numbering of the offenses done by Borachio and Conrad. What is the effect of having this wonderful comic moment immediately before the very serious revelation that Hero has been falsely accused?

have deceived even your very eyes. What your wisdoms could not discover, these shallow fools have brought to light, who in the night overheard me confessing to this man, how Don John your brother incensed° me to slander the Lady Hero; how you were brought into the orchard and saw me court Margaret in Hero's garments; how you disgraced her when you should marry her. My villainy they have upon record, which I had rather seal with my death than repeat over to my shame. The lady is dead upon mine and my master's false accusation, and briefly, I desire nothing but the reward of a villain.   **incensed:** incited   225   230

PEDRO   Runs not this speech like iron° through your blood?   **iron:** a sword   235

CLAUDIO   I have drunk poison whiles he uttered it.

PEDRO   But did my brother set thee on to this?

BORACHIO   Yea, and paid me richly for the practice° of it.   **practice:** accomplishment

PEDRO
He is composed and framed of treachery,   240
And fled he is upon this villainy.

CLAUDIO
Sweet Hero, now thy image doth appear
In the rare semblance° that I loved it first.   **semblance:** likeness

DOGBERRY   Come, bring away the plaintiffs.° By this time   **plaintiffs:** (for "defendants")
our sexton hath reformed° Signor Leonato of the matter.   **reformed:** (for "informed")   245
And, masters, do not forget to specify, when time and
place shall serve, that I am an ass.

VERGES   Here, here comes Master Signor Leonato, and
the sexton too.

       Enter Leonato, his brother [Antonio], and the Sexton.

LEONATO
Which is the villain? Let me see his eyes,   250
That, when I note another man like him,
I may avoid him. Which of these is he?

BORACHIO
If you would know your wronger, look on me.

LEONATO
Art thou the slave that with thy breath hast killed
Mine innocent child?   255

BORACHIO   Yea, even I alone.

LEONATO
No, not so, villain! thou beliest thyself.
Here stand a pair of honorable men —
A third is fled — that had a hand in it.
I thank you princes for my daughter's death.
Record it with your high and worthy deeds.   260
'Twas bravely done, if you bethink you of° it.   **bethink you of:** recall

CLAUDIO
I know not how to pray your patience;°   **pray your patience:** ask your forgiveness
Yet I must speak. Choose your revenge yourself;

DISCOVERING SHAKESPEARE

(100) Characterization [5.1.242]: When Claudio says "Sweet Hero, now thy image doth appear / In the rare semblance that I loved it first" (5.1.242–243), how do you feel about his expression of remorse? Do you forgive him for what he did to her? Why or why not?

Impose me to° what penance your invention
Can lay upon my sin. Yet sinned I not
But in mistaking.

PEDRO By my soul, nor I!
And yet, to satisfy this good old man,
I would bend under any heavy weight
That he'll enjoin me to.

LEONATO
I cannot bid you bid my daughter live –
That were impossible – but I pray you both,
Possess° the people in Messina here
How innocent she died, and if your love
Can labor aught in sad invention,
Hang her an epitaph upon her tomb,
And sing it to her bones – sing it tonight.
Tomorrow morning come you to my house,
And since you could not be my son-in-law,
Be yet my nephew. My brother hath a daughter,
Almost the copy of my child that's dead,
And she alone is heir to both of us.
Give her the right° you should have giv'n her cousin,
And so dies my revenge.

CLAUDIO O noble sir!
Your overkindness doth wring tears from me.
I do embrace your offer, and dispose°
For henceforth of poor Claudio.

LEONATO
Tomorrow then I will expect your coming;
Tonight I take my leave. This naughty° man
Shall face to face be brought to Margaret,
Who I believe was packed° in all this wrong,
Hired to it by your brother.

BORACHIO No, by my soul, she was not,
Nor knew not what she did when she spoke to me,
But always hath been just and virtuous
In anything that I do know by her.

DOGBERRY Moreover, sir, which indeed is not under white and black,° this plaintiff here, the offender, did call me ass. I beseech you let it be remembered in his punishment. And also the watch heard them talk of one Deformed. They say he wears a key in his ear, and a lock° hanging by it, and borrows money in God's name, the which he hath used so long and never paid that now men grow hardhearted and will lend nothing for God's sake. Pray you examine him upon that point.

LEONATO I thank thee for thy care and honest pains.

DOGBERRY Your worship speaks like a most thankful and reverent youth, and I praise God for you.

Impose me to: impose on me

Possess: inform

right: right of becoming your wife (perhaps with pun on "rite" of marriage)

dispose: you may dispose

naughty: evil

packed: in the pact, an accomplice

under . . . black: in writing

key, lock: (his misunderstanding of the *lock* of 3.3.168)

DISCOVERING SHAKESPEARE

(101) <u>Verse</u> [5.1.275]: Write your own verse epitaph for Hero; then find someone in class who can set it to music.

(102) Social Customs [5.1.300–301]: Dogberry's comment that Conrad borrows money "in God's name" (5.1.300–301) implies that the thief begs alms for charity and thereby ruins the practice for "honest" beggars. How common were beggars in Renaissance England?

LEONATO   There's for thy pains.
   [Gives money.]
DOGBERRY   God save the foundation!°
LEONATO   Go, I discharge° thee of thy prisoner, and I
   thank thee.
DOGBERRY   I leave an arrant knave with your worship,
   which I beseech your worship to correct yourself, for
   the example of others. God keep your worship! I wish
   your worship well. God restore you to health! I humbly
   give you leave° to depart, and if a merry meeting may be
   wished, God prohibit° it! Come, neighbor.
                    [Exeunt Dogberry and Verges.]
LEONATO
   Until tomorrow morning, lords, farewell.
ANTONIO
   Farewell, my lords. We look for you tomorrow.
PEDRO
   We will not fail.
CLAUDIO   Tonight I'll mourn with Hero.
                    [Exeunt Don Pedro and Claudio.]
LEONATO   *[To the Watch]*
   Bring you these fellows on. — We'll talk with Margaret,
   How her acquaintance grew with this lewd° fellow.
                    Exeunt.

God . . . foundation: (conventional phrase used by beggars receiving alms at the gates of religious or charitable foundations)   310
discharge: relieve

give you leave: (for "ask your leave")   315
prohibit: (for "grant")

    320
lewd: low, disreputable

❧ **5.2** *Enter Benedick and Margaret [meeting].*

BENEDICK   Pray thee, sweet Mistress Margaret, deserve
   well at my hands by helping me to the speech of
   Beatrice.
MARGARET   Will you then write me a sonnet in praise of
   my beauty?
BENEDICK   In so high a style,° Margaret, that no man living shall come over° it, for in most comely truth thou
   deservest it.
MARGARET   To have no man come over° me? Why, shall I
   always keep belowstairs?°
BENEDICK   Thy wit is as quick as the greyhound's
   mouth — it catches.
MARGARET   And yours as blunt as the fencer's foils,
   which hit but hurt not.
BENEDICK   A most manly wit, Margaret: it will not hurt
   a woman. And so I pray thee call Beatrice. I give thee
   the bucklers.°
MARGARET   Give us the swords;° we have bucklers° of our
   own.
BENEDICK   If you use them, Margaret, you must put in
   the pikes° with a vice,° and they are dangerous weapons
   for maids.

    5
style: i.e., of writing, but with a pun on "stile," stairs over a fence
come over: outdo

come over: have sex with
keep belowstairs: dwell in the servants' quarters   10
(i.e., never be mistress of a house by marrying a man of higher rank)

    15
bucklers: shields
swords: penises; **bucklers:** vulvas

    20
pikes: spikes in the center of the shields, penises;
vice: screw

DISCOVERING SHAKESPEARE

(103) Puns [5.2.1]: Find and explain all the sexual puns in the brief exchange between Benedick and Margaret at the beginning of 5.2.

MARGARET   Well, I will call Beatrice to you, who I think
  hath legs.   *Exit Margaret.*
BENEDICK   And therefore will come.   25

  [*Sings.*]   The god of love,
                  That sits above
              And knows me, and knows me,
                How pitiful I deserve —°   (lines from a popular song)

I mean in singing; but in loving, Leander° the good   **Leander:** (who swam the Hellespont every night   30
swimmer, Troilus° the first employer of panders, and a   to see another Hero until he was drowned in a
whole book full of these quondam carpetmongers,°   storm)
whose names yet run smoothly in the even road of a   **Troilus:** (who was helped to the love of Cressida
blank verse — why, they were never so truly turned over° by her uncle Pandarus)
and over as my poor self in love. Marry, I cannot show   **quondam carpetmongers:** ancient carpet
it in rhyme. I have tried. I can find out no rhyme to   knights (i.e., lovers rather than fighters)   35
"lady" but "baby" — an innocent° rhyme; for "scorn,"   **turned over and over:** head over heels
"horn"° — a hard rhyme; for "school," "fool" — a bab-   **innocent:** childish
bling rhyme. Very ominous endings! No, I was not   **horn:** (punning on a cuckold's horns or an
born under a rhyming planet, nor I cannot woo in   erection)
festival° terms.   40
  Enter Beatrice.   **festival:** elevated
Sweet Beatrice, wouldst thou come when I called thee?
BEATRICE   Yea, signor, and depart when you bid me.
BENEDICK   O, stay but till then!
BEATRICE   "Then" is spoken. Fare you well now. And yet,   45
  ere I go, let me go with that I came for, which is, with
  knowing what hath passed between you and Claudio.
BENEDICK   Only foul words, and thereupon I will kiss
  thee.
BEATRICE   Foul words is but foul wind, and foul wind is   50
  but foul breath, and foul breath is noisome.° Therefore I   **noisome:** offensive, bad-smelling
  will depart unkissed.
BENEDICK   Thou hast frighted the word out of his right
  sense,° so forcible is thy wit. But I must tell thee plainly,   **sense:** wits
  Claudio undergoes° my challenge, and either I must   **undergoes:** bears   55
  shortly hear from him or I will subscribe him° a coward.   **subscribe him:** write him down
  And I pray thee now tell me, for which of my bad parts
  didst thou first fall in love with me?
BEATRICE   For them all together, which maintained so
  politic° a state of evil that they will not admit any good   **politic:** well organized   60
  part to intermingle with them. But for which of my
  good parts did you first suffer° love for me?   **suffer:** experience, but also feel the pain
BENEDICK   Suffer love! — a good epithet. I do suffer love
  indeed, for I love thee against my will.
BEATRICE   In spite of your heart, I think. Alas, poor   65
  heart! If you spite it for my sake, I will spite it for yours,
  for I will never love that which my friend hates.

DISCOVERING SHAKESPEARE

(104) Teaser [5.2.42]: Find a situation in *The Taming of the Shrew* that echoes Benedick's "Sweet Beatrice, wouldst thou
come when I called thee?" (5.2.42–43).
(105) Language [5.2.59]: What does the word "politic" mean in Beatrice's phrase "so politic a state of evil" (5.2.59–60)?
Look up the word in the *Oxford English Dictionary* to see how many different meanings were available to Shakespeare and
his audience around the year 1600. Which definition seems most appropriate to you in this context?

BENEDICK   Thou and I are too wise to woo peaceably.

BEATRICE   It appears not in this confession. There's not one wise man among twenty that will praise himself.

BENEDICK   An old, an old instance, Beatrice, that lived in the time of good neighbors.° If a man do not erect in this age his own tomb ere he dies, he shall live no longer in monument than the bell rings and the widow weeps.

BEATRICE   And how long is that, think you?

BENEDICK   Question: why, an hour in clamor and a quarter in rheum.° Therefore it is most expedient for the wise, if Don Worm (his conscience) find no impediment to the contrary, to be the trumpet of his own virtues, as I am to myself. So much for praising myself, who, I myself will bear witness, is praiseworthy. And now tell me, how doth your cousin?

BEATRICE   Very ill.

BENEDICK   And how do you?

BEATRICE   Very ill too.

BENEDICK   Serve God, love me, and mend. There will I leave you too, for here comes one in haste.

Enter Ursula.

URSULA   Madam, you must come to your uncle. Yonder's old coil° at home. It is proved my Lady Hero hath been falsely accused, the prince and Claudio mightily abused,° and Don John is the author of all, who is fled and gone. Will you come presently?

BEATRICE   Will you go hear this news, signor?

BENEDICK   I will live in thy heart, die in thy lap,° and be buried in thy eyes, and moreover, I will go with thee to thy uncle's.   *Exit [with Beatrice and Ursula].*

๛ 5.3 *Enter Claudio, Prince [Don Pedro, Lord], and three or four [Attendants] with tapers° [followed by Musicians].*

CLAUDIO   Is this the monument of Leonato?

LORD   It is, my lord.

CLAUDIO   *[Reads from a scroll.]*

Epitaph.

Done to death by slanderous tongues°
    Was the Hero° that here lies.
Death, in guerdon° of her wrongs,
    Gives her fame which never dies.
So the life that died with shame
Lives in death with glorious fame.

time of good neighbors: i.e., golden age   70

75

rheum: tears

80

85

old coil: confusion   90

abused: deceived

die in thy lap: (punning on "have an orgasm")   95

tapers: candles (as a symbol of penitence)

(Q gives no speech prefix, and the epitaph might well be spoken by the Lord)
Hero: (pun intended)   5
guerdon: reward

DISCOVERING SHAKESPEARE

(106) Staging [5.2.89]: When Ursula enters to tell Beatrice and Benedick that Hero has been falsely accused, how do the two lovers react?

(107) Staging [5.3.1]: If you were directing a production of the play, how would you stage this scene at the monument? What specific design choices would you make in terms of <u>set</u>, lighting, music, <u>costuming</u>, and <u>props</u>?

[Hangs up the scroll.]
> Hang thou there upon the tomb,
> Praising her when I am dumb. 10
> Now, music, sound, and sing your solemn hymn.

       Song [by one or more Attendants].°   s.d. (perhaps Balthasar is one of the singers)

> Pardon, goddess of the night,°   **goddess of the night:** Diana, patroness of
> Those that slew thy virgin knight,°   chastity
> For the which, with songs of woe,   **virgin knight:** (still punning on "Hero")
> Round about her tomb they go. 15
> Midnight, assist our moan,
> Help us to sigh and groan
>   Heavily, heavily.
> Graves, yawn and yield your dead,
> Till death be utterèd°   **utterèd:** fully expressed 20
>   Heavily, heavily.

CLAUDIO   Now unto thy bones good night!
> Yearly will I do this rite.

PEDRO
> Good morrow, masters. Put your torches out.
>   The wolves have preyed, and look, the gentle day, 25
> Before the wheels of Phoebus,° round about   **Phoebus:** god who drives the chariot of the sun
>   Dapples the drowsy east with spots of gray.
> Thanks to you all, and leave us. Fare you well.

CLAUDIO
> Good morrow, masters. Each his several way.

PEDRO
> Come, let us hence and put on other weeds,°   **weeds:** clothes (they are in mourning) 30
> And then to Leonato's we will go.

CLAUDIO
> And Hymen° now with luckier issue speeds°   **Hymen:** god of marriage; **speeds:** (perhaps for
> Than this for whom we rendered up this woe.   "speed us")

                               Exeunt.

❧ **5.4** *Enter Leonato, Benedick, [Beatrice,] Margaret,
Ursula, Old Man [Antonio], Friar [Francis], Hero.*

FRIAR
> Did I not tell you she was innocent?

LEONATO
> So are the prince and Claudio, who accused her
> Upon° the error that you heard debated.   **Upon:** because of
> But Margaret was in some fault for this,
> Although against her will,° as it appears   **against her will:** unintentionally 5
> In the true course of all the question.°   **question:** investigation

---

DISCOVERING SHAKESPEARE

(108) <u>Verse</u> **[5.3.20]:** What is the <u>rhyme</u> scheme and <u>meter</u> of Claudio's epitaph? What part of it should be read, and what part sung? Why?

(109) <u>Themes</u> **[5.4.1]:** Act 5, scene 4 appears to take place the morning after Claudio's nighttime funeral epitaph. What is the <u>symbolic</u> significance of beginning the last scene of the play with a new day?

ANTONIO
   Well, I am glad that all things sorts° so well.   **sorts:** turn out

BENEDICK
   And so am I, being else by faith° enforced   **faith:** fidelity to my word
   To call young Claudio to a reckoning for it.

LEONATO
   Well, daughter, and you gentlewomen all,   10
   Withdraw into a chamber by yourselves,
   And when I send for you, come hither masked.
   The prince and Claudio promised by this hour
   To visit me. You know your office, brother:
   You must be father to your brother's daughter,   15
   And give her to young Claudio.   *Exeunt Ladies.*

ANTONIO
   Which I will do with confirmed countenance.°   **confirmed countenance:** straight face

BENEDICK
   Friar, I must entreat your pains, I think.

FRIAR
   To do what, signor?

BENEDICK
   To bind me, or undo me – one of them.   20
   Signor Leonato, truth it is, good signor,
   Your niece regards me with an eye of favor.

LEONATO
   That eye my daughter lent her. 'Tis most true.

BENEDICK
   And I do with an eye of love requite her.

LEONATO
   The sight whereof I think you had from me,   25
   From Claudio, and the prince; but what's your will?

BENEDICK
   Your answer, sir, is enigmatical;
   But, for my will, my will is your good will
   May stand with ours, this day to be conjoined
   In the state of honorable marriage,   30
   In which, good friar, I shall desire your help.

LEONATO
   My heart is with your liking.

FRIAR   And my help.
   Here comes the prince and Claudio.
   Enter Prince [Don Pedro] and Claudio and two or
   three other.

PEDRO
   Good morrow to this fair assembly.

LEONATO
   Good morrow, prince; good morrow, Claudio.   35
   We here attend you. Are you yet° determined   **yet:** still
   Today to marry with my brother's daughter?

CLAUDIO
   I'll hold my mind, were she an Ethiope.°   **Ethiope:** i.e., black, and hence ugly in the
                                      stereotypical comparison to blondes

DISCOVERING SHAKESPEARE

(110) Staging [5.4.25]: How does Benedick react to Leonato's "That eye my daughter lent her" (5.4.23) and "The sight whereof I think you had from me" (5.4.25)? Does he understand what Leonato means in the two lines? Why do you think so?

LEONATO
Call her forth, brother. Here's the friar ready.

[Exit Antonio.]

PEDRO
Good morrow, Benedick. Why, what's the matter   40
That you have such a February face,
So full of frost, of storm, and cloudiness?

CLAUDIO
I think he thinks upon the savage bull.
Tush, fear not, man! We'll tip thy horns with gold,
And all Europa° shall rejoice at thee,   45
As once Europa° did at lusty Jove
When he would play the noble beast in love.

BENEDICK
Bull Jove, sir, had an amiable low,
And some such strange bull leaped your father's cow
And got a calf° in that same noble feat   50
Much like to you, for you have just his bleat.
  Enter [Leonato's] brother [Antonio], Hero, Beatrice,
  Margaret, Ursula [the ladies wearing masks].

CLAUDIO
For this I owe you.° Here comes other reck'nings.°
Which is the lady I must seize upon?

LEONATO
This same is she, and I do give you her.°

CLAUDIO
Why then, she's mine. Sweet, let me see your face.   55

LEONATO
No, that you shall not till you take her hand
Before this friar and swear to marry her.

CLAUDIO
Give me your hand before this holy friar.
I am your husband if you like of me.

HERO *[Unmasks.]*
And when I lived I was your other wife;   60
And when you loved you were my other husband.

CLAUDIO
Another Hero!

HERO   Nothing certainer.
One Hero died defiled;° but I do live,
And surely as I live, I am a maid.

PEDRO
The former Hero! Hero that is dead!   65

LEONATO
She died, my lord, but whiles her slander lived.

FRIAR
All this amazement can I qualify,°

Europa: Europe

Europa: a girl who was wooed by Jove in the shape of a bull

calf: fool

I owe you: I will pay you later (Benedick has managed to call him both a calf and a bastard); **reck'nings:** bills to pay

This . . . her: (editors often reject Q and assign the speech to Antonio)

defiled: disgraced (by the false charge)

qualify: moderate, relieve

DISCOVERING SHAKESPEARE

(111) Metaphor [5.4.49]: Claudio's reference to "the savage bull" (5.4.43) reminds many readers of Don Pedro's earlier "In time the savage bull doth bear the yoke" (1.1.248–250), while Benedick's allusion to "your father's cow" (5.4.49) recalls Beatrice's earlier proof about why "God sends a curst cow short horns" (2.1.20–21). To what extent have both these lovers—Beatrice and Benedick—come full circle since the play's beginning?

(112) Characterization [5.4.63]: How can Claudio's attitude and behavior in the monument scene (5.3) and in the reconciliation scene (see especially 5.4.52–66) help the audience forgive his horrid treatment of Hero?

When, after that the holy rites are ended,
I'll tell you largely° of fair Hero's death.
Meantime let wonder seem familiar,°
And to the chapel let us presently.

BENEDICK
    Soft and fair, friar. Which is Beatrice?

BEATRICE *[Unmasks.]*
    I answer to that name. What is your will?

BENEDICK
    Do not you love me?

BEATRICE   Why, no, no more than reason.

BENEDICK
    Why, then your uncle, and the prince, and Claudio
    Have been deceived – they swore you did.

BEATRICE
    Do not you love me?

BENEDICK   Troth, no, no more than reason.

BEATRICE
    Why, then my cousin, Margaret, and Ursula
    Are much deceived, for they did swear you did.

BENEDICK
    They swore that you were almost sick for me.

BEATRICE
    They swore that you were well-nigh dead for me.

BENEDICK
    'Tis no such matter. Then you do not love me?

BEATRICE
    No, truly, but in friendly recompense.°

LEONATO
    Come, cousin, I am sure you love the gentleman.

CLAUDIO
    And I'll be sworn upon't that he loves her,
    For here's a paper written in his hand,
    A halting sonnet of his own pure brain,
    Fashioned to Beatrice.

HERO   And here's another,
    Writ in my cousin's hand, stol'n from her pocket,
    Containing her affection unto Benedick.

BENEDICK A miracle! Here's our own hands° against our
    hearts. Come, I will have thee; but, by this light, I take
    thee for pity.

BEATRICE I would not deny you; but, by this good day, I
    yield upon great persuasion, and partly to save your
    life, for I was told you were in a consumption.

BENEDICK Peace! I will stop your mouth.°
    [Kisses her.]

PEDRO How dost thou, Benedick, the married man?

BENEDICK I'll tell thee what, prince: a college of wit–
    crackers° cannot flout me out of my humor. Dost thou
    think I care for a satire or an epigram? No. If a man will

---

largely: in full
let . . . familiar: treat this marvel as if it were an   70
ordinary matter

75

80

friendly recompense: charitable repayment

85

90

hands: written testimony

95

Peace! . . . mouth: (Q assigns the line to
Leonato, who may be threatening to shut his niece
up)

college of wit-crackers: assembly of jokers   100

DISCOVERING SHAKESPEARE

(113) Plot [5.4.86]: What do Claudio and Hero do to keep Beatrice and Benedick together in 5.4.85–90?

be beaten with brains,° a shall wear nothing handsome about him. In brief, since I do purpose to marry, I will think nothing to any purpose that the world can say against it; and therefore never flout at me for what I have said against it, for man is a giddy° thing, and this is my conclusion. For thy part, Claudio, I did think to have beaten thee; but in that thou art like to be my kinsman, live unbruised, and love my cousin.

beaten with brains: defeated with witticisms (but with a play on the literal sense of having brains flung at him, which will spoil his clothes)

105

giddy: inconstant

CLAUDIO   I had well hoped thou wouldst have denied Beatrice, that I might have cudgeled thee out of thy single life, to make thee a double-dealer,° which out of question thou wilt be if my cousin do not look exceeding narrowly to thee.

110

double-dealer: married man, but also an unfaithful husband (a common newlywed joke)

BENEDICK   Come, come, we are friends. Let's have a dance ere we are married, that we may lighten our own hearts and our wives' heels.

115

LEONATO   We'll have dancing afterward.

BENEDICK   First, of° my word! Therefore play, music. Prince, thou art sad. Get thee a wife, get thee a wife! There is no staff° more reverend than one tipped with horn.°

of: upon

120

staff: rod of office, but also walking stick
tipped with horn: (the usual reference to horns and cuckoldry)

Enter Messenger.

MESSENGER
My lord, your brother John is ta'en in flight,
And brought with armèd men back to Messina.

BENEDICK   Think not on him till tomorrow. I'll devise thee brave punishments for him. Strike up, pipers!

125

Dance. [Exeunt.]

DISCOVERING SHAKESPEARE

(114) Characterization [5.4.109]: Why is Beatrice silent during the last thirty-two lines of the play? What should the actress be doing while she is on stage?

(115) Staging [5.4.125]: Devise a curtain call for the end of the play. Which characters should come out first? Which should be last? Would you underscore the curtain call with music in any way? If so, what song would you choose?

❧

Research and Discussion Topics

ACT I

1. Find each of the following cities on a map of Europe: Aragon (1.1.1), Messina (1.1.2), Florence (1.1.10), Padua (1.1.33), and Venice (1.1.258). Which of these cities is farthest from Messina?

2. Who was Cupid (1.1.37), and what was a "bird-bolt" (1.1.39)?

3. What was the difference between the "five wits" (1.1.61) and the five senses?

4. What were the four "humors" (1.1.124)?

5. What was a "flouting Jack" (1.1.175), and who was Vulcan (1.1.176)?

6. What were a "recheat" and a "baldrick" (1.1.229-230)?

7. What does Don John mean when he says he was "born under Saturn" (1.3.10)?

8. What was a "March chick" (1.3.50)?

9. What did a "perfumer" do (1.3.52)?

ACT II

1. Who was Philemon (2.1.90), and why does Don Pedro wear his visor?

2. What was the *Hundred Merry Tales* (2.1.124)? Why would Beatrice be upset at the suggestion that it was the source of her wit?

3. What was a "lieutenant's scarf" (2.1.182)?

4. Why was eating rabbit's meat supposedly a cause of melancholy (2.1.203–204)?

5. What pun is Beatrice making in the phrase "civil as an orange" (2.1.277)?

6. What was a "blazon" (2.1.279)?

7. Beatrice's pejorative reference to being "sunburned" (2.1.301) implies that Elizabethans did not appreciate the value of a good suntan. Why was this so?

8. What were the duties of a "waiting gentlewoman" like Margaret (2.2.12-13)?

9. How much would "a thousand ducats" (2.2.48) and "an angel" (2.3.31) be worth in today's currency?

ACT III

1. What does Ursula mean when she tells Hero that Beatrice is "limed" (3.1.104)?

2. How were "worms" (3.2.25) involved with toothaches?

3. What were "slops" (3.2.33)? Find a picture of them.

4. How many different services were performed at a "barbers" (3.2.40)?

5. What was "civet" (3.2.46), where did it come from, and what was it used for?

6. What kinds of cosmetics were used during the Renaissance (3.2.52)?

7. What was a "watch" (3.3.6)? What were the duties of a "constable" (3.3.10) and a "head-borough" (3.5.1 sd)? What were "bills" (3.3.42)?

8. Who was "Pharaoh" (3.3.133)? Who were "Bel's priests" (3.3.134)?

9. What was a "lock" (3.3.168) or a "lovelock"?

ACT IV

1. Research the Elizabethan marriage ceremony. How would it have differed from the "plain form of marriage" (4.1.2) requested by Leonato?

2. Consult William Lily's well-known grammar text (1538) on "interjections" (4.1.20), and provide some examples for your classmates.

3. Who were "Dian" and "Venus" (4.1.58–59)?

4. What does Hero mean by "catechizing" (4.1.77)? How does the meaning of the term relate to her name?

5. What were the duties of a friar (4.1.171)? What other Shakespearean plays feature friars?

6. Who was Hercules (4.1.319)?

7. What did a "sexton" do (4.2.2)?

ACT V

1. What is an "epitaph" (5.1.275)? Can you find any examples of sixteenth-century epitaphs?

2. Who were "Troilus" and "Leander" (5.2.30–31)?

3. What were the rules and customs regarding "challenges" (5.2.55) during the English Renaissance?

4. Why was a worm (5.2.79) or a serpent a traditional image for one's conscience?

5. Who was "Diana, the goddess of the night" (5.3.12)? Who is the "virgin knight" (5.3.13) mentioned in Balthasar's song? Who was "Phoebus" (5.3.26)?

6. Who were "Jove" and "Europa" (5.4.45–46)?

7. What was a "consumption" (5.4.96)?

8. What is a "satire" and an "epigram" (5.4.101)?

Filmography

1984
BBC
Rating:

Directed by: Stuart Burge

Cherie Lunghi as Beatrice
Robert Lindsay as Benedick
Michael Elphick as Dogberry
Katharine Levy as Hero
Vernon Dobtcheff as Don John
Jon Finch as Don Pedro
Lee Montague as Leonato
Robert Reynolds as Claudio

Lunghi's Beatrice and Lindsay's Benedick are nearly perfect and certainly seem perfect for each other. Television close-ups give an immediacy to their courtship that is hard to match on stage. The text is almost complete, allowing the two cleverest lovers in Shakespeare to shine as only they can. Most of the characters in the play declare that Beatrice is unattractive because she is independent. Cherie Lunghi is especially good at proving the opposite to be true. The rest of the cast is uniformly excellent, with a properly snobbish Leonato, unbearably and idiotically self-satisfied Dogberry, and a thoroughly clueless, moderately cruel Claudio. The production would be stronger, however, if it were more playful. The deception of Benedick is mostly humorless, with the tricking of Beatrice not much better.

1993
A Renaissance Films Production
Rating:

Directed by: Kenneth Branagh

Emma Thompson as Beatrice
Kenneth Branagh as Benedick

Michael Keaton as Dogberry
Kate Beckinsale as Hero
Keanu Reeves as Don John
Denzel Washington as Don Pedro
Richard Briers as Leonato
Robert Sean Leonard as Claudio

What should have been a definitive *Much Ado* is just another example of Shakespeare goes to Hollywood. Branagh and Thompson had the skills and experience to bring Benedick and Beatrice to life as never before on screen, but incredibly, Branagh so reduced their parts that they no longer seem to be the stars. He filled up time that might have been better occupied with great acting and greater lines with odd conceits such as Beatrice's sunburning and a cinematic reference to *The Magnificent Seven*. Other strange visual images include some of the most unappetizing nudity in a Shakespeare film since Polanski's *Macbeth*. Branagh did, however, do a much better (and more light-hearted) job of the deception of Benedick than the BBC managed. Kate Beckinsale and Robert Sean Leonard are physically appealing and dramatically effective. The production almost seems to belong to them. Keanu Reeves and Denzel Washington are adequate to their parts, but Michael Keaton, who plays Dogberry as a sadistic torturer, is unforgivably bad.

Annotated Bibliography

Allen, John A. "Dogberry." *Shakespeare Quarterly* 24:1 (Winter 1973): 37–53. journal PR 2885.S63.

> Challenging previous interpretations of Dogberry as a vapid and rather inconsequential character, Allen argues that the constable provides both comic relief and moral illumination in *Much Ado About Nothing*. In particular, Allen analyzes Dogberry's relationship with other characters and contends that the constable's foolishness mirrors frailties found in all human beings. In this manner, Allen believes, Shakespeare creates a character who reveals universal truths about human nature and who, in turn, makes *Much Ado About Nothing* much more than a merely "comic" play.

Berger, Harry, Jr. "Against the Sink-a-Pace: Sexual and Family Politics in *Much Ado About Nothing*." *Shakespeare Quarterly* 33:3 (Autumn 1982): 302–313. journal PR 2885.S63.

> Reading the marriage unions of *Much Ado About Nothing* as analogous to Sir Tobias Belch's description of the sink-a-pace dance in *Twelfth Night*, Berger contends that marriage in *Much Ado* is represented in sequential stages of excitement, boredom, and repentance. Focusing particularly on the ways males treat females in the play, Berger believes that men recognize the manner in which women are "abused" in marriage and therefore attempt to repent for their abuse once boredom has set into the relationship. Berger ultimately believes that *Much Ado* is a celebration of the end of happy marriages and suggests that the sink-a-pace, for all its pessimism

about the duration of frivolity, is a perfectly suited metaphor for this unique festivity.

Cook, Carol. " 'The Sign and Semblance of Her Honor': Reading Gender Difference" in *Much Ado About Nothing. Publications of the Modern Language Association* 101:2 (March 1986): 186–202. journal PB 6.M6.

In this gender studies reading of *Much Ado About Nothing,* Cook argues that the play supports patriarchal oppression of femininity. Contrary to previous criticism that suggests *Much Ado* is progressively pro-feminist, Cook contends that the play's apparent attempts to diffuse gender differences ultimately reinforce those differences and glorify masculine power. Focusing particularly on the cuckold jokes of the play's first scene, Cook argues that the script's comic tone is Shakespeare's artful way of diverting attention away from the gender contradictions inherent in the rest of the play.

Dennis, Carl. "Wit and Wisdom in *Much Ado About Nothing." Studies in English Literature: 1500–1900* 8:2 (Spring 1973): 223–237. journal PR 1.S82.

Agreeing with past critics who contend that *Much Ado About Nothing* is essentially a play about two worldviews, those informed by either wit or wisdom, Dennis argues that this distinction forms the foundation of the play's moral and intellectual vitality. With these two perspectives in mind, he analyzes the play's primary characters and examines how each follows life principles informed by either wit or wisdom. Ultimately, Dennis contends, *Much Ado About Nothing* is a play that urges us to forgo a worldview guided by wit in favor of one informed by wisdom.

Dobranski, Stephen B. "Children of the Mind: Miscarried Narratives in *Much Ado About Nothing." Studies in English Literature: 1500–1900* 38:1 (Winter 1998): 233–250. journal PR 1.S82.

Dobranski contends that Shakespeare creates a back-story within the central narrative of *Much Ado About Nothing* by alluding to but always avoiding direct discussion of a history of the past relationship between Beatrice and Benedick. Christening this literary technique "deflection," Dobranski argues that the absence of Beatrice and Benedick's child corresponds to this incomplete, undeveloped history at which the central story hints. In addition, Dobranski focuses on Beatrice's inability as a woman to speak explicitly of serious matters and the extent to which that inability contributes to the obscured past between the two lovers.

Friedman, Michael D. " 'For man is a giddy thing, and this is my conclusion': Fashion and *Much Ado About Nothing." Text and Performance Quarterly* 13:2 (July 1993): 267–282. journal PN 2.L69.

In this dramaturgical analysis of *Much Ado About Nothing,* Friedman argues that directors of the play can make creative use of costumes to illuminate some of the play's central topics, particularly the oppressive role of Messina's patriarchal social system. Suggesting that fashion is *Much Ado's* central metaphor, Friedman contends that clothing reflects social hierarchies and that, as fashion shifts, so too do Messina's social norms. As a result, Messina is forced to alter its traditional social order by integrating new fashions (and, therefore, social conventions) into more established behavioral patterns.

Friedman, Michael D. "'Hush'd on Purpose to Grace Harmony': Wives and Silence in *Much Ado About Nothing.*" *Theatre Journal* 42:3 (Oct 1990): 350–363. journal PN 3171.E38.

In this feminist reading of *Much Ado About Nothing,* Friedman contends that the play's wives must be silent in order for their marital relationships to be successful. In particular, he focuses on Beatrice as a vocal character who is progressively oppressed in order to create accord in her relationship with Benedick. Friedman argues that such silencing reinforces patriarchal forces and that the women are systematically stripped of their autonomy by the end of *Much Ado.*

Henze, Richard. "Deception in *Much Ado About Nothing.*" *Studies in English Literature: 1500–1900* 11:2 (Spring 1971): 187–201. journal PR 1.S82.

Arguing that deception is the play's unifying theme, Henze advances a Formalist reading of *Much Ado About Nothing* which analyzes imagery and dialogue to expose the varyingly "deceptive" natures of the play's primary characters. In particular, the critic considers images of eating, noting, fishing, and hunting to prove that Shakespeare illustrates the insidious nature of deception. Concluding that Beatrice, Benedick, and Don Pedro are too patently deceiving to mislead anyone else, Henze believes that Claudio represents deception's true danger, as Claudio masks his lies behind the artifice of integrity and loyalty.

Hunt, Maurice. "The Reclamation of Language in *Much Ado About Nothing.*" *Studies in Philology* 97:1 (Winter 2000): 165–191. journal P 25.S8.

In this Formalist reading of *Much Ado About Nothing,* Hunt argues that Shakespeare creates a world in which language is often disconnected from meaning. He believes that wordplay lends to the characters' shifting social prestige, as power strategies are often confused, misinterpreted, and manipulated because of language disconnects. Above all, Hunt focuses on the notion of truth in the play, arguing finally that patriarchal constructions of truth almost always win out in the struggle to determine what is "true."

Kehler, Dorothea. "*Much Ado About Nothing.* The Medieval Connection." *English Language Notes* 41:4 (June 2004): 11–15. journal PE 1.E53.

Kehler offers a short, concise, and engaging explanation of medieval customs observed within *Much Ado About Nothing.* Special attention is given to duels and dueling and the relationship to medieval "trial by combat." Kehler also explains why Shakespeare's use of medieval allusions is appropriate for this play.

King, Walter N. "Much Ado About Something." *Shakespeare Quarterly* 15 (1964): 143–155. journal PR 2885.S63.

Reacting to a mass of criticism that places *Much Ado About Nothing* among Shakespeare's lighter and more trivial works, King defends the play as an examination of the common human failing of acting illogically, imprudently, and inattentively. Central to this contention, King argues that *Much Ado* is a comedy of manners above all else and that reading the play as such reveals the satirical depth that many other Shakespeare scholars have overlooked. He focuses particularly upon the playwright's use of the word "nothing," suggesting that the play criticizes "a leisure-class world grown morally flabby by thoughtless acceptance of an inherited social code" (145).

Lewalski, B. K. "Love, Appearance, and Reality: Much Ado about Something." *Studies in English Literature* 8:1 (Winter 1968): 235–251. journal PR 1.S82.

> Positing that *Much Ado About Nothing* is intellectually more satisfying than most critics believe, Lewalski argues that *Much Ado* establishes a complex discussion of love. Calling upon previous criticism that indicates the theme of love as central to the characters' understanding of reality, the critic contends that Shakespeare relies upon neoplatonic and Christian themes in his suggestion that love elates and grounds the characters of *Much Ado.* In a Formalist reading of the play's action, structure, language, and imagery, Lewalski integrates Platonic and Christian philosophies to suggest that *Much Ado,* despite its comic overtones, is spiritually and intellectually rigorous.

McCollom, William. "The Role of Wit in *Much Ado About Nothing.*" *Shakespeare Quarterly* 14:2 (Spring 1968): 165–174. journal PR 2885.S63.

> Contending that many previous interpretations of *Much Ado About Nothing* have been reductive, often suggesting that the play is either satirical or trivial, McCollom argues for the concept of wit in *Much Ado* as a vital component of the play's meaning. In particular, the critic believes that wit defines characters in social and intellectual hierarchies, ranging from "truly witty and intelligent, inappropriately facetious, or ingeniously witless" (166). Furthermore, McCollom discusses how changes in the play's structure mirror changes in Shakespeare's use of wit.

McEachern, Claire. "Fathering Herself: A Source Study of Shakespeare's Feminism." *Shakespeare Quarterly* 39:3 (Autumn 1988): 269–290. journal PR 2885.S63.

> Attempting to mediate a debate among feminist critics who see Shakespeare as either a feminist or a misogynist, McEachern examines the playwright in his socio-historical context as a writer who both reacts to and subverts the patriarchal literary tradition of his forbearers. Focusing on Shakespeare's representations of daughters and fathers (particularly Leonato and Hero from *Much Ado About Nothing*), she contends that Shakespeare consistently represents women as defiant reactors to patriarchal oppression, particularly when they are commodities exchanged in the male marketplace. From this perspective, McEachern sees Shakespeare as a revolutionary writer who breaches social and literary conventions that depict women in marginalized ways.

Moses, Carol. "Kenneth Branagh's *Much Ado About Nothing.* Shakespearean Comedy as Shakespearean Romance." *Shakespeare Bulletin: A Journal of Performance Criticism and Scholarship* 14:1 (Winter 1996): 38–40. journal PR 3091.B77.

> In this analysis of Kenneth Branagh's film version of Shakespeare's *Much Ado About Nothing,* Moses contends that the film adapts the text by converting its sophisticated comedic foundation into material more suited to popular modern-day romance. Focusing particularly on Branagh's subdued Claudio, Moses disputes other critics' negative reactions to the film by suggesting that Branagh's interpretive variations are all textually based. Nevertheless, Moses takes pains to point out that Branagh's romantic interpretation of the play is but one of many possible ways of viewing *Much Ado About Nothing.*

Munro, Ian. "Shakespeare's Jestbook: Wit, Print, and Performance." *ELH* 71:1 (2004): 89–113. journal PR 1.E5.

> Munro studies Messina's economy of wit in *Much Ado About Nothing,* with specific attention to the characters who have wit (e.g. Beatrice and Benedick) and those who do not (Dogberry). He also relates the theme to the popular contemporary jestbook *A Hundred Merry Tales.*

Skrebels, Paul. "Transhistoricizing *Much Ado About Nothing.* Finding a Place for Shakespeare's Work in the Postmodern World." In *Teaching Shakespeare into the Twenty-First Century.* Ed. Ronald E. Salomone and James E. Davis. Athens: Ohio UP, 1997. 81–95. PR 2987.T364.

> Attempting to reinvigorate the study of Shakespeare in school curriculums, Skrebels contends that Shakespeare's plays are historically relevant to modern socio-political concerns. Focusing primarily on the association between *Much Ado About Nothing* and mid-1990s British royalty, the critic posits a "transhistorical" reading of Shakespeare that locates the playwright in his own historical context and relates that context to the lives of readers in a postmodern world. Skrebels' ultimate goal is to quell debate that suggests Shakespeare's writing should be "optional" despite its "universal human themes."

Spinrad, Phoebe S. "Dogberry Hero: Shakespeare's Comic Constables in Their Communal Context." *Studies in Philology* 84:1 (Winter 1992): 161–178. journal P 25.S8.

> Contrary to the majority of Shakespeare scholarship that sees Dogberry and Elbow as inefficient satirical characters, Spinrad contends that the constables of *Much Ado About Nothing* and *Measure for Measure* are effective creations whose inefficiency contributes to their dramatic reality. In particular, Spinrad believes that the plays' bumbling constables highlight the over-efficiency of high-quality enforcement organizations. By distinguishing between "efficiency" and "effectuality," she argues that Dogberry and Elbow represent two of the most satisfying characters within the field of Renaissance comedy.

Twelfth Night

Twelfth Night *at the Oregon Shakespearean Festival in Ashland, Oregon, with Ray Porter as Sir Toby Belch, G. Valmont Thomas as Feste, and Dan Donohue as Sir Andrew Aguecheek (2000). Photograph by Andree Lanthier.*

Like *A Midsummer Night's Dream, Twelfth Night* (1600–1601) is a holiday play. The traditional twelve-day festival, celebrated from Christmas Day through early January, offered Shakespeare's contemporaries the precious opportunity to escape their stern Elizabethan code of conduct through parties, plays, music, games, and other Renaissance entertainments. Descended from the Feast of the Epiphany, the Feast of the Magi, and ultimately from the Roman Saturnalia, this much loved holiday period licensed the inversion of authority through an appointed Lord of Misrule, whose sole responsibility was to make certain everyone was having a wonderful time. The actual "Twelfth Night" took place on the evening of January 6, which was the last opportunity everyone had to enjoy themselves before going back to their jobs the following day. One scholar, Leslie Hotson, even argues that the play was first produced at the court of Queen Elizabeth on January 6, 1601, to the delight of a visiting Italian nobleman named Don Virginio Orsino.

Shakespeare takes full advantage of this holiday atmosphere by featuring a cast of fascinating characters whose lives are all turned upside down through the comic progress of the play: Viola and Sebastian, two identical twins, are shipwrecked at the outset of the play, wander separately, provoke much mistaken identity, and are then reunited at the conclusion; the Count Orsino is in love with the beautiful Lady Olivia; Malvolio, Olivia's puritanical steward, fancies that his lady loves him; and a quirky, intriguing group of Olivia's kinsmen and servants round out the cast, including Sir Toby Belch, Sir Andrew Aguecheek, Fabian, and Feste the Jester.

Although Shakespeare borrowed plot elements from many different sources, including early Plautine comedies, Sir Philip Sidney's *Arcadia* (1590), Curzio Gonzaga's *Gl'Inganni* (*The Frauds,* 1592), and Emmanuel Forde's *Parismus* (1598), his primary source was Barnabe Riche's tale of "Apolonius and Silla" from *Riche His Farewell to Militarie Profession* (1581), which was in turn taken from Francois de Belleforest's 1571 French translation of Matteo Bandello's Italian *Novelle* of 1554. As always, Shakespeare's alterations from his sources tell us more about his concept for the play than the details he retained. Since Riche was a Puritan, his "Apolonius and Silla" is a stern, moralistic tale about the evils of lust. Shakespeare's revision of the plot, set in the mystical country of Illyria, omits the more sinister elements of the original source and focuses instead upon all the love, happiness, and camaraderie inherent in the Twelfth Night celebration. Through Shakespeare's comic genius, Feste represents the "festival" atmosphere of the play, Sir Toby Belch is its gregarious Lord of Misrule, and the reunion of the twins is a joyful moment that leads to love and marriage for most of the principal characters.

Not surprisingly, *Twelfth Night*'s main themes center around the play's holiday atmosphere, in particular Viola and Sebastian's comic movement from union to wandering to reunion, and include the festive inversion of authority through which Sir Toby and his rowdy friends ridicule the haughty Malvolio. At the same time, however, Shakespeare's script ends with Feste's somewhat melancholy song, which signals the end of holiday and a return to the mundane world of hard work and simple pleasures. Additional important themes feature the irrationality of love, the amorality of the world of Illyria, love as a "disease" (see especially Ovid's *De Remediis Amoris*), the wisdom of the fool vs. the insanity of society, and hostility toward the Puritans (who wished to close down the theatres). More recent scholarship has illuminated such subject areas as cross-dressing, homoerotic desire, sexual anxiety, social distinctions, marriage customs, stereotypes, and androgyny—all of which have helped enliven debate about this intriguing play.

Early productions of the script met with scant audience enthusiasm, though two notable adaptations—*The Plain-Dealer* by William Wycherley in 1674 and *Love Betray'd; or, The Agreable Disappointment* by William Burnaby in 1703—kept the spirit of the play alive until 1741, when Charles Macklin played Malvolio in a fairly traditional revival of the play at the Drury Lane Theatre in London. Nineteenth-century adapters began to add music and dance to the script, most notably in Frederic Reynolds' operatic version, which premiered at Covent Garden in 1820, in Augustin Daly's American production in 1895, and in the famous Beerbohm Tree extravaganza in 1901. E. H. Sothern's 1905 production at the Knickerbocker Theatre in New York returned the script to its original condition, which was soon followed by Ter-

ence Gray's Festival Theatre production at Cambridge (1926) featuring a revolving stage and a crowd-pleasing entrance by Sir Toby and Sir Andrew on
roller skates. Recent modern versions of the play have included several productions by the Royal Shakespeare Company—especially those by Peter Hall
(1958), Clifford Williams (1966), John Barton (1969), and Terry Hands
(1979)—plus a "smash-hit rock musical" version by Hal Hester and Danny
Aploinar in New York (1967).

Whatever theatrical trappings may accompany the play, Shakespeare's
Twelfth Night is a delightful <u>comedy</u> that investigates love, sex, gender expectations, holiday festivities, puritanical behavior, and other topics that are so
often staple ingredients of our everyday conversations. In this <u>script</u>, as in so
many others, Shakespeare proves himself our contemporary still by dramatiz-
ing modern issues that speak to our heads as well as to our hearts. If we listen
carefully, we can hear Feste's mournful tune at the play's conclusion lamenting our own lost innocence and inviting us to enjoy our holidays before life
passes us by forever.

*Twelfth Night at the Utah Shakespearean
Festival in Cedar City, Utah, with A. Bryan
Humphrey as Malvolio (1997). Photograph by
Karl Hugh.*

Twelfth Night

NAMES OF THE ACTORS

ORSINO, *Duke of Illyria*
SEBASTIAN, *brother of Viola*
ANTONIO, *a sea captain, friend to Sebastian*
A SEA CAPTAIN, *friend to Viola*
VALENTINE }
CURIO } *gentlemen attending on the duke*
SIR TOBY BELCH, *Olivia's kinsman*
SIR ANDREW AGUECHEEK
MALVOLIO, *steward to Olivia*
FABIAN, *servant to Olivia*
FESTE, *Olivia's jester*
OLIVIA, *a countess*
VIOLA, *sister of Sebastian*
MARIA, *Olivia's gentlewoman-in-waiting*
LORDS, A PRIEST, SAILORS, OFFICERS, MUSICIANS,
  AND ATTENDANTS

SCENE: *Illyria*

❧

1.1° *Enter Orsino Duke of Illyria, Curio, and other Lords [with Musicians].*

> **1.1:** The palace of Duke Orsino

DUKE
  If music be the food of love, play on,
  Give me excess of it, that, surfeiting,
  The appetite may sicken, and so die.
  That strain again, it had a dying fall;°   **fall:** cadence
  O, it came o'er my ear like the sweet sound   5
  That breathes upon a bank of violets,
  Stealing and giving odor. Enough, no more;
  'Tis not so sweet now as it was before.
  O spirit of love, how quick° and fresh art thou,   **quick:** alive
  That notwithstanding thy capacity   10
  Receiveth as the sea, naught enters there,
  Of what validity° and pitch° soe'er,   **validity:** value; **pitch:** i.e., worth (in falconry, high point of a falcon's flight)
  But falls into abatement and low price
  Even in a minute. So full of shapes° is fancy°   **shapes:** imagined forms; **fancy:** love
  That it alone is high fantastical.°   **high fantastical:** highly imaginative, extravagant   15

DISCOVERING SHAKESPEARE

(1) Themes [1.1.1-3]: Carefully read the first three lines of the script; then identify the most important eight or ten words spoken by Orsino. After examining these initial <u>images</u>, try to predict what the major <u>themes</u> of the play will be. Write down some preliminary thoughts about the possible <u>plot</u> and <u>themes</u>. After you have read a few more scenes, you may wish to come back to this question and revise your opinion based on the new information you have learned.

CURIO
  Will you go hunt, my lord?
DUKE
  What, Curio?
CURIO
  The hart.
DUKE
  Why, so I do, the noblest that I have.
  O, when mine eyes did see Olivia first,   20
  Methought she purged the air of pestilence.
  That instant was I turned into a hart,
  And my desires, like fell° and cruel hounds,   **fell:** savage
  E'er since pursue me.°   **hart . . . me:** (alluding to Ovid's story of
    Enter Valentine.   Actaeon, turned into a hart by Diana and killed by
                      How now? What news from her?   his own hounds)
VALENTINE
  So please my lord, I might not be admitted,   25
  But from her handmaid do return this answer:
  The element° itself, till seven years' heat,°   **element:** sky; **heat:** course
  Shall not behold her face at ample view;
  But like a cloistress° she will veilèd walk,   **cloistress:** nun
  And water once a day her chamber round   30
  With eye-offending brine:° all this to season°   **brine:** tears; **season:** preserve
  A brother's dead love, which she would keep fresh
  And lasting in her sad remembrance.
DUKE
  O, she that hath a heart of that fine frame
  To pay this debt of love but to a brother,   35
  How will she love when the rich golden shaft
  Hath killed the flock of all affections else°   **when . . . else:** i.e., when Cupid's arrow has slain
  That live in her; when liver, brain, and heart,   all emotions except love
  These sovereign thrones, are all supplied and filled,
  Her sweet perfections, with one self king.   40
  Away before me to sweet beds of flow'rs;
  Love thoughts lie rich when canopied with bow'rs.
                                          Exeunt.

❧ **1.2°** *Enter Viola, a Captain, and Sailors.*   **1.2:** The seacoast of Illyria

VIOLA
  What country, friends, is this?
CAPTAIN
  This is Illyria,° lady.   **Illyria:** on the east coast of the Adriatic
VIOLA
  And what should I do in Illyria?
  My brother he is in Elysium.°   **Elysium:** home of the blessed dead
  Perchance he is not drowned. What think you, sailors?   5
CAPTAIN
  It is perchance that you yourself were saved.

DISCOVERING SHAKESPEARE

(2) Language [1.1.31]: In what way do Olivia's tears "season" (1.1.31) her love for her dead brother? [*Hint:* See the definition for the word <u>metaphor</u> in the Glossary.)

VIOLA
O my poor brother, and so perchance may he be.

CAPTAIN
True, madam; and, to comfort you with chance,°   **chance:** what may have happened
Assure yourself, after our ship did split,
When you, and those poor number saved with you,   10
Hung on our driving° boat, I saw your brother,   **driving:** drifting
Most provident in peril, bind himself
(Courage and hope both teaching him the practice)
To a strong mast that lived° upon the sea;   **lived:** floated
Where, like Arion° on the dolphin's back,   **Arion:** a Greek bard who leapt overboard to   15
I saw him hold acquaintance with the waves   escape murderous sailors and charmed dolphins
So long as I could see.   with the music of his lyre so that they bore him to
     land

VIOLA
For saying so, there's gold.
Mine own escape unfoldeth to my hope,°   **unfoldeth to my hope:** gives me hope (for my
Whereto thy speech serves for authority   brother)   20
The like of him. Know'st thou this country?

CAPTAIN
Ay, madam, well, for I was bred and born
Not three hours' travel from this very place.

VIOLA
Who governs here?

CAPTAIN
A noble duke, in nature as in name.   25

VIOLA
What is his name?

CAPTAIN
Orsino.

VIOLA
Orsino! I have heard my father name him.
He was a bachelor then.

CAPTAIN
And so is now, or was so very late;   30
For but a month ago I went from hence,
And then 'twas fresh in murmur° (as you know   **fresh in murmur:** a current rumor
What great ones do, the less will prattle of)
That he did seek the love of fair Olivia.

VIOLA
What's she?   35

CAPTAIN
A virtuous maid, the daughter of a count
That died some twelvemonth since, then leaving her
In the protection of his son, her brother,
Who shortly also died; for whose dear love,
They say, she hath abjured° the sight   **abjured:** renounced   40
And company of men.

VIOLA   O that I served that lady,
And might not be delivered° to the world,   **delivered:** revealed
Till I had made mine own occasion mellow,°   **mellow:** ready to be revealed
What my estate° is.   **estate:** position in society

DISCOVERING SHAKESPEARE

(3) Mythology [1.2.15]: Who was Arion? How does this mythological story give Viola hope that her brother may still be alive?

CAPTAIN　　　　　　　That were hard to compass,° | **compass:** bring about | 45
Because she will admit no kind of suit,
No, not the duke's.

VIOLA
There is a fair behavior° in thee, captain, | **behavior:** both "conduct" and "appearance"
And though that nature with a beauteous wall
Doth oft close in pollution,° yet of thee | **pollution:** corruption | 50
I will believe thou hast a mind that suits
With this thy fair and outward character.° | **character:** personal appearance indicating moral qualities
I prithee (and I'll pay thee bounteously)
Conceal me what I am, and be my aid
For such disguise as haply° shall become | **haply:** by chance
The form of my intent.° I'll serve this duke. | **form of my intent:** my outward purpose | 55
Thou shalt present me as an eunuch° to him; | **eunuch:** castrato, or young male singer, emasculated to preserve his high voice
It may be worth thy pains. For I can sing
And speak to him in many sorts of music
That will allow me° very worth his service. | **allow me:** cause me to be considered
What else may hap, to time I will commit; | 60
Only shape thou thy silence to my wit.

CAPTAIN
Be you his eunuch, and your mute° I'll be; | **mute:** silent attendant
When my tongue blabs, then let mine eyes not see.

VIOLA
I thank thee. Lead me on.　　　　　　　*Exeunt.*

❧ **1.3**° *Enter Sir Toby and Maria.* | **1.3:** The house of Countess Olivia

TOBY　What a plague means my niece to take the death of her brother thus? I am sure care's an enemy to life.

MARIA　By my troth, Sir Toby, you must come in earlier o' nights. Your cousin,° my lady, takes great exceptions to your ill hours. | **cousin:** kinsman | 5

TOBY　Why, let her except before excepted.° | **except before excepted:** (cant legal phrase)

MARIA　Ay, but you must confine yourself within the modest limits of order.

TOBY　Confine? I'll confine myself no finer° than I am. These clothes are good enough to drink in, and so be these boots too. An° they be not, let them hang themselves in their own straps. | **finer:** both "tighter" and "better" | 10
An: if

MARIA　That quaffing and drinking will undo you. I heard my lady talk of it yesterday; and of a foolish knight that you brought in one night here to be her wooer. | 15

TOBY　Who? Sir Andrew Aguecheek?

DISCOVERING SHAKESPEARE

(4) Names [1.2.57–58]: Viola's boast that she can sing and speak to Orsino "in many sorts of music" betrays Shakespeare's <u>pun</u> on her name. In what way is she a "viola"? Examine such other names in the play as Sir Toby Belch, Feste the Clown, Sir Andrew Aguecheek, Valentine, and Malvolio; then predict how each of those characters will behave based solely on their names.

(5) <u>Verse</u> [1.3.1]: The first two scenes of the play are written in <u>verse</u>, while the third is in <u>prose</u>. What does this abrupt shift from <u>verse</u> to <u>prose</u> suggest about the characters and the dramatic situation in the third scene? In what important ways is this scene different from the two preceding it?

MARIA   Ay, he.

TOBY   He's as tall° a man as any's in Illyria.

MARIA   What's that to th' purpose?

TOBY   Why, he has three thousand ducats° a year.

MARIA   Ay, but he'll have but a year in all these ducats. He's a very fool and a prodigal.

TOBY   Fie that you'll say so! He plays o' th' viol-de-gamboys,° and speaks three or four languages word for word without book,° and hath all the good gifts of nature.

MARIA   He hath, indeed, almost natural;° for, besides that he's a fool, he's a great quarreler; and but that he hath the gift of a coward to allay the gust° he hath in quarreling, 'tis thought among the prudent he would quickly have the gift of a grave.

TOBY   By this hand, they are scoundrels and substractors° that say so of him. Who are they?

MARIA   They that add, moreover, he's drunk nightly in your company.

TOBY   With drinking healths to my niece. I'll drink to her as long as there is a passage in my throat and drink in Illyria. He's a coward and a coistrel° that will not drink to my niece till his brains turn o' th' toe like a parish top.° What, wench? *Castiliano vulgo;*° for here comes Sir Andrew Agueface.°

Enter Sir Andrew.

ANDREW   Sir Toby Belch. How now, Sir Toby Belch?

TOBY   Sweet Sir Andrew.

ANDREW   Bless you, fair shrew.

MARIA   And you too, sir.

TOBY   Accost,° Sir Andrew, accost.

ANDREW   What's that?

TOBY   My niece's chambermaid.

ANDREW   Good Mistress Accost, I desire better acquaintance.

MARIA   My name is Mary, sir.

ANDREW   Good Mistress Mary Accost —

TOBY   You mistake, knight. "Accost" is front° her, board° her, woo her, assail her.

ANDREW   By my troth, I would not undertake° her in this company. Is that the meaning of "accost"?

MARIA   Fare you well, gentlemen.

TOBY   An thou let part so, Sir Andrew, would thou mightst never draw sword again.

ANDREW   An you part so, mistress, I would I might never draw sword again! Fair lady, do you think you have fools in hand?

MARIA   Sir, I have not you by th' hand.

ANDREW   Marry,° but you shall have, and here's my hand.

---

tall: both "tall" and "brave"

ducats: Venetian gold coins

viol-de-gamboys: "leg-viola," predecessor of the violoncello
without book: by memory
natural: i.e., as a fool
gust: taste

substractors: detractors

coistrel: horse groom, base fellow

parish top: large top used for public amusement;
Castiliano vulgo: (of doubtful meaning; Castilians were noted for decorum, and this may be a plea for "common politeness")
Agueface: pale and thin-faced, like a man suffering from the acute fever of ague

Accost: make up to (her)

front: face; **board:** greet (literally, go on board, but here with sexual innuendo)
undertake: take on, with sexual implication of "take below"

Marry: indeed, to be sure (originally an oath on the name of the Virgin Mary)

20
25
30
35
40
45
50
55
60

DISCOVERING SHAKESPEARE

(6) Language [1.3.52]: What error does Sir Andrew make when he refers to Maria as "Mistress Mary Accost"? What other mistakes does Andrew commit in his conversation with Sir Toby? Why do you think Toby allows a fool like Andrew to associate with him? What evidence can you provide to support your claim?

MARIA   Now, sir, thought is free. I pray you, bring your hand to th' butt'ry bar° and let it° drink.

ANDREW   Wherefore, sweetheart? What's your metaphor?

MARIA   It's dry,° sir.

ANDREW   Why, I think so. I am not such an ass but I can keep my hand dry.° But what's your jest?

MARIA   A dry jest, sir.

ANDREW   Are you full of them?

MARIA   Ay, sir, I have them at my fingers' ends. Marry, now I let go your hand, I am barren.°   *Exit.*

TOBY   O knight, thou lack'st a cup of canary!° When did I see thee so put down?°

ANDREW   Never in your life, I think, unless you see canary put me down. Methinks sometimes I have no more wit than a Christian° or an ordinary man has. But I am a great eater of beef, and I believe that does harm to my wit.

TOBY   No question.

ANDREW   An I thought that, I'd forswear it. I'll ride home tomorrow, Sir Toby.

TOBY   *Pourquoi,°* my dear knight?

ANDREW   What is *"pourquoi"*? Do, or not do? I would I had bestowed that time in the tongues° that I have in fencing, dancing, and bearbaiting.° O, had I but followed the arts!°

TOBY   Then hadst thou had an excellent head of hair.

ANDREW   Why, would that have mended° my hair?

TOBY   Past question, for thou seest it will not curl by nature.

ANDREW   But it becomes me well enough, does't not?

TOBY   Excellent. It hangs like flax on a distaff;° and I hope to see a housewife take thee between her legs and spin it off.°

ANDREW   Faith, I'll home tomorrow, Sir Toby. Your niece will not be seen; or if she be, it's four to one she'll none of me. The count himself here hard by woos her.

TOBY   She'll none o' th' count. She'll not match above her degree,° neither in estate,° years, nor wit;° I have heard her swear't. Tut, there's life in't, man.

ANDREW   I'll stay a month longer. I am a fellow o' th' strangest mind i' th' world. I delight in masques and revels° sometimes altogether.°

TOBY   Art thou good at these kickshawses,° knight?

ANDREW   As any man in Illyria, whatsoever he be, under the degree of my betters, and yet I will not compare with an old man.°

TOBY   What is thy excellence in a galliard,° knight?

ANDREW   Faith, I can cut a caper.°

---

butt'ry bar: storeroom, from the bar of which liquor and provisions were served; here, too, Maria's breasts; **it:** i.e., your hand

dry: both "old" and "dryly humorous"

I am . . . dry: fools proverbially knew how to stay dry

barren: i.e., barren of jokes

canary: a sweet wine from the Canary Islands

put down: discomfited

Christian: i.e., humble, but perhaps humorless, too

Pourquoi: why

tongues: languages, perhaps with a pun on "tongs," curling irons

bearbaiting: popular spectacle in which a tied bear was tormented by dogs

arts: liberal arts such as languages

mended: improved

flax on a distaff: straight strings of flax, spun on a stick held between the spinning-woman's legs

spin it off: lose hair as a result of venereal disease

degree: rank in society; **estate:** fortune; **wit:** intelligence

masques and revels: court entertainments, involving masquerade, performance, and dancing

altogether: in all respects

kickshawses: trifles (French *quelque chose*)

old man: probably "experienced person"

galliard: quick dance in triple time

caper: frolicsome leap; also a spice used with mutton

65

70

75

80

85

90

95

100

105

110

DISCOVERING SHAKESPEARE

(7) Language [1.3.93–98]: What sexual joke does Sir Toby make about Sir Andrew's hair?

TOBY   And I can cut the mutton° to't. **cut the mutton:** i.e., the mutton served with capers, but also implying sex with a prostitute ("mutton" in Elizabethan slang)   115

ANDREW   And I think I have the back-trick° simply as strong as any man in Illyria. **back-trick:** backward step in a dance

TOBY   Wherefore are these things hid? Wherefore have these gifts a curtain before 'em? Are they like to take° dust, like Mistress Mall's picture?° Why dost thou not go to church in a galliard and come home in a coranto?° My very walk should be a jig. I would not so much as make water but in a sink-a-pace.° What dost thou mean? Is it a world to hide virtues in? I did think, by the excellent constitution of thy leg, it was formed under the star of a galliard.°

take: collect
Mistress Mall's picture: any woman's portrait   120
coranto: swift running dance

sink-a-pace: rapid dance of five steps (French *cinque-pas*)

under . . . galliard: i.e., under a dancing star   125

ANDREW   Ay, 'tis strong, and it does indifferent well in a dun-colored stock.° Shall we set about some revels? **stock:** stocking

TOBY   What shall we do else? Were we not born under Taurus?°

ANDREW   Taurus? That's sides and heart. **Taurus:** the Bull, one of the signs of the zodiac, which governed the nose and throat   130

TOBY   No, sir; it is legs and thighs. Let me see thee caper. Ha, higher; ha, ha, excellent!   *Exeunt.*

❧ **1.4°** *Enter Valentine, and Viola in man's attire.* **1.4:** The palace of Duke Orsino

VALENTINE   If the duke continue these favors towards you, Cesario, you are like to be much advanced.° He hath known you but three days and already you are no stranger. **advanced:** promoted

VIOLA   You either fear his humor° or my negligence, that you call in question the continuance of his love. Is he inconstant, sir, in his favors? **humor:** changeableness   5

VALENTINE   No, believe me.

Enter Duke, Curio, and Attendants.

VIOLA   I thank you. Here comes the count.

DUKE   Who saw Cesario, ho?   10

VIOLA   On your attendance, my lord, here.

DUKE   *[To Curio and Attendants]*
Stand you° awhile aloof. *[To Cesario]* Cesario,
Thou know'st no less but all.° I have unclasped
To thee the book even of my secret soul.
Therefore, good youth, address thy gait° unto her;
Be not denied access, stand at her doors,
And tell them there thy fixèd foot shall grow
Till thou have audience.

you: i.e., all except Cesario
no less but all: everything

address thy gait: direct your steps   15

VIOLA   Sure, my noble lord,
If she be so abandoned to her sorrow
As it is spoke, she never will admit me.   20

DUKE
Be clamorous and leap all civil bounds
Rather than make unprofited return.

DISCOVERING SHAKESPEARE

(8) Teaser [1.3.127]: Try to find out why this emphasis on stockings ("a dun-colored stock") is so important later in the play.

(9) Staging [1.4.1]: If Viola comes on stage a few seconds before Valentine enters, how could the actor indicate to the audience that she is a bit uncomfortable in men's clothing? Could there be any hint of jealousy in Valentine's first lines? Why or why not?

VIOLA
Say I do speak with her, my lord, what then?
DUKE
O, then unfold the passion of my love;
Surprise° her with discourse of my dear faith;   **Surprise:** ambush   25
It shall become thee well to act my woes.
She will attend it better in thy youth
Than in a nuncio's° of more grave aspect.   **nuncio's:** messenger's
VIOLA
I think not so, my lord.
DUKE   Dear lad, believe it;
                                                         30
For they shall yet belie thy happy years
That say thou art a man. Diana's° lip   **Diana:** Roman goddess of hunting and protector
Is not more smooth and rubious;° thy small pipe°   of women's chastity
Is as the maiden's organ, shrill and sound,°   **rubious:** ruby red; **pipe:** throat, voice
And all is semblative° a woman's part.   **shrill and sound:** high and clear
I know thy constellation° is right apt   **semblative:** like   35
For this affair. Some four or five attend him,   **constellation:** predestined nature
All, if you will; for I myself am best
When least in company. Prosper well in this,
And thou shalt live as freely as thy lord
To call his fortunes thine.   40
VIOLA   I'll do my best
To woo your lady. *[Aside]* Yet a barful strife!°   **barful strife:** conflict full of hindrances
Whoe'er I woo, myself would be his wife.   *Exeunt.*

❧ **1.5**° *Enter Maria and Feste.*   **1.5:** Within the house of Olivia

MARIA   Nay, either tell me where thou hast been, or I will
     not open my lips so wide as a bristle may enter in way
     of thy excuse. My lady will hang thee for thy absence.
FESTE   Let her hang me. He that is well hanged° in this   **well hanged:** (the hanged man proverbially has
     world needs to fear no colors.°   nothing more to fear, but here also "well hung")   5
MARIA   Make that good.°   **fear no colors:** fear nothing (proverbial)
FESTE   He shall see none to fear.   **Make that good:** "explain," but also "clean up
MARIA   A good lenten° answer. I can tell thee where that   your language"
     saying was born, of "I fear no colors."   **lenten:** scanty, chastened
FESTE   Where, good Mistress Mary?
MARIA   In the wars; and that may you be bold to say in   10
     your foolery.
FESTE   Well, God give them wisdom that have it, and
     those that are fools, let them use their talents.
MARIA   Yet you will be hanged for being so long absent.   15
     Or to be turned away: is not that as good as a hanging
     to you?

DISCOVERING SHAKESPEARE

(10) Gender [1.4.29–40]: During the speech that begins "Dear Lad, believe it," the Duke refers to several of Viola's "feminine" characteristics. How close to discovery is Viola in this scene? Try to find other important moments in the <u>script</u> when her disguise as a young man is nearly exposed.

(11) Staging [1.4.40–42]: How sudden is Viola's declaration of love for Orsino? Is there any indication that he hears her say these words? What is an <u>aside</u>? To what extent should the director prepare the audience for this sudden revelation of affection?

FESTE   Many a good hanging prevents a bad marriage, and for turning away, let summer bear it out.°

MARIA   You are resolute then?

FESTE   Not so, neither; but I am resolved on two points.°

MARIA   That if one break, the other will hold; or if both break, your gaskins° fall.°

FESTE   Apt, in good faith; very apt. Well, go thy way! If Sir Toby would leave drinking, thou wert as witty a piece of Eve's flesh° as any in Illyria.

MARIA   Peace, you rogue; no more o' that. Here comes my lady. Make your excuse wisely, you were best.° *[Exit.]*
Enter Lady Olivia with Malvolio.

FESTE   Wit, an't be thy will, put me into good fooling. Those wits that think they have thee do very oft prove fools, and I that am sure I lack thee may pass for a wise man. For what says Quinapalus?° "Better a witty fool than a foolish wit." God bless thee, lady.

OLIVIA   Take the fool away.

FESTE   Do you not hear, fellows? Take away the lady.

OLIVIA   Go to,° you're a dry° fool! I'll no more of you. Besides, you grow dishonest.°

FESTE   Two faults, madonna,° that drink and good counsel will amend. For give the dry fool drink, then is the fool not dry.° Bid the dishonest man mend himself: if he mend, he is no longer dishonest; if he cannot, let the botcher° mend him. Anything that's mended is but patched; virtue that transgresses is but patched with sin, and sin that amends is but patched with virtue. If that this simple syllogism° will serve, so; if it will not, what remedy? As there is no true cuckold but calamity, so beauty's a flower.° The lady bade take away the fool; therefore, I say again, take her away.

OLIVIA   Sir, I bade them take away you.

FESTE   Misprision° in the highest degree. Lady, *cucullus non facit monachum.*° That's as much to say as, I wear not motley° in my brain. Good madonna, give me leave to prove you a fool.

OLIVIA   Can you do it?

FESTE   Dexteriously,° good madonna.

OLIVIA   Make your proof.

FESTE   I must catechize° you for it, madonna. Good my mouse° of virtue,° answer me.

OLIVIA   Well, sir, for want of other idleness, I'll bide your proof.

FESTE   Good madonna, why mourn'st thou?

OLIVIA   Good fool, for my brother's death.

let . . . out: i.e., let mild weather make homelessness endurable

20

points: laces fastening hose to doublet

gaskins: loose breeches
if one . . . fall: (Maria puns on "points," l. 22)

25

Eve's flesh: erring woman

you were best: it would be best for you

30

Quinapalus: (an invention of the clown)

35

Go to: enough, cease; **dry:** dull
dishonest: unreliable
madonna: my lady (ironic)

40

dry: thirsty

botcher: mender of clothes

45

syllogism: three-step logical argument in set form
As . . . flower: (obscure, but apparently proverbial reassurance that the young and beautiful Olivia will not remain solitary)

50

Misprision: error
cucullus . . . monachum: the cowl doesn't make the monk
motley: clothing of a mixed color, worn by stage fools

55

Dexteriously: (variant of "dexterously")

catechize: question
mouse: (term of endearment); **of virtue:** virtuous

60

DISCOVERING SHAKESPEARE

(12) Characterization [1.5.30–34]: Immediately prior to Olivia's entrance, Feste the Clown prays for his "wit" to send him some good comic material. How much of this prayer do you think Olivia hears? What is her response to his first few jokes in lines 39–49? What jest in lines 61–66 finally earns her approval?

(13) Language [1.5.52]: What is the meaning of the Latin phrase "cucullus non facit monachum" (1.5.51–52)? How is the expression used by Feste as a defense of fools?

FESTE   I think his soul is in hell, madonna.

OLIVIA   I know his soul is in heaven, fool. 65

FESTE   The more fool, madonna, to mourn for your brother's soul, being in heaven. Take away the fool, gentlemen.

OLIVIA   What think you of this fool, Malvolio? Doth he not mend? 70

MALVOLIO   Yes, and shall do till the pangs of death shake him. Infirmity, that decays the wise, doth ever make the better fool.

FESTE   God send you, sir, a speedy infirmity, for the better increasing your folly. Sir Toby will be sworn that 75 I am no fox, but he will not pass his word for twopence that you are no fool.

OLIVIA   How say you to that, Malvolio?

MALVOLIO   I marvel your ladyship takes delight in such a barren rascal. I saw him put down the other day with 80 an ordinary fool that has no more brain than a stone. Look you now, he's out of his guard° already. Unless you laugh and minister occasion° to him, he is gagged. I protest I take these wise men that crow so at these set° 85 kind of fools no better than the fools' zanies.°

out of his guard: without a defense (of wit)
minister occasion: give an opportunity
set: with a rehearsed patter
zanies: i.e., fools' assistants

OLIVIA   O, you are sick of self-love, Malvolio, and taste with a distempered appetite. To be generous, guiltless, and of free disposition, is to take those things for bird-bolts° that you deem cannon bullets. There is no slander 90 in an allowed° fool, though he do nothing but rail; nor no railing in a known discreet man, though he do nothing but reprove.

bird-bolts: blunt-headed arrows for shooting birds
allowed: licensed

FESTE   Now Mercury° indue thee with leasing,° for thou speak'st well of fools.

Mercury: god of guile and tricks; **indue . . . leasing:** endow you with the art of casuistry

Enter Maria.

MARIA   Madam, there is at the gate a young gentleman 95 much desires to speak with you.

OLIVIA   From the count Orsino, is it?

MARIA   I know not, madam. 'Tis a fair young man, and well attended.

OLIVIA   Who of my people hold him in delay? 100

MARIA   Sir Toby, madam, your kinsman.

OLIVIA   Fetch him off, I pray you. He speaks nothing but madman. Fie on him! *[Exit Maria.]* Go you, Malvolio. If it be a suit from the count, I am sick, or not at home. What you will, to dismiss it.   *Exit Malvolio.* 105
Now you see, sir, how your fooling grows old,° and people dislike it.

old: stale

FESTE   Thou hast spoke for us, madonna, as if thy eldest son should be a fool; whose skull Jove cram with brains, for − here he comes − one of thy kin has a most 110 weak pia mater.°

pia mater: i.e., brain

Enter Sir Toby.

DISCOVERING SHAKESPEARE

(14) Metaphor [1.5.82]: What does Malvolio mean when he says that Feste is "out of his guard already" (1.5.82)?

(15) Language [1.5.111]: What was "pia mater" (1.5.111)? Why does Feste think that Sir Toby Belch's "pia mater" is "weak"?

OLIVIA   By mine honor, half drunk. What is he at the gate, cousin?

TOBY   A gentleman.

OLIVIA   A gentleman? What gentleman?   115

TOBY   'Tis a gentleman here. A plague o' these pickle-herring! How now, sot?

FESTE   Good Sir Toby.

OLIVIA   Cousin, cousin, how have you come so early by this lethargy?°

lethargy: sickness   120

TOBY   Lechery? I defy lechery. There's one at the gate.

OLIVIA   Ay, marry, what is he?

TOBY   Let him be the devil an he will, I care not. Give me faith,° say I. Well, it's all one.   *Exit.*

faith: i.e., to resist the devil   125

OLIVIA   What's a drunken man like, fool?

FESTE   Like a drowned man, a fool, and a madman. One draft above heat° makes him a fool, the second mads him, and a third drowns him.

above heat: above the amount to make him normally warm

OLIVIA   Go thou and seek the crowner,° and let him sit o' my coz;° for he's in the third degree of drink – he's drowned. Go look after him.

crowner: coroner
sit o' my coz: hold an inquest on my kinsman (Sir Toby)   130

FESTE   He is but mad yet, madonna, and the fool shall look to the madman.   *[Exit.]*
    Enter Malvolio.

MALVOLIO   Madam, yond young fellow swears he will speak with you. I told him you were sick; he takes on him to understand so much, and therefore comes to speak with you. I told him you were asleep; he seems to have a foreknowledge of that too, and therefore comes to speak with you. What is to be said to him, lady? He's fortified against any denial.   135

    140

OLIVIA   Tell him he shall not speak with me.

MALVOLIO   Has° been told so; and he says he'll stand at your door like a sheriff's post,° and be the supporter to a bench, but he'll speak with you.

Has: he has (from "h' has")
sheriff's post: post before a sheriff's house on which notices were posted

OLIVIA   What kind o' man is he?   145

MALVOLIO   Why, of mankind.

OLIVIA   What manner of man?

MALVOLIO   Of very ill manner. He'll speak with you, will you or no.

OLIVIA   Of what personage and years is he?   150

MALVOLIO   Not yet old enough for a man nor young enough for a boy; as a squash° is before 'tis a peasecod,° or a codling° when 'tis almost an apple. 'Tis with him in standing water,° between boy and man. He is very well-favored and he speaks very shrewishly. One would think his mother's milk were scarce out of him.

squash: unripe pea pod; **peasecod:** ripe pea pod
codling: unripe apple
standing water: the tide at ebb or flood when it flows neither way   155

OLIVIA   Let him approach. Call in my gentlewoman.

MALVOLIO   Gentlewoman, my lady calls.   *Exit.*
    Enter Maria.

DISCOVERING SHAKESPEARE

(16) Language [1.5.129]: What is the etymology of the word "coroner" (1.5.129)?

OLIVIA   Give me my veil; come, throw it o'er my face. We'll once more hear Orsino's embassy.   160

Enter Viola.

VIOLA   The honorable lady of the house, which is she?

OLIVIA   Speak to me; I shall answer for her. Your will?

VIOLA   Most radiant, exquisite, and unmatchable beauty – I pray you tell me if this be the lady of the house, for I never saw her – I would be loath to cast away my speech; for, besides that it is excellently well penned, I have taken great pains to con° it. Good beauties, let me sustain° no scorn. I am very comptible,° even to the least sinister usage.   165

con: memorize
sustain: endure; **comptible:** sensitive

OLIVIA   Whence came you, sir?   170

VIOLA   I can say little more than I have studied, and that question's out of my part. Good gentle one, give me modest assurance if you be the lady of the house, that I may proceed in my speech.

OLIVIA   Are you a comedian?°   175

comedian: actor

VIOLA   No, my profound heart; and yet (by the very fangs of malice I swear) I am not that I play. Are you the lady of the house?

OLIVIA   If I do not usurp° myself, I am.

usurp: supplant

VIOLA   Most certain, if you are she, you do usurp yourself; for what is yours to bestow is not yours to reserve. But this is from° my commission. I will on with my speech in your praise and then show you the heart of my message.   180

from: outside

OLIVIA   Come to what is important in't. I forgive° you the praise.   185

forgive: excuse

VIOLA   Alas, I took great pains to study it; and 'tis poetical.

OLIVIA   It is the more like to be feigned; I pray you keep it in. I heard you were saucy at my gates; and allowed your approach rather to wonder at you than to hear you. If you be not mad, be gone; if you have reason,° be brief. 'Tis not that time of moon with me° to make one in so skipping° a dialogue.   190

reason: sanity
'Tis . . . me: i.e., I am not in the mood
skipping: sprightly

MARIA   Will you hoist sail, sir? Here lies your way.   195

VIOLA   No, good swabber;° I am to hull° here a little longer. Some mollification for your giant,° sweet lady. Tell me your mind. I am a messenger.

swabber: one who washes decks; **hull:** float without sail
giant: i.e., the small Maria

OLIVIA   Sure you have some hideous matter to deliver, when the courtesy° of it is so fearful. Speak your office.°   200

courtesy: formality; **office:** business

VIOLA   It alone concerns your ear. I bring no overture° of war, no taxation° of homage. I hold the olive in my hand. My words are as full of peace as matter.

overture: declaration
taxation: demand

DISCOVERING SHAKESPEARE

(17) <u>Verse</u> [1.5.162]: Olivia shifts from <u>prose</u> to <u>verse</u> immediately prior to Viola's entrance, then the interview between them begins in <u>prose</u> and later moves back to <u>verse</u>. What does this alternation between <u>verse</u> and <u>prose</u> indicate in the scene?
(18) Language [1.5.187–188]: Viola has obviously memorized a speech in preparation for her visit to Olivia's house. When and why is she forced to deviate from her set speech and improvise in her <u>dialogue</u> with Olivia?

OLIVIA Yet you began rudely. What are you? What would you? 205

VIOLA The rudeness that hath appeared in me have I learned from my entertainment.° What I am, and what I would, are as secret as maidenhead: to your ears, divinity;° to any other's, profanation.

entertainment: reception

divinity: a holy message

OLIVIA Give us the place alone; we will hear this divinity. *[Exit Maria.]* Now, sir, what is your text? 210

VIOLA Most sweet lady –

OLIVIA A comfortable° doctrine, and much may be said of it. Where lies your text?

comfortable: comforting

VIOLA In Orsino's bosom. 215

OLIVIA In his bosom? In what chapter of his bosom?

VIOLA To answer by the method,° in the first of his heart.

To . . . method: to continue the figure

OLIVIA O, I have read it; it is heresy. Have you no more to say?

VIOLA Good madam, let me see your face. 220

OLIVIA Have you any commission from your lord to negotiate with my face? You are now out of your text. But we will draw the curtain and show you the picture. *[Unveils.]* Look you, sir, such a one I was this present.° Is't not well done?

this present: a minute ago

VIOLA Excellently done, if God did all. 225

OLIVIA 'Tis in grain,° sir; 'twill endure wind and weather.

in grain: fast dyed

VIOLA
'Tis beauty truly blent, whose red and white
Nature's own sweet and cunning° hand laid on.
Lady, you are the cruel'st she alive
If you will lead these graces to the grave, 230
And leave the world no copy.

cunning: skillful

OLIVIA O, sir, I will not be so hard-hearted. I will give out divers schedules° of my beauty. It shall be inventoried, and every particle and utensil° labeled to° my will: as, item,° two lips, indifferent° red; item, two gray eyes, with lids to them; item, one neck, one chin, and so forth. Were you sent hither to praise me?

schedules: lists
utensil: article; **labeled to:** added to 235
item: namely; **indifferent:** moderately

VIOLA
I see you what you are; you are too proud;
But if° you were the devil, you are fair.
My lord and master loves you. O, such love
Could be but recompensed though° you were crowned 240
The nonpareil° of beauty.

if: even if

but recompensed though: no more than repaid even though
nonpareil: unequaled one

OLIVIA   How does he love me?

VIOLA
With adorations, fertile° tears,
With groans that thunder love, with sighs of fire. 245

fertile: abundant

OLIVIA
Your lord does know my mind; I cannot love him.
Yet I suppose him virtuous, know him noble,

DISCOVERING SHAKESPEARE

(19) Characterization [1.5.210]: Viola and Olivia are very similar—both have apparently lost their parents, both mourn the death of a brother, and both are in love with someone who doesn't love them (see 1.5.279–287)—yet each woman tries to solve her problem in a different fashion. How and why are the two characters different in their approach to problem-solving?

Of great estate, of fresh and stainless youth;
In voices well divulged,° free, learned, and valiant,
And in dimension and the shape of nature
A gracious person. But yet I cannot love him.
He might have took his answer long ago.

VIOLA
If I did love you in my master's flame,
With such a suff'ring, such a deadly life,°
In your denial I would find no sense;
I would not understand it.

OLIVIA   Why, what would you?

VIOLA
Make me a willow° cabin at your gate
And call upon my soul within the house;
Write loyal cantons° of contemnèd° love
And sing them loud even in the dead of night;
Hallo your name to the reverberate hills
And make the babbling gossip° of the air
Cry out "Olivia!" O, you should not rest
Between the elements of air and earth
But you should pity me.

OLIVIA
You might do much. What is your parentage?

VIOLA
Above my fortunes, yet my state is well.
I am a gentleman.

OLIVIA   Get you to your lord.
I cannot love him. Let him send no more,
Unless, perchance, you come to me again
To tell me how he takes it. Fare you well.
I thank you for your pains. Spend this for me.

VIOLA
I am no fee'd post,° lady; keep your purse;
My master, not myself, lacks recompense.
Love make his heart of flint that you shall love;
And let your fervor, like my master's, be
Placed in contempt. Farewell, fair cruelty.   *Exit.*

OLIVIA
"What is your parentage?"
"Above my fortunes, yet my state is well.
I am a gentleman." I'll be sworn thou art.
Thy tongue, thy face, thy limbs, actions, and spirit
Do give thee fivefold blazon.° Not too fast; soft, soft,
Unless the master were the man.° How now?
Even so quickly may one catch the plague?
Methinks I feel this youth's perfections
With an invisible and subtle stealth
To creep in at mine eyes. Well, let it be.
What ho, Malvolio!
    Enter Malvolio.

In voices well divulged: in public opinion well reported   250

deadly life: life that is like death   255

willow: (symbol of grief for unrequited love)

cantons: songs; **contemnèd:** rejected   260

babbling gossip: echo

265

270

fee'd post: messenger to be paid or tipped

275

280

blazon: heraldic identification, as on a shield
Unless . . . man: i.e., unless Orsino were Cesario

285

DISCOVERING SHAKESPEARE

(20) Motivation [1.5.270–271]: At what point in this scene does Olivia become interested in Viola? What is it about Viola that intrigues her?

MALVOLIO   Here, madam, at your service.

OLIVIA

Run after that same peevish messenger,

The county's° man. He left this ring behind him,   **county:** count   290

Would I or not. Tell him I'll none of it.

Desire him not to flatter with° his lord   **flatter with:** encourage

Nor hold him up with hopes. I am not for him.

If that the youth will come this way tomorrow,

I'll give him reasons for't. Hie thee, Malvolio.   295

MALVOLIO

Madam, I will.   *Exit.*

OLIVIA

I do I know not what, and fear to find

Mine eye too great a flatterer for my mind.

Fate, show thy force; ourselves we do not owe.°   **owe:** own

What is decreed must be – and be this so!   *[Exit.]*   300

❧ **2.1**° *Enter Antonio and Sebastian.*   **2.1:** A lodging some distance from Orsino's court

ANTONIO   Will you stay no longer? Nor will you not that I go with you?

SEBASTIAN   By your patience,° no. My stars shine darkly   **patience:** leave
over me; the malignancy of my fate might perhaps dis-
temper° yours. Therefore I shall crave of you your leave,   **distemper:** disturb   5
that I may bear my evils alone. It were a bad recom-
pense for your love to lay any of them on you.

ANTONIO   Let me yet know of you whither you are
bound.

SEBASTIAN   No, sooth,° sir. My determinate° voyage is   **sooth:** truly; **determinate:** determined upon   10
mere extravagancy.° But I perceive in you so excellent a   **extravagancy:** wandering
touch of modesty that you will not extort from me
what I am willing to keep in; therefore it charges me in
manners° the rather to express myself. You must know   **it . . . manners:** I am compelled in good manners   15
of me then, Antonio, my name is Sebastian, which I
called Roderigo. My father was that Sebastian of Mes-
saline° whom I know you have heard of. He left behind   **Messaline:** Messina in Sicily
him myself and a sister, both born in an hour.° If the   **in an hour:** in the same hour
heavens had been pleased, would we had so ended! But
you, sir, altered that, for some hour before you took me   20
from the breach of the sea° was my sister drowned.   **the breach of the sea:** the breaking waves

ANTONIO   Alas the day!

SEBASTIAN   A lady, sir, though it was said she much resembled me, was yet of many accounted beautiful. But
though I could not with such estimable wonder° overfar   **estimable wonder:** admiring judgment   25
believe that, yet thus far I will boldly publish° her: she   **publish:** describe publicly
bore a mind that envy could not but call fair. She is
drowned already, sir, with salt water, though I seem to
drown her remembrance again with more.

ANTONIO   Pardon me, sir, your bad entertainment.°   **entertainment:** treatment as my guest   30

DISCOVERING SHAKESPEARE

(21) <u>Plot</u> **[1.5.290]:** Why does Olivia tell Malvolio that Viola left a ring with her? What does she hope to accomplish by this lie?

SEBASTIAN   O good Antonio, forgive me your trouble.°

ANTONIO   If you will not murder me for° my love, let me
be your servant.

SEBASTIAN   If you will not undo what you have done,
that is, kill him whom you have recovered,° desire it not.
Fare ye well at once. My bosom is full of kindness, and
I am yet so near the manners of my mother that, upon
the least occasion more, mine eyes will tell tales of me.°
I am bound to the Count Orsino's court. Farewell.

Exit.

ANTONIO
The gentleness of all the gods go with thee.
I have many enemies in Orsino's court,
Else would I very shortly see thee there.
But come what may, I do adore thee so
That danger shall seem sport, and I will go.   *Exit.*

❧ **2.2**° *Enter Viola and Malvolio at several° doors.*

MALVOLIO   Were not you ev'n now with the Countess
Olivia?

VIOLA   Even now, sir. On a moderate pace I have since
arrived but hither.

MALVOLIO   She returns this ring to you, sir. You might
have saved me my pains, to have taken it away yourself.
She adds, moreover, that you should put your lord into
a desperate° assurance she will none of him. And one
thing more, that you be never so hardy to come again
in his affairs, unless it be to report your lord's taking of
this. Receive it so.

VIOLA   She took the ring of me. I'll none of it.

MALVOLIO   Come, sir, you peevishly threw it to her, and
her will is, it should be so returned. If it be worth
stooping for, there it lies, in your eye; if not, be it his
that finds it.   *Exit.*

VIOLA
I left no ring with her. What means this lady?
Fortune forbid my outside have not charmed her.
She made good view of° me; indeed, so much
That, as methought, her eyes had lost° her tongue,
For she did speak in starts distractedly.°
She loves me sure; the cunning° of her passion
Invites me in this churlish messenger.
None of my lord's ring? Why, he sent her none.
I am the man. If it be so, as 'tis,

---

your trouble: for causing you trouble
murder me for: be my death in return for

recovered: saved   35

so near . . . tales of me: so effeminate I shall
weep

40

2.2: A street near Olivia's house;
several: different

5

desperate: without hope

10

15

made good view of: looked intently at
lost: caused her to lose   20
distractedly: madly
cunning: craftiness

25

DISCOVERING SHAKESPEARE

(22) Gender [2.1.43]: What is our first indication in this scene that Antonio is attracted to Sebastian? Can you think of any other same-sex attractions in the play so far? How would these relationships have been compounded on Shakespeare's stage by the fact that the parts of women were all played by boy actors? (For example, the part of Viola was played by a boy actor who was pretending to be a girl on stage who was disguised as a boy.)

(23) Verse [2.2.17–41]: Why does Viola shift from prose to verse when she is alone on stage? Notice that the scene ends with a couplet—a device Shakespeare often uses to punctuate the conclusions of scenes. Can you find other scenes in this play that end in a similar fashion?

Poor lady, she were better° love a dream.
Disguise, I see thou art a wickedness
Wherein the pregnant enemy° does much.
How easy is it for the proper false°
In women's waxen hearts to set their forms!°
Alas, our frailty is the cause, not we,
For such as we are made of, such we be.
How will this fadge?° My master loves her dearly;
And I (poor monster)° fond° as much on him;
And she (mistaken) seems to dote on me.
What will become of this? As I am man,
My state is desperate° for my master's love.
As I am woman (now alas the day!),
What thriftless° sighs shall poor Olivia breathe?
O Time, thou must untangle this, not I;
It is too hard a knot for me t' untie.   *[Exit.]*

were better: would do better to

pregnant enemy: resourceful Satan
the proper false: deceivers who are
prepossessing in appearance   30
forms: impressions (as of a seal)

fadge: turn out
monster: (because both man and woman);
fond: dote   35

desperate: hopeless

thriftless: unprofitable

                                                               40

& **2.3**° *Enter Sir Toby and Sir Andrew.*

TOBY   Approach, Sir Andrew. Not to be abed after midnight is to be up betimes; and "*diluculo surgere,*"° thou know'st.
ANDREW   Nay, by my troth, I know not, but I know to be up late is to be up late.
TOBY   A false conclusion; I hate it as an unfilled can.° To be up after midnight, and to go to bed then, is early; so that to go to bed after midnight is to go to bed betimes. Does not our lives consist of the four elements?
ANDREW   Faith, so they say; but I think it rather consists of eating and drinking.
TOBY   Thou'rt a scholar! Let us therefore eat and drink. Marian I say! a stoup° of wine!
    Enter Feste.
ANDREW   Here comes the fool, i' faith.
FESTE   How now, my hearts?° Did you never see the picture of We Three?°
TOBY   Welcome, ass. Now let's have a catch.°
ANDREW   By my troth, the fool has an excellent breast.° I had rather than forty shillings I had such a leg, and so sweet a breath to sing, as the fool has. In sooth, thou wast in very gracious° fooling last night, when thou spok'st of Pigrogromitus, of the Vapians passing the equinoctial of Queubus.° 'Twas very good, i' faith. I sent thee sixpence for thy leman.° Hadst it?
FESTE   I did impeticos° thy gratillity,° for Malvolio's nose is no whipstock.° My lady has a white hand, and the Myrmidons° are no bottle-ale houses.
ANDREW   Excellent. Why, this is the best fooling, when all is done. Now a song!
TOBY   Come on! there is sixpence for you. Let's have a song.
ANDREW   There's a testril° of me too. If one knight give a —
FESTE   Would you have a love song, or a song of good life?°

2.3: Within Olivia's house

diluculo surgere [saluberrimum est]: to get
up at dawn is healthful (Lily's *Latin Grammar*)

                                                               5
can: metal vessel for holding liquor

                                                               10

stoup: large drinking vessel

hearts: (term of endearment)   15
picture of We Three: picture showing two fools
or asses inscribed "We Three," the onlooker
making the third
catch: round song (such as "Three Blind Mice")
breast: voice
                                                               20
gracious: elegant

Pigrogromitus . . . Queubus: (meaningless
mock-learning)
leman: sweetheart   25
impeticos: put in pocket of gown; **gratillity:**
gratuity
for . . . whipstock: i.e., Malvolio sticks his nose
into everything (?)
Myrmidons: Thessalian warriors; i.e., not   30
mermaids on tavern signs (?)

testril: tester, sixpence

good life: virtuous living

TOBY   A love song, a love song.   35
ANDREW   Ay, ay, I care not for good life.

Feste sings.

O mistress mine, where are you roaming?
O, stay and hear! your true-love's coming,
    That can sing both high and low.
Trip no further, pretty sweeting;   40
Journeys end in lovers' meeting,
    Every wise man's son doth know.

ANDREW   Excellent good, i' faith.
TOBY   Good, good.

Feste [sings].

What is love? 'Tis not hereafter;   45
Present mirth hath present laughter;
    What's to come is still unsure:
In delay there lies no plenty;
Then come kiss me, sweet and twenty,   50
    Youth's a stuff will not endure.

ANDREW   A mellifluous voice, as I am true knight.
TOBY   A contagious breath.
ANDREW   Very sweet and contagious, i' faith.
TOBY   To hear by the nose, it is dulcet° in contagion. But shall we make the welkin° dance indeed? Shall we rouse the night owl in a catch that will draw three souls out of one weaver?° Shall we do that?
ANDREW   An you love me, let's do't. I am dog° at a catch.
FESTE   By'r Lady, sir, and some dogs will catch well.
ANDREW   Most certain. Let our catch be "Thou knave."
FESTE   "Hold thy peace, thou knave," knight? I shall be constrained in't to call thee knave, knight.
ANDREW   'Tis not the first time I have constrained one to call me knave. Begin, fool. It begins, "Hold thy peace."
FESTE   I shall never begin if I hold my peace.
ANDREW   Good, i' faith! Come, begin.

Catch sung. Enter Maria.

MARIA   What a caterwauling do you keep here? If my lady have not called up her steward Malvolio and bid him turn you out of doors, never trust me.
TOBY   My lady's a Cataian,° we are politicians,° Malvolio's a Peg-a-Ramsey,° and *[Sings.]* "Three merry men be we." Am not I consanguineous?° Am I not of her blood? Tilly-vally,° lady. *[Sings.]* "There dwelt° a man in Babylon, lady, lady."
FESTE   Beshrew me, the knight's in admirable fooling.
ANDREW   Ay, he does well enough if he be disposed, and so do I too. He does it with a better grace, but I do it more natural.°
TOBY   *[Sings.]*
"O the twelfth day of December."

---

dulcet: sweet
welkin: sky   55

weaver: (weavers were famous for psalm singing)
dog: good
                                                                  60
                                                                  65

Cataian: native of Cathay, trickster; **politicians:**   70
intriguers
Peg-a-Ramsey: disreputable woman in an old song
consanguineous: related
Tilly-vally: nonsense; **There dwelt . . . :** (from   75
an old song, "The Constancy of Susanna")

natural: naturally (but the word also means "like a fool")

DISCOVERING SHAKESPEARE

(24) History [2.3.55–57]: Calvinist weavers often sang psalms while they weaved, which they thought would help save their souls. Why does Sir Toby believe their "catch" (song) will save three souls?

MARIA   For the love o' God, peace!   80

Enter Malvolio.

MALVOLIO   My masters, are you mad? Or what are you? Have you no wit, manners, nor honesty, but to gabble like tinkers at this time of night? Do ye make an alehouse of my lady's house, that ye squeak out your coziers'° catches without any mitigation or remorse° of voice? Is there no respect of place, persons, nor time in you?   85

coziers': cobblers'
mitigation or remorse: i.e., considerate lowering

TOBY   We did keep time, sir, in our catches. Sneck up.°

Sneck up: go hang
round: plain

MALVOLIO   Sir Toby, I must be round° with you. My lady bade me tell you that, though she harbors you as her kinsman, she's nothing allied to your disorders. If you can separate yourself and your misdemeanors, you are welcome to the house. If not, and it would please you to take leave of her, she is very willing to bid you farewell.   90

TOBY   *[Sings.]*
"Farewell, dear heart, since I must needs be gone."°

Farewell, dear heart . . .: (from an old song, "Corydon's Farewell to Phyllis")   95

MARIA   Nay, good Sir Toby.

FESTE   *[Sings.]*
"His eyes do show his days are almost done."

MALVOLIO   Is't even so?

TOBY   *[Sings.]*
"But I will never die."

FESTE   *[Sings.]*
Sir Toby, there you lie.

MALVOLIO   This is much credit to you.   100

TOBY   *[Sings.]*
"Shall I bid him go?"

FESTE   *[Sings.]*
"What an if you do?"

TOBY   *[Sings.]*
"Shall I bid him go, and spare not?"

FESTE   *[Sings.]*
"O, no, no, no, no, you dare not!"

TOBY   Out o' tune, sir? Ye lie. Art any more than a steward? Dost thou think, because thou art virtuous, there shall be no more cakes and ale?   105

FESTE   Yes, by Saint Anne,° and ginger° shall be hot i' th' mouth too.

Saint Anne: mother of the Virgin Mary;
ginger: (used to spice ale)

TOBY   Thou'rt i' th' right. – Go, sir, rub your chain with crumbs.° A stoup° of wine, Maria!   110

rub . . . crumbs: (a contemptuous allusion to his steward's chain)
stoup: large drinking vessel

MALVOLIO   Mistress Mary, if you prized my lady's favor at anything more than contempt, you would not give means° for this uncivil rule. She shall know of it, by this hand.   *Exit.*

give means: i.e., bring the wine   115

MARIA   Go shake your ears.°

your ears: i.e., your ass's ears

DISCOVERING SHAKESPEARE

(25) History [2.3.81]: As a "steward," how much power would Malvolio have had in Olivia's household? Did he have any authority over Maria? What was his relationship with Sir Toby, Olivia's uncle?

(26) Language [2.3.106–107]: Explain what Sir Toby means by the following line: "Dost thou think, because thou art virtuous, there shall be no more cakes and ale?"

ANDREW 'Twere as good a deed as to drink when a man's ahungry, to challenge him the field, and then to break promise with him and make a fool of him.

TOBY Do't, knight. I'll write thee a challenge; or I'll deliver thy indignation to him by word of mouth. 120

MARIA Sweet Sir Toby, be patient for tonight. Since the youth of the count's was today with my lady, she is much out of quiet. For Monsieur Malvolio, let me alone with him. If I do not gull° him into a nayword,° **gull:** trick; **nayword:** byword 125 and make him a common recreation,° do not think I **recreation:** amusement have wit enough to lie straight in my bed. I know I can do it.

TOBY Possess us, possess us.° Tell us something of him. **Possess us:** give us the facts

MARIA Marry, sir, sometimes he is a kind of Puritan.° **Puritan:** member of a strict Protestant faction 130

ANDREW O, if I thought that, I'd beat him like a dog. generally opposed to playgoing, reveling, etc.

TOBY What, for being a Puritan? Thy exquisite reason, dear knight.

ANDREW I have no exquisite reason for't, but I have reason good enough. 135

MARIA The devil a Puritan that he is, or anything constantly but a time-pleaser;° an affectioned° ass, that cons **time-pleaser:** sycophant; **affectioned:** affected state without book° and utters it by great swarths;° the **cons . . . book:** learns statecraft best persuaded of himself; so crammed, as he thinks, **swarths:** quantities with excellencies that it is his grounds of faith that all that look on him love him; and on that vice in him will 140 my revenge find notable cause to work.

TOBY What wilt thou do?

MARIA I will drop in his way some obscure epistles of love, wherein by the color of his beard, the shape of his 145 leg, the manner of his gait, the expressure° of his eye, **expressure:** expression forehead, and complexion, he shall find himself most feelingly personated.° I can write very like my lady your **personated:** represented niece; on a forgotten matter we can hardly make distinction of our hands. 150

TOBY Excellent. I smell a device.° **device:** trick, stratagem

ANDREW I have't in my nose too.

TOBY He shall think by the letters that thou wilt drop that they come from my niece, and that she's in love with him. 155

MARIA My purpose is indeed a horse of that color.

ANDREW And your horse now would make him an ass.

MARIA Ass, I doubt not.

ANDREW O, 'twill be admirable.

MARIA Sport royal, I warrant you. I know my physic will 160 work with him. I will plant you two, and let the fool make a third, where he shall find the letter. Observe his construction° of it. For this night, to bed, and dream on **construction:** interpretation the event.° Farewell. *Exit.* **event:** outcome

TOBY Good night, Penthesilea.° **Penthesilea:** queen of the Amazons 165

ANDREW Before me,° she's a good wench. **Before me:** I swear by myself

---

DISCOVERING SHAKESPEARE

(27) Plot [2.3.144]: What is Maria's plan to ridicule Malvolio? Do you think it will work? Why or why not?

TOBY   She's a beagle° true-bred, and one that adores me. What o' that?

ANDREW   I was adored once too.

TOBY   Let's to bed, knight. Thou hadst need send for more money.

ANDREW   If I cannot recover° your niece, I am a foul way out.°

TOBY   Send for money, knight. If thou hast her not i' th' end, call me Cut.°

ANDREW   If I do not, never trust me, take it how you will.

TOBY   Come, come; I'll go burn some sack.° 'Tis too late to go to bed now. Come, knight; come, knight.

Exeunt.

beagle: small rabbit hound

170

recover: gain
out: out of money

Cut: horse with a docked tail; also, a gelding

175

burn some sack: warm some sherry

🞽 **2.4°** *Enter Duke, Viola, Curio, and others.*

2.4: Within the palace of Orsino

DUKE

Give me some music. Now good morrow, friends.
Now, good Cesario, but that piece of song,
That old and antic° song we heard last night.
Methought it did relieve my passion much,
More than light airs and recollected° terms
Of these most brisk and giddy-pacèd times.
Come, but one verse.

CURIO   He is not here, so please your lordship, that should sing it.

DUKE   Who was it?

CURIO   Feste the jester, my lord, a fool that the Lady Olivia's father took much delight in. He is about the house.

DUKE

Seek him out, and play the tune the while.

[Exit Curio.]

Music plays.
Come hither, boy. If ever thou shalt love,
In the sweet pangs of it remember me;
For such as I am all true lovers are,
Unstaid and skittish in all motions° else
Save in the constant image of the creature
That is beloved. How dost thou like this tune?

VIOLA

It gives a very echo to the seat
Where Love is thronèd.°

DUKE   Thou dost speak masterly.
My life upon't, young though thou art, thine eye
Hath stayed upon some favor° that it loves.
Hath it not, boy?

VIOLA   A little, by your favor.

antic: quaint

recollected: studied

5

10

15

motions: emotions

20

the seat . . . thronèd: i.e., the heart

favor: face

25

DISCOVERING SHAKESPEARE

(28) Language [2.3.172–173]: Why does Sir Andrew say to Toby, "If I cannot recover your niece, I am a foul way out"? What does he want from Olivia?

DUKE
  What kind of woman is't?
VIOLA   Of your complexion.
DUKE
  She is not worth thee then. What years, i' faith?
VIOLA
  About your years, my lord.
DUKE
  Too old, by heaven! Let still the woman take
  An elder than herself: so wears° she to him,   **wears:** adapts herself   30
  So sways she level in her husband's heart;°   **sways . . . heart:** she keeps constant her
  For, boy, however we do praise ourselves,   husband's love
  Our fancies° are more giddy and unfirm,   **fancies:** loves
  More longing, wavering, sooner lost and worn,
  Than women's are.   35
VIOLA   I think it well, my lord.
DUKE
  Then let thy love be younger than thyself,
  Or thy affection cannot hold the bent;°   **bent:** direction
  For women are as roses, whose fair flow'r,
  Being once displayed, doth fall that very hour.
VIOLA
  And so they are; alas, that they are so.   40
  To die, even when they to perfection grow.
    Enter Curio and Feste.
DUKE
  O, fellow, come, the song we had last night.
  Mark it, Cesario; it is old and plain.
  The spinsters° and the knitters in the sun,   **spinsters:** spinners
  And the free° maids that weave their thread with bones,° **free:** innocent; **bones:** bone bobbins   45
  Do use° to chant it. It is silly sooth,°   **Do use:** are accustomed; **silly sooth:** simple
  And dallies with the innocence of love,   truth
  Like the old age.°   **old age:** good old days
FESTE   Are you ready, sir?
DUKE   I prithee sing.   50
    Music.
                The Song.
    Come away, come away, death,
      And in sad cypress° let me be laid.   **cypress:** coffin of cypress wood
    Fly away, fly away, breath;
      I am slain by a fair cruel maid.
    My shroud of white, stuck all with yew,°   **yew:** yew sprigs, associated with mourning   55
      O, prepare it.
    My part° of death, no one so true   **part:** portion
      Did share it.

DISCOVERING SHAKESPEARE

(29) Language [2.4.30–31]: What does Orsino mean when he argues that a younger woman married to an older man "wears" to her husband and "sways level" in his heart? Do you think he is correct in his assumption that men's "fancies" are "more giddy and unfirm" (l. 33) than women's are? Why or why not?

(30) Metaphor [2.4.37]: How many different <u>metaphoric</u> meanings can you find in the phrase "Or thy affection cannot hold the bent"?

(31) Music [2.4.58]: How does this melancholy song affect each of the various characters on stage?

Not a flower, not a flower sweet,
    On my black coffin let there be strown;   60
Not a friend, not a friend greet
    My poor corpse, where my bones shall be thrown.
A thousand thousand sighs to save,
    Lay me, O, where
Sad true lover never find my grave,   65
    To weep there.

DUKE   There's for thy pains.   *[Giving him money]*

FESTE   No pains, sir. I take pleasure in singing, sir.

DUKE   I'll pay thy pleasure then.

FESTE   Truly, sir, and pleasure will be paid° one time or   **pleasure . . . paid:** indulgence exacts its penalty   70
another.

DUKE   Give me now leave to leave thee.

FESTE   Now the melancholy god° protect thee, and the   **melancholy god:** (usually identified by
tailor make thy doublet of changeable° taffeta, for thy   Elizabethans as Saturn)
mind is a very opal. I would have men of such con-   **changeable:** i.e., opalescent in effect   75
stancy put to sea, that their business might be every-
thing, and their intent everywhere; for that's it that
always makes a good voyage of nothing.° Farewell.   *Exit.*   **nothing:** bringing back nothing

DUKE
Let all the rest give place.°   **give place:** leave

              [Exeunt Curio and Attendants.]
              Once more, Cesario,
Get thee to yond same sovereign cruelty.°   **sovereign cruelty:** supremely cruel person   80
Tell her, my love, more noble than the world,
Prizes not quantity of dirty lands;
The parts° that fortune hath bestowed upon her   **parts:** possessions
Tell her I hold as giddily as fortune,
But 'tis that miracle and queen of gems   85
That nature pranks° her in attracts my soul.   **pranks:** decks

VIOLA
But if she cannot love you, sir?

DUKE
I cannot be so answered.

VIOLA   Sooth, but you must.
Say that some lady, as perhaps there is,
Hath for your love as great a pang of heart   90
As you have for Olivia. You cannot love her.
You tell her so. Must she not then be answered?

DUKE
There is no woman's sides
Can bide° the beating of so strong a passion   **bide:** withstand
As love doth give my heart; no woman's heart   95
So big to hold so much; they lack retention.°   **retention:** capacity of retaining
Alas, their love may be called appetite,
No motion° of the liver° but the palate,   **motion:** emotion; **liver:** seat of the emotion of
That suffers surfeit, cloyment, and revolt;°   love
But mine is all as hungry as the sea   **revolt:** revulsion
And can digest as much. Make no compare   100

DISCOVERING SHAKESPEARE

(32) <u>Imagery</u> **[2.4.93–103]:** Examine Orsino's food <u>imagery</u> here; then see how many other examples of food <u>metaphors</u> you can find in the play.

Between that love a woman can bear me
And that I owe° Olivia.   **owe:** have toward
VIOLA   Ay, but I know –
DUKE
What dost thou know?
VIOLA
Too well what love women to men may owe.   105
In faith, they are as true of heart as we.
My father had a daughter loved a man
As it might be perhaps, were I a woman,
I should your lordship.
DUKE   And what's her history?°   **history:** story
VIOLA
A blank, my lord. She never told her love,   110
But let concealment, like a worm i' th' bud,
Feed on her damask° cheek. She pined in thought;   **damask:** pink and white, as of a damask rose
And, with a green and yellow melancholy,
She sat like Patience on a monument,°   **Patience on a monument:** allegorical sculpture
Smiling at grief. Was not this love indeed?   of patience   115
We men may say more, swear more; but indeed
Our shows are more than will;° for still we prove   **will:** our passions
Much in our vows but little in our love.
DUKE
But died thy sister of her love, my boy?
VIOLA
I am all the daughters of my father's house,   120
And all the brothers too, and yet I know not.
Sir, shall I to this lady?
DUKE   Ay, that's the theme.
To her in haste. Give her this jewel. Say
My love can give no place,° bide no denay.°   *Exeunt.*   **can give no place:** cannot yield; **denay:** denial

❧ **2.5**° *Enter Sir Toby, Sir Andrew, and Fabian.*   **2.5:** The garden of Olivia's house

TOBY   Come thy ways, Signor Fabian.
FABIAN   Nay, I'll come. If I lose a scruple° of this sport, let   **scruple:** bit
me be boiled to death with melancholy.°   **boiled . . . melancholy:** (pun on "bile," the
TOBY   Wouldst thou not be glad to have the niggardly,°   cause of melancholy)
rascally sheep-biter° come by some notable shame?   **niggardly:** grudging   5
FABIAN   I would exult, man. You know he brought me   **sheep-biter:** dog that bites sheep, sneaking
out o' favor with my lady about a bearbaiting here.   fellow
TOBY   To anger him we'll have the bear again, and we
will fool him black and blue. Shall we not, Sir Andrew?
ANDREW   An we do not, it is pity of our lives.   10
    Enter Maria.
TOBY   Here comes the little villain. How now, my metal
of India?°   **my metal of India:** my golden one
MARIA   Get ye all three into the boxtree.° Malvolio's   **boxtree:** i.e., hedge
coming down this walk. He has been yonder i' the sun

DISCOVERING SHAKESPEARE

(33) Staging [2.4.122]: Can you find any occasions in 2.4 where Orsino might betray a subconscious attraction to Viola/Cesario? How important would such moments be to the final reconciliation scene in 5.1?

practicing behavior° to his own shadow this half hour. **behavior:** elegant conduct 15
Observe him, for the love of mockery, for I know this
letter will make a contemplative idiot° of him. Close,° in **contemplative idiot:** i.e., addled by his musings;
the name of jesting. *[The others hide.]* Lie thou there **Close:** hide
[Throws down a letter.]; for here comes the trout that
must be caught with tickling.° *Exit.* **tickling:** stroking about the gills 20
    Enter Malvolio.

MALVOLIO 'Tis but fortune; all is fortune. Maria once
told me she did affect me;° and I have heard herself **she did affect me:** Olivia liked me
come thus near, that, should she fancy, it should be one
of my complexion.° Besides, she uses me with a more **complexion:** personality
exalted respect than any one else that follows her.° What **that follows her:** in her service 25
should I think on't?

TOBY Here's an overweening rogue.

FABIAN O, peace! Contemplation makes a rare turkey
cock of him. How he jets° under his advanced plumes! **jets:** struts
                                                   'Slight: an oath (by God's light) 30

ANDREW 'Slight,° I could so beat the rogue.

TOBY Peace, I say.

MALVOLIO To be Count Malvolio.

TOBY Ah, rogue!

ANDREW Pistol him, pistol him.

TOBY Peace, peace. 35

MALVOLIO There is example for't. The Lady of the
Strachy° married the yeoman of the wardrobe. **Lady of the Strachy:** (unidentified allusion)

ANDREW Fie on him, Jezebel.° **Jezebel:** wicked queen of Israel

FABIAN O, peace! Now he's deeply in. Look how imagination blows him.° **blows him:** puffs him up 40

MALVOLIO Having been three months married to her,
sitting in my state –° **state:** chair of state

TOBY O for a stonebow,° to hit him in the eye! **stonebow:** stone shooter

MALVOLIO Calling my officers about me, in my
branched° velvet gown; having come from a daybed,° **branched:** embroidered; **daybed:** sofa 45
where I have left Olivia sleeping –

TOBY Fire and brimstone!

FABIAN O, peace, peace!

MALVOLIO And then to have the humor of state;° and **humor of state:** manner and disposition of
after a demure travel of regard,° telling them I know my authority 50
place, as I would they should do theirs, to ask for my **demure . . . regard:** grave survey
kinsman Toby –

TOBY Bolts and shackles!

FABIAN O peace, peace, peace, now, now.

MALVOLIO Seven of my people, with an obedient start, 55
make out for him. I frown the while, and perchance

DISCOVERING SHAKESPEARE

(34) Metaphor [2.5.18–20]: What does Maria mean when she metaphorically compares Malvolio to a "trout that must
be caught with tickling" (2.5.18–20)? Find other metaphors in this scene that describe the entrapment of Malvolio. How
many of them employ the feeding metaphors so prevalent in the play?

(35) Teaser [2.5.36–37]: When Malvolio cites the example of the Lady of the Strachy who married the yeoman of the
wardrobe, he is clearly attempting to rationalize the possibility that a wealthy and noble woman like Olivia might fall in
love with a commoner like himself. In literature, the "Cinderella" motif is more commonly seen: A poor girl marries a rich
prince and lives happily ever after. Can you discover any stories in literature or in the movies in which a wealthy woman
marries beneath her station in life? What is the result of these reverse-Cinderella marriages? What do these stories tell us
about gender inequalities in art and life?

wind up my watch, or play with my — some rich jewel.
Toby approaches; curtsies there to me —

TOBY   Shall this fellow live?

FABIAN   Though our silence be drawn from us with cars,°   **cars:** chariots   60
yet peace.

MALVOLIO   I extend my hand to him thus, quenching
my familiar smile with an austere regard of control —°   **regard of control:** look of authority

TOBY   And does not Toby take° you a blow o' the lips   **take:** give
then?   65

MALVOLIO   Saying, "Cousin Toby, my fortunes having
cast me on your niece, give me this prerogative of
speech."

TOBY   What, what?

MALVOLIO   "You must amend your drunkenness."   70

TOBY   Out, scab!

FABIAN   Nay, patience, or we break the sinews of our
plot.

MALVOLIO   "Besides, you waste the treasure of your time
with a foolish knight" —   75

ANDREW   That's me, I warrant you.

MALVOLIO   "One Sir Andrew" —

ANDREW   I knew 'twas I, for many do call me fool.

MALVOLIO   What employment have we here?
    [Takes up the letter.]

FABIAN   Now is the woodcock° near the gin.°   **woodcock:** (a stupid bird); **gin:** snare, trap   80

TOBY   O, peace, and the spirit of humors intimate reading aloud to him!

MALVOLIO   By my life, this is my lady's hand. These be
her very C's, her U's, and her T's;° and thus makes she   **C's . . . T's:** ("cut" is Elizabethan slang for women's genitals)   85
her great P's.° It is, in contempt of° question, her hand.   **great P's:** capital P's; also pun on urination; **in contempt of:** beyond

ANDREW   Her C's, her U's, and her T's? Why that?

MALVOLIO   *[Reads.]* "To the unknown beloved, this, and
my good wishes." Her very phrases! By your leave, wax.°   **By . . . wax:** (a conventional apology for breaking a seal)
Soft,° and the impressure° her Lucrece,° with which she   **Soft:** careful, slow; **impressure:** impression;   90
uses to seal. 'Tis my lady. To whom should this be?   **Lucrece:** chaste Roman heroine who commits suicide after being raped, pictured on Olivia's seal

FABIAN   This wins him, liver° and all.   **liver:** the seat of passion

MALVOLIO   *[Reads.]*
    "Jove knows I love,
      But who?
    Lips, do not move;
      No man must know."   95
"No man must know." What follows? The numbers° al-   **numbers:** meter
tered! "No man must know." If this should be thee,
Malvolio?

TOBY   Marry,° hang thee, brock!°   **Marry:** (corruption of "Mary"; mild oath); **brock:** badger

MALVOLIO   *[Reads.]*
    "I may command where I adore,   100
      But silence, like a Lucrece knife,

DISCOVERING SHAKESPEARE

(36) History [2.5.60–61]: What does Fabian mean when he refers to their silence being drawn from them "with cars"?
How many different torture devices were used during the Renaissance? Which seem most horrifying to you?

(37) Staging [2.5.81–82]: Why does Sir Toby want "the spirit of humors" to "intimate reading aloud" to Malvolio? How
would this scene be different if Malvolio read the letter silently?

With bloodless stroke my heart doth gore.
  M. O. A. I. doth sway my life."

FABIAN   A fustian° riddle.

TOBY   Excellent wench,° say I.

MALVOLIO   "M. O. A. I. doth sway my life." Nay, but first, let me see, let me see, let me see.

FABIAN   What dish o' poison has she dressed° him!

TOBY   And with what wing the staniel° checks° at it!

MALVOLIO   "I may command where I adore." Why, she may command me: I serve her; she is my lady. Why, this is evident to any formal° capacity. There is no obstruction° in this. And the end; what should that alphabetical position portend? If I could make that resemble something in me! Softly, "M. O. A. I."

TOBY   O, ay, make up that. He is now at a cold scent.°

FABIAN   Sowter will cry upon't° for all this, though it be as rank as a fox.

MALVOLIO   M — Malvolio. M — Why, that begins my name.

FABIAN   Did not I say he would work it out? The cur is excellent at faults.°

MALVOLIO   M — But then there is no consonancy° in the sequel. That suffers° under probation.° A should follow, but O does.

FABIAN   And O shall end, I hope.

TOBY   Ay, or I'll cudgel him, and make him cry O.

MALVOLIO   And then I comes behind.

FABIAN   Ay, an you had any eye behind you, you might see more detraction at your heels than fortunes before you.

MALVOLIO   M, O, A, I. This simulation° is not as the former; and yet, to crush° this a little, it would bow to me, for every one of these letters are in my name. Soft, here follows prose.

    [Reads.] "If this fall into thy hand, revolve.° In my stars° I am above thee, but be not afraid of greatness. Some are born great, some achieve greatness, and some have greatness thrust upon 'em. Thy Fates open their hands; let thy blood and spirit embrace them; and to inure° thyself to what thou art like to be, cast thy humble slough° and appear fresh. Be opposite with a kinsman, surly with servants. Let thy tongue tang° arguments of state; put thyself into the trick of singularity.° She thus advises thee that sighs for thee. Remember who commended thy yellow stockings and wished to see thee ever cross-gartered.° I say, remember. Go to, thou art made, if thou desir'st to be so. If not, let me see thee a steward still, the fellow of servants, and not worthy to

fustian: ridiculously elaborate	
Excellent wench: clever girl (Maria)	105
dressed: prepared	
staniel: an inferior hawk; **checks:** turns to pursue the wrong prey	110
formal: normal	
obstruction: difficulty	
	115
cold scent: difficult trail	
Sowter . . . upon't: the hound will pick up the scent	
	120
faults: gaps or breaks in the scent	
consonancy: agreement	
suffers: becomes strained; **probation:** testing	
	125
	130
simulation: hidden meaning	
crush: force	
revolve: consider; **stars:** fate	135
inure: accustom	
	140
slough: outer skin	
tang: sound with	
singularity: originality	
	145
cross-gartered: wearing hose garters crossed above and below the knee	

DISCOVERING SHAKESPEARE

(38) Language [2.5.103]: What do you think "M.O.A.I." stands for? Why does Maria include these initials in her letter?

(39) Staging [2.5.135]: What physical action could Malvolio perform to accompany the word "revolve"? What could the three conspirators be doing while he is reading the letter?

(40) Costuming [2.5.144–146]: Why does Maria include yellow stockings and cross-garters in her letter? How will the audience react when the puritanical Malvolio comes on stage dressed in this ridiculous fashion?

touch Fortune's fingers. Farewell. She that would alter services with thee,   150

The Fortunate Unhappy."°

Unhappy: unfortunate

Daylight and champian° discovers° not more! This is open. I will be proud, I will read politic authors,° I will baffle° Sir Toby, I will wash off gross acquaintance, I will be point-devise,° the very man. I do not now fool myself, to let imagination jade° me, for every reason excites to this, that my lady loves me. She did commend my yellow stockings of late, she did praise my leg being cross-gartered; and in this she manifests herself to my love, and with a kind of injunction drives me to these habits° of her liking. I thank my stars, I am happy. I will be strange,° stout,° in yellow stockings, and cross-gartered, even with the swiftness of putting on. Jove and my stars be praised. Here is yet a postscript. *[Reads.]* "Thou canst not choose but know who I am. If thou entertain'st° my love, let it appear in thy smiling. Thy smiles become thee well. Therefore in my presence still smile, dear my sweet, I prithee." Jove, I thank thee. I will smile; I will do everything that thou wilt have me.   *Exit.*

champian: open country; **discovers:** reveals, discloses
politic authors: writers on government
baffle: subject to disgrace   155
point-devise: perfectly correct
jade: trick

habits: attire   160
strange: aloof; **stout:** proud

entertain'st: accept   165

FABIAN   I will not give my part of this sport for a pension of thousands to be paid from the Sophy.°

Sophy: Shah of Persia

TOBY   I could marry this wench for this device.

ANDREW   So could I too.

TOBY   And ask no other dowry with her but such another jest.   175

Enter Maria.

ANDREW   Nor I neither.

FABIAN   Here comes my noble gull-catcher.°

gull-catcher: fool-catcher

TOBY   Wilt thou set thy foot o' my neck?

ANDREW   Or o' mine either?   180

TOBY   Shall I play° my freedom at tray-trip° and become thy bondslave?

play: gamble; **tray-trip:** a game of dice

ANDREW   I' faith, or I either?

TOBY   Why, thou hast put him in such a dream that, when the image of it leaves him, he must run mad.   185

MARIA   Nay, but say true, does it work upon him?

TOBY   Like aqua vitae° with a midwife.

aqua vitae: any distilled liquor

MARIA   If you will, then, see the fruits of the sport, mark his first approach before my lady. He will come to her in yellow stockings, and 'tis a color she abhors, and   190
cross-gartered, a fashion she detests; and he will smile upon her, which will now be so unsuitable to her disposition, being addicted to a melancholy as she is, that it cannot but turn him into a notable contempt. If you will see it, follow me.   195

DISCOVERING SHAKESPEARE

(41) Staging [2.5.168]: At what point in this speech should Malvolio smile to the audience? What other physical actions could he perform during this speech to imply that the letter excites him?

TOBY To the gates of Tartar,° thou most excellent devil of wit.

ANDREW I'll make one too.   *Exeunt.*

❧ **3.1**° *Enter Viola and Feste [with a tabor].*

VIOLA Save thee,° friend, and thy music. Dost thou live by° thy tabor?°

FESTE No, sir, I live by the church.

VIOLA Art thou a churchman?

FESTE No such matter, sir. I do live by the church; for I do live at my house, and my house doth stand by the church.

VIOLA So thou mayst say, the king lies° by a beggar, if a beggar dwell near him; or, the church stands by thy tabor, if thy tabor stand by the church.

FESTE You have said, sir. To see this age! A sentence is but a chev'ril° glove to a good wit. How quickly the wrong side may be turned outward!

VIOLA Nay, that's certain. They that dally nicely° with words may quickly make them wanton.°

FESTE I would therefore my sister had had no name, sir.

VIOLA Why, man?

FESTE Why, sir, her name's a word, and to dally with that word might make my sister wanton.° But indeed words are very rascals since bonds disgraced them.°

VIOLA Thy reason, man?

FESTE Troth, sir, I can yield you none without words, and words are grown so false I am loath to prove reason with them.

VIOLA I warrant thou art a merry fellow and car'st for nothing.

FESTE Not so, sir; I do care for something; but in my conscience, sir, I do not care for you. If that be to care for nothing, sir, I would it would make you invisible.

VIOLA Art not thou the Lady Olivia's fool?

FESTE No, indeed, sir. The Lady Olivia has no folly. She will keep no fool, sir, till she be married; and fools are as like husbands as pilchers° are to herrings, the husband's the bigger. I am indeed not her fool, but her corrupter of words.

VIOLA I saw thee late at the Count Orsino's.

FESTE Foolery, sir, does walk about the orb like the sun; it shines everywhere. I would be sorry, sir, but the fool should be as oft with your master as with my mistress. I think I saw your wisdom there.

Tartar: Tartarus, the section of hell reserved for the most evil

3.1: Before the house of Olivia

Save thee: God save thee
live by: make a living with
tabor: drum
                                                                    5

lies: dwells, here implying "sleeps with"
                                                                    10

chev'ril: kid

dally nicely: play subtly
wanton: capricious   15

wanton: abandoned   20
since . . . them: i.e., since bonds have been needed to guarantee them

                                                                    25

                                                                    30

pilchers: pilchards (small fish resembling herring)
                                                                    35

                                                                    40

DISCOVERING SHAKESPEARE

(42) Staging [2.5.197]: Most modern productions of the play put their intermission at the end of 2.5. Why would this be a particularly effective place to have it? Can you suggest a better moment in the play?

(43) Language [3.1.35–36]: Feste claims that he is Olivia's "corrupter of words" rather than her "fool." In what sense are all comedians "corrupters of words"? Find three of Feste's jokes and explain how words are "corrupted" in each of them.

VIOLA   Nay, an thou pass upon° me, I'll no more with thee. Hold, there's expenses for thee.
　　[Gives a coin.]

pass upon: jest at

FESTE   Now Jove, in his next commodity° of hair, send thee a beard.

commodity: shipment

45

VIOLA   By my troth, I'll tell thee, I am almost sick for one, though I would not have it grow on my chin. Is thy lady within?

FESTE   Would not a pair of these have bred, sir?

VIOLA   Yes, being kept together and put to use.°

put to use: put out at interest   50

FESTE   I would play Lord Pandarus° of Phrygia, sir, to bring a Cressida to this Troilus.

Pandarus: the go-between in the tale told by Chaucer and others

VIOLA   I understand you, sir. 'Tis well begged.
　　[Gives another coin.]

FESTE   The matter, I hope, is not great, sir, begging but a beggar: Cressida was a beggar.° My lady is within, sir. I will conster° to them whence you come. Who you are and what you would are out of my welkin;° I might say "element," but the word is overworn.　　*Exit.*

Cressida was a beggar: (she became a leprous beggar in Henryson's continuation of Chaucer's story)   55

conster: construe, explain

welkin: sky

VIOLA
This fellow is wise enough to play the fool,
And to do that well craves a kind of wit.°
He must observe their mood on whom he jests,
The quality of persons, and the time;
And like the haggard,° check at every feather°
That comes before his eye. This is a practice°
As full of labor as a wise man's art;
For folly that he wisely shows, is fit;
But wise men, folly-fall'n,° quite taint their wit.°
　　Enter Sir Toby and [Sir] Andrew.

wit: intelligence   60

haggard: untrained hawk; **check . . . feather:** forsake her quarry for other game

practice: skill   65

folly-fall'n: fallen into folly; **taint their wit:** ruin their reputation for intelligence

TOBY   Save you, gentleman.

VIOLA   And you, sir.

ANDREW   *Dieu vous garde, monsieur.*

70

VIOLA   *Et vous aussi; votre serviteur.*°

Dieu . . . serviteur: God protect you, sir . . . And you also; your servant

ANDREW   I hope, sir, you are, and I am yours.

TOBY   Will you encounter° the house? My niece is desirous you should enter, if your trade be to her.

encounter: meet—i.e., go into

VIOLA   I am bound to° your niece, sir; I mean, she is the list° of my voyage.

bound to: bound for   75
list: limit, destination

TOBY   Taste° your legs, sir; put them to motion.

Taste: try

VIOLA   My legs do better understand° me, sir, than I understand what you mean by bidding me taste my legs.

understand: both "comprehend" and "stand under"

TOBY   I mean, to go, sir, to enter.

80

VIOLA   I will answer you with gait and entrance. But we are prevented.°
　　Enter Olivia and Gentlewoman [Maria].
Most excellent accomplished lady, the heavens rain odors on you.

prevented: anticipated

ANDREW   That youth's a rare courtier. "Rain odors" — well!

85

DISCOVERING SHAKESPEARE

(44) Language [3.1.57]: Look up the word "welkin" in the *Oxford English Dictionary,* and list all the different meanings of the term available in 1600. What is the primary definition of the word in this particular dramatic context?

VIOLA   My matter hath no voice,° lady, but to your own
most pregnant° and vouchsafed° ear.

hath no voice: can be told to no one
pregnant: receptive; **vouchsafed:** willing

ANDREW   "Odors," "pregnant," and "vouchsafed" – I'll
get 'em all three all ready.

90

OLIVIA   Let the garden door be shut, and leave me to my
hearing. *[Exeunt Sir Toby, Sir Andrew, and Maria.]* Give
me your hand, sir.

VIOLA
My duty, madam, and most humble service.

OLIVIA
What is your name?

95

VIOLA
Cesario is your servant's name, fair princess.

OLIVIA
My servant, sir? 'Twas never merry world
Since lowly feigning° was called compliment.
You're servant to the Count Orsino, youth.

lowly feigning: false humility

VIOLA
And he is yours, and his must needs be yours.
Your servant's servant is your servant, madam.

100

OLIVIA
For him, I think not on him; for his thoughts,
Would they were blanks,° rather than filled with me.

blanks: blank sheets

VIOLA
Madam, I come to whet your gentle thoughts
On his behalf.

105

OLIVIA   O, by your leave, I pray you.
I bade you never speak again of him;
But, would you undertake another suit,
I had rather hear you to solicit that
Than music from the spheres.°

music from the spheres: celestial melody
believed to be produced by the several concentric
revolving spheres in which the planets and stars
were thought to be placed

VIOLA   Dear lady –

110

OLIVIA
Give me leave, beseech you. I did send,
After the last enchantment you did here,
A ring in chase of you. So did I abuse°
Myself, my servant, and, I fear me, you.
Under your hard construction° must I sit,
To force that on you in a shameful cunning
Which you knew none of yours. What might you think?
Have you not set mine honor at the stake
And baited° it with all th' unmuzzled thoughts
That tyrannous heart can think? To one of your receiving°
Enough is shown; a cypress,° not a bosom,
Hides my heart. So, let me hear you speak.

abuse: deceive

construction: interpretation

115

baited: harassed, as a chained bear by dogs
receiving: receptive capacity
cypress: transparent black cloth

120

VIOLA
I pity you.

OLIVIA   That's a degree to love.

DISCOVERING SHAKESPEARE

(45) Staging [3.1.89–90]: Imagine that Sir Andrew always carries a small notebook. Which important words in this scene
would he want to write down? Why? Can you find any other moments in the play when he might want to record certain
events or <u>dialogue</u>?

VIOLA
No, not a grize;° for 'tis a vulgar proof°
That very oft we pity enemies.

grize: degree; **vulgar proof:** common experience

OLIVIA
Why then, methinks 'tis time to smile again.   125
O world, how apt the poor are to be proud.
If one should be a prey, how much the better
To fall before the lion than the wolf.
   Clock strikes.
The clock upbraids me with the waste of time.
Be not afraid, good youth, I will not have you,   130
And yet, when wit and youth is come to harvest,
Your wife is like to reap a proper° man.

proper: handsome

There lies your way, due west.
VIOLA   Then westward ho!
Grace and good disposition attend your ladyship.
You'll nothing, madam, to my lord by me?   135
OLIVIA
Stay.
I prithee tell me what thou think'st of me.
VIOLA
That you do think you are not what you are.
OLIVIA
If I think so, I think the same of you.
VIOLA
Then think you right. I am not what I am.   140
OLIVIA
I would you were as I would have you be.
VIOLA
Would it be better, madam, than I am?
I wish it might, for now I am your fool.°

fool: butt

OLIVIA
O, what a deal of scorn looks beautiful
In the contempt and anger of his lip.   145
A murd'rous guilt shows not itself more soon
Than love that would seem hid: love's night is noon.
Cesario, by the roses of the spring,
By maidhood, honor, truth, and everything,
I love thee so that, maugre° all thy pride,   150

maugre: despite

Nor wit nor reason can my passion hide.
Do not extort thy reasons from this clause,
For that I woo, thou therefore hast no cause;
But rather reason thus with reason fetter,°

reason . . . fetter: bind reason with (stronger) reason

Love sought is good, but given unsought is better.   155

DISCOVERING SHAKESPEARE

(46) Characterization [3.1.125]: Olivia, who as mistress of her household is used to getting everything she desires, is in the uncomfortable position of pursuing Viola. How many other characters are, to borrow Feste's phrase, forced out of their "element" (3.1.58) by the action of the play? List the names of each principal character; then explain how Shakespeare's plot has placed them in unaccustomed circumstances.

(47) Verse [3.1.144–163]: At what point in her speech does Olivia shift into rhyming couplets? Why does she do so? Why does Viola answer her in couplets? Although most of the rhymes in this section are "perfect" (i.e., pride/hide, fetter/better), some of them exhibit what we call slant rhyme (none/alone, move/love). Why do we find these "slant" or off-key rhymes in Viola's speech in this particular section of the play?

VIOLA
By innocence I swear, and by my youth,
I have one heart, one bosom, and one truth,
And that no woman has; nor never none
Shall mistress be of it, save I alone.
And so adieu, good madam. Never more   160
Will I my master's tears to you deplore.
OLIVIA
Yet come again; for thou perhaps mayst move
That heart which now abhors to like his love.   *Exeunt.*

❧ **3.2**° *Enter Sir Toby, Sir Andrew, and Fabian.*   **3.2:** Within the house of Olivia

ANDREW   No, faith, I'll not stay a jot longer.
TOBY   Thy reason, dear venom;° give thy reason.   **venom:** (Sir Andrew is filled with venom)
FABIAN   You must needs yield your reason, Sir Andrew.
ANDREW   Marry, I saw your niece do more favors to the
    count's servingman than ever she bestowed upon me. I   5
    saw't i' th' orchard.°   **orchard:** probably "garden"
TOBY   Did she see thee the while, old boy? Tell me that.
ANDREW   As plain as I see you now.
FABIAN   This was a great argument° of love in her toward   **argument:** proof
    you.   10
ANDREW   'Slight! will you make an ass o' me?
FABIAN   I will prove it legitimate,° sir, upon the oaths° of   **legitimate:** true; **oaths:** testimony
    judgment and reason.
TOBY   And they have been grand-jury men since before
    Noah was a sailor.   15
FABIAN   She did show favor to the youth in your sight
    only to exasperate you, to awake your dormouse° valor,   **dormouse:** i.e., sleepy
    to put fire in your heart and brimstone in your liver.
    You should then have accosted her, and with some ex-
    cellent jests, fire-new from the mint, you should have   20
    banged the youth into dumbness. This was looked for
    at your hand, and this was balked.° The double gilt° of   **balked:** missed; **double gilt:** twice dipped in
    this opportunity you let time wash off, and you are   gold
    now sailed into the north° of my lady's opinion, where   **into the north:** i.e., out of the warmth
    you will hang like an icicle on a Dutchman's beard un-   25
    less you do redeem it by some laudable attempt either
    of valor or policy.
ANDREW   An't be any way, it must be with valor; for pol-
    icy I hate. I had as lief be a Brownist° as a politician.   **Brownist:** early Congregationalist
TOBY   Why then, build me thy fortunes upon the basis   30
    of valor. Challenge me the count's youth to fight with
    him; hurt him in eleven places. My niece shall take
    note of it, and assure thyself there is no love-broker in
    the world can more prevail in man's commendation
    with woman than report of valor.   35
FABIAN   There is no way but this, Sir Andrew.
ANDREW   Will either of you bear me a challenge to him?

DISCOVERING SHAKESPEARE

(48) Characterization [3.2.1]: Why does Sir Toby want Sir Andrew to stay with him rather than leaving Olivia's house?
Find one or more quotations elsewhere in the play that support your opinion.

TOBY Go, write it in a martial hand. Be curst° and brief; it is no matter how witty, so it be eloquent and full of invention. Taunt him with the license of ink.° If thou thou'st him° some thrice, it shall not be amiss; and as many lies as will lie in thy sheet of paper, although the sheet were big enough for the bed of Ware° in England, set 'em down. Go about it. Let there be gall enough in thy ink, though thou write with a goose pen, no matter. About it!

ANDREW Where shall I find you?

TOBY We'll call thee at the cubiculo.° Go.

Exit Sir Andrew.

FABIAN This is a dear manikin° to you, Sir Toby.

TOBY I have been dear to him, lad, some two thousand strong or so.

FABIAN We shall have a rare letter from him, but you'll not deliver't?

TOBY Never trust me then; and by all means stir on the youth to an answer. I think oxen and wainropes° cannot hale° them together. For Andrew, if he were opened, and you find so much blood in his liver as will clog the foot of a flea, I'll eat the rest of th' anatomy.

FABIAN And his opposite, the youth, bears in his visage no great presage of cruelty.

Enter Maria.

TOBY Look where the youngest wren° of mine comes.

MARIA If you desire the spleen,° and will laugh yourselves into stitches, follow me. Yond gull° Malvolio is turned heathen, a very renegado; for there is no Christian that means to be saved by believing rightly can ever believe such impossible passages of grossness.° He's in yellow stockings.

TOBY And cross-gartered?

MARIA Most villainously; like a pedant that keeps a school i' th' church.° I have dogged him like his murderer. He does obey every point of the letter that I dropped to betray him. He does smile his face into more lines than is in the new map with the augmentation of the Indies.° You have not seen such a thing as 'tis. I can hardly forbear hurling things at him. I know my lady will strike him. If she do, he'll smile, and take't for a great favor.

TOBY Come bring us, bring us where he is.

Exeunt omnes.

---

curst: perversely cross

license of ink: i.e., with the freedom possible in writing 40

thou'st him: call him "thou" instead of the polite "you"

bed of Ware: a famous bed, over ten feet wide

45

cubiculo: little chamber

manikin: puppet

50

wainropes: wagon ropes 55

hale: haul

60

youngest wren: smallest of small birds

spleen: a laughing fit

gull: dupe

65

passages of grossness: statements of exaggerated misinformation

like . . . church: i.e., like an unfashionable village schoolmaster 70

map . . . Indies: (Emerie Molyneux's map, c. 1599, which gave fuller details of the East Indies and North America, with meridian lines, etc.) 75

DISCOVERING SHAKESPEARE

(49) Language [3.2.41]: Why does Sir Toby tell Sir Andrew to insult Cesario by using the "thou" pronoun form in a letter to him? What was the difference between using "thou" and "you" in such a context? Can you find any other situations in the play where pronoun use offers a clue about the relationship between characters?

(50) Textual Emendation [3.2.61]: When Sir Toby calls Maria "the youngest wren of mine" (3.2.61), he implies that as the last bird hatched in a large brood, she is very tiny. What other references to her diminutive size can you find in the play? How would these references influence a director casting Maria's part in a production of the play? Instead of the word "mine" (which appeared in the 1623 <u>First Folio</u> edition of the play), an editor named Theobald emended the word to "nine." Which reading would you prefer: "nine" or "mine"? Why?

❧ **3.3**° *Enter Sebastian and Antonio.*   **3.3:** A street in the Illyrian capital

SEBASTIAN
  I would not by my will have troubled you;
  But since you make your pleasure of your pains,
  I will no further chide you.

ANTONIO
  I could not stay behind you. My desire
  (More sharp than filèd steel) did spur me forth;   5
  And not all° love to see you (though so much   **not all:** not only, not entirely
  As might have drawn one to a longer voyage)
  But jealousy° what might befall your travel,   **jealousy:** solicitude
  Being skill-less in° these parts; which to a stranger,   **skill-less in:** without knowledge of
  Unguided and unfriended, often prove   10
  Rough and unhospitable. My willing love,
  The rather by these arguments of fear,
  Set forth in your pursuit.

SEBASTIAN   My kind Antonio,
  I can no other answer make but thanks,
  And thanks, and ever oft good turns   15
  Are shuffled off with such uncurrent° pay.   **uncurrent:** valueless
  But, were my worth° as is my conscience° firm,   **worth:** wealth; **conscience:** right inclination
  You should find better dealing. What's to do?
  Shall we go see the relics° of this town?   **relics:** monuments

ANTONIO
  Tomorrow, sir; best first go see your lodging.   20

SEBASTIAN
  I am not weary, and 'tis long to night.
  I pray you let us satisfy our eyes
  With the memorials and the things of fame
  That do renown this city.

ANTONIO   Would you'd pardon me.
  I do not without danger walk these streets.   25
  Once in a sea fight 'gainst the count his galleys
  I did some service; of such note indeed
  That, were I ta'en here, it would scarce be answered.°   **answered:** atoned for

SEBASTIAN
  Belike you slew great number of his people?

ANTONIO
  Th' offense is not of such a bloody nature,   30
  Albeit the quality of the time and quarrel
  Might well have given us bloody argument.
  It might have since been answered in repaying
  What we took from them, which for traffic's° sake   **traffic's:** trade's
  Most of our city did. Only myself stood out;   35
  For which, if I be lapsèd° in this place,   **lapsèd:** surprised, pounced upon
  I shall pay dear.

SEBASTIAN   Do not then walk too open.

DISCOVERING SHAKESPEARE

(51) Arc [3.3.30]: If *Twelfth Night* is a play about "metamorphosis" (that is, about developing and changing one's personality), how do the characters of Sebastian and Antonio transform during the play? Write down some preliminary ideas now; then come back to this question after you have read the entire <u>script</u>, and revise your opinion based upon the new information you have learned.

ANTONIO
  It doth not fit me. Hold, sir, here's my purse.
  In the south suburbs at the Elephant°   **the Elephant:** an inn
  Is best to lodge. I will bespeak our diet,   40
  Whiles you beguile the time and feed your knowledge
  With viewing of the town. There shall you have me.
SEBASTIAN
  Why I your purse?
ANTONIO
  Haply your eye shall light upon some toy°   **toy:** trifle
  You have desire to purchase, and your store°   **store:** store of money   45
  I think is not for idle markets,° sir.   **idle markets:** useless purchasings
SEBASTIAN
  I'll be your purse-bearer, and leave you for
  An hour.
ANTONIO To th' Elephant.
SEBASTIAN   I do remember.   *Exeunt.*

❧ **3.4**° *Enter Olivia and Maria.*   **3.4:** The garden of Olivia's house

OLIVIA *[Aside]*
  I have sent after him; he says he'll come.
  How shall I feast him? What bestow of° him?   **of:** on
  For youth is bought more oft than begged or borrowed.
  I speak too loud. Where's Malvolio? He is sad and civil,°   **sad and civil:** serious and sedate
  And suits well for a servant with my fortunes.   5
  Where is Malvolio?
MARIA He's coming, madam, but in very strange man-
  ner. He is sure possessed,° madam.   **possessed:** mad
OLIVIA Why, what's the matter? Does he rave?
MARIA No, madam, he does nothing but smile. Your   10
  ladyship were best to have some guard about you if he
  come, for sure the man is tainted in's wits.
OLIVIA
  Go call him hither. *[Exit Maria.]* I am as mad as he,
  If sad and merry madness equal be.
    Enter Malvolio [with Maria].
  How now, Malvolio?   15
MALVOLIO Sweet lady, ho, ho!
OLIVIA Smil'st thou? I sent for thee upon a sad occasion.
MALVOLIO Sad, lady? I could be sad. This does make
  some obstruction in the blood, this cross-gartering; but
  what of that? If it please the eye of one, it is with me as   20
  the very true sonnet° is, "Please one, and please all."   **sonnet:** any short poem
OLIVIA Why, how dost thou, man? What is the matter
  with thee?

DISCOVERING SHAKESPEARE

(52) Verse [3.4.1–6]: At the top of 3.4, the <u>meter</u> of Olivia's first speech is irregular, while line 6 is extremely short. What does this disruption in the play's regular <u>iambic pentameter</u> indicate about her emotional state in this scene?

MALVOLIO Not black in my mind, though yellow in my legs. It did come to his hands, and commands shall be executed. I think we do know the sweet Roman hand.°   25

Roman hand: Italian style of handwriting

OLIVIA Wilt thou go to bed, Malvolio?

MALVOLIO To bed? Ay, sweetheart, and I'll come to thee.

OLIVIA God comfort thee: Why dost thou smile so, and kiss thy hand so oft?   30

MARIA How do you, Malvolio?

MALVOLIO At your request? Yes, nightingales answer daws!°

daws: small crows

MARIA Why appear you with this ridiculous boldness before my lady?   35

MALVOLIO "Be not afraid of greatness." 'Twas well writ.

OLIVIA What mean'st thou by that, Malvolio?

MALVOLIO "Some are born great."

OLIVIA Ha?

MALVOLIO "Some achieve greatness."   40

OLIVIA What say'st thou?

MALVOLIO "And some have greatness thrust upon them."

OLIVIA Heaven restore thee!

MALVOLIO "Remember who commended thy yellow stockings."   45

OLIVIA Thy yellow stockings?

MALVOLIO "And wished to see thee cross-gartered."

OLIVIA Cross-gartered?

MALVOLIO "Go to, thou art made, if thou desir'st to be so."

OLIVIA Am I made?   50

MALVOLIO "If not, let me see thee a servant still."

OLIVIA Why, this is very midsummer madness.°

Enter Servant.

midsummer madness: i.e., the height of madness

SERVANT Madam, the young gentleman of the Count Orsino's is returned. I could hardly entreat him back. He attends your ladyship's pleasure.   55

OLIVIA I'll come to him. *[Exit Servant.]* Good Maria, let this fellow be looked to. Where's my cousin Toby? Let some of my people have a special care of him. I would not have him miscarry° for the half of my dowry.

miscarry: come to harm

Exit [Olivia; then Maria].

MALVOLIO O ho, do you come near me now? No worse man than Sir Toby to look to me? This concurs directly with the letter. She sends him on purpose, that I may appear stubborn° to him; for she incites me to that in the letter. "Cast thy humble slough," says she; "be opposite with a kinsman, surly with servants; let thy tongue tang with arguments of state; put thyself into the trick of singularity." And consequently sets down the manner how: as, a sad face, a reverend carriage, a slow tongue, in   60   65

stubborn: hard, stiff, rigid

DISCOVERING SHAKESPEARE

(53) Language [3.4.24–28]: Notice the pronouns in these lines when Malvolio shifts abruptly from "my" to "his" and "we" to "I." What do these pronoun references suggest about Malvolio's mental condition in this scene? Which different roles is he trying to assimilate?

(54) Staging [3.4.49]: What references can you identify that would help a director <u>block</u> this scene? Underline in your <u>script</u> any "action" words that might suggest movement on stage.

the habit of some sir of note, and so forth. I have limed° her; but it is Jove's doing, and Jove make me thankful. And when she went away now, "Let this fellow be looked to." "Fellow."° Not "Malvolio," nor after my degree,° but "fellow." Why, everything adheres together, that no dram° of a scruple, no scruple of a scruple,° no obstacle, no incredulous° or unsafe circumstance – what can be said? Nothing that can be can come between me and the full prospect of my hopes. Well, Jove, not I, is the doer of this, and he is to be thanked.

Enter [Sir] Toby, Fabian, and Maria.

TOBY   Which way is he, in the name of sanctity? If all the devils of hell be drawn in little,° and Legion° himself possessed him, yet I'll speak to him.

FABIAN   Here he is, here he is! How is't with you, sir? How is't with you, man?

MALVOLIO   Go off; I discard you. Let me enjoy my private. Go off.

MARIA   Lo, how hollow the fiend speaks within him! Did not I tell you? Sir Toby, my lady prays you to have a care of him.

MALVOLIO   Aha! does she so?

TOBY   Go to, go to; peace, peace; we must deal gently with him. Let me alone. How do you, Malvolio? How is't with you? What, man, defy the devil! Consider, he's an enemy to mankind.

MALVOLIO   Do you know what you say?

MARIA   La you, an you speak ill of the devil, how he takes it at heart. Pray God he be not bewitched.

FABIAN   Carry his water° to th' wise woman.°

MARIA   Marry, and it shall be done tomorrow morning if I live. My lady would not lose him for more than I'll say.

MALVOLIO   How now, mistress?

MARIA   O Lord!

TOBY   Prithee hold thy peace. This is not the way. Do you not see you move° him? Let me alone with him.

FABIAN   No way but gentleness; gently, gently. The fiend is rough and will not be roughly used.

TOBY   Why, how now, my bawcock?° How dost thou, chuck?°

MALVOLIO   Sir!

TOBY   Ay, biddy,° come with me. What, man, 'tis not for gravity° to play at cherry pit° with Satan. Hang him, foul collier!°

MARIA   Get him to say his prayers; good Sir Toby, get him to pray.

---

limed: caught

Fellow: companion
after my degree: according to my position
dram: (1) small bit, (2) one eighth fluid ounce;
scruple: (1) doubt, (2) one third of a dram
incredulous: incredible

drawn in little: brought together in a small space; **Legion:** troop of fiends

water: urine for medical analysis; **wise woman:** herb woman

move: rouse

bawcock: fine fellow (French *beau coq*)
chuck: chick

biddy: chicken
gravity: dignity; **cherry pit:** a child's game
collier: coal peddler (Satan)

(line numbers: 70, 75, 80, 85, 90, 95, 100, 105, 110)

DISCOVERING SHAKESPEARE

(55) Staging [3.4.80]: What gestures and <u>props</u> could the conspirators use in their "exorcism" of Malvolio? For example, what action could accompany Fabian's "Carry his water to the wise woman" (97) and Maria's "Get him to say his prayers" (113)?

(56) Language [3.4.107–110]: What do the terms "bawcock" (107), "chuck" (108), and "biddy" (110) mean? What clues do these words offer us about the manner in which the conspirators are treating Malvolio in this scene?

MALVOLIO   My prayers, minx?   115

MARIA   No, I warrant you, he will not hear of godliness.

MALVOLIO   Go hang yourselves all! You are idle° shallow   **idle:** empty, trifling
   things; I am not of your element. You shall know more
   hereafter.   *Exit.*

TOBY   Is't possible?   120

FABIAN   If this were played upon a stage now, I could
   condemn it as an improbable fiction.

TOBY   His very genius° hath taken the infection of the de-   **genius:** nature
   vice, man.

MARIA   Nay, pursue him now, lest the device take air and   125
   taint.°   **take air and taint:** be exposed and thus
                                                              contaminated

FABIAN   Why, we shall make him mad indeed.

MARIA   The house will be the quieter.

TOBY   Come, we'll have him in a dark room and bound.
   My niece is already in the belief that he's mad. We may
   carry it° thus, for our pleasure and his penance, till our   **carry it:** carry the trick on   130
   very pastime, tired out of breath, prompt us to have
   mercy on him; at which time we will bring the device
   to the bar and crown thee for a finder of madmen. But
   see, but see!   135
      Enter Sir Andrew.

FABIAN   More matter for a May morning.°   **matter . . . morning:** material for a May Day
                                                      comedy

ANDREW   Here's the challenge; read it. I warrant there's
   vinegar and pepper in't.

FABIAN   Is't so saucy?°   **saucy:** (1) spicy, (2) impudent, sharp

ANDREW   Ay, is't, I warrant him. Do but read.   140

TOBY   Give me. *[Reads.]* "Youth, whatsoever thou art,
   thou art but a scurvy fellow."

FABIAN   Good, and valiant.

TOBY   *[Reads.]* "Wonder not nor admire° not in thy mind   **admire:** be amazed
   why I do call thee so, for I will show thee no reason
   for't."   145

FABIAN   A good note that keeps you from the blow of the
   law.

TOBY   *[Reads.]* "Thou com'st to the Lady Olivia, and in
   my sight she uses thee kindly. But thou liest in thy
   throat; that is not the matter I challenge thee for."   150

FABIAN   Very brief, and to exceeding good sense – less.

TOBY   *[Reads.]* "I will waylay thee going home; where if
   it be thy chance to kill me" –

FABIAN   Good.   155

TOBY   *[Reads.]* "Thou kill'st me like a rogue and a villain."

FABIAN   Still you keep o' th' windy° side of the law. Good.   **windy:** windward, safe

TOBY   *[Reads.]* "Fare thee well, and God have mercy upon
   one of our souls. He may have mercy upon mine, but
   my hope is better, and so look to thyself. Thy friend, as   160
   thou usest him, and thy sworn enemy,
                                        Andrew Aguecheek."

DISCOVERING SHAKESPEARE

(57) History [3.4.136]: When Fabian refers to Sir Andrew's letter as "More matter for a May morning," he is alluding to the well-known May Day holiday. What customs were followed in Renaissance England during May Day celebrations?

If this letter move him not, his legs cannot. I'll give't him.

MARIA   You may have very fit occasion for't. He is now in some commerce with my lady and will by and by depart.

TOBY   Go, Sir Andrew. Scout me for him at the corner of the orchard like a bum-baily.° So soon as ever thou seest him, draw; and as thou draw'st, swear horrible; for it comes to pass oft that a terrible oath, with a swaggering accent sharply twanged off, gives manhood more approbation° than ever proof° itself would have earned him. Away!

ANDREW   Nay, let me alone for swearing.°   *Exit.*

TOBY   Now will not I deliver his letter; for the behavior of the young gentleman gives him out to be of good capacity and breeding; his employment between his lord and my niece confirms no less. Therefore this letter, being so excellently ignorant, will breed no terror in the youth. He will find it comes from a clodpoll.° But, sir, I will deliver his challenge by word of mouth, set upon Aguecheek a notable report of valor, and drive the gentleman (as I know his youth will aptly receive it) into a most hideous opinion of his rage, skill, fury, and impetuosity. This will so fright them both that they will kill one another by the look, like cockatrices.°

Enter Olivia and Viola.

FABIAN   Here he comes with your niece. Give them way till he take leave, and presently after him.

TOBY   I will meditate the while upon some horrid message for a challenge.

[Exeunt Sir Toby, Fabian, and Maria.]

OLIVIA
I have said too much unto a heart of stone
And laid mine honor too unchary on't.°
There's something in me that reproves my fault;
But such a headstrong potent fault it is
That it but mocks reproof.

VIOLA
With the same havior° that your passion bears
Goes on my master's griefs.

OLIVIA
Here, wear this jewel° for me; 'tis my picture.
Refuse it not; it hath no tongue to vex you.
And I beseech you come again tomorrow.
What shall you ask of me that I'll deny,
That, honor saved, may upon asking give?

VIOLA
Nothing but this: your true love for my master.

---

bum-baily: an agent employed in making arrests

manhood more approbation: more reputation for courage; **proof:** testing

let . . . swearing: leave swearing to me

clodpoll: fool

cockatrices: basilisks, reptiles able to kill with a glance

unchary on't: carelessly on it (the *heart of stone*)

havior: behavior

jewel: any ornament or trinket; here perhaps "locket"

165

170

175

180

185

190

195

200

DISCOVERING SHAKESPEARE

(58) Characterization [3.4.165–167]: Why is Maria happy to report where Sir Toby and Sir Andrew can find Cesario? What has Cesario done to irritate Maria?

(59) Teaser [3.4.199]: When was the last time Olivia used the word "picture"? How is her situation different at this point in the play?

OLIVIA
  How with mine honor may I give him that   205
  Which I have given to you?
VIOLA   I will acquit you.
OLIVIA
  Well, come again tomorrow. Fare thee well.
  A fiend like thee° might bear my soul to hell.   *[Exit.]*   **like thee:** in your likeness
    Enter [Sir] Toby and Fabian.
TOBY   Gentleman, God save thee.
VIOLA   And you, sir.   210
TOBY   That defense thou hast, betake thee to't. Of what
  nature the wrongs are thou hast done him, I know not,
  but thy intercepter, full of despite,° bloody as the   **despite:** defiance
  hunter, attends thee at the orchard end. Dismount thy
  tuck,° be yare° in thy preparation, for thy assailant is   **Dismount thy tuck:** take out your rapier;   215
  quick, skillful, and deadly.   **yare:** quick
VIOLA   You mistake, sir. I am sure no man hath any quar-
  rel to me. My remembrance is very free and clear from
  any image of offense done to any man.
TOBY   You'll find it otherwise, I assure you. Therefore, if   220
  you hold your life at any price, betake you to your
  guard; for your opposite hath in him what youth,
  strength, skill, and wrath can furnish man withal.
VIOLA   I pray you, sir, what is he?
TOBY   He is knight, dubbed° with unhatched° rapier and   **dubbed:** knighted; **unhatched:** unhacked   225
  on carpet consideration,° but he is a devil in private   **on carpet consideration:** through court favor
  brawl. Souls and bodies hath he divorced three; and his
  incensement at this moment is so implacable that satisfaction can be none but by pangs of death and sepul-
  cher. "Hob, nob"° is his word; "give't or take't."   **Hob, nob:** have or have not   230
VIOLA   I will return again into the house and desire some
  conduct° of the lady. I am no fighter. I have heard of   **conduct:** protective escort
  some kind of men that put quarrels purposely on oth-
  ers to taste° their valor. Belike this is a man of that quirk.°   **taste:** test; **quirk:** peculiarity
TOBY   Sir, no. His indignation derives itself out of a very   235
  competent° injury; therefore get you on and give him   **competent:** sufficient
  his desire. Back you shall not to the house, unless you
  undertake that with me which with as much safety you
  might answer him. Therefore on, or strip your sword
  stark naked; for meddle° you must, that's certain, or for-   **meddle:** engage (in the fight)   240
  swear to wear iron° about you.   **forswear . . . iron:** repudiate on oath (your
VIOLA   This is as uncivil as strange. I beseech you do me   right) to wear a sword
  this courteous office, as to know of the knight what my
  offense to him is. It is something of my negligence,
  nothing of my purpose.   245
TOBY   I will do so. Signor Fabian, stay you by this gentle-
  man till my return.   *Exit.*

DISCOVERING SHAKESPEARE

(60) History [3.4.225–226]: When Sir Toby tells Viola that Sir Andrew has been "dubbed with unhatched rapier and on carpet consideration," is he bragging about Andrew's reputation as a swordsman or detracting from it? Why does he describe Andrew in this fashion?

(61) Language [3.4.240–241]: What pun is Shakespeare making in Sir Toby's "for meddle you must, that's certain, or forswear to wear iron about you"? Find another example of this pun later in the same scene.

VIOLA   Pray you, sir, do you know of this matter?

FABIAN   I know the knight is incensed against you, even to a mortal arbitrament;° but nothing of the circumstance more.

mortal arbitrament: deadly settlement   250

VIOLA   I beseech you, what manner of man is he?

FABIAN   Nothing of that wonderful promise, to read him by his form, as you are like to find him in the proof of his valor. He is indeed, sir, the most skillful, bloody, and fatal opposite that you could possibly have found in any part of Illyria. Will you walk towards him? I will make your peace with him if I can.

255

VIOLA   I shall be much bound to you for't. I am one that had rather go with sir priest than sir knight. I care not who knows so much of my mettle.   *Exeunt.*
    Enter [Sir] Toby and [Sir] Andrew.

260

TOBY   Why, man, he's a very devil; I have not seen such a firago.° I had a pass° with him, rapier, scabbard, and all, and he gives me the stuck-in° with such a mortal motion° that it is inevitable; and on the answer° he pays you as surely as your feet hits the ground they step on. They say he has been fencer to the Sophy.

firago: virago; **pass:** bout
stuck-in: thrust, lunge; **motion:** action
answer: return   265

ANDREW   Pox° on't, I'll not meddle with him.

Pox: syphilis

TOBY   Ay, but he will not now be pacified. Fabian can scarce hold him yonder.

270

ANDREW   Plague on't, an I thought he had been valiant, and so cunning in fence, I'd have seen him damned ere I'd have challenged him. Let him let the matter slip, and I'll give him my horse, gray Capilet.

TOBY   I'll make the motion.° Stand here; make a good show on't. This shall end without the perdition of souls.° *[Aside]* Marry, I'll ride your horse as well as I ride you.
    Enter Fabian and Viola.
I have his horse to take up° the quarrel. I have persuaded him the youth's a devil.

motion: offer   275
the perdition of souls: i.e., killing

take up: settle

FABIAN   He is as horribly conceited of him,° and pants and looks pale, as if a bear were at his heels.

He . . . him: he (Cesario) has just as frightening   280
a conception of him (Sir Andrew)

TOBY   There's no remedy, sir; he will fight with you for's oath sake. Marry, he hath better bethought him of his quarrel, and he finds that now scarce to be worth talking of. Therefore draw for the supportance of his vow. He protests he will not hurt you.

285

VIOLA   *[Aside]* Pray God defend me! A little thing would make me tell them how much I lack of a man.

FABIAN   Give ground if you see him furious.

TOBY   Come, Sir Andrew, there's no remedy. The gentleman will for his honor's sake have one bout with you; he cannot by the duello° avoid it; but he has promised me, as he is a gentleman and a soldier, he will not hurt you. Come on, to't.

290

duello: dueling code

DISCOVERING SHAKESPEARE

(62) Characterization [3.4.277]: What does Sir Toby mean when he says in an <u>aside</u> about Sir Andrew that he will "ride your horse as well as I ride you"?

ANDREW   Pray God he keep his oath!   295
 [Draws.]
 Enter Antonio.

VIOLA
 I do assure you 'tis against my will.
 [Draws.]

ANTONIO
 Put up your sword. If this young gentleman
 Have done offense, I take the fault on me;
 If you offend him, I for him defy you.

TOBY   You, sir? Why, what are you?   300

ANTONIO   *[Draws.]*
 One, sir, that for his love dares yet do more
 Than you have heard him brag to you he will.

TOBY   Nay, if you be an undertaker,° I am for you.   **undertaker:** one who takes up a challenge
 [Draws.]
 Enter Officers.

FABIAN   O good Sir Toby, hold. Here come the officers.

TOBY   *[To Antonio]* I'll be with you anon.   305

VIOLA   *[To Sir Andrew]* Pray, sir, put your sword up, if
 you please.

ANDREW   Marry, will I, sir; and for that° I promised you,   **that:** that which (i.e., the horse)
 I'll be as good as my word. He will bear you easily, and
 reins well.   310

FIRST OFFICER   This is the man; do thy office.

SECOND OFFICER
 Antonio, I arrest thee at the suit
 Of Count Orsino.

ANTONIO   You do mistake me, sir.

FIRST OFFICER
 No, sir, no jot. I know your favor° well,   **favor:** face
 Though now you have no sea cap on your head.   315
 Take him away. He knows I know him well.

ANTONIO
 I must obey. *[To Viola]* This comes with seeking you.
 But there's no remedy; I shall answer it.
 What will you do, now my necessity
 Makes me to ask you for my purse? It grieves me   320
 Much more for what I cannot do for you
 Than what befalls myself. You stand amazed,
 But be of comfort.

SECOND OFFICER   Come, sir, away.

ANTONIO
 I must entreat of you some of that money.   325

VIOLA
 What money, sir?
 For the fair kindness you have showed me here,
 And part being prompted by your present trouble,
 Out of my lean and low ability

DISCOVERING SHAKESPEARE

(63) Characterization [3.4.320–325]: How does Viola react during Antonio's request for money? What behavioral clues could the actress playing Viola find in his speech that would help govern her on-stage response? How does Antonio's demeanor change in his next six speeches?

I'll lend you something. My having is not much.
I'll make division of my present° with you.   **my present:** what I have now
Hold, there's half my coffer.°   **coffer:** money
ANTONIO   Will you deny me now?
  Is't possible that my deserts to you
  Can lack persuasion? Do not tempt my misery,
  Lest that it make me so unsound a man
  As to upbraid you with those kindnesses
  That I have done for you.
VIOLA   I know of none,
  Nor know I you by voice or any feature.
  I hate ingratitude more in a man
  Than lying, vainness, babbling, drunkenness,
  Or any taint of vice whose strong corruption
  Inhabits our frail blood.
ANTONIO   O heavens themselves!
SECOND OFFICER
  Come, sir, I pray you go.
ANTONIO
  Let me speak a little. This youth that you see here
  I snatched one half out of the jaws of death;
  Relieved him with such sanctity of love,
  And to his image, which methought did promise
  Most venerable° worth, did I devotion.   **venerable:** worthy of veneration
FIRST OFFICER
  What's that to us? The time goes by. Away!
ANTONIO
  But, O, how vile an idol proves this god!
  Thou hast, Sebastian, done good feature shame.
  In nature there's no blemish but the mind;
  None can be called deformed but the unkind.°   **unkind:** unnatural
  Virtue is beauty; but the beauteous° evil   **beauteous:** fair-seeming
  Are empty trunks,° o'erflourished° by the devil.   **trunks:** chests; **o'erflourished:** ornamented
FIRST OFFICER
  The man grows mad; away with him! Come, come, sir.
ANTONIO   Lead me on.   *Exit [with Officers].*
VIOLA
  Methinks his words do from such passion fly
  That he believes himself; so do not I.
  Prove true, imagination, O, prove true,
  That I, dear brother, be now ta'en for you!
TOBY   Come hither, knight; come hither, Fabian. We'll
  whisper o'er a couplet or two of most sage saws.°   **sage saws:** wise sayings
VIOLA
  He named Sebastian. I my brother know
  Yet living in my glass.° Even such and so   **Yet . . . glass:** i.e., whenever I look in the mirror
  In favor was my brother, and he went
  Still in this fashion, color, ornament,

330
335
340
345
350
355
360
365

DISCOVERING SHAKESPEARE

(64) Themes [3.4.354–355]: In these two lines, Antonio voices a common Shakespearean <u>theme</u>: the difference between appearance and reality. Look up the word "flourished" in the *Oxford English Dictionary,* and catalog all the different uses of the word available in the year 1600. Which of these do you think is Antonio's principal intended meaning? How do the words "o'erflourished" and "trunks" work together?

For him I imitate. O, if it prove,
Tempests are kind, and salt waves fresh in love!　　*[Exit.]*

TOBY　A very dishonest° paltry boy, and more a coward than a hare. His dishonesty appears in leaving his friend here in necessity and denying him; and for his cowardship, ask Fabian.

FABIAN　A coward, a most devout coward; religious° in it.

ANDREW　'Slid, I'll after him again and beat him.

TOBY　Do; cuff him soundly, but never draw thy sword.

ANDREW　An I do not –　　　　　　　　　　*[Exit.]*

FABIAN　Come, let's see the event.°

TOBY　I dare lay any money 'twill be nothing yet.°
　　　　　　　　　　　　　　　　　　Exeunt.

> **dishonest:** dishonorable　370
>
> **religious:** confirmed
> 　　　　　　375
>
> **event:** result
> **yet:** nevertheless

❧ **4.1**° *Enter Sebastian and Feste.*

FESTE　Will you make me believe that I am not sent for you?

SEBASTIAN　Go to, go to, thou art a foolish fellow. Let me be clear of thee.

FESTE　Well held out,° i' faith! No, I do not know you; nor I am not sent to you by my lady, to bid you come speak with her; nor your name is not Master Cesario; nor this is not my nose neither. Nothing that is so is so.

SEBASTIAN　I prithee vent thy folly somewhere else. Thou know'st not me.

FESTE　Vent my folly! He has heard that word of some great man, and now applies it to a fool. Vent my folly! I am afraid this great lubber,° the world, will prove a cockney.° I prithee now, ungird thy strangeness,° and tell me what I shall vent to my lady. Shall I vent to her that thou art coming?

SEBASTIAN　I prithee, foolish Greek,° depart from me. There's money for thee. If you tarry longer, I shall give worse payment.

FESTE　By my troth, thou hast an open hand. These wise men that give fools money get themselves a good report – after fourteen years' purchase.°
　　Enter [Sir] Andrew, [Sir] Toby, and Fabian.

ANDREW　Now, sir, have I met you again? There's for you!
　　[Strikes Sebastian.]

SEBASTIAN　Why, there's for thee, and there, and there!
　　[Strikes Sir Andrew.]
　　Are all the people mad?

TOBY　Hold, sir, or I'll throw your dagger o'er the house.
　　[Seizes Sebastian.]

FESTE　This will I tell my lady straight. I would not be in some of your coats for twopence.　　*Exit.*

> **4.1:** Before Olivia's house
>
> **held out:** kept up　5
>
> 　　　　　　10
>
> **lubber:** lout
> **cockney:** affected person; **ungird thy strangeness:** abandon your strange manner　15
>
> **Greek:** (proverbially "merry" nation)
>
> 　　　　　　20
>
> **after . . . purchase:** i.e., at a high price
>
> 　　　　　　25

DISCOVERING SHAKESPEARE

(65) Language [4.1.9–12]: At the outset of this scene, Feste ridicules Sebastian's use of the word "vent" as a form of linguistic affectation. Find three other words that the Clown objects to in this play. What words do you object to in your life?

TOBY   Come on, sir; hold.   30

ANDREW   Nay, let him alone. I'll go another way to work
with him. I'll have an action of battery° against him, if
there be any law in Illyria. Though I struck him first,
yet it's no matter for that.

action of battery: suit at law for beating (me)

SEBASTIAN   Let go thy hand.   35

TOBY   Come, sir, I will not let you go. Come, my young
soldier, put up° your iron. You are well fleshed.° Come on.

put up: put away; **well fleshed:** made eager by
a taste of blood

SEBASTIAN
I will be free from thee.
    [Frees himself.]   What wouldst thou now?
If thou dar'st tempt me further, draw thy sword.
    [Draws.]

TOBY   What, what? Nay then, I must have an ounce or   40
two of this malapert° blood from you.
    [Draws.]
    Enter Olivia.

malapert: impudent

OLIVIA
Hold, Toby! On thy life I charge thee hold!

TOBY   Madam.

OLIVIA
Will it be ever thus? Ungracious wretch,
Fit for the mountains and the barbarous caves,   45
Where manners ne'er were preached! Out of my sight!
Be not offended, dear Cesario.
Rudesby,° be gone.

Rudesby: unmannerly fellow

    [Exeunt Sir Toby, Sir Andrew, and Fabian.]
                    I prithee, gentle friend,
Let thy fair wisdom, not thy passion, sway
In this uncivil° and unjust extent°   50
Against thy peace. Go with me to my house,
And hear thou there how many fruitless pranks
This ruffian hath botched up,° that thou thereby
Mayst smile at this. Thou shalt not choose but go.
Do not deny. Beshrew° his soul for me,   55
He started° one poor heart° of mine, in thee.

uncivil: uncivilized; **extent:** intrusion

botched up: contrived

Beshrew: curse
started: startled; **heart:** (with a pun on "hart")

SEBASTIAN
What relish° is in this? How runs the stream?
Or I am mad, or else this is a dream.
Let fancy still my sense in Lethe° steep;
If it be thus to dream, still let me sleep!   60

relish: taste

Lethe: the river of forgetfulness in the
underworld

OLIVIA
Nay, come, I prithee. Would thou'dst be ruled by me!

SEBASTIAN
Madam, I will.

OLIVIA   O, say so, and so be.   *Exeunt.*

DISCOVERING SHAKESPEARE

(66) History [4.1.32]: What was an "action of battery," and why is Sir Andrew's mention of it so comical?

(67) Metaphor [4.1.59–60]: Why does Sebastian want his love for Olivia (his "fancy") to "steep" his sense in Lethe? Paraphrase this metaphor in modern English. Is your paraphrase longer or shorter than Shakespeare's image? Why do you think this is so?

❧ **4.2**° *Enter Maria and Feste.*

MARIA   Nay, I prithee put on this gown and this beard; make him believe thou art Sir° Topas° the curate. Do it quickly; I'll call Sir Toby the whilst.   *[Exit.]*

Sir: (common title of address for the clergy); **Topas:** comic knight in Chaucer (the topaz stone was thought to cure insanity)
dissemble: disguise   5

FESTE   Well, I'll put it on, and I will dissemble° myself in't, and I would I were the first that ever dissembled in such a gown. I am not tall enough to become the function° well, nor lean enough to be thought a good student; but to be said an honest man and a good housekeeper° goes as fairly as to say a careful man and a great scholar. The competitors° enter.

function: function of a cleric

good housekeeper: householder, neighbor
competitors: associates   10

   Enter [Sir] Toby [and Maria].

TOBY   Jove bless thee, Master Parson.

FESTE   *Bonos dies,*° Sir Toby; for, as the old hermit of Prague,° that never saw pen and ink, very wittily said to a niece of King Gorboduc,° "That that is is"; so, I, being Master Parson, am Master Parson; for what is "that" but that, and "is" but is?

Bonos dies: good day
the old hermit of Prague: (probably the clown's invention)
King Gorboduc: a legendary British king who   15
appeared in an early English tragedy

TOBY   To him, Sir Topas.

FESTE   What ho, I say. Peace in this prison!

TOBY   The knave counterfeits well; a good knave.°

knave: boy, fellow

   Malvolio within.

MALVOLIO   Who calls there?

20

FESTE   Sir Topas the curate, who comes to visit Malvolio the lunatic.

MALVOLIO   Sir Topas, Sir Topas, good Sir Topas, go to my lady.

FESTE   Out, hyperbolical° fiend! How vexest thou this man! Talkest thou nothing but of ladies?

hyperbolical: enormous   25

TOBY   Well said, Master Parson.

MALVOLIO   Sir Topas, never was man thus wronged. Good Sir Topas, do not think I am mad. They have laid me here in hideous darkness.

30

FESTE   Fie, thou dishonest° Satan! I call thee by the most modest terms, for I am one of those gentle ones that will use the devil himself with courtesy. Say'st thou that house° is dark?

dishonest: dishonorable

house: i.e., room

MALVOLIO   As hell, Sir Topas.

35

FESTE   Why, it hath bay windows transparent as barricadoes,° and the clerestories° toward the south north are as lustrous as ebony; and yet complainest thou of obstruction?

barricadoes: barricades
clerestories: upper windows

MALVOLIO   I am not mad, Sir Topas. I say to you this house is dark.

40

FESTE   Madman, thou errest. I say there is no darkness but ignorance, in which thou art more puzzled than the Egyptians in their fog.°

fog: (Moses brought a three-day fog on the Egyptians)
45

MALVOLIO   I say this house is as dark as ignorance, though ignorance were as dark as hell; and I say there

---

DISCOVERING SHAKESPEARE

(68) Staging [4.2.1–19]: Do you think Feste should put on a different <u>costume</u> when he plays the role of Sir Topas? Why or why not? How would Malvolio be imprisoned on stage, and how would his predicament affect Feste's use of a clerical <u>costume</u> in this scene?

was never man thus abused. I am no more mad than you are. Make the trial of it in any constant question.°

FESTE What is the opinion of Pythagoras° concerning wildfowl?

MALVOLIO That the soul of our grandam might happily° inhabit a bird.

FESTE What think'st thou of his opinion?

MALVOLIO I think nobly of the soul and no way approve his opinion.

FESTE Fare thee well. Remain thou still in darkness. Thou shalt hold th' opinion of Pythagoras ere I will allow of° thy wits, and fear to kill a woodcock, lest thou dispossess the soul of thy grandam. Fare thee well.

MALVOLIO Sir Topas, Sir Topas!

TOBY My most exquisite Sir Topas!

FESTE Nay, I am for all waters.°

MARIA Thou mightest have done this without thy beard and gown. He sees thee not.

TOBY To him in thine own voice, and bring me word how thou find'st him. *[To Maria]* I would we were well rid of this knavery. If he may be conveniently delivered, I would he were; for I am now so far in offense with my niece that I cannot pursue with any safety this sport to the upshot.° *[To the Clown]* Come by and by to my chamber.   *Exit [with Maria].*

FESTE *[Sings.]*
                  "Hey, Robin, jolly Robin,
                        Tell me how thy lady does."°

MALVOLIO Fool.

FESTE "My lady is unkind, perdie!"°

MALVOLIO Fool.

FESTE "Alas, why is she so?"

MALVOLIO Fool, I say.

FESTE "She loves another." Who calls, ha?

MALVOLIO Good fool, as ever thou wilt deserve well at my hand, help me to a candle, and pen, ink, and paper. As I am a gentleman, I will live to be thankful to thee for't.

FESTE Master Malvolio?

MALVOLIO Ay, good fool.

FESTE Alas, sir, how fell you besides your five wits?°

MALVOLIO Fool, there was never man so notoriously abused. I am as well in my wits, fool, as thou art.

FESTE But as well? Then you are mad indeed, if you be no better in your wits than a fool.

MALVOLIO They have here propertied me;° keep me in darkness, send ministers to me, asses, and do all they can to face me° out of my wits.

constant question: consistent discussion
Pythagoras: (who originated the doctrine of transmigration of souls)   50
happily: haply, by chance

55

allow of: acknowledge

60

for all waters: i.e., good for any trade

65

upshot: outcome   70

Hey, Robin . . . : (from an old song, sometimes attributed to Sir Thomas Wyatt)
perdie: certainly   75

80

85

besides your five wits: out of your mind

90

propertied me: made me a property, a mere thing
face me: brazen me

DISCOVERING SHAKESPEARE

(69) Teaser [4.2.47]: Where else in the play does Malvolio use the word "abused"? Who else uses the word to describe his mistreatment? Do you think Malvolio is "abused," or is he fairly punished for his arrogant behavior?

(70) Characterization [4.2.70–71]: When Sir Toby invites Maria to "Come by and by to my chamber," some scholars infer that the two are already married. What other indications in the script imply that Toby and Maria are in love?

FESTE   Advise you° what you say. The minister is here. – Malvolio, Malvolio, thy wits the heavens restore. Endeavor thyself to sleep and leave thy vain bibble-babble.

Advise you: be careful   95

MALVOLIO   Sir Topas.

FESTE   Maintain no words with him, good fellow. – Who, I, sir? Not I, sir. God b' wi' you, good Sir Topas. – Marry, amen. – I will, sir, I will.

100

MALVOLIO   Fool, fool, fool, I say!

FESTE   Alas, sir, be patient. What say you, sir? I am shent° for speaking to you.

shent: reproved

MALVOLIO   Good fool, help me to some light and some paper. I tell thee, I am as well in my wits as any man in Illyria.

105

FESTE   Welladay° that you were, sir.

Welladay: woe, alas

MALVOLIO   By this hand, I am. Good fool, some ink, paper, and light; and convey what I will set down to my lady. It shall advantage thee more than ever the bearing of letter did.

110

FESTE   I will help you to't. But tell me true, are you not mad indeed? or do you but counterfeit?

MALVOLIO   Believe me, I am not. I tell thee true.

FESTE   Nay, I'll ne'er believe a madman till I see his brains. I will fetch you light and paper and ink.

115

MALVOLIO   Fool, I'll requite it in the highest degree. I prithee be gone.

FESTE   *[Sings.]*
       I am gone, sir,
       And anon, sir,
   I'll be with you again,
       In a trice,
       Like to the old Vice,°
   Your need to sustain.
   Who with dagger of lath,°
   In his rage and his wrath,
       Cries "Ah ha" to the devil.
   Like a mad lad,
   "Pare thy nails, dad."°
       Adieu, goodman devil.   *Exit.*

120

Vice: comic character in old morality plays

lath: wood (i.e., stage dagger)   125

Pare . . . dad: (Vice defies his "father," Satan, in those terms)   130

❧ **4.3**° *Enter Sebastian.*

4.3: The house of Olivia

SEBASTIAN
   This is the air; that is the glorious sun;
   This pearl she gave me, I do feel't and see't;

DISCOVERING SHAKESPEARE

(71) Staging [4.2.96]: Write a brief catalog of all the supposed "remedies" used by Sir Toby and the other conspirators to cure Malvolio of his demonic possession.

(72) History [4.2.123]: Feste compares himself to the medieval "Vice" in his song at the end of the scene. Who or what was a Vice character, and why does Feste adopt this persona in his conversation with Malvolio?

(73) Language [4.3.1–21]: Sebastian's mention of "madness" in lines 4, 10, 15, and 16 of this speech at the top of 4.3 is in contrast to Malvolio's alleged madness in the previous scene. How many characters in this play are "mad"? And what is the nature of each character's lunacy?

And though 'tis wonder that enwraps me thus,
Yet 'tis not madness. Where's Antonio then?
I could not find him at the Elephant;   5
Yet there he was,° and there I found this credit,°   **was:** had been; **credit:** belief
That he did range the town to seek me out.
His counsel now might do me golden service;
For though my soul disputes well with my sense
That this may be some error, but no madness,   10
Yet doth this accident and flood of fortune
So far exceed all instance,° all discourse,°   **instance:** example; **discourse:** logic
That I am ready to distrust mine eyes
And wrangle° with my reason that persuades me   **wrangle:** dispute
To any other trust but that I am mad,   15
Or else the lady's mad. Yet, if 'twere so,
She could not sway° her house, command her followers,   **sway:** rule
Take and give back affairs and their dispatch°   **dispatch:** management
With such a smooth, discreet, and stable bearing
As I perceive she does. There's something in't   20
That is deceivable.° But here the lady comes.   **deceivable:** deceptive
    Enter Olivia and Priest.

OLIVIA
Blame not this haste of mine. If you mean well,
Now go with me and with this holy man
Into the chantry by.° There, before him,   **chantry by:** chapel nearby
And underneath that consecrated roof,   25
Plight me the full assurance of your faith,
That my most jealous° and too doubtful soul   **jealous:** anxious
May live at peace. He shall conceal it
Whiles° you are willing it shall come to note,   **Whiles:** until
What time we will our celebration keep   30
According to my birth. What do you say?

SEBASTIAN
I'll follow this good man and go with you
And having sworn truth, ever will be true.

OLIVIA
Then lead the way, good father, and heavens so shine
That they may fairly note this act of mine.   *Exeunt.*   35

  5.1° *Enter Feste and Fabian.*   **5.1:** Before Olivia's house

FABIAN   Now as thou lov'st me, let me see his letter.
FESTE   Good Master Fabian, grant me another request.
FABIAN   Anything.
FESTE   Do not desire to see this letter.
FABIAN   This is to give a dog, and in recompense desire   5
   my dog again.
    Enter Duke, Viola, Curio, and Lords.
DUKE   Belong you° to the Lady Olivia, friends?   **Belong you:** i.e., are you in the service of
FESTE   Ay, sir, we are some of her trappings.

DISCOVERING SHAKESPEARE

(74) Staging [4.3.22]: After Olivia dashes in with the priest in hand, she doesn't give anyone else in the scene a chance to speak till the end. What could Sebastian and the priest be doing while she speaks in lines 22–31?

DUKE   I know thee well. How dost thou, my good fellow?

10

FESTE   Truly, sir, the better for my foes, and the worse
for my friends.

DUKE   Just the contrary: the better for thy friends.

FESTE   No, sir, the worse.

DUKE   How can that be?

15

FESTE   Marry, sir, they praise me and make an ass of
me. Now my foes tell me plainly I am an ass; so that by
my foes, sir, I profit in the knowledge of myself, and by
my friends I am abused;° so that, conclusions to be as
kisses,° if your four negatives make your two affirma-
tives, why then, the worse for my friends, and the better for my foes.

abused: deceived

conclusions . . . kisses: with conclusions as
with kisses (i.e., the same rule applies)

20

DUKE   Why, this is excellent.

FESTE   By my troth, sir, no, though it please you to be
one of my friends.

25

DUKE   Thou shalt not be the worse for me. There's gold.

FESTE   But that it would be double-dealing,° sir, I
would you could make it another.

double-dealing: (1) double giving, (2) deceit

DUKE   O, you give me ill counsel.

FESTE   Put your grace° in your pocket, sir, for this once,
and let your flesh and blood obey it.

your grace: (1) title of address, (2) your
generosity

30

DUKE   Well, I will be so much a sinner to be a double-
dealer. There's another.

FESTE   *Primo, secundo, tertio* is a good play;° and the old
saying is "The third pays for all." The triplex,° sir, is a
good tripping measure; or the bells of Saint Bennet,° sir,
may put you in mind – one, two, three.

play: (probably a children's game)
triplex: triple time in music
Saint Bennet: Saint Benedict's church

35

DUKE   You can fool no more money out of me at this
throw.° If you will let your lady know I am here to speak
with her, and bring her along with you, it may awake
my bounty further.

throw: throw of the dice

40

FESTE   Marry, sir, lullaby to your bounty. Till I come
again, I go, sir; but I would not have you to think that
my desire of having is the sin of covetousness. But, as
you say, sir, let your bounty take a nap; I will awake it
anon.   *Exit.*

45

Enter Antonio and Officers.

VIOLA
Here comes the man, sir, that did rescue me.

DUKE
That face of his I do remember well;
Yet when I saw it last, it was besmeared
As black as Vulcan° in the smoke of war.
A baubling° vessel was he captain of,
For shallow draft and bulk unprizable,°
With which such scathful° grapple did he make
With the most noble bottom° of our fleet

Vulcan: Roman blacksmith god of fire and
patron of metalworkers
baubling: trifling
unprizable: unworthy of being taken as a prize
scathful: harmful
bottom: ship

50

DISCOVERING SHAKESPEARE

(75) Language [5.1.11–12]: Explain what Feste means when he says he is "the better for my foes, and the worse for my
friends" (11–12).

That very envy° and the tongue of loss°   **very envy:** even malice; **loss:** the losers   55
Cried fame and honor on him. What's the matter?

FIRST OFFICER
  Orsino, this is that Antonio
  That took the *Phoenix* and her fraught° from Candy;°   **fraught:** cargo; **Candy:** Candia (Crete)
  And this is he that did the *Tiger* board
  When your young nephew Titus lost his leg.   60
  Here in the streets, desperate° of shame and state,   **desperate:** reckless
  In private brabble° did we apprehend him.   **brabble:** brawl

VIOLA
  He did me kindness, sir; drew on my side;
  But in conclusion put strange speech upon me.
  I know not what 'twas but distraction.°   **distraction:** madness   65

DUKE
  Notable pirate, thou saltwater thief,
  What foolish boldness brought thee to their mercies
  Whom thou in terms so bloody and so dear°   **dear:** costly
  Hast made thine enemies?

ANTONIO   Orsino, noble sir,
  Be pleased that I shake off these names you give me.   70
  Antonio never yet was thief or pirate,
  Though I confess, on base and ground° enough,   **base and ground:** solid grounds
  Orsino's enemy. A witchcraft drew me hither.
  That most ingrateful boy there by your side
  From the rude sea's enraged and foamy mouth   75
  Did I redeem. A wrack past hope he was.
  His life I gave him, and did thereto add
  My love without retention or restraint,
  All his in dedication. For his sake
  Did I expose myself (pure° for his love)   **pure:** purely   80
  Into the danger of this adverse town;
  Drew to defend him when he was beset;
  Where being apprehended, his false cunning
  (Not meaning to partake with me in danger)
  Taught him to face me out of his acquaintance,°   **face . . . acquaintance:** pretend not to know   85
  And grew a twenty years removèd° thing   me
  While one would wink; denied me mine own purse,   **removèd:** estranged
  Which I had recommended° to his use   **recommended:** entrusted
  Not half an hour before.

VIOLA   How can this be?

DUKE
  When came he to this town?   90

ANTONIO
  Today, my lord; and for three months before,
  No int'rim, not a minute's vacancy,
  Both day and night did we keep company.
  Enter Olivia and Attendants.

DISCOVERING SHAKESPEARE

(76) Teaser [5.1.58]: The First Officer here accuses Antonio of having taken "the Phoenix [a ship] and her fraught [freight] from Candy [Crete]" (58). How far was Crete from Illyria? Find a map of the ancient world and plot the distance between the two countries.

(77) Chronology of the Play [5.1.91]: Antonio's claim that he has been with Sebastian for three straight months means that Viola has been in Orsino's service for the same length of time (line 96). Does the action of the play seem longer or shorter than three months to you? Why? What other references to the passage of time can you find in the script?

DUKE

    Here comes the countess; now heaven walks on earth.

    But for thee, fellow: fellow, thy words are madness.   95

    Three months this youth hath tended upon me;

    But more of that anon. Take him aside.

OLIVIA

    What would my lord, but that° he may not have,   **but that:** except what

    Wherein Olivia may seem serviceable?

    Cesario, you do not keep promise with me.   100

VIOLA

    Madam?

DUKE

    Gracious Olivia –

OLIVIA

    What do you say, Cesario? – Good my lord –

VIOLA

    My lord would speak; my duty hushes me.

OLIVIA

    If it be aught to the old tune, my lord,   105

    It is as fat° and fulsome° to mine ear   **fat:** superfluous; **fulsome:** offensive

    As howling after music.

DUKE   Still so cruel?

OLIVIA

    Still so constant, lord.

DUKE

    What, to perverseness? You uncivil lady,

    To whose ingrate and unauspicious altars   110

    My soul the faithfull'st off'rings have breathed out

    That e'er devotion tendered. What shall I do?

OLIVIA

    Even what it please my lord, that shall become him.

DUKE

    Why should I not, had I the heart to do it,

    Like to th' Egyptian thief° at point of death   **th' Egyptian thief:** Thyamis in the *Aethiopica,* a 115

    Kill what I love? (A savage jealously   Greek prose romance by Heliodorus

    That sometimes savors nobly.) But hear me this:

    Since you to non-regardance° cast my faith,   **non-regardance:** neglect

    And that I partly know the instrument

    That screws° me from my true place in your favor,   **screws:** pries   120

    Live you the marble-breasted tyrant still.

    But this your minion,° whom I know you love,   **minion:** favorite

    And whom, by heaven I swear, I tender° dearly,   **tender:** hold

    Him will I tear out of that cruel eye

    Where he sits crownèd in his master's spite.°   **in . . . spite:** despite his master   125

    Come, boy, with me. My thoughts are ripe in mischief.

    I'll sacrifice the lamb that I do love

    To spite a raven's heart within a dove.   *[Going]*

DISCOVERING SHAKESPEARE

(78) Characterization [5.1.100]: What "promise" does Olivia think Cesario has made to her? Who actually made this promise to the Lady? Why is Olivia surprised to see Cesario here in the company of the Duke?

(79) Metaphor [5.1.127–128]: Whom do the lamb, raven, and dove represent in Orsino's bitter speech to Olivia?

VIOLA
And I, most jocund, apt,° and willingly,
To do you rest° a thousand deaths would die.

                       [Following]

apt: properly

do you rest: give you peace   130

OLIVIA
Where goes Cesario?

VIOLA   After him I love
More than I love these eyes, more than my life,
More, by all mores,° than e'er I shall love wife.
If I do feign, you witnesses above
Punish my life for tainting of my love!

all mores: i.e., all conceivable comparisons

    135

OLIVIA
Ay me detested! How am I beguiled!

VIOLA
Who does beguile you? Who does do you wrong?

OLIVIA
Hast thou forgot thyself? Is it so long?
Call forth the holy father.   *[Exit an Attendant.]*

DUKE   *[To Viola]* Come, away!

OLIVIA
Whither, my lord? Cesario, husband, stay.   140

DUKE
Husband?

OLIVIA   Ay, husband. Can he that deny?

DUKE
Her husband, sirrah?

VIOLA   No, my lord, not I.

OLIVIA
Alas, it is the baseness of thy fear
That makes thee strangle thy propriety.°
Fear not, Cesario; take thy fortunes up;
Be that thou know'st thou art, and then thou art
As great as that thou fear'st.°
  Enter Priest.

strangle thy propriety: deny who and what you are   145

that thou fear'st: i.e., the duke

                O, welcome, father!
Father, I charge thee by thy reverence
Here to unfold – though lately we intended
To keep in darkness what occasion now
Reveals before 'tis ripe – what thou dost know
Hath newly passed between this youth and me.

    150

PRIEST
A contract of eternal bond of love,
Confirmed by mutual joinder of your hands,
Attested by the holy close° of lips,
Strengthened by interchangement of your rings;
And all the ceremony of this compact

close: meeting   155

DISCOVERING SHAKESPEARE

(80) Staging [5.1.130–137]: Does Orsino hear these three speeches by Viola to Olivia? If so, how could he react to Viola's admission that she loves Orsino more "than e'er I shall love wife" (133)? If not, how would you stage this part of the scene so that he does not hear her?

(81) Characterization [5.1.153–160]: When the Priest is finally allowed to speak here, the potential for comic characterization is nearly inescapable. Allowing for the fact that Shakespeare often <u>burlesqued</u> religious figures in his plays, what could the actor playing the part of the Priest do in <u>diction</u>, accent, body language, or other stage business to make his speech interesting (and perhaps funny)?

Sealed in my function, by my testimony;
Since when, my watch hath told me, toward my grave
I have traveled but two hours.   160

DUKE
O thou dissembling cub, what wilt thou be
When time hath sowed a grizzle° on thy case?°   **a grizzle:** gray hair; **case:** sheath, i.e., skin
Or will not else thy craft so quickly grow
That thine own trip° shall be thine overthrow?   **trip:** trickery
Farewell, and take her; but direct thy feet   165
Where thou and I, henceforth, may never meet.

VIOLA
My lord, I do protest –

OLIVIA   O, do not swear.
Hold little° faith, though thou hast too much fear.   **little:** a little
Enter Sir Andrew.

ANDREW   For the love of God, a surgeon! Send one
presently° to Sir Toby.   **presently:** at once   170

OLIVIA   What's the matter?

ANDREW   Has° broke my head across, and has given Sir   **Has:** he has
Toby a bloody coxcomb too. For the love of God, your
help! I had rather than forty pounds I were at home.

OLIVIA   Who has done this, Sir Andrew?   175

ANDREW   The count's gentleman, one Cesario. We took
him for a coward, but he's the very devil incardinate.°   **incardinate:** incarnate

DUKE   My gentleman Cesario?

ANDREW   Od's lifelings,° here he is! You broke my head   **Od's lifelings:** by God's little life
for nothing; and that that I did, I was set on to do't by   180
Sir Toby.

VIOLA
Why do you speak to me? I never hurt you.
You drew your sword upon me without cause,
But I bespake you fair and hurt you not.
Enter [Sir] Toby and Clown.

ANDREW   If a bloody coxcomb be a hurt, you have hurt   185
me. I think you set nothing by a bloody coxcomb. Here
comes Sir Toby halting;° you shall hear more. But if he   **halting:** limping
had not been in drink, he would have tickled you oth-
ergates° than he did.   **othergates:** otherwise

DUKE   How now, gentleman? How is't with you?   190

TOBY   That's all one! Has hurt me, and there's th' end
on't. Sot, didst see Dick Surgeon, sot?

FESTE   O, he's drunk, Sir Toby, an hour agone. His eyes
were set° at eight i' th' morning.   **set:** fixed or gone down

TOBY   Then he's a rogue and a passy measures pavin. I   195
hate a drunken rogue.

OLIVIA   Away with him! Who hath made this havoc with
them?

DISCOVERING SHAKESPEARE

(82) Teaser [5.1.193–194]: Feste explains here that the local doctor (Dick Surgeon) will be no help in tending to their wounds because he was dead drunk at eight o'clock in the morning. In addition to physicians, what other well-known professions does Shakespeare make fun of in this play? How does he treat these same occupations in his other plays? Which professions are most often ridiculed by the media these days?

ANDREW   I'll help you, Sir Toby, because we'll be dressed
together.   200

TOBY   Will you help? An ass-head and a coxcomb and a
knave, a thin-faced knave, a gull?

OLIVIA   Get him to bed, and let his hurt be looked to.
   [Exeunt Clown, Fabian, Sir Toby, and Sir Andrew.]
   Enter Sebastian.

SEBASTIAN
I am sorry, madam, I have hurt your kinsman;
But had it been the brother of my blood,   205
I must have done no less with wit and safety.°   **wit and safety:** intelligent regard for my safety
You throw a strange regard° upon me, and by that   **strange regard:** estranged look
I do perceive it hath offended you.
Pardon me, sweet one, even for the vows
We made each other but so late ago.   210

DUKE
One face, one voice, one habit,° and two persons –   **habit:** dress
A natural perspective° that is and is not.   **perspective:** glass producing an optical illusion

SEBASTIAN
Antonio, O my dear Antonio,
How have the hours racked and tortured me
Since I have lost thee!   215

ANTONIO
Sebastian are you?

SEBASTIAN   Fear'st thou that, Antonio?

ANTONIO
How have you made division of yourself?
An apple cleft in two is not more twin
Than these two creatures. Which is Sebastian?

OLIVIA
Most wonderful.   220

SEBASTIAN
Do I stand there? I never had a brother;
Nor can there be that deity in my nature
Of here and everywhere. I had a sister,
Whom the blind waves and surges have devoured.
Of charity, what kin are you to me?   225
What countryman? What name? What parentage?

VIOLA
Of Messaline; Sebastian was my father;
Such a Sebastian was my brother too;
So went he suited° to his watery tomb.   **suited:** dressed
If spirits can assume both form and suit,
You come to fright us.   230

SEBASTIAN   A spirit I am indeed,
But am in that dimension° grossly° clad   **dimension:** form; **grossly:** in the flesh
Which from the womb I did participate.°   **participate:** inherit
Were you a woman, as the rest goes even,°   **rest goes even:** other circumstances allow
                                                                               235

DISCOVERING SHAKESPEARE

(83) Characterization [5.1.221–253]: Why do Viola and Sebastian wait so long to embrace in this scene? Why do they cross-examine each other so strenuously about their home country, family name, parentage, and the mole on their father's brow? In short, why don't they immediately recognize each other?

I should my tears let fall upon your cheek
And say, "Thrice welcome, drownèd Viola!"

VIOLA
My father had a mole upon his brow.

SEBASTIAN
And so had mine.

VIOLA
And died that day when Viola from her birth
Had numbered thirteen years.   240

SEBASTIAN
O, that record° is lively in my soul!   **record:** memory
He finishèd indeed his mortal act
That day that made my sister thirteen years.

VIOLA
If nothing lets° to make us happy both   **lets:** hinders
But this my masculine usurped attire,   245
Do not embrace me till each circumstance
Of place, time, fortune do cohere and jump°   **jump:** agree completely
That I am Viola; which to confirm,
I'll bring you to a captain in this town,
Where lie my maiden weeds;° by whose gentle help   **weeds:** clothes   250
I was preserved to serve this noble count.
All the occurrence of my fortune since
Hath been between this lady and this lord.

SEBASTIAN   *[To Olivia]*
So comes it, lady, you have been mistook.
But nature to her bias drew° in that.   **to her bias drew:** i.e., drew you into a natural   255
You would have been contracted to a maid;   course (from bowls, in which a weighted ball
Nor are you therein, by my life, deceived: follows a curved path to its object)
You are betrothed both to a maid and man.

DUKE
Be not amazed; right noble is his blood.
If this be so, as yet the glass° seems true,   **glass:** perspective glass   260
I shall have share in this most happy wrack.
   [To Viola]
Boy, thou hast said to me a thousand times
Thou never shouldst love woman like to me.

VIOLA
And all those sayings will I over swear,°   **over swear:** swear over again
And all those swearings keep as true in soul   265
As doth that orbèd continent° the fire   **orbèd continent:** sphere of the sun
That severs day from night.

DUKE   Give me thy hand,
And let me see thee in thy woman's weeds.

VIOLA
The captain that did bring me first on shore
Hath my maid's garments. He upon some action°   **action:** legal charge   270
Is now in durance,° at Malvolio's suit,   **durance:** custody
A gentleman, and follower of my lady's.

DISCOVERING SHAKESPEARE

(84) Characterization [5.1.245]: How do Orsino and Olivia react to the sudden revelation that Viola/Cesario is a woman?
(85) Plot Development [5.1.271–272]: Why do you think Shakespeare adds the plot device of having the Sea Captain imprisoned ("in durance") at Malvolio's request? (*Hint:* What would happen at this point in the scene if all the characters simply left the stage?)

OLIVIA
He shall enlarge° him. Fetch Malvolio hither.
And yet alas, now I remember me,
They say, poor gentleman, he's much distract.
  Enter Clown with a letter, and Fabian.
A most extracting° frenzy of mine own
From my remembrance clearly banished his.
How does he, sirrah?

enlarge: free

275

extracting: distracting

FESTE Truly, madam, he holds Belzebub at the stave's
end° as well as a man in his case may do. Has here writ a
letter to you; I should have given't you today morning.
But as a madman's epistles are no gospels, so it skills° not
much when they are delivered.

holds . . . end: i.e., holds the devil off with a
long staff
skills: matters

280

OLIVIA Open't and read it.

FESTE Look then to be well edified, when the fool de-
livers° the madman. *[Reads in a loud voice.]* "By the
Lord, madam" –

285

delivers: speaks the words of

OLIVIA How now? Art thou mad?

FESTE No, madam, I do but read madness. An your
ladyship will have it as it ought to be, you must allow
vox.°

290

vox: amplification

OLIVIA Prithee read i' thy right wits.

FESTE So I do, madonna; but to read his right wits is to
read thus. Therefore perpend,° my princess, and give ear.

perpend: consider

OLIVIA *[To Fabian]* Read it you, sirrah.

295

FABIAN *[Reads.]* "By the Lord, madam, you wrong me,
and the world shall know it. Though you have put me
into darkness, and given your drunken cousin rule over
me, yet have I the benefit of my senses as well as your
ladyship. I have your own letter that induced me to the
semblance I put on; with the which I doubt not but to
do myself much right, or you much shame. Think of
me as you please. I leave my duty a little unthought of,
and speak out of my injury.
              The madly used Malvolio."

300

305

OLIVIA Did he write this?

FESTE Ay, madam.

DUKE This savors not much of distraction.°

distraction: insanity

OLIVIA
See him delivered, Fabian; bring him hither.
                     [Exit Fabian.]
My lord, so please you, these things further thought on,
To think me as well a sister as a wife,
One day shall crown th' alliance on't, so please you,
Here at my house and at my proper° cost.

310

proper: own

DUKE
Madam, I am most apt° t' embrace your offer.
  [To Viola]
Your master quits° you; and for your service done him,
So much against the mettle of your sex,

apt: ready

quits: releases

315

DISCOVERING SHAKESPEARE

(86) Motivation [5.1.315–320]: Why does Orsino take so long to propose to Viola (from 5.1.244–320)? Does his decision to marry her have anything to do with Olivia's conciliatory speech in 5.1.309–313?

So far beneath your soft and tender breeding,
And since you called me master for so long,
Here is my hand; you shall from this time be
Your master's mistress. 320

OLIVIA   A sister; you are she.
    Enter [Fabian, with] Malvolio.

DUKE
Is this the madman?

OLIVIA   Ay, my lord, this same.
How now, Malvolio?

MALVOLIO   Madam, you have done me wrong,
Notorious° wrong.   **Notorious:** scandalous

OLIVIA   Have I, Malvolio? No.

MALVOLIO
Lady, you have. Pray you peruse that letter.
You must not now deny it is your hand. 325
Write from it° if you can, in hand or phrase,   **from it:** differently
Or say 'tis not your seal, not your invention.°   **invention:** composition
You can say none of this. Well, grant it then,
And tell me, in the modesty of honor,°   **in . . . honor:** with honorable propriety
Why you have given me such clear lights of favor, 330
Bade me come smiling and cross-gartered to you,
To put on yellow stockings, and to frown
Upon Sir Toby and the lighter° people;   **lighter:** lesser
And, acting this in an obedient hope,
Why have you suffered me to be imprisoned, 335
Kept in a dark house, visited by the priest,
And made the most notorious geck and gull°   **geck and gull:** ludicrous dupe
That e'er invention played on? Tell me why.

OLIVIA
Alas, Malvolio, this is not my writing,
Though I confess much like the character;°   **character:** hand-writing 340
But, out of question, 'tis Maria's hand.
And now I do bethink me, it was she
First told me thou wast mad. Thou cam'st in smiling,
And in such forms which here were presupposed
Upon thee° in the letter. Prithee be content.   **presupposed/Upon thee:** put upon you 345
This practice hath most shrewdly passed° upon thee; beforehand
But when we know the grounds and authors of it,   **shrewdly passed:** maliciously been put
Thou shalt be both the plaintiff and the judge
Of thine own cause.

FABIAN   Good madam, hear me speak,
And let no quarrel, nor no brawl to come, 350
Taint the condition of this present hour,
Which I have wondered at. In hope it shall not.
Most freely I confess myself and Toby
Set this device against Malvolio here,

DISCOVERING SHAKESPEARE

(87) Staging [5.1.322]: How "mad" should Malvolio look when he comes on stage, especially in terms of his <u>costuming</u>, <u>make-up</u>, hair, and other design elements? Do you think he has been released from his "prison" recently, or has he been free for quite a while? Which would be the most effective choice for his final appearance?

(88) Characterization [5.1.339–341]: How does Malvolio react when he learns that Maria and Sir Toby were responsible for the plot against him?

Upon° some stubborn and uncourteous parts
We had conceived against him. Maria writ
The letter, at Sir Toby's great importance,°
In recompense whereof he hath married her.
How with a sportful malice it was followed
May rather pluck on laughter than revenge,
If that the injuries be justly weighed
That have on both sides passed.

OLIVIA
Alas, poor fool, how have they baffled thee!°

FESTE   Why, "some are born great, some achieve greatness, and some have greatness thrown upon them." I
was one, sir, in this interlude,° one Sir Topas, sir; but
that's all one. "By the Lord, fool, I am not mad!" But
do you remember, "Madam, why laugh you at such a
barren rascal? An you smile not, he's gagged"? And thus
the whirligig° of time brings in his revenges.

MALVOLIO   I'll be revenged on the whole pack of you!
                                                                    [Exit.]

OLIVIA
He hath been most notoriously abused.

DUKE
Pursue him and entreat him to a peace.
He hath not told us of the captain yet.
When that is known, and golden time convents,°
A solemn combination shall be made
Of our dear souls. Meantime, sweet sister,
We will not part from hence. Cesario, come –
For so you shall be while you are a man,
But when in other habits you are seen,
Orsino's mistress and his fancy's° queen.
                                              Exeunt [all but Feste].

                    Feste sings.
When that I was and a little tiny boy,
    With hey, ho, the wind and the rain,
A foolish thing was but a toy,
    For the rain it raineth every day.

But when I came to man's estate,
    With hey, ho, the wind and the rain,
'Gainst knaves and thieves men shut their gate,
    For the rain it raineth every day.

But when I came, alas, to wive,
    With hey, ho, the wind and the rain,
By swaggering° could I never thrive,
    For the rain it raineth every day.

Upon: on account of   355

importance: importunity

                                                                          360

baffled thee: disgraced you publicly

                                                                          365
interlude: an early form of dramatic
entertainment

whirligig: spinning top or similar toy   370

convents: is convenient   375

fancy's: love's   380

                                                                          385

                                                                          390
swaggering: bullying

DISCOVERING SHAKESPEARE

(89) Language [5.1.371]: In what way does Malvolio deliver his last line? Is he angry, or does he run off as if he were going to play practical jokes on his tormentors? If he is very angry, how does this one unresolved conflict influence the play's comic conclusion?

(90) Music [5.1.382]: Many different scholarly interpretations have been advanced to explain Feste's final song. What is your opinion of the song? Do the events described have anything to do with the plot of Shakespeare's play? Why do you think the play ends in such a melancholy fashion?

But when I came unto my beds,
    With hey, ho, the wind and the rain,   395
With tosspots° still had drunken heads,   **tosspots:** drunkards
    For the rain it raineth every day.

A great while ago the world begun,
    With hey, ho, the wind and the rain;
But that's all one, our play is done,   400
    And we'll strive to please you every day.

[Exit.]

Research and Discussion Topics

ACT I

1. What can you learn about the power of love during the Renaissance? Did people who were "love-sick" then behave differently from today's lovers?

2. In 1.1.20–24, Orsino compares himself to Actaeon, who was transformed into a stag by the Goddess Diana. What other information can you discover about this ancient myth?

3. What can you find out about the country of Illyria? Was it a real place, or did Shakespeare make up the name?

4. Some scholars believe that in 1.1 Orsino displays symptoms of love melancholy, which was considered to be a real disease during the Renaissance [*Hint:* See Robert Burton's *Anatomy of Melancholy*]. Can you name any other Shakespearean characters who suffer from this disease?

5. Why does Viola tell the Captain that she will present herself as an "eunuch" (1.2.56) to Orsino?

6. What was a "butt'ry bar" (1.3.66)? What sexual joke might Maria be playing on Sir Andrew here?

7. Find out as much as you can about the sport of bear-baiting (1.3.89).

8. Maria is undoubtedly a lady-in-waiting to Olivia, rather than a mere servant. What was the distinction between these two positions during the Renaissance?

9. How many different types of dances do Sir Toby and Sir Andrew refer to at the conclusion of 1.3? Learn to perform at least one of them.

10. Why is Feste described as a "clown" in 1.5? Find out everything you can about "fools" in Renaissance drama.

ACT II

1. Research the origin and customs of the Twelfth Night holiday, then explain how it is related to Shakespeare's play.

2. What can you learn about twins that would help you understand the relationship between Viola and Sebastian? Did Renaissance theories about twins differ greatly from those held by today's scientists?

3. Why does Viola describe Satan as "the pregnant enemy" in 2.2.28?

4. Sir Toby explains to Sir Andrew that getting up early in the morning is a healthy ritual ("diluculo surgere," 2.3.2). What else can you discover about Renaissance theories concerning good health?

5. Shakespeare's "O Mistress Mine" was a very popular song during the Renaissance. Who wrote the music to accompany his lyrics? Try to locate a copy of the sheet music and have someone play it for your class.

6. Several references in the comedy depict Malvolio as a "Puritan" (see, for example, 2.3.130). Locate as many of these quotes as possible; then find out all you can about Puritans in England at the beginning of the seventeenth century. Did they enjoy going to the theater? Why or why not? Why would Shakespeare have included a Puritan in his play?

7. In 2.3.160, Maria brags that her "physic" (medicine) will work with Malvolio. To what extent do Shakespeare's comedies attempt to "cure" characters of their anti-social behavior?

ACT III

1. Who were Troilus and Cressida (3.1.51–52)? What role did Pandarus play in bringing these two lovers together? In which play did Shakespeare write about their romance? Was it written before or after *Twelfth Night?*

2. What does Olivia mean when she refers to "music from the spheres" (3.1.109)?

3. What Renaissance sport does Olivia refer to in 3.1.117 when she accuses Viola of setting her "honor at the stake"? What other sports and pastimes were popular during Shakespeare's time? Which of these are still popular today?

4. What was a "Brownist" (3.2.29)? What were the most prominent religions in the early seventeenth century? To what religion did Queen Elizabeth belong? King James I? Shakespeare?

5. When Sir Toby counsels Sir Andrew to wound Cesario "in eleven places" (3.2.32), he refers to specific points of vulnerability in the "Code of the Duello." Find out everything you can about duels during the Renaissance (*Hint:* see 5.4.65–97 in *As You Like It*).

6. What was the Bed of Ware (3.2.43)? Does it still exist?

7. In 3.4.8, Maria claims that Malvolio is "possessed" by the devil. How frequently were people convicted of witchcraft at this time? What kind of "evidence" was allowed in court? What punishments were inflicted on those who were found guilty?

8. Find as many drawings or photographs of "cross-gartering" as you can (3.4.19).

9. When Malvolio refers to having "limed" Olivia (3.4.69), what hunting metaphor is he using? What animals were caught with "lime"?

10. What was a "bum-baily" (3.4.169)?

11. Define each of the following fencing terms in 3.4: "dismount thy tuck" (214), "betake you to your guard" (221–222), "unhatched rapier" (225), "meddle you must" (240), "forswear to wear iron" (240–241), "firago" (263), "scabbard" (263), and "stuck in" (264). What can you find out about each of these terms in addition to the information provided in the footnotes?

ACT IV

1. What was a "cockney" (4.1.13–14) and a "Greek" (17)?

2. Where was the River Lethe (4.1.59), and why is the allusion to it important at this point in the play?

3. What was a "curate" (4.2.2)? Look up the etymology of the word in the *Oxford English Dictionary.*

4. Why does Feste attempt to speak in Latin when he says "Bonos dies" to Sir Toby (4.2.12)? In which languages were the principal religious services conducted?

5. Who was Pythagoras, and what was his opinion about the soul (4.2.49–59)?

6. When Feste assumes his own persona again, he sings snatches from an old song written by Sir Thomas Wyatt. Try to locate a copy of the entire song, then determine which lines Shakespeare has excluded. What are some of Wyatt's most important poems?

7. What does the word "Topas" mean?

8. Why did the Vice character carry a "dagger of lath" in the old morality plays (4.2.125)?

9. What was a "chantry" (4.3.24)? Would Olivia have had one on her estate?

10. What was the difference in Renaissance England between plighting your "troth" to a loved one (4.3.26) and actually going through a marriage ceremony?

11. Why are Olivia and Sebastian married off stage? Can you think of any Shakespearean plays that feature on-stage marriages? (*Hint:* See *The Taming of the Shrew* and *Much Ado About Nothing,* in which characters almost get married on stage.)

ACT V

1. Who was Vulcan (5.1.50), and why would his face be black? Why was Antonio's face black the last time the Duke saw him?

2. Look up the story of the Egyptian thief Thyamis, recorded in Heliodorus' *Aethiopica,* and explain the Duke's metaphor (5.1.114–117).

3. What was a "bloody coxcomb" (5.1.173)?

4. Why would the surgeon move like a "passy measures pavin" (5.1.195)?

5. What is the "orbed continent the fire" that "severs day from night" (5.1.266–267)?

6. What was *vox* (5.1.291), and why does Feste need it to read Malvolio's letter properly?

7. Why does Malvolio compare himself to a "geck and gull" (5.1.337)?

8. Look up the word "baffle" (5.1.363) in the *Oxford English Dictionary,* and catalogue the primary meanings available in 1600. In what sense is Malvolio "baffled" by the conspirators?

Filmography

1980
BBC
Rating:

Directed by John Gorrie

Alec McCowen as Malvolio
Robert Hardy as Toby
Felicity Kendal as Viola
Annette Crosbie as Maria
Sinead Cusack as Olivia
Trevor Peacock as Feste
Clive Arrindell as Orsino
Michael Thomas as Sebastian
Ronnie Stevens as Andrew

The straightforward paths of tradition and attention to textual detail may not always lead to striking originality, but they can, as in this case, beget an appropriately humorous and a nearly definitive version. Filmed in and around an Elizabethan manor house, this production has the grace and authenticity of its setting. Feste is so believable that he seems to have come with the house, not the acting company. Felicity Kendall is reasonably boyish as Cesario, but attractive enough that we never lose sight of Viola. Toby has enough heft and charm to pass as Falstaff's younger brother. Malvolio is stuffy without becoming a caricature; Andrew is a dolt with touches of pathos; and Olivia is beautiful enough to excite the jealousy of any Viola.

1970
John Dexter Productions/Precision Video
Rating: 👤 👤 👤

Directed by John Dexter

Alec Guinness as Malvolio
Tommy Steele as Feste
Gary Raymond as Orsino
Joan Plowright as Viola/Cesario and Sebastian
Adrienne Corri as Olivia
Ralph Richardson as Toby
John Moffat as Andrew
Sheila Reid as Maria

This *Twelfth Night* is charmingly lighthearted; if it is also sometimes lightheaded, the lapse is usually forgivable. The production's greatest strengths and worst weaknesses are in the casting. Ralph Richardson's Toby Belch is too old, too thin, and too serious. While Joan Plowright is effective as Viola and Cesario, her Sebastian is just short of awful. Gary Raymond's Orsino looks and sounds like the amorous Duke, and Tommy Steele's Feste has a good singing voice plus the cheerful charm that belongs to a professional jester. The best player in a generally strong cast is Alec Guinness's gravel-voiced, slightly addled, superbly watchable Malvolio.

1998
Produced by Lincoln Center Theatre
Vivian Beaumont Theatre
Rating: 👤 👤 👤

Directed by Nicholas Hytner

Helen Hunt as Viola
Paul Rudd as Orsino
Kyra Sedgwick as Olivia
Philip Bosco as Malvolio

Max Wright as Andrew
Brian Murray as Toby
David Patrick Kelly as Feste
Rick Stear as Sebastian
Julio Monge as Antonio
Amy Hill as Maria

Although this production has a comparatively complete text, some good comic bits, and a number of well-known faces, the costumes and sets were peculiar, and the acting was inconsistent. Andrew was both pathetic and silly; Feste was the perfect fool who is not perfectly foolish; and Malvolio was so thoroughly serious that he became remarkably funny. Olivia, Viola, and Orsino were less successful. Orsino's readings were effective, but he lacked the romantic energy that makes the part believable; Viola's performance was acceptable but never electric; and Olivia overacted her way into high energy and almost out of the part. Still, as a filmed version of a stage production, it is humorous and occasionally touching.

1988
Renaissance Theatre Company
Rating: 🎭 🎭 🎭

Directed by Kenneth Branagh and Paul Kafno

James Simmons as Andrew
Anton Lesser as Feste
Richard Briers as Malvolio
Abigail McKern as Maria
Caroline Langrishe as Olivia
Christopher Ravenscroft as Orsino
Christopher Hollis as Sebastian
James Saxon as Toby
Frances Barber as Viola

Although the title of *Twelfth Night* refers to the Christmas season, it is not Shakespeare's version of *Miracle on 34th Street,* and setting it (as this production does) in a Victorian winter with Christmas trees makes nonsense of more than a few lines. Except for Olivia, who has the expected beauty and charm, the casting is somewhere between non-traditional and peculiar. Toby is too scruffy for even a down-at-heels aristocrat. Feste at times seems genuinely demented and disconcertingly angry. Sebastian and Viola looked convincingly alike, but oddly Sebastian seemed prettier. Malvolio and Andrew were closer to standard casting than most, with Andrew looking like a toy soldier brought to life.

1996
Renaissance Films
Rating: 👤 👤

Directed by Trevor Nunn

Ben Kingsley as Feste
Richard E. Grant as Andrew
Nigel Hawthorne as Malvolio
Imogen Stubbs as Viola
Toby Stephens as Orsino
Steven Makintosh as Sebastian
Imelda Staunton as Maria
Mel Smith as Toby
Helena Bonham Carter as Olivia

Trevor Nunn has rewritten Shakespeare so often in his directorial career that he should be better at it by now. This *Twelfth Night* adds a party on board ship, a shipwreck, the funeral of Olivia's brother, and a full-scale war between Illyria and Messaline. Not unexpectedly, it omits at least half the lines, re-arranges and intercuts scenes, and surgically removes the play's humor as though it were a dangerous growth. Sex, however, is consistently highlighted. Malvolio reads a magazine titled *Amour,* Viola/Cesario washes Orsino's back while he bathes, Malvolio reads the infamous letter while standing nose to torso with a naked Venus, and Orsino nearly kisses Viola as Cesario—moustache and all. Cesario's lip is supposed to be "smooth and rubious," yet this Viola seems too masculine. Feste is dark and cadaverous, and most of the cast (even Nigel Hawthorne) merely competent. Helena Bonham Carter's Olivia, though overly affectionate to everyone, is strong, and the whole last act is worth watching.

1955
A Lenfilm Studios Production
(Dubbed in English in an adaptation by Molly Stevens)
Rating: 👤 👤

Directed by Yakow Fried

K. Luchko as Viola/Sebastian
A. Larionova as Olivia
V. Medvediev as Orsino
V. Merkuriev as Malvolio
M. Yanshin as Toby
B. Freindlich as Feste
G. Vipin as Andrew
A. Lisyanskava as Maria

This black and white Russian version is probably of greater interest to Shakespearean film scholars than audience members looking for a watchable *Twelfth Night*. It has the feel, but not the studio slickness, of Hollywood Shakespeare from the thirties and forties. It begins with a shipwreck, uses the same actress to play Viola and Sebastian, and in spite of cutting the play to the bone (What else can one do in 88 minutes?), spends an amazing amount of time showing people walking silently. The actors do have plenty of energy, and where else does Feste sing in Russian?

Annotated Bibliography

Bloom, Harold, ed. *Modern Critical Interpretations: William Shakespeare's "Twelfth Night."* New York: Chelsea House Publishers, 1987. PR 2837.W54.
    This informative book provides an introduction by Harold Bloom and numerous essays on the play ranging in topics from music, class ideology, character, and nature. Among the authors are John Hollander, Elliot Krieger, Ruth Nevo, Coppelia Kahn, Camille Slights, Elizabeth M. Yearling, and Geoffrey H. Hartman.

Callaghan, Dympna. "'And All Is Semblative a Woman's Part': Body Politics and *Twelfth Night.*" *Textual Practice* 7:3 (Winter 1993): 428–452. journal PN 80.T49.
    Callaghan begins with a theoretical discussion of the body, explores the levels of cross-dressing in *Twelfth Night,* and notes the reaction of a Renaissance audience to transvestitism. The author then examines the exclusion of women actors on the Renaissance stage and the representation of the female body through the play's characterizations.

Carnegie, David. "Malvolio Within: Performance Perspectives on the Dark House." *Shakespeare Quarterly* 52:3 (Fall 2001): 393–404. journal PR 2885.S63.
    Carnegie discusses the history of the staging of Malvolio's dark house scene, taking into account (1) the lack of stage directions in the original folio, (2) additions made by directors through various theatrical interpretations, and (3) the issues of audibility and visibility for Malvolio. The author examines why the last would have been an issue and investigates why Shakespeare wanted Malvolio "within" in the first place.

Charles, Casey. "Gender Trouble in *Twelfth Night.*" *Theatre Journal* 49:2 (May 1997): 121–141. journal PN 3171.E38.
    Casey looks at the effects of Viola's cross-dressing, the same-sex relationships between Viola/Olivia and Sebastian/Antonio, and the "improbable" solutions of the last act in her analysis of gender theory and sexuality in *Twelfth Night.*

Coddon, Karin S. "'Slander in an Allow'd Fool': *Twelfth Night's* Crisis of the Aristocracy." *Studies in English Literature* 33:2 (Spring 1993): 309–325. journal PR 1.S82.
    This interesting article explores the violations of aristocratic rules by Malvolio and Feste in the play. Coddon provides the historic context in which the violations occur, focusing upon extravagances during a famine-plagued era, marrying above one's social status, and devotion to material goods.

Elam, Keir. "The Fertile Eunuch: *Twelfth Night,* Early Modern Intercourse, and the Fruits of Castration." *Shakespeare Quarterly* 47:1 (Spring 1996): 1–36. journal PR 2885.S63.

> Elam studies the language in *Twelfth Night,* interpreting passages (especially 1.2.55–63) that examine gender roles in the play. Elam argues that Shakespeare presents both views of a "eunuch" (castrated and fertile) in the character of Viola to "form a single, extraordinarily dense piece of role-playing."

Hunt, Maurice. "Malvolio, Viola, and the Question of Instrument: Defining Providence in *Twelfth Night.*" *Studies in Philology* 90:3 (Summer 1993): 277–297. journal P 25.S8.

> Providing interesting historical background about Providence (destiny guided by God) and a variety of Puritan beliefs, Hunt discusses the Puritanical Malvolio and the circumstances surrounding Viola and their roles in setting up Providence in the play.

Hutson, Lorna. "On Not Being Deceived: Rhetoric and the Body in *Twelfth Night.*" *Texas Studies in Literature and Language* 38:2 (Summer 1996): 140–174. journal AS 30.T4.

> Hutson argues extensively that the language use in the play helps us understand gender roles and sexuality in the Renaissance. Hutson compares *Twelfth Night* with *Gl'Inganni,* a possible source for the play, to show how Shakespeare uses gender for "the undoing of the social and sexual stereotyping."

King, Walter, N. *Twentieth Century Interpretations of "Twelfth Night."* Englewood Cliffs: Prentice Hall, Inc., 1968. PR 2837.A2.K48.

> This collection of essays is divided into two parts: "interpretations" and "viewpoints." In Part I, authors such as Joseph Summers, Porter Williams Jr., and Julian Markels discuss topics ranging from masks, design, and the alignment of plot and theme to the consummation of relationships. Part II considers plot and subplot, Toby Belch, theological punning, and word play in Feste's final song. Among the authors in this second section are G.K. Hunter, Mark Van Doren, W. Moelwyn Merchant, and Leslie Hotson.

Leech, Clifford. *"Twelfth Night" and Shakespearean Comedy.* Toronto: Dalhousie University Press, 1968. PR 2981.L4.

> This book is a series of three lectures given at the Neptune Theatre in Halifax, Nova Scotia. The first lecture explores Shakespeare's comedies and how his plays fit into the comedic realm of the Renaissance; the second lecture discusses more specifically the comic aspects of *Twelfth Night,* and the final lecture explains how Shakespeare's comedies change after *Twelfth Night.*

Logan, Thad Jenkins. "*Twelfth Night.* The Limits of Festivity." *Studies in English Literature* 22.2 (Spring 1982): 232–238. journal PR 1.S82.

> Logan examines sexuality in the main plot and "revelry" in the sub-plot as the source of festivity in *Twelfth Night.* He argues that the audience is the element in the play that makes the results of festivity ("violence and indiscriminate passion") especially humorous.

Marciano, Lisa. "The Serious Comedy of *Twelfth Night:* Dark Didacticism in Illyria." *Renascence* 56:1 (Fall 2003): 3–21. journal PN 2.R4.

> Marciano claims that all of Shakespeare's comedies use the theme of death as a learning device for the characters. In *"Twelfth Night"* in particular, each character learns that life is short and should be lived as fully as possible.

Potter, Lois. *"Twelfth Night": Text and Performance.* London: Macmillan Publishers LTD, 1985. PR 2837.P68.

> Potter divides her book into two parts: "Text" and "Performance." In Part I, she explores such topics as interpretations of the title, patterns of language, and a close analysis of 5.1. In Part II, Potter discusses possible settings for performances, the different romances onstage, and comedic elements as performed by various actors.

Preston, Dennis R. "The Minor Characters in *Twelfth Night."* *Shakespeare Quarterly* 25 (1970): 167–176. journal PR 2885.S63.

> Preston discusses the dramatic and linguistic functions of minor characters in *Twelfth Night,* creating a hierarchy of importance in their roles. Preston proves the significance of such minor characters as the First Officer, Curio, Valentine, and the Priest to the construction of events in the play.

Swander, Homer. "*Twelfth Night.* Critics, Players, and Script." *Educational Theatre Journal* 16 (1964): 114–121. journal PN 3171.E38.

> Swander makes two essential points: (1) *Twelfth Night* is often considered a dull play because of its characters and plot, even though productions often ignored textual hints from the playwright, and (2) people should not judge *Twelfth Night* based upon past performances because it has the potential to be a wonderfully exciting play.

Wells, Stanley, ed. *"Twelfth Night": Critical Essays.* New York: Garland Publishing, Inc., 1986. PR 2837.W45.

> This series of essays focuses on topics such as characterization, Feste, comic form, sources, and the ending of the play. It also provides numerous reviews of past performances of *Twelfth Night* by such authors as Henry Morley, Virginia Woolf, and Ray Walker. Other authors include A.C. Bradley, C.L. Barber, Harold Jenkins, and L.G. Salinger.

White, R.S., ed. *Twelfth Night.* New York: St. Martin's Press, 1996. PR 2837.T94.
> This book offers a group of essays that focus on politics in *Twelfth Night.* Various articles consider the treatment of the female body and the relationship of sexual politics, along with morality, gender, and genres. Authors include Stephen Greenblatt, Dympna Callaghan, Geoffrey Hartman, and Barbara Everett.

King Henry the Fourth, Part I

Henry IV, Parts I and II *at the Gutherie Theater in Minneapolis, Minnesota, with Stephen Yoakam as King Henry IV and Barton Tinapp as Prince Hal (1990). Photograph by Michal Daniel.*

England's stunning defeat of the Spanish Armada in 1588, coupled with the rising popularity of Queen Elizabeth, prompted a resurgence of nationalistic pride during the decade from 1590–1600 that was unprecedented in English history. One important consequence of this wave of patriotism was Shakespeare's creation of a series of plays celebrating the reigns of past kings and queens of England. These history plays were immensely popular with Shakespeare's audience, which was ravenous for information about its ancestral heritage and fascinated with political debates about the proper attributes of an ideal ruler. The closest twentieth-century parallel to this surge of national identity was Alex Haley's television series *Roots,* which prompted thousands of Americans in the late 1970s to research their families' genealogical charts.

Written in 1596–1597, *Henry IV, Part I* is the second part of a <u>tetralogy</u>—a series of four plays including *Richard II, Henry IV Parts I and II,* and *Henry V* that chronicle the rise to political power of Henry V (1387–1422), England's "ideal Christian king." Shakespeare's principal dramatic <u>source</u> was the 1587 edition of Raphael Holinshed's *Chronicles,* an extremely influential history of England, Ireland, and Scotland that would have been well known to audiences of the time. The play is also indebted to Samuel Daniel's *The First Four Books of the Civil Wars* (1595), John Stow's *The Chronicles of England* (1580), and an earlier anonymous play entitled *The Famous Victories of Henry V* (1587), which dramatizes popular mythology about Prince Hal as an unregenerate thief and womanizer who eventually sheds his dissolute behavior and ascends to the throne as Henry V. Shakespeare makes a number of important changes in these <u>sources</u> which include reducing Hotspur's age so he and Prince Hal can meet as equals at the Battle of Shrewsbury, exaggerating Glendower's fascination with magic and witchcraft, transforming the historical Sir John Oldcastle into Sir John Falstaff and greatly expanding his role, inventing Mistress Quickly and many of the minor characters in the <u>sub-plot</u>, and emphasizing the Machiavellian politics of the age.

By altering his <u>source</u> material in this fashion, Shakespeare crafted a <u>script</u> that dramatized a number of important <u>themes</u> and <u>images</u> common to all his history plays. The result is a series of dramatic "lessons" concerning politics, power, national pride, and heroism that have helped characterize England for the past four hundred years. Chief among these concepts is "the divine right of kings," which postulated that a ruler, as "God's viceroy on earth," was anointed by the Almighty and was, therefore, due absolute obedience by his subjects. Any disruption in this heavenly plan, such as the usurpation of Richard II's throne by Henry IV, would inevitably lead to civil war and divine retribution. A parallel <u>theme</u> is the Great Chain of Being, in which all of life was envisioned by Renaissance cosmologists as a long interlaced chain extending sequentially from God and the angels to mankind, animals, plants, rocks, and minerals. Men and women, suspended precariously between the angels and animals, were thought to contain aspects of both extremes: Just as their angelic natures pulled them upward toward heaven, so too did their innate bestiality drag them down to hell. Additional important <u>themes</u> reflected in *Henry IV, Part I* include the relationship between fathers and sons; the process of maturing into adulthood; the attractiveness of rebellion; and the conflict between the traditions of feudalism, represented by the rebellious Hotspur, and the new age of nationalism, symbolized by Prince Hal. Recent scholarship has investigated the relationship between memory and rebellion, homoerotic desire between Hal and Falstaff, censorship, historical narrative, theatricality, the uses and abuses of language, and the demystification of war.

The production history of *Henry IV, Part I* has focused principally on the success of the actors playing the <u>protagonist</u>, Prince Hal, and his three <u>antagonists</u>: Falstaff, Hotspur, and Henry IV. Early sixteenth-century attempts to conflate both *Henry IV* plays into a single production gave way to a seventeenth- and eighteenth-century tradition in which Falstaff became the central character. Acted most notably by James Quinn, Stephen Kemble, James Henry Hackett, and Herbert Beerbohm Tree, the famous fat knight and his comic companions in London's underworld made the play popular with several successive generations of theatergoers. Despite a lull in its appeal throughout most of the nineteenth century, the play began a triumphant theatrical comeback in 1864 at the Drury Lane Theatre with Samuel Phelps as Falstaff. Successful later productions were mounted by Frank Benson at Stratford (1901–1906), Barry Jackson at the Birmingham Repertory Theatre (1921), and John Burrell at the Old Vic (1945), featuring Laurence Olivier as Hotspur; Royal Shakespeare Company versions by Peter Hall, John Barton, Terry Hands, and Trevor Nunn kept the play alive from the 1960s through the 1980s. Important cinematic productions of the play have included the memorable Orson Welles film *Chimes at Midnight* (1965), which is a cut-and-paste adaptation of both *Henry IV* plays, and Cedric Messina's BBC television version (1979) starring Anthony Quayle as Falstaff.

Whether on stage or screen, *Henry IV, Part I* has charmed audiences for the past four hundred years through its unique blend of British history, patriotism, low comedy, vivid characters, and political intrigue. As Prince Hal matures, surrounded on each side by temptation, so too do we as audience members grow spiritually and emotionally through identification with England's future king. Shakespeare's consummate skill as storyteller is evident in all his history plays, whose immense popularity during the Renaissance speaks volumes about his audience's desire to find its "roots" during difficult and turbulent times. In fact, many of the playwright's lessons about life are still valuable today if we listen carefully as he speaks to us from centuries ago.

Henry IV, Part I *at the Oregon Shakespearean Festival in Ashland, Oregon, with Dan Donohue as Prince Hal (1998). Photograph by David Cooper.*

King Henry the Fourth, Part I

NAMES OF THE ACTORS

The Court:

KING HENRY THE FOURTH *(formerly Henry Bolingbroke)*
HENRY, PRINCE OF WALES
PRINCE JOHN OF LANCASTER } *the king's sons*
EARL OF WESTMORELAND
SIR WALTER BLUNT

The Rebel Camp:

THOMAS PERCY, *Earl of Worcester*
HENRY PERCY, *Earl of Northumberland*
HENRY PERCY ("HOTSPUR"), *his son*
EDMUND MORTIMER, *Earl of March*
RICHARD SCROOP, *Archbishop of York*
ARCHIBALD, *Earl of Douglas*
OWEN GLENDOWER
SIR RICHARD VERNON
SIR MICHAEL, *a friend of the Archbishop of York*
LADY PERCY, *Hotspur's wife and Mortimer's sister*
LADY MORTIMER, *Glendower's daughter*

The Tavern:

SIR JOHN FALSTAFF
POINS
GADSHILL
PETO
BARDOLPH
VINTNER *of an Eastcheap Tavern*
FRANCIS, *a waiter*
MISTRESS QUICKLY, *hostess of an Eastcheap tavern*

Others:

CHAMBERLAIN *of an inn at Rochester*
OSTLER
MUGS AND ANOTHER CARRIER
TRAVELERS *on the road from Rochester to London*
SHERIFF
HOTSPUR'S SERVANT
MESSENGER FROM NORTHUMBERLAND
TWO MESSENGERS *(soldiers in Hotspur's army)*

SCENE: *England and Wales*

❦ **1.1**° *Enter the King, Lord John of Lancaster, Earl of Westmoreland, [Sir Walter Blunt,] with others.*

1.1: London, the court of Henry IV

KING

So shaken as we are, so wan with care,
Find we° a time for frighted peace to pant
And breathe short-winded accents° of new broils°
To be commenced in stronds afar remote.°
No more the thirsty entrance° of this soil
Shall daub her lips with her own children's blood:
No more shall trenching° war channel her fields,
Nor bruise her flowerets with the armèd hoofs
Of hostile paces. Those opposèd eyes
Which, like the meteors of a troubled heaven,
All of one nature, of one substance bred,
Did lately meet in the intestine° shock
And furious close° of civil butchery,
Shall now in mutual well-beseeming ranks°
March all one way and be no more opposed
Against acquaintance, kindred, and allies.
The edge of war, like an ill-sheathèd knife,
No more shall cut his° master. Therefore, friends,
As far as to the sepulcher° of Christ –
Whose soldier now, under whose blessed cross
We are impressèd° and engaged to fight –
Forthwith a power° of English shall we levy,°
Whose arms were molded in their mother's womb
To chase these pagans° in those holy fields
Over whose acres walked those blessed feet
Which fourteen hundred years ago were nailed
For our advantage° on the bitter cross.
But this our purpose now is twelve month old,
And bootless° 'tis to tell you we will go.
Therefore we meet not° now. Then let me hear
Of you, my gentle cousin Westmoreland,
What yesternight our council did decree
In forwarding this dear expedience.°

WESTMORELAND

My liege,° this haste was hot in question°
And many limits of the charge° set down
But yesternight; when all athwart° there came
A post° from Wales, loaden with° heavy° news,
Whose worst was that the noble Mortimer,
Leading the men of Herefordshire to fight
Against the irregular° and wild Glendower,
Was by the rude hands of that Welshman taken,

Find we: let us find
accents: words; **broils:** battles
stronds afar remote: distant shores (strands)
entrance: openings, chasms   5

trenching: plowing

                                                           10

intestine: internal
close: hand-to-hand combat
mutual . . . ranks: unified, orderly army
formations   15

his: its
sepulcher: tomb (i.e., Jerusalem)
                                                           20

impressèd: conscripted
power: force, army; **levy:** raise

pagans: i.e., non-Christians
                                                           25

advantage: salvation

bootless: useless
Therefore . . . not: i.e., that is not why we meet   30

dear expedience: crucial (and perhaps
expensive) undertaking
liege: lord; **hot in question:** fiercely debated
limits of the charge: items of military duties   35
all athwart: in cross purpose
post: news, a messenger; **loaden with:**
carrying; **heavy:** sad

irregular: unruly, unpredictable   40

DISCOVERING SHAKESPEARE

(1) <u>Verse</u> [1.1.1]: <u>Scan</u> the first sixteen lines of the play, assigning either <u>stressed</u> or <u>unstressed</u> marks to each of the syllables. Which lines are in regular <u>iambic pentameter</u>? Which are irregular? To what extent does the <u>rhythm</u> of the lines match the subject matter of the King's speech?

(2) <u>Exposition</u> [1.1.29]: At the end of the first twenty-nine lines of the play, the King confesses that it has been "bootless" (useless) to tell his council members about his planned trip to the holy lands (1.1.29). If this is so, why do you think these first few lines are included in the play? What is their dramatic purpose?

A thousand of his° people butcherèd;
Upon whose dead corpse there was such misuse,
Such beastly shameless transformation,°
By those Welshwomen done as may not be
Without much shame retold or spoken of.

KING
It seems then that the tidings° of this broil
Brake off ° our business for the Holy Land.

WESTMORELAND
This, matched with other,° did, my gracious lord;
For more uneven° and unwelcome news
Came from the north, and thus it did import:
On Holy-Rood Day° the gallant Hotspur there,
Young Harry Percy, and brave Archibald,
That ever-valiant and approvèd° Scot,
At Holmedon° met,
Where they did spend a sad and bloody hour;
As by discharge of their artillery
And shape of likelihood° the news was told;
For he that brought them,° in the very heat
And pride° of their contention did take horse,
Uncertain of the issue° any way.

KING
Here is a dear, a true-industrious friend,
Sir Walter Blunt, new lighted° from his horse,
Stained with the variation° of each soil
Betwixt that Holmedon and this seat° of ours,
And he hath brought us smooth° and welcome news.
The Earl of Douglas is discomfited;°
Ten thousand bold Scots, two-and-twenty knights,
Balked° in their own blood did Sir Walter see
On Holmedon's plains. Of ° prisoners, Hotspur took
Mordake Earl of Fife and eldest son
To beaten Douglas, and the Earl of Athol,
Of Murray, Angus, and Menteith.
And is not this an honorable spoil?°
A gallant prize? Ha, cousin, is it not?

WESTMORELAND
In faith,
It is a conquest for a prince to boast of.

KING
Yea, there thou mak'st me sad, and mak'st me sin
In envy that my Lord Northumberland
Should be the father to so blest a son –
A son who is the theme of honor's tongue,
Amongst a grove the very straightest plant;
Who is sweet fortune's minion° and her pride;
Whilst I, by looking on the praise of him,

---

his: i.e., Mortimer's

transformation: mutilation (Welshwomen reputedly castrated enemy bodies in battle and placed the severed genitals in the mouth of the corpse)   45

tidings: news
Brake off: interrupt, call off

other: i.e., other news
uneven: disturbing   50

Holy-Rood Day: September 14 (the Roman Catholic feast of the exaltation of the Cross)
approvèd: of proven bravery
Holmedon: Humbleton, in Northumberland (in the north of England)   55

As . . . likelihood: judging from the sounds of their weapons and the probable outcome
them: i.e., news   60
heat . . . pride: midst and height
issue: outcome

new lighted: just dismounted
variation: different kinds
this seat: i.e., London   65
smooth: pleasant
discomfited: defeated

Balked: heaped up
Of: for   70

spoil: booty, winnings   75

80

minion: favorite

DISCOVERING SHAKESPEARE

(3) Parody [1.1.66]: In 1.1.66, the King parodies Westmoreland's "uneven and unwelcome news" (1.1.50) with the phrase "smooth and welcome news." How does this linguistic echo betray antagonism between the two men?

(4) Characterization [1.1.76]: How does Westmoreland's "In faith,/It is a conquest for a prince to boast of" (1.1.76–77) contribute to his quarrel with the King?

See riot and dishonor stain the brow   85
Of my young Harry. O, that it could be proved
That some night-tripping fairy had exchanged
In cradle clothes our children where they lay,
And called mine Percy, his Plantagenet!°   **Plantagenet:** family name of royalty since
Then would I have his Harry, and he mine.   Henry II   90
But let him from my thoughts. What think you, coz,
Of this young Percy's pride? The prisoners
Which he in this adventure hath surprised°   **surprised:** captured
To his own use he keeps, and sends me word
I shall have none but Mordake Earl of Fife.   95
WESTMORELAND
  This is his uncle's teaching, this is Worcester,
  Malevolent° to you in all aspects,   **Malevolent:** ill-willed
  Which makes him° prune° himself and bristle up   **him:** i.e., Hotspur; **prune:** preen (like a
  The crest of youth against your dignity.   predatory bird, with a feathered crest)
KING
  But I have sent for him to answer this;   100
  And for this cause awhile we must neglect
  Our holy purpose to Jerusalem.
  Cousin, on Wednesday next our council we
  Will hold at Windsor. So inform the lords;
  But come yourself with speed to us again;   105
  For more is to be said and to be done
  Than out of anger can be utterèd.
WESTMORELAND
  I will, my liege.   *Exeunt.*

🐱 **1.2°** *Enter Prince of Wales and Sir John Falstaff.*   **1.2:** London, a room of the prince's

FALSTAFF   Now, Hal, what time of day is it, lad?
PRINCE   Thou art so fat-witted° with drinking of old sack,°   **fat-witted:** thick-headed; **sack:** Spanish white
  and unbuttoning thee after supper, and sleeping upon   wine
  benches° after noon, that thou hast forgotten to demand   **benches:** privy seats
  that truly which thou wouldest truly know.° What a   **to demand . . . know:** how to ask what you   5
  devil hast thou to do with the time of the day? Unless   really want to know
  hours were cups of sack, and minutes capons,° and   **capons:** poultry (gelded male birds)
  clocks the tongues of bawds,° and dials the signs of leap-   **bawds:** prostitutes
  ing houses,° and the blessed sun himself a fair hot   **leaping houses:** brothels
  wench in flame-colored taffeta,° I see no reason why   **taffeta:** a stiff, shiny material favored by prostitutes 10
  thou shouldst be so superfluous° to demand the time of   **superfluous:** out of your way
  the day.
FALSTAFF   Indeed you come near me° now, Hal; for we   **you come near me:** you're on to me, you have
  that take purses° go by° the moon and the seven stars,°   me there
  and not by Phoebus,° he, that wand'ring knight so fair.   **take purses:** rob (with a pun on thieving   15
                                                               "Percies"?); **go by:** travel by the light of, tell
                                                               time by; **seven stars:** the Pleiades
                                                               Phoebus: the sun god (compared to a traveling
                                                               knight)

DISCOVERING SHAKESPEARE
(5) Metaphor [1.1.95]: Explain both metaphors that Westmoreland uses to describe Worcester in 1.1.96–99.
(6) Language [1.2.16]: Count the number of times in this scene that Falstaff uses the phrase "when thou art a king"
(1.2.16). Why do you think he is so obsessed with Hal ascending to the throne?

And I prithee, sweet wag,° when thou art a king, as, God save thy grace – majesty I should say, for grace° thou wilt have none –

PRINCE   What, none?

FALSTAFF   No, by my troth;° not so much as will serve to be prologue° to an egg and butter.°

PRINCE   Well, how then? Come, roundly, roundly.°

FALSTAFF   Marry,° then, sweet wag, when thou art king, let not us that are squires of the night's body be called thieves of the day's beauty.° Let us be Diana's° foresters, gentlemen of the shade, minions of the moon; and let men say we be men of good government, being governed as the sea° is, by our noble and chaste mistress the moon, under whose countenance° we steal.°

PRINCE   Thou sayest well, and it holds well° too; for the fortune° of us that are the moon's men doth ebb and flow like the sea, being governed, as the sea is, by the moon. As, for proof° now: a purse of gold most resolutely° snatched on Monday night and most dissolutely° spent on Tuesday morning; got with swearing "Lay by,"° and spent with crying "Bring in";° now in as low an ebb as the foot of the ladder,° and by-and-by in as high a flow as the ridge° of the gallows.

FALSTAFF   By the Lord, thou say'st true, lad – and is not my hostess of the tavern a most sweet wench?

PRINCE   As the honey of Hybla,° my old lad of the castle° – and is not a buff jerkin° a most sweet robe of durance?°

FALSTAFF   How now, how now, mad wag? What, in thy quips° and thy quiddities?° What a plague have I to do with a buff jerkin?

PRINCE   Why, what a pox° have I to do with my hostess of the tavern?

FALSTAFF   Well, thou hast called her to a reckoning° many a time and oft.

PRINCE   Did I ever call for thee to pay thy part?

FALSTAFF   No; I'll give thee thy due, thou hast paid all there.

PRINCE   Yea, and elsewhere, so far as my coin would stretch; and where it would not, I have used my credit.

FALSTAFF   Yea, and so used it that, were it not here apparent that thou art heir apparent° – But I prithee,° sweet wag, shall there be gallows standing in England when thou art king? and resolution thus fubbed° as it is with the rusty curb° of old father antic° the law? Do not thou, when thou art king, hang a thief.

PRINCE   No; thou shalt.

FALSTAFF   Shall I? O rare! By the Lord, I'll be a brave judge.

wag: fool, scamp

grace: (term for royalty, spiritual grace, and prayer before meals)

troth: truth   20

prologue: preface; **egg and butter:** i.e., a snack

roundly: out with it

Marry: indeed

squires . . . beauty: servants of the night be   25 accused of stealing daylight by sleeping during it

Diana: goddess of the moon, the hunt (and of chastity)

sea: i.e., tides, governed by the moon

countenance: (1) face, (2) approval; **steal:**   30 (1) move stealthily, (2) rob

holds well: is a good comparison

fortune: lot, fate

for proof: to demonstrate

resolutely: firmly   35

dissolutely: wastefully

Lay by: hands up; **Bring in:** bring me (spoken to a tavern waiter)

ladder: gallows ladder

ridge: ridgepole, crossbar (from which the noose   40 is hung)

Hybla: a town in Sicily famous for its honey

old lad of the castle: (a play on Falstaff's original historical name [Oldcastle], which was reputedly changed due to the objections of his descendants)   45

buff jerkin: leather jacket worn by law officers

durance: long-wearing, imprisoning

quips: clever remarks; **quiddities:** quibbles, finicky points

pox: venereal disease   50

called . . . reckoning: (1) settled the bill, (2) arranged a sexual encounter

    55

heir apparent: next in line to the throne; **prithee:** pray thee (please)

resolution thus fubbed: brave exploits (of criminals) thwarted, frustrated   60

curb: harsh bit (as for a horse); **antic:** buffoon

DISCOVERING SHAKESPEARE

(7) Characterization [1.2.38]: When Hal mentions the "gallows" in 1.2.38, how does Falstaff respond? What clues can you find in the next ten lines that exhibit Falstaff's nervousness? Why would the word "gallows" upset him?

PRINCE   Thou judgest false already. I mean, thou shalt have the hanging of the thieves and so become a rare hangman.   65

FALSTAFF   Well, Hal, well; and in some sort it jumps with° my humor° as well as waiting in the court,° I can tell you.

PRINCE   For obtaining of suits?°   70

FALSTAFF   Yea, for obtaining of suits, whereof the hangman hath no lean wardrobe.° 'Sblood,° I am as melancholy as a gib-cat° or a lugged° bear.

PRINCE   Or an old lion, or a lover's lute.

FALSTAFF   Yea, or the drone° of a Lincolnshire bagpipe.

PRINCE   What sayest thou to a hare,° or the melancholy of Moorditch?°

FALSTAFF   Thou hast the most unsavory similes, and art indeed the most comparative,° rascaliest, sweet young prince. But, Hal, I prithee trouble me no more with vanity.° I would to God thou and I knew where a commodity° of good names were to be bought. An old lord of the council rated° me the other day in the street about you, sir, but I marked him not; and yet he talked very wisely, but I regarded him not; and yet he talked wisely, and in the street too.

PRINCE   Thou didst well, for wisdom cries out in the streets, and no man regards it.°

FALSTAFF   O, thou hast damnable iteration,° and art indeed able to corrupt a saint. Thou hast done much harm upon me, Hal – God forgive thee for it! Before I knew thee, Hal, I knew nothing; and now am I, if a man should speak truly, little better than one of the wicked. I must give over this life, and I will give it over!° By the Lord, an° I do not, I am a villain!° I'll be damned for never a king's son in Christendom.

PRINCE   Where shall we take a purse tomorrow, Jack?

FALSTAFF   Zounds,° where thou wilt, lad! I'll make one.° An I do not, call me villain and baffle me.°

PRINCE   I see a good amendment of life in thee – from praying to purse-taking.

FALSTAFF   Why, Hal, 'tis my vocation, Hal. 'Tis no sin for a man to labor in his vocation.°

Enter Poins.

Poins! Now shall we know if Gadshill° have set a match.° O, if men were to be saved by merit,° what hole in hell were hot enough for him? This is the most omnipotent° villain that ever cried "stand!"° to a true man.

---

jumps with: suits

humor: nature; **waiting in the court:** being a courtier   70

obtaining of suits: (1) acquiring the clothes of the executed, (2) achieving answers to petitions to the king

wardrobe: (the hangman was entitled to the clothes of those hanged by him); **'Sblood:** by God's blood (an oath)   75

gib-cat: tomcat (hence randy); **lugged:** chained and baited by dogs

drone: keening bass sound

hare: proverbially melancholy   80

Moorditch: an open sewer draining Moorfields, outside London walls

comparative: given to bad comparisons

vanity: worldly concerns

commodity: supply, quantity   85

rated: berated, scolded

wisdom . . . it: Proverbs 1:20-24

iteration: repetition of Scripture   90

over: up   95

an: if; **villain:** (1) evil person, (2) peasant (villein)

Zounds: by God's wounds (an oath); **make one:** be there, be of the party   100

baffle me: disgrace in public

vocation: (religious) calling

Gadshill: (1) name of highway robber, (2) place on road from London to Canterbury; **set a match:** made a plan for a robbery   105

saved by merit: earn salvation, as opposed to having it freely granted by God

omnipotent: thorough, complete

stand!: hands up!

DISCOVERING SHAKESPEARE

(8) Puns [1.2.71]: How is Hal's phrase "For obtaining of suits" (1.2.71) a <u>pun</u> on the word "hangman" in 1.2.67? (*Hint:* See Falstaff's next speech, lines 72–74, for a partial explanation.)

(9) Language [1.2.79]: In 1.2.79–89, Hal and Falstaff play a word game that we might call "Name That <u>Proverb</u>," in which Falstaff tells a fictitious story, while Hal has to discover the <u>proverb</u> that his friend has described. Explain how the well-known Renaissance <u>proverb</u> "wisdom cries out in the streets, and no man regards it" (1.2.88–89) derives from Falstaff's previous story in lines 79–87.

PRINCE   Good morrow,° Ned.

POINS   Good morrow, sweet Hal. What says Monsieur Remorse?° What says Sir John Sack and Sugar? Jack, how agrees the devil and thee about thy soul, that thou soldest him on Good Friday last for a cup of Madeira° and a cold capon's leg?

PRINCE   Sir John stands to° his word, the devil shall have his bargain; for he was never yet a breaker of proverbs. He will give the devil his due.

POINS   Then art thou damned for keeping thy word with the devil.

PRINCE   Else he had been damned for cozening° the devil.

POINS   But, my lads, my lads, tomorrow morning, by four o'clock early, at Gad's Hill! There are pilgrims° going to Canterbury with rich offerings, and traders° riding to London with fat purses. I have vizards° for you all; you have horses for yourselves. Gadshill lies° tonight in Rochester. I have bespoke° supper tomorrow night in Eastcheap.° We may do it° as secure as sleep. If you will go, I will stuff your purses full of crowns; if you will not, tarry° at home and be hanged!

FALSTAFF   Hear ye, Yedward:° if I tarry at home and go not, I'll hang you for going.

POINS   You will, chops?°

FALSTAFF   Hal, wilt thou make one?°

PRINCE   Who, I rob? I a thief? Not I, by my faith.

FALSTAFF   There's neither honesty, manhood, nor good fellowship in thee, nor thou cam'st not of the blood royal if thou darest not stand for° ten shillings.

PRINCE   Well then, once in my days I'll be a madcap.°

FALSTAFF   Why, that's well said.

PRINCE   Well, come what will, I'll tarry at home.

FALSTAFF   By the Lord, I'll be a traitor then, when thou art king.

PRINCE   I care not.

POINS   Sir John, I prithee, leave the prince and me alone. I will lay him down such reasons for this adventure that he shall go.

FALSTAFF   Well, God give thee the spirit of persuasion and him the ears of profiting,° that what thou speakest may move° and what he hears may be believed, that the true prince may (for recreation sake) prove a false thief; for the poor abuses of the time want countenance.° Farewell; you shall find me in Eastcheap.

morrow: morning

110

Remorse: regret, penitence

Madeira: sweet Spanish wine

to: by   115

cozening: tricking, cheating   120

pilgrims: people traveling to a sacred place (here, the tomb of Thomas à Becket)
traders: merchants
vizards: masks, visors   125
lies: rests, stops
bespoke: ordered
Eastcheap: unsavory district of London; **it:** i.e., the robbery
tarry: stay   130
Yedward: nickname of (Edward) Poins
chops: fat cheeks, jaws
make one: be one of the party

135

stand for: (1) fight for, (2) be good for 10 shillings (value of a "royal," a denomination of coin)
madcap: reckless one   140

145

profiting: i.e., of persuasion
move: i.e., move him

150

countenance: encouragement

DISCOVERING SHAKESPEARE

(10) Social History [1.2.111]: Why does Poins use the phrase "sack-and-sugar" (1.2.111) to describe Falstaff? (*Hint:* See 2.4.455 for a clue about why some people put sugar in "sack" or white wine.)

(11) Source Material [1.2.134]: In one possible source for Shakespeare's plot, the anonymous *The Famous Victories of Henry IV,* Prince Hal actually participates in the robbery with Falstaff. Why do you think Shakespeare has his Prince Hal refuse to be a thief when he says "Who, I rob? I a thief? Not I, by my faith" (1.2.134)?

(12) Characterization [1.2.152]: In his speech in 1.2.147–152, Falstaff impersonates a Renaissance Puritan preacher whose rhetorical flourishes are reminiscent of some modern ministers. Try giving the speech in class, while your classmates shout "amen" at appropriate times.

PRINCE Farewell, thou latter spring!° farewell, All-
hallown summer!°   *[Exit Falstaff.]*

POINS Now, my good sweet honey lord, ride with us tomorrow. I have a jest to execute that I cannot manage
alone. Falstaff, Bardolph, Peto, and Gadshill shall rob
those men that we have already waylaid; yourself and I
will not be there; and when they have the booty, if you
and I do not rob them, cut this head off from my
shoulders.

PRINCE How shall we part with them in setting forth?

POINS Why, we will set forth before or after them and
appoint them a place of meeting, wherein it is at our
pleasure to fail;° and then will they adventure° upon the
exploit themselves, which they shall have no sooner
achieved, but we'll set upon them.

PRINCE Yea, but 'tis like that they will know us by our
horses, by our habits,° and by every other appointment,°
to be ourselves.

POINS Tut! our horses they shall not see – I'll tie them in
the wood; our vizards we will change after we leave
them; and, sirrah, I have cases of buckram for the
nonce,° to immask our noted° outward garments.

PRINCE Yea, but I doubt° they will be too hard° for us.

POINS Well, for two of them, I know them to be as true-
bred cowards as ever turned back;° and for the third, if
he fight longer than he sees reason, I'll forswear° arms.
The virtue of this jest will be the incomprehensible° lies
that this same fat rogue will tell us when we meet at
supper: how thirty, at least, he fought with; what wards,°
what blows, what extremities° he endured; and in the re-
proof° of this lives the jest.

PRINCE Well, I'll go with thee. Provide us all things necessary and meet me tomorrow night in Eastcheap.
There I'll sup.° Farewell.

POINS Farewell, my lord.   *Exit.*

PRINCE
I know you all, and will awhile uphold
The unyoked humor of your idleness.°
Yet herein° will I imitate the sun,
Who doth permit the base contagious° clouds
To smother up his beauty from the world,
That, when he please again to be himself,
Being wanted,° he may be more wondered at
By breaking through the foul and ugly mists
Of vapors that did seem to strangle him.
If all the year were playing holidays,°
To sport° would be as tedious as to work;
But when they seldom come, they wished-for come,
And nothing pleaseth but rare accidents.°
So, when this loose° behavior I throw off
And pay the debt I never promisèd,

---

latter spring: overgrown youth
Allhallown summer: Indian summer   155

160

to fail: to not show up; **adventure:** undertake   165

habits: clothes; **appointment:** detail of
appearance   170

nonce: this purpose; **noted:** known
doubt: fear; **hard:** much   175

turned back: turned their backs and ran
forswear: swear to give up
incomprehensible: unbelievable, unlimited
                                                         180

wards: parries (with a sword)
extremities: hardships
reproof: disproof

185

sup: dine (eat supper)

uphold . . . idleness: pretend to go along with
the unrestrained mood of your frivolity   190
herein: in this
base contagious: low (with a suggestion of
lower rank) and poisonous
wanted: missed

195

playing holidays: vacations
sport: play

rare accidents: unusual events   200
loose: unruly, irresponsible

DISCOVERING SHAKESPEARE

(13) Plot [1.2.180]: Explain Poins' plan to embarrass Falstaff. How will it work? Why will it be funny?

By how much better than my word I am,
By so much shall I falsify men's hopes;°
And, like bright metal on a sullen° ground,
My reformation, glitt'ring o'er my fault,
Shall show more goodly° and attract more eyes
Than that which hath no foil° to set it off.
I'll so offend to° make offense a skill,°
Redeeming time° when men think least I will.   *Exit.*

By . . . hopes: I will greatly surprise
expectations   205
sullen: dark

more goodly: to better advantage
foil: contrasting background
to: as to; **skill:** clever strategy
Redeeming time: making up for lost time   210

1.3° *Enter the King, Northumberland, Worcester,*
Hotspur, Sir Walter Blunt, with others.

1.3: The court

KING
My blood hath been too cold and temperate,
Unapt to stir at these indignities,°
And you have found me,° for accordingly
You tread upon my patience; but be sure
I will from henceforth rather be myself,°
Mighty and to be feared, than my condition,°
Which hath been smooth as oil, soft as young down,°
And therefore lost that title of respect
Which the proud soul ne'er pays but to the proud.

indignities: offenses
found me: found me to be so

myself: i.e., kingly   5
condition: i.e., mild temper
down: soft goose feathers, used for filling
cushions

WORCESTER
Our house,° my sovereign liege, little deserves
The scourge° of greatness to be used on it —
And that same greatness too which our own hands
Have holp° to make so portly.°

house: family, clan   10
scourge: punishment

holp: helped; **portly:** great (Worcester implies
that his family helped Henry to his throne)

NORTHUMBERLAND
My lord —

KING
Worcester, get thee gone, for I do see
Danger and disobedience in thine eye.
O, sir, your presence is too bold and peremptory,
And majesty might never yet endure
The moody frontier° of a servant° brow.
You have good leave° to leave us: when we need
Your use and counsel, we shall send for you.
                           Exit Worcester.
You were about to speak.

                 15

moody frontier: i.e., angry brow, forehead
("frontier" literally means fortification); **servant:**
i.e., subservient   20

good leave: permission

NORTHUMBERLAND   Yea, my good lord.
Those prisoners in your highness' name demanded
Which Harry Percy here at Holmedon took,
Were, as he says, not with such strength° denied
As is deliverèd° to your majesty.
Either envy, therefore, or misprision°
Is guilty of this fault, and not my son.

strength: i.e., vehemence   25
deliverèd: reported
misprision: mistake

DISCOVERING SHAKESPEARE

(14) <u>Rhyme</u> [1.2.210]: Why does this scene end with a <u>rhyme</u>? How many other scenes in the play end in <u>couplets</u>? Can
you find any pattern in the playwright's use of <u>rhyme</u> at the ends of scenes?
(15) <u>Plot</u> [1.3.15]: After Worcester accuses the King of ingratitude in 1.3.12–13, King Henry banishes Worcester from
the court. What advantage would the King have in negotiating with Hotspur if his uncle were absent from the proceedings?

HOTSPUR

My liege, I did deny no prisoners.
But I remember, when the fight was done,   30
When I was dry with rage and extreme toil,
Breathless and faint, leaning upon my sword,
Came there a certain lord, neat and trimly dressed,
Fresh as a bridegroom, and his chin new reaped°   **new reaped:** i.e., freshly (and perhaps
Showed like a stubble land at harvest home.   fashionably) shaven   35
He was perfumèd like a milliner,°   **milliner:** one who sells fashionable gloves and
And 'twixt his finger and his thumb he held   hats
A pouncet box,° which ever and anon°   **pouncet box:** perfumed box (sniffed to mask
He gave his nose, and took't away again;   unpleasant odors); **ever and anon:** now and
Who° therewith angry, when it next came there,   again   40
Took it° in snuff; and still he smiled and talked;   **Who:** i.e., his nose
And as the soldiers bore dead bodies by,   **Took it:** (1) inhaled it, (2) took offense (at the
He called them untaught knaves, unmannerly,   removal of the perfume)
To bring a slovenly unhandsome corse°   **corse:** corpse
Betwixt the wind and his nobility.   45
With many holiday and lady° terms   **holiday and lady:** elegant and effeminate
He questioned° me, amongst the rest° demanded   **questioned:** (1) interrogated, (2) kept on talking
My prisoners in your majesty's behalf.   to; **amongst the rest:** in the middle of which
I then, all smarting with my wounds being cold,
To be so pestered with a popinjay,°   **popinjay:** parrot   50
Out of my grief and my impatience
Answered neglectingly,° I know not what –   **neglectingly:** carelessly
He should, or he should not; for he made me mad
To see him shine so brisk, and smell so sweet,
And talk so like a waiting gentlewoman   55
Of guns and drums and wounds – God save the mark!° –   **God . . . mark!:** God forbid!
And telling me the sovereignest° thing on earth   **sovereignest:** most effective
Was parmacity° for an inward bruise,   **parmacity:** spermaceti, an oily ointment derived
And that it was great pity, so it was,   from the sperm whale thought to have curative
This villainous saltpeter° should be digged   properties
Out of the bowels° of the harmless earth,   **saltpeter:** potassium nitrate, mined to make   60
Which many a good tall fellow had destroyed   gunpowder
So cowardly, and but for these vile guns,   **bowels:** inmost parts
He would himself have been a soldier.
This bald unjointed° chat of his, my lord,   **bald unjointed:** frivolous and aimless   65
I answered indirectly, as I said,
And I beseech you, let not his report
Come current° for an accusation   **Come current:** stand as, be taken for
Betwixt my love and your high majesty.
BLUNT
The circumstance considered, good my lord,   70
Whate'er Lord Harry Percy then had said
To such a person, and in such a place,

DISCOVERING SHAKESPEARE

(16) Metaphor [1.3.40]: Examine Hotspur's use of figurative language in his long speech from 1.3.29–69 by identifying the tenor and vehicle of each metaphor. How many metaphors does Hotspur use in this speech? Which seems most effective to you?

(17) Social History [1.3.70]: Why are Hotspur and the King arguing over prisoners that Hotspur has captured in the King's name? What should Hotspur have done with the prisoners? Why? What are his "provisos" concerning Mortimer (1.3.78–80)?

At such a time, with all the rest retold,
May reasonably die, and never rise
To do him wrong,° or any way impeach°   **do him wrong:** harm him; **impeach:** discredit   75
What then he said, so he unsay it now.

KING
Why, yet he doth deny° his prisoners,   **deny:** deny me
But with proviso and exception,°   **proviso and exception:** qualification, stipulations
That we at our own charge° shall ransom straight°   **charge:** expense; **straight:** immediately   80
His brother-in-law, the foolish Mortimer;
Who, on my soul, hath willfully betrayed
The lives of those that he did lead to fight
Against that great magician, damned Glendower,
Whose daughter, as we hear, that Earl of March°   **that Earl of March:** i.e., Mortimer
Hath lately married. Shall our coffers,° then,   **coffers:** treasure chests   85
Be emptied to redeem a traitor home?
Shall we buy treason? and indent with fears°   **indent with fears:** bargain with potential traitors, cowards
When they have lost and forfeited themselves?
No, on the barren mountains let him starve!
For I shall never hold that man my friend   90
Whose tongue shall ask me for one penny cost
To ransom home revolted° Mortimer.   **revolted:** rebellious

HOTSPUR
Revolted Mortimer?
He never did fall off,° my sovereign liege,   **fall off:** betray loyalty
But by the chance of war. To prove that true   95
Needs no more but one tongue for all those wounds,
Those mouthèd° wounds, which valiantly he took   **mouthèd:** gaping (as if to speak)
When on the gentle Severn's° sedgy° bank,   **Severn:** river border of England and Wales; **sedgy:** weed-covered
In single opposition hand to hand,
He did confound° the best part of an hour   **confound:** spend, use   100
In changing hardiment° with great Glendower.   **changing hardiment:** exchanging blows
Three times, they breathed,° and three times did they drink,   **breathed:** paused, rested
Upon agreement, of swift Severn's flood;
Who then, affrighted with their bloody looks,
Ran fearfully among the trembling reeds   105
And hid his° crisp head in the hollow bank,   **his:** i.e., Severn's
Bloodstainèd with these valiant combatants.
Never did bare and rotten policy°   **policy:** statecraft
Color° her working with such deadly wounds;   **Color:** disguise
Nor never could the noble Mortimer   110
Receive so many, and all willingly.
Then let not him be slandered with revolt.

KING
Thou dost belie him, Percy, thou dost belie him!°   **belie:** tell lies about
He never did encounter with° Glendower.   **encounter with:** fight with
I tell thee   115

DISCOVERING SHAKESPEARE

(18) Verse [1.3.93]: How many syllables are in Hotspur's "Revolted Mortimer" (1.3.93)? Since these two words fill a space normally occupied by ten syllables, how many <u>beats</u> are omitted from the line? What do these missing syllables imply in terms of action or emotion at this point in the play? If you were acting out the line, would you pause before or after the words to flesh out the ten syllables?

(19) Verse [1.3.115]: Examine the King's speech in 1.3.113–124, paying similar attention to the number of syllables per line. When is he most angry? How can you tell?

He durst° as well have met the devil alone
As Owen Glendower for an enemy.
Art thou not ashamed? But, sirrah, henceforth
Let me not hear you speak of Mortimer.
Send me your prisoners with the speediest means,°
Or you shall hear in such a kind from me
As will displease you. My Lord Northumberland,
We license° your departure with your son. –
Send us your prisoners, or you will hear of it.

                    Exeunt King [, Blunt, and train].

HOTSPUR
An if the devil come and roar for them,
I will not send them. I will after straight°
And tell him so; for I will ease my heart,
Albeit I make a hazard of° my head.

NORTHUMBERLAND
What, drunk with choler?° Stay, and pause awhile.
Here comes your uncle.

    Enter Worcester.

HOTSPUR   Speak of Mortimer?
Zounds, I will speak of him, and let my soul
Want mercy° if I do not join with him!
Yea, on his part I'll empty all these veins,
And shed my dear blood drop by drop in the dust,
But I will lift the downtrod Mortimer
As high in the air as this unthankful king,
As this ingrate and cankered° Bolingbroke.°

NORTHUMBERLAND
Brother, the king hath made your nephew mad.

WORCESTER
Who struck this heat up after I was gone?

HOTSPUR
He will (forsooth) have all my prisoners;
And when I urged the ransom once again
Of my wife's brother, then his cheek looked pale,
And on my face he turned an eye of death,°
Trembling even at the name of Mortimer.

WORCESTER
I cannot blame him. Was not he proclaimed
By Richard° that dead is, the next of blood?

NORTHUMBERLAND
He was; I heard the proclamation.
And then it was when the unhappy king
(Whose wrongs in us° God pardon!) did set forth
Upon his Irish expedition;°
From whence he intercepted° did return
To be deposed, and shortly murderèd.

WORCESTER
And for whose death we in the world's wide mouth
Live scandalized° and foully spoken of.

durst: would have dared

with . . . means: in the speediest fashion   120

license: sanction, permit

                                                125

will after straight: will go to him immediately

Albeit . . . hazard of: even if I jeopardize

choler: anger

                                                130

Want mercy: be damned

                                                135

ingrate and cankered: ungrateful and corrupt;
Bolingbroke: the name of Henry IV prior to his
ascent to the throne

                                                140

of death: of deadly fear

                                                145

Richard: Richard II, the previous king,
murdered by order of Henry IV

wrongs in us: harms we caused
Irish expedition: wars in Ireland   150
whence . . . intercepted: where he was called
back

scandalized: covered with scandal (for helping
to depose)

DISCOVERING SHAKESPEARE

(20) Plot [1.3.145]: Worcester argues in 1.3.145–146 that King Richard proclaimed Mortimer next in line for the throne of England. Do you think this fact has influenced King Henry's refusal to pay Mortimer's ransom? Why or why not?

HOTSPUR

But soft,° I pray you. Did King Richard then | **soft:** wait a minute | 155
Proclaim my brother° Edmund Mortimer | **brother:** brother-in-law
Heir to the crown?

NORTHUMBERLAND He did; myself did hear it.

HOTSPUR

Nay, then I cannot blame his cousin° king, | **cousin:** with a pun on "cozen," to cheat
That wished him on the barren mountains° starve. | **barren mountains:** i.e., in Wales
But shall it be that you, that set the crown | 160
Upon the head of this forgetful man,
And for his sake wear the detested blot
Of murderous subornation° – shall it be | **murderous subornation:** urging him to murder Richard II
That you a world of curses undergo,
Being the agents or base second means,° | **base second means:** agents | 165
The cords, the ladder, or the hangman rather?
O, pardon me that I descend so low
To show the line° and the predicament | **line:** connection (with the crime), station
Wherein you range° under this subtle° king! | **range:** are situated; **subtle:** devious
Shall it for shame be spoken in these days, | 170
Or fill up chronicles° in time to come, | **chronicles:** histories
That men of your nobility and power
Did gage° them both in an unjust behalf° | **gage:** pledge themselves; **behalf:** cause
(As both of you, God pardon it! have done)
To put down Richard, that sweet lovely rose, | 175
And plant this thorn, this canker,° Bolingbroke? | **canker:** (1) wild rose, (2) ulcer
And shall it in more shame be further spoken
That you are fooled, discarded, and shook off
By him for whom these shames ye underwent?
No! yet time serves wherein you may redeem | 180
Your banished honors° and restore yourselves | **redeem . . . honors:** reclaim your lost reputation
Into the good thoughts of the world again;
Revenge the jeering and disdained° contempt | **disdained:** disdainful
Of this proud king, who studies day and night
To answer° all the debt he owes to you | **answer:** repay | 185
Even with the bloody payment of your deaths.
Therefore I say –

WORCESTER   Peace, cousin, say no more;
And now I will unclasp a secret book,° | **secret book:** plan
And to your quick-conceiving discontents° | **quick-conceiving discontents:** quick-witted grievances
I'll read you matter deep and dangerous, | 190
As full of peril and adventurous spirit
As to o'erwalk a current roaring loud
On the unsteadfast footing of a spear.° | **spear:** (spear laid over rushing water)

HOTSPUR

If he fall in, good night, or° sink or swim! | **or:** whether he
Send danger from the east unto the west, | 195
So° honor cross it from the north to south, | **So:** so long as, in order that

---

DISCOVERING SHAKESPEARE

(21) <u>Themes</u> **[1.3.166]:** Hotspur's mention of the "hangman" in 1.3.166 reminds us of a similar discussion of the "gallows" earlier in the play. When did the last reference occur, and how does it differ from Hotspur's <u>allusion</u> to the same <u>theme</u>?

(22) Punctuation [1.3.187]: In most productions of the play, Worcester breaks into Hotspur's long speech in 1.3.187 with "Peace, cousin, say no more." What clues does the <u>script</u> give us that Hotspur is interrupted here?

And let them grapple. O, the blood more stirs
To rouse a lion than to start a hare!

NORTHUMBERLAND
Imagination of some great exploit
Drives him° beyond the bounds of patience.   **him:** i.e., Hotspur   200

HOTSPUR
By heaven, methinks it were an easy leap
To pluck bright honor from the pale-faced moon,°   **moon:** a symbol of chastity
Or dive into the bottom of the deep,°   **deep:** ocean
Where fathom line° could never touch the ground,   **fathom line:** a weighted line marked every six
And pluck up drownèd honor by the locks,°   feet (a fathom), used to measure water   205
So he that doth redeem her thence° might wear   **locks:** hair
Without corrival° all her dignities;   **her thence:** her (honor) from there
But out upon this half-faced fellowship!°   **corrival:** partner, rival

WORCESTER   **half-faced fellowship:** sharing of honors
He apprehends a world of figures° here,   **figures:** figures of imagination, or of speech
But not the form of what he should attend.°   **attend:** pay attention to   210
Good cousin, give me audience° for a while.   **give me audience:** let me speak; listen to me

HOTSPUR
I cry you mercy.°   **cry you mercy:** I beg your pardon

WORCESTER   Those same noble Scots
That are your prisoners –

HOTSPUR   I'll keep them all.
By God, he shall not have a Scot° of them!   **a Scot:** a small amount
No, if a Scot would save his soul, he shall not.   215
I'll keep them, by this hand!

WORCESTER   You start away°   **start away:** jump into your own train of thought
And lend no ear unto my purposes.
Those prisoners you shall keep.

HOTSPUR   Nay, I will! That's flat!
He said he would not ransom Mortimer,
Forbade my tongue to speak of Mortimer,   220
But I will find him when he lies asleep,
And in his ear I'll hollow "Mortimer."
Nay, I'll have a starling shall be taught to speak
Nothing but "Mortimer," and give it him
To keep his anger still° in motion.   **still:** ever, constantly   225

WORCESTER
Hear you, cousin, a word.

HOTSPUR
All studies° here I solemnly defy°   **studies:** pursuits, interests; **defy:** renounce
Save how to gall° and pinch this Bolingbroke;   **gall:** make sore
And that same sword-and-buckler° Prince of Wales: **buckler:** small round shield (i.e., improperly,
But that° I think his father loves him not   basely armed; princes should carry rapiers and   230
And would be glad he met with some mischance,   daggers)
I would have him poisoned with a pot of ale.   **But that:** if it weren't that

---

DISCOVERING SHAKESPEARE

(23) Paraphrase [1.3.201]: Rewrite Hotspur's brilliant speech in 1.3.201–208 in your own words. What do these lines say about Hotspur's conception of honor? How do you think his sense of honor is different from Prince Hal's? From Falstaff's? Which is most like your own view of honor? Why?

(24) Verse [1.3.218]: Find a partner in class; then read aloud the Hotspur–Worcester exchange in 1.3.212–218. How do the half-lines affect the dialogue between the two characters? Do you feel the half-lines speed up the verse or slow it down? Why?

WORCESTER
Farewell, kinsman. I will talk to you
When you are better tempered° to attend.

tempered: disposed, self-controlled

NORTHUMBERLAND
Why, what a wasp-stung and impatient fool
Art thou to break into this woman's mood,°
Tying thine ear to no tongue but thine own!

235

woman's mood: quarrelsome, shrewish, or talkative mood

HOTSPUR
Why, look you, I am whipped and scourged° with rods,
Nettled,° and stung with pismires° when I hear
Of this vile politician,° Bolingbroke.
In Richard's time – what do you call the place?
A plague upon it! it is in Gloucestershire;
'Twas where the madcap duke his uncle kept,°
His uncle York – where I first bowed my knee
Unto this king of smiles, this Bolingbroke –
'Sblood! – when you and he came back from Ravens-
purgh° –

scourged: whipped
nettled: stung as if by thorns of the nettle plant;
pismires: ants

240

politician: one given to policy or cunning statecraft
kept: dwelled

245

NORTHUMBERLAND
At Berkeley Castle.°

Ravenspurgh: a port at the mouth of River Humber in Yorkshire (now under water) where Bolingbroke reentered England upon his return from exile
Berkeley Castle: castle near Bristol

HOTSPUR
You say true.
Why, what a candy deal° of courtesy
This fawning greyhound° then did proffer me!
"Look when his infant fortune came to age,"°
And "gentle Harry Percy," and "kind cousin" –
O, the devil take such cozeners!° – God forgive me!
Good uncle, tell your tale, for I have done.

candy deal: sugary amount
fawning greyhound: flattering house pet
"Look . . . age": as soon as his promise matured

250

cozeners: cheaters

WORCESTER
Nay, if you have not, to it again.
We will stay° your leisure.

255

stay: wait for

HOTSPUR   I have done, i' faith.

WORCESTER
Then once more to your Scottish prisoners.
Deliver them up without their ransom straight,
And make the Douglas' son° your only mean°
For powers in Scotland – which, for divers° reasons
Which I shall send you written, be assured
Will easily be granted.
[To Northumberland] You, my lord,
Your son in Scotland being thus employed,
Shall secretly into the bosom° creep
Of that same noble prelate well-beloved,
The archbishop.

the Douglas' son: i.e., Mordake (Murdoch);
mean: agent
divers: several

260

bosom: confidence

265

DISCOVERING SHAKESPEARE

(25) Social History [1.3.236]: When Northumberland accuses the talkative Hotspur of breaking into a "woman's mood" (1.3.236), the comment certainly seems anti-feminist. Can you find any other examples of Renaissance sexism in this play? Where? How sexist do you feel Shakespeare himself was? On what evidence do you base your decision?

(26) Names [1.3.256]: How many times does Hotspur interrupt other people in this scene? How appropriate is his name? Can you think of any other names in the play that accurately predict their characters' behavior? Explain how each of these is a perfect fit.

HOTSPUR   Of York, is it not?
WORCESTER
  True, who bears hard°
  His brother's death at Bristow, the Lord Scroop.
  I speak not this in estimation,°
  As what I think might be, but what I know
  Is ruminated, plotted, and set down,
  And only stays but to behold the face
  Of that occasion that shall bring it on.°
HOTSPUR
  I smell it. Upon my life, it will do well.
NORTHUMBERLAND
  Before the game is afoot thou still let'st slip.°
HOTSPUR
  Why, it cannot choose but be a noble plot.
  And then the power of Scotland and of York
  To join with Mortimer, ha?
WORCESTER   And so they shall.
HOTSPUR
  In faith, it is exceedingly well aimed.
WORCESTER
  And 'tis no little reason bids us speed
  To save our heads by raising of a head;°
  For, bear ourselves as even° as we can,
  The king will always think him in our debt,
  And think we think ourselves unsatisfied,
  Till he hath found a time to pay us home.°
  And see already how he doth begin
  To make us strangers to his looks of love.
HOTSPUR
  He does, he does! We'll be revenged on him.
WORCESTER
  Cousin, farewell. No further go in this
  Than I by letters shall direct your course.
  When time is ripe, which will be suddenly,°
  I'll steal to° Glendower and Lord Mortimer,
  Where you and Douglas, and our pow'rs at once,
  As I will fashion° it, shall happily meet,
  To bear our fortunes in our own strong arms,
  Which° now we hold at much uncertainty.
NORTHUMBERLAND
  Farewell, good brother. We shall thrive, I trust.
HOTSPUR
  Uncle, adieu. O, let the hours be short
  Till fields and blows and groans applaud our sport!

                             Exeunt.

Glosses:

bears hard: resents, begrudges

in estimation: by guessing
      270

And . . . on: and waits only for the sign of its opportunity to begin

let'st slip: i.e., release the dogs of war (i.e., you're 275 ready to start fighting even before the plan is in place)

      280

a head: army, force
as even: as carefully

home: completely (i.e., kill us)   285

      290

suddenly: soon
steal to: go secretly to

fashion: plan

      295
Which: i.e., our fortunes

DISCOVERING SHAKESPEARE

(27) <u>Plot</u> [1.3.273]: Describe in your own words Worcester's plan to overthrow the King.

❧ **2.1**° *Enter a Carrier with a lantern in his hand.*

FIRST CARRIER   Heigh-ho! an it be not four by the day,°
I'll be hanged. Charles' wain° is over the new chimney,
and yet° our horse° not packed. — What, ostler!°

OSTLER   *[Within]* Anon,° anon.

FIRST CARRIER   I prithee, Tom, beat° Cut's saddle, put a
few flocks° in the point.° Poor jade° is wrung in° the withers out of all cess.°
    Enter another Carrier.

SECOND CARRIER   Peas and beans° are as dank here as a
dog,° and that is the next° way to give poor jades the
bots.° This house is turned upside down since Robin
Ostler died.

FIRST CARRIER   Poor fellow never joyed since the price of
oats rose. It was the death of him.

SECOND CARRIER   I think this be the most villainous°
house in all London road for fleas. I am stung like a
tench.°

FIRST CARRIER   Like a tench? By the mass, there is ne'er a
king christen° could be better bit than I have been since
the first cock.°

SECOND CARRIER   Why, they will allow us ne'er a jordan,°
and then we leak in your chimney,° and your chamber-
lye° breeds fleas like a loach.°

FIRST CARRIER   What, ostler! come away and be hanged!°
come away!

SECOND CARRIER   I have a gammon° of bacon and two
razes° of ginger, to be delivered as far as Charing Cross.°

FIRST CARRIER   God's body! the turkeys in my pannier°
are quite starved. What, ostler! A plague on thee! hast
thou never an eye in thy head? Canst not hear? An
'twere not as good deed as drink to break the pate on
thee,° I am a very villain. Come, and be hanged! Hast
no faith in thee?°
    Enter Gadshill.

GADSHILL   Good morrow, carriers. What's o'clock?

FIRST CARRIER   I think it be two o'clock.

GADSHILL   I prithee lend me thy lantern to see my gelding in the stable.

FIRST CARRIER   Nay, by God, soft!° I know a trick worth
two of that, i' faith.

GADSHILL   I pray thee lend me thine.

SECOND CARRIER   Ay, when? canst tell?° Lend me thy
lantern, quoth he? Marry, I'll see thee hanged first!

GADSHILL   Sirrah° carrier, what time do you mean to
come to London?

SECOND CARRIER   Time enough to go to bed with a candle, I warrant thee.° Come, neighbor Mugs, we'll call up

---

2.1: A stable yard of an inn on the road between London and Canterbury

by the day: in the morning

Charles' wain: Charlemagne's wagon, or the constellation Ursa Major (the Big Dipper)

yet: still; **horse:** horses; **ostler:** (from hostler), one who handles horses   5

Anon: in a minute; be right there

beat: soften

flocks: sheepskin tufts; **point:** pommel of the saddle, the part that covers the horse's withers (the highest point of the shoulder at the base of the neck); **jade:** nag; **wrung in:** sore at

out . . . cess: beyond all measure   10

Peas and beans: horsefeed

dank . . . dog: very wet

next: quickest

bots: worms

villainous: worst (most evil)   15

tench: a red spotted fish

king christen: Christian king

first cock: midnight

jordan: chamber pot   20

leak in your chimney: piss in the fireplace

chamber-lye: urine (lye is a caustic alkaline solution)

loach: a small freshwater fish

come away and be hanged: come here or be hanged   25

gammon: a ham, or side of bacon

razes: roots; **Charing Cross:** a market town lying between London and Westminster

pannier: saddle bags or baskets   30

to . . . thee: to hit you on the head

Hast . . . thee?: Are you completely unreliable?

soft: hold on, wait   35

Ay . . . tell: i.e., never   40

Sirrah: mister

warrant thee: guarantee you   45

DISCOVERING SHAKESPEARE

(28) Social History [2.1.1]: What was a "carrier" (2.1.1 s.d.)? What modern job is most similar to this Renaissance occupation?

(29) Characterization [2.1.33]: What kind of character is Gadshill? Why does he want to know the carriers' schedule,
and what tricks does he use to discover it?

the gentlemen. They will along° with company, for they have great charge.°   *Exeunt [Carriers].*

GADSHILL   What, ho! chamberlain!°

    Enter Chamberlain.

CHAMBERLAIN   At hand, quoth pickpurse.°

GADSHILL   That's even as fair as° "at hand, quoth the chamberlain"; for thou variest no more from picking of purses than giving direction doth from laboring: thou layest the plot how.°

CHAMBERLAIN   Good morrow, Master Gadshill. It holds current that° I told you yesternight. There's a franklin° in the Weald° of Kent hath brought three hundred marks° with him in gold. I heard him tell it to one of his company° last night at supper – a kind of auditor, one that hath abundance of charge° too, God knows what. They are up already and call for eggs and butter. They will away presently.°

GADSHILL   Sirrah, if they meet not with Saint Nicholas' clerks,° I'll give thee this neck.

CHAMBERLAIN   No, I'll none of it. I pray thee keep that for the hangman; for I know thou worshippest Saint Nicholas as truly as a man of falsehood may.

GADSHILL   What talkest thou to me of the hangman? If I hang, I'll make a fat pair of gallows; for if I hang, old Sir John hangs with me, and thou knowest he is no starveling.° Tut! there are other Troyans° that thou dream'st not of, the which for sport° sake are content to do the profession° some grace;° that would (if matters should be looked into°) for their own credit sake make all whole.° I am joined with no foot land-rakers,° no long-staff sixpenny strikers,° none of these mad mustachio purple-hued maltworms;° but with nobility and tranquillity,° burgomasters° and great oneyers,° such as can hold in,° such as will strike sooner than speak,° and speak sooner than drink, and drink sooner than pray; and yet, zounds, I lie; for they pray continually to their saint, the commonwealth, or rather, not pray to her, but prey on her, for they ride up and down on her and make her their boots.°

CHAMBERLAIN   What, the commonwealth their boots? Will she hold out water in foul way?°

GADSHILL   She will, she will! Justice hath liquored her.° We steal as in a castle,° cocksure. We have the receipt° of fernseed,° we walk invisible.

CHAMBERLAIN   Nay, by my faith, I think you are more beholding° to the night than to fernseed for your walking invisible.

---

will along: will go
great charge: valuable luggage
chamberlain: male equivalent of a chambermaid

At . . . pickpurse: I'm right beside you, as the pickpurse said   50
as fair as: to say

variest . . . how: you differ no more from a pickpurse than giving orders does from laboring—i.e., you show how it's done   55
holds current that: is still true what
franklin: a small farmer who owns his own land
Weald: forest; **marks:** coins worth 13 shillings, 4 pence
company: companions   60
abundance of charge: valuable goods
presently: at once

St. Nicholas' clerks: highwaymen (Saint Nicholas was the patron saint of thieves; clerks are monks or clerics)   65

starveling: thin man; **Troyans:** playboys, sports   70
sport: fun's
the profession: i.e., of thieving
grace: credit
looked into: investigated; **make all whole:** repair any damage   75
foot land-rakers: foot-pads, thugs
long-staff sixpenny strikers: robbers with long staffs (a peasant's weapon) who knock down victims for a small amount of money
mustachio . . . maltworms: drunkards with beer-stained mustaches   80
tranquillity: those with an easy life
burgomasters: respectable citizens (chief magistrates); **great oneyers:** great ones; **hold in:** keep secret
speak: i.e., say "hands up!"   85
boots: booty
in foul way: in a bad road
liquored her: greased her, lubricated her (bribed)
as . . . castle: in safety; **receipt:** recipe
fernseed: (thought because of its own virtual invisibility to confer it)   90
more beholding to: owe more to

DISCOVERING SHAKESPEARE

(30) Prose [2.1.54]: Which characters in this play speak <u>prose</u>, and which speak <u>verse</u>? Can you find any connection between social status and pattern of speech?

(31) Language [2.1.77]: In 2.1.77, Gadshill refers to "burgomasters and great oneyers." Textual editors, confused by the word "oneyers," have variously <u>emended</u> the term to "moneyers," "owners," "mynheers," and "oyez-ers." What is your best guess about the meaning and/or spelling of the term?

GADSHILL   Give me thy hand. Thou shalt have a share in our purchase,° as I am a true man.

purchase: takings, loot

CHAMBERLAIN   Nay, rather let me have it,° as you are a false° thief.

it: all of it
false: pretend

GADSHILL   Go to; "homo"° is a common name to all men. Bid the ostler bring my gelding out of the stable. Farewell, you muddy° knave.   [Exeunt.]

homo: Latin for "man"   95

muddy: stupid

✖ **2.2°** Enter Prince, Poins, Peto [and Bardolph].

2.2: On the road at Gad's Hill

POINS   Come, shelter, shelter!° I have removed Falstaff's horse, and he frets° like a gummed velvet.°

shelter: hide
frets: chafes; **gummed velvet:** velvet made rigid with gum and liable to wear (a horse easily spooked)

PRINCE   Stand close.°   [They step aside.]
    Enter Falstaff.

close: aside

FALSTAFF   Poins! Poins, and be hanged! Poins!

PRINCE   [Comes forward.] Peace, ye fat-kidneyed rascal! What a brawling dost thou keep!°   5

keep: make, keep up

FALSTAFF   Where's Poins, Hal?

PRINCE   He is walked up to the top of the hill; I'll go seek him.   [Steps aside.]

FALSTAFF   I am accursed to rob in that thieve's° company. The rascal hath removed my horse and tied him I know not where. If I travel but four foot by the squire° further afoot, I shall break my wind.° Well, I doubt not but to die a fair death for all this, if I scape hanging for killing that rogue. I have forsworn his company hourly any time this two-and-twenty years, and yet I am bewitched with the rogue's company. If the rascal have not given me medicines° to make me love him, I'll be hanged. It could not be else: I have drunk medicines. Poins! Hal! A plague upon you both! Bardolph! Peto! I'll starve ere I'll rob a foot further. An 'twere not as good a deed as drink to turn true° man and to leave these rogues, I am the veriest varlet° that ever chewed with a tooth. Eight yards of uneven ground is threescore and ten° miles afoot with me, and the stony-hearted villains know it well enough. A plague upon it when thieves cannot be true one to another! (They whistle.) Whew!° A plague upon you all! Give me my horse, you rogues! give me my horse and be hanged!

thieve's: thief's   10

squire: a measuring instrument
break my wind: be totally out of breath (with scatological innuendo)

15

medicines: love potions

20

true: honest
veriest varlet: truest knave, rascal

threescore and ten: seventy

25

Whew!: (Falstaff either whistles in reply, mockingly, or gasps for breath)

PRINCE   [Comes forward.] Peace, ye fat-guts! Lie down, lay thine ear close to the ground, and list° if thou canst hear the tread° of travelers.

list: listen   30
tread: footfalls

FALSTAFF   Have you any levers to lift me up again, being down? 'Sblood, I'll not bear mine own flesh so far afoot again for all the coin in thy father's exchequer.° What a plague mean ye to colt° me thus?

exchequer: treasury
colt: trick (as by a young, unruly horse)   35

PRINCE   Thou liest; thou art not colted, thou art uncolted.

FALSTAFF   I prithee, good Prince Hal, help me to my horse, good king's son.

DISCOVERING SHAKESPEARE

(32) Soliloquy [2.2.10]: Read Falstaff's soliloquy in 2.2.10–28, then list five new "truths" about him that his speech reveals.

(33) Puns [2.2.36]: Explain all the "horse" puns in 2.2.32–40.

PRINCE   Out,° ye rogue! Shall I be your ostler? **Out:** get out of here   40

FALSTAFF   Go hang thyself in thine own heir-apparent garters!° If I be ta'en, I'll peach° for this. An I have not ballads made on you all, and sung to filthy tunes, let a cup of sack be my poison. When a jest is so forward° — and afoot° too — I hate it.

garters: straps that hold up stockings (with mocking reference to the Order of the Garter, a brotherhood of knights); **peach:** squeal, inform
so forward: so out of control; so far advanced   45
afoot: i.e., not on horseback

Enter Gadshill.

GADSHILL   Stand!

FALSTAFF   So I do, against my will.

POINS   *[Comes forward.]* O, 'tis our setter;° I know his voice.

setter: person who arranged the robbery

BARDOLPH   What news?   50

GADSHILL   Case ye,° case ye! On with your vizards! There's money of the king's coming down the hill; 'tis going to the king's exchequer.

Case ye: put on your masks

FALSTAFF   You lie, ye rogue! 'Tis going to the king's tavern.

GADSHILL   There's enough to make us° all.   **make us:** make our fortunes   55

FALSTAFF   To be hanged.

PRINCE   Sirs, you four shall front° them in the narrow lane; Ned Poins and I will walk lower. If they scape from your encounter, then they light on° us.

front: confront, accost

light on: find

PETO   How many be there of them?   60

GADSHILL   Some eight or ten.

FALSTAFF   Zounds, will they not rob us?

PRINCE   What, a coward, Sir John Paunch?

FALSTAFF   Indeed, I am not John of Gaunt,° your grandfather, but yet no coward, Hal.

Gaunt: with pun on thin   65

PRINCE   Well, we leave that to the proof.

POINS   Sirrah Jack, thy horse stands behind the hedge. When thou need'st him, there thou shalt find him. Farewell and stand fast.

FALSTAFF   Now cannot I strike him,° if I should be hanged.

cannot . . . him: I can't hit him   70

PRINCE   *[Aside to Poins]* Ned, where are our disguises?

POINS   *[Aside to Prince]* Here, hard by. Stand close.

[Exeunt Prince and Poins.]

FALSTAFF   Now, my masters, happy man be his dole,° say I. Every man to his business.

happy . . . dole: may all men find happiness   75

Enter the Travelers.

TRAVELER   Come, neighbor. The boy shall lead our horses down the hill; we'll walk afoot awhile and ease our legs.

THIEVES   Stand!

TRAVELER   Jesus bless us!   80

FALSTAFF   Strike! down with them! cut the villains' throats! Ah, whoreson° caterpillars!° bacon-fed° knaves! they hate us youth. Down with them! fleece° them!

whoreson: son of a whore; **caterpillars:** parasites; **bacon-fed:** well-fed
fleece: take all they have (as in shearing a sheep)

TRAVELER   O, we are undone,° both we and ours° forever!

undone: finished; **ours:** our families

DISCOVERING SHAKESPEARE

(34) Blocking [2.2.61]: How many characters are involved in this scene? When will they enter and exit the stage? What is the largest number of characters on stage at any one time? What is the smallest?

(35) Language [2.2.82]: In Falstaff's two speeches to the travelers in 2.2.81–83 and 2.2.85–88, how many of the epithets might refer to Falstaff himself? Why?

FALSTAFF Hang ye, gorbellied° knaves, are ye undone?
No, ye fat chuffs;° I would your store were here! On, ba-
cons, on! What, ye knaves! young men must live. You
are grandjurors,° are ye? We'll jure ye, faith!

Here they rob them and bind them. Exeunt.
Enter the Prince and Poins [in buckram suits].

PRINCE The thieves have bound the true men. Now
could thou and I rob the thieves and go merrily to London, it would be argument for a week, laughter for a
month, and a good jest forever.

POINS Stand close! I hear them coming.

[They stand aside.]
Enter the Thieves again.

FALSTAFF Come, my masters, let us share,° and then to
horse before day. An the prince and Poins be not two
arrant° cowards, there's no equity° stirring. There's no
more valor in that Poins than in a wild duck.°

PRINCE Your money!   *As they are sharing, the prince and
Poins set upon them. They all run
away, and Falstaff, after a blow or
two, runs away too, leaving the
booty behind them.*

POINS Villains!

PRINCE Got with much ease. Now merrily to horse. The
thieves are all scattered, and possessed with fear so
strongly that they dare not meet each other: each takes
his fellow for an officer.° Away, good Ned. Falstaff
sweats to death and lards° the lean earth as he walks
along. Were't not for laughing, I should pity him.

POINS How the fat rogue roared!   *Exeunt.*

❧ **2.3**° *Enter Hotspur [alone], reading a letter.*

HOTSPUR "But, for mine own part, my lord, I could be
well contented to be there, in respect of° the love I bear
your house."° He could be contented – why is he not
then? In respect of the love he bears our house! He
shows in this he loves his own barn better than he loves
our house. Let me see some more. "The purpose you
undertake is dangerous" – why, that's certain! 'Tis dangerous to take a cold, to sleep, to drink; but I tell you,
my lord fool, out of this nettle,° danger, we pluck this
flower, safety. "The purpose you undertake is dangerous, the friends you have named uncertain, the time itself unsorted,° and your whole plot too light for the
counterpoise of so great an opposition."° Say you so, say
you so? I say unto you again, you are a shallow, cowardly hind,° and you lie. What a lackbrain is this! By the

gorbellied: big-bellied   85
chuffs: churls, misers

grandjurors: men of wealth, able to serve on juries

90

share: divide the loot

95

arrant: out-and-out (with pun on "errant," as in wandering or runaway); **equity:** judgment
wild duck: (notoriously timid)

100

an officer: a constable
lards: greases

105

2.3: Hotspur's castle at Warkworth

in respect of: on account of
house: family

5

out of this nettle: (nettles are a prickly plant that must be grasped firmly to be plucked safely)   10

unsorted: unsuitable
too . . . opposition: too flimsy to meet so numerous an enemy
hind: peasant, rustic   15

DISCOVERING SHAKESPEARE

(36) <u>Characterization</u> [2.2.106]: What do you think Poins means at the end of this scene when he mentions how Falstaff "roared" (2.2.106)? Do you think Falstaff "roared" in terror or in anger? How could the staging of Falstaff's "roar" help
define his character in the play?

Lord, our plot is a good plot as ever was laid; our friends true and constant: a good plot, good friends, and full of expectation;° an excellent plot, very good friends. What a frosty-spirited rogue is this! Why, my Lord of York commends the plot and the general course of the action. Zounds, an I were now by° this rascal, I could brain him with his lady's fan. Is there not my father, my uncle, and myself; Lord Edmund Mortimer, my Lord of York, and Owen Glendower? Is there not, besides, the Douglas? Have I not all their letters to meet me in arms by the ninth of the next month, and are they not some of them set forward already? What a pagan° rascal is this! an infidel!° Ha! you shall see now, in very sincerity of fear and cold heart will he to the king and lay open all our proceedings. O, I could divide myself and go to buffets° for moving° such a dish of skim milk with so honorable an action! Hang him, let him tell the king! we are prepared. I will set forward tonight.

Enter his Lady.

How now, Kate? I must leave you within these two hours.

LADY PERCY
O my good lord, why are you thus alone?
For what offense have I this fortnight° been
A banished woman from my Harry's bed?
Tell me, sweet lord, what is't that takes from thee
Thy stomach,° pleasure, and thy golden sleep?
Why dost thou bend thine eyes upon the earth,
And start° so often when thou sit'st alone?
Why hast thou lost the fresh blood in thy cheeks
And given my treasures and my rights of thee°
To thick-eyed musing° and cursed melancholy?
In thy faint slumbers I by thee have watched,
And heard thee murmur tales of iron wars,
Speak terms of manage° to thy bounding steed,
Cry "Courage! to the field!" And thou hast talked
Of sallies° and retires,° of trenches, tents,
Of palisadoes,° frontiers,° parapets,°
Of basilisks,° of cannon, culverin,°
Of prisoners' ransom, and of soldiers slain,
And all the currents of a heady° fight.
Thy spirit within thee hath been so at war,
And thus hath so bestirred thee in thy sleep,
That beads of sweat have stood upon thy brow
Like bubbles in a late-disturbèd stream,
And in thy face strange motions have appeared,
Such as we see when the men restrain their breath

expectation: promise

20

an . . . by: if I were with

25

pagan: heretic, unbeliever; **infidel:** pagan

30

divide . . . buffets: fight with myself
moving: urging

35

fortnight: two weeks

stomach: appetite   40

start: jump involuntarily

treasures . . . thee: what I treasure and have a right to own   45
thick-eyed musing: vacant, dull-sighted thought

terms of manage: horsemanship commands

sallies: attack from a defensive position; **retires:** 50
retreats

palisadoes: stakes set in the ground for defense;
frontiers: defensive position; **parapets:** walls, ramparts

basilisks: large cannon; **culverin:** long cannon   55
heady: headlong

60

DISCOVERING SHAKESPEARE

(37) Plot [2.3.20]: What final command did Worcester give Hotspur in 1.3.289–290? Can you find any evidence in this scene that Hotspur has gone against Worcester's wishes? If so, what is it?

(38) Irony [2.3.47]: Most students of the play find Kate's long speech in 2.3.36–63 ironic to some extent. Do you think she is really asking questions about her husband's behavior, or does she already know what he has planned? Why do you feel this is so?

On some great sudden hest.° O, what portents° are these?   **hest:** command; **portents:** signs, prophecies
Some heavy° business hath my lord in hand,   **heavy:** serious, sorrowful
And I must know it, else he loves me not.
HOTSPUR
  What, ho!
    [Enter a Servant.]
           Is Gilliams with the packet gone?
SERVANT
  He is, my lord, an hour ago.   65
HOTSPUR
  Hath Butler brought those horses from the sheriff?
SERVANT
  One horse, my lord, he brought even now.
HOTSPUR
  What horse? A roan,° a crop-ear, is it not?   **roan:** usually a reddish horse (with red and white
SERVANT   hairs mixed)
  It is, my lord.
HOTSPUR   That roan shall be my throne.
  Well, I will back° him straight. O Esperance!°   **back:** mount; **Esperance:** hope (Percy family   70
  Bid Butler lead him forth into the park.   *[Exit Servant.]*   motto)
LADY PERCY
  But hear you, my lord.
HOTSPUR
  What say'st thou, my lady?
LADY PERCY
  What is it carries you away?
HOTSPUR
  Why, my horse, my love – my horse!   75
LADY PERCY
  Out, you mad-headed ape!
  A weasel hath not such a deal of spleen°   **spleen:** (thought to be the source of hasty and
  As you are tossed with.° In faith,   irritable behavior)
  I'll know your business, Harry; that I will!   **tossed with:** agitatedly moved by
  I fear my brother Mortimer doth stir   80
  About° his title° and hath sent for you   **stir/About:** make a move for
  To line° his enterprise; but if you go –   **title:** claim to the throne
HOTSPUR   **line:** strengthen
  So far afoot, I shall be weary, love.
LADY PERCY
  Come, come, you paraquito,° answer me   **paraquito:** parrot
  Directly unto this question that I ask.   85
  In faith, I'll break thy little finger, Harry,
  An if thou wilt not tell me all things true.
HOTSPUR
  Away, away, you trifler!° Love? I love thee not;   **trifler:** frivolous person
  I care not for thee, Kate. This is no world
  To play with mammets° and to tilt° with lips.   **mammets:** dolls; **tilt:** joust   90

DISCOVERING SHAKESPEARE

(39) Blocking [2.3.76]: In 2.3.76–87, what kind of <u>blocking</u> or stage business might accompany and enliven the <u>dialogue</u> between these two characters?

(40) Language [2.3.90]: What is a "mammet" (2.3.90)? [*Hint:* Consult the *Oxford English Dictionary* to determine the range of meanings available in 1598.] Why do you think Hotspur uses the term here? To what extent do you find the reference sexist?

We must have bloody noses and cracked crowns,°
And pass them current° too. Gods me,° my horse!
What say'st thou, Kate? What wouldst thou have with
    me?

crowns: (1) heads, (2) 5-shilling coins
pass them current: spend them; **Gods me:**
God save me

LADY PERCY
Do you not love me? do you not indeed?
Well, do not then; for since you love me not,   95
I will not love myself. Do you not love me?
Nay, tell me if you speak in jest or no.

HOTSPUR
Come, wilt thou see me ride?
And when I am a-horseback, I will swear
I love thee infinitely. But hark you, Kate: 100
I must not have you henceforth question me
Whither I go, nor reason whereabout.
Whither I must, I must, and to conclude,
This evening must I leave you, gentle Kate.
I know you wise, but yet no farther wise   105
Than Harry Percy's wife; constant° you are,   **constant:** trustworthy
But yet a woman; and for secrecy,
No lady closer,° for I well believe   **closer:** more close-mouthed
Thou wilt not utter what thou dost not know,
And so far will I trust thee, gentle Kate.   110

LADY PERCY
How? so far?

HOTSPUR
Not an inch further. But hark you, Kate:
Whither I go, thither shall you go too;
Today will I set forth, tomorrow you.
Will this content you, Kate?   115

LADY PERCY   It must of force.°   *Exeunt.*   **of force:** of necessity

☙ **2.4**° *Enter Prince and Poins.*   **2.4:** Eastcheap tavern

PRINCE   Ned, prithee come out of that fat° room and lend   **fat:** stuffy (or filled with vats)
    me thy hand to laugh a little.

POINS   Where hast been, Hal?

PRINCE   With three or four loggerheads° amongst three or   **loggerheads:** blockheads
    fourscore hogsheads.° I have sounded° the very bass-°   **hogsheads:** barrels; **sounded:** caused to sound   5
    string of humility. Sirrah, I am sworn brother to a leash° (i.e., strummed), measured the depths of; **bass:**
    of drawers° and can call them all by their christen°   with pun on "base," lowborn
    names, as Tom, Dick, and Francis. They take it already   **leash:** three
    upon their salvation° that, though I be but Prince of   **drawers:** waiters; **christen:** Christian (i.e., first,
    Wales, yet I am the king of courtesy, and tell me flatly I as opposed to family name)
    am no proud Jack like Falstaff, but a Corinthian,° a lad **upon their salvation:** as they hope to be   10
    of mettle,° a good boy (by the Lord, so they call me!),   eternally saved (as in swearing upon)
    and when I am King of England I shall command all   **Corinthian:** good sport
                                                             mettle: courage

---

DISCOVERING SHAKESPEARE

(41) Biblical Reference [2.3.113]: Hotspur's "Whither I go, thither shall you go too" (2.3.113) is clearly an echo of the promise Ruth makes to Naomi in Ruth 1:16. What is the effect of a Biblical <u>allusion</u> at precisely this point in the play? What insight does the reference give us about Hotspur and his relationship with Kate?

the good lads in Eastcheap. They call drinking deep, dyeing scarlet;° and when you breathe° in your watering,° they cry "hem!" and bid you play it off.° To conclude, I am so good a proficient° in one quarter of an hour that I can drink with any tinker° in his own language during my life. I tell thee, Ned, thou hast lost much honor that thou wert not with me in this action. But, sweet Ned – to sweeten which name of Ned, I give thee this penny-worth of sugar, clapped even now into my hand by an under-skinker,° one that never spake other English in his life than "Eight shillings and sixpence," and "You are welcome," with this shrill addition, "Anon,° anon, sir! Score° a pint of bastard° in the Half-moon,"° or so – but, Ned, to drive away the time till Falstaff come, I prithee° do thou stand in some by-room while I ques-tion my puny° drawer to what end he gave me the sugar; and do thou never leave calling "Francis!" that his tale to me may be nothing but "Anon!" Step aside, and I'll show thee a precedent.°

POINS Francis!

PRINCE Thou art perfect.

POINS Francis! *[Exit Poins.]*

Enter [Francis, a] Drawer.

FRANCIS Anon, anon, sir. – Look down into the Pom-garnet,° Ralph.

PRINCE Come hither, Francis.

FRANCIS My lord?

PRINCE How long hast thou to serve,° Francis?

FRANCIS Forsooth, five years, and as much as to –

POINS *[Within]* Francis!

FRANCIS Anon, anon, sir.

PRINCE Five year! by'r Lady,° a long lease for the clinking of pewter. But, Francis, darest thou be so valiant as to play the coward with thy indenture° and show it a fair pair of heels and run from it?

FRANCIS O Lord, sir, I'll be sworn upon all the books° in England I could find in my heart –

POINS *[Within]* Francis!

FRANCIS Anon, sir.

PRINCE How old art thou, Francis?

FRANCIS Let me see: about Michaelmas° next I shall be –

POINS *[Within]* Francis!

FRANCIS Anon, sir. Pray stay a little,° my lord.

PRINCE Nay, but hark you, Francis. For the sugar thou gavest me – 'twas a pennyworth, was't not?

FRANCIS O Lord! I would it had been two!

scarlet: dyes were best fixed with drunkards' urine (i.e., of high alcohol content); **breathe:** pause; **watering:** drinking   15

play it off: drink up

a proficient: an expert

tinker: vagabond, Gypsy   20

under-skinker: bartender's assistant

Anon: Coming! Be right there   25
Score: charge; **bastard:** sweet Spanish wine; **Half-moon:** a room in the tavern

prithee: pray thee (please)
puny: novice, subordinate

30

precedent: an example, something worth following

35

Pomgarnet: Pomegranate, a room in the tavern

serve: i.e., on his apprenticeship contract   40

by'r Lady: by our Lady

45

indenture: contract

books: Bibles

50

Michaelmas: September 29

stay a little: wait a moment   55

DISCOVERING SHAKESPEARE

(42) Pun [2.4.14]: Why would all the "good lads in Eastcheap" call "drinking deep, dyeing scarlet" (2.4.14–15)? How is the process of drinking alcohol associated with the color scarlet?

(43) Paraphrase [2.4.25]: Paraphrase the line "Score a pint of bastard in the Half-moon" (2.4.26); then explain how the line illuminates Renaissance pub customs.

(44) Staging [2.4.51]: What response from the audience do you think this scene between Hal and Poins (2.4.33–76) would bring forth in a theatrical production of the play? How effective is it at this particular moment in the script?

PRINCE   I will give thee for it a thousand pound. Ask me
when thou wilt, and thou shalt have it.   60

POINS   *[Within]* Francis!

FRANCIS   Anon, anon.

PRINCE   Anon, Francis? No, Francis; but tomorrow,
Francis; or, Francis, a Thursday; or indeed, Francis,
when thou wilt. But, Francis –   65

FRANCIS   My lord?

PRINCE   Wilt thou rob° this leathern-jerkin,° crystal-button,
not-pated, agate-ring, puke-stocking, caddis-garter,
smooth-tongue, Spanish-pouch° –

FRANCIS   O Lord, sir, who do you mean?

PRINCE   Why then, your brown bastard° is your only
drink; for look you, Francis, your white canvas doublet
will sully.° In Barbary, sir, it° cannot come to so much.

FRANCIS   What, sir?

POINS   *[Within]* Francis!

PRINCE   Away, you rogue! Dost thou not hear them call?
Here they both call him. The Drawer stands amazed,
not knowing which way to go.
Enter Vintner.

VINTNER   What, stand'st thou still, and hear'st such a
calling? Look to the guests within. *[Exit Francis.]* My
lord, old Sir John, with half-a-dozen more, are at the
door. Shall I let them in?   80

PRINCE   Let them alone awhile, and then open the door.
[Exit Vintner.] Poins!

POINS   *[Within]* Anon, anon, sir.
Enter Poins.

PRINCE   Sirrah, Falstaff and the rest of the thieves are at
the door. Shall we be merry?

POINS   As merry as crickets, my lad. But hark ye; what   85
cunning match° have you made with this jest of the
drawer? Come, what's the issue?°

PRINCE   I am now of all humors° that have showed themselves humors since the old days of goodman Adam to
the pupil age° of this present twelve o'clock at midnight.°   90
[Enter Francis.]
What's o'clock, Francis?

FRANCIS   Anon, anon, sir.   *[Exit.]*

PRINCE   That ever this fellow should have fewer words
than a parrot, and yet the son of a woman! His industry   95
is upstairs and downstairs, his eloquence the parcel of a
reckoning.° I am not yet of Percy's mind, the Hotspur of
the North; he that kills me° some six or seven dozen of
Scots at a breakfast, washes his hands, and says to his

rob: i.e., by running away; **leathern-jerkin:** close-fitting sleeveless leather jacket

not-pated . . . pouch: crop-haired, seal-ring-wearing, woolen-stockinged, worsted-gartered, smooth-talking, Spanish-leather-pouch-wearing   70

brown bastard: sweet Spanish wine

your . . . sully: you might as well remain a waiter

it: sugar, imported from Barbary   75

cunning match: sly game

issue: outcome, punch line

of all humors: in any moods

pupil age: i.e., most recent, youngest

since . . . midnight: since the days of farmer Adam to now (i.e., the whole history of the world)

parcel of a reckoning: items of a bill

kills me: kills

DISCOVERING SHAKESPEARE

(45) Plot [2.4.79]: What is the dramatic effect of delaying Falstaff's entrance till after the Hotspur–Kate scene in 2.3 and the first 107 lines of 2.4? How would the play have been different if Falstaff had confronted Hal immediately after the end of 2.2?

(46) Characterization [2.4.94]: In his brief speech in 2.4.94–106, why does Hal move logically into a discussion about Hotspur after he ridicules Francis, who has a vocabulary only slightly larger than that of a parrot? In Hal's mind, how are Francis and Hotspur similar?

wife, "Fie upon this quiet life! I want work." "O my
sweet Harry," says she, "how many hast thou killed
today?" "Give my roan horse a drench,"° says he, and
answers "Some fourteen," an hour after, "a trifle, a trifle." I prithee call in Falstaff. I'll play Percy, and that
damned brawn° shall play Dame Mortimer his wife.
"Rivo!"° says the drunkard. Call in ribs,° call in tallow.°

*Enter Falstaff [, Gadshill, Bardolph, and Peto; Francis
follows with wine].*

POINS   Welcome, Jack. Where hast thou been?

FALSTAFF   A plague of all cowards, I say, and a vengeance
too! Marry and amen! Give me a cup of sack, boy. Ere I
lead this life long, I'll sew netherstocks,° and mend them
and foot° them too. A plague of all cowards! Give me a
cup of sack, rogue. Is there no virtue extant?°

He drinketh.

PRINCE   Didst thou never see Titan° kiss a dish of butter (pitiful-hearted Titan!) that° melted at the sweet
tale of the sun's? If thou didst, then behold that compound.°

FALSTAFF   You rogue, here's lime° in this sack too! There is
nothing but roguery to be found in villainous man. Yet
a coward is worse than a cup of sack with lime in it — a
villainous coward! Go thy ways, old Jack, die when
thou wilt; if manhood, good manhood, be not forgot
upon the face of the earth, then am I a shotten herring.°
There lives not three good men unhanged in England;
and one of them is fat, and grows old. God help the
while!° A bad world, I say. I would I were a weaver;° I
could sing psalms or anything. A plague of all cowards,
I say still!

PRINCE   How now, woolsack? What mutter you?

FALSTAFF   A king's son! If I do not beat thee out of thy
kingdom with a dagger of lath° and drive all thy subjects
afore thee like a flock of wild geese, I'll never wear hair
on my face more. You Prince of Wales?

PRINCE   Why, you whoreson round man, what's the
matter?

FALSTAFF   Are not you a coward? Answer me to that —
and Poins there?

POINS   Zounds, ye fat paunch, an° ye call me coward, by
the Lord, I'll stab thee.

FALSTAFF   I call thee coward? I'll see thee damned ere I
call thee coward, but I would give a thousand pound I
could run as fast as thou canst. You are straight enough
in the shoulders; you care not who sees your back. Call
you that backing of your friends? A plague upon such

100

drench: drink

brawn: fat boar   105
Rivo!: (drinking cry, of uncertain meaning);
ribs: rib roast; **tallow:** grease

sew netherstocks: make stockings (a menial   110
occupation)
foot: make a new foot for
extant: still living

Titan: the sun
that: i.e., the butter

115

compound: sweating (melting) lump of butter
lime: caustic powder (calcium carbonate) added
to wine to make it sparkle

120

shotten herring: herring that has shed its eggs
and is thus thin, deflated

while: these times; **weaver:** (weavers were often   125
immigrants, known for Protestant devotion; with
some allusion to Falstaff's historical prototype?)

lath: thin strip of wood (the weapon of the vice   130
figure in a morality play)

135

an: if

140

DISCOVERING SHAKESPEARE

(47) Social History [2.4.117]: Why does Falstaff complain that the innkeeper has put lime (calcium oxide, also called
"quicklime") in his "sack" (wine)? What was the purpose of adding lime to wine?

(48) Stage History [2.4.130]: In 2.4.130, Falstaff compares himself to the Vice character from old morality plays who
carried a "dagger of lath" (i.e., wooden dagger). Spend some time researching the Vice character in medieval drama. [*Hint:*
See Bernard Spivack's *Shakespeare and the Allegory of Evil.*]

backing! Give me them that will face me. Give me a
cup of sack. I am a rogue if I drunk today.

PRINCE O villain! thy lips are scarce wiped since thou
drunk'st last. 145

FALSTAFF All is one° for that. *(He drinketh.)* A plague of
all cowards, still say I.

PRINCE What's the matter?

FALSTAFF What's the matter? There be four of us here
have ta'en a thousand pound this day morning. 150

PRINCE Where is it, Jack? where is it?

FALSTAFF Where is it? Taken from us it is. A hundred
upon poor four of us!

PRINCE What, a hundred, man? 155

FALSTAFF I am a rogue if I were not at half-sword° with a
dozen of them two hours together. I have scaped by
miracle. I am eight times thrust through the doublet,°
four through the hose°; my buckler° cut through and
through; my sword hacked like a handsaw – ecce 160
signum!° I never dealt° better since I was a man. All
would not do.° A plague of all cowards! Let them speak.
If they speak more or less than truth, they are villains
and the sons of darkness. 165

PRINCE Speak, sirs. How was it?

GADSHILL We four set upon some dozen –

FALSTAFF Sixteen at least, my lord.

GADSHILL And bound them.

PETO No, no, they were not bound. 170

FALSTAFF You rogue, they were bound, every man of
them, or I am a Jew else – an Ebrew° Jew.

GADSHILL As we were sharing, some six or seven fresh
men set upon us –

FALSTAFF And unbound the rest, and then come in the 175
other.°

PRINCE What, fought you with them all?

FALSTAFF All? I know not what you call all, but if I
fought not with fifty of them, I am a bunch of radish! If
there were not two or three and fifty upon poor old 180
Jack, then am I no two-legged creature.

PRINCE Pray God you have not murdered some of them.

FALSTAFF Nay, that's past praying for. I have peppered°
two of them. Two I am sure I have paid, two rogues in
buckram suits. I tell thee what, Hal – if I tell thee a lie, 185
spit in my face, call me horse.° Thou knowest my old
ward.° Here I lay,° and thus I bore my point.° Four rogues
in buckram let drive° at me.

PRINCE What, four? Thou saidst but two even now.

FALSTAFF Four, Hal. I told thee four. 190

POINS Ay, ay, he said four.

All is one: no matter

at half-sword: fighting at close quarters

doublet: a jacketlike garment
hose: close-fitting pants; **buckler:** shield

ecce signum: behold the proof (a term from the
liturgy); **dealt:** i.e., blows
All . . . do: but to no avail

Ebrew: Hebrew (a Christian term for the
faithless)

other: others

peppered: killed, made it hot for

horse: term of contempt
ward: defensive stance; **lay:** stood; **point:**
sword point
let drive: came at

DISCOVERING SHAKESPEARE

(49) Repetition [2.4.154]: What is the <u>rhetorical</u> purpose of all the repetition in 2.4.151–215?

(50) Imagery [2.4.179]: In 2.4.179, Falstaff calls himself "a bunch of radish," which is surely an effort to make himself
look thinner and more valiant in Hal's eyes. What other "skinny" <u>images</u> can you find in this scene? [*Hint:* Look especially
at 2.4.235–238 and later in the scene.]

FALSTAFF These four came all afront° and mainly thrust at me. I made me° no more ado but took all their seven points in my target,° thus.

PRINCE Seven? Why, there were but four even now.

FALSTAFF In buckram?

POINS Ay, four, in buckram suits.

FALSTAFF Seven, by these hilts, or I am a villain else.

PRINCE [Aside to Poins] Prithee let him alone. We shall have more anon.

FALSTAFF Dost thou hear me, Hal?

PRINCE Ay, and mark° thee too, Jack.

FALSTAFF Do so, for it is worth the list'ning to. These nine in buckram that I told thee of –

PRINCE So, two more already.

FALSTAFF Their points° being broken –

POINS Down fell their hose.

FALSTAFF Began to give me ground; but I followed me° close, came in,° foot and hand, and with a thought° seven of the eleven I paid.°

PRINCE O monstrous! Eleven buckram men grown out of two!

FALSTAFF But, as the devil would have it, three misbegotten knaves in Kendal° green came at my back and let drive at me; for it was so dark, Hal, that thou couldst not see thy hand.

PRINCE These lies are like their father that begets them – gross as a mountain, open, palpable.° Why, thou claybrained guts, thou knotty-pated° fool, thou whoreson obscene greasy tallow-keech° –

FALSTAFF What, art thou mad? art thou mad? Is not the truth the truth?

PRINCE Why, how couldst thou know these men in Kendal green when it was so dark thou couldst not see thy hand? Come, tell us your reason. What sayest thou to this?

POINS Come, your reason, Jack, your reason.

FALSTAFF What, upon compulsion? Zounds, an I were at the strappado° or all the racks° in the world, I would not tell you on compulsion. Give you a reason on compulsion? If reasons° were as plentiful as blackberries, I would give no reason upon compulsion, I.

PRINCE I'll be no longer guilty of this sin; this sanguine° coward, this bed-presser, this horseback-breaker, this huge hill of flesh –

FALSTAFF 'Sblood, you starveling, you eel-skin, you dried neat's°-tongue, you bull's pizzle,° you stockfish° – O

afront: abreast
made me: i.e., made
target: shield

195

200

mark: (1) pay attention to, (2) keep count

points: (1) sword points, (2) laces that hold up hose to doublet
followed me: followed
came in: advanced; **with a thought:** as quick as a thought
paid: beat

205

210

Kendal: a famous textile town

215

palpable: easily perceptible
knotty-pated: thick-headed
tallow-keech: lump of tallow

220

225

strappado: a torture in which the victim was hoisted by a rope and let drop its length; **racks:** a torture instrument upon which the body is stretched
reasons: (pun on "raisins")
sanguine: ruddy, confident

230

235

neat's: ox's; **pizzle:** penis; **stockfish:** dried cod

DISCOVERING SHAKESPEARE

(51) Hyperbole [2.4.201]: Count the number of assailants Falstaff claims to have fought with after the robbery. How do two men grow into eleven?

(52) Plot [2.4.213]: In his tall tale about the robbery, why does Falstaff specify the exact shade of green worn by his assailants: "three misbegotten knaves in Kendal green came at my back" (2.4.213)? How does this one precise detail force Hal to confront Falstaff about his story?

for breath to utter what is like thee! – you tailor's yard,° you sheath, you bowcase, you vile standing tuck!°

yard: yardstick
standing tuck: rigid rapier (which was supposed to be flexible)

PRINCE   Well, breathe awhile, and then to it again; and when thou hast tired thyself in base comparisons, hear me speak but this.

POINS   Mark, Jack.

PRINCE   We two saw you four set on four, and bound them and were masters of their wealth. Mark now how a plain tale shall put you down. Then did we two set on you four and, with a word,° outfaced° you from your prize, and have it; yea, and can show it you here in the house. And, Falstaff, you carried your guts away as nimbly, with as quick dexterity, and roared for mercy, and still run and roared, as ever I heard bullcalf. What a slave art thou to hack thy sword as thou hast done, and then say it was in fight! What trick, what device, what starting hole° canst thou now find out to hide thee from this open and apparent shame?

with a word: in short; **outfaced:** frightened

starting hole: subterfuge, (literally) refuge for hunted animals

POINS   Come, let's hear, Jack. What trick hast thou now?

FALSTAFF   By the Lord, I knew ye as well as he that made ye. Why, hear you, my masters. Was it for me to kill the heir apparent?° Should I turn upon the true prince? Why, thou knowest I am as valiant as Hercules,° but beware° instinct. The lion will not touch the true prince. Instinct is a great matter. I was now a coward on instinct. I shall think the better of myself, and thee, during my life – I for a valiant lion, and thou for a true prince. But, by the Lord, lads, I am glad you have the money. Hostess, clap to the doors. Watch tonight, pray tomorrow.° Gallants, lads, boys, hearts of gold, all the titles of good fellowship come to you! What, shall we be merry? Shall we have a play extempore?°

heir apparent: next in line to the throne
Hercules: legendary strong man
beware: watch out for

Watch . . . tomorrow: see Matthew 26:41

play extempore: an improvised play
argument: plot

PRINCE   Content – and the argument° shall be thy running away.

FALSTAFF   Ah, no more of that, Hal, an thou lovest me!

Enter Hostess.

HOSTESS   O Jesu, my lord the prince!

PRINCE   How now, my lady the hostess? What say'st thou to me?

HOSTESS   Marry, my lord, there is a noble man of the court at door would speak with you. He says he comes from your father.

PRINCE   Give him as much as will make him a royal man,° and send him back again to my mother.

a royal man: a royal was a coin worth 10 shillings; a noble, 6 shillings, 8 pence

FALSTAFF   What manner of man is he?

HOSTESS   An old man.

FALSTAFF   What doth gravity° out of his bed at midnight? Shall I give him his answer?

gravity: age, wisdom

240

245

250

255

260

265

270

275

280

DISCOVERING SHAKESPEARE

(53) Staging [2.4.249]: How would Hal's revelation in 2.4.249 that Falstaff "roared for mercy" help a director in staging the fight scene at the end of 2.2?

(54) Language [2.4.261]: Exactly what does Falstaff mean when he says he was "a coward on instinct" (2.4.261–262)? How does this statement help him save face with Hal and the others?

PRINCE   Prithee do, Jack.

FALSTAFF   Faith, and I'll send him packing.   *Exit.*   285

PRINCE   Now, sirs. By'r Lady, you fought fair;° so did you, Peto; so did you, Bardolph. You are lions too, you ran away upon instinct, you will not touch the true prince; no – fie!

BARDOLPH   Faith, I ran when I saw others run.   290

PRINCE   Tell me now in earnest, how came Falstaff's sword so hacked?

PETO   Why, he hacked it with his dagger, and said he would swear truth out of England but° he would make you believe it was done in fight, and persuaded us to do   295
the like.

BARDOLPH   Yea, and to tickle our noses with speargrass to make them bleed, and then to beslubber our garments with it and swear it was the blood of true men. I did that° I did not this seven year before – I blushed to   300
hear his monstrous devices.°

PRINCE   O villain! thou stolest a cup of sack eighteen years ago and wert taken with the manner,° and ever since thou hast blushed extempore.° Thou hadst fire° and   305
sword on thy side, and yet thou ran'st away. What instinct hadst thou for it?

BARDOLPH   My lord, do you see these meteors? Do you behold these exhalations?°

PRINCE   I do.

BARDOLPH   What think you they portend?   310

PRINCE   Hot livers and cold purses.°

BARDOLPH   Choler,° my lord, if rightly taken.°

PRINCE   No, if rightly taken, halter.°

Enter Falstaff.

Here comes lean Jack; here comes bare-bone. How now, my sweet creature of bombast?° How long is't ago,   315
Jack, since thou sawest thine own knee?

FALSTAFF   My own knee? When I was about thy years, Hal, I was not an eagle's talent° in the waist; I could have crept into any alderman's thumb-ring. A plague of   320
sighing and grief! It blows a man up like a bladder. There's villainous news abroad. Here was Sir John Bracy from your father. You must to the court in the morning. That same mad fellow of the north, Percy, and he of Wales that gave Amamon° the bastinado,° and   325
made Lucifer cuckold,° and swore the devil his true liegeman° upon the cross of a Welsh hook° – what a plague call you him?

POINS   Owen Glendower.

FALSTAFF   Owen, Owen – the same; and his son-in-law   330
Mortimer, and old Northumberland, and that sprightly

fair: well

but: if he didn't

that: what
devices: tricks

taken . . . manner: caught with the goods
extempore: without preparation; **fire:** i.e., Bardolph's nose, red from drinking

exhalations: meteors (i.e., red spots on Bardolph's face)

Hot livers and cold purses: i.e., drunkenness and poverty
Choler: anger, aggression; **taken:** understood
halter: i.e., collar (a play on choler), or hangman's noose
bombast: (1) cotton padding, (2) outrageous speech

talent: talon

Amamon: name of a demon; **bastinado:** beating on soles of the feet
made Lucifer cuckold: gave the devil his horns (a sign of cuckoldry)
liegeman: sworn subject; **Welsh hook:** a curved pike lacking the cross handle of a sword upon which oaths were usually sworn

---

DISCOVERING SHAKESPEARE

(55) Staging [2.4.285]: What is the purpose of having Falstaff leave the <u>stage</u> to talk with the nobleman in 2.4.285? What information do Hal and Poins learn from Bardolph while Falstaff is off-stage?

(56) Puns [2.4.310]: Explain Hal's triple pun on Bardolph's fiery complexion in 2.4.307–313. That is, each of the underlined words in the phrase "No, if <u>rightly taken, halter</u>" (2.4.313) has a double meaning. What are the meanings of these words?

Scot of Scots, Douglas, that runs a-horseback up a hill perpendicular –

PRINCE   He that rides at high speed and with his pistol kills a sparrow flying.

FALSTAFF   You have hit it.°   **hit it:** described it   335

PRINCE   So did he never the sparrow.

FALSTAFF   Well, that rascal hath good metal° in him; he will not run.   **metal:** mettle, temperament, courage

PRINCE   Why, what a rascal art thou then, to praise him so for running!   340

FALSTAFF   A-horseback, ye cuckoo! but afoot he will not budge a foot.

PRINCE   Yes, Jack, upon instinct.

FALSTAFF   I grant ye, upon instinct. Well, he is there too, and one Mordake,° and a thousand bluecaps° more. Worcester is stol'n away tonight; thy father's beard is turned white with the news; you may buy land now as cheap as stinking mack'rel.   **Mordake:** i.e., Murdoch; **bluecaps:** Scottish soldiers   345

PRINCE   Why then, it is like,° if there come a hot June, and this civil buffeting° hold, we shall buy maidenheads° as they buy hobnails,° by the hundreds.   **like:** likely / **buffeting:** war, fighting; **maidenheads:** hymens, or virginities, a spoil of war / **hobnails:** a short broad-headed nail sold in bulk   350

FALSTAFF   By the mass, lad, thou sayest true; it is like we shall have good trading that way.° But tell me, Hal, art not thou horrible afeard? Thou being heir apparent, could the world pick thee out three such enemies again as that fiend Douglas, that spirit Percy, and that devil Glendower? Art thou not horribly afraid? Doth not thy blood thrill° at it?   **good . . . way:** i.e., lots of women   355 / **thrill:** run cold

PRINCE   Not a whit, i' faith. I lack some of thy instinct.

FALSTAFF   Well, thou wilt be horribly chid° tomorrow when thou comest to thy father. If thou love me, practice an answer.   **chid:** reprimanded   360

PRINCE   Do thou stand for° my father and examine me upon the particulars of my life.   **stand for:** take the place of

FALSTAFF   Shall I? Content. This chair shall be my state,° this dagger my scepter, and this cushion my crown.   **state:** throne   365

PRINCE   Thy state is taken for° a joined-stool,° thy golden scepter for a leaden dagger, and thy precious rich crown° for a pitiful bald crown.   **taken for:** understood to be; **joined-stool:** a stool made of fitted parts (to "take someone for a joint stool" is an apology for overlooking them) / **crown:** (1) head, (2) coin   370

FALSTAFF   Well, an° the fire of grace be not quite out of thee, now shalt thou be moved. Give me a cup of sack to make my eyes look red, that it may be thought I have wept; for I must speak in passion, and I will do it in King Cambyses' vein.°   **an:** if / **King Cambyses' vein:** a ranting, an outdated theatrical style (from Thomas Preston's 1569 play)   375

PRINCE   Well, here is my leg.°   **leg:** bow

FALSTAFF   And here is my speech. Stand aside, nobility.

HOSTESS   O Jesu, this is excellent sport, i' faith!

FALSTAFF

Weep not, sweet queen, for trickling tears are vain.

DISCOVERING SHAKESPEARE

(57) Puns [2.4.337]: Explain Falstaff's pun on the word "mettle" in 2.4.337.

(58) Characterization [2.4.359]: Why is Hal's line "I lack some of thy instinct" (2.4.359) a criticism of Falstaff? What event is Hal referring to in this statement?

HOSTESS   O, the Father, how he holds his countenance!°

FALSTAFF

For God's sake, lords, convey° my tristful° queen! **convey:** escort away; **tristful:** sad   380
For tears do stop° the floodgates of her eyes.

HOSTESS   O Jesu, he doth it as like one of these harlotry°
players as ever I see!

FALSTAFF   Peace, good pintpot.° Peace, good ticklebrain.° — Harry, I do not only marvel where thou spend-
est thy time, but also how thou art accompanied. For
though the camomile,° the more it is trodden on, the
faster it grows, yet youth, the more it is wasted, the
sooner it wears. That thou art my son I have partly thy
mother's word, partly my own opinion, but chiefly a
villainous trick° of thine eye and a foolish hanging of
thy nether lip that doth warrant° me. If then thou be
son to me, here lies the point: why, being son to me, art
thou so pointed at? Shall the blessed sun of heaven
prove a micher° and eat blackberries? A question not to
be asked. Shall the son of England prove a thief and
take purses?° A question to be asked. There is a thing,
Harry, which thou hast often heard of, and it is known
to many in our land by the name of pitch. This pitch,°
as ancient writers do report, doth defile; so doth the
company thou keepest. For, Harry, now I do not speak
to thee in drink, but in tears; not in pleasure, but in
passion; not in words only, but in woes also. And yet
there is a virtuous man whom I have often noted in thy
company, but I know not his name.

PRINCE   What manner of man, an it like° your majesty?

FALSTAFF   A goodly° portly° man, i' faith, and a corpulent;°
of a cheerful look, a pleasing eye, and a most noble carriage;° and, as I think, his age some fifty, or, by'r Lady,
inclining to threescore;° and now I remember me, his
name is Falstaff. If that man should be lewdly given,° he
deceiveth me; for, Harry, I see° virtue in his looks. If
then the tree may be known by the fruit, as the fruit by
the tree, then, peremptorily° I speak it, there is virtue in
that Falstaff. Him keep with, the rest banish. And tell
me now, thou naughty varlet,° tell me where hast thou
been this month?

PRINCE   Dost thou speak like a king? Do thou stand for
me, and I'll play my father.

FALSTAFF   Depose me?° If thou dost it half so gravely, so
majestically, both in word and matter, hang me up by
the heels for a rabbit-sucker° or a poulter's° hare.

---

holds his countenance: keeps a straight face

stop: fill, overflow

harlotry: scurvy, vagabond

pintpot, ticklebrain: (nicknames based on the hostess's occupation)   385

camomile: an herb

390

trick: trait
warrant: assure

micher: truant   395

purses: (perhaps with a pun on "Percies")

pitch: a tar by-product (a reference to a proverb from Ecclesiastes 13:1)   400

405

an it like: if it please
goodly: (1) handsome, (2) sizable; **portly:** (1) large, (2) dignified; **corpulent:** fat
carriage: bearing, posture
threescore: sixty   410
lewdly given: disposed to wickedness
see: Matthew 12:33

peremptorily: decisively

415

varlet: rascal

Depose me?: (Falstaff jokes that Hal will force   420
him from the throne—much as Henry IV did
Richard II)

rabbit-sucker: unweaned rabbit; **poulter's:**
poulterer's (vendor of dead chickens and rabbits)

DISCOVERING SHAKESPEARE

(59) Literary History [2.4.385]: In 2.4.384–389, Falstaff speaks in a parody of the style of John Lyly's *Euphues* (1579), an extremely popular prose romance featuring excessive use of alliteration, balanced constructions, similes, and examples taken from mythology and natural history. Write a sentence of your own imitating this popular sixteenth-century prose style. [*Hint:* See also 2.4.412–415 for an additional example of this elaborate style of writing.]

(60) Plot [2.4.420]: At the end of the next play in the tetralogy, *Henry IV, Part II,* Hal does indeed "depose" (2.4.420) his old friend Falstaff. Read the conclusion of *Henry IV, Part II* to determine how Hal dismisses his friend. How do you feel about the fact that Hal banishes Falstaff from his life?

PRINCE   Well, here I am set.

FALSTAFF   And here I stand. Judge, my masters.

PRINCE   Now, Harry, whence come you?   425

FALSTAFF   My noble lord, from Eastcheap.

PRINCE   The complaints I hear of thee are grievous.

FALSTAFF   'Sblood,° my lord, they are false! Nay, I'll tickle ye for° a young prince, i' faith.

> **'Sblood:** by God's blood
> **tickle ye for:** amuse you in the role of

PRINCE   Swearest thou, ungracious boy? Henceforth   430
ne'er look on me. Thou art violently carried away from
grace.° There is a devil haunts thee in the likeness of
an old fat man; a tun° of man is thy companion. Why
dost thou converse° with that trunk of humors,° that
bolting hutch° of beastliness, that swoll'n parcel of   435
dropsies,° that huge bombard° of sack, that stuffed cloak-
bag of guts, that roasted Manningtree ox° with the pudding in his belly,° that reverend vice, that gray iniquity,°
that father ruffian, that vanity° in years? Wherein is he
good, but to taste sack and drink it? wherein neat and   440
cleanly, but to carve a capon and eat it? wherein cunning,° but in craft?° wherein crafty, but in villainy?
wherein villainous, but in all things? wherein worthy,
but in nothing?

> **grace:** (1) royalty, (2) divine grace
> **tun:** (1) ton, (2) barrel
> **converse:** talk with, associate with; **humors:** body fluids
> **bolting hutch:** large flour bin
> **dropsies:** watery swellings; **bombard:** leather drinking vessel
> **Manningtree ox:** notoriously large ox roasted whole in Essex, a town famous for fairs
> **pudding in his belly:** stuffing in intestines
> **reverend vice . . . iniquity:** name for chief tempter in morality plays
> **vanity:** worldly person
> **cunning:** skillful
> **craft:** trickery
> **take . . . you:** make yourself clear

FALSTAFF   I would your grace would take me with you.°
Whom means your grace?   445

PRINCE   That villainous abominable misleader of youth,
Falstaff, that old white-bearded Satan.

FALSTAFF   My lord, the man I know.

PRINCE   I know thou dost.

FALSTAFF   But to say I know more harm in him than in   450
myself were to say more than I know. That he is old
(the more the pity), his white hairs do witness it; but
that he is (saving your reverence)° a whoremaster,° that I
utterly deny. If sack and sugar be a fault, God help the
wicked! If to be old and merry be a sin, then many an   455
old host° that I know is damned. If to be fat be to be
hated, then Pharaoh's lean kine° are to be loved. No, my
good lord: banish Peto, banish Bardolph, banish Poins;
but for sweet Jack Falstaff, kind Jack Falstaff, true Jack
Falstaff, valiant Jack Falstaff, and therefore more valiant   460
being, as he is, old Jack Falstaff, banish not him thy
Harry's company, banish not him thy Harry's company.
Banish plump Jack, and banish all the world!

> **saving your reverence:** with my apologies for rough language; **whoremaster:** one who consorts with prostitutes
> **host:** innkeeper
> **Pharaoh's lean kine:** see Genesis 41:3-4; **kine:** cows

PRINCE   I do, I will.   465

[A knocking heard.]

[Exeunt Hostess, Francis, and Bardolph.]

Enter Bardolph, running.

BARDOLPH   O, my lord, my lord! the sheriff with a most
monstrous watch° is at the door.

> **watch:** constabulary

DISCOVERING SHAKESPEARE

(61) <u>**Imagery**</u> **[2.4.438]:** Read Hal's speech in 2.4.430–444, and underline all the references to Falstaff's immense size. Explain the meaning of each of these references.

(62) **Repetition [2.4.457]:** Identify all the repeated words and phrases in Falstaff's speech in 2.4.451–464. What is the <u>rhetorical</u> effect of this repetition?

FALSTAFF   Out, ye rogue! Play out the play. I have much to say in the behalf of that Falstaff.

Enter the Hostess.

HOSTESS   O Jesu, my lord, my lord! 470

PRINCE   Heigh, heigh, the devil rides upon a fiddlestick!° What's the matter?

HOSTESS   The sheriff and all the watch are at the door. They are come to search the house. Shall I let them in?

FALSTAFF   Dost thou hear, Hal? Never call a true piece of gold a counterfeit. Thou art essentially mad without seeming so.° 475

PRINCE   And thou a natural coward without instinct.

FALSTAFF   I deny your major.° If you will deny the sheriff,° so; if not, let him enter. If I become not a cart° as well as another man, a plague on my bringing up! I hope I shall as soon be strangled with a halter as another. 480

PRINCE   Go hide thee behind the arras.° The rest walk up above. Now, my masters, for a true° face and good conscience. 485

FALSTAFF   Both which I have had; but their date is out,° and therefore I'll hide me.   *Exit.*

PRINCE   Call in the sheriff.

[Exeunt. The Prince and Peto remain behind.]
Enter Sheriff and the Carrier.

Now, master sheriff, what is your will with me?

SHERIFF
First, pardon me, my lord. A hue and cry 490
Hath followed certain men unto this house.

PRINCE
What men?

SHERIFF
One of them is well known, my gracious lord –
A gross fat man.

CARRIER   As fat as butter.

PRINCE
The man, I do assure you, is not here, 495
For I myself at this time have employed him.
And, sheriff, I will engage° my word to thee
That I will by tomorrow dinnertime
Send him to answer thee, or any man,
For anything he shall be charged withal; 500
And so let me entreat° you leave the house.

SHERIFF
I will, my lord. There are two gentlemen
Have in this robbery lost three hundred marks.

PRINCE
It may be so. If he have robbed these men,
He shall be answerable; and so farewell. 505

devil . . . fiddlestick: here's much ado about nothing

Never . . . so: don't call me, a true fellow, false (i.e., betray me to the watch); you are one of us even though you don't seem it

major: major premise; **deny the sheriff:** refuse admittance to

a cart: a hangman's cart

arras: wall hanging

true: straight, honest

date is out: time is past

engage: promise

entreat: beg

DISCOVERING SHAKESPEARE

(63) Teaser [2.4.483]: Name another Shakespearean play in which an "arras" (2.4.483) figures prominently.

(64) Social Custom [4.2.490]: Why is the Sheriff so polite to Hal in 2.4.490? What specific information does the Carrier add to help identify Falstaff?

SHERIFF
Good night, my noble lord.
PRINCE
I think it is good morrow,° is it not?

morrow: tomorrow

SHERIFF
Indeed, my lord, I think it be two o'clock.

Exit [with Carrier].

PRINCE   This oily rascal is known as well as Paul's.° Go call him forth.

Paul's: Saint Paul's Cathedral, at the center of London   510

PETO   Falstaff! Fast asleep behind the arras, and snorting° like a horse.

snorting: snoring

PRINCE   Hark how hard he fetches breath. Search his pockets.

He searcheth his pockets and findeth certain papers.
What hast thou found?

515

PETO   Nothing but papers, my lord.
PRINCE   Let's see what they be. Read them.
PETO   *[Reads.]*
"Item,° A capon° .... ii s. ii d.°
Item, Sauce .... iiii d.
Item, Sack two gallons .... v s. viii d.
Item, Anchovies and sack after supper .. ii s. vi d.
Item, Bread .... ob."°

Item: a bill for goods; **capon:** male fowl; **ii s. ii d.:** two shillings twopence

520

ob: obulus, a halfpenny

PRINCE   O monstrous! but one halfpennyworth of bread to this intolerable deal of sack! What there is else, keep close;° we'll read it at more advantage.° There let him sleep till day. I'll to the court in the morning. We must all to the wars, and thy place shall be honorable. I'll procure this fat rogue a charge of foot,° and I know his death will be a march of twelve score.° The money shall be paid back again with advantage.° Be with me betimes° in the morning, and so good morrow, Peto.

close: secret, hidden; **at more advantage:** at better opportunity   525

charge of foot: command of a company of foot soldiers
twelve score: i.e., 240 yards   530
advantage: interest; **betimes:** early

PETO   Good morrow, good my lord.   *Exeunt.*

❧ **3.1**° *Enter Hotspur, Worcester, Lord Mortimer, Owen Glendower.*

3.1: Glendower's castle in Wales

MORTIMER
These promises are fair, the parties sure,°
And our induction° full of prosperous hope.°

the parties sure: the partners are certain, promised
induction: beginning; **prosperous hope:** hope of success

HOTSPUR   Lord Mortimer, and cousin Glendower, will you sit down? And uncle Worcester. A plague upon it! I have forgot the map.

5

GLENDOWER
No, here it is. Sit, cousin Percy;

DISCOVERING SHAKESPEARE

(65) Social Custom [2.4.518]: In the list of food and beverage items taken from Falstaff's pocket (2.4.517–522), what is the monetary differential between food and wine? Which did Falstaff spend more money on? What does this list tell us about Falstaff's social behavior?

(66) Set Design [3.1.1]: Where do you think this scene with Hotspur, Worcester, Mortimer, and Glendower takes place? What is the time of day? Are the characters inside a building or outside? What specific references in the scene can you identify to help support your conclusions?

Sit, good cousin Hotspur, for by that name
As oft as Lancaster° doth speak of you,   **Lancaster:** the king
His cheek looks pale, and with a rising sigh
He wisheth you in heaven.   10
HOTSPUR   And you in hell, as oft as he hears Owen Glen-
dower spoke of.
GLENDOWER
I cannot blame him. At my nativity°   **nativity:** birth
The front° of heaven was full of fiery shapes   **front:** brow
Of burning cressets,° and at my birth   **cressets:** lights burning in baskets atop poles (i.e., 15
The frame and huge foundation of the earth   meteors)
Shaked like a coward.
HOTSPUR   Why, so it would have done at the same sea-
son if your mother's cat had but kittened, though your-
self had never been born.   20
GLENDOWER
I say the earth did shake when I was born.
HOTSPUR
And I say the earth was not of my mind,
If you suppose as fearing you it shook.
GLENDOWER
The heavens were all on fire, the earth did tremble.
HOTSPUR
O, then the earth shook to see the heavens on fire,   25
And not in fear of your nativity.
Diseasèd nature oftentimes breaks forth
In strange eruptions; oft the teeming earth
Is with a kind of colic° pinched and vexed   **colic:** abdominal spasm
By the imprisoning of unruly wind   30
Within her womb, which, for enlargement° striving, **enlargement:** release, escape
Shakes the old beldame° earth and topples down **beldame:** grandmother
Steeples and mossgrown towers. At your birth
Our grandam earth, having this distemp'rature,° **distemp'rature:** ailment
In passion shook.   35
GLENDOWER   Cousin, of many men
I do not bear these crossings.° Give me leave   **crossings:** contradictions
To tell you once again that at my birth
The front of heaven was full of fiery shapes,
The goats ran from the mountains, and the herds
Were strangely clamorous° to the frighted fields. **clamorous:** confused outcry 40
These signs have marked me extraordinary,
And all the courses° of my life do show   **courses:** events
I am not in the roll° of common men.   **roll:** roster, rank
Where is he living, clipped in° with the sea   **clipped in:** surrounded by
That chides° the banks of England, Scotland, Wales, **chides:** lashes, rebukes 45
Which° calls me pupil or hath read to° me?   **Which:** who; **read to:** instructed
And bring him out that is but woman's son
Can trace° me in the tedious° ways of art°   **trace:** follow; **tedious:** laborious; **art:** magic
And hold me pace° in deep experiments.   **hold me pace:** keep up with me

---

DISCOVERING SHAKESPEARE

(67) <u>Paraphrase</u> [3.1.25]: <u>Paraphrase</u> Hotspur's speech in 3.1.25–35. Why do you think Glendower responds so angrily to Hotspur's comments?

HOTSPUR   I think there's no man speaks better Welsh.° I'll
to dinner.

Welsh: (derogatory term for boasting and/or nonsensical speech) 50

MORTIMER
Peace, cousin Percy; you will make him mad.

GLENDOWER
I can call spirits from the vasty deep.°

vasty deep: lower world

HOTSPUR
Why, so can I, or so can any man;
But will they come when you do call for them?

55

GLENDOWER   Why, I can teach you, cousin, to command the devil.

HOTSPUR
And I can teach thee, coz, to shame the devil –
By telling truth. Tell truth and shame the devil.
If thou have power to raise him, bring him hither,
And I'll be sworn I have power to shame him hence.
O, while you live, tell truth and shame the devil!

60

MORTIMER
Come, come, no more of this unprofitable chat.

GLENDOWER
Three times hath Henry Bolingbroke made head°
Against my power; thrice from the banks of Wye°
And sandy-bottomed Severn° have I sent him
Bootless° home and weather-beaten back.

made head: raised troops

65

Wye, Severn: rivers that border Wales
Bootless: without gain

HOTSPUR
Home without boots, and in foul weather too?
How scapes he agues,° in the devil's name?

agues: fevers

GLENDOWER
Come, here is the map. Shall we divide our right°
According to our threefold order ta'en?°

right: possession 70
order ta'en: arrangement

MORTIMER
The archdeacon° hath divided it
Into three limits very equally.
England, from Trent° and Severn hitherto,
By south and east is to my part assigned;
All westward, Wales beyond the Severn shore,
And all the fertile land within that bound,°
To Owen Glendower; and, dear coz,° to you
The remnant northward lying off° from Trent.
And our indentures tripartite are drawn,°
Which being° sealèd interchangeably
(A business that this night may execute),°
Tomorrow, cousin Percy, you and I
And my good Lord of Worcester will set forth
To meet your father and the Scottish power,
As is appointed us, at Shrewsbury.

archdeacon: i.e., of Bangor, whose house was the historical location for the meeting of the rebel leaders' deputies
Trent: river dividing England from Scotland (roughly speaking, Mortimer takes England; Hotspur, Scotland; and Glendower, Wales) 75
bound: boundary
coz: i.e., Hotspur
lying off: beyond
indentures . . . drawn: documents are drawn up in triplicate 80
Which being: which having been
may execute: may accomplish

85

DISCOVERING SHAKESPEARE

(68) <u>Verse</u> **[3.1.50]:** <u>Scan</u> Hotspur's two-line speech in 3.1.50–51; then explain how the <u>meter</u> of the speech helps betray his emotional state.

(69) <u>Staging</u> **[3.1.72]:** Mortimer's speech in 3.1.72–90 indicates that a map is brought on stage to symbolize the three-part division of England among the rebels. At what points in the following <u>dialogue</u> do the characters refer directly to the map? What kind of map would be most appropriate in a production of the play?

My father° Glendower is not ready yet,   **father:** i.e., father-in-law
Nor shall we need his help these fourteen days.
   [To Glendower]
Within that space you may° have drawn together   **may:** will
Your tenants, friends, and neighboring gentlemen.   90
GLENDOWER
A shorter time shall send me to you, lords;
And in my conduct° shall your ladies come,   **conduct:** safekeeping
From whom you now must steal° and take no leave,   **steal:** steal away
For there will be a world of water shed
Upon the parting of your wives and you.   95
HOTSPUR
Methinks my moiety,° north from Burton here,   **moiety:** share
In quantity equals not one of yours.
See how this river comes me cranking in°   **comes . . . in:** comes bending in
And cuts me from the best of all my land
A huge half-moon, a monstrous cantle° out.   **cantle:** piece   100
I'll have the current in this place dammed up,
And here the smug° and silver Trent shall run   **smug:** smooth
In a new channel fair and evenly.
It shall not wind with such a deep indent
To rob me of so rich a bottom° here.   **bottom:** valley   105
GLENDOWER
Not wind? It shall, it must! You see it doth.
MORTIMER
Yea, but
Mark how he° bears his course, and runs me° up   **he:** i.e., the Trent; **runs me:** runs
With like advantage on the other side,
Gelding the opposèd continent° as much   **Gelding . . . continent:** cutting off the land that   110
As on the other side it takes from you.   contains it on the opposite side
WORCESTER
Yea, but a little charge° will trench° him here   **charge:** expenditure; **trench:** dig a new
And on this north side win this cape° of land;   channel
And then he runs straight and even.   **cape:** peninsula
HOTSPUR
I'll have it so. A little charge will do it.   115
GLENDOWER
I will not have it altered.
HOTSPUR   Will not you?
GLENDOWER
No, nor you shall not.
HOTSPUR   Who shall say me nay?
GLENDOWER
Why, that will I.
HOTSPUR
Let me not understand you then; speak it in Welsh.

DISCOVERING SHAKESPEARE

(70) Teaser [3.1.98]: Find at least one other Shakespearean play in which a map appears on stage. How is that scene different from the one in 3.1 of *Henry IV, Part I*?

(71) <u>Verse</u> [3.1.118]: Select two students to play the roles of Hotspur and Glendower; then have them act out 3.1.115–125. How do these <u>short</u> and <u>shared lines</u> help dramatize the quarrel between the two men?

GLENDOWER

    I can speak English, lord, as well as you;   120

    For I was trained up in the English court,

    Where, being but young, I framèd to the harp°

    Many an English ditty° lovely well,

    And gave the tongue a helpful ornament° –

    A virtue that was never seen in you.

HOTSPUR

    Marry, and I am glad of it with all my heart!

    I had rather be a kitten and cry mew

    Than one of these same meter ballet-mongers.°

    I had rather hear a brazen canstick turned°

    Or a dry° wheel grate on the axletree,°

    And that would set my teeth nothing on edge,°

    Nothing so much as mincing poetry.

    'Tis like the forced gait of a shuffling° nag.

GLENDOWER

    Come, you shall have Trent turned.

HOTSPUR

    I do not care. I'll give thrice so much land   135

    To any well-deserving friend;

    But in the way of bargain, mark ye me,

    I'll cavil on the ninth part of a hair.°

    Are the indentures drawn? Shall we be gone?

GLENDOWER

    The moon shines fair; you may away by night.   140

    I'll haste° the writer, and withal°

    Break with° your wives of your departure hence.

    I am afraid my daughter will run mad,

    So much she doteth on her Mortimer.   *Exit.*

MORTIMER

    Fie, cousin Percy! how you cross my father!   145

HOTSPUR

    I cannot choose.° Sometimes he angers me

    With telling me of the moldwarp° and the ant,

    Of the dreamer Merlin° and his prophecies,

    And of a dragon and a finless fish,

    A clip-winged griffin° and a molten° raven,   150

    A couching° lion and a ramping° cat,

    And such a deal of skimble-skamble° stuff

    As puts me from my faith.° I tell you what –

    He held me last night at least nine hours

    In reckoning up the several° devils' names

    That were his lackeys.° I cried "hum," and "well, go to!"° 155

    But marked° him not a word. O, he is as tedious

    As a tired horse, a railing° wife;

    Worse than a smoky house. I had rather live

    With cheese and garlic in a windmill far

    Than feed on cates° and have him talk to me   160

    In any summer house in Christendom.

---

framèd . . . harp: set to the accompaniment of harp music

ditty: song

gave . . . ornament: (1) gave words a decoration of music, (2) gave a musicality to words

meter ballet-mongers: metrical (and hence unartful) ballad makers

brazen canstick turned: brass candlestick turned on a lathe

dry: lacking grease; **axletree:** axle

set . . . edge: not set my teeth on edge

shuffling: fettered

cavil . . . hair: argue the smallest detail

haste: hurry; **withal:** also

Break with: inform

choose: help it

moldwarp: mole

Merlin: mythical British (Celtic) magician and seer of the court of King Arthur

griffin: a fabulous beast, half lion, half eagle; **molten:** having moulted, featherless

couching: crouching (heraldic term); **ramping:** rampant, rearing on hind legs

skimble-skamble: nonsensical, foolish

faith: (1) Christian faith, (2) good faith toward him; patience

several: various

lackeys: servants; **go to:** you don't say

marked: paid attention to

railing: ranting

cates: delicacies

DISCOVERING SHAKESPEARE

(72) <u>Paraphrase</u> [3.1.138]: <u>Paraphrase</u> the following line by Hotspur: "I'll cavil on the ninth part of a hair" (3.1.138).

MORTIMER

In faith, he is a worthy gentleman,
Exceedingly well read, and profited°
In strange concealments,° valiant as a lion,
And wondrous affable, and as bountiful
As mines of India. Shall I tell you, cousin?
He holds your temper in a high respect
And curbs himself even of his natural scope°
When you come 'cross his humor.° Faith, he does.
I warrant you that man is not alive
Might so have tempted him as you have done
Without the taste of danger and reproof.
But do not use it° oft, let me entreat° you.

WORCESTER

In faith, my lord, you are too willful-blame,°
And since your coming hither have done enough
To put him quite besides° his patience.
You must needs learn, lord, to amend this fault.
Though sometimes it show greatness, courage, blood° —
And that's the dearest grace it renders you —
Yet oftentimes it doth present° harsh rage,
Defect of manners, want of government,°
Pride, haughtiness, opinion,° and disdain;
The least of which haunting a nobleman
Loseth men's hearts, and leaves behind a stain
Upon the beauty of all parts besides,°
Beguiling° them of commendation.°

HOTSPUR

Well, I am schooled.° Good manners be your speed!°
Here come our wives, and let us take our leave.
    Enter Glendower with the Ladies.

MORTIMER

This is the deadly spite° that angers me —
My wife can speak no English, I no Welsh.

GLENDOWER

My daughter weeps; she will not part with you;
She'll be a soldier too, she'll to the wars.

MORTIMER

Good father, tell her that she and my aunt° Percy
Shall follow in your conducts speedily.
    Glendower speaks to her in Welsh, and she answers
    him in the same.

GLENDOWER

She is desperate here.° A peevish self-willed harlotry,°
One that no persuasion can do good upon.
    The Lady speaks in Welsh.

MORTIMER

I understand thy looks. That pretty Welsh

---

profited: proficient
concealments: secrets   165

curbs . . . scope: checks himself from his usual
range of responses   170
come . . . humor: contradict his mood, temper

use it: do; **entreat:** beg

willful-blame: blameworthy for willfulness   175

besides: out of

blood: spirit, nobility
         180
present: represent
government: self-control
opinion: arrogance

         185
all parts besides: all other parts
Beguiling: robbing; **commendation:** praise

schooled: reprimanded; **be your speed:** give
you luck

spite: vexation   190

aunt: (to Edmund Mortimer, but sister-in-law to
Glendower's son-in-law)   195

here: on this score; **self-willed harlotry:**
willful wench

DISCOVERING SHAKESPEARE

(73) <u>Verse</u> [3.1.163]: Read Mortimer's speech in 3.1.163–174; then mark all the <u>caesuras</u> with a "C," <u>run-on lines</u> with
an "R," and <u>end-stopped lines</u> with an "E." Which lines exhibit the most regular <u>verse</u> form? Which seem closest to the
rhythm of <u>prose</u>? Why?
(74) <u>Verse</u> [3.1.192]: <u>Scan</u> 3.1.192. How does the <u>rhythm</u> of Glendower's line match the sense of what he is saying?

Which thou pourest down from these swelling heavens°
I am too perfect° in; and, but for shame,
In such a parley° should I answer thee.
   The Lady again in Welsh.
I understand thy kisses, and thou mine,
And that's a feeling disputation.°
But I will never be a truant,° love,
Till I have learnt thy language; for thy tongue
Makes Welsh as sweet as ditties highly penned,°
Sung by a fair queen in a summer's bow'r,
With ravishing division,° to her lute.

swelling heavens: tearful eyes
perfect: skilled   200
such a parley: a similar tongue (i.e., weeping)

feeling disputation: emotional conversation, exchange
truant: unfaithful man   205
highly penned: eloquently, nobly composed

division: musical variation

GLENDOWER
Nay, if you melt, then will she run mad.
   The Lady speaks again in Welsh.
MORTIMER
O, I am ignorance itself in this!   210
GLENDOWER
She bids you on the wanton° rushes° lay you down
And rest your gentle head upon her lap,
And she will sing the song that pleaseth you
And on your eyelids crown° the god of sleep,
Charming your blood° with pleasing heaviness,°
Making such difference 'twixt wake and sleep
As is the difference betwixt day and night
The hour before the heavenly-harnessed team°
Begins his golden progress in the east.

wanton: luxurious; **rushes:** reeds used for floor covering

crown: give dominion to
blood: mood; **heaviness:** sleepiness   215

team: (of horses drawing the chariot of the sun)

MORTIMER
With all my heart I'll sit and hear her sing.   220
By that time will our book,° I think, be drawn.

book: documents

GLENDOWER
Do so, and those musicians that shall play to you
Hang in the air a thousand leagues from hence,
And straight they shall be here. Sit, and attend.
HOTSPUR Come, Kate, thou art perfect° in lying down.°
Come, quick, quick, that I may lay my head in thy lap.

perfect: skilled; **lying down:** sexual congress   225

LADY PERCY Go, ye giddy goose.
   The music plays.
HOTSPUR
Now I perceive the devil understands Welsh.
And 'tis no marvel he is so humorous,°
By'r Lady, he is a good musician.

humorous: full of moods, whims
                                                         230

LADY PERCY Then should you be nothing but musical,
for you are altogether governed by humors. Lie still, ye
thief, and hear the lady sing in Welsh.
HOTSPUR I had rather hear Lady, my brach,° howl in
Irish.°

brach: female hound
Irish: (considered an even more contemptible   235
language than Welsh)

LADY PERCY Wouldst thou have thy head broken?
HOTSPUR No.
LADY PERCY Then be still.
HOTSPUR Neither!° 'Tis a woman's fault.

Neither: not that either

DISCOVERING SHAKESPEARE

(75) Music [3.1.222]: When Glendower calls for music, what type of instruments should begin playing? Should the song be live or recorded? Why?

LADY PERCY   Now God help thee! 240

HOTSPUR   To the Welsh lady's bed.

LADY PERCY   What's that?

HOTSPUR   Peace! she sings.

Here the Lady sings a Welsh song.

Come, Kate, I'll have your song too.

LADY PERCY   Not mine, in good sooth.° **sooth:** truth 245

HOTSPUR   Not yours, in good sooth? Heart!° you swear **Heart:** by Christ's heart
like a comfit-maker's° wife. "Not you, in good sooth!" **comfit-maker's:** candymaker's
and "as true as I live!" and "as God shall mend me!" and
"as sure as day!"
And givest such sarcenet° surety° for thy oaths **sarcenet:** flimsy (like the cloth); **surety:** 250
As if thou never walk'st further than Finsbury.° warrant, guarantee
Swear me, Kate, like a lady° as thou art, **Finsbury:** field on the outskirts of London
A good mouth-filling oath, and leave "in sooth" visited by London citizenry (Hotspur accuses Kate
And such protest of pepper gingerbread° of swearing genteel and pious oaths such as sworn
To velvet guards° and Sunday citizens. by sober citizens, instead of aristocratic and
Come, sing. soldierly oaths) 255

LADY PERCY   I will not sing. **lady:** i.e., noble

HOTSPUR   'Tis the next° way to turn tailor° or be red- **protest . . . gingerbread:** mealy-mouthed oaths
breast-teacher. An the indentures be drawn, I'll away **velvet guards:** velvet-trimmed housewives and
within these two hours; and so come in when ye will. citizens in Sunday finery

Exit. **next:** easiest; **turn tailor:** tailors were noted for 260
musical ability, which Hotspur considers
effeminate

GLENDOWER   Come, come, Lord Mortimer. You are as slow
As hot Lord Percy is on fire to go.
By this our book is drawn; we'll but seal,° **seal:** i.e., with wax seals denoting signatures
And then to horse immediately.

MORTIMER   With all my heart.

Exeunt.

❧ **3.2**° *Enter the King, Prince of Wales, and others.*   **3.2:** The palace of Henry IV

KING

Lords, give us leave: the Prince of Wales and I
Must have some private conference; but be near at
  hand,
For we shall presently have need of you.   *Exeunt Lords.*
I know not whether God will have it so
For some displeasing service I have done, 5
That, in his secret doom,° out of my blood **doom:** judgment
He'll breed revengement and a scourge° for me; **scourge:** punishment
But thou dost in thy passages° of life **passages:** conduct, actions
Make me believe that thou art only marked° **marked:** destined
For° the hot vengeance and the rod of heaven **For:** by, in order for 10
To punish my mistreadings.° Tell me else,° **mistreadings:** missteps, mistakes; **else:** how else

---

DISCOVERING SHAKESPEARE

(76) Social Custom [3.1.246–247]: Which oaths does Hotspur object to as being less appropriate to Kate than to a "comfit-maker's wife" (3.1.246–247)? Find two or three more "mouth-filling" (3.1.253) oaths elsewhere in the play. Which particular ingredients would make an oath worthy of Hotspur's praise?

(77) Verse [3.2.5]: When does Hal speak <u>verse</u> in this play, and when does he speak <u>prose</u>? Why does he switch from one dramatic medium to the other?

Could such inordinate° and low desires,
Such poor, such bare, such lewd, such mean attempts,°
Such barren pleasures, rude society,
As thou art matched withal and grafted° to,   15
Accompany the greatness of thy blood
And hold their level with° thy princely heart?

inordinate: immoderate, unworthy
mean attempts: base exploits, undertakings
grafted: joined
hold . . . with: be on equal terms with

PRINCE
So please your majesty, I would I could
Quit° all offenses with as clear excuse
As well as I am doubtless° I can purge°   20
Myself of many I am charged withal.
Yet such extenuation° let me beg
As, in reproof ° of many tales devised,
Which oft the ear of greatness needs must hear
By smiling pickthanks° and base newsmongers,°   25
I may, for some things true wherein my youth°
Hath faulty wandered and irregular,
Find pardon on my true submission.°

Quit: acquit myself of
doubtless: certain; **purge:** cleanse
extenuation: mitigation, justification
in reproof: upon disproof
pickthanks: flatterers; **newsmongers:** rumor spreaders, talebearers
youth: youthfulness
submission: admittance of fault, repentance

KING
God pardon thee! Yet let me wonder, Harry,
At thy affections, which do hold a wing°   30
Quite from° the flight of all thy ancestors.
Thy place in council° thou hast rudely° lost,
Which by thy younger brother is supplied,°
And art almost an alien to the hearts
Of all the court and princes of my blood.   35
The hope and expectation of thy time°
Is ruined, and the soul of every man
Prophetically do forethink thy fall.
Had I so lavish° of my presence been,
So common-hackneyed° in the eyes of men,   40
So stale and cheap to vulgar company,
Opinion,° that did help me to the crown,
Had still kept loyal to possession°
And left me in reputeless banishment,°
A fellow of no mark nor likelihood.°   45
By being seldom seen, I could not stir
But, like a comet, I was wondered at;
That men would tell their children, "This is he!"
Others would say, "Where? Which is Bolingbroke?"
And then I stole all courtesy° from heaven,   50
And dressed myself in such humility
That I did pluck allegiance from men's hearts,
Loud shouts and salutations° from their mouths
Even in the presence of the crownèd king.
Thus did I keep my person fresh and new,   55
My presence, like a robe pontifical,°
Ne'er seen but wondered at; and so my state,°

hold a wing: keep (fly a course)
from: away from
council: royal council; **rudely:** by violence (Hal was reputed to have punched the Lord Chief Justice, who imprisoned him for it)
supplied: replaced
time: youth
lavish: free
common-hackneyed: ordinary
Opinion: public opinion
to possession: i.e., that of Richard II, of the throne
reputeless banishment: abandoned exile
mark nor likelihood: name or prospects
stole all courtesy: appropriated all graciousness
salutations: greetings
pontifical: i.e., of the pope
state: pomp, presence

DISCOVERING SHAKESPEARE

(78) Metaphor [3.2.30]: Explain King Henry's metaphor in which he charges that Hal's affections "do hold a wing/Quite from the flight of all thy ancestors" (3.2.30–31).

(79) Paraphrase [3.2.55]: Put into your own words the King's principal argument in 3.2.39–59. How does the King think his behavior has been different from Hal's? Whose actions seem most "regal" to you? Whose are most "human"? Why?

Seldom but sumptuous,° showed like a feast
And won by rareness° such solemnity.°
The skipping king,° he ambled up and down
With shallow jesters and rash bavin° wits,
Soon kindled and soon burnt; carded° his state;
Mingled his royalty with cap'ring fools;
Had his great name profanèd° with their scorns°
And gave his countenance,° against his name,°
To laugh at gibing° boys and stand the push°
Of every beardless vain comparative;°
Grew a companion to the common streets,
Enfeoffed himself° to popularity;
That, being daily swallowed by men's eyes,
They surfeited° with honey and began
To loathe the taste of sweetness, whereof a little
More than a little is by much too much.
So, when he had occasion to be seen,
He was but as the cuckoo is in June,°
Heard, not regarded – seen, but with such eyes
As, sick and blunted with community,°
Afford no extraordinary° gaze,
Such as is bent° on sunlike majesty
When it shines seldom in admiring eyes;
But rather drowsed and hung their eyelids down,
Slept in his face, and rendered such aspect°
As cloudy° men use to their adversaries,
Being with his presence glutted, gorged, and full.
And in that very line,° Harry, standest thou;
For thou hast lost thy princely privilege
With vile participation.° Not an eye
But is aweary of thy common sight,
Save mine, which hath desired to see thee more;
Which now doth that° I would not have it do –
Make blind itself with foolish tenderness.°

PRINCE
I shall hereafter, my thrice-gracious lord,
Be more myself.

KING   For all the world,
As thou art to this hour was Richard then
When I from France set foot at Ravenspurgh;
And even as I was then is Percy now.
Now, by my scepter, and my soul to boot,°
He hath more worthy interest to the state°
Than thou, the shadow of succession;
For of no right, nor color like to° right,
He doth fill fields with harness° in the realm,
Turns head° against the lion's° armèd jaws,
And, being no more in debt to years° than thou,
Leads ancient° lords and reverend bishops on

Seldom but sumptuous: rare but rich
rareness: infrequency; **solemnity:** i.e., of a feast or holiday   60
skipping king: i.e., Richard II
rash bavin: highly flammable brushwood
carded: mixed (with the lower orders)
profanèd: debased; **their scorns:** (the scorns felt for the fools by the populace)   65
countenance: authority; **against his name:** contrary to his lineage and reputation
gibing: taunting; **stand the push:** tolerate the impudence
comparative: maker of comparisons   70
Enfeoffed himself: gave himself up to
surfeited: filled, sated

cuckoo is in June: i.e., nothing unusual   75

community: commonness, familiarity
extraordinary: wondering
bent: turned
                                                                                              80

rendered such aspect: showed a face
cloudy: sullen (the metaphor draws on that of the king as the sun)
very line: pattern, tradition   85

vile participation: consorting with low persons

that: that which   90
tenderness: tears

                                                                                              95

to boot: as well
worthy interest to the state: legitimate grounds to rule
color like to: anything resembling   100
harness: armored men
Turns head: leads an army; **lion's:** king's
in debt to years: older
ancient: time-honored

DISCOVERING SHAKESPEARE

(80) Symbolism [3.2.79]: In 3.2.79, as elsewhere in the play, the word "sun" is used symbolically. Here, the King suggests that Hal (his "son") is not behaving in a very princely fashion ("sun-like majesty"). Can you locate any other son–sun puns in the script? How does the repetition of these two related words achieve symbolic importance in the play?

To bloody battles and to bruising arms.   105
What never-dying honor hath he got
Against° renownèd Douglas! whose high deeds,   **Against:** from fighting
Whose hot incursions° and great name in arms   **incursions:** invasions
Holds from° all soldiers chief majority°   **from:** among; **majority:** preeminence
And military title capital°   **capital:** supreme   110
Through all the kingdoms that acknowledge Christ.
Thrice hath this Hotspur, Mars in swaddling clothes,
This infant warrior, in his enterprises
Discomfited° great Douglas; ta'en him once,   **Discomfited:** defeated
Enlargèd° him, and made a friend of him,   **Enlargèd:** set free   115
To fill the mouth of deep defiance up°   **To . . . up:** to increase the sound of defiance
And shake the peace and safety of our throne.
And what say you to this? Percy, Northumberland,
The Archbishop's grace of York, Douglas, Mortimer
Capitulate° against us and are up.°   **Capitulate:** draw up articles; **up:** in arms   120
But wherefore do I tell these news to thee?
Why, Harry, do I tell thee of my foes,
Which art my nearest and dearest enemy?
Thou that art like° enough, through vassal° fear,   **like:** likely; **vassal:** slavish, senile
Base inclination,° and the start of spleen,°   **Base inclination:** low tendencies; **spleen:** ill   125
To fight against me under Percy's pay,   temper
To dog his heels and curtsy at his frowns,
To show how much thou art degenerate.
PRINCE
Do not think so. You shall not find it so.
And God forgive them that so much have swayed   130
Your majesty's good thoughts away from me.
I will redeem° all this on Percy's head   **redeem:** make up for
And, in the closing° of some glorious day,   **closing:** end
Be bold to tell you that I am your son,
When I will wear a garment all of blood,   135
And stain my favors° in a bloody mask,   **favors:** features
Which, washed away, shall scour my shame with it.
And that shall be the day, whene'er it lights,°   **lights:** dawns
That this same child of honor and renown,
This gallant Hotspur, this all-praisèd knight,   140
And your unthought-of° Harry chance to meet.   **unthought-of:** ill-regarded, ignored
For every honor sitting on his helm,°   **helm:** helmet, head
Would they were multitudes, and on my head
My shames redoubled! For the time will come
That I shall make this northern youth exchange   145
His glorious deeds for my indignities.
Percy is but my factor,° good my lord,   **factor:** agent, instrument
To engross° up glorious deeds on my behalf;   **engross:** buy
And I will call him to so strict account
That he shall render° every glory up,   **render:** give   150
Yea, even the slightest worship° of his time,°   **worship:** honor; **time:** lifetime

---

DISCOVERING SHAKESPEARE

(81) Mythology [3.2.112]: Who was Mars in Roman mythology? Why does the King compare Hotspur to him in 3.2.112? How do you think this comparison affects Hal?

(82) Metaphor [3.2.135]: Analyze Hal's complex <u>metaphor</u> in 3.2.135–137 by identifying the <u>tenor</u> and <u>vehicle</u> of each element of the comparison.

Or I will tear the reckoning° from his heart.
This in the name of God I promise here;
The which if he° be pleased I shall perform,
I do beseech your majesty may salve°
The long-grown wounds of my intemperance.°
If not, the end of life cancels all bands,°
And I will die a hundred thousand deaths
Ere break the smallest parcel of this vow.

KING
A hundred thousand rebels die in this!°
Thou shalt have charge° and sovereign trust herein.
Enter Blunt.
How now, good Blunt? Thy looks are full of speed.

BLUNT
So hath the business that I come to speak of.
Lord Mortimer° of Scotland hath sent word
That Douglas and the English rebels met
The eleventh of this month at Shrewsbury.
A mighty and a fearful head° they are,
If promises be kept on every hand,
As ever offered foul play in a state.

KING
The Earl of Westmoreland set forth today;
With him my son, Lord John of Lancaster;
For this advertisement° is five days old.
On Wednesday next, Harry, you shall set forward;
On Thursday we ourselves will march. Our meeting°
Is Bridgenorth; and, Harry, you shall march
Through Gloucestershire; by which account,
Our business valuèd,° some twelve days hence
Our general forces at Bridgenorth shall meet.
Our hands are full of business. Let's away:
Advantage° feeds him° fat while men delay.   *Exeunt.*

❧ **3.3**° *Enter Falstaff and Bardolph.*

FALSTAFF   Bardolph, am I not fallen° away vilely since this
last action?° Do I not bate?° Do I not dwindle? Why, my
skin hangs about me like an old lady's loose gown! I am
withered like an old apple-john.° Well, I'll repent, and that
suddenly,° while I am in some liking.° I shall be out of heart°
shortly, and then I shall have no strength to repent. An I
have not forgotten what the inside of a church is made of,
I am a peppercorn,° a brewer's horse.° The inside of a
church! Company, villainous company, hath been the
spoil of me.

BARDOLPH   Sir John, you are so fretful you cannot live
long.

---

reckoning: amount owed

he: i.e., God
salve: heal   155
intemperance: wasteful behavior
bands: bonds, promises

this: this vow   160
charge: command

Lord Mortimer: a Scottish nobleman unrelated
to Edmund Mortimer, Glendower's son-in-law   165

head: force

170

advertisement: news

meeting: rendezvous

175

our business valuèd: depending upon how
long our business will take

Advantage: opportunity; **him:** himself   180

3.3: An Eastcheap tavern

fallen: wasted
action: (the robbery); **bate:** shrink

apple-john: shriveled eating apple
suddenly: immediately; **liking:** (1) inclination,   5
(2) good shape; **out of heart:** (1) disheartened,
(2) out of shape

peppercorn: i.e., very small; **brewer's horse:**
i.e., worn out

10

DISCOVERING SHAKESPEARE

(83) Plot [3.2.160]: When King Henry tells Hal "A hundred thousand rebels die in this" (3.2.160), he obviously trusts his son once again. What has Hal said or done in this scene to regain his father's confidence?

(84) Stage Business [3.3.1]: What are Falstaff and Bardolph doing at the beginning of 3.3? Suggest some possible activities that they might be engaged in at the top of the scene.

FALSTAFF   Why, there is it!° Come, sing me a bawdy° song; make me merry. I was as virtuously given° as a gentleman need to be, virtuous enough: swore little, diced not above seven times a week, went to a bawdy house° not above once in a quarter of an hour, paid money that I borrowed three or four times, lived well, and in good compass;° and now I live out of all order, out of all compass.

there is it: that's it; **bawdy:** lewd
virtuously given: given to good behavior

bawdy house: house of prostitution

compass: limit, girth

BARDOLPH   Why, you are so fat, Sir John, that you must needs be out of all compass — out of all reasonable compass, Sir John.

FALSTAFF   Do thou amend thy face,° and I'll amend my life. Thou art our admiral,° thou bearest the lantern° in the poop° — but 'tis in the nose of thee. Thou art the Knight of the Burning Lamp.°

face: (which is bright red from drinking)
admiral: flagship; **lantern:** i.e., for the fleet to follow
poop: rear deck
Burning Lamp: (Falstaff mockingly compares him to Amadis, knight of the Burning Sword)

BARDOLPH   Why, Sir John, my face does you no harm.

FALSTAFF   No, I'll be sworn. I make as good use of it as many a man doth of a death's-head or a memento mori.° I never see thy face but I think upon hellfire and Dives° that lived in purple; for there he is in his robes, burning, burning. If thou wert any way given to virtue, I would swear by thy face; my oath should be "By this fire, that's God's angel."° But thou art altogether given over,° and wert indeed, but for the light in thy face, the son of utter darkness. When thou ran'st up Gad's Hill in the night to catch my horse, if I did not think thou hadst been an ignus fatuus° or a ball of wildfire,° there's no purchase in money. O, thou art a perpetual triumph,° an everlasting bonfire-light! Thou hast saved me a thousand marks° in links° and torches, walking with thee in the night betwixt tavern and tavern; but the sack that thou hast drunk me° would have bought me lights as good cheap° at the dearest° chandler's° in Europe. I have maintained that salamander° of yours with fire any time this two-and-thirty years. God reward me for it!

death's-head or a memento mori: a skull and crossbones, or reminder of death
Dives: the rich man who went to hell, of Luke 26:19–31

By . . . angel: an echo of Exodus 3:2, Psalms 104:4, or Hebrews 1:7
given over: a lost cause

ignus fatuus: will-o'-the-wisp; **wildfire:** fireworks
triumph: torchlight procession
marks: silver coins; **links:** flares

drunk me: drunk off me
as good cheap: as cheap; **dearest:** most expensive; **chandler's:** candle maker's
salamander: lizard reputed to live in fire (because so cold-blooded)

BARDOLPH   'Sblood, I would my face were in your belly!°

FALSTAFF   God-a-mercy! so should I be sure to be heart-burnt.

I . . . belly: (a proverbial way of retorting to irritating remarks)

Enter Hostess.

How now, Dame Partlet° the hen? Have you enquired yet who picked my pocket?

Partlet: hen in animal stories

HOSTESS   Why, Sir John, what do you think, Sir John? Do you think I keep thieves in my house? I have searched, I have enquired, so has my husband, man by man, boy by boy, servant by servant. The tithe° of a hair was never lost in my house before.

tithe: tenth part

DISCOVERING SHAKESPEARE

(85) Imagery [3.3.24]: In 3.3.24–51, how many different references does Falstaff make to Bardolph's ruddy complexion? Which do you think is most creative? Why?

(86) Stage Business [3.3.53]: When did Falstaff have his pocket picked earlier in the script? Exactly what was found in his pocket? Did anyone take a "seal-ring" (3.3.81) from him? If so, who did it?

FALSTAFF   Ye lie, hostess. Bardolph was shaved and lost many a hair,° and I'll be sworn my pocket was picked. Go to,° you are a woman, go!

lost . . . hair: (1) from shaving, (2) from balding due to syphilis   60
Go to: go on, get out of here

HOSTESS   Who, I? No; I defy thee! God's light, I was never called so in mine own house before!

FALSTAFF   Go to, I know you well enough.

HOSTESS   No, Sir John; you do not know me, Sir John. I know you, Sir John. You owe me money, Sir John, and now you pick a quarrel to beguile° me of it. I bought you a dozen of shirts to your back.

65

beguile: hoodwink

FALSTAFF   Dowlas,° filthy dowlas! I have given them away to bakers' wives; they have made bolters° of them.

Dowlas: coarse cheap linen
bolters: flour-sifting cloths   70

HOSTESS   Now, as I am a true woman, holland° of eight shillings an ell.° You owe money here besides, Sir John, for your diet and by-drinkings,° and money lent you, four-and-twenty pound.

holland: fine lawn linen
ell: forty-five inches
by-drinkings: i.e., between meals

FALSTAFF   He° had his part of it; let him pay.

He: i.e., Bardolph   75

HOSTESS   He? Alas, he is poor; he hath nothing.

FALSTAFF   How? Poor? Look upon his face. What call you rich? Let them coin his nose, let them coin his cheeks. I'll not pay a denier.° What, will you make a younker° of me? Shall I not take mine ease° in mine inn but I shall have my pocket picked? I have lost a seal ring of my grandfather's worth forty mark.

denier: one twelfth of a French sou, a very small coin
younker: fool, gull, greenhorn; **ease:** relaxation   80

HOSTESS   O Jesu, I have heard the prince tell him, I know not how oft, that that ring was copper!

FALSTAFF   How? the prince is a Jack,° a sneak-up.° 'Sblood, an he were here, I would cudgel him° like a dog if he would say so.

Jack: knave, rascal; **sneak-up:** sneak   85
cudgel him: beat him with a stick

Enter the Prince [and Peto], marching, and Falstaff meets them, playing upon his truncheon° like a fife.

truncheon: club, stick

How now, lad? Is the wind in that door,° i' faith? Must we all march?

Is . . . door: Is that the way the wind blows

BARDOLPH   Yea, two and two, Newgate fashion.°

Newgate fashion: chained together like inmates of the London prison   90

HOSTESS   My lord, I pray you hear me.

PRINCE   What say'st thou, Mistress Quickly? How doth thy husband? I love him well; he is an honest man.

HOSTESS   Good my lord, hear me.

FALSTAFF   Prithee let her alone and list to me.

95

PRINCE   What say'st thou, Jack?

FALSTAFF   The other night I fell asleep here behind the arras and had my pocket picked. This house is turned bawdy house; they pick pockets.

PRINCE   What didst thou lose, Jack?

100

FALSTAFF   Wilt thou believe me, Hal, three or four bonds of forty pound apiece and a seal ring of my grandfather's.

PRINCE   A trifle,° some eightpenny matter.

trifle: cheap thing

DISCOVERING SHAKESPEARE

(87) Costume [3.3.72]: If you were a <u>costume</u> designer for a production of this play, how would you dress the Hostess? What colors, fabrics, and style of clothing would she wear? Why?

(88) Social History [3.3.90]: Where was Newgate Prison (3.3.90) located in London? What types of prisoners were incarcerated there? What were their principal crimes? How bad were conditions in the prison?

HOSTESS   So I told him, my lord, and I said I heard your grace say so; and, my lord, he speaks most vilely of you, like a foulmouthed man as he is, and said he would cudgel you.   105

PRINCE   What! he did not?

HOSTESS   There's neither faith, truth, nor womanhood in me else.   110

FALSTAFF   There's no more faith in thee than in a stewed prune,° nor no more truth in thee than in a drawn fox;° and for womanhood, Maid Marian may be the deputy's wife of the ward to thee.° Go, you thing, go!

> **stewed prune:** associated with brothels
> **a drawn fox:** hunted and drawn from cover
> **Maid Marian . . . thee:** compared to you, Maid Marian (a disreputable woman of folklore) would be respectable   115

HOSTESS   Say, what thing? what thing?

FALSTAFF   What thing? Why, a thing to thank God on.

HOSTESS   I am no thing to thank God on, I would thou shouldst know it! I am an honest man's wife, and, setting thy knighthood aside,° thou art a knave to call me so.

> **setting . . . aside:** the fact that you are a knight notwithstanding, not wishing to offend your knighthood   120

FALSTAFF   Setting thy womanhood aside, thou art a beast to say otherwise.

HOSTESS   Say, what beast, thou knave, thou?

FALSTAFF   What beast? Why, an otter.   125

PRINCE   An otter, Sir John? Why an otter?

FALSTAFF   Why? She's neither fish nor flesh; a man knows not where to have° her.

> **have:** take sexual possession of

HOSTESS   Thou art an unjust man in saying so. Thou or any man knows where to have me, thou knave, thou!   130

PRINCE   Thou say'st true, hostess, and he slanders thee most grossly.

HOSTESS   So he doth you, my lord, and said this other day you ought° him a thousand pound.°

> **ought:** owed; **pound:** currency

PRINCE   Sirrah, do I owe you a thousand pound?   135

FALSTAFF   A thousand pound, Hal? A million! Thy love is worth a million; thou owest me thy love.

HOSTESS   Nay, my lord, he called you Jack and said he would cudgel you.

FALSTAFF   Did I, Bardolph?   140

BARDOLPH   Indeed, Sir John, you said so.

FALSTAFF   Yea, if he said my ring was copper.

PRINCE   I say 'tis copper. Darest thou be as good as thy word now?

FALSTAFF   Why, Hal, thou knowest, as thou art but man, I dare; but as thou art prince, I fear thee as I fear the roaring of the lion's whelp.°   145

> **whelp:** offspring, cub

PRINCE   And why not as the lion?

FALSTAFF   The king himself is to be feared as the lion. Dost thou think I'll fear thee as I fear thy father? Nay, an I do, I pray God my girdle° break.   150

> **girdle:** belt-like article of dress

DISCOVERING SHAKESPEARE

(89) Language [3.3.129]: When the Hostess says to Falstaff "Thou or any man knows where to have me" (3.3.129–130), she seems unaware of the sexual double meaning of her statement. What does she intend the phrase to mean? How do you think Hal, Falstaff, and the others interpret her words?

(90) Symbolism [3.3.149]: In 3.3.145–151, Falstaff compares King Henry symbolically with a lion and Hal with the "lion's whelp" (3.3.147). What other animal references appear in this play? Why was the lion a traditional symbol for the King?

PRINCE   O, if it should, how would thy guts fall about thy knees! But, sirrah, there's no room for faith, truth, nor honesty in this bosom of thine. It is all filled up with guts and midriff. Charge an honest woman with picking thy pocket? Why, thou whoreson, impudent, embossed° rascal,° if there were anything in thy pocket but tavern reckonings,° memorandums° of bawdy houses, and one poor pennyworth of sugar candy to make thee long-winded — if thy pocket were enriched with any other injuries° but these, I am a villain. And yet you will stand° to it; you will not pocket up° wrong. Art thou not ashamed?

FALSTAFF   Dost thou hear, Hal? Thou knowest in the state of innocency Adam fell, and what should poor Jack Falstaff do in the days of villainy? Thou seest I have more flesh than another man, and therefore more frailty. You confess then, you picked my pocket?

PRINCE   It appears so by the story.

FALSTAFF   Hostess, I forgive thee. Go make ready breakfast. Love thy husband, look to thy servants, cherish thy guests. Thou shalt find me tractable to° any honest reason. Thou seest I am pacified still.° Nay, prithee be gone.   *Exit Hostess.*
Now, Hal, to the news at court. For the robbery, lad — how is that answered?

PRINCE   O my sweet beef, I must still be good angel to thee. The money is paid back again.

FALSTAFF   O, I do not like that paying back! 'Tis a double labor.

PRINCE   I am good friends with my father, and may do anything.

FALSTAFF   Rob me the exchequer° the first thing thou doest, and do it with unwashed hands° too.

BARDOLPH   Do, my lord.

PRINCE   I have procured thee, Jack, a charge of foot.°

FALSTAFF   I would it had been of horse.° Where shall I find one° that can steal well? O for a fine thief of the age of two-and-twenty° or thereabouts! I am heinously unprovided.° Well, God be thanked° for these rebels. They offend none but the virtuous. I laud them, I praise them.

PRINCE   Bardolph!

BARDOLPH   My lord?

PRINCE
Go bear this letter to Lord John of Lancaster,
To my brother John; this to my Lord of Westmoreland.
[Exit Bardolph.]
Go, Peto, to horse, to horse; for thou and I
Have thirty miles to ride yet ere dinnertime.
[Exit Peto.]

embossed: swollen; **rascal:** lean deer
reckonings: bills; **memorandums:** mementos

injuries: things you claim to have lost
stand to it: insist; **pocket up:** endure silently

tractable to: agreeable to, appeased by
still: always

exchequer: treasury
unwashed hands: without delay

charge of foot: command of a troop of infantry
horse: cavalry
one: a partner in crime
two-and-twenty: i.e., Hal's age
heinously unprovided: grievously unprepared
God be thanked: (Falstaff views the war as an opportunity)

155

160

165

170

175

180

185

190

195

DISCOVERING SHAKESPEARE

(91) Puns [3.3.179]: What does Falstaff mean when he complains that paying back the stolen money is "a double labor" (3.3.179–180)?

Jack, meet me tomorrow in the Temple Hall°
At two o'clock in the afternoon.
There shalt thou know thy charge, and there receive
Money and order for their furniture.°
The land is burning; Percy stands on high;
And either we or they must lower lie.   *[Exit.]*

Temple Hall: one of the Inns of Court (the law courts and schools)   200

furniture: equipment

FALSTAFF
Rare° words! brave world! Hostess, my breakfast, come.
O, I could wish this tavern were my drum!   *Exit.*

Rare: brave, splendid   205

 ❧ **4.1**° *[Enter Hotspur, Worcester, and Douglas.]*

4.1: The rebel camp at Shrewsbury

HOTSPUR
Well said, my noble Scot. If speaking truth
In this fine age were not thought flattery,
Such attribution° should the Douglas have
As not a soldier of this season's stamp°
Should go so general current° through the world.
By God, I cannot flatter, I do defy°
The tongues of soothers!° but a braver° place
In my heart's love hath no man than yourself.
Nay, task° me to my word; approve° me, lord.

attribution: tribute
stamp: coinage, pattern
go . . . current: be so universally esteemed and accepted   5
defy: despise
soothers: flatterers; **braver:** better
task: test, keep; **approve:** put to the test

DOUGLAS
Thou art the king of honor.
No man so potent° breathes upon the ground
But° I will beard° him.
    Enter one with letters.

10

potent: powerful
But: but that; **beard:** defy, best

HOTSPUR   Do so, and 'tis well. –
What letters hast thou there? – I can but thank you.
MESSENGER
These letters come from your father.
HOTSPUR
Letters from him? Why comes he not himself?

15

MESSENGER
He cannot come, my lord; he is grievous° sick.

grievous: grievously, terribly

HOTSPUR
Zounds!° how has he the leisure to be sick
In such a jostling time? Who leads his power?
Under whose government° come they along?

Zounds: God's wounds

government: command

MESSENGER
His letter bears his mind, not I, my lord.

20

WORCESTER
I prithee tell me, doth he keep° his bed?

keep: keep to

MESSENGER
He did, my lord, four days ere I set forth,
And at the time of my departure thence
He was much feared° by his physicians.

feared: feared for

DISCOVERING SHAKESPEARE

(92) Characterization [4.1.3]: How many different times in the play is Douglas praised by leaders of the two armies? Why is he referred to so frequently as "the Douglas"? How would all these different references help dictate an actor's approach to the role, including on-stage characterization, <u>blocking</u>, clothing, <u>diction</u>, and other theatrical details? What happens to the Douglas at the conclusion of the play?

WORCESTER
I would the state of time° had first been whole°
Ere he by sickness had been visited.
His health was never better worth° than now.

HOTSPUR
Sick now? droop now? This sickness doth infect
The very lifeblood of our enterprise.
'Tis catching hither, even to our camp.
He writes me here that inward sickness —
And that his friends by deputation° could not
So soon be drawn;° nor did he think it meet°
To lay so dangerous and dear a trust
On any soul removed° but on his own.
Yet doth he give us bold advertisement,°
That with our small conjunction° we should on,°
To see how fortune° is disposed to us;
For, as he writes, there is no quailing° now,
Because the king is certainly possessed°
Of all our purposes. What say you to it?

WORCESTER
Your father's sickness is a maim° to us.

HOTSPUR
A perilous gash, a very limb lopped off.
And yet, in faith, it is not! His present want°
Seems more than we shall find it. Were it good
To set the exact wealth of all our states°
All at one cast?° to set so rich a main°
On the nice° hazard° of one doubtful hour?
It were not good; for therein should we read°
The very bottom° and the soul of hope,
The very list,° the very utmost bound°
Of all our fortunes.

DOUGLAS   Faith, and so we should.
Where now remains a sweet reversion,°
We may boldly spend upon the hope of what
Is to come in.
A comfort of retirement° lives in this.

HOTSPUR
A rendezvous, a home to fly unto,
If that the devil and mischance look big°
Upon the maidenhead° of our affairs.

WORCESTER
But yet I would your father had been here.
The quality and hair° of our attempt
Brooks° no division. It will be thought
By some that know not why he is away,
That wisdom, loyalty,° and mere° dislike
Of our proceedings kept the earl from hence.

Glosses:

time: the times; **whole:** peaceful, ordered 25
better worth: worth more
30
deputation: deputies
drawn: assembled; **meet:** suitable
removed: other than himself 35
advertisement: advice
conjunction: conjoined forces; **on:** go on (to fight)
fortune: fate, divine will
quailing: backing down 40
possessed: informed
maim: injury
want: absence
45
states: (1) fortunes, (2) estates
cast: throw of the dice; **main:** stake, army
nice: delicate, chancy; **hazard:** (1) chance, peril, (2) dice game
read: learn 50
bottom: basis
list: limit; **bound:** boundary
reversion: future prospects, inheritance
55
retirement: something to fall back upon
big: threateningly
maidenhead: i.e., beginning (literally hymen, the physical marker of female virginity)
60
hair: nature
Brooks: tolerates
loyalty: i.e., to the king; **mere:** utter
65

DISCOVERING SHAKESPEARE

(93) Teaser [4.1.28]: What specific earlier line by Northumberland <u>foreshadowed</u> the fact that he might not join the rebellion?

(94) Metaphor [4.1.50]: Underline all the <u>metaphors</u> in Hotspur's speech in 4.1.43–52; then list the <u>tenor</u> and <u>vehicle</u> for each <u>metaphor</u>. Which seems most vivid and appropriate to you? Why?

And think how such an apprehension
May turn the tide of fearful° faction°
And breed a kind of question° in our cause.
For well you know we of the off'ring° side
Must keep aloof from strict arbitrament,°
And stop all sight-holes,° every loop from whence
The eye of reason may pry in upon us.
This absence of your father's draws° a curtain
That shows the ignorant a kind of fear
Before not dreamt of.
HOTSPUR   You strain° too far.
I rather of his absence make this use:
It lends a luster° and more great opinion,°
A larger dare° to our great enterprise,
Than if the earl were here; for men must think,
If we, without his help, can make a head°
To push against a kingdom, with his help
We shall o'erturn it topsy-turvy down.
Yet all goes well; yet all our joints° are whole.
DOUGLAS
As heart can think. There is not such a word
Spoke of in Scotland as this term of fear.
   Enter Sir Richard Vernon.
HOTSPUR
My cousin Vernon! welcome, by my soul.
VERNON
Pray God my news be worth a welcome, lord.
The Earl of Westmoreland, seven thousand strong,
Is marching hitherwards; with him Prince John.
HOTSPUR
No harm. What more?
VERNON   And further, I have learned
The king himself in person is set forth,
Or hitherwards intended° speedily,
With strong and mighty preparation.
HOTSPUR
He shall be welcome too. Where is his son,
The nimble-footed madcap Prince of Wales,
And his comrades, that daffed° the world aside
And bid it pass?
VERNON   All furnished,° all in arms;
All plumed like estridges° that with the wind
Bated° like eagles having lately bathed;
Glittering in golden coats° like images;°
As full of spirit as the month of May
And gorgeous as the sun at midsummer;
Wanton° as youthful goats, wild as young bulls.
I saw young Harry with his beaver° on,
His cuisses° on his thighs, gallantly armed,

fearful: timid; **faction:** support
question: doubt
off'ring: challenging
arbitrament: investigation, scrutiny   70
sight-holes: loopholes

draws: opens

    75

strain: reach, exaggerate

luster: shine; **opinion:** prestige
dare: daring

head: force, army   80

joints: limbs

    85

    90

intended: i.e., to come

    95
daffed: (1) put aside, (2) tipped his hat at

furnished: armed, equipped
estridges: ostriches
Bated: flapped wings
coats: (of armor); **images:** gilded statues   100

Wanton: frisky, sportive
beaver: armor
cuisses: thigh armor   105

DISCOVERING SHAKESPEARE

(95) <u>Themes</u> **[4.1.75]:** After reading Hotspur's speech in 4.1.75–83, explain how it expands and clarifies his concept of honor. Which other speeches by Hotspur help explain this chivalric ideal?
(96) **Language [4.1.98]:** What were "estridges" (4.1.98)? [*Hint:* See the *Oxford English Dictionary.*]

Rise from the ground like feathered Mercury,°
And vaulted° with such ease into his seat
As if an angel dropped down from the clouds
To turn and wind a fiery Pegasus°
And witch° the world with noble horsemanship.

HOTSPUR
No more, no more! Worse than the sun in March,
This praise doth nourish agues.° Let them come.
They come like sacrifices in their trim,°
And to the fire-eyed maid° of smoky war
All hot and bleeding will we offer them.
The mailèd° Mars° shall on his altar sit
Up to the ears in blood. I am on fire
To hear this rich reprisal° is so nigh,
And yet not ours. Come, let me taste° my horse,
Who is to bear me like a thunderbolt
Against the bosom of the Prince of Wales.
Harry to Harry shall, hot horse to horse,
Meet, and ne'er part till one drop down a corse.°
O that Glendower were come!

VERNON   There is more news.
I learned in Worcester, as I rode along,
He cannot draw° his power this° fourteen days.

DOUGLAS
That's the worst tidings that I hear of yet.

WORCESTER
Ay, by my faith, that bears a frosty sound.

HOTSPUR
What may the king's whole battle° reach unto?

VERNON
To thirty thousand.

HOTSPUR   Forty let it be.
My father and Glendower being both away,
The powers of us may serve° so great a day.
Come, let us take a muster speedily.
Doomsday is near. Die all, die merrily.

DOUGLAS
Talk not of dying. I am out of° fear
Of death or death's hand for this one half-year.   *Exeunt.*

❧ **4.2**° *Enter Falstaff and Bardolph.*

FALSTAFF Bardolph, get thee before° to Coventry; fill me
a bottle of sack. Our soldiers shall march through.
We'll to Sutton Co'fil'° tonight.

BARDOLPH Will you give me money, captain?

FALSTAFF Lay out,° lay out.

BARDOLPH This bottle makes an angel.°

Glossary (right column):

Mercury: messenger of the gods (with winged feet)
vaulted: jumped
Pegasus: winged horse of Greek mythology
witch: bewitch, charm   110

agues: shivery fear (believed to be caused by the vapors drawn by the spring sun)
trim: decoration, finery
maid: the goddess of war, Bellona   115
mailèd: i.e., chain-mail-wearing; **Mars:** god of war
reprisal: prize, booty
taste: feel
          120

corse: corpse
          125

draw: muster, gather; **this:** for

battle: army
          130

may serve: must be adequate to serve

out of: free from   135

4.2: The road to Coventry

get thee before: go ahead

Sutton Co'fil': (Sutton Coldfield is twenty miles beyond Coventry)

Lay out: pay for it yourself   5
makes an angel: ten shillings that you owe me, that I've spent for you

---

DISCOVERING SHAKESPEARE

(97) Rhyme [4.1.123]: What was a "corse" (4.1.123)? How does the rhyme between "horse" and "corse" help foreshadow Hotspur's death at Shrewsbury Field in 5.4?

FALSTAFF   An if it do,° take it for thy labor;° an if it make twenty, take them all; I'll answer° the coinage. Bid my lieutenant Peto meet me at town's end.

BARDOLPH   I will, captain. Farewell.   *Exit.*

FALSTAFF   If I be not ashamed of my soldiers, I am a soused gurnet.° I have misused the king's press° damnably. I have got, in exchange of° a hundred and fifty soldiers, three hundred and odd pounds. I press me none but good householders,° yeomen's° sons; inquire me out contracted° bachelors, such as had been asked twice on the banns° — such a commodity of warm slaves as had as lieve° hear the devil as a drum, such as fear the report of a caliver° worse than a struck fowl or a hurt wild duck. I pressed me none but such toasts-and-butter,° with hearts in their bellies no bigger than pins' heads, and they have bought out their services; and now my whole charge° consists of ancients,° corporals, lieutenants, gentlemen of companies° — slaves as ragged as Lazarus° in the painted cloth,° where the glutton's dogs licked his sores; and such as indeed were never soldiers, but discarded unjust° servingmen, younger sons° to younger brothers, revolted° tapsters, and ostlers trade-fallen;° the cankers° of a calm world and a long peace; ten times more dishonorable ragged than an old fazed ancient;° and such have I to fill up the rooms° of them as have bought out their services that you would think that I had a hundred and fifty tattered prodigals° lately come from swine-keeping, from eating draff° and husks. A mad fellow met me on the way, and told me I had unloaded all the gibbets° and pressed the dead bodies. No eye hath seen such scarecrows. I'll not march through Coventry with them, that's flat.° Nay, and the villains march wide betwixt the legs,° as if they had gyves° on, for indeed I had the most of them out of prison. There's not a shirt and a half in all my company, and the half-shirt is two napkins tacked together and thrown over the shoulders like a herald's coat without sleeves; and the shirt, to say the truth, stol'n from my host at Saint Alban's, or the red-nose innkeeper of Daventry. But that's all one; they'll find linen enough on every hedge.°

Enter the Prince and the Lord of Westmoreland.

PRINCE   How now, blown° Jack? How now, quilt?°

FALSTAFF   What, Hal? How now, mad wag? What a devil dost thou in Warwickshire? My good Lord of Westmoreland, I cry you mercy.° I thought your honor had already been at Shrewsbury.

An . . . do: (Falstaff pretends that "makes" means "creates"); **labor:** effort

answer: answer for, be responsible for (as if coinage were privately, illegally minted)   10

soused gurnet: pickled fish (with a large head and a slender body—i.e., the contrary of Falstaff); **press:** the right of conscription (drafting)

in exchange of: instead of (for allowing men to buy their way out of being drafted)   15

good householders: wealthy homeowners; **yeomen:** small freeholders

contracted: engaged to be married

banns: public announcements, made on three Sundays, of an intent to marry   20

lieve: rather

caliver: musket

toasts-and-butter: cowards, sissies (too elegant to fight)

charge: command; **ancients:** ensigns, or   25
standard-bearers (Falstaff has signed on men at more than the usual numbers of officers in order to collect—and pocket—their higher pay)

gentlemen of companies: volunteers

Lazarus: the beggar; **painted cloth:** a wall   30
decoration

unjust: dishonest; **younger sons:** i.e., with no hope of inheritance

revolted: run away from their apprenticeships

ostlers trade-fallen: horse handlers whose business has fallen off; **cankers:** worms   35

fazed ancient: frayed flag; **fill up the rooms:** take the place of

prodigals: i.e., prodigal sons; see Luke 15:15–16

draff: pig swill

gibbets: structures for hanging people   40

flat: for sure

wide . . . legs: with their legs apart

gyves: prisoner's chains

45

linen . . . hedge: washed clothes were dried on hedges

blown: swollen (with office); **quilt:** a soldier's quilted jacket was called a jack

50

cry you mercy: beg your pardon

DISCOVERING SHAKESPEARE

(98) Plot [4.2.11]: What illegal and unethical actions has Falstaff taken in recruiting his soldiers?

(99) Social History [4.2.36]: What can we learn from Falstaff's speeches in 4.2 about the conditions endured by English soldiers during the reign of King Henry IV (1366–1413)? What other interesting information can you discover about Medieval and Renaissance armies in your school library or online?

WESTMORELAND Faith, Sir John, 'tis more than time that I were there, and you too, but my powers° are there already. The king, I can tell you, looks for us all. We must away° all night.

powers: forces, soldiers

must away: march

55

FALSTAFF Tut, never fear° me: I am as vigilant as a cat to steal cream.

fear: worry about

PRINCE I think, to steal cream indeed, for thy theft hath already made thee butter. But tell me, Jack, whose fellows are these that come after?

60

FALSTAFF Mine, Hal, mine.

PRINCE I did never see such pitiful rascals.

FALSTAFF Tut, tut! good enough to toss;° food for powder,° food for powder. They'll fill a pit as well as better.° Tush,° man, mortal men, mortal men.

toss: i.e., on a pike (a sharp pole)

powder: gunpowder (i.e., cannon fodder)

better: i.e., their betters

Tush: a scoffing term

65

WESTMORELAND Ay, but, Sir John, methinks they are exceeding poor and bare – too beggarly.

FALSTAFF Faith, for their poverty, I know not where they had that, and for their bareness, I am sure they never learned that of me.

70

PRINCE No, I'll be sworn, unless you call three fingers° in the ribs bare. But, sirrah, make haste. Percy is already in the field.   *Exit.*

fingers: a finger was three quarters of an inch

FALSTAFF What, is the king encamped?

WESTMORELAND He is, Sir John. I fear we shall stay too long.   *[Exit.]*

FALSTAFF Well, to the latter end° of a fray° and the beginning of a feast fits a dull fighter and a keen° guest.
                    Exit.

latter end: finish; **fray:** fight

keen: eager

❧ **4.3**° *Enter Hotspur, Worcester, Douglas, Vernon.*

4.3: The rebel camp

HOTSPUR
We'll fight with him tonight.

WORCESTER   It may not be.

DOUGLAS
You give him then° advantage.

VERNON   Not a whit.°

then: i.e., if you wait

whit: small amount

HOTSPUR
Why say you so? Looks he not for supply?°

supply: reinforcements

VERNON
So do we.

HOTSPUR His is certain, ours is doubtful.

WORCESTER
Good cousin, be advised; stir not tonight.

5

VERNON
Do not, my lord.

DISCOVERING SHAKESPEARE

(100) Morality [4.2.64]: What does Falstaff mean when he says his soldiers are "good enough to toss; food for powder" (4.2.64–65)? How do you feel about his behavior? His morality?

(101) Teaser [4.3.5]: Compare the opening of 4.3.1–15 in *Henry IV, Part I* with the quarrel between Brutus and Cassius in *Julius Caesar*, 4.3.195–224. In each disagreement, which man ends up being right? Which play did Shakespeare write first? Do you think one of these situations is a deliberate echo of the other? Why or why not?

DOUGLAS   You do not counsel well.
You speak it out of fear and cold heart.
VERNON
Do me no slander, Douglas. By my life –
And I dare well maintain it with my life –
If well-respected° honor bid me on,°   **well-respected:** well-considered; **on:** i.e., to   10
I hold as little counsel° with weak fear   fight
As you, my lord, or any Scot that this day lives.   **counsel:** traffic, company
Let it be seen tomorrow in the battle
Which of us fears.
DOUGLAS   Yea, or tonight.
VERNON   Content.
HOTSPUR
Tonight, say I.   15
VERNON
Come, come, it may not be. I wonder much,
Being men of such great leading° as you are,   **leading:** leadership
That you foresee not what impediments
Drag back our expedition. Certain horse°   **horse:** i.e., cavalry
Of my cousin Vernon's are not yet come up.   20
Your uncle Worcester's horse came but today;
And now their pride and mettle° is asleep,   **pride and mettle:** spirit
Their courage with hard labor tame and dull,
That not a horse is half the half of himself.
HOTSPUR
So are the horses of the enemy   25
In general journey-bated° and brought low.   **journey-bated:** worn out from traveling
The better part of ours are full of rest.
WORCESTER
The number of the king exceedeth ours.
For God's sake, cousin, stay till all come in.
    The trumpet sounds a parley.
    Enter Sir Walter Blunt.
BLUNT
I come with gracious offers from the king,   30
If you vouchsafe° me hearing and respect.°   **vouchsafe:** grant, give; **respect:** attention
HOTSPUR
Welcome, Sir Walter Blunt, and would to God
You were of our determination.°   **determination:** mind, opinion
Some of us love you well; and even those some
Envy your great deservings° and good name,   **deservings:** reputation, honors   35
Because you are not of our quality,°   **quality:** party, number
But stand against us like an enemy.
BLUNT
And God defend° but still I should stand so,   **defend:** forbid
So long as out of limit° and true rule°   **limit:** bounds of allegiance and law; **rule:** law,
You stand against anointed majesty.   rulership   40
But to my charge. The king hath sent to know
The nature of your griefs,° and whereupon   **griefs:** grievances

---

DISCOVERING SHAKESPEARE

(102) <u>Themes</u> [4.3.40]: What does Sir Walter Blunt mean when he charges the rebels with fighting against "anointed majesty" (4.3.40)? What other lines can you point to in the play that refer to this concept of "the divine right of kings"?

You conjure from the breast of civil peace
Such bold hostility, teaching his duteous land
Audacious cruelty. If that the king   45
Have any way your good deserts° forgot,   **deserts:** deservings, what is owed to
Which he confesseth to be manifold,
He bids you name your griefs, and with all speed
You shall have your desires with interest,
And pardon absolute for yourself and these   50
Herein misled by your suggestion.°   **suggestion:** instigation

HOTSPUR
The king is kind, and well we know the king
Knows at what time to promise, when to pay.
My father and my uncle and myself
Did give him that same royalty he wears;   55
And when he was not six-and-twenty° strong,   **six-and-twenty:** i.e., twenty-six men
Sick° in the world's regard, wretched and low, **Sick:** unworthy, ill-esteemed
A poor unminded° outlaw sneaking home,   **unminded:** ignominious, ignored
My father gave him welcome to the shore;
And when he heard him swear and vow to God   60
He came but to be Duke of Lancaster,
To sue his livery° and beg his peace,   **sue his livery:** sue for his inheritance
With tears of innocency and terms of zeal,°   (confiscated by Richard II)
                                                 zeal: sincerity
My father, in kind heart and pity moved,
Swore him assistance, and performed it too.   65
Now when the lords and barons of the realm
Perceived Northumberland did lean to° him,   **lean to:** favor
The more and less° came in with cap and knee;° **more and less:** greater and lesser nobles; **cap
Met him in boroughs, cities, villages,   **and knee:** i.e., with cap off and bended knee
Attended° him on bridges, stood in lanes,   **Attended:** waited for   70
Laid gifts before him, proffered him their oaths,
Gave him their heirs as pages,° followed him   **pages:** young servants, attendants
Even at the heels in golden° multitudes.   **golden:** (1) richly dressed, (2) promising
He presently, as greatness knows itself,°   **knows itself:** feels its own strength
Steps me° a little higher than his vow°   **Steps me:** goes beyond; **vow:** (his promise to   75
Made to my father, while his blood° was poor,° seek no more than his inheritance)
Upon the naked shore at Ravenspurgh;   **blood:** spirit; **poor:** unambitious, without hope
And now, forsooth,° takes on him° to reform   **forsooth:** indeed; **takes on him:** takes it upon
Some certain edicts and some strait° decrees   himself
That lie too heavy on the commonwealth;   **strait:** strict   80
Cries out upon° abuses, seems to weep   **Cries out upon:** protests
Over his country's wrongs; and by this face,°   **face:** (1) appearance, (2) pretext
This seeming brow° of justice, did he win   **seeming brow:** pretense, face
The hearts of all that he did angle° for;   **angle:** fish
Proceeded further – cut me off ° the heads   **cut me off:** cut off   85
Of all the favorites° that the absent king   **favorites:** i.e., of the king
In deputation° left behind him here   **deputation:** as deputies
When he was personal° in the Irish war.   **personal:** in person

---

DISCOVERING SHAKESPEARE

(103) Renaissance History [4.3.64]: Hotspur's long speech to Blunt in 4.3.52–88 implies that Hotspur's family supported Bolingbroke (later King Henry IV) before he took the throne from Richard II. Compare Hotspur's allegations with the <u>narrative</u> told in Shakespeare's *Richard II*, 2.1.224–300 and 3.3.101–120.

BLUNT
Tut! I came not to hear this.
HOTSPUR   Then to the point.
In short time after, he deposed the king;   90
Soon after that deprived him of his life;
And in the neck of° that tasked° the whole state;
To make that worse, suffered° his kinsman March
(Who is, if every owner were well placed,°
Indeed his king) to be engaged° in Wales,
There without ransom to lie forfeited;°
Disgraced me in my happy° victories,
Sought to entrap me by intelligence;°
Rated° mine uncle from the council board;
In rage dismissed my father from the court;
Broke oath on oath, committed wrong on wrong;
And in conclusion drove us to seek out
This head of safety,° and withal° to pry
Into his title, the which we find
Too indirect° for long continuance.°
BLUNT
Shall I return this answer to the king?
HOTSPUR
Not so, Sir Walter. We'll withdraw awhile.
Go to the king; and let there be impawned°
Some surety° for a safe return again,
And in the morning early shall mine uncle
Bring him our purposes;° and so farewell.
BLUNT
I would you would accept of° grace and love.
HOTSPUR
And may be so we shall.
BLUNT   Pray God you do.   *Exeunt.*

in the neck of: immediately after; **tasked:** taxed
suffered: allowed
if . . . placed: if everyone were in their proper place   95
engaged: held as hostage
forfeited: unreclaimed
happy: fortunate
intelligence: spying
Rated: scolded   100

This head of safety: army of protection; **withal:** at the same time

indirect: i.e., unlawfully acquired;   105
continuance: possession, duration

impawned: pledged
surety: guarantee
          110
purposes: intentions, proposals, answer

accept of: accept (the king's forgiveness)

❧ **4.4**° *Enter the Archbishop of York and Sir Michael.*

ARCHBISHOP
Hie,° good Sir Michael; bear this sealèd brief °
With wingèd° haste to the lord marshal;°
This° to my cousin Scroop;° and all the rest
To whom they are directed. If you knew
How much they do import, you would make haste.
SIR MICHAEL
My good lord,
I guess their tenor.°
ARCHBISHOP   Like enough you do.
Tomorrow, good Sir Michael, is a day
Wherein the fortune of ten thousand men

4.4: York, the Archbishop's palace

Hie: go, hurry; **brief:** letter
wingèd: i.e., like Mercury, messenger of the gods; **lord marshal:** i.e., Thomas Mowbray, son of the Duke of Norfolk, an enemy of the king
This: this other letter; **Scroop:** i.e., perhaps Sir Stephen Scroop of *Richard II,* 3.2, or Lord Scroop of *Henry V,* 2.2   5

tenor: content

DISCOVERING SHAKESPEARE

(104) Language [4.3.89]: Exactly what "point" (4.3.89) does Hotspur make in his speech in 4.3.89–105?
(105) Plot [4.4.1]: Act 4, scene 4 involves two characters we have never met before. What necessary information does this scene add to the play? How would the script have been different without it?

Must bide the touch;° for, sir, at Shrewsbury,   **bide the touch:** withstand the test   10
As I am truly given to understand,
The king with mighty and quick-raisèd power
Meets with Lord Harry; and I fear, Sir Michael,
What with the sickness of Northumberland,
Whose power was in the first proportion,°   **first proportion:** greater magnitude   15
And what with Owen Glendower's absence thence,
Who with them was a rated sinew° too   **rated sinew:** valued source of strength, support
And comes not in, overruled by prophecies –
I fear the power of Percy is too weak
To wage° an instant° trial with the king.   **wage:** risk; **instant:** immediate   20

SIR MICHAEL
Why, my good lord, you need not fear;
There is Douglas and Lord Mortimer.

ARCHBISHOP
No, Mortimer is not there.

SIR MICHAEL
But there is Mordake, Vernon, Lord Harry Percy,
And there is my Lord of Worcester, and a head°   **head:** force   25
Of gallant warriors, noble gentlemen.

ARCHBISHOP
And so there is; but yet the king hath drawn
The special head of all the land together –
The Prince of Wales, Lord John of Lancaster,
The noble Westmoreland and warlike Blunt,   30
And many moe corrivals° and dear° men   **moe corrivals:** more allies; **dear:** valued
Of estimation and command in arms.

SIR MICHAEL
Doubt not, my lord, they shall be well opposed.

ARCHBISHOP
I hope no less, yet needful 'tis to fear;
And, to prevent the worst, Sir Michael, speed.   35
For if Lord Percy thrive° not, ere the king   **thrive:** succeed
Dismiss his power, he means to visit us,
For he hath heard of our confederacy,°   **confederacy:** alliance
And 'tis but wisdom to make strong° against him.   **make strong:** prepare ourselves
Therefore make haste. I must go write again   40
To other friends; and so farewell, Sir Michael.   *Exeunt.*

 5.1° *Enter the King, Prince of Wales, Lord John of*   **5.1:** Shrewsbury, the royal camp
Lancaster, Sir Walter Blunt, Falstaff.

KING
How bloodily the sun begins to peer
Above yon bulky° hill! The day looks pale   **bulky:** looming
At his distemp'rature.°   **distemp'rature:** unhealthy appearance

---

DISCOVERING SHAKESPEARE

(106) <u>Characterization</u> [4.4.16]: Were you surprised to learn in this scene that Glendower had decided not to join the rebels? What do you think has caused his "absence" (4.4.16)?

(107) <u>Lighting</u> [5.1.1]: At what time of day does this scene begin? Where are the King's forces? How could the characters' <u>costume</u> choices signal the season of the year and the weather?

PRINCE   The southern wind
  Doth play the trumpet° to his° purposes   **trumpet:** trumpeter, herald; **his:** i.e., the sun's
  And by his hollow whistling in the leaves   5
  Foretells a tempest and a blust'ring day.
KING
  Then with the losers let it sympathize,
  For nothing can seem foul to those that win.
    The trumpet sounds. Enter Worcester [and Vernon].
  How now, my Lord of Worcester? 'Tis not well
  That you and I should meet upon such terms   10
  As now we meet. You have deceived our trust
  And made us doff° our easy° robes of peace   **doff:** cast off, remove; **easy:** comfortable
  To crush our old limbs in ungentle steel.
  This is not well, my lord; this is not well.
  What say you to it? Will you again unknit   15
  This churlish knot of all-abhorrèd war,
  And move in that obedient orb° again   **orb:** orbit (the king's subjects are compared to
  Where you did give a fair and natural light,   revolving planets)
  And be no more an exhaled meteor,°   **exhaled meteor:** (meteors were thought to be
  A prodigy° of fear, and a portent   drawn up by the sun and ill omens)   20
  Of broachèd° mischief to the unborn times?   **prodigy:** sign, omen
WORCESTER   **broachèd:** launched, begun
  Hear me, my liege.
  For mine own part, I could be well content
  To entertain° the lag-end° of my life   **entertain:** occupy; **lag-end:** latter portion
  With quiet hours, for I do protest   25
  I have not sought the day of this dislike.°   **dislike:** discord, unrest
KING
  You have not sought it! How comes it then?
FALSTAFF
  Rebellion lay in his way, and he found it.
PRINCE
  Peace, chewet,° peace!   **chewet:** chatterer (jackdaw)
WORCESTER
  It pleased your majesty to turn your looks   30
  Of favor from myself and all our house;°   **house:** family
  And yet I must remember° you, my lord,   **remember:** remind
  We were the first and dearest of your friends.
  For you my staff of office° did I break   **staff of office:** i.e., the sign of his position
  In Richard's time, and posted° day and night   **posted:** rode swiftly   35
  To meet you on the way and kiss your hand
  When yet you were in place° and in account°   **place:** position; **account:** accounting,
  Nothing so strong and fortunate as I.   reckoning
  It was myself, my brother, and his son
  That brought you home and boldly did outdare°   **outdare:** defy   40
  The dangers of the time. You swore to us,
  And you did swear that oath at Doncaster,
  That you did nothing purpose° 'gainst the state,   **purpose:** intend
  Nor claim no further than your new-fallen° right,   **new-fallen:** recently inherited (from his father,
                                         John of Gaunt)

DISCOVERING SHAKESPEARE

(108) Verse [5.1.22]: Scan Worcester's speech in 5.1.22–26; then explain how a skilled actor could use the meter to help indicate the character's state of mind.

The seat of Gaunt, dukedom of Lancaster. 45
To this we swore our aid. But in short space
It rained down fortune show'ring on your head,
And such a flood of greatness fell on you –
What with our help, what with the absent king,
What with the injuries of a wanton° time, 50
The seeming sufferances° that you had borne,
And the contrarious° winds that held the king
So long in his unlucky Irish wars
That all in England did repute him dead –
And from this swarm of fair advantages 55
You took occasion° to be quickly wooed
To grip° the general sway° into your hand;
Forgot your oath to us at Doncaster;
And, being fed by us, you used us so
As that ungentle° gull,° the cuckoo's° bird, 60
Useth the sparrow – did oppress our nest;
Grew by our feeding to so great a bulk
That even our love durst not come near your sight
For fear of swallowing;° but with nimble wing 65
We were enforced for safety sake to fly
Out of your sight and raise this present head;°
Whereby we stand opposèd by such means°
As you yourself have forged against yourself
By unkind usage,° dangerous countenance,°
And violation of all faith and troth° 70
Sworn to us in your younger° enterprise.

KING
These things, indeed, you have articulate,°
Proclaimed at market crosses,° read in churches,
To face° the garment of rebellion
With some fine color° that may please the eye 75
Of fickle changelings° and poor discontents,°
Which gape° and rub the elbow° at the news
Of hurlyburly innovation.
And never yet did insurrection want
Such water colors° to impaint his cause, 80
Nor moody° beggars, starving° for a time
Of pell-mell havoc and confusion.

PRINCE
In both your° armies there is many a soul
Shall pay full dearly for this encounter,
If once they join in trial. Tell your nephew 85
The Prince of Wales doth join with all the world
In praise of Henry Percy. By my hopes,
This present enterprise set off his head,°
I do not think a braver gentleman,
More active-valiant or more valiant-young, 90

wanton: disordered, lawless
sufferances: distresses, injuries
contrarious: adverse

occasion: opportunity
grip: seize; **general sway:** i.e., the populace

ungentle: non-noble; **gull:** nestling; **cuckoo:** (a bird that lays its eggs in other birds' nests)

swallowing: i.e., being swallowed

head: army
means: causes, factors

usage: treatment; **countenance:** demeanor, behavior
troth: truth
younger: earlier, previous

articulate: specified
market crosses: crossways (or centers) or markets
face: trim, line
color: camouflage, excuse
changelings: turncoats, traitors; **discontents:** discontented persons
gape: open their mouths (in anticipation); **rub the elbow:** hug themselves (in delight)
water colors: thin pretexts
moody: angry, restless; **starving:** eager (but also literally hungry)

your: your and ours

off his head: discounted, not held against him

DISCOVERING SHAKESPEARE

(109) Renaissance History [5.1.45]: Who was John of Gaunt? [*Hint:* See act one of Shakespeare's *Richard II* for further information.)
(110) Metaphor [5.1.74]: Explain the King's <u>metaphoric</u> comment that the rebels have attempted to "face the garment of rebellion / With some fine color that may please the eye / Of fickle changelings and poor discontents" (5.1.74–76).

More daring or more bold, is now alive
To grace this latter° age with noble deeds.   **latter:** present
For my part, I may speak it to my shame,
I have a truant° been to chivalry;   **truant:** traitor, deserter
And so I hear he doth account° me too.   **account:** esteem   95
Yet this before° my father's majesty –   **this before:** i.e., sworn by
I am content that he shall take the odds
Of his great name and estimation,°   **estimation:** reputation
And will, to save the blood on either side,
Try fortune with him in a single fight.   100

KING
And, Prince of Wales, so dare° we venture° thee,   **dare:** would dare; **venture:** risk, gamble
Albeit° considerations infinite   **Albeit:** were it not that
Do make° against it. No, good Worcester, no!   **make:** argue, determine
We love our people well; even those we love
That are misled upon your cousin's part;   105
And, will they take the offer of our grace,
Both he, and they, and you, yea, every man
Shall be my friend again, and I'll be his.
So tell your cousin, and bring men word
What he will do. But if he will not yield,   110
Rebuke and dread correction wait on us,°   **wait on us:** are in attendance upon us
And they shall do their office. So be gone.
We will not now be troubled with reply.
We offer fair; take it advisedly.

Exit Worcester [with Vernon].

PRINCE
It will not be accepted, on my life.   115
The Douglas and the Hotspur both together
Are confident against the world in arms.

KING
Hence, therefore, every leader to his charge;
For, on their answer, will we set on them,
And God befriend us as our cause is just.   120

Exeunt. Prince, Falstaff [remain].

FALSTAFF   Hal, if thou see me down in the battle and be-
stride me, so!° 'Tis a point° of friendship.   **so:** good; **point:** aspect
PRINCE   Nothing but a colossus° can do thee that friend-   **colossus:** giant
ship. Say thy prayers, and farewell.
FALSTAFF   I would 'twere bedtime, Hal, and all well.   125
PRINCE   Why, thou owest God a death.°   *[Exit].*   **death:** (with pun on "debt")
FALSTAFF   'Tis not due yet: I would be loath° to pay him   **loath:** reluctant
before his day. What need I be so forward° with him   **forward:** eager
that calls not on me? Well, 'tis no matter; honor pricks°   **pricks:** urges
me on. Yea, but how if honor prick me off° when I come   **prick me off:** mark me (pick me) off for death   130

DISCOVERING SHAKESPEARE

(111) <u>Symbolism</u> **[5.1.100]:** When Prince Hal challenges Hotspur to single combat (5.1.100), these characters <u>symbolize</u> two strong, opposing forces in England's rise to nationalism during the fourteenth century. What specific abstract qualities do Hal and Hotspur each <u>symbolize</u>? Can you identify any other characters in the play who project <u>symbolic</u> meaning?

(112) <u>Soliloquy</u> **[5.1.127]:** Which characters have the most <u>soliloquies</u> in this play? Which don't have any? How does the assignment of these <u>soliloquies</u> help us determine who the principal characters are and where audience sympathy is focused?

on? How then? Can honor set to° a leg? No. Or an arm?
No. Or take away the grief of a wound? No. Honor
hath no skill in surgery° then? No. What is honor? A
word. What is that word honor? Air — a trim reckoning!° Who hath it? He that died a Wednesday. Doth he
feel it? No. Doth he hear it? No. 'Tis insensible° then?
Yea, to the dead. But will it not live with the living? No.
Why? Detraction° will not suffer it. Therefore I'll none
of it. Honor is a mere scutcheon° — and so ends my catechism.°   *Exit.*

> **set to:** set
>
> **surgery:** medicine
>
> **trim reckoning:** slender amount (slim thing)   135
> **insensible:** unable to be sensed
>
> **Detraction:** slander
> **scutcheon:** coat of arms borne at a funeral
> **catechism:** a question-and-answer rehearsal of   140
> the principles of faith

❧ **5.2**° *Enter Worcester and Sir Richard Vernon.*

> **5.2:** Shrewsbury battlefield, the rebel camp

WORCESTER
  O no, my nephew must not know, Sir Richard,
  The liberal° and kind offer of the king.

> **liberal:** generous

VERNON
  'Twere best he did.
WORCESTER   Then are we all undone.
  It is not possible, it cannot be,
  The king should keep his word in loving us.
  He will suspect us still° and find a time
  To punish this offense in other faults.
  Supposition° all our lives shall be stuck full° of eyes;
  For treason is but trusted like the fox,
  Who, ne'er so° tame, so cherished and locked up,
  Will have a wild trick° of his ancestors.
  Look° how we can, or sad or merrily,
  Interpretation will misquote° our looks,
  And we shall feed like oxen at a stall,
  The better cherished° still the nearer death,
  My nephew's trespass may be well forgot;
  It hath the excuse of youth and heat of blood,
  And an adopted name of privilege° —
  A hare-brained Hotspur, governed by a spleen.°
  All his offenses live upon my head
  And on his father's.° We did train° him on;
  And, his corruption° being ta'en° from us,
  We, as the spring° of all, shall pay for all.
  Therefore, good cousin, let not Harry know,
  In any case, the offer of the king.
    Enter Hotspur [and Douglas].
VERNON
  Deliver what you will, I'll say 'tis so.
  Here comes your cousin.
HOTSPUR   My uncle is returned.
  Deliver up° my Lord of Westmoreland.
  Uncle, what news?

>   5
>
> **still:** constantly
>
> **Supposition:** suspicion; **stuck full of:** have
> many
> **ne'er so:** be he never so   10
> **wild trick:** trait
> **Look:** behave
> **misquote:** misreport, misconstrue
>
> **cherished:** fed   15
>
> **adopted name of privilege:** i.e., a nickname
> **spleen:** fiery temper
> **All . . . father's:** his father and I will be held   20
> responsible for his offenses; **train:** lure
> **corruption:** guilt; **being ta'en:** being derived
> **spring:** source
>
>   25
>
> **Deliver up:** release (as a hostage)

DISCOVERING SHAKESPEARE

(113) Paraphrase [5.2.8]: Read Worcester's speech in 5.2.3–25; then paraphrase it in your own words. When Vernon
states "Deliver what you will, I'll say 'tis so" (5.2.26), precisely what is he agreeing to do?
(114) Staging [5.2.28]: Why has Westmoreland been held prisoner? And why does Hotspur tell Vernon to release him at
this moment of the play (5.2.28)?

WORCESTER
  The king will bid you battle presently.   30

DOUGLAS
  Defy him by° the Lord of Westmoreland.   **Defy him by:** send back your defiance with

HOTSPUR
  Lord Douglas, go you and tell him so.

DOUGLAS
  Marry,° and shall,° and very willingly.   *Exit.*   **Marry:** indeed; **and shall:** and I shall

WORCESTER
  There is no seeming mercy in the king.

HOTSPUR
  Did you beg any? God forbid!   35

WORCESTER
  I told him gently of our grievances,
  Of his oath-breaking, which he mended° thus,   **mended:** excused, made up for
  By now forswearing° that he is forsworn.°   **forswearing:** denying; **is forsworn:** broke a
  He calls us rebels, traitors, and will scourge°   promise
  With haughty arms this hateful name in us.   **scourge:** (1) cleanse, (2) brand   40
    Enter Douglas.

DOUGLAS
  Arm, gentlemen! to arms! for I have thrown
  A brave° defiance in King Henry's teeth,   **brave:** proud
  And Westmoreland, that was engaged,° did bear° it;   **engaged:** held hostage; **bear:** carry
  Which cannot choose° but bring him quickly on.   **choose:** help

WORCESTER
  The Prince of Wales stepped forth before the king   45
  And, nephew, challenged you to single fight.

HOTSPUR
  O, would the quarrel lay upon our heads,
  And that no man might draw short breath today
  But I and Harry Monmouth! Tell me, tell me,
  How showed his tasking?° Seemed it in contempt?   **tasking:** challenge   50

VERNON
  No, by my soul. I never in my life
  Did hear a challenge urged more modestly,
  Unless a brother should a brother dare
  To gentle exercise and proof° of arms.   **proof:** test
  He gave you all the duties° of a man;   **duties:** due merits   55
  Trimmed° up your praises with a princely tongue;   **Trimmed:** adorned
  Spoke your deservings like a chronicle;°   **chronicle:** historical record
  Making you ever better than his praise
  By still dispraising° praise valued° with you;   **dispraising:** disparaging; **valued:** compared
  And, which became him like a prince indeed,   60
  He made a blushing cital° of himself,   **cital:** citation, account
  And chid his truant youth with such a grace
  As if he mastered there a double spirit
  Of teaching and of learning instantly.°   **instantly:** at once, simultaneously
  There did he pause; but let me tell the world,   65
  If he outlive the envy° of this day,   **envy:** hostility

DISCOVERING SHAKESPEARE

(115) <u>Characterization</u> **[5.2.54]:** What is the significance of one of the rebels praising Hal, as Vernon does in 5.2.51–68? What is Hotspur's response to this heartfelt praise?

England did never owe° so sweet a hope,

So much misconstrued° in his wantonness.°

owe: own

misconstrued: misjudged; **wantonness:** sportiveness

HOTSPUR

Cousin, I think thou art enamorèd

Upon° his follies. Never did I hear

Of any prince so wild a liberty.°

But be he as he will, yet once ere night°

I will embrace him with a soldier's arm,

That he shall shrink under° my courtesy.°

Arm, arm with speed! and, fellows, soldiers, friends,

Better consider° what you have to do

Than I, that have not well the gift of tongue,

Can lift your blood up with persuasion.°

Enter a Messenger.

enamorèd/Upon: in love with   70

liberty: licentiousness

ere night: before nightfall

under: from; **courtesy:** (said ironically)

75

Better consider: you can better consider

Can . . . persuasion: can inspire you

MESSENGER

My lord, here are letters for you.

HOTSPUR

I cannot read them now. –   80

O gentlemen, the time of life is short!

To spend that shortness basely° were too long

If life did ride upon a dial's° point,

Still ending at the arrival of an hour.°

An° if we live, we live to tread on° kings;

If die, brave° death, when princes die with us!

Now for° our consciences, the arms are fair,

When the intent of bearing them is just.

Enter another Messenger.

basely: in a low manner, ignobly

dial's: clock's

Still . . . hour: if life were only an hour long

An: even; **tread on:** tread as   85

brave: glorious

Now for: now, as for

MESSENGER

My lord, prepare. The king comes on apace.°

HOTSPUR

I thank him that he cuts me° from my tale,

For I profess not° talking. Only this –

Let each man do his best; and here draw I

A sword whose temper° I intend to stain

With the best blood that I can meet withal

In the adventure of this perilous day.

Now, Esperance!° Percy! and set on.

Sound all the lofty instruments of war,

And by that music let us all embrace;

For, heaven to earth,° some of us never shall

A second time do such a courtesy.

Here they embrace. The trumpets sound. [Exeunt.]

apace: quickly

cuts me: cuts me short   90

profess not: am no good at, don't claim to be (a talker)

temper: steel

95

Esperance: hope (the Percy family battle cry)

heaven to earth: heaven bet against earth

100

✧ **5.3**° *The King enters with his power.° Alarum° to the battle. [Exeunt.] Then enter Douglas and Sir Walter Blunt.*

5.3: The battlefield

power: army; **Alarum:** trumpet

BLUNT

What is thy name, that in battle thus

DISCOVERING SHAKESPEARE

(116) <u>Metaphor</u> **[5.2.82]:** Explain Hotspur's complex <u>metaphor</u> about life riding "upon a dial's point" in 5.2.82–84.

(117) <u>Teaser</u> **[5.3.1]:** How is Sir Walter Blunt dressed on the battlefield? How does his choice of clothing lead to his death?

Thou crossest me? What honor dost thou seek
Upon° my head?

| | Upon: from |

DOUGLAS   Know then my name is Douglas,
And I do haunt thee in the battle thus
Because some tell me that thou art a king.°

| | a king: (several persons were disguised as the | 5 |
| | king in order to serve as decoys) |

BLUNT
They tell thee true.

DOUGLAS
The Lord of Stafford dear° today hath bought
Thy likeness,° for instead of thee, King Harry,
This sword hath ended° him. So shall it thee,
Unless thou yield thee as my prisoner.

	dear: dearly
	likeness: resemblance
	ended: finished, killed
		10

BLUNT
I was not born a yielder, thou proud Scot;
And thou shalt find a king that will revenge
Lord Stafford's death.
  They fight. Douglas kills Blunt. Then enter Hotspur.

HOTSPUR   O Douglas, hadst thou fought at Holmedon
thus, I never had triumphed upon a Scot.

| | | 15 |

DOUGLAS
All's done, all's won. Here breathless lies the king.

HOTSPUR   Where?

DOUGLAS   Here.

HOTSPUR
This, Douglas? No. I know this face full well.
A gallant knight he was, his name was Blunt;
Semblably furnished° like the king himself.

		20
	Semblably furnished: similarly equipped,
	dressed

DOUGLAS
A fool go with thy soul,° whither it goes!
A borrowed title hast thou bought too dear:
Why didst thou tell me that thou wert a king?

| | A fool . . . soul: may the name of fool go with |
| | your soul |

HOTSPUR
The king hath many marching in his coats.°

| | coats: vests worn over armor that display | 25 |
| | identifying coats of arms |

DOUGLAS
Now, by my sword, I will kill all his coats;
I'll murder all his wardrobe, piece by piece,
Until I meet the king.

HOTSPUR   Up and away!
Our soldiers stand full fairly° for the day.   *Exeunt.*
  Alarum. Enter Falstaff [alone].

| | fairly: in a good position |

FALSTAFF   Though I could scape shot-free° at London, I
fear the shot° here. Here's no scoring° but upon the pate.°
Soft!° who are you? Sir Walter Blunt. There's honor for
you! Here's no vanity!° I am as hot as molten lead, and as
heavy too. God keep lead out of me. I need no more
weight than mine own bowels. I have led my rag-of-
muffins where they are peppered.° There's not three of
my hundred and fifty left alive, and they are for the
town's end,° to beg during life. But who comes here?
  Enter the Prince.

	shot-free: unwounded, without paying bills	30
	shot: ammunition; scoring: (1) cutting,
	(2) tallying of expenses incurred; pate: head
	Soft!: hark, wait
	Here's no vanity: (if this isn't a good
	demonstration of honor's emptiness, then I don't	35
	know what is)
	peppered: i.e., with shot
	town's end: city gate

DISCOVERING SHAKESPEARE

(118) Puns [5.3.30]: How many different <u>puns</u> does Falstaff make in his speech in 5.3.30–38? List each one; then explain the double meaning involved in each.

PRINCE
What, stand'st thou idle here? Lend me thy sword.
Many a nobleman lies stark and stiff   40
Under the hoofs of vaunting° enemies,
Whose deaths are yet unrevenged. I prithee
Lend me thy sword.

vaunting: vanquishing, triumphant

FALSTAFF O Hal, I prithee give me leave to breathe
awhile. Turk Gregory° never did such deeds in arms as I
have done this day. I have paid° Percy; I have made him
sure.°

Turk Gregory: (Turk is a term for a tyrant;   45
Gregory refers either to Pope Gregory VII, who
was renowned for violence, or Gregory XIII
[1572–85], enemy of England and instigator of the
Saint Bartholomew's Day massacre in France in
1572)
paid: finished off
made him sure: made certain of his death   50

PRINCE
He is indeed, and living to kill thee.
I prithee lend me thy sword.

FALSTAFF Nay, before God, Hal, if Percy be alive, thou
get'st not my sword; but take my pistol, if thou wilt.

PRINCE Give it me. What, is it in the case?°

case: holster

FALSTAFF Ay, Hal. 'Tis hot, 'tis hot.° There's that will sack
a city.

hot: i.e., after much firing

The Prince draws it out and finds it to be a bottle of sack.

PRINCE
What, is it a time to jest and dally now?   55
He throws the bottle at him.   *Exit.*

FALSTAFF Well, if Percy° be alive, I'll pierce him. If he do
come in my way, so; if he do not, if I come in his willingly, let him make a carbonado° of me. I like not such
grinning honor as Sir Walter hath. Give me life; which
if I can save, so;° if not, honor comes unlooked for, and
there's an end.   *Exit.*

Percy: (pronounced "Perce")

carbonado: scored steak for broiling

so: well enough   60

   5.4 *Alarum. Excursions.° Enter the King, the Prince,
Lord John of Lancaster, Earl of Westmoreland.*

5.4 Excursions: sorties

KING
I prithee, Harry, withdraw thyself; thou bleedest too
much.
Lord John of Lancaster, go you with him.

JOHN
Not I, my lord, unless I did bleed too.

PRINCE
I do beseech your majesty make up,°
Lest your retirement° do amaze° your friends.°

KING
I will do so.
My Lord of Westmoreland, lead him to his tent.

make up: advance
retirement: retreat; **amaze:** alarm; **friends:**   5
allies, forces

WESTMORELAND
Come, my lord, I'll lead you to your tent.

PRINCE
Lead me, my lord? I do not need your help;

DISCOVERING SHAKESPEARE

(119) <u>Themes</u> **[5.3.55]:** How do Falstaff's speeches in 5.3.30–38 and 5.3.56–61 help refine and clarify his view of
honor? Write a brief paragraph in modern English prose explaining how he feels about the pursuit of honor.

And God forbid a shallow scratch should drive   10
The Prince of Wales from such a field as this,
Where stained nobility lies trodden on,
And rebels' arms triumph in massacres!

JOHN
We breathe° too long. Come, cousin Westmoreland,   **breathe:** pause to catch breath
Our duty this way lies. For God's sake, come.   15
     [Exeunt Prince John and Westmoreland.]

PRINCE
By God, thou hast deceived me, Lancaster!°   **Lancaster:** i.e., his brother John
I did not think thee lord of such a spirit.
Before, I loved thee as a brother, John;
But now, I do respect thee as my soul.

KING
I saw him hold Lord Percy at the point°   **point:** i.e., of his sword   20
With lustier maintenance° than I did look for   **lustier maintenance:** energetic bearing
Of such an ungrown warrior.

PRINCE   O, this boy
Lends mettle to us all!   *Exit.*
   [Enter Douglas.]

DOUGLAS
Another king? They grow like Hydra's heads.°   **Hydra's heads:** (the heads of the monster Hydra
I am the Douglas, fatal to all those   grew again, two for one, as fast as they were cut   25
That wear those colors on them. What art thou   off)
That counterfeit'st the person of a king?

KING
The king himself, who, Douglas, grieves at heart
So many° of his shadows° thou hast met,   **So many:** that so many; **shadows:** likeness
And not the very king. I have two boys   30
Seek° Percy and thyself about the field;   **Seek:** seeking
But, seeing thou fall'st on° me so luckily,   **fall'st on:** come upon
I will assay° thee. So defend thyself.   **assay:** challenge thee

DOUGLAS
I fear thou art another counterfeit;
And yet, in faith, thou bearest thee like a king.   35
But mine I am sure thou art, whoe'er thou be,
And thus I win thee.
   They fight. The King being in danger, enter Prince of
   Wales.

PRINCE
Hold up thy head, vile Scot, or thou art like°   **like:** likely
Never to hold it up again. The spirits
Of valiant Shirley, Stafford, Blunt are in my arms. 40
It is the Prince of Wales that threatens thee,
Who never promiseth but he means to pay.
   They fight. Douglas flieth.
Cheerly,° my lord. How fares your grace?   **Cheerly:** look cheerfully

---

DISCOVERING SHAKESPEARE

(120) Make Up [5.4.10]: At the top of 5.4, King Henry remarks that his son "bleedest too much" (5.4.1), and later Hal admits that he has received a "shallow scratch" (5.4.10) in battle. If you were directing a production of this play, would you use stage blood on Hal to make these lines more realistic? Which other characters should bleed on stage? What is stage blood made of?

(121) Renaissance History [5.4.26]: What were King Henry IV's "colors" (5.4.26)? What was his coat of arms?

Sir Nicholas Gawsey hath for succor° sent,
And so hath Clifton. I'll to Clifton straight.°

succor: aid, help
straight: straightaway   45

KING
Stay and breathe awhile.
Thou hast redeemed thy lost opinion,°
And showed thou mak'st some tender° of my life,
In this fair rescue thou hast brought to me.

opinion: reputation
tender: regard

PRINCE
O God, they did me too much injury   50
That ever said I hearkened° for your death.
If it were so, I might have let alone
The insulting° hand of Douglas over you,
Which would have been as speedy in your end
As all the poisonous potions in the world,   55
And saved the treacherous labor of your son.

hearkened: listened, waited

insulting: exulting, demeaning

KING
Make up° to Clifton; I'll to Sir Nicholas Gawsey.   *Exit.*
    Enter Hotspur.

Make up: advance to

HOTSPUR
If I mistake not, thou art Harry Monmouth.
PRINCE
Thou speak'st as if I would deny my name.
HOTSPUR
My name is Harry Percy.   60
PRINCE   Why, then I see
A very valiant rebel of the name.
I am the Prince of Wales, and think not, Percy,
To share with me in glory any more.
Two stars keep not their motion in one sphere,°
Nor can one England brook° a double reign   65
Of Harry Percy and the Prince of Wales.

sphere: orbit
brook: tolerate

HOTSPUR
Nor shall it, Harry, for the hour is come
To end the one of us; and would to God
Thy name in arms were now as great as mine!
PRINCE
I'll make it greater ere I part from thee,   70
And all the budding honors on thy crest°
I'll crop° to make a garland for my head.

crest: helmet
crop: pluck

HOTSPUR
I can no longer brook thy vanities.°
    They fight. Enter Falstaff.

vanities: boasts

FALSTAFF   Well said, Hal! to it, Hal! Nay, you shall find
no boy's play here, I can tell you.   75
    *Enter Douglas. He fighteth with Falstaff, who falls
    down as if he were dead. [Exit Douglas.] The Prince
    killeth Percy.*
HOTSPUR
O Harry, thou hast robbed me of my youth!

DISCOVERING SHAKESPEARE

(122) <u>Plot</u> **[5.4.47]:** When King Henry IV tells Hal that he has "redeemed" his "lost opinion" (5.4.47) by his bravery on the battlefield, exactly what is he referring to? Which specific line or speech earlier in the play most clearly expresses the King's low opinion of his son?

I better brook the loss of brittle life
Than those proud titles thou hast won of me.
They wound my thoughts worse than thy sword in flesh.
But thoughts the° slaves of life, and life time's fool,°   **thoughts the:** thoughts that are; **fool:** plaything   80
And time, that takes survey° of all the world,   **takes survey:** oversees
Must have a stop. O, I could prophesy,
But that the earthy and cold hand of death
Lies on my tongue. No, Percy, thou art dust,
And food for –   85
    [Dies.]
PRINCE
For worms, brave Percy. Fare thee well, great heart.
Ill-weaved ambition, how much art thou shrunk!
When that this body did contain a spirit,
A kingdom for it was too small a bound;°   **bound:** territory, limit
But now two paces of the vilest earth   90
Is room enough. This earth that bears thee dead
Bears not alive so stout° a gentleman.   **stout:** brave, valiant
If thou wert sensible of° courtesy,   **sensible of:** able to sense
I should not make so dear a show of zeal.°   **so . . . zeal:** so enthusiastic a demonstration of admiration
But let my favors° hide thy mangled face;   **favors:** plumes, scarf   95
And, even in thy behalf, I'll thank myself
For doing these fair rites of tenderness.
Adieu, and take thy praise with thee to heaven.
Thy ignominy sleep with thee in the grave,
But not remembered in thy epitaph.   100
    He spieth Falstaff on the ground.
What, old acquaintance? Could not all this flesh
Keep in a little life? Poor Jack, farewell!
I could have better spared a better man.
O, I should have a heavy° miss of thee   **heavy:** (1) severe, (2) weighty
If I were much in love with vanity.°   **vanity:** frivolity   105
Death hath not struck so fat a deer today,
Though many dearer, in this bloody fray.
Emboweled° will I see thee by-and-by;   **Emboweled:** eviscerated, preparatory to embalming a corpse
Till then in blood by noble Percy lie.   *Exit.*
    Falstaff riseth up.
FALSTAFF   Emboweled? If thou embowel me today, I'll   110
give you leave to powder° me and eat me too tomorrow.   **powder:** pickle in salt
'Sblood, 'twas time to counterfeit, or that hot terma-
gant° Scot had paid° me scot and lot° too. Counterfeit? I   **termagant:** violent   **paid:** i.e., killed; **scot and lot:** thoroughly
lie; I am no counterfeit. To die is to be a counterfeit, for   115
he is but the counterfeit of a man who hath not the life
of a man; but to counterfeit dying when a man thereby
liveth, is to be no counterfeit, but the true and perfect

DISCOVERING SHAKESPEARE

(123) Alliteration [5.4.77]: Circle all the alliterative words in the following line: "I better brook the loss of brittle life" (5.4.77). In addition to these explosive consonants, what other rhetorical effects in Hotspur's speech in 5.4.76–85 allow us to see that he is dying?

(124) Stage Business [5.4.101]: In order to escape being killed by Douglas, Falstaff pretends to be dead (see the stage direction following 5.4.75). When Hal spies Falstaff on the ground in 5.4.101, his old friend is still feigning death. How do you think Falstaff fakes his own death?

image of life indeed. The better part° of valor is discretion, in the which better part I have saved my life.
Zounds, I am afraid of this gunpowder Percy, though 120
he be dead. How if he should counterfeit too, and rise?
By my faith, I am afraid he would prove the better
counterfeit. Therefore I'll make him sure; yea, and I'll
swear I killed him. Why may not he rise as well as I?
Nothing confutes me but eyes,° and nobody sees me. 125
Therefore, sirrah *[Stabs him.],* with a new wound in
your thigh, come you along with me.
   He takes up Hotspur on his back. Enter Prince, and
   John of Lancaster.

PRINCE
Come, brother John; full bravely hast thou fleshed°
Thy maiden° sword.
JOHN   But, soft! whom have we here?
Did you not tell me this fat man was dead? 130
PRINCE
I did; I saw him dead,
Breathless and bleeding on the ground. Art thou alive?
Or is it fantasy° that plays upon our eyesight?
I prithee speak. We will not trust our eyes
Without our ears. Thou art not what thou seem'st. 135
FALSTAFF   No, that's certain, I am not a double man;° but
if I be not Jack Falstaff, then am I a Jack.° There is Percy.
If your father will do me any honor, so; if not, let him
kill the next Percy himself. I look to be either earl or
duke, I can assure you. 140
PRINCE   Why, Percy I killed myself, and saw thee dead!
FALSTAFF   Didst thou? Lord, Lord, how this world is
given to lying. I grant you I was down, and out of
breath, and so was he; but we rose both at an instant
and fought a long hour by Shrewsbury clock. If I may 145
be believed, so; if not, let them that should reward valor
bear the sin upon their own heads. I'll take it upon my
death, I gave him this wound in the thigh. If the man
were alive and would deny it, zounds! I would make
him eat a piece of my sword. 150
JOHN
This is the strangest tale that ever I heard.
PRINCE
This is the strangest fellow, brother John.
Come, bring your luggage nobly on your back.
For my part, if a lie may do thee grace,°
I'll gild it with the happiest terms I have. 155
   A retreat is sounded.
The trumpet sounds retreat; the day is ours.

part: quality, role

confutes . . . eyes: stops me but an eyewitness

fleshed: initiated
maiden: virgin

fantasy: hallucination

double man: (1) ghost, (2) two men
Jack: knave

grace: credit

DISCOVERING SHAKESPEARE

(125) Paraphrase [5.4.118]: When Falstaff explains in <u>soliloquy</u> that "The better part of valor is discretion"
(5.4.118–119), what does he mean? <u>Paraphrase</u> his statement in modern English. What does this sentiment have to do with
his action of stabbing the dead Hotspur in his thigh (5.4.126)?

(126) Themes [5.4.152]: Read Hal's speech in 5.4.152–155; then contrast his sense of honor with Falstaff's.

Come, brother, let's to the highest of the field,
To see what friends are living, who are dead.

Exeunt [Prince Henry and Prince John].

FALSTAFF   I'll follow, as they say, for reward. He that rewards me, God reward him. If I do grow great,° I'll grow
less; for I'll purge,° and leave sack, and live cleanly, as a
nobleman should do.   *Exit [bearing off the body].*

great: i.e., in status, size, or funds   160
purge: (1) diet with laxatives, (2) repent

₴ **5.5**° *The trumpets sound. Enter the King, Prince of
Wales, Lord John of Lancaster, Earl of Westmoreland,
with Worcester and Vernon prisoners.*

5.5: The king's command post

KING
Thus ever did rebellion find rebuke.
Ill-spirited Worcester, did not we send grace,°
Pardon, and terms of love to all of you?
And wouldst thou turn our offers contrary?°
Misuse the tenor of thy kinsman's trust?°
Three knights upon our party slain today,
A noble earl, and many a creature else
Had been alive this hour,
If like a Christian thou hadst truly borne
Betwixt our armies true intelligence.°

grace: mercy

contrary: away
Misuse . . . trust: abuse Hotspur's trust by   5
concealing my offer of mercy from him

intelligence: report   10

WORCESTER
What I have done my safety urged me to;
And I embrace this fortune patiently,
Since not to be avoided it falls on me.

KING
Bear Worcester to the death, and Vernon too;
Other offenders we will pause° upon.

pause: wait   15

[Exeunt Worcester and Vernon, guarded.]

How goes the field?

PRINCE
The noble Scot, Lord Douglas, when he saw
The fortune of the day quite turned from him,
The noble Percy slain, and all his men
Upon the foot of fear,° fled with the rest;
And falling from a hill, he was so bruised
That the pursuers took him. At my tent
The Douglas is, and I beseech your grace
I may dispose of him.

Upon the foot of fear: in flight for fear   20

KING   With all my heart.

PRINCE
Then, brother John of Lancaster, to you
This honorable bounty° shall belong.
Go to the Douglas and deliver° him
Up to his pleasure, ransomless and free.
His valors shown upon our crests today
Have taught us how to cherish such high deeds,
Even in the bosom of our adversaries.

bounty: act of benevolence   25
deliver: free

30

DISCOVERING SHAKESPEARE

(127) **Plot** [5.5.9]: In the first speech in 5.5, King Henry accuses Worcester of not acting "like a Christian" (5.5.9). Exactly what has Worcester done that seems irreligious to the King? With whom do you most agree: Worcester or the King?

JOHN
   I thank your grace for this high courtesy,
   Which I shall give away immediately.
KING
   Then this remains, that we divide our power.
   You, son John, and my cousin Westmoreland,   35
   Towards York shall bend° you with your dearest speed   **bend:** direct
   To meet Northumberland and the prelate Scroop,
   Who, as we hear, are busily in arms.
   Myself and you, son Harry, will towards Wales
   To fight with Glendower and the Earl of March.   40
   Rebellion in this land shall lose his sway,
   Meeting the check of such another day;
   And since this business so fair is done,
   Let us not leave° till all our own be won.   *Exeunt.*   **leave:** cease

---

DISCOVERING SHAKESPEARE

(128) <u>Rhyme</u> [5.5.41]: How many <u>rhyming</u> couplets end this play? Are they <u>slant rhymes</u> or <u>perfect rhymes</u>? Do these <u>rhymes</u> conclude the play on a note of finality? Why or why not?

❧

Research and Discussion Topics

ACT I

1. What were the dates of Henry IV's reign as King of England? How accurate is his statement that Christ's feet were nailed to the cross "fourteen hundred years ago" (1.1.26)?

2. Locate the following places on a map of England and Wales: Herefordshire (1.1.39), Holmedon (1.1.55), Windsor (1.1.104), Lincolnshire (1.2.76), Canterbury (1.2.123), London (1.2.124), Rochester (1.2.126), Eastcheap (1.2.127), Ravenspurgh (1.3.246), York (1.3.266), Charing Cross (2.1.26), Kent (2.1.56), Burton (3.1.96), Finsbury (3.1.251), Shrewsbury (3.2.166), Bridgenorth (3.2.175), Gloucestershire (3.2.176), Coventry (4.2.1), Saint Alban's (4.2.45), Daventry (4.2.45), Warwickshire (4.2.50), Doncaster (5.1.42), and Lancaster (5.1.45).

3. Find the following rivers on the same map: Wye (3.1.65), Severn (3.1.66), and Trent (3.1.74).

4. What was Holy Rood Day (1.1.52)?

5. Find a family tree for the Plantagenets (1.1.89).

6. What was a leaping house (1.2.8)?

7. Who was Phoebus (1.2.15)?

8. What was Moorditch (1.2.78)? Why does Falstaff refer to the place as "unsavory"?

9. How much money was a "royal" worth (1.2.137)?

10. Why were clouds thought to be "contagious" (1.2.191)?

11. What were parmacity and saltpeter used for (1.3.58–60)?

12. What was choler (1.3.129)?

ACT II

1. What were a carrier and an ostler (2.1.1–3)? What were their duties?

2. Why were robbers called "Saint Nicholas' clerks" (2.1.62–63)?

3. What was a Troyan (2.1.70)?

4. What were foot-land rakers, long-staff six-penny strikers, and mad mustachio purple-hued maltworms (2.1.74–76)?

5. What kind of measuring tool was a "squire" (2.2.12)?

6. What was a setter (2.2.48)?

7. Who was John of Gaunt (2.2.64)? What was his relationship to Bolingbroke (King Henry IV)?

8. Define the following military terms: sallies, retires, palisadoes, frontiers, parapets, basilisks, and culverin (2.3.50–52).

9. What were mammets (2.3.90)?

10. Explain the following tavern terms: hogsheads (2.4.5), under-skinker (2.4.23), a pint of bastard (2.4.26), indenture (2.4.46), and sack (2.4.112).

11. What was a shotten herring (2.4.122)?

12. What sort of punishment was the bastinado (2.4.324)?

13. Who was King Cambyses (2.4.374)?

14. What was a Manningtree ox (2.4.437)?

15. Why did unscrupulous tavern owners put sugar in sack (2.4.455)?

16. Where was St. Paul's (2.4.509)?

ACT III

1. Compare Shakespeare's version of the meeting of the conspirators in 3.1 with his source material in Holinshed's *Chronicles*.

2. What was a comfit-maker (3.1.247)?

3. What were pickthanks and newsmongers (3.2.25)?

4. Who was Mars (3.2.112)? Why does King Henry compare Hotspur to Mars?

5. What was spleen (3.2.125)?

6. Who was Dame Partlet (3.3.52)? Why does Falstaff compare the Hostess to her?

7. How long was an ell (3.3.72)? What was it used to measure?

8. What was a seal ring (3.3.81)?

9. Who was Maid Marian (3.3.114)?

ACT IV

1. Who was Mercury (4.1.106)?

2. Who was Pegasus (4.1.109)?

3. What was an ague (4.1.112)?

4. What was a caliver (4.2.19)? Research the word in the *Oxford English Dictionary* and find out its relationship to "caliber."

5. How has Falstaff misused his power to conscript soldiers (4.2.11–74)? How has he attempted to make money in the process?

6. Who was Lazarus (4.2.25)? Why is he compared to Falstaff's soldiers?

7. Why does Sir Walter Blunt refer to King Henry's "anointed majesty" (4.3.40)? What ceremonies were used when kings were newly crowned?

ACT V

1. Why does Worcester call the cuckoo an "ungentle gull" (5.1.60)? What comparison is he making between King Henry and the cuckoo?

2. What was a colossus (5.1.123)?

3. What was a scutcheon (5.1.139)?

4. What were considered to be the musical "instruments of war" (5.2.97)?

5. Who was Turk Gregory (5.3.45)?

6. What was a carbonado (5.3.58)?

7. What was Hydra (5.4.24)? How many heads did it have?

8. Why does Hotspur call Prince Hal "Monmouth" (5.4.58)? Why is this term of address an insult?

9. What does Prince Hal mean when he says he will see Falstaff "Emboweled" (5.4.108)?

Filmography
Chimes at Midnight (Falstaff)

1966
Arthur Cantor Films
Rating:

Directed by: Orson Welles

Orson Welles as Falstaff
Keith Baxter as Prince Hal
John Gielgud as King Henry IV
Margaret Rutherford as Hostess Quickly
Fernando Rey as Worcester
Alan Webb as Justice Shallow
Tony Beckley as Poins
Jeanne Moreau as Doll Tearsheet

This is the best of Orson Welles' Shakespeare films, and with the possible exception of *Citizen Kane,* the best of Orson Welles' films. As usual, the budget was limited, but the visual images are extraordinary, the battle scene brilliant, and the touches of humor (such as Prince Hal detecting that Falstaff is still alive by the frosty breath that rises from his visor) superb. Welles has taken material from *Richard II, 1 Henry IV, 2 Henry IV, Henry V,* and *The Merry Wives of Windsor* to tell the story of Falstaff and Prince Hal. Their complex relationship—made from equal parts of friendship and exploitation—has never been better demonstrated. The rejection of Falstaff shows Hal feeling pain as he banishes his best friend and Falstaff taking pride in the foster son he has always loved. Keith

Baxter's Hal has a knowing innocence that perfectly balances Welles' wide-eyed lies. Welles' famous friends trooped dutifully in to help him make this movie. John Gielgud as Henry IV is the epitome of upright, fatherly disapproval, and Jeanne Moreau as Doll Tearsheet seems truly to care for the old, fat knight.

1980
BBC
Rating:

Directed by: David Giles

Anthony Quayle as Falstaff
David Gwillim as Henry Prince of Wales
Jon Finch as King Henry IV
Jack Galloway as Poins
Brenda Bruce as Mistress Quickly
Tim Pigott-Smith as Henry Percy, Hotspur
Richard Owens as Owen Glendower

Anthony Quayle has been one of this century's most effective Falstaffs on stage. His performance here is brilliant but encumbered by the overall interpretation. David Giles called the second tetralogy a "Henriad," the story of how Hal grows up to be Henry V, and the plays are cut accordingly. For instance, Falstaff's words to Hal, "thy love is worth a million, thou owest me thy love," are gone, as is much of the warmth between the old knight and the young prince. As a result, Falstaff becomes a secondary character who hums and haws with nervousness. David Gwillim is engagingly ingenuous as Hal, and he very nearly succeeds in carrying the additional weight that Giles has loaded on him. The rest of the cast is also strong, with Jon Finch a guilt-ridden usurper, Tim Pigott-Smith a fiercely mock-heroic Hotspur, and Richard Owens a pompously magical Glendower.

1990
Portman Classics
Rating:

Directed by: Michael Bogdnov

Barry Stanton as Falstaff
Michael Pennington as Henry Prince of Wales
Michael Cronin as Henry IV
Charles Dale as Poins
June Watson as Mistress Quickly
Andrew Jarvis as Hotspur
Sion Probert as Owen Glendower

The great strength of the English Shakespeare Company's *Henry IV* is its eclecticism. The costumes include chain mail, Victorian-Edwardian formal dress, and battle fatigues. In *Henry IV Part II,* Pistol wears a leather motorcycle jacket with "Hal's Angels" on the back. The production began on stage and was filmed with an audience. There is an aura of fluidity and improvisation about the whole film, which gives a simultaneous sense of freshness and timelessness. The great weakness of the English Shakespeare Company's *Henry IV* is its incoherence. This is in some fashion anti-Shakespeare or at least anti-traditionalist Shakespeare, and in some cases (the cutting of set-piece speeches) the result is the weakening of the play. Too many modern issues and interpretations tug at the text—often, it seems, from different directions. However, the cast is uniformly excellent, and the readings are interesting even when they are ill advised.

Annotated Bibliography

Barker, Roberta. "Tragical-Comical-Historical Hotspur." *Shakespeare Quarterly* 54:3 (Fall 2003): 288–307. journal PR 2885.S63.

> Barker traces the gradual evolution in the performance of Hotspur's character in *Henry IV Part 1* from tragic hero in the original theatrical context to a comic foil for Hal and eventually to a historical emblem of feudal chivalry. The author's goal for this reevaluation is to help "deepen the sense of interaction between the text and performance."

Bevington, David, ed. *"Henry the Fourth Parts I and II": Critical Essays.* New York: Garland Publishing, 1986. PR 2809.H46.

> This collection of essays on *Henry IV* includes criticism from the eighteenth century to 1983 and features work from such luminaries as Samuel Johnson, Samuel Taylor Coleridge, and A. C. Bradley. Mapping the historical variations in criticism of *Henry IV,* Bevington's book outlines the major critical shifts in discussion of the play and provides a useful introduction to *Henry IV* studies.

Calderwood, James L. *Metadrama in Shakespeare's Henriad: "Richard II" to "Henry V."* Berkeley: University of California Press, 1979. PR 2982.C28.

> Calderwood examines the connection between the events in three of Shakespeare's histories—*Richard II, Henry IV,* and *Henry V*—and the historical facts of those events. The author advances close textual readings of each play, linking the imagery and poetic language of Shakespeare's dramas to the actual events to which the playwright refers. In particular, Calderwood considers the fall of Richard II, the "legitimacy" of language and authority in Henry IV's rule, and the restoration of valid rule with Henry V.

Campbell, Lily B. *Shakespeare's "Histories": Mirrors of Elizabethan Policy.* London: Methuen, 1964. PR 2982.C3.

> Campbell analyzes Shakespeare's second tetralogy in relation to its historical and political backdrop, arguing that the plays parallel the social and political issues of Elizabethan England. Frequently referring to Elizabethan texts on history, politics, and morality, Campbell attempts to locate Shakespeare's history plays in a distinctive historical moment and cultural atmosphere. For example, in her study of *Richard II* the author examines the similarities in temperament between Richard and Queen Elizabeth;

considering the *Henry IV* plays, Campbell highlights the parallels between Prince Hal and James I; and relating *Henry V*'s allusions to contemporary concerns, Campbell notes the correlation between Henry's heroism and the Elizabethan preoccupation with the morality of war.

Evans, Barbara. "The Fatness of Falstaff: Shakespeare and Character." *Proceedings of the British Academy* 76 (1990): 109–128. journal AS 122.L5.

In this detailed study of *Henry IV,* Evans defends serious literary criticism of Falstaff, a character whom she thinks is often overlooked as a "minor" member of the play's subplot. Charting the character's historical reception, the author observes that Falstaff has long been considered only a comic character with little relation to the play's overarching themes of rebellion and heroism. Evans, however, contends that Falstaff is essential to Shakespeare's ability to humanize history, to depict the tension inherent in the characters' relationships, and to make that tension the crux of the play's most important action.

Hodgdon, Barbara. *The End Crowns All: Closure and Contradiction in Shakespeare's History.* Princeton, Princeton University Press, 1991. PR 2982.H56.

In this fascinating essay, Hodgdon argues that all ten of Shakespeare's history plays have ambiguous endings that can provide a wide array of interpretations in performance. To prove her contention, the author reflects upon various productions as well as the folio versions of all ten of the Bard's English histories and notes how various stagings have resulted in radically varied interpretations of the plays' endings. In a particularly interesting connection, Hodgdon even goes so far as to argue that *Henry V*'s ending is a precursor to Bertolt Brecht's plays of the modern period.

Howard, Jean E., and Phyllis Rackin. *Engendering a Nation: A Feminist Account of Shakespeare's English Histories.* New York: Routledge, 1997. PR 2982.H67.

This book claims that Shakespeare's English histories reflect a change in social and gender roles that occurred in England during the Elizabethan age. The authors investigate how the Elizabethan history play reflected contemporary issues, discuss women's conventional gender roles in Elizabethan England, and note the theater's importance as a cultural institution in Shakespeare's time.

Kastan, David Scott. "'The King Hath Many Marching in His Coats,' or, What Did You Do in the War, Daddy?" *Shakespeare Left and Right.* Ivo Kamps, ed. New York: Routledge, 1991. 241–258. PR 2970.S52.

Placing *Henry IV* within the cultural and political context of Elizabethan England, Kastan discusses the similarities between King Henry's ability to maintain authority and Queen Elizabeth's occasionally troubled rule. In particular, the author notes how each ruler created an illusion of unity within their countries in order to maintain power. Such illusory unity, however, reveals a level of uncertainty in the ruler's authority that Kastan finds quite interesting.

McMillin, Scott. *Shakespeare in Performance: "Henry IV, Part One."* Manchester: Manchester University, 1991. PR 2810.M36.

This book examines six modern film productions of Shakespeare's *1 Henry IV* and documents the films' movements from a focus on Falstaff and Hotspur to a concentration on political concerns and Prince Hal.

Scott's volume is well respected for its attention to both the literary and theatrical aspects of each production. The author closes the book with a helpful filmography and an index of major modern productions of 1 *Henry IV.*

Ornstein, Robert. *A Kingdom for a Stage: The Achievement of Shakespeare's History Plays.* Cambridge: Harvard University Press, 1972. PR 2982.O7.
> Offering a fascinating perspective on Shakespeare's second tetralogy, Ornstein contends that the histories are less an examination of the Tudor dynasty than they are a framework that underlies all social and personal interaction. The author devotes a chapter to each of the ten histories, building his argument on a case-by-case basis. Ornstein's primary goal is to reveal the multidimensional qualities of the plays and their characters.

Peat, Derek. "Falstaff Gets the Sack." *Shakespeare Quarterly* 53:3 (Fall 2002): 379–385. journal PR 2885.S63.
> This article explores the staging of the scene in the final act where Hal throws a bottle at Falstaff. Two different scenarios utilizing several Royal Shakespeare Company productions are explored in depth to illustrate how this single act can change the balance of the scene, redefine the relationship between the two men, and perhaps affect the entire play.

Pilkington, Ace G. *Screening Shakespeare from "Richard II" to "Henry V."* Newark: University of Delaware Press, 1991. PR 3093.P55.
> An extremely helpful guide to film versions of Shakespeare's history plays, Pilkington's book argues that films should be analyzed with the same attention to detail and depth as is given to literary texts. The author believes that films should not be "reviewed" critically, but rather studied with the actors' and directors' intentions in mind. In this volume, Pilkington considers the following film adaptations of Shakespeare's plays: the BBC *Richard II* (1978); the BBC *1* and *2 Henry IV* (1979); Laurence Olivier's *Henry V* (1944); and Orson Welles' *Chimes at Midnight* (1966).

Ribner, Irving. *The English History Play in the Age of Shakespeare.* London: Methuen, 1965. PR 658.H5.R5.
> In his discussion of Shakespeare's second tetralogy, Ribner outlines the political and historical correlations between the playwright's dramas and factual events. Unlike similar historical accounts, however, Ribner's volume discusses the plays' literary correlations as well. For example, the author notes the presence of the folk hero archetype in *Henry V* and argues for Falstaff's didactic purpose in *Henry IV.*

Saccio, Peter. *Shakespeare's English Kings: History, Chronicle, and Drama.* New York: Oxford University Press, 1977. PR 2982.S2.
> In this revealing book, Saccio discusses each of Shakespeare's ten English histories in relation to the real-life historical circumstances that gave rise to the plays. For example, concerning *Henry IV* Saccio discusses the Percies' rebellion and the Welsh uprising and compares the actual historical events with Shakespeare's account of them. The author points out how Shakespeare does not choose sides in his plays so much as he allows all positions represented in these historical conflicts to speak their voices; in this manner, Saccio argues, the playwright enlivens history and creates works of lasting impact.

Tillyard, E.M.W. "The Second Tetralogy." In *Shakespeare's History Plays.* London: Chatto and Windus, 1944. 234–314. PR 2982.T5.

> Considered one of the most authoritative discussions of the second tetralogy, Tillyard's essay examines Shakespeare's history plays (including *Macbeth*) in relation to the "Tudor Myth": the notion that the House of Tudor was destined to reign as a result of celestial or divine circumstances. The author also discusses the epic characteristics of the plays, often alluding to historical circumstances and other literary works to examine Shakespeare's use of epic conventions. Tillyard concludes his review by arguing that *Henry V* is inferior to the other histories and is therefore a sign of the Bard's growing apathy toward the dramatic epic.

Traversi, Derek A. *Shakespeare: From "Richard II" to "Henry V."* Stanford: Stanford University Press, 1957. PR 2982.T7.

> In his examination of Shakespeare's English histories, Traversi considers the plays in sequence and argues that they document the results of disruption in rule established by the divine right of kings. The author's argument is primarily made from the New Critical approach; that is, he builds his contention by making close readings of each of Shakespeare's ten history plays, analyzing symbolism, poetic language, and themes. Traversi concludes his argument by noting how *Henry V*'s plot institutes a sense of order after the chaos of the previous history plays.

Wilson, J. Dover. *The Fortunes of Falstaff.* Cambridge: Cambridge University Press, 1944. PR 2993.F2.W5.

> In this interesting collection of lectures, Wilson challenges popular interpretations of Falstaff by charting the character's development throughout the histories, particularly his movement from a disreputable but friendly companion to Prince Hal to an unsympathetic, conceited drunkard. This volume is considered particularly important for its illumination of Prince Hal's reactions toward Falstaff.

Hamlet

Hamlet *at the Colorado Shakespeare Festival in Boulder, Colorado, with Val Kilmer* *as Hamlet (1988). Photograph by J. Martin Natvig.*

First performed near the end of Queen Elizabeth's reign during the midst of the plague years in London, *Hamlet* is a fascinating excursion into melancholia and death. At the same time, it is a morally and spiritually re-generative story about a brilliant, inquisitive young man grappling with pro-found questions about his purpose in life and the meaning of existence in a sinful and corrupt world. Written sometime between 1599 and 1603, this mag-nificent play has a tangled textual history. The first published <u>script</u> was a <u>bad quarto</u> of 1603, which was followed soon after by a <u>good quarto</u> of 1604, two additional <u>quarto</u> editions, and the <u>First Folio</u> in 1623. The <u>copy text</u> for most modern editions is the 1604 Second Quarto, corrected by references to the <u>First Folio</u>. Many scholars believe these different textual states of the <u>script</u> indi-cate frequent authorial revisions, perhaps for various early productions of the play. Shakespeare's primary <u>source</u> for the <u>plot</u> of *Hamlet* was Saxo Grammati-cus' *Historia Danica* (1180–1208), which may have been supplemented by

Francois de Belleforest's *Histoires Tragiques* (1576) and a lost play referred to as the *Ur-Hamlet*. Shakespeare's plot faithfully follows the story by Grammaticus, which chronicles the tale of a brother's murder and the vengeance of a devoted son who pretends madness to help uncover the truth about his father's death.

Properly classified as a <u>revenge tragedy</u>, *Hamlet* exists within a well-defined tradition that extends from the Latin playwright Seneca, through Thomas Kyd's *Spanish Tragedy* (1586), and into such contemporary dramas as Shakespeare's own *Titus Andronicus* (c. 1590), Marston's *Antonio's Revenge* (1602), and Tourneur's *Atheist's Tragedy* (1611). Shakespeare makes skillful use of the stock ingredients of the <u>genre</u>, including a sensational murder, a ghost demanding revenge, delay of the avenger, feigned madness, philosophical speculation about man's place in the universe, a surrender to fate, and a bloody, spectacular conclusion.

Within this traditional context, however, the dramatist introduces an acutely self-aware protagonist who distinguishes the play and its status within the <u>genre</u> by his thoughtful analysis of the world around him. Keenly aware that "Something is rotten in the state of Denmark" (1.4.90), Hamlet sets out to avenge his father's murder. Plagued by a melancholic disposition and an obsessive pursuit of the truth, he delays killing Claudius in order to be absolutely certain of his stepfather's guilt. Consequently, Hamlet, Claudius, Gertrude, Laertes, Polonius, Ophelia, Rosencrantz, and Guildenstern all die before the end of the play. As is the case in all Shakespearean <u>tragedies</u>, however, the <u>protagonist's</u> demise is counterbalanced by the spiritual and psychological insights he gains prior to his death. For Hamlet, the price of truth is the loss of his life.

Under the surface of this conventional <u>revenge tragedy</u> are a number of important <u>themes</u> and <u>images</u> that elevate the <u>script</u> far above its dramatic counterparts. Gravedigging, for example, is a central <u>symbol</u> in a play so deeply concerned with uncovering the truth and unearthing cultural memories. Likewise, poison is an important <u>theme</u> which surfaces not only in the macabre murder of Old Hamlet, but also in the poisoned sword and drink and in the way venomous words are poured into so many people's ears in the play. Madness is also a recurrent <u>image</u>, as is playacting, incest, suicide, the weakness of women, the relationship between fathers and sons, the divine right of kings, fate vs. free will, and the socialization of revenge. Most important, perhaps, is the extent to which the script exists within the *ars moriendi* tradition ("the art of dying well"), which encouraged devout Christians to practice a number of spiritual exercises during the plague years through which they readied themselves for death and life everlasting. As Hamlet prepares to die, so too does the audience by watching the production. In this sense, the play provides a theatrical defense against our own mortality. Like Hamlet brooding over the skull of Yorick, we stare directly into the face of death and are forever strengthened by the experience. More recent scholarship has opened up a number of additional topics in the play, including scriptural echoes, epistemology, purgatory, figures of rhetoric, proverbs, gender issues, patriarchy, and even the question of whether Hamlet was a woman.

Not surprisingly, *Hamlet* was successful on stage from the start. Although we have no evidence of early productions at the Globe Theatre and only two references to stagings at court, the many different <u>quarto</u> editions testify to its initial popularity with seventeenth-century audiences. The popular tragedian Richard Burbage was apparently the first to act the title character, whose allure exerted a strong influence on later dramatists like Tourneur, Chapman,

Marston, Jonson, and other contemporary playwrights intrigued by the <u>genre</u>. Unlike many Shakespearean <u>scripts</u> that were altered, updated, and savagely <u>cut</u> in performance after the Restoration, *Hamlet* has seldom been "adapted for the stage." Following a German-language production titled *Der bestrafte Brudermord* ("Fratricide Punished") and a version during the Puritan Interregnum called *The Grave-Makers,* the <u>script</u> profited from a number of leading actors in the title role, extending from David Garrick, Charles Kemble, Edmund Kean, Edwin Booth, and Henry Irving in the early years to the more recent triumphs of John Barrymore, John Gielgud, Laurence Olivier, Richard Burton, and Kenneth Branagh. Popular and influential cinematic versions of the play have included Olivier's 1948 film, Grigori Kozintsev's in 1964, Franco Zeffirelli's 1990 production starring Mel Gibson, Branagh's in 1996, and Michael Almereyda's modern-dress version in 2000 featuring Ethan Hawke as a brooding New York businessman confronted by a spectral Sam Shepard.

What has made *Hamlet* such an incredibly popular theatrical experience for so many years? For the <u>groundlings</u> among us, the lure of the play has much to do with ghosts, pirate ships, sword fights, young love, and comic gravediggers. For those who want a little more intellectual stimulation with their <u>revenge tragedies,</u> the <u>script</u> offers audiences the chance to communicate with one of literature's most intriguing characters. As Hamlet grapples with his fate, we see our own, ghostlike, dancing before us. This is a great play, in part, because it invites us to consider a number of profound and often disturbing questions that help define us as human beings within a complex and often frustrating world. Our response to these theatrical inquiries shapes our consciousness and determines our destiny. As a result, Hamlet asks a great deal of us as audience members, but rewards us richly for our effort.

Hamlet *at the Huntington Theater in Boston, Massachusetts, with Campbell Scott as Hamlet (foreground) and Jack Willis as the Ghost (1996). Photograph by T. Charles Erickson.*

Hamlet

NAMES OF THE ACTORS

KING CLAUDIUS, *of Denmark*
HAMLET, *son of the late, and nephew of the present, King*
POLONIUS, *Danish councillor*
HORATIO, *Hamlet's friend*
LAERTES, *Polonius' son*
VOLTEMAND
CORNELIUS
ROSENCRANTZ
GUILDENSTERN   } *courtiers*
OSRIC
A GENTLEMAN
A PRIEST
MARCELLUS
BARNARDO   } *soldiers*
FRANCISCO
REYNALDO, *servant in Polonius' household*
PLAYERS, *including Player King, Player Queen, Player Lucianus*
TWO CLOWNS, *one a gravedigger*
FORTINBRAS, *Prince of Norway*
A NORWEGIAN CAPTAIN, *in Fortinbras' army*
ENGLISH AMBASSADORS
QUEEN GERTRUDE, *of Denmark, Hamlet's mother*
OPHELIA, *Polonius' daughter*
GHOST OF HAMLET'S FATHER
LORDS, LADIES, OFFICERS, SOLDIERS, SAILORS, MESSENGERS, ATTENDANTS

SCENE: *Denmark*

1.1° *Enter Barnardo and Francisco, two sentinels.*

1.1: Elsinore Castle, Denmark: the battlements

BARNARDO   Who's there?
FRANCISCO
   Nay, answer me. Stand and unfold yourself.
BARNARDO   Long live the king!
FRANCISCO   Barnardo?
BARNARDO   He.
FRANCISCO
   You come most carefully upon your hour.°   **upon your hour:** right on time

5

DISCOVERING SHAKESPEARE

(1) <u>Meter</u> [1.1.1]: <u>Scan</u> the first thirteen lines of the play. How many are in <u>verse</u>? How many in <u>prose</u>? What does this rapid-fire exchange of <u>dialogue</u> tell us about the intensity of the situation?

BARNARDO
    'Tis now struck twelve. Get thee to bed, Francisco.
FRANCISCO
    For this relief much thanks. 'Tis bitter cold,
    And I am sick at heart.
BARNARDO
    Have you had quiet guard?   10
FRANCISCO   Not a mouse stirring.
BARNARDO
    Well, good night.
    If you do meet Horatio and Marcellus,
    The rivals° of my watch, bid them make haste.   **rivals:** sharers
      Enter Horatio and Marcellus.
FRANCISCO
    I think I hear them. Stand, ho! Who is there?
HORATIO
    Friends to this ground.   15
MARCELLUS   And liegemen° to the Dane.°   **liegemen:** sworn followers; **Dane:** King of
FRANCISCO   Denmark
    Give you good night.
MARCELLUS   O, farewell, honest soldier.
    Who hath relieved you?
FRANCISCO   Barnardo hath my place.
    Give you good night.   *Exit Francisco.*
MARCELLUS   Holla, Barnardo!
BARNARDO   Say −
    What, is Horatio there?
HORATIO   A piece of him.
BARNARDO
    Welcome, Horatio. Welcome, good Marcellus.   20
HORATIO
    What, has this thing appeared again tonight?
BARNARDO
    I have seen nothing.
MARCELLUS
    Horatio says 'tis but our fantasy,°   **fantasy:** imagination
    And will not let belief take hold of him
    Touching this dreaded sight twice seen of us.   25
    Therefore I have entreated him along
    With us to watch the minutes of this night,
    That, if again this apparition come,
    He may approve° our eyes and speak to it.   **approve:** confirm
HORATIO
    Tush, tush, 'twill not appear.   30
BARNARDO   Sit down awhile,
    And let us once again assail your ears,
    That are so fortified against our story,
    What we have two nights seen.

DISCOVERING SHAKESPEARE

(2) Paraphrase [1.1.29]: <u>Paraphrase</u> the following comment by Marcellus concerning Horatio and the Ghost: "That, if again this apparition come, / He may approve our eyes and speak to it" (1.1.28–29). What do these lines tell us about Marcellus? About Horatio?

HORATIO   Well, sit we down,
And let us hear Barnardo speak of this.

BARNARDO
Last night of all,   35
When yond same star that's westward from the pole°   **pole:** polestar
Had made his course t' illume that part of heaven
Where now it burns, Marcellus and myself,
The bell then beating one –
    Enter Ghost.

MARCELLUS
Peace, break thee off. Look where it comes again.   40

BARNARDO
In the same figure like the king that's dead.

MARCELLUS
Thou art a scholar; speak to it, Horatio.

BARNARDO
Looks a° not like the king? Mark it, Horatio.   **a:** he

HORATIO
Most like. It harrows me with fear and wonder.

BARNARDO
It would be spoke to.   45

MARCELLUS   Speak to it, Horatio.

HORATIO
What art thou that usurp'st this time of night
Together with that fair and warlike form
In which the majesty of buried Denmark°   **buried Denmark:** the buried King of Denmark
Did sometimes° march? By heaven I charge thee, speak.   (old Hamlet)
                                                           sometimes: formerly

MARCELLUS
It is offended.   50

BARNARDO   See, it stalks away.

HORATIO
Stay. Speak, speak. I charge thee, speak.   *Exit Ghost.*

MARCELLUS
'Tis gone and will not answer.

BARNARDO
How now, Horatio? You tremble and look pale.
Is not this something more than fantasy?
What think you on't?   55

HORATIO
Before my God, I might not this believe
Without the sensible and true avouch°   **avouch:** assurance
Of mine own eyes.

MARCELLUS   Is it not like the king?

HORATIO
As thou art to thyself.
Such was the very armor he had on   60
When he the ambitious Norway° combated.   **Norway:** King of Norway
So frowned he once when, in an angry parle,°   **parle:** parley, negotiation under truce (said
He smote the sledded Polacks on the ice.   ironically)
'Tis strange.

DISCOVERING SHAKESPEARE

(3) Characterization [1.1.51]: Whom does the Ghost look like? Why is this information significant to Horatio?

MARCELLUS
Thus twice before, and jump° at this dead hour,
With martial stalk hath he gone by our watch.

jump: just, exactly 65

HORATIO
In what particular thought to work I know not;
But, in the gross and scope° of my opinion,
This bodes some strange eruption° to our state.

gross and scope: gross scope, general view
strange eruption: unexpected, destructive change

MARCELLUS
Good now, sit down, and tell me he that knows,
Why this same strict and most observant watch

70

So nightly toils° the subject° of the land,
And why such daily cast of brazen cannon

toils: makes toil; **subject:** subjects

And foreign mart° for implements of war,

mart: trading

Why such impress° of shipwrights, whose sore task

impress: conscription 75

Does not divide the Sunday from the week.
What might be toward° that this sweaty haste

toward: in preparation, coming on

Doth make the night joint laborer with the day?
Who is't that can inform me?

HORATIO   That can I.

80

At least the whisper goes so. Our last king,
Whose image even but now appeared to us,
Was as you know by Fortinbras of Norway,°

Fortinbras of Norway: i.e., father of *young Fortinbras* (l. 95)

Thereto pricked on by a most emulate° pride,

emulate: jealously rivaling

Dared to the combat; in which our valiant Hamlet
(For so this side of our known world esteemed him)

85

Did slay this Fortinbras; who, by a sealed compact
Well ratified by law and heraldry,°

law and heraldry: law of heralds regulating combat

Did forfeit, with his life, all those his lands
Which he stood seized° of to the conqueror;

seized: possessed

Against the which a moiety competent°

moiety competent: sufficient portion 90

Was gagèd° by our king, which had returned

gagèd: engaged, staked

To the inheritance of Fortinbras
Had he been vanquisher, as, by the same comart°

comart: joint bargain

And carriage° of the article designed,

carriage: purport

His° fell to Hamlet. Now, sir, young Fortinbras,

His: i.e., old Fortinbras' share, had he won 95

Of unimprovèd° mettle hot and full,

unimprovèd: unused

Hath in the skirts of Norway here and there
Sharked° up a list° of lawless resolutes°

Sharked: snatched indiscriminately; **list:** roll call; **resolutes:** determined people

For food and diet to some enterprise
That hath a stomach° in't; which is no other,

stomach: promise of danger 100

As it doth well appear unto our state,
But to recover of us by strong hand
And terms compulsatory those foresaid lands
So by his father lost; and this, I take it,
Is the main motive of our preparations,

105

The source of this our watch, and the chief head°

head: fountainhead, source

Of this posthaste° and rummage° in the land.

posthaste: bustle, urgency; **rummage:** disorder, ransacking

---

DISCOVERING SHAKESPEARE

(4) Paraphrase [1.1.75]: Paraphrase lines 1.1.70–79. Exactly what kinds of problems in Denmark is Marcellus describing?

(5) Plot [1.1.105]: At what intervals does the Ghost enter in 1.1? How does Shakespeare use the Ghost's entrances to break up the long exposition at the beginning of the play?

BARNARDO
I think it be no other but e'en so.
Well may it sort° that this portentous° figure
Comes armèd through our watch so like the king
That was and is the question of these wars.

HORATIO
A mote° it is to trouble the mind's eye.
In the most high and palmy° state of Rome,
A little ere the mightiest Julius fell,
The graves stood tenantless and the sheeted° dead
Did squeak and gibber in the Roman streets;
As° stars with trains of fire and dews of blood,
Disasters° in the sun; and the moist star°
Upon whose influence Neptune's empire stands°
Was sick almost to doomsday° with eclipse.
And even the like precurse° of feared events,
As harbingers° preceding still° the fates
And prologue to the omen° coming on,
Have heaven and earth together demonstrated
Unto our climatures° and countrymen.
    Enter Ghost.
But soft, behold, lo where it comes again!
I'll cross it,° though it blast me. – Stay, illusion.
    [He] spreads his arms.
If thou hast any sound or use of voice,
Speak to me.
If there be any good thing to be done
That may to thee do ease and grace to me,
Speak to me.
If thou art privy to thy country's fate,
Which happily° foreknowing may avoid,
O, speak!
Or if thou hast uphoarded in thy life
Extorted treasure in the womb of earth,
For which, they say, your° spirits oft walk in death,
    The cock crows.
Speak of it. Stay and speak. Stop it, Marcellus.

MARCELLUS
Shall I strike it with my partisan?°

HORATIO
Do, if it will not stand.°

BARNARDO   'Tis here.
HORATIO   'Tis here.
MARCELLUS
'Tis gone.   *[Exit Ghost.]*
We do it wrong, being so majestical,
To offer it the show of violence,
For it is as the air invulnerable,
And our vain blows malicious mockery.

BARNARDO
It was about to speak when the cock crew.

---

sort: be fitting; **portentous:** ominous

110

mote: speck of dust
palmy: successful, victorious

sheeted: in burial shrouds   115

As: (this line does not follow grammatically from the preceding one, although it continues to list dangerous portents; some words have probably been omitted accidentally)
Disasters: omens; **moist star:** moon   120
stands: depends
sick almost to doomsday: almost as terrible as the Christian Apocalypse
precurse: foreshadowing
harbingers: forerunners; **still:** constantly   125
omen: calamity
climatures: regions
cross it: cross its path, confront it

130

happily: haply, perchance

135

your: (an indefinite usage referring to hearers in general, not a specific interlocutor; F reads "you")

partisan: pike (a spearlike weapon)   140

stand: stop, stand still

145

DISCOVERING SHAKESPEARE

(6) Mythology [1.1.147]: Why does the Ghost vanish "when the cock crew" (1.1.147)?

HORATIO

And then it started, like a guilty thing
Upon a fearful summons. I have heard
The cock, that is the trumpet to the morn,   150
Doth with his lofty and shrill-sounding throat
Awake the god of day,° and at his warning,   **god of day:** i.e., sun
Whether in sea or fire, in earth or air,
Th' extravagant° and erring° spirit hies   **extravagant:** wandering beyond bounds;
To his confine; and of the truth herein   **erring:** wandering   155
This present object made probation.°   **probation:** test

MARCELLUS

It faded on the crowing of the cock.
Some say that ever 'gainst° that season comes   **'gainst:** just before
Wherein our Savior's birth is celebrated,°   **season . . . celebrated:** i.e., Christmastime
This bird of dawning singeth all night long,
And then, they say, no spirit dare stir abroad,   160
The nights are wholesome, then no planets strike,°   **strike:** work evil by influence
No fairy takes,° nor witch hath power to charm,   **takes:** bewitches
So hallowed and so gracious° is that time.   **gracious:** full of (divine) grace

HORATIO

So have I heard and do in part believe it.   165
But look, the morn in russet° mantle clad   **russet:** reddish brown rough cloth
Walks o'er the dew of yon high eastward hill.
Break we our watch up, and by my advice
Let us impart what we have seen tonight
Unto young Hamlet, for upon my life   170
This spirit, dumb° to us, will speak to him.   **dumb:** silent
Do you consent we shall acquaint him with it,
As needful in our loves, fitting our duty?

MARCELLUS

Let's do't, I pray, and I this morning know
Where we shall find him most convenient.°   *Exeunt.*   **convenient:** i.e., conveniently (Shakespeare often   175
uses adjectives for adverbs)

❧ **1.2**° *Flourish. Enter Claudius, King of Denmark,*   **1.2:** Elsinore
Gertrude the Queen, Councillors, Polonius and his son
Laertes, Hamlet, cum aliis° *[including Voltemand and*   **cum aliis:** with others
Cornelius].

KING

Though yet of Hamlet our° dear brother's death   **our:** my (the royal plural)
The memory be green, and that it us befitted
To bear our hearts in grief, and our whole kingdom
To be contracted in one brow of woe,
Yet so far hath discretion fought with nature   5
That we with wisest sorrow think on him
Together with remembrance of ourselves.
Therefore our sometime sister,° now our queen,   **sometime sister:** former sister-in-law
Th' imperial jointress° to this warlike state,   **jointress:** widow who has a jointure, or joint
Have we, as 'twere with a defeated joy,   tenancy, of an estate (with this word and *imperial,*   10
Claudius acknowledges Gertrude as co-sovereign)

DISCOVERING SHAKESPEARE

(7) Characterization [1.2.1]: Write a brief description of Claudius based solely on the <u>rhetoric</u> and <u>diction</u> in his first speech (1.2.1–39).

With an auspicious and a dropping eye,
With mirth in funeral and with dirge in marriage,
In equal scale weighing delight and dole,
Taken to wife. Nor have we herein barred°   **barred:** excluded
Your better wisdoms, which have freely gone   15
With this affair along. For all, our thanks.
Now follows, that you know, young Fortinbras,
Holding a weak supposal of our worth,
Or thinking by our late dear brother's death
Our state to be disjoint and out of frame,   20
Colleaguèd° with this dream of his advantage,   **Colleaguèd:** united
He hath not failed to pester us with message
Importing the surrender of those lands
Lost by his father, with all bands° of law,   **bands:** bonds
To our most valiant brother. So much for him.   25
Now for ourself and for this time of meeting.
Thus much the business is: we have here writ
To Norway, uncle of young Fortinbras –
Who, impotent and bedrid, scarcely hears
Of this his nephew's purpose – to suppress   30
His further gait° herein, in that the levies,   **gait:** going
The lists, and full proportions° are all made   **proportions:** amounts of forces and supplies
Out of his subject; and we here dispatch
You, good Cornelius, and you, Voltemand,
For bearers of this greeting to old Norway,   35
Giving to you no further personal power
To business with the king, more than the scope
Of these delated° articles allow.   **delated:** (1) expressly stated, (2) conveyed
Farewell, and let your haste commend your duty.
CORNELIUS, VOLTEMAND
In that, and all things, will we show our duty.   40
KING
We doubt it nothing. Heartily farewell.
                  [Exeunt Voltemand and Cornelius.]
And now, Laertes, what's the news with you?
You told us of some suit.° What is't, Laertes?   **suit:** request
You cannot speak of reason to the Dane°   **Dane:** King of Denmark
And lose your voice.° What wouldst thou beg, Laertes,   **lose your voice:** speak in vain   45
That shall not be my offer, not thy asking?
The head is not more native° to the heart,   **native:** joined by nature
The hand more instrumental° to the mouth,   **instrumental:** serviceable
Than is the throne of Denmark to thy father.
What wouldst thou have, Laertes?   50
LAERTES   My dread lord,
Your leave and favor to return to France,
From whence though willingly I came to Denmark
To show my duty in your coronation,

DISCOVERING SHAKESPEARE

(8) Plot [1.2.25]: According to Claudius' first speech, what is the quarrel between Denmark and Norway? How does the king propose to solve it? Why do you think this information is important in the play?

(9) Paraphrase [1.2.48]: Paraphrase lines 47–50, where Claudius pledges his loyalty to Polonius and Laertes. Do you think the king is sincere in his statements? Why or why not?

Yet now I must confess, that duty done,
My thoughts and wishes bend again toward France   55
And bow them to your gracious leave and pardon.

KING
Have you your father's leave? What says Polonius?

POLONIUS
He hath, my lord, wrung from me my slow leave
By laborsome petition, and at last
Upon his will I sealed my hard° consent.   60
I do beseech you give him leave to go.

KING
Take thy fair hour, Laertes. Time be thine,
And thy best graces spend it at thy will.
But now, my cousin° Hamlet, and my son –

HAMLET *[Aside]*
A little more than kin,° and less than kind!°

KING
How is it that the clouds still hang on you?

HAMLET
Not so, my lord. I am too much in the sun.°

QUEEN
Good Hamlet, cast thy nighted color off,
And let thine eye look like a friend on Denmark.
Do not for ever with thy vailèd° lids   70
Seek for thy noble father in the dust.
Thou know'st 'tis common. All that lives must die,
Passing through nature to eternity.

HAMLET
Ay, madam, it is common.

QUEEN   If it be,
Why seems it so particular with thee?   75

HAMLET
Seems, madam? Nay, it is. I know not "seems."
'Tis not alone my inky cloak, good mother,
Nor customary suits of solemn black,
Nor windy suspiration of forced breath,
No, nor the fruitful river in the eye,   80
Nor the dejected havior° of the visage,
Together with all forms, moods, shapes of grief,
That can denote me truly. These indeed seem,
For they are actions that a man might play,°
But I have that within which passes show –   85
These but the trappings and the suits of woe.

KING
'Tis sweet and commendable in your nature, Hamlet,
To give these mourning duties to your father,
But you must know your father lost a father,
That father lost, lost his, and the survivor bound   90
In filial obligation for some term

Glosses (right margin):

hard: i.e., hard-won

cousin: kinsman more distant than parent, child, brother, or sister

kin: related as nephew; **kind:** (1) natural, (2) kindly, affectionate, (3) related by direct descent, member of the immediate family

sun: sunshine of the king's unwanted favor (with wordplay on "place of a son")

vailèd: downcast

havior: behavior, demeanor

play: feign, playact

DISCOVERING SHAKESPEARE

(10) <u>Diction</u> [1.2.75]: Which word in the Queen's speech in 1.2.75 sparks Hamlet's <u>monologue</u> in 1.2.76–86? Why does he object to this particular word?

To do obsequious° sorrow. But to persever°
In obstinate condolement is a course
Of impious stubbornness. 'Tis unmanly grief.
It shows a will most incorrect to heaven,
A heart unfortified, or mind impatient,
An understanding simple and unschooled.
For what we know must be and is as common
As any the most vulgar thing to sense,
Why should we in our peevish opposition
Take it to heart? Fie, 'tis a fault to heaven,
A fault against the dead, a fault to nature,
To reason most absurd, whose common theme
Is death of fathers, and who still hath cried,
From the first corpse till he that died today,
"This must be so." We pray you throw to earth
This unprevailing woe, and think of us
As of a father, for let the world take note
You are the most immediate to° our throne,
And with no less nobility of love
Than that which dearest father bears his son
Do I impart toward you. For your intent
In going back to school in Wittenberg,
It is most retrograde° to our desire,
And we beseech you, bend you to remain
Here in the cheer and comfort of our eye,
Our chiefest courtier, cousin, and our son.

QUEEN
Let not thy mother lose her prayers, Hamlet.
I pray thee stay with us, go not to Wittenberg.

HAMLET
I shall in all my best obey you, madam.

KING
Why, 'tis a loving and a fair reply.
Be as ourself in Denmark. Madam, come.
This gentle and unforced accord of Hamlet
Sits smiling to my heart, in grace whereof
No jocund health that Denmark drinks today
But the great cannon to the clouds shall tell,
And the king's rouse° the heaven shall bruit° again,
Respeaking earthly thunder. Come away.
                    Flourish. Exeunt all but Hamlet.

HAMLET
O that this too too sullied° flesh would melt,
Thaw, and resolve° itself into a dew,
Or that the Everlasting had not fixed
His canon° 'gainst self-slaughter. O God, God,
How weary, stale, flat, and unprofitable
Seem to me all the uses of this world!

obsequious: proper to obsequies (funerals);
persever: persevere (accented on the second syllable, as always in Shakespeare)

95

100

105

most immediate to: i.e., next to inherit

110

retrograde: contrary

115

120

125

rouse: toast drunk in wine; **bruit:** echo, make noise

sullied: dirtied, discolored
resolve: dissolve   130

canon: law

DISCOVERING SHAKESPEARE

(11) <u>Plot</u> [1.2.100]: How long ago did Hamlet's father die? How does Claudius feel about the length of time Hamlet has been in mourning?

(12) <u>Soliloquy</u> [1.2.129]: Read Hamlet's first <u>soliloquy</u> (1.2.129–159); then write down what effect you think it would have on an audience.

Fie on't, ah, fie, 'tis an unweeded garden   135
That grows to seed. Things rank and gross in nature
Possess it merely.° That it should come to this,   **merely:** completely
But two months dead, nay, not so much, not two,
So excellent a king, that was to this
Hyperion° to a satyr, so loving to my mother   **Hyperion:** the sun god   140
That he might not beteem° the winds of heaven   **beteem:** allow
Visit her face too roughly. Heaven and earth,
Must I remember? Why, she would hang on him
As if increase of appetite had grown
By what it fed on, and yet within a month –
Let me not think on't; frailty, thy name is woman –   145
A little month, or ere those shoes were old
With which she followed my poor father's body
Like Niobe,° all tears, why she –   **Niobe:** (in Greek myth, after Niobe boasted she
O God, a beast that wants discourse° of reason   had more children than Leto, Niobe's children   150
Would have mourned longer – married with my uncle,   were killed by Apollo and Artemis, Leto's children;
My father's brother, but no more like my father   Zeus transformed the grieving Niobe into a stone
Than I to Hercules. Within a month,   that continually dropped tears)
Ere yet the salt of most unrighteous tears   **discourse:** logical power or process
Had left the flushing in her gallèd° eyes,   **gallèd:** irritated   155
She married. O, most wicked speed, to post
With such dexterity to incestuous sheets!
It is not nor it cannot come to good.
But break my heart, for I must hold my tongue.°   **But . . . tongue:** (Hamlet alludes to a Latin and
  Enter Horatio, Marcellus, and Barnardo.   an English proverb claiming that unspoken griefs
HORATIO   crush the heart)
  Hail to your lordship!   160
HAMLET   I am glad to see you well.
  Horatio – or I do forget myself.
HORATIO
  The same, my lord, and your poor servant ever.
HAMLET
  Sir, my good friend, I'll change° that name with you.   **change:** exchange
  And what make° you from Wittenberg, Horatio?   **make:** do
  Marcellus?   165
MARCELLUS   My good lord!
HAMLET
  I am very glad to see you. *[To Barnardo]* Good even, sir.
  But what, in faith, make you from Wittenberg?
HORATIO
  A truant disposition, good my lord.
HAMLET
  I would not hear your enemy say so,   170
  Nor shall you do my ear that violence
  To make it truster of your own report
  Against yourself. I know you are no truant.
  But what is your affair in Elsinore?
  We'll teach you for to° drink ere you depart.   **for to:** to (archaic phrase)   175

DISCOVERING SHAKESPEARE
(13) Mythology [1.2.149]: Who was Niobe (1.2.149)? Why was she crying? What do mythological references like this tell us about the literacy level of Shakespeare's audience?

HORATIO
My lord, I came to see your father's funeral.
HAMLET
I prithee do not mock me, fellow student.
I think it was to see my mother's wedding.
HORATIO
Indeed, my lord, it followed hard upon.
HAMLET
Thrift, thrift, Horatio. The funeral baked meats   180
Did coldly furnish forth the marriage tables.
Would I had met my dearest° foe in heaven   **dearest:** direst, bitterest
Or ever I had seen that day, Horatio!
My father – methinks I see my father.
HORATIO
Where, my lord?   185
HAMLET   In my mind's eye, Horatio.
HORATIO
I saw him once. A was a goodly king.
HAMLET
A° was a man, take him for all in all,   **A:** he
I shall not look upon his like again.
HORATIO
My lord, I think I saw him yesternight.
HAMLET   Saw? Who?   190
HORATIO
My lord, the king your father.
HAMLET   The king my father?
HORATIO
Season your admiration° for a while   **Season your admiration:** control your wonder
With an attent° ear till I may deliver   **attent:** attentive, alert
Upon the witness of these gentlemen
This marvel to you.   195
HAMLET   For God's love let me hear!
HORATIO
Two nights together had these gentlemen,
Marcellus and Barnardo, on their watch
In the dead waste and middle of the night
Been thus encountered. A figure like your father,
Armèd at point° exactly, cap-à-pie,°   **at point:** completely; **cap-à-pie:** from head to   200
                                                            foot
Appears before them and with solemn march
Goes slow and stately by them. Thrice he walked
By their oppressed and fear-surprisèd eyes
Within his truncheon's° length, whilst they, distilled   **truncheon:** military commander's baton
Almost to jelly with the act of fear,
Stand dumb and speak not to him. This to me   205
In dreadful° secrecy impart they did,   **dreadful:** full of dread, fearful
And I with them the third night kept the watch,

DISCOVERING SHAKESPEARE

(14) Plot [1.2.178]: How soon after her husband's funeral did Gertrude marry Claudius? (*Hint:* See also 1.2.146.) What joke does Hamlet make in 1.2.180–181 about his mother's haste in remarrying?

(15) Metaphor [1.2.205]: Explain Horatio's metaphor in 1.2.204–205 in which he claims that the guards, after seeing the Ghost, were "distilled/Almost to jelly with the act of fear."

Where, as they had delivered, both in time,
Form of the thing, each word made true and good,   210
The apparition comes. I knew your father.
These hands are not more like.
HAMLET   But where was this?
MARCELLUS
My lord, upon the platform° where we watched.   **platform:** battlement
HAMLET
Did you not speak to it?
HORATIO   My lord, I did,   215
But answer made it none. Yet once methought
It lifted up it° head and did address   **it:** its (archaic, but common in Shakespeare)
Itself to motion° like as it would speak.   **did address . . . motion:** began to move
But even then the morning cock crew loud,
And at the sound it shrunk in haste away
And vanished from our sight.   220
HAMLET   'Tis very strange.
HORATIO
As I do live, my honored lord, 'tis true,
And we did think it writ down in our duty
To let you know of it.
HAMLET
Indeed, sirs, but this troubles me.
Hold you the watch tonight?   225
ALL   We do, my lord.
HAMLET   Armed, say you?
ALL   Armed, my lord.
HAMLET
From top to toe?
ALL   My lord, from head to foot.
HAMLET
Then saw you not his face?
HORATIO
O, yes, my lord. He wore his beaver° up.   **beaver:** movable face guard of the helmet   230
HAMLET
What, looked he frowningly?
HORATIO
A countenance more in sorrow than in anger.
HAMLET   Pale or red?
HORATIO
Nay, very pale.
HAMLET   And fixed his eyes upon you?
HORATIO
Most constantly.   235
HAMLET   I would I had been there.
HORATIO
It would have much amazed you.
HAMLET
Very like. Stayed it long?

DISCOVERING SHAKESPEARE

(16) Verse [1.2.231]: <u>Scan</u> lines 1.2.225–243. Which are in <u>verse</u>, and which are <u>prose</u>? What is the <u>rhetorical</u> effect of all these <u>short lines</u>? How are <u>short lines</u> in <u>verse</u> different from <u>short lines</u> in <u>prose</u>?

HORATIO
While one with moderate haste might tell° a hundred.   **tell:** count
BOTH   Longer, longer.
HORATIO
Not when I saw't.   240
HAMLET   His beard was grizzled,° no?   **grizzled:** gray
HORATIO
It was as I have seen it in his life,
A sable silvered.°   **sable silvered:** black mixed with white
HAMLET   I will watch tonight.
Perchance 'twill walk again.
HORATIO   I warr'nt it will.
HAMLET
If it assume my noble father's person,
I'll speak to it though hell itself should gape   245
And bid me hold my peace. I pray you all,
If you have hitherto concealed this sight,
Let it be tenable° in your silence still,   **tenable:** held firmly
And whatsomever else shall hap tonight,
Give it an understanding but no tongue.   250
I will requite your loves. So fare you well.
Upon the platform, 'twixt eleven and twelve
I'll visit you.
ALL   Our duty to your honor.
HAMLET
Your loves, as mine to you. Farewell.
                              Exeunt [all but Hamlet].
My father's spirit – in arms? All is not well.   255
I doubt° some foul play. Would the night were come!   **doubt:** suspect, fear
Till then sit still, my soul. Foul deeds will rise
Though all the earth o'erwhelm them to men's eyes.°   **Foul . . . eyes:** (proverbially, murder cannot be
                              Exit.   hidden)

❧ **1.3**° *Enter Laertes and Ophelia, his sister.*   **1.3:** Elsinore Castle: Polonius' rooms

LAERTES
My necessaries are embarked. Farewell.
And, sister, as the winds give benefit
And convoy° is assistant, do not sleep,   **convoy:** means of transport
But let me hear from you.
OPHELIA   Do you doubt that?
LAERTES
For Hamlet, and the trifling of his favor,   5
Hold it a fashion and a toy° in blood,   **toy:** passing fancy
A violet in the youth of primy° nature,   **of primy:** of the springtime
Forward,° not permanent, sweet, not lasting,   **Forward:** blooming early
The perfume and suppliance° of a minute,   **perfume and suppliance:** filling sweetness
No more.   10
OPHELIA   No more but so?

DISCOVERING SHAKESPEARE

(17) Paraphrase [1.2.250]: Paraphrase Hamlet's instruction to the guards that they give their knowledge of the Ghost "an understanding but no tongue" (1.2.250). Why does Hamlet make the guards agree to do this?

LAERTES   Think it no more.

For nature crescent° does not grow alone

In thews and bulk, but as this temple° waxes

The inward service of the mind and soul

Grows wide withal. Perhaps he loves you now,

And now no soil nor cautel° doth besmirch   15

The virtue° of his will,° but you must fear,

His greatness weighed,° his will is not his own.

He may not, as unvalued persons do,

Carve° for himself, for on his choice depends

The safety and health of this whole state,   20

And therefore must his choice be circumscribed

Unto the voice and yielding° of that body

Whereof he is the head. Then if he says he loves you,

It fits your wisdom so far to believe it

As he in his particular act and place   25

May give his saying deed, which is no further

Than the main voice of Denmark goes withal.

Then weigh what loss your honor may sustain

If with too credent° ear you list° his songs,

Or lose your heart, or your chaste treasure open   30

To his unmastered importunity.

Fear it, Ophelia, fear it, my dear sister,

And keep you in the rear of your affection,°

Out of the shot and danger of desire.

The chariest° maid is prodigal enough   35

If she unmask her beauty to the moon.

Virtue itself scapes not calumnious strokes.

The canker° galls° the infants of the spring

Too oft before their buttons° be disclosed,

And in the morn and liquid dew of youth   40

Contagious blastments° are most imminent.

Be wary then; best safety lies in fear.

Youth to itself rebels, though none else near.

OPHELIA

I shall the effect of this good lesson keep

As watchman to my heart, but, good my brother,   45

Do not as some ungracious pastors do,

Show me the steep and thorny way to heaven,

Whiles like a puffed and reckless libertine

Himself the primrose path of dalliance treads

And recks° not his own rede.°   50

     Enter Polonius.

LAERTES   O, fear me not.

I stay too long. But here my father comes.

A double blessing is a double grace;

Occasion smiles upon a second leave.

POLONIUS

Yet here, Laertes? Aboard, aboard, for shame!

Glosses:

crescent: growing
this temple: the body
cautel: deceit
virtue: (1) strength, (2) virtuousness; **will:** desire
greatness weighed: high position considered
Carve: choose (with romantic or erotic choice implied)
yielding: assent
credent: credulous; **list:** listen to
affection: feelings (which rashly lead into dangers)
chariest: most careful
canker: rose worm; **galls:** injures
buttons: buds
blastments: blights
recks: regards; **rede:** counsel

DISCOVERING SHAKESPEARE

(18) Characterization [1.3.15]: What kind of person is Laertes? Describe his relationship with Ophelia.

(19) Plot [1.3.45]: What advice does Laertes give his sister about her relationship with Hamlet? Do you feel this is good counsel? Why or why not?

The wind sits in the shoulder of your sail,   55
And you are stayed for. There – my blessing with thee,
And these few precepts in thy memory
Look thou character.° Give thy thoughts no tongue,   **character:** inscribe, write
Nor any unproportioned° thought his act.   **unproportioned:** distorted from what is right
Be thou familiar, but by no means vulgar.   60
Those friends thou hast, and their adoption tried,
Grapple them unto thy soul with hoops of steel,
But do not dull thy palm with entertainment
Of each new-hatched, unfledged courage.° Beware   **courage:** man of spirit, young blood
Of entrance to a quarrel; but being in,   65
Bear't that th' opposèd may beware of thee.
Give every man thy ear, but few thy voice;
Take each man's censure,° but reserve thy judgment.   **censure:** judgment
Costly thy habit as thy purse can buy,
But not expressed in fancy; rich, not gaudy,   70
For the apparel oft proclaims the man,
And they in France of the best rank and station
Are of a most select and generous chief° in that.   **chief:** eminence (English prejudice found the
Neither a borrower nor a lender be,   French overly fashion-conscious)
For loan oft loses both itself and friend,   75
And borrowing dulleth edge of husbandry.°   **husbandry:** thriftiness
This above all, to thine own self be true,
And it must follow as the night the day
Thou canst not then be false to any man.
Farewell. My blessing season° this in thee!   **season:** ripen and make fruitful   80
LAERTES
Most humbly do I take my leave, my lord.
POLONIUS
The time invites you. Go, your servants tend.°   **tend:** wait
LAERTES
Farewell, Ophelia, and remember well
What I have said to you.
OPHELIA   'Tis in my memory locked,
And you yourself shall keep the key of it.   85
LAERTES   Farewell.   *Exit Laertes.*
POLONIUS
What is't, Ophelia, he hath said to you?
OPHELIA
So please you, something touching the Lord Hamlet.
POLONIUS
Marry,° well bethought.   **Marry:** by (the Virgin) Mary (a weak oath)
'Tis told me he hath very oft of late   90
Given private time to you, and you yourself
Have of your audience been most free and bounteous.
If it be so – as so 'tis put on me,
And that in way of caution – I must tell you
You do not understand yourself so clearly   95
As it behooves my daughter and your honor.
What is between you? Give me up the truth.

DISCOVERING SHAKESPEARE

(20) Characterization [1.3.69]: What do you think of the advice Polonius gives Laertes prior to his departure for France? How many of these suggestions do you think were clichés by the time Shakespeare wrote them? If the entire speech is nothing but a collection of hackneyed suggestions, what does this tell us about Polonius' role as a father?

OPHELIA

He hath, my lord, of late made many tenders°
Of his affection to me.

tenders: offers

POLONIUS

Affection? Pooh! You speak like a green girl,
Unsifted° in such perilous circumstance.
Do you believe his tenders, as you call them?

Unsifted: untested

100

OPHELIA

I do not know, my lord, what I should think.

POLONIUS

Marry, I will teach you. Think yourself a baby
That you have ta'en these tenders for true pay
Which are not sterling. Tender yourself more dearly,
Or (not to crack the wind of° the poor phrase,
Running it thus) you'll tender° me a fool.

105

crack . . . of: make wheeze like a horse driven too hard

tenders . . . Tender . . . tender: offers . . . hold in regard . . . present (wordplay runs through these three meanings; the last use of the word yields further complexity with its implication that she will show herself to Polonius as a *fool* [1.108], will show him to the world as a fool, and may go so far as to present him with a fool, an Elizabethan term of endearment especially applied to an infant)

110

OPHELIA

My lord, he hath importuned me with love
In honorable fashion.

POLONIUS

Ay, fashion you may call it. Go to,° go to.

Go to: go away, go on (an expression of impatience)

OPHELIA

And hath given countenance to his speech, my lord,
With almost all the holy vows of heaven.

POLONIUS

Ay, springes° to catch woodcocks.° I do know,
When the blood burns, how prodigal the soul
Lends the tongue vows. These blazes, daughter,
Giving more light than heat, extinct in both
Even in their promise, as it is a-making,
You must not take for fire. From this time
Be something scanter of your maiden presence.
Set your entreatments° at a higher rate
Than a command to parley.° For Lord Hamlet,
Believe so much in him that he is young,
And with a larger tether may he walk
Than may be given you. In few, Ophelia,
Do not believe his vows, for they are brokers,°
Not of that dye which their investments° show,
But mere implorators of unholy suits,
Breathing like sanctified and pious bawds
The better to beguile. This is for all:
I would not, in plain terms, from this time forth
Have you so slander° any moment° leisure
As to give words or talk with the Lord Hamlet.
Look to't, I charge you. Come your ways.

springes: snares; **woodcocks:** (birds believed to be foolish)

115

120

entreatments: military negotiations for surrender
parley: confer with a besieger

125

brokers: middlemen, panders
investments: clothes

130

slander: use disgracefully; **moment:** momentary

OPHELIA

I shall obey, my lord.

Exeunt.

135

─────────────────────────────

DISCOVERING SHAKESPEARE

(21) Characterization [1.3.99]: On a separate sheet of paper, write a brief description of the relationship between Polonius and Ophelia.

(22) Metaphor [1.3.121]: Paraphrase the following admonition by Polonius: "Set your entreatments at a higher rate/Than a command to parley" (1.3.121–122). Can you detect any hint of military language in Polonius' diction? What would these metaphors tell us about his character?

❧ **1.4**° *Enter Hamlet, Horatio, and Marcellus.*

HAMLET
  The air bites shrewdly;° it is very cold.

HORATIO
  It is a nipping and an eager° air.

HAMLET
  What hour now?

HORATIO   I think it lacks of twelve.

MARCELLUS   No, it is struck.

HORATIO
  Indeed? I heard it not. It then draws near the season
  Wherein the spirit held his wont to walk.

    A flourish of trumpets, and two pieces° goes off.
  What does this mean, my lord?

HAMLET
  The king doth wake tonight and takes his rouse,°
  Keeps wassail, and the swaggering upspring° reels,
  And as he drains his draughts° of Rhenish° down
  The kettledrum and trumpet thus bray out
  The triumph° of his pledge.

HORATIO   Is it a custom?

HAMLET
  Ay, marry, is't,
  But to my mind, though I am native here
  And to the manner born, it is a custom
  More honored in the breach than the observance.°
  This heavy-headed revel east and west
  Makes us traduced and taxed° of other nations.
  They clepe° us drunkards and with swinish phrase
  Soil our addition,° and indeed it takes
  From our achievements, though performed at height,
  The pith and marrow of our attribute.°
  So oft it chances in particular men
  That (for some vicious mole° of nature in them,
  As in their birth, wherein they are not guilty,
  Since nature cannot choose his° origin)
  By the o'ergrowth of some complexion,°
  Oft breaking down the pales° and forts of reason,
  Or by some habit that too much o'erleavens°
  The form of plausive° manners – that (these men
  Carrying, I say, the stamp of one defect,
  Being nature's livery,° or fortune's star)°
  His virtues else, be they as pure as grace,
  As infinite as man may undergo,
  Shall in the general censure take corruption
  From that particular fault. The dram of evil
  Doth all the noble substance often dout,°
  To his own scandal.
    Enter Ghost.

1.4: Elsinore: the battlements

shrewdly: wickedly, bitterly

an eager: a sharp

5

pieces: cannon

rouse: carousal
upspring: German dance
draughts: gulps; **Rhenish:** Rhine wine   10

triumph: achievement, feat (in downing a cup of wine at one gulp)

15

More . . . observance: better broken than observed

taxed of: censured by
clepe: call
addition: reputation, title added as a distinction   20

attribute: reputation, what is attributed

mole: blemish, flaw

25

his: its
complexion: part of an individual's human nature
pales: barriers, fences
o'erleavens: works change throughout, as yeast ferments dough   30
plausive: pleasing
livery: (1) badge or other identifying token, (2) provision
star: astrologically determined human nature
35

dout: extinguish, put out

DISCOVERING SHAKESPEARE

(23) Sound Effects [1.4.10]: What sound effects are mentioned in 1.4.1–16? How do these help introduce the appearance of the Ghost?

HORATIO   Look, my lord, it comes.

HAMLET

Angels and ministers of grace defend us!

Be thou a spirit of health° or goblin° damned,   **of health:** sound, good; **goblin:** fiend   40

Bring with thee airs from heaven or blasts from hell,

Be thy intents wicked or charitable,

Thou com'st in such a questionable shape

That I will speak to thee. I'll call thee Hamlet,

King, father, royal Dane. O, answer me!   45

Let me not burst in ignorance, but tell

Why thy canonized° bones, hearsèd in death,   **canonized:** buried with the established rites of

Have burst their cerements,° why the sepulchre   the church

Wherein we saw thee quietly interred   **cerements:** waxed grave cloths

Hath oped his ponderous and marble jaws   50

To cast thee up again. What may this mean

That thou, dead corpse, again in complete steel,

Revisits thus the glimpses of the moon,

Making night hideous, and we fools of nature°   **fools of nature:** men made conscious of natural

So horridly to shake our disposition°   limitations by a supernatural manifestation   55

With thoughts beyond the reaches of our souls?   **disposition:** mental constitution

Say, why is this? wherefore? what should we do?

   [Ghost] beckons.

HORATIO

It beckons you to go away with it,

As if it some impartment° did desire   **some impartment:** something to impart, to say

To you alone.   60

MARCELLUS   Look with what courteous action

It waves you to a more removèd° ground.   **removèd:** farther away, more remote

But do not go with it.

HORATIO   No, by no means.

HAMLET

It will not speak. Then I will follow it.

HORATIO

Do not, my lord.

HAMLET   Why, what should be the fear?

I do not set my life at a pin's fee,°   **a pin's fee:** the value of a pin (i.e., very little)   65

And for my soul, what can it do to that,

Being a thing immortal as itself?

It waves me forth again. I'll follow it.

HORATIO

What if it tempt you toward the flood, my lord,

Or to the dreadful summit of the cliff   70

That beetles° o'er his base into the sea,   **beetles:** juts out

And there assume some other horrible form,

Which might deprive° your sovereignty of reason°   **deprive:** take away; **sovereignty of reason:**

And draw you into madness? Think of it.   state of being ruled by reason

The very place puts toys° of desperation,   **toys:** fancies   75

Without more motive, into every brain

That looks so many fathoms to the sea

And hears it roar beneath.

DISCOVERING SHAKESPEARE

(24) Half-Lines [1.4.58]: Examine the <u>half-lines</u> and <u>shared lines</u> in 1.4.58–64; then analyze how they would affect the delivery of these speeches by the actors and the intensity of this portion of the <u>scene</u>.

HAMLET   It waves me still.
  Go on. I'll follow thee.
MARCELLUS
  You shall not go, my lord.   80
HAMLET   Hold off your hands.
HORATIO
  Be ruled. You shall not go.
HAMLET   My fate cries out
  And makes each petty artire° in this body   **artire:** artery
  As hardy as the Nemean lion's° nerve.°   **Nemean lion:** lion Hercules killed in the first of
  Still am I called. Unhand me, gentlemen.   his twelve labors; **nerve:** sinew
  By heaven, I'll make a ghost of him that lets° me!   **lets:** hinders   85
  I say, away! Go on. I'll follow thee.
                                   Exit Ghost and Hamlet.
HORATIO
  He waxes desperate with imagination.
MARCELLUS
  Let's follow. 'Tis not fit thus to obey him.
HORATIO
  Have after. To what issue will this come?
MARCELLUS
  Something is rotten in the state of Denmark.   90
HORATIO
  Heaven will direct it.
MARCELLUS   Nay, let's follow him.   *Exeunt.*

❧ **1.5**° *Enter Ghost and Hamlet.*   **1.5:** Elsinore: the battlements

HAMLET
  Whither wilt thou lead me? Speak. I'll go no further.
GHOST
  Mark me.
HAMLET   I will.
GHOST   My hour° is almost come,   **My hour:** daybreak
  When I to sulph'rous and tormenting flames°   **flames:** sufferings in purgatory (not hell)
  Must render up myself.
HAMLET   Alas, poor ghost!
GHOST
  Pity me not, but lend thy serious hearing   5
  To what I shall unfold.
HAMLET   Speak. I am bound to hear.
GHOST
  So art thou to revenge, when thou shalt hear.
HAMLET   What?
GHOST
  I am thy father's spirit,

DISCOVERING SHAKESPEARE

(25) Staging [1.4.86]: When the Ghost beckons to Hamlet and then leaves the stage with him, where do the two characters exit? Will they exit up center and then reappear on the <u>upper stage</u>? Will they exit stage right and then return to the main stage? If you were directing this <u>scene</u>, where would you put Hamlet and the Ghost for their long discussion in 1.5?
(26) Teaser [1.5.7]: Find out the titles of some other <u>revenge tragedies</u> that would have been popular during Shakespeare's time. Which of these plays is most well known? Why do you think this is so?

Doomed for a certain term to walk the night, 10
And for the day confined to fast° in fires,   **fast:** do penance
Till the foul crimes done in my days of nature
Are burnt and purged away. But that I am forbid
To tell the secrets of my prison house,
I could a tale unfold whose lightest word 15
Would harrow up thy soul, freeze thy young blood,
Make thy two eyes like stars start from their spheres,°   **spheres:** transparent revolving shells in each of
Thy knotted and combinèd locks to part,   which, according to Ptolemaic astronomy, a planet
And each particular hair to stand an° end   or other heavenly body was placed
Like quills upon the fearful° porcupine.   **an:** on
But this eternal blazon° must not be   **fearful:** (1) frightened, (2) frightening   20
To ears of flesh and blood. List, list, O, list!   **eternal blazon:** depiction of eternity
If thou didst ever thy dear father love –
HAMLET   O God!
GHOST
Revenge his foul and most unnatural murder. 25
HAMLET   Murder?
GHOST
Murder most foul, as in the best it is,
But this most foul, strange, and unnatural.
HAMLET
Haste me to know't, that I, with wings as swift
As meditation° or the thoughts of love,   **meditation:** thought   30
May sweep to my revenge.
GHOST   I find thee apt,
And duller shouldst thou be than the fat weed
That roots itself in ease on Lethe° wharf,   **Lethe:** a river in Hades (drinking from it
Wouldst thou not stir in this. Now, Hamlet, hear.   produced forgetfulness of one's past life)
'Tis given out that, sleeping in my orchard, 35
A serpent stung me. So the whole ear of Denmark
Is by a forgèd process° of my death   **forgèd process:** fabricated official report
Rankly abused. But know, thou noble youth,
The serpent that did sting thy father's life
Now wears his crown. 40
HAMLET   O my prophetic soul!
My uncle?
GHOST
Ay, that incestuous, that adulterate° beast,   **adulterate:** adulterous
With witchcraft of his wit, with traitorous gifts –
O wicked wit and gifts, that have the power
So to seduce! – won to his shameful lust 45
The will of my most seeming-virtuous queen.
O Hamlet, what a falling off was there
From me, whose love was of that dignity
That it went hand in hand even with the vow
I made to her in marriage, and to decline 50
Upon a wretch whose natural gifts were poor
To those of mine!
But virtue, as it never will be moved,

DISCOVERING SHAKESPEARE

(27) <u>Staging</u> [1.5.41]: The missing seven beats in Hamlet's line "My uncle" (1.5.41) seem to invite some stage action on the part of Hamlet or the Ghost. What do you think that action is? Why?

Though lewdness court it in a shape of heaven,°   **a shape of heaven:** angelic disguise

So lust, though to a radiant angel linked,   55

Will sate itself in a celestial bed

And prey on garbage.

But soft, methinks I scent the morning air.

Brief let me be. Sleeping within my orchard,°   **orchard:** garden

My custom always of the afternoon,   60

Upon my secure° hour thy uncle stole   **secure:** carefree, unsuspecting

With juice of cursed hebona° in a vial,   **hebona:** poisonous plant

And in the porches of my ears did pour

The leperous distillment, whose effect

Holds such an enmity with blood of man   65

That swift as quicksilver it courses through

The natural gates and alleys of the body

And with a sudden vigor it doth posset°   **posset:** curdle

And curd, like eager° droppings into milk,   **eager:** sour

The thin and wholesome blood. So did it mine,   70

And a most instant tetter° barked° about   **tetter:** eruption; **barked:** covered as with bark

Most lazarlike° with vile and loathsome crust   **lazarlike:** leperlike

All my smooth body.

Thus was I sleeping by a brother's hand

Of life, of crown, of queen at once dispatched,   75

Cut off even in the blossoms of my sin,

Unhouseled,° disappointed,° unaneled,°   **Unhouseled:** without the Christian Eucharist; **disappointed:** unprepared spiritually; **unaneled:** without extreme unction (a Christian rite involving holy oil, given at the end of a believer's life)

No reck'ning made, but sent to my account

With all my imperfections on my head.

O, horrible! O, horrible! most horrible!   80

If thou hast nature in thee, bear it not.

Let not the royal bed of Denmark be

A couch for luxury° and damnèd incest.   **luxury:** lust

But howsomever thou pursues this act,

Taint not thy mind, nor let thy soul contrive   85

Against thy mother aught. Leave her to heaven

And to those thorns that in her bosom lodge

To prick and sting her. Fare thee well at once.

The glowworm shows the matin° to be near   **matin:** morning

And gins to pale his uneffectual fire.   90

Adieu, adieu, adieu. Remember me.   *[Exit.]*

HAMLET

O all you host of heaven! O earth! What else?

And shall I couple° hell? O fie! Hold, hold, my heart,   **couple:** join with, marry

And you, my sinews, grow not instant old,

But bear me stiffly up. Remember thee?   95

Ay, thou poor ghost, while memory holds a seat

In this distracted globe.° Remember thee?   **globe:** head

Yea, from the table° of my memory   **table:** writing tablet, record book

I'll wipe away all trivial fond° records,   **fond:** foolish

---

DISCOVERING SHAKESPEARE

(28) Teaser [1.5.65]: Who was Bartolommeo Eustachio? What did he discover in approximately 1570 that Shakespeare made use of in 1.5.59–79?

(29) Diction [1.5.91]: What is the importance of the Ghost's departing words: "Remember me" (1.5.91)? How do they help introduce the revenge motif?

All saws° of books, all forms,° all pressures° past   **saws:** wise sayings; **forms:** mental images, 100
That youth and observation copied there,   concepts; **pressures:** impressions
And thy commandment all alone shall live
Within the book and volume of my brain,
Unmixed with baser matter. Yes, by heaven!   105
O most pernicious woman!
O villain, villain, smiling, damnèd villain!
My tables – meet° it is I set it down   **meet:** appropriate
That one may smile, and smile, and be a villain.
At least I am sure it may be so in Denmark.
    [Writes.]
So, uncle, there you are. Now to my word: 110
It is "Adieu, adieu, remember me."
I have sworn't.
    Enter Horatio and Marcellus.
HORATIO
  My lord, my lord!
MARCELLUS   Lord Hamlet!
HORATIO   Heavens secure him!
HAMLET   So be it!
MARCELLUS
  Illo, ho, ho,° my lord!   **Illo, ho, ho:** (cry of the falconer to summon his 115
HAMLET   hunting bird)
  Hillo, ho, ho, boy! Come and come.
MARCELLUS
  How is't, my noble lord?
HORATIO   What news, my lord?
HAMLET   O, wonderful!°   **wonderful:** full of wonder, amazing
HORATIO
  Good my lord, tell it.
HAMLET   No, you will reveal it.
HORATIO
  Not I, my lord, by heaven.   120
MARCELLUS   Nor I, my lord.
HAMLET
  How say you then? Would heart of man once think it?
  But you'll be secret?
BOTH   Ay, by heaven.
HAMLET
  There's never a villain dwelling in all Denmark
  But he's an arrant knave.
HORATIO
  There needs no ghost, my lord, come from the grave   125
  To tell us this.
HAMLET   Why, right, you are in the right,
  And so, without more circumstance° at all,   **circumstance:** ceremony
  I hold it fit that we shake hands and part:
  You, as your business and desire shall point you,
  For every man hath business and desire   130

DISCOVERING SHAKESPEARE

(30) Verse [1.5.120]: Why does the fairly regular verse of this scene change abruptly to half-lines in 1.5.113–126. What is happening on stage to cause this transformation in the dialogue?

Such as it is, and for my own poor part,
I will go pray.
HORATIO
These are but wild and whirling words, my lord.
HAMLET
I am sorry they offend you, heartily;
Yes, faith, heartily.   135
HORATIO   There's no offense, my lord.
HAMLET
Yes, by Saint Patrick,° but there is, Horatio,   **Saint Patrick:** the legendary keeper of
And much offense too. Touching this vision here,   purgatory
It is an honest ghost,° that let me tell you.   **an honest ghost:** a genuine ghost (not a
For your desire to know what is between us,   disguised demon)
O'ermaster't as you may. And now, good friends,   140
As you are friends, scholars, and soldiers,
Give me one poor request.
HORATIO
What is't, my lord? We will.
HAMLET
Never make known what you have seen tonight.
BOTH   My lord, we will not.   145
HAMLET   Nay, but swear't.
HORATIO   In faith, my lord, not I.
MARCELLUS   Nor I, my lord – in faith.
HAMLET   Upon my sword.°   **sword:** i.e., upon the cross formed by the sword
MARCELLUS   We have sworn, my lord, already.   hilt   150
HAMLET   Indeed, upon my sword, indeed.
     Ghost cries under the stage.
GHOST   Swear.
HAMLET
Ha, ha, boy, say'st thou so? Art thou there, truepenny?°   **truepenny:** honest old fellow
Come on. You hear this fellow in the cellarage.
Consent to swear.   155
HORATIO   Propose the oath, my lord.
HAMLET
Never to speak of this that you have seen,
Swear by my sword.
GHOST   *[Beneath]* Swear.
HAMLET
Hic et ubique?° Then we'll shift our ground.   **Hic et ubique:** here and everywhere (Latin)
Come hither, gentlemen,   160
And lay your hands again upon my sword.
Swear by my sword
Never to speak of this that you have heard.
GHOST   *[Beneath]* Swear by his sword.

DISCOVERING SHAKESPEARE

(31) Staging [1.5.150]: If you were directing a production of this play, how would you interpret the stage direction that the Ghost "cries" under the stage" (1.5.152)? How would the word "pioner" in line 166 help suggest staging options?

(32) Alliteration [1.5.160]: Underline all the alliteration, word repetition, and slant rhymes in 1.5.157–164. Why is the language so distinctive at this particular point in the play?

HAMLET
  Well said, old mole! Canst work i' th' earth so fast?   165
  A worthy pioner!° Once more remove, good friends.
HORATIO
  O day and night, but this is wondrous strange!
HAMLET
  And therefore as a stranger give it welcome.
  There are more things in heaven and earth, Horatio,
  Than are dreamt of in your philosophy.°   170
  But come:
  Here as before, never, so help you mercy,
  How strange or odd some'er I bear myself
  (As I perchance hereafter shall think meet
  To put an antic° disposition on),   175
  That you, at such times seeing me, never shall,
  With arms encumbered° thus, or this headshake,
  Or by pronouncing of some doubtful phrase,
  As "Well, well, we know," or "We could, an if° we would,"
  Or "If we list to speak," or "There be, an if they might,"   180
  Or such ambiguous giving out, to note
  That you know aught of me – this do swear,
  So grace and mercy at your most need help you.
GHOST   *[Beneath]* Swear.
    [They swear.]
HAMLET
  Rest, rest, perturbèd spirit! So, gentlemen,   185
  With all my love I do commend° me to you,
  And what so poor a man as Hamlet is
  May do t' express his love and friending to you,
  God willing, shall not lack. Let us go in together,
  And still° your fingers on your lips, I pray.   190
  The time is out of joint. O cursèd spite
  That ever I was born to set it right!
  Nay, come, let's go together.   *Exeunt.*

❧ **2.1**° *Enter old Polonius, with his man [Reynaldo].*

POLONIUS
  Give him this money and these notes, Reynaldo.
REYNALDO
  I will, my lord.
POLONIUS
  You shall do marvelous wisely, good Reynaldo,
  Before you visit him, to make inquire
  Of his behavior.   5
REYNALDO   My lord, I did intend it.
POLONIUS
  Marry, well said, very well said. Look you, sir,
  Inquire me first what Danskers° are in Paris,

Glosses (right column):

pioner: pioneer, miner (the archaic spelling is stressed on the first syllable)

your philosophy: this philosophizing one hears about

antic: grotesque, mad

encumbered: folded

an if: if

commend: entrust

still: always

2.1: Polonius' rooms in Elsinore

Danskers: Danes

DISCOVERING SHAKESPEARE
(33) <u>Staging</u> [2.1.1]: Where do you think this <u>scene</u> should take place on stage? Why?

And how, and who, what means,° and where they keep,°   **what means:** what their wealth; **keep:** dwell
What company, at what expense; and finding
By this encompassment° and drift of question   **encompassment:** roundabout means   10
That they do know my son, come you more nearer
Than your particular demands° will touch it.   **particular demands:** definite questions
Take you as 'twere some distant knowledge of him,
As thus, "I know his father and his friends,
And in part him" – do you mark this, Reynaldo?   15
REYNALDO
   Ay, very well, my lord.
POLONIUS
   "And in part him, but," you may say, "not well,
But if't be he I mean, he's very wild,
Addicted so and so." And there put on him
What forgeries° you please; marry, none so rank°   **forgeries:** invented wrongdoings; **rank:**   20
As may dishonor him – take heed of that –   exaggerated, terrible
But, sir, such wanton, wild, and usual slips
As are companions noted and most known
To youth and liberty.
REYNALDO   As gaming, my lord.
POLONIUS
   Ay, or drinking, fencing, swearing, quarreling,   25
Drabbing.° You may go so far.   **Drabbing:** whoring
REYNALDO
   My lord, that would dishonor him.
POLONIUS
   Faith,° as you may season° it in the charge.   **Faith:** (a mild oath; F reads "Faith, no,"); **season:**
You must not put another scandal on him,   soften
That he is open to incontinency.°   **incontinency:** extreme promiscuity   30
That's not my meaning. But breathe his faults so quaintly°   **quaintly:** artfully
That they may seem the taints of liberty,
The flash and outbreak of a fiery mind,
A savageness in unreclaimèd° blood,   **unreclaimèd:** untamed
Of general assault.°   **Of general assault:** assailing all young men   35
REYNALDO   But, my good lord –
POLONIUS
   Wherefore should you do this?
REYNALDO   Ay, my lord,
   I would know that.
POLONIUS   Marry, sir, here's my drift,
And I believe it is a fetch of wit.°   **fetch of wit:** clever trick
You laying these slight sullies on my son
As 'twere a thing a little soiled with working,   40
Mark you,
Your party in converse, him you would sound,
Having ever° seen in the prenominate° crimes   **Having ever:** if he has ever; **prenominate:**
The youth you breathe of guilty, be assured   aforementioned
He closes with° you in this consequence:°   **closes with:** agrees with; **consequence:**   45
"Good sir," or so, or "friend," or "gentleman" –   following way

---

DISCOVERING SHAKESPEARE

(34) Plot [2.1.26]: What was "drabbing" (2.1.26)? Why do you think Polonius wants Reynaldo to slander Laertes?

According to the phrase or the addition°
Of man and country –
REYNALDO   Very good, my lord.
POLONIUS
And then, sir, does a this – a° does –
What was I about to say? By the mass, I was about to
say something! Where did I leave?
REYNALDO   At "closes in the consequence."
POLONIUS
At "closes in the consequence" – Ay, marry!
He closes thus: "I know the gentleman;
I saw him yesterday, or th' other day,
Or then, or then, with such or such, and, as you say,
There was a° gaming, there o'ertook° in's rouse,°
There falling out° at tennis"; or perchance,
"I saw him enter such a house of sale,"
Videlicet,° a brothel, or so forth.
See you now –
Your bait of falsehood takes this carp of truth,
And thus do we of wisdom and of reach,°
With windlasses° and with assays of bias,°
By indirections find directions° out.
So, by my former lecture and advice,
Shall you my son. You have me,° have you not?
REYNALDO
My lord, I have.
POLONIUS   God buy ye,° fare ye well.
REYNALDO   Good my lord.
POLONIUS
Observe his inclination in yourself.
REYNALDO   I shall, my lord.
POLONIUS
And let him ply his music.
REYNALDO   Well, my lord.
POLONIUS
Farewell.   *Exit Reynaldo.*
  Enter Ophelia.
                    How now, Ophelia, what's the matter?
OPHELIA
O my lord, my lord, I have been so affrighted!
POLONIUS
With what, i' th' name of God?
OPHELIA
My lord, as I was sewing in my closet,°
Lord Hamlet, with his doublet° all unbraced,°
No hat upon his head, his stockings fouled,
Ungartered, and down-gyvèd° to his ankle,
Pale as his shirt, his knees knocking each other,

addition: title

a: he   50

                                                                 55

a: he; **o'ertook:** overcome with drunkenness;
rouse: carousal
falling out: quarreling
Videlicet: namely (Latin)   60

reach: far-reaching comprehension
windlasses: roundabout courses; **assays of
bias:** devious attacks (metaphors from the game   65
of bowls, in which balls are weighted or "biased")
directions: ways of procedure
have me: understand me

God buy ye: God be with you, good-bye

                                                                 70

closet: private room
doublet: jacket; **unbraced:** unlaced

down-gyvèd: fallen down like gyves (chains) on
a prisoner's legs   80

DISCOVERING SHAKESPEARE

(35) <u>Verse</u> [2.1.51]: Why does this <u>verse</u> scene between Polonius and Reynaldo shift into <u>prose</u> in lines 49–51?
(36) <u>Blocking</u> [2.1.73]: How does Ophelia enter in 2.1.73? Is she calm, assured, frantic, angry? What clues in the follow-ing lines suggest her mood and behavior?

And with a look so piteous in purport
As if he had been loosèd out of hell
To speak of horrors – he comes before me.
POLONIUS
Mad for thy love?
OPHELIA   My lord, I do not know,
But truly I do fear it.   85
POLONIUS   What said he?
OPHELIA
He took me by the wrist and held me hard.
Then goes he to the length of all his arm,
And with his other hand thus o'er his brow
He falls to such perusal of my face
As a would draw it. Long stayed he so.   90
At last, a little shaking of mine arm
And thrice his head thus waving up and down,
He raised a sigh so piteous and profound
As it did seem to shatter all his bulk
And end his being. That done, he lets me go,   95
And with his head over his shoulder turned
He seemed to find his way without his eyes,
For out o' doors he went without their helps
And to the last bended their light on me.
POLONIUS
Come, go with me. I will go seek the king.   100
This is the very ecstasy° of love,
Whose violent property° fordoes° itself
And leads the will to desperate undertakings
As oft as any passion under heaven
That does afflict our natures. I am sorry.   105
What, have you given him any hard words of late?
OPHELIA
No, my good lord; but as you did command
I did repel his letters and denied
His access to me.
POLONIUS   That hath made him mad.
I am sorry that with better heed and judgment   110
I had not quoted° him. I feared he did but trifle
And meant to wrack° thee; but beshrew° my jealousy.
By heaven, it is as proper to our age
To cast beyond ourselves° in our opinions
As it is common for the younger sort   115
To lack discretion. Come, go we to the king.
This must be known, which, being kept close,° might
 move°
More grief to hide than hate to utter love.°
Come.   *Exeunt.*

ecstasy: madness

property: quality; **fordoes:** destroys

quoted: observed

wrack: ruin (by sexual seduction); **beshrew:** curse

cast beyond ourselves: pay more attention to (or, suppose more significance in) something than we ought to

close: secret; **move:** cause

to hide . . . love: i.e., more grief will come from concealing Hamlet's supposed love for Ophelia than hate will come from making that love public

---

DISCOVERING SHAKESPEARE

(37) Metaphor [2.1.98]: Explain the following metaphor in 2.1.97–99: "He seemed to find his way without his eyes, / For out o' doors he went without their helps / And to the last bended their light on me."

ᶘ **2.2°** *Flourish. Enter King and Queen, Rosencrantz,*
and Guildenstern [with others].

2.2: Elsinore

KING
 Welcome, dear Rosencrantz and Guildenstern.
 Moreover° that we° much did long to see you,   **Moreover:** besides; **we:** (the royal plural)
 The need we have to use you did provoke
 Our hasty sending. Something have you heard
 Of Hamlet's transformation – so call it,   5
 Sith° nor th' exterior nor the inward man   **Sith:** since
 Resembles that it was. What it should be,
 More than his father's death, that thus hath put him
 So much from th' understanding of himself,
 I cannot dream of.° I entreat you both   **dream of:** imagine   10
 That, being of so young days brought up with him,
 And sith so neighbored to his youth and havior,°   **youth and havior:** youthful ways of life ("behavior")
 That you vouchsafe your rest° here in our court   **vouchsafe your rest:** agree to stay
 Some little time, so by your companies
 To draw him on to pleasures, and to gather   15
 So much as from occasion you may glean,
 Whether aught to us unknown afflicts him thus,
 That opened° lies within our remedy.   **opened:** revealed
QUEEN
 Good gentlemen, he hath much talked of you,
 And sure I am two men there is° not living   **is:** (a singular verb with a plural subject is   20
 To whom he more adheres.° If it will please you   common in Shakespeare's period)
 To show us so much gentry° and good will   **more adheres:** is more attached
 As to expend your time with us a while   **gentry:** courtesy
 For the supply and profit of our hope,
 Your visitation shall receive such thanks   25
 As fits a king's remembrance.
ROSENCRANTZ   Both your majesties
 Might, by the sovereign power you have of us,
 Put your dread pleasures more into command
 Than to entreaty.
GUILDENSTERN   But we both obey,
 And here give up ourselves in the full bent°   **in the full bent:** to full capacity (a metaphor   30
 To lay our service freely at your feet,   from the *bent* bow)
 To be commanded.
KING
 Thanks, Rosencrantz and gentle Guildenstern.
QUEEN
 Thanks, Guildenstern and gentle Rosencrantz.
 And I beseech you instantly to visit   35
 My too much changèd son. – Go, some of you,
 And bring these gentlemen where Hamlet is.

DISCOVERING SHAKESPEARE

(38) Teaser [2.2.1]: Who wrote a play entitled *Rosencrantz and Guildenstern Are Dead?* From whose point of view is the play written? Which characters are most sympathetic to the audience? How is this version of the "Hamlet" story different from Shakespeare's play?

(39) Costuming [2.2.33]: The king and queen seem to confuse Rosencrantz and Guildenstern in 2.2.33–34. If you were casting the roles and costuming the actors, would you want the two characters to look alike or different? Why?

GUILDENSTERN
Heavens make our presence and our practices
Pleasant and helpful to him!
QUEEN   Ay, amen!
           Exeunt Rosencrantz and Guildenstern
                   [with some Attendants].

    Enter Polonius.
POLONIUS
Th' ambassadors from Norway, my good lord,   40
Are joyfully returned.
KING
Thou still° hast been the father of good news.   **still:** always
POLONIUS
Have I, my lord? I assure my good liege
I hold my duty as I hold my soul,
Both to my God and to my gracious king,   45
And I do think – or else this brain of mine
Hunts not the trail of policy so sure
As it hath used to do – that I have found
The very cause of Hamlet's lunacy.
KING
O, speak of that! That do I long to hear.   50
POLONIUS
Give first admittance to th' ambassadors.
My news shall be the fruit° to that great feast.   **fruit:** dessert
KING
Thyself do grace° to them and bring them in.   **grace:** honor
                    [Exit Polonius.]
He tells me, my dear Gertrude, he hath found
The head and source of all your son's distemper.   55
QUEEN
I doubt° it is no other but the main,   **doubt:** suspect
His father's death and our o'erhasty marriage.
KING
Well, we shall sift him.
    Enter Ambassadors [Voltemand and Cornelius, with
    Polonius].
                   Welcome, my good friends.
Say, Voltemand, what from our brother Norway?
VOLTEMAND
Most fair return of greetings and desires.   60
Upon our first,° he sent out to suppress   **our first:** our first words about the matter
His nephew's levies, which to him appeared
To be a preparation 'gainst the Polack,
But better looked into, he truly found
It was against your highness, whereat grieved,   65
That so his sickness, age, and impotence
Was falsely borne in hand,° sends out arrests   **borne in hand:** deceived
On Fortinbras, which he in brief obeys,
Receives rebuke from Norway, and in fine°   **in fine:** in the end

---

DISCOVERING SHAKESPEARE

(40) Geography [2.2.40]: Where is Norway in relation to Denmark? How long would it have taken ambassadors to travel from one country to the other? How is this time lapse important to Shakespeare's play?

Makes vow before his uncle never more   70
To give th' assay° of arms against your majesty.   **assay:** trial, test
Whereon old Norway, overcome with joy,
Gives him threescore thousand crowns in annual fee
And his commission to employ those soldiers,
So levied as before, against the Polack,   75
With an entreaty, herein further shown,
   [Gives a paper.]
That it might please you to give quiet pass
Through your dominions for this enterprise,
On such regards° of safety and allowance   **regards:** terms
As therein are set down.   80
KING   It likes us well;°   **It . . . well:** (see 4.4)
And at our more considered time° we'll read,   **considered time:** convenient time for
Answer, and think upon this business.   consideration
Meantime we thank you for your well-took labor.
Go to your rest; at night we'll feast together.
Most welcome home!   *Exeunt Ambassadors.*   85
POLONIUS   This business is well ended.
My liege and madam, to expostulate°   **expostulate:** discuss
What majesty should be, what duty is,
Why day is day, night night, and time is time,
Were nothing but to waste night, day, and time.
Therefore, since brevity is the soul of wit,°   **wit:** understanding   90
And tediousness the limbs and outward flourishes,
I will be brief. Your noble son is mad.
Mad call I it, for, to define true madness,
What is't but to be nothing else but mad?
But let that go.   95
QUEEN   More matter, with less art.
POLONIUS
Madam, I swear I use no art at all.
That he's mad, 'tis true: 'tis true 'tis pity,
And pity 'tis 'tis true – a foolish figure.°   **figure:** figure of speech
But farewell it, for I will use no art.
Mad let us grant him then, and now remains   100
That we find out the cause of this effect –
Or rather say, the cause of this defect,
For this effect defective comes by cause.
Thus it remains, and the remainder thus.
Perpend.°   **Perpend:** consider, think about (this)   105
I have a daughter (have while she is mine),
Who in her duty and obedience, mark,
Hath given me this. Now gather and surmise.
   [Reads the] letter.
"To the celestial, and my soul's idol, the most beauti-
fied Ophelia" –   110
That's an ill phrase, a vile phrase; "beautified" is a vile
phrase. But you shall hear. Thus:
   [Reads.]

DISCOVERING SHAKESPEARE

(41) Characterization [2.2.70]: Based upon his long speech in 2.2.60–80, what kind of character do you think Voltemand is? What clues in his <u>diction</u> and <u>syntax</u> lead you to that conclusion?
(42) <u>Irony</u> [2.2.90]: Why is Polonius' comment about brevity being "the soul of wit" (2.2.90) <u>ironic</u> in this context?

"In her excellent white bosom, these, etc."°

QUEEN
Came this from Hamlet to her?

POLONIUS
Good madam, stay a while. I will be faithful.°
   [Reads.]

       "Doubt° thou the stars are fire;
         Doubt that the sun doth move;
       Doubt truth to be a liar;
         But never doubt I love.

O dear Ophelia, I am ill at these numbers.° I have not
art to reckon my groans, but that I love thee best, O
most best, believe it. Adieu.

     Thine evermore, most dear lady,
       whilst this machine° is to° him, Hamlet."

This in obedience hath my daughter shown me,
And more above° hath his solicitings,
As they fell out° by time, by means, and place,
All given to mine ear.

KING   But how hath she
Received his love?

POLONIUS   What do you think of me?

KING
As of a man faithful and honorable.

POLONIUS
I would fain° prove so. But what might you think,
When I had seen this hot love on the wing
(As I perceived it, I must tell you that,
Before my daughter told me), what might you,
Or my dear majesty your queen here, think,
If I had played the desk or table book,°
Or given my heart a winking,° mute and dumb,
Or looked upon this love with idle sight?
What might you think? No, I went round° to work
And my young mistress° thus I did bespeak:
"Lord Hamlet is a prince, out of thy star.°
This must not be." And then I prescripts° gave her
That she should lock herself from his resort,
Admit no messengers, receive no tokens.
Which done, she took the fruits of my advice,
And he, repelled, a short tale to make,
Fell into a sadness, then into a fast,
Thence to a watch,° thence into a weakness,
Thence to a lightness,° and, by this declension,
Into the madness wherein now he raves,
And all we mourn for.

KING   Do you think this?

---

etc.: (i.e., other conventional words of greeting: early modern letters often include "etc." for such common, formalized greetings)

faithful: i.e., true to the text   115

Doubt: suspect

numbers: verses   120

machine: body; **to:** attached to

     125

above: besides
fell out: came about

     130

fain: wish to, prefer to

     135

desk or table book: i.e., silent receptacle
winking: closing of the eyes

round: plainly
mistress: i.e., "miss" (a dismissive term for his daughter)   140
star: status determined by stellar influence
prescripts: instructions

     145

watch: sleepless state
lightness: light-headedness

     150

DISCOVERING SHAKESPEARE

(43) <u>Verse</u> [2.2.116]: What is the <u>meter</u> and <u>rhyme</u> scheme of Hamlet's four-line poem in 2.2.116–119? How are they different from the <u>meter</u> and <u>verse</u> of Shakespeare's play?

(44) <u>Diction</u> [2.2.142]: Look up the word "prescripts" (2.2.142) in the *Oxford English Dictionary*. What range of meanings did it have in the year 1600? What do you think its primary meaning is in this context?

QUEEN
  It may be, very like.
POLONIUS
  Hath there been such a time – I would fain know
    that –
  That I have positively said "'Tis so,"
  When it proved otherwise? 155
KING   Not that I know.
POLONIUS
  Take this from this,° if this be otherwise.
  If circumstances lead me, I will find
  Where truth is hid, though it were hid indeed
  Within the center.°
KING   How may we try it further?
POLONIUS
  You know sometimes he walks four hours together 160
  Here in the lobby.
QUEEN   So he does indeed.
POLONIUS
  At such a time I'll loose° my daughter to him.
  Be you and I behind an arras° then.
  Mark the encounter. If he love her not,
  And be not from his reason fallen thereon,° 165
  Let me be no assistant for a state
  But keep a farm and carters.
KING   We will try it.
    Enter Hamlet [reading on a book].
QUEEN
  But look where sadly° the poor wretch comes reading.
POLONIUS
  Away, I do beseech you both, away.
                Exit King and Queen [with Attendants].
  I'll board° him presently.° O, give me leave. 170
  How does my good Lord Hamlet?
HAMLET   Well, God-a-mercy.°
POLONIUS   Do you know me, my lord?
HAMLET   Excellent well. You are a fishmonger.°
POLONIUS   Not I, my lord. 175
HAMLET   Then I would you were so honest a man.
POLONIUS   Honest, my lord?
HAMLET   Ay, sir. To be honest, as this world goes, is to be one man picked out of ten thousand.
POLONIUS   That's very true, my lord. 180
HAMLET   For if the sun breed maggots in a dead dog, being a good kissing carrion° – Have you a daughter?
POLONIUS   I have, my lord.
HAMLET   Let her not walk i' th' sun. Conception is a blessing, but as your daughter may conceive, friend, look to't. 185

Take . . . from this: i.e., behead me (traditionally the actor is directed to gesture to head and neck or shoulder)

center: center of the earth

loose: release (the word refers specifically to the breeding of domesticated animals and hence is coarse when used of humans, much less one's daughter)

an arras: a hanging tapestry

thereon: on that account

sadly: seriously

board: greet; **presently:** at once

God-a-mercy: thank you (literally, "God have mercy!")

fishmonger: seller of fish (but also slang for procurer: Ophelia is "bait")

a good kissing carrion: flesh good for kissing

DISCOVERING SHAKESPEARE

(45) Scansion [2.2.160]: Scan 2.2.156–162 to determine the number of syllables per line and the amount of feminine endings. Why does the verse pattern break down somewhat in these lines?

(46) Puns [2.2.184]: What pun is Hamlet making on the words "conception" and "conceive" in 2.2.184–185?

POLONIUS   *[Aside]* How say you by that? Still harping on my daughter. Yet he knew me not at first. A said I was a fishmonger. A is far gone. And truly in my youth I suffered much extremity for love, very near this. I'll speak to him again. – What do you read, my lord?

HAMLET   Words, words, words.

POLONIUS   What is the matter, my lord?

HAMLET   Between who?°

POLONIUS   I mean the matter that you read, my lord.

HAMLET   Slanders, sir, for the satirical rogue says here that old men have gray beards, that their faces are wrinkled, their eyes purging thick amber and plum-tree gum,° and that they have a plentiful lack of wit, together with most weak hams.° All which, sir, though I most powerfully and potently believe, yet I hold it not honesty to have it thus set down, for yourself, sir, shall grow old as I am if, like a crab, you could go backward.°

POLONIUS   *[Aside]* Though this be madness, yet there is method in't. – Will you walk out of the air, my lord?

HAMLET   Into my grave.

POLONIUS   Indeed, that's out of the air. *[Aside]* How pregnant° sometimes his replies are! a happiness° that often madness hits on, which reason and sanity could not so prosperously be delivered of. I will leave him [and suddenly contrive the means of meeting between him]° and my daughter. – My lord, I will take my leave of you.

HAMLET   You cannot take from me anything that I will not° more willingly part withal° – except my life, except my life, except my life.

   Enter Guildenstern and Rosencrantz.

POLONIUS   Fare you well, my lord.

HAMLET   These tedious old fools!

POLONIUS   You go to seek the Lord Hamlet. There he is.

ROSENCRANTZ   *[To Polonius]* God save you, sir.

   [Exit Polonius.]

GUILDENSTERN   My honored lord!

ROSENCRANTZ   My most dear lord!

HAMLET   My excellent good friends! How dost thou, Guildenstern? Ah, Rosencrantz! Good lads, how do you both?

ROSENCRANTZ
As the indifferent° children of the earth.

GUILDENSTERN   Happy in that we are not overhappy on Fortune's cap. We are not the very button.

HAMLET   Nor the soles of her shoe?

ROSENCRANTZ   Neither, my lord.

HAMLET   Then you live about her waist or in the middle of her favors?

190

Between who: (Hamlet jokingly misunderstands *matter* as the subject of a quarrel or a lawsuit)   195

gum: resin (?)
hams: legs   200

shall . . . backward: you will be as old as I am if you could age backward
205

pregnant: full of meaning; **a happiness:** an aptness of expression
210

and . . . him: (this phrase from F was probably omitted accidentally from Q2 when the compositor's eye skipped from *him* to *him*)

cannot . . . not: (a common double negative); **withal:** with   215

220

225

indifferent: average

230

DISCOVERING SHAKESPEARE

(47) **Paraphrase** [2.2.205]: Paraphrase the following famous line by Polonius: "Though this be madness, yet there is method in't" (2.2.204–205). Does Hamlet want Polonius to think he is mad? Why or why not?

GUILDENSTERN   Faith, her privates° we.

HAMLET   In the secret parts of Fortune? O, most true; she is a strumpet. What news?

ROSENCRANTZ   None, my lord, but the world's grown honest.

HAMLET   Then is doomsday near. But your news is not true.° But in the beaten° way of friendship, what make° you at Elsinore?

ROSENCRANTZ   To visit you, my lord; no other occasion.

HAMLET   Beggar that I am, I am ever poor in thanks, but I thank you; and sure, dear friends, my thanks are too dear a halfpenny.° Were you not sent for? Is it your own inclining? Is it a free visitation? Come, come, deal justly with me. Come, come. Nay, speak.

GUILDENSTERN   What should we say, my lord?

HAMLET   Anything but to th' purpose. You were sent for, and there is a kind of confession in your looks, which your modesties have not craft enough to color.° I know the good king and queen have sent for you.

ROSENCRANTZ   To what end, my lord?

HAMLET   That you must teach me. But let me conjure you by the rights of our fellowship, by the consonancy° of our youth, by the obligation of our ever-preserved love, and by what more dear a better proposer° can charge you withal,° be even° and direct with me whether you were sent for or no.

ROSENCRANTZ   [Aside to Guildenstern] What say you?

HAMLET   [Aside] Nay then, I have an eye of you. – If you love me, hold not off.

GUILDENSTERN   My lord, we were sent for.

HAMLET   I will tell you why. So shall my anticipation prevent° your discovery,° and your secrecy to the king and queen molt no feather.° I have of late – but wherefore I know not – lost all my mirth, forgone all custom of exercises; and indeed, it goes so heavily with my disposition that this goodly frame the earth seems to me a sterile promontory; this most excellent canopy, the air, look you, this brave o'erhanging firmament,° this majestical roof fretted° with golden fire – why, it appeareth nothing to me but a foul and pestilent congregation of vapors. What piece of work is a man, how noble in reason, how infinite in faculties, in form and moving how express° and admirable, in action how like an angel, in apprehension how like a god: the beauty of the world, the paragon of animals! And yet to me what is this

---

privates: ordinary men in private, not public, life (with wordplay on "private parts," which Hamlet emphasizes with *secret parts*)   235

true: (after this word F includes a substantial passage not in Q2; **beaten:** well-trodden, well-worn; **make:** do   240

a halfpenny: at a halfpenny   245

color: conceal, cover up with deceptive colorings   250

consonancy: accord (in sameness of age)   255

proposer: propounder
withal: with; **even:** straight

260

prevent: forestall; **discovery:** disclosure
molt no feather: let fall no feather (i.e., be left whole)   265

firmament: sky   270
fretted: decorated with fretwork (it is traditionally supposed that the original actor of Hamlet here gestured toward the roof of the Globe's stage, which was painted with *golden fire,* the zodiac and stars)
express: well-framed   275

DISCOVERING SHAKESPEARE

(48) Teaser [2.2.233]: Find three more examples in Shakespeare's plays where Fortune is <u>personified</u> as a woman. Is Fortune's effect in those plays different than in *Hamlet*? If so, how?

(49) History [2.2.240]: Where was Elsinore (2.2.240) located in Denmark? What famous castle is there?

(50) Teaser [2.2.263]: The infamous 1960's musical *Hair* uses part of Hamlet's <u>monologue</u> in 2.2.263–280 for one of its songs. Find the lyrics to this song and compare them to Hamlet's speech. Does the meaning of the words change from *Hamlet* to *Hair*? If so, how and why?

quintessence° of dust?° Man delights not me – nor woman neither, though by your smiling you seem to say so.

ROSENCRANTZ   My lord, there was no such stuff in my thoughts.

HAMLET   Why did ye laugh then, when I said "Man delights not me"?

ROSENCRANTZ   To think, my lord, if you delight not in man, what Lenten° entertainment the players shall receive from you. We coted° them on the way, and hither are they coming to offer you service.

HAMLET   He that plays the king shall be welcome – his majesty shall have tribute of me –, the adventurous knight shall use his foil and target,° the lover shall not sigh gratis, the humorous man° shall end his part in peace, [the clown shall make those laugh whose lungs are tickle o' th' sere,]° and the lady shall say her mind freely, or the blank verse shall halt° for't. What players are they?

ROSENCRANTZ   Even those you were wont to take such delight in, the tragedians of the city.

HAMLET   How chances it they travel? Their residence,° both in reputation and profit, was better both ways.

ROSENCRANTZ   I think their inhibition comes by the means of the late innovation.°

HAMLET   Do they hold the same estimation they did when I was in the city?° Are they so followed?

ROSENCRANTZ   No indeed, are they not.°

HAMLET   It is not very strange, for my uncle is King of Denmark, and those that would make mouths at him° while my father lived give twenty, forty, fifty, a hundred ducats apiece for his picture in little.° 'Sblood,° there is something in this more than natural, if philosophy could find it out.

   A flourish.

GUILDENSTERN   There are the players.

HAMLET   Gentlemen, you are welcome to Elsinore. Your hands, come then. Th' appurtenance of welcome is fashion and ceremony. Let me comply with you in this garb,° lest my extent° to the players (which I tell you must show fairly outwards) should more appear like entertainment than yours. You are welcome. But my uncle-father and aunt-mother are deceived.

GUILDENSTERN   In what, my dear lord?

HAMLET   I am but mad north-northwest. When the wind is southerly I know a hawk° from a handsaw.°

   Enter Polonius.

POLONIUS   Well be with you, gentlemen.

---

quintessence: fifth (*quint-*) and finest essence (an alchemical term for something superior to the four essences or elements—fire, air, earth, water— that constituted all earthly life); **dust:** the earth of which humankind is created according to the Judeo-Christian Scriptures (see 5.1.187 ff.)

Lenten: scanty (from "Lent," the forty-day period of abstinence and repentance before the Christian Easter)

coted: overtook

foil and target: sword and shield

the humorous man: an eccentric character

the clown . . . sere,: (versions of this phrase appear in Q1 and F; it seems accidentally absent from Q2); **tickle o' th' sere:** hair-triggered for the discharge of laughter (*sere* = part of a gunlock)

halt: go lame (a joke on metrical "feet" in verse)

residence: (for Shakespeare and his audience, this word would evoke the theatrical center, London)

late innovation: new fashion (possibly the companies of boy actors who had reappeared circa 1601 as competitors for adult companies such as Shakespeare's; possibly a reference to political upheaval)

city: (as in ll. 297–300, presumably *city* = London for Shakespeare's original audiences)

not: (after this word F has a lengthy passage)

make mouths at him: make faces at him, ridicule him

his picture in little: a miniature; **'Sblood:** by God's [i.e., Christ's] blood

garb: manner; **extent:** showing, behavior

hawk: mattock or pickax (also called "hack"; here used apparently with a play on *hawk,* the bird); **handsaw:** carpenter's tool (apparently with a play on some form of "hernshaw," the heron)

280

285

290

295

300

305

310

315

320

DISCOVERING SHAKESPEARE

(51) Verse [2.2.295]: What is blank verse (2.2.295)? Find an example from this scene and write it on a separate sheet of paper. Then scan the line to find out how many syllables it has and where the accents fall.

(52) Music [2.2.311]: What is the difference between a "flourish" (2.2.311 s.d.) and a "tucket"? (*Hint:* See the *Oxford English Dictionary.*)

HAMLET   Hark you, Guildenstern – and you too – at each ear a hearer. That great baby you see there is not yet out of his swaddling clouts.° 325

clouts: clothes

ROSENCRANTZ   Happily° he is the second time come to them, for they say an old man is twice a child.

Happily: haply, perhaps

HAMLET   I will prophesy he comes to tell me of the players. Mark it. – You say right, sir; a Monday morning, 'twas then indeed. 330

POLONIUS   My lord, I have news to tell you.

HAMLET   My lord, I have news to tell you. When Roscius° was an actor in Rome –

Roscius: a legendary Roman comic actor

POLONIUS   The actors are come hither, my lord. 335

HAMLET   Buzz, buzz.

POLONIUS   Upon my honor –

HAMLET   Then came each actor on his ass –

POLONIUS   The best actors in the world, either for tragedy, comedy, history, pastoral, pastoral-comical, historical-pastoral; scene individable,° or poem unlimited.° Seneca° cannot be too heavy,° nor Plautus° too light.° For the law of writ° and the liberty,° these are the only men. 340

scene individable: drama observing the unity of place (?)

poem unlimited: drama not observing the unity of place (?); **Seneca:** classical Roman writer of tragedies; **heavy:** serious; **Plautus:** classical Roman writer of comedies; **light:** unserious

HAMLET   O Jephthah,° judge of Israel, what a treasure hadst thou! 345

law of writ: drama written (as Shakespeare's was not) according to classical or neoclassical rules; **liberty:** freedom from such rule-based orthodoxy

POLONIUS   What a treasure had he, my lord?

HAMLET   Why,
        "One fair daughter, and no more,
        The which he lovèd passing° well."

Jephthah: biblical father whose rash vow compelled him to sacrifice his beloved daughter (Judges 11:30–40) 350

POLONIUS   [Aside] Still on my daughter.

HAMLET   Am I not i' th' right, old Jephthah?

passing: surpassingly (the verses are from a surviving ballad on Jephthah)

POLONIUS   If you call me Jephthah, my lord, I have a daughter that I love passing well.

HAMLET   Nay, that follows not. 355

POLONIUS   What follows then, my lord?

HAMLET   Why,
        "As by lot, God wot,"
and then, you know,
        "It came to pass, as most like it was." 360
The first row° of the pious chanson° will show you more, for look where my abridgment° comes.

row: stanza; **chanson:** song (French)
my abridgment: something that shortens my talk

        Enter the Players.

You are welcome, masters, welcome, all. – I am glad to see thee well. – Welcome, good friends. – O, old friend, why, thy face is valanced° since I saw thee last. Com'st thou to beard me in Denmark? – What, my young lady° and mistress? By'r Lady, your ladyship is nearer to heaven than when I saw you last by the altitude of a chopine.° Pray God your voice, like a piece of uncurrent° gold, be 365

valanced: fringed (with a *beard*)
young lady: boy who plays women's parts

chopine: woman's thick-soled shoe
uncurrent: not legal tender

DISCOVERING SHAKESPEARE

(53) History [2.2.333]: Who was Roscius? Why was he famous?
(54) Diction [2.2.361]: What was a "pious chanson" (2.2.361)? How many other times does Shakespeare use the word "chanson" in his plays? (*Hint:* See *The Harvard Concordance to Shakespeare.*)

not cracked within the ring.° – Masters, you are all welcome. We'll e'en to't like French falconers, fly at anything we see. We'll have a speech straight. Come, give us a taste of your quality. Come, a passionate speech.

PLAYER   What speech, my good lord?

HAMLET   I heard thee speak me a speech once, but it was never acted, or if it was, not above once, for the play, I remember, pleased not the million; 'twas caviar to the general,° but it was (as I received it, and others, whose judgments in such matters cried in the top of° mine) an excellent play, well digested in the scenes, set down with as much modesty as cunning. I remember one said there were no sallets° in the lines to make the matter savory, nor no matter in the phrase that might indict the author of affection,° but called it an honest method, as wholesome as sweet, and by very much more handsome than fine. One speech in't I chiefly loved. 'Twas Aeneas' tale to Dido, and thereabout of it especially when he speaks of Priam's slaughter.° If it live in your memory, begin at this line – let me see, let me see:
    "The rugged Pyrrhus, like th' Hyrcanian beast° –"
'Tis not so; it begins with Pyrrhus:
    "The rugged Pyrrhus, he whose sable° arms,
    Black as his purpose, did the night resemble
    When he lay couchèd in the ominous° horse,°
    Hath now this dread and black complexion smeared
    With heraldry more dismal.° Head to foot
    Now is he total gules,° horridly tricked°
    With blood of fathers, mothers, daughters, sons,
    Baked and impasted with the parching° streets,
    That lend a tyrannous and a damnèd light
    To their lord's murder. Roasted in wrath and fire,
    And thus o'ersizèd° with coagulate° gore,
    With eyes like carbuncles, the hellish Pyrrhus
    Old grandsire Priam seeks."
So, proceed you.

POLONIUS   'Fore God, my lord, well spoken, with good accent and good discretion.

PLAYER   "Anon he finds him,
    Striking too short at Greeks. His antique sword,
    Rebellious to his arm, lies where it falls,
    Repugnant to command. Unequal matched,
    Pyrrhus at Priam drives, in rage strikes wide,
    But° with the whiff and wind of his fell° sword
    Th' unnervèd father falls. [Then senseless° Ilium,]
    Seeming to feel this blow, with flaming top
    Stoops to his° base, and with a hideous crash
    Takes prisoner Pyrrhus' ear. For lo! his sword,
    Which was declining on the milky head

---

a piece . . . cracked within the ring: i.e., 370 literally, a coin that has had precious metal removed from within the *ring* surrounding the sovereign's image; figuratively, the boy actor's voice, which has *cracked,* making him unsuitable for women's roles; finally there is bawdy wordplay on the *ring* of a woman's (or female character's) 375 vagina, *cracked* by sexual intercourse

general: multitude
in the top of: more authoritatively than
380

sallets: salads (metaphorically: highly seasoned literary passages)
affection: affectation
385

Priam's slaughter: i.e., at the fall of Troy (Virgil, *Aeneid* II, 506 ff.; *Priam* was King of Troy, *Aeneas* his son-in-law, *Hecuba* his wife; after Troy's fall, Aeneas wandered the Mediterranean Sea and 390 visited Carthage, whose queen was *Dido*)
Hyrcanian beast: tiger (Hyrcania is on the southern shores of the Caspian Sea)
sable: black
ominous: fateful; **horse:** wooden horse by 395 which the Greeks gained entrance to Troy
dismal: ill-omened
gules: red (a heraldic term); **tricked:** decorated in color (another heraldic term)
parching: drying (i.e., because Troy is burning) 400

o'ersizèd: covered as with "size," a glutinous material used for filling, for example, pores of plaster or gaps in cloth; **coagulate:** clotted
405

410

But: even (i.e., with only the sword's movement); **fell:** cruel
senseless: without feeling 415
his: its

DISCOVERING SHAKESPEARE

(55) Teaser [2.2.377]: When was caviar (2.2.377) introduced into England? Why is its mention here important to the play?
(56) Mythology [2.2.390]: Where was Hyrcania? What was a "Hyrcanian beast" (2.2.390)?

Of reverend Priam, seemed i' th' air to stick.
So as a painted° tyrant Pyrrhus stood, · **painted:** pictured · 420
And like a neutral to his will and matter° · **will and matter:** desire and aim (between
Did nothing. · which he stands *neutral,* motionless)
But as we often see, against° some storm, · **against:** just before
A silence in the heavens, the rack° stand still, · **rack:** clouds
The bold winds speechless, and the orb below · 425
As hush as death, anon the dreadful thunder
Doth rend the region,° so after Pyrrhus' pause, · **region:** sky
Arousèd vengeance sets him new awork,
And never did the Cyclops'° hammers fall · **Cyclops:** giant workmen who made armor in
On Mars's armor, forged for proof eterne,° · Vulcan's forge · 430
With less remorse° than Pyrrhus' bleeding sword · **proof eterne:** eternal protection
Now falls on Priam. · **remorse:** pity, compassion
Out, out, thou strumpet Fortune! All you gods,
In general synod take away her power,
Break all the spokes and fellies° from her wheel, · **fellies:** segments of the rim of a wheel · 435
And bowl the round nave° down the hill of heaven, · **nave:** hub of a wheel
As low as to the fiends."

POLONIUS   This is too long.

HAMLET   It shall to the barber's, with your beard. –
Prithee say on. He's for a jig° or a tale of bawdry, or he · **a jig:** comic singing and dancing often · 440
sleeps. Say on; come to Hecuba. · performed following a play in the public theaters

PLAYER
"But who (ah woe!) had seen the mobled° queen – " · **mobled:** muffled (the archaic word's

HAMLET   "The mobled queen"? · pronunciation is uncertain, "mobled" or

POLONIUS   That's good. · "mobbled," short or long *o*)

PLAYER
"Run barefoot up and down, threat'ning the flames · 445
With bisson rheum;° a clout° upon that head · **bisson rheum:** blinding tears; **clout:** cloth
Where late the diadem stood, and for a robe,
About her lank and all o'erteemèd° loins, · **o'erteemèd:** overproductive of children
A blanket in the alarm of fear caught up –
Who this had seen, with tongue in venom steeped · 450
'Gainst Fortune's state° would treason have pro- · **state:** government of worldly events
    nounced.
But if the gods themselves did see her then,
When she saw Pyrrhus make malicious sport
In mincing with his sword her husband's limbs, · 455
The instant burst of clamor that she made
(Unless things mortal move them not at all)
Would have made milch° the burning eyes° of heaven · **milch:** tearful (milk-giving); **eyes:** i.e., stars
And passion in the gods."

POLONIUS   Look, where° he has not turned his color, and · **where:** whether
has tears in's eyes. Prithee no more. · 460

HAMLET   'Tis well. I'll have thee speak out the rest of this
soon. – Good my lord, will you see the players well be-
stowed?° Do you hear? Let them be well used, for they · **bestowed:** lodged

---

DISCOVERING SHAKESPEARE

(57) Verse [2.2.422]: The First Player has a three-syllable line in 2.2.422. What on-stage action might take place in these seven missing beats?

(58) Language [2.2.442]: What does the word "mobled" (2.2.442) mean? Does Shakespeare use the word elsewhere in his plays? What is the earliest recorded use of the word according to the *Oxford English Dictionary*?

are the abstract and brief chronicles of the time.° After your death you were better have a bad epitaph than their ill report while you live.

POLONIUS My lord, I will use them according to their desert.

HAMLET God's bodkin,° man, much better! Use every man after his desert, and who shall scape whipping? Use them after your own honor and dignity. The less they deserve, the more merit is in your bounty. Take them in.

POLONIUS Come, sirs.

HAMLET Follow him, friends. We'll hear a play tomorrow. *[Aside to Player]* Dost thou hear me, old friend? Can you play "The Murder of Gonzago"?

PLAYER Ay, my lord.

HAMLET We'll ha't tomorrow night. You could for a need° study a speech of some dozen or sixteen lines which I would set down and insert in't, could you not?

PLAYER Ay, my lord.

HAMLET Very well. Follow that lord, and look you mock him not. – My good friends, I'll leave you till night. You are welcome to Elsinore.   *Exeunt Polonius and Players.*

ROSENCRANTZ Good my lord.
                          Exeunt [Rosencrantz and Guildenstern].

HAMLET
Ay, so, God buy to you. – Now I am alone.
O, what a rogue and peasant slave am I!
Is it not monstrous that this player here,
But in a fiction, in a dream of passion,
Could force his soul so to his own conceit°
That from her working all his visage wanned,°
Tears in his eyes, distraction in his aspect,
A broken voice, and his whole function° suiting
With forms to his conceit? And all for nothing,
For Hecuba!
What's Hecuba to him, or he to her,
That he should weep for her? What would he do
Had he the motive and the cue for passion
That I have? He would drown the stage with tears
And cleave the general ear with horrid speech,
Make mad the guilty and appall the free,
Confound the ignorant, and amaze indeed
The very faculties of eyes and ears.
Yet I,
A dull and muddy-mettled° rascal, peak°
Like John-a-dreams,° unpregnant° of my cause,
And can say nothing. No, not for a king,
Upon whose property° and most dear life

they . . . time: i.e., the players tell the stories of our times   465

God's bodkin: by God's little body (an oath)   470

475

for a need: if necessary   480

485

490

conceit: conception, idea
wanned: paled

function: action of bodily powers

495

500

505

muddy-mettled: dull-spirited; **peak:** mope
John-a-dreams: a lazy dawdler; **unpregnant:** barren of realization

property: proper (own) person (?)

DISCOVERING SHAKESPEARE

(59) Stage Direction [2.2.476]: On a separate piece of paper, write a description of what happens on stage while Hamlet talks privately to the First Player, beginning at 2.2.476.

(60) Paraphrase [2.2.496]: Paraphrase lines 489–496 in Hamlet's 2.2.487–544 soliloquy. What important comparison does he make between himself and the player?

A damned defeat was made. Am I a coward?   510
Who calls me villain? breaks my pate° across?   **pate:** head
Plucks off my beard and blows it in my face?
Tweaks me by the nose? gives me the lie i' th' throat
As deep as to the lungs? Who does me this?
Ha, 'swounds,° I should take it, for it cannot be   **'swounds:** by God's [i.e., Christ's] wounds (an   515
But I am pigeon-livered° and lack gall   oath)
To make oppression bitter, or ere this   **pigeon-livered:** unaggressive (pigeons were
I should ha' fatted all the region kites°   supposed to lack a *gall* bladder and hence to be
With this slave's offal.° Bloody, bawdy villain!   meek)
Remorseless, treacherous, lecherous, kindless° villain! **region kites:** kites (scavenging birds) of the air   520
Why, what an ass am I! This is most brave,   **offal:** guts
That I, the son of a dear father murdered,   **kindless:** unnatural
Prompted to my revenge by heaven and hell,
Must like a whore unpack my heart with words
And fall a-cursing like a very drab,   525
A stallion!° Fie upon 't, foh! About,° my brains.   **stallion:** (slang for "prostitute," male or female);
Hum –   **About:** get working, get going
I have heard that guilty creatures sitting at a play
Have by the very cunning of the scene
Been struck so to the soul that presently°   **presently:** immediately   530
They have proclaimed their malefactions.°   **guilty . . . malefactions:** (popular belief held
For murder, though it have no tongue, will speak   that such incidents occurred)
With most miraculous organ. I'll have these players
Play something like the murder of my father
Before mine uncle. I'll observe his looks.   535
I'll tent° him to the quick. If a° do blench,°   **tent:** probe; **a:** he; **blench:** flinch
I know my course. The spirit that I have seen
May be a devil, and the devil hath power
T' assume a pleasing shape, yea, and perhaps
Out of my weakness and my melancholy,   540
As he is very potent with such spirits,
Abuses° me to damn me. I'll have grounds   **Abuses:** deludes
More relative° than this. The play's the thing   **relative:** cogent
Wherein I'll catch the conscience of the king.   *Exit.*

❧ **3.1**° *Enter King, Queen, Polonius, Ophelia,*   **3.1:** Elsinore
Rosencrantz, Guildenstern, Lords.

KING
And can you by no drift of conference°   **drift of conference:** course of conversation
Get from him why he puts on this confusion,
Grating so harshly all his days of quiet
With turbulent and dangerous lunacy?
ROSENCRANTZ
He does confess he feels himself distracted,   5
But from what cause a° will by no means speak.   **a:** he

DISCOVERING SHAKESPEARE

(61) <u>Diction</u> [2.2.520]: What is the meaning of the word "kindless" in 2.2.520? (*Hint:* See the *Oxford English Dictionary*.) In 2.2.527, what stage action could take place during the missing nine syllables in the line "Hum—"?
(62) <u>Diction</u> [2.2.536]: When Hamlet says he will "tent" Claudius "to the quick" (2.2.536), what does he mean? Look up the definitions of "tent" and "quick" in the *Oxford English Dictionary*, and write their meanings on a separate sheet of paper. What is the <u>etymology</u> of each word?

GUILDENSTERN
  Nor do we find him forward to be sounded,°   **forward . . . sounded:** willing to be
  But with a crafty madness keeps aloof   (thoroughly) understood
  When we would bring him on to some confession
  Of his true state.   10
QUEEN   Did he receive you well?
ROSENCRANTZ
  Most like a gentleman.
GUILDENSTERN
  But with much forcing of his disposition.
ROSENCRANTZ
  Niggard of° question, but of our demands   **Niggard of:** chary of, not forthcoming with
  Most free in his reply.
QUEEN   Did you assay° him   **assay:** try to win
  To any pastime?   15
ROSENCRANTZ
  Madam, it so fell out that certain players
  We o'erraught° on the way. Of these we told him,   **o'erraught:** overtook
  And there did seem in him a kind of joy
  To hear of it. They are here about the court,
  And, as I think, they have already order   20
  This night to play before him.
POLONIUS   'Tis most true,
  And he beseeched me to entreat your majesties
  To hear and see the matter.
KING
  With all my heart, and it doth much content me
  To hear him so inclined.   25
  Good gentlemen, give him a further edge°   **edge:** keen desire
  And drive his purpose into these delights.
ROSENCRANTZ
  We shall, my lord.

             Exeunt Rosencrantz and Guildenstern.
KING   Sweet Gertrude, leave us too,
  For we have closely° sent for Hamlet hither,   **closely:** privately
  That he, as 'twere by accident, may here   30
  Affront° Ophelia.   **Affront:** come face to face with
  Her father and myself, lawful espials,°   **espials:** spies
  We'll so bestow ourselves that, seeing unseen,
  We may of their encounter frankly judge
  And gather by him, as he is behaved,   35
  If 't be th' affliction of his love or no
  That thus he suffers for.
QUEEN   I shall obey you. —
  And for your part, Ophelia, I do wish
  That your good beauties be the happy cause
  Of Hamlet's wildness. So shall I hope your virtues   40
  Will bring him to his wonted way again,
  To both your honors.

DISCOVERING SHAKESPEARE

(63) Half Lines [3.1.21]: In 3.1.21–23, Polonius and Rosencrantz share a line; then Polonius has a seven-syllable line. How do the shared line and short line speed up the verse in this section of the scene? Can you think of any action or stage movement that Polonius or Claudius could perform during the missing three beats of line 23?

OPHELIA   Madam, I wish it may.

[Exit Queen.]

POLONIUS

Ophelia, walk you here. – Gracious, so please you,
We will bestow ourselves.
   [To Ophelia]   Read on this book,
That show of such an exercise° may color°
Your loneliness.° We are oft to blame in this,
'Tis too much proved, that with devotion's visage
And pious action we do sugar o'er°
The devil himself.

KING   *[Aside]*   O, 'tis too true.
How smart a lash that speech doth give my conscience!
The harlot's cheek, beautied with plast'ring art,
Is not more ugly to° the thing that helps it
Than is my deed to my most painted word.
O heavy burden!

POLONIUS

I hear him coming. Let's withdraw, my lord.

[Exeunt King and Polonius.]

   Enter Hamlet.

HAMLET

To be, or not to be – that is the question:
Whether 'tis nobler in the mind to suffer
The slings and arrows of outrageous fortune
Or to take arms against a sea of troubles
And by opposing end them. To die, to sleep
No more, and by a sleep to say we end
The heartache, and the thousand natural shocks
That flesh is heir to. 'Tis a consummation
Devoutly to be wished. To die, to sleep,
To sleep – perchance to dream – ay, there's the rub,°
For in that sleep of death what dreams may come
When we have shuffled° off this mortal coil°
Must give us pause. There's the respect°
That makes calamity of so long life.°
For who would bear the whips and scorns of time,°
Th' oppressor's wrong, the proud man's contumely,°
The pangs of despised love, the law's delay,
The insolence of office, and the spurns
That patient merit of th' unworthy takes,
When he himself might his quietus° make
With a bare bodkin?° Who would fardels° bear,
To grunt and sweat under a weary life,
But that the dread of something after death,
The undiscovered country, from whose bourn°
No traveler returns, puzzles the will,
And makes us rather bear those ills we have

45 **an exercise:** a religious exercise (the *book* is apparently a devotional text); **color:** give an appearance of naturalness to
loneliness: solitude
sugar o'er: conceal beneath sweetness

50

to: compared to

55

60

65 **rub:** obstacle (literally, obstruction encountered by a lawn bowler's ball)
shuffled: cast; **coil:** to-do, turmoil
respect: consideration, regard
of so long life: so long-lived (but also, perhaps, *long life* as a *calamity*)
70 **time:** the world as we experience it
contumely: rudeness, contempt

75 **quietus:** settlement (literally, release, "quit," from debt)
bodkin: short dagger; **fardels:** burdens

bourn: region

80

DISCOVERING SHAKESPEARE

(64) Aside [3.1.49]: What is an aside? Why do you think Claudius has one at this precise moment in the script? What effect will this aside have on the audience?

(65) Paraphrase [3.1.74]: Paraphrase any ten lines of Hamlet's famous soliloquy in 3.1.56–90. Why do you think this speech is so important in the play?

Than fly to others that we know not of?
Thus conscience° does make cowards of us all,
And thus the native hue of resolution
Is sicklied o'er with the pale cast of thought,
And enterprises of great pitch° and moment
With this regard° their currents turn awry
And lose the name of action. – Soft you now,°
The fair Ophelia! – Nymph, in thy orisons°
Be all my sins remembered.

OPHELIA   Good my lord,
How does your honor for this many a day?

HAMLET
I humbly thank you, well.

OPHELIA
My lord, I have remembrances of yours
That I have longèd long to redeliver.
I pray you, now receive them.

HAMLET   No, not I,
I never gave you aught.

OPHELIA
My honored lord, you know right well you did,
And with them words of so sweet breath composed
As made the things more rich. Their perfume lost,
Take these again, for to the noble mind
Rich gifts wax poor when givers prove unkind.
There, my lord.

HAMLET   Ha, ha! Are you honest?°

OPHELIA   My lord?

HAMLET   Are you fair?

OPHELIA   What means your lordship?

HAMLET   That if you be honest and fair, your honesty
should admit no discourse to your beauty.

OPHELIA   Could beauty, my lord, have better commerce°
than with honesty?

HAMLET   Ay, truly; for the power of beauty will sooner
transform honesty from what it is to a bawd than the
force of honesty can translate beauty into his likeness.
This was sometime a paradox,° but now the time gives it
proof. I did love you once.

OPHELIA   Indeed, my lord, you made me believe so.

HAMLET   You should not have believed me, for virtue
cannot so inoculate° our old stock but we shall relish° of
it. I loved you not.

OPHELIA   I was the more deceived.

HAMLET   Get thee to a nunnery.° Why wouldst thou be a
breeder of sinners? I am myself indifferent honest,° but
yet I could accuse me of such things that it were better

---

conscience: (1) inner moral sense, (2) consciousness

85

pitch: height (of a soaring falcon's flight)
regard: consideration
Soft you now: be quiet, stop talking
orisons: prayers

90

95

100

honest: (1) truthful, (2) chaste

105

commerce: intercourse

110

a paradox: an idea contrary to common opinion

115

inoculate: graft (in horticulture); **relish:** have a flavor

120

nunnery: house of nuns (but also slang, by opposition, for "whorehouse")
indifferent honest: moderately respectable

DISCOVERING SHAKESPEARE

(66) <u>Verse</u> [3.1.100]: Where do Hamlet and Ophelia shift from <u>verse</u> to <u>prose</u> in their brief <u>scene</u> in 3.1.88–149? Why do you think the shift occurs at this point in the <u>scene</u>? When does the <u>scene</u> shift back into <u>verse</u> again? Why does it do so?
(67) <u>Diction</u> [3.1.121]: Why does Hamlet use the word "nunnery" in this scene? What does the word mean? Does its definition change during the scene? Why or why not? (*Hint:* See the *Oxford English Dictionary*.)

my mother had not borne me: I am very proud, re- 125
vengeful, ambitious, with more offenses at my beck
than I have thoughts to put them in, imagination to
give them shape, or time to act them in. What should
such fellows as I do crawling between earth and
heaven? We are arrant knaves all; believe none of us. Go
thy ways to a nunnery. Where's your father? 130

OPHELIA   At home, my lord.

HAMLET   Let the doors be shut upon him, that he may
play the fool nowhere but in's own house. Farewell.

OPHELIA   O, help him, you sweet heavens!

HAMLET   If thou dost marry, I'll give thee this plague for 135
thy dowry: be thou as chaste as ice, as pure as snow,
thou shalt not escape calumny. Get thee to a nunnery,
farewell. Or if thou wilt needs marry, marry a fool, for
wise men know well enough what monsters° you make   **monsters:** cuckolds
of them. To a nunnery, go, and quickly too. Farewell. 140

OPHELIA   Heavenly powers, restore him!

HAMLET   I have heard of your paintings well enough.
God hath given you one face, and you make yourselves
another. You jig and amble, and you lisp; you nick-
name God's creatures and make your wantonness° your   **wantonness:** affectation 145
ignorance.° Go to, I'll no more on't; it hath made me   **your ignorance:** something you pretend you
mad. I say we will have no more marriage. Those that   don't know better than to do
are married already — all but one — shall live. The rest
shall keep as they are. To a nunnery, go.   *Exit.*

OPHELIA
O, what a noble mind is here o'erthrown! 150
The courtier's, soldier's, scholar's, eye, tongue, sword,
Th' expectancy and rose° of the fair state,   **expectancy and rose:** fair hope
The glass° of fashion and the mold of form,   **glass:** mirror
Th' observed of all observers, quite, quite down!
And I, of ladies most deject and wretched, 155
That sucked the honey of his music vows,
Now see that noble and most sovereign reason
Like sweet bells jangled, out of time and harsh,
That unmatched form and feature of blown° youth   **blown:** in full flower
Blasted° with ecstasy.° O, woe is me   **Blasted:** destroyed (as of a decayed flower); 160
T' have seen what I have seen, see what I see.   **ecstasy:** madness
    Enter King and Polonius.

KING
Love? his affections° do not that way tend,   **affections:** emotions
Nor what he spake, though it lacked form a little,
Was not like madness. There's something in his soul
O'er which his melancholy sits on brood, 165
And I do doubt° the hatch and the disclose°   **doubt:** fear; **hatch and the disclose:**
Will be some danger; which for to prevent,   revealing, outcome (as of birds emerging from
I have in quick determination   eggs)

DISCOVERING SHAKESPEARE

(68) <u>Syntax</u> **[3.1.151]:** Examine the relationships between pairs of words in 3.1.151 (for example, is the soldier associated with his "tongue" or "sword"?). What do these disrupted associations suggest about Ophelia's deteriorating mental condition?

Thus set it down: he shall with speed to England
For the demand of our neglected tribute. 170
Haply the seas, and countries different,
With variable objects, shall expel
This something-settled° matter in his heart, **something-settled:** somewhat settled
Whereon his brains still° beating puts him thus **still:** constantly
From fashion of himself.° What think you on't? **fashion of himself:** Hamlet's normal behavior 175

POLONIUS
It shall do well. But yet do I believe
The origin and commencement of his grief
Sprung from neglected love. – How now, Ophelia?
You need not tell us what Lord Hamlet said.
We heard it all. – My lord, do as you please, 180
But if you hold it fit, after the play
Let his queen mother all alone entreat him
To show his grief. Let her be round° with him, **round:** plainspoken
And I'll be placed, so please you, in the ear
Of all their conference. If she find him not, 185
To England send him, or confine him where
Your wisdom best shall think.

KING   It shall be so.
Madness in great ones must not unwatched go.

Exeunt.

❧ **3.2°** *Enter Hamlet and three of the Players.* **3.2:** Elsinore

HAMLET   Speak the speech, I pray you, as I pronounced
it to you, trippingly° on the tongue. But if you mouth it, **trippingly:** easily
as many of our players do, I had as lief the town crier
spoke my lines. Nor do not saw the air too much with
your hand, thus, but use all gently, for in the very tor- 5
rent, tempest, and (as I may say) whirlwind of your
passion, you must acquire and beget a temperance that
may give it smoothness. O, it offends me to the soul to
hear a robustious° periwig-pated° fellow tear a passion to **robustious:** boisterous; **periwig-pated:** wig-
tatters, to very rags, to split the ears of the groundlings,° wearing (as contemporary actors were) 10
who for the most part are capable of nothing but inex- **groundlings:** spectators who paid least and stood
plicable dumb shows° and noise. I would have such a in the yard of the open-air theater
fellow whipped for o'erdoing Termagant.° It out-Herods **dumb shows:** brief pantomimes sketching
Herod.° Pray you avoid it. dramatic matter to follow

PLAYER   I warrant your honor. **Termagant:** a Saracen "god" in medieval
romance and drama 15

HAMLET   Be not too tame neither, but let your own dis- **Herod:** a stereotypical tyrant, based on the
cretion be your tutor. Suit the action to the word, the biblical kings of that name and a common
word to the action, with this special observance, that character in pre-Shakespearean religious plays
you o'erstep not the modesty of nature. For anything

DISCOVERING SHAKESPEARE

(69) Geography [3.1.169]: How far away is Denmark from England? How much time do you think a sea voyage between the two countries would have taken? Why would this information be important to our understanding of the play?

(70) Language [3.2.2]: What does Hamlet mean when he counsels the players not to "mouth" their lines or "saw the air
too much" (3.2.2–4)?

(71) Paraphrase [3.2.17]: Paraphrase the following advice that Hamlet gives to the actors: "Suit the action to the word,
the word to the action" (3.2.17–18). In what other professions would this be a good recommendation?

so overdone is from° the purpose of playing, whose end, both at the first and now, was and is, to hold, as 'twere, the mirror up to nature, to show virtue her feature, scorn her own image, and the very age and body of the time his form and pressure.° Now this overdone, or come tardy off,° though it makes the unskillful laugh, cannot but make the judicious grieve, the censure of the which one° must in your allowance o'erweigh a whole theater of others. O, there be players that I have seen play, and heard others praise, and that highly (not to speak it profanely), that neither having th' accent of Christians, nor the gait of Christian, pagan, nor man, have so strutted and bellowed that I have thought some of Nature's journeymen° had made men, and not made them well, they imitated humanity so abominably.

PLAYER   I hope we have reformed that indifferently° with us.

HAMLET   O, reform it altogether! And let those that play your clowns° speak no more than is set down for them, for there be of them° that will themselves laugh, to set on some quantity of barren spectators to laugh too, though in the meantime some necessary question of the play be then to be considered. That's villainous and shows a most pitiful ambition in the fool that uses it. Go make you ready.   [Exeunt Players.]

  Enter Polonius, Guildenstern, and Rosencrantz.

How now, my lord? Will the king hear this piece of work?

POLONIUS   And the queen too, and that presently.°

HAMLET   Bid the players make haste.   [Exit Polonius.]
Will you two help to hasten them?

ROSENCRANTZ   Ay, my lord.   Exeunt they two.

HAMLET   What, ho, Horatio!

  Enter Horatio.

HORATIO
Here, sweet lord, at your service.

HAMLET
Horatio, thou art e'en as just° a man
As e'er my conversation coped withal.°

HORATIO
O, my dear lord –

HAMLET   Nay, do not think I flatter.
For what advancement may I hope from thee,
That no revenue hast but thy good spirits
To feed and clothe thee? Why should the poor be flat-
  tered?
No, let the candied tongue lick absurd pomp,
And crook the pregnant° hinges of the knee
Where thrift° may follow fawning. Dost thou hear?
Since my dear soul was mistress of her choice

from: apart from   20

pressure: impression (as of a stamp in wax or on a coin)   25
come tardy off: brought off slowly and badly
the censure of the which one: the judgment of even one of whom (note Hamlet's elitist streak)

                                                                30

journeymen: workmen not yet masters of their trade
indifferently: fairly well   35

clowns: comic actors
of them: some of them
                                                                40

                                                                45

presently: at once

                                                                50

just: well-balanced
conversation coped withal: dealings (not just talk) with men encountered
                                                                55

pregnant: quick to move   60
thrift: profit

DISCOVERING SHAKESPEARE

(72) <u>Staging</u> [3.2.45]: Draw a picture of the stage on a separate sheet of paper; then, using letters for characters, diagram the exits and entrances of all the actors.

And could of men distinguish her election,
S' hath sealed° thee for herself, for thou hast been
As one in suff'ring all that suffers nothing,
A man that Fortune's buffets and rewards
Hast ta'en with equal thanks; and blessed are those
Whose blood° and judgment are so well commeddled°
That they are not a pipe° for Fortune's finger
To sound what stop she please. Give me that man
That is not passion's slave, and I will wear him
In my heart's core, ay, in my heart of heart,
As I do thee. Something too much of this –
There is a play tonight before the king.
One scene of it comes near the circumstance
Which I have told thee, of my father's death.
I prithee, when thou seest that act afoot,
Even with the very comment of thy soul°
Observe my uncle. If his occulted° guilt
Do not itself unkennel° in one speech,
It is a damnèd ghost° that we have seen,
And my imaginations are as foul
As Vulcan's stithy.° Give him heedful note,
For I mine eyes will rivet to his face,
And after we will both our judgments join
In censure° of his seeming.

HORATIO   Well, my lord.
If a° steal aught the whilst this play is playing,
And scape detecting, I will pay the theft.°

*Enter Trumpets and Kettledrums, King, Queen,
Polonius, Ophelia [, Rosencrantz, Guildenstern, and
other Lords attendant].*

HAMLET   They are coming to the play. I must be idle.°
Get you a place.

KING   How fares our cousin° Hamlet?

HAMLET   Excellent, i' faith, of the chameleon's dish.° I eat
the air, promise-crammed. You cannot feed capons so.

KING   I have nothing with this answer, Hamlet. These
words are not mine.°

HAMLET   No, nor mine now. *[To Polonius]* My lord, you
played once i' th' university, you say?

POLONIUS   That did I, my lord, and was accounted a
good actor.

HAMLET   What did you enact?

POLONIUS   I did enact Julius Caesar. I was killed i' th'
Capitol;° Brutus killed me.

HAMLET   It was a brute part of him to kill so capital a calf
there. Be the players ready?

ROSENCRANTZ   Ay, my lord. They stay upon your patience.°

QUEEN   Come hither, my dear Hamlet, sit by me.

S' hath sealed: she (the soul) has marked

65

blood: passion; **commeddled:** mingled
a pipe: an instrument like a recorder or flute

70

75

the very . . . soul: thy deepest consideration
occulted: hidden
unkennel: dislodge, come out (literally, *unkennel* 80
is to drive a fox from its hole; *kennel* also means
"gutter")
a damnèd ghost: an evil spirit, a devil (as
thought of in 2.2.537 ff.)
stithy: smithy (hence, "black," "hellish")

85

censure of: sentence upon

a: he
If . . . theft: (Horatio analogizes Claudius with
the pickpockets who haunted the Elizabethan
public theater)

be idle: be foolish, act like the madman

90

cousin: nephew
chameleon's dish: i.e., air (which was believed
the chameleon's food; Hamlet jokingly
misunderstands *fares*)

not mine: not for me as the asker of my   95
question

100

Capitol: (on the summit of the Capitoline hill,
overlooking classical Rome's Forum)

105

stay upon your patience: await your
indulgence

DISCOVERING SHAKESPEARE

(73) <u>Pun</u> **[3.2.72]:** What <u>pun</u> is Hamlet making on the word "heart" (3.2.72)? (*Hint:* What is the word's Latin origin?)
(74) Mythology [3.2.92]: What was "the chameleon's dish" (3.2.92)? What other facts can you learn about the alleged
properties of this famous lizard?

HAMLET   No, good mother. Here's metal more attractive.

POLONIUS   *[To the King]* O ho! do you mark that?

HAMLET   Lady, shall I lie in your lap?°

OPHELIA   No, my lord.

HAMLET   Do you think I meant country° matters?

OPHELIA   I think nothing, my lord.

HAMLET   That's a fair thought to lie between maids' legs.

OPHELIA   What is, my lord?

HAMLET   Nothing.

OPHELIA   You are merry, my lord.

HAMLET   Who, I?

OPHELIA   Ay, my lord.

HAMLET   O God, your only jig-maker!° What should a man do but be merry? For look you how cheerfully my mother looks, and my father died within's two hours.

OPHELIA   Nay, 'tis twice two months, my lord.

HAMLET   So long? Nay then, let the devil wear black, for I'll have a suit of sables.° O heavens! die two months ago, and not forgotten yet? Then there's hope a great man's memory may outlive his life half a year. But, by'r Lady, a must build churches then, or else shall a suffer not thinking on, with the hobbyhorse,° whose epitaph is "For O, for O, the hobbyhorse is forgot!"

The trumpet sounds. Dumb show follows.
Enter a King and a Queen [very lovingly], the Queen embracing him, and he her. [She kneels; and makes show of protestation unto him.] He takes her up, and declines his head upon her neck. He lies him down upon a bank of flowers. She, seeing him asleep, leaves him. Anon come in another man: takes off his crown, kisses it, pours poison in the sleeper's ears, and leaves him. The Queen returns, finds the King dead, makes passionate action. The poisoner, with some three or four, come in again, seem to condole with her. The dead body is carried away. The poisoner woos the Queen with gifts; she seems harsh awhile, but in the end accepts love.
[Exeunt.]

OPHELIA   What means this, my lord?

HAMLET   Marry, this is miching mallecho;° it means mischief.

OPHELIA   Belike this show imports the argument° of the play.

Enter Prologue.

HAMLET   We shall know by this fellow. The players cannot keep counsel; they'll tell all.

OPHELIA   Will a tell us what this show meant?

HAMLET   Ay, or any show that you will show him. Be not you ashamed to show, he'll not shame to tell you what it means.

---

lie . . . lap: have sexual intercourse with you   110

country: rustic (with a bawdy pun on the first syllable:"cunt-try")

115

jig-maker: writer of jigs (see 2.2.440)   120

sables: black furs (luxurious garb, not for mourning)   125

hobbyhorse: (an imitation horse worn by a performer in May games and morris dances so the performer appeared to ride the horse suspended from his own shoulders)   130

miching mallecho: sneaking iniquity

argument: (1) subject, (2) plot outline

135

140

DISCOVERING SHAKESPEARE

(75) Diction [3.2.112]: What sexual reference is Hamlet making with the term "country matters" (3.2.112)? Explain the following phallic pun in the word "Nothing" (3.2.116).

(76) Etymology [3.2.130]: What was a dumb show? According to the *Oxford English Dictionary*, what is the origin of the term?

OPHELIA You are naught,° you are naught. I'll mark the
play.

naught: indecent, offensive

PROLOGUE

For us and for our tragedy,
Here stooping to your clemency,
We beg your hearing patiently. *[Exit.]*

145

HAMLET Is this a prologue, or the posy° of a ring?

posy: brief motto in rhyme often engraved inside
a *ring*

OPHELIA 'Tis brief, my lord.

HAMLET As woman's love.

Enter [two Players as] King and Queen.

PLAYER KING

Full thirty times hath Phoebus' cart° gone round
Neptune's salt wash and Tellus'° orbèd ground,
And thirty dozen moons with borrowed° sheen
About the world have times twelve thirties° been,
Since love our hearts, and Hymen° did our hands,
Unite commutual° in most sacred bands.

Phoebus' cart: the sun's chariot — 150
Tellus: Roman goddess of the earth
borrowed: i.e., taken from the sun
twelve thirties: i.e., thirty years
Hymen: the Greek god of marriage
commutual: mutually — 155

PLAYER QUEEN

So many journeys may the sun and moon
Make us again count o'er ere love be done!
But woe is me, you are so sick of late,
So far from cheer and from your former state,
That I distrust you.° Yet, though I distrust,
Discomfort you, my lord, it nothing must.
For women fear too much, even as they love,
And women's fear and love hold quantity,°
In neither aught, or in extremity.
Now what my love is, proof hath made you know,
And as my love is sized, my fear is so.
Where love is great, the littlest doubts are fear;
Where little fears grow great, great love grows there.

distrust you: fear for you — 160

quantity: proportion

165

PLAYER KING

Faith, I must leave thee, love, and shortly too;
My operant powers° their functions leave to do.
And thou shalt live in this fair world behind,
Honored, beloved, and haply one as kind
For husband shalt thou –

operant powers: active bodily forces — 170

PLAYER QUEEN   O, confound the rest!
Such love must needs be treason in my breast.
In second husband let me be accurst!
None wed the second but who killed the first.°

175

HAMLET *[Aside]* That's wormwood.°

None . . . first: (a general statement: *None* is
plural)
wormwood: a bitter herb

PLAYER QUEEN

The instances° that second marriage move
Are base respects of thrift, but none of love.
A second time I kill my husband dead
When second husband kisses me in bed.

instances: motives

180

PLAYER KING

I do believe you think what now you speak,

DISCOVERING SHAKESPEARE

(77) Teaser [3.2.154]: Who was Hymen? In which Shakespearean play does he actually appear?

(78) Paraphrase [3.2.180]: Paraphrase the following lines by the Player Queen: "A second time I kill my husband dead / When second husband kisses me in bed" (3.2.180–181). What is the relationship of these lines to the plot of *Hamlet*?

But what we do determine oft we break.
Purpose is but the slave to° memory,°
Of violent birth, but poor validity,°
Which now, the fruit unripe, sticks on the tree,
But fall unshaken when they mellow be.°
Most necessary 'tis that we forget
To pay ourselves what to ourselves is debt.
What to ourselves in passion we propose,
The passion ending, doth the purpose lose.
The violence of either grief or joy
Their own enactures° with themselves destroy.
Where joy most revels, grief doth most lament;
Grief joys, joy grieves, on slender accident.
This world is not for aye, nor 'tis not strange
That even our loves should with our fortunes change,
For 'tis a question left us yet to prove,°
Whether love lead fortune, or else fortune love.
The great man down, you mark his favorite flies,
The poor advanced makes friends of enemies;
And hitherto doth love on fortune tend,
For who not needs shall never lack a friend,
And who in want a hollow friend doth try,
Directly seasons him° his enemy.
But, orderly to end where I begun,
Our wills° and fates do so contrary run
That our devices still° are overthrown;
Our thoughts are ours, their ends none of our own.
So think thou wilt no second husband wed,
But die thy thoughts when thy first lord is dead.

PLAYER QUEEN
Nor earth to me give food, nor heaven light,
Sport and repose lock from me day and night,
To desperation turn my trust and hope,
An anchor's cheer° in prison be my scope,°
Each opposite that blanks° the face of joy
Meet what I would have well, and it destroy,
Both here and hence° pursue me lasting strife,
If, once a widow, ever I be wife!

HAMLET　If she should break it now!

PLAYER KING
'Tis deeply sworn. Sweet, leave me here a while.
My spirits grow dull, and fain I would beguile
The tedious day with sleep.

PLAYER QUEEN　　　　　　Sleep rock thy brain,　*[He sleeps.]*
And never come mischance between us twain!　*[Exit.]*

HAMLET　Madam, how like you this play?

QUEEN　The lady doth protest too much, methinks.

---

slave to: i.e., dependent on; **Purpose . . . memory:** i.e., fulfilling our intentions depends upon our remembering them, and memory may be faulty (see ll. 190–91, 209)　185
validity: strength
Which . . . be: i.e., as time passes, the *fruit* ripens and falls, just as *purpose* fails when not sustained by *memory*　190

enactures: fulfillments

195

prove: test

200

seasons him: ripens him into　205

wills: desires, intentions
still: always

210

An anchor's cheer: a hermit's way of life (*anchor* is an anchorite—i.e., hermit); **scope:** limit, all I may have　215
blanks: blanches, makes pale
hence: in the next world

220

225

DISCOVERING SHAKESPEARE

(79) Rhyme [3.2.203]: What is the rhyme scheme in 3.2.178–219? Which of these rhymes are perfect? Which are slant? How many are couplets? Can you see any pattern in the rhyme scheme in this section of the scene? If so, what is it?

(80) Paraphrase [3.2.226]: Paraphrase Gertrude's observation that "The lady protests too much, methinks" (3.2.226). What does Hamlet's reply in line 227 mean? In early texts of the play, the First Folio and First Quarto have "protests," while the Second Quarto prints "doth protest." Which reading do you prefer? Why?

HAMLET   O, but she'll keep her word.

KING   Have you heard the argument?° Is there no offense in't?

HAMLET   No, no, they do but jest, poison in jest; no offense i' th' world.

KING   What do you call the play?

HAMLET   "The Mousetrap." Marry, how? Tropically.° This play is the image of a murder done in Vienna. Gonzago is the duke's name; his wife, Baptista. You shall see anon. 'Tis a knavish piece of work, but what of that? Your majesty, and we that have free° souls, it touches us not. Let the galled° jade° wince; our withers° are unwrung.

Enter [a Player as] Lucianus.

This is one Lucianus, nephew to the king.

OPHELIA   You are as good as a chorus,° my lord.

HAMLET   I could interpret between you and your love, if I could see the puppets° dallying.

OPHELIA   You are keen, my lord, you are keen.

HAMLET   It would cost you a groaning to take off mine edge.°

OPHELIA   Still better, and worse.

HAMLET   So you mis-take your husbands. Begin, murderer. Leave thy damnable faces and begin. Come, the croaking raven doth bellow for revenge.

PLAYER LUCIANUS
   Thoughts black, hands apt, drugs fit, and time agreeing,
   Confederate season,° else no creature seeing,
   Thou mixture rank, of midnight weeds collected,
   With Hecate's° ban° thrice blasted, thrice infected,
   Thy natural magic and dire property
   On wholesome life usurps immediately.
      [Pours the poison in his ears.]

HAMLET   A° poisons him i' th' garden for his estate. His name's Gonzago. The story is extant, and written in very choice Italian. You shall see anon how the murderer gets the love of Gonzago's wife.

OPHELIA   The king rises.

QUEEN   How fares my lord?

POLONIUS   Give o'er the play.

KING   Give me some light. Away!

POLONIUS   Lights, lights, lights!

Exeunt all but Hamlet and Horatio.

HAMLET
   Why, let the stricken deer go weep,
      The hart ungallèd play.
   For some must watch,° while some must sleep;
      Thus runs the world away.
   Would not this, sir, and a forest of feathers° – if the rest

argument: (1) subject, (2) plot outline

230

Tropically: in the way of a "trope" or rhetorical figure (with a play on "trapically"—as in *The Mousetrap*)

235

free: guiltless
galled: sore-backed; **jade:** horse; **withers:** shoulders (of a horse)

240

a chorus: one in a play who explains the action

puppets: i.e., you and your lover as in a puppet show

245

keen . . . edge: (Hamlet turns *keen* wit into the bite of sexual desire whose gratification might bring *groaning* in sexual pleasure and/or pain in childbirth)

250

Confederate season: the moment agreeing with my plan

Hecate: the goddess of magic arts; **ban:** curse

255

A: he

260

265

watch: stay awake at night

feathers: plumes for actors' costumes

270

DISCOVERING SHAKESPEARE

(81) Puns [3.2.245–246]: What sexual <u>pun</u> does Hamlet make when he tells Ophelia, "It would cost you a groaning to take off mine edge" (3.2.245–246)?

(82) Teaser [3.2.254]: Who was Hecate (3.2.254)? In which Shakespearean play does Hecate actually appear?

of my fortunes turn Turk° with me – with Provincial
roses° on my razed° shoes, get me a fellowship° in a cry° of
players?

HORATIO   Half a share.

HAMLET   A whole one, I.
       For thou dost know, O Damon° dear,
         This realm dismantled was
       Of Jove himself; and now reigns here
         A very, very – pajock.°

HORATIO   You might have rhymed.

HAMLET   O good Horatio, I'll take the ghost's word for a
thousand pound. Didst perceive?

HORATIO   Very well, my lord.

HAMLET   Upon the talk of the poisoning?

HORATIO   I did very well note him.

HAMLET   Aha! Come, some music! Come, the recorders!°
       For if the king like not the comedy,°
       Why then, belike he likes it not, perdy.°
Come, some music!

Enter Rosencrantz and Guildenstern.

GUILDENSTERN   Good my lord, vouchsafe me a word
with you.

HAMLET   Sir, a whole history.°

GUILDENSTERN   The king, sir –

HAMLET   Ay, sir, what of him?

GUILDENSTERN   Is in his retirement marvelous distempered.°

HAMLET   With drink, sir?

GUILDENSTERN   No, my lord, with choler.°

HAMLET   Your wisdom should show itself more richer to
signify this to the doctor, for for me to put him to his
purgation would perhaps plunge him into more choler.

GUILDENSTERN   Good my lord, put your discourse into
some frame,° and start not so wildly from my affair.

HAMLET   I am tame,° sir; pronounce.

GUILDENSTERN   The queen, your mother, in most great
affliction of spirit hath sent me to you.

HAMLET   You are welcome.

GUILDENSTERN   Nay, good my lord, this courtesy is not
of the right breed. If it shall please you to make me a
wholesome° answer, I will do your mother's commandment. If not, your pardon and my return shall be the
end of my business.

HAMLET   Sir, I cannot.

ROSENCRANTZ   What, my lord?

HAMLET   Make you a wholesome answer; my wit's diseased. But, sir, such answer as I can make, you shall
command, or rather, as you say, my mother. Therefore
no more, but to the matter. My mother, you say –

turn Turk: turn renegade, like a Christian
turning Muslim

Provincial roses: rosettes that covered shoelaces
in fashionable garb (the Provençal rose is a large-
blossomed cabbage rose)

razed: decorated with slashed patterns;
fellowship: financial partnership (such as
Shakespeare had) in a theatrical company, a *share*
(l. 274); **cry:** pack (of hounds)

Damon: (conventional name for a shepherd-
friend in classical Greco-Roman and early
modern pastoral literature)

pajock: patchock, disreputable fellow

recorders: wind instruments (cf. l. 69)
comedy: i.e., any drama (Latin: *comoedia*), not just
one meant to amuse

perdy: by God (French: *pardieu*)

history: lengthy discourse

distempered: out of temper, vexed (twisted by
Hamlet into "drunk")

choler: anger

frame: logical order
tame: calm (i.e., quietly awaiting your speech)

wholesome: i.e., rational

275

280

285

290

295

300

305

310

315

DISCOVERING SHAKESPEARE

(83) <u>Rhyme</u> [3.2.279]: What bawdy <u>rhyme</u> with the word "was" does Horatio expect Hamlet to make instead of using
the nonsense word "pajock" (3.2.279)?

(84) History [3.2.298]: What was "choler" (3.2.298)? Why does Guildenstern imply that the king is "drunk" with it?

ROSENCRANTZ   Then thus she says: your behavior hath struck her into amazement and admiration.°

HAMLET   O wonderful son, that can so stonish a mother! But is there no sequel at the heels of this mother's admiration? Impart.

ROSENCRANTZ   She desires to speak with you in her closet° ere you go to bed.

HAMLET   We shall obey, were she ten times our mother. Have you any further trade° with us?

ROSENCRANTZ   My lord, you once did love me.

HAMLET   And do still, by these pickers and stealers.°

ROSENCRANTZ   Good my lord,° what is your cause of distemper? You do surely bar the door upon your own liberty, if you deny your griefs to your friend.

HAMLET   Sir, I lack advancement.

ROSENCRANTZ   How can that be, when you have the voice of the king himself for your succession° in Denmark?

HAMLET   Ay, sir, but "while the grass grows"° – the proverb is something musty.

Enter the Players with recorders.

O, the recorders. Let me see one. To withdraw° with you – why do you go about to recover the wind° of me, as if you would drive me into a toil?°

GUILDENSTERN   O my lord, if my duty be too bold, my love is too unmannerly.°

HAMLET   I do not well understand that. Will you play upon this pipe?

GUILDENSTERN   My lord, I cannot.

HAMLET   I pray you.

GUILDENSTERN   Believe me, I cannot.

HAMLET   I do beseech you.

GUILDENSTERN   I know no touch of it, my lord.

HAMLET   It is as easy as lying. Govern these ventages° with your fingers and thumb, give it breath with your mouth, and it will discourse most eloquent music. Look you, these are the stops.

GUILDENSTERN   But these cannot I command to any utterance of harmony. I have not the skill.

HAMLET   Why, look you now, how unworthy a thing you make of me! You would play upon me, you would seem to know my stops, you would pluck out the heart of my mystery, you would sound me from my lowest note to the top of my compass;° and there is much music, excellent voice, in this little organ, yet cannot you make it speak. 'Sblood, do you think I am easier to

admiration: wonder, astonishment (cf. *stonish,* l. 321)   320

closet: private room   325

trade: business

pickers and stealers: i.e., hands (a quotation from the Anglican catechism)   330
Good my lord: my good lord

voice . . . succession: (cf. 1.2.109)   335

while the grass grows: (a proverb, ending: "the horse starves")

withdraw: step aside
recover the wind: come up to windward (as a hunter might in order to drive game into the *toil*)   340
toil: snare
is too unmannerly: leads me beyond the restraint of good manners

345

350
ventages: holes, vents

355

360
compass: range

DISCOVERING SHAKESPEARE

(85) **Diction** [3.2.327]: Why does Hamlet use the word "trade" (3.2.327) to describe his dealings with Rosencrantz and Guildenstern? How contemptuous is the remark?

(86) **Metaphor** [3.2.351]: What <u>metaphoric</u> use is Hamlet making of the "pipe" (recorder) in 3.2.351? How does he employ the musical instrument to describe his relationship with Rosencrantz and Guildenstern?

be played on than a pipe? Call me what instrument you
will, though you can fret° me, you cannot play upon me.

fret: irritate (with wordplay on the fingering of some stringed musical instruments)   365

Enter Polonius.

God bless you, sir!

POLONIUS   My lord, the queen would speak with you,
and presently.°

presently: at once

HAMLET   Do you see yonder cloud that's almost in shape
of a camel?   370

POLONIUS   By th' mass and 'tis, like a camel indeed.

HAMLET   Methinks it is like a weasel.

POLONIUS   It is backed like a weasel.

HAMLET   Or like a whale.

POLONIUS   Very like a whale.   375

HAMLET   Then I will come to my mother by and by.°
[Aside] They fool me to the top of my bent.° – I will
come by and by.

by and by: immediately
bent: (see 2.2.30 n.)

POLONIUS   I will say so.   *[Exit.]*   380

HAMLET   "By and by" is easily said. Leave me, friends.

[Exeunt all but Hamlet.]

'Tis now the very witching° time of night,

witching: i.e., associated with witches

When churchyards yawn, and hell itself breathes out
Contagion to this world. Now could I drink hot blood
And do such bitter business as the day
Would quake to look on. Soft, now to my mother.   385
O heart, lose not thy nature;° let not ever

nature: filial love

The soul of Nero° enter this firm bosom.

Nero: Roman emperor and murderer of his mother, Agrippina

Let me be cruel, not unnatural;
I will speak daggers to her, but use none.
My tongue and soul in this be hypocrites: 390
How in my words somever she be shent,°

shent: reproved

To give them seals° never,° my soul, consent!   *Exit.*

seals: authentications in actions; **never:** may never

🙚 **3.3°** *Enter King, Rosencrantz, and Guildenstern.*

3.3: Elsinore

KING
I like him not, nor stands it safe with us
To let his madness range. Therefore prepare you.
I your commission° will forthwith dispatch,

commission: written order

And he to England shall along with you.
The terms° of our estate° may not endure

terms: circumstances; **estate:** royal position   5

Hazard so near's as doth hourly grow
Out of his brows.°

brows: (1) frowns, (2) head (i.e., Hamlet's plans)

GUILDENSTERN   We will ourselves provide.
Most holy and religious fear it is
To keep those many many bodies safe
That live and feed upon your majesty.   10

DISCOVERING SHAKESPEARE

(87) Time [3.2.381]: What clues in Hamlet's speech in 3.2.381–392 imply the time of day in this scene? Why does he wish to "drink hot blood" (3.2.383)?

ROSENCRANTZ

The single and peculiar° life is bound   **peculiar:** individual
With all the strength and armor of the mind
To keep itself from noyance,° but much more   **noyance:** harm
That spirit upon whose weal° depends and rests   **weal:** health
The lives of many. The cess° of majesty   **cess:** decease, cessation   15
Dies not alone, but like a gulf° doth draw   **gulf:** whirlpool
What's near it with it; or it is a massy wheel
Fixed on the summit of the highest mount,
To whose huge spokes ten thousand lesser things
Are mortised and adjoined, which when it falls,   20
Each small annexment, petty consequence,
Attends° the boist'rous ruin. Never alone   **Attends:** joins in (like a royal attendant)
Did the king sigh, but with a general groan.

KING

Arm° you, I pray you, to this speedy° voyage,   **Arm:** prepare; **speedy:** immediate
For we will fetters put about this fear,   25
Which now goes too free-footed.

ROSENCRANTZ   We will haste us.
                 Exeunt Gentlemen.

   Enter Polonius.

POLONIUS

My lord, he's going to his mother's closet.
Behind the arras° I'll convey myself   **arras:** cloth wall hanging
To hear the process.° I'll warrant she'll tax him home,°   **process:** proceedings; **tax him home:**
And, as you said, and wisely was it said,   reprimand him severely   30
'Tis meet that some more audience than a mother,
Since nature makes them partial, should o'erhear
The speech, of vantage.° Fare you well, my liege.   **of vantage:** from an advantageous position
I'll call upon you ere you go to bed
And tell you what I know.   35

KING   Thanks, dear my lord.°   **dear my lord:** my dear lord
                 Exit [Polonius].

O, my offense is rank, it smells to heaven;
It hath the primal eldest curse° upon't,   **primal eldest curse:** God's curse on the biblical
A brother's murder. Pray can I not,   Cain, who also murdered a brother (Genesis
Though inclination be as sharp as will.   4:11–12)
My stronger guilt defeats my strong intent,   40
And like a man to double business bound
I stand in pause where I shall first begin,
And both neglect. What if this cursèd hand
Were thicker than itself with brother's blood,
Is there not rain° enough in the sweet heavens   **rain:** i.e., heavenly mercy (see Ecclesiasticus   45
To wash it white as snow? Whereto serves mercy   35:20 and *The Merchant of Venice,* 4.1.182–83)
But to confront the visage of offense?°   **offense:** sin
And what's in prayer but this twofold force,
To be forestallèd ere we come to fall,
Or pardoned being down? Then I'll look up.   50

DISCOVERING SHAKESPEARE

(88) Staging [3.3.11]: Where does 3.3 take place in the castle? If you were directing a production of the play, where would you put the <u>scene</u> on <u>stage</u>? Why? What <u>set</u> design elements and/or <u>props</u> could signal this specific location to an audience?

(89) Bible [3.3.37]: When Claudius <u>alludes</u> to "the primal eldest curse" (3.3.37), what Biblical reference is he making to the *Book of Genesis*? To which character in this Biblical story is he comparing himself?

My fault is past, but, O, what form of prayer
Can serve my turn? "Forgive me my foul murder"?
That cannot be, since I am still possessed
Of those effects° for which I did the murder,   **effects:** things I acquired
My crown, mine own ambition, and my queen.   55
May one be pardoned and retain th' offense?°   **offense:** i.e., what Claudius has gained by
In the corrupted currents of this world   murdering old Hamlet
Offense's gilded° hand may shove by justice,   **gilded:** gold-laden
And oft 'tis seen the wicked prize itself
Buys out the law. But 'tis not so above.   60
There is no shuffling;° there the action° lies   **shuffling:** cheating; **action:** legal proceeding
In his true nature, and we ourselves compelled,   (in heaven's court)
Even to the teeth and forehead° of our faults,   **to the teeth and forehead:** face-to-face
To give in evidence. What then? What rests?
Try what repentance can. What can it not?   65
Yet what can it when one cannot repent?
O wretched state! O bosom black as death!
O limèd° soul, that struggling to be free   **limèd:** caught in birdlime, a gluey material
Art more engaged!° Help, angels! Make assay.°   spread as a bird snare
Bow, stubborn knees, and, heart with strings of steel,   **engaged:** embedded; **assay:** essay, attempt   70
Be soft as sinews of the newborn babe.
All may be well.
    [He kneels.]
    Enter Hamlet.
HAMLET
Now might I do it pat,° now a is a-praying,   **pat:** opportunely
And now I'll do't. And so a° goes to heaven,   **a:** he
And so am I revenged. That would be scanned.°   **scanned:** studied, thought about   75
A villain kills my father, and for that
I, his sole son, do this same villain send
To heaven.
Why, this is [hire and salary,] not revenge.
A took my father grossly,° full of bread,°   **grossly:** morally unprepared; **full of bread:**   80
With all his crimes broad blown,° as flush° as May;   i.e., sensually gratified (hence not ready for a
And how his audit° stands, who knows save heaven?   purified death)
But in our circumstance and course of thought,   **broad blown:** fully blossomed; **flush:** vigorous
'Tis heavy with him; and am I then revenged,   **audit:** account
To take him in the purging of his soul,
When he is fit and seasoned for his passage?   85
No.
Up, sword, and know thou a more horrid hent.°   **hent:** occasion
When he is drunk asleep, or in his rage,
Or in th' incestuous pleasure of his bed,   90
At game a-swearing, or about some act
That has no relish° of salvation in't –   **relish:** flavor

DISCOVERING SHAKESPEARE

(90) <u>**Paraphrase**</u> **[3.3.57]:** <u>Paraphrase</u> the following lines by Claudius: "In the corrupted currents of this world/Offense's gilded hand may shove by justice" (3.3.57–58). What do these lines tell us about Claudius' sense of guilt?
(91) <u>**Paraphrase**</u> **[3.3.64]:** <u>Paraphrase</u> 3.3.61–63. What does Claudius mean by "shuffling," "even to the teeth," and "forehead of our faults"? To what extent does he feel guilty for killing Hamlet's father?
(92) <u>**History**</u> **[3.3.80]:** When Hamlet complains that Claudius killed his father "full of bread" (3.3.80), what does he mean? What does the condition of Old Hamlet's digestion have to do with repentance and spiritual preparedness, according to Catholic doctrine?

Then trip him, that his heels may kick at heaven,
And that his soul may be as damned and black
As hell, whereto it goes. My mother stays.   95
This physic but prolongs thy sickly days.   *Exit.*
KING *[Rises.]*
  My words fly up, my thoughts remain below.
  Words without thoughts never to heaven go.   *Exit.*

❧ **3.4°** *Enter [Queen] Gertrude and Polonius.*   **3.4:** Elsinore: Gertrude's private rooms

POLONIUS
  A° will come straight. Look you lay home to° him.   **A:** he; **lay home to:** tax (see 3.3.29)
  Tell him his pranks have been too broad° to bear with,   **broad:** unrestrained
  And that your grace hath screened and stood between
  Much heat and him. I'll silence me even here.
  Pray you be round.°   **round:** plainspoken   5
QUEEN   I'll warrant you; fear me not. Withdraw; I hear
  him coming.
    [Polonius hides behind the arras.]
    Enter Hamlet.
HAMLET
  Now, mother, what's the matter?
QUEEN
  Hamlet, thou hast thy father much offended.
HAMLET
  Mother, you have my father much offended.   10
QUEEN
  Come, come, you answer with an idle° tongue.   **an idle:** a foolish
HAMLET
  Go, go, you question with a wicked tongue.
QUEEN
  Why, how now, Hamlet?
HAMLET   What's the matter° now?   **matter:** subject, point of our discussion
QUEEN
  Have you forgot me?
HAMLET   No, by the rood,° not so!   **rood:** cross
  You are the queen, your husband's brother's wife,   15
  And (would it were not so) you are my mother.
QUEEN
  Nay, then I'll set those to you that can speak.
HAMLET
  Come, come, and sit you down. You shall not budge.
  You go not till I set you up a glass°   **glass:** mirror
  Where you may see the inmost part of you.   20
QUEEN
  What wilt thou do? Thou wilt not murder me?
  Help, ho!
POLONIUS   *[Behind]°* What, ho! help!   **Behind:** (for the action here, see 4.1.8-12)

DISCOVERING SHAKESPEARE

(93) Language [3.4.9]: Read 3.4.8–14 out loud, paying special attention to the way in which the <u>stichomythia</u> and <u>half lines</u> speed up the <u>verse</u>. What is the difference between Shakespeare's use of <u>stichomythia</u> here and in 1.1.194–201 of *A Midsummer Night's Dream*?

HAMLET   *[Draws.]*
   How now? a rat? Dead for a ducat, dead!
   [Thrusts through the arras and kills Polonius.]
POLONIUS   *[Behind]*
   O, I am slain!   25
QUEEN   O me, what hast thou done?
HAMLET
   Nay, I know not. Is it the king?
QUEEN
   O, what a rash and bloody deed is this!
HAMLET
   A bloody deed – almost as bad, good mother,
   As kill a king, and marry with his brother.
QUEEN
   As kill a king?   30
HAMLET   Ay, lady, it was my word.
   [Looks behind the arras and sees Polonius.]
   Thou wretched, rash, intruding fool, farewell!
   I took thee for thy better. Take thy fortune.
   Thou find'st to be too busy is some danger. –
   Leave wringing of your hands. Peace, sit you down
   And let me wring your heart, for so I shall   35
   If it be made of penetrable stuff,
   If damnèd custom° have not brazed° it so
   That it be proof° and bulwark against sense.°
QUEEN
   What have I done that thou dar'st wag thy tongue
   In noise so rude against me?   40
HAMLET   Such an act
   That blurs the grace and blush of modesty,
   Calls virtue hypocrite, takes off the rose
   From the fair forehead of an innocent love,
   And sets a blister° there, makes marriage vows
   As false as dicers' oaths. O, such a deed   45
   As from the body of contraction° plucks
   The very soul, and sweet religion° makes
   A rhapsody° of words! Heaven's face does glow,
   O'er this solidity and compound mass,°
   With heated visage, as against° the doom,°   50
   Is thought-sick at the act.
QUEEN   Ay me, what act,
   That roars so loud and thunders in the index?°
HAMLET
   Look here upon this picture, and on this,
   The counterfeit presentment° of two brothers.
   See what a grace was seated on this brow: 55
   Hyperion's° curls, the front° of Jove himself,
   An eye like Mars, to threaten and command,

custom: habit; **brazed:** hardened like brass
proof: armor; **sense:** feeling

blister: brand (in the early modern period, convicted prostitutes were sometimes branded on the forehead; see 4.5.118–19)
contraction: the category, contract-making, of which marriage is an instance
religion: i.e., sacred marriage vows
rhapsody: confused heap
compound mass: the earth as compounded of the four elements (see 2.2.278 n.)
against: in expectation of; **doom:** Day of Judgment
index: table of contents preceding the body of a book, prefatory matter
counterfeit presentment: representation in a portrait
Hyperion: the sun god; **front:** forehead

DISCOVERING SHAKESPEARE

(94) Shared Lines [3.4.24]: How do the <u>shared lines</u> in 3.4.24–30 affect the timing of the scene? Exactly when does Hamlet stab Polonius?

(95) Mythology [3.4.56]: Who were the following mythological characters in 3.4.56–58: Hyperion, Mars, and Mercury? How is Hamlet using them to influence his mother?

A station° like the herald Mercury°
New lighted on a heaven-kissing hill –
A combination and a form indeed
Where every god did seem to set his seal
To give the world assurance of a man.
This was your husband. Look you now what follows.
Here is your husband, like a mildewed ear
Blasting his wholesome brother. Have you eyes?
Could you on this fair mountain leave to feed,
And batten° on this moor? Ha! have you eyes?
You cannot call it love, for at your age
The heyday° in the blood is tame, it's humble,
And waits upon° the judgment, and what judgment
Would step from this to this? Sense° sure you have,
Else could you not have motion,° but sure that sense
Is apoplexed,° for madness would not err,
Nor sense to ecstasy° was ne'er so thralled
But it reserved some quantity of choice
To serve in such a difference.° What devil was't
That thus hath cozened° you at hoodman-blind?°
Eyes without feeling, feeling without sight,
Ears without hands or eyes, smelling sans° all,
Or but a sickly part of one true sense
Could not so mope.°
O shame, where is thy blush? Rebellious hell,
If thou canst mutine° in a matron's bones,
To flaming youth let virtue be as wax
And melt in her own fire. Proclaim no shame
When the compulsive° ardor gives the charge,°
Since frost itself as actively doth burn,
And reason panders will.°

QUEEN   O Hamlet, speak no more.
Thou turn'st my eyes into my very soul,
And there I see such black and grainèd° spots
As will leave there° their tinct.°

HAMLET   Nay, but to live
In the rank sweat of an enseamèd° bed,
Stewed in corruption, honeying and making love
Over the nasty sty –

QUEEN   O, speak to me no more.
These words like daggers enter in my ears.
No more, sweet Hamlet.

HAMLET   A murderer and a villain,
A slave that is not twentieth part the tithe°
Of your precedent lord, a vice° of kings,
A cutpurse° of the empire and the rule,
That from a shelf the precious diadem stole
And put it in his pocket –

QUEEN   No more.
Enter [the] Ghost [in his nightgown].°

---

station: stance; **herald Mercury:** messenger of the Olympian gods, typifying grace

60

65

batten: feed greedily

heyday: excitement of passion
waits upon: yields to   70
Sense: feeling
motion: desire, impulse
apoplexed: paralyzed
ecstasy: madness
                                              75
serve . . . difference: i.e., make a choice where there is such great difference
cozened: cheated; **hoodman-blind:** blindman's buff
sans: without (French)   80
mope: be in a daze

mutine: mutiny

                                              85
compulsive: compelling; **gives the charge:** delivers the attack
panders will: acts as procurer for desire (implied: *reason* should control *will*—desire in general, sexual desire in particular)
grainèd: indelibly dyed ("grain" is dye)   90
leave there: (F reads "not leave," which amounts to the same thing); **tinct:** color
enseamèd: grease-laden ("seam" is grease)

                                              95

tithe: tenth part
vice: clownish rogue (like the Vice, a staple character of the earlier morality plays)
cutpurse: skulking thief   100

nightgown: dressing gown

DISCOVERING SHAKESPEARE

(96) Shared Lines [3.4.93]: How do the shared lines in 3.4.88–115 tell an audience that the scene is reaching its climax? At what point does the Ghost enter? Why do you think so?

HAMLET
A king of shreds and patches –
Save me and hover o'er me with your wings,
You heavenly guards!° What would your gracious figure?

Save . . . guards: (cf. 1.4.39)

QUEEN
Alas, he's mad.   105

HAMLET
Do you not come your tardy son to chide,
That, lapsed in time and passion,° lets go by
Th' important acting of your dread command?
O, say!

lapsed . . . passion: having let both the moment and passionate purpose slip

GHOST
Do not forget. This visitation   110
Is but to whet thy almost blunted purpose.
But look, amazement° on thy mother sits.
O, step between her and her fighting soul!
Conceit° in weakest bodies strongest works.
Speak to her, Hamlet.   115

amazement: bewilderment (literally, "in a maze")
Conceit: imagination

HAMLET   How is it with you, lady?

QUEEN
Alas, how is't with you,
That you do bend your eye on vacancy,
And with th' incorporal° air do hold discourse?
Forth at your eyes your spirits wildly peep,
And as the sleeping soldiers in th' alarm°   120
Your bedded hair, like life in excrements,°
Start up and stand an° end. O gentle son,
Upon the heat and flame of thy distemper°
Sprinkle cool patience. Whereon do you look?

incorporal: bodiless

alarm: call to arms
excrements: outgrowths
an: on
distemper: mental disorder

HAMLET
On him, on him! Look you, how pale he glares!   125
His form and cause conjoined, preaching to stones,
Would make them capable.° – Do not look upon me,
Lest with this piteous action you convert
My stern effects.° Then what I have to do
Will want° true color° – tears perchance for blood.   130

capable: responsive, able to comprehend

effects: planned actions
want: lack; **color:** (1) character, distinguishing quality, (2) tincture (i.e., red *blood* rather than colorless *tears*)

QUEEN
To whom do you speak this?

HAMLET   Do you see nothing there?

QUEEN
Nothing at all; yet all that is I see.

HAMLET
Nor did you nothing hear?

QUEEN   No, nothing but ourselves.

HAMLET
Why, look you there! Look how it steals away!
My father, in his habit as he lived!   135
Look where he goes even now out at the portal!

Exit Ghost.

DISCOVERING SHAKESPEARE

(97) Paraphrase [3.4.116]: Paraphrase the following lines by Gertrude: "Alas, how is't with you, / That you do bend your eye on vacancy, / And with th' incorporal air do hold discourse?" (3.4.116–118). Does she see the Ghost, as Hamlet does?

QUEEN

  This is the very coinage of your brain.
  This bodiless creation ecstasy°
  Is very cunning in.

HAMLET

  My pulse as yours doth temperately keep time   140
  And makes as healthful music. It is not madness
  That I have uttered. Bring me to the test,
  And I the matter will reword, which madness
  Would gambol° from. Mother, for love of grace,
  Lay not that flattering unction° to your soul,   145
  That not your trespass but my madness speaks.
  It will but skin and film the ulcerous place
  Whiles rank corruption, mining° all within,
  Infects unseen. Confess yourself to heaven,
  Repent what's past, avoid what is to come,   150
  And do not spread the compost on the weeds
  To make them ranker. Forgive me this my virtue.
  For in the fatness° of these pursy° times
  Virtue itself of vice must pardon beg,
  Yea, curb° and woo for leave to do him good.   155

QUEEN

  O Hamlet, thou hast cleft my heart in twain.

HAMLET

  O, throw away the worser part of it,
  And live the purer with the other half.
  Good night – but go not to my uncle's bed.
  Assume a virtue, if you have it not.   160
  That monster custom, who all sense doth eat
  Of habits evil,° is angel yet in this,
  That to the use of actions fair and good
  He likewise gives a frock or livery°
  That aptly is put on. Refrain tonight,   165
  And that shall lend a kind of easiness
  To the next abstinence; the next more easy;
  For use° almost can change the stamp° of nature,
  And either [lodge]° the devil, or throw him out
  With wondrous potency. Once more, good night,   170
  And when you are desirous to be blessed,
  I'll blessing beg of you. – For this same lord,
  I do repent; but heaven hath pleased it so,
  To punish me with this, and this with me,
  That I must be their scourge and minister.   175
  I will bestow° him and will answer° well
  The death I gave him. So again, good night.
  I must be cruel only to be kind.
  This° bad begins, and worse remains behind.°
  One word more, good lady.   180

ecstasy: madness

gambol: shy (like a startled horse)
unction: ointment

mining: undermining

fatness: grossness (physical and moral); **pursy:** corpulent (derived from "purse")

curb: bow to

custom . . . evil: i.e., long continuance (*custom*) deprives us of knowing that our behavior is *evil* (the next lines explain that we may also become habituated to good behavior)
livery: characteristic dress

use: habit; **stamp:** impression, form
lodge: (a conjectural addition to Q2, which lacks a verb to parallel *throw*)

bestow: stow, hide; **answer:** be responsible for

This: i.e., the killing of Polonius; **behind:** to come

DISCOVERING SHAKESPEARE

(98) <u>Verse</u> **[3.4.139]:** Scan Gertrude's lines in 3.4.138–139: "This bodiless creation ecstasy / Is very cunning in." What stage action could fill the missing <u>beats</u> in these two lines?

(99) <u>Diction</u> **[3.4.175]:** Look up the words "scourge" and "minister" (3.4.175) in the *Oxford English Dictionary*. What definitions would have been most prominent during the year 1600? How would you define the words based on their context in Hamlet's speech in 3.4.157–180?

QUEEN   What shall I do?

HAMLET
Not this, by no means, that I bid you do:
Let the bloat° king tempt you again to bed,   **bloat:** flabby
Pinch wanton on your cheek, call you his mouse,
And let him, for a pair of reechy° kisses,   **reechy:** filthy (i.e., "reeky")
Or paddling in your neck with his damned fingers,   185
Make you to ravel all this matter out,°   **ravel . . . out:** disentangle
That I essentially am not in madness,
But mad in craft. 'Twere good you let him know,
For who that's but a queen, fair, sober, wise,
Would from a paddock,° from a bat, a gib,°   **paddock:** toad; **gib:** tomcat   190
Such dear concernings° hide? Who would do so?   **dear concernings:** matters so personally important
No, in despite of sense and secrecy,
Unpeg the basket on the house's top,
Let the birds fly, and like the famous ape,°   **famous ape:** (the story, if there was one, is now unknown)
To try conclusions,° in the basket creep   195
And break your own neck down.   **conclusions:** experiments

QUEEN
Be thou assured, if words be made of breath,
And breath of life, I have no life to breathe
What thou hast said to me.

HAMLET
I must to England; you know that?   200

QUEEN   Alack,
I had forgot. 'Tis so concluded on.

HAMLET
There's letters sealed, and my two schoolfellows,
Whom I will trust as I will adders fanged,
They bear the mandate;° they must sweep my way   **mandate:** order
And marshal° me to knavery. Let it work.   **marshal:** conduct, lead   205
For 'tis the sport to have the enginer°   **enginer:** maker of military engines (the spelling, from Q2, indicates stress on the first syllable)
Hoist° with his own petard,° and't shall go hard **Hoist:** blown up; **petard:** bomb or mine
But I will delve one yard below their mines
And blow them at the moon. O, 'tis most sweet
When in one line two crafts directly meet.   210
This man shall set me packing.°   **packing:** (1) traveling in a hurry, (2) carrying Polonius' body, (3) plotting, contriving
I'll lug the guts into the neighbor room.
Mother, good night. Indeed, this counselor
Is now most still, most secret, and most grave,
Who was in life a foolish prating knave.   215
Come, sir, to draw toward an end with you.
Good night, mother.

[Exit the Queen. Then] exit [Hamlet,
lugging in Polonius].

DISCOVERING SHAKESPEARE

(100) Mythology [3.4.190]: What were a "paddock," a "bat," and a "gib" (3.4.190)? What did all these animals have to do with witchcraft?

(101) <u>Rhyme</u> [3.4.215]: How does Hamlet's <u>rhyme</u> between "grave" and "knave" (3.4.214–215) help punctuate Polonius' death? What stage action could occur in the missing six <u>beats</u> in Hamlet's final line, "Good night, mother" (3.4.217)?

❧ **4.1°** *Enter King and Queen, with Rosencrantz and Guildenstern.*

KING
  There's matter in these sighs. These profound heaves
  You must translate; 'tis fit we understand them.
  Where is your son?
QUEEN
  Bestow this place on us° a little while.
                        [Exeunt Rosencrantz and Guildenstern.]
  Ah, mine own lord, what have I seen tonight!
KING
  What, Gertrude? How does Hamlet?
QUEEN
  Mad as the sea and wind when both contend
  Which is the mightier. In his lawless fit,
  Behind the arras hearing something stir,
  Whips out his rapier, cries "A rat, a rat!"
  And in this brainish° apprehension kills
  The unseen good old man.
KING   O heavy deed!
  It had been so with us,° had we been there.
  His liberty is full of threats to all,
  To you yourself, to us, to every one.
  Alas, how shall this bloody deed be answered?
  It will be laid to us, whose providence°
  Should have kept short,° restrained, and out of haunt°
  This mad young man. But so much was our love
  We would not understand what was most fit,
  But, like the owner of a foul disease,
  To keep it from divulging,° let it feed
  Even on the pith of life. Where is he gone?
QUEEN
  To draw apart the body he hath killed;
  O'er whom his very madness, like some° ore°
  Among a mineral° of metals base,
  Shows itself pure. A° weeps for what is done.
KING
  O Gertrude, come away!
  The sun no sooner shall the mountains touch
  But we will ship him hence, and this vile deed
  We must with all our majesty and skill
  Both countenance and excuse.° Ho, Guildenstern!
    Enter Rosencrantz and Guildenstern.
  Friends both, go join you with some further aid.
  Hamlet in madness hath Polonius slain,
  And from his mother's closet hath he dragged him.
  Go seek him out; speak fair, and bring the body
  Into the chapel. I pray you haste in this.
               [Exeunt Rosencrantz and Guildenstern.]

4.1: Elsinore (the act break here is not in Q2 or F, and Gertrude remains onstage)

Bestow this place on us: give us privacy (a polite formula)

5

brainish: deluded, crazed

10

us: me (the royal plural and so throughout the scene)

15

providence: foresight
short: i.e., on a short leash; **haunt:** association with others

20

divulging: becoming known

some: (the printer's manuscript might have read "fine"); **ore:** vein of gold   25
mineral: mine
A: he

30

majesty . . . excuse: i.e., royal power will *countenance,* make publicly acceptable, and *skill,* political savvy, will make palatable

35

DISCOVERING SHAKESPEARE

(102) Characterization [4.1.25]: When Gertrude refers to Hamlet's "very madness" (4.1.25), do you think she believes her son is truly mad? Why or why not?

Come, Gertrude, we'll call up our wisest friends
And let them know both what we mean to do
And what's untimely done.°
Whose whisper o'er the world's diameter,
As level° as the cannon to his blank°
Transports his poisoned shot, may miss our name
And hit the woundless air. O, come away!
My soul is full of discord and dismay.   *Exeunt.*

And . . . done: (some words seem to be missing   40
after this partial line; two editorial guesses: "So,
haply, slander" [Capell]; "So envious slander"
[Jenkins])
As level: with as direct aim; **blank:** mark,
central white spot on a target   45

❧ **4.2**° *Enter Hamlet.*

4.2: Elsinore

HAMLET   Safely stowed. *[Calling within]*° But soft, what
noise? Who calls on Hamlet? O, here they come.
   [Enter] Rosencrantz, [Guildenstern,] and others.

Calling within: (in F, "Gentlemen within" call
Hamlet's name after *stowed*)

ROSENCRANTZ
What have you done, my lord, with the dead body?
HAMLET
Compounded it with dust, whereto 'tis kin.°
ROSENCRANTZ
Tell us where 'tis, that we may take it thence
And bear it to the chapel.
HAMLET   Do not believe it.
ROSENCRANTZ   Believe what?
HAMLET   That I can keep your counsel and not mine
own. Besides, to be demanded of a sponge,° what repli-
cation° should be made by the son of a king?
ROSENCRANTZ   Take you me for a sponge, my lord?
HAMLET   Ay, sir, that soaks up the king's countenance,°
his rewards, his authorities. But such officers do the
king best service in the end. He keeps them, like an
ape, in the corner of his jaw, first mouthed, to be last
swallowed. When he needs what you have gleaned, it is
but squeezing you and, sponge, you shall be dry again.
ROSENCRANTZ   I understand you not, my lord.
HAMLET   I am glad of it. A knavish speech sleeps in° a
foolish ear.
ROSENCRANTZ   My lord, you must tell us where the body
is and go with us to the king.
HAMLET   The body is with the king, but the king is not
with the body. The king is a thing –
GUILDENSTERN   A thing, my lord?
HAMLET   Of nothing.° Bring me to him.   *Exeunt.*

dust . . . kin: (see Genesis 3:19: ". . . dust thou
art, and unto dust shalt thou return")
  5

sponge: i.e., something that absorbs (e.g.,   10
counsel) and may also be squeezed dry (i.e., by
Claudius)
replication: reply (a legal term)
countenance: favor

  15

sleeps in: means nothing to   20

  25

Of nothing: (cf. the Anglican Book of Common
Prayer, Psalm 144:4, "Man is like a thing of
naught: his time passeth away like a shadow")

❧ **4.3**° *Enter King, and two or three.*

4.3: Elsinore

KING
I have sent to seek him and to find the body.
How dangerous is it that this man goes loose!
Yet must not we put the strong law on him;
He's loved of the distracted° multitude,

distracted: confused

DISCOVERING SHAKESPEARE
(103) Diction [4.2.10]: Why does Hamlet call Rosencrantz a "sponge" (4.2.10)? Do you agree with his satirical description?

Who like not in their judgment, but their eyes,   5
And where 'tis so, th' offender's scourge° is weighed,   **scourge:** punishment
But never the offense. To bear all smooth and even,
This sudden sending him away must seem
Deliberate pause.° Diseases desperate grown   **Deliberate pause:** i.e., something thoughtfully
By desperate appliance° are relieved,   deliberated   10
Or not at all.   **appliance:** treatment

           Enter Rosencrantz [, Guildenstern,] and all the rest.
        How now? What hath befallen?
ROSENCRANTZ
Where the dead body is bestowed, my lord,
We cannot get from him.
KING   But where is he?
ROSENCRANTZ
Without, my lord; guarded, to know your pleasure.
KING
Bring him before us.   15
ROSENCRANTZ   Ho! Bring in the lord.
   They enter [with Hamlet].
KING   Now, Hamlet, where's Polonius?
HAMLET   At supper.
KING   At supper? Where?
HAMLET   Not where he eats, but where a° is eaten. A cer-   **a:** he
tain convocation of politic worms° are e'en at him. Your   **politic worms:** craftily scheming worms (just as   20
worm is your only emperor for diet.° We fat all creatures   Polonius was a schemer)
else to fat us, and we fat ourselves for maggots. Your fat   **diet:** food and drink (perhaps with a play upon a
king and your lean beggar is but variable service° – two   famous *convocation,* the Diet [Council] of Worms
dishes, but to one table. That's the end.   opened by Charles V on 28 January 1521, before
KING   Alas, alas!   which the Protestant reformer Martin Luther
                                                                                                                appeared)   25
HAMLET   A man may fish with the worm that hath eat° of   **variable service:** different servings of one food
a king, and eat of the fish that hath fed of that worm.   **eat:** (past tense, pronounced "et")
KING   What dost thou mean by this?
HAMLET   Nothing but to show you how a king may go a
progress° through the guts of a beggar.   **progress:** royal journey through the hinterlands   30
KING   Where is Polonius?
HAMLET   In heaven. Send thither to see. If your messen-
ger find him not there, seek him i' th' other place your-
self. But if indeed you find him not within this month,
you shall nose him as you go up the stairs into the   35
lobby.
KING   *[To Attendants]* Go seek him there.
HAMLET   A will stay till you come.   *[Exeunt Attendants.]*
KING
Hamlet, this deed, for thine especial safety,
Which we do tender° as we dearly° grieve   **tender:** hold dear; **dearly:** intensely   40
For that which thou hast done, must send thee hence
With fiery quickness. Therefore prepare thyself.
The bark° is ready and the wind at help,   **bark:** ship
Th' associates tend,° and everything is bent°   **tend:** wait; **bent:** set in readiness (like a bent
For England.   bow)   45

DISCOVERING SHAKESPEARE

(104) Short Lines [4.3.11]: What is the rhetorical effect of all the short lines in 4.3.11–18?

(105) Paraphrase [4.3.32]: Paraphrase the following advice when Hamlet urges Claudius to look for Polonius in heaven: "If your messenger find him not there, seek him i' th' other place yourself" (4.3.32–34).

HAMLET   For England?
KING   Ay, Hamlet.
HAMLET   Good.
KING
So is it, if thou knew'st our purposes.
HAMLET   I see a cherub° that sees them. But come, for   **cherub:** one of the cherubim, second in the nine
England! Farewell, dear mother.   orders of angels
KING   Thy loving father, Hamlet.
HAMLET   My mother – father and mother is man and   50
wife, man and wife is one flesh;° so, my mother. Come,   **one flesh:** (many biblical passages endorse this
for England!   *Exit.*   claim; see Genesis 2:24, Matthew 19:5–6, Mark
KING   10:8)
Follow him at foot;° tempt him with speed aboard.   **at foot:** closely
Delay it not; I'll have him hence tonight.
Away! for everything is sealed and done   55
That else° leans on° th' affair. Pray you make haste.   **else:** otherwise; **leans on:** is connected with
                            [Exeunt all but the King.]
And, England,° if my love thou hold'st at aught° –   **England:** King of England; **aught:** anything,
As my great power thereof may give thee sense,   any value
Since yet thy cicatrice° looks raw and red   **cicatrice:** scar
After the Danish sword, and thy free awe°   **free awe:** voluntary respect   60
Pays homage to us – thou mayst not coldly set°   **set:** esteem
Our sovereign process,° which imports at full   **process:** formal command
By letters congruing° to that effect   **congruing:** agreeing
The present° death of Hamlet. Do it, England,   **present:** instant
For like the hectic° in my blood he rages,   **the hectic:** a continuous fever   65
And thou must cure me. Till I know 'tis done,
Howe'er my haps,° my joys will ne'er begin.   *Exit.*   **haps:** fortunes

❧ **4.4°** *Enter Fortinbras with his Army [including a*   **4.4:** Somewhere in Denmark's territories
Norwegian Captain, marching] over the stage.

FORTINBRAS
Go, captain, from me greet the Danish king.
Tell him that by his license Fortinbras
Craves the conveyance° of a promised° march   **conveyance:** escort; **promised:** i.e., agreed
Over his kingdom. You know the rendezvous.   upon by diplomats (see 2.2.77–80)
If that his majesty would aught with us,   5
We shall express our duty in his eye;°   **eye:** presence
And let him know so.
NORWEGIAN CAPTAIN   I will do't, my lord.
FORTINBRAS
Go softly° on.   *[Exeunt all but the Captain.]*   **softly:** slowly
   Enter Hamlet, Rosencrantz, [Guildenstern,]
   and others.
HAMLET
Good sir, whose powers° are these?   **powers:** forces
NORWEGIAN CAPTAIN
They are of Norway, sir.   10

DISCOVERING SHAKESPEARE

(106) Diction [4.3.59]: What was a "cicatrice" (4.3.59)? What use is being made of the term in this particular context?

HAMLET
How purposed, sir, I pray you?
NORWEGIAN CAPTAIN
Against some part of Poland.
HAMLET
Who commands them, sir?
NORWEGIAN CAPTAIN
The nephew to old Norway, Fortinbras.
HAMLET
Goes it against the main° of Poland, sir,   **main:** main body   15
Or for some frontier?
NORWEGIAN CAPTAIN
Truly to speak, and with no addition,°   **addition:** exaggeration
We go to gain a little patch of ground
That hath in it no profit but the name.
To pay° five ducats, five, I would not farm it,   **To pay:** (i.e., as rent)   20
Nor will it yield to Norway or the Pole
A ranker° rate, should it be sold in fee.°   **ranker:** more lavish; **in fee:** outright
HAMLET
Why, then the Polack never will defend it.
NORWEGIAN CAPTAIN
Yes, it is already garrisoned.°   **garrisoned:** guarded by soldiers
HAMLET
Two thousand souls and twenty thousand ducats   25
Will not debate the question of this straw.
This is th' imposthume° of much wealth and peace,   **imposthume:** abscess
That inward breaks, and shows no cause without
Why the man dies. I humbly thank you, sir.
NORWEGIAN CAPTAIN
God buy you, sir.   *[Exit.]*   30
ROSENCRANTZ   Will't please you go, my lord?
HAMLET
I'll be with you straight. Go a little before.
                              [Exeunt all but Hamlet.]
How all occasions do inform° against me   **inform:** take shape
And spur my dull revenge! What is a man,
If his chief good and market of° his time   **market of:** compensation for
Be but to sleep and feed? A beast, no more.   35
Sure he that made us with such large discourse,°   **discourse:** power of thought
Looking before and after, gave us not
That capability and godlike reason
To fust° in us unused. Now, whether it be   **fust:** mold
Bestial oblivion,° or some craven scruple   **oblivion:** forgetfulness   40
Of thinking too precisely on th' event° –   **event:** outcome (see l. 50)
A thought which, quartered,° hath but one part wisdom   **quartered:** divided in four (see the many earlier
And ever three parts coward – I do not know   mathematical divisions: e.g., 3.4.97)
Why yet I live to say "This thing's to do,"
Sith I have cause, and will, and strength, and means   45
To do't. Examples gross° as earth exhort me.   **gross:** large and evident
Witness this army of such mass and charge,°   **charge:** expense
Led by a delicate and tender prince,
Whose spirit, with divine ambition puffed,
Makes mouths° at the invisible event,   **Makes mouths:** makes scornful faces   50
Exposing what is mortal and unsure
To all that fortune, death, and danger dare,

Even for an eggshell. Rightly to be great
Is not to stir without great argument,
But greatly to find quarrel in a straw°   **greatly . . . straw:** to recognize the *great*   55
When honor's at the stake. How stand I then,   *argument* even in some small matter
That have a father killed, a mother stained,
Excitements of my reason and my blood,
And let all sleep, while to my shame I see
The imminent death of twenty thousand men   60
That for a fantasy° and trick° of fame   **fantasy:** fanciful image; **trick:** something
Go to their graves like beds, fight for a plot   negligible
Whereon the numbers cannot try the cause,°   **try the cause:** fight to a conclusion the issue in
Which is not tomb enough and continent   contention
To hide the slain? O, from this time forth,   65
My thoughts be bloody, or be nothing worth!   *Exit.*

❧ **4.5**° *Enter Horatio, [Queen] Gertrude, and*   **4.5:** Elsinore
a Gentleman.

QUEEN
  I will not speak with her.
GENTLEMAN
  She is importunate, indeed distract.°   **distract:** insane
  Her mood will needs be pitied.
QUEEN   What would she have?
GENTLEMAN
  She speaks much of her father, says she hears
  There's tricks° i' th' world, and hems, and beats her heart,   **tricks:** deceits   5
  Spurns enviously° at straws,° speaks things in doubt   **Spurns enviously:** kicks spitefully, takes offense;
  That carry but half sense. Her speech is nothing,   **straws:** trifles
  Yet the unshapèd use° of it doth move   **unshapèd use:** disordered manner
  The hearers to collection;° they aim° at it,   **collection:** attempts at making her *speech*
  And botch° the words up fit to their own thoughts,   coherent; **aim:** guess   10
  Which, as her winks and nods and gestures yield them,   **botch:** patch
  Indeed would make one think there might be thought,
  Though nothing sure, yet much unhappily.
HORATIO
  'Twere good she were spoken with, for she may strew
  Dangerous conjectures in ill-breeding minds.   15
QUEEN
  Let her come in.   *[Exit Gentleman.]*
    [Aside]
  To my sick soul (as sin's true nature is)
  Each toy° seems prologue to some great amiss.°   **toy:** trifle; **amiss:** misdeed, evil deed
  So full of artless° jealousy° is guilt   **artless:** unskillfully managed; **jealousy:** suspicion
  It spills° itself in fearing to be spilt.°   **spills:** destroys   20
    Enter Ophelia [distracted].   **To my . . . spilt:** (in Q2, each of these lines
OPHELIA   begins with a quotation mark, indicating
  Where is the beauteous majesty of Denmark?   sententious sayings)

DISCOVERING SHAKESPEARE

(107) Paraphrase [4.5.6]: What does Horatio mean when he claims that Ophelia "Spurns enviously at straws" (4.5.6)? Paraphrase the line into modern English. How does Horatio's comment help characterize Ophelia's madness? To what extent would it assist an actor playing the role?

QUEEN　How now, Ophelia?

OPHELIA

She sings.

> How should I your truelove know
>   From another one?
> By his cockle hat° and staff
>   And his sandal shoon.°

cockle hat: hat bearing a cockleshell, worn by a pilgrim who had been to the shrine of Saint James of Compostela in northwestern Spain 25

shoon: shoes

QUEEN

Alas, sweet lady, what imports this song?

OPHELIA　Say you? Nay, pray you mark.

> *Song.*
> He is dead and gone, lady,
>   He is dead and gone;
> At his head a grass-green turf,
>   At his heels a stone.

30

O, ho!

QUEEN　Nay, but Ophelia —

OPHELIA　Pray you mark.

35

[Sings.]

> White his shroud as the mountain snow —

Enter King.

QUEEN　Alas, look here, my lord.

OPHELIA

> *Song.*
> Larded° all with sweet flowers;
> Which bewept to the ground did not go
>   With truelove showers.

Larded: bedecked

40

KING　How do you, pretty lady?

OPHELIA　Well, good dild° you! They say the owl° was a baker's daughter. Lord, we know what we are, but know not what we may be. God be at your table!

good dild: (a colloquial form of "God yield," or repay); **the owl:** (according to a folktale, a baker's daughter was transformed into an owl because she wasn't generous when Christ asked for bread)

KING　Conceit upon° her father.

OPHELIA　Pray let's have no words of this, but when they ask you what it means, say you this:

Conceit upon: fantasies about 45

> *Song.*
> Tomorrow is Saint Valentine's day.
>   All in the morning betime,°
> And I a maid at your window,
>   To be your Valentine.
> Then up he rose and donned his clo'es
>   And dupped° the chamber door,
> Let in the maid, that out a maid
>   Never departed more.

betime: early

50

dupped: opened

55

KING　Pretty Ophelia!

OPHELIA　Indeed without an oath, I'll make an end on't:

DISCOVERING SHAKESPEARE

(108) <u>Verse</u> [4.5.30]: What is a <u>ballad</u>? Write your own four-line <u>ballad</u>. Why does Ophelia sing so many of them in this scene?

[Sings.]

> By Gis° and by Saint Charity,°
>   Alack, and fie for shame!
> Young men will do't if they come to't.
>   By Cock,° they are to blame.
> Quoth she, "Before you tumbled me,
>   You promised me to wed."

He answers:

> "So would I 'a' done, by yonder sun,
>   And thou hadst not come to my bed."

KING   How long hath she been thus?

OPHELIA   I hope all will be well. We must be patient, but I cannot choose but weep to think they would lay him i' th' cold ground. My brother shall know of it; and so I thank you for your good counsel. Come, my coach! Good night, ladies, good night. Sweet ladies, good night, good night.   *[Exit.]*

KING
Follow her close; give her good watch, I pray you.
                               [Exit Horatio.]
O, this is the poison of deep grief; it springs
All from her father's death and now behold,
O Gertrude, Gertrude,
When sorrows come, they come not single spies,°
But in battalions: first, her father slain;
Next, your son gone, and he most violent author
Of his own just remove; the people muddied,°
Thick and unwholesome in their thoughts and whispers
For good Polonius' death, and we have done but greenly°
In hugger-mugger° to inter him; poor Ophelia
Divided from herself and her fair judgment,
Without the which we are pictures° or mere° beasts;
Last, and as much containing as all these,
Her brother is in secret come from France,
Feeds on this wonder, keeps himself in clouds,°
And wants° not buzzers° to infect his ear
With pestilent speeches of his father's death,
Wherein necessity, of matter beggared,°
Will nothing stick° our person to arraign°
In ear and ear. O my dear Gertrude, this,
Like to a murd'ring piece,° in many places
Gives me superfluous° death.
    A noise within.   Attend!
Where is my Switzers?° Let them guard the door.
What is the matter?
    Enter a Messenger.
MESSENGER   Save yourself, my lord.
The ocean, overpeering of° his list,°
Eats not the flats with more impetuous° haste

Gis: Jesus; **Saint Charity:** (not a recognized saint, but a common saying)

60

Cock: (1) God (a common verbal corruption), (2) penis (?)

65

70

75

spies: scouts (the entire idea is proverbial; cf. 4.7.161–62)

80

muddied: stirred up and confused

greenly: foolishly
hugger-mugger: secrecy

85

pictures: soulless images, vacant forms; **mere:** solely

clouds: obscurity
wants: lacks; **buzzers:** rumor bearers   90

of matter beggared: unprovided with facts
Will nothing stick: doesn't hesitate; **arraign:** accuse

murd'ring piece: cannon loaded with shot   95
meant to scatter
superfluous: (since one *death* would suffice)
Switzers: Swiss mercenaries

overpeering of: rising above; **list:** boundary
impetuous: violent (Q2's "impitious" is an old   100
spelling, not a different modern word)

DISCOVERING SHAKESPEARE

(109) Diction [4.5.58]: Examine Ophelia's brief song in 4.5.58–66, and find all the bawdy references. What does this song tell us about her degenerating mental state?

(110) History [4.5.97]: What was a "Switzer" (4.5.97)? What did they do in the castle?

Than young Laertes, in a riotous head,°   **head:** armed force
O'erbears your officers. The rabble call him lord,
And, as the world were now but to begin,
Antiquity forgot, custom not known,
The ratifiers and props of every word,°   **word:** motto, slogan   105
They cry, "Choose we! Laertes shall be king!"
Caps, hands, and tongues applaud it to the clouds,
"Laertes shall be king! Laertes king!"
    A noise within.
QUEEN
How cheerfully on the false trail they cry!°   **cry:** bellow (i.e., like a pack of hounds)
O, this is counter,° you false Danish dogs!   **counter:** hunting the scent backward   110
KING
The doors are broke.
    Enter Laertes with others.
LAERTES
Where is this king? – Sirs, stand you all without.
ALL
No, let's come in.
LAERTES   I pray you give me leave.
ALL   We will, we will.
LAERTES
I thank you. Keep the door.   *[Exeunt his Followers.]*   115
                O thou vile king,
Give me my father.
QUEEN   Calmly, good Laertes.
LAERTES
That drop of blood that's calm proclaims me bastard,
Cries cuckold to my father, brands the harlot
Even here between the chaste unsmirchèd brow
Of my true mother.   120
KING   What is the cause, Laertes,
That thy rebellion looks so giantlike?°   **giantlike:** (an allusion to the war the giants made
Let him go, Gertrude. Do not fear° our person.   on Olympus: see Ovid, *Metamorphoses* I, and
There's such divinity doth hedge a king°   mentions of Pelion and Ossa here at 5.1.243 and
That treason can but peep to° what it would,   273)
Acts little of his will. Tell me, Laertes,   **fear:** fear for
Why thou art thus incensed. – Let him go, Gertrude. –   **divinity . . . king:** (an allusion to the   125
Speak, man.   contemporary theory that God appointed and
LAERTES   protected earthly monarchs)
Where is my father?   **peep to:** i.e., through the barrier
KING   Dead.
QUEEN   But not by him.
KING
Let him demand his fill.
LAERTES
How came he dead? I'll not be juggled with.   130
To hell allegiance, vows to the blackest devil,
Conscience and grace to the profoundest pit!
I dare damnation. To this point I stand,

DISCOVERING SHAKESPEARE

(111) Irony [4.5.123]: Why are the following lines by Claudius <u>ironic</u>: "There's such divinity doth hedge a king / That treason can but peep to what it would" (4.5.123–124)?

That both the worlds° I give to negligence,°
Let come what comes, only I'll be revenged
Most throughly° for my father.

KING   Who shall stay you?

LAERTES
My will, not all the world's.
And for my means, I'll husband them so well
They shall go far with little.

KING   Good Laertes,
If you desire to know the certainty
Of your dear father, is't writ in your revenge
That sweepstake° you will draw both friend and foe,
Winner and loser?

LAERTES
None but his enemies.

KING   Will you know them then?

LAERTES
To his good friends thus wide I'll ope my arms
And like the kind life-rend'ring° pelican
Repast them with my blood.

KING   Why, now you speak
Like a good child and a true gentleman.
That I am guiltless of your father's death,
And am most sensibly° in grief for it,
It shall as level° to your judgment 'pear
As day does to your eye.

    A noise within [: "Let her come in."]

LAERTES
How now? What noise is that?

    Enter Ophelia.

O heat, dry up my brains; tears seven times salt
Burn out the sense and virtue of mine eye!
By heaven, thy madness shall be paid with weight
Till our scale turn the beam.° O rose of May,
Dear maid, kind sister, sweet Ophelia!
O heavens, is't possible a young maid's wits
Should be as mortal as an old man's life?

OPHELIA
                            Song.
        They bore him barefaced on the bier
        And in his grave rained many a tear –
        Fare you well, my dove!

LAERTES
Hadst thou thy wits, and didst persuade revenge,
It could not move thus.

OPHELIA   You must sing "A-down a-down, and you call
him a-down-a." O, how the wheel° becomes it! It is the
false steward, that stole his master's daughter.

both the worlds: this world and the next; **give to negligence:** disregard   135
throughly: thoroughly

sweepstake: taking all stakes on the gambling table

life-rend'ring: life-yielding (fable held that the mother pelican took blood from her breast to feed her young)

sensibly: feelingly   150
level: plain

beam: bar of a balance

wheel: refrain

140

145

155

160

165

DISCOVERING SHAKESPEARE

(112) Mythology [4.5.146]: To what mythic qualities of the pelican does Laertes refer in 4.5.146?
(113) Teaser [4.5.166]: Compare and contrast Shakespeare's use of flowers in this scene with similar references in 4.4.73–127 of *The Winter's Tale*.

LAERTES   This nothing's more than matter.°

OPHELIA   There's rosemary, that's for remembrance. Pray you, love, remember. And there is pansies, that's for thoughts.°

LAERTES   A document° in madness, thoughts and remembrance fitted.

OPHELIA   There's fennel° for you, and columbines.° There's rue° for you, and here's some for me. We may call it herb of grace o' Sundays. You must wear your rue with a difference. There's a daisy.° I would give you some violets,° but they withered all when my father died. They say a made a good end.

   [Sings.]
          For bonny sweet Robin is all my joy.

LAERTES
Thought and afflictions, passion, hell itself,
She turns to favor° and to prettiness.

OPHELIA

                    Song.
          And will a not come again?
          And will a not come again?
             No, no, he is dead;
             Go to thy deathbed;
          He never will come again.
          His beard was as white as snow,
          Flaxen was his poll.°
             He is gone, he is gone,
             And we cast away moan.
          God 'a' mercy on his soul.
And of° all Christian souls, God buy you.   *[Exit.]*

LAERTES
Do you see this, O God?

KING
Laertes, I must commune with your grief,
Or you deny me right. Go but apart,
Make choice of whom your wisest friends you will,
And they shall hear and judge 'twixt you and me.
If by direct or by collateral° hand
They find us touched,° we will our kingdom give,
Our crown, our life, and all that we call ours,
To you in satisfaction; but if not,
Be you content to lend your patience to us,
And we shall jointly labor with your soul
To give it due content.

LAERTES   Let this be so.
His means of death, his obscure funeral –
No trophy,° sword, nor hatchment° o'er his bones,
No noble rite nor formal ostentation° –
Cry to be heard, as 'twere from heaven to earth,
That° I must call't in question.

---

more than matter: more meaningful than sane speech   170

pansies . . . for thoughts: (*pansies* derives from French *pensées*—i.e., *thoughts*)

document: lesson

fennel: (symbol of flattery or deceit);   175
columbines: (symbol of infidelity)

rue: (symbol of regret)

daisy: (symbol of dissembling [?])

rosemary . . . violets: (to whom Ophelia distributes which flowers and herbs is uncertain;   180
perhaps: rosemary and pansies to Laertes, fennel and columbines to Gertrude, rue to Claudius, with daisy kept for herself)

favor: charm

185

poll: head   190

of: on

195

collateral: indirect   200
touched: i.e., with the crime

205

trophy: memorial; **hatchment:** coat of arms (hung up as a memorial)

ostentation: ceremony   210

That: so that

DISCOVERING SHAKESPEARE

(114) <u>Rhyme</u> [4.5.189]: Analyze the <u>rhyme</u> scheme in 4.5.184–193. How do the <u>slant rhymes</u> help <u>foreshadow</u> Ophelia's tragic death?

KING   So you shall;
And where th' offense is, let the great ax fall.
I pray you go with me.   *Exeunt.*

❧ **4.6**° *Enter Horatio and others.*   **4.6:** Elsinore

HORATIO   What are they that would speak with me?
GENTLEMAN   Seafaring men, sir. They say they have let-
ters for you.
HORATIO   Let them come in.   *[Exit Attendant.]*   5
I do not know from what part of the world
I should be greeted, if not from Lord Hamlet.
    Enter Sailors.
SAILOR   God bless you, sir.
HORATIO   Let him bless thee too.
SAILOR   A° shall, sir, and't please him. There's a letter for   **A:** he
you, sir – it came from th' ambassador that was bound   10
for England – if your name be Horatio, as I am let to
know it is.
HORATIO   *[Reads the letter.]* "Horatio, when thou shalt
have overlooked° this, give these fellows some means° to   **overlooked:** scanned; **means:** i.e., of access
the king. They have letters for him. Ere we were two   15
days old at sea, a pirate° of very warlike appointment°   **pirate:** i.e., pirate ship; **appointment:**
gave us chase. Finding ourselves too slow of sail, we put   equipment
on a compelled valor, and in the grapple I boarded
them. On the instant they got clear of our ship; so I
alone became their prisoner. They have dealt with me   20
like thieves of mercy,° but they knew what they did: I   **thieves of mercy:** merciful thieves
am to do a turn° for them. Let the king have the letters I   **turn:** i.e., an act responding to the sailors' (good)
have sent, and repair thou to me with as much speed as   act
thou wouldest fly death. I have words to speak in thine
ear will make thee dumb;° yet are they much too light   **dumb:** silent, dumbstruck   25
for the bore° of the matter. These good fellows will bring   **bore:** caliber (as of a gun)
thee where I am. Rosencrantz and Guildenstern hold
their course for England. Of them I have much to tell
thee. Farewell.
                        He that thou knowest thine, Hamlet."   30
Come, I will give you way for these your letters,
And do't the speedier that you may direct me
To him from whom you brought them.   *Exeunt.*

❧ **4.7**° *Enter King and Laertes.*   **4.7:** Elsinore

KING
Now must your conscience my acquittance seal,
And you must put me in your heart for friend,
Sith you have heard, and with a knowing ear,
That he which hath your noble father slain
Pursued my life.

DISCOVERING SHAKESPEARE
(115) <u>Costuming</u> **[4.6.6]:** How should the sailors be <u>costumed</u>? How should they talk and act?
(116) <u>Plot</u> **[4.7.1]:** How much time has passed between the end of 4.6 and the beginning of 4.7? Why does Shakespeare
gloss over this passage of time?

LAERTES It well appears. But tell me
Why you proceeded not against these feats°   **feats:** acts   5
So criminal and so capital° in nature,   **capital:** punishable by death
As by your safety, wisdom, all things else,
You mainly° were stirred up.   **mainly:** powerfully
KING O, for two special reasons,
Which may to you perhaps seem much unsinewed,   10
But yet to me th' are strong. The queen his mother
Lives almost by his looks, and for myself –
My virtue or my plague, be it either which –
She is so conjunctive° to my life and soul   **conjunctive:** closely united
That, as the star moves not but in his° sphere,   **his:** its   15
I could not but by her. The other motive
Why to a public count° I might not go   **count:** trial, accounting
Is the great love the general gender° bear him,   **general gender:** ordinary people
Who, dipping all his faults in their affection,
Work like the spring that turneth wood to stone,   20
Convert his gyves° to graces; so that my arrows,   **gyves:** chains
Too slightly timbered for so loud a wind,
Would have reverted to my bow again,
But not where I had aimed them.
LAERTES
And so have I a noble father lost,   25
A sister driven into desp'rate terms,°   **terms:** circumstances
Whose worth, if praises may go back again,°   **back again:** i.e., to her former (sane) self
Stood challenger on mount° of all the age   **on mount:** on a height
For her perfections. But my revenge will come.
KING
Break not your sleeps for that. You must not think   30
That we are made of stuff so flat and dull
That we can let our beard be shook with danger,
And think it pastime. You shortly shall hear more.
I loved your father, and we love ourself,
And that, I hope, will teach you to imagine –   35
     Enter a Messenger with letters.
MESSENGER
These to your majesty, this to the queen.
KING
From Hamlet? Who brought them?
MESSENGER
Sailors, my lord, they say; I saw them not.
They were given me by Claudio; he received them
Of him that brought them.   40
KING Laertes, you shall hear them. –
Leave us.   *[Exit Messenger.]*
     [Reads.] "High and mighty, you shall know I am set
naked° on your kingdom. Tomorrow shall I beg leave to   **naked:** i.e., without a princely entourage (cf. *rest,*
see your kingly eyes; when I shall (first asking your par-   l. 47)
don thereunto) recount the occasion of my sudden   45
return."

DISCOVERING SHAKESPEARE

(117) Paraphrase [4.7.26]: Paraphrase this description of Ophelia by Laertes: "A sister driven into desp'rate terms, / Whose worth, if praises may go back again, / Stood challenger on mount of all the age / For her perfections" (4.7.26–29). How would this brief description help an actor play the role of Ophelia on stage?

What should this mean? Are all the rest come back?
Or is it some abuse,° and no such thing? — **abuse:** deception

LAERTES
Know you the hand?° — **hand:** handwriting

KING   'Tis Hamlet's character.° "Naked"! — **character:** handwriting
And in a postscript here, he says "alone."   50
Can you devise° me? — **devise:** explain to

LAERTES
I am lost in it, my lord. But let him come.
It warms the very sickness in my heart
That I shall live and tell him to his teeth,
"Thus didest thou."   55

KING   If it be so, Laertes –
As how should it be so? how otherwise? –
Will you be ruled by me?

LAERTES   Ay, my lord,
So you will not o'errule me to a peace.

KING
To thine own peace. If he be now returned,
As checking° at his voyage, and that he means — **checking:** shying   60
No more to undertake it, I will work him
To an exploit now ripe in my device,
Under the which he shall not choose but fall;
And for his death no wind of blame shall breathe,
But even his mother shall uncharge the practice° — **uncharge the practice:** acquit the stratagem of   65
And call it accident. — being a plot

LAERTES   My lord, I will be ruled;
The rather if you could devise it so
That I might be the organ.° — **organ:** instrument

KING   It falls right.
You have been talked of since your travel much,
And that in Hamlet's hearing, for a quality   70
Wherein they say you shine. Your sum of parts
Did not together pluck such envy from him
As did that one, and that, in my regard,
Of the unworthiest siege.° — **siege:** status, rank

LAERTES   What part is that, my lord?

KING
A very ribbon° in the cap of youth, — **ribbon:** decoration   75
Yet needful too, for youth no less becomes
The light and careless livery° that it wears — **livery:** distinctive attire
Than settled age his sables° and his weeds° — **sables:** richly furred robes; **weeds:** garments
Importing health° and graveness. Two months since — **health:** prosperity
Here was a gentleman of Normandy.   80
I have seen myself and served against the French,
And they can well° on horseback, but this gallant — **well:** perform well
Had witchcraft in't. He grew unto his seat,
And to such wondrous doing brought his horse
As had he been incorpsed° and deminatured° — **incorpsed:** made one body; **deminatured:**   85
made sharer of nature half and half (as man shares
with horse in the centaur)

DISCOVERING SHAKESPEARE

(118) <u>Verse</u> **[4.7.49]:** What is happening in the <u>verse</u> from 4.7.51–58? <u>Scan</u> the <u>meter</u> in these lines in order to find out where the missing syllables are. What, if any, <u>stage</u> action occurs during these missing <u>beats</u>?

With the brave beast. So far he topped° my thought°
That I, in forgery° of shapes and tricks,°
Come short of what he did.

topped: excelled; **thought:** imagination of possibilities

forgery: invention; **shapes and tricks:** i.e., various show-stopping exercises

LAERTES   A Norman was't?

KING   A Norman.

LAERTES
Upon my life, Lamord.°

Lamord: i.e., "the death" (French; *la mort*)   90

KING   The very same.

LAERTES
I know him well. He is the brooch° indeed
And gem of all the nation.

brooch: jewel, decorative ornament

KING
He made confession of° you,
And gave you such a masterly report
For art and exercise in your defense
And for your rapier most especial,
That he cried out 'twould be a sight indeed
If one could match you. The scrimers° of their nation
He swore had neither motion, guard, nor eye,
If you opposed them. Sir, this report of his
Did Hamlet so envenom with his envy
That he could nothing do but wish and beg
Your sudden coming o'er to play with you.
Now, out of this –

made confession of: testified to

95

scrimers: fencers

100

LAERTES   What out of this, my lord?

KING
Laertes, was your father dear to you?
Or are you like the painting of a sorrow,
A face without a heart?°

105

painting . . . heart: (cf. 4.5.86 and n.)

LAERTES   Why ask you this?

KING
Not that I think you did not love your father,
But that I know love is begun by time,
And that I see, in passages of proof,°
Time qualifies° the spark and fire of it.°
There lives within the very flame of love
A kind of wick or snuff° that will abate it,
And nothing is at a like goodness still,°
For goodness, growing to a plurisy,°
Dies in his own too-much. That we would do
We should do when we would, for this "would" changes,
And hath abatements and delays as many
As there are tongues, are hands, are accidents,
And then this "should" is like a spendthrift sigh,
That hurts° by easing. But to the quick° of th' ulcer –
Hamlet comes back; what would you undertake
To show yourself in deed your father's son
More than in words?

passages of proof: experience   110
qualifies: weakens
But . . . it: (cf. 3.2.178 ff.)
snuff: unconsumed portion of burned *wick*
still: always
a plurisy: an excess   115

120

hurts: i.e., shortens life by drawing blood from the heart (as was believed); **quick:** sensitive flesh

LAERTES   To cut his throat i' th' church!

DISCOVERING SHAKESPEARE

(119) <u>Shared Lines</u> [4.7.90]: How do the <u>shared lines</u> in 4.7.88–90 affect the delivery of these speeches? What does the <u>verse</u> in this section of the <u>scene</u> tell us about the recent alliance between Claudius and Laertes?

(120) <u>Irony</u> [4.7.124]: Why is Laertes' willingness to cut Hamlet's "throat i' th' church" (4.7.124) <u>ironic</u>?

KING
No place indeed should murder sanctuarize;°   **sanctuarize:** protect from punishment   125
Revenge should have no bounds. But, good Laertes,
Will you do this? Keep close within your chamber.
Hamlet returned shall know you are come home.
We'll put on° those shall praise your excellence   **put on:** instigate
And set a double varnish on the fame   130
The Frenchman gave you, bring you in fine° together   **in fine:** at the end (*fine* derives from Latin *finis,*
And wager o'er your heads. He, being remiss,°   the end; cf. the jokes on *fine* at 5.1.99 ff.)
Most generous, and free from all contriving,   **remiss:** negligent
Will not peruse° the foils, so that with ease,   **peruse:** examine
Or with a little shuffling, you may choose   135
A sword unbated,° and, in a pass of practice,°   **unbated:** not blunted; **pass of practice:** thrust
Requite him for your father.   made effective by trickery
LAERTES   I will do't,
And for that purpose I'll anoint my sword.
I bought an unction° of a mountebank,°   **unction:** ointment; **mountebank:** snake oil
So mortal that, but dip a knife in it,   salesman, quack   140
Where it draws blood no cataplasm° so rare,   **cataplasm:** poultice
Collected from all simples° that have virtue   **simples:** herbs
Under the moon, can save the thing from death
That is but scratched withal.° I'll touch my point   **withal:** with it
With this contagion, that, if I gall° him slightly,   **gall:** scratch   145
It may be death.
KING   Let's further think of this,
Weigh what convenience both of time and means
May fit us to our shape.° If this should fail,   **shape:** plan
And that our drift° look° through our bad performance,   **drift:** scheme; **look:** be seen
'Twere better not assayed. Therefore this project   150
Should have a back or second, that might hold
If this did blast in proof.° Soft, let me see.   **blast in proof:** blow up during trial (like a faulty
We'll make a solemn wager on your cunnings° –   cannon?)
I ha't!   **cunnings:** respective skills (i.e., how you do and
When in your motion you are hot and dry –   how he does)
As make your bouts more violent to that end –   155
And that he calls for drink, I'll have prepared him
A chalice for the nonce,° whereon but sipping,   **nonce:** occasion
If he by chance escape your venomed stuck,°   **stuck:** thrust
Our purpose may hold there. – But stay, what noise?
    Enter Queen.   160
QUEEN
One woe doth tread upon another's heel,
So fast they follow. Your sister's drowned, Laertes.
LAERTES   Drowned! O, where?
QUEEN
There is a willow grows askant° the brook,   **askant:** alongside
That shows his° hoary° leaves in the glassy stream.   **his:** its; **hoary:** gray   165
Therewith fantastic garlands did she make

DISCOVERING SHAKESPEARE

(121) History [4.7.139]: What was a "mountebank" (4.7.139)? What principal poisons were available during the Renaissance?

Of crowflowers, nettles, daisies, and long purples,
That liberal° shepherds give a grosser name,
But our cold maids do dead-men's-fingers call them.
There on the pendent boughs her crownet° weeds
Clamb'ring to hang, an envious sliver broke,
When down her weedy trophies and herself
Fell in the weeping brook. Her clothes spread wide,
And mermaidlike awhile they bore her up,
Which time she chanted snatches of old lauds,°
As one incapable° of her own distress,
Or like a creature native and indued°
Unto that element. But long it could not be
Till that her garments, heavy with their drink,
Pulled the poor wretch from her melodious lay
To muddy death.

LAERTES   Alas, then she is drowned?

QUEEN   Drowned, drowned.

LAERTES
Too much of water hast thou, poor Ophelia,
And therefore I forbid my tears; but yet
It is our trick;° nature her custom holds,
Let shame say what it will. When these are gone,
The woman will be out. Adieu, my lord.
I have a speech o' fire, that fain would blaze
But that this folly drowns it.   *Exit.*

KING   Let's follow, Gertrude.
How much I had to do to calm his rage!
Now fear I this will give it start again;
Therefore let's follow.   *Exeunt.*

> **liberal:** free-spoken, licentious
>
> **crownet:** coronet (a small crown)   170
>
> **lauds:** hymns   175
> **incapable of:** insensible to
> **indued:** endowed
>
>   180
>
> **trick:** (human) way (i.e., to shed tears when   185
> sorrowful)
>
>   190

& **5.1**° *Enter two Clowns° [, one a gravedigger].*

CLOWN   Is she to be buried in Christian burial° when she
willfully seeks her own salvation?

OTHER   I tell thee she is. Therefore make her grave
straight.° The crowner° hath sat on her, and finds it
Christian burial.

CLOWN   How can that be, unless she drowned herself in
her own defense?

OTHER   Why, 'tis found so.

CLOWN   It must be *se offendendo;*° it cannot be else. For
here lies the point: if I drown myself wittingly, it argues
an act, and an act hath three branches – it is to act, to
do, to perform. Argal,° she drowned herself wittingly.

OTHER   Nay, but hear you, Goodman Delver.°

CLOWN   Give me leave. Here lies the water – good. Here
stands the man – good. If the man go to this water and

> **5.1:** A churchyard; **Clowns:** humble rural folk
> (the gravedigger probably here carries a spade and
> pickax; see l. 88)
>
> **Christian burial:** consecrated ground with the
> prescribed service of the church (a burial denied
> to suicides)
>
> **straight:** straightaway, at once; **crowner:**   5
> coroner
>
> **se offendendo:** (a misspeaking of Latin *se*
> *defendendo*, in "self-defense")   10
>
> **Argal:** (a comic mispronunciation of Latin *ergo,*
> "therefore")
>
> **Delver:** Digger (spoken as if the gravedigger's   15
> occupation was also his family name)

DISCOVERING SHAKESPEARE

(122) Teaser [4.7.168]: What "grosser name" (4.7.168) was given to the "long purples" (4.7.167) or *Orchis mascula*?

(123) Paraphrase [4.7.188]: Paraphrase the following lines by Laertes: "I have a speech o' fire that fain would blaze / But that this folly drowns it" (4.7.188–189).

(124) History [5.1.15]: Explain the First Clown's legal quibble concerning death by water.

drown himself, it is, will he nill he,° he goes, mark you that. But if the water come to him and drown him, he drowns not himself. Argal, he that is not guilty of his own death shortens not his own life.

will he nill he: willy-nilly

20

OTHER   But is this law?

CLOWN   Ay marry, is't – crowner's quest° law.

quest: inquest

OTHER   Will you ha' the truth on't? If this had not been a gentlewoman, she should have been buried out o' Christian burial.

25

CLOWN   Why, there thou say'st.° And the more pity that great folk should have countenance° in this world to drown or hang themselves more than their even-Christian.° Come, my spade. There is no ancient gentlemen but gard'ners, ditchers, and gravemakers. They hold up Adam's profession.

thou say'st: you're right
countenance: privilege

even-Christian: fellow Christians

30

OTHER   Was he a gentleman?

CLOWN   A° was the first that ever bore arms. I'll put another question to thee. If thou answerest me not to the purpose, confess thyself –

A: he

35

OTHER   Go to.

CLOWN   What is he that builds stronger than either the mason, the shipwright, or the carpenter?

OTHER   The gallowsmaker, for that frame outlives a thousand tenants.

40

CLOWN   I like thy wit well, in good faith. The gallows does well. But how does it well? It does well to those that do ill. Now thou dost ill to say the gallows is built stronger than the church. Argal, the gallows may do well to thee. To't again, come.

45

OTHER   Who builds stronger than a mason, a shipwright, or a carpenter?

CLOWN   Ay, tell me that, and unyoke.°

unyoke: i.e., unharness your powers of thought after a good day's work

OTHER   Marry, now I can tell.

CLOWN   To't.

50

OTHER   Mass,° I cannot tell.

Mass: by the mass

CLOWN   Cudgel thy brains no more about it, for your dull ass will not mend his pace with beating. And when you are asked this question next, say "a gravemaker." The houses he makes lasts till doomsday. Go, get thee in, and fetch me a stoup° of liquor.

55

stoup: tankard

[Exit Other Clown.]

Enter Hamlet and Horatio [as Clown digs and sings].

Song.
In youth when I did love, did love,
    Methought it was very sweet
To contract – O – the time for – a –
    my behove,°
    O, methought there – a – was nothing –
    a – meet.

behove: behoof, advantage

60

DISCOVERING SHAKESPEARE
(125) <u>Diction</u> [5.1.31]: What joke does the First Clown make about Adam?
(126) Teaser [5.1.56]: What was a "stoup" of liquor (5.1.56)? What is the word's <u>etymology</u>?

HAMLET Has this fellow no feeling of his business? A°
sings in gravemaking.

HORATIO Custom hath made it in him a property of easiness.°

HAMLET 'Tis e'en so. The hand of little employment
hath the daintier sense.°

CLOWN

Song.
But age with his stealing steps
    Hath clawed me in his clutch,
And hath shipped me into the land,
    As if I had never been such.

[Throws up a skull.]

HAMLET That skull had a tongue in it, and could sing
once. How the knave jowls° it to the ground, as if 'twere
Cain's jawbone,° that did the first murder! This might
be the pate of a politician,° which this ass now o'erreaches;° one that would circumvent God, might it not?

HORATIO It might, my lord.

HAMLET Or of a courtier, which could say "Good morrow, sweet lord! How dost thou, sweet lord?" This
might be my Lord Such-a-one, that praised my Lord
Such-a-one's horse when a° meant to beg it, might it
not?

HORATIO Ay, my lord.

HAMLET Why, e'en so, and now my Lady Worm's, chopless,° and knocked about the mazard° with a sexton's
spade. Here's fine revolution, an we had the trick to
see't. Did these bones cost no more the breeding but to
play at loggets° with them? Mine ache to think on't.

CLOWN

Song.
A pickax and a spade, a spade,
    For and° a shrouding sheet;
O, a pit of clay for to be made
    For such a guest is meet.

[Throws up another skull.]

HAMLET There's another. Why may not that be the skull
of a lawyer? Where be his quiddities° now, his quillities,°
his cases, his tenures,° and his tricks? Why does he suffer
this mad knave now to knock him about the sconce°
with a dirty shovel, and will not tell him of his action of
battery? Hum! This fellow might be in's time a great
buyer of land, with his statutes,° his recognizances,° his
fines, his double vouchers,° his recoveries. [Is this the

A: he

property of easiness: matter of indifference

65

daintier sense: more delicate feeling (because
the *hand* is less callused)

70

jowls: hurls
Cain's jawbone: (according to Genesis 4, Cain
killed his brother, Abel—traditionally, but not
biblically, using the jawbone of an ass)   75
politician: crafty schemer; **o'erreaches:** gets
the better of (with a play on the literal meaning)

a: he   80

chopless: lacking the lower chop, or jaw;
mazard: head (a jocular, slangy word)   85

loggets: small pieces of wood thrown in a game

For and: and moreover

90

quiddities: subtleties (from medieval scholastic
terminology, "quidditas," meaning the distinctive
nature of anything); **quillities:** nice distinctions   95
(variant of *quiddities*)
tenures: holdings of property
sconce: head (another slang term)
statutes, recognizances: (two forms of legal
acknowledgments of debt)
vouchers: persons called on ("vouched") to
warrant a legal title

DISCOVERING SHAKESPEARE

(127) History [5.1.93]: Look up the following legal terms from 5.1.93–106 in the *Oxford English Dictionary*: "quiddities,"
"quillities," "tenures," "action of battery," "statutes," "recognizances," "fines," "double vouchers," "recoveries," and "indentures." How would a knowledge of the meaning of each term help us understand Hamlet's speech about "the skull of a
lawyer"?

fine° of his fines, and the recovery of his recoveries,°] to have his fine pate full of fine dirt? Will his vouchers vouch him no more of his purchases, and double ones too, than the length and breadth of a pair of indentures?° The very conveyances° of his lands will scarcely lie in this box, and must th' inheritor himself have no more, ha?

HORATIO   Not a jot more, my lord.

HAMLET   Is not parchment made of sheepskins?

HORATIO   Ay, my lord, and of calfskins too.

HAMLET   They are sheep and calves which seek out assurance in that. I will speak to this fellow. Whose grave's this, sirrah?

CLOWN   Mine, sir.

    [Sings.]

                  O, a pit of clay for to be made –

HAMLET   I think it be thine indeed, for thou liest in't.

CLOWN   You lie out on't, sir, and therefore 'tis not yours. For my part, I do not lie in't, yet it is mine.

HAMLET   Thou dost lie in't, to be in't and say it is thine. 'Tis for the dead, not for the quick;° therefore thou liest.

CLOWN   'Tis a quick lie, sir; 'twill away again from me to you.

HAMLET   What man dost thou dig it for?

CLOWN   For no man, sir.

HAMLET   What woman then?

CLOWN   For none neither.

HAMLET   Who is to be buried in't?

CLOWN   One that was a woman, sir; but, rest her soul, she's dead.

HAMLET   How absolute° the knave is! We must speak by the card,° or equivocation° will undo us. By the Lord, Horatio, this three years I have took note of it, the age is grown so picked° that the toe of the peasant comes so near the heel of the courtier he galls° his kibe.° – How long hast thou been gravemaker?

CLOWN   Of all the days i' th' year, I came to't that day that our last king Hamlet overcame Fortinbras.

HAMLET   How long is that since?

CLOWN   Cannot you tell that? Every fool can tell that. It was that very day that young Hamlet was born – he that is mad, and sent into England.

HAMLET   Ay, marry, why was he sent into England?

CLOWN   Why, because a was mad. A shall recover his wits there; or, if a do not, 'tis no great matter there.

HAMLET   Why?

CLOWN   'Twill not be seen in him there. There the men are as mad as he.

HAMLET   How came he mad?

CLOWN   Very strangely, they say.

fine: conclusion, end (the word introduces wordplay punning on four meanings of *fine*); **fines, recoveries:** (legal ways of converting from a limited to a more absolute form of property ownership)
pair of indentures: deed or legal agreement in duplicate
conveyances: deeds

quick: living

How absolute: how strict, what a stickler for accuracy
by the card: accurately (*card* is a mariner's chart?), to the point; **equivocation:** ambiguity
picked: refined, spruce
galls: chafes; **kibe:** chilblain (the analogy means the peasant affects a courtier's garb and hence diminishes the latter's status)

100
105
110
115
120
125
130
135
140
145

DISCOVERING SHAKESPEARE

(128) Characterization [5.1.120]: What is your opinion of the "working class" characters, like the gravediggers, in this play? Can you make any generalizations about working class characters throughout Shakespeare's plays?

HAMLET   How strangely?

CLOWN   Faith, e'en with losing his wits.   150

HAMLET   Upon what ground?

CLOWN   Why, here in Denmark. I have been sexton
here, man and boy, thirty years.

HAMLET   How long will a man lie i' th' earth ere he rot?

CLOWN   Faith, if a be not rotten before a die (as we have   155
many pocky° corpses nowadays that will scarce hold the
laying in),° a will last you some eight year or nine year. A
tanner will last you nine year.

pocky: rotten by pox (syphilis)
laying in: i.e., in the ground

HAMLET   Why he more than another?

CLOWN   Why, sir, his hide is so tanned with his trade   160
that a will keep out water a great while, and your water
is a sore decayer of your whoreson° dead body. Here's a
skull now hath lien you i' th' earth three and twenty
years.

whoreson: (coarse, here jocular, term of
familiarity, perhaps of contempt)

HAMLET   Whose was it?   165

CLOWN   A whoreson mad fellow's it was. Whose do you
think it was?

HAMLET   Nay, I know not.

CLOWN   A pestilence on him for a mad rogue! A poured
a flagon of Rhenish° on my head once. This same skull,   170
sir, was Sir,° Yorick's skull, the king's jester.

Rhenish: Rhine wine
Sir: (the title is ironic, affectionate, and a
common Shakespearean quip; cf. "Lady Worm,"
l. 83)

HAMLET   This? [*Takes the skull.*]

CLOWN   E'en that.

HAMLET   Alas, poor Yorick! I knew him, Horatio, a fellow of infinite jest, of most excellent fancy. He hath   175
bore me on his back a thousand times. And now how
abhorred in my imagination it is! My gorge rises at it.
Here hung those lips that I have kissed I know not how
oft. Where be your gibes now? Your gambols, your
songs, your flashes of merriment that were wont to set   180
the table on a roar? Not one now to mock your own
grinning? Quite chopfallen?° Now get you to my lady's
table,° and tell her, let her paint an inch thick, to this
favor° she must come. Make her laugh at that. Prithee,   185
Horatio, tell me one thing.

chopfallen: lacking the lower chop, or jaw (also
"down in the mouth," "dejected")
table: (1) piece of furniture, (2) painted portrait
favor: countenance, aspect

HORATIO   What's that, my lord?

HAMLET   Dost thou think Alexander looked o' this fashion i' th' earth?

HORATIO   E'en so.

HAMLET   And smelt so? Pah!   190
[*Puts down the skull.*]

HORATIO   E'en so, my lord.

HAMLET   To what base uses we may return, Horatio!
Why may not imagination trace the noble dust of
Alexander till a find it stopping a bunghole?°

a bunghole: an opening in a barrel (e.g., of wine
or beer)

DISCOVERING SHAKESPEARE

(129) Teaser [5.1.153]: If Yorick's skull has lain in the earth "three and twenty years" (5.1.163–164), and Yorick carried young Hamlet on his back "a thousand times" (5.1.176), approximately how old is Hamlet now? The First Quarto says that the skull has been in the earth "this dozen years." How would this small textual detail change Hamlet's age?

(130) Staging [5.1.174]: Where is the grave located on stage? Do most modern theaters have traps? If so, where are they?

(131) History [5.1.194]: Who was "Alexander" (5.1.194)? Why was he famous?

HORATIO 'Twere to consider too curiously,° to consider so.

HAMLET No, faith, not a jot, but to follow him thither with modesty° enough, and likelihood to lead it. Alexander died, Alexander was buried, Alexander returneth to dust; the dust is earth; of earth we make loam; and why of that loam° whereto he was converted might they not stop a beer barrel?
Imperious° Caesar, dead and turned to clay,
Might stop a hole to keep the wind away.
O, that that earth which kept the world in awe
Should patch a wall t' expel the winter's flaw!°
But soft, but soft awhile! Here comes the king –
    Enter King, Queen, Laertes, and the Corpse [with Lords attendant and a Doctor of Divinity as Priest].
The queen, the courtiers. Who is this they follow?
And with such maimed rites? This doth betoken
The corpse they follow did with desp'rate hand
Fordo° it° own life. 'Twas of some estate.°
Couch° we awhile, and mark.

LAERTES
What ceremony else?

HAMLET   That is Laertes,
A very noble youth. Mark.

LAERTES
What ceremony else?

DOCTOR
Her obsequies have been as far enlarged
As we have warranty. Her death was doubtful,
And, but that great command o'ersways the order,
She should in ground unsanctified have lodged
Till the last trumpet. For charitable prayers,
Flints and pebbles should be thrown on her.
Yet here she is allowed her virgin crants,°
Her maiden strewments,° and the bringing home°
Of bell and burial.

LAERTES
Must there no more be done?

DOCTOR   No more be done.
We should profane the service of the dead
To sing a requiem and such rest to her
As to peace-parted souls.

LAERTES   Lay her i' th' earth,
And from her fair and unpolluted flesh
May violets spring! I tell thee, churlish priest,
A minist'ring angel shall my sister be
When thou liest howling.°

HAMLET   What, the fair Ophelia?

QUEEN
Sweets to the sweet! Farewell.
    [Scatters flowers.]

---

curiously: (1) minutely, (2) ingeniously   195

modesty: moderation

                                                              200

loam: clay or cement (called "lute" in archaic English) used to seal an opening (in a barrel, l. 194, or a *wall,* l. 206)
Imperious: imperial

                                                              205

flaw: gust of wind

                                                              210

Fordo: destroy; **it:** its; **estate:** rank
Couch: hide (Hamlet and Horatio are not seen or heard by the other characters until l. 244)

                                                              215

                                                              220

crants: garlands, chaplets
strewments: strewings of the grave with flowers;
bringing home: laying to rest

                                                              225

                                                              230

howling: i.e., in hell (see Matthew 13:42)

DISCOVERING SHAKESPEARE

(132) Characterization [5.1.230]: Why is Laertes so angry with the priest?

I hoped thou shouldst have been my Hamlet's wife.
I thought thy bridebed to have decked, sweet maid, 235
And not have strewed thy grave.

LAERTES   O, treble woe
Fall ten times double on that cursèd head
Whose wicked deed thy most ingenious° sense — **most ingenious:** of quickest apprehension
Deprived thee of! Hold off the earth awhile,
Till I have caught her once more in mine arms. 240
   [Leaps in the grave.]
Now pile your dust upon the quick and dead
Till of this flat a mountain you have made
T' o'ertop old Pelion° or the skyish head
Of blue Olympus.

Pelion: (a mountain in Thessaly, as are *Olympus*, l. 244, and *Ossa*, l. 273; when the Titans fought the gods [cf. 4.5.121 n.], the Titans attempted to heap Ossa and Olympus on Pelion, or Pelion and Ossa on Olympus, in order to scale heaven) 245

HAMLET   What is he whose grief
Bears such an emphasis?° whose phrase of sorrow — **an emphasis:** violent, exaggerated language
Conjures° the wand'ring stars,° and makes them stand — **Conjures:** charms, puts a spell upon; **wand'ring stars:** planets
Like wonder-wounded hearers? This is I,
Hamlet the Dane.°

Hamlet . . . Dane: (Q1 directs Hamlet to join Laertes in the "grave" following this line, and near-contemporary comment supports a struggle there—perhaps an open trapdoor—but many different stagings have been tried, and precisely what happened in early performances is unknown) 250

LAERTES   The devil take thy soul!
   [Grapples with him.]

HAMLET
Thou pray'st not well.
I prithee take thy fingers from my throat,
For, though I am not splenitive° and rash, — **splenitive:** hot-tempered (the spleen was considered the seat of anger)
Yet have I in me something dangerous,
Which let thy wisdom fear. Hold off thy hand.

KING
Pluck them asunder.

QUEEN   Hamlet, Hamlet!

ALL
Gentlemen! 255

HORATIO   Good my lord, be quiet.

HAMLET
Why, I will fight with him upon this theme
Until my eyelids will no longer wag.

QUEEN
O my son, what theme?

HAMLET
I loved Ophelia. Forty thousand brothers
Could not with all their quantity° of love — **quantity:** (used here as a contemptuous term: "a small amount") 260
Make up my sum. What wilt thou do for her?

KING
O, he is mad, Laertes.

QUEEN
For love of God, forbear him.° — **forbear him:** leave him alone

HAMLET
'Swounds, show me what thou't do.
Woo't° weep? woo't fight? woo't fast? woo't tear thyself? — **Woo't:** wilt (thou) 265
Woo't drink up eisel?° eat a crocodile? — **eisel:** vinegar
I'll do't. Dost come here to whine?

DISCOVERING SHAKESPEARE

(133) Etymology [5.1.251]: What is the origin of the word "splenitive" (5.1.251)? What is the meaning of the term in this particular context?

To outface me with leaping in her grave?
Be buried quick with her, and so will I.
And if thou prate of mountains, let them throw   270
Millions of acres on us, till our ground,
Singeing his pate against the burning zone,°   **burning zone:** i.e., where the sun is
Make Ossa like a wart! Nay, an thou'lt mouth,
I'll rant as well as thou.
QUEEN   This is mere° madness;   **mere:** absolute
And thus a while the fit will work on him.   275
Anon, as patient as the female dove
When that her golden couplets° are disclosed,°   **couplets:** pair of fledgling birds; **disclosed:** hatched
His silence will sit drooping.
HAMLET   Hear you, sir.
What is the reason that you use me thus?
I loved you ever. But it is no matter.   280
Let Hercules° himself do what he may,   **Hercules:** (1) a legendary and mighty demigod, (2) literarily famous as a boastful ranter (Hamlet casts Laertes as Hercules)
The cat will mew, and dog will have his day.°   *Exit.*   **dog . . . day:** (proverbially, even the least creature will have a turn at success and happiness: Hamlet views himself as *cat* and *dog*); s.d. *Exit* (Q2's exit s.d. is on two lines in the margin and seems to demand the separate exits indicated here)
KING
I pray thee, good Horatio, wait upon him.
                                        Exit Horatio.

[To Laertes]
Strengthen your patience in° our last night's speech.   **in:** in the thought of, by calling to mind   285
We'll put the matter to the present push.° –   **the present push:** immediate action
Good Gertrude, set some watch over your son. –
This grave shall have a living monument.
An hour of quiet shortly shall we see;
Till then in patience our proceeding be.   *Exeunt.*

❧ **5.2°** *Enter Hamlet and Horatio.*   **5.2:** Elsinore

HAMLET
So much for this, sir; now shall you see the other.
You do remember all the circumstance?
HORATIO
Remember it, my lord!
HAMLET
Sir, in my heart there was a kind of fighting
That would not let me sleep. Methought I lay   5
Worse than the mutines° in the bilboes.° Rashly,   **mutines:** mutineers; **the bilboes:** chains
And praised be rashness for it – let us know,
Our indiscretion sometimes serves us well
When our deep plots do pall,° and that should learn us   **pall:** fail
There's a divinity that shapes our ends,°   **ends:** (1) purposes, (2) outcomes
Rough-hew° them how we will –   **Rough-hew:** shape roughly in trial form   10
HORATIO   That is most certain.
HAMLET
Up from my cabin,
My sea gown scarfed about me, in the dark

DISCOVERING SHAKESPEARE

(134) Mythology [5.1.281]: Who was Hercules (5.1.281)? Why does Hamlet <u>allude</u> to him here?
(135) <u>Paraphrase</u> [5.2.10]: <u>Paraphrase</u> Hamlet's contention that "There's a divinity that shapes our ends, / Rough-hew them how we will" (5.2.10–11). Do you agree with him? Why or why not?

Groped I to find out them, had my desire,
Fingered° their packet, and in fine° withdrew
To mine own room again, making so bold,
My fears forgetting manners, to unseal
Their grand commission; where I found, Horatio –
Ah, royal knavery! – an exact command,
Larded° with many several sorts of reasons,
Importing° Denmark's health, and England's too,
With, ho! such bugs° and goblins in my life,°
That on the supervise,° no leisure bated,°
No, not to stay the grinding of the ax,
My head should be struck off.

HORATIO   Is't possible?

HAMLET
Here's the commission; read it at more leisure.
But wilt thou hear now how I did proceed?

HORATIO   I beseech you.

HAMLET
Being thus benetted round with villainies,
Or° I could make a prologue to my brains,
They had begun the play. I sat me down,
Devised a new commission, wrote it fair.°
I once did hold it, as our statists° do,
A baseness to write fair, and labored much
How to forget that learning, but, sir, now
It did me yeoman's service.° Wilt thou know
Th' effect° of what I wrote?

HORATIO   Ay, good my lord.

HAMLET
An earnest conjuration from the king,
As England was his faithful tributary,°
As love between them like the palm might flourish,°
As peace should still her wheaten garland° wear
And stand a comma° 'tween their amities,
And many suchlike as's of great charge,°
That on the view and knowing of these contents,
Without debatement further, more or less,
He should those bearers put to sudden death,
Not shriving time° allowed.

HORATIO   How was this sealed?

HAMLET
Why, even in that was heaven ordinant.°
I had my father's signet in my purse,
Which was the model° of that Danish seal,
Folded the writ° up in the form of th' other,
Subscribed it, gave't th' impression,° placed it safely,
The changeling never known. Now, the next day
Was our sea fight, and what to this was sequent°
Thou knowest already.

Fingered: filched; **in fine:** finally	15
Larded: garnished (a metaphor from cooking)	20
Importing: relating to	
bugs: bugbears, bogeymen; **in my life:** i.e., in my (Hamlet's) being allowed to live	
supervise: perusal; **no leisure bated:** no time allowed	
	25
Or: ere, before	30
fair: with professional clarity (like a scrivener, not like a gentleman: see l. 34)	
statists: statesmen, politicians	
	35
yeoman's service: brave service such as yeomen foot soldiers gave as archers	
effect: purport	
tributary: one who pays tribute	
palm . . . flourish: (see Psalm 92:12, "The righteous shall flourish like the palm tree")	40
wheaten garland: (traditional symbol of peace)	
comma: i.e., something small	
charge: burden (with a double meaning to fit wordplay that makes *as's* into "asses")	
	45
shriving time: time for confession and absolution	
ordinant: ordaining	
model: likeness	50
writ: writing	
impression: i.e., of the signet (a seal)	
sequent: subsequent, following	
	55

DISCOVERING SHAKESPEARE

(136) Plot [5.2.35]: Exactly how did Hamlet cause the deaths of Rosencrantz and Guildenstern? Do you think his two college friends deserved to die? Why or why not?

HORATIO
  So Guildenstern and Rosencrantz go to't.
HAMLET
  They are not near my conscience; their defeat
  Does by their own insinuation° grow.
  'Tis dangerous when the baser nature comes
  Between the pass° and fell° incensèd points
  Of mighty opposites.
HORATIO   Why, what a king is this!
HAMLET
  Does it not, think thee, stand me now upon° –
  He that hath killed my king and whored my mother,
  Popped in between th' election° and my hopes,
  Thrown out his angle° for my proper° life,
  And with such coz'nage° – is't not perfect conscience?
    Enter [Osric,]° a courtier.
OSRIC   Your lordship is right welcome back to Denmark.
HAMLET   I humbly thank you, sir. *[Aside to Horatio]* Dost know this waterfly?°
HORATIO   *[Aside to Hamlet]* No, my good lord.
HAMLET   *[Aside to Horatio]* Thy state is the more gracious, for 'tis a vice to know him. He hath much land, and fertile. Let a beast be lord of beasts, and his crib shall stand at the king's mess.° 'Tis a chough,° but, as I say,° spacious in the possession of dirt.°
OSRIC   Sweet lord, if your lordship were at leisure, I should impart a thing to you from his majesty.
HAMLET   I will receive it, sir, with all diligence of spirit. Your bonnet to his right use. 'Tis for the head.
OSRIC   I thank your lordship, it is very hot.
HAMLET   No, believe me, 'tis very cold; the wind is northerly.
OSRIC   It is indifferent° cold, my lord, indeed.
HAMLET   But yet methinks it is very sultry and hot for my complexion.°
OSRIC   Exceedingly, my lord; it is very sultry, as 'twere – I cannot tell how. My lord, his majesty bade me signify to you that a° has laid a great wager on your head. Sir, this is the matter –
HAMLET   I beseech you remember.°
OSRIC   Nay, good my lord; for my ease,° in good faith. Sir, here is newly come to court Laertes – believe me, an absolute° gentleman, full of most excellent differences,° of very soft society° and great showing.° Indeed, to speak feelingly° of him, he is the card° or calendar° of gentry;° for

---

insinuation: slipping in

pass: sword thrust; **fell:** fierce   60

stand me now upon: am I now obliged (i.e., to do something about these facts)

election: i.e., to the kingship (the Danish kingship was elective, not inherited, as the English and Scottish crowns were in Shakespeare's day)   65

angle: fishhook; **proper:** own

coz'nage: cozenage, trickery

Osric: (here, this character's name is from F; in Q1, "a Bragart Gentleman"; in Q2, "a Courtier"; Q2 later uses "Ostricke" at l. 176)

waterfly: dragonfly (?)—some gaudy insect   70

mess: table; **chough:** jackdaw (a screeching bird), chatterer   75
as I say: I'd guess; **spacious in . . . dirt:** (he) owns a lot of land

  80

indifferent: somewhat

complexion: temperament   85

a: he

remember: i.e., to put on your hat (see l. 79)   90
for my ease: i.e., I keep my hat off just for comfort (a conventional polite phrase)

an absolute: a complete, flawless; **differences:** differentiating qualities
soft society: refined manners; **great showing:**   95 noble appearance
feelingly: appropriately; **card:** map; **calendar:** guide; **gentry:** gentlemanliness

---

DISCOVERING SHAKESPEARE

(137) <u>Paraphrase</u> [5.2.59]: <u>Paraphrase</u> the following lines by Hamlet: "'Tis dangerous when the baser nature comes / Between the pass and fell incensèd points / Of mighty opposites" (5.2.59–61). How do these lines help us understand Hamlet's attitude towards Rosencrantz and Guildenstern?
(138) Characterization [5.2.67]: What kind of person is Osric? What type of clothes should he be wearing? What kinds of gestures would he make?

you shall find in him the continent° of what part a gentleman would see.

HAMLET   Sir, his definement° suffers no perdition° in you, though, I know, to divide him inventorially would dozy° th' arithmetic of memory, and yet but yaw° neither° in respect of° his quick sail. But, in the verity of extolment, I take him to be a soul of great article,° and his infusion° of such dearth° and rareness as, to make true diction of him, his semblable° is his mirror, and who else would trace° him, his umbrage,° nothing more.

OSRIC   Your lordship speaks most infallibly of him.

HAMLET   The concernancy,° sir? Why do we wrap the gentleman in our more rawer breath?°

OSRIC   Sir?

HORATIO   Is't not possible to understand in another tongue? You will to't,° sir, really.

HAMLET   What imports the nomination° of this gentleman?

OSRIC   Of Laertes?

HORATIO   *[Aside to Hamlet]* His purse is empty already. All's golden words are spent.

HAMLET   Of him, sir.

OSRIC   I know you are not ignorant –

HAMLET   I would you did, sir; yet, in faith, if you did, it would not much approve° me. Well, sir?

OSRIC   You are not ignorant of what excellence Laertes is –

HAMLET   I dare not confess that, lest I should compare° with him in excellence; but to know a man well were to know himself.

OSRIC   I mean, sir, for his weapon; but in the imputation laid on him by them, in his meed° he's unfellowed.

HAMLET   What's his weapon?

OSRIC   Rapier and dagger.

HAMLET   That's two of his weapons – but well.

OSRIC   The king, sir, hath wagered with him six Barbary horses, against the which he has impawned,° as I take it, six French rapiers and poniards, with their assigns,° as girdle, hanger,° and so. Three of the carriages, in faith, are very dear to fancy,° very responsive° to the hilts, most delicate carriages, and of very liberal conceit.°

HAMLET   What call you the carriages?

HORATIO   *[Aside to Hamlet]* I knew you must be edified by the margent° ere you had done.

OSRIC   The carriage, sir, are the hangers.

HAMLET   The phrase would be more germane to the matter if we could carry a cannon by our sides. I would it might be hangers till then. But on! Six Barbary horses against six French swords, their assigns, and three liberal-

continent: containment (but with wordplay on *card*)

definement: definition; **perdition:** loss

dozy: dizzy; **yaw:** veer like a ship that steers wild; **neither:** for all that   100
in respect of: in comparison with
article: scope, importance
infusion: essence; **dearth:** scarcity
semblable: likeness   105
trace: follow (from hunting terminology);
umbrage: shadow
concernancy: relevance
rawer breath: cruder speech

110
to't: i.e., get to an understanding
nomination: mention

115

approve: commend   120

compare: compete

125

meed: reward

130
impawned: staked
assigns: appurtenances
hanger: straps by which the sword hangs from the belt   135
dear to fancy: finely designed; **responsive:** corresponding closely
liberal conceit: tasteful design, refined conception
margent: margin (i.e., explanatory notes printed in the margin of a page)   140

DISCOVERING SHAKESPEARE

(139) Paraphrase [5.2.100]: What does Hamlet mean when he says that trying to divide Laertes "inventorially" would "dozy th' arithmetic of memory" (5.2.99–100)?

(140) History [5.2.129]: What was the difference between a "rapier" and a "dagger" (5.2.129)?

conceited carriages – that's the French bet against the Danish. Why is this all impawned, as you call it?° 145

impawned . . . it: (in F, Hamlet seems to mock Osric's *impawned*, but in Q2 the compositor apparently misunderstood the word here, but not at l. 132)

OSRIC   The king, sir, hath laid, sir, that in a dozen passes between yourself and him he shall not exceed you three hits; he hath laid on twelve for nine, and it would come to immediate trial if your lordship would vouchsafe the answer. 150

HAMLET   How if I answer no?

OSRIC   I mean, my lord, the opposition of your person in trial.

HAMLET   Sir, I will walk here in the hall. If it please his majesty, it is the breathing time° of day with me. Let the foils be brought, the gentleman willing, and the king hold his purpose, I will win for him and° I can; if not, I will gain nothing but my shame and the odd hits. 155

breathing time: exercise hour

and: if

OSRIC   Shall I deliver you so? 160

HAMLET   To this effect, sir, after what flourish your nature will.

OSRIC   I commend my duty to your lordship.

HAMLET   Yours. *[Exit Osric.]* He does well to commend it himself; there are no tongues else for's turn. 165

HORATIO   This lapwing° runs away with the shell on his head.

lapwing: (a bird reputed to be so precocious as to run as soon as hatched)

HAMLET   A did comply° with his dug° before a sucked it. Thus has he, and many more of the same breed that I know the drossy° age dotes on, only got the tune of the time and, out of an habit of encounter, a kind of yeasty collection, which carries them through and through the most [fanned] and [winnowed]° opinions; and do but blow them to their trial, the bubbles are out. 170

comply: observe formalities of courtesy; **dug:** nipple

drossy: frivolous

fanned and winnowed: select and refined

Enter a Lord.

LORD   My lord, his majesty commended him to you by young Osric, who brings back to him that you attend him in the hall. He sends to know if your pleasure hold to play with Laertes, or that you will take longer time. 175

HAMLET   I am constant to my purposes; they follow the king's pleasure. If his fitness speaks, mine is ready; now or whensoever, provided I be so able as now. 180

LORD   The king and queen and all are coming down.

HAMLET   In happy time.°

In happy time: I am happy (a polite response)

LORD   The queen desires you to use some gentle entertainment° to Laertes before you fall to play.

entertainment: courtesy 185

HAMLET   She well instructs me.   *[Exit Lord.]*

HORATIO   You will lose, my lord.

HAMLET   I do not think so. Since he went into France I have been in continual practice. I shall win at the odds. Thou wouldst not think how ill all's here about my heart, but it is no matter. 190

HORATIO   Nay, good my lord –

DISCOVERING SHAKESPEARE

(141) Plot [5.2.147]: Explain the wager the King has made on the fencing match (see 5.2.147–151). What are the odds? Whom do they favor?

(142) Mythology [5.2.166]: What was a "lapwing" (5.2.166)? Why would it run away with its shell on its head?

HAMLET   It is but foolery, but it is such a kind of gain-giving° as would perhaps trouble a woman.

gaingiving: misgiving

HORATIO   If your mind dislike anything, obey it. I will forestall their repair hither and say you are not fit.

195

HAMLET   Not a whit, we defy augury. There is special providence in the fall of a sparrow. If it be now, 'tis not to come; if it be not to come, it will be now; if it be not now, yet it will come. The readiness is all.° Since no man of aught he leaves knows, what is't to leave betimes? Let be.

all: all that matters

200

A table prepared. [Enter] Trumpets, Drums, and Officers with cushions; King, Queen, [Osric,] and all the State,° [with] foils, daggers, and Laertes.

State: court and courtiers (there must also be props for serving wine)

KING

Come, Hamlet, come, and take this hand° from me.

this hand: i.e., Laertes' hand

HAMLET

Give me your pardon, sir. I have done you wrong,

But pardon't, as you are a gentleman.

205

This presence° knows, and you must needs have heard,

presence: assembly

How I am punished with a sore distraction.

What I have done

That might your nature, honor, and exception°

exception: disapproval

Roughly awake, I here proclaim was madness.

210

Was't Hamlet wronged Laertes? Never Hamlet.

If Hamlet from himself be ta'en away,

And when he's not himself does wrong Laertes,

Then Hamlet does it not, Hamlet denies it.

Who does it then? His madness. If't be so,

215

Hamlet is of the faction° that is wronged;

faction: political group in opposition to another group

His madness is poor Hamlet's enemy.

[Sir, in this audience,]

Let my disclaiming from a purposed evil

Free me so far in your most generous thoughts

220

That I have shot my arrow o'er the house

And hurt my brother.

LAERTES   I am satisfied in nature,°

nature: natural feeling

Whose motive in this case should stir me most

To my revenge. But in my terms of honor°

terms of honor: position as a man of honor

I stand aloof, and will no reconcilement

225

Till by some elder masters of known honor

I have a voice° and precedent of peace

a voice: an authoritative statement

To keep my name ungored.° But till that time

ungored: uninjured

I do receive your offered love like love,

And will not wrong it.

230

HAMLET   I embrace it freely,

And will this brother's wager frankly play.

Give us the foils.

LAERTES   Come, one for me.

DISCOVERING SHAKESPEARE

(143) <u>Paraphrase</u> [5.2.197]: Paraphrase Hamlet's speech in 5.2.197–202. What does he mean by the sentence "The readiness is all" (5.2.200)? Do you agree with this philosophy of life? Why or why not?

(144) Language [5.2.217]: How does Hamlet explain the killing of Polonius (see 5.2.204–222)? To what extent does Laertes forgive him (see lines 222–230)?

HAMLET
  I'll be your foil,° Laertes. In mine ignorance
  Your skill shall, like a star i' th' darkest night,
  Stick fiery off° indeed.   You mock me, sir.
LAERTES
HAMLET
  No, by this hand.
KING
  Give them the foils, young Osric. Cousin Hamlet,
  You know the wager?   Very well, my lord.
HAMLET
  Your grace has laid the odds o' th' weaker side.
KING
  I do not fear it, I have seen you both;
  But since he is bettered,° we have therefore odds.
LAERTES
  This is too heavy; let me see another.
HAMLET
  This likes me well. These foils have all a length?
    [Prepare to play.]
OSRIC
  Ay, my good lord.
KING
  Set me the stoups of wine upon that table.
  If Hamlet give the first or second hit,
  Or quit° in answer of the third exchange,
  Let all the battlements their ordnance fire.
  The king shall drink to Hamlet's better breath,
  And in the cup an union° shall he throw
  Richer than that which four successive kings
  In Denmark's crown have worn. Give me the cups,
  And let the kettle° to the trumpet speak,
  The trumpet to the cannoneer without,
  The cannons to the heavens, the heaven to earth,
  "Now the king drinks to Hamlet." Come, begin.
    Trumpets the while.
  And you, the judges, bear a wary eye.
HAMLET   Come on, sir.
LAERTES   Come, my lord.
    [They play.]
HAMLET   One.
LAERTES   No.
HAMLET   Judgment?
OSRIC   A hit, a very palpable hit.
    Drum, trumpets, and shot. Flourish; a piece° goes off.
LAERTES   Well, again.
KING
  Stay, give me drink. Hamlet, this pearl is thine.
  Here's to thy health. Give him the cup.

foil: setting that displays a jewel advantageously (punning on *foil* as a weapon)
Stick fiery off: show off in brilliant relief   235

bettered: said to be better by public opinion

quit: repay by a hit

an union: a pearl

kettle: kettledrum

piece: cannon

240

245

250

255

260

265

DISCOVERING SHAKESPEARE

(145) Verse [5.2.236]: In 5.2.232–239, the <u>verse</u> breaks down into several <u>half lines</u> and <u>shared lines</u>. What is the effect of this deviation from the play's normal <u>verse</u> pattern of ten-syllable lines of <u>iambic pentameter</u>?

(146) Plot [5.2.250]: Exactly when does the King poison the wine? Why do you believe he does it at this precise moment in the play? Do you think the audience is aware of what is happening? Why or why not?

HAMLET
I'll play this bout first; set it by awhile.
Come. *[They play.]* Another hit. What say you?
LAERTES   I do confess't.
KING
Our son shall win.   270
QUEEN   He's fat,° and scant of breath.   **fat:** (1) not physically fit, (2) sweaty
Here, Hamlet, take my napkin,° rub thy brows.   **napkin:** handkerchief
The queen carouses° to thy fortune, Hamlet.   **carouses:** drinks a toast
HAMLET
Good madam!
KING   Gertrude, do not drink.
QUEEN
I will, my lord; I pray you pardon me.
[Drinks.]
KING   *[Aside]*
It is the poisoned cup; it is too late.   275
HAMLET
I dare not drink yet, madam – by and by.
QUEEN
Come, let me wipe thy face.
LAERTES
My lord, I'll hit him now.
KING   I do not think't.
LAERTES   *[Aside]*
And yet it is almost against my conscience.
HAMLET
Come for the third, Laertes. You do but dally.   280
I pray you pass° with your best violence;   **pass:** thrust (with a sword)
I am sure you make a wanton° of me.   **wanton:** spoiled child
LAERTES
Say you so? Come on.
[They play.]
OSRIC
Nothing neither way.
LAERTES
Have at you now!   285
[In scuffling they change rapiers.]
KING   Part them. They are incensed.
HAMLET
Nay, come – again!
[The Queen falls.]
OSRIC   Look to the queen there, ho!
HORATIO
They bleed on both sides. How is it, my lord?
OSRIC
How is't, Laertes?
LAERTES
Why, as a woodcock° to mine own springe,° Osric.   **woodcock:** (a bird reputed to be stupid and
I am justly killed with mine own treachery.   easily trapped); **springe:** trap   290

DISCOVERING SHAKESPEARE
(147) Plot [5.2.273]: When Claudius begs Gertrude not to drink the wine (5.2.273), what is his dilemma?

HAMLET
How does the queen?
KING   She swoons to see them bleed.
QUEEN
No, no, the drink, the drink! O my dear Hamlet!
The drink, the drink! I am poisoned.
    [Dies.]
HAMLET
O villainy! Ho! let the door be locked.
Treachery! Seek it out.   *[Exit Osric.]*   295
LAERTES
It is here, Hamlet. Hamlet, thou art slain;
No med'cine in the world can do thee good.
In thee there is not half an hour's life.
The treacherous instrument is in thy hand,
Unbated° and envenomed. The foul practice°   **Unbated:** unblunted; **practice:** trick   300
Hath turned itself on me. Lo, here I lie,
Never to rise again. Thy mother's poisoned.
I can no more. The king, the king's to blame.
HAMLET
The point envenomed too?
Then venom, to thy work.   305
    [Wounds the King.]
ALL   Treason! treason!
KING
O, yet defend me, friends. I am but hurt.
HAMLET
Here, thou incestuous, murd'rous, damnèd Dane,
Drink off this potion. Is thy union° here?   **union:** (1) pearl, (2) marriage to Gertrude
Follow my mother.   310
    [King dies.]
LAERTES   He is justly served.
It is a poison tempered° by himself.   **tempered:** mixed
Exchange forgiveness with me, noble Hamlet.
Mine and my father's death come not upon thee,
Nor thine on me!
    [Dies.]
HAMLET
Heaven make thee free of it! I follow thee.   315
I am dead, Horatio. Wretched queen, adieu!
You that look pale and tremble at this chance,
That are but mutes° or audience to this act,   **mutes:** actors without speaking parts
Had I but time — as this fell sergeant,° Death, **sergeant:** court officer with power of arrest
Is strict° in his arrest — O, I could tell you — **strict:** (1) just, (2) inescapable   320
But let it be. Horatio, I am dead;
Thou livest; report me and my cause aright
To the unsatisfied.
HORATIO   Never believe it.
I am more an antique Roman° than a Dane.   **antique Roman:** i.e., someone who prefers
Here's yet some liquor left.   suicide to a dishonored life   325

DISCOVERING SHAKESPEARE

(148) <u>Plot</u> **[5.2.291]:** Why does Claudius say that Gertrude "swoons to see them bleed" (5.2.291)?
(149) <u>Verse</u> **[5.2.320]:** What does the breakdown in the <u>verse</u> pattern in 5.2.315–323 tell us about Hamlet's physical condition? How does the punctuation help the actor deliver his lines?

HAMLET   As th' art a man,
　Give me the cup. Let go. By heaven, I'll ha't!
　O God, Horatio, what a wounded name,
　Things standing thus unknown, shall I leave behind
　　me!
　If thou didst ever hold me in thy heart,
　Absent thee from felicity awhile,   330
　And in this harsh world draw thy breath in pain,
　To tell my story.
　　A march afar off.
　　　　　　　　What warlike noise is this?
　　Enter Osric.
OSRIC
　Young Fortinbras, with conquest come from Poland,
　To the ambassadors of England gives
　This warlike volley.   335
HAMLET   O, I die, Horatio!
　The potent poison quite o'ercrows° my spirit.
　I cannot live to hear the news from England,
　But I do prophesy th' election° lights
　On Fortinbras. He has my dying voice.°   340
　So tell him, with th' occurrents,° more and less,
　Which have solicited° – the rest is silence.
　　[Dies.]
HORATIO
　Now cracks a noble heart. Good night, sweet prince,
　And flights of angels sing thee to thy rest!
　　[March within.]
　Why does the drum come hither?
　　Enter Fortinbras, with the Ambassadors [and Drum,
　　Colors, and Attendants].
FORTINBRAS
　Where is this sight?   345
HORATIO   What is it you would see?
　If aught of woe or wonder,° cease your search.
FORTINBRAS
　This quarry° cries on° havoc.° O proud Death,
　What feast is toward° in thine eternal cell
　That thou so many princes at a shot   350
　So bloodily hast struck?
AMBASSADOR   The sight is dismal;
　And our affairs from England come too late.
　The ears are senseless that should give us hearing
　To tell him his commandment is fulfilled,
　That Rosencrantz and Guildenstern are dead.
　Where should we have our thanks?   355
HORATIO   Not from his mouth,
　Had it th' ability of life to thank you.
　He never gave commandment for their death.

o'ercrows: triumphs over (as a crow does over its meal? as a cock does in a cockfight?)

election: i.e., for the throne of Denmark (cf. l. 64)

voice: vote

occurrents: occurrences

solicited: incited, provoked

wonder: disaster (an archaic meaning in Shakespeare's day?)

quarry: pile of dead (literally, killed deer gathered after the hunt); **cries on:** proclaims loudly; **havoc:** indiscriminate killing and destruction

toward: forthcoming, about to occur (i.e., *Death* will feast on *so many princes*)

DISCOVERING SHAKESPEARE

(150) <u>Puns</u> **[5.2.341]:** What <u>pun</u> is Hamlet making in his final line, "The rest is silence" (5.2.341)?

(151) <u>Plot</u> **[5.2.357]:** Is Horatio correct that Hamlet "never gave commandment" (5.2.357) for the deaths of Rosencrantz and Guildenstern?

But since, so jump° upon this bloody question,   **jump:** precisely
You from the Polack wars, and you from England,
Are here arrived, give order that these bodies   360
High on a stage° be placèd to the view,   **stage:** platform (the meaning for performance or
And let me speak to th' yet unknowing world   the early modern audience is uncertain)
How these things came about. So shall you hear
Of carnal, bloody, and unnatural acts,
Of accidental° judgments,° casual° slaughters,   **accidental:** i.e., inscrutable to human eyes;   365
Of deaths put on° by cunning and forced° cause,   **judgments:** retributions; **casual:** not humanly
And, in this upshot, purposes mistook   planned (the word reinforces *accidental*)
Fall'n on th' inventors' heads. All this can I   **put on:** instigated; **forced:** contrived
Truly deliver.
FORTINBRAS   Let us haste to hear it,
And call the noblest to the audience.   370
For me, with sorrow I embrace my fortune.
I have some rights of memory° in this kingdom,   **of memory:** unforgotten
Which now to claim my vantage° doth invite me.   **vantage:** advantageous opportunity
HORATIO
Of that I shall have also cause to speak,
And from his mouth whose voice will draw on more.°   **more:** i.e., more voices, or votes, for the kingship   375
But let this same be presently° performed,   **presently:** immediately
Even while men's minds are wild, lest more mischance
On° plots and errors happen.   **On:** on the basis of
FORTINBRAS   Let four captains
Bear Hamlet like a soldier to the stage,
For he was likely, had he been put on,°   **put on:** set to perform in office   380
To have proved most royal; and for his passage°   **passage:** death
The soldiers' music and the rite of war
Speak loudly for him.
Take up the bodies. Such a sight as this
Becomes the field, but here shows much amiss.   385
Go, bid the soldiers shoot.

*Exeunt [marching; after the which
a peal of ordnance is shot off].*

DISCOVERING SHAKESPEARE

(152) <u>Short Lines</u> [5.2.383]: Fortinbras has <u>short lines</u> in 5.2.383 and 386. What stage action might be happening during the missing <u>beats</u> in those two lines?

❧

Research and Discussion Topics

ACT I

1. Research the history of Denmark. What use was Shakespeare making of actual historical events in *Hamlet*? What details does he change in his fictional account of Danish history?

2. In writing *Hamlet*, Shakespeare was working within a well-defined tradition of revenge tragedy stretching back as far as the Latin playwright Seneca. Research one or more of the revenge tragedies written during the English Renaissance. Which stock elements of the genre did Shakespeare use in *Hamlet*? What additions to the tradition did he invent?

3. What was a "liegeman" (1.1.15)?

4. What would Danish armor have looked like (1.1.39 ff.)? What was a "truncheon" (1.1.39 s.d.)? A "partisan" (1.1.140)?

5. Why would a "scholar" be particularly well qualified to speak to ghosts (1.1.42)?

6. Find a map of Europe and locate Denmark, Norway, Poland, Germany, and France. How far apart are these countries from each other?

7. What were the legal and moral consequences of suicide during the Renaissance (see 1.2.132)?

8. What was the definition of incest during the Renaissance? If a woman married her husband's brother, was she guilty of incest (see 1.2.157, 1.5.42, and elsewhere in the play)?

9. How were birds caught during Shakespeare's time (see 1.3.114)?

10. What were the most prominent Renaissance beliefs about hell and eternal damnation (see 1.5.3 ff.)?

11. Name some popular Renaissance poisons.

12. What sort of work did "pioners" do (1.5.166)?

13. What was an "antic" disposition (1.5.175)? How was madness diagnosed and treated during the Renaissance?

ACT II

1. What was "drabbing" (see 2.1.26 and 2.2.525)?

2. When was "tennis" (2.1.58) first played? How was it different from today's game?

3. What was a "windlass" (2.1.64)?

4. Research the "art" of rhetoric (2.2.96). Who were the most famous rhetoricians studied during the Renaissance?

5. What is the difference between a "sadness," a "fast," a "watch," a "weakness," a "lightness," and a "madness" (2.2.147–150)?

6. What was a "carter" (2.2.167)?

7. What was "Lenten entertainment" (2.2.286)?

8. Investigate the different categories of plays that Polonius mentions in 2.2.339–344.

9. Who was "Jephthah, judge of Israel" (2.2.345)?

10. What was a "chopine" (2.2.368)?

ACT III

1. What types of perfumes were used during the Renaissance (3.1.99)? What cosmetics were available (cf. 3.1.142 ff.)?

2. What were "nunneries" like during Shakespeare's time? How many women were housed in them? What was their social and religious hierarchy?

3. What was a "periwig" (3.2.9)?

4. Who was Herod (3.2.13)? What was he known for in pre-Shakespearean drama?

5. Who was Vulcan (3.2.83)?

6. Who was Julius Caesar (3.2.101 and 5.1.203)?

7. Who were Phoebus, Neptune, and Tellus (3.2.150–151)?

8. What were the most popular English Renaissance proverbs (cf. 3.2.337 and elsewhere)?

9. What was the game of "hoodman-blind" (3.4.77)?

ACT IV

1. What was a "cherub" (4.3.47)?

2. What was the origin of Saint Valentine's Day (4.5.48)? Has it always been on February 14th? Is it celebrated differently in England than it is in the United States?

3. What was the "Great Chain of Being" (4.5.86 and elsewhere)?

4. What was the sport of hunting like during the Renaissance (4.5.109–110)? How were dogs used in hunting? What types of game were pursued?

5. What were the duties of sailors during Shakespeare's time (see 4.6.1–6)?

ACT V

1. What did a "crowner" do (5.1.4)? What is our modern version of that word?

2. What does "se offendendo" (5.1.9) mean?

3. Who was Cain (5.1.73)?

4. What is the meaning of the following legal terms: "quiddities," "quillities," "cases," "tenures," "tricks," "statutes," "recognizances," "fines," "double vouchers," "recoveries," and "indentures" (5.1.93–106)?

5. What were Pelion, Olympus, and Ossa (5.1.243–244 and 5.1.273)?

6. What was "eisel" (5.1.266)?

7. What were "mutines in the bilboes" (5.2.6)?

8. What was Elizabethan Secretary Hand (5.2.51–53)?

9. What was a "signet" (5.2.49)? For what was it used?

10. Was Denmark an elective monarchy at this time (see 5.2.64)?

11. What was "augury" (5.2.197)? How was it used?

12. What were "foils" (5.2.202 s.d.)?

13. What was a "union" (5.2.250)?

14. What were the rules of fencing contests? What were some of the principal thrusts and parries?

Filmography

1980
BBC
Rating:

Directed by: Rodney Bennett

Derek Jacobi as Hamlet
Patrick Stewart as Claudius
Claire Bloom as Gertrude
Lalla Ward as Ophelia
Eric Porter as Polonius

David Robb as Laertes
Robert Swann as Horatio

The BBC has presented a more complex and complete *Hamlet* than most film-makers dare attempt. While alternative versions may provide a more spectacular and fantastic setting, Jacobi's Hamlet possesses the intelligence and clarity such an intricate and difficult character requires. Notwithstanding talent such as Claire Bloom and Patrick Stewart, viewers are more likely to gravitate toward Jacobi's solar pull as the principal character, making satellites of his co-stars. Stewart's Claudius is sometimes sympathetic for the audience, while simultaneously contemptuous toward his nephew–son. Claire Bloom plays Gertrude with a grace and maturity often lacking in the part, while Ophelia is portrayed as a weak and submissive character—a sensible interpretive choice ignored by most performers. Overall, Horatio and the ghost are the most off-key characters in this finely tuned orchestration.

1996
Castle Rock Entertainment
Rating:

Directed by: Kenneth Branagh
Kenneth Branagh as Hamlet
Derek Jacobi as Claudius
Julie Christie as Gertrude
Kate Winslet as Ophelia
Richard Briers as Polonius
Michael Maloney as Laertes
Nicholas Farrell as Horatio

Branagh has embellished his *Hamlet* with nineteenth-century decor, and the tragic prince's prison is transformed into a wintry party palace wherein every room has a hidden passage to admit prostitutes and conceal secrets. Scholars will appreciate that this time-skewed *Hamlet* delivers every line, although the words are sometimes spoon-fed through flashbacks and reenacted scenes illustrating the dialogue. The questions which *Hamlet* should leave its audience pondering are all answered through such inserted clips as Claudius and Gertrude's affair previous to the king's death, Hamlet and Ophelia's physical intimacy, and Ophelia's sexual gestures in her strait-jacketed lunacy. Branagh's portrayal of Hamlet lacks the intellect to outwit his wicked stepfather–uncle, as he adopts faux madness throughout the film. Jacobi's Claudius, the highlight of this production, appears too complex against Branagh's simplified Hamlet, and Richard Briers' Polonius is not so much nosy and intrusive as he is sleazy and cunning. Winslet as Ophelia is weak, but not in the way the character should be. She seems an actress unable to carry the part, not a girl unable to bear her father's death and her lover's madness. Branagh is seldom subtle either as actor or director. He announces his soliloquies as though he is motivating an army before an attack, and the final scene, which involves swinging from the balcony and crushing the king under a chandelier belongs with *The Last Action Hero*'s parody of *Hamlet* by Arnold Schwarzenegger.

1969
Columbia Pictures
Rating:

Directed by: Tony Richardson
Nicol Williamson as Hamlet
Anthony Hopkins as Claudius
Judy Parfitt as Gertrude
Marianne Faithfull as Ophelia
Mark Dignam as Polonius
Michael Pennington as Laertes
Gordon Jackson as Horatio

Tony Richardson's film started as a stage production in London, and it still has much of the ambiance of London's Roundhouse Theatre and the second half of the 1960s. Nicol Williamson's Hamlet is edgy, frenetic, and sometimes downright peculiar. This is Hamlet as angry young man, except that Williamson does not look all that young in comparison to Anthony Hopkins as Claudius and Judy Parfitt as Gertrude. Williamson's unusual appearance, strange energy, and North country accent mark him as a rebel who means to bring down the establishment. Hopkins and Parfitt as the morally, politically, and sexually corrupt Claudius and Gertrude provide a sufficiently wicked establishment to justify any amount of self-righteous rebellion.

1990
Great Performances
Rating:

Directed by: Kevin Kline
Kevin Kline as Hamlet
Brian Murray as Claudius
Dana Ivey as Gertrude
Diane Venora as Ophelia
Josef Sommer as Polonius
Michael Cumpsty as Laertes
Peter Francis James as Horatio

The New York Shakespearean Festival (and its *Great Performances* filmed version) may have hit their market, but they missed the mark, beginning with the casting of the primary character. From uncertainties of where his hands should go to his tight and nervous movements, Kline's weepy Hamlet is awkward, much like some of the Hollywood characters he plays. Michael Cumpsty's Laertes is unsettling, appearing to be the younger brother of Ophelia, his spunky sister. She insists on Hamlet's honorable intentions and screams uncontrollably. The costumes appear to be dressy-casual wear the cast found in their closets, though Claudius looks like a survival from the days of the British Raj, while Laertes seems a strange cross between yuppie and wise guy. Oddly, Gertrude encourages Hamlet to "cast off [his] nighted color," while she herself is clad in a black evening dress. The set is so bare it's almost naked. Polonius is the greatest strength in this adapted stage performance, simply because he tends to be the only actor who fully understands the humor and dialogue. While individual moments and even scenes in this production are strong, on the whole it is somewhat dry, and for students, it may be slightly more effective as an aid to sleep than as a guide to the play.

1990
Warner/Nelson Entertainment
Rating:

Directed by: Franco Zeffirelli
Mel Gibson as Hamlet
Alan Bates as Claudius
Glenn Close as Gertrude
Helena Bonham Carter as Ophelia
Ian Holm as Polonius
Nathaniel Parker as Laertes
Stephen Dillane as Horatio

Zeffirelli intended this to be the most action-packed *Hamlet* ever filmed, but ultimately his interpretation of this Shakespeare classic is not much more than an update of Olivier's 1948 version. Mel Gibson's action-hero Hamlet is the most considerable contrast with the Olivier film. Gibson's Hamlet is unquestionably unstable and unstoppable from the first moment the camera meets his eyes, while Olivier is a brooding, dull Hamlet. Zeffirelli begins in medieval Denmark with the funeral of the murdered king and flashes forward to the widow's wedding with her former brother-in-law. The political and military struggle with Norway is completely cut from the film, as well as the rich opportunity for character development that can come from actually performing those lines. Close's Gertrude is an irrational little girl in her second adolescence. She literally skips toward Claudius and nearly entices her only son to bed. Polonius is too darkly serious, depriving the play of the comic relief the character usually provides. Bonham Carter's Ophelia is convincing in her madness, but mainly as an extension of the ghost-like instability she communicates through the entire picture. Horatio's part is underplayed, particularly when he is unable to proclaim himself "more an ancient Roman than a Dane" by threatening suicide to follow the prince. And without Fortinbras, of course, Denmark is left to no one.

1948
Rank/Two Cities
Rating:

Directed by: Laurence Olivier
Laurence Olivier as Hamlet
Basil Sydney as Claudius
Eileen Herlie as Gertrude

Jean Simmons as Ophelia
Felix Aylmer as Polonius
Terence Morgan as Laertes
Norman Wooland as Horatio

Olivier could have produced an extraordinarily vigorous Hamlet, bursting with energy and boasting a physical panache that few others could equal. Instead, he has, unfortunately, deprived Hamlet of more than half his lines and many of his actions. He is more the paperweight of Denmark than its prince. Scenes are rearranged, lines rewritten, and words changed. There is no trace of politics: Rosencrantz, Guildenstern, and even Fortinbras vanish. Olivier's voice-over, "This is the tragedy of a man who could not make up his mind" (from the Gary Cooper film *Souls at Sea*), might more appropriately have been, "This is the tragedy of *Hamlet* made simpleminded." Hamlet becomes an immobile young man troubled by the twin demons of indecision and incest. In this cut-up, cut-down *Hamlet*, the prince cannot act until he resolves his feelings for his mother and his girlfriend and determines they are not one and the same. Sadly, the strength of the film is not in the text or the actors, but in the questing, fluid camera, and the confining, claustrophobic set.

2000
Miramax Films
Rating:

Directed by: Michael Almereyda
Ethan Hawke as Hamlet
Kyle Machlachlan as Claudius
Diane Venora as Gertrude
Julia Stiles as Ophelia
Bill Murray as Polonius
Liev Schreiber as Laertes
Karl Geary as Horatio

Ethan Hawke makes an incapable, uninvolved Hamlet. Almereyda's film lacks not only important lines, continuity, and style, but also the complexity viewers expect from Shakespeare's greatest (or at least longest) play. Ethan Hawke's slacker Hamlet sports a Peruvian wool cap through most major scenes, including the "To-be-or-not-to-be" soliloquy, which takes place in the action section of a Blockbuster Video store. Many of Hamlet's pivotal lines are shouted into answering machines or over telephones. However, it matters little since Hawke doesn't understand his part anyway, and he would probably be as unintelligible in contemporary prose as he is in Shakespeare's verse. Murray's Polonius is just short of pathetic and never laughable or ridiculous as the character should sometimes be. Stiles' Ophelia is a dramatic undergraduate obsessed with Polaroids, who contemplates drowning herself long before Hamlet's madness, her father's murder, and her brother's absence cause a psychological overload. Diane Venora as Gertrude is the most interesting character in this film: jealous of Ophelia, ultimately disloyal to Claudius, and protective of her son (even to the point of deliberately drinking the poisoned wine). The theme of poison in the play is drowned out by the sound of firearms, which seem to both exhilarate and terrify Hawke's Hamlet, keeping him at a safe emotional and physical distance from confrontation. The blood-splattered final scene violently sprays bullets into Hamlet, Laertes, and Claudius.

Annotated Bibliography

Bevington, David, ed. *Twentieth-Century Interpretations of "Hamlet."* Englewood Cliffs, New Jersey: Prentice Hall, 1968. PR 2807.B46.
> Divided into two sections, this collection of seventeen essays features work by Bradley, Eliot, Spencer, Mack, and Knights. While the first section, ("Interpretations") includes full-length essays on *Hamlet*, the second section, ("Viewpoints") contains portions of essays that analyze the play's themes and characters. Bevington also appends a bibliography of secondary resources on the play.

Bloom, Harold, ed. *William Shakespeare's "Hamlet": Modern Critical Interpretations.* New York: Chelsea House, 1986. PR 2807.W456.
> A compilation of contemporary interpretations of *Hamlet,* Bloom's collection features work by Nevo, Danson, Lanham, Felperin, and Rose, as well as an essay by Bloom himself. The critical approaches featured in the collection range throughout formalist, metadramatic, Foucaultian, and historicist critical approaches. Also included are a chronology and a concise bibliography of the books and articles that Bloom feels offer the most distinguished analyses of *Hamlet*.

Bradley, A. C. *Shakespearean Tragedy: Lectures on "Hamlet," "Othello," "King Lear," and "Macbeth."* London: Macmillan, 1904. Lecture Three, 71–108. PR 2983.B7.
> Responding to Coleridge and Schlegel's interpretations of Hamlet, Bradley argues that the prince suffers from melancholy and is therefore prone to inaction. Further, he points to Hamlet's intelligence and moral integrity as factors in his tragically doomed relationship with Ophelia. Bradley also makes careful examinations of Claudius, Gertrude, and Ophelia, noting each of these major characters' primary flaws. Considered a seminal essay on the play, Bradley's commentary on *Hamlet* marked a new standard for Shakespearean criticism characterized by objective rather than subjective analysis.

Branagh, Kenneth. *"Hamlet," by William Shakespeare: Screenplay, Introduction, and Film Diary.* New York: W. W. Norton, 1996. PN 1997.H254.B7.
> In this extensive discussion of his 1996 film version of *Hamlet*, Branagh notes that he wanted to create both an intimate examination of the play's characters as well as an epic representation of a country and royal empire in ruin. Included in the book are an introduction by the director himself and the film's screenplay, as well as a diary of the film's production written by screenwriter Russell Jackson. In addition to discussing the intricate details of the film's production, this book features thirty pages of color photographs of the actors and scenes from the movie.

Calderwood, James L. *To Be and Not to Be: Negation and Metadrama in "Hamlet."* New York: Columbia University Press, 1983. PR 2807.C24.

> Discussing the play's negations, erasures, and disjunctures, Calderwood advances an intricate argument that *Hamlet* inherently deconstructs and reconstructs itself. The critic focuses primarily upon Hamlet's crisis of being, suggesting that the prince's ability to reclaim his sense of identity is vital to the reconstruction of the play's universe. Drawing on poststructuralist philosophers like Jacques Derrida and such structuralist writers as Ferdinand de Saussure, Calderwood contends that *Hamlet*'s missing material leaves its own trace, which is the origin of the play's central meaning.

Charney, Maurice. *Style in "Hamlet."* Princeton: Princeton University Press, 1969. PR 2807.C28.

> Attempting to move away from psychoanalytic readings of the play, Charney displays both formalist and performance-oriented readings of *Hamlet* to suggest that style above all else informs the play's central meaning. Divided into three parts, Charney's study considers the interrelation of image and idea in the play and how both the text itself and the performance of the text rely upon one another for meaning, as image and idea are expressed differently in each medium. The critic pays particular attention to characters' speeches, while exposing the paradoxes and complexities of the play's language.

Dawson, Anthony B. *"Hamlet": Shakespeare in Performance.* Manchester: Manchester University Press, 1995. PR 2807.D35.

> In this comprehensive discussion of *Hamlet* in performance, Dawson attempts to account for the play's major stage adaptations and suggests that the wide swath of interpretations exhibited in these productions indicates *Hamlet*'s slipperiness and complexity. Divided into nine chapters, Dawson's book examines both classic and modern productions of *Hamlet* and includes an index of those productions' actors and directors. Ultimately, Dawson argues, the variety of productions indicates *Hamlet*'s status as a play about representation and as an artifact of representation itself.

Fergusson, Francis. *"Hamlet, Prince of Denmark: The Analogy of Action."* In *The Idea of a Theater: A Study of Ten Plays.* Princeton: Princeton University Press, 1949. PN 1661.F4.

> Likening the play to the ritual drama of ancient Greece, Fergusson contends that *Hamlet* was as important for Elizabethan England as a cultural artifact as plays like *Antigone* and *Oedipus Rex* were for ancient civilizations. Fergusson suggests that the play is structured by a series of ritual scenes. Many subsequent critics have criticized Fergusson for his vague definition of ritual and his anachronistic imposition of the value of Greek rites on Elizabethan culture.

Freud, Sigmund. "Hamlet." In vol. 4 of *The Standard Edition of the Complete Psychological Works of Sigmund Freud.* James Strachey et al., eds. London: 1953. 264–66. BF 173.F6253.

> In this seminal study of *Hamlet*, Freud argues that the prince is driven by a repressed Oedipal fantasy that makes his erratic behavior "hysterical." An important influence on T. S. Eliot, E. E. Jones, and myriad actors, di-

rectors, and scholars, Freud's essay changed forever the way the world viewed *Hamlet*. It is still considered one of the principal works written on the play within the great mass of Shakespearean scholarship.

Frye, Roland Mushat. *The Renaissance "Hamlet": Issues and Responses in 1600.* Princeton: Princeton University Press, 1984. PR 2807.F79.

> In this historical reading of *Hamlet*, Frye attempts to describe the reactions Shakespeare must have anticipated from audiences in the early 1600s. He particularly considers the issues of regicide, incest, revenge, and rebellion, while arguing that Hamlet is not an indecisive character but a man dealing with sensitive contemporary issues in Renaissance England. The book includes many illustrations and photographs of Renaissance artwork and woodcuts that offer visual representations of the issues examined within the text.

Granville-Barker, Harley. "*Hamlet.*" In vol. 1 of *Preface to Shakespeare.* London: Sidgewick and Jackson, 1936. 24–260. PR 2976.G674.

> Primarily concerned with *Hamlet* as a script for stage production, Granville-Barker devotes much of his discussion to the play's language, action, and characters. Above all, he argues, since Shakespeare uses poetic style to realize character, this style must be recognized in stage productions of the play. Granville-Barker's use of the terms "Place-structure" and "Time-structure" (38–46) have often been cited, and his essay is considered to be a profoundly useful reading of *Hamlet*'s language and characters.

Holland, Norman N. *Psychoanalysis and Shakespeare.* New York: McGraw-Hill, 1964. PR 2976.H55.

> In this comprehensive review of psychoanalytical perspectives on *Hamlet,* Holland discusses the work of Freud, Jones, and other major psychoanalytic critics on the play and its characters. The author pays particular attention to views on Hamlet's melancholia, interpretations that suggest matricide as the play's central conflict, as well as discussions focusing on Hamlet's inaction. Holland also discusses Freud's reading of Hamlet's Oedipal complex.

Jones, Ernest. *Hamlet and Oedipus.* London: Gollancz, 1976. PR 2807.J63.

> Separated into eight chapters, Jones' analysis of Hamlet's Oedipal complex was initially a footnote to Freud's original discussion of the subject. Jones considers the psychological states of both Hamlet and Shakespeare, utilizing Freud's method of "depth psychology" throughout his examination. A seminal study of *Hamlet,* Jones' essay is believed to have been extremely influential on T. S. Eliot as well as Sir Laurence Olivier, who made a film adaptation of the play in 1948.

Kastan, David Scott, ed. *Critical Essays on Shakespeare's "Hamlet."* New York: G. K. Hall, 1995. PR 2807.K33.

> In this brief but helpful collection of essays, Kastan offers an introduction, "Very Like a Whale," that considers *Hamlet*'s critical heritage, as well as several modern interpretations of the play. Subsequent essays include work by such authors as Stephen Booth, Michael Goldman, Inga-Stina Ewbank, George T. Wright, and Paul Werstine.

Kinney, Arthur F., ed. *"Hamlet": New Critical Essays.* New York & London: Routledge, 2002. PR 2807.H2657.

> Arthur Kinney provides an excellent introduction to *Hamlet* that covers numerous sources, productions, and criticism regarding the play since the seventeenth century. This work includes many excellent essays divided into three sections: 1) Tudor-Stuart *Hamlet,* 2) Subsequent *Hamlet*s, and 3) *Hamlet* after Theory. Contributing authors include R. A. Foakes, Philip Edwards, Paul Werstine, Catherine Belsey, and Richard Levin.

Knight, G. Wilson. "The Embassy of Death: an Essay on *Hamlet.*" In *The Wheel of Fire: Interpretations of Shakespearian Tragedy, with Three New Essays.* Oxford: Oxford University Press, 1930. 17–46. PR 2983.K6.

> A foremost Shakespearean scholar, Knight analyzes *Hamlet*'s poetic–symbolic imagery and argues that the play is above all a meditation on death. Citing Hamlet's preoccupation with existence and meaninglessness, the author contends that the play's core theme is its concern with the prince's spiritual and physical death. Considered a defining study of *Hamlet*, Knight's essay established a precedent for future studies of the play that discuss its spatial structure, personification, and poetic symbolism.

Knights, L. C. *An Approach to "Hamlet."* London: Chatto & Windus, 1960. PR 2807.K58.

> Finding fault with Hamlet's inability to act on behalf of both his father and his own moral conscience, Knights argues that *Hamlet* is primarily a play concerned with man's self-deception and his incapacity to deal with death and evil. Referring to G. Wilson Knight's essay that highlights the importance of death and corruption in the play, the author suggests that Hamlet is obsessed with facing death and insufficiently committed to the task of avenging his father's murder. Knights attributes such paralysis to the evil of the Ghost, who tempts Hamlet to "gaze with fascinated horror at an abyss" (47) of evil, corruption, and death.

Leavenworth, Russell E., ed. *Interpreting "Hamlet": Materials for Analysis.* San Francisco: Chandler, 1960. PR 2807.L355.

> Compiled specifically for student use, Leavenworth's collection of essays features work on *Hamlet* by such luminaries as Eliot, Jones, Goethe, Knight, Bradley, and Shaw. The collection also includes recommendations to teachers for writing assignments, forms for footnotes, and an extensive bibliography of secondary resources on *Hamlet*.

Prosser, Eleanor. *"Hamlet" and Revenge.* Stanford: Stanford University Press, 1967. PR 2807.P77.

> Considering the theme of revenge in *Hamlet*, Prosser divides her examination into two parts: In the first, she discusses Elizabethan attitudes toward revenge; in the second, she analyzes Hamlet's revenge. Prosser focuses in particular on the role of the ghost of Hamlet's father in the play, arguing that the predominant Elizabethan interpretation of the ghost was that it is a demonic, malevolent phantom. Furthermore, the critic suggests that Hamlet felt no moral obligation to avenge his father, and

that the prince nobly risks all (i.e., spiritual and physical death) to exact his revenge.

Reynolds, Peter. "*Hamlet.*" In *Shakespeare: Text Into Performance.* London: Penguin, 1991. 67–75. PR 3091.R48.

> In this pedagogical resource for ideas on teaching Shakespeare, Reynolds discusses how teachers can best help their students understand *Hamlet* (the rest of the book is devoted to Shakespeare's other plays). Focusing specifically on teaching about the character Ophelia, Reynolds believes students should act out the scenes in which Ophelia is present in order to get the most complete idea of the emotion behind the character's words. Furthermore, the author suggests that teachers bring a copy of Millais' painting *Ophelia* to class, and that students have the opportunity to watch filmed versions of the play, particularly act 4, scene 7.

Rosenberg, Marvin. *The Masks of "Hamlet."* Newark, DE: University of Delaware Press, 1992. PR 2807.R656.

> Considering both textual and theatrical analyses of the play, Rosenberg reviews the body of existing *Hamlet* scholarship in this comprehensive study. In his own formalist analysis, Rosenberg contends that Hamlet is the embodiment of the complex and multifarious nature of human identity, and that no one interpretation of the prince can be pronounced "valid" or "correct." The critic uses this idea of multiplicity to account for the varying and often divergent reactions to and interpretations of Shakespeare's masterpiece.

Shakespeare Quarterly 46 (1995). PR 2885.S63.

> Devoted entirely to strategies for teaching Shakespeare, this special edition of *Shakespeare Quarterly* is divided into three sections: viewpoint, methods, and tools. While only one essay focuses exclusively on *Hamlet*, many of the issue's guides for teaching Shakespeare touch upon elements specific to *Hamlet* in conjunction with other plays. Guest-edited by Ralph Alan Cohen, this special issue of the journal features many strategies for teaching Shakespeare through performance.

Spurgeon, Caroline F. E. *Shakespeare's Imagery and What It Tells Us.* Cambridge: Cambridge University Press, 1935. PR 3081.S64.

> Anticipating the New Criticism movement of the mid-twentieth century, Spurgeon makes a close reading of *Hamlet* and other plays to expose the presence of Shakespeare's own personality within his writing. Particularly considering the play's food and illness imagery, the critic suggests that Shakespeare creates a world of sickness and corruption in *Hamlet* that must be cleansed and purged of all impurities. In addition to a thorough analysis of *Hamlet*'s imagery, Spurgeon makes a close reading of *Troilus and Cressida,* particularly to link the two plays' disease imagery.

Watson, Elizabeth. "Old King, New King, Eclipsed Sons and Abandoned Altars." *Sixteenth Century Journal* 35.2 (Summer 2004): 475–501. journal D 219.S55.

> According to the author, the wordplay present in Shakespeare's *Hamlet* creates "patterns of doubling, splitting, and loss that mimic . . . the condition of the changing English church of the Reformation period" as well

as the dramatic condition of the characters themselves. Watson draws on ecclesiastical history from both the old Roman rites and the new language of the Church of England, as well as strong textual evidence.

Wilson, J. Dover. *What Happens in "Hamlet."* Cambridge: Cambridge University Press, 1935. PR 2807.W48.

> Responding to an article by W. W. Greg, Wilson attempts to demonstrate *Hamlet*'s artistic unity, arguing that Shakespeare creates parallel sub-plots and character dilemmas that allow the play to cohere with elegance and precision. In particular, the critic cites the dumb show and the allegory of Gonzago to suggest that the play is riddled with unifying elements. Divided into seven chapters, Wilson's book offers a comprehensive study of *Hamlet* and even discusses the work that authors like T. S. Eliot have completed on the play.

Wofford, Susanne L., ed. *William Shakespeare: "Hamlet." Case Studies in Contemporary Criticism.* New York: St. Martin's Press, 1993. PR 2807.A2.W64.

> Divided into two sections, Wofford's casebook is designed for student study and contains a glossary of critical and theoretical terms in addition to critical essays and bibliographies of critical works in major theoretical areas. Part one of the casebook includes a discussion of *Hamlet*'s biographical and historical contexts as well as the full text of the Riverside edition. Part two contains the aforementioned critical heritage of *Hamlet*, including critical essays, five theoretical perspectives, and bibliographies of essays on each of those perspectives. Essays included in this collection include work by Showalter, Adelman, Gerber, Bristol, and Coddon.

Othello

Othello at the Oregon Shakespearean Festival in Ashland, Oregon, with Anthony Heald (head in water) as Iago and Derrick Lee Weeden as Othello (1999). Photograph by David Cooper.

Othello is an exquisitely painful play to watch, since it deals with the destruction of a good man and his beautiful, loyal wife by one of the most inherently evil characters ever to inhabit the world of theater. Written in 1603–1604, it was first published in a 1621 <u>quarto</u> edition as "The Tragedie of Othello, the Moore of Venice," then subsequently revised in the 1623 <u>First Folio</u>, which is now regarded by most scholars as the <u>copy text</u> of the play. Shakespeare's principal <u>source</u> was the seventh story from the third "decade" of Giraldi Cinthio's *Hecatommithi,* originally published in Italian in 1565 and later translated into French. An additional topical influence on the play was the ascension of James I to the throne of England in 1603. The newly crowned king was fascinated with Turkish history, while his wife, Queen Anne, once asked Ben Jonson to write a play about Moors (*The Masque of Blackness*) in which she played a role in "dusky" <u>makeup</u>.

Based on an actual incident that occurred in Venice in the early sixteenth century, Shakespeare's play is heavily indebted to Cinthio's plot, including the marriage of a valiant Moor to a noble Venetian lady, his voyage to suppress a Turkish invasion in Cyprus, the treacherous insinuations of his ensign, the Moor's jealous rage, and the eventual murder of Desdemona in her bed. To this sparse <u>plot</u> outline Shakespeare adds a distraught father, the gullible <u>foil</u> Roderigo, a devoted and courageous Emilia, and, most importantly, enough depth and complexity in Iago to turn him into one of the most fascinating villains ever created by the playwright.

While the play is clearly a tragedy, its narrow focus and psychological sophistication set it apart from most other dramas of its kind. The cast is relatively small, for example, with an unrelenting emphasis on the actions of its central characters. Unlike many other great tragedies, *Othello* has no <u>sub-plot</u> to dilute the dramatic experience, nor does it feature frequent appeals to divine justice (as in *King Lear*) or the intrusion of supernatural elements (*Hamlet* and *Macbeth*). In addition, *Othello* is the most contemporary of Shakespeare's tragedies; since the Turks had attacked Cyprus as recently as 1570, the specter of an infidel invasion was still fresh in the minds of his audience.

The character of Iago is most changed from Shakespeare's <u>source</u> material, where the one-dimensional ensign truly loves Desdemona and eventually bludgeons her to death with a sock full of sand. While Shakespeare's villain provides several reasons for his hatred of the Moor (frustration over his lack of military promotion, suspicion that his wife has been unfaithful with Othello, and unvarnished racism), Iago is also driven by what Samuel Taylor Coleridge called "motiveless malignity," which seems to ally his insidious nature with the Vice character of the medieval morality plays, whose delight in evil for its own sake was a staple ingredient of the <u>genre</u>. As such, Iago has offered students of the play a unique opportunity to investigate the pathology of evil through a psychological examination of his behavior in the script. Ultimately, however, Iago's silence at the end of the play is the final unsettling answer: The most horrifying evil in the world transcends rational analysis.

Several additional important <u>themes</u> arise from this troubling <u>script</u>. For instance, the concept of geographical dichotomy, so prominent in other Shakespearean plays, is of crucial significance here. When Othello and Desdemona move from the urbane, civilized, and somewhat depraved city-state of Venice to Cyprus, they enter a barren military encampment whose claustrophobic confines intensify Iago's unrelenting psychological assault. Prejudice and racism are also key elements in the drama, not only in Iago's hatred of Othello, but also in the Moor's naiveté concerning the subtle charms of Venetian ladies. Enlivened by such other significant topics as the changing roles of women, the uses of verbal and psychological poison, the lust for revenge, images of foreignness, the tempest at sea and in Othello's mind, the isolation of an island universe, the reversion to brutish behavior, cultural relativism, sexual and racial anxiety, eloquence, and the <u>ironic</u> importance of the handkerchief, *Othello* is a play filled with profound insights into the flawed and intriguing world around us.

Early productions of *Othello* at the Globe and Blackfriars theatres featured Richard Burbage as the Moor and a succession of boy actors as Desdemona. Not until the Restoration, in fact, was the first actress allowed to play the role of Othello's wife. Eighteenth-century audiences endured numerous <u>cuts</u> in the script (including the epileptic fit in act four), which were intended to emphasize the nobility and dignity of the central character. Such well-known actors as Thomas Betterton, Barton Booth, and Spranger Barry all played Othello in black-face, as did Edmund Keane and Tommaso Salvini in the nineteenth century. The first African-American actor to play the title role was Ira Aldridge in the 1850s, who was followed in the twentieth century by the brilliant performances of Earle Hyman, James Earl Jones, Paul Robeson, and Willard White. Other notable modern Othellos have included John Neville, Richard Burton, Orson Welles, and Laurence Olivier, while Emrys James, José Ferrer, Alfred Drake, and Leo McKern played memorable Iagos. The script's romance, passion, and eloquence spawned nineteenth-century operas of *Otello* by two great Italian composers, Rossini and Verdi, as well as twentieth-century films by Orson Welles, Trevor Nunn, Jonathan Miller, and Oliver Parker (whose 1995 movie starred Laurence Fishburne as Othello and Kenneth Branagh as Iago).

Regardless of the actors playing the principal roles and the centuries they inhabit, well-crafted productions of this play take us on a geographic and psychological journey into the human heart. Othello gains self-knowledge at a terrible price, for he loses everything dear to him as a result of Iago's villainy. The goodness that Desdemona represents, however, rises above the heart-breaking conclusion of the play, as does Othello's eventual awareness of his disastrous actions. Like all great tragedies, *Othello* provides this spiritual and emotional uplift to counterbalance the sadness of defeat on the physical level. Although the deep and inspiring love between Othello and Desdemona is destroyed by Iago, it is resurrected during each new production of the play as proof that such perfect unions can exist outside of space, time, and the evils of racism—at least in the idealistic and regenerative world of theatre.

Othello at the Guthrie Theatre in Minneapolis, Minnesota, with Melissa Brown as Desdemona, Robert Foxworth as Iago, and Sally Wingert as Emilia (1994). Photograph by Michal Daniel.

Othello

THE NAMES OF THE ACTORS

OTHELLO, *the Moor, leader of the Venetian armed forces*
BRABANTIO, *father to Desdemona*
CASSIO, *an honorable lieutenant*
IAGO, *a villain*
RODERIGO, *a gulled gentleman*
DUKE OF VENICE
SENATORS
MONTANO, *Governor of Cyprus*
GENTLEMEN OF CYPRUS
LODOVICO *and* GRATIANO, *two noble Venetians*
SAILORS
CLOWN
DESDEMONA, *wife to Othello*
EMILIA, *wife to Iago*
BIANCA, *a courtesan*
MESSENGER, HERALD, OFFICERS, VENETIAN GENTLEMEN,
   MUSICIANS, ATTENDANTS

SCENE: *Venice and Cyprus*

1.1° *Enter Roderigo and Iago.*

1.1: A street in Venice

RODERIGO
  Tush, never tell me! I take it much unkindly
  That thou, Iago, who hast had my purse
  As if the strings were thine, shouldst know of this.
IAGO
  'Sblood,° but you'll not hear me!
  If ever I did dream of such a matter,
  Abhor me.

'Sblood: (an oath; originally "by God's [i.e., Christ's] blood")

5

RODERIGO
  Thou told'st me thou didst hold him in thy hate.
IAGO
  Despise me if I do not. Three great ones° of the city,
  In personal suit to make me his lieutenant,
  Off-capped to him; and, by the faith of man,
  I know my price; I am worth no worse a place.
  But he, as loving his own pride and purposes,

great ones: influential men

10

DISCOVERING SHAKESPEARE

(1) Plot [1.1.1]: Like all plays, *Othello* begins *in medias res* ("in the middle of things"). On a separate sheet of paper, write a description of what you think Iago and Roderigo have been talking about before the play begins.

Evades them, with a bombast circumstance°
Horribly stuffed with epithets of war,
Nonsuits° my mediators; for, "Certes," says he,
"I have already chose my officer."
And what was he?
Forsooth, a great arithmetician,°
One Michael Cassio, a Florentine
(A fellow almost damned in a fair wife°)
That never set a squadron in the field,
Nor the division of a battle° knows
More than a spinster, unless the bookish theoric,°
Wherein the tonguèd consuls° can propose
As masterly as he. Mere prattle without practice
Is all his soldiership. But he, sir, had th' election;
And I (of whom his eyes had seen the proof
At Rhodes, at Cyprus, and on other grounds
Christened and heathen) must be beleed and calmed°
By debitor and creditor.° This countercaster,°
He, in good time, must his lieutenant be,
And I – God bless the mark!° – his Moorship's ancient.°

RODERIGO
By heaven, I rather would have been his hangman.

IAGO
Why, there's no remedy; 'tis the curse of service.
Preferment goes by letter and affection,
And not by old gradation,° where each second
Stood heir to th' first. Now, sir, be judge yourself,
Whether I in any just term am affined°
To love the Moor.

RODERIGO   I would not follow him then.

IAGO
O, sir, content you;
I follow him to serve my turn upon him.
We cannot all be masters, nor all masters
Cannot be truly followed. You shall mark
Many a duteous and knee-crooking° knave
That, doting on his own obsequious bondage,°
Wears out his time, much like his master's ass,
For nought but provender,° and when he's old,
cashiered.°
Whip me such honest knaves!° Others there are
Who, trimmed° in forms and visages° of duty,
Keep yet° their hearts attending on themselves,
And, throwing but shows of service on their lords,
Do well thrive by them, and when they have lined their
coats,
Do themselves homage.° These fellows have some soul,
And such a one do I profess myself. For, sir,

---

bombast circumstance: pompous evasion, roundabout excuses (*bombast* is cotton stuffing; see *stuffed,* l. 14)
Nonsuits: denies   15

arithmetician: theorist, bean counter

almost . . . wife: (a mystifying reference, perhaps   20
a result of error in textual transmission; although
Cassio is unmarried, the line links him with
women early in the play)
division of a battle: arrangement of troops
unless . . . theoric: except hypothetically
tonguèd consuls: i.e., those who advise but   25
don't actually fight

beleed and calmed: i.e., left behind; a nautical
metaphor for frustration ("belee" = "to place   30
under the lee, or unfavorably to the wind")
debitor and creditor: bookkeeper;
countercaster: accountant

God . . . mark: (an exclamation of impatience);
ancient: ensign, standard-bearer (an officer
inferior to lieutenant)

                                                        35

Preferment . . . gradation: i.e., promotion
now depends on favoritism or whom you know,
not on the old system of rising through the ranks
affined: bound

                                                        40

knee-crooking: i.e., constantly bowing
doting . . . bondage: i.e., loving the role of the   45
fawning servant
provender: provisions, especially dry food for
animals; **cashiered:** dismissed
Whip me . . . knaves: (a common early modern
construction, the ethical dative, meaning "As for
me, I say whip such men")   50
trimmed: dressed up; **visages:** masks,
appearances
yet: still
Do . . . homage: honor themselves by looking
out for themselves

DISCOVERING SHAKESPEARE

(2) Teaser [1.1.20]: In Iago's description of Cassio, what does the following line mean: "A fellow almost damned in a fair wife" (1.1.20)? Is Cassio married? Why do you have this opinion? Come back to this question after you have read further in the play.
(3) Verse [1.1.54]: What does the irregular <u>verse</u> in lines 48–64 tell us about Iago's emotional state during this long speech?

It is as sure as you are Roderigo,   55
Were I the Moor, I would not be Iago.
In following him, I follow but myself.
Heaven is my judge, not I for love and duty,
But seeming so, for my peculiar end,°   **peculiar end:** private purpose
For when my outward action doth demonstrate   60
The native act and figure of my heart
In complement extern,° 'tis not long after   **my outward . . . complement extern:** i.e.,
But I will wear my heart upon my sleeve   when my behavior corresponds to my real feelings
For daws° to peck at. I am not what I am.   **daws:** jackdaws (proverbially foolish birds)
RODERIGO
What a full fortune does the thick-lips° owe°   **the thick-lips:** (a racist slur on Othello's African   65
If he can carry't thus!°   heritage); **owe:** own
IAGO   Call up her father,   **carry't thus:** bring it off (i.e., succeed)
Rouse him. Make after him, poison his delight,
Proclaim him in the streets. Incense her kinsmen,
And though he in a fertile climate dwell,
Plague him with flies. Though that his joy be joy,   70
Yet throw such chances of vexation° on't   **chances of vexation:** possibilities for misery and
As it may lose some color.°   embarrassment
RODERIGO   **lose some color:** i.e., his *joy* will fade
Here is her father's house. I'll call aloud.
IAGO
Do, with like timorous° accent and dire yell   **timorous:** frightening
As when, by night and negligence, the fire
Is spied in populous cities.   75
RODERIGO
What, ho, Brabantio! Signor Brabantio, ho!
IAGO
Awake! What, ho, Brabantio! Thieves! thieves!
Look to your house, your daughter, and your bags!
Thieves! thieves!   80
    [Enter Brabantio] above.
BRABANTIO
What is the reason of this terrible summons?
What is the matter there?
RODERIGO
Signor, is all your family within?
IAGO
Are your doors locked?
BRABANTIO   Why, wherefore ask you this?
IAGO
Zounds,° sir, you're robbed! For shame, put on your   **Zounds:** (an oath; originally "by God's [i.e.,   85
    gown!   Christ's] wounds")
Your heart is burst; you have lost half your soul.
Even now, now, very now,° an old black ram   **very now:** at this very moment
Is tupping° your white ewe. Arise, arise!   **tupping:** copulating with (used specifically of
Awake the snorting° citizens with the bell,   rams)
Or else the devil will make a grandsire of you.   **snorting:** snoring   90
Arise, I say!

DISCOVERING SHAKESPEARE

(4) Staging [1.1.73]: How would you stage this section of the scene when Iago and Roderigo rouse Brabantio from his bed?

BRABANTIO What, have you lost your wits?

RODERIGO

Most reverend signor, do you know my voice?

BRABANTIO

Not I. What are you?

RODERIGO

My name is Roderigo.

BRABANTIO   The worser welcome!

I have charged thee not to haunt about my doors.   95

In honest plainness thou hast heard me say

My daughter is not for thee. And now, in madness,

Being full of supper and distemp'ring draughts,°   **distemp'ring draughts:** intoxicating drinks

Upon malicious knavery dost thou come

To start my quiet.°   **start my quiet:** disturb my peace   100

RODERIGO

Sir, sir, sir —

BRABANTIO   But thou must needs be sure

My spirits° and my place have in their power   **spirits:** emotions (i.e., anger)

To make this bitter to thee.

RODERIGO   Patience, good sir.

BRABANTIO

What tell'st thou me of robbing? This is Venice;

My house is not a grange.°   **grange:** farmhouse   105

RODERIGO   Most grave Brabantio,

In simple and pure soul I come to you.

IAGO Zounds, sir, you are one of those that will not
serve God if the devil bid you. Because we come to do
you service, and you think we are ruffians, you'll have
your daughter covered with a Barbary horse;° you'll have   **covered . . . horse:** (another figure for bestial   110
your nephews° neigh to you; you'll have coursers for   copulation; Barbary was the home of Berbers, or
cousins,° and jennets for germans.°   Moors)

                                                    nephews: (kinsmen generally; here grandsons)

BRABANTIO   **coursers for cousins:** racehorses for relatives;

What profane wretch art thou?   **jennets for germans:** small Spanish horses for

IAGO I am one, sir, that comes to tell you your daughter   near kinsmen
and the Moor are making the beast with two backs.°   **beast with two backs:** (a visual symbol of   115

BRABANTIO   sexual intercourse)

Thou art a villain.

IAGO   You are — a senator.

BRABANTIO

This thou shalt answer. I know thee, Roderigo.

RODERIGO

Sir, I will answer anything. But I beseech you,

If 't be your pleasure and most wise consent,

As partly I find it is, that your fair daughter,

At this odd-even and dull watch° o' th' night,   120

Transported, with no worse nor better guard   **odd-even and dull watch:** i.e., in-between and

But with a knave of common hire, a gondolier,   sleepy hour, perhaps midnight (between evening
                                                      and morning)

DISCOVERING SHAKESPEARE

(5) <u>Shared Lines</u> [1.1.101]: How do the <u>shared lines</u> in 1.1.100–105 help suggest how the <u>verse</u> should be spoken by the actors?

To the gross clasps of a lascivious Moor –
If this be known to you, and your allowance,°   **allowance:** approval   125
We then have done you bold and saucy wrongs.
But if you know not this, my manners tell me,
We have your wrong rebuke. Do not believe
That, from the sense of° all civility,   **from the sense of:** against
I thus would play and trifle with your reverence.   130
Your daughter, if you have not given her leave,
I say again, hath made a gross revolt,
Tying her duty, beauty, wit, and fortunes
In an extravagant and wheeling° stranger   **extravagant and wheeling:** i.e., far from home
Of here and everywhere. Straight° satisfy yourself.   and rootless, roving   135
If she be in her chamber, or your house,   **Straight:** straightaway, immediately
Let loose on me the justice of the state
For thus deluding you.
BRABANTIO   Strike on the tinder,° ho!   **tinder:** tinderbox (for a light)
Give me a taper! Call up all my people!
This accident° is not unlike my dream.   **accident:** occurrence   140
Belief of it oppresses me already.
Light, I say! light!   *Exit [above].*
IAGO   Farewell, for I must leave you.
It seems not meet, nor wholesome to my place,
To be producted° – as, if I stay, I shall –   **producted:** produced (i.e., called as a witness)
Against the Moor. For I do know the state,   145
However this may gall him with some check,°   **check:** reprimand
Cannot with safety cast° him; for he's embarked   **cast:** dismiss
With such loud reason to the Cyprus wars,
Which even now stands in act,° that for their souls°   **stands in act:** is imminent; **for their souls:**
Another of his fathom° they have none   i.e., to save their souls   150
To lead their business; in which regard,   **fathom:** deep capacity (i.e., talent)
Though I do hate him as I do hell pains,
Yet, for necessity of present life,
I must show out a flag and sign of love,
Which is indeed but sign. That you shall surely find
  him,   155
Lead to the Sagittary° the raisèd search;   **the Sagittary:** (an inn)
And there will I be with him. So farewell.   *Exit.*
  Enter Brabantio [below, in his nightgown],° with   **nightgown:** dressing gown; **Torches:**
  Servants and Torches.°   torchbearers
BRABANTIO
It is too true an evil. Gone she is,
And what's to come of my despisèd time°   **despisèd time:** unfortunate life
Is nought but bitterness. Now, Roderigo,   160
Where didst thou see her? – O unhappy girl! –
With the Moor, say'st thou? – Who would be a father?–
How didst thou know 'twas she? – O, she deceives me

DISCOVERING SHAKESPEARE

(6) History [1.1.124]: Using the *Oxford English Dictionary* and/or other standard reference sources, look up the word "Moor" (1.1.124). What was the definition of the word in the early seventeenth century? Has its meaning changed substantially since that time?

(7) Metaphor [1.1.152]: As you read through the script, underline any references to "hell" or "the devil" made by or about Iago (cf. "I do hate him as I do hell pains" in 1.1.152). Why do you think the play exhibits such a strong metaphorical relationship between Iago and infernal punishment?

Past thought! – What said she to you? – Get more ta-
    pers!
Raise all my kindred! – Are they married, think you?   165

RODERIGO
Truly I think they are.

BRABANTIO
O heaven! How got she out? O treason of the blood!
Fathers, from hence trust not your daughters' minds
By what you see them act. Is there not charms
By which the property° of youth and maidhood   **property:** natural behavior   170
May be abused? Have you not read, Roderigo,
Of some such thing?

RODERIGO   Yes, sir, I have indeed.

BRABANTIO
Call up my brother. – O, would you had had her! –
Some one way, some another. – Do you know
Where we may apprehend her and the Moor?   175

RODERIGO
I think I can discover him, if you please
To get good guard and go along with me.

BRABANTIO
Pray you lead on. At every house I'll call;
I may command at most. – Get weapons, ho!
And raise some special officers of night.° –   **special . . . night:** (a famous Venetian nocturnal 180
On, good Roderigo; I will deserve° your pains.   *Exeunt.*   patrol)
                                      deserve: repay

♠ **1.2**° *Enter Othello, Iago, Attendants, with Torches.*   **1.2:** The street in front of the Sagittary

IAGO
Though in the trade of war I have slain men,
Yet do I hold it very stuff° o' th' conscience   **very stuff:** the essence
To do no contrived murder. I lack iniquity
Sometime to do me service. Nine or ten times
I had thought t' have yerked° him here under the ribs.   **yerked:** struck or (as with a horse) kicked *under* 5
                                        the ribs

OTHELLO
'Tis better as it is.

IAGO   Nay, but he prated,°   **prated:** babbled
And spoke such scurvy and provoking terms
Against your honor
That with the little godliness I have
I did full hard forbear° him. But I pray you, sir,   **did full hard forbear:** i.e., barely tolerated 10
Are you fast° married? Be assured of this,   **fast:** securely
That the magnifico° is much beloved,   **magnifico:** aristocrat (i.e., Brabantio)
And hath in his effect a voice potential
As double as the duke's.° He will divorce you,   **a voice . . . duke's:** i.e., an influence twice as
Or put upon you what restraint or grievance   great as the duke's 15
The law, with all his might to enforce it on,
Will give him cable.°   **give him cable:** i.e., allow him freedom

---

DISCOVERING SHAKESPEARE

(8) Characterization [1.1.173]: What kind of character is Brabantio? How old do you think he is? What type of clothes is he wearing? How does he feel about Desdemona marrying Othello?

OTHELLO   Let him do his spite.
My services which I have done the signory°
Shall out-tongue his complaints. 'Tis yet to know° –
Which, when I know that boasting is an honor,
I shall promulgate° – I fetch my life and being
From men of royal siege,° and my demerits°
May speak unbonneted to as proud a fortune
As this that I have reached.° For know, Iago,
But that I love the gentle Desdemona,
I would not my unhousèd free condition
Put into circumscription and confine°
For the sea's worth. But look, what lights come yond?
   Enter Cassio [and Officers] with Torches.

IAGO
Those are the raisèd° father and his friends.
You were best go in.

OTHELLO   Not I; I must be found.
My parts,° my title, and my perfect soul°
Shall manifest me° rightly. Is it they?

IAGO
By Janus,° I think no.

OTHELLO
The servants of the duke? And my lieutenant?
The goodness of the night upon you, friends!
What is the news?

CASSIO   The duke does greet you, general,
And he requires your haste-posthaste appearance
Even on the instant.

OTHELLO   What is the matter, think you?

CASSIO
Something from Cyprus, as I may divine.°
It is a business of some heat.° The galleys
Have sent a dozen sequent° messengers
This very night at one another's heels,
And many of the consuls, raised and met,
Are at the duke's already. You have been hotly called for;
When being not at your lodging to be found,
The Senate hath sent about° three several° quests
To search you out.

OTHELLO   'Tis well I am found by you.
I will but spend a word here in the house,
And go with you.   *[Exit.]*

CASSIO   Ancient, what makes he here?

IAGO
Faith,° he tonight hath boarded a land carrack.°
If it prove lawful prize, he's made forever.

CASSIO
I do not understand.

---

signory: Venetian political establishment
yet to know: still not generally known

promulgate: broadcast, make known
siege: seat (i.e., rank or status); **demerits:** merits, deserts (obsolete form)

May speak . . . have reached: i.e., can without boasting claim worldly success equal to that of Desdemona's family (*this that I have reached*)

my unhousèd . . . and confine: i.e., trade the outdoors for domesticity, my independence for limits

raisèd: roused, alarmed

parts: abilities; **perfect soul:** clear conscience
manifest me: i.e., make my case

Janus: the two-faced Roman god

as I may divine: i.e., I suppose
heat: intensity or urgency
sequent: consecutive

sent about: sent out; **several:** separate

Faith: by my faith, in faith (a mild oath); **carrack:** treasure ship

(Line numbers: 20, 25, 30, 35, 40, 45, 50)

DISCOVERING SHAKESPEARE

(9) Paraphrase [1.2.21]: Paraphrase the following lines by Othello: "I fetch my life and being/From men of royal siege, and my demerits/May speak unbonneted to as proud a fortune/As this that I have reached" (1.2.21–24). Why does he make this statement?

(10) History [1.2.49]: What was an "Ancient" (1.2.49)? What were his duties?

IAGO   He's married.
CASSIO   To who?
    [Enter Othello.]
IAGO
    Marry,° to – Come, captain, will you go?   **Marry:** (a mild form of the oath "By the Virgin
OTHELLO   Have with you.   Mary")
CASSIO
    Here comes another troop to seek for you.
    Enter Brabantio, Roderigo, with Officers and Torches.
IAGO
    It is Brabantio. General, be advised.   55
    He comes to bad intent.
OTHELLO   Holla! stand there!
RODERIGO
    Signor, it is the Moor.
BRABANTIO   Down with him, thief!
    [They draw on both sides.]
IAGO
    You, Roderigo! Come, sir, I am for you.°   **am for you:** challenge you
OTHELLO
    Keep up° your bright swords, for the dew will rust them.   **Keep up:** i.e., sheathe, put away
    Good signor, you shall more command with years   60
    Than with your weapons.
BRABANTIO
    O thou foul thief, where hast thou stowed my daugh-
       ter?
    Damned as thou art, thou hast enchanted her!
    For I'll refer me to all things of sense,
    If she in chains of magic were not bound,   65
    Whether a maid so tender, fair, and happy,
    So opposite to marriage that she shunned
    The wealthy curlèd darlings of our nation,
    Would ever have, t' incur a general mock,°   **a general mock:** universal laughter
    Run from her guardage to the sooty bosom   70
    Of such a thing as thou – to fear, not to delight.
    Judge me the world if 'tis not gross in sense°   **gross in sense:** obvious
    That thou hast practiced on her with foul charms,
    Abused her delicate youth with drugs or minerals
    That weakens motion.° I'll have't disputed on;°   **motion:** perception; **disputed on:** brought to   75
    'Tis probable, and palpable to thinking.   law
    I therefore apprehend and do attach° thee   **attach:** arrest
    For an abuser of the world, a practicer
    Of arts inhibited and out of warrant.
    Lay hold upon him. If he do resist,   80
    Subdue him at his peril.
OTHELLO   Hold your hands,
    Both you of my inclining and the rest.
    Were it my cue to fight, I should have known it
    Without a prompter. Where will you that I go
    To answer this your charge?   85

DISCOVERING SHAKESPEARE

(11) <u>Diction</u> [1.2.71]: Underline in your <u>script</u> the number of specific words like "magic" and "charms" that Brabantio uses to charge Othello with enchanting his daughter. How do these accusations help characterize Desdemona's father? (*Hint:* See not only 1.2.62–81, but also 1.3.60 ff. and 1.3.94 ff.)

BRABANTIO   To prison, till fit time
Of law and course of direct session°   **direct session:** regular trial
Call thee to answer.
OTHELLO   What if I do obey?
How may the duke be therewith satisfied,
Whose messengers are here about my side
Upon some present business of the state   90
To bring me to him?
OFFICER   'Tis true, most worthy signor.
The duke's in council, and your noble self
I am sure is sent for.
BRABANTIO   How? The duke in council?
In this time of the night? Bring him away.
Mine's not an idle° cause. The duke himself,   **idle:** inconsequential   95
Or any of my brothers of the state,
Cannot but feel this wrong as 'twere their own;
For if such actions may have passage free,
Bondslaves and pagans shall our statesmen be.   *Exeunt.*

&ea; **1.3**°   *Enter Duke, Senators, and Officers [with lights].*   **1.3:** The Venetian Senate Chamber

DUKE
There's no composition° in this news°   **composition:** consistency; **news:** newly
That gives them credit.   received information
FIRST SENATOR   Indeed they are disproportioned.
My letters say a hundred and seven galleys.
DUKE
And mine a hundred forty.
SECOND SENATOR   And mine two hundred.
But though they jump° not on a just account° –   **jump:** agree; **just account:** precise estimate   5
As in these cases where the aim° reports   **aim:** guess
'Tis oft with difference – yet do they all confirm
A Turkish fleet, and bearing up to Cyprus.
DUKE
Nay, it is possible enough to judgment.
I do not so secure me in the error   10
But the main article I do approve
In fearful sense.°   **I do not . . . sense:** the discrepancies of the
SAILOR   *Within*   reports aren't enough to cancel the frightening
            What, ho! what, ho! what, ho!   substance (*main article*) of them
   Enter Sailor.
OFFICER
A messenger from the galleys.
DUKE   Now, what's the business?
SAILOR
The Turkish preparation° makes for Rhodes.   **preparation:** forces, assembled fleet
So was I bid report here to the state   15
By Signor Angelo.

DISCOVERING SHAKESPEARE

(12) Geography [1.3.1]: Locate Venice, Cyprus, Turkey, and Rhodes on a map. Are the boundaries the same today as they were during the Renaissance? How long do you think sailing from one place to another would have taken? Which is closer to Cyprus: Venice or Turkey? Why would this information be important in the script?

DUKE
How say you by this change?
FIRST SENATOR   This cannot be
By no assay° of reason. 'Tis a pageant°

assay: test, effort; **pageant:** sideshow

To keep us in false gaze.° When we consider

in false gaze: looking the wrong way

Th' importancy of Cyprus to the Turk,   20
And let ourselves again but understand
That, as it more concerns the Turk than Rhodes,
So may he with more facile question bear it,°

with . . . it: capture it more easily

For that it stands not in such warlike brace,°

brace: state of defense

But altogether lacks th' abilities   25
That Rhodes is dressed in — if we make thought of this,
We must not think the Turk is so unskillful
To leave that latest° which concerns him first,

latest: last

Neglecting an attempt of ease and gain
To wake and wage° a danger profitless.

wake and wage: rouse and risk   30

DUKE
Nay, in all confidence, he's not for Rhodes.
OFFICER
Here is more news.
    Enter a Messenger.
MESSENGER
The Ottomites,° reverend and gracious,°

Ottomites: Turkish fleet (Turks and Ottomites
seem to have been identified in the Elizabethan

Steering with due° course toward the isle of Rhodes,

mind); **reverend and gracious:** (honorific term   35
of address to the assembly)

Have there injointed° them with an after fleet.°

due: direct
injointed: combined (themselves); **after fleet:**
a subordinate or secondary navy

FIRST SENATOR
Ay, so I thought. How many, as you guess?
MESSENGER
Of thirty sail; and now they do restem°

restem: steer again

Their backward course, bearing with frank appearance°

with frank appearance: openly, without deceit

Their purposes toward Cyprus. Signor Montano,
Your trusty and most valiant servitor,   40
With his free duty° recommends° you thus

free duty: unlimited loyalty; **recommends:**
informs

And prays you to believe him.
DUKE
'Tis certain then for Cyprus.
Marcus Luccicos, is not he in town?
FIRST SENATOR
He's now in Florence.   45
DUKE
Write from us to him post-posthaste. Dispatch!
FIRST SENATOR
Here comes Brabantio and the valiant Moor.
    Enter Brabantio, Othello, Cassio, Iago, Roderigo, and
    Officers.
DUKE
Valiant Othello, we must straight° employ you

straight: straightaway, immediately

Against the general enemy Ottoman.
    [To Brabantio]

DISCOVERING SHAKESPEARE

(13) History [1.3.20]: What religion were most people in Turkey during the Renaissance? Why does the Duke refer to them as "the general enemy Ottoman" (1.3.49)?

I did not see you. Welcome, gentle signor.   50
We lacked your counsel and your help tonight.
BRABANTIO
So did I yours. Good your grace, pardon me.
Neither my place,° nor aught I heard of business,   **place:** position (as senator)
Hath raised me from my bed; nor doth the general care
Take hold on me; for my particular grief   55
Is of so floodgate° and o'erbearing nature   **of so floodgate:** so torrential
That it engluts° and swallows other sorrows,   **engluts:** gulps down
And it is still itself.
DUKE   Why, what's the matter?
BRABANTIO
My daughter! O, my daughter!
ALL   Dead?
BRABANTIO   Ay, to me.
She is abused,° stol'n from me, and corrupted   **abused:** deceived   60
By spells and medicines bought of mountebanks;°   **mountebanks:** quacks or scam artists (for which
For nature so prepost'rously to err,   Venice was notorious)
Being not deficient,° blind, or lame of sense,   **deficient:** feebleminded
Sans witchcraft could not.
DUKE
Whoe'er he be that in this foul proceeding   65
Hath thus beguiled your daughter of herself,
And you of her, the bloody book of law
You shall yourself read in the bitter letter
After your own sense;° yea, though our proper° son   **bloody . . . sense:** i.e., you may interpret the law
Stood in your action.°   in the strictest sense that suits you; **our proper:**   70
                                                      my own
BRABANTIO   Humbly I thank your grace.   **Stood in your action:** were the object of your
Here is the man – this Moor, whom now, it seems,   charges
Your special mandate for the state affairs
Hath hither brought.
ALL   We are very sorry for't.
DUKE   [To Othello]
What, in your own part, can you say to this?
BRABANTIO
Nothing, but this is so.   75
OTHELLO
Most potent, grave, and reverend signors,
My very noble and approved° good masters,   **approved:** tested by experience
That I have ta'en away this old man's daughter,
It is most true; true I have married her.
The very head and front of my offending   80
Hath this extent, no more. Rude° am I in my speech,   **Rude:** unskilled, unpolished
And little blessed with the soft phrase of peace;
For since these arms of mine had seven years' pith°   **pith:** strength
Till now some nine moons wasted,° they have used   **wasted:** gone by
Their dearest° action in the tented field;   **dearest:** most valuable   85
And little of this great world can I speak

DISCOVERING SHAKESPEARE
(14) <u>Metaphor</u> [1.3.56]: Explain Brabantio's "floodgate" <u>image</u> in 1.3.56–58.
(15) <u>Diction</u> [1.3.76]: According to the *Oxford English Dictionary*, how did the meanings of the words "potent," "grave," and "reverend" (1.3.76) differ around the year 1605? Why does Othello use each of these terms in the opening of his speech to the Duke and his senators?

More than pertains to feats of broils° and battle;   **broils:** strife, hurly-burly
And therefore little shall I grace my cause
In speaking for myself. Yet, by your gracious patience,
I will a round° unvarnished tale deliver   **round:** plain   90
Of my whole course of love – what drugs, what
   charms,
What conjuration, and what mighty magic
(For such proceeding I am charged withal)
I won his daughter.

BRABANTIO   A maiden never bold;   95
Of spirit so still and quiet that her motion
Blushed° at herself; and she – in spite of nature,   **her motion / Blushed:** her own feelings caused
Of years, of country, credit,° everything –   her to blush
To fall in love with what she feared to look on!   **credit:** reputation
It is a judgment maimed and most imperfect
That will confess perfection so could err   100
Against all rules of nature, and must be driven
To find out practices of cunning hell°   **must be driven . . . hell:** i.e., the reasonable
Why this should be. I therefore vouch° again   mind must seek diabolical plots
That with some mixtures pow'rful o'er the blood,°   **vouch:** claim
Or with some dram,° conjured° to this effect,   **blood:** passions, sexual appetite   105
He wrought upon her.   **dram:** small portion; **conjured:** bewitched,
    magically produced (accent on second syllable)

DUKE   To vouch this is no proof,
Without more wider and more overt° test   **more wider . . . overt:** more thorough and
Than these thin habits and poor likelihoods   manifest (i.e., convincing)
Of modern seeming° do prefer against him.   **these thin . . . seeming:** i.e., these flimsy signs
    and conclusions drawn from ordinary appearances

SENATOR   110
But, Othello, speak.
Did you by indirect and forcèd° courses
Subdue and poison this young maid's affections?   **forcèd:** (1) unnatural, (2) coercive
Or came it by request, and such fair question°
As soul to soul affordeth?   **question:** talk, conversation

OTHELLO   I do beseech you,   115
Send for the lady to the Sagittary
And let her speak of me before her father.
If you do find me foul° in her report,   **foul:** ugly (also "dark," perhaps Othello's ironic
The trust, the office, I do hold of you   reference to his own color)
Not only take away, but let your sentence
Even fall upon my life.   120

DUKE   Fetch Desdemona hither.

OTHELLO
Ancient, conduct them; you best know the place.
        [Exit two or three Officers with Iago.]
And till she come, as truly as to heaven
I do confess the vices of my blood,
So justly to your grave ears I'll present
How I did thrive in this fair lady's love,   125
And she in mine.

DISCOVERING SHAKESPEARE

(16) Characterization [1.3.100]: Write a brief description of Desdemona based on Brabantio's speech about her in 1.3.94–106. Then create another image of her taken from Othello's long speech in 1.3.128–170. How do these two accounts of the same woman differ? Why does each man paint a different verbal portrait of her?

DUKE

  Say it, Othello.

OTHELLO

  Her father loved me, oft invited me,

  Still° questioned me the story of my life

  From year to year – the battles, sieges, fortunes

  That I have passed.

  I ran it through, even from my boyish days

  To th' very moment that he bade me tell it.

  Wherein I spoke of most disastrous° chances,

  Of moving accidents by flood and field;°

  Of hairbreadth scapes i' th' imminent deadly breach;°

  Of being taken by the insolent° foe

  And sold to slavery. Of my redemption thence

  And portance° in my traveler's history,°

  Wherein of anters° vast and deserts idle,

  Rough quarries, rocks, and hills whose heads touch
    heaven,

  It was my hint° to speak – such was my process;°

  And of the cannibals that each other eat,

  The anthropophagi,° and men whose heads

  Do grow beneath their shoulders. These things to hear

  Would Desdemona seriously incline;

  But still the house affairs would draw her thence,

  Which ever as she could with haste dispatch,

  She'd come again, and with a greedy ear

  Devour up my discourse. Which I observing,

  Took once a pliant° hour, and found good means

  To draw from her a prayer of earnest heart

  That I would all my pilgrimage dilate,°

  Whereof by parcels° she had something heard,

  But not intentively.° I did consent,

  And often did beguile her of her tears

  When I did speak of some distressful stroke

  That my youth suffered. My story being done,

  She gave me for my pains a world of kisses.

  She swore in faith 'twas strange, 'twas passing strange;

  'Twas pitiful, 'twas wondrous pitiful.

  She wished she had not heard it, yet she wished

  That heaven had made her such a man. She thanked
    me,

  And bade me, if I had a friend that loved her,

  I should but teach him how to tell my story,

  And that would woo her. Upon this hint° I spake.

  She loved me for the dangers I had passed,

  And I loved her that she did pity them.

  This only is the witchcraft I have used.

Still: constantly

130

disastrous: unlucky (Latin "ill-starred")

accidents by flood and field: occurrences on   135
sea and land

in . . . deadly breach: gap in a defense inviting
immediate disaster

insolent: (1) arrogant, (2) insulting

portance: behavior, bearing; **traveler's history:**   140
(a minor sub-genre of writing c. 1600, often
containing tall tales)

anters: caves

hint: occasion, opportunity; **process:** drift

anthropophagi: man-eaters

145

150

pliant: convenient

dilate: expand upon

by parcels: in bits and pieces

intentively: i.e., with her full attention   155

160

hint: opportunity (as at l. 142)   165

DISCOVERING SHAKESPEARE

(17) <u>Verse</u> **[1.3.131]:** Othello's <u>short line</u> in 1.3.131 ("That I have passed") implies that some stage action covers the missing six <u>beats</u> in the line. What could he do in terms of <u>blocking</u> or gesture to fill up this gap in the <u>verse</u> line?

(18) History [1.3.144]: What were the "anthropophagi" (1.3.144)? Why does Othello mention them at this point in his speech?

(19) <u>Plot</u> **[1.3.167]:** Reread Othello's claim that Desdemona "loved me for the dangers I had passed, / And I loved her that she did pity them" (1.3.167–168). Do you think this explanation predicts a stable foundation for their marriage?

Here comes the lady. Let her witness it.   170
  Enter Desdemona, Iago, Attendants.

DUKE
I think this tale would win my daughter too.
Good Brabantio,
Take up this mangled matter at the best.
Men do their broken weapons rather use
Than their bare hands.   175

BRABANTIO   I pray you hear her speak.
If she confess that she was half the wooer,
Destruction on my head if my bad blame
Light on the man! Come hither, gentle mistress.
Do you perceive in all this noble company
Where most you owe obedience?   180

DESDEMONA   My noble father,
I do perceive here a divided duty.
To you I am bound for life and education.°   **education:** rearing
My life and education both do learn me
How to respect you: you are the lord of duty;
I am hitherto your daughter. But here's my husband;   185
And so much duty as my mother showed
To you, preferring you before her father,
So much I challenge° that I may profess   **challenge:** assert the right
Due to the Moor my lord.

BRABANTIO   God be with you! I have done.
Please it your grace, on to the state affairs.   190
I had rather to adopt a child than get° it.   **get:** beget
Come hither, Moor.
I here do give thee that with all my heart
Which, but thou hast already,° with all my heart   **but thou hast already:** if you didn't have it already
I would keep from thee. For your sake,° jewel,   195
I am glad at soul I have no other child,   **For your sake:** thanks to you
For thy escape° would teach me tyranny,   **escape:** transgression, escapade
To hang clogs° on them. I have done, my lord.   **clogs:** weights (of the kind attached to prisoners; in the seventeenth century they were made of blocks of wood)

DUKE
Let me speak like yourself° and lay a sentence°   **like yourself:** as you should; **sentence:** brief sermon or maxim (i.e., the following rhymed couplets of advice)
Which, as a grece° or step, may help these lovers   200
Into your favor.
When remedies are past, the griefs are ended   **grece:** stairstep
By seeing the worst, which late on hopes depended.°   **When remedies . . . depended:** i.e., disappointment is best mended by facing the unhappy outcome that you feared
To mourn a mischief that is past and gone
Is the next way to draw new mischief on.   205
What cannot be preserved when fortune takes,
Patience her injury a mock'ry makes.°   **What cannot . . . mock'ry makes:** to show *patience* when one is unfortunate is to ridicule and thus show superiority to *fortune*
The robbed that smiles steals something from the thief;
He robs himself that spends a bootless grief.°   **spends a bootless grief:** indulges in worthless lamentation

BRABANTIO
So° let the Turk of Cyprus us beguile:°   **So:** in that case; **of Cyprus us beguile:** cheat us out of possession of Cyprus   210

DISCOVERING SHAKESPEARE

(20) Paraphrase [1.3.191]: Paraphrase into modern English Brabantio's lament that he would rather adopt a child "than get it" (1.3.191). How does he feel about fatherhood at this point in the play?

(21) Rhyme [1.3.210]: Compare the rhyme scheme of the Duke's speech in 1.3.202–209 with the subsequent lines by Brabantio in 210–219. To what extent is Brabantio mimicking the rhyme, rhythm, and sententiousness of the Duke's speech? Why does he do so?

We lose it not so long as we can smile.
He bears the sentence well that nothing bears
But the free comfort which from thence he hears;
But he bears both the sentence and the sorrow
That to pay grief must of poor patience borrow.°
These sentences, to sugar, or to gall,
Being strong on both sides, are equivocal.
But words are words. I never yet did hear
That the bruised heart was pierced° through the ear.
I humbly beseech you proceed to th' affairs of state.

DUKE   The Turk with a most mighty preparation makes
for Cyprus. Othello, the fortitude° of the place is best
known to you; and though we have there a substitute° of
most allowed° sufficiency, yet opinion,° a more sovereign
mistress of effects,° throws a more safer voice on you.
You must therefore be content to slubber° the gloss
of your new fortunes with this more stubborn° and
boist'rous expedition.

OTHELLO
The tyrant custom, most grave senators,
Hath made the flinty and steel couch of war
My thrice-driven bed of down.° I do agnize
A natural and prompt alacrity
I find in hardness;° and do undertake
This present wars against the Ottomites.
Most humbly, therefore, bending to your state,°
I crave fit disposition° for my wife,
Due reference of place,° and exhibition,°
With such accommodation and besort°
As levels with° her breeding.

DUKE
Why, at her father's.

BRABANTIO   I will not have it so.

OTHELLO
Nor I.

DESDEMONA   Nor would I there reside,
To put my father in impatient thoughts
By being in his eye. Most gracious duke,
To my unfolding lend your prosperous° ear,
And let me find a charter° in your voice,
T' assist my simpleness.°

DUKE
What would you, Desdemona?

DESDEMONA
That I did love the Moor to live with him,
My downright violence,° and storm of fortunes,°
May trumpet to the world. My heart's subdued
Even to the very quality° of my lord.

He bears . . . borrow: i.e., he who can simply 215
take the advice and forget the injury is lucky, but
he who is still sorrowful (who has to borrow from
patience to *pay* a debt to *grief*) has to put up with
the lecture and the misery

pierced: (some editors emend to "pieced"—i.e., 220
"mended")

fortitude: defensive strength, fortification
substitute: governor or deputy (another instance
of replacement in the play)
allowed: acknowledged; **opinion:** reputation 225
more sovereign mistress of effects: better
predictor of outcomes
slubber: stain or darken
stubborn: untamable

230

thrice-driven bed of down: feather bed
winnowed three times to make it supersoft
agnize . . . hardness: i.e., recognize in myself a
taste (*alacrity*) for hardship or challenge
bending to your state: i.e., bowing to your 235
position
fit disposition: appropriate arrangements
reference of place: assignment of residence;
exhibition: allowance
besort: companions
levels with: matches 240

prosperous: favorable
a charter: license, authority 245
simpleness: inexperience

downright violence: obvious unconventionality
(*violence* against propriety); **storm of fortunes:** 250
i.e., the tempestuous results of that
unconventionality
quality: essential nature

DISCOVERING SHAKESPEARE

(22) Plot [1.3.240]: Why are Othello and Brabantio in agreement that Desdemona should not continue to live with her father?

I saw Othello's visage in his mind,°
And to his honors and his valiant parts°
Did I my soul and fortunes consecrate.
So that, dear lords, if I be left behind,
A moth of peace, and he go to the war,
The rites° for why I love him are bereft me,
And I a heavy interim shall support
By his dear° absence. Let me go with him.

OTHELLO
Let her have your voice.
Vouch with me, heaven, I therefore beg it not
To please the palate of my appetite,
Nor to comply with heat° – the young affects°
In me defunct – and proper satisfaction;
But to be free and bounteous to her mind.
And heaven defend your good souls that you think
I will your serious and great business scant
When she is with me. No, when light-winged toys
Of feathered Cupid° seel with wanton dullness
My speculative and officed instruments,°
That° my disports° corrupt and taint my business,
Let housewives make a skillet of my helm,
And all indign° and base adversities
Make head° against my estimation!°

DUKE
Be it as you shall privately determine,
Either for her stay or going. Th' affair cries haste,
And speed must answer it.

SENATOR
You must away tonight.

OTHELLO   With all my heart.

DUKE
At nine i' th' morning here we'll meet again.
Othello, leave some officer behind,
And he shall our commission bring to you,
And such things else of quality and respect
As doth import° you.

OTHELLO   So please your grace, my ancient;
A man he is of honesty and trust.
To his conveyance° I assign my wife,
With what else needful your good grace shall think
To be sent after me.

DUKE   Let it be so.
Good night to every one.
   [To Brabantio]   And, noble signor,
If virtue no delighted beauty lack,°
Your son-in-law is far more fair than black.

SENATOR
Adieu, brave Moor. Use Desdemona well.

I saw . . . his mind: i.e., I looked within Othello, replacing his dark face (*visage*) with his *mind*
parts: talents, gifts   255

rites: ceremonies or perhaps also "rights," privileges of marriage
dear: costly, grievous

                                                   260

comply with heat: follow the dictates of passion; **young affects:** youthful desires

                                                   265

light-winged toys . . . Cupid: trivial sports of love   270
seel . . . instruments: i.e., blind my vision (*speculative and officed instruments*) with the low desires of the body
That: such that; **disports:** i.e., sexual pleasures
indign: shameful
Make head: mount an attack; **estimation:** reputation   275

import: concern

conveyance: escorting   285

If virtue . . . lack: if worthiness (*virtue*) has the power to be delightful (*delighted*)   290

DISCOVERING SHAKESPEARE

(23) Characterization [1.3.278]: How does Othello respond to the Senator's command that he and Desdemona must leave for Cyprus immediately (1.3.278)? What do you make of the fact that Desdemona does not speak at this moment?

BRABANTIO
Look to her, Moor, if thou hast eyes to see:
She has deceived her father, and may thee.
                    Exit [Duke, with Senators, Officers, etc.].

OTHELLO
My life upon her faith!° – Honest Iago,   **faith:** fidelity, faithfulness
My Desdemona must I leave to thee.   295
I prithee let thy wife attend on her,
And bring them after in the best advantage.°   **in the best advantage:** at the most opportune
Come, Desdemona. I have but an hour   time
Of love, of worldly matters and direction,°   **direction:** overseeing business
To spend with thee. We must obey the time.   300
                    Exit [Othello with Desdemona].

RODERIGO   Iago –
IAGO   What say'st thou, noble heart?
RODERIGO   What will I do, think'st thou?
IAGO   Why, go to bed and sleep.
RODERIGO   I will incontinently° drown myself.   **incontinently:** immediately   305
IAGO   If thou dost, I shall never love thee after. Why,
    thou silly gentleman?
RODERIGO   It is silliness to live when to live is torment,
    and then have we a prescription to die when death is
    our physician.°   **have . . . physician:** ancient custom (*prescription*)   310
                                                                leads us to kill ourselves if doing so will cure our
                                                                ills
IAGO   O villainous! I have looked upon the world for
    four times seven years, and since I could distinguish be-
    twixt a benefit and an injury, I never found man that
    knew how to love himself. Ere I would say I would
    drown myself for the love of a guinea hen,° I would   **guinea hen:** bird (figuratively, slang term for a   315
    change my humanity with a baboon.   woman; cf. "chick")
RODERIGO   What should I do? I confess it is my shame
    to be so fond, but it is not in my virtue° to amend it.   **virtue:** power, ability
IAGO   Virtue? a fig! 'Tis in ourselves that we are thus or
    thus. Our bodies are our gardens, to the which our   320
    wills° are gardeners; so that if we will plant nettles or **wills:** desires (but the term is sexually loaded: in
    sow lettuce, set hyssop and weed up thyme, supply   the period its specific sense of "erotic desire" was
    it with one gender° of herbs or distract° it with many –   supplemented with numerous connotations, from
    either to have it sterile with idleness or manured with   "penis" to "vagina")
    industry° – why, the power and corrigible authority° of   **gender:** kind (cf. "genre"); **distract:** divide
    this lies in our wills. If the beam of our lives had not   **sterile . . . industry:** either unproductive or   325
    one scale of reason to poise° another of sensuality, the   richly cultivated; **corrigible authority:** power
    blood and baseness° of our natures would conduct us to   to correct
    most prepost'rous conclusions. But we have reason to   **poise:** counterbalance
    cool our raging motions,° our carnal stings or unbitted°   **blood and baseness:** bestial instincts
    lusts; whereof I take this that you call love to be a sect **motions:** impulses; **unbitted:** uncontrolled,   330
    or scion.°   unbridled
RODERIGO   It cannot be.   **a sect or scion:** an offshoot or a cutting
IAGO   It is merely° a lust of the blood and a permission of **merely:** completely (i.e., nothing more than)
    the will. Come, be a man! Drown thyself? Drown cats   335
    and blind puppies! I have professed me thy friend, and

DISCOVERING SHAKESPEARE

(24) **Prose** [1.3.301]: Why does the scene shift from <u>verse</u> to <u>prose</u> after the departure of Desdemona and Othello in 1.3.300?

(25) **Paraphrase** [1.3.327]: <u>Paraphrase</u> the last two sentences in Iago's speech to Roderigo in 1.3.326–332. What does he mean by the terms "raging motions," "carnal stings," and "unbitted lusts"?

I confess me knit to thy deserving with cables of per-
durable° toughness. I could never better stead° thee than
now. Put money in thy purse. Follow thou the wars; defeat thy favor° with an usurped beard. I say, put money
in thy purse. It cannot be long that Desdemona should
continue her love to the Moor – put money in thy
purse – nor he his to her. It was a violent commencement in her, and thou shalt see an answerable seques-
tration° – put but money in thy purse. These Moors are
changeable in their wills – fill thy purse with money.
The food that to him now is as luscious as locusts° shall
be to him shortly as bitter as coloquintida.° She must
change for youth: when she is sated with his body, she
will find the errors of her choice. Therefore put money
in thy purse. If thou wilt needs damn thyself, do it a
more delicate° way than drowning. Make° all the money
thou canst. If sanctimony° and a frail vow betwixt an
erring° barbarian and supersubtle Venetian be not too
hard for my wits and all the tribe of hell, thou shalt
enjoy her. Therefore make money. A pox of° drowning
thyself! – it is clean out of the way.° Seek thou rather to
be hanged in compassing thy joy than to be drowned
and go without her.°

RODERIGO   Wilt thou be fast° to my hopes, if I depend on
the issue?°

IAGO   Thou art sure of me. Go, make money. I have told
thee often, and I retell thee again and again, I hate the
Moor. My cause is hearted;° thine hath no less reason.
Let us be conjunctive° in our revenge against him. If
thou canst cuckold him,° thou dost thyself a pleasure,
me a sport. There are many events in the womb of
time, which will be delivered. Traverse,° go, provide thy
money! We will have more of this tomorrow. Adieu.

RODERIGO   Where shall we meet i' th' morning?

IAGO   At my lodging.

RODERIGO   I'll be with thee betimes.°

IAGO   Go to,° farewell. – Do you hear, Roderigo?

RODERIGO   I'll sell all my land.   *Exit.*

IAGO
Thus do I ever make my fool my purse;
For I mine own gained knowledge should profane
If I would time expend with such a snipe°
But for my sport and profit. I hate the Moor,
And it is thought abroad that 'twixt my sheets
H'as done my office.° I know not if 't be true,
But I, for mere suspicion in that kind,
Will do as if for surety. He holds me well;°
The better shall my purpose work on him.

perdurable: unbreakable; **stead:** help

defeat thy favor: undo your facial appearance   340
(i.e., disguise yourself by putting on *an usurped*
[counterfeit] *beard*)

answerable sequestration: equivalent   345
separation

locusts: carobs, known for their sweet juice
coloquintida: medicine made from the
colocynth, a bitter apple

                                                         350

delicate: pleasant; **Make:** raise
sanctimony: holiness (here false virtue or
faithfulness?)
erring: wandering   355
A pox of: i.e., "a curse on," "to hell with"
(*pox*=venereal disease)
clean out of the way: i.e., out of the question
Seek thou . . . without her: i.e., risk death in
trying to win her rather than die and have no   360
chance
fast: faithful
depend on the issue: i.e., wait to see the
outcome
hearted: i.e., lodged deep in my heart
                                                         365
conjunctive: united
cuckold him: commit adultery with his wife

Traverse: i.e., get moving, onward

                                                         370

betimes: early
Go to: (conventional expression of impatience or
agreement—"all right, then" or "you see")

                                                         375

snipe: dupe, fool

office: business (i.e., sexual)   380

holds me well: thinks highly of me

DISCOVERING SHAKESPEARE

(26) <u>Plot</u> [1.3.356]: How many times in this scene does Iago tell Roderigo to "put money in thy purse" (1.3.339) or "make money" (1.3.356)? Why is Iago so concerned with the amount of money Roderigo has?

(27) <u>Paraphrase</u> [1.3.379]: What does Iago mean when he says that "it is thought abroad that 'twixt my sheets [the Moor has] done my office" (1.3.379–380)? Do you think this is true? Why or why not?

Cassio's a proper° man. Let me see now:
To get his place,° and to plume up my will°
In double knavery – How, how? – Let's see: –
After some time, to abuse Othello's ears
That he is too familiar with his wife.
He hath a person and a smooth dispose°
To be suspected – framed to make women false.
The Moor is of a free° and open nature
That thinks men honest that but seem to be so;
And will as tenderly be led by th' nose
As asses are.
I have't! It is engendered! Hell and night
Must bring this monstrous birth to the world's light.

[Exit.]

proper: (1) good-looking, (2) dutiful, responsible
place: position, job; **plume up my will:** i.e., 385
pride myself on getting what I want (*to plume* is to
show self-satisfaction, to preen)

dispose: manner
390

free: unreserved, unsuspicious

395

❧ **2.1°** *Enter Montano and two Gentlemen.*

2.1: Cyprus, near the harbor

MONTANO
 What from the cape can you discern at sea?
FIRST GENTLEMAN
 Nothing at all: it is a high-wrought flood.°
 I cannot 'twixt the heaven and the main°
 Descry° a sail.
MONTANO
 Methinks the wind hath spoke aloud at land;
 A fuller blast ne'er shook our battlements.
 If it hath ruffianed so upon the sea,
 What ribs of oak,° when mountains melt on them,
 Can hold the mortise?° What shall we hear of this?
SECOND [GENTLEMAN]
 A segregation° of the Turkish fleet.
 For do but stand upon the foaming shore,
 The chidden billow° seems to pelt the clouds;
 The wind-shaked surge, with high and monstrous
  mane,°
 Seems to cast water on the burning Bear°
 And quench the Guards of th' ever-fixèd pole.°
 I never did like molestation° view
 On the enchafèd° flood.
MONTANO   If that the Turkish fleet
 Be not ensheltered and embayed, they are drowned;
 It is impossible to bear it out.
  Enter a [third] Gentleman.
THIRD [GENTLEMAN]
 News, lads! Our wars are done.
 The desperate tempest hath so banged the Turks
 That their designment halts.° A noble ship of Venice
 Hath seen a grievous wrack and sufferance°
 On most part of their fleet.

high-wrought flood: turbulent sea
main: sea
Descry: discern, make out

5

ribs of oak: curved frame of a ship's hull
hold the mortise: hold their joints together

segregation: scattering (i.e., defeat) 10

chidden billow: i.e., driven wave (past tense of
"chide," to scold or compel by scolding)
mane: (figuratively the foam of the *surge* is like a
monster's mane; with a pun on "main," sea)
burning Bear: constellation Ursa Minor 15
Guards . . . pole: two attendant stars, known as
the "guardians" of the polestar
molestation: turmoil
enchafèd: furious, enraged

20

designment halts: naval plan limps
wrack and sufferance: devastation and injury

DISCOVERING SHAKESPEARE

(28) Teaser [2.1.14]: What were "the burning Bear" and "th' ever-fixèd pole" (2.1.14–15)? How were stars and constellations used for navigation during the Renaissance?

MONTANO
    How? Is this true?   25

THIRD [GENTLEMAN]   The ship is here put in,
    A Veronesa.° Michael Cassio,
    Lieutenant to the warlike Moor, Othello,
    Is come on shore; the Moor himself at sea,
    And is in full commission here for Cyprus.

Veronesa: (probably a ship supplied by the city of Verona, but perhaps a particular kind of vessel)

MONTANO
    I am glad on't. 'Tis a worthy governor.   30

THIRD [GENTLEMAN]
    But this same Cassio, though he speak of comfort°
    Touching the Turkish loss, yet he looks sadly
    And prays the Moor be safe, for they were parted
    With foul and violent tempest.

of comfort: i.e., with relief

MONTANO   Pray heavens he be;
    For I have served him, and the man commands
    Like a full soldier. Let's to the seaside – ho! –   35
    As well to see the vessel that's come in
    As to throw out our eyes for brave Othello,
    Even till we make the main and th' aerial blue
    An indistinct regard.°

Even till . . . regard: until we can't distinguish the blues of sea and sky   40

GENTLEMAN   Come, let's do so;
    For every minute is expectancy
    Of more arrivance.
       Enter Cassio.

CASSIO
    Thanks, you the valiant of the warlike isle,
    That so approve° the Moor! O, let the heavens
    Give him defense against the elements,   45
    For I have lost him on a dangerous sea!

approve: admire, support

MONTANO
    Is he well shipped?

CASSIO
    His bark is stoutly timbered, and his pilot
    Of very expert and approved allowance;
    Therefore my hopes, not surfeited to death,   50
    Stand in bold cure.°

my hopes . . . bold cure: i.e., since I haven't allowed myself to hope too much (*hopes, not surfeited to death*), the chances of my getting my wish are good (*Stand in bold cure*)

[VOICES]   *(Within)* A sail, a sail, a sail!

CASSIO
    What noise?

GENTLEMAN
    The town is empty; on the brow o' th' sea
    Stand ranks of people, and they cry "A sail!"

CASSIO
    My hopes do shape him for the governor.°   55
     [A shot.]

My . . . governor: i.e., "I hope this is Othello's ship"

GENTLEMAN
    They do discharge their shot of courtesy:
    Our friends at least.

DISCOVERING SHAKESPEARE

(29) <u>Staging</u> [2.1.34]: Find as many references as possible in the first 51 lines of 2.1 that suggest the severity of the storm at sea. If you were directing a production of the play, how would you indicate the foul weather through lighting, sound effects, music, and/or stage movement?

CASSIO   I pray you, sir, go forth
And give us truth who 'tis that is arrived.

GENTLEMAN
I shall.   *Exit.*

MONTANO
But, good lieutenant, is your general wived?   60

CASSIO
Most fortunately. He hath achieved a maid
That paragons description and wild fame;°   **paragons . . . fame:** surpasses the wildest praise
One that excels the quirks° of blazoning° pens,   **quirks:** turns of phrase; **blazoning:** descriptive (with the suggestion of praise)
And in th' essential vesture of creation
Does tire the ingener.°   **essential vesture . . . ingener:** i.e., her native   65
    Enter Gentleman.   excellence wearies the would-be inventor (*ingener*)
             How now? Who has put in?   of praise

GENTLEMAN
'Tis one Iago, ancient to the general.

CASSIO
H'as had most favorable and happy speed:°   **happy speed:** good fortune (as well as pace)
Tempests themselves, high seas, and howling winds,
The guttered° rocks and congregated sands,   **guttered:** grooved, jagged
Traitors ensteeped° to enclog the guiltless keel,   **ensteeped:** submerged   70
As having sense of beauty, do omit
Their mortal° natures, letting go safely by   **mortal:** deadly
The divine Desdemona.

MONTANO   What is she?

CASSIO
She that I spake of, our great captain's captain,
Left in the conduct of the bold Iago,   75
Whose footing° here anticipates our thoughts   **footing:** landing
A sennight's° speed. Great Jove, Othello guard,   **sennight's:** week's
And swell his sail with thine own pow'rful breath,
That he may bless this bay with his tall ship,
Make love's quick pants° in Desdemona's arms,   **That . . . Make love's quick pants:** i.e., that he   80
Give renewed fire to our extincted° spirits,   may experience the rapid breathing of joyous love
And bring all Cyprus comfort!   **extincted:** extinguished, dampened
    Enter Desdemona, Iago, Roderigo, and Emilia [with
    Attendants].   O, behold!
The riches of the ship is come on shore!
You men of Cyprus, let her have your knees.°   **let her have your knees:** i.e., bow to her
Hail to thee, lady! and the grace of heaven,
Before, behind thee, and on every hand,   85
Enwheel thee round!

DESDEMONA   I thank you, valiant Cassio.
What tidings can you tell me of my lord?

CASSIO
He is not yet arrived, nor know I aught
But that he's well and will be shortly here.   90

DESDEMONA
O but I fear! How lost you company?

DISCOVERING SHAKESPEARE

(30) Characterization [2.1.60]: Write a characterization of Cassio based principally on his speeches in the first 99 lines of 2.1. On what weakness or peculiarity in Cassio's behavior does Iago focus to help initiate his revenge?

(31) Epithets [2.1.87]: Find as many epithets as you can in 2.1, such as "the warlike Moor" (2.1.27), "The divine Desdemona" (73), and "valiant Cassio" (87). To what extent do these descriptors help form our opinions of the characters?

CASSIO
  The great contention of sea and skies
  Parted our fellowship.
[VOICES]   *(Within)* A sail, a sail! *[A shot.]*
CASSIO   But hark. A sail!
GENTLEMAN
  They give their greeting to the citadel;
  This likewise is a friend.   95
CASSIO   See for the news.
                      [Exit Gentleman.]
  Good ancient, you are welcome.
    [To Emilia]   Welcome, mistress. –
  Let it not gall your patience, good Iago,
  That I extend my manners.° 'Tis my breeding   **extend my manners:** i.e., as far as Emilia
  That gives me this bold show of courtesy.
    [Kisses Emilia.]°   **Kisses Emilia:** (a social custom among the Elizabethans)
IAGO
  Sir, would she give you so much of her lips   100
  As of her tongue° she oft bestows on me,   **tongue:** (in the sense of scolding)
  You would have enough.
DESDEMONA   Alas, she has no speech!
IAGO
  In faith, too much.
  I find it still° when I have leave° to sleep.   **still:** always (i.e., even); **have leave:** am allowed (and should be able)   105
  Marry, before your ladyship, I grant,
  She puts her tongue a little in her heart
  And chides with thinking.°   **She puts . . . thinking:** i.e., she scolds me silently
EMILIA
  You have little cause to say so.
IAGO
  Come on, come on! You are pictures out of door,
  Bells° in your parlors, wildcats in your kitchens,   **Bells:** i.e., noisemakers   110
  Saints in your injuries,° devils being offended,   **Saints in your injuries:** i.e., pretenders of innocence when harming others
  Players in your huswifery,° and huswives in your beds.°   **Players in your huswifery:** actors (i.e., not real workers at your housekeeping); **huswives in your beds:** i.e., (1) in control of your husbands, (2) hussies, wantons
DESDEMONA
  O, fie upon thee, slanderer!
IAGO
  Nay, it is true, or else I am a Turk:
  You rise to play, and go to bed to work.   115
EMILIA
  You shall not write my praise.
IAGO   No, let me not.
DESDEMONA
  What wouldst write of me, if thou shouldst praise me?
IAGO
  O gentle lady, do not put me to't,
  For I am nothing if not critical.
DESDEMONA
  Come on, assay.° – There's one gone to the harbor?   **assay:** try   120
IAGO
  Ay, madam.

DISCOVERING SHAKESPEARE

(32) Characterization [2.1.110]: Read Iago's diatribe against females in 2.1.100–160; then explain how you think he feels about women. How well does he treat his wife in the play? Why do you think so?

DESDEMONA
  I am not merry; but I do beguile°
  The thing I am° by seeming otherwise. –
  Come, how wouldst thou praise me?
IAGO
  I am about it; but indeed my invention°
  Comes from my pate° as birdlime does from frieze° –
  It plucks out brains and all. But my muse labors,
  And thus she is delivered:
  If she be fair and wise, fairness and wit –
  The one's for use, the other useth it.
DESDEMONA
  Well praised! How if she be black° and witty?
IAGO
  If she be black, and thereto have a wit,
  She'll find a white that shall her blackness fit.°
DESDEMONA
  Worse and worse!
EMILIA
  How if fair and foolish?
IAGO
  She never yet was foolish that was fair,
  For even her folly° helped her to an heir.
DESDEMONA These are old fond° paradoxes to make fools laugh i' th' alehouse. What miserable praise hast thou for her that's foul° and foolish?
IAGO
  There's none so foul, and foolish thereunto,
  But does foul pranks which fair and wise ones do.
DESDEMONA O heavy° ignorance! Thou praisest the worst best. But what praise couldst thou bestow on a deserving woman indeed – one that in the authority of her merit did justly put on the vouch° of very malice itself?
IAGO
  She that was ever fair, and never proud;
  Had tongue at will, and yet was never loud;
  Never lacked gold, and yet went never gay;°
  Fled from her wish, and yet said "Now I may";°
  She that, being angered, her revenge being nigh,
  Bade her wrong stay, and her displeasure fly;°
  She that in wisdom never was so frail
  To change the cod's head for the salmon's tail;°
  She that could think, and ne'er disclose her mind;
  See suitors following, and not look behind:
  She was a wight° (if ever such wights were) –
DESDEMONA To do what?
IAGO
  To suckle° fools and chronicle small beer.°

beguile: charm away
The thing I am: i.e., my nervousness about my husband's arrival

invention: idea (i.e, the praise)   125
pate: head; **as birdlime . . . frieze:** with as much difficulty as getting *birdlime* (a sticky white paste used to trap birds) out of *frieze* (a coarse woolen cloth)

  130

black: brunet or dark-complexioned

find a white . . . fit: (a complex pun: *white* = "wight" or "man," but also the "white" was the center of a target — i.e., "she'll find a matching fair-skinned man who likes her dark skin")

  135

folly: sexual looseness (as well as foolishness)
fond: foolish

foul: ugly   140

heavy: grievous

  145
put on the vouch: win the approval

gay: extravagantly dressed   150
Fled . . . I may: i.e., did not allow herself to do what she could have

Bade her . . . fly: i.e., put up with her trouble and dismissed her anger about it

To change . . . tail: i.e., not so foolish (*never . . .*   155 *so frail*) as to exchange something worthless—*the cod's head*—for something precious—*the salmon's tail* (cod [scrotum] and *tail* also have sexual connotations)
wight: person

suckle: take care of; **chronicle small beer:**   160 keep a tally of trivialities

---

DISCOVERING SHAKESPEARE

(33) Language [2.1.137]: In 2.1.131–166, which characters speak mostly in <u>verse</u> and which in <u>prose</u>? Why does the scene alternate between these two linguistic styles?

DESDEMONA   O most lame and impotent conclusion!
Do not learn of him, Emilia, though he be thy husband. How say you, Cassio? Is he not a most profane
and liberal° counselor?

CASSIO   He speaks home,° madam. You may relish him
more in the soldier than in the scholar.

IAGO   *[Aside]* He takes her by the palm. Ay, well said,°
whisper! With as little a web as this will I ensnare as
great a fly as Cassio. Ay, smile upon her, do! I will gyve
thee° in thine own courtship. — You say true; 'tis so, indeed! — If such tricks as these strip you out of your lieu-
tenantry, it had been better you had not kissed your
three fingers so oft — which now again you are most apt
to play the sir in.° Very good! well kissed! and excellent
courtesy! 'Tis so, indeed. Yet again your fingers to your
lips? Would they were clyster pipes° for your sake!
[Trumpet within.] The Moor! I know his trumpet.

CASSIO   'Tis truly so.

DESDEMONA   Let's meet him and receive him.

CASSIO   Lo, where he comes.

    Enter Othello and Attendants.

OTHELLO
  O my fair warrior!

DESDEMONA   My dear Othello!

OTHELLO
  It gives me wonder great as my content
  To see you here before me. O my soul's joy!
  If after every tempest come such calms,
  May the winds blow till they have wakened death!
  And let the laboring bark climb hills of seas
  Olympus-high, and duck again as low
  As hell's from heaven! If it were now° to die,
  'Twere now to be most happy,° for I fear
  My soul hath her content so absolute
  That not another comfort° like to this
  Succeeds in unknown fate.

DESDEMONA   The heavens forbid
  But that our loves and comforts should increase
  Even as our days do grow.

OTHELLO   Amen to that, sweet powers!
  I cannot speak enough of this content;
  It stops me here;° it is too much of joy.
  And this, and this, the greatest discords be
    [They kiss.]
  That e'er our hearts shall make!

IAGO   *[Aside]*   O, you are well tuned now!
  But I'll set down° the pegs that make this music,
  As honest as I am.

---

profane and liberal: lewd and free-talking
home: bluntly   165

well said: i.e., well done, good work

gyve thee: chain you up, entrap you   170

play the sir in: act the courtier
        175
clyster pipes: tubes for enemas or vaginal
insertions

        180

        185

If it were now: if it were now my fate
happy: fortunate
        190
comfort: satisfaction

        195
here: (presumably he indicates his heart)

set down: i.e., loosen, untune
        200

DISCOVERING SHAKESPEARE

(34) <u>**Paraphrase**</u> **[2.1.165]:** <u>Paraphrase</u> Cassio's remark about Iago that "you may relish him more in the soldier than in the scholar" (2.1.165–166). What does this comment imply about Iago? What does it tell us about Cassio himself?

(35) <u>**Staging**</u> **[2.1.197]:** How many times does Othello kiss Desdemona immediately after he arrives in Cyprus? (*Hint:* See 2.1.197.)

OTHELLO   Come, let us to the castle.
News, friends! Our wars are done; the Turks are
  drowned.
How does my old acquaintance of this isle? –
Honey, you shall be well desired° in Cyprus;
I have found great love amongst them. O my sweet,
I prattle out of fashion,° and I dote
In mine own comforts. I prithee, good Iago,
Go to the bay and disembark my coffers.°
Bring thou the master° to the citadel;
He is a good one, and his worthiness
Does challenge° much respect. – Come, Desdemona,
Once more well met at Cyprus.

        Exit Othello and Desdemona
        [with all but Iago and Roderigo].

IAGO *[To an Attendant going out]* Do thou meet me
presently at the harbor. *[To Roderigo]* Come hither. If
thou be'st valiant (as they say base men being in love
have then a nobility in their natures more than is native
to them), list° me. The lieutenant tonight watches on
the court of guard.° First, I must tell thee this: Desdemona is directly in love with him.

RODERIGO   With him? Why, 'tis not possible.

IAGO   Lay thy finger thus,° and let thy soul be instructed.
Mark me with what violence she first loved the Moor,
but for bragging and telling her fantastical lies. To love
him still for prating? Let not thy discreet° heart think it.
Her eye must be fed; and what delight shall she have to
look on the devil?° When the blood is made dull with
the act of sport,° there should be, again to inflame it and
to give satiety a fresh appetite, loveliness in favor,° sympathy in years, manners, and beauties; all which the
Moor is defective in. Now for want of these required
conveniences,° her delicate tenderness will find itself
abused, begin to heave the gorge,° disrelish and abhor
the Moor. Very nature will instruct her in it and compel her to some second choice. Now sir, this granted –
as it is a most pregnant° and unforced position – who
stands so eminent in the degree of this fortune as Cassio does? A knave very voluble;° no further conscionable
than in putting on the mere form of civil and humane
seeming for the better compass of his salt and most hidden loose affection?° Why, none! why, none! A slipper°
and subtle knave, a finder of occasion,° that has an eye
can stamp and counterfeit advantages,° though true advantage never present itself; a devilish knave! Besides,
the knave is handsome, young, and hath all those req-
uisites in him that folly and green° minds look after.° A
pestilent complete knave! and the woman hath found
him already.

well desired: sought after, welcomed

out of fashion: i.e., as I shouldn't at this time   205

disembark my coffers: bring my luggage ashore (*coffers* = trunks)
master: i.e., ship master
challenge: demand, deserve   210

  215

list: listen to
watches . . . guard: i.e., is on duty with the *corps de garde,* the patrol assigned to headquarters

thus: i.e., on your lips, for silence   220

discreet: discerning

the devil: (traditionally represented as dark)   225
act of sport: i.e., copulation
favor: appearance, especially of the face

conveniences: points of agreement (literally, "comings together")   230
heave the gorge: vomit

pregnant: apparent

  235
voluble: smooth-talking (also "inconstant")

no . . . affection: i.e., his conscience requires him to do no more than to assume good manners   240 *(form of civil and humane seeming)* in order to succeed sexually *(salt* = salacious, sexy);
slipper: slippery

finder of occasion: i.e., an opportunist

stamp . . . advantages: invent opportunities by fraudulent *(counterfeit)* means   245
green: young, naive; **look after:** i.e., go for

DISCOVERING SHAKESPEARE

(36) Plot [2.1.223]: What is Iago's principal argument in 2.1.220–281? Why does he try to convince Roderigo that this is true? How does this assertion help further his plan to seek revenge against Othello?

RODERIGO   I cannot believe that in her; she's full of most blessed condition.°

IAGO   Blessed fig's-end!° The wine she drinks is made of grapes. If she had been blessed, she would never have loved the Moor. Blessed pudding!° Didst thou not see her paddle with the palm of his hand? Didst not mark that?

RODERIGO   Yes, that I did; but that was but courtesy.

IAGO   Lechery, by this hand! an index° and obscure° prologue to the history of lust and foul thoughts. They met so near with their lips that their breaths embraced together. Villainous thoughts, Roderigo! When these mutualities so marshal the way, hard at hand comes the master and main exercise, th' incorporate conclusion.° Pish!° But, sir, be you ruled by me: I have brought you from Venice. Watch you° tonight. For the command, I'll lay't upon you.° Cassio knows you not. I'll not be far from you: do you find some occasion to anger Cassio, either by speaking too loud, or tainting his discipline,° or from what other course you please which the time shall more favorably minister.

RODERIGO   Well.

IAGO   Sir, he's rash and very sudden in choler,° and haply° may strike at you. Provoke him that he may;° for even out of that will I cause these of Cyprus to mutiny;° whose qualification shall come into no true taste° again but by the displanting of Cassio. So shall you have a shorter journey to your desires by the means I shall then have to prefer° them; and the impediment most profitably removed without the which there were no expectation of our prosperity.

RODERIGO   I will do this if you can bring it to any opportunity.

IAGO   I warrant thee. Meet me by and by at the citadel; I must fetch his necessaries ashore. Farewell.

RODERIGO   Adieu.   *Exit.*

IAGO
That Cassio loves her, I do well believe't;
That she loves him, 'tis apt° and of great credit.°
The Moor, howbeit that I endure him not,
Is of a constant, loving, noble nature,
And I dare think he'll prove to Desdemona
A most dear husband. Now I do love her too;
Not out of absolute lust, though peradventure
I stand accountant° for as great a sin,
But partly led to diet° my revenge,
For that I do suspect the lusty Moor
Hath leaped into my seat,° the thought whereof

---

blessed condition: holy character

fig's-end: (a crude turn on the preceding phrase; see 1.3.319)   250

pudding: sausage

an index: a table of contents; **obscure:** hidden, secret   255

mutualities . . . conclusion: polite exchanges   260
(*mutualities*) initiate a figurative parade, with hand-kissing as those who lead (*marshal the way*) followed immediately (*hard at hand*) by the main event (*master and main exercise*), the sexual act (*incorporate conclusion*)

Pish: (expression of disgust)   265

Watch you: i.e., you join the watch

lay't upon you: i.e., arrange for your participation

tainting his discipline: belittling his professionalism   270

sudden in choler: quick to anger; **haply:** perhaps

Provoke . . . may: i.e., do something to ensure that he will

mutiny: riot

qualification . . . taste: (a drinking metaphor   275
concerning diluted or altered wine; i.e., the disturbed Cypriots won't be back to normal until Cassio is fired)

prefer: advance

                    280

apt: likely; **of great credit:** easily credible

                    285

accountant: accountable   290
diet: feed, nourish

leaped into my seat: i.e., done my (sexual) job

DISCOVERING SHAKESPEARE

(37) Staging [2.1.251]: How do Iago's speeches in 2.1.249–258 suggest earlier stage action for the actors playing Desdemona and Cassio?

(38) Soliloquies [2.1.283]: Count the number of soliloquies each character has in the play. Who has the most? Which major characters don't have any soliloquies? How do soliloquies usually affect an audience?

Doth, like a poisonous mineral, gnaw my inwards,
And nothing can or shall content my soul   295
Till I am evened with him, wife for wife;
Or failing so, yet that I put the Moor
At least into a jealousy so strong
That judgment cannot cure. Which thing to do,
If this poor trash of Venice, whom I trace°   300
For his quick hunting,° stand the putting on,°
I'll have our Michael Cassio on the hip,°
Abuse him to the Moor in the rank garb°
(For I fear Cassio with my nightcap too),
Make the Moor thank me, love me, and reward me   305
For making him egregiously° an ass
And practicing upon° his peace and quiet
Even to madness. 'Tis here, but yet° confused:
Knavery's plain face is never seen till used.   *Exit.*

trace: pursue (with a pun on *trash* earlier in the line)
For his quick hunting: i.e., because he goes after what I tell him to; **stand the putting on:** tolerates my using him as I do
on the hip: i.e., where I want him (term from wrestling)
rank garb: nasty fashion
egregiously: exceptionally, spectacularly
practicing upon: plotting against
yet: so far

& **2.2°** *Enter Othello's Herald, with a proclamation.*

2.2: Cyprus, a public area

HERALD   It is Othello's pleasure, our noble and valiant general, that, upon certain tidings now arrived, importing the mere perdition° of the Turkish fleet, every man put himself into triumph; some to dance, some to make bonfires, each man to what sport and revels his addition° leads him. For, besides these beneficial news, it is the celebration of his nuptial. So much was his pleasure should be proclaimed. All offices° are open, and there is full liberty of feasting from this present hour of five till the bell have told° eleven. Heaven bless the isle of Cyprus and our noble general Othello!   *Exit.*

mere perdition: total loss

addition: rank, position   5

offices: military storehouses

told: tolled (with pun on "tell" = count)   10

& **2.3°** *Enter Othello, Desdemona, Cassio, and Attendants.*

2.3: The area in front of the Cyprian castle

OTHELLO
Good Michael, look you to the guard tonight.
Let's teach ourselves that honorable stop,
Not to outsport° discretion.
CASSIO
Iago hath direction what to do;
But notwithstanding, with my personal eye   5
Will I look to't.
OTHELLO   Iago is most honest.
Michael, good night. Tomorrow with your earliest°
Let me have speech with you.
   [To Desdemona]   Come, my dear love.
The purchase made, the fruits are to ensue;

outsport: overrun, violate

with your earliest: at your earliest convenience

DISCOVERING SHAKESPEARE

(39) Metaphor [2.1.302]: What does Iago mean when he plans to have Cassio "on the hip" (2.1.302)? What is the literal meaning of the metaphor? Why is it particularly appropriate at this moment of the play?
(40) Plot [2.2.11]: Act 2, scene 2 is often omitted in modern productions of the play. If you were directing *Othello*, would you cut the scene? Why or why not? What is its purpose in the play?

That profit's yet to come 'tween me and you. – 10
Good night.
        Exit [Othello with Desdemona and Attendants].
    Enter Iago.
CASSIO   Welcome, Iago. We must to the watch.
IAGO   Not this hour, lieutenant; 'tis not yet ten o' th'
clock. Our general cast° us thus early for the love of his   **cast:** dismissed, "cast us off"
Desdemona, who let us not therefore blame. He hath   15
not yet made wanton the night with her, and she is
sport for Jove.
CASSIO   She's a most exquisite lady.
IAGO   And, I'll warrant her, full of game.°   **full of game:** i.e., sexually eager
CASSIO   Indeed, she's a most fresh and delicate creature.   20
IAGO   What an eye she has! Methinks it sounds a parley   **a parley to provocation:** a signal to a sexual
to provocation.°   encounter (a military metaphor)
CASSIO   An inviting eye, and yet methinks right modest.
IAGO   And when she speaks, is it not an alarum° to love?   **an alarum:** a call (again, a military signal)
CASSIO   She is indeed perfection.   25
IAGO   Well, happiness to their sheets! Come, lieutenant,
I have a stoup° of wine, and here without are a brace° of   **stoup:** tankard, container; **brace:** pair
Cyprus gallants that would fain have a measure° to the   **would . . . measure:** desire to drink a toast
health of black Othello.
CASSIO   Not tonight, good Iago. I have very poor and   30
unhappy brains for drinking. I could well wish courtesy
would invent some other custom of entertainment.
IAGO   O, they are our friends. But one cup! I'll drink for
you.
CASSIO   I have drunk but one cup tonight, and that was   35
craftily qualified° too, and behold what innovation° it   **craftily qualified:** carefully diluted;
makes here. I am unfortunate in the infirmity and dare   **innovation:** disturbance, revolution
not task° my weakness with any more.   **task:** endanger, overtax
IAGO   What, man! 'Tis a night of revels: the gallants de-
sire it.   40
CASSIO   Where are they?
IAGO   Here at the door; I pray you call them in.
CASSIO   I'll do't, but it dislikes me.   *Exit.*
IAGO
If I can fasten but one cup upon him
With that which he hath drunk tonight already,   45
He'll be as full of quarrel and offense
As my young mistress' dog. Now my sick fool
  Roderigo,
Whom love hath turned almost the wrong side out,
To Desdemona hath tonight caroused
Potations pottle-deep;° and he's to watch.   **caroused/Potations pottle-deep:** drunk gulps 50
Three else° of Cyprus – noble swelling° spirits,   to the bottom of the *pottle* or cup
That hold their honors in a wary distance,°   **else:** others; **swelling:** proud
                                                                hold . . . distance: are vain and sensitive about
                                                                their honor

---

DISCOVERING SHAKESPEARE

(41) Diction [2.3.20]: What are the primary differences between the descriptors Cassio and Iago use for Desdemona in 2.3.12–26? Which character is more chivalrous in his portrayal of her? Why?
(42) Verse [2.3.49]: After a lengthy discussion in <u>prose</u> with Cassio, why does Iago shift immediately into <u>verse</u> when the lieutenant leaves the stage (2.3.44)?

The very elements° of this warlike isle –
Have I tonight flustered with flowing cups,
And they watch too. Now, 'mongst this flock of drunk-
    ards
Am I to put our Cassio in some action
That may offend the isle.
    Enter Cassio, Montano, and Gentlemen [with Servants
    bringing wine].
                            But here they come.
If consequence° do but approve° my dream,
My boat sails freely, both with wind and stream.
CASSIO   'Fore God, they have given me a rouse° already.
MONTANO   Good faith, a little one; not past a pint, as I
    am a soldier.
IAGO   Some wine, ho!
    [Sings.]
            And let me the cannikin° clink, clink;°
            And let me the cannikin clink.
                A soldier's a man;
                O man's life's but a span,
            Why then, let a soldier drink.
    Some wine, boys!
CASSIO   'Fore God, an excellent song!
IAGO   I learned it in England, where indeed they are
    most potent in potting. Your Dane, your German, and
    your swagbellied° Hollander – Drink, ho! – are nothing
    to your English.
CASSIO   Is your Englishman so exquisite° in his drinking?
IAGO   Why, he drinks you with facility° your Dane dead
    drunk; he sweats not to overthrow your Almain;° he
    gives your Hollander a vomit° ere the next pottle can be
    filled.
CASSIO   To the health of our general!
MONTANO   I am for it, lieutenant, and I'll do you justice.
IAGO   O sweet England!
    [Sings.]
            King Stephen was and-a worthy peer,
                His breeches cost him but a crown;
            He held them sixpence all too dear,
                With that he called the tailor lown.°
            He was a wight of high renown,
                And thou art but of low degree.
            'Tis pride that pulls the country down;
                Then take thine auld° cloak about thee.
    Some wine, ho!
CASSIO   'Fore God, this is a more exquisite song than the
    other.
IAGO   Will you hear't again?

very elements: i.e., the proud soldiers represent the essential defensiveness of the islanders   55

consequence: what follows; **approve:** bear out

a rouse: a carouse (i.e., a drink)   60

cannikin: (diminutive of "can"); **clink:** i.e., against another in a toast   65

    70

swagbellied: with a stomach draped over the belt

exquisite: (1) accomplished, (2) extreme   75
with facility: easily
Almain: German (French *Allemagne,* Germany)
gives . . . vomit: i.e., causes the Dutchman to throw up

    80

    85

lown: rascal, lout

auld: old   90

DISCOVERING SHAKESPEARE

(43) Music [2.3.65]: Compose a tune for Iago's songs (2.3.64–68 and 2.3.83–90); then experiment with singing each of them. Why do you think Cassio says the second is "more exquisite" (2.3.92) than the first? How do the two songs differ in music and lyrics?

CASSIO   No, for I hold him to be unworthy of his place
that does those things.° Well, God's above all; and there
be souls must be saved, and there be souls must not be
saved.

does those things: behaves in that way

IAGO   It's true, good lieutenant.

CASSIO   For mine own part – no offense to the general,
nor any man of quality° – I hope to be saved.

man of quality: person of high rank or station

IAGO   And so do I too, lieutenant.

CASSIO   Ay, but, by your leave, not before me. The lieutenant is to be saved before the ancient. Let's have no
more of this; let's to our affairs. – God forgive us our
sins! – Gentlemen, let's look to our business. Do not
think, gentlemen, I am drunk. This is my ancient; this
is my right hand, and this is my left. I am not drunk
now. I can stand well enough, and I speak well enough.

GENTLEMEN   Excellent well!

CASSIO   Why, very well then. You must not think then
that I am drunk.   *Exit.*

MONTANO
To th' platform, masters. Come, let's set the watch.
                          [Exeunt some Gentlemen.]

IAGO
You see this fellow° that is gone before.°
He's a soldier fit to stand by Caesar
And give direction, and do but see his vice.
'Tis to his virtue a just equinox,°
The one as long as th' other. 'Tis pity of him.
I fear the trust Othello puts him in,
On some odd time of his infirmity,
Will shake this island.

fellow: person (but sometimes, perhaps here,
with a contemptuous undertone); **is gone
before:** just left

just equinox: precise equivalent

MONTANO   But is he often thus?

IAGO
'Tis evermore his prologue to his sleep:
He'll watch the horologe a double set
If drink rock not his cradle.°

watch . . . cradle: stay awake twice around the
clock unless he has a drink (i.e., Cassio can't sleep
without drinking first)

MONTANO   It were well
The general were put in mind of it.
Perhaps he sees it not, or his good nature
Prizes the virtue that appears in Cassio
And looks not on his evils. Is not this true?
   Enter Roderigo.

IAGO   *[Aside to him]*
How now, Roderigo?
I pray you after the lieutenant, go!   *[Exit Roderigo.]*

MONTANO
And 'tis great pity that the noble Moor
Should hazard such a place as his own second
With one of an engraffed° infirmity.

an engraffed: a built-in

95

100

105

110

115

120

125

130

DISCOVERING SHAKESPEARE

(44) Characterization [2.3.103]: How do you think Iago responds when Cassio explains that "the lieutenant is to be saved before the ancient" (2.3.103–104)?

(45) Plot [2.3.130]: Why does Iago send Roderigo after Cassio (2.3.130)? What does he hope to accomplish by doing this?

It were an honest action to say
So to the Moor.   135

IAGO   Not I, for this fair island!
I do love Cassio well and would do much
To cure him of this evil.

[VOICE]   *(Within)* Help! help!

IAGO   But hark! What noise?

Enter Cassio pursuing Roderigo.

CASSIO
Zounds, you rogue! you rascal!

MONTANO
What's the matter, lieutenant?

CASSIO   A knave teach me my duty?
I'll beat the knave into a twiggen bottle.°   **twiggen bottle:** wicker-covered bottle (i.e.,   140
                                                          Cassio threatens crisscross stripes on his victim's
RODERIGO   skin)
Beat me?

CASSIO   Dost thou prate, rogue?
[Strikes Roderigo.]

MONTANO   Nay, good lieutenant!
[Stays Cassio.]
I pray you, sir, hold your hand.

CASSIO   Let me go, sir,
Or I'll knock you o'er the mazard.°   **mazard:** head

MONTANO   Come, come, you're
drunk!

CASSIO   Drunk?
[They fight.]

IAGO   *[Aside to Roderigo]*
Away, I say! Go out and cry a mutiny! *[Exit Roderigo.]*   145
Nay, good lieutenant. God's will, gentlemen!
[A bell rung.]
Help, ho! – lieutenant – sir – Montano!
Help, masters! – Here's a goodly watch indeed!
Who's that which rings the bell? Diablo,° ho!   **Diablo:** devil (an oath)
The town will rise.° God's will, lieutenant, hold!   **rise:** i.e., rise up, riot   150
You'll be ashamed forever.
Enter Othello and Attendants.

OTHELLO   What is the matter here?

MONTANO
Zounds, I bleed still. I am hurt to th' death.
He dies!

OTHELLO
Hold for your lives!

IAGO
Hold, ho! Lieutenant – sir – Montano – gentlemen!   155
Have you forgot all place of sense and duty?
Hold! The general speaks to you. Hold, for shame!

OTHELLO
Why, how now, ho? From whence ariseth this?
Are we turned Turks,° and to ourselves do that   **Are . . . turned Turks:** have we become
                                                          barbarous (proverbial in the period)

DISCOVERING SHAKESPEARE

(46) <u>Shared Lines</u> [2.3.144]: How do the <u>shared lines</u> between Cassio, Roderigo, and Montano (2.3.140–144) help accelerate the speed of the scene? Can you find any irregular <u>verse</u> lines in this section of the scene that imply heightened action or <u>dialogue</u>?

Which heaven hath forbid the Ottomites?°
For Christian shame put by this barbarous brawl!
He that stirs next to carve for his own rage°
Holds his soul light;° he dies upon his motion.
Silence that dreadful bell! It frights the isle
From her propriety.° What is the matter, masters?
Honest Iago, that looks dead with grieving,
Speak. Who began this? On thy love, I charge thee.

IAGO
I do not know. Friends all, but now, even now,
In quarter,° and in terms° like bride and groom
Devesting them for bed; and then, but now —
As if some planet had unwitted men —
Swords out, and tilting° one at others' breasts
In opposition bloody. I cannot speak
Any beginning to this peevish odds,°
And would in action glorious I had lost
Those legs that brought me to a part of it!

OTHELLO
How comes it, Michael, you are thus forgot?

CASSIO
I pray you pardon me. I cannot speak.

OTHELLO
Worthy Montano, you were wont to be civil;
The gravity and stillness of your youth
The world hath noted, and your name is great
In mouths of wisest censure.° What's the matter
That you unlace° your reputation thus
And spend your rich opinion° for the name
Of a night brawler? Give me answer to it.

MONTANO
Worthy Othello, I am hurt to danger.
Your officer, Iago, can inform you,
While I spare speech, which something now offends me,°
Of all that I do know; nor know I aught
By me that's said or done amiss this night,
Unless self-charity° be sometimes a vice,
And to defend ourselves it be a sin
When violence assails us.

OTHELLO   Now, by heaven,
My blood° begins my safer guides to rule,
And passion, having my best judgment collied,°
Assays to lead the way. Zounds, if I stir
Or do but lift this arm, the best of you
Shall sink in my rebuke. Give me to know
How this foul rout began, who set it on,
And he that is approved in° this offense,
Though he had twinned with me, both at a birth,
Shall lose me. What! in a town of war,
Yet wild, the people's hearts brimful of fear,
To manage° private and domestic quarrel?

Glossary	Line
hath forbid the Ottomites: i.e., to defeat ourselves (which they could not)	160
carve for his own rage: indulge his anger	
Holds his soul light: doesn't value his own soul (i.e., will die)	
propriety: proper state (i.e., calm)	165
quarter: conduct toward; **terms:** language	
	170
tilting: aiming, thrusting	
peevish odds: headstrong, childish strife	
	175
	180
censure: judgment	
unlace: undo, remove	
spend your rich opinion: squander your reputation	185
something now offends me: i.e., somewhat pains me, is difficult for me	
	190
self-charity: self-protection	
blood: passion (as elsewhere in the play)	
collied: darkened, obscured (covered with coal dust?)	195
approved in: found guilty of	200
manage: conduct	
	205

DISCOVERING SHAKESPEARE

(47) Paraphrase [2.3.181]: Paraphrase into modern English Othello's assertion that Montano's name "is great / In mouths of wisest censure" (2.3.181–182). Is Othello complimenting or criticizing Montano here? Why do you think so?

In night, and on the court and guard of safety?
'Tis monstrous. Iago, who began't?

MONTANO
If partially affined, or leagued in office,°   **partially . . . office:** bound by partiality or
Thou dost deliver more or less than truth,   soldierly affiliation
Thou art no soldier.

IAGO   Touch° me not so near.   **Touch:** charge
I had rather have this tongue cut from my mouth   210
Than it should do offense to Michael Cassio;
Yet I persuade myself, to speak the truth
Shall nothing wrong him. This it is, general.
Montano and myself being in speech,
There comes a fellow crying out for help   215
And Cassio following him with determined sword
To execute upon° him. Sir, this gentleman   **execute upon:** take action against
Steps in to Cassio and entreats his pause.
Myself the crying fellow did pursue,
Lest by his clamor (as it so fell out)   220
The town might fall in fright. He, swift of foot,
Outran my purpose; and I returned then rather
For that I heard the clink and fall of swords,
And Cassio high in oath;° which till tonight   **high in oath:** in a fit of cursing
I ne'er might say before. When I came back –   225
For this was brief – I found them close together
At blow and thrust, even as again they were
When you yourself did part them.
More of this matter cannot I report.
But men are men; the best sometimes forget.   230
Though Cassio did some little wrong to him,
As men in rage strike those that wish them best,
Yet surely Cassio I believe received
From him that fled some strange indignity,
Which patience could not pass.°   **pass:** i.e., pass over, let go by   235

OTHELLO   I know, Iago,
Thy honesty and love° doth mince° this matter,   **love:** i.e., affection for your colleague; **mince:**
Making it light to Cassio. Cassio, I love° thee,   reduce, minimize
But never more be officer of mine.   **love:** respect and feel affection for
     Enter Desdemona, attended.
Look if my gentle love be not raised up!
I'll make thee an example.   240

DESDEMONA
What is the matter, dear?

OTHELLO   All's well, sweeting.°   **sweeting:** sweetheart
Come away to bed. *[To Montano]* Sir, for your hurts,
Myself will be your surgeon. Lead him off.
                [Montano is led off.]
Iago, look with care about the town
And silence those whom this vile brawl distracted.°   **distracted:** excited, disturbed   245

DISCOVERING SHAKESPEARE

(48) <u>Diction</u> [2.3.210]: In Iago's long speech in 2.3.209–235, what details does he exaggerate or omit to make Cassio look especially guilty?

(49) <u>Metaphor</u> [2.3.236]: What does Othello mean when he tells Iago that "Thy honesty and love doth mince this matter" (2.3.236)? Look up the word "mince" in the *Oxford English Dictionary* to determine its literal meaning in this <u>metaphoric</u> context.

Come, Desdemona, 'tis the soldiers' life
To have their balmy slumbers waked with strife.

Exit [with all but Iago and Cassio].

IAGO What, are you hurt, lieutenant?

CASSIO Ay, past all surgery.

IAGO Marry, God forbid! 250

CASSIO Reputation, reputation, reputation! O, I have lost my reputation! I have lost the immortal part of myself, and what remains is bestial. My reputation, Iago, my reputation!

IAGO As I am an honest man, I had thought you had received some bodily wound. There is more sense° in that than in reputation. Reputation is an idle and most false imposition,° oft got without merit and lost without deserving. You have lost no reputation at all unless you repute yourself such a loser. What, man! there are more ways to recover the general° again. You are but now cast in his mood° – a punishment more in policy° than in malice, even so as one would beat his offenseless dog to affright an imperious° lion.° Sue to° him again, and he's yours. 255

sense: material reality

imposition: something imposed from without 260

recover the general: i.e., recuperate your standing with Othello
cast in his mood: dismissed owing to his anger; **in policy:** i.e., a strategic punishment
imperious: powerful; **beat . . . lion:** i.e., make an example of you to frighten others; **Sue to:** petition 265

CASSIO I will rather sue to be despised than to deceive so good a commander with so slight, so drunken, and so indiscreet an officer. Drunk! and speak parrot!° and squabble! swagger! swear! and discourse fustian° with one's own shadow! O thou invisible spirit of wine, if thou hast no name to be known by, let us call thee devil!

speak parrot: babble idiotically
discourse fustian: speak bombastic nonsense 270

IAGO What was he that you followed with your sword? What had he done to you?

CASSIO I know not. 275

IAGO Is't possible?

CASSIO I remember a mass of things, but nothing distinctly; a quarrel, but nothing wherefore.° O God, that men should put an enemy in their mouths to steal away their brains! that we should with joy, pleasance, revel, and applause° transform ourselves into beasts!

nothing wherefore: not why 280

applause: approval (i.e., social approbation)

IAGO Why, but you are now well enough. How came you thus recovered?

CASSIO It hath pleased the devil drunkenness to give place to the devil wrath. One unperfectness° shows me another, to make me frankly despise myself.

unperfectness: failing 285

IAGO Come, you are too severe a moraler. As the time, the place, and the condition of this country stands, I could heartily wish this had not befall'n; but since it is as it is, mend it for your own good. 290

CASSIO I will ask him for my place again: he shall tell me I am a drunkard! Had I as many mouths as Hydra,° such

Hydra: the legendary multiheaded monster

DISCOVERING SHAKESPEARE

(50) Teaser [2.3.259]: What was the theory of the great chain of being during the Renaissance? Underline all the animal references in the scene between Iago and Cassio (2.3.248–323); then show how they help illustrate Cassio's portrayal of himself as a sub-human entity on the chain.

(51) Mythology [2.3.292]: What was "Hydra" (2.3.292) in Greek mythology? Why does Cassio compare himself to it in this scene?

an answer would stop them all. To be now a sensible man, by and by a fool, and presently a beast! O strange! Every inordinate° cup is unblessed, and the ingredient is a devil.

IAGO   Come, come, good wine is a good familiar creature° if it be well used. Exclaim no more against it. And, good lieutenant, I think you think I love you.

CASSIO   I have well approved° it, sir. I drunk!

IAGO   You or any man living may be drunk at a time, man. I tell you what you shall do. Our general's wife is now the general.° I may say so in this respect, for that he hath devoted and given up himself to the contemplation, mark, and denotement of her parts° and graces. Confess yourself freely to her; importune her help to put you in your place again. She is of so free,° so kind, so apt, so blessed a disposition she holds it a vice in her goodness not to do more than she is requested. This broken joint between you and her husband entreat her to splinter;° and my fortunes against any lay° worth naming, this crack of° your love shall grow stronger than it was before.

CASSIO   You advise me well.

IAGO   I protest,° in the sincerity of love and honest kindness.

CASSIO   I think it freely; and betimes in the morning I will beseech the virtuous Desdemona to undertake for me.° I am desperate of my fortunes° if they check me° here.

IAGO   You are in the right. Good night, lieutenant; I must to the watch.

CASSIO   Good night, honest Iago.   *Exit Cassio.*

IAGO
And what's he then that says I play the villain,
When this advice is free I give and honest,
Probal° to thinking, and indeed the course
To win the Moor again? For 'tis most easy
Th' inclining Desdemona to subdue°
In any honest suit; she's framed as fruitful°
As the free elements. And then for her
To win the Moor – were't to renounce his baptism,
All seals and symbols of redeemèd sin° –
His soul is so enfettered° to her love
That she may make, unmake, do what she list,
Even as her appetite shall play the god
With his weak function.° How am I then a villain
To counsel Cassio to this parallel° course,
Directly to his good? Divinity° of hell!
When devils will the blackest sins put on,°
They do suggest at first with heavenly shows,

---

inordinate: immoderate   295

familiar creature: friendly thing (but with pun on *familiar* in the sense of an evil spirit)

approved: demonstrated, proved   300

general's wife . . . general: i.e., Desdemona rules her husband

parts: gifts, abilities   305

free: generous

     310

entreat her to splinter: i.e., ask her to set with a splint; **lay:** wager

crack of: division in

protest: affirm   315

undertake for me: take up my plea; **desperate of my fortunes:** in despair about my future;   320
check me: stop me

     325

Probal: plausible

subdue: convince
fruitful: generous

     330

were't . . . redeemèd sin: i.e., she could make him go as far as to renounce his faith

enfettered: bound, enslaved

     335

Even as . . . weak function: i.e., he is helpless to deny whatever she wants

parallel: similar, related
Divinity: theology
put on: bring about   340

DISCOVERING SHAKESPEARE

(52) <u>**Paraphrase**</u> **[2.3.310]:** <u>Paraphrase</u> Iago's advice to Cassio: "This broken joint between you and her husband entreat her to splinter" (2.3.309–311). To whom does each of the pronouns refer?

(53) <u>**Oxymoron**</u> **[2.3.317]:** The phrase "Divinity of hell" (2.3.338) is an <u>oxymoron</u> like "jumbo shrimp." How does this contradiction in terms make sense within the context of Iago's soliloquy in 2.3.324–350?

As I do now. For whiles this honest fool
Plies° Desdemona to repair his fortune,
And she for him pleads strongly to the Moor,
I'll pour this pestilence into his ear,
That she repeals° him for her body's lust;
And by how much she strives to do him good,
She shall undo her credit with the Moor.
So will I turn her virtue into pitch,
And out of her own goodness make the net
That shall enmesh them all.
    Enter Roderigo.   How, now, Roderigo?

RODERIGO   I do follow here in the chase, not like a hound
that hunts, but one that fills up the cry.° My money is
almost spent; I have been tonight exceedingly well
cudgeled;° and I think the issue° will be — I shall have so
much experience for my pains, and so, with no money
at all, and a little more wit, return again to Venice.

IAGO
How poor are they that have not patience!
What wound did ever heal but by degrees?
Thou know'st we work by wit° and not by witchcraft,
And wit depends on dilatory° time.
Does't not go well? Cassio hath beaten thee,
And thou by that small hurt hast cashiered° Cassio.
Though other things grow fair against the sun,
Yet fruits that blossom first will first be ripe.°
Content thyself awhile. By the mass, 'tis morning!
Pleasure and action make the hours seem short.
Retire thee; go where thou art billeted.°
Away, I say! Thou shalt know more hereafter.
Nay, get thee gone!   *Exit Roderigo.*
           Two things are to be done:
My wife must move° for Cassio to her mistress —
I'll set her on —
Myself a while to draw the Moor apart
And bring him jump° when he may Cassio find
Soliciting his wife. Ay, that's the way!
Dull not device° by coldness and delay.   *Exit.*

Plies: petitions

repeals: i.e., tries to get him reinstated (literally,   345
"recalls")

350

cry: pack of dogs

cudgeled: beaten (with a cudgel); **issue:**
outcome   355

wit: cunning, mind
dilatory: slow-moving, unfolding   360

cashiered: dismissed (i.e., got him fired)

Though . . . ripe: i.e., although it looks as if
others are prospering, our plan (*fruits that blossom*   365
first) will soon bear fruit (*first be ripe*)

billeted: assigned lodging

move: plead   370

jump: just, exactly

Dull not device: don't hold up the scheme   375

3.1° *Enter Cassio, Musicians, and Clown.*

CASSIO
Masters, play here, I will content your pains:°
Something that's brief; and bid "Good morrow, general."
   [They play.]

CLOWN   Why, masters, have your instruments been in
Naples, that they speak i' th' nose thus?°

MUSICIAN   How, sir, how?

3.1: The grounds of the castle

content your pains: reward you for your labor

in Naples . . . thus: i.e., why do your musical
instruments whine so (Have they been in Naples,   5
associated with venereal disease, and caught
syphilis, thus causing their noses to fall off and
produce such a sound?)

DISCOVERING SHAKESPEARE

(54) Plot [2.3.375]: What is Iago's plan at the end of 2.3? Do you think he will succeed? Why or why not?

CLOWN   Are these, I pray you, wind instruments?° | **wind instruments:** (the following lines initiate a series of puns on *wind,* or flatulence, and *tail*)

MUSICIAN   Ay, marry, are they, sir.

CLOWN   O, thereby hangs a tail.

MUSICIAN   Whereby hangs a tale, sir?

CLOWN   Marry, sir, by many a wind instrument that I know. But, masters, here's money for you; and the general so likes your music that he desires you, for love's sake, to make no more noise with it.   [10]

MUSICIAN   Well, sir, we will not.

CLOWN   If you have any music that may not be heard, to't again: but, as they say, to hear music the general does not greatly care.   [15]

MUSICIAN   We have none such,° sir. | **none such:** ("Nonesuch" was the name of a popular tune)

CLOWN   Then put up your pipes in your bag, for I'll away. Go, vanish into air, away!   *Exit Musicians.*   [20]

CASSIO   Dost thou hear, mine honest friend?

CLOWN   No, I hear not your honest friend. I hear you.

CASSIO   Prithee keep up° thy quillets.° There's a poor piece of gold for thee. If the gentlewoman that attends the general's wife be stirring,° tell her there's one Cassio entreats her a little favor of speech. Wilt thou do this? | **keep up:** put away; **quillets:** quips, jokes | **be stirring:** i.e., is moving around, awake   [25]

CLOWN   She is stirring, sir. If she will stir hither, I shall seem to notify unto her.

CASSIO
Do, good my friend.   *Exit Clown.*
    Enter Iago.   In happy° time, Iago. | **happy:** fortunate (i.e., "good to see you")

IAGO
You have not been abed then?   [30]

CASSIO
Why, no; the day had broke
Before we parted. I have made bold, Iago,
To send in to your wife. My suit to her
Is that she will to virtuous Desdemona
Procure me some access.   [35]

IAGO   I'll send her to you presently,
And I'll devise a mean° to draw the Moor
Out of the way, that your converse and business
May be more free. | **devise a mean:** invent a way

CASSIO
I humbly thank you for't.   *Exit [Iago].*
                 I never knew
A Florentine more kind and honest.° | **Florentine . . . honest:** i.e., even my own countrymen aren't so honest (Cassio comes from Florence, Iago from Venice, notorious for trickery)   [40]
    Enter Emilia.

EMILIA
Good morrow, good lieutenant. I am sorry
For your displeasure, but all will sure be well.
The general and his wife are talking of it,
And she speaks for you stoutly.° The Moor replies | **stoutly:** strongly
That he you hurt is of great fame in Cyprus   [45]

DISCOVERING SHAKESPEARE

(55) Puns [3.1.15]: Identify and explain all the bawdy puns in the Musicians' scene (3.1.1–20).

(56) Characterization [3.1.42]: Write a brief characterization of Emilia. How well do she and Desdemona know each other? What do you think her relationship with Iago is like?

And great affinity,° and that in wholesome wisdom
He might not but refuse you;° but he protests he loves
 you,
And needs no other suitor but his likings°
To bring you in again.

great affinity: i.e., is well-connected

in wholesome . . . refuse you: i.e., common sense forbids him to reinstate you

no . . . likings: i.e., his own inclination would be sufficient by itself

CASSIO   Yet I beseech you,
If you think fit, or that it may be done,
Give me advantage of some brief discourse
With Desdemon alone.   50

EMILIA   Pray you come in.
I will bestow you where you shall have time
To speak your bosom° freely.

bosom: i.e., inmost feelings

CASSIO   I am much bound to you.

[Exeunt.]

❧ **3.2°** *Enter Othello, Iago, and Gentlemen.*

3.2: The grounds of the castle

OTHELLO
These letters give, Iago, to the pilot
And by him do my duties to the Senate.
That done, I will be walking on the works;°
Repair° there to me.

works: breastworks, fortifications
Repair: return

IAGO   Well, my good lord, I'll do't.

OTHELLO
This fortification, gentlemen, shall we see't?   5

GENTLEMEN
We'll wait upon your lordship.   *Exeunt.*

❧ **3.3°** *Enter Desdemona, Cassio, and Emilia.*

3.3: The grounds of the castle

DESDEMONA
Be thou assured, good Cassio, I will do
All my abilities in thy behalf.

EMILIA
Good madam, do. I warrant it grieves my husband
As if the cause were his.

DESDEMONA
O, that's an honest fellow. Do not doubt, Cassio,   5
But I will have my lord and you again
As friendly as you were.

CASSIO   Bounteous madam,
Whatever shall become of Michael Cassio,
He's never anything but your true servant.

DESDEMONA
I know't; I thank you. You do love my lord;   10
You have known him long; and be you well assured
He shall in strangeness° stand no farther off
Than in a politic distance.°

strangeness: aloofness
Than . . . distance: than wise policy demands

DISCOVERING SHAKESPEARE

(57) Plot [3.2.1]: The brief scene between Othello, Iago, and the Gentlemen in 3.2 is usually <u>cut</u> in productions of the play. Why do you think the scene is in the play? If you were a director, would you include or omit it? Why?

CASSIO   Ay, but, lady,
  That policy may either last so long,
  Or feed upon such nice and waterish diet,°   **feed . . . diet:** i.e., have so little to nourish it   15
  Or breed itself so out of circumstances,°   **breed . . . circumstances:** i.e., get so far away
  That, I being absent, and my place supplied,°   from the original point
  My general will forget my love and service.   **place supplied:** position filled by someone else
DESDEMONA
  Do not doubt° that. Before Emilia here   **doubt:** suspect, fear
  I give thee warrant of thy place. Assure thee,
  If I do vow a friendship, I'll perform it   20
  To the last article. My lord shall never rest;
  I'll watch him tame° and talk him out of patience;   **watch him tame:** i.e., keep him awake until he
  His bed shall seem a school, his board a shrift;°   does what I want
  I'll intermingle everything he does   **board a shrift:** i.e., his dining table will seem a   25
  With Cassio's suit. Therefore be merry, Cassio,   confessional (where he receives spiritual advice)
  For thy solicitor shall rather die
  Than give thy cause away.
      Enter Othello and Iago [at a distance].
EMILIA
  Madam, here comes my lord.
CASSIO
  Madam, I'll take my leave.   30
DESDEMONA
  Why, stay, and hear me speak.
CASSIO
  Madam, not now: I am very ill at ease,
  Unfit for mine own purposes.
DESDEMONA
  Well, do your discretion.   *Exit Cassio.*
IAGO
  Ha! I like not that.   35
OTHELLO   What dost thou say?
IAGO
  Nothing, my lord; or if – I know not what.
OTHELLO
  Was not that Cassio parted from my wife?
IAGO
  Cassio, my lord? No, sure, I cannot think it,
  That he would steal away so guiltylike,
  Seeing your coming.   40
OTHELLO   I do believe 'twas he.
DESDEMONA
  How now, my lord?
  I have been talking with a suitor here,
  A man that languishes in your displeasure.
OTHELLO
  Who is't you mean?
DESDEMONA
  Why, your lieutenant, Cassio. Good my lord,   45
  If I have any grace or power to move you,

DISCOVERING SHAKESPEARE

(58) Plot [3.3.30]: Why is Cassio uneasy about being seen with Desdemona (3.3.30)? How does his nervousness advance Iago's plot?

His present reconciliation take.°
For if he be not one that truly loves you,
That errs in ignorance, and not in cunning,
I have no judgment in an honest face.
I prithee call him back.

OTHELLO   Went he hence now?

DESDEMONA
Yes, faith; so humbled
That he hath left part of his grief with me
To suffer with him. Good love, call him back.

OTHELLO
Not now, sweet Desdemon; some other time.

DESDEMONA
But shall't be shortly?

OTHELLO   The sooner, sweet, for you.

DESDEMONA
Shall't be tonight at supper?

OTHELLO   No, not tonight.

DESDEMONA
Tomorrow dinner then?

OTHELLO   I shall not dine at home;
I meet the captains at the citadel.

DESDEMONA
Why then, tomorrow night, on Tuesday morn,
On Tuesday noon or night, on Wednesday morn.
I prithee name the time, but let it not
Exceed three days. In faith, he's penitent;
And yet his trespass, in our common reason°
(Save that they say the wars must make example
Out of her best), is not almost° a fault
T' incur a private check.° When shall he come?
Tell me, Othello. I wonder in my soul
What you would ask me that I should deny
Or stand so mamm'ring on.° What? Michael Cassio,
That came a-wooing with you, and so many a time,
When I have spoke of you dispraisingly,
Hath ta'en your part — to have so much to do
To bring him in?° By'r Lady, I could do much —

OTHELLO
Prithee no more. Let him come when he will!
I will deny thee nothing.

DESDEMONA   Why, this is not a boon;°
'Tis as I should entreat you wear your gloves,
Or feed on nourishing dishes, or keep you warm,
Or sue to you to do a peculiar° profit
To your own person. Nay, when I have a suit
Wherein I mean to touch° your love indeed,
It shall be full of poise and difficult weight,
And fearful to be granted.°

His . . . take: immediately restore him to your good graces

50

55

in . . . reason: i.e., looked at by normal standards

60

not almost: scarcely

65

a private check: even a private reprimand

mamm'ring on: hesitating about or perhaps stuttering

70

bring him in: i.e., into your favor

75

boon: personal favor (i.e., I'm not asking you to do something for me, but rather for your own good)

peculiar: particular, special

80

touch: test

full . . . granted: i.e., something hard to agree to

DISCOVERING SHAKESPEARE

(59) <u>Plot</u> **[3.3.57]:** Why is Desdemona so persistent in asking Othello to reinstate Cassio? What effect do her entreaties have on the Moor?

OTHELLO   I will deny thee nothing!
  Whereon I do beseech thee grant me this,
  To leave me but a little to myself.   85
DESDEMONA
  Shall I deny you? No. Farewell, my lord.
OTHELLO
  Farewell, my Desdemona: I'll come to thee straight.
DESDEMONA
  Emilia, come. – Be as your fancies teach you;°   **as . . . you:** i.e., as your whims suggest
  Whate'er you be, I am obedient.   *Exit [with Emilia].*
OTHELLO
  Excellent wretch!° Perdition catch my soul   **wretch:** (a term of affection, but the opposite is   90
  But I do love thee!° and when I love thee not,   also current in the period)
  Chaos is come again.   **Perdition . . . thee:** i.e., I'll be damned if I don't
IAGO   love you
  My noble lord –
OTHELLO   What dost thou say, Iago?
IAGO
  Did Michael Cassio, when you wooed my lady,
  Know of your love?   95
OTHELLO
  He did, from first to last. Why dost thou ask?
IAGO
  But for a satisfaction of my thought;
  No further harm.
OTHELLO   Why of thy thought, Iago?
IAGO
  I did not think he had been acquainted with her.
OTHELLO
  O, yes, and went between us° very oft.   **went between us:** i.e., served as a go-between   100
IAGO
  Indeed?
OTHELLO
  Indeed? Ay, indeed! Discern'st thou aught in that?
  Is he not honest?
IAGO   Honest, my lord?
OTHELLO   Honest. Ay, honest.
IAGO
  My lord, for aught I know.
OTHELLO
  What dost thou think?   105
IAGO   Think, my lord?
OTHELLO   Think, my lord?
  By heaven, thou echo'st me
  As if there were some monster in thy thought
  Too hideous to be shown. Thou dost mean something:
  I heard thee say even now, thou lik'st not that,
  When Cassio left my wife. What didst not like?   110
  And when I told thee he was of my counsel°   **of my counsel:** my confidant (i.e., knew my
  In my whole course of wooing, thou cried'st "Indeed?"   plans)

DISCOVERING SHAKESPEARE

(60) Foreshadowing [3.3.90]: To what extent do Othello's lines in 3.3.90–92 help foreshadow the play's tragic conclusion? Do you think Desdemona hears the lines? Why or why not?

And didst contract and purse thy brow together,
As if thou then hadst shut up in thy brain
Some horrible conceit.° If thou dost love me,   **conceit:** fancy or idea (Italian *concetto*, concept)   115
Show me thy thought.
IAGO
My lord, you know I love you.
OTHELLO   I think thou dost,
And, for I know thou'rt full of love and honesty
And weigh'st thy words before thou giv'st them breath,
Therefore these stops° of thine fright me the more.   **stops:** hesitations, refusals   120
For such things in a false disloyal knave
Are tricks of custom,° but in a man that's just°   **tricks of custom:** tricks of the trade; **just:**
They're close dilations,° working from the heart   honest, good
That passion cannot rule.   **close dilations:** secret swellings ("dilate"=
IAGO   For Michael Cassio,   expand) of emotion that can't be controlled
I dare be sworn I think that he is honest.   125
OTHELLO
I think so too.
IAGO   Men should be what they seem;
Or those that be not, would they might seem none!°   **seem none:** i.e., not pretend to be men but be
OTHELLO   instead the monsters that they are
Certain, men should be what they seem.
IAGO
Why then, I think Cassio's an honest man.
OTHELLO
Nay, yet there's more in this.   130
I prithee speak to me as to thy thinkings,
As thou dost ruminate, and give thy worst of thoughts
The worst of words.
IAGO   Good my lord, pardon me:
Though I am bound to every act of duty,
I am not bound to that. All slaves are free –   135
Utter my thoughts? Why, say they are vile and false,
As where's that palace whereinto foul things
Sometimes intrude not? Who has that breast so pure
But some uncleanly apprehensions
Keep leets and law days, and in sessions sit   140
With meditations lawful?°   **uncleanly apprehensions . . . lawful:** i.e., evil
OTHELLO   thoughts that do legal business (*leets* = courts)
Thou dost conspire against thy friend, Iago,   alongside honorable ideas
If thou but think'st him wronged, and mak'st his ear
A stranger to thy thoughts.
IAGO   I do beseech you –
Though I perchance am vicious in my guess   145
(As I confess it is my nature's plague
To spy into abuses, and oft my jealousy°   **jealousy:** suspicion
Shapes faults that are not) – that your wisdom°   **your wisdom:** i.e., you

---

DISCOVERING SHAKESPEARE

(61) <u>Irony</u> [3.3.125]: How do Iago's lines "I dare be sworn I think that he is honest" (3.3.125) and "Men should be what they seem" (3.3.126) use <u>irony</u> to help awaken Othello's suspicion of Cassio? What other lines can you find in this scene that function in the same <u>rhetorical</u> manner?

(62) <u>Paraphrase</u> [3.3.143]: <u>Paraphrase</u> Othello's speech to Iago in 3.3.142–144. How do these lines give Iago permission to proceed in his accusations against Cassio?

From one that so imperfectly conceits
Would take no notice,° nor build yourself a trouble
Out of his scattering and unsure observance.°   **150**
It were not for your quiet nor your good,
Nor for my manhood, honesty, and wisdom,
To let you know my thoughts.

OTHELLO   What dost thou mean?

IAGO
Good name in man and woman, dear my lord,   **155**
Is the immediate° jewel of their souls.
Who steals my purse steals trash; 'tis something, noth-
  ing;
'Twas mine, 'tis his, and has been slave to thousands.
But he that filches from me my good name
Robs me of that which not enriches him   **160**
And makes me poor indeed.

OTHELLO
By heaven, I'll know thy thoughts!

IAGO
You cannot, if my heart were in your hand,
Nor shall not whilst 'tis in my custody.

OTHELLO
Ha!

IAGO   O, beware, my lord, of jealousy!   **165**
It is the green-eyed monster, which doth mock
The meat it feeds on.° That cuckold lives in bliss
Who, certain of his fate, loves not his wronger;°
But O, what damnèd minutes tells° he o'er
Who dotes,° yet doubts – suspects, yet soundly° loves!   **170**

OTHELLO
O misery!

IAGO
Poor and content is rich, and rich enough;
But riches fineless° is as poor as winter
To him that ever fears he shall be poor.
Good God, the souls of all my tribe defend   **175**
From jealousy!

OTHELLO   Why, why is this?
Think'st thou I'd make a life of jealousy,
To follow still° the changes of the moon
With fresh suspicions? No! To be once in doubt
Is once to be resolved.° Exchange me for a goat   **180**
When I shall turn the business of my soul
To such exsufflicate and blowed surmises,°
Matching thy inference. 'Tis not to make me jealous
To say my wife is fair, feeds well, loves company,
Is free of speech, sings, plays, and dances;   **185**
Where virtue is, these are more virtuous.
Nor from mine own weak merits will I draw

From one . . . notice: i.e., wouldn't pay any attention to me, who unreliably conjectures about things

scattering . . . observance: random and unfounded observations

immediate: inmost

doth mock . . . on: toys with the prey it is about to consume

cuckold . . . wronger: i.e., a wronged husband doesn't resent an adulterous wife if he doesn't love her

tells: counts

dotes: loves dotingly; **soundly:** profoundly

fineless: unlimited

still: always

resolved: determined to act

exsufflicate and blowed surmises: (1) spat out and flyblown (i.e., disgusting) speculations, (2) inflated and blown abroad (rumored) notions

---

DISCOVERING SHAKESPEARE

(63) Language [3.3.162]: Contrast Iago's speech to Othello in 3.3.155–161 with his earlier advice to Cassio in 2.3.255–265. What does the difference between the two <u>monologues</u> tell us about Iago's character? About his ability to manipulate language and truth?

The smallest fear or doubt of her revolt,°   **revolt:** turning away (i.e., infidelity)
For she had eyes, and chose me. No, Iago;
I'll see before I doubt; when I doubt, prove;   190
And on the proof there is no more but this –
Away at once with love or jealousy!
IAGO
I am glad of this; for now I shall have reason
To show the love and duty that I bear you
With franker° spirit. Therefore, as I am bound,   **franker:** more candid   195
Receive it from me. I speak not yet of proof.
Look to your wife; observe her well with Cassio;
Wear your eyes thus, not jealous nor secure.°   **secure:** overconfident
I would not have your free and noble nature,
Out of self-bounty,° be abused. Look to't.   **self-bounty:** i.e., your own natural generosity   200
I know our country disposition° well: **our country disposition:** i.e., the secret habits
In Venice they do let God see the pranks   of Venetian women (indicated in ll. 202–4)
They dare not show their husbands; their best con-
    science
Is not to leave't undone, but keep't unknown.
OTHELLO
Dost thou say so?   205
IAGO
She did deceive her father, marrying you;
And when she seemed to shake and fear your looks,
She loved them most.
OTHELLO   And so she did.
IAGO   Why, go to then!
She that, so young, could give out such a seeming
To seel her father's eyes° up° close as oak° –   **seel . . . up:** shut; **as oak:** (referring to the *close*   210
He thought 'twas witchcraft – but I am much to blame.   grain of oak—i.e., completely opaque)
I humbly do beseech you of your pardon
For too much loving you.
OTHELLO   I am bound to thee forever.
IAGO
I see this hath a little dashed your spirits.
OTHELLO
Not a jot, not a jot.   215
IAGO   I' faith, I fear it has.
I hope you will consider what is spoke
Comes from my love. But I do see you're moved.°   **moved:** upset
I am to pray you not to strain my speech
To grosser issues° nor to larger reach   **strain . . . issues:** constrain me to speak of
Than to suspicion.   potentially ugly outcomes   220
OTHELLO
I will not.

DISCOVERING SHAKESPEARE

(64) Beat Change [3.3.193]: Most directors and actors see Iago's "I am glad of this" in 3.3.193 as a beat change that shifts this section of the scene into a deeper and more malevolent mode. What has Othello said to Iago that gives him permission to speak to the Moor "With franker spirit" (3.3.195) in the following lines?

(65) Verse [3.3.218]: In 3.3.213–225, the verse form breaks down–not only in the shared lines between Iago and Othello, but in a disruption of the normal iambic pentameter. Scan lines 213–225 to determine where the irregularities occur. Why does the verse degenerate at this particular moment in the scene? How could accomplished actors use the erratic verse to convey emotion on stage?

IAGO   Should you do so, my lord,
My speech should fall into such vile success°
Which my thoughts aimed not. Cassio's my worthy
    friend –
My lord, I see you're moved.

vile success: evil result

OTHELLO   No, not much moved:
I do not think but Desdemona's honest.°

honest: (primarily "chaste," but with the 225
suggestion of "honorable")

IAGO
Long live she so! and long live you to think so!

OTHELLO
And yet, how nature erring from itself –

IAGO
Ay, there's the point! as (to be bold with you)
Not to affect many proposed matches
Of her own clime, complexion, and degree,°
Whereto we see in all things nature tends –
Foh!° one may smell in such° a will° most rank,
Foul disproportions,° thoughts unnatural –
But pardon me – I do not in position°
Distinctly speak of her; though I may fear
Her will, recoiling° to her better judgment,
May fall to match you with her country forms,°
And happily° repent.

affect . . . degree: care for proposed husbands 230
from her own background

Foh: (expression of disgust); **in such:** i.e., in
such a headstrong woman; **will:** sexual appetite
(as elsewhere)
disproportions: lack of balance   235
in position: i.e., in proposing this
characterization
recoiling: yielding
fall . . . forms: i.e., happen to compare you with
the Venetian men
happily: perhaps
Set on: instruct, arrange for   240

OTHELLO   Farewell, farewell!
If more thou dost perceive, let me know more.
Set on° thy wife to observe. Leave me, Iago.

IAGO   *[Going]*
My lord, I take my leave.

OTHELLO
Why did I marry? This honest creature doubtless
Sees and knows more, much more, than he unfolds.

IAGO   *[Returning]*
My lord, I would I might entreat your honor°
To scan° this thing no farther: leave it to time.
Although 'tis fit that Cassio have his place,
For sure he fills it up with great ability,
Yet, if you please to hold him off awhile,
You shall by that perceive him and his means.
Note if your lady strain his entertainment°
With any strong or vehement importunity;°
Much will be seen in that. In the meantime
Let me be thought too busy° in my fears
(As worthy cause° I have to fear I am)
And hold her free,° I do beseech your honor.

entreat your honor: request you
scan: inspect, consider   245

strain his entertainment: i.e., insists on   250
discussing his treatment
importunity: begging, pressure
too busy: i.e., too meddlesome
worthy cause: good reason
hold her free: consider her innocent   255

OTHELLO
Fear not my government.°

government: behavior, self-control

IAGO
I once more take my leave.   *Exit.*

OTHELLO
This fellow's of exceeding honesty,

DISCOVERING SHAKESPEARE

(66) Plot [3.3.244]: Why does Iago return to Othello after leaving the stage in 3.3.243? What <u>objective</u> does he accomplish in his following speech (3.3.244–255)?

And knows all qualities,° with a learned spirit°
Of human dealings. If I do prove her haggard,°
Though that her jesses° were my dear heartstrings,
I'd whistle her off and let her down the wind
To prey at fortune.° Haply,° for I am black
And have not those soft parts of conversation°
That chamberers° have, or for I am declined
Into the vale of years – yet that's not much –
She's gone. I am abused, and my relief
Must be to loathe her. O curse of marriage,
That we can call these delicate creatures ours,
And not their appetites! I had rather be a toad
And live upon the vapor of a dungeon
Than keep a corner in the thing I love
For others' uses. Yet 'tis the plague of great ones;°
Prerogatived° are they less than the base.°
'Tis destiny unshunnable, like death.
Even then this forkèd plague° is fated to us
When we do quicken.° Look where she comes.
   Enter Desdemona and Emilia.
If she be false, O, then heaven mocks itself!
I'll not believe't.
DESDEMONA   How now, my dear Othello?
Your dinner, and the generous° islanders
By you invited, do attend your presence.
OTHELLO
I am to blame.
DESDEMONA   Why do you speak so faintly?
Are you not well?
OTHELLO
I have a pain upon my forehead, here.
DESDEMONA
Faith, that's with watching;° 'twill away again.
Let me but bind it hard, within this hour
It will be well.
OTHELLO   Your napkin° is too little;
   [He pushes the handkerchief from him, and it falls
   unnoticed.]
Let it alone.° Come, I'll go in with you.
DESDEMONA
I am very sorry that you are not well.
              Exit [with Othello].
EMILIA
I am glad I have found this napkin;
This was her first remembrance from the Moor.
My wayward husband hath a hundred times
Wooed me to steal it; but she so loves the token

qualities: natures; **a learned spirit:** an informed understanding — 260
haggard: a wild hawk (beginning a metaphor of Desdemona as an uncontrolled bird)
her jesses: the leather straps for controlling the hawk
whistle . . . fortune: i.e., send her away and let her take care of herself; **Haply:** perhaps — 265
soft . . . conversation: refined manners
chamberers: courtiers

— 270

great ones: prominent people
Prerogatived: privileged; **the base:** i.e., those of the lower class — 275
forkèd plague: curse of being a cuckold (i.e., with horns on the forehead)
do quicken: are born

generous: noble — 280

watching: staying up late (i.e., sleeplessness) — 285

napkin: handkerchief

Let it alone: i.e., never mind about the headache

— 290

DISCOVERING SHAKESPEARE

(67) Metaphor [3.3.263]: Underline and explain all the metaphoric references to hawking in 3.3.260–277. Why does Othello refer to Desdemona as a wayward hawk in this speech? What do these metaphors tell us about Othello's view of women?

(68) Plot [3.3.287]: What is the importance of the handkerchief (3.3.287) to the plot of the play? Come back to this question later, and revise your answer if necessary.

(For he conjured her° she should ever keep it)
That she reserves it evermore about her
To kiss and talk to. I'll have the work ta'en out°
And give't Iago. What he will do with it
Heaven knows, not I;
I nothing but to please his fantasy.°
    Enter Iago.

IAGO
How now? What do you here alone?

EMILIA
Do not you chide; I have a thing° for you.

IAGO
You have a thing for me? It is a common thing° –

EMILIA   Ha?

IAGO
To have a foolish wife.

EMILIA
O, is that all? What will you give me now
For that same handkerchief?

IAGO   What handkerchief?

EMILIA
What handkerchief?
Why, that the Moor first gave to Desdemona;
That which so often you did bid me steal.

IAGO
Hast stol'n it from her?

EMILIA
No, faith; she let it drop by negligence,
And to th' advantage,° I, being here, took't up.
Look, here 'tis.

IAGO   A good wench! Give it me.

EMILIA
What will you do with't, that you have been so earnest
To have me filch it?

IAGO   Why, what is that to you?
    [Snatches it.]

EMILIA
If it be not for some purpose of import,°
Give't me again. Poor lady, she'll run mad
When she shall lack it.

IAGO
Be not acknown on't;° I have use for it.
Go, leave me.   *Exit Emilia.*
I will in Cassio's lodging lose this napkin
And let him find it. Trifles light as air
Are to the jealous confirmations strong
As proofs of holy writ.° This may do something.
The Moor already changes with my poison:
Dangerous conceits° are in their natures poisons,
Which at the first are scarce found to distaste,°

conjured her: made her swear (in *conjured,* the accent is on the second syllable)   295

work ta'en out: pattern copied

I nothing . . . fantasy: I do nothing but please his whims

300

a thing: an object (but with sexual connotations in the following lines)

common thing: i.e., sexual organ used by everybody

305

310

to th' advantage: opportunely

315

import: great importance

Be . . . on't: don't acknowledge it

320

proofs of holy writ: biblical truth

325

conceits: ideas, conceptions

at . . . distaste: initially aren't perceived to taste bitter

---

DISCOVERING SHAKESPEARE

(69) Characterization [3.3.313]: How do you think Emilia behaves with Iago in this scene (3.3.300–320)? How sensual is their relationship? Do you believe Iago changes his behavior once he has the handkerchief? Why or why not?

But with a little act upon the blood
Burn like the mines of sulphur.°
   Enter Othello.   I did say so.
Look where he comes! Not poppy nor mandragora,°
Nor all the drowsy° syrups of the world,
Shall ever med'cine° thee to that sweet sleep
Which thou owedst° yesterday.

OTHELLO   Ha! ha! false to me?

IAGO
Why, how now, general? No more of that!

OTHELLO
Avaunt!° be gone! Thou hast set me on the rack.°
I swear 'tis better to be much abused
Than but to know't a little.

IAGO   How now, my lord?

OTHELLO
What sense had I in her stol'n hours of lust?
I saw't not, thought it not, it harmed not me;
I slept the next night well, fed well, was free° and merry;
I found not Cassio's kisses on her lips.
He that is robbed, not wanting° what is stol'n,
Let him not know't, and he's not robbed at all.

IAGO
I am sorry to hear this.

OTHELLO
I had been happy if the general camp,
Pioners° and all, had tasted her sweet body,
So I had nothing known. O, now forever
Farewell the tranquil mind! farewell content!
Farewell the plumèd troops,° and the big wars°
That makes ambition virtue!° O, farewell!
Farewell the neighing steed and the shrill trump,
The spirit-stirring drum, th' ear-piercing fife,
The royal banner, and all quality,
Pride, pomp, and circumstance° of glorious war!
And O you mortal engines° whose rude throats
Th' immortal Jove's dread clamors counterfeit,°
Farewell! Othello's occupation's gone!

IAGO
Is't possible, my lord?

OTHELLO
Villain, be sure thou prove my love a whore!
Be sure of it; give me the ocular° proof;
Or, by the worth of mine eternal soul,
Thou hadst been better have been born a dog
Than answer my waked wrath!

IAGO   Is't come to this?

OTHELLO
Make me to see't; or at the least so prove it

Burn . . . sulphur: i.e., are difficult to extinguish

mandragora: a narcotic   330
drowsy: soporific, sleep-inducing
med'cine: i.e., help by drugs
owedst: owned, enjoyed

Avaunt: away (a command to a devil); **the rack:** 335
an instrument of torture

free: carefree   340

wanting: missing

   345
Pioners: ditchdiggers, laborers

plumèd troops: uniformed (*plumèd* = feathered)
soldiers; **big wars:** mighty conflicts   350
makes ambition virtue: i.e., that justify the
desire for glory

circumstance: surrounding pageantry
mortal engines: deadly weapons   355
rude . . . counterfeit: i.e., noises imitate the
thunder (*dread clamors*) of the heavens

ocular: visible   360

DISCOVERING SHAKESPEARE

(70) Teaser [3.3.339]: Compare Othello's language in 3.3.338–343 with a similar speech by Leontes in *The Winter's Tale* (1.2.179–207). Which play did Shakespeare write first? Which man is most jealous of his wife? Why do you think so? Does the fact that one play is a <u>romance</u> while the other is a <u>tragedy</u> influence this comparison?

That the probation bear no hinge nor loop°
To hang a doubt on – or woe upon thy life!

IAGO
My noble lord –

OTHELLO
If thou dost slander her and torture me,
Never pray more; abandon all remorse;
On horror's head horrors accumulate,
Do deeds to make heaven weep, all earth amazed;
For nothing canst thou to damnation add
Greater than that.

IAGO   O grace! O heaven forgive me!
Are you a man? Have you a soul or sense? –
God buy you!° take mine office. O wretched fool,
That lov'st to make thine honesty a vice!°
O monstrous world! Take note, take note, O world,
To be direct and honest is not safe.
I thank you for this profit,° and from hence
I'll love no friend, sith° love breeds such offense.

OTHELLO
Nay, stay. Thou shouldst be° honest.

IAGO
I should be wise; for honesty's a fool
And loses that it works for.

OTHELLO   By the world,
I think my wife be honest, and think she is not;
I think that thou art just,° and think thou art not.
I'll have some proof. My name,° that was as fresh
As Dian's visage,° is now begrimed and black
As mine own face. If there be cords, or knives,
Poison, or fire, or suffocating streams,
I'll not endure it. Would I were satisfied!°

IAGO
I see you are eaten up with passion:
I do repent me that I put it to you.°
You would be satisfied?

OTHELLO   Would? Nay, and I will.

IAGO
And may; but how? how satisfied, my lord?
Would you, the supervisor,° grossly gape on?
Behold her topped?°

OTHELLO   Death and damnation! O!

IAGO
It were a tedious difficulty, I think,
To bring them to that prospect.° Damn them then,
If ever mortal eyes do see them bolster°
More than their own! What then? How then?
What shall I say? Where's satisfaction?

---

probation . . . loop: i.e., proof allows no loophole   365

God buy you: (abbreviation for "God be with   375
you"—i.e., "good-bye")
That lov'st . . . vice: i.e., who holds so dearly to
his honesty as to make it a liability

profit: beneficial insight

sith: since   380

shouldst be: (1) ought to be, (2) i.e., all right, I
believe you are honest

just: upright, honorable   385
My name: (Q reads "Her name," which is tidier
metaphorically)
Dian's visage: the image of Diana, goddess of
chastity

satisfied: absolutely certain (with, in the next   390
four lines, sexual undertones)

put it to you: proposed it

supervisor: spectator, one who looks down   395
upon
topped: (a visual image for sexual intercourse;
"top" is perhaps a homophone of "tup" [see
tupping in 1.1.88])

prospect: view, sight to be seen
bolster: couch (i.e., copulate)

400

DISCOVERING SHAKESPEARE

(71) Punctuation [3.3.367]: The dash at the end of Iago's "My noble lord—" (3.3.367) implies that Othello interrupts Iago's speech. Why does Othello break into his friend's sentence? What do you think Iago was about to say?

(72) Mythology [3.3.387]: Who was Diana? Why does Othello <u>allude</u> to this mythological deity here?

It is impossible you should see this,
Were they as prime° as goats, as hot as monkeys,
As salt as wolves in pride,° and fools as gross°
As ignorance made drunk. But yet, I say,
If imputation° and strong circumstances°
Which lead directly to the door of truth
Will give you satisfaction, you might have't.

OTHELLO
Give me a living reason she's disloyal.

IAGO
I do not like the office.°
But sith I am entered in this cause so far,
Pricked° to't by foolish honesty and love,
I will go on. I lay° with Cassio lately,
And being troubled with a raging tooth,
I could not sleep.
There are a kind of men so loose of soul
That in their sleeps will mutter their affairs.
One of this kind is Cassio.
In sleep I heard him say "Sweet Desdemona,
Let us be wary, let us hide our loves!"
And then, sir, would he gripe° and wring my hand,
Cry "O sweet creature!" then kiss me hard,
As if he plucked up kisses by the roots
That grew upon my lips, lay his leg o'er my thigh,
And sigh, and kiss, and then cry "Cursèd fate
That gave thee to the Moor."

OTHELLO
O monstrous! monstrous!

IAGO   Nay, this was but his dream.

OTHELLO
But this denoted a foregone conclusion:°
'Tis a shrewd doubt,° though it be but a dream.

IAGO
And this may help to thicken° other proofs
That do demonstrate thinly.

OTHELLO   I'll tear her all to pieces!

IAGO
Nay, yet be wise. Yet we see nothing done;
She may be honest yet. Tell me but this –
Have you not sometimes seen a handkerchief,
Spotted with strawberries, in your wife's hand?

OTHELLO
I gave her such a one; 'twas my first gift.

IAGO
I know not that; but such a handkerchief –
I am sure it was your wife's – did I today
See Cassio wipe his beard with.

prime: sexually eager
salt as wolves in pride: lecherous as wolves in heat; **gross:** indecent, coarse — 405

imputation: charge, accusation;
circumstances: circumstantial evidence

office: task — 410

Pricked: spurred (but the obscene meaning of "prick" is also audible)
lay: i.e., shared lodgings (sexual undertones are present here as well) — 415

420

gripe: grip

425

foregone conclusion: deed already concluded
shrewd doubt: piercing suspicion

thicken: give substance to — 430

435

DISCOVERING SHAKESPEARE

(73) <u>Plot</u> **[3.3.412]:** What reason does Iago give for telling the story about his "raging tooth" (3.3.414)?

OTHELLO   If it be that —
IAGO
  If it be that, or any that was hers,   440
  It speaks against her with the other proofs.
OTHELLO
  O, that the slave° had forty thousand lives!   **slave:** i.e., Cassio (the word here means "villain")
  One is too poor, too weak for my revenge.
  Now do I see 'tis true. Look here, Iago:
  All my fond love thus do I blow to heaven.   445
  'Tis gone.
  Arise, black vengeance, from the hollow hell!
  Yield up, O love, thy crown and hearted throne°   **hearted throne:** i.e., *love* sits royally in the heart
  To tyrannous hate! Swell, bosom, with thy fraught,°   **fraught:** burden, freight
  For 'tis of aspics' tongues!°   **aspics' tongues:** fangs of asps, venomous snakes   450
IAGO   Yet be content.
OTHELLO
  O, blood, blood, blood!
IAGO
  Patience, I say. Your mind may change.
OTHELLO
  Never, Iago. Like to the Pontic Sea,°   **Pontic Sea:** Black Sea
  Whose icy current and compulsive course
  Ne'er feels retiring ebb, but keeps due on   455
  To the Propontic and the Hellespont,
  Even so my bloody thoughts, with violent pace,
  Shall ne'er look back, ne'er ebb to humble love,
  Till that a capable° and wide revenge   **capable:** all-embracing, capacious
  Swallow them up.   460
    [He kneels.]   Now, by yond marble° heaven, **marble:** i.e., shining or perhaps constant
  In the due reverence of a sacred vow
  I here engage° my words.   **engage:** pledge, guarantee
IAGO   Do not rise yet.
    [Iago kneels.]
  Witness, you ever-burning lights above,
  You elements that clip° us round about,   **clip:** clasp, embrace
  Witness that here Iago doth give up   465
  The execution° of his wit, hands, heart   **execution:** employment, action
  To wrongèd Othello's service! Let him command,
  And to obey shall be in me remorse,
  What bloody business ever.°   **to . . . ever:** i.e., whatever *bloody business* I'm
    [They rise.]   required to do, I'll perform it in pity of Othello
OTHELLO   I greet thy love,
  Not with vain thanks but with acceptance bounteous,   470
  And will upon the instant put thee to't.°   **put thee to't:** i.e., to the test
  Within these three days let me hear thee say
  That Cassio's not alive.

DISCOVERING SHAKESPEARE

(74) Plot [3.3.439]: Why does Iago add to his fictitious story the specific detail about Cassio wiping his beard with Othello's handkerchief (3.3.437–439)?

(75) Geography [3.3.457]: Locate a map of the region and find the Pontic Sea (Black Sea), the Propontic (Sea of Marmora), and the Hellespont (Dardenelles) (3.3.453–456). What do these wide-ranging geographical references tell us about Othello's travels? About his resolve to murder Desdemona and Cassio?

IAGO
My friend is dead; 'tis done at your request.
But let her live.   475

OTHELLO
Damn her, lewd minx! O, damn her! damn her!
Come, go with me apart. I will withdraw
To furnish me with some swift means of death
For the fair devil. Now art thou my lieutenant.

IAGO
I am your own forever.   *Exeunt.*   480

☙ **3.4**° *Enter Desdemona, Emilia, and Clown.*

3.4: An area outside the castle

DESDEMONA   Do you know, sirrah,° where Lieutenant
Cassio lies?°

sirrah: (a form of "sir" used toward social inferiors or servants)
lies: lives, stays

CLOWN   I dare not say he lies anywhere.

DESDEMONA   Why, man?

CLOWN   He's a soldier, and for me to say a soldier lies, 'tis
stabbing.°   5

'tis stabbing: i.e., it puts me in danger

DESDEMONA   Go to. Where lodges he?

CLOWN   To tell you where he lodges is to tell you where I
lie.

DESDEMONA   Can anything be made of this?   10

CLOWN   I know not where he lodges; and for me to de-
vise° a lodging, and say he lies here or he lies there, were
to lie in mine own throat.°

devise: make up
lie . . . throat: lie deeply or foully

DESDEMONA   Can you inquire him out, and be edified
by report?°

edified by report: i.e., instructed (with religious connotations) by what you hear   15

CLOWN   I will catechize° the world for him – that is, make
questions, and by them answer.

catechize: interrogate, search (playing on Desdemona's religious discourse)

DESDEMONA   Seek him, bid him come hither. Tell him I
have moved° my lord on his behalf and hope all will be
well.

moved: solicited   20

CLOWN   To do this is within the compass of man's wit,
and therefore I will attempt the doing it.   *Exit Clown.*

DESDEMONA
Where should I lose the handkerchief, Emilia?

EMILIA
I know not, madam.

DESDEMONA
Believe me, I had rather have lost my purse   25
Full of crusadoes.° And but° my noble Moor
Is true of mind, and made of no such baseness
As jealous creatures are, it were enough
To put him to ill thinking.

crusadoes: gold coins (with a figure of the cross, *crux*); **And but:** i.e., if it were not that

EMILIA   Is he not jealous?

DESDEMONA
Who? he? I think the sun where he was born   30
Drew all such humors° from him.
    Enter Othello.

humors: bodily fluids governing temperament

DISCOVERING SHAKESPEARE

(76) Language [3.3.480]: What does Iago mean in the final line of the scene when he says to Othello "I am your own
forever" (3.3.480)?

EMILIA   Look where he comes.

DESDEMONA
I will not leave him now till Cassio
Be called to him. – How is't with you, my lord?

OTHELLO
Well, my good lady. *[Aside]* O, hardness to dissemble! –
How do you, Desdemona?   35

DESDEMONA   Well, my good lord.

OTHELLO
Give me your hand. This hand is moist, my lady.

DESDEMONA
It hath felt no age nor known no sorrow.

OTHELLO
This argues fruitfulness and liberal heart.°   **argues . . . heart:** signifies fertility, sexual
Hot, hot, and moist. This hand of yours requires   abundance, and licentiousness
A sequester° from liberty; fasting and prayer,   **sequester:** separation   40
Much castigation,° exercise devout;   **castigation:** holy correction
For here's a young and sweating devil here
That commonly rebels. 'Tis a good hand,
A frank° one.   **frank:** free, open (with sexual sense)

DESDEMONA   You may, indeed, say so;   45
For 'twas that hand that gave away my heart.

OTHELLO
A liberal hand! The hearts of old gave hands,
But our new heraldry is hands, not hearts.°   **The hearts . . . hearts:** i.e., in better days
                                                people pledged their hearts with their hands, but

DESDEMONA   now, in modern symbols of courtship (*heraldry*),
I cannot speak of this. Come now, your promise!   the two no longer go together

OTHELLO
What promise, chuck?°   **chuck:** (a term of affection; cf. *wretch,* 3.3.90)

DESDEMONA   50
I have sent to bid Cassio come speak with you.

OTHELLO
I have a salt and sorry rheum° offends me.   **salt and sorry rheum:** painful running cold
Lend me thy handkerchief.

DESDEMONA   Here, my lord.

OTHELLO
That which I gave you.

DESDEMONA   I have it not about me.

OTHELLO
Not?

DESDEMONA   No, faith, my lord.

OTHELLO   That's a fault.
That handkerchief   55
Did an Egyptian° to my mother give.   **Egyptian:** (probably "gypsy")
She was a charmer,° and could almost read   **charmer:** sorceress
The thoughts of people. She told her, while she kept it,
'Twould make her amiable° and subdue my father   **amiable:** desirable
Entirely to her love; but if she lost it   60

DISCOVERING SHAKESPEARE

(77) Teaser [3.4.36]: Why is Desdemona's "moist" hand (3.4.36) significant to Othello?

(78) <u>Themes</u> [3.4.56]: Compare Othello's speeches in 3.4.55–75 about the "magic in the web" of the handkerchief with Brabantio's charge in 1.2 and 1.3 that his daughter has been "enchanted" by the Moor. How would Brabantio respond to this speech by Othello?

Or made a gift of it, my father's eye
Should hold her loathèd, and his spirits should hunt
After new fancies.° She, dying, gave it me,   **fancies:** loves, attractions
And bid me, when my fate would have me wived,
To give it her.° I did so; and take heed on't;   **her:** i.e., the intended bride   65
Make it a darling° like your precious eye.°   **darling:** beloved thing; **eye:** (early modern
To lose't or give't away were such perdition°   slang for the vagina, a sense that may pertain here)
As nothing else could match.   **perdition:** loss, disaster

DESDEMONA   Is't possible?

OTHELLO
'Tis true. There's magic in the web° of it.   **web:** fabric
A sibyl° that had numbered in the world   **sibyl:** prophetess   70
The sun to course two hundred compasses,°   **sun . . . compasses:** i.e., two hundred years
In her prophetic fury sewed the work;
The worms were hallowed that did breed the silk;
And it was dyed in mummy which the skillful
Conserved of maidens' hearts.°   **mummy . . . hearts:** a drug distilled (*Conserved*)   75
     from mummified bodies, here from *maidens' hearts*

DESDEMONA   I' faith? Is't true?

OTHELLO
Most veritable. Therefore look to't well.

DESDEMONA
Then would to God that I had never seen't!

OTHELLO   Ha! Wherefore?

DESDEMONA
Why do you speak so startingly° and rash?   **startingly:** by starts, fitfully

OTHELLO
Is't lost? Is't gone? Speak, is't out o' th' way?   80

DESDEMONA   Heaven bless us!

OTHELLO   Say you?

DESDEMONA
It is not lost. But what an if° it were?   **an if:** if

OTHELLO   How?

DESDEMONA
I say it is not lost.   85

OTHELLO   Fetch't, let me see't!

DESDEMONA
Why, so I can, but I will not now.
This is a trick to put me from° my suit: **put me from:** distract me from
Pray you let Cassio be received again.

OTHELLO
Fetch me the handkerchief! My mind misgives.°   **misgives:** feels doubt or regret

DESDEMONA
Come, come!   90
You'll never meet a more sufficient° man.   **sufficient:** thoroughly capable

OTHELLO
The handkerchief!

DESDEMONA   A man that all his time°   **all his time:** throughout his career
Hath founded his good fortunes on your love,
Shared dangers with you —

DISCOVERING SHAKESPEARE

(79) <u>Verse</u> [3.4.75]: <u>Scan</u> Othello's speech in 3.4.69–75 to determine how regular the <u>verse</u> is. What is the relationship between the regularity of the <u>meter</u> and the subject matter of the lines?

OTHELLO
 The handkerchief!   95
DESDEMONA
 I' faith, you are to blame.
OTHELLO   Zounds!   *Exit Othello.*
EMILIA   Is not this man jealous?
DESDEMONA
 I ne'er saw this before.
 Sure there's some wonder in this handkerchief;   100
 I am most unhappy in the loss of it.
EMILIA
 'Tis not a year or two shows us a man.°
 They are all but° stomachs, and we all but food;
 They eat us hungrily, and when they are full,
 They belch us.
     Enter Iago and Cassio.
                    Look you – Cassio and my husband!
IAGO
 There is no other way; 'tis she must do't.
 And lo the happiness!° Go and importune° her.
DESDEMONA
 How now, good Cassio? What's the news with you?
CASSIO
 Madam, my former suit. I do beseech you
 That by your virtuous means I may again   110
 Exist, and be a member of his love
 Whom I with all the office° of my heart
 Entirely honor. I would not be delayed.
 If my offense be of such mortal° kind
 That nor my service past, nor present sorrows,   115
 Nor purposed merit in futurity,
 Can ransom me into his love again,
 But to know so must be my benefit.°
 So° shall I clothe me in a forced content,°
 And shut myself up in° some other course,   120
 To fortune's alms.°
DESDEMONA   Alas, thrice-gentle Cassio!
 My advocation° is not now in tune.
 My lord is not my lord; nor should I know him,
 Were he in favor° as in humor° altered.
 So help me every spirit sanctified   125
 As I have spoken for you all my best
 And stood within the blank° of his displeasure
 For my free speech! You must awhile be patient.
 What I can do I will; and more I will
 Than for myself I dare. Let that suffice you.   130
IAGO
 Is my lord angry?

'Tis not . . . man: i.e., it takes a long time to know a man's real self (or perhaps "good men don't come along very often")
all but: nothing except

lo the happiness: i.e., and what luck that she is here; **importune:** ask

office: devoted service

mortal: i.e., hopeless

But . . . benefit: merely to know it will be helpful
So: in that case; **forced content:** necessary contentment (i.e., being resigned to it)
shut myself up in: limit myself to
fortune's alms: the best I can get from fortune
advocation: advocacy

favor: appearance; **humor:** mood, temperament

blank: center of a target (also known as the "white")

DISCOVERING SHAKESPEARE

(80) Objectives [3.4.97]: How do the objectives of Desdemona and Othello differ in 3.4.88–97? What primary goal is each of them trying to achieve?

(81) Irony [3.4.122]: What does Desdemona mean when she tells Cassio that her "advocation is not now in tune" (3.4.122)? To what extent is this line ironic?

EMILIA He went hence but now,
And certainly in strange unquietness.

IAGO
Can he be angry? I have seen the cannon
When it hath blown his ranks into the air
And, like the devil, from his very arm   135
Puffed his own brother – and is he angry?
Something of moment° then. I will go meet him.   **of moment:** momentous, significant
There's matter in't indeed if he be angry.

DESDEMONA
I prithee do so.   *Exit [Iago].*
        Something sure of state,°   **of state:** having to do with politics
Either from Venice or some unhatched practice°   **unhatched practice:** still-hidden plot   140
Made demonstrable here in Cyprus to him,
Hath puddled° his clear spirit; and in such cases   **puddled:** disturbed, muddied
Men's natures wrangle with inferior things,
Though great ones are their object.° 'Tis even so;   **wrangle . . . object:** i.e., bicker over or debate
For let our finger ache, and it endues°   about trivia when they are really concerned with 145
Our other, healthful members even to a sense   major topics
Of pain. Nay, we must think men are not gods,   **endues:** introduces
Nor of them look for such observancy
As fits the bridal.° Beshrew me° much, Emilia,   **observancy . . . bridal:** i.e., attentiveness
I was, unhandsome warrior° as I am,   expected on the wedding day; **Beshrew me:** (a 150
Arraigning his unkindness° with my soul;   mild oath, the equivalent of "I'll be darned")
But now I find I had suborned the witness,°   **unhandsome warrior:** poor soldier
And he's indicted falsely.   **Arraigning his unkindness:** indicting his
                                                     abnormal (not according to kind) behavior toward
EMILIA   me
Pray heaven it be state matters, as you think,   **suborned the witness:** bribed the witness (i.e.,
And no conception° nor no jealous toy°   herself) to lie   155
Concerning you.   **conception:** fantasy, wild idea; **toy:** whim,
                                                     foolish fancy
DESDEMONA
Alas the day!° I never gave him cause.   **Alas the day:** (conventional lament—"What a
                                                     shame")
EMILIA
But jealous souls will not be answered so;
They are not ever jealous for the cause,
But jealous for° they're jealous. It is a monster   **for:** because   160
Begot upon itself,° born on itself.   **Begot upon itself:** self-engendered

DESDEMONA
Heaven keep the monster from Othello's mind!

EMILIA Lady, amen.

DESDEMONA
I will go seek him. Cassio, walk hereabout:
If I do find him fit,° I'll move your suit   **fit:** receptive, fit to listen   165
And seek to effect it to my uttermost.

CASSIO
I humbly thank your ladyship.
                    Exit [Desdemona with Emilia].
        Enter Bianca.

BIANCA
Save you,° friend Cassio!   **Save you:** God save you

DISCOVERING SHAKESPEARE

(82) Paraphrase [3.4.147]: Paraphrase Desdemona's admission that "we must think men are not gods, / Nor of them look for such observancy / As fits the bridal" (3.4.147–149). Is she blaming or excusing Othello for his behavior?

CASSIO   What make you from home?°
How is't with you, my most fair Bianca?
I' faith, sweet love, I was coming to your house.

BIANCA
And I was going to your lodging, Cassio.
What, keep a week away? seven days and nights?
Eightscore eight hours?° and lovers' absent hours,
More tedious than the dial° eightscore times?
O weary reck'ning!

CASSIO   Pardon me, Bianca:
I have this while with leaden thoughts been pressed,
But I shall in a more continuate° time
Strike off this score° of absence. Sweet Bianca,
[Gives her Desdemona's handkerchief.]
Take me this work out.°

BIANCA   O Cassio, whence came this?
This is some token from a newer friend.
To the felt absence now I feel a cause.°
Is't come to this? Well, well.

CASSIO   Go to, woman!
Throw your vile guesses in the devil's teeth,
From whence you have them. You are jealous now
That this is from some mistress, some remembrance.
No, by my faith, Bianca.

BIANCA   Why, whose is it?

CASSIO
I know not, neither; I found it in my chamber.
I like the work well; ere it be demanded,°
As like enough it will, I would have it copied.
Take it and do't, and leave me for this time.

BIANCA
Leave you? Wherefore?

CASSIO
I do attend here on the general
And think it no addition,° nor my wish,
To have him see me womaned.

BIANCA   Why, I pray you?

CASSIO
Not that I love you not.

BIANCA   But that you do not love me!
I pray you bring me° on the way a little,
And say if I shall see you soon at night.

CASSIO
'Tis but a little way that I can bring you,
For I attend° here, but I'll see you soon.

BIANCA
'Tis very good. I must be circumstanced.°
                         Exeunt omnes.°

What make you from: what are you doing away from

Eightscore eight hours: one hundred sixty-eight hours, the number in a week
dial: clock

more continuate: less interrupted, less fretful
Strike off this score: pay this bill

Take . . . out: copy this embroidery (*work* = needlework) for me

To . . . cause: i.e., I can now explain your absence from me

ere it be demanded: i.e., before somebody claims it

no addition: no bonus—i.e., not beneficial to my standing

bring me: go along with me

attend: am waiting

circumstanced: governed by things as they are;
omnes: all

170

175

180

185

190

195

200

DISCOVERING SHAKESPEARE

(83) Plot [3.4.171]: Why is Bianca upset with Cassio in 3.4.179–182? See also 4.1.146–153.

❧ 4.1° *Enter Othello and Iago.*

4.1: An area outside Othello's quarters

IAGO
  Will you think so?
OTHELLO   Think so, Iago?
IAGO   What,
  To kiss in private?
OTHELLO   An unauthorized kiss.
IAGO
  Or to be naked with her friend in bed
  An hour or more, not meaning any harm?
OTHELLO
  Naked in bed, Iago, and not mean harm?   5
  It is hypocrisy against the devil.°
  They that mean virtuously, and yet do so,°
  The devil their virtue tempts, and they tempt heaven.
IAGO
  If they do nothing, 'tis a venial slip.°
  But if I give my wife a handkerchief –   10
OTHELLO
  What then?
IAGO
  Why, then 'tis hers, my lord, and being hers,
  She may, I think, bestow't on any man.
OTHELLO
  She is protectress of her honor too;
  May she give that?   15
IAGO
  Her honor is an essence that's not seen;
  They have it very oft that have it not.°
  But for the handkerchief –
OTHELLO
  By heaven, I would most gladly have forgot it!
  Thou said'st – O, it comes o'er my memory   20
  As doth the raven o'er the infectious° house,
  Boding° to all! – he had my handkerchief.
IAGO
  Ay, what of that?
OTHELLO   That's not so good now.
IAGO   What
  If I had said I had seen him do you wrong?
  Or heard him say – as knaves be such abroad°   25
  Who having, by their own importunate suit,
  Or voluntary dotage of some mistress,
  Convincèd or supplied them,° cannot choose
  But they must blab –
OTHELLO   Hath he said anything?

hypocrisy against the devil: i.e., apparent evil concealing good (ironic)

yet do so: i.e., still allow themselves to be naked in bed

venial slip: minor sin

They . . . not: many people who seem to have it in fact do not

infectious: plague-ridden
Boding: prophesying (ill)

knaves . . . abroad: there are men around

by . . . them: i.e., achieved satisfaction either by insistent wooing or by the irresistible attraction they exert over a woman

---

DISCOVERING SHAKESPEARE

(84) Language [4.1.1]: Act 4, scene 1 starts in the middle of a conversation between Iago and Othello (*in medias res*). What do you think the two have been talking about immediately before the scene begins? Write out six or eight lines of <u>dialogue</u> to represent their prior discussion.

(85) Metaphor [4.1.21]: Why does Othello compare his recollection of the handkerchief with a raven hovering over a sick person's home (4.1.21)?

IAGO
He hath, my lord; but be you well assured,
No more than he'll unswear.   30
OTHELLO   What hath he said?
IAGO
Faith, that he did – I know not what he did.
OTHELLO   What? what?
IAGO
Lie –
OTHELLO   With her?
IAGO   With her, on her; what you will.°
OTHELLO   Lie with her? lie on her? – We say lie on her
when they belie° her. – Lie with her! Zounds, that's ful-
some.° – Handkerchief – confessions – handkerchief! –
To confess, and be hanged for his labor – first to be
hanged, and then to confess!° I tremble at it. Nature
would not invest herself in such shadowing passion
without some instruction.° It is not words° that shakes
me thus. – Pish! Noses, ears, and lips? Is't possible? –
Confess? – Handkerchief? – O devil!
        Falls in a trance.
IAGO   Work on,
My medicine° works! Thus credulous fools are caught,
And many worthy and chaste dames even thus,
All guiltless, meet reproach. – What, ho! my lord!
My lord, I say! Othello!
        Enter Cassio.   How now, Cassio?
CASSIO
What's the matter?
IAGO
My lord is fall'n into an epilepsy.   50
This is his second fit; he had one yesterday.
CASSIO
Rub him about the temples.
IAGO   No, forbear.
The lethargy° must have his° quiet course.
If not, he foams at mouth, and by and by
Breaks out to savage madness. Look, he stirs.   55
Do you withdraw yourself a little while.
He will recover straight. When he is gone,
I would on great occasion° speak with you.
        [Exit Cassio.]
How is it, general? Have you not hurt your head?
OTHELLO
Dost thou mock me?°   60
IAGO   I mock you not, by heaven.
Would you would bear your fortune like a man!

what you will: (a conventional phrase—"as you like it"—ending with the sexually charged *will*)   35

belie: slander

fulsome: foul

To confess . . . confess: ("To confess and be hanged" was a proverbial phrase; Othello uses and then inverts it)   40

Nature . . . instruction: nature wouldn't permit such strong emotion that produces these images (*shadowing passion*) without a basis for it; words: i.e., words only

medicine: (1) poison, (2) medicine   45

lethargy: state of unconsciousness; his: its

great occasion: significant matter

mock me: (Othello reads Iago's *hurt your head,* l. 59, as a joke about cuckoldry, wearing horns; also see l. 62)   60

DISCOVERING SHAKESPEARE

(86) Staging [4.1.43]: If you were playing the role of Othello, how would you interpret the stage direction that the character falls into a "trance" (4.1.43)? Most actors infer that Othello has an epileptic fit here (4.1.50). Do you agree? Why or why not? What do you think the primary symptoms of such a seizure would be?

OTHELLO
A hornèd man's a monster and a beast.

IAGO
There's many a beast then in a populous city,
And many a civil° monster.

> **civil:** civilized, domesticated

OTHELLO
Did he confess it?

IAGO   Good sir, be a man.
Think every bearded fellow that's but yoked°
May draw° with you. There's millions now alive
That nightly lie in those unproper° beds
Which they dare swear peculiar:° your case is better.°
O, 'tis the spite of hell, the fiend's arch-mock,
To lip a wanton in a secure couch,°
And to suppose her chaste! No, let me know;
And knowing what I am, I know what she shall be.°

> **yoked:** married (but also yoked like an ox; the image introduces a series of puns on marriage, yoking, and horned beasts)
> **draw:** (1) compare, (2) pull a cart
> **unproper:** not exclusively their own
> **peculiar:** theirs alone; **your . . . better:** i.e., at least you know
> **lip . . . couch:** kiss a whore in an apparently untainted bed (*secure couch*)
> **No . . . be:** i.e., I'd rather know that I'm a cuckold, and then I can take action against her

OTHELLO
O, thou art wise! 'Tis certain.

IAGO   Stand you awhile apart;
Confine yourself but in a patient list.°
Whilst you were here, o'erwhelmèd with your grief –
A passion most unsuiting such a man –
Cassio came hither. I shifted him away
And laid good 'scuses upon your ecstasy;°
Bade him anon° return, and here speak with me;
The which he promised. Do but encave° yourself
And mark the fleers,° the gibes, and notable scorns
That dwell in every region of his face;
For I will make him tell the tale anew –
Where, how, how oft, how long ago, and when
He hath, and is again to cope° your wife.
I say, but mark his gesture. Marry, patience!
Or I shall say you're all in all in spleen,°
And nothing of a man.

> **Confine . . . list:** stay within the limits of self-control
>
> **ecstasy:** trance (*ec-stasy* = out of one's natural state)
> **anon:** shortly
> **encave:** conceal
> **fleers:** sneers
>
> **cope:** get together with (in both senses)
>
> **all in all in spleen:** flooded entirely with choler (the humor of the *spleen*, seat of passionate anger)

OTHELLO   Dost thou hear, Iago?
I will be found most cunning in my patience;
But – dost thou hear? – most bloody.

IAGO   That's not amiss;
But yet keep time in all. Will you withdraw?
    [Othello retires.]
Now will I question Cassio of Bianca,
A huswife° that by selling her desires
Buys herself bread and cloth. It is a creature
That dotes on Cassio, as 'tis the strumpet's plague
To beguile° many and be beguiled by one.
He, when he hears of her, cannot restrain
From the excess of laughter. Here he comes.
    Enter Cassio.

> **huswife:** (not only "hussy" or "prostitute" but also "a woman who manages her household with skill and thrift, a domestic economist" [*OED*]; see the dispute with Emilia, 5.1.123–24)
> **beguile:** enchant, deceive

DISCOVERING SHAKESPEARE

(87) Teaser [4.1.62]: Why does Othello refer to himself as a "hornèd man" (4.1.62)? (*Hint:* See the word "cuckold" in the *Oxford English Dictionary*.)

(88) Characterization [4.1.94]: What is Bianca's occupation? What textual evidence can you give to support your opinion?

As he shall smile, Othello shall go mad,   100
And his unbookish° jealousy must conster°   **unbookish:** naive; **conster:** construe, interpret
Poor Cassio's smiles, gestures, and light° behaviors   **light:** cheerful, casual
Quite in the wrong. How do you now, lieutenant?

CASSIO
The worser that you give me the addition°   **addition:** title, rank
Whose want° even kills me.   **want:** lack   105

IAGO
Ply Desdemona well, and you are sure on 't.
Now, if this suit lay in Bianca's power,
How quickly should you speed!°   **speed:** succeed;

CASSIO   Alas, poor caitiff!°   **caitiff:** wretch

OTHELLO
Look how he laughs already!

IAGO
I never knew a woman love man so.   110

CASSIO
Alas, poor rogue!° I think, i' faith, she loves me.   **rogue:** rascal (a term of endearment)

OTHELLO
Now he denies it faintly,° and laughs it out.   **denies it faintly:** i.e., doesn't strenuously object
                                                   to the suggestion

IAGO
Do you hear, Cassio?

OTHELLO   Now he importunes him
To tell it o'er. Go to! Well said,° well said!   **Well said:** i.e., well done, good work

IAGO
She gives it out that you shall marry her.   115
Do you intend it?

CASSIO   Ha, ha, ha!

OTHELLO
Do ye triumph, Roman?° Do you triumph?   **Roman:** i.e., victor, associated with *triumph*

CASSIO   I marry? What, a customer?° Prithee bear some   **customer:** prostitute, one who sells herself
charity to my wit; do not think it so unwholesome. Ha,   120
ha, ha!

OTHELLO   So, so, so, so! They laugh that wins!

IAGO
Faith, the cry° goes that you marry her.   **cry:** rumor

CASSIO   Prithee say true.

IAGO   I am a very villain else.   125

OTHELLO   Have you scored° me? Well.   **scored:** beaten, scored off

CASSIO   This is the monkey's own giving out. She is persuaded I will marry her out of her own love and flattery,
not out of my promise.

OTHELLO   Iago beckons° me; now he begins the story.   **beckons:** signals   130

CASSIO   She was here even now; she haunts me in every
place. I was the other day talking on the sea bank with
certain Venetians, and thither comes the bauble,° and   **bauble:** playtoy
falls me thus about my neck –

OTHELLO   Crying "O dear Cassio!" as it were. His ges-   135
ture imports it.

DISCOVERING SHAKESPEARE

(89) Staging [4.1.122]: Imagine that you are Othello overhearing this scene between Iago and Cassio. What inferences would you make from seeing the two together and hearing bits of their conversation? Write your impressions on a separate piece of paper.

CASSIO So hangs, and lolls, and weeps upon me; so shakes and pulls me! Ha, ha, ha!

OTHELLO Now he tells how she plucked him to my chamber. O, I see that nose° of yours, but not that dog I shall throw it to.°

CASSIO Well, I must leave her company.

Enter Bianca.

IAGO Before me! Look where she comes.

CASSIO 'Tis such another fitchew!° marry, a perfumed° one. What do you mean by this haunting of me?

BIANCA Let the devil and his dam° haunt you! What did you mean by that same handkerchief you gave me even now? I was a fine fool to take it. I must take out the work? A likely piece of work° that you should find it in your chamber and know not who left it there! This is some minx's token,° and I must take out the work? There! Give it your hobbyhorse.° Wheresoever you had it, I'll take out no work on't.

CASSIO How now, my sweet Bianca? How now? how now?

OTHELLO By heaven, that should° be my handkerchief!

BIANCA If you'll come to supper tonight, you may; if you will not, come when you are next prepared for.°

Exit.

IAGO After her, after her!

CASSIO Faith, I must; she'll rail° in the streets else.

IAGO Will you sup there?

CASSIO Faith, I intend so.

IAGO Well, I may chance to see you; for I would very fain° speak with you.

CASSIO Prithee come. Will you?

IAGO Go to! say no more. *[Exit Cassio.]*

OTHELLO *[Comes forward.]* How shall I murder him, Iago?

IAGO Did you perceive how he laughed at his vice?°

OTHELLO O Iago!

IAGO And did you see the handkerchief?

OTHELLO Was that mine?

IAGO Yours, by this hand!° And to see how he prizes° the foolish woman your wife! She gave it him, and he hath given it his whore.

OTHELLO I would have him nine years a-killing! – A fine woman! a fair woman! a sweet woman!

IAGO Nay, you must forget that.

OTHELLO Ay, let her rot, and perish, and be damned tonight, for she shall not live. No, my heart is turned to stone; I strike it, and it hurts my hand. O, the world hath not a sweeter creature! She might lie by an emperor's side and command him tasks.°

nose: could be a euphemism for "penis") 140
I . . . to: (Othello imagines dismembering Cassio)

such another fitchew: just such a (notoriously lecherous) polecat (i.e., prostitute) as we were 145
talking of; **perfumed:** (alluding to the odor of the polecat)
dam: mother ("devil's dam" was a proverbial phrase)
likely piece of work: likely story, fiction 150
minx's token: present from a whore
your hobbyhorse: i.e., to whatever slut gave it to you

155

should: i.e., must

next prepared for: i.e., the next time you are invited (which will be never)

rail: complain shrewishly 160

fain: eagerly

165

vice: i.e., his weakness for women

170

by this hand: i.e., I swear by this hand; **prizes:** values

175

180

command him tasks: give him orders

DISCOVERING SHAKESPEARE

(90) Metaphor [4.1.152]: What does Bianca mean when she tells Cassio to give the handkerchief to his "hobbyhorse" (4.1.152)? Why is she angry with him?

(91) Paraphrase [4.1.175]: Paraphrase Othello's comment that he would like to have Cassio "nine years a-killing" (4.1.175). What does this line tell us about the Moor?

IAGO   Nay, that's not your way.

OTHELLO   Hang her! I do but say what she is. So delicate
with her needle! an admirable musician! O, she will
sing the savageness out of a bear! Of so high and plen-
teous wit and invention° –   185

invention: imagination

IAGO   She's the worse for all this.

OTHELLO   O, a thousand, a thousand times! And then,
of so gentle a condition!°   190

gentle a condition: (1) pleasant temperament,
(2) genteel social position

IAGO   Ay, too gentle.

OTHELLO   Nay, that's certain. But yet the pity of it, Iago!
O Iago, the pity of it, Iago!

IAGO   If you are so fond over her iniquity, give her patent°
to offend; for if it touch not you,° it comes near nobody.   195

patent: license
touch not you: doesn't concern you

OTHELLO   I will chop her into messes!° Cuckold me!

messes: pieces of food suitable for meals (i.e., "to
bits")

IAGO   O, 'tis foul in her.

OTHELLO   With mine officer!

IAGO   That's fouler.

OTHELLO   Get me some poison, Iago, this night. I'll not   200
expostulate° with her, lest her body and beauty unpro-
vide my mind° again. This night, Iago!

expostulate: converse, dispute
unprovide my mind: i.e., change my
determination

IAGO   Do it not with poison. Strangle her in her bed,
even the bed she hath contaminated.

OTHELLO   Good, good! The justice of it pleases. Very   205
good!

IAGO   And for Cassio, let me be his undertaker:° you shall
hear more by midnight.

his undertaker: (1) one who acts as security for
another (i.e., "I'll take care of him"), (2) one who
takes up a challenge (probably not yet in the
modern sense of funeral director)

OTHELLO
Excellent good!
   [A trumpet.]
What trumpet is that same?

IAGO
I warrant° something from Venice.   210
   Enter Lodovico, Desdemona, and Attendants.
                                    'Tis Lodovico.
This comes from the duke. See, your wife's with him.

warrant: feel sure

LODOVICO
God save you, worthy general!

OTHELLO   With all my heart,° sir.

With all my heart: (a reciprocal compliment to
Lodovico's greeting)

LODOVICO
The duke and the senators of Venice greet you.
   [Gives him a letter.]

OTHELLO
I kiss the instrument° of their pleasures.
   [Opens the letter and reads.]

instrument: i.e., letter

DESDEMONA
And what's the news, good cousin Lodovico?   215

IAGO
I am very glad to see you, signor.
Welcome to Cyprus.

DISCOVERING SHAKESPEARE

(92) Plot [4.1.203]: Why do you think Iago wants Othello to strangle Desdemona in her bed? Why is Othello pleased by
the suggestion?

LODOVICO
    I thank you. How does Lieutenant Cassio?
IAGO   Lives, sir.
DESDEMONA
    Cousin, there's fall'n between him and my lord
    An unkind breach; but you shall make all well.   220
OTHELLO   Are you sure of that?
DESDEMONA   My lord?
OTHELLO   *[Reads.]* "This fail you not to do, as you will —"
LODOVICO
    He did not call; he's busy in the paper.
    Is there division 'twixt my lord and Cassio?   225
DESDEMONA
    A most unhappy one. I would do much
    T' atone them,° for the love I bear to Cassio.
OTHELLO
    Fire and brimstone!
DESDEMONA   My lord?
OTHELLO   Are you wise?
DESDEMONA
    What, is he angry?
LODOVICO   May be the letter moved him;
    For, as I think, they do command him home,
    Deputing Cassio in his government.°   230
DESDEMONA
    By my troth, I am glad on't.
OTHELLO   Indeed?
DESDEMONA   My lord?
OTHELLO
    I am glad to see you mad.°
DESDEMONA   Why, sweet Othello?
OTHELLO   Devil!
    [Strikes her.]
DESDEMONA   I have not deserved this.   235
LODOVICO
    My lord, this would not be believed in Venice,
    Though I should swear I saw't. 'Tis very much.°
    Make her amends; she weeps.
OTHELLO   O devil, devil!
    If that the earth could teem° with woman's tears,
    Each drop she falls would prove a crocodile.°   240
    Out of my sight!
DESDEMONA   I will not stay to offend you.   *[Going]*
LODOVICO
    Truly, an obedient lady.
    I do beseech your lordship call her back.
OTHELLO
    Mistress!

atone them: reconcile them, make them united ("at one")

Deputing . . . government: i.e., giving Othello's office to Cassio

glad . . . mad: i.e., I am pleased that you are foolish enough to rejoice in this news (with a possible pun on "maid")

very much: i.e., too much, unbelievable

teem: breed
crocodile: (notorious for weeping false tears as a means of ensnaring human victims)

DISCOVERING SHAKESPEARE

(93) Staging [4.1.220]: In 4.1.219–234, which of Desdemona's comments to Lodovico does Othello respond to? Why do these statements make him angry?

(94) Teaser [4.1.239]: What does the expression "crocodile tears" (4.1.239–240) mean? When did it originate?

DESDEMONA   My lord?

OTHELLO   What would you with her, sir?

LODOVICO

Who? I, my lord?   245

OTHELLO

Ay! You did wish that I would make her turn.°
Sir, she can turn, and turn, and yet go on
And turn again; and she can weep, sir, weep;
And she's obedient;° as you say, obedient,
Very obedient. – Proceed you in your tears. –   250
Concerning this, sir – O well-painted passion! –°
I am commanded home. – Get you away;
I'll send for you anon. – Sir, I obey the mandate
And will return to Venice. – Hence, avaunt!

[Exit Desdemona.]

Cassio shall have my place. And, sir, tonight   255
I do entreat that we may sup together.
You are welcome, sir, to Cyprus. – Goats and monkeys!°

Exit.

LODOVICO

Is this the noble Moor whom our full Senate
Call all in all sufficient? Is this the nature
Whom passion could not shake? whose solid virtue   260
The shot of accident nor dart of chance
Could neither graze nor pierce?

IAGO   He is much changed.

LODOVICO

Are his wits safe?° Is he not light of brain?

IAGO

He's that he is; I may not breathe my censure.°
What he might be – if what he might he is not –   265
I would to heaven he were!°

LODOVICO   What, strike his wife?

IAGO

Faith, that was not so well; yet would I knew
That stroke would prove the worst!

LODOVICO   Is it his use?°
Or did the letters work upon his blood
And new create his fault?   270

IAGO   Alas, alas!
It is not honesty in me to speak
What I have seen and known. You shall observe him,
And his own courses° will denote him so
That I may save my speech. Do but go after
And mark how he continues.   275

LODOVICO

I am sorry that I am deceived in him.   *Exeunt.*

---

turn: turn back (but with a multiple pun, repeated in the following lines, on *turn* as [1] change indiscriminately, [2] pursue sexual encounters, as in the modern "turn tricks")

obedient: (Othello twists Lodovico's use of the word in l. 242 to suggest "easy," "yielding"—i.e., sexually pliant)   250

well-painted passion: artfully counterfeited sorrow

Goats and monkeys: (apparently a muttered reference to the lecherous animals mentioned in 3.3.403–4)

safe: sound, normal

censure: opinion, judgment   265

What . . . were: i.e., if he's not insane, then he ought to be (to explain this behavior)

use: custom   270

courses: modes of action   275

DISCOVERING SHAKESPEARE

(95) Language [4.1.262]: When Iago tells Lodovico that Othello is "much changed" (4.1.262) and says "I may not breathe my censure. / What he might be" (4.1.264–265), he proves himself a master of understatement and innuendo. Find three other examples of Iago's use of this <u>rhetorical</u> technique in the play.

❧ **4.2**° *Enter Othello and Emilia.*

4.2: A room in the castle

OTHELLO
You have seen nothing then?
EMILIA
Nor ever heard, nor ever did suspect.
OTHELLO
Yes, you have seen Cassio and she together.
EMILIA
But then I saw no harm, and then I heard
Each syllable that breath made up between them.   5
OTHELLO
What, did they never whisper?
EMILIA   Never, my lord.
OTHELLO
Nor send you out o' th' way?
EMILIA   Never.
OTHELLO
To fetch her fan, her gloves, her mask, nor nothing?
EMILIA   Never, my lord.   10
OTHELLO   That's strange.
EMILIA
I durst,° my lord, to wager she is honest,
Lay down my soul at stake. If you think other,
Remove your thought; it doth abuse your bosom.°
If any wretch have put this in your head,
Let heaven requite it with the serpent's curse!°
For if she be not honest, chaste, and true,
There's no man happy; the purest of their wives
Is foul as slander.
OTHELLO   Bid her come hither. Go.   *Exit Emilia.*
She says enough; yet she's a simple bawd°   20
That cannot say as much. This° is a subtle whore,
A closet lock and key° of villainous secrets;
And yet she'll kneel and pray; I have seen her do't.
    Enter Desdemona and Emilia.
DESDEMONA
My lord, what is your will?°
OTHELLO   Pray you, chuck, come hither.
DESDEMONA
What is your pleasure?
OTHELLO   Let me see your eyes.   25
Look in my face.
DESDEMONA   What horrible fancy's this?
OTHELLO   *[To Emilia]*
Some of your function, mistress.°
Leave procreants° alone and shut the door;
Cough or cry hem if anybody come.
Your mystery,° your mystery! Nay, dispatch!   30
    Exit Emilia.

durst: would dare

abuse your bosom: deceive your heart   15

with the serpent's curse: i.e., by making him move eternally on his belly (see Genesis 3:14)

simple bawd: foolish pimp (Othello figures Emilia as a brothel keeper protecting her merchandise, the whore)
This: i.e., Desdemona
closet lock and key: i.e., a closed cabinet

what is your will: (Desdemona's words resemble the greeting of a courtesan seeking to please her client; see note to *wills* at 1.3.321)

Some . . . mistress: i.e., do your job by leaving us alone and watching the door
procreants: procreators, copulators
mystery: trade

DISCOVERING SHAKESPEARE

(96) History [4.2.16]: What was "the serpent's curse" (4.2.16)? Why does Othello refer to it at this moment in the play?

DESDEMONA
Upon my knee, what doth your speech import?
I understand a fury in your words,
But not the words.
OTHELLO
Why, what art thou?
DESDEMONA   Your wife, my lord, your true
And loyal wife.   35
OTHELLO   Come, swear it, damn thyself;
Lest, being like one of heaven,° the devils themselves   **being . . . heaven:** looking like an angel as you
Should fear to seize thee. Therefore be double-   do
    damned –
Swear thou art honest.°   **honest:** chaste
DESDEMONA   Heaven doth truly know it.
OTHELLO
Heaven truly knows that thou art false as hell.
DESDEMONA
To whom, my lord? With whom? How am I false?   40
OTHELLO
Ah, Desdemon! away! away! away!
DESDEMONA
Alas the heavy day! Why do you weep?
Am I the motive of these tears, my lord?
If haply you my father do suspect
An instrument° of this your calling back,   **An instrument:** a means   45
Lay not your blame on me. If you have lost him,
I have lost him too.
OTHELLO   Had it pleased heaven
To try me with affliction, had they rained
All kinds of sores and shames on my bare head,
Steeped me in poverty to the very lips,   50
Given to captivity me and my utmost hopes,
I should have found in some place of my soul
A drop of patience. But, alas, to make me
The fixèd figure for the time of scorn
To point his slow and moving finger at!°   **fixèd . . . at:** object of ridicule for a scornful age,   55
Yet could I bear that too; well, very well.   which is figured as a clock; the dial moves without
But there where I have garnered up° my heart,   appearing to (*slow and moving finger*)
Where either I must live or bear no life,   **garnered up:** stored, put for safekeeping
The fountain° from the which my current runs   **fountain:** spring
Or else dries up – to be discarded thence,   60
Or keep it as a cistern° for foul toads   **cistern:** cesspool, filthy sink
To knot and gender° in – turn thy complexion there,   **knot and gender:** copulate, reproduce
Patience, thou young and rose-lipped cherubin!
Ay, here look grim as hell!°   **turn . . . hell:** i.e., if you, Patience, look on that,
DESDEMONA   your cherubic appearance will become as *grim as
I hope my noble lord esteems me honest.   hell*   65
OTHELLO
O, ay, as summer flies are in the shambles,°   **shambles:** slaughterhouse

---

DISCOVERING SHAKESPEARE

(97) Language [4.2.35]: What does Othello mean when he tells Desdemona to "Come, swear it, damn thyself" (4.2.35)?
(98) <u>Metaphor</u> [4.2.61]: Compare 4.2.61 with a similar line in *Antony and Cleopatra,* 2.5.96–99. Which play did Shakespeare write first? How do the two <u>metaphors</u> differ?

That quicken even with blowing.° O thou weed,°
Who art so lovely fair, and smell'st so sweet,
That the sense aches at thee, would thou hadst never
    been born!

DESDEMONA
Alas, what ignorant sin have I committed?°

OTHELLO
Was this fair paper, this most goodly book,
Made to write "whore" upon? What committed?
Committed? O thou public commoner!°
I should make very forges of my cheeks
That would to cinders burn up modesty,°
Did I but speak thy deeds. What committed?
Heaven stops the nose at it, and the moon winks;°
The bawdy wind,° that kisses all it meets,
Is hushed within the hollow mine of earth
And will not hear't. What committed?
Impudent strumpet!

DESDEMONA   By heaven, you do me wrong!

OTHELLO
Are not you a strumpet?

DESDEMONA   No, as I am a Christian!
If to preserve this vessel° for my lord
From any other foul unlawful touch
Be not to be a strumpet, I am none.

OTHELLO
What, not a whore?

DESDEMONA   No, as I shall be saved!

OTHELLO   Is't possible?

DESDEMONA
O, heaven forgive us!

OTHELLO   I cry you mercy° then.
I took you for that cunning whore of Venice
That married with Othello. – *[Calling]* You, mistress,
That have the office opposite to Saint Peter
And keeps the gate of hell!°
   Enter Emilia.   You, you, ay, you!
We have done our course;° there's money for your pains:
I pray you turn the key, and keep our counsel.   *Exit.*

EMILIA
Alas, what does this gentleman conceive?
How do you, madam? How do you, my good lady?

DESDEMONA   Faith, half asleep.°

EMILIA
Good madam, what's the matter with my lord?

DESDEMONA   With who?

EMILIA   Why, with my lord, madam.

DESDEMONA
Who is thy lord?

EMILIA   He that is yours, sweet lady.

---

quicken . . . blowing: i.e., that spring to life as soon as they are deposited; **weed:** i.e., the wild thing she is, as against, in the next lines, the beautiful flower she appears to be

committed: (Desdemona's neutral sense of the word—i.e., "done"—is corrupted by Othello in ll. 72, 73, 76, and 80 to mean only "commit adultery")   70

commoner: prostitute, woman used in common

forges . . . modesty: (an image of blushing)   75

winks: closes her eyes in shame (the moon symbolizes chastity)
bawdy wind: i.e., indiscriminately lustful, pleasuring everybody   80

vessel: body

   85

cry you mercy: beg your pardon

   90

have . . . hell: (the brothel keeper, the infernal counterpart of Saint Peter, welcomes men to *hell,* another term for the female genitalia)
done our course: finished our business, "had a go"

   95

half asleep: i.e., dazed

   100

DISCOVERING SHAKESPEARE

(99) Shared Lines [4.2.86]: How do the <u>shared lines</u> between Othello and Desdemona in 4.2.81–88 suggest on-stage action and rapid-fire <u>dialogue</u>?

DESDEMONA
  I have none. Do not talk to me, Emilia.
  I cannot weep, nor answers have I none
  But what should go by water.° Prithee tonight   **go by water:** be expressed in tears
  Lay on my bed my wedding sheets – remember –   105
  And call thy husband hither.
EMILIA   Here's a change indeed!

                                     Exit.

DESDEMONA
  'Tis meet I should be used so, very meet.°   **meet:** proper (referring to Emilia's kindness as
  How have I been behaved, that he might stick   opposed to Othello's brutality?)
  The small'st opinion° on my least misuse?°   **small'st opinion:** worst interpretation (i.e.,
    Enter Iago and Emilia.   sexual suspicion); **least misuse:** slightest
                                misconduct
IAGO
  What is your pleasure, madam? How is't with you?   110
DESDEMONA
  I cannot tell. Those that do teach young babes
  Do it with gentle means and easy tasks:
  He might have chid me so; for, in good faith,
  I am a child to chiding.°   **a child to chiding:** unused to being scolded
IAGO   What is the matter, lady?
EMILIA
  Alas, Iago, my lord hath so bewhored her,°   **bewhored her:** (1) called her "whore,"   115
  Thrown such despite° and heavy terms upon her   (2) treated her like a whore
  That true hearts cannot bear it.   **despite:** abuse
DESDEMONA
  Am I that name, Iago?
IAGO   What name, fair lady?
DESDEMONA
  Such as she said my lord did say I was.
EMILIA
  He called her whore. A beggar in his drink   120
  Could not have laid such terms upon his callet.°   **callet:** slut
IAGO
  Why did he so?
DESDEMONA
  I do not know; I am sure I am none such.
IAGO
  Do not weep, do not weep. Alas the day!
EMILIA
  Hath she forsook° so many noble matches,°   **forsook:** refused; **matches:** marriages   125
  Her father and her country, and her friends,
  To be called whore? Would it not make one weep?
DESDEMONA
  It is my wretched fortune.
IAGO   Beshrew him for't!
  How comes this trick° upon him?   **trick:** (1) eccentric behavior, (2) fantasy
DESDEMONA   Nay, heaven doth know.
EMILIA
  I will be hanged if some eternal° villain,   **eternal:** i.e., incorrigible, never-changing   130

DISCOVERING SHAKESPEARE

(100) <u>Paraphrase</u> [4.2.114]: <u>Paraphrase</u> Desdemona's "I am a child to chiding" in 4.2.114. What are the meanings of the words "child" and "chiding"?

Some busy and insinuating rogue,
Some cogging, cozening° slave, to get some office,
Have not devised this slander. I will be hanged else.

IAGO
Fie, there is no such man! It is impossible.

DESACEMONA
If any such there be, heaven pardon him!

EMILIA
A halter° pardon him! and hell gnaw his bones!
Why should he call her whore? Who keeps her company?
What place? what time? what form? what likelihood?
The Moor's abused by some most villainous knave,
Some base notorious knave, some scurvy° fellow.
O heaven, that such companions° thou'dst unfold,°
And put in every honest hand a whip
To lash the rascals naked through the world
Even from the east to th' west!

IAGO   Speak within door.°

EMILIA
O, fie upon them! Some such squire° he was
That turned your wit the seamy side without°
And made you to suspect me with the Moor.

IAGO
You are a fool. Go to.

DESDEMONA   Alas, Iago,
What shall I do to win my lord again?
Good friend, go to him; for, by this light of heaven,
I know not how I lost him. Here I kneel:
If e'er my will° did trespass 'gainst his love
Either in discourse of thought° or actual deed,
Or that mine eyes, mine ears, or any sense
Delighted them° in any other form,°
Or that I do not yet,° and ever did,
And ever will (though he do shake me off
To beggarly divorcement) love him dearly,
Comfort forswear° me! Unkindness° may do much,
And his unkindness may defeat° my life,
But never taint my love. I cannot say "whore."
It does abhor° me now I speak the word;
To do the act that might the addition° earn
Not the world's mass of vanity° could make me.

IAGO
I pray you be content. 'Tis but his humor.
The business of the state does him offense,
And he does chide with you.

DESDEMONA
If 'twere no other –

cogging, cozening: cheating, deceiving

135

halter: noose

scurvy: disgusting, contemptible   140
companions: rogues, base men (like *fellow* in previous line); **unfold:** expose

within door: with greater restraint (i.e., not so loud)

squire: fellow (used contemptuously)   145
seamy side without: wrong side out

150

will: desire (with explicit sexual meaning; see note to 1.3.321)
discourse of thought: process of thinking
Delighted them: took delight; **form:** image,   155
appearance
yet: still, even now

Comfort forswear: let happiness forsake;
Unkindness: unnaturalness (as elsewhere), but   160
also "loss of love"
defeat: destroy
abhor: disgust (with pun on "turn into a whore")
addition: label (i.e., "whore")
vanity: temptations, splendor   165

DISCOVERING SHAKESPEARE

(101) Irony [4.2.133]: When Emilia unknowingly criticizes her husband as "some eternal villain . . ." in 4.2.130–133, how do you think Iago should behave during his wife's tirade?

(102) Syntax [4.2.159]: Find the main clause in Desdemona's long sentence in 4.2.152–159. Can you punctuate the sentence so that it reads more clearly?

IAGO   It is but so, I warrant.

[Trumpets within.]

Hark how these instruments summon to supper.

The messengers of Venice stays the meat:°   **stays the meat:** await their meal   170

Go in, and weep not. All things shall be well.

                     Exeunt Desdemona and Emilia.

   Enter Roderigo.

How now, Roderigo?

RODERIGO   I do not find that thou deal'st justly with me.

IAGO   What in the contrary?

RODERIGO   Every day thou daff'st me with some device,°   **daff'st . . . device:** put me off ("daff" = "doff,"   175
Iago, and rather, as it seems to me now, keep'st from me   remove) with some trick
all conveniency° than suppliest me with the least advan-   **conveniency:** advantage, opportunity
tage of hope. I will indeed no longer endure it, nor am
I yet persuaded to put up in peace what already I have   180
foolishly suffered.

IAGO   Will you hear me, Roderigo?

RODERIGO   Faith, I have heard too much; and your
words and performances are no kin together.

IAGO   You charge me most unjustly.

RODERIGO   With nought but truth. I have wasted myself   185
out of my means. The jewels you have had from me to
deliver Desdemona would half have corrupted a
votarist.° You have told me she hath received them, and   **votarist:** nun
returned me expectations and comforts of sudden re-
spect° and acquaintance; but I find none.   **sudden respect:** immediate attention   190

IAGO   Well, go to; very well.

RODERIGO   Very well! go to! I cannot go to,° man; nor 'tis   **cannot go to:** (Roderigo turns Iago's cliché [*go*
not very well. Nay, I think it is scurvy, and begin to find   *to*] into a sexual phrase—i.e., I can't get anywhere
myself fopped° in it.   with her)

IAGO   Very well.   **fopped:** made a fool of, duped   195

RODERIGO   I tell you 'tis not very well. I will make myself
known to Desdemona. If she will return me my jewels,
I will give over my suit and repent my unlawful solici-
tation; if not, assure yourself I will seek satisfaction° of   **satisfaction:** i.e., "my money back" or equivalent
you.   punishment   200

IAGO   You have said now.

RODERIGO   Ay, and said nothing but what I protest in-
tendment of doing.

IAGO   Why, now I see there's mettle° in thee; and even   **mettle:** spirit, bravery (with pun on "metal,"
from this instant do build on thee a better opinion than   gold)   205
ever before. Give me thy hand, Roderigo. Thou hast
taken against me a most just exception, but yet I
protest I have dealt most directly° in thy affair.   **directly:** straightforwardly

RODERIGO   It hath not appeared.

IAGO   I grant indeed it hath not appeared, and your   210
suspicion is not without wit and judgment. But,
Roderigo, if thou hast that in thee indeed which I have
greater reason to believe now than ever — I mean purpose, courage, and valor — this night show it. If thou

---

DISCOVERING SHAKESPEARE

(103) Plot [4.2.185]: Why is Roderigo so angry with Iago? What "jewels" is he talking about in 4.2.185–190?

(104) Characterization [4.2.209]: Write a characterization of Roderigo at this point in the play.

the next night following enjoy not Desdemona, take me from this world with treachery and devise engines for° my life.

RODERIGO   Well, what is it? Is it within reason and compass?°

IAGO   Sir, there is especial commission come from Venice to depute Cassio in Othello's place.

RODERIGO   Is that true? Why, then Othello and Desdemona return again to Venice.

IAGO   O, no; he goes into Mauritania° and taketh away with him the fair Desdemona, unless his abode be lingered here° by some accident; wherein none can be so determinate° as the removing of Cassio.

RODERIGO   How do you mean removing him?

IAGO   Why, by making him uncapable of Othello's place – knocking out his brains.

RODERIGO   And that you would have me to do?

IAGO   Ay, if you dare do yourself a profit and a right. He sups tonight with a harlotry,° and thither will I go to him. He knows not yet of his honorable fortune. If you will watch his going thence, which I will fashion to fall out between twelve and one, you may take him at your pleasure. I will be near to second your attempt, and he shall fall between us.° Come, stand not amazed at it, but go along with me. I will show you such a necessity in his death that you shall think yourself bound to put it on him. It is now high suppertime, and the night grows to waste. About it!

RODERIGO   I will hear further reason for this.

IAGO   And you shall be satisfied.   *Exeunt.*

❧ **4.3**° *Enter Othello, Lodovico, Desdemona, Emilia, and Attendants.*

LODOVICO
I do beseech you, sir, trouble yourself no further.

OTHELLO
O, pardon me; 'twill do me good to walk.

LODOVICO
Madam, good night. I humbly thank your ladyship.

DESDEMONA
Your honor is most welcome.

OTHELLO   Will you walk, sir?
O, Desdemona –

DESDEMONA   My lord?

OTHELLO   Get you to bed on th' instant; I will be returned forthwith.° Dismiss your attendant there. Look 't be done.

engines for: i.e., weapons to take

compass: possibility

Mauritania: a North African realm, home of the Moors
abode be lingered here: stay here be extended
determinate: effective

harlotry: harlot (i.e., Bianca)

he . . . us: i.e., between the two of us, we can take care of him

4.3: A room in the castle

forthwith: right away

215

220

225

230

235

240

5

DISCOVERING SHAKESPEARE

(105) Plot [4.2.238]: How does Iago convince Roderigo to kill Cassio? In 5.1.9, Roderigo tells the audience that Iago "hath given me satisfying reasons." What do you think those reasons were? How many acts of violence does Iago himself commit in the play?

DESDEMONA   I will, my lord.   10

       Exit [Othello, with Lodovico and Attendants].

EMILIA   How goes it now? He looks gentler than he did.

DESDEMONA

He says he will return incontinent,°   **incontinent:** immediately

And hath commanded me to go to bed,

And bid me to dismiss you.

EMILIA   Dismiss me?

DESDEMONA

It was his bidding; therefore, good Emilia,   15

Give me my nightly wearing, and adieu.

We must not now displease him.

EMILIA   Ay −° would you had never seen him!   **Ay − :** (most editions read "I would . . .": in the
                                                                                        folio "I" can signify both "I" and "Ay")

DESDEMONA

So would not I. My love doth so approve him

That even his stubbornness,° his checks,° his frowns −   **stubbornness:** roughness; **checks:** complaints,   20

Prithee unpin me − have grace and favor.   rebukes

EMILIA   I have laid those sheets you bade me on the bed.

DESDEMONA

All's one.° Good faith, how foolish are our minds!   **All's one:** it doesn't matter

If I do die before thee, prithee shroud me°   **shroud me:** i.e., wrap my corpse

In one of these same sheets.   25

EMILIA   Come, come! You talk.

DESDEMONA

My mother had a maid called Barbary.°   **Barbary:** (variant of "Barbara")

She was in love; and he she loved proved mad°   **mad:** wild, unsteady

And did forsake her. She had a song of "Willow";

An old thing 'twas; but it expressed her fortune,

And she died singing it. That song tonight   30

Will not go from my mind; I have much to do

But° to go hang my head all at one side   **I have much to do / But:** i.e., it's all I can do
                                                                                        not

And sing it like poor Barbary. Prithee dispatch.°   **Prithee dispatch:** please hurry

EMILIA

Shall I go fetch your nightgown?

DESDEMONA   No, unpin me here.

This Lodovico is a proper° man.   **proper:** (1) good-looking, (2) well-behaved   35

EMILIA   A very handsome man.

DESDEMONA   He speaks well.

EMILIA   I know a lady in Venice would have walked bare-

foot to Palestine for a touch of his nether lip.

DESDEMONA   *[Sings.]*

"The poor soul sat sighing by a sycamore tree,   40

  Sing all a green willow;°   **willow:** ("weeping" tree identified with
                                                                                        unrequited love)
Her hand on her bosom, her head on her knee,

  Sing willow, willow, willow.

The fresh streams ran by her and murmured her

    moans;

  Sing willow, willow, willow;   45

DISCOVERING SHAKESPEARE

(106) Teaser [4.3.23]: What were "shroud sheets" (4.3.23–25) during the Renaissance? Which sheets has Desdemona asked Emilia to put on her bed? Why is this action <u>ironic</u>?

Her salt tears fell from her, and softened the stones,
   Sing willow, willow, willow."
Lay by these. – "Willow, willow."
Prithee hie thee;° he'll come anon.   **hie thee:** hurry   50
   "Sing all a green willow must be my garland.
   Let nobody blame him; his scorn I approve" –
Nay, that's not next. Hark! who is't that knocks?

EMILIA   It's the wind.

DESDEMONA   *[Sings.]*
   "I called my love false love, but what said he then?
     Sing willow, willow, willow: 55
   If I court more women, you'll couch with more men."
So, get thee gone; good night. Mine eyes do itch.
Doth that bode weeping?

EMILIA   'Tis neither here nor there.

DESDEMONA
I have heard it said so. O, these men, these men!
Dost thou in conscience think – tell me, Emilia –   60
That there be women do abuse° their husbands   **abuse:** mistreat (i.e., betray)
In such gross kind?°   **In such gross kind:** in this wicked way—i.e.,
                                        carnally

EMILIA   There be some such, no question.

DESDEMONA
Wouldst thou do such a deed for all the world?

EMILIA
Why, would not you?

DESDEMONA   No, by this heavenly light!

EMILIA
Nor I neither by this heavenly light.   65
I might do't as well i' th' dark.

DESDEMONA
Wouldst thou do such a deed for all the world?

EMILIA   The world's a huge thing; it is a great price for a
small vice.

DESDEMONA
In troth,° I think thou wouldst not.   **In troth:** by my truth—i.e., faith (a mild oath)   70

EMILIA   In troth, I think I should; and undo't when I had
done. Marry, I would not do such a thing for a joint
ring,° nor for measures of lawn,° nor for gowns, petti-   **joint ring:** ring made in two halves; **lawn:**
coats, nor caps, nor any petty exhibition;° but, for all the   linen fabric
whole world – 'Ud's° pity! who would not make her   **exhibition:** gift   75
husband a cuckold to make him a monarch? I should   **'Ud's:** God's
venture purgatory for't.

DESDEMONA
Beshrew me if I would do such a wrong
For the whole world.

EMILIA   Why, the wrong is but a wrong i' th' world; and   80
having the world for your labor, 'tis a wrong in your
own world, and you might quickly make it right.

DISCOVERING SHAKESPEARE

(107) Music [4.3.46]: What is the purpose of Desdemona's song in 4.3.40–51? If you were directing a production of the play, would you include the song or omit it? Why?
(108) Characterization [4.3.66]: Read Emilia's lines in 4.3.62–77; then summarize her opinion of infidelity. How does her view differ from Desdemona's philosophy?

DESDEMONA   I do not think there is any such woman.

EMILIA   Yes, a dozen;° and as many to th' vantage° as
would store° the world they played° for.
But I do think it is their husbands' faults
If wives do fall. Say that they slack their duties
And pour our treasures into foreign° laps;
Or else break out in peevish° jealousies,
Throwing restraint upon us;° or say they strike us,
Or scant our former having° in despite –
Why, we have galls,° and though we have some grace,
Yet have we some revenge. Let husbands know
Their wives have sense° like them. They see, and smell,
And have their palates both for sweet and sour,
As husbands have. What is it that they do
When they change us for others? Is it sport?
I think it is. And doth affection° breed it?
I think it doth. Is't frailty that thus errs?
It is so too. And have not we affections,
Desires for sport, and frailty, as men have?
Then let them use us well; else let them know,
The ills we do, their ills instruct us so.

DESDEMONA
Good night, good night. God me such uses° send,
Not to pick° bad from bad, but by bad mend!   *Exeunt.*

dozen: (a hyperbolic understatement); **to th' vantage:** in addition   85
store: populate; **played:** gambled (with sexual undertone)

foreign: i.e., strangers'

peevish: unreasonable

Throwing restraint upon us: limiting our freedom, locking us up   90

scant our former having: reduce our allowance

galls: resentment

sense: sensual feelings   95

affection: passion, lust

100

uses: behavior, habits

pick: i.e., pick up, learn   105

⁓ **5.1°** *Enter Iago and Roderigo.*

5.1: A street in Cyprus

IAGO
Here, stand behind this bulk;° straight will he come.
Wear thy good rapier bare, and put it home.
Quick, quick! Fear nothing; I'll be at thy elbow.
It makes us, or it mars us – think on that,
And fix most firm thy resolution.

bulk: stall-like structure projecting from a shop

RODERIGO
Be near at hand; I may miscarry in't.

5

IAGO
Here, at thy hand. Be bold, and take thy stand.
[Stands aside.]

RODERIGO
I have no great devotion to the deed,
And yet he hath given me satisfying reasons.
'Tis but a man gone. Forth my sword! He dies!

10

IAGO
I have rubbed this young quat° almost to the sense,°
And he grows angry. Now whether he kill Cassio,
Or Cassio him, or each do kill the other,
Every way makes my gain. Live Roderigo,°
He calls me to a restitution large

quat: boil, pimple; **sense:** quick

Live Roderigo: i.e., if Roderigo lives

15

DISCOVERING SHAKESPEARE

(109) Paraphrase [4.3.89]: Paraphrase Emilia's lines from 4.3.86–96. Do you agree with her? Why or why not?

(110) Plot [5.1.11]: Why will Iago benefit regardless of whether Roderigo kills Cassio or Cassio kills Roderigo (5.1.11–22)?

Of gold and jewels that I bobbed° from him

bobbed: swindled

As gifts to Desdemona.
It must not be. If Cassio do remain,
He hath a daily beauty in his life
That makes me ugly; and besides, the Moor   20
May unfold me to him; there stand I in much peril.
No, he must die. But so! I heard him coming.
    Enter Cassio.

RODERIGO
I know his gait. 'Tis he. Villain, thou diest!
    [Makes a pass at Cassio.]

CASSIO
That thrust had been mine enemy indeed
But that my coat° is better than thou know'st.   25

coat: i.e., soldier's undercoat of mail

I will make proof of thine.
    [Draws, and wounds Roderigo.]

RODERIGO   O, I am slain!
    [Iago leaps at Cassio from behind,
    wounds him in the leg, and exits.]

CASSIO
I am maimed forever. Help, ho! Murder! murder!
    [Falls.]
    Enter Othello.

OTHELLO
The voice of Cassio. Iago keeps his word.

RODERIGO
O, villain that I am!

OTHELLO   It is even so.

CASSIO
O, help, ho! light! a surgeon!   30

OTHELLO
'Tis he. O brave Iago, honest and just,
That hast such noble sense of thy friend's wrong!
Thou teachest me. Minion,° your dear lies dead,

Minion: darling, favorite (here addressed contemptuously to Desdemona)

And your unblessed fate hies.° Strumpet, I come.

hies: comes quickly

Forth of° my heart those charms, thine eyes, are blotted.   35

Forth of: i.e., out of

Thy bed, lust-stained, shall with lust's blood be spotted.   *Exit Othello.*
    Enter Lodovico and Gratiano.

CASSIO
What, ho? No watch?° No passage?° Murder! murder!

watch: night watchmen; **passage:** traffic, passersby

GRATIANO
'Tis some mischance. The voice is very direful.

CASSIO   O, help!

LODOVICO   Hark!   40

RODERIGO   O wretched villain!

LODOVICO
Two or three groan. 'Tis heavy° night.

heavy: dismal, dark

These may be counterfeits. Let's think't unsafe
To come into the cry without more help.

DISCOVERING SHAKESPEARE

(111) Plot [5.1.31]: How does Othello's belief that Iago has murdered Cassio (5.1.31–37) help the Moor decide to kill Desdemona?

RODERIGO
Nobody come? Then shall I bleed to death.   45
LODOVICO   Hark!
    Enter Iago [with a light].
GRATIANO
Here's one comes in his shirt,° with light and weapons.   **shirt:** i.e., without his jacket, not fully dressed
IAGO
Who's there? Whose noise is this that cries on° murder?   **on:** of
LODOVICO
We do not know.
IAGO   Do not you hear a cry?
CASSIO
Here, here! For heaven sake, help me!   50
IAGO   What's the matter?
GRATIANO
This is Othello's ancient, as I take it.
LODOVICO
The same indeed, a very valiant fellow.
IAGO
What are you here that cry so grievously?
CASSIO
Iago? O, I am spoiled,° undone by villains!   **spoiled:** ruined (i.e., injured)
Give me some help.   55
IAGO
O me, lieutenant! What villains have done this?
CASSIO
I think that one of them is hereabout
And cannot make away.°   **make away:** escape
IAGO   O treacherous villains!
    [To Lodovico and Gratiano]
What are you there? Come in, and give some help.
RODERIGO
O, help me there!   60
CASSIO
That's one of them.
IAGO   O murd'rous slave! O villain!
    [Stabs Roderigo.]
RODERIGO
O damned Iago! O inhuman dog!
IAGO
Kill men i' th' dark? — Where be these bloody thieves? —
How silent is this town! — Ho! murder! murder! —
What may you be? Are you of good or evil?   65
LODOVICO
As you shall prove us, praise us.°   **prove us, praise us:** i.e., put us to the test and
IAGO   Signor Lodovico?   you'll see (*praise* = appraise)
LODOVICO   He, sir.
IAGO
I cry you mercy. Here's Cassio hurt by villains!
GRATIANO   Cassio?   70

DISCOVERING SHAKESPEARE

(112) Shared Lines [5.1.58]: How do the short and <u>shared lines</u> in 5.1.55–99 help suggest stage action in this frantic scene?

IAGO   How is't, brother?

CASSIO
My leg is cut in two.

IAGO   Marry, heaven forbid!
Light, gentlemen. I'll bind it with my shirt.
  Enter Bianca.

BIANCA
What is the matter, ho? Who is't that cried?

IAGO
Who is't that cried?   75

BIANCA
O my dear Cassio! my sweet Cassio!
O Cassio, Cassio, Cassio!

IAGO
O notable strumpet! – Cassio, may you suspect
Who they should be that have thus mangled you?

CASSIO   No.   80

GRATIANO   I am sorry to find you thus. I have been to
seek you.

IAGO
Lend me a garter.° So. – O for a chair°
To bear him easily hence!

| | garter: i.e., for a tourniquet; **chair:** litter (a framework couch for carrying the wounded) |

BIANCA
Alas, he faints! O Cassio, Cassio, Cassio!   85

IAGO
Gentlemen all, I do suspect this trash°
To be a party in this injury. –
Patience awhile, good Cassio. – Come, come!
Lend me a light. Know we this face or no?
Alas, my friend and my dear countryman   90
Roderigo? No. – Yes, sure. – O heaven, Roderigo!

| | trash: i.e., Bianca |

GRATIANO   What, of Venice?

IAGO
Even he, sir. Did you know him?

GRATIANO   Know him? Ay.

IAGO
Signor Gratiano? I cry° your gentle pardon.
These bloody accidents° must excuse my manners   95
That so neglected you.

| | **cry:** beg **accidents:** sudden events |

GRATIANO   I am glad to see you.

IAGO
How do you, Cassio? – O, a chair, a chair!

GRATIANO   Roderigo?

IAGO
He, he, 'tis he!
  [A litter brought in.]
                O, that's well said;° the chair.
Some good man bear him carefully from hence.   100
I'll fetch the general's surgeon.
  [To Bianca]   For you, mistress,

| | **well said:** i.e., well done |

DISCOVERING SHAKESPEARE

(113) <u>Verse</u> **[5.1.86]:** <u>Scan</u> lines 86–97 in 5.1 to determine where and why the <u>iambic</u> <u>pentameter</u> <u>verse</u> breaks down.

Save you your labor.° – He that lies slain here, Cassio,
Was my dear friend. What malice was between you?

CASSIO
None in the world, nor do I know the man.

IAGO   *[To Bianca]*
What, look you pale? – O, bear him out o' th' air.
                              [Cassio and Roderigo are borne off.]
Stay you, good gentlemen. – Look you pale, mistress? –
Do you perceive the gastness° of her eye? –
Nay, if you stare, we shall hear more anon.
Behold her well; I pray you look upon her.
Do you see, gentlemen? Nay, guiltiness will speak,
Though tongues were out of use.
    [Enter Emilia.]

EMILIA
Alas, what is the matter? What is the matter, husband?

IAGO
Cassio hath here been set on in the dark
By Roderigo, and fellows that are scaped.
He's almost slain, and Roderigo quite dead.

EMILIA
Alas, good gentleman! alas, good Cassio!

IAGO
This is the fruits of whoring. Prithee, Emilia,
Go know of Cassio where he supped tonight.
    [To Bianca]
What, do you shake at that?

BIANCA
He supped at my house; but I therefore shake not.

IAGO
O did he so? I charge you go with me.

EMILIA
O, fie° upon thee, strumpet!

BIANCA
I am no strumpet, but of life as honest°
As you that thus abuse me.

EMILIA   As I? Fie upon thee!

IAGO
Kind gentlemen, let's go see poor Cassio dressed.°
    [To Bianca]
Come, mistress, you must tell's another tale.
Emilia, run you to the citadel
And tell my lord and lady what hath happed.
                                        [Exit Emilia.]
Will you go on afore?   *Exeunt [all but Iago].*
            This is the night
That either makes me or fordoes° me quite.   *[Exit.]*

Save . . . labor: i.e., you needn't fuss about him anymore; leave him alone

105

gastness: ghastly look, fear

110

115

fie: i.e., shame

honest: chaste

120

dressed: bandaged   125

fordoes: destroys, undoes   130

DISCOVERING SHAKESPEARE

(114) **Plot** [5.1.116]: Why does Iago try to throw suspicion on Bianca in 5.1.113–126?

❧ **5.2°** *Enter Othello [with a light], and Desdemona [asleep] in her bed.*

OTHELLO
It is the cause,° it is the cause, my soul.°
Let me not name it to you, you chaste stars!
It is the cause. Yet I'll not shed her blood,
Nor scar that whiter skin of hers than snow,
And smooth as monumental alabaster.°
Yet she must die, else she'll betray more men.
Put out the light, and then put out the light.
If I quench thee, thou flaming minister,°
I can again thy former light restore,
Should I repent me; but once put out thy light,
Thou cunning'st pattern of excelling nature,°
I know not where is that Promethean heat°
That can thy light relume.° When I have plucked thy
    rose,
I cannot give it vital growth again;
It needs must wither. I'll smell thee on the tree.
    [He kisses her.]
O balmy breath, that dost almost persuade
Justice to break her sword! One more, one more!
Be thus when thou art dead, and I will kill thee,
And love thee after. One more, and that's the last!
So sweet was ne'er so fatal. I must weep,
But they are cruel° tears. This sorrow's heavenly;
It strikes where it doth love.° She wakes.
DESDEMONA
Who's there? Othello?
OTHELLO   Ay, Desdemona.
DESDEMONA
Will you come to bed, my lord?
OTHELLO
Have you prayed tonight, Desdemon?
DESDEMONA   Ay, my lord.
OTHELLO
If you bethink yourself of any crime°
Unreconciled as yet to heaven and grace,
Solicit° for it straight.
DESDEMONA
Alack, my lord, what may you mean by that?
OTHELLO
Well, do it, and be brief; I will walk by.
I would not kill thy unpreparèd spirit.
No, heavens forfend!° I would not kill thy soul.

5.2: A bedroom in the castle

cause: (1) legal matter or "case" (here, the crime of adultery), (2) principle (i.e., not merely a personal grievance); **my soul:** (conventional form of self-address)

alabaster: alabaster, white marble (the archaic form retained here for its sound)   5

flaming minister: i.e., the torch or candle that, as *minister* or servant, lights the chamber

10

Thou . . . nature: i.e., Desdemona (*cunning'st* = beautifully made)
Promethean heat: divine spark (Prometheus legendarily stole fire from heaven)
relume: rekindle

15

20

cruel: i.e., unmerciful, but perhaps "painful" or "distressing"
sorrow's . . . love: (see Hebrews 12:6, "whom the Lord loveth he chasteneth")

25

crime: sin

Solicit: i.e., pray for forgiveness

30

forfend: forbid

DISCOVERING SHAKESPEARE

(115) Staging [5.2.7]: When does Othello put out the candle at the beginning of 5.2? Why do you think this would be an appropriate moment to do so?

(116) Paraphrase [5.2.31]: What does Othello mean when he tells Desdemona that "I would not kill thy unpreparèd spirit" (5.2.31)?

DESDEMONA
  Talk you of killing?
OTHELLO   Ay, I do.
DESDEMONA   Then heaven
  Have mercy on me!
OTHELLO   Amen, with all my heart!
DESDEMONA
  If you say so, I hope you will not kill me.   35
OTHELLO Humh.
DESDEMONA
  And yet I fear you; for you're fatal° then   **fatal:** ominous, frightening
  When your eyes roll so. Why I should fear I know not,
  Since guiltiness I know not; but yet I feel I fear.
OTHELLO
  Think on thy sins.   40
DESDEMONA   They are loves I bear to you.°   **They . . . you:** i.e., my only sin is in loving you
OTHELLO   too much (more than God)
  Ay, and for that thou diest.
DESDEMONA
  That death's unnatural that kills for loving.
  Alas, why gnaw you so your nether lip?
  Some bloody passion shakes your very frame.
  These are portents;° but yet I hope, I hope,   **portents:** omens, usually bad   45
  They do not point on me.
OTHELLO   Peace and be still!°   **still:** quiet
DESDEMONA
  I will so. What's the matter?
OTHELLO
  That handkerchief which I so loved and gave thee
  Thou gav'st to Cassio.
DESDEMONA   No, by my life and soul!
  Send for the man and ask him.   50
OTHELLO   Sweet soul, take heed,
  Take heed of perjury; thou art on thy deathbed.°   **deathbed:** (i.e., women were sometimes buried
DESDEMONA   in their wedding sheets)
  Ay, but not yet to die.
OTHELLO   Presently.°   **Presently:** right away
  Therefore confess thee freely of thy sin,
  For to deny each article with oath
  Cannot remove nor choke the strong conception°   **conception:** belief, or perhaps "plan,"   55
  That I do groan° withal. Thou art to die.   "intention," preparing for the metaphor in the
DESDEMONA   next line of aborted childbirth
  Then Lord have mercy on me!   **groan withal:** i.e., labor to give birth to (but
OTHELLO   I say amen.   with the modern sense of "moan in sorrow")
DESDEMONA
  And have you mercy too! I never did
  Offend° you in my life; never loved Cassio   **Offend:** wrong
  But with such general warranty of heaven
  As I might love. I never gave him token.   60

DISCOVERING SHAKESPEARE

(117) Language [5.2.55]: Underline in your text all the legal jargon Othello uses in 5.2.26–84. To what extent does he make himself judge, jury, and executioner in this scene?

OTHELLO
By heaven, I saw my handkerchief in's hand!
O perjured woman! thou dost stone my heart,°   **stone my heart:** i.e., turn it to stone
And makes me call what I intend to do
A murder, which I thought a sacrifice.   65
I saw the handkerchief.
DESDEMONA   He found it then.
I never gave it him. Send for him hither.
Let him confess a truth.
OTHELLO   He hath confessed.
DESDEMONA
What, my lord?
OTHELLO
That he hath used thee.   70
DESDEMONA   How? unlawfully?
OTHELLO   Ay.
DESDEMONA
He will not say so.
OTHELLO   No, his mouth is stopped.
Honest Iago hath ta'en order° for't.   **ta'en order:** arranged
DESDEMONA
O, my fear interprets.° What, is he dead?   **interprets:** guesses (the worst)
OTHELLO
Had all his hairs been lives, my great revenge
Had stomach° for them all.   **stomach:** appetite, desire   75
DESDEMONA
Alas, he is betrayed, and I undone!
OTHELLO
Out, strumpet! Weep'st thou for him to my face?
DESDEMONA
O, banish me, my lord, but kill me not!
OTHELLO
Down, strumpet!
DESDEMONA
Kill me tomorrow; let me live tonight!   80
OTHELLO
Nay, if you strive° –   **strive:** struggle
DESDEMONA
But half an hour!
OTHELLO   Being done,° there is no pause.   **Being done:** i.e., since the case is over
DESDEMONA
But while I say one prayer!
OTHELLO   It is too late.
Smothers her.
DESDEMONA   O Lord, Lord, Lord!
Emilia at the door.
EMILIA   *[Calls within.]*
My lord, my lord! What, ho! my lord, my lord!   85

DISCOVERING SHAKESPEARE

(118) Staging [5.2.85]: Imagine four different ways Othello might smother Desdemona. Which would be most "dramatic" on stage? Why?

OTHELLO
What noise is this? Not dead? not yet quite dead?
I that am cruel am yet merciful;
I would not have thee linger in thy pain.
So, so.

EMILIA *Within*
What, ho! my lord, my lord!

OTHELLO   Who's there?

EMILIA *[Within]*
O, good my lord, I would speak a word with you!   90

OTHELLO
Yes, 'tis Emilia. – By and by.° – She's dead. –   **By and by:** coming, just a moment (to Emilia)
'Tis like she comes to speak of Cassio's death.
The noise was high.° Ha! no more moving?   **high:** loud
Still as the grave. – Shall she come in? Were't good? –   95
I think she stirs again. No. – What's best to do?
If she come in, she'll sure speak to my wife.
My wife! my wife! what wife? I have no wife.
O, insupportable! O heavy hour!
Methinks it should be now a huge eclipse   100
Of sun and moon, and that th' affrighted globe
Did yawn at alteration.°   **yawn at alteration:** split open (in an
                                                         earthquake) at the change brought on by
                                                         Desdemona's death

EMILIA *[Within]*   I do beseech you
That I may speak with you, O good my lord!

OTHELLO
I had forgot thee. O, come in, Emilia.
Soft, by and by. – Let me the curtains draw. –   105
[Closes the bed curtains.]
Where art thou?
[Opens the door.]
Enter Emilia.
                    What's the matter with thee now?

EMILIA
O my good lord, yonder's foul murders done!

OTHELLO What? Now?

EMILIA But° now, my lord.   **But:** just

OTHELLO
It is the very error° of the moon.   **error:** wandering, errancy, with dire earthly   110
She comes more nearer earth than she was wont°   consequences
And makes men mad.   **was wont:** was formerly accustomed to do

EMILIA
Cassio, my lord, hath killed a young Venetian
Called Roderigo.

OTHELLO   Roderigo killed?
And Cassio killed?   115

EMILIA   No, Cassio is not killed.

OTHELLO
Not Cassio killed? Then murder's out of tune,
And sweet revenge grows harsh.

DISCOVERING SHAKESPEARE

(119) Characterization [5.2.101]: Why does Othello think "th' affrighted globe / Did yawn at alteration" (5.2.101–102)? What has been "altered"?

(120) Paraphrase [5.2.116]: What does Othello mean when he says "Then murder's out of tune, / And sweet revenge grows harsh" (5.2.116–117)?

DESDEMONA
  O, falsely, falsely murdered!
EMILIA   O Lord! what cry is that?
OTHELLO   That? What?
EMILIA
  Out and alas! that was my lady's voice.   120
  Help! help, ho! help! O lady, speak again!
  Sweet Desdemona! O sweet mistress, speak!
DESDEMONA
  A guiltless death I die.
EMILIA
  O, who hath done this deed?
DESDEMONA
  Nobody – I myself. Farewell.   125
  Commend° me to my kind lord. O, farewell!   **Commend:** remember, speak of
  [She dies.]
OTHELLO
  Why, how should she be murdered?
EMILIA   Alas, who knows?
OTHELLO
  You heard her say herself, it was not I.
EMILIA
  She said so. I must needs report the truth.
OTHELLO
  She's like a liar gone to burning hell!   130
  'Twas I that killed her.
EMILIA   O, the more angel she,
  And you the blacker devil!
OTHELLO
  She turned to folly, and she was a whore.
EMILIA
  Thou dost belie her, and thou art a devil.
OTHELLO
  She was false as water.°   **water:** (considered unstable or changing)   135
EMILIA   Thou art rash as fire to say
  That she was false. O, she was heavenly true!
OTHELLO
  Cassio did top° her. Ask thy husband else.°   **top:** (see *tupping*, 1.1.88); **else:** i.e., if you want
  O, I were damned beneath all depth in hell   to know more (*else*)
  But that I did proceed upon just grounds°   **But that . . . grounds:** i.e., if I had acted
  To this extremity. Thy husband knew it all.   without justification   140
EMILIA   My husband?
OTHELLO   Thy husband.
EMILIA
  That she was false to wedlock?
OTHELLO
  Ay, with Cassio. Had she been true,
  If heaven would make me such another world°   **such another world:** i.e., another world like this 145
  Of one entire and perfect chrysolite,°   one
  I'd not have sold her for it.   **chrysolite:** precious gem
EMILIA
  My husband?
OTHELLO   Ay, 'twas he that told me on her first.
  An honest man he is, and hates the slime

That sticks on filthy deeds.	150

EMILIA   My husband?

OTHELLO
What needs this iterance,° woman? I say thy husband.

iterance: repetition

EMILIA
O mistress, villainy hath made mocks° with love!
My husband say she was false?

made mocks with: played games with

OTHELLO   He, woman.
I say, thy husband. Dost understand the word?
My friend, thy husband; honest, honest Iago.

155

EMILIA
If he say so, may his pernicious soul
Rot half a grain a day!° he lies to th' heart.
She was too fond of her most filthy bargain.°

half a grain a day: i.e., slowly and painfully
fond . . . bargain: i.e., devoted to her vows to you

OTHELLO   Ha!

EMILIA   Do thy worst.
This deed of thine is no more worthy heaven
Than thou wast worthy her.

160

OTHELLO   Peace, you were best.

EMILIA
Thou hast not half that power to do me harm
As I have to be hurt.° O gull!° O dolt!
As ignorant as dirt! thou has done a deed –
I care not for thy sword; I'll make thee known,
Though I lost twenty lives. Help! help! ho! help!
The Moor hath killed my mistress! Murder! murder!

to be hurt: to endure pain; **gull:** (common word for a dupe, someone easy to cheat)

165

Enter Montano, Gratiano, and Iago [with others].

MONTANO
What is the matter? How now, general?

EMILIA
O, are you come, Iago? You have done well,
That men must lay their murders on your neck.°

lay . . . neck: charge you with murder

170

GRATIANO
What is the matter?

EMILIA
Disprove this villain, if thou be'st a man.
He says thou told'st him that his wife was false.
I know thou didst not; thou'rt not such a villain.
Speak, for my heart is full.

175

IAGO
I told him what I thought, and told no more
Than what he found himself was apt and true.

EMILIA
But did you ever tell him she was false?

IAGO   I did.

180

EMILIA
You told a lie, an odious damnèd lie!

DISCOVERING SHAKESPEARE

(121) Language [5.2.150]: How could the actress playing Emilia change her intonation and delivery of the words "My husband?" so that each utterance has a different effect?

(122) Blocking [5.2.172]: Draw a diagram of the stage with letters (like O, I, and E) denoting the position of each of the characters. Where is the bed in your set design? How is it brought on and off stage?

Upon my soul, a lie! a wicked lie!
She false with Cassio? Did you say with Cassio?

IAGO
With Cassio, mistress. Go to, charm° your tongue.

charm: cast a spell on (i.e., silence)

EMILIA
I will not charm my tongue; I am bound to speak: 185
My mistress here lies murdered in her bed –

ALL
O heavens forfend!

EMILIA
And your reports have set the murder on.

OTHELLO
Nay, stare not, masters. It is true indeed.

GRATIANO
'Tis a strange truth.   190

MONTANO
O monstrous act!

EMILIA   Villainy, villainy, villainy!
I think upon't – I think I smell't! – O villainy!
I thought so then. – I'll kill myself for grief. –
O villainy, villainy!

IAGO
What, are you mad? I charge you get you home.   195

EMILIA
Good gentlemen, let me have leave to speak.
'Tis proper I obey him, but not now.
Perchance, Iago, I will ne'er go home.

OTHELLO
O! O! O!
    [Falls on the bed.]

EMILIA   Nay, lay thee down and roar!
For thou hast killed the sweetest innocent   200
That e'er did lift up eye.°

lift up eye: i.e., to heaven in prayer

OTHELLO   O, she was foul!
    [Rises.]
I scarce did know you, uncle. There lies your niece,
Whose breath, indeed, these hands have newly stopped.
I know this act shows° horrible and grim.

shows: appears

GRATIANO
Poor Desdemon! I am glad thy father's dead.   205
Thy match was mortal to him, and pure grief
Shore° his old thread in twain. Did he live now,

Shore: cut

This sight would make him do a desperate turn,°

turn: act

Yea, curse his better angel from his side,
And fall to reprobance.°

reprobance: the state of rejection by God   210

OTHELLO
'Tis pitiful; but yet Iago knows
That she with Cassio hath the act of shame
A thousand times committed. Cassio confessed it,
And she did gratify his amorous works°

gratify . . . works: reward his sexual acts

DISCOVERING SHAKESPEARE

(123) Characterization [5.2.198]: Why does Othello cry "O! O! O!" (5.2.198) at this moment in the scene? Why does he fall upon the bed?

With that recognizance° and pledge of love   **recognizance:** token   215
Which I first gave her. I saw it in his hand.
It was a handkerchief, an antique token
My father gave my mother.

EMILIA
O God! O heavenly God!

IAGO
Zounds, hold your peace!   220

EMILIA   'Twill out, 'twill out! I peace?
No, I will speak as liberal as the north.°   **as liberal as the north:** as freely as the north
Let heaven and men and devils, let them all,   wind blows
All, all, cry shame against me, yet I'll speak.

IAGO
Be wise, and get you home.

EMILIA   I will not.
    [Iago draws and threatens Emilia.]

GRATIANO   Fie!
Your sword upon a woman?   225

EMILIA
O thou dull Moor, that handkerchief thou speak'st of
I found by fortune, and did give my husband;
For often with a solemn earnestness –
More than indeed belonged to such a trifle –
He begged of me to steal't.   230

IAGO   Villainous whore!

EMILIA
She give it Cassio? No, alas, I found it,
And I did give't my husband.

IAGO   Filth, thou liest!

EMILIA
By heaven, I do not, I do not, gentlemen.
O murd'rous coxcomb!° what should such a fool   **coxcomb:** jester, fool (i.e., Othello)
Do with so good a wife?   235

OTHELLO   Are there no stones in heaven
But what serves for the thunder?° Precious° villain!   **Are there . . . the thunder:** i.e., why doesn't
    [The Moor runs at Iago but is disarmed.   heaven rain down stones on this villain;
    Iago stabs his wife.]   **Precious:** utter, complete

GRATIANO
The woman falls. Sure he hath killed his wife.

EMILIA
Ay, ay. O, lay me by my mistress' side.   *[Exit Iago.]*

GRATIANO
He's gone, but his wife's killed.

MONTANO
'Tis a notorious° villain. Take you this weapon,   **a notorious:** an extraordinary, incredible (i.e.,   240
Which I have here recovered from the Moor.   not the modern "well-known")
Come, guard the door without. Let him not pass,
But kill him rather. I'll after that same villain,
For 'tis a damnèd slave.
        Exit [Montano, with all but Othello and Emilia].

DISCOVERING SHAKESPEARE

(124) <u>Shared Lines</u> [5.2.224]: In 5.2.224, three actors (Iago, Emilia, and Gratiano) share the same line, and in the same ten syllables Iago draws his sword upon his wife. Count out the <u>beats</u> of the line; then determine at which moment Iago threatens Emilia with his sword.

OTHELLO   I am not valiant neither;
But every puny whipster° gets my sword.
But why should honor° outlive honesty?°
Let it go all.

EMILIA   What did thy song bode, lady?
Hark, canst thou hear me? I will play the swan,
And die in music.° [Sings.] "Willow, willow, willow."
Moor, she was chaste. She loved thee, cruel Moor:
So come my soul to bliss as I speak true.
So speaking as I think, alas, I die.
    [She dies.]

OTHELLO
I have another weapon in this chamber;
It was a sword of Spain, the ice brook's temper.°
O, here it is. – Uncle, I must come forth.

GRATIANO   [Within]
If thou attempt it, it will cost thee dear.
Thou hast no weapon, and perforce must suffer.

OTHELLO
Look in upon me then and speak with me,
Or, naked° as I am, I will assault thee.
    [Enter Gratiano.]

GRATIANO
What is the matter?

OTHELLO   Behold, I have a weapon;
A better never did itself sustain
Upon a soldier's thigh. I have seen the day
That with this little arm and this good sword
I have made my way through more impediments
Than twenty times your stop.° But O vain boast!
Who can control his fate? 'Tis not so now.
Be not afraid, though you do see me weaponed.
Here is my journey's end, here is my butt°
And very seamark of my utmost sail:°
Do you go back dismayed? 'Tis a lost° fear.
Man but a rush° against Othello's breast
And he retires.° Where should Othello go?
Now, how dost thou look now? O ill-starred wench!
Pale as thy smock! When we shall meet at compt,°
This look of thine will hurl my soul from heaven,
And fiends will snatch at it. Cold, cold, my girl?
Even like thy chastity.
O cursèd, cursèd slave! Whip me, ye devils,
From the possession of this heavenly sight!
Blow me about in winds! roast me in sulphur!
Wash me in steep-down gulfs of liquid fire!
Oh Desdemon! dead Desdemon! dead! Oh! Oh!
    Enter Lodovico, Cassio [in a litter], Montano, and
    Iago, with Officers.

---

puny whipster: foolish, insignificant person (cf. whippersnapper)   245
honor: i.e., military achievement; **honesty:** chastity

swan . . . music: (according to legend, the ordinarily mute swan sang beautifully just before death)   250

sword . . . temper: i.e., Spanish sword hardened or "tempered" in freezing water   255

naked: unarmed

260

your stop: i.e., the obstacle you impose   265

butt: target (from archery)
seamark . . . sail: beacon or destination of my last voyage   270
lost: wasted
Man but a rush: i.e., use only a reed
retires: withdraws, retreats (a military term)
compt: i.e., final accounting (Last Judgment)

275

280

DISCOVERING SHAKESPEARE

(125) Teaser [5.2.248]: What is the origin of the myth that swans sing as they die (5.2.248–249)?

LODOVICO
Where is this rash and most unfortunate man?
OTHELLO
That's he that was Othello. Here I am.
LODOVICO
Where is that viper? Bring the villain forth.   285
OTHELLO
I look down towards his feet – but that's a fable.°   **I . . . fable:** (Othello inspects Iago's feet to test
If that thou be'st a devil, I cannot kill thee.   the legend that the devil's feet are cloven)
  [Wounds Iago.]
LODOVICO
Wrench his sword from him.
  [Othello is disarmed.]
IAGO   I bleed, sir, but not killed.
OTHELLO
I am not sorry neither. I'd have thee live,
For in my sense, 'tis happiness to die.   290
LODOVICO
O thou Othello that was once so good,
Fall'n in the practice° of a damnèd slave,   **practice:** plot
What shall be said to thee?
OTHELLO   Why, anything:
An honorable murderer, if you will;
For nought I did in hate, but all in honor.   295
LODOVICO
This wretch hath part confessed his villainy.
Did you and he consent in° Cassio's death?   **consent in:** agree (in planning)
OTHELLO   Ay.
CASSIO
Dear general, I never gave you cause.
OTHELLO
I do believe it, and I ask your pardon.   300
Will you, I pray, demand that demidevil°   **demidevil:** half demon, almost a devil
Why he hath thus ensnared my soul and body?
IAGO
Demand me nothing. What you know, you know.
From this time forth I never will speak word.
LODOVICO
What, not to pray?   305
GRATIANO   Torments will ope your lips.
OTHELLO
Well, thou dost best.
LODOVICO
Sir, you shall understand what hath befall'n,
Which, as I think, you know not. Here is a letter
Found in the pocket of the slain Roderigo,
And here another. The one of them imports   310
The death of Cassio to be undertook
By Roderigo.

DISCOVERING SHAKESPEARE

(126) Characterization [5.2.283]: When Lodovico enters this chaotic scene in 5.2.283, he immediately takes charge.
Find at least three indications in the text that he seizes control of the scene.

(127) Props [5.2.307]: How many letters are discovered at the conclusion of this final scene (5.2.307–329)?

OTHELLO
  O villain!

CASSIO   Most heathenish and most gross!°   **gross:** monstrous

LODOVICO
  Now here's another discontented paper
  Found in his pocket too, and this, it seems,   315
  Roderigo meant t' have sent this damnèd villain;
  But that, belike, Iago in the interim
  Came in and satisfied him.

OTHELLO   O thou pernicious caitiff!° –   **caitiff:** villain
  How came you, Cassio, by that handkerchief
  That was my wife's?   320

CASSIO   I found it in my chamber;
  And he himself confessed it but even now
  That there he dropped it for a special purpose
  Which wrought to his desire.

OTHELLO   O fool! fool! fool!

CASSIO
  There is besides in Roderigo's letter,
  How he upbraids Iago that he made him   325
  Brave° me upon the watch, whereon it came   **Brave:** defy, challenge
  That I was cast;° and even but now he spake,   **cast:** dismissed
  After long seeming dead – Iago hurt him,
  Iago set him on.

LODOVICO
  You must forsake this room and go with us.
  Your power and your command is taken off,   330
  And Cassio rules in Cyprus. For this slave,
  If there be any cunning cruelty
  That can torment him much and hold him long,°   **hold him long:** i.e., keep him alive through
  It shall be his. You shall close prisoner rest°   torture   335
  Till that the nature of your fault be known   **close prisoner rest:** i.e., remain closely guarded,
  To the Venetian state. Come, bring away.   confined

OTHELLO
  Soft you!° a word or two before you go.   **Soft you:** one moment, wait
  I have done the state some service, and they know't.
  No more of that. I pray you, in your letters,   340
  When you shall these unlucky° deeds relate,   **unlucky:** unfortunate
  Speak of me as I am. Nothing extenuate,°   **extenuate:** soft-pedal (literally, "thin out")
  Nor set down aught in malice. Then must you speak
  Of one that loved not wisely, but too well;
  Of one not easily jealous, but, being wrought,°   **wrought:** worked up, worked on   345
  Perplexed° in the extreme; of one whose hand,   **Perplexed:** desperate, bewildered
  Like the base Judean,° threw a pearl away   **base Judean:** (perhaps Judas Iscariot, betrayer of
  Richer than all his tribe; of one whose subdued° eyes,   Christ, or Herod, who impulsively killed his wife;
  Albeit unusèd to the melting mood,   Q reads "Indian")
  Drops tears as fast as the Arabian trees   **subdued:** conquered, overcome with grief
  Their medicinable gum.° Set you down this.   350
  And say besides that in Aleppo once,   **gum:** i.e., myrrh
  Where a malignant and a turbaned Turk
  Beat a Venetian and traduced° the state,   **traduced:** betrayed

---

DISCOVERING SHAKESPEARE

(128) Renaissance History [5.2.334]: What were the primary tortures used in Italy around the year 1600?

I took by th' throat the circumcisèd dog   355
And smote him – thus.
[He stabs himself.]
LODOVICO
  O bloody period!°   **period:** ending
GRATIANO   All that is spoke is marred.
OTHELLO
  I kissed thee ere I killed thee. No way but this,
  Killing myself, to die upon a kiss.
  [He] dies.
CASSIO
  This did I fear, but thought he had no weapon;   360
  For he was great of heart.
LODOVICO   *[To Iago]*   O Spartan dog,°   **Spartan dog:** (bloodhound known for silence)
  More fell° than anguish, hunger, or the sea!   **fell:** merciless, inhuman
  Look on the tragic loading of this bed.
  This is thy work. The object poisons sight;
  Let it be hid.° Gratiano, keep° the house,   **Let it be hid:** i.e., draw the bed curtains;   365
  And seize upon° the fortunes of the Moor,   **keep:** guard
  For they succeed on° you. To you, lord governor,   **seize upon:** take legal control of
  Remains the censure° of this hellish villain,   **succeed on:** pass to you (as Desdemona's uncle)
  The time, the place, the torture. O, enforce it!   by inheritance
  Myself will straight aboard, and to the state   **censure:** judgment, passing sentence   370
  This heavy act with heavy heart relate.   *Exeunt.*

DISCOVERING SHAKESPEARE

(129) Characterization [5.2.370]: In Shakespearean tragedies and history plays, convention dictates that the most powerful character speaks last. Is that rule followed in this play? Why or why not?

❧

Research and Discussion Topics

ACT I

1. Research the history of Venice and Cyprus during the Renaissance.

2. What was a "Moor"?

3. Where was Mauritania?

4. What were the duties of the Duke (Doge) of Venice?

5. What was an "ancient"?

6. What is the importance of Michael Cassio being a "Florentine" (1.1.19)?

7. Locate the following places on a map: Rhodes (1.1.28), Cyprus (1.1.28), Venice, and Florence.

8. What was a "Sagittary" (1.1.156)?

9. What was a "magnifico" (1.2.12)?

10. What was a "galley" (1.3.3)?

11. Who were the "Ottomites" (1.3.33)?

12. What was a "mountebank" (1.3.61)?

13. Who were the "anthropophagi" (1.3.144)?

14. What sort of "education" (1.3.182) were women given during the Renaissance?

15. Research the following herbs: nettles, lettuce, hyssop, and thyme (1.3.321–322).

16. What was "coloquintida" (1.3.348)?

17. What was a "cuckold" (1.3.366)?

ACT II

1. Research Giraldi Cinthio's *Hecatommithi* (1566), where Shakespeare's <u>source</u> for *Othello* is contained in the seventh "story" of the third "decade." What principal changes did Shakespeare make in his <u>source</u> material? Why did he make these alterations?

2. In how many different <u>quarto</u> and <u>folio</u> editions was *Othello* published during the early 1600s? Which text is now considered the most authoritative?

3. What important political and social events were occurring in England around the year 1604, when *Othello* was written and first performed?

4. Who was "Jove" (2.1.77), and why does Cassio refer to him at this moment in the play?

5. What were "birdlime" and "frieze" (2.1.126)?

6. What was "choler" (2.1.269)?

7. What were "clyster pipes" (2.1.176)?

8. What type of wines did soldiers drink during the Renaissance (2.3.44–69 ff.)?

9. What was the "watch" (2.3.113)?

10. Who was "Caesar" (2.3.115)?

11. What was an "horologue" (2.3.123) and a "mazard" (2.3.143)?

12. What were the duties of a "surgeon" (2.3.243)? How were they trained?

ACT III

1. What was a "clown" (3.1.3) within the context of a Shakespearean play?

2. What were the "works" (3.2.3) of a fort?

3. What did the moon (3.3.178) symbolize during the Renaissance?

4. What was the "forked plague" (3.3.276)?

5. Where were the mines of sulphur (3.3.329)?

6. What were the medicinal properties of "poppy" and "mandragora" (3.3.330)?

7. What kind of work did "pioners" do (3.3.346)?

8. What were the duties of early dentists (3.3.414)?

9. What were "crusadoes" (3.4.26)?

10. What was a "sibyl" (3.4.70)? What was "mummy" (3.4.74)?

11. What was a "dial" (3.4.174)?

ACT IV

1. What sins were considered "venial" (4.1.9) by the Catholic Church?

2. What was a "fitchew" (4.1.144)?

3. What is the origin of the phrase to "sing the savageness out of a bear" (4.1.185–186)?

4. What was "the serpent's curse" (4.2.16)?

5. Why does Othello call prostitution a "mystery" (4.2.30)?

6. What were "cherubin" (4.2.62)?

7. What was a "shambles" (4.2.66)? What is the origin of the word?

8. Who was "Saint Peter" (4.2.91)? What was his occupation?

9. What was a "callet" (4.2.121)?

10. What was a "votarist" (4.2.188)?

11. What was a "joint ring" (4.3.72)?

ACT V

1. What was a "rapier" (5.1.2)?

2. What was a "minion" (5.1.33)? What is the word's linguistic origin?

3. What was "alabaster" (5.2.5)?

4. Who was Prometheus? What was "Promethean heat" (5.2.12)?

5. Why did Lady Justice have a sword (5.2.17)?

6. What was an "error of the moon" (5.2.110)?

7. What were the four elements (5.2.135)?

8. What was a "chrysolite" (5.2.146)?

9. What was a "seamark" (5.2.269)?

10. What was "compt" (5.2.274)?

11. In the Quarto, Othello describes a "base Indian" who "threw a pearl away / Richer than all his tribe" (5.2.347), but in the 1623 First Folio the line is changed to "base Judean" (i.e., Judas, who betrayed Christ). What does each reading mean? Which do you prefer? Why?

Filmography

1981
Bard Productions
Rating:

Directed by: Franklin Melton

William Marshall as Othello
Ron Moody as Iago
Jenny Agutter as Desdemona
DeVeren Bookwalter as Cassio

William Marshall's Othello is the noble Moor, with no trace of the bluster and ostentation that are sometimes imposed on the part. He is an heroic soldier and faithful lover destroyed during the course of the play by his mistakes and those of his friends and by the villainy of his chief enemy. Marshall's deep, flexible voice and natural dignity are especially impressive. Jenny Agutter's Desdemona is beautiful and self-possessed, a believable senator's daughter. While she seems more knowing than perhaps Desdemona should be, her sympathy for Othello and absolute loyalty to him are clear. Ron Moody is effective as a blunt, unattractive but trustworthy Iago, who is, of course, deception personified. If this production has a fault, it is that not all of the actors live up to the high standard set by the main characters.

1965
B.H.E. Production from The National Theatre of Great Britain
Rating:

Directed by: Stuart Burge

Laurence Olivier as Othello
Frank Finlay as Iago
Maggie Smith as Desdemona
Derek Jacobi as Cassio

Brilliant and infuriating in almost equal measure, this production is always watchable. Olivier's Othello is part charlatan and part champion, and his portrayal of a Moor has been attacked as racist and praised as perfection. Olivier lowered his voice, lifted weights, and invented a rolling walk for the performance, but he says the walk was designed to keep his big toes from standing straight up, not as any sort of African stride. Ultimately, this Othello is a large reading, less noble, more passionate, and sooner jealous than most. Maggie Smith's Desdemona is charismatic if not especially innocent, and Frank Finlay's Iago (criticized for underacting in the National Theatre production from which the film came) has the right mix of restraint and villainy.

1995
Dakota Films/Imminent Films Production
(R—Restricted)
Rating:

Directed by: Oliver Parker

Laurence Fishburne as Othello
Kenneth Branagh as Iago
Irene Jacob as Desdemona
Nathaniel Parker as Cassio

Making Shakespeare into a movie is a tricky business. Oliver Parker has succeeded in keeping the main outlines of the characters and the central emotions of the play. The visual images are strong and the musical score effective. However, two-thirds of the lines are gone and with them has gone some of Othello's breadth of soul and largeness of purpose, some of the depth of Iago's malice, and some of the pity and pain in Desdemona's death. Laurence Fishburne brings an intense realism to Othello, but he is sometimes less than adept at handling the longer speeches. Irene Jacob is a picture of desirable innocence, but her accent slows and encumbers her lines. Kenneth Branagh is the most effective actor in the film, combining charm, malice, and subtlety to create an entirely believable (and still horrifying) Iago.

1952
A Mercury Production
(Black and White)
Rating:

Directed by: Orson Welles

Orson Welles as Othello
Micheàl MacLiammoir as Iago
Suzanne Cloutier as Desdemona
Michael Laurence as Cassio

The term "flawed masterpiece" should have been invented for Orson Welles. His Othello is visually enthralling, filled as it is with vast spaces that somehow seem to constrict and confine the humans who move through them. Welles' juxtapositions are as sharp as jealousies—the faces of Othello and Desdemona picked out of the dark or Desdemona talking to Emilia and looking through a window filled with spikes. The film begins with funerals and with perhaps the most striking of all the visuals, Iago hanging in a metal cage as the crowds and corpses go by below. Orson Welles is a fascinating rather than believable Othello. His great strength as an actor is not the portrayal of innocence, but his voice is often magical. Suzanne Cloutier is a pattern for all pure and elegant Desdemonas, and Micheàl MacLiammoir (who seems to be working up to Richard III) for villainous Iagos.

1981
BBC
Rating:

Directed by: Jonathan Miller

Anthony Hopkins as Othello
Bob Hoskins as Iago
Penelope Wilton as Desdemona
David Yelland as Cassio

James Earl Jones was supposed to be the BBC's Othello, but British Actors' Equity objected to an American in the part. Anthony Hopkins as an Arab (not African) Othello so underplays and minimizes the role that the result seems to be something other than tragedy. The sets, which are Jonathan Miller's usual cluttered interiors with references to paintings, are part of the problem. Penelope Wilton's Desdemona appears unattractive and willful. Bob Hoskins' Iago is the most interesting part of the production, realistic and vicious, scheming and low-class, funny and angry. If Iago were meant to act the villain at every moment in the play, this would be a nearly definitive performance.

Annotated Bibliography

Adamson, W.D. "Unpinned or Undone? Desdemona's Critics and the Problem of Sexual Innocence." *Shakespeare Studies* 13 (1980): 169–186. journal PR 2885.S63.

> Adamson does a character study of Desdemona, noting the complex emotions that keep her from being easily categorized. Adamson focuses on Desdemona's sexuality, which is deemed deliberate in nature. The author also discusses Desdemona's fall to be an important part of the play's tragedy.

Calderwood, James L. "Appalling Property of *Othello.*" *University of Toronto Quarterly* 57 (1987–1988): 353-75. journal AP 5.U55.

> In Calderwood's analysis of the theme of propriety in the play, he argues that Othello displays an attitude of ownership over Desdemona, whose reaction to his claim is surprisingly indifferent. Calderwood also discusses Emilia as a foil to Desdemona in her rebellion against patriarchal ownership of women.

Elliott, G.R. *Flaming Minister: A Study of "Othello" as a Tragedy of Love and Hate.* Durham, NC: Duke University Press, 1953. PR 2829.E6.

> Elliott establishes how pride, a significant theme in the play, has the power to destroy even the strongest virtues of love. In his argument, Elliott focuses on Iago as a great facilitator in enabling pride to enact these changes. The author also discusses the manner in which these issues lead to visual performance.

Garner, S.N. "Shakespeare's Desdemona." *Shakespeare Studies* 9 (1976): 233–252. journal PR 2885.S63.

> Garner analyzes Desdemona's depth of character as she displays the emotions of both rebellion and desire. Desdemona's problem recognizing her own flaws, particularly her inability to see Othello as a man with human failures, converts her into a submissive character and prevents reconciliation between them.

Heilman, Robert B. *Magic in the Web: Action and Language in "Othello."* Lexington: University of Kentucky Press, 1956. PR 2829.H4.

> Heilman notes that the play's language and plot blend to form an effective expression of meaning. Iago's public image is known through a façade he has constructed through implication and deception. Heilman further discusses how Othello's contrary actions reflect his inner conflict between defending what is just and his own less-than-noble human emotions.

Jones, Eldred D. *Othello's Countrymen: The African in English Renaissance Drama.* London: Oxford University Press, 1965. PR 658.A4.J6.

> Jones establishes that Othello's failures are due to his human weakness, which opposes the typical racist Elizabethan view of the Moor as evil. The author further argues that in contrast to Othello, Iago's character more clearly portrays the characteristics of evil. Jones also reviews the stage appearance of Moors in Elizabethan times.

Kolin, Philip C. ed. *"Othello": New Critical Essays.* New York & London: Routledge, 2002. PR2829.O855.

> This book contains many useful articles ranging from the topics of marriage, racism, and sexuality to discussions on images of water, murder trials,

and morality/ethics. Peter Erickson has an especially interesting interdisciplinary article that draws connections between depictions of black and white in Renaissance art and *Othello*. Other notable authors in the collection include David Bevington, Jay L. Halio, and Clifford Ronan.

Loomba, Ania. "'Delicious Traffick': Alterity and Exchange on Early Modern Stages." *Shakespeare Survey* 52 (1999): 201–214. journal PR 2888.C3.
> In this well-researched essay, the author looks back to a historical period when "color was not the primary marker of difference" to examine linkages between blackness and devilry, the sexuality of Muslims and blacks, intercourse between members of different racial groups, and the relationship between visible difference and moral difference.

Mafe, Diana A. "From Ogun to *Othello*: (Re)Aquainting Yoruba Myth and Shakespeare's Moor." *Research in African Literature* 35.3 (2004): 46–61. journal PL 8010.R46.
> Mafe acknowledges the years of criticism regarding Othello and his African connections, but the goal of this article is to make specific connections between Othello and Yoruba culture and myth. The author also explores the implications of the term "moor," as well as perceptions of Africa and Africans held by the English based on early travel literature and contemporary personal accounts.

Orkin, Martin. "Othello and the Plain Face of Racism." *Shakespeare Quarterly* 38 (1987): 166–88. journal PR 2885.S63.
> Orkin states that South African criticism has produced a profound silence about the racist references in this play. He argues that this silence actually reinforces racism. The play is not in itself racist, but rather uses racist language to demonstrate the evils of racism. Ultimately, racism/hate is depicted as a destructive evil that destroys lives.

Rosenberg, Marvin. *The Masks of "Othello."* Berkeley: University of California Press, 1961. PR 2829.R6.
> Rosenberg examines the limitations of interpreting *Othello* exclusively as a morality play. He asserts that stage tradition can greatly influence ideas about characterization. The author traces *Othello*'s production history from the Restoration into the twentieth century, followed by interviews with several notable modern actors. He reasons that a focus on the humanity depicted in the play is central to the best performances. His interviews include Earle Hyman, Sir Laurence Olivier, Anthony Quayle, Paul Robeson, Abraham Sofaer, Wilifred Walter, and Sir Donald Wolfit.

Spivack, Bernard. *Shakespeare and the Allegory of Evil.* New York: Columbia University Press, 1958. PR 2992.V5S6.
> Spivack, much like E. E. Stoll, approaches characterization in relation to the theatrical appetites of an Elizabethan audience. Spivack's focus is on Iago and his kinship to the Vice character of medieval morality plays.

Stoll, E. E. *"Othello": A Historical and Comparative Study.* Cambridge University Press, 1915. PR 2829.S75 1967
> Stoll approaches the characters as fictional entities created for an Elizabethan audience rather than as realistic human beings on stage. He therefore focuses on the expectations of this audience in relation to

characterization. Stoll focuses on the language in the play as well as on the literary traditions and stage conventions of the time.

Wain, John. "Introduction," *"Othello": A Casebook.* London: MacMillan, 1971, pp. 1–33. PR 2829.W28

In addition to discussing issues of setting and race, Wain mainly concentrates on the theme of misunderstanding. He concludes that *Othello* is ultimately a tragedy based on this theme. He also cites various examples of how misunderstanding is a force driving the action of the characters.

King Lear

King Lear *at the Guthrie Theater in Minneapolis, Minnesota, with Stephen Yoakam as the Earl of Kent, Richard Ooms as King Lear, Isabell Monk as the Fool, and Christopher Bayes as Edgar (1995). Photograph by Michal Daniel.*

Once upon a time, an old man had three daughters. Within the simple structure of this mythic narrative, Shakespeare's *King Lear* speaks to us through the centuries about such enduring <u>themes</u> as old age, filial in-gratitude, self-knowledge, and the constantly shifting relationship between wisdom and maturity. Written between 1604 and 1606, the <u>script</u> of the play has an intriguing history. After publication of the so-called "Pied Bull" <u>quarto</u> edition of the play in 1608 (named after the sign of the publishing house), a second <u>quarto</u> followed in 1619 and the <u>First Folio</u> text in 1623. Current scholarly opinion holds that the 1608 <u>quarto</u> <u>script</u>, on which this edition is based, is an authorial revision of Shakespeare's earlier manuscript which was submitted to his acting company to be readied for production; the <u>folio</u> <u>script</u> represents an edited and emended theatrical version of the play intended for a specific performance by Shakespeare's actors.

Though the story of *King Lear* originates in ancient legend, Shakespeare's immediate <u>source</u> was an old play entitled *The True Chronicle History of King Leir,* which was first published in 1605, but may have existed as early as 1590 in manuscript form. Unlike Shakespeare's version of the <u>script</u>, *Leir* ends happily with the old king restored to the throne. Shakespeare's <u>narrative</u> omits the <u>comic</u> ending, makes Cornwall a villain, creates the brilliant storm scenes, and adds the Gloucester <u>sub-plot</u>. Sir Philip Sidney's *Arcadia* may have inspired the episode in which Edgar leads his blind, aged father, as well as the disguise <u>motif</u> that appears throughout the play and the drama's <u>tragic</u> conclusion. Essentially the same story of King Lear appears in a number of earlier works, including Geoffrey of Monmouth's *Historia Regum Britanniae, The Mirror for Magistrates, Albion's England,* Spenser's *The Faerie Queen,* and Raphael Holinshed's *Chronicles,* although Shakespeare's retelling of these pseudo-historical events is the only <u>narrative</u> that does not retain the happy ending.

Shakespeare's <u>tragic</u> retelling of this traditionally <u>comic</u> narrative elevates the <u>script</u> from a mildly enjoyable romance to a brilliant dramatic parable about man's place in the cosmos, including an epic battle between good and evil over the characters' souls. The relationship between parents and children is another important <u>theme</u>, especially in the complex double <u>plot</u> juxtaposing Lear and his three daughters with Gloucester and his two sons, as are such other topics as the suffering of innocents, the quest for self-knowledge, the "illness" of old age, the wheel of fortune, appearance vs. reality, the paradox of the "wise fool," literal vs. spiritual blindness, and the difference between madness and sanity. Although Lear's progress through the play ends in defeat on the physical level, most viewers rejoice in the <u>cathartic</u> spiritual reunion between Cordelia and her aged father that counterbalances their deaths at the end of the <u>script</u>. Recent scholarship, though still content with investigating these principal <u>themes</u>, has moved into new areas of inquiry such as death consciousness, resistance to authority, politics, divinity, emotional and spiritual renewal, the relationship between the past and present, and the love between parents and children.

Despite its immense popularity with modern audiences, *King Lear* was not an immediate theatrical success. After a sparse performance history during the early seventeenth century, the play was revived in a 1680s adaptation by Nahum Tate, which cut over eight hundred lines from the <u>script</u>, fabricated a love story between Edgar and Cordelia, omitted the characters of France and the Fool, and ended happily with Lear, Gloucester, and Kent still alive. This truncated version of the play held the stage for over one hundred and fifty years, until William Charles Macready's 1838 production returned to an abbreviated Shakespearean <u>script</u> and restored the Fool (played by Priscilla Horton). Similarly abridged and unsuccessful presentations of the play held the stage through the nineteenth century, most notably Tommaso Salvini's Italian production in 1882, Henry Irving's 1892 version that cut nearly half the lines, and Andre Antoine's 1904 French translation in Paris—all of which seemed to justify the famous comment by essayist Charles Lamb that "*Lear* is essentially impossible to be represented on a stage" because of its epic scope and mythic geography.

The rebirth of *King Lear* began in the early twentieth century through innovations in continuous staging by William Poel and Harley Granville-Barker, who directed John Gielgud as Lear in a 1940 production at the Old Vic Theatre in London. Other seminal modern presentations of the play have included Donald Wolfit's appearance in the title role in the 1940s and 50s, Peter Brook's Stratford production with Paul Scofield as Lear in 1962, Peter Zadek's 1974 German translation set in circus tents, Ingmar Bergman's 1984 expressionistic adaptation in Stockholm, Deborah Warner's 1990 British version (where Lear screeched into the first scene in a wheelchair wearing a red nose in celebration of his eightieth birthday), Ian Holm's modern-dress performance at the National Theatre in 1997, and Helena Kaut-Howson's Leicester Haymarket production that presented the play as the dreamvision of a terminally ill patient in a geriatric ward. Interesting modern cinematic productions include Grigori Kozintsev's 1969 barren landscape version, Peter Brook's 1971 movie set in ice and snow, Michael Elliott's film for Granada Television in 1983 featuring the seventy-five-year-old Laurence Olivier, Akira Kurosawa's 1985 Japanese adaptation entitled *Ran,* and Jonathan Miller's 1982 BBC-TV production with Michael Hordern playing the lead.

Although we suffer terribly with Lear as he is rejected by his daughters and tormented by the tempest within his mind, we are edified and elevated by the nobility of his struggle to regain his sanity against such fierce opposition. After dying with the old king, we are reborn into a life made richer and more "human" by our experience with the play. This is the special triumph of *King Lear* for modern audiences: The painful reality of Lear's descent into madness and the divine reconciliation with his beloved Cordelia resonate deeply within contemporary psyches that have been sensitized to the specter of mental illness and scarred by the indignity of warfare, terrorist attacks, and the thousand natural shocks that flesh is heir to. For a brief moment, the play allows us to see truth within the chaos that surrounds us. Such gifts are precious indeed.

King Lear *at the Oregon Shakespearean Festival in Ashland, Oregon, with James Edmondson (top) as King Lear and Dennis Robertson (bottom) as Gloucester (1997). Photograph by Andree Lanthier.*

King Lear

ⓒ⅋⅋⅋❧

NAMES OF THE ACTORS

LEAR, *King of Britain*
KING OF FRANCE
GONERIL, *Lear's eldest daughter*
DUKE OF ALBANY, *Goneril's husband*
REGAN, *Lear's second daughter*
DUKE OF CORNWALL, *Regan's husband*
CORDELIA, *Lear's youngest daughter*
DUKE OF BURGUNDY
EARL OF KENT
EARL OF GLOUCESTER
EDGAR, *Gloucester's elder son, later disguised as Tom o' Bedlam*
EDMUND, *Gloucester's younger, bastard son*
OSWALD, *Goneril's steward*
OLD MAN, *Gloucester's tenant*
CURAN, *Gloucester's servant*
FOOL, *attending on Lear*
DOCTOR
SERVANTS, CAPTAINS, HERALD, KNIGHT,
MESSENGER, GENTLEMEN, SOLDIERS, *etc.*

SCENE: *Britain*

❧

❧ **1.1°** *Enter Kent, Gloucester,° and Bastard [Edmund].*

KENT   I thought the king had more affected the Duke of Albany° than° Cornwall.

GLOUCESTER   It did always seem so to us, but now in the division of the kingdoms, it appears not which of the dukes he values most, for equalities are so weighed° that curiosity in neither can make choice of either's moiety.°

KENT   Is not this your son, my lord?

GLOUCESTER   His breeding, sir, hath been at my charge. I have so often blushed to acknowledge him that now I am brazed° to it.

KENT   I cannot conceive° you.

GLOUCESTER   Sir, this young fellow's mother could, whereupon she grew round-wombed and had indeed,

1.1: Lear's palace; **Gloucester:** (pronounced "Gloster")

Albany: i.e., Scotland; **more affected . . . than:** preferred . . . to

equalities . . . weighed: their qualities are so equal   5

curiosity . . . moiety: thorough examination cannot find either's share preferable

brazed: brazened   10
conceive: understand

DISCOVERING SHAKESPEARE

(1) Geography [1.1.1]: Find Albany and Cornwall on a map of Britain. How far apart are they? How far is each from London?

sir, a son for her cradle ere she had a husband for her bed. Do you smell a fault? 15

KENT I cannot wish the fault undone, the issue of it being so proper.°

GLOUCESTER But I have, sir, a son by order of law,° some year elder than this, who yet is no dearer in my account.° Though this knave came something saucily° into the world before he was sent for, yet was his mother fair; there was good sport at his making, and the whoreson° must be acknowledged. Do you know this noble gentleman, Edmund?

EDMUND No, my lord.

GLOUCESTER My lord of Kent. Remember him hereafter as my honorable friend.

EDMUND My services to your lordship.

KENT I must love you, and sue° to know you better.

EDMUND Sir, I shall study deserving.°

GLOUCESTER He hath been out° nine years, and away he shall again. The king is coming.

Sound a sennet.° Enter one bearing a coronet, then Lear, then the Dukes of Albany and Cornwall; next Goneril, Regan, Cordelia, with Followers.

LEAR
Attend my lords of France and Burgundy, Gloucester.

GLOUCESTER I shall, my liege. *Exit.*

LEAR
Meantime we will express our darker purposes.° 35
The map there. Know we have divided
In three our kingdom, and 'tis our first intent
To shake all cares and business of our state,
Confirming them on younger years.
The two great princes, France and Burgundy, 40
Great rivals in our youngest daughter's love,
Long in our court have made their amorous sojourn,
And here are to be answered. Tell me, my daughters,
Which of you shall we say doth love us most,
That we our largest bounty may extend 45
Where merit doth most challenge it?
Goneril, our eldest born, speak first.

GONERIL
Sir, I do love you more than words can wield the matter,°
Dearer than eyesight, space,° or liberty,
Beyond what can be valued rich or rare, 50
No less than life, with grace, health, beauty, honor;
As much as child e'er loved, or father, friend;
A love that makes breath° poor and speech unable.
Beyond all manner of so much I love you.

CORDELIA *[Aside]*
What shall Cordelia do? Love and be silent. 55

---

proper: handsome
by . . . law: legitimate

account: esteem; **something saucily:** 20
somewhat impertinently

whoreson: (literally "bastard," but the word was
also an affectionate term, like "scamp")

25

sue: seek
study deserving: undertake to deserve it 30
out: away

sennet: trumpet fanfare

darker purposes: secret plan

wield the matter: express the subject
space: scope (to enjoy *liberty*)

breath: voice

DISCOVERING SHAKESPEARE

(2) History [1.1.27]: How does Gloucester treat his bastard son, Edmund, before the King's entrance in 1.1.32? What does his attitude toward Edmund tell us about Gloucester? About Edmund?

(3) Subtext [1.1.48]: What do you suppose Goneril is thinking while she is speaking to Lear in 1.1.48–54? Write your opinion of her subtext on a separate piece of paper.

LEAR
Of all these bounds, even from this line to this,
With shady forests and wide-skirted meads,°   **wide-skirted meads:** spreading meadows
We make thee lady. To thine and Albany's issue°   **issue:** heirs
Be this perpetual. What says our second daughter,
Our dearest Regan, wife to Cornwall? Speak.   60

REGAN
Sir, I am made
Of the selfsame mettle that my sister is,
And prize me° at her worth in my true heart.   **prize me:** value myself
I find she names my very deed of love;
Only she came short, that° I profess   **that:** in that   65
Myself an enemy to all other joys
Which the most precious square of sense possesses,°   **most . . . possesses:** measure of perception
And find I am alone felicitate°   holds to be most precious
In your dear highness' love.   **felicitate:** made happy

CORDELIA   *[Aside]*   Then poor Cordelia!
And yet not so, since I am sure my love's   70
More richer than my tongue.

LEAR
To thee and thine hereditary ever
Remain this ample third of our fair kingdom,
No less in space, validity,° and pleasure   **validity:** value
Than that confirmed on Goneril. But now, our joy,   75
Although the last, not least in our dear love,
What can you say to win a third more opulent
Than your sisters?

CORDELIA   Nothing, my lord.

LEAR   How!
Nothing can come of nothing;° speak again.   **Nothing . . . nothing:** (quoting a famous
      scholastic maxim derived from Aristotle, *nihil ex*

CORDELIA   *nihilo fit*)
Unhappy that I am, I cannot heave   80
My heart into my mouth. I love you majesty
According to my bond,° nor more nor less.   **bond:** duty

LEAR
Go to, go to, mend your speech a little
Lest it may mar your fortunes.

CORDELIA   Good my lord,
You have begot me, bred me, loved me.   85
I return those duties back as are right fit,°   **I . . . fit:** I am properly dutiful in return
Obey you, love you, and most honor you.
Why have my sisters husbands, if they say
They love you all? Happily when I shall wed
That lord whose hand must take my plight° shall carry   **plight:** marriage vow   90
Half my love with him, half my care and duty.
Sure I shall never marry like my sisters,
To love my father all.

LEAR
But goes this with thy heart?

CORDELIA   Ay, good my lord.

DISCOVERING SHAKESPEARE

(4) Paraphrase [1.1.80]: Paraphrase the following lines by Cordelia in 1.1.80–81: "Unhappy that I am, I cannot heave / My heart into my mouth."

LEAR
So young and so untender? 95

CORDELIA
So young, my lord, and true.° **true:** honest

LEAR
Well, let it be so. Thy truth then be thy dower,
For by the sacred radiance of the sun,
The mysteries of Hecate° and the night, **Hecate:** goddess of the underworld, patron of witchcraft 100
By all the operation of the orbs,° **operation . . . orbs:** astrological influences
From whom we do exist and cease to be,
Here I disclaim all my paternal care,
Propinquity, and property of blood,° **Propinquity . . . blood:** blood relationship
And as a stranger to my heart and me
Hold thee from this° forever. The barbarous Scythian,° **this:** this time; **Scythian:** Crimean tribesman, notorious for cruelty 105
Or he that makes his generation
Messes° to gorge his appetite, shall be **makes . . . Messes:** devours his children
As well neighbored, pitied, and relieved
As thou my sometime daughter.

KENT   Good my liege –

LEAR
Peace, Kent! Come not between the dragon and his wrath. 110
I loved her most, and thought to set my rest
On her kind nursery.° *[To Cordelia]* Hence, and avoid my sight! **nursery:** care
So be my grave my peace° as here I give **So . . . peace:** let my peace be in my grave
Her father's heart from her. Call France – who stirs?
Call Burgundy. Cornwall and Albany, 115
With my two daughters' dowers digest this third.
Let pride, which she calls plainness, marry her.
I do invest you jointly in my power,
Preeminence, and all the large effects° **large effects:** rich trappings
That troop with° majesty. Ourself by monthly course, **troop with:** accompany 120
With reservation of° an hundred knights, **With reservation of:** legally retaining
By you to be sustained, shall our abode
Make with you by due turns. Only we still retain
The name and all the additions° to a king. **all the additions:** i.e., the honors and prerogatives
The sway,° revenue, execution of the rest, **sway:** authority 125
Belovèd sons, be yours; which to confirm,
This coronet° part betwixt you. **coronet:** (which would have crowned Cordelia)

KENT   Royal Lear,
Whom I have ever honored as my king,
Loved as my father, as my master followed,
As my great patron thought on in my prayers – 130

LEAR
The bow is bent and drawn; make from° the shaft. **make from:** get out of the way of

KENT
Let it fall° rather, though the fork° invade **fall:** strike; **fork:** (two-pronged) arrowhead
The region of my heart. Be Kent unmannerly

DISCOVERING SHAKESPEARE

(5) Teaser [1.1.99]: In which other Shakespearean plays is Hecate (1.1.99) mentioned? Who was she? Why does Lear invoke her name at this particular moment in the play?

(6) Characterization [1.1.127]: How would you characterize Lear thus far in the play? How is he behaving?

When Lear is mad. What wilt thou do, old man?
Think'st thou that duty shall have dread to speak   135
When power to flattery bows? To plainness° honor's   **plainness:** straight talk
  bound
When majesty stoops to folly. Reverse thy doom,°   **doom:** decision
And in thy best consideration check
This hideous rashness. Answer my life° my judgment: **Answer my life:** I stake my life on
Thy youngest daughter does not love thee least,   140
Nor are those empty-hearted whose low sound
Reverbs no hollowness.°   **Reverbs no hollowness:** does not resonate
                                                            hollowly
LEAR   Kent, on thy life, no more.
KENT
My life I never held but as a pawn°   **pawn:** (1) stake, (2) the least valuable chess piece
To wage° against thy enemies, nor fear to lose it,   **wage:** wager, risk   145
Thy safety being the motive.°   **motive:** motivation
LEAR   Out of my sight!
KENT
See better, Lear, and let me still° remain   **still:** always
The true blank° of thine eye.   **true blank:** exact bull's-eye
LEAR   Now by Apollo —
KENT
Now by Apollo,° king, thou swearest thy gods in vain.   **Apollo:** the sun god
LEAR   Vassal, recreant!°   **recreant:** (1) traitor, (2) infidel   150
KENT
Do, kill thy physician,
And the fee bestow upon the foul disease.
Revoke thy doom, or whilst I can vent clamor
From my throat, I'll tell thee thou dost evil.
LEAR
Hear me, on thy allegiance hear me!   155
Since thou hast sought to make us break our vow,
Which we durst never yet and with strayed° pride   **strayed:** undutiful
To come between our sentence and our power,°   **our power:** the power to execute them
Which nor our nature nor our place° can bear,   **place:** royal office
Our potency made good,° take thy reward: **Our . . . good:** hereby demonstrating my power   160
Four days we do allot thee for provision
To shield thee from diseases of the world,
And on the fifth to turn thy hated back
Upon our kingdom. If on the tenth day following
Thy banished trunk° be found in our dominions,   **trunk:** body   165
The moment is thy death. Away! By Jupiter,
This shall not be revoked.
KENT
Why, fare thee well, king; since thus thou wilt appear,
Friendship lives hence, and banishment is here.
  [To Cordelia]
The gods to their protection take thee, maid,   170
That rightly thinks, and hast most justly said.
  [To Goneril and Regan]
And your large speeches may your deeds approve,°   **your . . . approve:** i.e., may your actions justify
                                                            your words

DISCOVERING SHAKESPEARE

(7) Chronology [1.1.149]: As Lear's reference to Apollo (1.1.149) and other mythological gods implies, the play is set in pre-Christian Britain. What information can you find about the dates of King Lear's reign?

That good effects may spring from words of love.
Thus Kent, O princes, bids you all adieu;
He'll shape his old course in a country new.   *[Exit.]*   175
    Enter [the King of] France and [the Duke of]
    Burgundy, with Gloucester.
GLOUCESTER
Here's France and Burgundy, my noble lord.
LEAR
My lord of Burgundy,
We first address towards you, who with a king
Hath rivaled for our daughter. What in the least
Will you require in present dower with her,   180
Or cease your quest of love?
BURGUNDY   Royal majesty,
I crave no more than what your highness offered,
Nor will you tender° less.   **tender:** offer
LEAR   Right noble Burgundy,
When she was dear to us we did hold her so;
But now her price is fallen. Sir, there she stands.   185
If aught° within that little seeming substance,°   **aught:** anything; **little . . . substance:** (1) mere
Or all of it, with our displeasure pieced°   shell of a person, (2) person with few pretensions
And nothing else, may fitly like° your grace,   **pieced:** joined
She's there, and she is yours.   **like:** please
BURGUNDY   I know no answer.
LEAR
Sir, will you with those infirmities she owes,°   **owes:** owns   190
Unfriended, new-adopted to our hate,
Covered with our curse, and strangered with° our oath, **strangered with:** made a stranger by
Take her or leave her?
BURGUNDY   Pardon me, royal sir;
Election makes not up on such conditions.°   **Election . . . conditions:** choice is impossible
                              on such terms
LEAR
Then leave her, sir; for, by the power that made me,   195
I tell you all her wealth. *[To France]* For you, great king,
I would not from your love make such a stray°   **make . . . stray:** stray so far as
To match you where I hate; therefore beseech you
To avert° your liking a more worthier way   **avert:** turn
Than on a wretch whom nature is ashamed   200
Almost to acknowledge hers.
FRANCE   This is most strange,
That she that even but now was your best object,
The argument° of your praise, balm of your age,   **argument:** theme
Most best, most dearest, should in this trice of time
Commit a thing so monstrous to dismantle°   **to dismantle:** as to strip off   205
So many folds of favor. Sure her offense
Must be of such unnatural degree
That monsters it,° or you fore-vouched affections   **monsters it:** makes it monstrous
Fall'n into taint;° which to believe of her   **you . . . taint:** you previously swore a love that
                              must now appear suspect

DISCOVERING SHAKESPEARE

(8) Geography [1.1.176]: Locate Burgundy on a map of France. What was the area known for?
(9) <u>Metaphor</u> [1.1.204]: When France expresses surprise that Cordelia "should in this trice of time / Commit a thing so monstrous to dismantle / So many folds of favor" (1.1.204–206), what is he saying to Lear? What are the "tenor" and the "vehicle" of his <u>metaphor</u>?

Must be a faith that reason without miracle   210
  Could never plant in me.
CORDELIA *[To Lear]*
  I yet beseech your majesty,
  If for I want° that glib and oily art   **for I want:** because I lack
  To speak and purpose not − since what I well intend
  I'll do't before I speak − that you may know°   **you . . . know:** (addressed to France)   215
  It is no vicious blot, murder, or foulness,
  No unclean action or dishonored step
  That hath deprived me of your grace and favor,
  But even for want of that for which I am rich:
  A still-soliciting° eye, and such a tongue   **still-soliciting:** always begging   220
  As I am glad I have not, though not to have it
  Hath lost me in your liking.
LEAR   Go to, go to.
  Better thou hadst not been born than not to have
    pleased me better.
FRANCE
  Is it no more but this? A tardiness in nature,
  That often leaves the history unspoke   225
  That it intends to do? My lord of Burgundy,
  What say you to the lady? Love is not love
  When it is mingled with respects that stands
  Aloof from the entire point.° Will you have her?   **respects . . . point:** considerations irrelevant to
  She is herself a dower.   love   230
BURGUNDY   Royal Lear,
  Give but that portion which yourself proposed,
  And here I take Cordelia by the hand,
  Duchess of Burgundy.
LEAR   Nothing; I have sworn.
BURGUNDY *[To Cordelia]*
  I am sorry, then, you have so lost a father
  That you must lose a husband.   235
CORDELIA
  Peace be with Burgundy.
  Since that respects of fortune° are his love,   **respects . . . fortune:** considerations of wealth
  I shall not be his wife.
FRANCE
  Fairest Cordelia, that art most rich being poor,
  Most choice forsaken, and most loved despised,   240
  Thee and thy virtues here I seize upon.
  Be it lawful I take up what's cast away.
  Gods, gods! 'Tis strange that from their cold'st neglect
  My love should kindle to inflamed respect.°   **inflamed respect:** ardent admiration
  Thy dowerless daughter, king, thrown to thy chance,   245
  Is queen of us, of ours, and our fair France.
  Not all the dukes in wat'rish° Burgundy   **wat'rish:** (1) well-irrigated, (2) weak, wishy-
  Shall buy this unprized° precious maid of me.   washy
  Bid them farewell, Cordelia, though unkind;   **unprized:** unappreciated
  Thou losest here, a better where° to find.   **where:** elsewhere   250

DISCOVERING SHAKESPEARE
(10) Paraphrase [1.1.227]: Paraphrase the following lines by France: "Love is not love / When it is mingled with respects that stands / Aloof from the entire point" (1.1.227–229). What do his vocabulary and syntax imply about his attitude toward King Lear?

LEAR
  Thou hast her, France. Let her be thine, for we
  Have no such daughter, nor shall ever see
  That face of hers again. Therefore be gone,
  Without our grace, our love, our benison.°   **benison:** blessing
  Come, noble Burgundy.   255
           Exeunt Lear and Burgundy [, Albany, Cornwall,
                 Gloucester, Edmund, and followers].
FRANCE   *[To Cordelia]*
  Bid farewell to your sisters.
CORDELIA
  The jewels of our father, with washed° eyes   **washed:** tearful
  Cordelia leaves you. I know you what you are,
  And, like a sister, am most loath to call
  Your faults as they are named.° Use well our father.   **as . . . named:** by their real names   260
  To your professèd bosoms° I commit him;   **professèd bosoms:** proclaimed love
  But yet, alas, stood I within his grace,
  I would prefer° him to a better place.   **prefer:** promote
  So, farewell to you both.
GONERIL
  Prescribe not us our duties.   265
REGAN   Let your study
  Be to content your lord, who hath received you
  At fortune's alms.° You have obedience scanted,   **At . . . alms:** as charity from fortune
  And well are worth the worth that you have wanted.° **well . . . wanted:** are properly deprived of what
                                          you yourself have lacked
CORDELIA
  Time shall unfold what pleated cunning hides;
  Who covers faults, at last shame them derides.°   **Who . . . derides:** i.e., time finally exposes   270
  Well may you prosper.   hidden faults to shame
FRANCE   Come, fair Cordelia.
                Exeunt France and Cordelia.
GONERIL   Sister, it is not a little I have to say of what
most nearly appertains to us both. I think our father
will hence tonight.
REGAN   That's most certain, and with you; next month   275
with us.
GONERIL   You see how full of changes his age is. The observation we have made of it hath not been little. He always loved our sister most, and with what poor
judgment he hath now cast her off appears too gross.°   **gross:** obvious   280
REGAN   'Tis the infirmity of his age; yet he hath ever but
slenderly known himself.
GONERIL   The best and soundest of his time hath been°   **The . . . been:** even at his best he was
but rash; then° must we look to receive from his age not   **then:** therefore
alone the imperfection of long-engrafted° condition,   **long-engrafted:** deep-seated   285
but therewithal° unruly waywardness that infirm and   **therewithal:** along with that
choleric years bring with them.
REGAN   Such unconstant starts° are we like to have from   **unconstant starts:** fits of impulsiveness
him at this of Kent's banishment.

DISCOVERING SHAKESPEARE

(11) Language [1.1.254]: Give the meaning and the etymological origin of the word "benison" (1.1.254).
(12) Prose [1.1.272]: Why do Goneril and Regan shift from <u>verse</u> to <u>prose</u> in 1.1.272–295 after the departure of France and Cordelia?

GONERIL   There is further compliment° of leave-taking between France and him. Pray, let's hit° together. If our father carry authority with such dispositions as he bears, this last surrender° of his will but offend us. 290

REGAN   We shall further think on't.

GONERIL   We must do something, and i' th' heat.° 295

Exeunt.

❧ **1.2**° *Enter Bastard [Edmund] solus.*°

EDMUND

Thou, Nature, art my goddess. To thy law
My services are bound. Wherefore should I
Stand in the plague of custom° and permit
The curiosity° of nations to deprive me
For that° I am some twelve or fourteen moonshines° 5
Lag of° a brother? Why bastard? Wherefore base,
When my dimensions are as well compact,°
My mind as generous,° and my shape as true
As honest° madam's issue?
Why brand they us with base, base bastardy, 10
Who in the lusty stealth of nature° take
More composition° and fierce° quality
Than doth within a stale, dull-eyed bed
Go to the creating of a whole tribe of fops°
Got° 'tween asleep and wake? Well then, 15
Legitimate Edgar, I must have your land.°
Our father's love is to the bastard Edmund
As to the legitimate. Well, my legitimate, if
This letter speed° and my invention° thrive,
Edmund the base shall to° th' legitimate. 20
I grow, I prosper. Now gods, stand up for bastards!

Enter Gloucester. [Edmund reads a letter.]

GLOUCESTER

Kent banished thus, and France in choler parted,°
And the king gone tonight,° subscribed° his power,
Confined to exhibition° – all this done 25
Upon the gad?° – Edmund, how now? What news?

EDMUND   So please your lordship, none.

GLOUCESTER   Why so earnestly seek you to put up that letter?

EDMUND   I know no news, my lord.

GLOUCESTER   What paper were you reading? 30

EDMUND   Nothing, my lord.

GLOUCESTER   No? What needs then that terrible° dispatch of it into your pocket? The quality of nothing hath not such need to hide itself. Let's see. Come, if it be nothing I shall not need spectacles. 35

---

compliment: formality
hit: consult

last surrender: recent abdication

i' th' heat: immediately ("while the iron is hot")

1.2: Gloucester's house; **solus:** alone

Stand . . . custom: submit to the affliction of convention (whereby the eldest son inherits everything, and illegitimate sons have no claim on the estate)
curiosity: (legal) technicalities
For that: because; **moonshines:** months
Lag of: younger than
compact: composed
My . . . generous: I am as well supplied with intelligence
honest: chaste (i.e., married)
the . . . nature: natural lust practiced in secret
composition: physical excellence; **fierce:** vigorous
fops: fools, sissies
Got: begotten
land: i.e., inheritance
speed: succeed; **invention:** scheme
to: rise to, equal

in . . . parted: departed in anger
tonight: i.e., last night; **subscribed:** given up
Confined . . . exhibition: limited to an allowance
Upon . . . gad: suddenly, impulsively

terrible: frightened

DISCOVERING SHAKESPEARE

(13) Plot [1.2.1]: Why does Edmund worship Nature as his "goddess" (see 1.2.1–21)? How is his reverence for Nature related to his illegitimate birth?

(14) Language [1.2.22]: What is the meaning of the word "choler" (1.2.22)? How does the term help dictate France's behavior as he leaves the stage in 1.1.271?

EDMUND   I beseech you, sir, pardon me. It is a letter from my brother that I have not all o'er-read; for so much as I have perused, I find it not fit for your liking.

GLOUCESTER   Give me the letter, sir.

EDMUND   I shall offend either to detain or give it. The contents, as in part I understand them, are to blame.°   **to blame:** blameworthy   40

GLOUCESTER   Let's see, let's see.

EDMUND   I hope for my brother's justification he wrote this but as an essay or taste° of my virtue.   **essay or taste:** (both words mean "test")

[He gives Gloucester] a letter.

GLOUCESTER   *Reads.* "This policy of age makes the world   45 bitter to the best of our times,° keeps our fortunes from   **to ... times:** in the prime of our lives us till our oldness cannot relish them. I begin to find an idle and fond° bondage in the oppression of aged   **idle ... fond:** worthless and foolish tyranny, who sways not as it hath power but as it is suf-fered.° Come to me, that of this I may speak more. If   **suffered:** allowed to do so   50 our father would sleep till I waked him, you should enjoy half his revenue forever, and live the beloved of your brother Edgar."

Hum, conspiracy! "Slept till I waked him, you should enjoy half his revenue" – my son Edgar! Had he a hand   55 to write this, a heart and brain to breed it in? When came this to you? Who brought it?

EDMUND   It was not brought me, my lord, there's the cunning of it. I found it thrown in at the casement of my closet.°   **casement ... closet:** window of my bedroom   60

GLOUCESTER   You know the character° to be your   **character:** handwriting brother's?

EDMUND   If the matter° were good, my lord, I durst swear   **matter:** substance it were his; but in respect of that,° I would fain° think it   **in ... that:** i.e., considering the content; **fain:** were not.   prefer to   65

GLOUCESTER   It is his.

EDMUND   It is his hand, my lord, but I hope his heart is not in the contents.

GLOUCESTER   Hath he never heretofore sounded you° in   **sounded you:** sounded you out this business?   70

EDMUND   Never, my lord; but I have often heard him maintain it to be fit that, sons at perfect age° and fathers   **sons ... age:** when sons are mature declining, his father should be as ward to° the son, and   **as ... to:** placed under the guardianship of the son manage the revenue.

GLOUCESTER   O villain, villain – his very opinion in the   75 letter. Abhorred villain, unnatural, detested, brutish vil-lain – worse than brutish! Go, sir, seek him. I appre-hend him, abominable villain! Where is he?

EDMUND   I do not well know, my lord. If it shall please you to suspend your indignation against my brother till   80

DISCOVERING SHAKESPEARE

(15) Paraphrase [1.2.50]: Paraphrase the following statement from the letter allegedly written by Edgar: "If our father would sleep till I waked him, you should enjoy half his revenue forever . . ." (1.2.50–52). Why is Gloucester so outraged by the letter?

(16) Characterization [1.2.75]: Characterize both Gloucester and Edmund based on their behavior in this scene.

you can derive from him better testimony of this intent, you should run a certain course;° where° if you violently proceed against him, mistaking his purpose, it would make a great gap in your own honor and shake in pieces the heart of his obedience. I dare pawn down° my life for him he hath wrote this to feel° my affection to your honor, and to no further pretense of danger.°

run . . . course: be sure of your course of action; **where:** whereas

pawn down: stake 85
feel: test
pretense of danger: intent to do harm

GLOUCESTER   Think you so?

EDMUND   If your honor judge it meet,° I will place you where you shall hear us confer of this, and by an auricular assurance° have your satisfaction, and that without any further delay than this very evening.

meet: appropriate
90
an . . . assurance: the testimony of your own ears

GLOUCESTER   He cannot be such a monster.

EDMUND   Nor is not, sure.

GLOUCESTER   To his father, that so tenderly and entirely loves him. Heaven and earth! Edmund, seek him out, wind me into him.° I pray you, frame° your business after your own wisdom. I would unstate myself to be in a due resolution.°

95

wind . . . him: worm your way into his confidence for me; **frame:** arrange
unstate . . . resolution: give up everything to resolve my doubts
100

EDMUND   I shall seek him, sir, presently,° convey° the business as I shall see means, and acquaint you withal.°

presently: immediately; **convey:** conduct
withal: with the result

GLOUCESTER   These late° eclipses in the sun and moon portend no good to us. Though the wisdom of nature can reason thus and thus,° yet nature finds itself scourged by the sequent effects.° Love cools, friendship falls off, brothers divide; in cities mutinies,° in countries discords, palaces treason, the bond cracked between son and father. Find out this villain, Edmund. It shall lose thee nothing. Do it carefully. And the noble and true-hearted Kent banished, his offense honesty – strange, strange.   *[Exit.]*

late: recent
wisdom . . . thus: natural science can supply various explanations
105
nature . . . effects: humanity ("nature") suffers the consequences
mutinies: rebellions

110

EDMUND   This is the excellent foppery° of the world, that when we are sick in fortune – often the surfeit° of our own behavior – we make guilty of our disasters the sun, the moon, and the stars, as if we were villains by necessity, fools by heavenly compulsion, knaves, thieves, and treacherers° by spherical predominance,° drunkards, liars, and adulterers by an enforced obedience of° planetary influence; and all that we are evil in by a divine thrusting on.° An admirable° evasion of whoremaster man, to lay his goatish° disposition to the charge of stars! My father compounded° with my mother under the Dragon's tail, and my nativity was under Ursa Major,° so that it follows I am rough and lecherous. Fut!

foppery: foolishness
surfeit: overindulgence

115

treacherers: traitors; **spherical predominance:** astrological influence
of: to
thrusting on: enforcement; **admirable:** 120
astonishing
goatish: lecherous
compounded: had sex
Dragon's tail, Ursa Major: the constellations of Draco and the Great Bear

---

DISCOVERING SHAKESPEARE

(17) Paraphrase [1.2.103]: Paraphrase the following statement by Gloucester: "Though the wisdom of nature can reason thus and thus, yet nature finds itself scourged by the sequent effects" (1.2.103–105). How do Gloucester and Edmund differ in their opinion of Nature?

(18) Characterization [1.2.122]: What is Edmund's opinion of astrology (1.2.112–126)? Why is it important in the plot?

I should have been that I am had the maidenliest star of   125
the firmament twinkled on my bastardy. Edgar –
Enter Edgar.
and out he comes, like the catastrophe of the old com-
edy;° mine° is villainous° melancholy, with a sigh like   **catastrophe . . . comedy:** conclusion in early
them of Bedlam.° O these eclipses do portend these di-   comedy (i.e., often arbitrary or unmotivated, but
visions° –   at the appointed time); **mine:** my role;   130
                                                                villainous: severe
EDGAR   How now, brother Edmund, what serious con-   **Bedlam:** Bedlam (Bethlehem) Hospital, the
templation are you in?   London madhouse
EDMUND   I am thinking, brother, of a prediction I read   **divisions:** (1) conflicts, (2) musical phrases
this other day, what should follow these eclipses.
EDGAR   Do you busy yourself about that?   135
EDMUND   I promise you the effects he writ of succeed°   **succeed:** conclude
unhappily, as of unnaturalness between the child and
the parent, death, dearth, dissolutions of ancient amities, divisions in state, menaces and maledictions
against king and nobles, needless diffidences,° banish-   **diffidences:** mistrust   140
ment of friends, dissipation of cohorts,° nuptial   **dissipation of cohorts:** disbanding of armies
breaches, and I know not what.
EDGAR   How long have you been a sectary astronomical?°   **sectary astronomical:** astrological expert
EDMUND   Come, come, when saw you my father last?
EDGAR   Why, the night gone by.   145
EDMUND   Spake you with him?
EDGAR   Two hours together.
EDMUND   Parted you in good terms? Found you no dis-
pleasure in him by word or countenance?°   **countenance:** look
EDGAR   None at all.   150
EDMUND   Bethink yourself wherein you may have of-
fended him, and at my entreaty forbear his presence till
some little time hath qualified° the heat of his displea-   **qualified:** moderated
sure, which at this instant so rageth in him that with
the mischief of° your person it would scarce allay.°   **the mischief of:** injury to; **allay:** be allayed   155
EDGAR   Some villain hath done me wrong.
EDMUND   That's my fear, brother. I advise you to the
best. Go armed. I am no honest man if there be any
good meaning towards you. I have told you what I have
seen and heard but faintly, nothing like the image and   160
horror of it.° Pray you, away.   **image . . . it:** as horrible as it seemed
EDGAR   Shall I hear from you anon?
EDMUND   I do serve you in this business.
                                             Exit Edgar.
A credulous father, and a brother noble,
Whose nature is so far from doing harms   165
That he suspects none, on whose foolish honesty
My practices° ride easy. I see the business.°   **practices:** plots; **I . . . business:** the plan is
Let me, if not by birth, have lands by wit.°   now clear
All with me's meet° that I can fashion fit.°   *Exit.*   **wit:** intelligence
                                                               with . . . meet: suits me; **fashion fit:** shape to
                                                               serve my purpose

---

DISCOVERING SHAKESPEARE

(19) Plot [1.2.150]: Why doesn't Edgar simply go to his father and ask him why he is angry? What does his reluctance to
do so tell us about his relationship with his father?

1.3° *Enter Goneril and Steward [Oswald].*

                                     1.3: Albany's castle

GONERIL
Did my father strike my gentleman
For chiding of his fool?
OSWALD   Yes, madam.
GONERIL
By day and night he wrongs me. Every hour
He flashes into one gross crime° or other   **crime:** offense
That sets us all at odds. I'll not endure it.
His knights grow riotous, and himself upbraids us   5
On every trifle. When he returns from hunting
I will not speak with him. Say I am sick.
If you come slack of former services°   **come . . . services:** serve him less well than
You shall do well; the fault of it I'll answer.°   usual   10
  [Horns within.]   **answer:** answer for
OSWALD   He's coming, madam, I hear him.
GONERIL
Put on what weary negligence you please,
You and your fellow servants. I'd have it come in ques-
  tion.°   **come . . . question:** made an issue
If he dislike it, let him to our sister,
Whose mind and mine I know in that are one,   15
Not to be overruled. Idle old man,
That still would manage those authorities
That he hath given away! Now, by my life,
Old fools are babes again, and must be used
With checks as flatteries,° when they are seen° abused.   **checks . . . flatteries:** rebukes as well as   20
Remember what I tell you.   compliments; **they . . . seen:** the compliments
OSWALD   Very well, madam.   are
GONERIL
And let his knights have colder looks among you;
What grows of it, no matter. Advise your fellows so.
I would breed from hence occasions,° and I shall   **breed . . . occasions:** use this to provoke scenes   25
That I may speak.° I'll write straight to my sister   **speak:** speak my mind
To hold my very course.° Go prepare for dinner.   **hold . . . course:** pursue the same course I do
                                 [Exeunt separately.]

1.4 *Enter Kent [disguised].*

KENT
If but as well I other accents borrow°   **If . . . borrow:** i.e., If I disguise my voice as
That can my speech defuse,° my good intent   effectively as I do my appearance
May carry through itself to that full issue°   **defuse:** confuse, disguise
For which I razed my likeness.° Now, banished Kent,   **issue:** outcome
If thou canst serve where thou dost stand condemned,   **razed . . . likeness:** erased my appearance   5
Thy master, whom thou lov'st, shall find thee full of   (including "razoring" his beard)
  labor.°   **full . . . labor:** i.e., hard at work
  Enter Lear [and Knights from hunting].

DISCOVERING SHAKESPEARE

(20) Characterization [1.3.5]: Why is Goneril so upset with her father? Explain her point of view as objectively as possible.
(21) <u>Staging</u> [1.4.1]: If you were directing a production of *King Lear*, how would you have Kent disguise himself in 1.4?

LEAR Let me not stay° a jot for dinner. Go get it ready.	**stay:** wait
[Exit Knight.]	
How now, what° art thou?	**what:** who
KENT A man, sir.	
LEAR What dost thou profess?° What wouldst thou with us?	**dost . . . profess:** is your trade 10
KENT I do profess to be no less than I seem, to serve him truly that will put me in trust, to love him that is honest, to converse° with him that is wise and says little, to fear judgment,° to fight when I cannot choose,° and to eat no fish.°	**converse:** associate **fear judgment:** show respect for authority; 15 **choose:** avoid it **eat no fish:** (A joke whose point has obviously been lost: not to be Catholic, and thus forbidden to eat meat on Fridays? To be a meat-eater only—i.e., manly?)
LEAR What art thou?	
KENT A very honest-hearted fellow, and as poor as the king.	20
LEAR If thou be as poor for a subject as he is for a king, thou'rt poor enough. What wouldst thou?	
KENT Service.	
LEAR Who wouldst thou serve?	
KENT You.	
LEAR Dost thou know me, fellow?	25
KENT No, sir, but you have that in your countenance which I would fain° call master.	**fain:** like to
LEAR What's that?	
KENT Authority.	
LEAR What services canst do?	30
KENT I can keep honest counsel,° ride, run, mar a curious° tale in telling it, and deliver a plain message bluntly. That which ordinary men are fit for I am qualified in, and the best of me is diligence.	**keep . . . counsel:** respect confidences **curious:** complicated
LEAR How old art thou?	35
KENT Not so young to love a woman for singing nor so old to dote on her for anything. I have years on my back forty-eight.	
LEAR Follow me. Thou shalt serve me. If I like thee no worse after dinner, I will not part from thee yet. Dinner, ho, dinner! Where's my knave,° my fool? Go you and call my fool hither. *[Exit Knight.]*	40 **knave:** boy (the term could be affectionate)
Enter Steward [Oswald].	
You, sirrah,° where's my daughter?	**sirrah:** (term of address used to a social inferior)
OSWALD So please you. *[Exit.]*	
LEAR What says the fellow there? Call the clotpoll° back.	**clotpoll:** blockhead 45
[Exeunt Kent and Knight.]	
Where's my fool, ho! I think the world's asleep.	
[Reenter Kent and Knight.]	
How now, where's that mongrel?	
KENT He says, my lord, your daughter is not well.	
LEAR Why came not the slave back to me when I called him?	50
KNIGHT Sir, he answered me in the roundest° manner he would not.	**roundest:** rudest

---

DISCOVERING SHAKESPEARE

(22) **Metaphor** [1.4.37]: Why does Kent tell Lear that "I have years on my back forty-eight" (1.4.37–38)? What is the metaphoric meaning of this statement?

(23) **Plot** [1.4.51]: What has Oswald done to be rude to the King and his knights? Why has he acted this way?

LEAR   A° would not?

KNIGHT   My lord, I know not what the matter is, but to my judgment your highness is not entertained° with that ceremonious affection as you were wont.° There's a great abatement appears as well in the general dependents,° as in the duke himself also, and your daughter.

LEAR   Ha, sayst thou so?

KNIGHT   I beseech you pardon me, my lord, if I be mistaken, for my duty cannot be silent when I think your highness wronged.

LEAR   Thou but rememb'rest° me of mine own conception.° I have perceived a most faint neglect of late, which I have rather blamed as mine own jealous curiosity° than as a very pretense° and purport of unkindness. I will look further into't. But where's this fool? I have not seen him this two days.

KNIGHT   Since my young lady's going into France, sir, the fool hath much pined away.

LEAR   No more of that, I have noted it. Go you and tell my daughter I would speak with her.

[Exit Knight.]

Go you, call hither my fool.

[Exit another Knight.]

[Enter Oswald.]

O, you sir, you sir, come you hither. Who am I, sir?

OSWALD   My lady's father.

LEAR   My lady's father? My lord's knave, you whoreson dog, you slave, you cur!

OSWALD   I am none of this, my lord; I beseech you, pardon me.

LEAR   Do you bandy looks with me, you rascal? *[Strikes him.]*

OSWALD   I'll not be struck, my lord.

KENT   *[Tripping him]* Nor tripped neither, you base football player.°

LEAR   *[To Kent]* I thank thee, fellow; thou serv'st me, and I'll love thee.

KENT   *[To Oswald]* Come, sir, I'll teach you differences.° Away, away. If you will measure your lubber's° length° again, tarry; but away, if you have wisdom.

[Exit Oswald.]

LEAR   Now, friendly knave, I thank thee. There's earnest of° thy service.

[Lear gives Kent money.] Enter Fool.

FOOL   Let me hire him, too. *[To Kent]* Here's my coxcomb.°

LEAR   How now, my pretty knave, how dost thou?

FOOL   Sirrah, you were best take my coxcomb.

KENT   Why, fool?

FOOL   Why, for taking one's part that's out of favor. Nay, an° thou canst not smile as the wind sits, thou'lt catch

---

A: he

entertained: treated
wont: accustomed to

the . . . dependents: all the servants

rememb'rest: remind
conception: perception

jealous curiosity: hypersensitiveness; **very pretense:** real intention

football player: (soccer was a lower-class street game)

differences: distinctions of rank
lubber: oaf; **measure . . . length:** i.e., have me trip you up again

earnest of: a down payment on

coxcomb: fool's cap

an: if

55

60

65

70

75

80

85

90

95

DISCOVERING SHAKESPEARE

(24) Staging [1.4.80]: How does Kent's treatment of Oswald earn Lear's praise?

cold shortly.° There, take my coxcomb. Why, this fellow hath banished° two on's° daughters and done the third a blessing against his will. If thou follow him, thou must needs wear my coxcomb. How now, nuncle?° Would I had two coxcombs and two daughters.

LEAR Why, my boy?

FOOL If I gave them my living° I'd keep my coxcombs myself.° There's mine; beg another of thy daughters.

LEAR Take heed, sirrah: the whip.

FOOL Truth is a dog that must to kennel. He must be whipped out° when lady the brach° may stand by the fire and stink.°

LEAR A pestilent gall° to me!

FOOL Sirrah, I'll teach thee a speech.

LEAR Do.

FOOL Mark it, uncle:

> Have more than thou showest,
> Speak less than thou knowest,
> Lend less than thou owest,°
> Ride more than thou goest,°
> Learn more than thou trowest,°
> Set less than thou throwest,°
> Leave thy drink and thy whore,
> And keep in-a-door,
> And thou shalt have more
> Than two tens to a score.°

LEAR This is nothing, fool.

FOOL Then, like the breath° of an unfeed° lawyer, you gave me nothing for't. Can you make no use of nothing, uncle?

LEAR Why no, boy. Nothing can be made out of nothing.

FOOL *[To Kent]* Prithee, tell him so much the rent of his land comes to.° He will not believe a fool.

LEAR A bitter fool.

FOOL Dost know the difference, my boy, between a bitter fool and a sweet fool?

LEAR No, lad, teach me.

FOOL

> That lord that counseled thee
>   To give away thy land,
> Come, place him here by me;
>   Do thou for him stand.
> The sweet and bitter fool
>   Will presently appear,°
> The one in motley° here,
>   The other found out there.

an . . . shortly: if you can't please those in power, you'll soon be out in the cold
banished: (as Kent says, "banishment is here," (1.1.169); **on's:** of his   100
nuncle: (mine) uncle

living: possessions
I'd . . . myself: I'd be a double fool   105

out: out of doors; **brach:** bitch
when . . . stink: i.e., as Goneril and Regan are favored and the truthful Cordelia exiled   110
gall: bitterness, sore

115

owest: own
goest: walk
trowest: believe (i.e., don't believe everything you hear)
Set . . . throwest: bet less than you win (at dice)   120

score: twenty (i.e., you'll do better than break even)

breath: speech; **unfeed:** unpaid (lawyers proverbially will not plead without a fee)   125

so . . . to: i.e., he no longer has any land, and therefore no income from it   130

135

Will . . . appear: i.e., it will be immediately apparent which is which   140
motley: the jester's parti-colored costume

DISCOVERING SHAKESPEARE

(25) Language [1.4.98]: What was a "coxcomb" (1.4.98)? Why did fools wear them? (*Hint:* See the *Oxford English Dictionary*.)

(26) Language [1.4.128]: How many times has the word "nothing" (1.4.128) been used so far in the script? In what way is the word <u>ironic</u> within this particular context?

LEAR   Dost thou call me fool, boy?

FOOL   All thy other titles thou hast given away; that   145
thou wast born with.

KENT   This is not altogether fool, my lord.

FOOL   No, faith, lords and great men will not let me.° If
I had a monopoly out, they would have part on't, and
ladies too: they will not let me have all the fool to my-   150
self; they'll be snatching. Give me an egg, nuncle, and
I'll give thee two crowns.

LEAR   What two crowns shall they be?

FOOL   Why, after I have cut the egg in the middle and
eat up the meat, the two crowns of the egg.° When thou   155
clovest thy crown i' th' middle and gavest away both
parts, thou borest thy ass at° th' back o'er the dirt. Thou
hadst little wit in thy bald crown when thou gavest thy
golden one away. If I speak like myself° in this, let him   160
be whipped that first finds it so.°

   [Sings.]
      Fools had ne'er less wit in a year,°
         For wise men are grown foppish,°
      They know not how their wits do wear,°
         Their manners are so apish.°   165

LEAR   When were you wont° to be so full of songs, sirrah?

FOOL   I have used it, nuncle, ever since thou madest thy
daughters thy mother; for when thou gavest them the
rod and putt'st down thine own breeches,

   [Sings.]
      Then they for sudden joy did weep,   170
         And I for sorrow sung,
      That such a king should play bopeep°
         And go the fools among.

Prithee, nuncle, keep a schoolmaster that can teach thy
fool to lie. I would fain° learn to lie.

LEAR   An° you lie, we'll have you whipped.   175

FOOL   I marvel what kin thou and thy daughters are.
They'll have me whipped for speaking true, thou wilt
have me whipped for lying, and sometime I am
whipped for holding my peace. I had rather be any
kind of thing than a fool; and yet I would not be thee,   180
nuncle. Thou hast pared thy wit o' both sides, and left
nothing in the middle.

   Enter Goneril.

Here comes one of the parings.

LEAR
How now, daughter, what makes that frontlet° on?°
Methinks you are too much o' late i' th' frown.   185

FOOL   Thou wast a pretty fellow when thou hadst no
need to care for her frown. Now thou art an O without
a figure.° I am better than thou art now; I am a fool,

Glosses (right margin):

let me: i.e., let me have all the foolishness, be "altogether fool"

two . . . egg: i.e., the empty shell

at: on

like myself: i.e., like a fool
that . . . so: i.e., for being a fool himself

had . . . year: are now out of fashion
foppish: foolish
their . . . wear: to use their heads
apish: (1) stupid, (2) imitative
wont: accustomed

play bopeep: i.e., act like a child

fain: gladly
An: if

frontlet: forehead or a headband worn on it;
what . . . on: why are you wearing such a face

an . . . figure: a zero with no number in front of it—i.e., nothing

---

DISCOVERING SHAKESPEARE

(27) <u>Puns</u> **[1.4.153]:** In 1.4.148–160, the Fool puns on the two "crowns" of an egg broken in the middle. What serious message does he have for Lear within this little joke?

(28) Language [1.4.183]: Why does the Fool call Goneril "one of the parings" (1.4.183)?

thou art nothing. *[To Goneril]* Yes, forsooth, I will hold
my tongue; so your face bids me, though you say noth-   190
ing.
      Mum, mum.
       He that keeps neither crust nor crumb,
       Weary of all, shall want some.
That's a shelled peasecod.°   **shelled peasecod:** empty pea pod   195

GONERIL
    Not only, sir, this your all-licensed° fool,   **all-licensed:** allowed to do anything
    But other of your insolent retinue
    Do hourly carp and quarrel, breaking forth
    In rank° and not-to-be-endurèd riots.   **rank:** gross
    Sir, I had thought by making this well known unto you   200
    To have found a safe redress,° but now grow fearful,   **safe redress:** sure remedy
    By what yourself too late° have spoke and done,   **too late:** lately
    That you protect this course, and put on°   **put on:** encourage it
    By your allowance; which if you should, the fault
    Would not scape censure nor the redress sleep,°   **redress sleep:** punishment lie dormant   205
    Which in the tender of a wholesome weal°   **tender ... weal:** government of a healthy
    Might in their working do you that offense   commonwealth
    That else were shame, that then necessity°   **necessity:** what the situation demands
    Must call discreet proceedings.°   **Must ... proceedings:** might humiliate you,
                         but, being necessary, would be merely prudent   210
FOOL   For you trow, nuncle,
       The hedge-sparrow fed the cuckoo so long
       That it had it head bit off by it° young;°   **it ... it:** its ... its; **The ... young:** (the
    So out went the candle, and we were left darkling.°   cuckoo lays its eggs in other birds' nests; the young
LEAR   Are you our daughter?   cuckoos eventually destroy the sparrow that has
                         been feeding them)
GONERIL
    Come, sir, I would you would make use of that good   **darkling:** in darkness
      wisdom   215
    Whereof I know you are fraught,° and put away   **fraught:** full
    These dispositions° that of late transform you   **dispositions:** moods
    From what you rightly are.
FOOL   May not an ass know when the cart draws the
    horse? *[Sings.]* Whoop, Jug,° I love thee.   **Jug:** Joan (generic name for a whore)   220
LEAR
    Doth any here know me? Why, this is not Lear.
    Doth Lear walk thus? Speak thus? Where are his eyes?
    Either his notion° weakens, or his discernings°   **notion:** mind; **discernings:** perceptions
    Are lethargied. Sleeping or waking,° ha?   **Sleeping or waking:** am I asleep or awake
    Sure 'tis not so.   225
    Who is it that can tell me who I am?
    Lear's shadow? I would learn that, for by the marks
    Of sovereignty, knowledge, and reason
    I should be false persuaded I had daughters.
FOOL   Which they will make an obedient father.   230
LEAR
    Your name, fair gentlewoman?

DISCOVERING SHAKESPEARE

(29) Paraphrase [1.4.203]: Paraphrase Goneril's complaint against her father, his knights, and the Fool in 1.4.196–209. In
your opinion, to what extent are her grievances justifiable?

(30) Verse [1.4.225]: What is the purpose of Lear's short line in 1.4.225? How does the line signal a change in the King's
emotion or demeanor?

GONERIL   Come, sir,
This admiration° is much of the savor
Of other your new pranks. I do beseech you
Understand my purposes aright.
As you are old and reverend, should be wise.   235
Here do you keep a hundred knights and squires,
Men so disordered, so debauched and bold°
That this our court, infected with their manners,
Shows° like a riotous inn, epicurism°
And lust make more like a tavern or brothel   240
Than a great palace. The shame itself doth speak
For instant remedy. Be thou desired
By her that else will take the thing she begs
A little to disquantity your train,°
And the remainder that shall still depend°   245
To be such men as may besort° your age,
That know themselves and you.
LEAR   Darkness and devils!
Saddle my horses, call my train together!°
Degenerate bastard, I'll not trouble thee;   250
Yet have I left a daughter.
GONERIL
You strike my people, and your disordered rabble
Make servants of their betters.
Enter Albany.
LEAR
Woe that too late repents – O, sir, are you come?
Is it your will that we – prepare my horses!   255
Ingratitude, thou marble-hearted fiend,
More hideous when thou showest thee in a child
Than the sea monster. *[To Goneril]* Detested kite,° thou
    liest.
My train are men of choice and rarest parts,°
That all particulars of duty know,
And in the most exact regard° support   260
The worships° of their name. O most small fault,
How ugly didst thou in Cordelia show,
That, like an engine,° wrenched my frame of nature
From the fixed place,° drew from my heart all love
And added to the gall. O Lear, Lear!   265
Beat at this gate° that let thy folly in
And thy dear judgment out. Go, go, my people!
ALBANY
My lord, I am guiltless as I am ignorant –
LEAR
It may be so, my lord. Hark, Nature; hear,
Dear goddess: suspend thy purpose if   270
Thou didst intend to make this creature fruitful.
Into her womb convey sterility;

admiration: spectacle (something to be wondered at)

bold: impudent

Shows: looks; **epicurism:** gluttony

disquantity . . . train: reduce the size of your retinue
depend: be your dependents
besort: befit

Saddle . . . together: (Most editors send some knights off to do Lear's bidding, but it is more likely that everyone is immobilized with astonishment: he has to order the horses saddled again at l. 254.)

Detested kite: detestable bird of prey

parts: qualities

in . . . regard: with the most scrupulous attention
worships: honor
engine: machine
my . . . place: the structure of my being from its foundations
this gate: (presumably his head)

DISCOVERING SHAKESPEARE

(31) <u>Paraphrase</u> [1.4.242]: <u>Paraphrase</u> the following lines by Goneril to Lear: "Be thou desired / By her that else will take the thing she begs / A little to disquantity your train" (1.4.242–244). To what extent is this statement an implicit threat by Goneril?

Dry up in her the organs of increase,
And from her derogate° body never spring   **derogate:** debased
A babe to honor her. If she must teem,°   **teem:** breed   275
Create her child of spleen,° that it may live   **spleen:** malice
And be a thwart disnatured° torment to her.   **thwart disnatured:** perverse unnatural
Let it stamp wrinkles in her brow of youth,
With cadent° tears fret° channels in her cheeks,   **cadent:** falling; **fret:** wear
Turn all her mother's pains° and benefits   **pains:** care   280
To laughter and contempt, that she may feel —
That she may feel
How sharper than a serpent's tooth it is
To have a thankless child. Go, go, my people!
          [Exeunt Lear, Kent, and Attendants.]°   **s.d.:** The Fool apparently remains onstage.
ALBANY
Now gods that we adore, whereof comes this?   285
GONERIL
Never afflict yourself to know the cause,
But let his disposition° have that scope   **disposition:** mood
That dotage gives it.
    [Reenter Lear.]
LEAR
What, fifty of my followers at a clap,
Within a fortnight?   290
ALBANY   What is the matter, sir?
LEAR
I'll tell thee. *[To Goneril]* Life and death! I am ashamed
That thou hast power to shake my manhood thus,
That these hot tears that break from me perforce,°   **perforce:** i.e., against my will
Should make — the worst blasts and fogs upon thee!
Untented woundings° of a father's curse   **Untented woundings:** wounds too deep to be   295
Pierce every sense about thee! Old fond° eyes,   probed
Beweep° this cause again I'll pluck you out   **fond:** foolish
And you cast with the waters that you make   **Beweep:** if you weep over
To temper° clay. Yea, is't come to this?   **temper:** soften
Yet have I left a daughter   300
Whom, I am sure, is kind and comfortable.°   **comfortable:** comforting
When she shall hear this of thee, with her nails
She'll flay thy wolvish visage. Thou shalt find
That I'll resume the shape which thou dost think
I have cast off forever; thou shalt, I warrant thee.   305
          [Exit Lear.]
GONERIL
Do you mark that, my lord?
ALBANY
I cannot be so partial, Goneril,
To° the great love I bear you —   **partial . . . To:** biased . . . by
GONERIL   Come, sir, no more.
    [To Fool]
You, more knave than fool, after your master!

DISCOVERING SHAKESPEARE

(32) Metaphor [1.4.283]: Explain the "tenor" and "vehicle" in the following metaphor by Lear: "How sharper than a serpent's tooth it is / To have a thankless child" (1.4.283–284).

(33) Characterization [1.4.307]: Based on your limited acquaintance with Albany so far in the script, write a characterization of him on a separate sheet of paper.

FOOL   Nuncle Lear, nuncle Lear, tarry, and take the fool   310
with.

      A fox, when one has caught her,
      And such a daughter,
      Should sure° to the slaughter,   **sure:** surely be sent
      If my cap would buy a halter.°   **halter:** noose   315
      So the fool follows after.   *[Exit.]*

GONERIL   What, Oswald, ho!
   [Enter Oswald.]
OSWALD   Here, madam.
GONERIL   What, have you writ this letter to my sister?
OSWALD   Yes, madam.   320
GONERIL

Take you some company, and away to horse.
Inform her full of my particular fears,
And thereto add such reasons of your own
As may compact° it more. Get you gone,   **compact:** confirm
And hasten your return.   325

                 [Exit Oswald.]
            Now, my lord,
This milky gentleness and course° of yours,   **milky . . . course:** mild and gentle way
Though I dislike not, yet under pardon,°   **under pardon:** if you'll pardon me
You're much more atasked° for want of wisdom   **atasked:** taken to task
Than praised for harmful mildness.

ALBANY

How far your eyes may pierce I cannot tell;   330
Striving to better aught, we mar what's well.
GONERIL   Nay, then –
ALBANY   Well, well, the event.°   *Exeunt.*   **the event:** let's await the outcome

❧ **1.5** *Enter Lear [, Kent disguised, and Fool].*

LEAR   *[To Kent]* Go you before° to Gloucester° with these   **before:** ahead of me; **Gloucester:** (apparently
letters.° Acquaint my daughter no further with anything   not the earl but the town, which would therefore
you know than comes from her demand out of° the let-   be the location of Regan and Cornwall's castle)
ter. If your diligence be not speedy, I shall be there be-   **these letters:** this letter (i.e., the letters that
fore you.   constitute one message; cf. "these words")
    demand . . . of: questions prompted by   5
KENT   I will not sleep, my lord, till I have delivered your
letter.   *Exit.*
FOOL   If a man's brains were in his heels, were't not in
danger of kibes?°   **kibes:** chilblains, ulcers of the skin
LEAR   Ay, boy.   10
FOOL   Then I prithee be merry; thy wit shall ne'er go
slipshod.°   **shall . . . slipshod:** will not have to wear slippers
    because of chilblains (the point is that feet with
LEAR   Ha, ha, ha!   brains would not make this journey)
FOOL   Shalt° see thy other daughter will use thee kindly,   **Shalt:** thou shalt
for though she's as like this as a crab° is like an apple, yet   **crab:** crab apple (proverbially sour)   15
I con° what I can tell.   **con:** know
LEAR   Why, what canst thou tell, my boy?

DISCOVERING SHAKESPEARE

(34) <u>Metaphor</u> [1.4.326]: Why does Goneril refer to her husband's behavior as "milky gentleness" (1.4.326)? How does this description help us understand the difference between Albany and his wife?

FOOL   She'll taste as like this as a crab doth to a crab.
Thou canst not tell why one's nose stand in the middle
of his face?   20

LEAR   No.

FOOL   Why, to keep his eyes on either side's nose, that
what a man cannot smell out, a may° spy into.

a may: he may

LEAR   I did her° wrong.

her: Cordelia

FOOL   Canst tell how an oyster makes his shell?   25

LEAR   No.

FOOL   Nor I neither; but I can tell why a snail has a
house.

LEAR   Why?   30

FOOL   Why, to put his head in, not to give it away to his
daughter and leave his horns° without a case.

horns: (with a quibble on the cuckold's horns,
implying that Goneril and Regan are illegitimate)

LEAR   I will forget my nature.° So kind a father! Be my
horses ready?

nature: paternal instincts

FOOL   Thy asses are gone about them. The reason why
the seven stars° are no more than seven is a pretty rea-
son.   35

the seven stars: the constellation the Pleiades

LEAR   Because they are not eight.

FOOL   Yes. Thou wouldst make a good fool.

LEAR   To take't again perforce!° Monster ingratitude!

To . . . perforce: to take it back forcibly (Lear
either rages at Goneril's revocation of his
privileges or contemplates reasserting his power)   40

FOOL   If thou wert my fool, nuncle, I'd have thee beaten
for being old before thy time.

LEAR   How's that?

FOOL   Thou shouldst not have been old before thou
hadst been wise.

LEAR
O, let me not be mad, sweet heaven!   45
I would not be mad.
Keep me in temper;° I would not be mad.

in temper: temperate, sane

    [Enter a Servant.]
Are the horses ready?

SERVANT   Ready, my lord.

LEAR   [To Fool] Come, boy.   50

            [Exeunt Lear and Servant.]

FOOL
She that is maid now, and laughs at my departure,
Shall not be a maid long, except things be cut shorter.°

            Exit.

She . . . shorter: i.e., the maid who laughed at
my leaving would be a fool, and would not remain
a virgin unless men were castrated

❧ **2.1**° Enter Bastard [Edmund] and Curan, meeting.

2.1: Gloucester's house

EDMUND   Save thee,° Curan.

Save thee: God save thee (a casual greeting like
"good day")

CURAN   And you, sir. I have been with your father, and
given him notice that the Duke of Cornwall and his
duchess will be here with him tonight.

EDMUND   How comes that?   5

DISCOVERING SHAKESPEARE

(35) Language [1.5.24]: Whom do you think Lear is referring to when he says "I did her wrong" (1.5.24)? Why is he reminded of this person at this particular moment in the play?

(36) Characterization [2.1.1]: Who is Curan? What is his purpose in this scene?

CURAN Nay, I know not. You have heard of the news abroad? I mean, the whispered ones, for there are yet but ear-bussing arguments.°

ear-bussing arguments: ear-kissing (i.e., whispered) matters

EDMUND Not I. Pray you, what are they?

CURAN Have you heard of no likely wars towards° 'twixt the two Dukes of Cornwall and Albany?

towards: impending 10

EDMUND Not a word.

CURAN You may then in time. Fare you well, sir. *[Exit.]*

EDMUND

The duke be here tonight! The better best.°

This weaves itself perforce° into my business.

My father hath set guard to take my brother,

And I have one thing of a queasy question°

Which must ask briefness and fortune help.°

Brother, a word! Descend,° brother, I say.

  Enter Edgar.

My father watches. O, fly this place!

Intelligence° is given where you are hid.

You have now the good advantage of the night.

Have you not spoken 'gainst the Duke of Cornwall aught?

He's coming hither now, in the night, i' th' haste,

And Regan with him. Have you nothing said

Upon his party against° the Duke of Albany?

Advise your —

better best: very best

perforce: necessarily 15

queasy question: delicate problem

must . . . help: requires the aid of speed and luck

Descend: (possibly Edgar has appeared on the upper-stage gallery)

Intelligence: information 20

Upon . . . against: relating to his quarrel with 25

EDGAR   I am sure on't,° not a word.

on't: of it

EDMUND

I hear my father coming. Pardon me

In craving I must draw my sword upon you.

Seem to defend yourself. Now, quit you° well.

  [They fight.]

Yield, come before my father! Light here, here!

(Fly, brother, fly!) Torches, torches! (So, farewell.)

                    [Exit Edgar.]

Some blood drawn on me would beget opinion

Of my more fierce endeavor.°

  [He cuts his arm.]

                    I have seen drunkards

Do more than this in sport. Father, father!

Stop, stop! No help?

  Enter Gloucester [and Servants].

quit you: acquit yourself 30

beget . . . endeavor: give the impression that I fought fiercely 35

GLOUCESTER   Now Edmund, where is the villain?

EDMUND

Here stood he in the dark, his sharp sword out,

Warbling of wicked charms, conjuring the moon

To stand's° auspicious mistress.

stand's: act as his

GLOUCESTER   But where is he?

EDMUND

Look, sir, I bleed.

GLOUCESTER   Where is the villain, Edmund? 40

DISCOVERING SHAKESPEARE

(37) Plot [2.1.29]: Why does Edmund draw his sword in 2.1.29? Why does he fight with Edgar?

EDMUND
 Fled this way, sir, when by no means he could –
GLOUCESTER
 Pursue him, go after.

[Exeunt Servants.]
      By no means what?
EDMUND
 Persuade me to the murder of your lordship,
 But that° I told him the revengive gods   **But that:** however
 'Gainst parricides did all their thunders bend,°   **thunders bend:** thunderbolts aim   45
 Spoke with how manifold and strong a bond
 The child was bound to the father. Sir, in fine,°   **in fine:** finally
 Seeing how loathly opposite° I stood   **loathly opposite:** loathingly opposed
 To his unnatural purpose, with fell motion°   **fell motion:** deadly action
 With his preparèd sword he charges home°   **charges home:** thrusts directly at   50
 My unprovided° body, lanched° mine arm;   **unprovided:** unprotected; **lanched:** lanced
 But when he saw my best alarumed° spirits   **best alarumed:** fully aroused
 Bold in the quarrel's rights° roused to the encounter,   **quarrel's rights:** justice of the cause
 Or whether ghasted° by the noise I made,   **ghasted:** frightened
 But suddenly he fled.
GLOUCESTER   Let him fly far.   55
 Not in this land shall he remain uncaught;
 And found, dispatch!° The noble duke my master,   **found, dispatch!:** once found, death!
 My worthy arch and patron,° comes tonight.   **arch . . . patron:** chief patron
 By his authority I will proclaim it
 That he which finds him shall deserve our thanks,   60
 Bringing the murderous caitiff° to the stake;   **caitiff:** villain, wretch
 He that conceals him, death.
EDMUND
 When I dissuaded him from his intent,
 And found him pight° to do it, with curst° speech   **pight:** determined; **curst:** angry
 I threatened to discover° him. He replied,   **discover:** expose   65
 "Thou unpossessing° bastard, dost thou think   **unpossessing:** unpropertied, landless
 If I would stand against thee, could the reposure°   **reposure:** placing
 Of any trust, virtue, or worth in thee
 Make thy words faithed?° No, what I should° deny –   **faithed:** believed; **what . . . should:** whatever I
 As this I would, ay, though thou didst produce   would   70
 My very character° – I'd turn° it all   **character:** handwriting (i.e., evidence in my
 To thy suggestion, plot, and damned pretense;°   own hand); **turn:** ascribe
 And thou must make a dullard of the world°   **pretense:** evil schemes
 If they not thought the profits of my death   **make . . . world:** consider everyone stupid
 Were very pregnant and potential spurs°   **pregnant . . . spurs:** meaningful and powerful   75
 To make thee seek it."   motives
GLOUCESTER   Strong and fastened° villain!   **fastened:** hardened
 Would he deny his letter? I never got° him.   **got:** fathered
  [Tucket° within.]   **Tucket:** trumpet signal
 Hark, the duke's trumpets. I know not why he comes.
 All ports° I'll bar; the villain shall not scape;   **ports:** (1) seaports, (2) town gates
 The duke must grant me that. Besides, his picture   80

DISCOVERING SHAKESPEARE

(38) <u>Plot</u> [2.1.51]: Why does Edmund cut himself in this scene? If you were the <u>make-up</u> designer for a production of this play, what other blood effects would the script require?
(39) Stage Direction [2.1.77]: What is a "tucket" (s.d. 2.1.77)? Whose arrival is announced here?

I will send far and near that all the kingdom
May have note of him; and of my land,
Loyal and natural boy, I'll work the means
To make thee capable.°　　　　　　　　　　　　　　　　　　　**capable:** legally able to inherit
　　Enter the Duke of Cornwall [, Regan, and
　　Attendants].
CORNWALL
　　How now, my noble friend? Since I came hither,　　　　　　　　　　　　85
　　Which I can call but° now, I have heard strange news.　　**call but:** say was only
REGAN
　　If it be true, all vengeance comes too short
　　Which can pursue the offender. How dost, my lord?
GLOUCESTER
　　Madam, my old heart is cracked, is cracked.
REGAN
　　What, did my father's godson seek your life?　　　　　　　　　　　　90
　　He whom my father named, your Edgar?
GLOUCESTER
　　Ay, lady, lady, shame would have it hid.
REGAN
　　Was he not companion with the riotous knights
　　That tends upon my father?
GLOUCESTER
　　I know not, madam. 'Tis too bad, too bad.　　　　　　　　　　　　95
EDMUND　　Yes, madam, he was.
REGAN
　　No marvel then though° he were ill affected.°　　　　　**though:** that; **ill affected:** disposed to evil
　　'Tis they have put° him on the old man's death,　　　　**put:** set
　　To have the spoil and waste° of his revenues.　　　　　**waste:** plunder
　　I have this present evening from my sister
　　Been well informed of them, and with such cautions　　　　　　　　100
　　That if they come to sojourn at my house
　　I'll not be there.
CORNWALL　　Nor I, assure thee, Regan.
　　Edmund, I heard that you have shown your father　　　　　　　　105
　　A childlike office.
EDMUND　　　　　　'Twas my duty, sir.
GLOUCESTER
　　He did betray his practice,° and received　　　　　　　**betray . . . practice:** expose Edgar's plot
　　This hurt you see striving to apprehend him.
CORNWALL
　　Is he pursued?
GLOUCESTER　　Ay, my good lord.　　　　　　　　　　　　110
CORNWALL
　　If he be taken, he shall never more
　　Be feared of doing harm. Make your own purpose
　　How in my strength you please.° For you, Edmund,　　**Make . . . please:** carry out your intentions
　　Whose virtue and obedience doth this instant　　　　　making what use you wish of my powers
　　So much commend itself, you shall be ours.　　　　　　　　　　　115
　　Natures of such deep trust we shall much need.
　　You we first seize on.

DISCOVERING SHAKESPEARE

(40) <u>Staging</u> **[2.1.100]:** Since Regan and Edmund eventually become lovers in the script, how could a production of the play indicate in this early scene that the two find each other attractive?

EDMUND   I shall serve you truly,
  However else.°

However else: if nothing else

GLOUCESTER
  For him I thank your grace.

CORNWALL
  You know not why we came to visit you?   120

REGAN
  Thus out-of-season,° threat'ning dark-eyed night?°
  Occasions, noble Gloucester, of some poise,°
  Wherein we must have use of your advice.
  Our father he hath writ, so hath our sister,
  Of differences° which I least thought it fit
  To answer from our home.° The several° messengers
  From hence attend° dispatch. Our good old friend,
  Lay comforts to your bosom, and bestow
  Your needful° counsel to our business
  Which craves the instant use.°

out-of-season: untimely (i.e., traveling at night);
threat'ning . . . night: with the dark night
threatening us
poise: weight

differences: quarrels   125
least . . . home: i.e., thought it best to respond
by being away from home; **several:** various

attend: await
needful: needed
the . . . use: immediate action   130

GLOUCESTER
                          I serve you, madam;
  Your graces are right welcome.   *Exeunt.*

& **2.2** *Enter Kent [disguised] and Steward [Oswald].*

OSWALD   Good even° to thee, friend. Art of° the house?
KENT   Ay.°
OSWALD   Where may we set our horses?
KENT   I' th' mire.
OSWALD   Prithee, if thou love me,° tell me.
KENT   I love thee not.
OSWALD   Why then, I care not for thee.
KENT   If I had thee in Lipsbury Pinfold° I would make
  thee care for me.
OSWALD   Why dost thou use° me thus? I know thee not.
KENT   Fellow, I know thee.
OSWALD   What dost thou know me for?
KENT   A knave, a rascal, an eater of broken meats,° a base,
  proud, shallow, beggarly, three-suited,° hundred-pound,°
  filthy worsted-stocking° knave; a lily-livered,° action-
  taking° knave; a whoreson, glass-gazing, superfinical°
  rogue; one-trunk-inheriting° slave; one that wouldst be
  a bawd in way of good service,° and art nothing but the
  composition° of a knave, beggar, coward, pander, and
  the son and heir of a mongrel bitch, whom I will beat
  into clamorous whining if thou deny the least syllable
  of the addition.°
OSWALD   What a monstrous fellow art thou, thus to rail
  on one that's neither known of thee nor knows thee!
KENT   What a brazen-faced varlet° art thou, to deny thou
  knowest me! Is it two days ago since I beat thee and
  tripped up thy heels before the king? Draw, you rogue,

even: evening; **Art of:** are you a servant in
Ay: (since the house is Gloucester's, Kent is lying,
presumably as a way of picking a fight with
Oswald)

if . . . me: i.e., be kind enough to   5

Lipsbury Pinfold: in the pen of my lips (i.e.,
between my teeth—treated jocularly as a place-
name)
use: treat   10
broken meats: leftover food, fit for menials
three-suited: (male household servants were
furnished with three suits per year: Kent attacks
Oswald's pretensions to gentility); **hundred-
pound:** (the minimum annual income for a   15
gentleman)
worsted-stocking: coarse wool stocking (a
gentleman would wear silk); **lily-livered:**
cowardly
action-taking: litigious (resorting to legal action
instead of fighting); **glass-gazing, superfinical:**   20
vain, toadying, fussy
one-trunk-inheriting: owning no more than
will fit in a single trunk
a bawd . . . service: a pimp if asked
composition: composite   25
addition: title (i.e., the names I have just called you)
varlet: rogue

DISCOVERING SHAKESPEARE
(41) **Plot** **[2.2.2]:** Why does Kent lie in 2.2.2 when Oswald asks him if he is a servant in Gloucester's house?

for though it be night, the moon shines. *[Kent draws his sword.]* I'll make a sop of the moonshine° o' you. Draw, you whoreson, cullionly° barbermonger,° draw!

OSWALD   Away, I have nothing to do with thee.

KENT   Draw, you rascal. You bring letters against the king, and take Vanity the puppet's part° against the royalty of her father. Draw, you rogue, or I'll so carbonado° your shanks – draw, you rascal, come your ways!°

OSWALD   Help, ho, murder, help!

[Kent attacks Oswald, who tries to escape.]

KENT   Strike, you slave! Stand, rogue! Stand, you neat° slave, strike!

OSWALD   Help, ho, murder, help!

Enter Edmund with his rapier drawn, Gloucester, [Servants, then] the duke [Cornwall] and duchess [Regan].

EDMUND   How now, what's the matter?

KENT   With you, goodman° boy.° An you please come, I'll flesh you.° Come on, young master.

GLOUCESTER   Weapons? Arms? What's the matter here?

CORNWALL   Keep peace, upon your lives. He dies that strikes again. What's the matter?

REGAN   The messengers from our sister and the king.

CORNWALL   What's your difference?° Speak.

OSWALD   I am scarce in breath, my lord.

KENT   No marvel, you have so bestirred your valor, you cowardly rascal. Nature disclaims in° thee; a tailor made thee.

CORNWALL   Thou art a strange fellow – a tailor make a man?

KENT   Ay, a tailor, sir. A stonecutter or a painter could not have made him so ill° though he had been but two hours at the trade.

GLOUCESTER   Speak yet; how grew your quarrel?

OSWALD   This ancient ruffian, sir, whose life I have spared at suit° of his gray beard –

KENT   Thou whoreson zed,° thou unnecessary letter! My lord, if you'll give me leave, I will tread this unbolted° villain into mortar and daub the walls of a jakes° with him. *[To Oswald]* Spare my gray beard, you wagtail?°

CORNWALL   Peace, sir! You beastly knave, you have no reverence.

KENT   Yes, sir, but anger has a privilege.

CORNWALL   Why art thou angry?

KENT
That such a slave as this should wear a sword,
That wears no honesty. Such smiling rogues as these,
Like rats, oft bite those cords° in twain

make . . . moonshine: fill you with holes so your body will sop up moonshine   30

cullionly: despicable (cullions are testicles; the insult is analogous to calling someone a "prick");

barbermonger: (a particularly inventive insult: on the model of whoremonger, a pimp for barbers, one who supplies them with clients, hence who caters to the needs of effeminate men)   35

take . . . part: support the vain, overdressed Goneril

carbonado: slash

come . . . ways: come on, get to it

neat: prissy

40

goodman: yeoman or farmer; **goodman boy:** (both are deliberate insults to Edmund as a gentleman)

flesh you: give you your first taste of blood

45

difference: quarrel

disclaims in: disowns   50

ill: badly   55

at suit: at the plea

zed: the letter *z* ("unnecessary" because its sound   60 is also represented by *s,* and because it is not used in Latin)

unbolted: unsifted (as flour or plaster)

jakes: toilet

wagtail: (a bird that constantly wags its tail; hence a nervous or effeminate person)   65

cords: bonds   70

DISCOVERING SHAKESPEARE

(42) Paraphrase [2.2.29]: Paraphrase the following lines by Kent: "I'll make a sop of the moonshine o' you. Draw, you whoreson, cullionly barbermonger, draw!" (2.2.29–30).

(43) Language [2.2.50]: Why does Kent tell Oswald that "a tailor made thee" (2.2.50–51)? Translate this insult into modern English.

Which are too entrenched° to unloose; smooth° every
  passion

entrenched: intertwined; **smooth:** flatter

That in the natures of their lords rebel,°

rebel: i.e., against reason

Bring oil to fire, snow to their colder moods,
Renege,° affirm, and turn their halcyon° beaks

Renege: deny; **halcyon:** kingfisher (its beak
was said to be usable as a weather vane)

With every gale and vary° of their masters,

gale . . . vary: changing wind

Knowing naught, like dogs, but following.
  [To Oswald]
A plague upon your epileptic° visage!

epileptic: grinning

Smile you° my speeches as° I were a fool?

Smile you: do you smile at; **as:** as if

Goose, an° I had you upon Sarum Plain°

an: if; **Sarum Plain:** Salisbury Plain, near
Winchester (Oswald is a goose because he is
laughing, but it is not clear why Shakespeare
associates geese with Salisbury Plain)

I'd send you cackling home to Camelot.°

Camelot: (legendary capital of King Arthur,
thought to have been on the site of Winchester)

CORNWALL   What, art thou mad, old fellow?
GLOUCESTER   How fell you out? Say that.
KENT

No contraries° hold more antipathy

contraries: opposites

Than I and such a knave.
CORNWALL

Why dost thou call him knave? What's his offense?
KENT

His countenance likes me not.°

His . . . not: I don't like his face

CORNWALL

No more perchance does mine, or his, or hers.
KENT

Sir, 'tis my occupation to be plain:
I have seen better faces in my time
Than stands on any shoulder that I see
Before me at this instant.
CORNWALL   This is a fellow
Who, having been praised for bluntness, doth affect°

affect: adopt

A saucy roughness, and constrains the garb°

garb: style of speech

Quite from his° nature.° He cannot flatter, he;

his: its; **constrains . . . nature:** forces plain
speaking away from its proper function

He must be plain, he must speak truth.
An they will take't, so;° if not, he's plain.°

so: well and good; **he's plain:** his excuse is his
bluntness

These kind of knaves I know, which in this plainness
Harbor more craft and more corrupter ends
Than twenty silly-ducking observants°

silly . . . observants: bowing attendants

That stretch their duties nicely.°

nicely: excessively

KENT

Sir, in good sooth, or in sincere verity,
Under the allowance of your grand aspect,
Whose influence, like the wreath of radiant fire
In flickering Phoebus' front° –

Phoebus' front: the sun god's forehead

CORNWALL   What mean'st thou by this?
KENT   To go out of my dialect,° which you discommend
so much. I know, sir, I am no flatterer. He that beguiled
you° in a plain accent was a plain knave, which for my

go . . . dialect: depart from my usual way of
speaking

He . . . you: whoever deceived you

DISCOVERING SHAKESPEARE

(44) Language [2.2.77]: What was the meaning of the word "epileptic" (2.2.77) in the year 1600? (*Hint:* See the *Oxford English Dictionary.*) How has the word changed from Shakespeare's time to the present day?
(45) Verse [2.2.101]: Why does Kent move from <u>verse</u> in 2.2.101–104 to <u>prose</u> in 2.2.105–109? How does each mode of communication serve his purpose in these two speeches?

part I will not be, though I should win your displeasure
to entreat me to't.°

CORNWALL   *[To Oswald]*
What's the offense you gave him?   110

OSWALD
I never gave him any.
It pleased the king his master very late°
To strike at me upon his misconstruction,°
When he, conjunct,° and flattering his displeasure,
Tripped me behind; being down, insulted, railed,   115
And put upon him such a deal of man°
That worthied him,° got praises of the king
For him attempting who was self-subdued,°
And in the fleshment° of this dread exploit,
Drew on me here again.   120

KENT
None of these rogues and cowards
But Ajax is their fool.°

CORNWALL   Bring forth the stocks, ho!
You stubborn, ancient knave, you reverend braggart,
We'll teach you.

KENT   I am too old to learn.
Call not your stocks for me; I serve the king,   125
On whose employments I was sent to you.
You should do small respect, show too bold malice
Against the grace and person of my master,
Stocking his messenger.

CORNWALL   Fetch forth the stocks!
As I have life and honor, there shall he sit till noon.   130

REGAN
Till noon? Till night, my lord, and all night too.

KENT
Why, madam, if I were your father's dog
You could not use me so.

REGAN
Sir, being° his knave, I will.
   [Stocks brought out.]

CORNWALL
This is a fellow of the selfsame nature   135
Our sister speaks of. Come, bring away° the stocks.

GLOUCESTER
Let me beseech your grace not to do so.
His fault is much, and the good king his master
Will check him for't. Your purposed low correction
Is such as basest and contemnèd'st wretches   140
For pilf'rings and most common trespasses
Are punished with. The king must take it ill
That he's so slightly valued in his messenger,
Should have him thus restrained.

CORNWALL   I'll answer° that.

Glosses (right column)

to . . . to't: i.e., even if you begged me to be a knave

very late: recently
misconstruction: misunderstanding me
conjunct: in league with (the king)

deal . . . man: macho act
worthied him: made him a hero
For . . . self-subdued: for attacking a man who refused to fight
fleshment: excitement

None . . . fool: i.e., Oswald is making a fool out of Cornwall, whom Kent identifies with the dull-witted and boastful Greek hero Ajax

being: as you are

away: forward

answer: answer for

DISCOVERING SHAKESPEARE

(46) Half Lines [2.2.122]: How do the <u>half lines</u> and <u>shared lines</u> between Kent and Cornwall in 2.2.121–129 help indicate the speed and intensity of this section of the scene?

REGAN
My sister may receive it much more worse   145
To have her gentlemen abused, assaulted,
For following her affairs. Put in his legs.
[Kent is put in the stocks.]
[To Gloucester]
Come, my good lord, away!
                                    [Exeunt all but Kent and Gloucester.]
GLOUCESTER
I am sorry for thee, friend. 'Tis the duke's pleasure,
Whose disposition, all the world well knows,   150
Will not be rubbed° nor stopped. I'll entreat for thee.   **rubbed:** deflected (term from the game of bowls)
KENT
Pray you, do not, sir. I have watched° and traveled hard.   **watched:** stayed awake
Some time I shall sleep out; the rest I'll whistle.
A good man's fortune may grow out at heels.°   **grow . . . heels:** wear thin
Give you good morrow.   155
GLOUCESTER
The duke's to blame in this; 'twill be ill took.   *[Exit.]*
KENT
Good king, that must approve the common saw:°   **approve . . . saw:** prove the truth of the old saying
Thou out of heaven's benediction comest   **Thou . . . sun:** you go from God's blessing into the hot sun (i.e., you go from good to bad)
To the warm sun.°
Approach, thou beacon° to this under globe,   **beacon:** (presumably the moon, since it is night)   160
That by thy comfortable° beams I may   **comfortable:** comforting
Peruse this letter. Nothing almost sees miracles   **Nothing . . . misery:** miracles are rarely seen by any but the miserable
But misery.° I know 'tis from Cordelia,
Who hath most fortunately been informed
Of my obscurèd° course. "– And shall find time   **obscurèd:** disguised   165
From this enormous state,° seeking to give   **enormous state:** terrible situation
Losses their remedies."° All weary and overwatched,°   **And . . . remedies:** (a famously incoherent crux: is Kent reading a bit of Cordelia's letter?); **overwatched:** too long without sleep
Take vantage,° heavy eyes, not to behold   **Take vantage:** take advantage (by falling asleep)
This shameful lodging. Fortune, good night;
Smile; once more turn thy wheel.°   *Sleeps.*   **turn . . . wheel:** change my luck (The goddess   170
                                                          Fortuna is depicted with a large vertical wheel,
                                                          which she turns arbitrarily; Kent is now at the
                                                          bottom.)

❧ **2.3**° *Enter Edgar.*   **2.3:** Kent remains onstage in the stocks, asleep,
                                                          but he and Edgar are clearly not part of the same
                                                          scene

EDGAR
I hear myself proclaimed,°   **proclaimed:** i.e., as an outlaw
And by the happy hollow° of a tree   **happy hollow:** i.e., lucky hiding place
Escaped the hunt. No port is free, no place
That guard and most unusual vigilance
Does not attend my taking.° While I may scape   **attend . . . taking:** prepare to arrest me   5
I will preserve myself, and am bethought°   **am bethought:** have a plan
To take the basest and most poorest shape
That ever penury in contempt of° man   **of:** for
Brought near to beast. My face I'll grime with filth,
Blanket my loins, elf° all my hair with knots,   **elf:** tangle (into "elf locks")   10

DISCOVERING SHAKESPEARE

(47) History [2.2.147]: What kind of discipline is Kent subjected to? How harsh do you think his punishment is?
(48) Costuming [2.3.10]: What clues in 2.3 help suggest the type of costume Edgar wears as Tom o'Bedlam? (*Hint:* See also 3.6.74–75.)

And with presented° nakedness outface
The wind and persecution of the sky.
The country gives me proof° and precedent
Of Bedlam beggars° who with roaring voices
Strike° in their numbed and mortified° bare arms
Pins, wooden pricks, nails, sprigs of rosemary,
And with this horrible object° from low service,°
Poor pelting° villages, sheepcotes, and mills
Sometime with lunatic bans,° sometime with prayers
Enforce their charity. "Poor Turlygod!° poor Tom!"
That's something yet. Edgar° I nothing am.   *Exit.*

presented: the show of

proof: experience
Bedlam beggars: (see 1.2.129)
Strike: stick; **mortified:** dead to pain   15

object: spectacle; **low service:** menial servants
pelting: paltry
bans: curses
Turlygod: (unexplained, but evidently another   20
name for a Bedlam beggar)
Edgar: i.e., as Edgar

& **2.4** *Enter Lear [, Fool, and Knight. Kent still in the stocks].*

LEAR
'Tis strange that they should so depart from home
And not send back my messenger.
KNIGHT   As I learned,
The night before there was no purpose
Of his remove.°
KENT   Hail to thee, noble master.
LEAR
How! Mak'st thou this shame thy pastime?
FOOL   Ha, ha, look, he wears cruel° garters. Horses are
tied by the heads, dogs and bears by th' neck, monkeys
by th' loins, and men by th' legs. When a man's over-
lusty at legs,° then he wears wooden netherstocks.°
LEAR
What's he that hath so much thy place mistook
To set thee here?
KENT
It is both he and she,
Your son° and daughter.
LEAR
                              No.
KENT
                                    Yes.
LEAR
                                          No, I say.
KENT
I say yea.
LEAR
            No, no, they would not.
KENT
                                          Yes, they have.
LEAR
By Jupiter, I swear no. They durst not do't,
They would not, could not do't. 'Tis worse than murder
To do upon respect° such violent outrage.
Resolve° me with all modest° haste which way

there . . . remove: the duke had no intention of
leaving

                                                                        5

cruel: (punning on "crewel," worsted cloth)

overlusty . . . legs: too eager to run;
netherstocks: stockings

                                                                        10

son: i.e., son-in-law

                                                                        15

upon respect: to one who should be respected
(as the king's messenger)
Resolve: explain to; **modest:** decent

DISCOVERING SHAKESPEARE
(49) Shared Lines [2.4.13]: What is the effect of the shared lines in 2.4.13–14?

Thou mayst deserve or they purpose this usage,
Coming from us.   20
KENT   My lord, when at their home
I did commend° your highness' letters to them,   **commend:** deliver
Ere I was risen from the place that showed
My duty kneeling, came there a reeking post
Stewed° in his haste, half breathless, panting forth   **reeking . . . Stewed:** hot and sweaty messenger
From Goneril his mistress salutations;   25
Delivered letters spite of intermission,°   **spite . . . intermission:** though he was interrupting me
Which presently° they read, on whose contents   **presently:** immediately
They summoned up their men, straight took horse,
Commanded me to follow and attend
The leisure of their answer, gave me cold looks;   30
And meeting here the other messenger,
Whose welcome I perceived had poisoned mine,
Being the very fellow that of late
Displayed° so saucily against your highness,   **Displayed:** behaved
Having more man than wit° about me, drew.°   **wit:** sense; **drew:** drew my sword   35
He raised the house with loud and coward cries.
Your son and daughter found this trespass worth
This shame which here it suffers.
LEAR
O, how this mother° swells up toward my heart!   **mother:** hysteria
Hysterica passio,° down, thou climbing sorrow,   *Hysterica passio:* (the medical term for hysteria)   40
Thy element's below.° Where is this daughter?   **Thy . . . below:** (hysteria's natural place, "element," was said to be the abdomen or, in women, the womb)
KENT
With the earl, sir, within.
LEAR
    [*To Attendants*]
Follow me not; stay there.   [*Exit.*]
KNIGHT Made you no more offense than what you
speak of?   45
KENT No. How chance the king comes with so small a
train?
FOOL An° thou hadst been set in the stocks for that ques-   **An:** if
tion, thou hadst well deserved it.
KENT Why, fool?   50
FOOL We'll set thee to school to an ant, to teach thee
there's no laboring in the winter.° All that follow their   **We'll . . . winter:** (ants proverbially do not work in winter—implying that working for Lear is now unprofitable)
noses are led by their eyes but blind men, and there's
not a nose among a hundred but can smell him that's
stinking. Let go thy hold when a great wheel runs down   55
a hill, lest it break thy neck with following it; but the
great one that goes up the hill, let him draw thee after.
When a wise man gives thee better counsel, give me
mine again.° I would have none but knaves follow it,   **again:** back
since a fool gives it.   60
        That sir that serves for gain
            And follows but for form,°   **form:** show
        Will pack° when it begin to rain,   **pack:** leave

DISCOVERING SHAKESPEARE
(50) History [2.4.40]: What was "*hysterica passio*" (2.4.40)? What other diseases are mentioned in the play? In what sense is "disease" a major <u>theme</u> in the play?

And leave thee in the storm.
But I will tarry, the fool will stay,   65
    And let the wise man fly.
The knave turns fool that runs away,°   **knave . . . away:** i.e., disloyalty is the real folly
    The fool no knave, perdy.°   **perdy:** by God (*par Dieu*)
KENT   Where learnt you this, fool?
FOOL   Not in the stocks.   70
    Enter Lear and Gloucester.
LEAR
Deny to speak with me? They're sick, they're weary,
They traveled hard tonight? Mere justice?°   **Mere justice:** (presumably Cornwall's
Ay, the images° of revolt and flying off.°   explanation for why Kent is in the stocks)
Fetch me a better answer.   **images:** signs; **flying off:** insurrection
GLOUCESTER   My dear lord,
You know the fiery quality° of the duke,   **quality:** disposition   75
How unremovable and fixed he is
In his own course.
LEAR
Vengeance, death, plague, confusion!
What "fiery quality"? Why, Gloucester, Gloucester,
I'd speak with the Duke of Cornwall and his wife.   80
GLOUCESTER   Ay, my good lord.
LEAR
The king would speak with Cornwall; the dear father
Would with his daughter speak, commands her service.
Fiery duke? Tell the hot duke that Lear —
No, but not yet; maybe he is not well.   85
Infirmity doth still neglect all office°   **still . . . office:** always neglects duty
Whereto our health is bound.° We are not ourselves **Whereto . . . bound:** which in health we are
When nature, being oppressed, commands the mind bound to obey
To suffer with the body. I'll forbear,
And am fallen out° with my more headier° will, **fallen out:** angry; **headier:** headstrong   90
To take° the indisposed and sickly fit   **To take:** that mistook
For the sound man. — Death on my state!° wherefore **Death . . . state:** (the expletive is ironic: "Let my
Should he° sit here? This act persuades me   royal power die")
That this remotion° of the duke and her   **he:** Kent
Is practice° only. Give me my servant forth.°   **remotion:** (1) removal (from their home),   95
Tell the duke and's wife I'll speak with them,   (2) aloofness (from Lear)
Now, presently.° Bid them come forth and hear me, **practice:** trickery; **Give . . . forth:** release my
Or at their chamber door I'll beat the drum   servant
Till it cry sleep to death.°   **presently:** instantly
GLOUCESTER   I would have all well betwixt you.   *[Exit.]* **Till . . . death:** till it kills sleep with the noise 100
LEAR   O, my heart, my heart!
FOOL   Cry to it, nuncle, as the cockney° did to the eels **cockney:** Londoner (i.e., a city dweller)
    when she put 'em i' th' paste° alive. She rapped 'em o' th' **paste:** pastry
    coxcombs° with a stick, and cried "Down, wantons,° **coxcombs:** heads; **wantons:** rascals (with a
                                                      quibble on lechers, and on deflating erections)

DISCOVERING SHAKESPEARE

(51) Verse [2.4.65]: Scan the Fool's song in 2.4.61–68; then write down the meter and rhyme scheme. How is the verse form of this song different from some of his other songs in the play?

(52) Monologue [2.4.92]: In his monologue in 2.4.82–99, Lear reasons with himself about why the Duke of Cornwall will not come speak with him. What excuses does he offer for the Duke? What conclusion does Lear come to at the end of this speech?

down!" 'Twas her brother that, in pure kindness to his
horse, buttered his hay.°   105

> *Enter Cornwall and Regan [, followed by Gloucester*
> *and Servants].*

LEAR   Good morrow to you both.
CORNWALL   Hail to your grace.
REGAN
  I am glad to see your highness.
  [Kent is set free.]
LEAR
  Regan, I think you are. I know what reason
  I have to think so. If thou shouldst not be glad   110
  I would divorce me from thy mother's tomb,
  Sepulch'ring an adult'ress.° *[To Kent]* Yea, are you free?
  Some other time for that. Belovèd Regan,
  Thy sister is naught.° O, Regan, she hath tied
  Sharp-toothed unkindness like a vulture here.   115
  I can scarce speak to thee. Thou'lt not believe
  Of how depraved a quality – O Regan!
REGAN
  I pray, sir, take patience. I have hope
  You less know how to value her desert
  Than she to slack her duty.°   120
LEAR
  My curses on her.
REGAN   O, sir, you are old;
  Nature in you stands on the very verge
  Of her confine.° You should be ruled and led
  By some discretion that discerns your state°   125
  Better than you yourself. Therefore I pray
  That to our sister you do make return;
  Say you have wronged her, sir.
LEAR   Ask her forgiveness?
  Do you mark how this becomes the house?°
  [Kneels.]
  "Dear daughter, I confess that I am old;
  Age is° unnecessary. On my knees I beg   130
  That you'll vouchsafe me raiment, bed, and food."
REGAN
  Good sir, no more. These are unsightly tricks.
  Return you to my sister.
LEAR   *[Rising]*   No, Regan.
  She hath abated° me of half my train,
  Looked black upon me, struck me with her tongue   135
  Most serpentlike upon the very heart.
  All the stored vengeances of heaven fall
  On her ingrateful top!° Strike her young bones,
  You taking airs,° with lameness.
CORNWALL   Fie, fie, sir.

---

buttered . . . hay: (misguided kindness: horses will not eat grease)

Sepulch'ring . . . adult'ress: i.e., it would prove you were not my daughter
naught: wicked (cf. "naughty")

You . . . duty: the problem is that you are unable to evaluate her merit rather than that she has failed in her duty

Nature . . . confine: your life stands at the very edge of its allotted space
discretion . . . state: discerning person who understands your condition

house: family

Age is: old people are

abated: deprived

top: head
taking airs: infectious vapors

DISCOVERING SHAKESPEARE

(53) Meter [2.4.114]: What metrical clues can you find in Lear's speech to Regan in 2.4.109–117 that illustrate how upset he is?

LEAR
You nimble lightnings, dart your blinding flames 140
Into her scornful eyes. Infect her beauty,
You fen-sucked fogs drawn by the pow'rful sun° **fen-sucked . . . sun:** (the sun was believed to draw infectious vapors from swamps)
To fall and blast her pride.

REGAN   O the blest gods!
So will you wish on me when the rash mood —

LEAR
No, Regan, thou shalt never have my curse. 145
Thy tender-hefted° nature shall not give **tender-hefted:** gently disposed
Thee o'er to harshness. Her eyes are fierce, but thine
Do comfort and not burn. 'Tis not in thee
To grudge my pleasures, to cut off my train,
To bandy hasty words, to scant my sizes,° **sizes:** allowance 150
And, in conclusion, to oppose the bolt° **oppose the bolt:** bolt the door
Against my coming in. Thou better knowest
The offices° of nature, bond of childhood, **offices:** duties
Effects° of courtesy, dues of gratitude; **Effects:** obligations
Thy half of the kingdom hast thou not forgot, 155
Wherein I thee endowed.

REGAN   Good sir, to th' purpose.° **to . . . purpose:** get to the point

LEAR
Who put my man i' th' stocks?
    [Tucket within.]

CORNWALL   What trumpet's that?
    Enter Steward [Oswald].

REGAN
I know't, my sister's. This approves° her letters **approves:** confirms
That she would soon be here. *[To Oswald]* Is your lady come?

LEAR
This is a slave whose easy,° borrowed° pride **easy:** impudent; **borrowed:** assumed 160
Dwells in the fickle grace of her a° follows. **a:** he
    [Strikes Oswald.]
Out, varlet,° from my sight! **varlet:** scoundrel

CORNWALL   What means your grace?
    Enter Goneril.

GONERIL
Who struck my servant? Regan, I have good hope
Thou didst not know on't.° **on't:** of it

LEAR   Who comes here? O heavens,
If you do love old men, if you sweet sway 165
Allow obedience,° if yourselves are old, **If . . . obedience:** if you permit gentle rule to be obeyed
Make it your cause; send down and take my part.
    [To Goneril]
Art not ashamed to look upon this beard?
O Regan, wilt thou take her by the hand?

DISCOVERING SHAKESPEARE

(54) Alliteration [2.4.140]: Find all the alliteration in Lear's speech in 2.4.140–143. What is the purpose of this rhetorical device?

(55) Blocking [2.4.168]: What blocking clues can you find in Lear's speech in 2.4.164–169? What other staging suggestions can you discover after Goneril's entrance in line 162 until the end of the scene?

GONERIL

  Why not by the hand, sir? How have I offended?   170

  All's not offense that indiscretion° finds   **indiscretion:** poor judgment

  And dotage terms so.

LEAR   O sides,° you are too tough!   **sides:** breast (which should burst with grief)

  Will you yet hold? How came my man i' th' stocks?

CORNWALL

  I set him there, sir, but his own disorders

  Deserved much less advancement.°   **less advancement:** less of a promotion (i.e., a   175
                                       worse punishment)

LEAR   You? Did you?

REGAN

  I pray you, father, being weak, seem so.

  If till the expiration of your month

  You will return and sojourn with my sister,

  Dismissing half your train, come then to me.

  I am now from° home, and out of that provision   **from:** away from   180

  Which shall be needful for your entertainment.°   **entertainment:** reception

LEAR

  Return to her, and fifty men dismissed?

  No, rather I abjure all roofs, and choose

  To wage° against the enmity of the air,   **wage:** fight

  To be a comrade with the wolf and owl –   185

  Necessity's sharp pinch. Return with her?

  Why, the hot-blood in France that dowerless took

  Our youngest born – I could as well be brought

  To knee° his throne and, squirelike, pension beg   **knee:** kneel to

  To keep base life afoot. Return with her?   190

  Persuade me rather to be slave and sumpter°   **sumpter:** pack-horse

  To this detested groom.   *[Points at Oswald.]*

GONERIL   At your choice, sir.

LEAR

  Now I prithee, daughter, do not make me mad.

  I will not trouble thee, my child. Farewell;

  We'll no more meet, no more see one another.   195

  But yet thou art my flesh, my blood, my daughter,

  Or rather a disease that lies within my flesh,

  Which I must needs call mine. Thou art a boil,

  A plague-sore, an embossèd carbuncle°   **embossèd carbuncle:** swollen tumor

  In my corrupted blood. But I'll not chide thee.   200

  Let shame come when it will, I do not call it.

  I do not bid the thunder-bearer° shoot,   **the thunder-bearer:** Jove

  Nor tell tales of thee to high-judging Jove.

  Mend when thou canst; be better at thy leisure.

  I can be patient, I can stay with Regan,   205

  I and my hundred knights.

REGAN

  Not altogether so, sir;

  I look not for you yet, nor am provided

  For your fit welcome. Give ear, sir, to my sister;

  For those that mingle reason with your passion°   **mingle . . . passion:** deal rationally with your   210
                                       intemperate behavior

  Must be content to think you are old, and so –

  But she knows what she does.

DISCOVERING SHAKESPEARE

(56) Language [2.4.192]: Why does Lear refer to Oswald as a "groom" in 2.4.192? To what extent is his remark an insult?

LEAR
Is this well spoken now?

REGAN
I dare avouch° it, sir. What, fifty followers?
Is it not well? What should you need of more,
Yea, or so many, sith that° both charge° and danger
Speaks 'gainst so great a number? How in a house
Should many people under two commands
Hold amity? 'Tis hard, almost impossible.

GONERIL
Why might not you, my lord, receive attendance
From those that she calls servants, or from mine?

REGAN
Why not, my lord? If then they chanced to slack° you,
We could control them. If you will come to me,
For now I spy a danger, I entreat you
To bring but five-and-twenty; to no more
Will I give place or notice.°

LEAR
I gave you all.

REGAN   And in good time you gave it.

LEAR
Made you my guardians, my depositaries,°
But kept a reservation to be° followed
With such a number. What, must I come to you
With five-and-twenty, Regan? Said you so?

REGAN
And speak't again, my lord. No more with me.

LEAR
Those wicked creatures yet do seem well favored°
When others are more wicked. Not being the worst
Stands in some rank of° praise. *[To Goneril]* I'll go with
  thee.
Thy fifty yet doth double five-and-twenty,
And thou art twice her love.°

GONERIL   Hear me, my lord:
What need you five-and-twenty, ten, or five,
To follow in a house where twice so many
Have a command to tend you?

REGAN   What needs one?

LEAR
O reason° not the need! Our basest beggars
Are in the poorest thing superfluous.°
Allow not° nature more than nature needs,
Man's life is cheap as beasts'. Thou art a lady;
If only to go warm were gorgeous,°
Why, nature needs not what thou gorgeous wearest,
Which scarcely keeps thee warm. But for true need —
You heavens, give me that patience, patience I need.

avouch: swear

215

sith that: since; **charge:** expense

220

slack: neglect

225
notice: recognition

depositaries: trustees
kept . . . be: stipulated that I be
230

well favored: attractive

Stands . . . of: deserves at least some   235

twice . . . love: twice as loving as she

240

reason: calculate
Are . . . superfluous: have something more than
is absolutely necessary
Allow not: if you do not grant
If . . . gorgeous: if warmth were the measure of   245
fashionable dress

DISCOVERING SHAKESPEARE

(57) Paraphrase [2.4.214]: Paraphrase Regan's argument in 2.4.214–219. Why do you think Lear's knights are so important to him?

(58) Logic [2.4.236]: Why does Lear say that Goneril's love for him is "twice" as much as Regan's in 2.4.236–237? What is his reasoning?

You see me here, you gods, a poor old fellow,
As full of grief as age, wretched in both. 250
If it be you that stirs these daughters' hearts
Against their father, fool me not so much
To° bear it tamely. Touch me with noble anger.   **fool . . . To:** don't make me such a fool as to
O, let not women's weapons, waterdrops,
Stain my man's cheeks! No, you unnatural hags, 255
I will have such revenges on you both
That all the world shall – I will do such things,
What they are, yet I know not; but they shall be
The terrors of the earth. You think I'll weep:
No, I'll not weep. 260
   [Storm and tempest.]
I have full cause of weeping, but this heart
Shall break in a hundred thousand flaws°   **flaws:** fragments
Or ere° I'll weep. O fool, I shall go mad!   **Or ere:** before
     Exeunt Lear, Gloucester, Kent, [Knight,] and Fool.

CORNWALL
Let us withdraw; 'twill be a storm.

REGAN
This house is little: the old man and his people 265
Cannot be well bestowed.

GONERIL
'Tis his own blame hath put himself from rest,
And must needs taste his folly.

REGAN
For his particular° I'll receive him gladly,   **his particular:** himself alone
But not one follower. 270

CORNWALL   So am I purposed.
Where is my lord of Gloucester?

REGAN
Followed the old man forth.
   Enter Gloucester.
                He is returned.

GLOUCESTER
The king is in high rage, and will I know not whither.

REGAN
'Tis good to give him way. He leads himself.

GONERIL
My lord, entreat him by no means to stay. 275

GLOUCESTER
Alack, the night comes on, and the bleak winds
Do sorely ruffle.° For many miles about   **ruffle:** rage
There's not a bush.

REGAN   O sir, to willful men
The injuries that they themselves procure
Must be their schoolmasters. Shut up your doors. 280
He is attended with a desperate train,°   **desperate train:** violent troop

---

DISCOVERING SHAKESPEARE

(59) Short Lines [2.4.258]: How does the use of dashes, <u>short lines</u>, and irregular <u>meter</u> in 2.4.241–263 help indicate Lear's heightened emotion?

(60) Paraphrase [2.4.280]: <u>Paraphrase</u> Regan's assertion that "to willful men / The injuries that they themselves procure/ Must be their schoolmasters" (2.4.278–280). Do you agree with her in this case? Why or why not?

And what they may incense him to, being apt
To have his ear abused,° wisdom bids fear.   **apt . . . abused:** i.e., likely to be misled
CORNWALL
Shut up your doors, my lord; 'tis a wild night.
My Regan counsels well. Come out o' th' storm.   285

                                Exeunt.

& **3.1°** *[Storm still.] Enter Kent [disguised] and a*   **3.1:** A heath
Gentleman at several° doors.   **several:** different

KENT
What's here beside foul weather?
GENTLEMAN
One minded like the weather, most unquietly.
KENT
I know you. Where's the king?
GENTLEMAN
Contending with the fretful element;°   **fretful element:** angry sky
Bids the wind blow the earth into the sea   5
Or quell the curlèd waters 'bove the main,°   **main:** mainland
That things might change or cease; tears his white hair,
Which the impetuous blasts, with eyeless° rage,   **eyeless:** blind
Catch in their fury and make nothing of;
Strives in his little world of man to outscorn   10
The to-and-fro conflicting wind and rain.
This night, wherein the cub-drawn° bear would couch,°   **cub-drawn:** sucked dry by her cubs, and
The lion and the belly-pinchèd° wolf   therefore ravenous; **couch:** stay inside
Keep their fur dry, unbonneted he runs,   **belly-pinchèd:** starving
And bids what will° take all.   **bids . . . will:** commands whatever wishes to   15
KENT   But who is with him?
GENTLEMAN
None but the fool, who labors to outjest°   **outjest:** overcome with jesting
His heart-struck injuries.
KENT   Sir, I do know you,
And dare upon the warrant of my art°   **art:** judgment
Commend a dear thing° to you. There is division,°   **Commend . . . thing:** entrust a precious matter;
Although as yet the face of it be covered   **division:** dissension   20
With mutual cunning, 'twixt Albany and Cornwall;
But true it is. From France there comes a power
Into this scattered kingdom, who already,
Wise in° our negligence, have secret feet°   **Wise in:** knowing of; **secret feet:** secretly set
In some of our best ports, and are at point°   foot   25
To show their open banner. Now to you: **at point:** ready
If on my credit you dare build° so far   **If . . . build:** if you trust me
To make your speed to Dover, you shall find
Some that will thank you, making just report
Of how unnatural and bemadding sorrow   30
The king hath cause to plain.°   **plain:** complain
I am a gentleman of blood and breeding,

DISCOVERING SHAKESPEARE

(61) Plot [3.1.20]: What is the purpose of this short scene (3.1) between Kent and the Gentleman? What information is
delivered that audiences must know?

And from some knowledge and assurance offer
This office° to you.   **office:** undertaking

GENTLEMAN
I will talk farther with you.   35

KENT   No, do not.
For confirmation that I am much more
Than my outwall,° open this purse and take   **outwall:** outward appearance
What it contains. If you shall see Cordelia,
As fear not but you shall, show her this ring,
And she will tell you who your fellow is°   **who . . . is:** i.e., who I am   40
That yet you do not know. Fie on this storm!
I will go seek the king.

GENTLEMAN
Give me your hand. Have you no more to say?

KENT
Few words, but to effect° more than all yet: **to effect:** in importance
That when we have found the king – I'll this way,   45
You that – he that first lights on him
Holla the other.   *Exeunt [in different directions].*

❧ **3.2**° *[Storm still.] Enter Lear and Fool.*   **3.2:** Elsewhere on the heath

LEAR
Blow, wind, and crack your cheeks!° Rage, blow,   **crack . . . cheeks:** (as winds are represented on
You cataracts and hurricanoes,° spout   old maps, heads with cheeks puffed out)
Till you have drenched the steeples, drowned the cocks!°   **cataracts . . . hurricanoes:** torrential rains and
You sulphurous and thought-executing° fires,   hurricanes
Vaunt-couriers° to oak-cleaving thunderbolts,   **cocks:** weather vanes   5
Singe my white head; and thou all-shaking thunder,   **thought-executing:** either annihilating thought
Smite flat the thick rotundity of the world,   or acting as fast as thought
Crack nature's mold,° all germens° spill at once   **Vaunt-couriers:** heralds
That make ingrateful man.   **nature's mold:** (in which life is given form);
                                                                          germens: seeds
FOOL   O nuncle, court holy water° in a dry house is bet-   **court holy water:** flattery   10
ter than this rainwater out o' door. Good nuncle, in,
and ask thy daughters' blessing. Here's a night pities
neither wise man nor fool.

LEAR
Rumble thy bellyful! Spit, fire; spout, rain!
Nor rain, wind, thunder, fire are my daughters.   15
I tax° not you, you elements, with unkindness.   **tax:** charge
I never gave you kingdom, called you children.
You owe me no subscription.° Why then, let fall   **subscription:** deference
Your horrible pleasure. Here I stand your slave,
A poor, infirm, weak, and despised old man,   20
But yet I call you servile ministers,°   **ministers:** agents
That have with two pernicious daughters joined
Your high-engendered battle° 'gainst a head   **high-engendered battle:** heavenly battalion
So old and white as this. O, 'tis foul!

DISCOVERING SHAKESPEARE

(62) <u>Staging</u> [3.2.1]: Where does 3.2 take place geographically? What clues does the <u>script</u> give us about the location of
the scene?

FOOL He that has a house to put his head in has a good   25
headpiece.°

> The codpiece° that will house°
>> Before the head has any,
> The head and he shall louse,
>> So beggars marry many.°
> The man that makes his toe
>> What he his heart should make°
> Shall have a corn, cry woe,
>> And turn his sleep to wake.

For there was never yet fair woman but she made
mouths in a glass.°

LEAR
No, I will be the pattern of all patience.
Enter Kent [disguised].
I will say nothing. *[He sits.]*

KENT Who's there?

FOOL Marry,° here's grace and a codpiece, that's a wise   40
man and a fool.

KENT
Alas, sir, sit you here? Things that love night
Love not such nights as these. The wrathful skies
Gallow° the very wanderers of the dark
And makes them keep° their caves. Since I was man   45
Such sheets of fire, such bursts of horrid thunder,
Such groans of roaring wind and rain I ne'er
Remember to have heard. Man's nature cannot carry°
The affliction nor the force.

LEAR   Let the great gods,
That keep this dreadful pother° o'er our heads,   50
Find out their enemies now. Tremble, thou wretch
That hast within thee undivulgèd crimes
Unwhipped of° justice; hide thee, thou bloody hand,
Thou perjured and thou simular man of° virtue
That art incestuous; caitiff,° in pieces shake,   55
That under covert and convenient seeming°
Hast practiced on° man's life;
Close° pent-up guilts, rive° your concealèd centers,
And cry these dreadful summoners grace.°
I am a man more sinned against than sinning.   60

KENT
Alack, bareheaded?
Gracious my lord, hard° by here is a hovel.
Some friendship will it lend you 'gainst the tempest.
Repose you there whilst I to this hard house –
More hard than is the stone whereof 'tis raised,   65
Which even but now, demanding° after you,
Denied me to come in – return and force
Their scanted° courtesy.

---

headpiece: (1) helmet, (2) brain

codpiece: the pouch for the genitals on men's breeches (here used for the penis); **house:** lodge (in copulation)

The . . . many: will infest both the head and the codpiece with lice, and end in married poverty

The . . . make: (a parallel instance of preferring the lower part to the higher)

made . . . glass: practiced smiling in a mirror (i.e., was afflicted with vanity)

Marry: (a mild exclamation, originally an oath on the name of the Virgin)

Gallow: frighten
keep: stay inside

carry: endure

pother: tumult

of: by
simular . . . of: pretender to
caitiff: wretch
seeming: hypocrisy
practiced on: plotted against
Close: secret; **rive:** split open
cry . . . grace: beg for mercy from these terrible agents of justice (summoners are officers of church courts)

hard: close

demanding: as I was asking

scanted: deficient

*****

DISCOVERING SHAKESPEARE

(63) <u>Puns</u> [3.2.27]: What obscene <u>puns</u> does the Fool make in his little song in 3.2.27–34? What gestures could the actor use to clarify the meaning of these lines?

(64) <u>Meter</u> [3.2.50]: <u>Scan</u> the <u>meter</u> in 3.2.49–60. Why is Lear's <u>verse</u> form so irregular in these lines? What do you think is happening in this scene in terms of lighting and sound effects?

LEAR
My wit begins to turn.
Come on, my boy. How dost, my boy? Art cold?   70
I am cold myself. Where is this straw, my fellow?
The art of our necessities is strange,
That can make vile things precious. Come, your hovel.
Poor fool and knave, I have one part of my heart
That sorrows yet for thee.   75

FOOL
        He that has a little tiny wit,
            With heigh-ho, the wind and the rain,
        Must make content with his fortunes fit,°   **make . . . fit:** be content with his lot
            For the rain it raineth every day.

LEAR
True, my good boy. Come, bring us to this hovel.   80
                                        [*Exeunt.*]

❧ **3.3**° *Enter Gloucester and the Bastard [Edmund]*   **3.3:** Gloucester's house
with lights.

GLOUCESTER   Alack, alack, Edmund, I like not this unnatural dealing. When I desired their leave that I might
pity° him, they took from me the use of mine own   **pity:** take pity on
house, charged me on pain of their displeasure neither
to speak of him, entreat for him, nor any way sustain   5
him.
EDMUND   Most savage and unnatural!
GLOUCESTER   Go to,° say you nothing. There's a division   **Go to:** be quiet
betwixt the dukes, and a worse matter than that. I have
received a letter this night – 'tis dangerous to be spo-   10
ken. I have locked the letter in my closet.° These injuries   **closet:** (any private room: study, bedroom)
the king now bears will be revenged home.° There's part   **home:** thoroughly
of a power° already landed. We must incline to° the king.   **power:** army; **incline to:** side with
I will seek him and privily° relieve him. Go you and   **privily:** secretly
maintain talk with the duke, that my charity be not of°   **of:** by   15
him perceived. If he ask for me, I am ill and gone to
bed. Though I die for't – as no less is threatened me –
the king my old master must be relieved. There is some
strange thing toward,° Edmund. Pray you, be careful.   **toward:** impending
                                        Exit.

EDMUND
This courtesy, forbid thee,° shall the duke   **courtesy . . . thee:** kindness you have been   20
Instantly know, and of that letter too.   forbidden to show
This seems a fair deserving,° and must draw me   **fair deserving:** action that would deserve a fair
That which my father loses: no less than all.   reward
Then younger rises when the old do fall.   *Exit.*

DISCOVERING SHAKESPEARE

(65) Teaser [3.2.76]: The Fool's song in 3.2.76–79, particularly the line "For the rain it raineth every day," is an echo of a song from what earlier play by Shakespeare?
(66) Plot [3.3.22]: Why does Edmund decide to tell Cornwall about the letter that Gloucester received? What reward does he hope to get for doing so?

❧ **3.4**° *[Storm still.] Enter Lear, Kent [disguised], and Fool.*

3.4: Before a hovel on the heath

KENT
Here is the place, my lord; good my lord, enter.
The tyranny of the open night's too rough
For nature° to endure.

nature: humanity, human frailty

LEAR   Let me alone.
KENT
Good my lord, enter.
LEAR
Wilt break my heart?   5
KENT
I had rather break mine own. Good my lord, enter.
LEAR
Thou think'st 'tis much that this contentious storm
Invades us to the skin; so 'tis to thee,
But where the greater malady is fixed,°

fixed: lodged

The lesser is scarce felt. Thou'dst shun a bear,   10
But if thy flight lay toward the roaring sea
Thou'dst meet the bear i' th' mouth.° When the mind's
    free,°

i' th' mouth: head-on
When . . . free: only when the mind is untroubled

The body's delicate.° This tempest in my mind

delicate: sensitive to pain

Doth from my senses take all feeling else
Save what beats there: filial ingratitude.   15
Is it not as° this mouth should tear this hand

as: as if

For lifting food to't? But I will punish sure.
No, I will weep no more. – In such a night as this!
O Regan, Goneril, your old kind father,
Whose frank heart gave you all. – O, that way mad-   20
    ness lies.
Let me shun that; no more of that.
KENT
Good my lord, enter.
LEAR
Prithee, go in thyself; seek thy own ease.
This tempest will not give me leave to ponder
On things would° hurt me more; but I'll go in.

would: that would   25

                                        [Exit Fool.]
Poor naked wretches, wheresoe'er you are,
That bide° the pelting of this pitiless night,

bide: endure, wait out

How shall your houseless heads and unfed sides,
Your looped and windowed° raggedness, defend you

looped, windowed: (both mean "full of holes")

From seasons° such as these? O, I have ta'en

seasons: weather   30

Too little care of this. Take physic, pomp,°

Take . . . pomp: grandeur, purge yourself

Expose thyself to feel what wretches feel,
That thou mayst shake the superflux° to them

shake . . . superflux: pour out your surplus

And show the heavens more just.
    [Enter Fool.]

DISCOVERING SHAKESPEARE

(67) <u>Plot</u> **[3.4.26]:** What important discovery does Lear make in 3.4.26–34 that helps him grow emotionally and spiritually?

FOOL   Come not in here, nuncle; here's a spirit! Help   35
me, help me!

KENT   Give me thy hand. Who's there?

FOOL   A spirit. He says his name's Poor Tom.

KENT
What art thou that dost grumble there in the straw?
Come forth.   40

[Enter Edgar disguised as a madman.]

EDGAR   Away, the foul fiend follows me. "Through the
sharp hawthorn blows the cold wind."° Go to thy cold
bed and warm thee.

LEAR   Hast thou given all to thy two daughters, and art
thou come to this?   45

EDGAR   Who gives anything to Poor Tom, whom the
foul fiend hath led through fire and through ford and
whirlypool, o'er bog and quagmire; that has laid knives
under his pillow and halters in his pew,° set ratsbane° by
his pottage, made him proud of heart to ride on a bay   50
trotting horse over four-inched bridges,° to course his
own shadow for a traitor.° Bless thy five wits,° Tom's
acold! Bless thee from whirlwinds, star-blasting,° and   55
taking.° Do Poor Tom some charity, whom the foul
fiend vexes. There could I have him now – and there –
and there again.

LEAR
What, his daughters brought him to this pass?

[To Edgar]
Couldst thou save nothing? Didst thou give them all?

FOOL   Nay, he reserved a blanket, else we had been all   60
shamed.

LEAR   *[To Edgar]*
Now all the plagues that in the pendulous° air
Hang fated° o'er men's faults fall on thy daughters!

KENT   He hath no daughters, sir.

LEAR
Death, traitor! Nothing could have subdued nature   65
To such a lowness but his unkind daughters.
Is it the fashion that discarded fathers
Should have thus little mercy on their flesh?
Judicious punishment: 'twas this flesh begot
Those pelican° daughters.   70

EDGAR   Pillicock° sat on pillicock's hill, a lo, lo, lo.°

FOOL   This cold night will turn us all to fools and madmen.

EDGAR   Take heed° o' th' foul fiend; obey thy parents;°
keep thy words justly;° swear not; commit not° with

Through . . . wind: (apparently a fragment of a ballad, quoted again at ll. 90–91)

halters . . . pew: nooses on his balcony; **knives, halters, ratsbane:** (all temptations to suicide)
made . . . bridges: i.e., made him take mad risks
course . . . traitor: hunt his own shadow as if it were an enemy; **five wits:** (the constituent parts of intelligence in Renaissance theories of cognition: common wit, imagination, fantasy, estimation, memory)
star-blasting: malignant stars
taking: infection

pendulous: overhanging
fated: ominously

pelican: cannibalistic (young pelicans were said to feed on their mother's blood)
Pillicock: (1) an endearment, (2) baby talk for penis; **Pillicock . . . lo:** (a fragment of a nursery rhyme)
Take heed: beware; **obey . . . parents:** (this and the following injunctions are from the Ten Commandments)
keep . . . justly: i.e., do not lie; **commit not:** i.e., do not commit adultery

---

DISCOVERING SHAKESPEARE

(68) Metaphor [3.4.57]: Why does Lear think that Edgar's daughters have "brought him to this pass" (3.4.57)? What is the meaning of this metaphor?

man's sworn spouse; set not thy sweet heart on proud array.° Tom's acold.

LEAR   What hast thou been?

EDGAR   A servingman proud in heart and mind, that curled my hair, wore gloves in my cap,° served the lust of my mistress' heart, and did the act of darkness with her; swore as many oaths as I spake words, and broke them in the sweet face of heaven; one that slept in the contriving of lust,° and waked to do it. Wine loved I deeply, dice dearly, and in woman out-paramoured the Turk.° False of heart, light of ear,° bloody of hand; hog in sloth, fox in stealth, wolf in greediness, dog in madness, lion in prey. Let not the creaking of shoes nor the rustlings of silks° betray thy poor heart to women. Keep thy foot out of brothel, thy hand out of placket,° thy pen from lender's book,° and defy the foul fiend. "Still through the hawthorn blows the cold wind. Heigh no nonny." Dolphin my boy, my boy! cease,° let him trot by.

LEAR   Why, thou wert better in thy grave than to answer° with thy uncovered body this extremity of the skies. Is man no more but this? Consider him well. Thou owest the worm no silk, the beast no hide, the sheep no wool, the cat° no perfume. Here's three on's° are sophisticated.° Thou art the thing itself. Unaccommodated° man is no more but such a poor, bare, forked animal as thou art. *[Removing his clothes]* Off, off, you lendings,° come on.

FOOL   Prithee, nuncle, be content. This is a naughty° night to swim in. Now a little fire in a wild field were like an old lecher's heart, a small spark, all the rest in body cold. Look, here comes a walking fire.

Enter Gloucester [with a torch].

EDGAR   This is the foul fiend Flibbertigibbet.° He begins at curfew° and walks till the first cock.° He gives the web and the pin,° squinies° the eye, and makes the harelip; mildews the white° wheat, and hurts the poor creature of earth.

     Swithold° footed thrice the wold,°
     He met the night mare° and her ninefold;°
       Bid her alight°
       And her troth plight,°
     And aroint thee,° witch, aroint thee!

KENT   How fares your grace?

LEAR   *[Pointing to Gloucester]* What's he?

KENT   *[To Gloucester]* Who's there? What is't you seek?

GLOUCESTER   What are you there? Your names?

EDGAR   Poor Tom, that eats the swimming frog, the toad, the tadpole, the wall newt° and the water;° that in the fury of his heart, when the foul fiend rages, eats cow dung for sallets,° swallows the old rat and the ditch dog,°

75

proud array: luxurious clothing

wore . . . cap: (as courtly lovers did with tokens from their mistresses)

80

slept . . . lust: went to sleep planning acts of lechery

out-paramoured . . . Turk: had more lovers than the sultan has in his harem

85

light of ear: attentive to gossip and slander

creaking . . . silks: (both fashionable in women)

placket: a slit in women's skirts (hence, the vagina)

90

pen . . . book: i.e., stay out of debt

Dolphin . . . cease: (Unexplained; possibly a bit of a ballad, possibly a hunting call. Dolphin is usually taken to refer to the French crown prince, the "dauphin," but it sounds more like a hunting dog's name.)

95

answer: experience

cat: civet cat (from whose secretions perfume was made); **on's:** of us; **sophisticated:** artificial

Unaccommodated: unadorned, unfurnished

lendings: borrowed articles (because not part of his body)

100

naughty: evil

Flibbertigibbet: (in Elizabethan folklore, a dancing devil)

105

curfew: 9 P.M.; **first cock:** midnight

the web . . . pin: eye cataracts; **squinies:** makes squint

white: almost ripe

110

Swithold: Saint Withold (invoked as a general protector against harm); **footed . . . wold:** walked the plain three times

night mare: incubus, female demon; **ninefold:** nine offspring

Bid . . . alight: ordered her to get off (the sleeper's chest)

115

her troth plight: give her promise (not to do it again)

aroint thee: be gone

wall newt: lizard; **water:** i.e., water newt

120

sallets: delicacies; **ditch dog:** dead dog thrown in a ditch

---

DISCOVERING SHAKESPEARE

(69) <u>Verse</u> [3.4.75]: Why does Lear oscillate from <u>verse</u> to <u>prose</u> in his conversations with Edgar in 3.4.61–173?

(70) Mythology [3.4.105]: Who was "Flibbertigibbet" in Elizabethan folklore? What was the <u>etymological</u> origin of the name?

drinks the green mantle° of the standing° pool; who is
whipped from tithing to tithing,° and stock-punished,°
and imprisoned; who hath had three suits to his back,
six shirts to his body,

    Horse to ride, and weapon to wear,
    But mice and rats and such small deer°
    Hath been Tom's food for seven long year.

Beware my follower. Peace, Smulkin;° peace, thou
fiend!

GLOUCESTER
What, hath your grace no better company?

EDGAR
The Prince of Darkness is a gentleman;
Modo he's called, and Mahu –

GLOUCESTER   *[To Lear]*
Our flesh and blood is grown so vile, my lord,
That it doth hate what gets° it.

EDGAR   Poor Tom's acold.

GLOUCESTER
Go in with me. My duty cannot suffer°
To obey in all your daughters' hard commands.
Though their injunction be to bar my doors
And let this tyrannous night take hold upon you,
Yet have I ventured to come seek you out
And bring you where both food and fire is ready.

LEAR
First let me talk with this philosopher.
What is the cause of thunder?

KENT   My good lord,
Take his offer; go into the house.

LEAR
I'll talk a word with this most learnèd Theban.°
What is your study?°

EDGAR
How to prevent° the fiend, and to kill vermin.

LEAR   Let me ask you one word in private.
   [They talk aside.]

KENT
Importune him to go, my lord;
His wits begin to unsettle.

GLOUCESTER   Canst thou blame him?
His daughters seek his death. O, that good Kent,
He said it would be thus, poor banished man!
Thou sayest the king grows mad; I'll tell thee, friend,
I am almost mad myself. I had a son,
Now outlawed from my blood;° a° sought my life
But lately, very late.° I loved him, friend;
No father his son dearer. True to tell thee,

green mantle: scum; **standing:** stagnant
tithing: parish; **stock-punished:** put in the
stocks   125

deer: game (the jingle is adapted from the
popular romance *Bevis of Hampton*)

Smulkin: (like Modo and Mahu below, devils   130
identified in Samuel Harsnett's *Declaration of
Egregious Popish Impostures,* 1603)

135

gets: begets

suffer: allow me

140

145

learnèd Theban: Greek scholar
study: field of study

prevent: thwart

150

155

outlawed . . . blood: disowned, disinherited;
a: he
late: recently

DISCOVERING SHAKESPEARE

(71) Staging [3.4.128]: When Gloucester enters this scene in 3.4.104, do you think Edgar is nervous that his father
might recognize him? Why or why not? Does Edgar behave differently after his father arrives? If so, how?

(72) Irony [3.4.153]: Why is Gloucester's line about "that good Kent" (3.4.153) <u>ironic</u>?

The grief hath crazed my wits. What a night's this!   160
I do beseech your grace –
LEAR   O, cry you mercy!°   **cry . . . mercy:** I beg your pardon
   [To Edgar]
Noble philosopher, your company.
EDGAR   Tom's acold.
GLOUCESTER
In, fellow, there in t' hovel; keep thee warm.
LEAR
Come, let's in all.   165
KENT   This way, my lord.
LEAR   With him;
I will keep still with my philosopher.
KENT   Good my lord, soothe° him; let him take the fellow.   **soothe:** humor
GLOUCESTER   Take him you on.°   **you on:** along with you
KENT   Sirrah, come on. Go along with us.
LEAR   Come, good Athenian.°   **Athenian:** philosopher   170
GLOUCESTER   No words, no words, hush!
EDGAR
   Child° Roland to the dark tower come,°   **Child:** a knight in training; **Child . . . come:**
   His word° was still° "Fie, fo, and fum;   (presumably from a ballad about the hero of *La*
   I smell the blood of a British man."°   *Chanson de Roland*)
                Exeunt.   **word:** motto; **still:** always

His . . . man: (Edgar switches to a ballad about
Jack the Giant Killer)

❧ **3.5°** *Enter Cornwall and Bastard [Edmund].*   **3.5:** Gloucester's house

CORNWALL   I will have my revenge ere I depart the house.
EDMUND   How, my lord, I may be censured° that nature   **censured:** criticized
   thus gives way to loyalty,° something fears me° to think of.   **nature . . . loyalty:** (the contrast is between
CORNWALL   I now perceive it was not altogether your   familial and political bonds); **something . . .**
   brother's evil disposition made him seek his° death, but   **me:** I am almost afraid
   a provoking merit set awork° by a reprovable badness in   **his:** Gloucester's   5
   himself.°   **a . . . awork:** a virtue incited to work
EDMUND   How malicious is my fortune that I must re-   **himself:** Gloucester (i.e., however wicked
   pent to be just! This is the letter he spoke of, which ap-   parricide is, Gloucester got what he deserved)
   proves° him an intelligent party to the advantages of°
   France. O heavens, that his treason were not, or not I   **approves:** proves; **intelligent . . . of:** spy on   10
   the detector!   behalf of
CORNWALL   Go with me to the duchess.
EDMUND   If the matter of this paper be certain, you have
   mighty business in hand.   15
CORNWALL   True or false, it hath made thee Earl of
   Gloucester. Seek out where thy father is, that he may be
   ready for our apprehension.°   **apprehension:** arrest
EDMUND   *[Aside]* If I find him comforting° the king, it   **comforting:** abetting
   will stuff his suspicion more fully. *[To Cornwall]* I will
   persever in my course of loyalty, though the conflict be   20
   sore between that and my blood.°   **blood:** family ties
CORNWALL   I will lay trust upon thee, and thou shalt
   find a dearer father in my love.   *Exeunt.*

DISCOVERING SHAKESPEARE

(73) <u>Plot</u> **[3.5.1]:** Upon whom does Cornwall vow revenge in 3.5.1? Why is he so furious at this person?

❧ **3.6**° *Enter Gloucester and Lear, Kent [disguised],*
Fool, and [Edgar as] Tom.

3.6: Within the hovel

GLOUCESTER   Here is better than the open air; take it
thankfully. I will piece out° the comfort with what addition I can. I will not be long from you.

piece out: augment

KENT   All the power of his wits have given way to impatience;° the gods deserve your kindness!°

impatience: passion, rage; **deserve . . .** 5
kindness: give your kindness what it deserves

[Exit Gloucester.]

EDGAR   Frateretto° calls me, and tells me Nero° is an an-
gler in the Lake of Darkness. Pray, innocent; beware
the foul fiend.

Frateretto: (another devil from Harsnett's
Declaration; see 3.4. 130); **Nero:** (the diabolical
Roman emperor, here condemned, following
Chaucer's "Monk's Tale," to fish in the lake of
Hell)

FOOL   Prithee, nuncle, tell me whether a madman be a
gentleman or a yeoman.°

yeoman: a landowner, but not a gentleman 10

LEAR   A king, a king! To have a thousand with red burning spits come hissing in upon them!

EDGAR   The foul fiend bites my back.

FOOL   He's mad that trusts in the tameness of a wolf, a
horse's health, a boy's love, or a whore's oath.

15

LEAR
It shall be done. I will arraign them straight.°

arraign . . . straight: put them on trial
immediately

[To Edgar]
Come, sit thou here, most learnèd justicer.
[To Fool]
Thou sapient sir, sit here. – No, you she-foxes –

EDGAR   Look where he stands and glares. Want'st thou
eyes° at trial, madam?

Want'st . . . eyes: do you lack for spectators (?); 20
are you blind (?)

[Sings.]
    Come o'er the burn,° Bessy, to me.°

burn: stream. (The Fool's continuation is an
obscene parody, punning on "burn" as the pain of
venereal disease.); **Come . . . me:** from a
popular ballad

FOOL
[Sings.]
    Her boat hath a leak,°
    And she must not speak
    Why she dares not come over to thee.

Her boat . . . leak: i.e., (1) from the effects of
the disease, (2) because women are proverbially
"leaky vessels"

EDGAR   The foul fiend haunts Poor Tom in the voice of a
nightingale. Hoppedance° cries in Tom's belly for two
white° herring. Croak not,° black angel: I have no food
for thee.

25

Hoppedance: (another devil from Harsnett)
white: fresh; **Croak not:** i.e., stop rumbling,
belly

KENT
How do you, sir? Stand you not so amazed.°
Will you lie down and rest upon the cushions?

amazed: bewildered

30

LEAR
I'll see their trial first. Bring in their evidence.
[To Edgar]
Thou robèd man of justice, take thy place;
[To fool]
And thou, his yokefellow of equity,°
Bench° by his side. *[To Kent]* You are o' th' commission,°
Sit you, too.

yokefellow . . . equity: fellow judge
Bench: preside; **o' th' commission:** i.e.,
presiding as a judge

35

DISCOVERING SHAKESPEARE

(74) Setting [3.6.1]: If Lear, Gloucester, Kent, the Fool, and Edgar are not in "the open air" (3.6.1) at the beginning of
3.6, where are they geographically? Where are they on stage? Why do you think this is so?

(75) Teaser [3.6.22]: The Fool's song in 3.6.22–24 is an obscene parody of a popular ballad. What was the ballad about?
What verbal changes has the Fool made to turn it bawdy?

EDGAR   Let us deal justly.
  [*Sings.*]
        Sleepest or wakest thou, jolly shepherd?
          Thy sheep be in the corn,°
        And for one blast of thy minikin° mouth
          Thy sheep shall take no harm.
    Pur the cat° is gray.

corn: wheat	
minikin: pretty little	

40

Pur the cat: (another Harsnett devil, here taking the form of a cat)

LEAR   Arraign her first. 'Tis Goneril. I here take my oath before this honorable assembly she kicked the poor king her father.

FOOL   Come hither, mistress. Is your name Goneril?

45

LEAR   She cannot deny it.

FOOL   Cry you mercy, I took you for a joint stool.°

Cry . . . stool: I beg your pardon, I mistook you for a stool—i.e., I didn't notice you (but the stool here is standing in for Goneril)

LEAR
  And here's another, whose warped looks proclaim
  What store° her heart is made on.° Stop her there!
  Arms, arms, sword, fire! Corruption in the place!°
  False justicer, why hast thou let her scape?

store: material; **on:** of

Corruption . . . place: i.e., there's bribery in the court

50

EDGAR   Bless thy five wits.

KENT
  O pity, sir, where is the patience now
  That you so oft have boasted to retain?

EDGAR   [*Aside*]
  My tears begin to take his part so much
  They'll mar my counterfeiting.

55

LEAR
  The little dogs and all,°
  Trey, Blanch, and Sweetheart, see, they bark at me.

The . . . all: even the lapdogs

EDGAR   Tom will throw° his head at them. Avaunt,° you curs!

throw: shake; **Avaunt:** get away

60

        Be thy mouth or° black or white,
        Tooth that poisons if it bite,
        Mastiff, greyhound, mongrel grim,
        Hound or spaniel, brach or him,°
        Bobtail tyke or trundle-tail,°
        Tom will make them weep and wail;
        For with throwing thus my head,
        Dogs leap the hatch,° and all are fled.

or: either

brach . . . him: bitch or male

Bobtail . . . trundle-tail: short- or long-tailed mongrel

65

  Loudla, doodla! Come, march to wakes° and fairs
  And market towns. Poor Tom, thy horn is dry.°

hatch: (lower half of a Dutch door)
wakes: festivals

horn is dry: drinking horn is empty (i.e., "I've run out of steam")

70

LEAR   Then let them anatomize° Regan, see what breeds about her heart. Is there any cause in nature that makes this hardness? [*To Edgar*]° You, sir, I entertain° you for one of my hundred, only I do not like the fashion of your garments. You'll say they are Persian° attire; but let them be changed.

anatomize: dissect

[*To Edgar*]: or perhaps addressed to Kent, who has, ironically, been in Lear's service; **entertain:** employ

Persian: luxurious

75

KENT   Now, good my lord, lie here awhile.

LEAR   Make no noise, make no noise; draw the curtains.°
  So, so, so. We'll go to supper i' th' morning. So, so, so.
    Enter Gloucester.

curtains: i.e., about an imaginary four-poster bed

DISCOVERING SHAKESPEARE

(76) <u>Verse</u> [3.6.50]: How could the actor playing Lear use the alternation between <u>verse</u> and <u>prose</u> in 3.6.42–79 to his advantage?

(77) <u>Language</u> [3.6.75]: What does Lear mean when he refers to Edgar's "Persian attire" (3.6.75)?

GLOUCESTER
   [To Kent]
   Come hither, friend. Where is the king my master?   80
KENT
   Here, sir, but trouble him not; his wits are gone.
GLOUCESTER
   Good friend, I prithee take him in thy arms.
   I have o'erheard a plot of death upon° him.   **upon:** against
   There is a litter ready. Lay him in't
   And drive towards Dover, friend, where thou shalt meet   85
   Both welcome and protection. Take up thy master.
   If thou shouldst dally half an hour, his life,
   With thine and all that offer to defend him,
   Stand in assurèd loss.° Take up the king,   **Stand . . . loss:** will surely be lost
   And follow me, that will to some provision   90
   Give thee quick conduct.°   **to . . . conduct:** will quickly lead you to provisions for the journey
KENT   Oppressèd nature sleeps.
   This rest might yet have balmed thy broken sinews
   Which, if convenience° will not allow,   **convenience:** circumstances
   Stand in hard cure.° *[To Fool]* Come, help to bear thy   **Stand . . . cure:** will be hard to cure
     master.
   Thou must not stay behind.   95
GLOUCESTER   Come, come away.
         Exeunt [carrying Lear. Edgar remains].
EDGAR
   When we our betters see bearing our woes,°   **bearing . . . woes:** enduring the same suffering as we do
   We scarcely think our miseries our foes.
   Who alone suffers, suffers most i' th' mind,
   Leaving free° things and happy shows° behind.   **free:** carefree; **shows:** scenes
   But then the mind much sufferance doth o'erskip   100
   When grief hath mates, and bearing fellowship.°   **bearing fellowship:** endurance has company
   How light and portable° my pain seems now,   **portable:** bearable
   When that which makes me bend makes the king bow.
   He° childed as I fathered. Tom, away.   **He:** he is
   Mark the high noises,° and thyself bewray°   **Mark . . . noises:** follow the news of those in power; **bewray:** reveal   105
   When false opinion, whose wrong thoughts defile thee,
   In thy just proof repeals° and reconciles thee.   **When . . . repeals:** when proof of your innocence vindicates
   What will hap more° tonight, safe scape the king!   **What . . . more:** whatever more happens
   Lurk, lurk.   *[Exit.]*

🔖 **3.7**° *Enter Cornwall and Regan, and Goneril, and Bastard [Edmund, and Servants].*   **3.7:** Gloucester's house

CORNWALL   *[To Goneril]* Post° speedily to my lord your   **Post:** ride
    husband; show him this letter. The army of France is
    landed. *[To Servants]* Seek out the villain Gloucester.
           [Exeunt some Servants.]
REGAN   Hang him instantly!
GONERIL   Pluck out his eyes!   5

DISCOVERING SHAKESPEARE

(78) Setting [3.7.1]: What clues can you find in the first few lines of 3.7 that tell us where we are in the kingdom? Where would this scene be <u>set</u> on <u>stage</u>?

CORNWALL   Leave him to my displeasure. Edmund, keep
you our sister° company. The revenges we are bound to
take upon your traitorous father are not fit for your beholding. Advise the duke where you are going to a most
festinate preparation;° we are bound to° the like. Our
post° shall be swift, and intelligence° betwixt us.
Farewell, dear sister. Farewell, my lord of Gloucester.°
   Enter Steward [Oswald].
How now, where's the king?

OSWALD
My lord of Gloucester hath conveyed him hence.
Some five or six and thirty of his knights,
Hot questrists° after him, met him at gate,
Who, with some other of the lord's dependents,
Are gone with him towards Dover, where they boast
To have well-armèd friends.

CORNWALL
Get horses for your mistress.   *[Exit Oswald.]*

GONERIL
Farewell, sweet lord, and sister.

CORNWALL   Edmund, farewell.
           Exeunt Goneril and Edmund.
Go, seek the traitor Gloucester.
Pinion him° like a thief; bring him before us.
           [Exeunt Servants.]
Though we may not pass° upon his life
Without the form of justice, yet our power
Shall do a curtsy to° our wrath, which men
May blame but not control.
   Enter Gloucester brought in by two or three [Servants].
          Who's there? The traitor?

REGAN
Ingrateful fox, 'tis he.

CORNWALL *[To Servants]*
Bind fast his corky° arms.

GLOUCESTER
What means your graces? Good my friends, consider
You are my guests. Do me no foul play, friends.

CORNWALL *[To Servants]*
Bind him, I say.

REGAN   Hard, hard! O filthy traitor!

GLOUCESTER
Unmerciful lady as you are, I am true.°

CORNWALL
To this chair bind him. *[To Gloucester]* Villain, thou
  shalt find –
   [Regan plucks Gloucester's beard.]

GLOUCESTER
By the kind gods, 'tis most ignobly done
To pluck me by the beard.°

---

sister: i.e., Goneril

to . . . preparation: to prepare himself quickly; 10
are . . . to: must do

post: messenger; **intelligence:** i.e., information
will pass swiftly

my . . . Gloucester: (Edmund has been given
his father's title)

                         15

questrists: searchers

                         20

Pinion him: tie him up

pass: pass sentence
                         25
do . . . to: defer to

corky: dry, withered

                         30

true: loyal

                         35

To . . . beard: (considered an extreme insult)

DISCOVERING SHAKESPEARE

(79) Paraphrase [3.7.25]: <u>Paraphrase</u> the following lines by Cornwall: "yet our power / Shall do a curtsy to our wrath, which men / May blame but not control" (3.7.25–27).

REGAN
  So white, and such a traitor!
GLOUCESTER   Naughty° lady,   **Naughty:** evil
  These hairs which thou dost ravish from my chin
  Will quicken° and accuse thee. I am your host.   **quicken:** come to life
  With robbers' hands my hospitable favors°   **hospitable favors:** welcoming face   40
  You should not ruffle° thus. What will you do?   **ruffle:** tear at
CORNWALL
  Come, sir, what letters had you late° from France?   **late:** lately
REGAN
  Be simple, answerer,° for we know the truth.   **Be simple, answerer:** answer plainly
CORNWALL
  And what confederacy have you with the traitors
  Late footed° in the kingdom?   **Late footed:** lately landed   45
REGAN   To whose hands
  You have sent the lunatic king, speak!
GLOUCESTER
  I have a letter guessingly° set down,   **guessingly:** speculatively
  Which came from one that's of a neutral heart,
  And not from one opposed.
CORNWALL   Cunning.
REGAN   And false.
CORNWALL   Where hast thou sent the king?   50
GLOUCESTER   To Dover.
REGAN   Wherefore to Dover? Wast thou not charged at
  peril – °   **charged at peril:** ordered at peril of your life
CORNWALL   Wherefore to Dover? Let him first answer
  that.   55
GLOUCESTER   I am tied to th' stake, and I must stand the
  course.°   **I . . . course:** (the image is from bearbaiting, in
REGAN   Wherefore to Dover, sir?   which the animal is tied to a stake and attacked by
GLOUCESTER   dogs)
  Because I would not see thy cruel nails
  Pluck out his poor old eyes, nor thy fierce sister   60
  In his anointed° flesh rash° boarish fangs.   **anointed:** consecrated; **rash:** tear
  The sea, with such a storm on his bowed head
  In hell-black night endured, would have buoyed° up   **buoyed:** swelled
  And quenched the stellèd° fires.   **stellèd:** stellar
  Yet, poor old heart, he holped° the heavens to rage. **holped:** helped   65
  If wolves had at thy gate howled that dern° time,   **dern:** dreadful
  Thou shouldst have said "Good porter, turn the key" – ° **turn the key:** open the door
  All cruels else subscribe.° But I shall see   **All . . . subscribe:** all other cruel creatures
  The wingèd vengeance° overtake such children.   submit (to feelings of compassion)
CORNWALL   **wingèd vengeance:** avenging Furies
  See't shalt thou never. Fellows, hold the chair.   70
  Upon those eyes of thine I'll set my foot.
GLOUCESTER
  He that will think to live till he be old
  Give me some help. O, cruel! O ye gods!
  [Cornwall puts out one of Gloucester's eyes.]

DISCOVERING SHAKESPEARE

(80) Half Lines [3.7.47]: What is the effect of all the half lines and short lines in 3.7.28–58? How does the verse suggest stage action?

REGAN
One side will mock another; t'other too.

CORNWALL
If you see vengeance –   75

SERVANT   Hold your hand, my lord.
I have served ever since I was a child,
But better service have I never done you
Than now to bid you hold.

REGAN   How now, you dog!

SERVANT
If you did wear a beard upon your chin
I'd shake it on this quarrel.° What do you mean?°   **shake . . . quarrel:** pluck it in this cause; **What**   80
                                                                              . . . mean?: i.e., how dare you?

CORNWALL   My villain!°   **villain:** (the word retained some of its original
                                                                              meaning of "serf" or "servant")

SERVANT
Why then, come on, and take the chance of anger.°   **chance . . . anger:** risk of an angry fight
[They] draw and fight. [Cornwall is wounded.]

REGAN
[To another Servant]
Give me thy sword. A peasant stand up thus!
She takes a sword and runs at him behind.

SERVANT
O, I am slain! My lord, yet have you one eye left
To see some mischief on him. Oh!   *[He dies.]*   85

CORNWALL
Lest it see more, prevent it. Out, vile jelly!
[He puts out Gloucester's other eye.]
Where is thy luster now?

GLOUCESTER
All dark and comfortless. Where's my son Edmund?
Edmund, unbridle all the sparks of nature
To quit° this horrid act.   **quit:** avenge   90

REGAN   Out, villain!
Thou call'st on him that hates thee. It was he
That made the overture of° thy treasons to us,   **made . . . of:** revealed
Who is too good to pity thee.

GLOUCESTER
O my follies! Then Edgar was abused.°   **abused:** wronged
Kind gods, forgive me that and prosper him!   95

REGAN
Go thrust him out at gates, and let him smell
His way to Dover.
                        [Exit a Servant with Gloucester.]
How is't, my lord, how look you?°   **How . . . you:** how do you feel

CORNWALL
I have received a hurt. Follow me, lady.
[To Servants]
Turn out that eyeless villain. Throw this slave   100

DISCOVERING SHAKESPEARE

(81) <u>Irony</u> [3.7.76]: What is the <u>irony</u> of Cornwall's own servant trying to protect Gloucester in 3.7.76–85? What does this brave and altruistic action suggest about working-class characters in Shakespeare?

(82) <u>Plot</u> [3.7.99]: How has Cornwall been hurt? How does his wound help choreograph the staging of the fight between him and the servant?

Upon the dunghill. Regan, I bleed apace.
Untimely comes this hurt. Give me your arm.
        Exeunt [Cornwall and Regan].

SECOND SERVANT
 I'll never care what wickedness I do
 If this man come to good.
THIRD SERVANT   If she live long
 And in the end meet the old course of death,°   **meet . . . death:** i.e., die a natural death   105
 Women will all turn monsters.
SECOND SERVANT
 Let's follow the old earl and get the Bedlam
 To lead him where he would. His roguish madness
 Allows itself to anything.
THIRD SERVANT
 Go thou. I'll fetch some flax and whites of eggs   110
 To apply to his bleeding face. Now heaven help him!
               Exeunt.

4.1 ❧ *Enter Edgar [as Poor Tom].*°   **4.1:** Open country

EDGAR
 Yet better thus and known to be contemned°   **contemned:** despised
 Than still° contemned and flattered. To be worst,   **still:** always
 The lowest and most dejected thing of fortune,
 Stands still in esperance,° lives not in fear.   **Stands . . . esperance:** always has hope (because
 The lamentable change is from the best,   he has no fear of falling lower)   5
 The worst returns to laughter.°   **returns to laughter:** i.e., can only get better
  Enter Gloucester led by an Old Man.
 Who's here? My father parti-eyed?° World, world, O   **parti-eyed:** with parti-colored eyes (because of
 world!   the blood on the bandages)
 But° that thy strange mutations make us hate thee,   **But:** except
 Life would not yield to age.°   *[Stands aside.]*   **yield to age:** be reconciled to growing old
OLD MAN   O my good lord,
 I have been your tenant and your father's tenant   10
 This fourscore –
GLOUCESTER
 Away, get thee away, good friend, begone.
 Thy comforts can do me no good at all,
 Thee they may hurt.
OLD MAN
 Alack, sir, you cannot see your way.   15
GLOUCESTER
 I have no way, and therefore want no eyes.
 I stumbled when I saw. Full oft 'tis seen
 Our means secure us,° and our mere defects°   **Our . . . us:** our prosperity makes us
 Prove our commodities.° Ah dear son Edgar,   overconfident; **mere defects:** utter deprivation
 The food° of thy abusèd father's wrath,   **commodities:** advantages   20
 Might I but live to see thee in my touch,   **food:** prey
 I'd say I had eyes again.

DISCOVERING SHAKESPEARE

(83) Paraphrase [4.1.17]: Paraphrase Gloucester's line "I stumbled when I saw" (4.1.17). To what extent is the realization ironic in this context?

OLD MAN   How now, who's there?

EDGAR   *[Aside]*
  O gods, who is't can say "I am at the worst"?
  I am worse than e'er I was.

OLD MAN   'Tis poor mad Tom.

EDGAR   *[Aside]*
  And worse I may be yet. The worst is not   25
  As long as we can say "This is the worst."

OLD MAN
  Fellow, where goest?

GLOUCESTER   Is it a beggarman?

OLD MAN   Madman and beggar too.

GLOUCESTER
  A° has some reason,° else he could not beg.   **A:** he; **reason:** sanity
  In the last night's storm I such a fellow saw,   30
  Which made me think a man a worm. My son
  Came then into my mind, and yet my mind
  Was then scarce friends with him. I have heard more
    since.
  As flies are to th' wanton° boys are we to th' gods: **wanton:** playful, irresponsible
  They kill us for their sport.   35

EDGAR   *[Aside]*   How should this be?
  Bad is the trade that must play the fool to sorrow,°   **Bad . . . sorrow:** playing the fool in the
  Ang'ring itself and others. – Bless thee, master.   presence of grief is a bad business

GLOUCESTER
  Is that the naked fellow?

OLD MAN   Ay, my lord.

GLOUCESTER
  Then, prithee, get thee gone. If for my sake
  Thou wilt o'ertake us here a mile or twain,   40
  I' th' way toward Dover, do it for ancient love,°   **ancient love:** our long relationship (as lord and
  And bring some covering for this naked soul,   tenant)
  Who I'll entreat to lead me.

OLD MAN
  Alack, sir, he is mad.

GLOUCESTER
  'Tis the times' plague° when madmen lead the blind.   **times' plague:** sickness of the times   45
  Do as I bid thee, or rather do thy pleasure.
  Above the rest,° begone.   **Above . . . rest:** above all

OLD MAN
  I'll bring him the best 'parel° that I have,   **'parel:** apparel
  Come on't what will.°   *[Exit.]*   **Come . . . will:** whatever may come of it

GLOUCESTER   Sirrah, naked fellow!

EDGAR   Poor Tom's acold. *[Aside]* I cannot dance it far-   50
  ther.°   **dance . . . farther:** continue the masquerade

GLOUCESTER   Come hither, fellow.

EDGAR   Bless thy sweet eyes, they bleed.

GLOUCESTER   Know'st thou the way to Dover?

EDGAR   Both stile and gate, horseway and footpath. Poor   55
  Tom hath been scared out of his good wits. Bless thee,

DISCOVERING SHAKESPEARE

(84) Geography [4.1.41]: How far is Dover (4.1.41) from London? How long would it take someone to walk from one place to the other?

goodman, from the foul fiend. Five fiends have been in
Poor Tom at once, of lust as Obidicut, Hobbididence,
prince of dumbness, Mahu of stealing, Modo of mur-
der, Flibbertigibbet of mopping and mowing,° who   **mopping . . . mowing:** making faces   60
since possesses chambermaids and waiting-women. So
bless thee, master.

GLOUCESTER
Here, take this purse, thou whom the heavens' plagues
Have humbled to° all strokes. That I am wretched   **humbled to:** reduced to bearing meekly
Makes thee the happier. Heavens deal so still.   65
Let the superfluous and lust-dieted man°   **superfluous . . . man:** man who has too much
That stands your ordinance,° that will not see   and feeds his desires
Because he does not feel, feel your power quickly.   **stands . . . ordinance:** resists (stands) heaven's
So distribution should undo excess,   command (to give to the poor)
And each man have enough. Dost thou know Dover?   70

EDGAR   Ay, master.

GLOUCESTER
There is a cliff whose high and bending° head   **bending:** overhanging
Looks firmly in the confinèd deep.°   **in . . . deep:** over the straits (of the English
Bring me but to the very brim of it   Channel) below
And I'll repair the misery thou dost bear
With something rich about me. From that place   75
I shall no leading need.

EDGAR   Give me thy arm;
Poor Tom shall lead thee.   *[Exeunt.]*

❧ **4.2**° *Enter Goneril and Bastard [Edmund].*   **4.2:** Before Albany's castle

GONERIL
Welcome, my lord. I marvel our mild husband
Not° met us on the way.   **Not:** has not
  Enter Steward [Oswald].
               Now, where's your master?

OSWALD
Madam, within; but never man so changed.
I told him of the army that was landed;
He smiled at it. I told him you were coming;   5
His answer was "The worse." Of Gloucester's treachery
And of the loyal service of his son
When I informed him, then he called me sot,°   **sot:** fool
And told me I had turned the wrong side out.
What he should most dislike seems pleasant to him;   10
What like, offensive.

GONERIL   *[To Edmund]*
Then shall you go no further.
It is the cowish° terror of his spirit   **cowish:** cowardly
That dares not undertake.° He'll not feel wrongs   **undertake:** commit himself to action

---

DISCOVERING SHAKESPEARE

(85) Plot [4.1.60]: Why is Edgar still pretending to be Tom o'Bedlam (4.1.55–56 ff.)? Why doesn't he reveal himself to his father?

(86) Characterization [4.2.8]: What kind of character is Oswald? Write a description of him on a separate piece of paper.

Which tie him to an answer.° Our wishes on the way

    He'll . . . answer: he'll ignore injuries that require him to retaliate   15

May prove effects.° Back, Edmund, to my brother.°

    prove effects: be fulfilled; **brother:** brother-in-law, Cornwall

Hasten his musters° and conduct his powers.°

    musters: the muster of his troops; **conduct . . . powers:** guide his forces

I must change arms at home, and give the distaff

Into my husband's hands.° This trusty servant

    give . . . hands: give my husband the housewife's spinning staff   20

Shall pass between us. Ere long you are like° to hear,

    like: likely

If you dare venture in your own behalf,

A mistress' command. Wear this.° Spare speech.

    Wear this: (Goneril gives Edmund a lover's token, such as a handkerchief or a glove)

Decline your head. This kiss, if it durst speak,

Would stretch thy spirits up into the air.

Conceive,° and fare you well.

    Conceive: understand me   25

EDMUND

Yours in the ranks of° death.

    in the ranks of: even up to

GONERIL   My most dear Gloucester!

                     [Exit Edmund.]

To thee a woman's services are due;

A fool usurps my bed.°

    A . . . bed: i.e., my fool of a husband wrongfully possesses me

OSWALD

Madam, here comes my lord.   *Exit Steward [Oswald].*

  [Enter Albany.]

GONERIL

I have been worth the whistling.°

    I . . . whistling: I used to be worth welcoming home (alluding to the proverbial poor dog who is "not worth the whistling")   30

ALBANY   O Goneril,

You are not worth the dust which the rude wind

Blows in your face. I fear your disposition.

That nature which contemns it° origin

    contemns it: despises its

Cannot be bordered certain° in itself.

    Cannot . . . certain: can have no secure boundaries

She that herself will sliver and disbranch°

    sliver and disbranch: cut herself off and split away   35

From her material sap perforce must wither,

And come to deadly use.°

    deadly use: destructiveness

GONERIL

No more, the text is foolish.

ALBANY

Wisdom and goodness to the vile seem vile;

Filths savor but themselves. What have you done?

   40

Tigers, not daughters, what have you performed?

A father, and a gracious agèd man,

Whose reverence even the head-lugged° bear would lick,

    head-lugged: dragged by a chain around its neck (and thus ill-tempered)

Most barbarous, most degenerate, have you madded.°

    madded: driven mad   45

Could my good brother° suffer you to do it,

    brother: brother-in-law

A man, a prince, by him so benefited?

If that the heavens do not their visible spirits

Send quickly down to tame these vile offenses,

It will come —

Humanity must perforce prey on itself

   50

Like monsters of the deep.

GONERIL   Milk-livered° man,

    Milk-livered: cowardly

That bear'st a cheek for° blows, a head for wrongs;

    for: fit for

Who hast not in thy brows an eye discerning

Thine honor from thy suffering;° that not know'st

    discerning . . . suffering: that can distinguish what affects your honor (and thus must be resisted) from what must be endured

---

DISCOVERING SHAKESPEARE

(87) Metaphor [4.2.30]: What metaphor is Goneril using when she tells Albany, "I have been worth the whistling" (4.2.30)? What well-known proverb is being alluded to in this comment?

Fools° do those villains pity who are punished   **Fools:** i.e., only fools   55
Ere they have done their mischief. Where's thy drum?°   **drum:** i.e., why are you not mustering your army
France° spreads his banners in our noiseless° land,   **France:** the King of France; **noiseless:** silent
With plumèd helm; thy state begins thereat,°   (without the sound of military drums)
Whilst thou, a moral° fool, sits still and cries   **thy . . . thereat:** i.e., this is where the exercise of
"Alack, why does he so?"   your power should begin (a famous crux, much   60
ALBANY   See thyself, devil.   emended)
Proper deformity shows not° in the fiend   **moral:** moralizing
So horrid as in woman.   **Proper . . . not:** a deformed nature does not
GONERIL   O vain° fool!   appear
ALBANY   **vain:** silly, worthless
Thou changèd and self-covered° thing, for shame,   **self-covered:** hiding your true nature
Bemonster not thy feature. Were't my fitness°   **Were't . . . fitness:** if it were appropriate for me
To let these hands obey my blood,°   **blood:** passion   65
They are apt enough to dislocate and tear
Thy flesh and bones. Howe'er° thou art a fiend,   **Howe'er:** although
A woman's shape doth shield thee.
GONERIL
Marry,° your manhood mew –°   **Marry:** (an interjection, originally an oath on the
    Enter a Gentleman.   name of the Virgin); **your manhood mew:**
ALBANY   What news?   lock up your manhood   70
GENTLEMAN
O my good lord, the Duke of Cornwall's dead,
Slain by his servant, going to put out
The other eye of Gloucester.
ALBANY   Gloucester's eyes?
GENTLEMAN
A servant that he bred, thralled with remorse,°   **thralled . . . remorse:** seized with pity
Opposed against the act, bending his sword
To his great master, who thereat enraged   75
Flew on him, and amongst them felled him dead,
But not without that harmful stroke which since
Hath plucked him after.
ALBANY   This shows you are above,
You justicers,° that these our nether crimes   **justicers:** (heavenly) judges   80
So speedily can venge. But O, poor Gloucester,
Lost he his other eye?
GENTLEMAN   Both, both, my lord.
This letter, madam, craves a speedy answer.
'Tis from your sister.
GONERIL   *[Aside]* One way I like this well;
But being° widow, and my Gloucester with her,   **being:** she being   85
May all the building on my fancy pluck°   **all . . . pluck:** pull down my dream castles
Upon my hateful life. Another way°   **Another way:** i.e., returning to the "One way"
The news is not so took.° I'll read and answer.   *Exit.*   of l. 84
ALBANY   **not . . . took:** may be taken differently
Where was his son when they did take his eyes?

DISCOVERING SHAKESPEARE

(88) Imagery [4.2.57]: Why does Goneril refer to Britain as a "noiseless land" in 4.2.57? Why does she call Albany a "moral fool" two lines later?

(89) Plot [4.2.84]: Goneril's aside about Cornwall's death in 4.2.84 ("One way I like this well") implies that she is happy about the news. Then she immediately senses danger in Regan's widowhood. In what way is Cornwall's demise both a blessing and a threat to Goneril?

GENTLEMAN
  Come with my lady hither. 90
ALBANY   He is not here.
GENTLEMAN
  No, my good lord, I met him back° again. **back:** returning
ALBANY
  Knows he the wickedness?
GENTLEMAN
  Ay, my good lord; 'twas he informed against him,
  And quit the house on purpose that their punishment
  Might have the freer course. 95
ALBANY   Gloucester, I live
  To thank thee for the love thou showed'st the king,
  And to revenge thy eyes. Come hither, friend,
  Tell me what more thou knowest. *Exeunt.*

  4.3° *Enter Kent [disguised] and a Gentleman.* **4.3:** Near Dover

KENT   Why the King of France is so suddenly gone back
  know you no reason?
GENTLEMAN   Something he left imperfect° in the state **imperfect:** incomplete
  which since his coming forth is thought of, which im-
  ports° to the kingdom so much fear and danger that his **imports:** threatens 5
  personal return was most required and necessary.
KENT   Who hath he left behind him general?
GENTLEMAN   The Marshal of France, Monsieur La Far.
KENT   Did your letters pierce the queen to any demon-
  stration of grief? 10
GENTLEMAN
  Ay, sir. She took them, read them in my presence,
  And now and then an ample tear trilled down
  Her delicate cheek. It seemed she was a queen
  Over her passion who,° most rebel-like, **who:** which
  Sought to be king o'er her. 15
KENT   O, then it moved her.
GENTLEMAN
  Not to a rage. Patience and sorrow strove
  Who should express her goodliest.° You have seen **Who . . . goodliest:** which should best express her feelings
  Sunshine and rain at once; her smiles and tears
  Were like, a better way.° Those happy smilets **like . . . way:** like that, only better
  That played on her ripe lip seem not to know 20
  What guests were in her eyes, which parted thence
  As pearls from diamonds dropped. In brief,
  Sorrow would be a rarity° most beloved **rarity:** jewel
  If all could so become it.° **all . . . it:** everyone wore it so well
KENT
  Made she no verbal question? 25
GENTLEMAN
  Faith, once or twice she heaved the name of father

DISCOVERING SHAKESPEARE
(90) Metaphor [4.3.12]: Explain the Gentleman's <u>metaphor</u> in which Cordelia's tears "trilled down / Her delicate cheek" (4.3.12–13). In what way does the word "trilled" help characterize Cordelia? What does his use of <u>figurative language</u> tell us about the Gentleman?

Pantingly forth, as if it pressed her heart,
Cried "Sisters, sisters, shame of ladies, sisters,
Kent, father, sisters, what, i' th' storm, i' th' night?
Let pity not be believed!"° There she shook
The holy water from her heavenly eyes
And clamor moistened;° then away she started
To deal with grief alone.

KENT   It is the stars,
The stars above us govern our conditions,
Else one self mate and make° could not beget
Such different issues.° You spoke not with her since?

GENTLEMAN   No.

KENT
Was this before the king returned?

GENTLEMAN   No, since.

KENT
Well, sir, the poor distressèd Lear's i' th' town,
Who sometime in his better tune° remembers
What we are come about, and by no means
Will yield to see his daughter.

GENTLEMAN   Why, good sir?

KENT
A sovereign shame so elbows him: his own unkindness,
That stripped her from his benediction, turned her
To foreign casualties,° gave her dear° rights
To his dog-hearted daughters, these things sting
His mind so venomously that burning shame
Detains him from Cordelia.

GENTLEMAN
Alack, poor gentleman.

KENT
Of Albany's and Cornwall's powers° you heard not?

GENTLEMAN
'Tis so, they are afoot.

KENT
Well, sir, I'll bring you to our master Lear,
And leave you to attend him. Some dear° cause
Will in concealment wrap me up awhile.
When I am known aright you shall not grieve°
Lending me this acquaintance. I pray you go
Along with me.   *Exeunt.*

❧ **4.4**° *Enter Cordelia, Doctor, and others.*

CORDELIA
Alack, 'tis he. Why, he was met even now,
As mad as the vexed sea, singing aloud,
Crowned with rank fumiter° and furrow weeds,

Let . . . believed: never trust in pity (or, how can pity be believed to exist)   30

clamor moistened: moistened her grief with tears

one . . . make: one married couple ("mate" and   35 "make" both mean "spouse")
issues: offspring

better tune: more rational state   40

casualties: dangers; **dear:** valuable   45

powers: forces   50

dear: important

grieve: regret   55

4.4: The French camp

fumiter: fumitory (this and the following are all field weeds)

DISCOVERING SHAKESPEARE

(91) Themes [4.3.33]: Kent's "It is the stars, / The stars above us govern our conditions" (4.3.33–34) states his view that fate controls our lives. How many other references to the theme of fate can you discover in the script? Which characters refer to it most often? Which do so the least? What does the focus on this particular theme tell us about the play?

With hardocks, hemlock, nettles, cuckooflowers,
Darnel, and all the idle° weeds that grow
In our sustaining corn.° A century° is sent forth.
Search every acre in the high-grown field,
And bring him to our eye. What can man's wisdom°
In the restoring his bereavèd sense,
He that can help him, take all my outward worth.°

DOCTOR
There is means, madam.
Our foster nurse of nature° is repose,
The which he lacks; that to provoke° in him
Are many simples operative,° whose power
Will close the eye of anguish.

CORDELIA   All blest secrets,
All you unpublished virtues° of the earth,
Spring with my tears, be aidant and remediate°
In the good man's distress! Seek, seek for him,
Lest his ungoverned rage dissolve the life
That wants° the means to lead it.

        Enter Messenger.

MESSENGER   News, madam.
The British powers are marching hitherward.

CORDELIA
'Tis known before; our preparation stands
In expectation of them. O dear father,
It is thy business that I go about;
Therefore great France°
My mourning and important° tears hath pitied.
No blown° ambition doth our arms incite,
But love, dear love, and our agèd father's right.
Soon may I hear and see him!   *Exeunt.*

idle: useless, uncultivated   5
sustaining corn: life-sustaining wheat;
century: troop of one hundred soldiers
What . . . wisdom: whatever man's wisdom can
do
outward worth: material possessions   10

Our . . . nature: what naturally cares for us
provoke: induce
simples operative: herbal remedies
                                                            15

unpublished virtues: secret powers
be . . . remediate: aid and heal

wants: lacks   20

France: the King of France   25
important: urgent, of great import
blown: presumptuous

❧ **4.5**° *Enter Regan and Steward [Oswald].*

REGAN
But are my brother's powers° set forth?
OSWALD   Ay, madam.
REGAN
Himself in person?
OSWALD   Madam with much ado.°
Your sister is the better soldier.
REGAN   Lord Edmund spake not with your lady at
     home?
OSWALD   No, madam.
REGAN   What might import my sister's letters to him?
OSWALD   I know not, lady.
REGAN
Faith, he is posted hence° on serious matter.

4.5: Gloucester's house

brother's powers: Albany's forces

ado: difficulty

                                                            5

is posted hence: rushed away from here

DISCOVERING SHAKESPEARE

(92)Teaser [4.4.12]: What does the Doctor mean when he says "Our foster nurse of nature is repose" (4.4.12)? How many other references to the curative power of sleep can you find in Shakespeare's plays?

(93) Plot [4.5.7]: Why is Regan so interested in Goneril's letters to Edmund (4.5.7)? What sort of blocking and gestures could she use in this scene to gain the information she desires from Oswald?

It was great ignorance, Gloucester's eyes being out,   10
To let him live; where he arrives he moves
All hearts against us, and now, I think, is gone,
In pity of his misery, to dispatch
His nighted° life; moreover to descry°
The strength o' th' army.

nighted: (1) benighted, (2) blind; **descry:** spy out   15

OSWALD
I must needs after him with my letters.

REGAN
Our troop sets forth tomorrow. Stay with us.
The ways are dangerous.

OSWALD   I may not, madam;
My lady charged° my duty in this business.

charged: strictly commanded

REGAN
Why should she write to Edmund? Might not you   20
Transport her purposes by word? Belike° –
Something, I know not what. I'll love thee much;
Let me unseal the letter.

Belike: perhaps

OSWALD   Madam I'd rather –

REGAN
I know your lady does not love her husband;
I am sure of that, and at her late° being here   25
She gave strange oeillades° and most speaking looks
To noble Edmund. I know you are of her bosom.°

late: recently
oeillades: amorous glances
of . . . bosom: in her confidence (with a sexual overtone)

OSWALD   I, madam?

REGAN
I speak in understanding,° for I know't.
Therefore I do advise you take this note.°   30
My lord is dead; Edmund and I have talked,
And more convenient° is he for my hand
Than for your lady's – you may gather more.°
If you do find him, pray you give him this;°
And when your mistress hears thus much from you,   35
I pray desire her call her wisdom to her.°
So, farewell.
If you do chance to hear of that blind traitor,
Preferment falls on him that cuts him off.°

understanding: certain knowledge
take . . . note: take note of this

convenient: appropriate
gather more: infer more (from what I say)
this: (Perhaps a token; perhaps a letter: Edgar finds only Goneril's letter in Oswald's pockets in 4.5.253 ff., but Oswald, dying, speaks of "letters," so perhaps Edgar misses one. "Letters," on the other hand, could be singular.)
wisdom to her: back to reason
cuts him off: cuts short his life

OSWALD
Would I could meet him, madam. I would show   40
What lady I do follow.

REGAN   Fare thee well.   *Exeunt.*

❧ **4.6°** *Enter Gloucester and Edgar [disguised as a peasant].*

4.6: Open country near Dover

GLOUCESTER
When shall we come to th' top of that same hill?

EDGAR
You do climb it up now; look how we labor!

GLOUCESTER
Methinks the ground is even.

DISCOVERING SHAKESPEARE

(94) Staging [4.6.1]: How could Edgar convince his father that they are climbing a steep hill when they are in fact on level ground?

EDGAR   Horrible steep.
  Hark, do you hear the sea?
GLOUCESTER   No, truly.
EDGAR
  Why then your other senses grow imperfect   5
  By your eyes' anguish.
GLOUCESTER   So may it be indeed.
  Methinks thy voice is altered, and thou speakest
  With better phrase and matter than thou didst.
EDGAR
  You're much deceived: in nothing am I changed
  But in my garments.   10
GLOUCESTER   Methinks you're better spoken.
EDGAR
  Come on, sir, here's the place. Stand still. How fearful
  And dizzy 'tis to cast one's eyes so low!
  The crows and choughs° that wing the midway air
  Show° scarce so gross° as beetles. Halfway down
  Hangs one that gathers samphire,° dreadful trade!   15
  Methinks he seems no bigger than his head.
  The fishermen that walk upon the beach
  Appear like mice, and yon tall anchoring bark°
  Diminished to her cock, her cock° a buoy
  Almost too small for sight. The murmuring surge   20
  That on the unnumbered idle pebble° chafes
  Cannot be heard, it's so high. I'll look no more,
  Lest my brain turn and the deficient sight
  Topple° down headlong.
GLOUCESTER   Set me where you stand.
EDGAR
  Give me your hand. You are now within a foot   25
  Of th' extreme verge. For all beneath the moon
  Would I not leap upright.°
GLOUCESTER   Let go my hand.
  Here, friend, 's another purse; in it a jewel
  Well worth a poor man's taking. Fairies and gods
  Prosper° it with thee! Go thou farther off;   30
  Bid me farewell, and let me hear thee going.
EDGAR
  Now fare you well, good sir.
GLOUCESTER   With all my heart.
EDGAR *[Aside]*
  Why I do trifle thus with his despair
  Is done to cure it.
GLOUCESTER   O you mighty gods.
    He kneels.
  This world I do renounce, and in your sights   35
  Shake patiently my great affliction off.
  If I could bear it longer, and not fall
  To quarrel with your great opposeless wills,
  My snuff° and loathèd part of nature° should

choughs: jackdaws (pronounced "chuffs")
Show: appear; **gross:** large
samphire: (Saint Peter's herb, used in pickling; it grows on steep cliffs, hence the danger in gathering it)

bark: ship
cock: dinghy

unnumbered . . . pebble: barren reach of innumerable pebbles

Topple: topple me

leap upright: jump upward (to jump forward would reveal to Gloucester that he is not on the edge of a cliff)

Prosper: increase

snuff: burnt-out candle end; **loathèd . . . nature:** despised remnant of life

---

DISCOVERING SHAKESPEARE

(95) Plot [4.6.33]: When Edgar explains to us that he "trifles" with his father's despair in order to "cure" it (4.6.33–34), do you agree with his strategy? Why or why not?

Burn itself out. If Edgar live, O bless him!   40
Now, fellow, fare thee well.
EDGAR   Gone, sir, farewell.
    [Gloucester falls forward.]
    [Aside]
And yet I know not how conceit° may rob   **conceit:** illusion, imagination
The treasury of life, when life itself
Yields to° the theft. Had he been where he thought,   **Yields to:** accedes to, welcomes
By this° had thought been past. – Alive or dead?   **this:** this time   45
Ho you, sir! Hear you, sir? Speak!
    [Aside]
Thus might he pass indeed.° Yet he revives.   **pass indeed:** really die
  – What are you, sir?
GLOUCESTER   Away, and let me die.
EDGAR
Hadst thou been aught° but gossamer, feathers, air,   **aught:** anything
So many fathom down precipitating,   50
Thou hadst shivered° like an egg; but thou dost breathe, **shivered:** shattered
Hast heavy substance, bleed'st not, speak'st, art sound.
Ten masts at each° make not the altitude   **at each:** placed end to end
Which thou hast perpendicularly fell.
Thy life's a miracle. Speak yet again.   55
GLOUCESTER
But have I fallen or no?
EDGAR
From the dread summit of this chalky bourn.°   **chalky bourn:** chalk cliff (the White Cliffs of
Look up a-height. The shrill-gorged° lark so far   Dover)
Cannot be seen or heard. Do but look up.   **shrill-gorged:** shrill-voiced
GLOUCESTER
Alack, I have no eyes.   60
Is wretchedness deprived° that benefit   **deprived:** denied
To end itself by death? 'Twas yet some comfort
When misery could beguile° the tyrant's rage   **beguile:** cheat
And frustrate his proud will.
EDGAR   Give me your arm.
Up; so. How feel you your legs? You stand.   65
GLOUCESTER
Too well, too well.
EDGAR   This is above all strangeness.
Upon the crown of the cliff what thing was that
Which parted from you?
GLOUCESTER   A poor unfortunate beggar.
EDGAR   As I stood here below, methoughts his eyes
Were two full moons. A° had a thousand noses,   **A:** he   70
Horns whelked° and waved like the enridgèd sea.   **whelked:** twisted
It was some fiend. Therefore, thou happy father,°   **happy father:** lucky old man
Think that the clearest° gods, who made their honors   **clearest:** wisest, most glorious
Of men's impossibilities,° have preserved thee.   **who . . . impossibilities:** whose glory consists
                                           in performing miracles

---

DISCOVERING SHAKESPEARE

(96) <u>Staging</u> [4.6.49]: Why does Edgar use a different voice after his father's "fall" from the Cliffs of Dover? How many accents does the actor playing Edgar use throughout the play?

GLOUCESTER
I do remember now. Henceforth I'll bear   75
Affliction till it do cry out itself
"Enough, enough," and die. That thing you speak of,
I took it for a man. Often would it say
"The fiend, the fiend." He led me to that place.

EDGAR
Bear free and patient thoughts.   80

Enter Lear mad [, crowned with weeds].

                    But who comes here?
The safer sense° will ne'er accommodate°
His master thus.

    The . . . sense: a sane mind; accommodate: array

LEAR   No, they cannot touch° me for coining;° I am the
king himself.

    touch: arrest; coining: counterfeiting (because minting money was a royal prerogative)

EDGAR   O thou side-piercing sight!

LEAR   Nature is above art in that respect.° There's your   85
press money.° That fellow handles his bow like a
crowkeeper.° Draw me a clothier's yard.° Look, look, a
mouse! Peace, peace, this toasted cheese will do it.°
There's my gauntlet.° I'll prove it on° a giant. Bring up   90
the brown bills.° O, well flown bird,° in the air. Ha! Give
the word.°

    Nature . . . respect: i.e., kings are born, not made

    press money: payment for volunteering or being drafted to fight (Lear is conscripting an imaginary army)

    crowkeeper: scarecrow; Draw . . . yard: draw the bow out fully (a clothier's yard, 37 inches, was the length of an arrow)

    do it: catch the mouse

    gauntlet: armored glove (thrown down as a challenge); prove it on: uphold my cause against

    brown bills: pike carriers (Lear continues to assemble his army); bird: arrow

    word: password

EDGAR   Sweet marjoram.

LEAR   Pass.

GLOUCESTER   I know that voice.

LEAR   Ha, Goneril! Ha, Regan! They flattered me like a
dog,° and told me I had white hairs in my beard° ere the   100
black ones were there. To say "ay" and "no" to everything I said "ay" and "no" to was no good divinity.°
When the rain came to wet me once, and the wind to
make me chatter, when the thunder would not peace at
my bidding, there I found them,° there I smelt them
out. Go to, they are not men of their words. They told
me I was everything. 'Tis a lie; I am not ague-proof.°

    like a dog: as a dog does (i.e., they fawned on me); white . . . beard: i.e., the wisdom of age

    no . . . divinity: bad theology

    found them: found them out

    ague-proof: immune to fever

GLOUCESTER
The trick° of that voice I do well remember.   105
Is't not the king?

    trick: special quality

LEAR   Ay, every inch a king.
When I do stare, see how the subject quakes.
I pardon that man's life. What was thy cause?°
Adultery? Thou shalt not die for adultery.
No, the wren goes to't, and the small gilded fly   110
Does lecher in my sight.
Let copulation thrive, for Gloucester's bastard son
Was kinder to his father than my daughters
Got° 'tween the lawful sheets. To't, luxury,° pell-mell,
For I lack soldiers. Behold yon simp'ring dame   115
Whose face between her forks° presageth snow,°

    cause: offense

    Got: begotten; luxury: lechery

    face . . . forks: (1) her face between the combs that hold her hair in place, (2) her genitals between her forked legs; snow: sexual coldness, frigidity

---

DISCOVERING SHAKESPEARE

(97) Plot [4.6.75]: What is Gloucester's new attitude in 4.6.75-79? Why has he changed?

(98) Verse [4.6.106]: Why does Lear shift from prose to verse at 4.6.106 ff? What realization does he have at this moment in the play that prompts him to speak differently?

That minces° virtue, and does shake the head
To hear of pleasure's name:
The fitchew° nor the soilèd° horse goes to't
With a more riotous appetite. Down from the waist
They're centaurs,° though women all above;
But to the girdle° do the gods inherit,°
Beneath is all the fiend's: there's hell, there's darkness,
There's the sulphury pit, burning, scalding,
Stench, consummation. Fie, fie, fie; pah, pah!
Give me an ounce of civet,° good apothecary,
To sweeten my imagination.
There's money for thee.
GLOUCESTER   O, let me kiss that hand.
LEAR   Here, wipe it first; it smells of mortality.
GLOUCESTER
O ruined piece° of nature! This great world
Should so wear out to naught.° Do you know me?
LEAR   I remember thy eyes well enough. Dost thou
squiny° on me? No, do thy worst, blind Cupid, I'll not
love. Read thou that challenge. Mark the penning of 't.
GLOUCESTER
Were all the letters suns, I could not see one.
EDGAR
I would not take° this from report. It is,°
And my heart breaks at it.
LEAR   Read.
GLOUCESTER   What, with the case° of eyes?
LEAR   O, ho, are you there with me?° No eyes in your
head, nor no money in your purse? Your eyes are in a
heavy case,° your purse in a light; yet you see how this
world goes.
GLOUCESTER   I see it feelingly.
LEAR   What, art mad? A man may see how the world
goes with no eyes. Look with thy ears. See how yon jus-
tice rails upon yon simple° thief. Hark in thy ear:
handy-dandy,° which is the thief, which is the justice?
Thou hast seen a farmer's dog bark at a beggar?
GLOUCESTER   Ay, sir.
LEAR   And the creature° run from the cur? There thou
mightst behold the great image of authority: a dog's
obeyed in office.°
Thou rascal beadle,° hold thy bloody hand.
Why dost thou lash that whore? Strip thine own back.
Thy blood hotly lusts to use her in that kind°
For which thou whipp'st her. The usurer° hangs the
cozener.°
Through tattered rags small vices do appear;
Robes and furred gowns hides all. Get thee glass eyes,°
And like a scurvy politician° seem
To see the things thou dost not. No. Now,   [Sits.]
Pull off my boots; harder, harder! So.

minces: affects

fitchew: (1) polecat, (2) prostitute; **soilèd:** pastured, well-fed   120

centaurs: (the classical centaurs were men to the waist and horses below, and were notoriously lustful)

But . . . girdle: only down to the waist; **inherit:** possess   125

civet: perfume

130

piece: masterpiece
so. . . naught: decay to nothing in the same way

squiny: squint
135

take: believe; **is:** is actually happening

case: sockets   140
are . . . me: is that what you mean (with an overtone of "Are we both blind?")
heavy case: sad situation

145

simple: mere
handy-dandy: the child's game "choose a hand"
150

creature: man

in office: in a position of power
beadle: church constable   155

kind: way
usurer: money-lender; **usurer . . . cozener:** i.e., the big thief hangs the little one; **cozener:** cheat

glass eyes: eyeglasses   160
scurvy politician: vile Machiavel

DISCOVERING SHAKESPEARE

(99) <u>Paraphrase</u> **[4.6.145]:** What does Gloucester mean when he says he sees the world "feelingly" (4.6.145)? Does Lear agree or disagree with him in the next speech?

EDGAR   *[Aside]*
　O matter and impertinency° mixed,
　Reason in madness.

matter . . . impertinency: sense and nonsense   165

LEAR
　If thou wilt weep my fortune, take my eyes.
　I know thee well enough; thy name is Gloucester.
　Thou must be patient; we came crying hither.
　Thou knowest the first time that we smell the air,
　We wail and cry. I will preach to thee: mark me.   170
GLOUCESTER   Alack, alack, the day.
LEAR
　When we are born, we cry that we are come
　To this great stage of fools. This'° a good block.°
　It were a delicate stratagem to shoe
　A troop of horse with felt;° and when I have stole upon
　These son-in-laws, then kill, kill, kill, kill, kill, kill!
　　　Enter three Gentlemen.

This': this is; **block:** felt hat (either the hat decked with weeds, which he removes to begin his sermon, or an imaginary hat suggested by the crown of weeds)   175

shoe . . . felt: (and thus enable them to approach silently)

GENTLEMAN
　O, here he is. Lay hands upon him, sirs.
　　　[To Lear]
　Your most dear –
LEAR
　No rescue? What, a prisoner? I am e'en
　The natural fool° of fortune. Use° me well.
　You shall have ransom. Let me have a surgeon;
　I am cut to the brains.

natural fool: born plaything; **Use:** treat   180

GENTLEMAN   You shall have anything.
LEAR
　No seconds?° all myself?
　Why, this would make a man of salt,°
　To use his eyes for garden waterpots,°
　Ay, and laying autumn's dust.

seconds: supporters
salt: tears   185
waterpots: watering cans

GENTLEMAN   Good sir –
LEAR
　I will die° bravely,° like a bridegroom.
　What, I will be jovial. Come, come,
　I am a king, my masters, know you that?

die: (with a quibble on the sexual sense, have an orgasm); **bravely:** (1) courageously, (2) handsomely   190

GENTLEMAN
　You are a royal one, and we obey you.
LEAR   Then there's life in't.° Nay, an° you get it, you shall
　get it with running.
　　　Exit King [Lear] running [pursued by two Gentlemen].

there's . . . in't: i.e., there's still hope; **an:** if

GENTLEMAN
　A sight most pitiful in the meanest wretch,
　Past speaking of in a king. Thou hast one daughter   195
　Who redeems nature from the general curse
　Which twain hath brought her to.°

general . . . to: the universal disruption caused by your other two daughters (but also the original sin caused by the filial ingratitude of the original pair, Adam and Eve)

DISCOVERING SHAKESPEARE

(100) Metaphor [4.6.172]: In what way is Lear's reference to "this great stage of fools" (4.6.172–173) metatheatrical? What does the Latin phrase "theatrum mundi" mean? Where else is this same theme expressed in the play?
(101) Pun [4.6.188]: What sexual pun is suggested in Lear's "I will die bravely, like a bridegroom" (4.6.188)?

EDGAR Hail, gentle° sir.	**gentle:** noble
GENTLEMAN	
Sir, speed° you; what's your will?	**speed:** God prosper
EDGAR	
Do you hear aught of a battle toward?°	**toward:** impending
GENTLEMAN	
Most sure and vulgar;° everyone hears that	**vulgar:** common knowledge 200
That° can distinguish sense.	**That:** who
EDGAR But, by your favor,	
How near's the other army?	
GENTLEMAN	
Near and on speed° for't; the main descries	**on speed:** in haste
Stands on the hourly thoughts.°	**the . . . thoughts:** the sight of the main body is expected hourly
EDGAR	
I thank you, sir; that's all.	205
GENTLEMAN	
Though that° the queen on special cause° is here,	**Though that:** however; **on . . . cause:** for a particular reason
Her army is moved on.	
EDGAR I thank you, sir.	
Exit [Gentleman].	
GLOUCESTER	
You ever gentle gods, take my breath from me.	
Let not my worser spirit° tempt me again	**worser spirit:** "bad side"
To die before you please.	210
EDGAR Well pray you, father.°	**father:** old man
GLOUCESTER	
Now, good sir, what are you?	
EDGAR	
A most poor man made lame by fortune's blows,	
Who, by the art of known and feeling sorrows,°	**art . . . sorrows:** lesson of sorrows experienced and deeply felt
Am pregnant° to good pity. Give me your hand,	**pregnant:** prone 215
I'll lead you to some biding.°	**biding:** dwelling
GLOUCESTER Hearty thanks.	
The bounty and the benison of heaven	
To boot, to boot.°	**bounty . . . boot:** may it bring you the bounty and a blessing of heaven in addition
Enter Steward [Oswald].	
OSWALD	
A proclaimed prize!° Most happy!°	**proclaimed prize:** criminal with a price on his head; **happy:** lucky
That eyeless head of thine was first framed flesh°	**framed flesh:** made human 220
To raise my fortunes. Thou most unhappy traitor,	
Briefly thyself remember.° The sword is out	**thyself remember:** i.e., remember your sins and pray
That must destroy thee.	
GLOUCESTER Now let thy friendly hand	
Put strength enough to't.	
[Edgar interposes.]	
OSWALD Wherefore, bold peasant,	
Durst thou support a published° traitor? Hence,	**published:** proclaimed
Lest the infection of his fortune take	225
Like hold on thee. Let go his arm.	

DISCOVERING SHAKESPEARE

(102) <u>Plot</u> **[4.6.218]:** Why is Oswald so happy to find Gloucester (4.6.218)? Why does Edgar adopt yet another dialectical accent in his fight with Oswald?

EDGAR 'Chill° not let go, sir, without 'cagion.°

OSWALD Let go, slave, or thou diest.

EDGAR Good gentleman, go your gate.° Let poor volk pass. An 'chud have been swaggered° out of my life, it would not have been so long by a vortnight. Nay, come not near the old man. Keep out, 'che vor' ye,° or I'll try whether your costard or my bat° be the harder, I'll be plain with you.

OSWALD Out, dunghill!

They fight.

EDGAR 'Chill pick your teeth,° sir. Come, no matter for your foins.°

[Oswald falls.]

OSWALD
Slave, thou hast slain me. Villain, take my purse.
If ever thou wilt thrive, bury my body,
And give the letters° which thou find'st about me
To Edmund, Earl of Gloucester. Seek him out
Upon° the British party. O untimely death! Death –

He dies.

EDGAR
I know thee well: a serviceable villain,
As duteous to the vices of thy mistress
As badness would desire.

GLOUCESTER   What, is he dead?

EDGAR
Sit you down, father, rest you.
Let's see his pockets. These letters that he speaks of
May be my friends. He's dead; I am only sorrow°
He had no other deathsman. Let us see.
Leave, gentle wax,° and manners blame us not.
To know our enemies' minds we'd rip their hearts;
Their° papers is more lawful.

[Reads] a letter.

"Let your reciprocal vows be remembered. You have many opportunities to cut him° off. If your will want not,° time and place will be fruitfully° offered. There is nothing done° if he return the conqueror; then am I the prisoner, and his bed my jail, from the loathed warmth whereof deliver me, and supply° the place for your labor.

  Your wife – so I would say – your affectionate servant, and for you her own for venture,

                          Goneril."

O indistinguished° space of woman's wit!°
A plot upon her virtuous husband's life,
And the exchange my brother! – Here in the sands
Thee I'll rake up,° the post unsanctified°
Of murderous lechers, and in the mature time°
With this ungracious paper strike the sight

'Chill: I'll (Edgar adopts a west country dialect); **'cagion:** occasion, cause

go your gate: be on your way

An . . . swaggered: if I could have been bullied   230

'che vor' ye: I warn you

your . . . bat: your head or my cudgel

   235

pick . . . teeth: i.e., with my club

foins: sword thrusts

letters: (Oswald has a letter for Edmund from   240 Goneril; if he has indeed been given one by Regan too, as is implied at 4.4.34, Edgar fails to find it. But "letters" may be singular—the letters that together compose one letter—as at 1.5.2.)

Upon: among

   245

I . . . sorrow: my only sorrow is

Leave . . . wax: by your leave, kind seal   250

Their: to rip their

him: Albany

If . . . not: if you do not lack the will;   255 **fruitfully:** i.e., promising success

done: accomplished

supply: fill

   260

indistinguished: unlimited; **wit:** cunning

   265

rake up: cover over; **post unsanctified:** unholy messenger

in . . . time: when the time is ripe

DISCOVERING SHAKESPEARE

(103) Characterization [4.6.242]: What does Oswald's dying request tell us about this character? Do you have more or less respect for him at this point in the play? Why?

Of the death-practiced° duke. For him 'tis well
That of thy death and business I can tell.

                [Exit with Oswald's body.]°

GLOUCESTER
The king is mad. How stiff is my vile sense,°
That I stand up and have ingenious° feeling
Of my huge sorrows! Better I were distract,°
So should my thoughts be fencèd from my griefs,
And woes by wrong imaginations° lose
The knowledge of themselves.
   [Enter Edgar.] A drum afar off.

EDGAR   Give me your hand.
Far off, methinks, I hear the beaten drum.
Come, father, I'll bestow you with a friend.   *Exeunt.*

death-practiced: whose death is plotted

270

s.d.: None of the original texts makes any provision for the removal of Oswald's body. Editors since the eighteenth century have had Edgar exit here dragging it offstage, and then return six lines later. The very awkward alternative is for him to remove it while he is also leading Gloucester offstage.

How . . . sense: how obstinate is my hateful consciousness

275

ingenious: rational, intelligent
distract: mad
wrong imaginations: delusions

❧ **4.7**° *Enter Cordelia, [and] Kent [disguised].*

4.7: The French camp

CORDELIA
O thou good Kent,
How shall I live and work to match thy goodness?
My life will be too short, and every measure fail me.

KENT
To be acknowledged, madam, is o'erpaid.°
All my reports go° with the modest truth,
Nor more, nor clipped,° but so.

o'erpaid: more than sufficient
go: accord   5
clipped: less; **suited:** dressed

CORDELIA   Be better suited.°
These weeds° are memories° of those worser hours;
I prithee put them off.

weeds: clothes; **memories:** reminders

KENT   Pardon me, dear madam.
Yet to be known shortens my made intent.°
My boon I make it° that you know me not
Till time and I think meet.°

Yet . . . intent: to reveal myself now would spoil my plan (for Lear to recognize him as Kent)   10
My . . . it: I ask as my reward
meet: suitable

CORDELIA
Then be't so, my good lord.
   [Enter Doctor and Gentleman.]
                  – How does the king?

DOCTOR   Madam, sleeps still.

CORDELIA
O you kind gods,
Cure this great breach in his abusèd nature;
The untuned and jarring° senses O wind up°
Of this child-changèd° father.

15

jarring: discordant; **wind up:** put in tune
child-changèd: (1) changed by his children, (2) changed into a child

DOCTOR   So please your majesty
That we may wake the king? He hath slept long.

CORDELIA
Be governed by your knowledge, and proceed
I' th' sway of your own will.° Is he arrayed?°

I' th' sway . . . will: as you see fit; **arrayed:**   20
properly dressed

DISCOVERING SHAKESPEARE

(104) Staging [4.6.270]: In 4.6.270–278, Edgar carries Oswald's dead body off stage and then enters again immediately to lead his father to safety. How many other characters are killed on stage in this play? How is each taken off stage?

(105) Paraphrase [4.7.9]: What does Kent mean when he says to Cordelia "Yet to be known shortens my made intent" (4.7.9)? Paraphrase the line into modern English.

GENTLEMAN
Ay, madam. In the heaviness of his sleep
We put fresh garments on him.

DOCTOR
Good madam, be by when we do awake him.
I doubt not of his temperance.°   **temperance:** self-control

CORDELIA   Very well.
[Music.]

DOCTOR
Please you draw near. Louder the music there.   25
[Lear is revealed asleep.]

CORDELIA
O my dear father, restoration hang
Thy medicine on my lips, and let this kiss
Repair those violent harms that my two sisters
Have in thy reverence° made.   **in . . . reverence:** on the dignity of your age

KENT   Kind and dear princess!

CORDELIA
Had you not been their father, these white flakes°   **flakes:** hairs   30
Had challenged° pity of them. Was this a face   **challenged:** demanded
To be exposed against the warring winds,
To stand against the deep dread-bolted thunder
In the most terrible and nimble stroke
Of quick cross-lightning, to watch,° poor *perdu,*°   **watch:** stand guard; **perdu:** exposed (and   35
With this thin helm?° Mine injurious dog,   expendable) sentry
Though he had bit me, should have stood that night   **helm:** helmet (i.e., his white hair)
Against° my fire; and wast thou fain,° poor father,   **Against:** beside; **fain:** obliged
To hovel thee with swine and rogues forlorn
In short° and musty straw? Alack, alack,   **short:** broken   40
'Tis wonder that thy life and wits at once
Had not concluded all. – He wakes. Speak to him.

DOCTOR
Madam, do you; 'tis fittest.

CORDELIA
How does my royal lord? How fares your majesty?

LEAR
You do me wrong to take me out o' th' grave.   45
Thou art a soul in bliss, but I am bound
Upon a wheel of fire,° that mine own tears   **wheel of fire:** (the image combines the wheel
Do scald like molten lead.   on which prisoners were bound for beatings with
                                              the burning of heretics or of souls in hell)

CORDELIA   Sir, know me.

LEAR
You're a spirit, I know. Where did you die?

CORDELIA
Still, still far wide.°   **wide:** wide of the mark   50

DOCTOR
He's scarce awake. Let him alone awhile.

LEAR
Where have I been? Where am I? Fair daylight?
I am mightily abused.° I should e'en die with pity   **abused:** ill-used, deceived

---

DISCOVERING SHAKESPEARE

(106) Language [4.7.35]: What does the phrase "poor *perdu*" (4.7.35) mean? Why would Cordelia use a French word here?

To see another thus. I know not what to say.
I will not swear these are my hands. Let's see: 55
I feel this pin prick. Would I were assured
Of my condition.
CORDELIA   O look upon me, sir,
And hold your hands in benediction o'er me.
No, sir, you must not kneel.
LEAR   Pray do not mock.
I am a very foolish fond° old man,   **fond:** (the word also means "foolish")   60
Fourscore and upward, and, to deal plainly,
I fear I am not in my perfect mind.
Methinks I should know you, and know this man;
Yet I am doubtful, for I am mainly° ignorant   **mainly:** entirely
What place this is; and all the skill I have   65
Remembers not these garments; nor I know not
Where I did lodge last night. Do not laugh at me,
For, as I am a man, I think this lady
To be my child Cordelia.
CORDELIA   And so I am.
LEAR
Be your tears wet? Yes, faith. I pray, weep not.   70
If you have poison for me, I will drink it.
I know you do not love me, for your sisters
Have, as I do remember, done me wrong.
You have some cause, they have not.
CORDELIA   No cause, no cause.
LEAR
Am I in France?   75
KENT   In your own kingdom, sir.
LEAR
Do not abuse° me.   **abuse:** deceive
DOCTOR
Be comforted, good madam. The great rage,
You see, is cured in him, and yet it is danger
To make him even o'er° the time he has lost.   **even o'er:** fill in
Desire him to go in; trouble him no more   80
Till further settling.°   **settling:** calm sets in
CORDELIA
Will't please your highness walk?
LEAR   You must bear with me.
Pray now, forget and forgive. I am old and foolish.
    Exeunt [Lear, Cordelia, and Doctor]. Kent and Gentle-
    man remain.
GENTLEMAN   Holds it true, sir, that the Duke of Corn-
wall was so slain?   85
KENT   Most certain, sir.
GENTLEMAN   Who is conductor of his people?°   **conductor . . . people:** commander of his
KENT   As 'tis said, the bastard son of Gloucester.   forces

DISCOVERING SHAKESPEARE

(107) Staging [4.7.59]: At what moment does Lear kneel to Cordelia in this scene? Why is this action <u>ironic</u>?
(108) Plot [4.7.77]: What medical advice does the Doctor give Cordelia in 4.7.77–81? Does she follow his prescription?
How does Shakespeare usually depict doctors in his plays?

GENTLEMAN   They say Edgar, his banished son, is with
the Earl of Kent in Germany.

KENT   Report° is changeable. 'Tis time to look about.° The
powers° of the kingdom approach apace.

Report: rumor; **look about:** see to our preparations
powers: forces

GENTLEMAN   The arbitrament° is like to be bloody. Fare
you well, sir.   *[Exit.]*

arbitrament: action

KENT
My point and period will be throughly wrought,°
Or° well or ill, as this day's battle's fought.   *Exit.*

My . . . wrought: my purpose and end will be fully completed
Or: either

❧ **5.1**°   *Enter Edmund, Regan, and their powers.*

5.1: The British camp

EDMUND   *[To a Gentleman]*
Know of the duke if his last purpose hold,°
Or whether since° he is advised by aught
To change the course. He's full of alteration
And self-reproving. Bring his constant pleasure.°
                                                    [Exit Gentleman.]

Know . . . hold: find out from Albany if his most recent intention (to join in the fight against Cordelia's forces) still holds good
since: since then
constant pleasure: firm decision

REGAN
Our sister's man° is certainly miscarried.°

sister's man: Oswald; **is . . . miscarried:** has certainly met with an accident

EDMUND
'Tis to be doubted,° madam.

doubted: feared

REGAN   Now, sweet lord,
You know the goodness I intend upon you.
Tell me but truly, but then speak the truth,
Do you not love my sister?

EDMUND   Ay, honored° love.

honored: honorable

REGAN
But have you never found my brother's° way
To the forfended° place?

brother's: Albany's
forfended: forbidden

EDMUND   That thought abuses° you.

abuses: is unworthy of

REGAN
I am doubtful° that you have been conjunct
And bosomed with her,° as far as we call hers.°

doubtful: suspicious
conjunct . . . her: in complicity with her, and her lover; **as . . . hers:** as completely hers as you can be

EDMUND
No, by mine honor, madam.

REGAN
I never shall endure her. Dear my lord,
Be not familiar° with her.

familiar: intimate

EDMUND   Fear° me not
She and the duke her husband —
Enter Albany and Goneril with troops.

Fear: doubt

GONERIL   *[Aside]*
I had rather lose the battle than that sister
Should loosen him and me.

ALBANY
Our very loving sister, well bemet,
For this I hear: the king is come to his daughter,
With others whom the rigor of our state°

rigor . . . state: harshness of our rule

DISCOVERING SHAKESPEARE

(109) Language [5.1.11]: What does Regan mean when she asks Edmund if he has ever found his way to "the forfended place" (5.1.11)? Why is she so obsessed with Edmund's behavior?

Forced to cry out. Where I could not be honest°
I never yet was valiant. For this business,
It touches° us as France invades our land,
Not bolds° the king, with others whom, I fear,
Most just and heavy° causes make oppose.

be honest: behave honorably

touches: concerns 25
Not bolds: not because he emboldens
heavy: serious

EDMUND
Sir, you speak nobly.

REGAN   Why is this reasoned?°

Why . . . reasoned?: i.e., why are you telling us this

GONERIL
Combine together° 'gainst the enemy,
For these domestic door particulars°
Are not to question° here.

Combine together: let us join our forces
domestic . . . particulars: household matters 30
to question: the issue

ALBANY   Let us then determine
With the ensign of war° on our proceedings.

ensign of war: experienced senior officers

EDMUND
I shall attend you presently at your tent.   *[Exit.]*

REGAN   Sister, you'll go with us?

GONERIL   No.   35

REGAN
'Tis most convenient;° pray you, go with us.

convenient: proper that you do

GONERIL   *[Aside]*
O, ho, I know the riddle.° I will go.
        Enter Edgar [disguised].

I . . . riddle: I get the point (which is not to leave her alone with Edmund)

EDGAR
If e'er your grace had speech with man so poor,
Hear me one word.
                    Exeunt [all except Edgar and Albany].

ALBANY   *[To the departing forces]*
I'll overtake you. *[To Edgar]* Speak.   40

EDGAR
Before you fight the battle, ope this letter.
If you have victory, let the trumpet sound
For him that brought it. Wretched though I seem,
I can produce a champion that will prove°
What is avouchèd° there. If you miscarry,°
Your business of the world hath so an end.
Fortune love you.

prove: establish as true (in a trial by single combat) 45
avouchèd: asserted; **miscarry:** lose the battle

ALBANY
Stay till I have read the letter.

EDGAR
I was forbid it.
When time shall serve, let but the herald cry,
And I'll appear again.   *Exit.*   50

ALBANY
Why, fare thee well. I will o'erlook the paper.°
        Enter Edmund.

paper: presumably Albany has no time to read Oswald's letter before Edmund's entrance

---

DISCOVERING SHAKESPEARE

(110) Plot [5.1.36]: Why does Regan want Goneril to leave with her (5.1.36)? What "riddle" does Goneril learn the answer to in 5.1.37?

EDMUND
The enemy's in view; draw up our powers.
Here is the guess° of their great strength and forces   **guess:** estimate
By diligent discovery;° but your haste   **discovery:** spying   55
Is now urged on you.

ALBANY   We will greet the time.°   *Exit.*   **greet the time:** be ready when the time comes

EDMUND
To both these sisters have I sworn my love,
Each jealous° of the other as the stung°   **jealous:** suspicious; **stung:** those who have
Are of the adder. Which of them shall I take?   been bitten
Both, one, or neither? Neither can be enjoyed   60
If both remain alive. To take the widow
Exasperates, makes mad, her sister Goneril,
And hardly shall I carry out my side,°   **carry . . . side:** accomplish my plan
Her husband being alive. Now then, we'll use
His countenance° for the battle, which being done,   **countenance:** authority, backing   65
Let her that would be rid of him devise
His speedy taking off.° As for his mercy   **taking off:** murder
Which he intends to Lear and to Cordelia,
The battle done, and they within our power,
Shall° never see his pardon; for my state   **Shall:** they shall   70
Stands on me° to defend, not to debate.   *Exit.*   **state . . . me:** situation requires me

  🙠 **5.2**° *Alarum.*° *Enter the powers of France over the stage,*   **5.2:** A field; **Alarum:** trumpets; **with . . .**
Cordelia with her father in her hand.° *[Exeunt.] Enter*   **hand:** leading her father by the hand
Edgar [disguised] and Gloucester.

EDGAR
Here, father,° take the shadow of this bush   **father:** old man (Edgar still has not revealed his
For your good host;° pray that the right may thrive.   identity to Gloucester)
If ever I return to you again   **host:** shelter
I'll bring you comfort.

GLOUCESTER   Grace go with you, sir.
    Exit [Edgar]. Alarum and [sound of] retreat.
    [Enter Edgar.]

EDGAR
Away, old man – give me thy hand, away!   5
King Lear hath lost, he and his daughter ta'en.
Give me thy hand. Come on.

GLOUCESTER
No farther, sir; a man may rot even here.

EDGAR
What, in ill thoughts again? Men must endure
Their going hence even as their coming hither.   10
Ripeness is all.° Come on.   *[Exeunt.]*   **Ripeness is all:** i.e., the gods decree when fruit
    is ripe and falls; coming to that ripeness is all that
    matters

DISCOVERING SHAKESPEARE

(111) Metaphor [5.1.58]: Explain Edmund's metaphor when he says that Goneril and Regan are "Each jealous of the other as the stung / Are of the adder" (5.1.58–59). What are the "tenor" and "vehicle" of this figurative expression?

5.3° *Enter Edmund, with Lear and Cordelia prisoners [, a Captain, and Soldiers].*

5.3: The British camp

EDMUND
Some officers take them away. Good guard,
Until their greater pleasures° best be known
That are to censure° them.

their . . . pleasures: the wishes of those in command
censure: pass judgment on

CORDELIA   We are not the first
Who with best meaning° have incurred the worst.
For thee, oppressèd king, am I cast down,
Myself could else° outfrown false fortune's frown.
Shall we not see these daughters and these sisters?

meaning: intentions

5

else: otherwise

LEAR
No, no. Come, let's away to prison.
We two alone will sing like birds i' th' cage.
When thou dost ask me blessing, I'll kneel down
And ask of thee forgiveness; so we'll live,
And pray, and sing, and tell old tales, and laugh
At gilded butterflies, and hear poor rogues
Talk of court news, and we'll talk with them too,
Who loses and who wins, who's in, who's out,
And take upon's the mystery of things
As if we were God's spies; and we'll wear out°
In a walled prison packs and sects° of great ones
That ebb and flow by th' moon.°

10

15

wear out: outlast
packs and sects: parties and factions
That . . . moon: whose power changes monthly

EDMUND   Take them away.

LEAR

20

Upon such sacrifices, my Cordelia,
The gods themselves throw incense.° Have I caught
    thee?°
He that parts us shall bring a brand° from heaven
And fire us hence like foxes. Wipe thine eyes.
The good years° shall devour 'em, flesh and fell,°
Ere they shall make us weep. We'll see 'em starve first.
    Come.

throw incense: are celebrants; **Have . . . thee?:** i.e., do I really have you again?
brand: torch (i.e., it will take divine powers to separate us now)
good years: passage of time, old age; **flesh . . . fell:** meat and skin, entirely

25

[Exeunt Lear and Cordelia with Soldiers.]

EDMUND
Come hither, captain, hark.
Take thou this note; go follow them to prison.
One step I have advanced° thee; if thou dost
As this instructs thee, thou dost make thy way
To noble fortunes. Know thou this, that men
Are as the time is;° to be tender-minded
Does not become a sword.° Thy great employment
Will not bear question.° Either say thou'lt do't,
Or thrive by other means.

advanced: promoted

30

Are . . . is: i.e., must seize their opportunities
sword: i.e., soldier
question: discussion

CAPTAIN   I'll do't, my lord.

DISCOVERING SHAKESPEARE

(112) Characterization [5.3.8]: Read Lear's speech in 5.3.8–19; then explain your opinion of his mental and emotional condition at this moment in the play.

(113) Paraphrase [5.3.33]: Rephrase in modern English Edmund's command to the Captain: "Either say thou'lt do't, / Or thrive by other means" (5.3.33–34). What implicit threat is carried by Edmund's words?

EDMUND
About it; and write happy° when thou hast done.   **write happy:** call yourself fortunate   35
Mark, I say instantly, and carry it° so   **carry it:** carry it out
As I have set it down.

CAPTAIN
I cannot draw a cart,
Nor eat dried oats.° If it be man's work, I'll do't. *[Exit.]*   **draw . . . oats:** i.e., I'm a man, not a horse
Enter Duke [Albany], the two ladies [Goneril and Regan] and
Others [, Officers and Soldiers].

ALBANY
Sir, you have showed today your valiant strain,°   **strain:** (1) qualities, (2) lineage   40
And fortune led you well. You have the captives
That were the opposites of° this day's strife.   **opposites of:** opponents in
We do require then of you so to use° them   **use:** treat
As we shall find their merits and our safety
May equally determine.   45

EDMUND   Sir, I thought it fit
To send the old and miserable king
To some retention° and appointed guard;   **retention:** detention
Whose age has charms in it, whose title more,
To pluck the common bosom on° his side   **pluck . . . on:** draw popular sympathy to
And turn our impressed lances° in our eyes°   **impressed lances:** drafted pikemen; **turn . . .**   50
Which do command them. With him I sent the queen,   **eyes:** i.e., turn our soldiers against us
My reason all the same; and they are ready
Tomorrow, or at further space,° to appear   **further space:** a later time
Where you shall hold your session.° At this time   **session:** court hearing
We sweat and bleed. The friend hath lost his friend,   55
And the best quarrels in the heat° are cursed   **best . . . heat:** most just wars in the heat of
By those that feel their sharpness.°   battle
The question of Cordelia and her father   **feel . . . sharpness:** endure their pain
Requires a fitter place.

ALBANY   Sir, by your patience,
I hold you but a subject of° this war,   **subject of:** subordinate in   60
Not as a brother.

REGAN   That's as we list° to grace him.   **we list:** I please
Methinks our pleasure should have been demanded°   **pleasure . . . demanded:** wishes should have
Ere you had spoke so far. He led our powers,   been consulted
Bore the commission of my place and person,°   **Bore . . . person:** i.e., acted with my authority
The which immediate° may well stand up   **immediate:** present status (as my deputy)   65
And call itself your brother.

GONERIL   Not so hot.°   **hot:** fast
In his own grace° he doth exalt himself   **grace:** merit
More than in your advancement.°   **your advancement:** the honors conferred by
                                                          you
REGAN   In my right
By me invested, he compeers° the best.   **compeers:** equals

GONERIL
That were the most° if he should husband you.   **the most:** i.e., the most complete investiture   70
                                                          with your rights
REGAN
Jesters do oft prove prophets.

DISCOVERING SHAKESPEARE

(114) <u>Plot</u> **[5.3.60]:** Why does Albany tell Edmund, "I hold you but a subject of this war, / Not as a brother" (5.3.60–61)? Explain Regan's response in lines 61–66.

GONERIL   Holla, holla –
  That eye that told you so looked but asquint.°   **asquint:** cross-eyed (i.e., jealously)
REGAN
  Lady, I am not well, else I should answer
  From a full-flowing stomach.° *[To Edmund]* General,   **stomach:** anger
  Take thou my soldiers, prisoners, patrimony.°   **patrimony:** inheritance   75
  Witness the world that I create thee here
  My lord and master.
GONERIL   Mean you to enjoy him then?
ALBANY
  The let-alone° lies not in your good will.   **let-alone:** (1) permission, (2) veto
EDMUND
  Nor in thine, lord.
ALBANY   Half-blooded° fellow, yes.   **Half-blooded:** illegitimate (and only half noble)
EDMUND
  Let the drum strike° and prove my title good.   **drum strike:** (as a signal to prepare for battle)   80
ALBANY
  Stay yet, hear reason. Edmund, I arrest thee
  On capital treason, and in thine attaint°   **in . . . attaint:** in complicity with your crimes
    [Indicating Goneril]
  This gilded serpent. For your claim, fair sister,
  I bar it in the interest of my wife.
  'Tis she is subcontracted° to this lord,   **subcontracted:** (because she is already   85
  And I, her husband, contradict the banns.°   contracted, by marriage, to Albany)
  If you will marry, make your love to° me.   **banns:** declaration of an intention to marry
  My lady is bespoke.° – Thou art armed, Gloucester.   **make . . . to:** woo
  If none appear to prove upon thy head   **bespoke:** already spoken for
  Thy heinous, manifest, and many treasons,   90
  There is my pledge. *[Throws down a glove.]* I'll prove it
    on thy heart,
  Ere I taste bread, thou art in nothing less°   **nothing less:** no way less guilty
  Than I have here proclaimed thee.
REGAN   Sick, O sick!
GONERIL *[Aside]*
  If not, I'll ne'er trust poison.
EDMUND *[Throws his glove.]*
  There's my exchange. What in the world° he is   **What . . . world:** whoever   95
  That names me traitor, villainlike he lies.
  Call by thy trumpet. He that dares approach,
  On him, on you – who not? – I will maintain
  My truth and honor firmly.
ALBANY   A herald, ho!
EDMUND
  A herald, ho, a herald!   100
ALBANY
  Trust to thy single virtue,° for thy soldiers,   **single virtue:** unaided strength
  All levied in my name, have in my name
  Took their discharge.
REGAN   This sickness grows upon me.

DISCOVERING SHAKESPEARE

(115) <u>Plot</u> **[5.3.73]:** Why is Regan feeling ill (5.3.73–74)? (*Hint:* Read further in the scene to answer this question.)
(116) <u>Teaser</u> **[5.3.95]:** In 5.3.95, Edmund throws down his glove as a challenge. When did this custom first appear?

ALBANY
    She is not well. Convey her to my tent.
    [Regan is led out. Enter a Herald and a Trumpeter.]
    Come hither, herald. Let the trumpet sound,   105
    And read out this.

CAPTAIN   Sound, trumpet! *[Trumpet sounds.]*

HERALD   "If any man of quality or degree in the host of
    the army will maintain upon Edmund, supposed Earl
    of Gloucester, that he's a manifold traitor, let him appear   110
    at the third sound of the trumpet. He is bold in his
    defense."

EDMUND   Sound! *[Trumpet sounds.]* Again! *[Trumpet
    sounds.]*
    Enter Edgar [armed]° at the third sound, a
    Trumpet[er] before him.

armed: (Edgar wears a helmet with the beaver down, covering his face)

ALBANY
    Ask him his purposes, why he appears
    Upon this call o' th' trumpet.   115

HERALD   What are you?
    Your name and quality,° and why you answer
    This present summons?

quality: rank

EDGAR   O, know my name is lost,
    By treason's° tooth bare-gnawn and canker-bit.°
    Yet ere I move't,° where is the adversary
    I come to cope° withal?

treason's: treachery's; **canker-bit:** eaten away by worms
ere . . . move't: before I make my declaration   120
cope: encounter

ALBANY   Which is that adversary?

EDGAR
    What's he that speaks for Edmund, Earl of Gloucester?

EDMUND
    Himself. What sayest thou to him?

EDGAR   Draw thy sword,
    That if my speech offend a noble heart
    Thy arm may do thee justice. Here is mine.
    Behold, it is the privilege of my tongue,   125
    My oath, and my profession.° I protest,
    Maugre° thy strength, youth, place, and eminence,
    Despite thy victor sword and fire-new° fortune,
    Thy valor and thy heart,° thou art a traitor,
    False to thy gods, thy brother, and thy father,   130
    Conspirant° 'gainst this high illustrious prince,
    And from th' extremest upward° of thy head
    To the descent° and dust beneath thy feet
    A most toad-spotted° traitor. Say thou no,
    This sword, this arm, and my best spirits are bent   135
    To prove upon thy heart, whereto I speak,
    Thou liest.

profession: i.e., as a knight
Maugre: despite
fire-new: newly forged
heart: courage

Conspirant: conspirator
upward: top
descent: lowest part
toad-spotted: venomous, reptilian

EDMUND   In wisdom I should ask thy name,°
    But since thy outside looks so fair and warlike,
    And that thy being° some say of breeding breathes,

In . . . name: (because one was not obliged to fight with an inferior, nor with an unknown adversary)
being: nature

DISCOVERING SHAKESPEARE

(117) Language [5.3.117]: Why does Edgar tell the Herald that his name is "lost" (5.3.117)? Why doesn't he want Edmund to know whom he is fighting against?

By right of knighthood I disdain and spurn.°
Here do I toss those treasons to thy head,
With the hell-hated° lie o'erturn thy heart,
Which, for they° yet glance by and scarcely bruise,
This sword of mine shall give them instant way°
Where they shall rest forever. Trumpets, speak!
    [Alarums. They fight. Edmund falls.]

ALBANY
Save him,° save him.

GONERIL   This is mere practice,° Gloucester.
By the law of arms thou art not bound to answer
An unknown opposite.° Thou art not vanquished,
But cozened° and beguiled.

ALBANY   Stop your mouth, dame,
Or with this paper shall I stopple it.
Thou worse than anything, read thine own evil.
Nay, no tearing, lady. I perceive you know't.

GONERIL
Say if I do, the laws are mine,° not thine.
Who shall arraign° me for't?

ALBANY
Most monstrous! Know'st thou this paper?

GONERIL
Ask me not what I know.   Exit.

ALBANY
Go after her. She's desperate; govern° her.
                                    [Exit an Officer.]

EDMUND
What you have charged me with, that have I done,
And more, much more. The time will bring it out.
'Tis past, and so am I. But what art thou
That hast this fortune on° me? If thou beest noble,
I do forgive thee.

EDGAR   Let's exchange charity.°
I am no less in blood than thou art, Edmund;
If more, the more thou hast wronged me.
    [Removing his helmet]
My name is Edgar, and thy father's son.
The gods are just, and of our pleasant virtues°
Make instruments to scourge us.
The dark and vicious place° where thee he got°
Cost him his eyes.

EDMUND   Thou hast spoken truth.
The wheel is come full circled; I am here.°

ALBANY
Methought thy very gait did prophesy
A royal nobleness. I must embrace thee.
Let sorrow split my heart if I did ever hate
Thee or thy father.

---

disdain and spurn: i.e., ask what I am entitled to know   140

hell-hated: hateful as hell

Which, for they: since those treasons

way: access

   145

Save him: i.e., don't kill him

This is mere practice: i.e., you've been tricked

opposite: opponent

cozened: cheated

   150

the . . . mine: (Goneril is queen; Albany is her consort)

arraign: try (the monarch, having no peers, could not be prosecuted)   155

govern: take care of

   160

fortune on: victory over

charity: forgiveness

   165

pleasant virtues: e.g., sexual prowess: what we are good at in the realm of pleasure (F's "pleasant vices" is an obvious revision, clarifying the sense but muting the irony; Q's "vertues" cannot have been a compositor's misreading of "vices.")

dark . . . place: adulterous bed, illicit genitals; **got:** begot   170

I . . . here: i.e., at the bottom of Fortune's wheel again

DISCOVERING SHAKESPEARE

(118) <u>Staging</u> **[5.3.146]:** If you were directing a production of this play, how long would you want the fight between Edmund and Edgar to last? What weapons would they use? How would Edgar defeat his brother?

(119) <u>Staging</u> **[5.3.169]:** Why does Goneril exit so rapidly from the stage in 5.3.156?

EDGAR   Worthy prince, I know't.
ALBANY
  Where have you hid yourself?   175
  How have you known the miseries of your father?
EDGAR
  By nursing them, my lord. List° a brief tale,   **List:** hear
  And when 'tis told, O that my heart would burst!
  The bloody proclamation° to escape   **bloody proclamation:** (declaring him an
  That followed me so near – O our lives' sweetness,°   outlaw)   180
  That with the pain of death would hourly die   **our . . . sweetness:** how sweet life is to us
  Rather than die at once! – taught me to shift
  Into a madman's rags, to assume a semblance
  That very dogs disdained; and in this habit
  Met I my father with his bleeding rings,°   **rings:** sockets   185
  The precious stones new lost; became his guide,
  Led him, begged for him, saved him from despair,
  Never – O father! – revealed myself unto him
  Until some half hour past, when I was armed.
  Not sure, though hoping of this good success,   190
  I asked his blessing, and from first to last
  Told him my pilgrimage; but his flawed heart,
  Alack too weak the conflict to support,
  'Twixt two extremes of passion, joy and grief,
  Burst smilingly.   195
EDMUND   This speech of yours hath moved me,
  And shall perchance do good. But speak you on;
  You look as you had something more to say.
ALBANY
  If there be more, more woeful, hold it in,
  For I am almost ready to dissolve,°   **dissolve:** (in tears)
  Hearing of this.   200
EDGAR   This would have seemed a period°   **a period:** the limit
  To such as love not sorrow; but another
  To amplify too much would make much more,
  And top extremity.°   **another . . . extremity:** to describe another
  Whilst I was big in clamor° came there in a man   sorrow too fully would exceed the limit
  Who, having seen me in my worst estate,°   **big in clamor:** loudly lamenting   205
  Shunned my abhorred society; but then, finding   **in . . . estate:** at my worst
  Who 'twas that so endured, with his strong arms
  He fastened on my neck and bellowed out
  As° he'd burst heaven; threw him° on my father,   **As:** as if; **him:** himself
  Told the most piteous tale of Lear and him
  That ever ear received, which in recounting   210
  His grief grew puissant° and the strings of life   **puissant:** powerful
  Began to crack. Twice then the trumpets sounded,
  And there I left him tranced.
ALBANY   But who was this?
EDGAR
  Kent, sir, the banished Kent, who in disguise   215
  Followed his enemy king, and did him service

DISCOVERING SHAKESPEARE

(120) Plot [5.3.190]: According to Edgar's speech in 5.3.177–195, what has happened to Gloucester? Why do you think this event occurs off stage rather than on stage?

Improper for a slave.

Enter [a Gentleman] with a bloody knife.

GENTLEMAN   Help, help!

ALBANY
What kind of help?
What means that bloody knife?   220

GENTLEMAN   It's hot, it smokes;
It came even from the heart of –

ALBANY   Who, man? speak!

GENTLEMAN
Your lady, sir, your lady; and her sister
By her is poisonèd – she hath confessed it.

EDMUND
I was contracted to them both; all three
Now marry° in an instant.   **marry:** unite   225

ALBANY
Produce their bodies, be they alive or dead.
                                        [Exit Attendant.]
This justice of the heavens that makes us tremble
Touches us not with pity.

EDGAR
Here comes Kent, sir.
            Enter Kent [as himself].

ALBANY
O, 'tis he. The time will not allow   230
The compliment that very manners urges.

KENT
I am come
To bid my king and master aye° good night.   **aye:** forever
Is he not here?

ALBANY   Great thing of us forgot!
Speak, Edmund, where's the king, and where's Cordelia?   235
            The bodies of Goneril and Regan are brought in.
Seest thou this object,° Kent?   **object:** sight, spectacle

KENT   Alack, why thus?

EDMUND
Yet Edmund was beloved.
The one the other poisoned for my sake,
And after slew herself.

ALBANY   Even so. Cover their faces.   240

EDMUND
I pant for life. Some good I mean to do,
Despite of my own nature. Quickly send –
Be brief° in't – to th' castle, for my writ°   **brief:** quick; **writ:** order of execution
Is on the life of Lear and on Cordelia.
Nay, send in time.   245

ALBANY   Run, run, O run!

DISCOVERING SHAKESPEARE

(121) Irony [5.3.224]: What does Edmund mean when he says that he, Goneril, and Regan "Now marry in an instant" (5.3.224–225)? How is this statement ironic?

(122) Plot [5.3.241]: What "good" does Edmund try to do before he dies (5.3.241)? What does this action tell us about his character?

EDGAR
　　To who, my lord? Who hath the office?° Send　　　　　**office:** commission
　　Thy token of reprieve.
EDMUND
　　Well thought on. Take my sword. The captain,
　　Give it the captain.　　　　　　　　　　　　　　　　　　　　　　　250
ALBANY　　　　　　　　Haste thee for thy life.
　　　　　　　　　　　　　　　　　[Exit Captain.]
EDMUND
　　He hath commission from thy wife and me
　　To hang Cordelia in the prison, and
　　To lay the blame upon her own despair,
　　That she fordid° herself.　　　　　　　　　　　　**fordid:** destroyed
ALBANY
　　The gods defend her! Bear him hence awhile.　　　　　　　255
　　　　　　　　　　　　　　　[Edmund is borne off.]
　　Enter Lear with Cordelia in his arms [followed by
　　Captain].
LEAR
　　Howl, howl, howl, howl! O you are men of stones.
　　Had I your tongues and eyes, I would use them so
　　That heaven's vault should crack. She's gone forever.
　　I know when one is dead and when one lives.
　　She's dead as earth. Lend me a looking glass;　　　　　　　　260
　　If that her breath will mist or stain the stone,°　　　**stone:** mirror of polished stone
　　Why, then she lives.
KENT　　　　　　　Is this the promised end?°　　　　**promised end:** Judgment Day
EDGAR
　　Or image of that horror?
ALBANY　　　　　　Fall and cease.°　　　　　　　　**Fall . . . cease:** let the world end
LEAR
　　This feather stirs. She lives. If it be so,
　　It is a chance which does redeem all sorrows　　　　　　　265
　　That ever I have felt.
KENT　　　　　　　　Ah, my good master –
LEAR
　　Prithee, away.
EDGAR　　　　　'Tis noble Kent, your friend.
LEAR
　　A plague upon you, murderous traitors all!
　　I might have saved her; now she's gone forever.
　　Cordelia, Cordelia, stay a little. Ha?　　　　　　　　　270
　　What is't thou sayest? – Her voice was ever soft,
　　Gentle and low, an excellent thing in women.
　　I killed the slave that was a-hanging thee.
CAPTAIN
　　'Tis true, my lords, he did.
LEAR　　　　　　　　Did I not, fellow?
　　I have seen the day, with my good biting falchion°　　**falchion:** small sword　275
　　I would have made them skip. I am old now,

DISCOVERING SHAKESPEARE

(123) History [5.3.260]: Why does Lear call for a "looking glass" in 5.3.260? Why does he refer to it as a "stone" in the following line? When were mirrors first invented?

And these same crosses spoil° me.
   [To Kent]

                        Who are you?
Mine eyes are not o' the best, I'll tell you straight.

crosses spoil: vexations weaken

KENT
If fortune bragged of two she loved or hated,°
One of them we behold.

loved or hated: first loved, then hated (Lear and a hypothetical other? Lear and Cordelia? Lear and Kent, who are looking at each other?)

                      Are not you Kent?

280

LEAR

KENT
The same, your servant Kent. Where is your servant
   Caius?°

Caius: (obviously Kent's alias; but the name appears nowhere else in the play)

LEAR
He's a good fellow, I can tell you that.
He'll strike, and quickly too. He's dead and rotten.

KENT
No, my good lord, I am the very man –

LEAR
I'll see that straight.°

I'll . . . straight: I'll attend to it shortly

285

KENT
That from your first of difference and decay°
Have followed your sad steps.

difference and decay: quarrel and decline

LEAR
               You're welcome hither.°

You're . . . hither: (Lear fails to make the connection)

KENT
Nor no man else.° All's cheerless, dark, and deadly.
Your eldest daughters have fordone° themselves,
And desperately° are dead.

Nor . . . else: i.e., no one is welcome here
fordone: killed
desperately: in despair

290

LEAR
              So think I, too.

ALBANY
He knows not what he sees, and vain it is
That we present us to him.

EDGAR
             Very bootless.°
   Enter Captain.

bootless: pointless

CAPTAIN
Edmund is dead, my lord.

ALBANY
That's but a trifle here.
You lords and noble friends, know our intent.
What comfort to this decay° may come
Shall be applied; for us, we will resign
During the life of this old majesty
To him our absolute power. *[To Edgar and Kent]* You
   to your rights,
With boot° and such addition° as your honors
Have more than merited. All friends shall taste
The wages of their virtue, and all foes
The cup of their deservings. O see, see!

295

decay: ruin (i.e., Lear)

boot: reward; **addition:** advancement in rank

300

LEAR
And my poor fool° is hanged. No, no life?

fool: (A term of endearment; here, Cordelia. The Fool disappears after 3.6.)

DISCOVERING SHAKESPEARE

(124) Plot [5.3.282]: Why does Kent ask Lear about "Caius" in 5.3.282? Why is this reference <u>ironic</u>?

(125) Language [5.3.304]: Lear's agonizing cry that "my poor fool is hanged" (5.3.304) is a famous crux in the play. Whom is he referring to here: The Fool or Cordelia? What did the word "fool" mean during Shakespeare's time? What do you think happens to the Fool when he disappears after 3.6?

Why should a dog, a horse, a rat have life,   305
And thou no breath at all? O, thou wilt come no more.
Never, never, never. – Pray you, undo
This button. Thank you, sir. O, O, O, O!
EDGAR
He faints. My lord, my lord!
LEAR
Break, heart, I prithee break.   310
   [He dies.]
EDGAR   Look up, my lord.
KENT
Vex not his ghost.° O, let him pass. He hates him   **ghost:** spirit
That would upon the rack° of this tough world   **rack:** i.e., a torture instrument
Stretch him out longer.
EDGAR   O, he is gone indeed.
KENT
The wonder is he hath endured so long.
He but usurped his life.   315
ALBANY
Bear them from hence. Our present business
Is to general woe. *[To Edgar and Kent]* Friends of my
  soul, you twain
Rule in this kingdom, and the gored° state sustain.   **gored:** wounded
KENT
I have a journey, sir, shortly to go;
My master calls, and I must not say no.   320
ALBANY
The weight of this sad time we must obey,°   **obey:** Albany speaks the final lines as the highest-
Speak what we feel, not what we ought to say.   ranking person left alive. In the folio, Edgar speaks
The oldest have borne most; we that are young   them as the inheritor of Lear's kingdom.
Shall never see so much, nor live so long.

                       [Exeunt.]

DISCOVERING SHAKESPEARE

(126) Language [5.3.319]: Why does Kent tell Albany that he has a journey to take? What does he mean when he explains, "My master calls, and I must not say no" (5.3.320)?

        ❧

Research and Discussion Topics

ACT I

1. How did people during Shakespeare's time feel about the division of a kingdom (1.1.4)? What happened during the War of the Roses, and what effect did these events have on the Renaissance concept of divided kingdoms?

2. What were the laws regarding bastardy and legitimacy (1.1.18) during Shakespeare's time? Could bastard children inherit land and titles?

3. What was a "sennet" (1.1.32 s.d.)?

4. What was a "coronet" (1.1.32 s.d.)?

5. What was a "Scythian" (1.1.105)?

6. In mythology, who were Apollo and Jupiter (1.1.148 and 166)? What kinds of power and authority did each have?

7. How were spectacles made during the Renaissance (1.2.35)?

8. What was "the catastrophe of the old comedy" (1.2.127–128)?

9. What was "Bedlam" (1.2.129)? What does the word mean now?

10. What were the cuckoo's nesting and feeding habits (1.4.211)?

11. What was "spleen" (1.4.276)?

12. What were "kibes" (1.5.9)?

13. What were "the seven stars" (1.5.35)?

ACT II

1. Look up and define all the derogatory terms that Kent calls Oswald in 2.2.13–35.

2. What was a "carbonado" (2.2.34)?

3. What was a "jakes" (2.2.62)? Why would Kent want to "daub the walls" with Oswald (2.2.62)? In which of his plays does Shakespeare use character names that pun on the word "jakes"?

4. What were Sarum Plain and Camelot (2.2.79–80)?

5. Who was Ajax (2.2.122)?

6. What was the Wheel of Fortune (2.2.170)?

7. What was a "carbuncle" (2.4.199)?

8. Who were "depositaries" (2.4.228)? What were their legal duties?

ACT III

1. What were "cataracts" and "hurricanoes" (3.2.2)?

2. What was a "codpiece" (3.2.27)? Who wore them? During what years were they fashionable?

3. What peculiar feeding rituals did pelicans have (3.4.69)?

4. What was a "placket" (3.4.89)?

5. Who was Swithold? (3.4.110)?

6. Who were Smulkin (3.4.130), Modo (134), and Mahu (134)?

7. Who was a Theban (3.4.147)? Who was Child Roland (3.4.171)? What is *La Chanson de Roland* (3.4.171)?

8. Who was Nero (3.6.6)? What was he famous for?

ACT IV

1. What was a "distaff" (4.2.18)?

2. What were "oeillades" (4.5.26)? What is the etymological origin of the word?

3. What were "choughs" (4.6.13)?

4. What was "samphire" (4.6.15)? Who was it gathered? What was it used for?

5. What was "press money" (4.6.87)?

6. What was a "gauntlet" (4.6.90)? What were "brown bills" (4.6.91)?

7. What was an "ague" (4.6.104). Which Shakespearean character is named after this illness?

8. What was "civet" (4.6.126)? Where did it come from? What was it used for?

9. What was a "beadle" (4.6.155)?

ACT V

1. What were "domestic door particulars" (5.1.30)?

2. What types of "adders" (5.1.59) were known during Shakespeare's time?

3. What does Edgar's sentence "Ripeness is all" mean (5.2.11)?

4. What types of poison (5.3.93) were available during the Renaissance?

5. What was the definition of treason in 1600s England (5.3.141)?

6. What was "the law of arms" (5.3.147) to which Goneril refers?

7. What was a "writ" (5.3.243)?

8. What was a "falchion" (5.3.275)?

Filmography

1983
Rating:

Granada Television

Directed by: Michael Elliott

Laurence Olivier as King Lear
Anna Calder-Marshall as Cordelia
Dorothy Tutin as Goneril
Diana Rigg as Regan
Robert Lindsay as Edmund
David Threfal as Edgar
Leo McKern as Gloucester
John Hurt as the Fool

There is laughter in *King Lear* as well as suffering, but suffering eclipses everything in this production. Too much is cut; too many elements are added, including the mad king ripping up a rabbit and eating it raw. Olivier appears too fragile for the part, ready to collapse at any moment under no greater weight than his wispy white hair. However, he bears his burdens successfully, and if this is not Olivier's greatest Shakespearean role, it may be his most endearing. He is joined by an extraordinarily watchable cast, an object lesson in the ability of film to assemble a more powerful ensemble than the stage can reasonably match. After Olivier, Leo McKern and John Hurt are the most memorable. If the performances have a fault, it is that some of the deference the other actors felt for Olivier comes through in their characterizations. The bright, pastoral colors of the film offer an effective contrast to the script's dark messages.

1982
BBC
Rating:

Directed by: Jonathan Miller

Michael Hordern as King Lear
Brenda Blethyn as Cordelia
Gillian Barge as Goneril
Penelope Wilton as Regan
Michael Kitchen as Edmund
Anton Lesser as Edgar
Norman Rodway as Gloucester
Frank Middlemass as the Fool

The BBC *King Lear* is, overall, a solid production that presents the play in a traditional, straightforward fashion and retains most of Shakespeare's lines. This production manages to explore much of the darkness inherent in the script without eradicating the humor. Michael Hordern's Lear, who is all doddering pomposity, becomes so obnoxious that many viewers sympathize with Goneril and Regan when they give him the boot. Cordelia is, in dress and manner, a humorless puritan; she seems petty and jealous of the approval Lear bestows upon her sisters in the dowry scene. Michael Kitchen's Edmund makes an entertaining villain, and Frank Middlemass' Fool, costumed in black with a large, oddly shaped hat and clown-like make-up, is a strange combination of a witty fool and an old country bumpkin.

1997
Mobil Masterpiece Theatre
Rating:

Directed by: Richard Eyre

Ian Holm as King Lear
Victoria Hamilton as Cordelia
Barbara Flynn as Goneril
Amanda Redman as Regan
Finbar Lynch as Edmund

Paul Rhys as Edgar
Timothy West as Gloucester
Michael Bryant as the Fool
David Burke as Kent

King Lear is about old age, but not everyone in it is old or should appear to be so. David Burke's Kent seems of an age with Ian Holm's King Lear. Finbar Lynch's Edmund and Victoria Hamilton's Cordelia, though they do not look like contemporaries of Kent and Lear, do not look young either. Clearly visual impact was less important than other considerations. Some of the sets, for example, are orange, and some actors wear matching costumes, a choice more distracting than edifying. Some of the readings too have a sameness about them, and Holm's Lear is too often simply angry, too seldom the victim of terribly mixed emotions. Nevertheless, the production has strengths. The storm scene, for example, is quite believable. Ian Holm, as he did in the National Theatre production on which this film is based, removes his clothes (or almost all of them—the water and the camera's distance make it difficult to be sure). Throughout, the passions that activate these characters seem newly minted, not worn by their centuries of use. The production is professional, and if no actor (except for Holm) stands out as extraordinary, no one falls below that uniformly high standard either.

1971
Filmways Pictures
Rating:

Directed by: Peter Brook

Paul Scofield as King Lear
Anne-Lise Gabold as Cordelia
Irene Worth as Goneril
Susan Engel as Regan
Ian Hogg as Edmund
Robert Lloyd as Edgar
Alan Webb as Gloucester
Jack MacGowran as the Fool

Peter Brook dressed his characters in animal skins, loaded them into wagons, and set them in a black-and-white, minimalist world. The verse is lopped and hacked rather than merely cut, and it is spoken with a brutality that sometimes seems to smash it into prose. This *Lear* is expressionist and absurdist, cruel and bleak. Except for the Fool's songs and some electronic sounds, the film features no music, only harsh human voices. Sometimes beautiful, sometimes hateful, this production at times reaches the levels of pain that Shakespeare built into the play. However, the bleakness is so uninterrupted that it occasionally becomes boring. The cast is powerful, with Paul Scofield especially impressive.

1953
Orson Welles
(b/w)
Rating:

Directed by: Andrew McCullough & Peter Brook

Orson Welles as King Lear
Natasha Parry as Cordelia
Beatrice Straight as Goneril
Margaret Phillips as Regan
Michael McLiammoir as Poor Tom
Frederic Worlock as Gloucester
Alan Badel as the Fool

This production of *King Lear,* which seems to be the fairy-tale version of Shakespeare's play, eliminates large portions of the script and some of the characters, and fails to achieve the emotional intensity of the text. The costuming is rather outlandish, the ladies wearing Elizabethan ruffs and Lear sporting a cartoonish cape and crown. Edgar does not exist except as Poor Tom, and Edmund has been eliminated entirely. Orson Welles—large, surly, and fierce—is neither overblown nor understated; the rest of the actors, however, are frequently melodramatic in their readings. The sets are stylized, and the film creates little real feeling of Lear being exposed to the elements; the only concession to realism is an occasional token gust of wind. The violence is also surrealistic, with slow-motion stabbings and bloodless eye-gouging.

Annotated Bibliography

Adelman, Janet, ed. *Twentieth-Century Interpretations of "King Lear": A Collection of Critical Essays.* Englewood Cliffs, NJ: Prentice Hall, 1978. PR 2819.T9.
This collection of essays features work by such renowned scholars as Bradley, Knight, Danby, Mack, Cavell, and Rosenberg in the first section titled "Interpretations." In the second section, "Viewpoints," the editor presents several excerpts from influential essays on *King Lear* by Maud Bodkin, Kenneth Muir, Phyllis Rackin, Nicholas Brooke and others. Adelman's introduction discusses the concept of "spectators," which includes both the play's audience as well as spectators within the play (such as the dual character of Edgar, who is both a participant in and a spectator of the play's action). A brief annotated bibliography is also included.

Brayton, Dan. "Angling in the Lake of Darkness: Possession, Dispossession, and the Politics of Discovery in *King Lear.*" *ELH* 70.2 (2003): 399–426. journal PR 1.E5.
Brayton argues that the issues of social alienation and political dissolution in *King Lear* are spatial problems similar to territories on a map such as the one used in the first act to divide up the kingdom. According to Brayton, the play then becomes a metaphor for the discovery and critique of these "new lands."

Danby, John F. *Shakespeare's Doctrine of Nature: A Study of "King Lear."* London: Faber and Faber, 1949. PR 2819.D33.

> In this historicist analysis of *King Lear,* Danby argues that Shakespeare deviates from two well-known Renaissance conceptions of nature and reason, those held by Hobbes and Hooker. Danby divides his book into two separate sections, defining these views of nature (one as malevolent, the other as harmless) in the first part and discussing Shakespeare's deviation from these definitions in the second half. Danby incorporates his notion of "Shakespeare's Inner Biography up to 1606" in this discussion of *Lear,* suggesting that the playwright varies his representations of the machiavel throughout his plays.

Elton, William R. *"King Lear" and the Gods.* San Marino, CA: Huntington Library, 1966. PR 2819.E4.

> Rebuking interpretations of *King Lear* as "Christian" drama, Elton contends that the play is built upon pagan ritual and is absent any whiff of organized religion. In particular, Elton points to the four representations of Providence in Sir Philip Sidney's *Arcadia:* the virtuous heathen (Cordelia and Edgar); the atheist (Goneril, Regan, and Edmund); the superstitious (Gloucester); and the theory of hidden providence (Lear). Elton concludes his argument by suggesting that the play denies all hope of salvation, as the variety of religious perspectives in *Lear*'s pagan world preclude any possibility of Christian redemption.

Heilman, Robert Bechtold. *This Great Stage: Image and Structure in "King Lear."* Baton Rouge: Louisiana State University Press, 1948. PR 2819.H4.

> Advancing a formalist reading of the play, Heilman examines patterned language and imagery in *King Lear,* contending that repeated images form the basis of *Lear*'s central themes. Of particular interest to him are images of nature (both as law and as the basis of individual drives and impulses), age and justice, as well as representations of sight and clothing. Heilman concludes his eleven-chapter study by arguing that *Lear* is not a fatalistic or optimistic play, but that it lauds the individual's imagination above all else.

Hopkins, Lisa. "'Base-football Player': This Sporting Life in *King Lear.*" *English Language Notes* 37.4 (June 2000): 8–17. journal PE 1.E53.

> Hopkins offers several interesting insights into the multiple meanings of the sporting terms found throughout *King Lear,* asserting that the sporting terminology (mainly pertaining to tennis) creates intriguing competitive relationships between characters. The language also leaves a trail of historic political references that connect the script back to the fictional kingdom of Lear.

Knight, G. Wilson. *The Wheel of Fire: Interpretations of Shakespearean Tragedy with Three New Essays.* Oxford: Oxford University Press, 1930, pp. 160–206. PR 2983.K6.

> In this collection of essays, Knight includes two studies of *King Lear.* In the first, titled "*King Lear* and the Comedy of the Grotesque," he contends that the play is filled with grotesque, imaginative, and bizarre humor that makes a farce of humanity. In the second essay, "The *Lear*

Universe," Knight discusses the play's naturalism, pagan sensibility, justice, truth, and "apocalyptic beauty" (179) to establish a description of the play's unspoken central philosophy.

Leggatt, Alexander. *"King Lear." Shakespeare in Performance*. Manchester: Manchester University Press, 1991. PR 2819.L4.

Examining several modern productions of *King Lear*, Leggatt argues that all theatrical interpretations of the play struggle to integrate the dueling elements of "abstraction and humanity." Divided into eight chapters, Leggatt's book examines performances ranging from those of John Gielgud, Paul Scofield, and Peter Ustinov, and the directorial efforts of Peter Brooks, Robin Phillips, and Adrian Nobles. The book concludes with a bibliography of secondary reading material on the play.

Mack, Maynard. *"King Lear" in Our Time*. Berkeley: University of California Press, 1965. PR 2819.M3.

Examining how the play can be received in our post-World War II atmosphere, Mack discusses *King Lear*'s relevance to a postmodern audience. In particular, he considers the play's stage history and critical heritage, arguing that *Lear* is an unrealistic psychological examination because of its link to folktales, morality plays, and pastoral romances. Mack concludes his book by noting aspects of *Lear* that particularly appeal to modern audiences, including the play's violence, its ambiguity, and its discussion of suffering as essential to humanity.

Rosenberg, Marvin. *The Masks of "King Lear."* Berkeley: University of California Press, 1972. PR 2819.R65.

In this comprehensive examination of productions of *King Lear*, Rosenberg contends that the play's intricate and complex messages can only be fully realized through performance. He discusses every scene of the play and cross-references several different productions to describe how each scene is most successfully performed. Rosenberg concludes his examination with information on *Lear*'s folklore antecedents, the play's poetic language, and the role of the Fool. A bibliography featuring a list of productions and actors is appended.

Welsford, Enid. *The Fool: His Social and Literary History*. London: Faber and Faber, 1935. GT 3670.W4.

In this anthropological study of *King Lear*, Welsford considers cross-cultural and historical representations of the fool in literature. She classifies three types of fools: the comic joker, the real and imaginary court fool, and the stage clown. In her analysis of *Lear*'s Fool, Welsford draws several comparisons with Shakespeare's other fools, particularly Touchstone in *As You Like It* and Feste in *Twelfth Night*. The author concludes her argument by suggesting that in *King Lear* Shakespeare moves away from the medieval Saturnalia when the King is invested with "motley" (271).

Macbeth

❧

Macbeth *at the Oregon Shakespearean Festival in Ashland, Oregon, with Michael
J. Hume as Macbeth (1998). Photograph by David Cooper.*

Enlivened by witches, apparitions, prophecies, sword fights, sensational
murders, and a bloody, severed head, *Macbeth* is one of Shakespeare's
most spectacular and frequently produced plays. It also provides a fascinating glimpse into two important chronological periods: the history of medieval Scotland and the reign of James I. Shakespeare's principal <u>source</u> for his
<u>plot</u> was Raphael Holinshed's *Chronicles of Scotland* (1587), which was itself in-
debted to earlier histories by Hector Boece, John of Fordun, and Andrew of
Wyntoun. By the time the story of Macbeth's reign (1040–1057) reached
Holinshed, it had become more fiction than fact. Shakespeare's <u>script</u> omits,
for example, Macbeth's legitimate claim to the throne and his ten years as a
good ruler between the murders of Duncan and Banquo, while the play makes
Duncan older and more reverent in order to blacken the guilt of the usurper
and his murderous wife. Enough historical similarities remain, however, to
allow audiences an unflinching look at the brutality and lust for power extant
in eleventh-century Scotland.

Written soon after the death of Queen Elizabeth in 1603, the script commemorates the accession of her successor to the throne of England through its focus on the Scottish heritage of James I, his notorious bouts with insomnia, and his interest in witchcraft and magic (evidenced by the king's publication of a treatise entitled *Demonology* in 1597). Shakespeare even provides a fictitious genealogical line of descent through which James becomes a descendant of Banquo's son, Fleance, thereby dignifying his reign through antiquity. Although not published until the 1623 First Folio edition of Shakespeare's plays, *Macbeth* was probably written and first performed in 1606, soon after the infamous Gunpowder Plot, a conspiracy by Catholic extremists to blow up the Parliament building and all the heads of state on November 5, 1605. The many references to Jesuits, equivocation, and the role of divine providence in protecting the realm all point to Shakespeare's use of this specific historical event, which is now celebrated throughout England as Guy Fawkes Day.

Shakespeare's semi-fictional account of Macbeth's reign becomes brilliant drama through the playwright's vivid portrayal of ambition gone berserk. Among the script's principal themes, fate plays a major role—especially as it relates to the characterization of the witches. The more supernatural and powerful the "weïrd sisters" appear on stage, the less Macbeth seems to be responsible for his own actions. Conversely, in productions featuring more "human" witches, the play becomes a tragedy in which Macbeth's murderous actions bring about his own demise. Oxymorons are also paramount in the play, particularly those alternating between dark/light, sin/grace, salvation/damnation, good/evil, and, of course, fair/foul. Additional important themes include clarity of vision, controlling the future, ill-fitting garments, surrogate fathers and sons, pregnancy, the power of women, omens, sleeplessness, sexual inversion, the psychology of evil, and the corruption of authority. The brevity of the play (it is the shortest of Shakespeare's tragedies) suggests the text may have been taken from a script edited for performance, perhaps with the Hecate scenes added later by Thomas Middleton, a rival playwright. Recent scholarship has also delved into such new topics as chaos theory, demonism, impotence, the passage of time, militarism, Christian virtue, and the oppressiveness of power.

Although the play was initially produced in 1606, the first historical evidence of a performance at the Globe Theatre occurs in April, 1611, when the astrologer Simon Forman recorded it in his diary. In the early 1660s, Sir William Davenant rewrote the play for Restoration audiences, featuring several songs, flying witches, Hecate's entrance on a cloud, and a symbolic parallel between Macbeth as Oliver Cromwell and Malcolm as the restored Charles II. The production also cut the Porter and the Doctor, did away with the murder of Macduff's children, and simplified much of the diction of the play. In 1744, David Garrick produced his own version of the script that retained Davenant's operatic witches and provided Macbeth with a penitent death speech. Adaptations by Charles Macklin (1773), Edmund Keane (1814), Charles Macready (1820–1848), Samuel Phelps (1844–1865), and Henry Irving (1875) gradually restored Shakespeare's script to the stage, although none was seen as remarkably successful. Notable twentieth century productions have included those featuring John Gielgud (1930), Laurence Olivier and Judith Anderson (1937), Peter Hall and John Russell Brown (1967), and Trevor Nunn's Royal Shakespeare Company production starring Ian McKellen and Judi Dench (1976). Orson Welles' famous "voodoo" *Macbeth* in 1936 and Peter O'Toole's melodramatic treatment in 1976 were two of the most disastrous productions during the same time period.

Cinematic versions of the play have generally fared better than their stage counterparts, with Orson Welles' *Macbeth* (1948), Akira Kurosawa's *Throne of Blood* (1957), and Roman Polanski's "Playboy" *Macbeth* (1971) all generating a good deal of controversy. The <u>script</u> also spawned an American gangster film, *Men of Respect* (1991), which updates and remains faithful to the play's central themes and images. George Schaefer's television adaptation (1954) starring Maurice Evans and Judith Anderson was somewhat less successful than Trevor Nunn's televised Royal Shakespeare Company in-the-round production (1979), though both have been judged superior to the lackluster 1982 BBC-TV production featuring Nicol Williamson and Jane Lapotaire.

As its prolific stage and screen history implies, *Macbeth* has remained one of Shakespeare's most popular plays for nearly four hundred years. It even has its own superstitious mystique, which forbids actors from saying the name "Macbeth" inside a theatre lest it bring down a curse upon them. The <u>script</u> not only offers access to two intriguing historical periods—primitive Scotland and early seventeenth-century England—but it also provides a detailed psychological study of the moral degeneration of two brilliant and noble minds. Driven by ambition for the throne, Macbeth and his fiendish queen provide a vision of evil that alternately intrigues and frightens audiences of the play. If we were in Macbeth's place, could we, like Macduff and Banquo, resist the temptation of the throne? What secret witches sing to us of kingdoms to conquer and seductive crowns to seize? As with all of Shakespeare's best plays, the answer lies not in the <u>script</u>, but deep within our souls.

Macbeth at the Utah Shakespearean Festival in Cedar City, Utah, with Angela Iannone as Lady Macbeth and Robert Martini as Macbeth (1996). Photograph by Wilkes and Bernard.

Macbeth

NAMES OF THE ACTORS

DUNCAN, *King of Scotland*

MALCOLM } *his sons*
DONALBAIN

MACBETH
BANQUO
MACDUFF
LENNOX
ROSS *Scottish thanes*
MENTEITH
ANGUS
CAITHNESS

FLEANCE, *son to Banquo*
SIWARD, *Earl of Northumberland*
YOUNG SIWARD, *his son*
SEYTON, *an officer attending on Macbeth*
BOY, *son to Macduff*
A CAPTAIN
AN ENGLISH DOCTOR
A SCOTTISH DOCTOR
A PORTER
AN OLD MAN
THREE MURDERERS
LADY MACBETH
LADY MACDUFF
A GENTLEWOMAN, *attending on Lady Macbeth*
THE WEÏRD SISTERS, *witches*
HECATE
APPARITIONS
LORDS, OFFICERS, SOLDIERS, MESSENGERS, ATTENDANTS

SCENE: *Scotland and England*

1.1° *Thunder and lightning. Enter three Witches.*

1.1: An open field

FIRST WITCH
When shall we three meet again?
In thunder, lightning, or in rain?
SECOND WITCH
When the hurly-burly's° done,

hurly-burly: turmoil

When the battle's lost and won.
THIRD WITCH   That will be ere the set of sun.   5
FIRST WITCH   Where the place?
SECOND WITCH   Upon the heath.
THIRD WITCH   There to meet with Macbeth.
FIRST WITCH   I come, Graymalkin!°

Graymalkin: gray cat, her familiar spirit

SECOND WITCH   Paddock° calls.

Paddock: toad   10

THIRD WITCH   Anon!°

Anon: at once

ALL
Fair is foul, and foul is fair.
Hover through the fog and filthy air.   *Exeunt.*

1.2° *Alarum within.° Enter King [Duncan], Malcolm,
Donalbain, Lennox, with Attendants, meeting a
bleeding Captain.*

1.2: Duncan's camp; **within:** offstage

KING DUNCAN
What bloody man is that? He can report,
As seemeth by his plight, of the revolt
The newest state.
MALCOLM   This is the sergeant°

sergeant: (generic term for a military officer; he ranks as a captain)

Who like a good and hardy soldier fought
'Gainst my captivity. Hail, brave friend;
Say to the king the knowledge of the broil   5
As thou didst leave it.
CAPTAIN   Doubtful it stood,
As two spent swimmers that do cling together
And choke their art. The merciless Macdonwald –
Worthy to be a rebel, for to that°

to that: to that end   10

The multiplying villainies of nature
Do swarm upon him – from the Western Isles°

Western Isles: the Hebrides and Ireland

Of kerns and galloglasses° is supplied;

kerns and galloglasses: Irish mercenary soldiers

And Fortune, on his damnèd quarrel smiling,
Showed like a rebel's whore. But all's too weak: 15
For brave Macbeth – well he deserves that name –
Disdaining Fortune, with his brandished steel,
Which smoked with bloody execution,
Like valor's minion° carved out his passage

minion: darling

Till he faced the slave;
Which ne'er shook hands nor bade farewell to him   20

DISCOVERING SHAKESPEARE

(1) Characterization [1.1.1]: Find as many clues as possible in the first twelve lines of the play that help to characterize the Witches. Who are they? What special powers do they have? How much control do you think they will exert over the action of the play? Come back to this question after you have read further in the play, and revise your answer if necessary.
(2) Costuming [1.2.13]: How is the Captain dressed? How would the phrase "bloody man" (1.2.1) affect his theatrical make-up? How would he speak to King Duncan?

Till he unseamed him from the nave° to th' chaps°   **nave:** navel; **chaps:** jaws
And fixed his head upon our battlements.
KING DUNCAN
  O valiant cousin, worthy gentleman!
CAPTAIN
  As whence the sun 'gins his reflection   25
  Shipwracking storms and direful thunders,
  So from that spring whence comfort seemed to come
  Discomfort swells. Mark, King of Scotland, mark.
  No sooner justice had, with valor armed,
  Compelled these skipping kerns to trust their heels   30
  But the Norwegian lord, surveying vantage,°   **surveying vantage:** seeing an opportunity
  With furbished arms and new supplies of men,
  Began a fresh assault.
KING DUNCAN   Dismayed not this
  Our captains, Macbeth and Banquo?
CAPTAIN   Yes,
  As sparrows eagles, or the hare the lion.   35
  If I say sooth, I must report they were
  As cannons overcharged with double cracks,°   **cracks:** explosives
  So they doubly redoubled strokes upon the foe.
  Except° they meant to bathe in reeking wounds,   **Except:** unless
  Or memorize another Golgotha,°   **memorize another Golgotha:** make as 40
  I cannot tell –   memorable as Calvary (where the Crucifixion
  But I am faint; my gashes cry for help.   took place)
KING DUNCAN
  So well thy words become thee as thy wounds,
  They smack of honor both. Go get him surgeons.
                   [Exit Captain, attended.]

  Enter Ross and Angus.
  Who comes here?   45
MALCOLM   The worthy Thane° of Ross.   **Thane:** (a Scottish lord, equivalent to the English
LENNOX   earl)
  What a haste looks through° his eyes! So should he look   **looks through:** appears in
  That seems to° speak things strange.   **seems to:** is ready to
ROSS   God save the king.
KING DUNCAN
  Whence cam'st thou, worthy thane?
ROSS   From Fife, great king,
  Where the Norwegian banners flout the sky
  And fan our people cold.   50
  Norway° himself, with terrible numbers,   **Norway:** the King of Norway
  Assisted by that most disloyal traitor
  The Thane of Cawdor, began a dismal° conflict,   **dismal:** ominous
  Till that Bellona's° bridegroom, lapped in proof,°   **Bellona:** goddess of war; **lapped in proof:**
  Confronted him with self-comparisons,°   (1) protected by experience, (2) wearing proven 55
  Point° against point, rebellious arm 'gainst arm,   armor
  Curbing his lavish spirit; and to conclude,
  The victory fell on us.   **self-comparisons:** power comparable with his
KING DUNCAN   Great happiness!   own
                                  Point: sword

DISCOVERING SHAKESPEARE

(3) <u>Syntax</u> **[1.2.40]:** What is the <u>etymology</u> of the word "Golgotha" (1.2.40)? (*Hint:* See the *Oxford English Dictionary*.) Why is this a particularly effective word in this context?

ROSS
    That now
    Sweno, the Norways' king, craves composition;°   **composition:** terms of surrender   60
    Nor would we deign him burial of his men
    Till he disbursèd, at Saint Colme's Inch,°   **Saint Colme's Inch:** Inchcolm, an island near Edinburgh (Inch means "island")
    Ten thousand dollars° to our general use.   **dollars:** (the German thaler was a pan-European silver currency)

KING DUNCAN
    No more that Thane of Cawdor shall deceive
    Our bosom interest.° Go pronounce his present° death   **bosom interest:** heart's trust; **present:**   65
    And with his former title greet Macbeth.   immediate

ROSS
    I'll see it done.

KING DUNCAN
    What he hath lost noble Macbeth hath won.   *Exeunt.*

❧ **1.3°** *Thunder. Enter the three Witches.*   **1.3:** A heath

FIRST WITCH   Where hast thou been, sister?
SECOND WITCH   Killing swine.
THIRD WITCH   Sister, where thou?
FIRST WITCH
    A sailor's wife had chestnuts in her lap
    And munched and munched and munched. "Give me,"   5
        quoth I.
    "Aroint thee,° witch!" the rump-fed runnion° cries.   **Aroint thee:** get thee gone; **rump-fed runnion:** fat-rumped slut
    Her husband's to Aleppo gone, master° o' th' *Tiger:*°   **master:** captain; **Tiger:** (name of his ship)
    But in a sieve I'll thither sail
    And, like a rat without a tail,
    I'll do, I'll do, and I'll do.   10
SECOND WITCH   I'll give thee a wind.
FIRST WITCH   Thou'rt kind.
THIRD WITCH   And I another.
FIRST WITCH
    I myself have all the other,
    And the very ports they blow,°   **ports they blow:** safe havens they afflict with   15
    All the quarters that they know   storms
    I' th' shipman's card.°   **shipman's card:** nautical chart
    I'll drain him dry as hay.
    Sleep shall neither night nor day
    Hang upon his penthouse lid.°   **penthouse lid:** eyelid (what overhangs the eye)   20
    He shall live a man forbid.°   **forbid:** accursed
    Weary sev'nights, nine times nine,
    Shall he dwindle, peak,° and pine.   **peak:** waste away
    Though his bark cannot be lost,
    Yet it shall be tempest-tossed.   25
    Look what I have.
SECOND WITCH   Show me, show me.

DISCOVERING SHAKESPEARE

(4) Staging [1.3.1]: Do you think the Witches appear in the same place on <u>stage</u> as they did in 1.1? Or is this an entirely new location? Why do you feel this way?

(5) Meter [1.3.25]: Analyze the <u>meter</u> and <u>rhyme</u> scheme of the Witches' speeches. Do all three of them speak alike, or can you find subtle differences in the <u>verse</u> that distinguish each character?

FIRST WITCH
   Here I have a pilot's thumb,
   Wrecked as homeward he did come.
    Drum within.
THIRD WITCH
   A drum, a drum;   30
   Macbeth doth come.
ALL
   The weïrd° sisters, hand in hand,
   Posters° of the sea and land,
   Thus do go about, about,
   Thrice to thine, and thrice to mine,
   And thrice again, to make up nine.
   Peace, the charm's wound up.
    Enter Macbeth and Banquo.
MACBETH
   So foul and fair a day I have not seen.
BANQUO
   How far is't called° to Forres? What are these,
   So withered and so wild in their attire
   That look not like th' inhabitants o' th' earth
   And yet are on't? Live you, or are you aught
   That man may question? You seem to understand me,
   By each at once her choppy° finger laying
   Upon her skinny lips. You should be women,
   And yet your beards forbid me to interpret
   That you are so.
MACBETH   Speak, if you can. What are you?
FIRST WITCH
   All hail, Macbeth! Hail to thee, Thane of Glamis!°
SECOND WITCH
   All hail, Macbeth! Hail to thee, Thane of Cawdor!
THIRD WITCH
   All hail, Macbeth, that shalt be king hereafter!   50
BANQUO
   Good sir, why do you start and seem to fear
   Things that do sound so fair? *[To the Witches]* I' th'
    name of truth,
   Are ye fantastical,° or that indeed
   Which outwardly ye show? My noble partner
   You greet with present grace° and great prediction
   Of noble having and of royal hope,
   That he seems rapt withal.° To me you speak not.
   If you can look into the seeds of time°
   And say which grain will grow and which will not,
   Speak then to me, who neither beg nor fear
   Your favors nor your hate.
FIRST WITCH   Hail!
SECOND WITCH   Hail!
THIRD WITCH   Hail!

weïrd: (two syllables: from Old English "wyrd," "fate," hence "supernatural," associated with fate, with an overtone of the uncanny, suggested by F's spelling "weyward")
35
Posters: swift travelers

is't called: do they say it is
40

choppy: chapped
45

Glamis: (one syllable)

fantastical: imaginary, hallucinations

grace: honor
55

rapt withal: spellbound at the thought
seeds of time: sources of future events
60

DISCOVERING SHAKESPEARE

(6) Language [1.3.44]: How does Banquo's use of the word "choppy" (1.3.44) offer a clue about the occupation and behavior of these women?

FIRST WITCH
    Lesser than Macbeth, and greater.   65
SECOND WITCH
    Not so happy,° yet much happier.   **happy:** fortunate
THIRD WITCH
    Thou shalt get° kings, though thou be none.   **get:** beget
    So all hail, Macbeth and Banquo!
FIRST WITCH
    Banquo and Macbeth, all hail!
MACBETH
    Stay, you imperfect° speakers, tell me more: **imperfect:** incomplete   70
    By Finel's° death I know I am Thane of Glamis,   **Finel:** or Finley, Macbeth's father
    But how of Cawdor? The Thane of Cawdor lives,
    A prosperous gentleman; and to be king
    Stands not within the prospect of belief,
    No more than to be Cawdor. Say from whence   75
    You owe this strange intelligence, or why
    Upon this blasted heath you stop our way
    With such prophetic greeting. Speak, I charge you.
                            Witches vanish.
BANQUO
    The earth hath bubbles as the water has,
    And these are of them. Whither are they vanished?   80
MACBETH
    Into the air, and what seemed corporal° melted   **corporal:** corporeal
    As breath into the wind. Would they had stayed!
BANQUO
    Were such things here as we do speak about?
    Or have we eaten on the insane° root   **insane:** inducing insanity
    That takes the reason prisoner?   85
MACBETH
    Your children shall be kings.
BANQUO   You shall be king.
MACBETH
    And Thane of Cawdor too. Went it not so?
BANQUO
    To th' selfsame tune and words. Who's here?
    Enter Ross and Angus.
ROSS
    The king hath happily received, Macbeth,
    The news of thy success; and when he reads°   **reads:** considers   90
    Thy personal venture in the rebels' fight,
    His wonders and his praises do contend
    Which should be thine or his.° Silenced with that,   **His wonders . . . or his:** i.e., dumbstruck
    In viewing o'er the rest o' th' selfsame day,   admiration makes him keep your praises to
    He finds thee in the stout Norwegian ranks,   himself   95
    Nothing afeard of what thyself didst make,
    Strange images of death. As thick as tale°   **thick as tale:** as fast as they can be counted
    Came post with post,° and everyone did bear   **post with post:** messenger after messenger

---

DISCOVERING SHAKESPEARE

(7) <u>Theme</u> [1.3.70]: Why do you think Macbeth calls the Witches "imperfect speakers" (1.3.70)? Write your response on a separate piece of paper; then come back to this question after you have read the entire play and, if necessary, revise your answer.

Thy praises in his kingdom's great defense
And poured them down before him.   100
ANGUS   We are sent
To give thee from our royal master thanks;
Only to herald thee into his sight,
Not pay thee.
ROSS
And for an earnest of a greater honor,
He bade me, from him, call thee Thane of Cawdor;   105
In which addition,° hail, most worthy thane,   **addition:** title
For it is thine.
BANQUO   What, can the devil speak true?
MACBETH
The Thane of Cawdor lives. Why do you dress me
In borrowed robes?
ANGUS   Who was the thane lives yet,
But under heavy judgment bears that life   110
Which he deserves to lose. Whether he was combined°   **combined:** leagued
With those of Norway, or did line° the rebel   **line:** support
With hidden help and vantage,° or that with both   **vantage:** assistance
He labored in his country's wrack, I know not;
But treasons capital, confessed and proved,   115
Have overthrown him.
MACBETH   [Aside]   Glamis, and Thane of Cawdor –
The greatest is behind.°   **behind:** still to come
    [To Ross and Angus] Thanks for your pains.
    [Aside to Banquo]
Do you not hope your children shall be kings,
When those that gave the Thane of Cawdor to me
Promised no less to them?   120
BANQUO   [To Macbeth] That, trusted home,°   **home:** all the way
Might yet enkindle you unto the crown,
Besides the Thane of Cawdor. But 'tis strange;
And oftentimes, to win us to our harm,
The instruments of darkness tell us truths,
Win us with honest trifles, to betray's   125
In deepest consequence.° –   **deepest consequence:** the crucial sequel
Cousins,° a word, I pray you.   **Cousins:** i.e., fellow lords
MACBETH   [Aside]   Two truths are told,
As happy prologues to the swelling act°   **swelling act:** developing drama
Of the imperial theme. – I thank you, gentlemen. –
    [Aside]
This supernatural soliciting   130
Cannot be ill, cannot be good. If ill,
Why hath it given me earnest of success
Commencing in a truth? I am Thane of Cawdor.
If good, why do I yield to that suggestion
Whose horrid image doth unfix my hair   135

DISCOVERING SHAKESPEARE

(8) Plot [1.3.105]: What is the importance of Ross addressing Macbeth as the "Thane of Cawdor" (1.3.105) so soon after the Witches' prophecy? How would the play be different if more time had elapsed between the two events?

(9) Language [1.3.127]: Which "two truths" (1.3.127) have been told to Macbeth? What third truth does he describe as "the swelling act / Of the imperial theme" (1.3.128–129)?

And make my seated° heart knock at my ribs
Against the use° of nature? Present fears
Are less than horrible imaginings:
My thought, whose murder yet is but fantastical,°
Shakes so my single state of man° that function°
Is smothered in surmise and nothing is
But what is not.
BANQUO   Look how our partner's rapt.
MACBETH   [Aside]
If chance will have me king, why, chance may crown
  me
Without my stir.
BANQUO   New honors come upon him,
Like our strange° garments, cleave not to their mold
But with the aid of use.
MACBETH   [Aside]   Come what come may,
Time and the hour runs through the roughest day.°
BANQUO
Worthy Macbeth, we stay upon your leisure.
MACBETH
Give me your favor.° My dull brain was wrought
With things forgotten. Kind gentlemen, your pains
Are registered where every day I turn
The leaf to read them. Let us toward the king.
  [Aside to Banquo]
Think upon what hath chanced, and at more time,
The interim having weighed it, let us speak
Our free hearts° each to other.
BANQUO   Very gladly.
MACBETH
Till then, enough. – Come, friends.   Exeunt.

seated: fixed	
use: normal habit	
fantastical: imaginary	
single state of man: both undivided and weak	140
human condition; **function:** the power to act	

strange: new — 145

Time . . . day: i.e., the worst day comes to an end

favor: pardon — 150

free hearts: thoughts freely — 155

❦ **1.4°** *Flourish. Enter King [Duncan], Lennox,*
Malcolm, Donalbain, and Attendants.

KING DUNCAN
Is execution done on Cawdor? Are not
Those in commission° yet returned?
MALCOLM   My liege,
They are not yet come back. But I have spoke
With one that saw him die, who did report
That very frankly he confessed his treasons,
Implored your highness' pardon, and set forth
A deep repentance. Nothing in his life
Became him like the leaving it. He died
As one that had been studied° in his death
To throw away the dearest thing he owed°
As 'twere a careless trifle.

1.4: Duncan's camp

in commission: commissioned to carry out the execution

5

studied: rehearsed
owed: owned — 10

DISCOVERING SHAKESPEARE

(10) Teaser [1.4.8]: Look up the Latin term "contemplatio mortis." How does the concept help explain Malcolm's comment that Cawdor died "As one that had been studied in his death" (1.4.9)?

KING DUNCAN   There's no art
  To find the mind's construction in the face.
  He was a gentleman on whom I built
  An absolute trust.
    Enter Macbeth, Banquo, Ross, and Angus.
    [To Macbeth]   O worthiest cousin,   15
  The sin of my ingratitude even now
  Was heavy on me. Thou art so far before°   **before:** ahead in deserving
  That swiftest wing of recompense is slow
  To overtake thee. Would thou hadst less deserved,
  That the proportion° both of thanks and payment   **proportion:** satisfactory apportioning
  Might have been mine. Only I have left to say,   20
  More is thy due than more than all can pay.
MACBETH
  The service and the loyalty I owe,
  In doing it pays itself. Your highness' part
  Is to receive our duties, and our duties
  Are to your throne and state children and servants,   25
  Which do but what they should by doing everything
  Safe° toward your love and honor.   **Safe:** fitting
KING DUNCAN   Welcome hither.
  I have begun to plant° thee and will labor   **plant:** nurture
  To make thee full of growing. Noble Banquo,
  That hast no less deserved nor must be known   30
  No less to have done so, let me enfold thee
  And hold thee to my heart.
BANQUO   There if I grow,
  The harvest is your own.
KING DUNCAN   My plenteous joys,
  Wanton° in fullness, seek to hide themselves   **Wanton:** unrestrained
  In drops of sorrow. Sons, kinsmen, thanes,   35
  And you whose places are the nearest, know
  We will establish our estate upon
  Our eldest, Malcolm, whom we name hereafter
  The Prince of Cumberland;° which honor must   **Prince of Cumberland:** (equivalent to the
  Not unaccompanied invest him only,   English Prince of Wales, the designated heir to the 40
  But signs of nobleness, like stars, shall shine   throne)
  On all deservers. From hence to Inverness,
  And bind us further to you.
MACBETH
  The rest is labor which is not used for you.
  I'll be myself the harbinger, and make joyful   45
  The hearing of my wife with your approach;
  So, humbly take my leave.
KING DUNCAN   My worthy Cawdor!
MACBETH   *[Aside]*
  The Prince of Cumberland – that is a step
  On which I must fall down or else o'erleap,
  For in my way it lies. Stars, hide your fires;   50
  Let not light see my black and deep desires.

DISCOVERING SHAKESPEARE

(11) __Plot__ **[1.4.38]:** Why does Malcolm's sudden promotion to "Prince of Cumberland" (1.4.38–39) present an obstacle to Macbeth?

The eye wink at the hand;° yet let that be
Which the eye fears, when it is done, to see.   *Exit.*

wink at the hand: disregard what the hand does

KING DUNCAN
True, worthy Banquo: he is full so valiant,
And in his commendations I am fed;
It is a banquet to me. Let's after him,
Whose care is gone before to bid us welcome.
It is a peerless kinsman.   *Flourish. Exeunt.*

55

1.5° *Enter Macbeth's Wife, alone, with a letter.*

1.5: Within Macbeth's castle at Inverness

LADY MACBETH   *[Reads.]* "They met me in the day of success; and I have learned by the perfect'st report° they have more in them than mortal knowledge. When I burned in desire to question them further, they made themselves air, into which they vanished. Whiles I stood rapt in the wonder of it, came missives° from the king, who all-hailed me Thane of Cawdor, by which title, before, these weïrd sisters saluted me, and referred me to the coming on of time with 'Hail, king that shalt be!' This have I thought good to deliver thee, my dearest partner of greatness, that thou mightst not lose the dues of rejoicing by being ignorant of what greatness is promised thee. Lay it to thy heart, and farewell."

perfect'st report: most reliable evidence

5

missives: messengers

10

Glamis thou art, and Cawdor, and shalt be
What thou art promised. Yet do I fear thy nature.
It is too full o' th' milk of human kindness
To catch the nearest way.° Thou wouldst be great,
Art not without ambition, but without
The illness° should attend it. What thou wouldst highly,
That wouldst thou holily; wouldst not play false,
And yet wouldst wrongly win. Thou'dst have, great
 Glamis,
That which cries "Thus thou must do" if thou have it;
And that which rather thou dost fear to do
Than wishest should be undone. Hie thee hither,
That I may pour my spirits in thine ear
And chastise with the valor of my tongue
All that impedes thee from the golden round°
Which fate and metaphysical° aid doth seem
To have thee crowned withal.°
 Enter Messenger.   What is your tidings?
MESSENGER
The king comes here tonight.
LADY MACBETH   Thou'rt mad to say it!
Is not thy master with him? who, were't so,
Would have informed for preparation.

15

catch . . . way: take the most direct roure

illness: wickedness

20

25

round: crown
metaphysical: supernatural
withal: with

30

DISCOVERING SHAKESPEARE

(12) Staging [1.5.8]: Where in the castle does 1.5 take place? What clues in Lady Macbeth's initial soliloquy hint at this location?

(13) Shared Lines [1.5.29]: How do the shared lines between Lady Macbeth and the Messenger in 1.5.29–36 help suggest the speed and delivery of the verse?

MESSENGER
 So please you, it is true. Our thane is coming.
 One of my fellows had the speed of him,
 Who, almost dead for breath,° had scarcely more   **breath:** want of breath   35
 Than would make up his message.
LADY MACBETH   Give him tending;
 He brings great news.   *Exit Messenger.*
       The raven himself is hoarse
 That croaks the fatal entrance of Duncan
 Under my battlements. Come, you spirits
 That tend on mortal° thoughts, unsex me here,   **mortal:** deadly   40
 And fill me from the crown to the toe topful
 Of direst cruelty. Make thick my blood;
 Stop up th' access and passage to remorse,°   **remorse:** pity
 That no compunctious visitings of nature°   **nature:** natural feeling
 Shake my fell° purpose nor keep peace between   **fell:** fierce   45
 Th' effect and it.° Come to my woman's breasts   **keep peace . . . and it:** i.e., lull it from achieving its end
 And take my milk for gall,° you murd'ring ministers,°   **take . . . gall:** exchange my milk for gall; **ministers:** agents
 Wherever in your sightless° substances   **sightless:** invisible   50
 You wait on° nature's mischief. Come, thick night,   **wait on:** aid
 And pall thee° in the dunnest° smoke of hell,   **pall thee:** shroud thyself; **dunnest:** darkest
 That my keen knife see not the wound it makes,
 Nor heaven peep through the blanket of the dark
 To cry "Hold, hold."
  Enter Macbeth.   Great Glamis, worthy Cawdor,
 Greater than both, by the all-hail hereafter,
 Thy letters have transported me beyond   55
 This ignorant° present, and I feel now   **ignorant:** unaware
 The future in the instant.
MACBETH   My dearest love,
 Duncan comes here tonight.
LADY MACBETH   And when goes hence?
MACBETH
 Tomorrow, as he purposes.
LADY MACBETH   O, never
 Shall sun that morrow see.   60
 Your face, my thane, is as a book where men
 May read strange matters. To beguile° the time,   **beguile:** deceive
 Look like the time;° bear welcome in your eye,   **Look . . . time:** act as the occasion requires
 Your hand, your tongue; look like th' innocent flower,
 But be the serpent under't. He that's coming   65
 Must be provided for; and you shall put
 This night's great business into my dispatch,°   **dispatch:** efficient management
 Which shall to all our nights and days to come
 Give solely sovereign sway and masterdom.
MACBETH
 We will speak further.   70

DISCOVERING SHAKESPEARE

(14) <u>Staging</u> [1.5.54]: How does Lady Macbeth know her husband has arrived? Does she see him coming, or does she somehow instinctively feel his presence before he enters the room?

(15) <u>Paraphrase</u> [1.5.70]: <u>Paraphrase</u> the following lines by Lady Macbeth: "Only look up clear./To alter favor ever is to fear" (1.5.70–71). How does the <u>rhyme</u> at the ends of the lines help punctuate the meaning of the words?

LADY MACBETH   Only look up clear.°
  To alter favor° ever is to fear.
  Leave all the rest to me.   *Exeunt.*

look up clear: appear untroubled
alter favor: change your countenance

❧ **1.6**° *Hautboys° and torches. Enter King [Duncan],*
Malcolm, Donalbain, Banquo, Lennox, Macduff,
Ross, Angus, and Attendants.

1.6: Before Inverness Castle; **Hautboys:** treble shawms (ancestors of the modern oboe)

KING DUNCAN
  This castle hath a pleasant seat.° The air
  Nimbly and sweetly recommends itself
  Unto our gentle° senses.

seat: site

gentle: soothed

BANQUO   This guest of summer,
  The temple-haunting° martlet,° does approve°
  By his loved mansionry° that the heaven's breath
  Smells wooingly here. No jutty,° frieze,
  Buttress, nor coign of vantage,° but this bird
  Hath made his pendent bed and procreant cradle.°
  Where they most breed and haunt, I have observed
  The air is delicate.
    Enter Lady [Macbeth].

temple-haunting: nesting around churches;
martlet: swallow, house martin; **approve:** demonstrate   5

loved mansionry: beloved nest
jutty: projection
coign of vantage: convenient corner
procreant cradle: cradle for breeding   10

KING DUNCAN
  See, see, our honored hostess!
  The love that follows us sometime is our trouble,
  Which still we thank as love.° Herein I teach you
  How you shall bid God 'ield us° for your pains
  And thank us for your trouble.

The love . . . as love: our subjects' love sometimes inconveniences us, but we still acknowledge it as love   15
God 'ield us: God reward me

LADY MACBETH   All our service
  In every point twice done, and then done double,
  Were poor and single business° to contend
  Against those honors deep and broad wherewith
  Your majesty loads our house. For those of old,
  And the late° dignities heaped up to them,
  We rest your hermits.°

single business: simple effort

late: recent   20
hermits: beadsmen (who are obligated to pray for a benefactor's welfare)

KING DUNCAN   Where's the Thane of Cawdor?
  We coursed him at the heels and had a purpose
  To be his purveyor;° but he rides well,
  And his great love, sharp as his spur, hath holp° him
  To his home before us. Fair and noble hostess,
  We are your guest tonight.

had . . . purveyor: (the purveyor was the chief logistical officer in the royal household, arranging for lodging and supplies; Duncan had wished to provide this service for Macbeth)   25
holp: helped

LADY MACBETH   Your servants ever
  Have theirs,° themselves, and what is theirs,° in count,°
  To make their audit at your highness' pleasure,
  Still° to return your own.

Have theirs: have their servants; **what is theirs:** their possessions; **in count:** in trust
Still: always

KING DUNCAN   Give me your hand.
  Conduct me to mine host; we love him highly
  And shall continue our graces towards him.
  By your leave, hostess.   *Exeunt.*

    30

DISCOVERING SHAKESPEARE

(16) Language [1.6.27]: Why is Lady Macbeth's speech to King Duncan in 1.6.26–29 phrased in such elevated <u>diction</u>? Which words seem particularly lofty? Explain the monetary <u>metaphor</u> running through the lines.

❧ **1.7°** *Hautboys. Torches. Enter a Sewer,° and divers Servants with dishes and service over the stage. Then enter Macbeth.*

1.7: A room off the great hall in Macbeth's castle;
Sewer: chief waiter

MACBETH
If it were done when 'tis done,° then 'twere well
It were done quickly. If th' assassination
Could trammel up the consequence,° and catch
With his surcease° success, that but this blow
Might be the be-all and the end-all – here,
But here upon this bank and shoal° of time,
We'd jump° the life to come. But in these cases
We still have judgment here, that° we but teach
Bloody instructions,° which, being taught, return
To plague th' inventor. This evenhanded° justice
Commends th' ingredience° of our poisoned chalice
To our own lips. He's here in double trust:
First, as I am his kinsman and his subject,
Strong both against the deed; then, as his host,
Who should against his murderer shut the door,
Not bear the knife myself. Besides, this Duncan
Hath borne his faculties° so meek, hath been
So clear° in his great office, that his virtues
Will plead like angels, trumpet-tongued against
The deep damnation of his taking-off;
And pity, like a naked newborn babe
Striding the blast, or heaven's cherubin horsed
Upon the sightless couriers° of the air,
Shall blow the horrid deed in every eye
That° tears shall drown the wind. I have no spur
To prick the sides of my intent, but only
Vaulting ambition, which o'erleaps itself
And falls on th' other –
    Enter Lady [Macbeth].
                        How now? What news?
LADY MACBETH
He has almost supped. Why have you left the chamber?
MACBETH
Hath he asked for me?
LADY MACBETH   Know you not he has?
MACBETH
We will proceed no further in this business.
He hath honored me of late, and I have bought°
Golden opinions from all sorts of people,
Which would be worn now in their newest gloss,
Not cast aside so soon.
LADY MACBETH   Was the hope drunk
Wherein you dressed yourself? Hath it slept since?
And wakes it now to look so green° and pale
At what it did so freely? From this time
Such I account thy love. Art thou afeard

done when 'tis done: over and done with when the act is performed
trammel . . . consequence: entrap the consequences as in a net
his surcease: Duncan's death   5
bank and shoal: sandbank and shallows
jump: risk
that: because
instructions: lessons
evenhanded: impartial   10
ingredience: contents (the ingredients collectively)

                                                                    15

faculties: power
clear: innocent

                                                                    20

sightless couriers: invisible messengers (the winds)
That: so that   25

                                                                    30

bought: acquired

                                                                    35

green: bilious

DISCOVERING SHAKESPEARE

(17) <u>**Shared Lines**</u> **[1.7.29]:** What is the tone of Lady Macbeth's question in 1.7.29? Is this a gentle inquiry or an angry accusation? Why do you think so?

To be the same in thine own act and valor   40
As thou art in desire? Wouldst thou have that
Which thou esteem'st the ornament of life,
And live a coward in thine own esteem,
Letting "I dare not" wait upon° "I would,"   **wait upon:** preempt
Like the poor cat i' th' adage?°   **cat i' th' adage:** (the adage says, "The cat would   45
           eat fish but will not wet her feet")
MACBETH   Prithee peace.
I dare do all that may become a man;
Who dares do more is none.°   **none:** not a man
LADY MACBETH   What beast was't then
That made you break° this enterprise to me?   **break:** broach
When you durst do it, then you were a man;
And to be more than what you were, you would   50
Be so much more the man. Nor time nor place
Did then adhere,° and yet you would make both.   **adhere:** agree
They have made themselves, and that their fitness° now   **that their fitness:** their very fitness
Does unmake you. I have given suck, and know
How tender 'tis to love the babe that milks me: 55
I would, while it was smiling in my face,
Have plucked my nipple from his boneless gums
And dashed the brains out, had I so sworn as you
Have done to this.
MACBETH   If we should fail?°   **fail? . . . fail?:** (F's punctuation mark could
LADY MACBETH   We fail?   represent both modern ? and !; it is thus not clear   60
But° screw your courage to the sticking place°   whether Lady Macbeth is acknowledging the
And we'll not fail. When Duncan is asleep,   possibility of failure)
Whereto the rather° shall his day's hard journey   **But:** (1) however, (2) merely; **sticking place:**
Soundly invite him, his two chamberlains   (the notch holding the string taut, on either a
Will I with wine and wassail° so convince°   crossbow or a musical instrument)
That memory, the warder° of the brain,   **the rather:** the sooner   65
Shall be a fume,° and the receipt° of reason   **wassail:** liquor; **convince:** overwhelm
A limbeck° only. When in swinish sleep   **warder:** guardian
Their drenchèd natures lies as in a death,   **fume:** vapor; **receipt:** receptacle
What cannot you and I perform upon   **limbeck:** distilling device
Th' unguarded Duncan? what not put upon   70
His spongy officers, who shall bear the guilt
Of our great quell?°   **quell:** killing
MACBETH   Bring forth men-children only;
For thy undaunted mettle° should compose   **mettle:** valor
Nothing but males. Will it not be received,   75
When we have marked with blood those sleepy two
Of his own chamber and used their very daggers,
That they have done't?
LADY MACBETH   Who dares receive it other,°   **other:** otherwise
As we shall make our griefs and clamor roar
Upon his death?
MACBETH   I am settled, and bend up   80
Each corporal agent to this terrible feat.

DISCOVERING SHAKESPEARE

(18) Metaphor [1.7.49]: In 1.7.49, Lady Macbeth attacks her husband's masculinity when she says, "When you durst do it, then you were a man." Where else in the scene does she use this same tactic? What effect does it have on Macbeth?

(19) Verse [1.7.73]: At which point in this scene does Macbeth change his mind about killing Duncan? How does the verse help the actor arrive at this new decision?

Away, and mock° the time with fairest show;

mock: delude

False face must hide what the false heart doth know.

Exeunt.

❧ **2.1°** *Enter Banquo, and Fleance, with a torch before him.*

2.1: Another room in Macbeth's castle

BANQUO

How goes the night, boy?

FLEANCE

The moon is down; I have not heard the clock.

BANQUO

And she goes down at twelve.

FLEANCE

I take't, 'tis later, sir.

BANQUO

Hold, take my sword. There's husbandry° in heaven;   **husbandry:** economy   5

Their candles are all out. Take thee that too.

A heavy summons° lies like lead upon me,   **summons:** signal to sleep

And yet I would not sleep. Merciful powers,

Restrain in me the cursèd thoughts that nature

Gives way to in repose.   10

Enter Macbeth, and a Servant with a torch.

Give me my sword!

Who's there?

MACBETH

A friend.

BANQUO

What, sir, not yet at rest? The king's abed.

He hath been in unusual pleasure and

Sent forth great largess to your offices.°   **largess . . . offices:** gifts to your household staff   15

This diamond he greets your wife withal

By the name of most kind hostess, and shut up°   **shut up:** concluded

In measureless content.

MACBETH   Being unprepared,

Our will° became the servant to defect,°   **will:** good will; **defect:** deficient means

Which else should free have wrought.°   **should . . . wrought:** would have worked liberally   20

BANQUO   All's well.

I dreamt last night of the three weïrd sisters.

To you they have showed some truth.

MACBETH   I think not of them.

Yet when we can entreat an hour to serve,

We would spend it in some words upon that business,

If you would grant the time.   25

BANQUO   At your kind'st leisure.

DISCOVERING SHAKESPEARE

(20) Plot [2.1.22]: Many scholars feel that during the brief conversation between Banquo and Macbeth in 2.1.21–31, Macbeth realizes he will eventually have to kill his good friend. What happens during this discussion that might lead Macbeth to such a bloody conclusion?

MACBETH
  If you shall cleave to my consent, when 'tis,°
  It shall make honor for you.

cleave . . . 'tis: support my interests at the proper time

BANQUO   So I lose none
  In seeking to augment it, but still keep
  My bosom franchised° and allegiance clear,
  I shall be counseled.°

franchised: free of obligations
be counseled: take your advice   30

MACBETH   Good repose the while.
BANQUO
  Thanks, sir. The like to you.

Exeunt Banquo [and Fleance].

MACBETH   *[To Servant]*
  Go bid thy mistress, when my drink is ready,
  She strike upon the bell. Get thee to bed. *Exit [Servant].*
  Is this a dagger which I see before me,
  The handle toward my hand? Come, let me clutch thee.   35
  I have thee not, and yet I see thee still.
  Art thou not, fatal vision, sensible
  To feeling as to sight? or art thou but
  A dagger of the mind, a false creation
  Proceeding from the heat-oppressèd° brain?

heat-oppressèd: overheated   40

  I see thee yet, in form as palpable
  As this which now I draw.
  Thou marshal'st me the way that I was going,
  And such an instrument I was to use.
  Mine eyes are made the fools o'° th' other senses,

made the fools o': playing tricks on   45

  Or else worth all the rest. I see thee still,
  And on thy blade and dudgeon° gouts° of blood,

dudgeon: handle; **gouts:** spots

  Which was not so before. There's no such thing.
  It is the bloody business which informs°

informs: (1) reports, (2) takes shape

  Thus to mine eyes. Now o'er the one half-world   50
  Nature seems dead, and wicked dreams abuse
  The curtained sleep. Witchcraft celebrates
  Pale Hecate's offerings;° and withered murder,

Hecate's offerings: worship of Hecate, goddess of the moon and of witchcraft

  Alarumed° by his sentinel, the wolf,

Alarumed: given the signal   55

  Whose howl's his watch, thus with his stealthy pace,
  With Tarquin's° ravishing side,° towards his design

Tarquin: Sextus Tarquinius, the ancient Roman king who raped the chaste Lucretia (the story is recounted in Shakespeare's poem *The Rape of Lucrece*); **side:** arrogance

  Moves like a ghost. Thou sure and firm-set earth,
  Hear not my steps which way they walk, for fear
  Thy very stones prate of my whereabout
  And take the present horror from the time,°

take . . . time: i.e., break the silence and thus disrupt the horror appropriate to the moment   60

  Which now suits with it. Whiles I threat, he lives;
  Words to the heat of deeds too cold breath gives.
  A bell rings.
  I go, and it is done. The bell invites me.
  Hear it not, Duncan, for it is a knell
  That summons thee to heaven, or to hell.   *Exit.*   65

DISCOVERING SHAKESPEARE

(21) Staging [2.1.50]: How do you think this "dagger scene" (2.1.34–65) should be staged? Does Macbeth actually see a dagger? If so, is it a projection on stage, a part of the set, or is it drawn from his own scabbard? Or is the dagger an illusion, a product of his vivid imagination? How would each of these theatrical choices affect an audience? Which choice would be best?

🔊 **2.2** *Enter Lady [Macbeth].*

LADY MACBETH
  That which hath made them drunk hath made me bold;
  What hath quenched them hath given me fire. *[An owl*
    shrieks.] Hark! Peace.
  It was the owl that shrieked, the fatal bellman°   **bellman:** night watchman
  Which gives the stern'st good-night. He is about it.
  The doors are open, and the surfeited grooms   5
  Do mock their charge with snores. I have drugged their
    possets,°   **possets:** warm milk with spices and liquor
  That° death and nature do contend about them   **That:** so that
  Whether they live or die.
MACBETH *[Within]*   Who's there? What, ho?
LADY MACBETH
  Alack, I am afraid they have awaked,
  And 'tis not done. Th' attempt, and not the deed,   10
  Confounds° us. Hark! I laid their daggers ready –   **Confounds:** defeats
  He could not miss 'em. Had he not resembled
  My father as he slept, I had done't.
    Enter Macbeth [with two bloody daggers].   My husband!
MACBETH
  I have done the deed. Didst thou not hear a noise?
LADY MACBETH
  I heard the owl scream and the crickets cry.   15
  Did not you speak?
MACBETH When?
LADY MACBETH Now.
MACBETH As I descended?
LADY MACBETH Ay.   20
MACBETH Hark! Who lies i' th' second chamber?
LADY MACBETH Donalbain.
MACBETH This is a sorry sight.
LADY MACBETH
  A foolish thought to say a sorry sight.
MACBETH
  There's one did laugh in's sleep, and one cried "Murder!"   25
  That° they did wake each other. I stood and heard them.   **That:** so that
  But they did say their prayers and addressed them°   **addressed them:** prepared
  Again to sleep.
LADY MACBETH   There are two lodged together.
MACBETH
  One cried "God bless us" and "Amen" the other,
  As° they had seen me with these hangman's hands.°   **As:** as if; **hangman's hands:** executioner's   30
  List'ning their fear, I could not say "Amen"   hands (hence, bloody)
  When they did say "God bless us."
LADY MACBETH   Consider it not so deeply.

DISCOVERING SHAKESPEARE

(22) Shared Lines [2.2.16]: In 2.2.13–24, Shakespeare again uses shared lines for theatrical effect. Try reading these lines with a partner. What impact do they have on the relationship between Macbeth and Lady Macbeth? Where does this scene speed up, and where does it slow down? Why?

MACBETH
But wherefore could not I pronounce "Amen"?
I had most need of blessing, and "Amen"
Stuck in my throat.   35
LADY MACBETH   These deeds must not be thought
After these ways; so, it will make us mad.
MACBETH
Methought I heard a voice cry "Sleep no more!
Macbeth does murder sleep" – the innocent sleep,
Sleep that knits up the raveled sleave° of care,   **knits . . . sleave:** smoothes the tangled skein   40
The death of each day's life, sore labor's bath,
Balm of hurt minds, great nature's second course,°   **second course:** the main, and most satisfying
Chief nourisher in life's feast.   course (sleep, after labor)
LADY MACBETH   What do you mean?
MACBETH
Still it cried "Sleep no more!" to all the house;
"Glamis hath murdered sleep, and therefore Cawdor   45
Shall sleep no more, Macbeth shall sleep no more."
LADY MACBETH
Who was it that thus cried? Why, worthy thane,
You do unbend° your noble strength to think   **unbend:** slacken
So brainsickly of things. Go get some water
And wash this filthy witness° from your hand.   **witness:** evidence   50
Why did you bring these daggers from the place?
They must lie there: go carry them and smear
The sleepy grooms with blood.
MACBETH   I'll go no more.
I am afraid to think what I have done;
Look on't again I dare not.   55
LADY MACBETH   Infirm of purpose!
Give me the daggers. The sleeping and the dead
Are but as pictures. 'Tis the eye of childhood
That fears a painted devil. If he do bleed,
I'll gild° the faces of the grooms withal,   **gild:** paint
For it must seem their guilt.   *Exit.*   60
     Knock within.
MACBETH   Whence is that knocking?
How is't with me when every noise appalls me?
What hands are here? Ha! they pluck out mine eyes.
Will all great Neptune's ocean wash this blood
Clean from my hand? No, this my hand will rather
The multitudinous seas incarnadine,°   **incarnadine:** redden   65
Making the green one° red.   **the green one:** Neptune's ocean (l. 63); most
     Enter Lady [Macbeth].   editors, following Johnson, take "one" to mean
LADY MACBETH   "uniformly," but F has a comma after "one"
My hands are of your color, but I shame

DISCOVERING SHAKESPEARE

(23) Imagery [2.2.38]: In this scene, Macbeth introduces the <u>theme</u> of "sleep" (2.2.38), which reappears frequently throughout the play. As you read through the rest of the script, record every instance of the <u>theme</u> that you find. How do these sleep <u>images</u> change as the play progresses?

(24) Teaser [2.2.65]: In 2.2.65, Macbeth complains that the blood on his hands is enough to stain "The multitudinous seas incarnadine." Did Shakespeare originate this concept of guilt incapable of being washed clean, or was the expression proverbial by his time?

To wear a heart so white.
  Knock.   I hear a knocking
At the south entry. Retire we to our chamber.
A little water clears us of this deed.   70
How easy is it then! Your constancy
Hath left you unattended.°   **left you unattended:** deserted you
  Knock.   Hark, more knocking.
Get on your nightgown,° lest occasion call us   **nightgown:** dressing gown
And show us to be watchers.° Be not lost   **watchers:** i.e., awake
So poorly in your thoughts.   75
MACBETH
To know my deed, 'twere best not know myself.
  Knock.
Wake Duncan with thy knocking – I would thou
couldst.   *Exeunt.*

ሴ **2.3** *Enter a Porter. Knocking within.*

PORTER   Here's a knocking indeed. If a man were porter
of hell gate, he should have old° turning the key.   **old:** too much
(Knock.) Knock, knock, knock. Who's there, i' th' name
of Beelzebub?° Here's a farmer that hanged himself on th'   **Beelzebub:** one of the biblical devils
expectation of plenty.° Come in time° – have napkins   **farmer . . . plenty:** (because a crop surplus   5
enow° about you; here you'll sweat for't. *(Knock.)* Knock,   would lower prices and diminish his profit);
knock. Who's there, in th' other devil's name? Faith,   **Come in time:** you've come at the right time
here's an equivocator,° that could swear in both the scales   **napkins enow:** enough handkerchiefs (to wipe
against either scale; who committed treason enough for   away the sweat caused by hellfire)
God's sake, yet could not equivocate to heaven. O come   **equivocator:** deceiver, prevaricator (here
in, equivocator. *(Knock.)* Knock, knock, knock. Who's   alluding to the equivocating testimony given by   10
there? Faith, here's an English tailor come hither for   the Jesuit conspirators in the Gunpowder Plot,
stealing out of a French hose.° Come in, tailor. Here you   1605)
may roast your goose.°   *(Knock.)* Knock, knock. Never at   **stealing . . . hose:** (probably skimping on
quiet! What are you? – But this place is too cold for hell.   material in the making of French hose, which
I'll devil-porter it no further. I had thought to have let   were tight-fitting, and hence would lead to
in some of all professions that go the primrose way to th'   discovery)   15
everlasting bonfire. *(Knock.)* Anon, anon! *[Opens the*   **roast your goose:** heat your iron (a goose is a
door.] I pray you remember° the porter.   long-handled tailor's iron)
  Enter Macduff and Lennox.   **remember:** i.e., tip
MACDUFF
Was it so late, friend, ere you went to bed,   20
That you do lie so late?
PORTER   Faith, sir, we were carousing till the second
cock;° and drink, sir, is a great provoker of three things.   **second cock:** second crowing of the cock (i.e.,
MACDUFF   What three things does drink especially pro-   till early morning)
voke?
                                                                 25
PORTER   Marry, sir, nose-painting,° sleep, and urine.   **nose-painting:** i.e., a red nose (from habitual
Lechery, sir, it provokes, and unprovokes: it provokes   drunkenness)
the desire, but it takes away the performance. Therefore

DISCOVERING SHAKESPEARE

(25) <u>Staging</u> [2.3.10]: How should the Porter scene (2.3) be staged? What does the Porter look like? How is he dressed?
How does he act on stage? How bawdy should he be? And which references in his opening speech could be directed to
specific people in the audience (i.e., "Here's a farmer . . .")?

much drink may be said to be an equivocator with lechery: it makes him, and it mars him; it sets him on, and it takes him off; it persuades him, and disheartens him; makes him stand to,° and not stand to; in conclusion, equivocates him in a sleep,° and, giving him the lie,° leaves him.

MACDUFF   I believe drink gave thee the lie° last night.

PORTER   That it did, sir, i' the very throat° on me; but I requited him for his lie; and, I think, being too strong for him, though he took up my legs° sometime, yet made a shift to cast° him.

MACDUFF   Is thy master stirring?

Enter Macbeth.

Our knocking has awaked him: here he comes.

LENNOX

Good morrow, noble sir.

MACBETH   Good morrow, both.

MACDUFF

Is the king stirring, worthy thane?

MACBETH   Not yet.

MACDUFF

He did command me to call timely° on him;
I have almost slipped° the hour.

MACBETH   I'll bring you to him.

MACDUFF

I know this is a joyful trouble to you;
But yet 'tis one.

MACBETH

The labor we delight in physics pain.°
This is the door.

MACDUFF   I'll make so bold to call,
For 'tis my limited° service.   *Exit Macduff.*

LENNOX

Goes the king hence today?

MACBETH   He does – he did appoint so.

LENNOX

The night has been unruly. Where we lay,
Our chimneys were blown down; and, as they say,
Lamentings heard i' th' air, strange screams of death,
And prophesying, with accents terrible,
Of dire combustion° and confused events
New hatched to th' woeful time. The obscure bird°
Clamored the livelong night. Some say the earth
Was feverous and did shake.

MACBETH   'Twas a rough night.

LENNOX

My young remembrance cannot parallel
A fellow to it.

Enter Macduff.

30	

stand to: grow erect
equivocates . . . sleep: i.e., satisfies him only by putting him to sleep;
giving . . . lie: (1) deceiving him (because he cannot perform sexually), (2) overthrowing him, (3) making him lose his erection, (4) accusing him of lying
gave thee the lie: (1) made you a liar, (2) made you fall down
i' the very throat: (to lie in the throat was to lie egregiously)
took up my legs: (1) made me fall down from drunkenness, (2) overthrew me in wrestling
cast: throw

timely: early
slipped: missed

physics pain: cures the trouble it gives us

limited: appointed

combustion: tumult
obscure bird: i.e., the owl

DISCOVERING SHAKESPEARE

(26) Characterization [2.3.40]: How should Macbeth behave when he enters this scene at line 40? How long ago did the murders occur? How much time has he had to change his clothes and wash off Duncan's blood?

MACDUFF

O horror, horror, horror –
Tongue nor heart cannot conceive nor name thee!

MACBETH AND LENNOX   What's the matter?

MACDUFF

Confusion° now hath made his masterpiece:
Most sacrilegious murder hath broke ope
The Lord's anointed temple and stole thence
The life o' th' building!

Confusion: destruction   65

MACBETH   What is't you say? the life?

LENNOX

Mean you his majesty?

MACDUFF

Approach the chamber and destroy your sight   70
With a new Gorgon.° Do not bid me speak.
See, and then speak yourselves.

Gorgon: Medusa, a mythical monster whose
terrible aspect turned those who saw her to stone

                    Exeunt Macbeth and Lennox.
                    Awake, awake!
Ring the alarum bell! Murder and treason!
Banquo and Donalbain! Malcolm, awake!
Shake off this downy sleep, death's counterfeit,   75
And look on death itself. Up, up, and see
The great doom's° image. Malcolm! Banquo!
As from your graves rise up and walk like sprites°
To countenance° this horror.

great doom: the Last Judgment
sprites: ghosts
countenance: appear in keeping with

    Bell rings. Enter Lady [Macbeth].

LADY MACBETH   What's the business,
That such a hideous trumpet calls to parley   80
The sleepers of the house? Speak, speak!

MACDUFF   O gentle lady,
'Tis not for you to hear what I can speak:
The repetition in a woman's ear
Would murder as it fell.

    Enter Banquo.   O Banquo, Banquo,
Our royal master's murdered!   85

LADY MACBETH   Woe, alas –
What, in our house?

BANQUO   Too cruel anywhere.
Dear Duff, I prithee contradict thyself
And say it is not so.

    Enter Macbeth, Lennox, and Ross.

MACBETH

Had I but died an hour before this chance,
I had lived a blessèd time; for from this instant   90
There's nothing serious in mortality:°
All is but toys.° Renown and grace is dead,
The wine of life is drawn, and the mere lees°
Is left this vault° to brag of.

    Enter Malcolm and Donalbain.

mortality: human life
toys: trifles
lees: dregs
vault: (1) world (with its *vault* the sky), (2) wine
cellar

DISCOVERING SHAKESPEARE

(27) Language [2.3.65]: After Macduff has discovered Duncan's slain body (2.3.65), why is his language so stilted? How could an actor make these lines sound fresh and natural on stage?

(28) Irony [2.3.84]: In 2.3.82–84, Macduff refuses to tell Lady Macbeth that Duncan is dead because "The repetition in a woman's ear / Would murder as it fell." To what extent is this statement <u>ironic</u>? How sexist is it?

DONALBAIN
  What is amiss?   95

MACBETH   You are, and do not know't.
  The spring, the head, the fountain of your blood
  Is stopped, the very source of it is stopped.

MACDUFF
  Your royal father's murdered.

MALCOLM   O, by whom?

LENNOX
  Those of his chamber, as it seemed, had done't.
  Their hands and faces were all badged° with blood;   **badged:** marked   100
  So were their daggers, which unwiped we found
  Upon their pillows. They stared and were distracted.
  No man's life was to be trusted with them.

MACBETH
  O, yet I do repent me of my fury
  That I did kill them.   105

MACDUFF   Wherefore did you so?

MACBETH
  Who can be wise, amazed, temp'rate and furious,
  Loyal and neutral,° in a moment? No man.   **Loyal and neutral:** loyal to Duncan and
  The expedition° of my violent love   impartial on the question of the grooms' guilt
  Outrun the pauser, reason. Here lay Duncan,   **expedition:** haste
  His silver skin laced with his golden blood;   110
  And his gashed stabs looked like a breach in nature
  For ruin's wasteful entrance: there, the murderers,
  Steeped in the colors of their trade, their daggers
  Unmannerly breeched° with gore. Who could refrain   **Unmannerly breeched:** indecently garbed
  That had a heart to love, and in that heart   115
  Courage to make's love known?

LADY MACBETH   Help me hence, ho!

MACDUFF
  Look to° the lady.   **Look to:** look after

MALCOLM   *[Aside to Donalbain]*
                Why do we hold our tongues,
  That most may claim this argument for ours?°   **argument for ours:** matter as chiefly our
                                                        concern

DONALBAIN   *[To Malcolm]*
  What should be spoken here,
  Where our fate, hid in an auger hole,°   **auger hole:** i.e., any tiny cranny   120
  May rush and seize us? Let's away:
  Our tears are not yet brewed.

MALCOLM   *[To Donalbain]*   Nor our strong sorrow
  Upon the foot of motion.°   **Upon . . . motion:** yet in motion

BANQUO   Look to the lady.
                [Lady Macbeth is assisted out.]
  And when we have our naked frailties hid,°   **frailties hid:** bodies clothed
  That suffer in exposure, let us meet   125
  And question° this most bloody piece of work,   **question:** discuss
  To know it further. Fears and scruples° shake us.   **scruples:** doubts
  In the great hand of God I stand, and thence
  Against the undivulged pretense° I fight   **undivulged pretense:** secret purposes
  Of treasonous malice.   130

DISCOVERING SHAKESPEARE

(29) Plot [2.3.116]: Why does Lady Macbeth faint in 2.3.116? What is she trying to cover up?

MACDUFF　　　　　　And so do I.

ALL　　　　　　　　　　So all.

MACBETH
Let's briefly put on manly readiness
And meet i' th' hall together.

ALL　　　　　　　　Well contented.

Exeunt [all but Malcolm and Donalbain].

MALCOLM
What will you do? Let's not consort with them.
To show an unfelt sorrow is an office
Which the false man does easy. I'll to England.　　　　　　135

DONALBAIN
To Ireland I. Our separated fortune
Shall keep us both the safer. Where we are
There's daggers in men's smiles; the near° in blood,
The nearer bloody.°

MALCOLM　　　　　This murderous shaft that's shot
Hath not yet lighted,° and our safest way
Is to avoid the aim. Therefore to horse,
And let us not be dainty of° leave-taking
But shift° away. There's warrant° in that theft
Which steals itself when there's no mercy left.　　　*Exeunt.*

near: nearer
the near . . . bloody: i.e., the closer we are to Duncan in blood, the more likely we are to be killed　　140
lighted: landed

dainty of: scrupulous about
shift: steal; **warrant:** justification

❧ **2.4**° *Enter Ross with an Old Man.*

2.4: Somewhere outside the castle

OLD MAN
Threescore and ten° I can remember well;
Within the volume of which time I have seen
Hours dreadful and things strange, but this sore night
Hath trifled former knowings.°

ROSS　　　　　　Ha, good father,
Thou seest the heavens, as troubled with man's act,°
Threatens his bloody stage. By th' clock 'tis day,
And yet dark night strangles the traveling lamp.°
Is't night's predominance,° or the day's shame,
That darkness does the face of earth entomb
When living light should kiss it?

OLD MAN　　　　　　　　　'Tis unnatural,
Even like the deed that's done. On Tuesday last
A falcon, tow'ring° in her pride of place,
Was by a mousing owl° hawked at° and killed.

ROSS
And Duncan's horses – a thing most strange and
　certain –
Beauteous and swift, the minions° of their race,
Turned wild in nature, broke their stalls, flung out,°
Contending 'gainst obedience, as they would make
War with mankind.

Threescore and ten: seventy years

trifled . . . knowings: made former experiences seem trifling
as . . . act: as if troubled by the actions of men　　5

traveling lamp: i.e., the sun
predominance: powerful influence

10

tow'ring: soaring
mousing owl: owl that preys on mice (a mere domestic predator); **hawked at:** caught on the wing

minions: favorites (the most highly prized)　　15
flung out: lunged about

DISCOVERING SHAKESPEARE

(30) Paraphrase [2.3.138]: Paraphrase the following lines by Donalbain: "the near in blood, / The nearer bloody" (2.3.138–139). How do these lines help us understand why Malcolm and Donalbain decide to flee Scotland?

(31) Verse [2.4.10]: Scan lines 2.4.10–21 by the Old Man and Ross; then analyze how the fractured meter of these lines mimics the chaos in the natural world described in these speeches.

OLD MAN   'Tis said they ate each other.
ROSS
  They did so, to th' amazement of mine eyes
  That looked upon't.
    Enter Macduff.   Here comes the good Macduff.   20
  How goes the world, sir, now?
MACDUFF   Why, see you not?
ROSS
  Is't known who did this more than bloody deed?
MACDUFF
  Those that Macbeth hath slain.
ROSS   Alas the day,
  What good could they pretend?°   **pretend:** expect
MACDUFF   They were suborned.°   **suborned:** bribed
  Malcolm and Donalbain, the king's two sons,   25
  Are stol'n away and fled, which puts upon them
  Suspicion of the deed.
ROSS   'Gainst nature still.
  Thriftless° ambition, that will ravin up°   **Thriftless:** wasteful; **ravin up:** greedily devour
  Thine own life's means! Then 'tis most like°   **like:** likely
  The sovereignty will fall upon Macbeth.   30
MACDUFF
  He is already named,° and gone to Scone°   **named:** chosen; **Scone:** (where Scottish kings
  To be invested.°   traditionally were crowned; near Perth)
ROSS   Where is Duncan's body?   **invested:** crowned
MACDUFF
  Carried to Colmekill,°   **Colmekill:** (the island of Iona, in the Hebrides,
  The sacred storehouse of his predecessors   burial place of the ancient Scottish kings)
  And guardian of their bones.
ROSS   Will you to Scone?   35
MACDUFF
  No, cousin, I'll to Fife.
ROSS   Well, I will thither.
MACDUFF
  Well, may you see things well done there. Adieu,
  Lest our old robes sit easier than our new.
ROSS
  Farewell, father.
OLD MAN
  God's benison° go with you, and with those   **benison:** blessing   40
  That would make good of bad, and friends of foes.
                                   Exeunt omnes.

❧ **3.1**° *Enter Banquo.*   **3.1:** The royal castle at Forres

BANQUO
  Thou hast it now – king, Cawdor, Glamis, all,
  As the weïrd women promised; and I fear
  Thou play'dst most foully for't. Yet it was said
  It should not stand in thy posterity,°   **stand . . . posterity:** continue through your heirs

---

DISCOVERING SHAKESPEARE

(32) Paraphrase [3.1.1]: Paraphrase Banquo's soliloquy at the top of 3.1 (lines 1–10). How does he feel about the Witches' prophecy? Does he suspect Macbeth of foul play? Why do you think so?

But that myself should be the root and father   5
Of many kings. If there come truth from them –
As upon thee, Macbeth, their speeches shine° –   **shine:** look auspicious
Why, by the verities on thee made good,
May they not be my oracles as well
And set me up in hope? But hush, no more.   10
   Sennet° sounded. Enter Macbeth as King, Lady   **Sennet:** trumpet salute
   [Macbeth as Queen], Lennox, Ross, Lords, and
   Attendants.
MACBETH
   Here's our chief guest.
LADY MACBETH   If he had been forgotten,
   It had been as a gap in our great feast,
   And all-thing° unbecoming.   **all-thing:** altogether
MACBETH
   Tonight we hold a solemn supper,° sir,   **solemn supper:** formal banquet
   And I'll request your presence.   15
BANQUO   Let your highness
   Command upon me, to the which my duties
   Are with a most indissoluble tie
   Forever knit.
MACBETH   Ride you this afternoon?
BANQUO
   Ay, my good lord.
MACBETH
   We should have else desired your good advice,   20
   Which still° hath been both grave and prosperous,°   **still:** always; **prosperous:** profitable
   In this day's council; but we'll take tomorrow.
   Is't far you ride?
BANQUO
   As far, my lord, as will fill up the time
   'Twixt this and supper. Go not my horse the better,°   **Go . . . better:** i.e., unless my horse goes faster   25
   I must become a borrower of° the night   than anticipated
   For a dark hour or twain.   **borrower of:** i.e., borrower of time from
MACBETH   Fail not our feast.
BANQUO
   My lord, I will not.
MACBETH
   We hear our bloody cousins are bestowed
   In England and in Ireland, not confessing   30
   Their cruel parricide, filling their hearers
   With strange invention.° But of that tomorrow,   **invention:** falsehoods
   When therewithal we shall have cause of state
   Craving us jointly.° Hie you to horse. Adieu,   **cause . . . jointly:** state business requiring our
   Till you return at night. Goes Fleance with you?   joint attention   35
BANQUO
   Ay, my good lord. Our time does call upon's.
MACBETH
   I wish your horses swift and sure of foot,
   And so I do commend you to their backs.

DISCOVERING SHAKESPEARE

(33) Plot [3.1.29]: Whom does Macbeth blame for the murder of Duncan? How has he used their flight from Scotland to his advantage?

Farewell.   *Exit Banquo.*
Let every man be master of his time   40
Till seven at night. To make society
The sweeter welcome, we will keep ourself
Till suppertime alone. While° then, God be with you.   **While:** until
                        Exeunt Lords [and others].
[To Servant]
Sirrah,° a word with you. Attend those men   **Sirrah:** (form of address to an inferior)
Our pleasure?°   **Attend . . . pleasure:** are those men awaiting   45
                                                    my orders
SERVANT
They are, my lord, without the palace gate.
MACBETH
Bring them before us.   *Exit Servant.*
To be thus is nothing, but° to be safely thus.   **but:** unless
Our fears in Banquo° stick deep,°   **in Banquo:** about Banquo; **stick deep:** are
And in his royalty of nature° reigns that   deep-seated   50
Which would be° feared. 'Tis much he dares;   **royalty of nature:** royal nature
And to that dauntless temper of his mind   **would be:** deserves to be
He hath a wisdom that doth guide his valor
To act in safety. There is none but he
Whose being I do fear; and under him   55
My genius is rebuked,° as it is said   **genius is rebuked:** guiding spirit is daunted
Mark Antony's was by Caesar. He chid the sisters
When first they put the name of king upon me,
And bade them speak to him. Then, prophetlike,
They hailed him father to a line of kings.   60
Upon my head they placed a fruitless crown
And put a barren scepter in my grip,
Thence to be wrenched with an unlineal hand,
No son of mine succeeding. If't be so,
For Banquo's issue have I filed° my mind;   **filed:** defiled   65
For them the gracious Duncan have I murdered;
Put rancors° in the vessel of my peace   **rancors:** hatreds
Only for them, and mine eternal jewel°   **eternal jewel:** immortal soul
Given to the common enemy of man°   **common enemy of man:** i.e., Satan
To make them kings – the seeds of Banquo kings.   70
Rather than so, come, Fate, into the list,°   **list:** lists (the tournament field where knights
And champion° me to th' utterance.° Who's there?   answered challenges)
                                                    champion: (1) defend, (2) challenge;
Enter Servant and two Murderers.   **champion . . . utterance:** (1) support me to the
[To Servant]   utmost, (2) fight with me to the death;
Now go to the door and stay there till we call.
                        Exit Servant.
Was it not yesterday we spoke together?
MURDERERS
It was, so please your highness.   75
MACBETH   Well then, now
Have you considered of my speeches? Know
That it was he, in the times past, which held you
So under fortune,° which you thought had been   **under fortune:** out of favor with fortune
Our innocent self. This I made good to you

DISCOVERING SHAKESPEARE

(34) Teaser [3.1.56]: In which Shakespearean play is Mark Antony "rebuked" by Octavius Caesar (3.1.56)? (*Hint:* The correct answer is not *Julius Caesar.*)

In our last conference, passed in probation with° you | **passed in probation with:** proved to | 80
How you were borne in hand,° how crossed;° the instru- | **borne in hand:** manipulated, deceived;
ments;° | **crossed:** thwarted; **instruments:** agents
Who wrought° with them; and all things else that might | **wrought:** worked
To half a soul° and to a notion crazed° | **half a soul:** (even) a half-wit; **notion crazed:** insane mind
Say "Thus did Banquo."

FIRST MURDERER   You made it known to us.

MACBETH
I did so; and went further, which is now | | 85
Our point of° second meeting. Do you find | **Our point of:** the point of our
Your patience so predominant in your nature
That you can let this go? Are you so gospeled° | **gospeled:** religious
To pray for this good man and for his issue,
Whose heavy hand hath bowed you to the grave | | 90
And beggared yours° forever? | **yours:** your families

FIRST MURDERER   We are men, my liege.

MACBETH
Ay, in the catalogue° ye go for men, | **catalogue:** inventory, classification
As hounds and greyhounds, mongrels, spaniels, curs,° | **curs:** watchdogs or sheep dogs
Shoughs,° waterrugs,° and demiwolves are clept° | **shoughs:** lapdogs; **waterrugs:** long-haired water dogs; **clept:** called
All by the name of dogs. The valued file° | **valued file:** list of valued qualities | 95
Distinguishes the swift, the slow, the subtle,
The housekeeper,° the hunter, every one | **housekeeper:** watchdog
According to the gift which bounteous nature
Hath in him closed,° whereby he does receive | **closed:** incorporated
Particular addition, from the bill° | **addition . . . bill:** distinction, contrary to the catalogue | 100
That writes them all alike; and so of men.
Now, if you have a station in the file,° | **station . . . file:** place on the list
Not i' th' worst rank of manhood, say't;
And I will put that business in your bosoms° | **bosoms:** trust
Whose execution takes your enemy off,° | **execution . . . off:** accomplishment kills your enemy | 105
Grapples you to the heart and love of us,
Who wear our health but sickly in his life,
Which in his death were perfect.

SECOND MURDERER   I am one, my liege,
Whom the vile blows and buffets of the world
Have so incensed that I am reckless what | | 110
I do to spite the world.

FIRST MURDERER   And I another,
So weary with disasters, tugged with fortune,
That I would set° my life on any chance | **set:** risk
To mend it or be rid on't.° | **on't:** of it

MACBETH   Both of you
Know Banquo was your enemy. | | 115

MURDERERS   True, my lord.

MACBETH
So is he mine, and in such bloody distance° | **distance:** enmity
That every minute of his being thrusts

DISCOVERING SHAKESPEARE

(35) History [3.1.92]: Look up the names of dogs mentioned by Macbeth in 3.1.92–95. How many of these were used for hunting?

(36) Shared Lines [3.1.109]: To what extent do the shared lines between Macbeth and the Murderers in 3.1.109–115 foreshadow their willingness to kill Banquo?

Against my near'st of life;° and though I could
With barefaced power sweep him from my sight
And bid my will avouch° it, yet I must not,
For° certain friends that are both his and mine,
Whose loves I may not drop, but wail° his fall
Who I myself struck down. And thence it is
That I to your assistance do make love,
Masking the business from the common eye
For sundry weighty reasons.

SECOND MURDERER   We shall, my lord,
Perform what you command us.

FIRST MURDERER   Though our lives –

MACBETH
Your spirits shine through you. Within this hour a most
I will advise you where to plant yourselves,
Acquaint you with the perfect spy o' th' time°
The moment on't, for't must be done tonight
And something° from the palace – always thought°
That I require a clearness;° and with him,
To leave no rubs nor botches° in the work,
Fleance his son, that keeps him company,
Whose absence is no less material to me
Than is his father's, must embrace the fate
Of that dark hour. Resolve yourselves apart;
I'll come to you anon.

MURDERERS   We are resolved, my lord.

MACBETH
I'll call upon you straight. Abide within.
It is concluded. Banquo, thy soul's flight,
If it find heaven, must find it out tonight.   *Exeunt.*

❧ **3.2**° *Enter Macbeth's Lady and a Servant.*

LADY MACBETH
Is Banquo gone from court?

SERVANT
Ay, madam, but returns again tonight.

LADY MACBETH
Say to the king I would attend his leisure
For a few words.

SERVANT   Madam, I will.   *Exit.*

LADY MACBETH
Naught's had, all's spent,
Where our desire is got without content.
'Tis safer to be that which we destroy
Than by destruction dwell in doubtful joy.
    Enter Macbeth.
How now, my lord? Why do you keep alone,

---

near'st of life: vital parts

avouch: justify   120
For: because of
wail: I must bewail

                                                         125

Acquaint . . . time: (a famous crux: the general   130
sense is "spy out the perfect time and inform you
of it," but the syntax has not been satisfactorily
explained)
something: some distance; **thought:** bearing
in mind
clearness: alibi   135
rubs nor botches: problems or flaws

                                                         140

3.2: A private chamber in the castle

                                                           5

DISCOVERING SHAKESPEARE

(37) Plot [3.2.3]: The fact that Lady Macbeth must ask a servant to see her husband (3.2.3–4) suggests a growing distance between the two central characters. Can you find any other examples of the separation between Macbeth and Lady Macbeth following the murder of Duncan? What do you think this distance means symbolically in the play?

Of sorriest fancies° your companions making,
Using those thoughts which should indeed have died
With them they think on? Things without all° remedy
Should be without regard. What's done is done.

MACBETH
We have scorched° the snake, not killed it.
She'll close° and be herself, whilst our poor malice°
Remains in danger of her former tooth.
But let the frame of things disjoint,° both the worlds° suffer,
Ere we will eat our meal in fear, and sleep
In the affliction of these terrible dreams
That shake us nightly. Better be with the dead,
Whom we, to gain our peace, have sent to peace,
Than on the torture° of the mind to lie
In restless ecstasy.° Duncan is in his grave;
After life's fitful fever he sleeps well.
Treason has done his worst: nor steel nor poison,
Malice domestic,° foreign levy, nothing,
Can touch him further.

LADY MACBETH   Come on.
Gentle my lord, sleek o'er your rugged looks;
Be bright and jovial among your guests tonight.

MACBETH
So shall I, love; and so, I pray, be you.
Let your remembrance° apply to Banquo;
Present him eminence° both with eye and tongue:
Unsafe the while, that° we must lave°
Our honors in these flattering streams
And make our faces vizards° to our hearts,
Disguising what they are.

LADY MACBETH   You must leave° this.

MACBETH
O, full of scorpions is my mind, dear wife.
Thou know'st that Banquo, and his Fleance, lives.

LADY MACBETH
But in them Nature's copy's° not eterne.°

MACBETH
There's comfort yet; they are assailable.
Then be thou jocund. Ere the bat hath flown
His cloistered flight, ere to black Hecate's summons
The shard-born° beetle with his drowsy hums
Hath rung night's yawning peal, there shall be done
A deed of dreadful note.

LADY MACBETH   What's to be done?

MACBETH
Be innocent of the knowledge, dearest chuck,°
Till thou applaud the deed. Come, seeling° night,

---

sorriest fancies: most painful delusions   10

all: any

scorched: slashed
close: heal; **poor malice:** inadequate evil   15

frame . . . disjoint: structure of the universe collapse; **both the worlds:** heaven and earth

20

torture: rack
ecstasy: frenzy

25

Malice domestic: native evil (rebellion)

30

remembrance: reminder
Present him eminence: do him honor
Unsafe . . . that: while we are unsafe; **lave:** wash
vizards: masks   35

leave: leave off, stop

Nature's copy: Nature's copyhold (their lease on life); **eterne:** eternal

40

shard-born: born in dung

45

chuck: chick (term of affection)
seeling: sewing up, hooding (from falconry)

DISCOVERING SHAKESPEARE

(38) Verse [3.2.25]: In 3.2.25–26, Macbeth's verse expands into eleven-syllable lines. Where else is the verse distorted in this section of the play? Why is it so irregular here?

(39) Paraphrase [3.2.47]: Paraphrase Macbeth's speech in 3.2.46–57, beginning with the phrase "Come, seeling night." How does Macbeth hint at the impending murder of Banquo without actually telling his wife what will happen? Why doesn't he want her to know his specific plan?

Scarf up° the tender eye of pitiful° day,   **Scarf up:** blindfold; **pitiful:** pitying,
And with thy bloody and invisible hand   compassionate
Cancel and tear to pieces that great bond°   **bond:** contract (Banquo's tenure of life)   50
Which keeps me pale. Light thickens, and the crow
Makes wing to th' rooky° wood.   **rooky:** i.e., full of birds
Good things of day begin to droop and drowse,
Whiles night's black agents to their preys do rouse.
Thou marvel'st at my words, but hold thee still;   55
Things bad begun make strong themselves by ill.
So prithee go with me.   *Exeunt.*

❧ **3.3**° *Enter three Murderers.*   **3.3:** Outside the castle

FIRST MURDERER
  But who did bid thee join with us?
THIRD MURDERER   Macbeth.
SECOND MURDERER
  He needs not our mistrust,° since he delivers   **He . . . mistrust:** we need not mistrust this man
  Our offices° and what we have to do   **offices:** duties
  To the direction just.°   **To . . . just:** according to the precise instructions
FIRST MURDERER   Then stand with us.
  The west yet glimmers with some streaks of day.   5
  Now spurs the lated° traveler apace   **lated:** belated
  To gain the timely inn,° and near approaches   **gain . . . inn:** reach the inn in good time
  The subject of our watch.
THIRD MURDERER   Hark, I hear horses.
BANQUO   *[Within]*
  Give us a light there, ho!
SECOND MURDERER
  Then 'tis he: the rest   10
  That are within the note of expectation°   **within . . . expectation:** on the list of those
  Already are i' th' court.   invited
FIRST MURDERER   His horses go about.°   **His . . . about:** i.e., he's walking his horses
THIRD MURDERER
  Almost a mile; but he does usually,
  So all men do, from hence to th' palace gate
  Make it their walk.   15
    Enter Banquo and Fleance, with a torch.
SECOND MURDERER   A light, a light!
THIRD MURDERER   'Tis he.
FIRST MURDERER   Stand to't.
BANQUO
  It will be rain tonight.   20
FIRST MURDERER   Let it come down!
BANQUO
  O, treachery! Fly, good Fleance, fly, fly, fly!
                     [Exit Fleance.]
  Thou mayst revenge – O slave!
  [Banquo slain.]

DISCOVERING SHAKESPEARE

(40) <u>Staging</u> [3.3.15]: Where do the Murderers hide on stage? How is Banquo killed? How does Fleance escape? Draw a diagram of all the entrances and exits during this <u>scene</u>. Where does the murder actually take place on stage?

THIRD MURDERER
Who did strike out the light?
FIRST MURDERER   Was't not the way?°

Was't . . . way: wasn't that the plan

THIRD MURDERER
There's but one down: the son is fled.
SECOND MURDERER
We have lost best half of our affair.

25

FIRST MURDERER
Well, let's away, and say how much is done.   *Exeunt.*

❧ **3.4**° *Banquet prepared. Enter Macbeth, Lady [Macbeth], Ross, Lennox, Lords, and Attendants.*

3.4: The great hall of the palace

MACBETH
You know your own degrees° – sit down:
At first and last the hearty welcome.

degrees: relative rank, order of precedence

LORDS
Thanks to your majesty.
MACBETH
Ourself will mingle with society°
And play the humble host.

society: the company

5

Our hostess keeps her state,° but in best time
We will require her welcome.

keeps her state: remains seared in her chair of state

LADY MACBETH
Pronounce it for me, sir, to all our friends,
For my heart speaks they are welcome.
        Enter First Murderer.
MACBETH
See, they encounter° thee with their hearts' thanks.

encounter: greet

10

Both sides are even. Here I'll sit i' th' midst.
Be large in mirth; anon we'll drink a measure
The table round.
        [Goes to Murderer.]
There's blood upon thy face.
FIRST MURDERER   'Tis Banquo's then.
MACBETH
'Tis better thee without than he within.
Is he dispatched?

15

FIRST MURDERER   My lord, his throat is cut:
That I did for him.
MACBETH   Thou art the best o' th' cutthroats.
Yet he's good that did the like for Fleance:
If thou didst it, thou art the nonpareil.°

nonpareil: absolute best

FIRST MURDERER
Most royal sir, Fleance is scaped.

20

MACBETH
Then comes my fit again. I had else been perfect;°
Whole as the marble, founded° as the rock,
As broad and general° as the casing° air.

perfect: flawless
founded: solidly based
broad and general: unconfined and omnipresent; **casing:** enveloping

---

DISCOVERING SHAKESPEARE

(41) <u>Shared Lines</u> [3.4.16]: What physical action or gesture could the First Murderer do during his speech to Macbeth in 3.4.16–17? Why do you think that would be appropriate?

But now I am cabined,° cribbed,° confined, bound in
To saucy° doubts and fears. But Banquo's safe?°

FIRST MURDERER
Ay, my good lord. Safe in a ditch he bides,
With twenty trenchèd° gashes on his head,
The least a death to nature.

MACBETH   Thanks for that.
There the grown serpent lies; the worm° that's fled
Hath nature that in time will venom breed,
No teeth for th' present. Get thee gone. Tomorrow
We'll hear ourselves° again.   *Exit Murderer.*

LADY MACBETH   My royal lord,
You do not give the cheer.° The feast is sold°
That is not often vouched,° while 'tis a-making,
'Tis given with welcome. To feed were best at home;°
From thence,° the sauce to meat is ceremony:
Meeting were bare without it.

MACBETH   Sweet remembrancer!
Now good digestion wait on appetite,
And health on both.

LENNOX   May't please your highness sit.

MACBETH
Here had we now our country's honor roofed
Were the graced person of our Banquo present –
Enter the Ghost of Banquo, and sits in Macbeth's place.
Who may I rather challenge for° unkindness
Than pity for mischance.

ROSS   His absence, sir,
Lays blame upon his promise. Please't your highness
To grace us with your royal company?

MACBETH
The table's full.

LENNOX   Here is a place reserved, sir.

MACBETH
Where?

LENNOX
Here, my good lord. What is't that moves your highness?

MACBETH
Which of you have done this?

LORDS
What, my good lord?

MACBETH
Thou canst not say I did it. Never shake
Thy gory locks at me.

ROSS
Gentlemen, rise. His highness is not well.

LADY MACBETH
Sit, worthy friends. My lord is often thus,
And hath been from his youth. Pray you keep seat.
The fit is momentary; upon a thought

---

cabined: pent up; **cribbed:** boxed in
saucy: insolent; **safe:** safely disposed of (i.e., dead)   25

trenchèd: deep-furrowed

worm: snake
                                          30

hear ourselves: speak together

give the cheer: toast the company; **sold:** i.e., not freely given
vouched: affirmed   35
To . . . home: i.e., mere eating is best done at home
From thence: away from home

                                          40

challenge for: accuse of

                                          45

                                          50

                                          55

DISCOVERING SHAKESPEARE

(42) Shared Lines [3.4.46]: How do the shared lines and short lines in 3.4.46–54 help increase the tension in this scene?

He will again be well. If much you note him,
You shall offend him and extend his passion.°   **extend his passion:** prolong his seizure
Feed, and regard him not. – Are you a man?

MACBETH
Ay, and a bold one, that dare look on that   60
Which might appall the devil.

LADY MACBETH   O proper stuff!
This is the very painting of your fear.
This is the air-drawn° dagger which you said   **air-drawn:** i.e., fashioned of air
Led you to Duncan. O, these flaws° and starts,   **flaws:** outbursts
Impostors to° true fear, would well become   **to:** in comparison with   65
A woman's story at a winter's fire,
Authorized° by her grandam. Shame itself!   **Authorized:** told on the authority of
Why do you make such faces? When all's done,
You look but on a stool.

MACBETH   Prithee see there!
Behold! Look! Lo! – How say you?   70
Why, what care I? If thou canst nod, speak too.
If charnel houses and our graves must send
Those that we bury back, our monuments°   **our monuments:** i.e., our only tombs
Shall be the maws of kites.°   *[Exit Ghost.]*   **maws of kites:** bellies of ravens

LADY MACBETH   What, quite unmanned in folly?

MACBETH
If I stand here, I saw him.   75

LADY MACBETH   Fie, for shame!

MACBETH
Blood hath been shed ere now, i' th' olden time,
Ere humane statute purged the gentle weal;°   **purged . . . weal:** rendered the state civilized
Ay, and since too, murders have been performed
Too terrible for the ear. The time has been
That, when the brains were out, the man would die,   80
And there an end. But now they rise again,
With twenty mortal murders on their crowns,°   **murders on their crowns:** murderous wounds
And push us from our stools. This is more strange   on their heads
Than such a murder is.

LADY MACBETH   My worthy lord,
Your noble friends do lack you.   85

MACBETH   I do forget.
Do not muse at me, my most worthy friends:
I have a strange infirmity, which is nothing
To those that know me. Come, love and health to all,
Then I'll sit down. Give me some wine, fill full.
I drink to th' general joy o' th' whole table,   90
And to our dear friend Banquo, whom we miss.
Would he were here!   *Enter Ghost.*
                    To all, and him we thirst,°   **him we thirst:** him whom we long for
And all to all.°   **all to all:** each toast the others

LORDS   Our duties, and the pledge.

MACBETH
Avaunt, and quit my sight! Let the earth hide thee!

DISCOVERING SHAKESPEARE

(43) History [3.4.72]: What were "charnel houses" (3.4.72)? Why does Macbeth refer to them when talking to Banquo's Ghost?

Thy bones are marrowless, thy blood is cold;
Thou hast no speculation° in those eyes
Which thou dost glare with.

speculation: vision

95

LADY MACBETH   Think of this, good peers,
But as a thing of custom.° 'Tis no other.
Only it spoils the pleasure of the time.

thing of custom: i.e., nothing out of the ordinary

MACBETH
What man dare, I dare.
Approach thou like the rugged Russian bear,
The armed rhinoceros, or th' Hyrcan° tiger;
Take any shape but that,° and my firm nerves
Shall never tremble. Or be alive again
And dare me to the desert° with thy sword.
If trembling I inhabit° then, protest me
The baby of a girl.° Hence, horrible shadow!
Unreal mock'ry, hence!   [Exit Ghost.]
                    Why, so; being gone,
I am a man again. – Pray you sit still.

100

Hyrcan: from Hyrcania (classical name for the area on the south coast of the Caspian Sea; its tigers were proverbially fierce)
but that: i.e., but that of Banquo's ghost
dare . . . desert: challenge me to fight you in the desert
If . . . inhabit: if I make a habit of trembling
The . . . girl: a baby girl, or a girl's doll

105

LADY MACBETH
You have displaced the mirth, broke the good meeting
With most admired° disorder.

admired: amazing

110

MACBETH   Can such things be,
And overcome° us like a summer's cloud
Without our special wonder? You make me strange
Even to the disposition that I owe,°
When now I think you can behold such sights
And keep the natural ruby of your cheeks
When mine is blanched with fear.

overcome: pass over

You . . . owe: you estrange me from my true nature (as a brave man); owe: own

115

ROSS   What sights, my lord?
LADY MACBETH
I pray you speak not: he grows worse and worse;
Question enrages him. At once, good night.
Stand not upon the order of your going,°
But go at once.

Stand . . . going: i.e., don't bother about precedence

120

LENNOX   Good night and better health
Attend his majesty.
LADY MACBETH   A kind good night to all.
                    Exeunt Lords.

MACBETH
It will have blood, they say: blood will have blood.
Stones have been known to move and trees to speak;
Augurs° and understood relations° have
By maggotpies and choughs° and rooks brought forth
The secret'st man of blood.° What is the night?

Augurs: auguries; understood relations: comprehensible relations of causes to effects

maggotpies and choughs: magpies, crows (both, like rooks, capable of imitating speech, and all three birds of ill omen)

secret'st man of blood: best-hidden murderer

125

LADY MACBETH
Almost at odds with morning, which is which.
MACBETH
How say'st thou, that Macduff denies his person
At our great bidding?

130

LADY MACBETH   Did you send to him, sir?

DISCOVERING SHAKESPEARE

(44) Teaser [3.4.102]: What was a "Hyrcan tiger" (3.4.102)? How many other Shakespearean plays mention them?
(45) Language [3.4.123]: What is the antecedent of the pronoun "It" in 3.4.123? What will have blood?

MACBETH
I hear it by the way;° but I will send.°
There's not a one of them but in his house
I keep a servant fee'd.° I will tomorrow,
And betimes° I will, to the weïrd sisters.
More shall they speak, for now I am bent° to know
By the worst means the worst. For mine own good
All causes shall give way. I am in blood
Stepped in so far that, should I wade no more,
Returning were as tedious as go o'er.
Strange things I have in head, that will to hand,
Which must be acted ere they may be scanned.°

LADY MACBETH
You lack the season° of all natures, sleep.

MACBETH
Come, we'll to sleep. My strange and self-abuse°
Is the initiate° fear that wants hard use.°
We are yet but young in deed.   *Exeunt.*

by the way: casually; **send:** send a messenger

fee'd: paid to spy
betimes: (1) speedily, (2) early
bent: determined   135

                                                            140

scanned: analyzed

season: (1) the best time (when nature is "in season"), (2) the seasoning (what makes life palatable)
self-abuse: delusion, hallucination
initiate: beginner's; **wants hard use:** needs much practice   145

✒ **3.5°** *Thunder. Enter the three Witches, meeting Hecate.*

3.5: An open place (a non-Shakespearean scene)

FIRST WITCH
Why, how now, Hecate? You look angerly.

HECATE
Have I not reason, beldams° as you are,
Saucy and overbold? How did you dare
To trade and traffic with Macbeth
In riddles and affairs of death;
And I, the mistress of your charms,
The close° contriver of all harms,
Was never called to bear my part°
Or show the glory of our art?
And, which is worse, all you have done
Hath been but for a wayward° son,
Spiteful and wrathful, who, as others do,
Loves for his own ends, not for you.
But make amends now: get you gone
And at the pit of Acheron°
Meet me i' th' morning. Thither he
Will come to know his destiny.
Your vessels° and your spells provide,
Your charms and everything beside.
I am for th' air. This night I'll spend
Unto a dismal and a fatal end.
Great business must be wrought ere noon.
Upon the corner of the moon

beldams: hags, witches

                                                            5

close: secret
bear my part: participate

                                                            10
wayward: willful, disobedient

Acheron: one of the rivers of Hades   15

vessels: cauldrons

                                                            20

DISCOVERING SHAKESPEARE

(46) Plot [3.5.1]: Often <u>cut</u> in modern productions of the play, 3.5 is viewed by many editors and scholars as an addition to the <u>script</u> by Thomas Middleton, one of Shakespeare's contemporaries. Can you find any information in 3.5 necessary for the development of the <u>plot</u> that would, if <u>cut</u>, be confusing to an audience?

There hangs a vap'rous drop profound;°   **a vap'rous drop profound:** a misty
I'll catch it ere it come to ground;   "exhalation" with deep, hidden properties   25
And that, distilled by magic sleights,°   **sleights:** artifices
Shall raise such artificial° sprites   **artificial:** (1) deceitful, (2) produced by artifice
As by the strength of their illusion
Shall draw him on to his confusion.°   **confusion:** damnation
He shall spurn fate, scorn death, and bear   30
His hopes 'bove wisdom, grace, and fear;
And you all know security°   **security:** overconfidence
Is mortals' chiefest enemy.
   Music, and a song.
FIRST SPIRIT   *[Within]*
  Hecate, Hecate, Hecate, O come away!
HECATE
  Hark, I am called. My little spirit, see,   35
  Sits in a foggy cloud and stays for me.
FIRST SPIRIT   *[Within]*
  Come away, Hecate, Hecate, O come away!
HECATE
  I come, I come, with all the speed I may.
  Where's Stadling?
SECOND SPIRIT   *[Within]*
          Here.
HECATE   Where's Puckle?
SECOND SPIRIT   *[Within]*   Here.
FIRST SPIRIT   *[Within]*
  And Hopper too, and Hellway too;   40
  We want but you, we want but you!°   **We . . . you:** only you are missing
  Come away, make up the count.
HECATE
  I will but 'noint,° and then I mount;   **'noint:** anoint myself (with a magic ointment)
  I will but 'noint, and then I mount.
FIRST SPIRIT   *[Within]*
  Here comes down one to fetch his due,   45
  A kiss, a cull,° a sip of blood;   **cull:** hug
  And why thou stay'st so long I muse,
  Since the air's so sweet and good.
HECATE
  O, art thou come? What news?
SECOND SPIRIT   *[Within]*
  All goes for our delight.   50
  Either come, or else refuse.
  Now I am furnished for the flight;
  Now I go, and now I fly,
  Malkin my sweet spirit and I.
THIRD SPIRIT   *[Within]*
  O what a dainty pleasure's this,   55
  To sail i' th' air while the moon shines fair,
  To sing, to toy, to dance, and kiss.
  Over woods, high rocks and mountains,

DISCOVERING SHAKESPEARE

(47) Verse [3.5.25]: Scan Hecate's verse in 3.5.1–33. What is the predominant meter of these lines?
(48) Rhyme [3.5.47]: Analyze the rhyme scheme in 3.5. Can you detect any patterns that distinguish the different speakers?

  Over hills and misty fountains,
  Over steeples, towers and turrets   60
  We fly by night 'mongst troops of spirits.
  No ring of bells to our ears sounds,
  No howls of wolves nor yelps of hounds,
  No, nor the noise of water's breach,°   **water's breach:** breaking waves
  Nor cannons' throats our height can reach.   65
FIRST SPIRIT *[Within]*   *[Exit Hecate.]*
  Come, let's make haste, she'll soon be back again.
SECOND SPIRIT *[Within]*
  But whilst she moves through the foggy air,
  Let's to the cave and our dire charms prepare.

                 Exeunt.

❧ **3.6**° *Enter Lennox and another Lord.*   **3.6:** Somewhere in Scotland

LENNOX
  My former speeches° have but hit° your thoughts, **My former speeches:** what I have just said;
  Which can interpret farther.° Only I say   **hit:** coincided with
  Things have been strangely borne. The gracious Duncan **interpret farther:** draw their own conclusions
  Was pitied of Macbeth. Marry, he was dead.
  And the right valiant Banquo walked too late;   5
  Whom, you may say, if't please you, Fleance killed,
  For Fleance fled. Men must not walk too late.
  Who cannot want the thought° how monstrous **cannot . . . thought:** can avoid thinking
  It was for Malcolm and for Donalbain
  To kill their gracious father? Damnèd fact,° **fact:** crime   10
  How it did grieve Macbeth! Did he not straight,
  In pious rage, the two delinquents tear
  That were the slaves of drink and thralls° of sleep? **thralls:** slaves
  Was not that nobly done? Ay, and wisely too,
  For 'twould have angered any heart alive   15
  To hear the men deny't. So that I say
  He has borne° all things well; and I do think **borne:** carried off
  That, had he Duncan's sons under his key –
  As, an't° please heaven, he shall not – they should find **an't:** if it
  What 'twere to kill a father. So should Fleance.   20
  But peace; for from broad words,° and 'cause he failed **from broad words:** because of his blunt speech
  His presence at the tyrant's feast, I hear
  Macduff lives in disgrace. Sir, can you tell
  Where he bestows himself?
LORD   The son of Duncan,
  From whom this tyrant holds the due of birth,° **holds . . . birth:** withholds his birthright 25
  Lives in the English court, and is received
  Of the most pious Edward with such grace
  That the malevolence of fortune nothing
  Takes from his high respect.° Thither Macduff **his high respect:** the great esteem for him
  Is gone to pray the holy king upon his aid° **upon his aid:** on Malcolm's behalf 30
  To wake Northumberland and warlike Siward;° **Northumberland . . . Siward:** (the English
                  county bordering Scotland, and the family name
                  of the Earl of Northumberland)

DISCOVERING SHAKESPEARE

(49) Language [3.6.10]: How does Lennox use questions in 3.6.1–24 to betray his point of view? How much of what he says is <u>ironic</u>?

That by the help of these (with Him above
To ratify the work) we may again
Give to our tables meat, sleep to our nights, 35
Free from our feasts and banquets bloody knives,
Do faithful homage and receive free° honors –   **free:** untainted
All which we pine for now. And this report
Hath so exasperate the king that he
Prepares for some attempt of war.

LENNOX   Sent he to Macduff? 40

LORD
He did; and with an absolute "Sir, not I,"
The cloudy° messenger turns me his back   **cloudy:** angry
And hums, as who should say, "You'll rue the time
That clogs° me with this answer."   **clogs:** burdens

LENNOX   And that well might
Advise him to a caution t' hold what distance 45
His wisdom can provide.° Some holy angel   **Advise . . . provide:** caution him to keep as safe
Fly to the court of England and unfold   a distance as he can manage
His message ere he come, that a swift blessing
May soon return to this our suffering country
Under a hand accursed. 50

LORD   I'll send my prayers with him.

                        Exeunt.

❦ **4.1°** *Thunder. Enter the three Witches.*   **4.1:** The Witches' cave

FIRST WITCH
Thrice the brindled° cat hath mewed.   **brindled:** striped

SECOND WITCH
Thrice, and once the hedgepig whined.

THIRD WITCH
Harpier° cries – 'Tis time, 'tis time!   **Harpier:** (a familiar spirit, like Graymalkin and
        Paddock)

FIRST WITCH
Round about the cauldron go;
In the poisoned entrails throw. 5
Toad, that under cold stone
Days and nights has thirty-one
Sweltered venom sleeping got,°   **Sweltered . . . got:** poisonous sweat generated
Boil thou first i' th' charmèd pot.   while asleep

ALL
Double, double toil and trouble, 10
Fire burn and cauldron bubble.

SECOND WITCH
Fillet of a fenny° snake,   **fenny:** marsh
In the cauldron boil and bake;
Eye of newt, and toe of frog,
Wool of bat, and tongue of dog, 15
Adder's fork,° and blindworm's° sting,   **fork:** forked tongue; **blindworm:** adder

---

DISCOVERING SHAKESPEARE

(50) Paraphrase [3.6.41]: Paraphrase the Lord's speech in 3.6.41–44. What was Macduff's answer when the king's messenger asked him to return to Scotland?

(51) Verse [4.1.10]: Scan the Witches' verse in 4.1.1–69. Which of the lines are not written in trochaic tetrameter? Why do you think these lines are different from the rest?

Lizard's leg, and owlet's wing –
For a charm of powerful trouble
Like a hellbroth boil and bubble.

ALL

Double, double toil and trouble,   20
Fire burn and cauldron bubble.

THIRD WITCH

Scale of dragon, tooth of wolf,
Witch's mummy,° maw and gulf°   **mummy:** mummified flesh; **maw and gulf:**
Of the ravined° salt-sea shark,   devouring stomach; **gulf:** anything voracious
Root of hemlock digged i' th' dark,   **ravined:** ravenous   25
Liver of blaspheming Jew,
Gall of goat, and slips of yew
Slivered in the moon's eclipse,
Nose of Turk, and Tartar's lips,
Finger of birth-strangled babe   30
Ditch-delivered° by a drab°   **Ditch-delivered:** born in a ditch; **drab:** whore
Make the gruel thick and slab.°   **slab:** thick, semiliquid
Add thereto a tiger's chawdron°   **chawdron:** guts
For th' ingredient of our cauldron.

ALL

Double, double toil and trouble,   35
Fire burn and cauldron bubble.

SECOND WITCH

Cool it with a baboon's blood,
Then the charm is firm and good.
Enter Hecate and the other three Witches.°   **s.d.** (ll. 40–65) (the Hecate section is a non-
                                               Shakespearean addition)

HECATE

O, well done! I commend your pains,
And every one shall share i' th' gains.   40
And now about the cauldron sing
Like elves and fairies in a ring,
Enchanting all that you put in.
Music and a song.

HECATE

Black spirits and white,
Red spirits and gray   45
Mingle,° mingle, mingle,   **Mingle:** mix together (but with an obscene
You that mingle may.   overtone: have intercourse; see l. 49)

FOURTH WITCH

Tiffin, Tiffin,
Keep it stiff in.

FIFTH WITCH

Firedrake° Pucky,   **Firedrake:** will-o'-the-wisp   50
Make it lucky.

HECATE

Liar Robin,
You must bob in.

CHORUS

Around, around, around, about, about,
All ill come running in, all good keep out.   55

DISCOVERING SHAKESPEARE

(52) Music [4.1.43]: When Hecate calls for music in 4.1.43, is it vocal, instrumental, or both? Does the music come from onstage or offstage? What kinds of instruments play it?

FOURTH WITCH
Here's the blood of a bat.
HECATE
O put in that, put in that.
FIFTH WITCH
Here's lizard's brain.
HECATE
Put in a grain.
FOURTH WITCH
Here's juice of toad, here's oil of adder,   60
That will make the charm grow madder.
FIFTH WITCH
Put in all these, 'twill raise the stench.
HECATE
Nay, here's three ounces of a red-haired wench.
CHORUS
Around, around, around, about, about,
All ill come running in, all good keep out.   65
    [Exeunt Hecate and the three Singers.]
SECOND WITCH
By the pricking of my thumbs,
Something wicked this way comes.
Open locks,
Whoever knocks!
 Enter Macbeth.
MACBETH
How now, you secret, black,° and midnight hags, **black:** evil, malevolent 70
What is't you do?
ALL   A deed without a name.
MACBETH
I conjure you by that which you profess,°   **that . . . profess:** your profession, witchcraft
Howe'er you come to know it, answer me.
Though you untie the winds and let them fight
Against the churches, though the yeasty° waves **yeasty:** foaming 75
Confound and swallow navigation up,
Though bladed corn be lodged° and trees blown down, **bladed . . . lodged:** ripe wheat be flattened
Though castles topple on their warders' heads,
Though palaces and pyramids do slope°   **slope:** bend
Their heads to their foundations, though the treasure   80
Of Nature's germens° tumble all together   **Nature's germens:** the essential seeds of nature
Even till destruction sicken,° answer me   **sicken:** surfeit
To what I ask you.
FIRST WITCH   Speak.
SECOND WITCH   Demand.
THIRD WITCH   We'll answer.
FIRST WITCH
Say if thou'dst rather hear it from our mouths
Or from our masters.°   **masters:** instruments, agents, experts (the spirits 85
MACBETH   Call 'em. Let me see 'em. through whom they communicate with the occult
               world—a *master* is a skilled workman)

DISCOVERING SHAKESPEARE

(53) <u>Verse</u> [4.1.72]: What is the difference in <u>verse</u> form between the way the Witches talk to Macbeth and the manner in which he answers them? Does the Witches' use of language sound more supernatural? If so, why?

FIRST WITCH
Pour in sow's blood, that hath eaten
Her nine farrow;° grease that's sweaten°   **nine farrow:** litter of nine; **sweaten:** exuded
From the murderer's gibbet throw
Into the flame.
ALL   Come, high or low,
Thyself and office° deftly show.   **office:** function   90
Thunder. First Apparition, an Armed Head.
MACBETH
Tell me, thou unknown power –
FIRST WITCH   He knows thy thought:
Hear his speech, but say thou naught.
FIRST APPARITION
Macbeth, Macbeth, Macbeth, beware Macduff,
Beware the Thane of Fife. Dismiss me. Enough.
                              He descends.
MACBETH
Whate'er thou art, for thy good caution thanks: 95
Thou hast harped° my fear aright. But one word more –   **harped:** hit the tune of
FIRST WITCH
He will not be commanded. Here's another,
More potent than the first.
Thunder. Second Apparition, a Bloody Child.
SECOND APPARITION
Macbeth, Macbeth, Macbeth –
MACBETH
Had I three ears, I'd hear thee.   100
SECOND APPARITION
Be bloody, bold, and resolute. Laugh to scorn
The pow'r of man, for none of woman born
Shall harm Macbeth.   *Descends.*
MACBETH
Then live, Macduff, what need I fear of thee?
But yet I'll make assurance double sure   105
And take a bond of° fate. Thou shalt not live,   **take a bond of:** secure a guarantee from
That I may tell pale-hearted fear it lies
And sleep in spite of thunder.
Thunder. Third Apparition, a Child Crowned, with a
tree in his hand.
                              What is this
That rises like the issue of a king
And wears upon his baby brow the round   110
And top° of sovereignty?   **round . . . top:** crown
ALL   Listen, but speak not to't.
THIRD APPARITION
Be lion-mettled, proud, and take no care
Who chafes, who frets, or where conspirers are.
Macbeth shall never vanquished be until
Great Birnam Wood to high Dunsinane Hill   115
Shall come against him.   *Descends.*

DISCOVERING SHAKESPEARE

(54) <u>Rhyme</u> **[4.1.93]:** What is the <u>rhyme</u> scheme of the Apparitions' prophecies? Are all the <u>rhymes</u> <u>perfect</u>, or are some of then <u>slant</u>? How do these different <u>rhymes</u> affect the audience?

MACBETH   That will never be.
  Who can impress° the forest, bid the tree
  Unfix his earthbound root? Sweet bodements,° good.
  Rebellious dead rise never till the Wood
  Of Birnam rise, and our high-placed Macbeth
  Shall live the lease of nature,° pay his breath
  To time and mortal custom.° Yet my heart
  Throbs to know one thing. Tell me, if your art
  Can tell so much: Shall Banquo's issue° ever
  Reign in this kingdom?
ALL   Seek to know no more.
MACBETH
  I will be satisfied. Deny me this,
  And an eternal curse fall on you! Let me know.
  Why sinks that cauldron? and what noise is this?
    Hautboys.
FIRST WITCH   Show!
SECOND WITCH   Show!
THIRD WITCH   Show!
ALL
        Show his eyes, and grieve his heart,
        Come like shadows, so depart.
  A show of eight Kings and Banquo, last [King] with a
  glass° in his hand.
MACBETH
  Thou art too like the spirit of Banquo. Down!
  Thy crown does sear mine eyeballs. And thy hair,
  Thou other gold-bound brow, is like the first.
  A third is like the former. Filthy hags,
  Why do you show me this? A fourth? Start,° eyes!
  What, will the line stretch out to th' crack of doom?
  Another yet? A seventh? I'll see no more.
  And yet the eighth appears, who bears a glass
  Which shows me many more; and some I see
  That twofold balls and treble scepters° carry.
  Horrible sight! Now I see 'tis true;
  For the blood-boltered° Banquo smiles upon me
  And points at them for his. What? Is this so?
    [Exeunt Apparitions.]
FIRST WITCH
  Ay, sir, all this is so. But why
  Stands Macbeth thus amazedly?
  Come, sisters, cheer we up his sprites°
  And show the best of our delights.
  I'll charm the air to give a sound
  While you perform your antic round,°
  That this great king may kindly say
  Our duties did his welcome pay.
    Music. The Witches dance, and vanish.

Glossary (margin):

impress: conscript
bodements: prophecies

120

lease of nature: full life span
pay . . . custom: be obligated only to age and normal death
issue: offspring

125

130

glass: mirror

135

Start: burst, start from your sockets

140

twofold . . . scepters: two orbs and three scepters (the British royal insignia)
blood-boltered: matted with blood   145

sprites: spirits

150

antic round: grotesque dance

s.d.: (a non-Shakespearean addition)

DISCOVERING SHAKESPEARE

(55) Music [4.1.128]: What are "Hautboys" (4.1.128 s.d.)? What specific ambiance or feeling would these instruments bring to the scene?

(56) Rhyme [4.1.147]: How does the First Witch's rhyme scheme in 4.1.147–154 attempt to calm Macbeth's fears? How successful is she in doing so?

MACBETH
   Where are they? Gone? Let this pernicious hour   155
   Stand aye accursèd in the calendar.
   Come in, without there!
     Enter Lennox.
LENNOX   What's your grace's will?
MACBETH
   Saw you the weïrd sisters?
LENNOX   No, my lord.
MACBETH
   Came they not by you?
LENNOX   No indeed, my lord.
MACBETH
   Infected be the air whereon they ride,   160
   And damned all those that trust them! I did hear
   The galloping of horse. Who was't came by?
LENNOX
   'Tis two or three, my lord, that bring you word
   Macduff is fled to England.
MACBETH   Fled to England?
LENNOX
   Ay, my good lord.   165

MACBETH   *[Aside]*

   Time, thou anticipat'st° my dread exploits.   **anticipat'st:** forestall
   The flighty° purpose never is o'ertook   **flighty:** fleeting
   Unless the deed go with it. From this moment
   The very firstlings of my heart shall be
   The firstlings of my hand.° And even now,   **firstlings . . . my hand:** i.e., I shall act at the   170
   To crown my thoughts with acts, be it thought and   moment I feel the first impulse
     done:
   The castle of Macduff I will surprise,
   Seize upon Fife, give to th' edge o' th' sword
   His wife, his babes, and all unfortunate souls
   That trace° him in his line.° No boasting like a fool; **trace:** follow; **line:** family line   175
   This deed I'll do before this purpose cool.
   But no more sights. *[To Lennox]* Where are these gen-
     tlemen?
   Come, bring me where they are.   *Exeunt.*

🐚 **4.2°** *Enter Macduff's Wife, her Son, and Ross.*   **4.2:** Macduff's castle at Fife

LADY MACDUFF
   What had he done to make him fly the land?
ROSS
   You must have patience, madam.
LADY MACDUFF   He had none.
   His flight was madness. When our actions do not,
   Our fears do make us traitors.°   **traitors:** i.e., betray our interests
ROSS   You know not
   Whether it was his wisdom or his fear.   5

DISCOVERING SHAKESPEARE

(57) Staging [4.2.1]: Where does 4.2 take place on stage? What <u>props</u> or <u>set</u> design elements might indicate to an audience that the scene is in Macduff's castle?

LADY MACDUFF
Wisdom? To leave his wife, to leave his babes,
His mansion and his titles° in a place   **titles:** rights, what he is entitled to
From whence himself does fly? He loves us not,
He wants° the natural touch. For the poor wren,   **wants:** lacks
The most diminutive of birds, will fight,   10
Her young ones in her nest, against the owl.
All is the fear and nothing is the love,
As little is the wisdom, where the flight
So runs against all reason.
ROSS   My dearest coz,°   **coz:** (from "cousin," an affectionate diminutive)
I pray you school° yourself. But for your husband,   **school:** control   15
He is noble, wise, judicious, and best knows
The fits o' th' season.° I dare not speak much further,   **knows . . . season:** understands the violent
But cruel are the times when we are traitors   conditions of the time
And do not know ourselves;° when we hold rumor   **we . . . ourselves:** we are considered traitors and
From what we fear, yet know not what we fear,°   do not know that we are   20
But float upon a wild and violent sea   **hold . . . fear:** believe rumors based on what we
Each way and none.° I take my leave of you,   fear
Shall not be long but I'll be here again.   **Each way and none:** i.e., move every which
Things at the worst will cease,° or else climb upward   way but in no settled direction
To what they were before. *[To the Son]* My pretty cousin,   **will cease:** i.e., can get no worse   25
Blessing upon you.
LADY MACDUFF
Fathered he is, and yet he's fatherless.
ROSS
I am so much a fool, should I stay longer
It would be my disgrace° and your discomfort.   **my disgrace:** (because he would weep)
I take my leave at once.   *Exit.*   30
LADY MACDUFF
Sirrah, your father's dead;
And what will you do now? How will you live?
SON
As birds do, mother.
LADY MACDUFF   What, with worms and flies?
SON
With what I get, I mean; and so do they.
LADY MACDUFF
Poor bird, thou'dst never fear the net nor lime,°   **lime:** birdlime (a sticky substance used to catch   35
The pitfall nor the gin.°   birds)
SON   **gin:** trap
Why should I, mother? Poor birds they are not set for.
My father is not dead for all your saying.
LADY MACDUFF
Yes, he is dead. How wilt thou do for a father?
SON   Nay, how will you do for a husband?   40
LADY MACDUFF   Why, I can buy me twenty at any market.
SON   Then you'll buy 'em to sell° again.   **sell:** deceive them
LADY MACDUFF
Thou speak'st with all thy wit; and yet, i' faith,
With wit enough for thee.°   **with . . . thee:** indeed, you are witty enough

---

DISCOVERING SHAKESPEARE

(58) Characterization [4.2.30]: How old do you think Lady Macduff's son is? What clues in the <u>dialogue</u> between the two lead you to this conclusion?

SON   Was my father a traitor, mother?   45

LADY MACDUFF   Ay, that he was.

SON   What is a traitor?

LADY MACDUFF   Why, one that swears and lies.°   **swears and lies:** takes a vow and violates it

SON   And be all traitors that do so?

LADY MACDUFF   Every one that does so is a traitor and   50
must be hanged.

SON   And must they all be hanged that swear and lie?

LADY MACDUFF   Every one.

SON   Who must hang them?

LADY MACDUFF   Why, the honest men.   55

SON   They the liars and swearers are fools, for there are
liars and swearers enow° to beat the honest men and   **enow:** enough
hang up them.

LADY MACDUFF   Now God help thee, poor monkey! But
how wilt thou do for a father?   60

SON   If he were dead, you'd weep for him. If you would
not, it were a good sign that I should quickly have a
new father.

LADY MACDUFF   Poor prattler, how thou talk'st!
    Enter a Messenger.

MESSENGER
Bless you, fair dame. I am not to you known,   65
Though in your state of honor° I am perfect.°   **state of honor:** (1) high status, (2) honorable
I doubt° some danger does approach you nearly.   character; **in . . . perfect:** I am well aware of
If you will take a homely° man's advice,   your nobility and virtue;
Be not found here. Hence with your little ones.
To fright you thus methinks I am too savage;   **doubt:** fear   70
To do worse to you were fell° cruelty,   **homely:** plain
Which is too nigh° your person. Heaven preserve you!   **fell:** deadly
I dare abide no longer.   *Exit.*   **nigh:** near (i.e., I frighten you to save you from
LADY MACDUFF   Whither should I fly?   the worse cruelty threatening you)
I have done no harm. But I remember now
I am in this earthly world, where to do harm   75
Is often laudable, to do good sometime
Accounted dangerous folly. Why then, alas,
Do I put up that womanly defense
To say I have done no harm?
    Enter Murderers.   What are these faces?

MURDERER
Where is your husband?   80

LADY MACDUFF
I hope in no place so unsanctified
Where such as thou mayst find him.

MURDERER   He's a traitor.

SON
Thou liest, thou shag-haired° villain!   **shag-haired:** unkempt, uncouth

---

DISCOVERING SHAKESPEARE

(59) Logic [4.2.56]: What is the boy's logic in arguing that "the liars and swearers are fools" (4.2.56)? Does he think his father is "honest"? Do you think so? Why?

(60) Verse [4.2.81]: Lady Macduff's irregular line "To say I have done no harm" (4.2.79) implies panic at the approach of the Murderers. How many <u>beats</u> are in the line? What stage action might take place during these syllables?

MURDERER   What, you egg!
   [Stabs him.]
   Young fry° of treachery!   **egg. . . fry:** offspring of birds and fish,
SON   He has killed me, mother.   respectively
   Run away, I pray you!   85
   [Dies.]   *Exit [Lady Macduff], crying "Murder"*
                                                [pursued by Murderers]

❧ **4.3**° *Enter Malcolm and Macduff.*   **4.3:** In England, at the court of King Edward the
                                                 Confessor

MALCOLM
   Let us seek out some desolate shade, and there
   Weep our sad bosoms empty.
MACDUFF   Let us rather
   Hold fast° the mortal° sword and, like good men,   **fast:** tightly; **mortal:** deadly
   Bestride our downfall° birthdom.° Each new morn   **downfall:** fallen; **birthdom:** (1) homeland,
   New widows howl, new orphans cry, new sorrows   (2) inheritance   5
   Strike heaven on the face, that it resounds
   As if it felt with Scotland and yelled out
   Like syllable of dolor.°   **Like . . . dolor:** the same cry of grief
MALCOLM   What I believe, I'll wail;
   What know, believe; and what I can redress,
   As I shall find the time to friend,° I will.   **to friend:** befriending me (i.e., propitious)   10
   What you have spoke, it may be so perchance.
   This tyrant, whose sole name° blisters our tongues,   **sole name:** name alone
   Was once thought honest; you have loved him well;
   He hath not touched you yet. I am young, but some-
     thing
   You may deserve of him through me, and wisdom°   **wisdom:** you may consider it wise   15
   To offer up a weak, poor, innocent lamb
   T' appease an angry god.
MACDUFF
   I am not treacherous.
MALCOLM   But Macbeth is.
   A good and virtuous nature may recoil°   **recoil:** hold back, withdraw
   In an imperial charge.° But I shall crave your pardon.   **In . . . charge:** (1) in an imperial military   20
   That which you are, my thoughts cannot transpose:°   engagement, (2) under royal orders
   Angels are bright still though the brightest° fell;   **transpose:** change
   Though all things foul would wear the brows of grace,°   **the brightest:** Lucifer
   Yet grace must still look so.   **wear . . . grace:** put on the appearance of
MACDUFF   I have lost my hopes.   goodness
MALCOLM
   Perchance even there where I did find my doubts.   25
   Why in that rawness° left you wife and child,   **rawness:** suddenness, rudeness
   Those precious motives, those strong knots of love,
   Without leave-taking? I pray you,
   Let not my jealousies° be your dishonors,   **jealousies:** suspicions
   But mine own safeties. You may be rightly just   30
   Whatever I shall think.

DISCOVERING SHAKESPEARE

(61) <u>**Paraphrase**</u> **[4.3.19]:** <u>Paraphrase</u> Malcolm's "A good and virtuous nature may recoil / In an imperial charge"
(4.3.19–20). How do these lines help betray Malcolm's fear of Macduff?

MACDUFF   Bleed, bleed, poor country!
Great tyranny, lay thou thy basis° sure,   **basis:** foundation
For goodness dare not check thee; wear thou thy
   wrongs,
The title is affeered!° Fare thee well, lord.   **The title is affeered:** (1) your claim is legally
I would not be the villain that thou think'st   confirmed, (2) the valid claimant is frightened   35
For the whole space that's in the tyrant's grasp   (afeard) of you
And the rich East to boot.
MALCOLM   Be not offended.
I speak not as in absolute fear° of you.   **as . . . fear:** entirely in fear
I think our country sinks beneath the yoke,
It weeps, it bleeds, and each new day a gash   40
Is added to her wounds. I think withal°   **withal:** moreover
There would be hands uplifted in my right;
And here from gracious England° have I offer   **England:** the King of England
Of goodly thousands. But, for all this,
When I shall tread upon the tyrant's head   45
Or wear it on my sword, yet my poor country
Shall have more vices than it had before,
More suffer, and more sundry ways than ever,
By him that shall succeed.
MACDUFF   What should he be?
MALCOLM   50
It is myself I mean, in whom I know
All the particulars° of vice so grafted°   **particulars:** varieties; **grafted:** implanted
That, when they shall be opened,° black Macbeth   **opened:** revealed
Will seem as pure as snow, and the poor state
Esteem him as a lamb, being compared
With my confineless° harms.   **confineless:** limitless   55
MACDUFF   Not in the legions
Of horrid hell can come a devil more damned
In evils to top Macbeth.
MALCOLM   I grant him bloody,
Luxurious,° avaricious, false, deceitful,   **Luxurious:** lecherous
Sudden,° malicious, smacking of every sin   **Sudden:** violent
That has a name. But there's no bottom, none,   60
In my voluptuousness. Your wives, your daughters,
Your matrons, and your maids could not fill up
The cistern of my lust; and my desire
All continent° impediments would o'erbear   **continent:** restraining
That did oppose my will. Better Macbeth   65
Than such an one to reign.
MACDUFF   Boundless intemperance
In nature° is a tyranny. It hath been   **nature:** human nature
Th' untimely emptying of the happy throne
And fall of many kings. But fear not yet
To take upon you what is yours. You may   70
Convey° your pleasures in a spacious plenty   **Convey:** manage
And yet seem cold — the time you may so hoodwink.

DISCOVERING SHAKESPEARE

(62) Plot [4.3.50]: What is Malcolm's strategy for testing the loyalty of Macduff in this scene? How successful is his attempt to do so? Exactly when does Malcolm realize that Macduff is a true and loyal countryman not under the control of Macbeth?

We have willing dames enough. There cannot be
That vulture in you to devour so many
As will to greatness dedicate themselves,   75
Finding it so inclined.°
MALCOLM   With this there grows
In my most ill-composed affection° such
A stanchless° avarice that, were I king,
I should cut off° the nobles for their lands,
Desire his jewels, and this other's house,   80
And my more-having would be as a sauce
To make me hunger more, that I should forge°
Quarrels unjust against the good and loyal,
Destroying them for wealth.
MACDUFF   This avarice
Sticks deeper, grows with more pernicious root   85
Than summer-seeming° lust, and it hath been
The sword of our slain° kings. Yet do not fear.
Scotland hath foisons° to fill up your will
Of your mere° own. All these are portable,°
With other graces weighed.   90
MALCOLM
But I have none. The king-becoming graces,
As justice, verity, temp'rance, stableness,
Bounty, perseverance, mercy, lowliness,°
Devotion, patience, courage, fortitude,
I have no relish° of them, but abound   95
In the division° of each several crime,
Acting in many ways. Nay, had I pow'r, I should
Pour the sweet milk of concord into hell,
Uproar° the universal peace, confound
All unity on earth.   100
MACDUFF   O Scotland, Scotland!
MALCOLM
If such a one be fit to govern, speak.
I am as I have spoken.
MACDUFF   Fit to govern?
No, not to live! O nation miserable,
With an untitled° tyrant bloody-sceptered,   105
When shalt thou see thy wholesome days again,
Since that the truest issue of thy throne
By his own interdiction° stands accursed
And does blaspheme his breed?° Thy royal father
Was a most sainted king; the queen that bore thee,
Oft'ner upon her knees than on her feet,   110
Died° every day she lived. Fare thee well.
These evils thou repeat'st upon thyself

There ... inclined: i.e., when you are king, more women will willingly offer to serve your lust than you can possibly consume

ill-composed affection: ill-regulated passion

stanchless: insatiable

cut off: execute

that I should forge: so that I would fabricate

summer-seeming: i.e., transitory and hot

sword ... slain: cause of death of our

foisons: plenty

mere: very; **portable:** bearable

lowliness: humility

relish: trace

division: variations

Uproar: throw into chaos

untitled: not entitled to rule

interdiction: prohibition

blaspheme his breed: slander his heritage

Died: i.e., turned away from this life

DISCOVERING SHAKESPEARE

(63) Paraphrase [4.3.73]: Paraphrase Macduff's claim to Malcolm that "There cannot be / That vulture in you to devour so many / As will to greatness dedicate themselves, / Finding it so inclined" (4.3.73–76). What sexual pun is implied in Macduff's words?

(64) Shared Lines [4.3.100]: How do the shared lines in 4.3.100–102 indicate Macduff's strongly negative opinion of Malcolm's suitability as a ruler of Scotland? How would this moment in the play be different if each character spoke regular ten-syllable lines instead of half-lines?

Hath banished me from Scotland. O my breast,
Thy hope ends here.
MALCOLM   Macduff, this noble passion,
  Child of integrity, hath from my soul   115
  Wiped the black scruples,° reconciled my thoughts   **scruples:** doubts
  To thy good truth and honor. Devilish Macbeth
  By many of these trains° hath sought to win me   **trains:** plots
  Into his power; and modest° wisdom plucks° me   **modest:** cautious; **plucks:** restrains
  From overcredulous haste; but God above   120
  Deal between thee and me, for even now
  I put myself to thy direction and
  Unspeak mine own detraction, here abjure
  The taints and blames I laid upon myself
  For° strangers to my nature. I am yet   **For:** as   125
  Unknown to woman,° never was forsworn,   **am . . . woman:** have never slept with a woman
  Scarcely have coveted what was mine own,
  At no time broke my faith, would not betray
  The devil to his fellow, and delight
  No less in truth than life. My first false speaking   130
  Was this upon myself. What I am truly
  Is thine and my poor country's to command;
  Whither indeed, before thy here-approach,
  Old Siward with ten thousand warlike men
  Already at a point° was setting forth.   **at a point:** fully prepared   135
  Now we'll together;° and the chance of goodness   **we'll together:** we'll go on together
  Be like our warranted quarrel.° Why are you silent?   **the chance . . . quarrel:** let our good fortune
MACDUFF   match our just cause
  Such welcome and unwelcome things at once
  'Tis hard to reconcile.
    Enter a Doctor.
MALCOLM
  Well, more anon.° – Comes the king forth, I pray you?   **anon:** soon   140
DOCTOR
  Ay, sir. There are a crew of wretched souls
  That stay° his cure. Their malady convinces°   **stay:** await; **convinces:** overwhelms
  The great assay of art;° but at his touch,   **assay of art:** attempts of (medical) science
  Such sanctity hath heaven given his hand,
  They presently amend.   145
MALCOLM   I thank you, doctor.
    Exit [Doctor].
MACDUFF
  What's the disease he means?
MALCOLM   'Tis called the evil.°   **the evil:** the King's Evil, scrofula (a painful
  A most miraculous work in this good king,   inflammation of the lymph nodes, often
  Which often since my here-remain in England   accompanied by ulcerations)
  I have seen him do: how he solicits heaven

DISCOVERING SHAKESPEARE

(65) <u>Staging</u> [4.3.125]: Malcolm's long <u>monologue</u> in 4.3.114–137 seems to require some stage movement whereby the actor delivering the lines can break up the speech. What kind of <u>blocking</u> and/or gestures do you think would be most effective at this point in the play?
(66) History [4.3.146]: What was the king's "evil" (see 4.3.146)? In what medicinal way did English monarchs practice "touching" their subjects?

Himself best knows, but strangely visited° people,   strangely visited: seriously afflicted   150
All swoll'n and ulcerous, pitiful to the eye,
The mere° despair of surgery, he cures,   mere: utter
Hanging a golden stamp° about their necks,   stamp: coin or medal
Put on with holy prayers, and 'tis spoken
To the succeeding royalty he leaves   155
The healing benediction.° With this strange virtue,°   'tis . . . benediction: it is said that he bequeaths the healing power to the monarchs who succeed him; virtue: power
He hath a heavenly gift of prophecy,
And sundry blessings hang about his throne
That speak° him full of grace.   speak: declare
    Enter Ross.

MACDUFF   See who comes here.

MALCOLM
My countryman; but yet I know him not.   160

MACDUFF
My ever gentle cousin, welcome hither.

MALCOLM
I know him now. Good God betimes° remove   betimes: quickly
The means that makes us strangers.

ROSS   Sir, amen.

MACDUFF
Stands Scotland where it did?

ROSS   Alas, poor country,
Almost afraid to know itself. It cannot   165
Be called our mother but our grave, where nothing°   nothing: no one
But who knows nothing is once seen to smile;
Where sighs and groans, and shrieks that rend the air,
Are made, not marked;° where violent sorrow seems   marked: noticed
A modern ecstasy.° The dead man's knell   modern ecstasy: commonplace emotion   170
Is there scarce asked for who,° and good men's lives   for who: for whom it tolls
Expire before the flowers in their caps,
Dying or ere° they sicken.   or ere: before; relation: report

MACDUFF   O, relation°
Too nice,° and yet too true!   nice: particular

MALCOLM   What's the newest grief?

ROSS
That of an hour's age doth hiss° the speaker;   hiss: mock   175
Each minute teems° a new one.   teems: brings forth

MACDUFF   How does my wife?

ROSS
Why, well.

MACDUFF   And all my children?

ROSS   Well too.

MACDUFF
The tyrant has not battered at their peace?

ROSS
No, they were well at peace when I did leave 'em.

MACDUFF
Be not a niggard of your speech. How goes't?   180

DISCOVERING SHAKESPEARE

(67) Shared Lines [4.3.173]: Once again Shakespeare uses <u>shared lines</u> in 4.3.173–180, this time to indicate tension and <u>foreshadowing</u> in the scene. What terrible event does Ross delay telling Macduff? What happens to the <u>verse</u> in 4.3.204 when Ross actually delivers his bad news?

ROSS
When I came hither to transport the tidings
Which I have heavily borne,° there ran a rumor
Of many worthy fellows that were out,°
Which was to my belief witnessed the rather
For that I saw the tyrant's power afoot.°
Now is the time of help. Your eye in Scotland
Would create soldiers, make our women fight
To doff their dire distresses.
MALCOLM   Be't their comfort
We are coming thither. Gracious England hath
Lent us good Siward and ten thousand men,
An older and a better soldier none
That Christendom gives out.
ROSS   Would I could answer
This comfort with the like. But I have words
That would be howled out in the desert air,
Where hearing should not latch° them.
MACDUFF   What concern they?
The general cause or is it a fee-grief
Due° to some single breast?
ROSS   No mind that's honest
But in it shares some woe, though the main part
Pertains to you alone.
MACDUFF   If it be mine,
Keep it not from me; quickly let me have it.
ROSS
Let not your ears despise my tongue forever,
Which shall possess them with the heaviest sound
That ever yet they heard.
MACDUFF   Hmm – I guess at it.
ROSS
Your castle is surprised, your wife and babes
Savagely slaughtered. To relate the manner
Were, on the quarry° of these murdered deer,
To add the death of you.
MALCOLM   Merciful heaven –
    [To Macduff]
What, man, ne'er pull your hat upon your brows.°
Give sorrow words. The grief that does not speak°
Whispers° the o'erfraught heart and bids it break.
MACDUFF
My children too?
ROSS   Wife, children, servants, all
That could be found.
MACDUFF   And I must be from thence?°
My wife killed too?
ROSS   I have said.

heavily borne: sadly brought	
out: in arms	
Which . . . afoot: i.e., the fact that I saw Macbeth's troops on the march confirms my belief that his enemies, too, are mobilized	185
	190
latch: catch	195
fee-grief/Due: private grief belonging (from "fee simple," absolute legal possession)	
	200
	205
quarry: heap of game	
upon your brows: down over your eyes	
speak: i.e., speak to other people	
Whispers: whispers to	210
from thence: away from home	

DISCOVERING SHAKESPEARE

(68) <u>Plot</u> **[4.3.201]:** Why do you think Ross lied earlier when he told Macduff his wife and children were all well (4.3.177)? What was his motivation for doing so?

MALCOLM   Be comforted.
Let's make us med'cines of our great revenge
To cure this deadly grief.   215

MACDUFF
He has no children. All my pretty ones?
Did you say all? O hellkite! All?
What, all my pretty chickens and their dam
At one fell° swoop?   **fell:** savage

MALCOLM
Dispute° it like a man.   **Dispute:** confront, contend with   220

MACDUFF   I shall do so;
But I must also feel it as a man.
I cannot but remember such things were
That were most precious to me. Did heaven look on
And would not take their part? Sinful Macduff,
They were all struck for thee. Naught° that I am,   **Naught:** wicked   225
Not for their own demerits but for mine
Fell slaughter on their souls. Heaven rest them now.

MALCOLM
Be this the whetstone of your sword. Let grief
Convert to anger; blunt not the heart, enrage it.

MACDUFF
O, I could play the woman with mine eyes°   **play . . . eyes:** weep   230
And braggart with my tongue. But, gentle heavens,
Cut short all intermission.° Front to front°   **intermission:** interval; **Front to front:** face to
Bring thou this fiend of Scotland and myself.   face
Within my sword's length set him. If he scape,
Heaven forgive him too.   235

MALCOLM   This tune goes manly.
Come, go we to the king. Our power° is ready;   **power:** army
Our lack is nothing but our leave.° Macbeth   **Our . . . leave:** we lack only formal permission
Is ripe for shaking, and the pow'rs above   to depart
Put on their instruments.° Receive what cheer you may   **Put . . . instruments:** urge on their agents
The night is long that never finds the day.   *Exeunt.*   240

       5.1° *Enter a Doctor of Physic and a Waiting Gentlewoman.*   **5.1:** Macbeth's castle at Dunsinane

DOCTOR   I have two nights watched with you, but can
perceive no truth in your report. When was it she last
walked?

GENTLEWOMAN   Since his majesty went into the field I
have seen her rise from her bed, throw her nightgown°
upon her, unlock her closet,° take forth paper, fold it,   5
write upon't, read it, afterwards seal it, and again return   **nightgown:** dressing gown
to bed; yet all this while in a most fast sleep.   **closet:** chest or cabinet

---

DISCOVERING SHAKESPEARE

(69) Staging [4.3.220]: What do you think Macduff does during his speech beginning in 4.3.220? Does some stage action take place?

(70) History [5.1.1]: What was a "Doctor of Physic" (5.1.1 s.d.)? What kind of training did such "doctors" have? What were their duties?

DOCTOR   A great perturbation in nature, to receive at once the benefit of sleep and do the effects of watching.° In this slumb'ry agitation, besides her walking and other actual performances, what at any time have you heard her say?

do . . . watching: act as if awake   10

GENTLEWOMAN   That, sir, which I will not report after her.

15

DOCTOR   You may to me, and 'tis most meet° you should.

meet: fitting

GENTLEWOMAN   Neither to you nor anyone, having no witness to confirm my speech.°

having . . . speech: (the gentlewoman's report would amount to charging the king with murder, which would be treasonable)

Enter Lady [Macbeth], with a taper.

Lo you, here she comes. This is her very guise,° and, upon my life, fast asleep. Observe her; stand close.°

guise: custom
close: concealed   20

DOCTOR   How came she by that light?

GENTLEWOMAN   Why, it stood by her. She has light by her continually. 'Tis her command.

DOCTOR   You see her eyes are open.

GENTLEWOMAN   Ay, but their sense are shut.   25

DOCTOR   What is it she does now? Look how she rubs her hands.

GENTLEWOMAN   It is an accustomed action with her, to seem thus washing her hands. I have known her continue in this a quarter of an hour.   30

LADY MACBETH   Yet here's a spot.

DOCTOR   Hark, she speaks. I will set down what comes from her, to satisfy my remembrance the more strongly.

LADY MACBETH   Out, damned spot! Out, I say! One — two — why then 'tis time to do't. Hell is murky. Fie, my lord, fie! a soldier and afeard? What need we fear who knows it, when none can call our power to account? Yet who would have thought the old man to have had so much blood in him?   35

40

DOCTOR   Do you mark that?

LADY MACBETH   The Thane of Fife° had a wife. Where is she now? What, will these hands ne'er be clean? No more o' that, my lord, no more o' that. You mar all with this starting.°

Thane of Fife: Macduff

starting: flinching   45

DOCTOR   Go to, go to!° You have known what you should not.

Go to, go to: come, come

GENTLEWOMAN   She has spoke what she should not, I am sure of that. Heaven knows what she has known.

LADY MACBETH   Here's the smell of the blood still. All the perfumes of Arabia will not sweeten this little hand Oh, oh, oh!   50

DOCTOR   What a sigh is there. The heart is sorely charged.°

sorely charged: heavily burdened

GENTLEWOMAN   I would not have such a heart in my bosom for the dignity° of the whole body.

dignity: high rank (i.e., as queen)   55

DOCTOR   Well, well, well.

DISCOVERING SHAKESPEARE

(71) <u>Staging</u> **[5.1.31]:** Why is Lady Macbeth rubbing her hands (5.1.31)? What <u>props</u> would be required in this scene? Why?

(72) <u>Paraphrase</u> **[5.1.58]:** Why does the Doctor say, "This disease is beyond my practice" (5.1.58)? Paraphrase this line into modern English. What "disease" does he think Lady Macbeth has?

GENTLEWOMAN   Pray God it be, sir.

DOCTOR   This disease is beyond my practice.° Yet I have
known those which have walked in their sleep who
have died holily in their beds.

LADY MACBETH   Wash your hands, put on your nightgown, look not so pale. I tell you yet again, Banquo's
buried. He cannot come out on's grave.

DOCTOR   Even so?

LADY MACBETH   To bed, to bed; there's knocking at the
gate. Come, come, come, come, give me your hand.
What's done cannot be undone. To bed, to bed, to bed.

Exit.

DOCTOR   Will she go now to bed?

GENTLEWOMAN   Directly.

DOCTOR
Foul whisp'rings are abroad. Unnatural deeds
Do breed unnatural troubles. Infected minds
To their deaf pillows will discharge their secrets.
More needs she the divine than the physician.
God, God forgive us all. Look after her;
Remove from her the means of all annoyance,°
And still keep eyes upon her. So good night.
My mind she has mated,° and amazed my sight.
I think, but dare not speak.

GENTLEWOMAN   Good night, good doctor.

Exeunt.

❧ **5.2°** *Drum and Colors.° Enter Menteith, Caithness,*
Angus, Lennox, Soldiers.

MENTEITH
The English pow'r is near, led on by Malcolm,
His uncle Siward, and the good Macduff.
Revenges burn° in them; for their dear causes
Would to the bleeding° and the grim alarm
Excite° the mortified° man.

ANGUS   Near Birnam Wood
Shall we well meet them; that way are they coming.

CAITHNESS
Who knows if Donalbain be with his brother?

LENNOX
For certain, sir, he is not. I have a file°
Of all the gentry. There is Siward's son
And many unrough° youths that even now
Protest° their first of manhood.

MENTEITH   What does the tyrant?

CAITHNESS
Great Dunsinane he strongly fortifies.
Some say he's mad; others that lesser hate him

practice: professional skill

60

65

70

annoyance: harm, trouble   75

mated: defeated (cf. checkmate)

5.2: Open country near Dunsinane; **Drum and Colors:** drummers and standard-bearers

Revenges burn: desire for revenge burns
bleeding: shedding of blood
Excite: incite; **mortified:** dead   5

file: list

unrough: beardless   10
Protest: assert

DISCOVERING SHAKESPEARE

(73) Staging [5.2.1]: How do you think 5.2 should be presented? How many actors should be on stage? What costumes
would they wear? What weapons and flags would they carry? Would they be accompanied by music of any kind?

Do call it valiant fury; but for certain
He cannot buckle his distempered° cause   **distempered:** diseased   15
Within the belt of rule.°   **rule:** authority

ANGUS   Now does he feel
His secret murders sticking on his hands.
Now minutely° revolts° upbraid his faith breach.°   **minutely:** every minute; **revolts:** rebellions;
Those he commands move only in command,°   **faith breach:** broken faith
Nothing in love. Now does he feel his title   **in command:** under orders   20
Hang loose about him, like a giant's robe
Upon a dwarfish thief.

MENTEITH   Who then shall blame
His pestered° senses to recoil and start,   **pestered:** tormented
When all that is within him does condemn
Itself for being there?   25

CAITHNESS   Well, march we on
To give obedience where 'tis truly owed.
Meet we the med'cine° of the sickly weal;°   **med'cine:** physician (i.e., Malcolm); **weal:** state
And with him pour we in our country's purge
Each drop of us.

LENNOX   Or so much as it needs
To dew° the sovereign flower and drown the weeds.   **dew:** water   30
Make we our march towards Birnam.

                        Exeunt, marching.

* **5.3**° *Enter Macbeth, Doctor, and Attendants.*   **5.3:** Within Macbeth's castle at Dunsinane

MACBETH
Bring me no more reports. Let them fly all.
Till Birnam Wood remove to Dunsinane,
I cannot taint° with fear. What's the boy Malcolm?   **taint:** grow weak
Was he not born of woman? The spirits that know
All mortal consequences° have pronounced me thus: **mortal consequences:** human eventualities   5
"Fear not, Macbeth. No man that's born of woman
Shall e'er have power upon thee." Then fly, false thanes,
And mingle with the English epicures.°   **English epicures:** pleasure-loving English
The mind I sway by° and the heart I bear   **I sway by:** (1) that rules me, (2) that I rule by
Shall never sag with doubt nor shake with fear.
   Enter Servant.   10
The devil damn thee black, thou cream-faced° loon!°   **cream-faced:** pale (with fear); **loon:** scoundrel
Where got'st thou that goose° look?   **goose:** foolish

SERVANT
There is ten thousand –

MACBETH   Geese, villain?

SERVANT   Soldiers, sir.   15

MACBETH
Go prick thy face and over-red° thy fear,   **over-red:** paint red (i.e., with ruddy courage)
Thou lily-livered boy. What soldiers, patch?°   **patch:** fool

---

DISCOVERING SHAKESPEARE

(74) Imagery [5.2.21]: The reference by Angus to "a giant's robe / Upon a dwarfish thief" (5.2.21–22) is only one of many prominent clothing <u>images</u> in the play. Find at least two others and list them on a separate piece of paper.

(75) Language [5.3.16]: What does Macbeth mean when he tells the Servant to "Go prick thy face and over-red thy fear" (5.3.16)? Why does he call the man a "goose" (5.3.12)?

Death of thy soul! those linen cheeks of thine
Are counselors to fear. What soldiers, whey-face?

SERVANT
The English force, so please you.   20

MACBETH
Take thy face hence.   *[Exit Servant.]*
                 Seyton! – I am sick at heart,
When I behold – Seyton, I say! – This push°   **push:** attack
Will cheer me ever, or disseat° me now.   **disseat:** unseat
I have lived long enough. My way of life
Is fall'n into the sere,° the yellow leaf,   **sere:** dry, withered   25
And that which should accompany old age,
As honor, love, obedience, troops of friends,
I must not look to have; but, in their stead,
Curses not loud but deep, mouth-honor, breath,
Which the poor heart would fain deny, and dare not.   30
Seyton!
   Enter Seyton.

SEYTON
What's your gracious pleasure?

MACBETH   What news more?

SEYTON
All is confirmed, my lord, which was reported.

MACBETH
I'll fight till from my bones my flesh be hacked.
Give me my armor.   35

SEYTON   'Tis not needed yet.

MACBETH
I'll put it on.
Send out more horses,° skirr° the country round,   **horses:** horsemen; **skirr:** scour
Hang those that talk of fear. Give me mine armor.
How does your patient, doctor?

DOCTOR   Not so sick, my lord,
As she is troubled with thick-coming fancies   40
That keep her from her rest.

MACBETH   Cure her of that.
Canst thou not minister to a mind diseased,
Pluck from the memory a rooted sorrow,
Raze out° the written troubles of the brain,   **Raze out:** erase
And with some sweet oblivious° antidote   **oblivious:** causing forgetfulness   45
Cleanse the stuffed bosom of that perilous stuff
Which weighs upon the heart?

DOCTOR   Therein the patient
Must minister to himself.

MACBETH
Throw physic° to the dogs, I'll none of it.   **physic:** medicine
   [To an Attendant]
Come, put mine armor on. Give me my staff.   50
Seyton, send out. – Doctor, the thanes fly from me. –
Come, sir, dispatch.° – If thou couldst, doctor, cast   **dispatch:** hurry

---

DISCOVERING SHAKESPEARE

(76) Language [5.3.37]: What is the meaning of the word "skirr" (5.3.37) in this context? (*Hint:* See the *Oxford English Dictionary.*)

The water° of my land, find her disease,
And purge it to a sound and pristine health,
I would applaud thee to the very echo,
That should applaud again. – Pull't off, I say. –
What rhubarb, senna, or what purgative drug
Would scour these English hence? Hear'st thou of them?

cast . . . water: analyze the urine (as a way of diagnosing illness)

55

DOCTOR
Ay, my good lord. Your royal preparation
Makes us hear something.

60

MACBETH   Bring it° after me.
I will not be afraid of death and bane°
Till Birnam Forest come to Dunsinane.

it: i.e., the remaining armor
bane: destruction

Exeunt [all but the Doctor].

DOCTOR
Were I from Dunsinane away and clear,
Profit again should hardly draw me here.   *[Exit.]*

⚜ **5.4°** *Drum and Colors. Enter Malcolm, Siward, Macduff, Siward's Son, Menteith, Caithness, Angus,
[Lennox, Ross,] and Soldiers, marching.*

5.4: Before Birnam Wood

MALCOLM
Cousins, I hope the days are near at hand
That chambers° will be safe.

chambers: private rooms (i.e., our homes);
nothing: not at all

MENTEITH   We doubt it nothing.°
SIWARD
What wood is this before us?
MENTEITH   The Wood of Birnam.
MALCOLM
Let every soldier hew him down a bough
And bear't before him. Thereby shall we shadow°
The numbers of our host and make discovery°
Err in report of us.

shadow: conceal
discovery: (Macbeth's) reconnaissance

5

SOLDIER   It shall be done.
SIWARD
We learn no other but the confident tyrant
Keeps still in Dunsinane and will endure
Our setting down before't.°

setting down before: laying siege to

10

MALCOLM   'Tis his main hope,
For where there is advantage to be given°
Both more and less have given him the revolt,°
And none serve with him but constrainèd things
Whose hearts are absent too.

where . . . given: as the opportunity presents itself
more . . . revolt: high and low (i.e., nobility and commoners) have rebelled against him

MACDUFF   Let our just censures°
Attend the true event,° and put we on
Industrious soldiership.

just censures: impartial judgment
Attend . . . event: await the actual result

15

DISCOVERING SHAKESPEARE

(77) History [5.3.63]: Can you make an educated guess about the Renaissance opinion of doctors based on the depiction of this particular one? (*Hint:* See especially 5.3.63–64.)
(78) Paraphrase [5.4.13]: Paraphrase the following lines by Malcolm: "And none serve with him but constrainèd things/ Whose hearts are absent too" (5.4.13–14). How strong and loyal does Malcolm think Macbeth's army is?

SIWARD   The time approaches
That will with due decision make us know
What we shall say we have and what we owe.
Thoughts speculative their unsure hopes relate,
But certain issue strokes must arbitrate° –   **certain . . . arbitrate:** blows must decide the   20
                                                  final outcome
Towards which advance the war.°   *Exeunt, marching.*   **war:** army

5.5° *Enter Macbeth, Seyton, and Soldiers, with Drum*   **5.5:** Inside Macbeth's castle
and Colors.

MACBETH
Hang out our banners on the outward walls.
The cry is still, "They come." Our castle's strength
Will laugh a siege to scorn. Here let them lie
Till famine and the ague° eat them up.   **ague:** fever
Were they not forced° with those that should be ours,   **forced:** reinforced   5
We might have met them dareful,° beard to beard,   **dareful:** defiant
And beat them backward home.
   A cry within of women.   What is that noise?
SEYTON
It is the cry of women, my good lord.   *[Exit.]*
MACBETH
I have almost forgot the taste of fears.
The time has been my senses would have cooled   10
To hear a night-shriek, and my fell° of hair   **fell:** head
Would at a dismal treatise° rouse and stir   **dismal treatise:** frightening story
As life were in't. I have supped full with horrors.
Direness,° familiar to my slaughterous thoughts,   **Direness:** horror
Cannot once start° me.   **start:** frighten   15
   [Enter Seyton.]   Wherefore was that cry?
SEYTON
The queen, my lord, is dead.
MACBETH
She should have died hereafter:
There would have been a time° for such a word.   **a time:** i.e., an appropriate time
Tomorrow, and tomorrow, and tomorrow
Creeps in this petty pace from day to day   20
To the last syllable of recorded time,
And all our yesterdays have lighted fools
The way to dusty death. Out, out, brief candle,
Life's but a walking shadow, a poor player
That struts and frets his hour upon the stage   25
And then is heard no more. It is a tale
Told by an idiot, full of sound and fury,
Signifying nothing.
   Enter a Messenger.
Thou com'st to use thy tongue: thy story quickly.
MESSENGER
Gracious my lord,   30

DISCOVERING SHAKESPEARE

(79) <u>Imagery</u> [5.5.17]: Why does Macbeth say his wife "should have died hereafter" (5.5.17)? What other important references to time can you find in the play? Can you discover any progression in these <u>images</u>?

I should report that which I say° I saw,
But know not how to do't.

say: insist

MACBETH   Well, say, sir.

MESSENGER
As I did stand my watch upon the hill,
I looked toward Birnam, and anon methought
The wood began to move.   35

MACBETH   Liar and slave!

MESSENGER
Let me endure your wrath if't be not so.
Within this three mile may you see it coming.
I say, a moving grove.

MACBETH   If thou speak'st false,
Upon the next tree shalt thou hang alive
Till famine cling° thee. If thy speech be sooth,°   **cling:** shrivel; **sooth:** truth   40
I care not if thou dost for me as much.
I pull in° resolution, and begin   **pull in:** curb, check
To doubt° th' equivocation° of the fiend   **doubt:** suspect; **equivocation:** double-talk
That lies like truth. "Fear not, till Birnam Wood
Do come to Dunsinane," and now a wood   45
Comes toward Dunsinane. Arm, arm, and out!
If this which he avouches° does appear,   **avouches:** affirms
There is nor flying hence nor tarrying here.
I 'gin to be aweary of the sun,
And wish th' estate° o' th' world were now undone.   **estate:** order   50
Ring the alarum bell! Blow wind, come wrack,
At least we'll die with harness° on our back.   *Exeunt.*   **harness:** armor

❧ **5.6**° *Drum and Colors. Enter Malcolm, Siward, Mac-*   **5.6:** Fields outside Dunsinane Castle
duff, and their Army, with boughs.

MALCOLM
Now near enough. Your leafy screens throw down
And show like those you are. You, worthy uncle,
Shall with my cousin, your right noble son,
Lead our first battle.° Worthy Macduff and we   **battle:** battalion
Shall take upon's what else remains to do,   5
According to our order.°   **order:** battle plan

SIWARD   Fare you well.
Do we but find the tyrant's power° tonight,   **power:** forces
Let us be beaten if we cannot fight.

MACDUFF
Make all our trumpets speak, give them all breath,
Those clamorous harbingers of blood and death.   10
             Exeunt. Alarums continued.

DISCOVERING SHAKESPEARE

(80) Language [5.5.43]: What does Macbeth mean by the "equivocation" of the fiend (5.5.43)? See also 5.8.19–22 for another view of this same paradox.

❧ **5.7**° *Enter Macbeth.*

MACBETH
    They have tied me to a stake. I cannot fly,
    But bearlike I must fight the course.° What's he
    That was not born of woman? Such a one
    Am I to fear, or none.
      Enter Young Siward.

course: attack (like a bear tied to a stake and baited by dogs)

YOUNG SIWARD
    What is thy name?   5
MACBETH   Thou'lt be afraid to hear it.
YOUNG SIWARD
    No, though thou call'st thyself a hotter name
    Than any is in hell.
MACBETH   My name's Macbeth.
YOUNG SIWARD
    The devil himself could not pronounce a title
    More hateful to mine ear.
MACBETH   No, nor more fearful.
YOUNG SIWARD
    Thou liest, abhorrèd tyrant! With my sword   10
    I'll prove the lie thou speak'st.
      Fight, and Young Siward slain.
MACBETH   Thou wast born of woman
    But swords I smile at, weapons laugh to scorn,
    Brandished by man that's of a woman born.
                    Exit [with Young Siward's body.]
      Alarums. Enter Macduff.
MACDUFF
    That way the noise is. Tyrant, show thy face!
    If thou beest slain and with no stroke of mine,   15
    My wife and children's ghosts will haunt me still.
    I cannot strike at wretched kerns,° whose arms
    Are hired to bear their staves.° Either thou, Macbeth,
    Or else my sword with an unbattered edge
    I sheathe again undeeded.° There thou shouldst be;   20
    By this great clatter one of greatest note°
    Seems bruited.° Let me find him, Fortune,
    And more I beg not.   *Exit. Alarums.*
      Enter Malcolm and Siward.

kerns: mercenary foot soldiers
staves: lances

undeeded: having done nothing
note: importance
bruited: indicated, noised

SIWARD
    This way, my lord. The castle's gently rendered:°
    The tyrant's people on both sides do fight,
    The noble thanes do bravely in the war,   25
    The day almost itself professes° yours
    And little is to do.

gently rendered: surrendered calmly (or nobly)

itself professes: declares itself

DISCOVERING SHAKESPEARE

(81) History [5.7.2]: What was the Renaissance sport of "bear baiting"? How would a knowledge of this pastime help explain Macbeth's "They have tied me to a stake. I cannot fly, / But bearlike I must fight the course" (5.7.1–2)?

(82) Paraphrase [5.7.20]: Paraphrase Macduff's anxiousness to find Macbeth in the battle: "There thou shouldst be;/ By this great clatter one of greatest note / Seems bruited" (5.7.20–22). Why is he so desperate to locate him?

MALCOLM   We have met with foes
   That strike beside us.°
SIWARD   Enter, sir, the castle.

Exeunt. Alarum.

strike beside us: (1) fight on our side, (2) strike to one side of us

---

5.8 *Enter Macbeth.*

MACBETH
   Why should I play the Roman fool and die
   On mine own sword? Whiles I see lives,° the gashes
   Do better upon them.
     Enter Macduff.
MACDUFF   Turn, hellhound, turn!
MACBETH
   Of all men else I have avoided thee.
   But get thee back. My soul is too much charged°
   With blood of thine already.
MACDUFF   I have no words;
   My voice is in my sword, thou bloodier villain
   Than terms can give thee out.°
    Fight. Alarum.
MACBETH   Thou losest labor.
   As easy mayst thou the intrenchant° air
   With thy keen sword impress° as make me bleed.
   Let fall thy blade on vulnerable crests.
   I bear a charmèd life, which must not yield
   To one of woman born.
MACDUFF   Despair thy charm,°
   And let the angel° whom thou still° hast served
   Tell thee, Macduff was from his mother's womb
   Untimely ripped.
MACBETH
   Accursèd be that tongue that tells me so,
   For it hath cowed° my better part of man;°
   And be these juggling° fiends no more believed,
   That palter with us° in a double sense,
   That keep the word of promise to our ear
   And break it to our hope. I'll not fight with thee.
MACDUFF
   Then yield thee coward,°
   And live to be the show and gaze o' th' time.
   We'll have thee, as our rarer monsters° are,
   Painted upon a pole,° and underwrit
   "Here may you see the tyrant."
MACBETH   I will not yield,
   To kiss the ground before young Malcolm's feet
   And to be baited with the rabble's curse.
   Though Birnam Wood be come to Dunsinane,
   And thou opposed, being of no woman born,

Whiles . . . lives: as long as I see living creatures

charged: burdened   5

give thee out: describe you

intrenchant: incapable of being cut
impress: mark   10

charm: magic
angel: guardian spirit; **still:** always
     15

cowed: made cowardly; **better . . . man:** most of what makes me a man
juggling: deceiving, quibbling   20
palter with us: equivocate to us, trick us

yield thee coward: surrender as, or concede that you are, a coward
monsters: freaks   25
Painted . . . pole: depicted on a signboard

     30

DISCOVERING SHAKESPEARE

(83) Plot [5.8.8]: Why does Macbeth say to Macduff in the middle of their fight, "Thou losest labor" (5.8.8)? How does Macduff answer him?

Yet I will try the last. Before my body
I throw my warlike shield. Lay on, Macduff,
And damned be him that first cries "Hold, enough!"
Exeunt fighting. Alarums. [Re]enter fighting, and
Macbeth slain. [Exit Macduff with Macbeth's body.]

Retreat and flourish. Enter, with Drum and Colors,
Malcolm, Siward, Ross, Thanes, and Soldiers.

MALCOLM
I would the friends we miss were safe arrived.   35
SIWARD
Some must go off;° and yet, by these° I see,
So great a day as this is cheaply bought.

> go off: perish; these: i.e., these here assembled

MALCOLM
Macduff is missing, and your noble son.
ROSS
Your son, my lord, has paid a soldier's debt.
He only lived but till he was a man,   40
The which no sooner had his prowess confirmed
In the unshrinking station° where he fought
But like a man he died.

> unshrinking station: place from which he did not retreat

SIWARD   Then he is dead?
ROSS
Ay, and brought off the field. Your cause of sorrow
Must not be measured by his worth, for then   45
It hath no end.
SIWARD   Had he his hurts before?°

> Had . . . before?: were his wounds on the front of his body (i.e., was he running away?)

ROSS
Ay, on the front.
SIWARD   Why then, God's soldier be he.
Had I as many sons as I have hairs,
I would not wish them to a fairer death:
And so his knell is knolled.°

> knolled: tolled   50

MALCOLM   He's worth more sorrow,
And that I'll spend for him.
SIWARD   He's worth no more.
They say he parted well and paid his score,°
And so, God be with him. Here comes newer comfort.

> score: reckoning

Enter Macduff, with Macbeth's head.
MACDUFF
Hail, king, for so thou art. Behold where stands
Th' usurper's cursèd head. The time is free.   55
I see thee compassed° with thy kingdom's pearl,°
That speak my salutation in their minds,
Whose voices I desire aloud with mine –
Hail, King of Scotland!

> compassed: surrounded; kingdom's pearl: what is most valuable in the kingdom (i.e., the assembled nobility)

ALL   Hail, King of Scotland!
Flourish.

DISCOVERING SHAKESPEARE

(84) Language [5.8.46]: Why does Old Siward ask if his dead son had "his hurts before" (5.8.46)? What pun on the word "hair" is he making when he says, "Had I as many sons as I have hairs, / I would not wish them to a fairer death" (5.8.48–49)?

MALCOLM

We shall not spend a large expense of time   60
Before we reckon° with your several loves   **reckon:** settle accounts
And make us even with° you. My thanes and kinsmen,   **make . . . with:** repay our debts to
Henceforth be earls, the first that ever Scotland
In such an honor named. What's more to do
Which would be planted newly with the time° –   **planted . . . time:** done at the beginning of the   65
As calling home our exiled friends abroad   new era
That fled the snares of watchful tyranny,
Producing forth the cruel ministers°   **ministers:** agents
Of this dead butcher and his fiendlike queen,
Who, as 'tis thought, by self and violent° hands   **self and violent:** her own violent   70
Took off her life – this, and what needful else
That calls upon us, by the grace of Grace
We will perform in measure, time,° and place.   **perform in measure, time:** duly perform at
So thanks to all at once and to each one,   the appropriate time
Whom we invite to see us crowned at Scone.   75

Flourish. Exeunt omnes.

DISCOVERING SHAKESPEARE

(85) Rhyme [5.8.72]: How many rhyming couplets end the play? Are these perfect or slant rhymes? Can you make any predictions about the stability of Malcolm's reign based on these final couplets?

❧

Research and Discussion Topics

ACT I

1. What were the most common beliefs regarding witchcraft during the Renaissance? How were witches discovered and punished? What special powers did they have? What were their "familiars"?

2. What was a "heath" (1.1.7)?

3. What were "kerns" and "galloglasses" (1.2.13)?

4. How did Shakespeare's audience perceive of Fortune (1.2.14)?

5. Find a map of Scotland. What were the major cities during Shakespeare's time? How was Scotland governed?

6. Where was Norway (1.2.31) in relation to Scotland?

7. What was a "thane" (1.2.45)?

8. Where were Cawdor (1.2.53), Glamis (1.3.48), Cumberland (1.4.39), Inverness (1.4.42), Colmekill (2.4.33), Scone (2.4.31 and 5.8.75), and Fife (2.4.36)?

9. Where was Saint Colme's Inch (1.2.62)?

10. What was the "shipman's card" (1.3.17)?

11. What was the "insane root" (1.3.84)?

12. How were criminals executed in Renaissance Scotland (1.4.1)?

13. What were "heaven's cherubin" (1.7.22)?

14. Who was the "poor cat i' th' adage" (1.7.45)?

15. What was a "limbeck" (1.7.68)?

ACT II

1. What type of clocks (2.1.2) were used during the Renaissance?

2. What are the "weïrd sisters" (2.1.21)? Where does the name "weïrd" come from?

3. What was a "dudgeon" (2.1.47)?

4. Who were Hecate (2.1.53) and Tarquin (2.1.56)?

5. What was a "bellman" (2.2.3)?

6. What was a "posset" (2.2.6)?

7. What did "grooms" (2.2.53) do?

8. Who was Neptune (2.2.63)?

9. What were a porter's duties (2.3.1)?

10. Who was Beelzebub (2.3.3)?

11. What was an "equivocator" (2.3.8)?

12. What was "French hose" (2.3.13)?

13. What time did the "second cock" crow (2.3.22)?

14. What was a Gorgon (2.3.71)?

ACT III

1. Does Banquo become "the root and father / Of many kings" (3.1.5–6)? What was the historical relationship between Fleance and James I?

2. What was an "oracle" (3.1.9)?

3. What was a "parricide" (3.1.31)?

4. What was a "vizard" (3.2.35)?

5. Did "scorpions" (3.2.37) exist in Scotland at this time?

6. Who is the Third Murderer (3.3.1)?

7. What were "Augurs" (3.4.125)?

8. What were maggotpies, choughs, and rooks (3.4.126)?

9. What were "beldams" (3.5.2)?

10. Where was Acheron (3.5.15)?

11. Who are Stadling, Puckle, Hopper, and Hellway (3.5.39–40)?

12. Who was "the most pious Edward" (3.6.27)?

13. What was the Gunpowder Plot? How did it influence *Macbeth?*

14. Who were the Jesuits? Why were they called "equivocators"?

ACT IV

1. Who is Harpier (4.1.3)?

2. Explain the following cauldron ingredients: fenny snake, newt, blindworm, howlet, mummy, slips of yew, tiger's chawdron (4.1.12–34).

3. What was a "murderer's gibbet" (4.1.88)?

4. In which other Shakespearean plays do "apparitions" appear?

5. Which other Renaissance plays feature a magic "glass" (4.1.133)?

6. What was the meaning of "twofold balls, and treble scepters" (4.1.143)?

7. How were "lime" and a "gin" used to catch birds (4.2.35)?

8. Who was the "brightest" angel (4.3.22)? How did he fall?

ACT V

1. What types of writing instruments were available during the Renaissance (5.1.7)?

2. Were most perfumes manufactured in "Arabia" (5.1.51)? What were they made of?

3. Where was Birnam Wood (5.2.5)?

4. How close was it to Dunsinane (5.2.12)?

5. What were "epicures" (5.3.8)?

6. What was "whey" (5.3.19)?

7. What kinds of diseases could physicians diagnose from urinalysis (5.3.53)?

8. What were "rhubarb" and "senna" (5.3.57)?

9. What was the "ague" (5.5.4)?

10. When were "earls" (5.8.63) first created in Scotland? How were people rewarded for becoming earls?

Filmography

1982
Lincoln Center Theater Company
Rating:

Directed by: Sarah Caldwell and Kirk Browning

Philip Anglim as Macbeth
Maureen Anderman as Lady Macbeth
Kenneth Campbell as Macduff
Fritz Sperberg as Banquo
Kelsey Grammer as Ross
Heard Cordis as Witch
Ellen Gould as Witch
Dana Ivey as Witch

The Lincoln Center *Macbeth* is a filmed stage production full of energy; it has a few minor problems of picture and sound quality resulting from this format, but the dialogue is clear, and the acting is good throughout. The witches, one male and two female, sing most of their lines. The Macbeths are an attractive, younger couple, full of ambition even before the witches' prophecies. Philip Anglim's Macbeth is slightly pompous and has shifty brown eyes, which sometimes appear unfocused, making him seem mentally unbalanced. Kenneth Campbell's performance as Macduff is particularly strong. At the end of the play, when Macduff fights Macbeth, Anglim, full of regret for the slaughter of Macduff's family, refuses to draw his sword to fight; Campbell, however, kills him anyway, afterward placing the cross he wears on Macbeth's chest.

1981
Bard Productions, Ltd.
Rating:

Directed by: Arthur Allan Seidelman

Jeremy Brett as Macbeth
Piper Laurie as Lady Macbeth
Barry Primus as Banquo
Simon MacCorkindale as Macduff
Brad David Stockton as Ross
Alan Oppenheimer as Duncan
Richard Alfieri as Malcolm
Michael Augenstein as Donalbain
Johnny Crawford as Seyton
Jay Robinson as Porter

The Bard versions of Shakespeare's plays are filmed on a mostly bare wooden stage without an audience, and this one is no exception. However, using fog (dry ice), fire, and the swirling draperies of the witches (which vaguely resemble multicolored moss), this production creates an atmosphere suitable for *Macbeth*. If there is nothing extraordinary about it, there is nothing substandard about it either. The acting is uniformly professional, and even those choices that might seem questionable, such as Piper Laurie's cold-blooded, sometimes detached Lady Macbeth, can certainly find support in the text. Jeremy Brett is as emotional as Laurie is emotionless. His is a compelling, ultimately believable portrait of a good man gone almost completely bad. The witches, who appear with their familiars and are young and attractive, give an interesting spin to the play's "Fair is foul and foul is fair."

1982
B B C
(color)
Rating:

Directed by: Jack Gold

Nicol Williamson as Macbeth
Jane Lapotaire as Lady Macbeth
Mark Dignam as Duncan
Ian Hogg as Banquo
Tony Doyle as Macduff
James Bolam as the Porter

Brenda Bruce as First Witch
Eileen Way as Second Witch
Anne Dyson as Third Witch

As with most of the BBC Shakespeare films, this *Macbeth* is a straightforward representation of Shakespeare's play, largely faithful to the text, but it is not without its flaws. The acting style in this production is very subdued, often depriving the play of its energy. The cast (with few exceptions) is singularly unattractive, including Lady Macbeth; she is, however, young, and her reading of the "unsex me now" scene is sexually charged. Nicol Williamson's Macbeth is alternately dour, growling out his lines, and agitated, with the labored breathing of an asthmatic. The Porter is not perceivably drunk and is certainly not funny. The witches, however, are excellent; old crones in shabby, hooded cloaks, with gnarled hands, their lines are clearly articulated, not drowned by sound effects, as is often the case.

1971
Columbia Pictures Industries, Inc. & Playboy Productions, Inc.
Rating:

Directed by: Roman Polanski

Jon Finch as Macbeth
Francesca Annis as Lady Macbeth
Martin Shaw as Banquo
Terence Bayler as Macduff
John Stride as Ross
Nicholas Selby as Duncan
Stephen Chase as Malcolm
Paul Shelley as Donalbain
Noel Davis as Seyton
Sydney Bromley as Porter

Polanski has directed *Macbeth* as an R-rated horror film. Blood is more than a physical presence here; it has almost become a character. Many of the images are either terrible or grotesque. The witches bury a severed human hand, and there are extra, added witches whose nudity is truly repulsive. However, many of the realistic details, including animals such as the bear being brought in for bear baiting, help to energize the story and even to actualize some of Shakespeare's metaphors. Jon Finch as Macbeth and Francesca Annis as Lady Macbeth are much younger than is usual and, therefore, much more believable as lovers whose passion for each other becomes a poison for Scotland. Finch, who had never acted in Shakespeare before but went on to appear in two BBC Shakespeare films, gives his most natural performance here, aided perhaps by the voice-over soliloquies. Because of Playboy's participation in the project and Francesca Annis' nudity, many reviewers have underestimated this production.

1948
Republic Pictures
(b/w)
Rating:

Directed by: Orson Welles

Orson Welles as Macbeth
Jeanette Nolan as Lady Macbeth
Dan O'Herlihy as Macduff
Roddy McDowall as Malcolm
Edgar Barrier as Banquo
Peggy Webber as Lady Macduff/Witch
Brainerd Duffield as First Witch/First Murderer
Christopher Welles as Young Macduff
Alan Napier as Holy Father

This production is notable for its crisp cinematography, voice-over soliloquies, distracting Scottish accents, and brutal pruning of Shakespeare's text. The elimination of entire scenes made way for new scenes not often in the play, including horses galloping across the countryside, the execution of Cawdor, an elaborate procession to Macbeth's castle, Lady Macbeth dispensing drugged wine to Duncan's guards, Birnam Wood creeping along to Dunsinane, and Lady Macbeth running around screaming like a loon. Welles also added a new character called "Holy Father" in order to make the play seem a more direct struggle between good and evil. Unfortunately, the character has the hairstyle of Heidi and the screen presence of a large wooden door. Nevertheless, Orson Welles makes a charismatic and commanding Macbeth, and Jeanette Nolan (in her screen debut) is lovely and quietly scheming as his lady. The witches (one male and two female) are costumed traditionally as hags with long gray hair. Welles as always used black and white film to good effect, producing an eerie and expressionistic film.

1954
Hallmark Hall of Fame
(b/w)
Rating:

Directed by: George Schaefer

Maurice Evans as Macbeth
Judith Anderson as Lady Macbeth
House Jameson as Duncan
Richard Waring as Macduff
Staats Cotsworth as Banquo
Pat O'Malley as the Porter
Jane Rose as First Witch
Frieda Altman as Second Witch
Maud Sheerer as Third Witch

This Hallmark Hall of Fame production of *Macbeth* is poorly lit; the actors appear either over-exposed by a bright spotlight or lost in shadow, and in both cases, facial expressions are difficult to read. The soundtrack also has its flaws, with the actors throwing away some lines in too-soft whispers. The style of performance is overly theatrical, a caricature of Shakespearean acting. The costumes and hairstyles are Hollywood-medieval, and the fight scenes, filmed with what sounds like wooden swords, are unrealistic, to say the least. The witches are played as old hags in black robes. The Macbeths are not a young couple, and Lady Macbeth could easily have doubled as one of the witches, particularly in the "unsex me now" scene, which is complete with music that is meant to be (but is not) unnerving. The only outstanding aspect of the film is Pat O'Malley's performance as the Porter in the knocking-at-the-gate scene.

Annotated Bibliography

Bloom, Harold, ed. *Modern Critical Interpretations: William Shakespeare's "Macbeth."* New York: Chelsea House, 1987. PR 2823.W48.

> In this collection of contemporary essays on *Macbeth,* Bloom includes articles by such notable critics as Mack, Felperin, and Watson. In addition, in his own brief introduction, the critic examines the play's Oedipal aspects and takes into account critical work by Goddard, Knights, and Levin.

Brown, John Russell, ed. *Focus on "Macbeth."* London: Routledge, 1982. PR 2823.F65.

> Attempting to provide a comprehensive review of modern interpretations of *Macbeth,* Brown divides his collection into four parts: a focus on the play's structure and themes, a history of productions of the play, recent performance criticism, and a "special studies" section on *Macbeth.* Contained in the first group are classic essays by Hawkins, Stallybrass, Rosenberg, Hall, and Evans. Topics discussed under the special studies category include vision and spectacle in the play, *Macbeth* as a tragedy of guilt, the Witches' "musical" language, and the psychopathology of murder.

Calderwood, James L. *If It Were Done: "Macbeth" and Tragic Action.* Amherst: University of Massachusetts Press, 1986. PR 2823.C28.

> In this hybrid poststructuralist, anthropological, and psychoanalytic reading of the play, Calderwood presents three analyses of *Macbeth.* The first compares *Macbeth* and *Hamlet,* in particular the plays' discussions of time and space, their high theatricality, and their ambiguous meanings. In the second essay, Calderwood examines *Macbeth* from an Aristotelian perspective, considering the play's elements of tragic action, off-stage occurrences, and mixture of sexuality and violence. The third and final essay considers *Macbeth* using Rene Girard's concept of sacrificial violence and Freud's notion of the Oedipus complex to suggest that violence forms the core of Macbeth's self-concept.

Elliott, G. R. *Dramatic Providence in "Macbeth": A Study of Shakespeare's Tragic Theme of Humanity and Grace with a Supplementary Essay on King Lear*. Princeton: Princeton University Press, 1960. PR 2823.E4.

> Advancing a Formalist analysis of *King Lear*, Elliott reads the play as a dramatic poem and scrutinizes uses of imagery, characterization, and language. He contends that the play's central theme revolves around the notions of divine grace and sincere charity, qualities exhibited primarily in the character of Duncan. Elliott then examines the play's other central figures for these same qualities, suggesting ultimately that Malcolm, Banquo, the Doctor, and Ross all exhibit some "good" characteristics.

Jorgens, Jack J. *Shakespeare on Film*. Bloomington: Indiana University Press, 1977, pp.148–74. PR 3093.J6.

> In the first of these two chapters on cinematic versions of *Macbeth*, Jorgens compares the film adaptations of George Schaefer, Orson Welles, and Akira Kurosawa. He highlights the films' central differences, arguing that Schaefer's version focuses on the unnatural, Welles' completely on the play's dark and evil elements, and Kurosawa's on the drama's "tragedy of fate." Jorgens devotes all of chapter eleven to a discussion of Roman Polanski's 1971 adaptation of the play, arguing that the director successfully depicts *Macbeth*'s nihilistic, violent qualities within a naturalistic framework.

Jorgensen, Paul A. *Our Naked Frailties: Sensational Art and Meaning in "Macbeth."* Berkeley: University of California Press, 1971. PR 2823.J6.

> Focusing on the play's "sensational" qualities, Jorgensen argues that *Macbeth* evokes an indescribable sense of terror within the audience in its portrayal of crime and punishment. Suggesting that the play's images of evil, blood, murder, and the supernatural mirror elements in Senecan tragedy, the critic argues that *Macbeth* is a historical play in which punishment befits early modern standards. In particular, Jorgensen notes Macbeth's self-destructive fear and deems such paralyzing anxiety a traditionally appropriate punishment for his crimes.

Kliman, Bernice W. *"Macbeth": Shakespeare in Performance*. Manchester: Manchester University Press, 1992. PR 2823.K58.

> Examining a relatively small number of productions, Kliman classifies performances of *Macbeth* into either actor- or director-controlled categories. Exemplifying actor-dominated types, the critic compares early productions that focused on the protagonist with recent productions that focus more on the actors, such as Laurence Olivier and Vivien Leigh's 1955 theatrical version, Maurice Evans and Judith Anderson's 1960 television production, and two BBC television versions. In her discussion of director-dominated productions, Kliman considers versions by Orson Welles, Roman Polanski, and Trevor Nunn. The critic includes some literary criticism in her evaluation of these productions.

Lemon, Rebecca. "Scaffolds of Treason in *Macbeth*." *Theatre Journal* 54.1 (2002): 25–43. journal PN 3171.E38.

> This intriguing article draws on the history of scaffold speeches by traitors which were compelled in order to teach the public not to be treasonous. Specifically mentioned is the actual speech given by the Thane of

Cawdor. Lemon's goal is to demonstrate how the language of Cawdor is present in the language of all treasonous figures and, more controversially, in the language of Malcolm.

Levin, Joanna. "Lady Macbeth and the Daemonologie of Hysteria." *ELH* 69.1 (2002): 21–55. journal PR 1.E5.
> Levin explores the characterization of Lady Macbeth with regard to the evolution in early modern England concerning the view of bewitched women from demon-possessed to suffering from hysteria (or "suffocated mother" syndrome). Drawing on abundant textual evidence, Levin claims that Lady Macbeth is the embodiment of this change, since she is connected to both witchcraft and motherhood.

Rosenberg, Marvin. *The Masks of "Macbeth."* Berkeley: University of California Press, 1978. PR 2823.R67.
> In this extensive scene-by-scene examination of *Macbeth*'s imagery, values, and language, Rosenberg suggests that the play contains a complex and ambiguous mix of themes and symbols. Evaluating the play's stage history, he discusses various performances to support his notion that *Macbeth* is centrally a play about conflict among nature, the individual, and society. Rosenberg advances particularly close readings of Macbeth, Lady Macbeth, and the Witches. Also included in this volume is a list of criticism; an index of actors, actresses, and directors; and lists of performances in non–English-speaking countries.

Schoenbaum, S. *"Macbeth": Critical Essays.* New York: Garland Press, 1991. PR 2823.S345.
> In this examination of *Macbeth*'s critical heritage, Schoenbaum includes seminal analyses of the play by such authors as Bradley, Knight, Brooks, Holloway, Rosenberg, and Wickham. The editor also incorporates comments by Samuel Johnson and Hazlett to offer a broad historical swath of critical interpretations. Furthermore, Schoenbaum includes a wide array of twentieth-century examinations of *Macbeth,* featuring work by Derek Traversi, Mark Van Doren, Donald A. Stauffer, Kenneth Muir, Harold C. Goddard, Richard David, and others.

Sinfield, Alan, ed. *"Macbeth": New Casebooks.* New York: St. Martin's, 1992. PR 2823.M237.
> Focusing primarily on contemporary interpretations of *Macbeth,* Sinfield includes essays by Stallybrass, Freud, Adelman, Evans, Goldberg, and Mullaney. Additionally, the editor features excerpts from work by French, Eagleton, Dollimore, Belsey, and Holderness. A brief annotated bibliography is also included in this casebook.

Wills, Garry. *Witches and Jesuits: Shakespeare's "Macbeth."* Oxford: Oxford University Press, 1995. PR 2823.W49.
> In this historicist reading of the play, Wills contends that *Macbeth* is a response to the Gunpowder Plot of 1605. Concentrating on the play's allusions to demonology, regicide, and Jesuitical equivocation, the critic reads Macbeth's character as a kind of warlock. Wills concludes his argument with the suggestion that *Macbeth*'s topicality makes the play less successful in modern productions, but that its aspects of demonology might offer intriguing material for new performances.

The Tempest

The Tempest at the American Repertory Theater in Cambridge, Massachusetts, with Benjamin Evett as Ariel and Alvin Epstein as Gonzalo (1995). Photograph by T. Charles Erickson.

Originally performed at the court of James I on November 1, 1611, *The Tempest* was not published until the 1623 First Folio, where it stands as the first play in the collection. Although no single source has been found for Shakespeare's plot, several important influences on the script have been identified by scholars. Travel literature by such fashionable authors as Sir Walter Ralegh, Richard Hakluyt, and Thomas Harriot, for example, had awakened the public's fascination with exploring new worlds, as did the sensational shipwreck of the *Sea Venture* in 1609 in the Bermudas, which was described by a contemporary author as "a most prodigious and enchanted place" thought to be populated by devils, evil spirits, and primitive, bloodthirsty natives. Michel de Montaigne's well-known essay "Of the Cannibals" (translated by John Florio in 1603) was not only the inspiration for Gonzalo's monologue on the ideal commonwealth in 2.1, but was no doubt also the stimulus for the play's ironic debate juxtaposing noble savages against the evils of Western civilization and colonial imperialism. Additional <u>sources</u> including Ovid's *Metamorphoses,* English fairy lore, and the courtly <u>masque</u> tradition round out the principal influences on Shakespeare's <u>script</u>.

The play's unique <u>genre</u> is best described as a "revenge comedy," with side glances at the popular <u>romance</u> tradition. The <u>comic</u> pattern of the play moves from society to wilderness to improved society as it oscillates between the usurped duchy of Milan to Prospero's island and back to the prospect of Milan again, finally restored to its rightful ruler. Prospero's lust for revenge, turned to benign forgiveness by Ariel's pity, dissolves into comic <u>catharsis</u> as he discards his "rough magic" and resolves to drown his book "deeper than did ever plummet sound" (5.1.50–57).

Although *The Tempest* is not the last play written by Shakespeare (most scholars feel it is followed by *King Henry VIII* and *The Two Noble Kinsmen*), tradition dictates that Prospero's renunciation of magic is a dramatic <u>metaphor</u> for Shakespeare's own farewell to the stage, in which he gives up the excitement and power of theatre for quiet retirement in his home town of Stratford-upon-Avon. Written around the same time as *Cymbeline, The Winter's Tale,* and *Pericles, The Tempest* also betrays the influence of the playwright's late <u>romances</u>, which feature improbable fictions, separation and reunion, apparent death and miraculous resurrection, lost children, magic, riddles, and prophecies.

The <u>themes</u> and <u>symbols</u> that rise from Shakespeare's <u>script</u> are some of the most profound and enduring in all his plays. Chief among them is a fascination with the unknown—not only in the exploration of new and exotic civilizations, but also through psychological and sociological inquiries into the human psyche. The vision of an idyllic island universe is set against the corrupt, unregenerate world of Naples, just as Caliban's innocence and vulnerability is in contrast to the power and deceit of Prospero and his fellow Europeans. The <u>plot</u> also investigates the proper duties of rulers to their subjects: a debate personified by Prospero's control over Ariel, Caliban, and the various bands of "conspirators" on the island. Additional <u>themes</u> investigated by recent scholarship include patriarchy, race and colonialism, magic as a precursor of Baconian science, the versatility of language, piety, the practices of slavery, geography, the many different meanings of the word "monster," the ideal balance between the active and contemplative life, the value of utopian societies, the uses of music, and the regenerative power of water.

Although *The Tempest* was apparently not one of Shakespeare's most popular plays during the Renaissance, it was reintroduced by William Davenant in 1667 in a drastic revision that cut two-thirds of Shakespeare's text, expanded the comic scenes, reduced Prospero's role, and provided Miranda and Caliban with sisters named Dorinda and Sycorax. Thomas Shadwell's operatic version of the play in 1674, complete with elaborate set machinery and newly written songs, held the stage for nearly seventy years before being replaced by productions mounted by James Lacy (1746) and David Garrick (1756), which advertised "the play as written by Shakespeare," although both versions included a fifth-act "Masque of Neptune" and several characters alien to the original <u>script</u>. Later productions by Richard Sheridan (1777), John Philip Kemble (1789), and William Macready (1838) relied more heavily on Shakespeare's text, but retained most of the spectacular effects, stage machinery, and vocal music that had made the play so popular a century earlier. The extent of these extra-textual materials is nowhere more apparent than in Charles Kean's 1857 London production, which was heavily cut, yet employed 140 stage hands and ran more than five hours. Twentieth-century landmark productions have included those by Beerbohm Tree (1904), Harcourt Williams (1934), Peter Brook (1957), Jonathan Miller (1970), Peter Hall (1973), and Nicholas Hytner (1988).

Not surprisingly, the characters of Ariel, Caliban, and Prospero show most evolution over the past four hundred years. Although Ariel had been a male role throughout the seventeenth century, the part was gradually taken over by women until an Old Vic production in 1930, when a male actor in the role re-opened the possibility of androgynous casting. Likewise, Caliban debuted as a comic caricature, then gradually morphed into a more malign, human, and tragic figure in the Victorian period and beyond. And Prospero, who had tradi-tionally been presented as an aged, kindly wizard, has developed through the brilliance of such actors as John Gielgud, Derek Jacobi, and Michael Hordern into a fascinating and ambiguous figure who skillfully combines vengeance and compassion within the play. Among the most arresting film versions of the script are Dallas Bower's 1939 production featuring Peggy Ashcroft as Miranda, the 1960 American Hallmark Series *Tempest* (with Maurice Evans, Lee Remick, and Richard Burton), Derek Jarman's darkly seductive 1980 adaptation, and Peter Greenaway's wildly inventive *Prospero's Books* (1991)—a fictitious, symbolic re-creation based on the volumes Gonzalo furnishes for Prospero's exile.

Regardless of whether *The Tempest* is the author's farewell to the stage, the script serves as a fitting tribute to the brilliance of the playwright's astounding career. With its emphasis on the magic of theatre, Shakespeare's play confirms the power of "art to enchant" (5.1.332) through the divine and communal mystery of drama. Suspended as we are between the extremes of Ariel and Caliban, we need the regenerative influence of theatre to help us aspire to our more heavenly selves. For this wonderful gift, all we have to do is enclose ourselves in the enchanted circle of Shakespeare's plays.

The Tempest *at the Oregon Shakespearean Festi-val in Ashland, Oregon, with John Pribyl as Cal-iban (2001). Photograph by Andree Lanthier.*

The Tempest

NAMES OF THE ACTORS

ALONSO, *King of Naples*
SEBASTIAN, *his brother*
PROSPERO, *the right Duke of Milan*
ANTONIO, *his brother, the usurping Duke of Milan*
FERDINAND, *son to the King of Naples*
GONZALO, *an honest old councilor*
ADRIAN AND FRANCISCO, *lords*
CALIBAN, *a savage and deformed slave*
TRINCULO, *a jester*
STEPHANO, *a drunken butler*
MASTER OF A SHIP
BOATSWAIN
MARINERS
MIRANDA, *daughter to Prospero*
ARIEL, *an airy spirit*
IRIS ⎤
CERES ⎥
JUNO ⎬ *[personated by] spirits*
NYMPHS ⎥
REAPERS ⎦
[OTHER SPIRITS ATTENDING ON PROSPERO]

SCENE: *An uninhabited Island*

1.1° *A tempestuous noise of thunder and lightning heard. Enter a Shipmaster and a Boatswain.*

1.1: The deck of a ship at sea

MASTER   Boatswain!
BOATSWAIN   Here, master. What cheer?
MASTER   Good,° speak to th' mariners; fall to't yarely,° or we run ourselves aground. Bestir, bestir!   *Exit.*
   Enter Mariners.

Good: good fellow; **yarely:** quickly

BOATSWAIN   Heigh, my hearts! Cheerly, cheerly, my hearts! Yare, yare! Take in the topsail! Tend° to th' master's whistle! Blow till thou burst thy wind,° if room enough!°
   Enter Alonso, Sebastian, Antonio, Ferdinand, Gonzalo, and others.

5

Tend: attend

Blow . . . wind: (addressed to the storm)
if room enough: i.e., so long as we have sea room

DISCOVERING SHAKESPEARE

(1) History [1.1.1]: In nautical terminology, what was the difference between a "master" and a "boatswain" (1.1.2)?

ALONSO   Good boatswain, have care. Where's the master? Play the men.°

Play the men: act like men   10

BOATSWAIN   I pray now, keep below.

ANTONIO   Where is the master, bos'n?

BOATSWAIN   Do you not hear him? You mar our labor.
Keep your cabins: you do assist the storm.

GONZALO   Nay, good, be patient.   15

BOATSWAIN   When the sea is. Hence! What cares these
roarers° for the name of king? To cabin! Silence! Trouble
us not!

roarers: (1) waves, (2) rioters

GONZALO   Good, yet remember whom thou hast
aboard.   20

BOATSWAIN   None that I more love than myself. You are
a councilor: if you can command these elements to silence and work the peace of the present, we will not
hand° a rope more; use your authority. If you cannot,
give thanks you have lived so long, and make yourself
ready in your cabin for the mischance of the hour, if it
so hap. – Cheerly, good hearts! – Out of our way, I say.

hand: handle   25

Exit.

GONZALO   I have great comfort from this fellow: methinks he hath no drowning mark upon him; his com-
plexion° is perfect gallows.° Stand fast, good Fate, to his
hanging! Make the rope of his destiny our cable,° for
our own doth little advantage.° If he be not born to be
hanged, our case is miserable.   *Exeunt.*

complexion: indication of character in
appearance of face; **gallows:** (alluding to the
proverb "He that's born to be hanged need fear no
drowning")   30

cable: anchor cable

doth little advantage: doesn't help us much

Enter Boatswain.

BOATSWAIN   Down with the topmast! Yare! Lower, lower!
Bring her to try with main course!° *(A cry within.)* A
plague° upon this howling! They are louder than the
weather or our office.°

try with main course: lie hove-to (close to the
wind) with only the mainsail   35

plague: (followed by a dash in F, possibly
indicating a string of oaths censored out of the
text; cf. l. 40, and 5.1.218–19)

our office: (the noise we make at) our work

Enter Sebastian, Antonio, and Gonzalo.

Yet again? What do you here? Shall we give o'er and
drown? Have you a mind to sink?

SEBASTIAN   A pox o' your throat, you bawling, blasphe-
mous, incharitable dog!   40

BOATSWAIN   Work you, then.

ANTONIO   Hang, cur, hang, you whoreson, insolent
noisemaker! We are less afraid to be drowned than thou
art.

GONZALO   I'll warrant him for° drowning, though the
ship were no stronger than a nutshell and as leaky as an
unstanched wench.°

warrant . . . for: guarantee . . . against   45

as leaky . . . wench: (a joke probably about a
woman menstruating without using any absorbent
padding, but possibly about her being unsatisfied
though sexually aroused)   50

BOATSWAIN   Lay her ahold, ahold!° Set her two courses!°
Off to sea again! Lay her off!°

Lay her ahold: bring the ship close to the wind
(this would hold it away from the rocks but would
require more sail); **two courses:** foresail and
mainsail

Enter Mariners wet.

MARINERS   All lost! To prayers, to prayers! All lost!

[Exeunt.]

BOATSWAIN   What, must our mouths be cold?

Lay her off: take the ship out to sea

DISCOVERING SHAKESPEARE

(2) Paraphrase [1.1.31]: What does Gonzalo mean when he looks at the Boatswain and begs, "make the rope of his destiny our cable" (1.1.31)? Paraphrase the line into modern English.

GONZALO
 The king and prince at prayers! Let's assist them,
 For our case is as theirs.
SEBASTIAN   I am out of patience.
ANTONIO
 We are merely° cheated of our lives by drunkards.   **merely:** completely   55
 This wide-chopped° rascal – would thou mightst lie **wide-chopped:** wide-jawed
 drowning
 The washing of ten tides!°   **ten tides:** (pirates were hanged on shore and left
                    until three tides washed over them)
GONZALO   He'll be hanged yet,
 Though every drop of water swear against it
 And gape at wid'st to glut° him.   **glut:** swallow
  A confused noise within: "Mercy on us! –
 We split, we split! – Farewell, my wife and children! –   60
 Farewell, brother! – We split, we split, we split!"
            [Exit Boatswain.]
ANTONIO
 Let's all sink with th' king.
SEBASTIAN   Let's take leave of him.
           Exit [with Antonio].
GONZALO Now would I give a thousand furlongs of sea
 for an acre of barren ground – long heath, brown furze,° **long heath, brown furze:** heather and gorse
 anything. The wills above be done, but I would fain die   65
 a dry death.   *Exit.*

❧ **1.2**° *Enter Prospero and Miranda.*   **1.2:** The Island

MIRANDA
 If by your art,° my dearest father, you have   **art:** magic, skill
 Put the wild waters in this roar, allay them.
 The sky, it seems, would pour down stinking pitch
 But that the sea, mounting to th' welkin's cheek,°   **welkin's cheek:** sky's face
 Dashes the fire out. O, I have suffered   5
 With those that I saw suffer! A brave° vessel   **brave:** fine, noble, handsome (and so elsewhere
 (Who had no doubt some noble creature in her)   throughout the play)
 Dashed all to pieces! O, the cry did knock
 Against my very heart! Poor souls, they perished!
 Had I been any god of power, I would   10
 Have sunk the sea within the earth or ere°   **or ere:** before
 It should the good ship so have swallowed and
 The fraughting° souls within her.   **fraughting:** forming the cargo; **collected:**
PROSPERO   Be collected.°   composed
 No more amazement.° Tell your piteous° heart   **amazement:** fear, wonder; **piteous:** pitying
 There's no harm done.   15
MIRANDA   O, woe the day!
PROSPERO   No harm.
 I have done nothing but in care of thee,
 Of thee my dear one, thee my daughter, who

DISCOVERING SHAKESPEARE

(3) Shared Lines [1.1.54]: How do the shared lines in 1.1.54–62 influence the pacing of this portion of the scene?
(4) Names [1.2.15]: What do the names "Prospero" and "Miranda" mean? How does the etymology of each word help us understand these two important characters in the play?

Art ignorant of what thou art, naught knowing
Of whence I am; nor that I am more better
Than Prospero, master of a full poor cell,°   **cell:** a hermit's or poor person's dwelling or small   20
And thy no greater father.   cottage (not a prison cell)
MIRANDA   More to know
Did never meddle° with my thoughts.   **meddle:** mingle, interfere
PROSPERO   'Tis time
I should inform thee farther. Lend thy hand
And pluck my magic garment from me. *[Miranda
helps Prospero to take off his magic robe.]* So,
Lie there, my art.° Wipe thou thine eyes; have comfort.   **art:** i.e., his robe   25
The direful spectacle of the wrack, which touched
The very virtue of compassion in thee,
I have with such provision° in mine art   **provision:** foresight
So safely ordered that there is no soul –
No, not so much perdition° as an hair   **perdition:** loss   30
Betid° to any creature in the vessel   **Betid:** happened
Which thou heard'st cry, which thou saw'st sink. Sit
   down;
For thou must now know farther.
MIRANDA   You have often
Begun to tell me what I am; but stopped
And left me to a bootless inquisition,°   **bootless inquisition:** fruitless inquiry   35
Concluding, "Stay: not yet."
PROSPERO   The hour's now come;
The very minute bids thee ope thine ear.
Obey, and be attentive. Canst thou remember
A time before we came unto this cell?
I do not think thou canst, for then thou wast not   40
Out° three years old.   **Out:** fully
MIRANDA   Certainly, sir, I can.
PROSPERO
By what? By any other house or person?
Of anything the image tell me° that   **tell me:** i.e., describe for me
Hath kept with thy remembrance.
MIRANDA   'Tis far off,
And rather like a dream than an assurance   45
That my remembrance warrants.° Had I not   **remembrance warrants:** memory guarantees
Four or five women once that tended me?
PROSPERO
Thou hadst, and more, Miranda. But how is it
That this lives in thy mind? What seest thou else
In the dark backward° and abysm° of time?   **backward:** past; **abysm:** abyss   50
If thou remember'st aught ere thou cam'st here,
How thou cam'st here thou mayst.
MIRANDA   But that I do not.
PROSPERO
Twelve year since, Miranda, twelve year since,
Thy father was the Duke of Milan and
A prince of power.   55

DISCOVERING SHAKESPEARE

(5) Characterization [1.2.38]: How many times in this scene does Prospero tell Miranda to pay attention to him? How does this clue help us understand Prospero's character?

MIRANDA   Sir, are not you my father?

PROSPERO
Thy mother was a piece° of virtue, and   **piece:** masterpiece
She said thou wast my daughter; and thy father
Was Duke of Milan;° and his only heir   **Milan:** (stressed on first syllable)
And princess – no worse issued.°   **no worse issued:** no meaner in descent

MIRANDA   O the heavens!
What foul play had we that we came from thence?   60
Or blessèd was't we did?

PROSPERO   Both, both, my girl!
By foul play, as thou say'st, were we heaved thence,
But blessedly holp° hither.   **blessedly holp:** providentially helped

MIRANDA   O, my heart bleeds
To think o' th' teen° that I have turned you to,°   **teen:** trouble; **turned you to:** put you in mind of
Which is from° my remembrance! Please you, farther.   65
                                        from: out of

PROSPERO
My brother and thy uncle, called Antonio –
I pray thee mark me – that a brother should
Be so perfidious! – he whom next thyself
Of all the world I loved, and to him put
The manage of my state,° as at that time   **put . . . state:** entrusted the administration of my   70
Through all the signories° it was the first   dukedom
And Prospero the prime duke, being so reputed   **signories:** states of northern Italy
In dignity, and for the liberal arts
Without a parallel; those being all my study,
The government I cast upon my brother   75
And to my state grew stranger, being transported
And rapt in secret studies. Thy false uncle –
Dost thou attend me?

MIRANDA   Sir, most heedfully.

PROSPERO
Being once perfected° how to grant suits,   **Being . . . perfected:** having once mastered the
How to deny them, who t' advance, and who   skills of   80
To trash for overtopping,° new-created   **trash for overtopping:** check, as hounds, for
The creatures that were mine, I say, or° changed 'em,   going too fast
Or else new-formed 'em; having both the key°   **or:** either
Of officer and office, set all hearts i' th' state   **key:** (used with pun on its musical sense, leading
To what tune pleased his ear, that now he was   to the metaphor of *tune*)   85
The ivy which had hid my princely trunk
And sucked my verdure° out on't. Thou attend'st not?   **verdure:** sap, vitality

MIRANDA
O, good sir, I do.

PROSPERO   I pray thee mark me.
I thus neglecting worldly ends, all dedicated
To closeness,° and the bettering of my mind   **closeness:** seclusion   90
With that which, but° by being so retired,   **but:** merely
O'erprized all popular rate,° in my false brother   **O'erprized . . . rate:** exceeded the people's
Awaked an evil nature, and my trust,   understanding

DISCOVERING SHAKESPEARE

(6) Characterization [1.2.63]: On a separate piece of paper, write a character sketch of Miranda. How old is she? What kind of relationship does she have with her father? What specific lines and actions in 1.2 suggest these conclusions?

(7) <u>Verse</u> [1.2.88]: <u>Scan</u> Prospero's speech in 1.2.88–106. In which particular lines does the irregularity of the <u>verse</u> betray his emotional turmoil?

Like a good parent,° did beget of him
A falsehood in its contrary as great
As my trust was, which had indeed no limit,
A confidence sans bound.° He being thus lorded,
Not only with what my revenue yielded
But what my power might else exact,° like one
Who having unto truth, by telling of it,°
Made such a sinner of his memory
To° credit his own lie, he did believe
He was indeed the duke, out° o' th' substitution
And executing th' outward face of royalty
With all prerogative. Hence his ambition growing –
Dost thou hear?

MIRANDA   Your tale, sir, would cure deafness.

PROSPERO
To have no screen between this part he played
And him he played it for, he needs will be
Absolute Milan.° Me° (poor man) my library
Was dukedom large enough. Of temporal royalties°
He thinks me now incapable; confederates°
(So dry° he was for sway) with th' King of Naples
To give him annual tribute, do him homage,
Subject his coronet to his crown, and bend
The dukedom yet° unbowed (alas, poor Milan!)
To most ignoble stooping.

MIRANDA   O the heavens!

PROSPERO
Mark his condition,° and th' event;° then tell me
If this might be a brother.

MIRANDA   I should sin
To think but nobly of my grandmother.
Good wombs have borne bad sons.

PROSPERO   Now the condition.
This King of Naples, being an enemy
To me inveterate, hearkens my brother's suit;
Which was, that he, in lieu o' th' premises°
Of homage and I know not how much tribute,
Should presently° extirpate° me and mine
Out of the dukedom and confer fair Milan,
With all the honors, on my brother. Whereon,
A treacherous army levied, one midnight
Fated° to th' purpose, did Antonio open
The gates of Milan; and i' th' dead of darkness,
The ministers° for th' purpose hurried thence
Me and thy crying self.

MIRANDA   Alack, for pity!
I, not rememb'ring how I cried out then,
Will cry it o'er again; it is a hint°
That wrings mine eyes to't.

---

good parent: (alluding to the same proverb cited by Miranda in l. 120)   95

sans bound: unlimited

He . . . exact: (the sense is that Antonio had the prerogatives as well as the income of the duke)   100
it: i.e., the lie

To: as to
out: as a result

  105

Absolute Milan: Duke of Milan completely;
Me: as for me   110
temporal royalties: practical rule
confederates: joins in league with
dry: thirsty, eager

yet: hitherto   115

condition: pact; **event:** outcome

  120

in lieu o' th' premises: in return for the guarantees
presently: immediately; **extirpate:** remove   125

Fated: chosen by fate
  130
ministers: agents

hint: occasion
  135

DISCOVERING SHAKESPEARE

(8) Teaser [1.2.118]: Contrast Miranda's defense of her grandmother ("Good wombs have borne bad sons" in 1.2.120) with Don Pedro's lines about Hero's father in 1.1.105–108 of *Much Ado About Nothing*. Which character offers a better argument in favor of parents?

PROSPERO Hear a little further,
And then I'll bring thee to the present business
Which now's upon's; without the which this story
Were most impertinent.°   **impertinent:** irrelevant
MIRANDA   Wherefore did they not
That hour destroy us?
PROSPERO   Well demanded, wench.
My tale provokes that question. Dear, they durst not,   140
So dear the love my people bore me; nor set
A mark so bloody on the business; but
With colors fairer painted their foul ends.
In few,° they hurried us aboard a bark,   **few:** few words
Bore us some leagues to sea; where they prepared   145
A rotten carcass of a butt,° not rigged,   **butt:** tub
Nor tackle, sail, nor mast; the very rats
Instinctively have quit it. There they hoist us,
To cry to th' sea that roared to us; to sigh
To th' winds, whose pity, sighing back again,   150
Did us but loving wrong.
MIRANDA   Alack, what trouble
Was I then to you!
PROSPERO   O, a cherubin
Thou wast that did preserve me! Thou didst smile,
Infusèd with a fortitude from heaven,
When I have decked° the sea with drops full salt,   **decked:** adorned   155
Under my burden groaned: which raised in me
An undergoing stomach,° to bear up   **undergoing stomach:** determination to endure
Against what should ensue.
MIRANDA   How came we ashore?
PROSPERO
By providence divine.
Some food we had, and some fresh water, that   160
A noble Neapolitan, Gonzalo,
Out of his charity, who being then appointed
Master of this design, did give us, with
Rich garments, linens, stuffs, and necessaries
Which since have steaded° much. So, of his gentleness,   **steaded:** been of use   165
Knowing I loved my books, he furnished me
From mine own library with volumes that
I prize above my dukedom.
MIRANDA   Would I might
But ever see that man!
PROSPERO   Now I arise.
Sit still, and hear the last of our sea sorrow.   170
Here in this island we arrived; and here
Have I, thy schoolmaster, made thee more profit°   **more profit:** profit more

---

DISCOVERING SHAKESPEARE

(9) Tense [1.2.148]: In 1.2.148, Prospero shifts to present tense in order to give his story more dramatic emphasis ("There they hoist us . . ."). Where else in 1.2 does he use the present tense for similar rhetorical effect?

(10) Foreshadowing [1.2.168]: Miranda's wish to meet Gonzalo ("Would I might / But ever see that man" in 1.2.168–169) foreshadows the play's conclusion. Come back to this question after you have read further into the play, and write down any other examples of foreshadowing that you find.

Than other princes° can, that have more time
For vainer hours, and tutors not so careful.

MIRANDA
Heavens thank you for't! And now I pray you, sir – 175
For still 'tis beating in my mind – your reason
For raising this sea storm?

PROSPERO   Know thus far forth.
By accident most strange, bountiful Fortune
(Now, my dear lady) hath mine enemies 180
Brought to this shore; and by my prescience
I find my zenith° doth depend upon
A most auspicious star, whose influence
If now I court not, but omit,° my fortunes
Will ever after droop. Here cease more questions. 185
Thou art inclined to sleep. 'Tis a good dullness,°
And give it way. I know thou canst not choose.
    [Miranda sleeps.]
Come away,° servant, come! I am ready now.
Approach, my Ariel:° come!
    Enter Ariel.

ARIEL
All hail, great master! Grave sir, hail! I come
To answer thy best pleasure; be't to fly, 190
To swim, to dive into the fire, to ride
On the curled clouds. To thy strong bidding task
Ariel and all his quality.°

PROSPERO   Hast thou, spirit,
Performed to point° the tempest that I bade thee?

ARIEL
To every article. 195
I boarded the king's ship: now on the beak,°
Now in the waist,° the deck,° in every cabin,
I flamed amazement:° sometime I'd divide
And burn in many places; on the topmast,
The yards, and bowsprit would I flame distinctly,° 200
Then meet and join. Jove's lightnings, the precursors
O' th' dreadful thunderclaps, more momentary
And sight-outrunning were not. The fire and cracks
Of sulphurous roaring the most mighty Neptune
Seem to besiege and make his bold waves tremble; 205
Yea, his dread trident shake.

PROSPERO   My brave spirit!
Who was so firm, so constant, that this coil°
Would not infect his reason?

ARIEL   Not a soul
But felt a fever of the mad° and played
Some tricks of desperation. All but mariners 210
Plunged in the foaming brine and quit the vessel,

princes: (royal children of either gender)

zenith: apex of fortune

omit: neglect

dullness: drowsiness

Come away: come here
Ariel: (in Hebrew, it means "Lion of God"; a common name for a spirit in magical texts)

quality: cohorts (Ariel is leader of a band of elemental spirits)
to point: in detail

beak: prow
waist: amidships; **deck:** poop
flamed amazement: struck terror by appearing as (Saint Elmo's) fire
distinctly: in different places

coil: uproar

of the mad: such as madmen have

DISCOVERING SHAKESPEARE

(11) Costuming [1.2.187]: If you were designing <u>costumes</u> for a production of the play, what would Prospero's magic cloak look like? Draw a sketch of the cloak, or find a picture in a book or magazine that you might use as inspiration.

Then all afire with me;° the king's son Ferdinand,
With hair upstaring° (then like reeds, not hair),
Was the first man that leapt, cried "Hell is empty,
And all the devils are here!"

PROSPERO   Why, that's my spirit!
But was not this nigh shore?

ARIEL   Close by, my master.

PROSPERO
But are they, Ariel, safe?

ARIEL   Not a hair perished.
On their sustaining° garments not a blemish,
But fresher than before; and as thou bad'st me,
In troops I have dispersed them 'bout the isle.
The king's son have I landed by himself,
Whom I left cooling of the air with sighs
In an odd angle of the isle, and sitting,
His arms in this° sad knot.

PROSPERO   Of the king's ship
The mariners say how thou hast disposed,
And all the rest o' th' fleet.

ARIEL   Safely in harbor
Is the king's ship; in the deep nook where once
Thou call'dst me up at midnight to fetch dew
From the still-vexed° Bermudas, there she's hid;
The mariners all under hatches stowed,
Who, with a charm joined to their suffered° labor,
I have left asleep; and for the rest o' th' fleet,
Which I dispersed, they all have met again,
And are upon the Mediterranean float°
Bound sadly home for Naples,
Supposing that they saw the king's ship wracked
And his great person perish.

PROSPERO   Ariel, thy charge
Exactly is performed; but there's more work.
What is the time o' th' day?

ARIEL   Past the midseason.°

PROSPERO
At least two glasses.° The time 'twixt six and now
Must by us both be spent most preciously.

ARIEL
Is there more toil? Since thou dost give me pains,
Let me remember° thee what thou hast promised,
Which is not yet performed me.

PROSPERO   How now? moody?
What is't thou canst demand?

ARIEL   My liberty.

PROSPERO   Before the time° be out? No more!

---

afire with me: (refers either to the vessel or, possibly, to Ferdinand, depending on the punctuation; F suggests the latter)
upstaring: standing on end   215

sustaining: buoying them up in the water

220

this: (illustrated by a gesture)

225

still-vexed: always stormy

230
suffered: undergone

float: sea

235

midseason: noon

glasses: hours   240

remember: remind

245

time: period of service

DISCOVERING SHAKESPEARE

(12) Verse [1.2.212]: Scan several lines by Ariel. How is this character's verse different from Prospero's?
(13) Time [1.2.240]: What is the time of day in 1.2.240? Come back to this question after you have read the final scene, and calculate the passage of time throughout the entire play.

ARIEL   I prithee,
  Remember I have done thee worthy service,
  Told thee no lies, made no mistakes, served
  Without or grudge or grumblings. Thou did promise
  To bate me° a full year.   **bate me:** shorten my term of service   250
PROSPERO   Dost thou forget
  From what a torment I did free thee?
ARIEL   No.
PROSPERO
  Thou dost; and think'st it much to tread the ooze
  Of the salt deep,
  To run upon the sharp wind of the North,
  To do me business in the veins° o' th' earth   **veins:** streams   255
  When it is baked° with frost.   **baked:** hardened
ARIEL   I do not, sir.
PROSPERO
  Thou liest, malignant thing! Hast thou forgot
  The foul witch Sycorax,° who with age and envy°   **Sycorax:** (name not found elsewhere; usually
  Was grown into a hoop? Hast thou forgot her?   connected with Greek *sys,* sow, and *korax,* which
ARIEL   means both "raven"—cf. l. 322—and "curved,"
  No, sir.   hence perhaps *hoop*); **envy:** malice
PROSPERO   Thou hast. Where was she born? Speak!   260
  Tell me!
ARIEL
  Sir, in Argier.°   **Argier:** Algiers
PROSPERO   O, was she so? I must
  Once in a month recount what thou hast been,
  Which thou forget'st. This damned witch Sycorax,
  For mischiefs manifold, and sorceries terrible
  To enter human hearing, from Argier,   265
  Thou know'st, was banished. For one thing she did°   **one thing she did:** (being pregnant, her
  They would not take her life. Is not this true?   sentence was commuted from death to exile)
ARIEL
  Ay, sir.
PROSPERO
  This blue-eyed° hag was hither brought with child   **blue-eyed:** (blue eyelids were held to be a sign of
  And here was left by th' sailors. Thou, my slave,   pregnancy)   270
  As thou report'st thyself, wast then her servant;
  And, for thou wast a spirit too delicate
  To act her earthy and abhorred commands,
  Refusing her grand hests,° she did confine thee,   **hests:** commands
  By help of her more potent ministers,
  And in her most unmitigable rage,   275
  Into a cloven pine; within which rift
  Imprisoned thou didst painfully remain
  A dozen years; within which space she died
  And left thee there, where thou didst vent thy groans   280
  As fast as mill wheels° strike. Then was this island   **mill wheels:** the blades of waterwheels
  (Save for the son that she did litter here,

DISCOVERING SHAKESPEARE

(14) Teaser [1.2.266]: Why was Sycorax banished from Algiers rather than being executed? What "thing" (1.2.266) did she do that saved her life?

A freckled whelp, hag-born) not honored with
A human shape.
ARIEL   Yes, Caliban her son.
PROSPERO
  Dull thing, I say so: he, that Caliban   285
  Whom now I keep in service. Thou best know'st
  What torment I did find thee in: thy groans
  Did make wolves howl and penetrate the breasts°   **penetrate the breasts:** (and arouse sympathy in)
  Of ever-angry bears. It was a torment
  To lay upon the damned, which Sycorax   290
  Could not again undo. It was mine art,
  When I arrived and heard thee, that made gape
  The pine, and let thee out.
ARIEL   I thank thee, master.
PROSPERO
  If thou more murmur'st, I will rend an oak
  And peg thee in his° knotty entrails till   **his:** its   295
  Thou hast howled away twelve° winters.   **twelve:** (the same length of time that Ariel has
ARIEL   Pardon, master.   been released)
  I will be correspondent° to command   **correspondent:** obedient
  And do my spriting gently.°   **spriting gently:** office as a spirit graciously
PROSPERO   Do so; and after two days
  I will discharge thee.
ARIEL   That's my noble master!
  What shall I do? Say what? What shall I do?   300
PROSPERO
  Go make thyself like a nymph o' th' sea. Be subject
  To no sight but thine and mine, invisible
  To every eyeball else. Go take this shape
  And hither come in't. Go! Hence with diligence!
                                Exit [Ariel].
  Awake, dear heart, awake! Thou hast slept well.   305
  Awake!
MIRANDA   The strangeness of your story put
  Heaviness in me.
PROSPERO   Shake it off. Come on.
  We'll visit Caliban, my slave, who never
  Yields us kind answer.
MIRANDA   'Tis a villain, sir,
  I do not love to look on.   310
PROSPERO   But as 'tis,
  We cannot miss° him: he does make our fire,   **miss:** do without
  Fetch in our wood, and serves in offices
  That profit us. What, ho! slave! Caliban!
  Thou earth, thou! Speak!
CALIBAN   *[Within]*   There's wood enough within.

DISCOVERING SHAKESPEARE

(15) <u>Anagram</u> [1.2.284]: If you scramble the letters in the name "Caliban" (1.2.284), what other words can you get? Do any of these <u>anagrams</u> or near-<u>anagrams</u> help predict the behavior of this character?

(16) Characterization [1.2.310]: Miranda's depiction of Caliban as "a villain, sir, / I do not love to look on" (1.2.309–310) seems to imply that he is ugly or misshapen in some way. Find as many other clues as possible about Caliban's physical appearance; then write or draw a description of him on a separate piece of paper.

PROSPERO
Come forth, I say! There's other business for thee.   315
Come, thou tortoise! When?°
    Enter Ariel like a water nymph.
Fine apparition! My quaint° Ariel,
Hark in thine ear.

When: (expression of impatience)

quaint: ingenious

ARIEL   My lord, it shall be done.   *Exit.*

PROSPERO
Thou poisonous slave, got by the devil himself
Upon thy wicked dam, come forth!   320
    Enter Caliban.

CALIBAN
As wicked dew° as e'er my mother brushed
With raven's feather from unwholesome fen
Drop on you both! A southwest° blow on ye
And blister you all o'er!

dew: (often used in magic; see l. 228)

southwest: (a wind linked to warm, damp, and unhealthy weather)

PROSPERO
For this, be sure, tonight thou shalt have cramps,   325
Side stitches that shall pen thy breath up; urchins°
Shall, for that vast° of night that they may work,°
All exercise on thee; thou shalt be pinched
As thick as honeycomb, each pinch more stinging
Than bees that made 'em.

urchins: goblins in the shape of hedgehogs
vast: void; **that they may work:** (referring to the belief that malignant spirits had power only during darkness)

    330

CALIBAN   I must eat my dinner.
This island's mine by Sycorax my mother,
Which thou tak'st from me. When thou cam'st first,
Thou strok'st me and made much of me; wouldst give me
Water with berries in't; and teach me how
To name the bigger light, and how the less,   335
That burn by day and night; and then I loved thee
And showed thee all the qualities° o' th' isle,
The fresh springs, brine pits, barren place and fertile.
Cursèd be I that did so! All the charms°
Of Sycorax – toads, beetles, bats, light on you!   340
For I am all the subjects that you have,
Which first was mine own king; and here you sty me
In this hard rock, whiles you do keep from me
The rest o' th' island.

qualities: resources

charms: spells

PROSPERO   Thou most lying slave,
Whom stripes° may move, not kindness! I have used thee   345
(Filth as thou art) with humane care, and lodged thee
In mine own cell till thou didst seek to violate
The honor of my child.

stripes: lashes

CALIBAN
O ho, O ho! Would't had been done!
Thou didst prevent me; I had peopled else   350
This isle with Calibans.

MIRANDA°   Abhorrèd slave,
Which any print of goodness wilt not take,

Miranda: (so F; early editors often gave the speech to Prospero)

DISCOVERING SHAKESPEARE

(17) Teaser [1.2.331]: To what extent would Caliban's claim to the island (1.2.331) be affected by whether or not he was a legitimate child?

(18) Metaphor [1.2.352]: What does Miranda mean when she says that Caliban will not take any "print of goodness" (1.2.352)? How many different metaphoric meanings can you find in the word "print"?

Being capable of all ill! I pitied thee,
Took pains to make thee speak, taught thee each hour
One thing or other: when thou didst not, savage,   355
Know thine own meaning, but wouldst gabble like
A thing most brutish, I endowed thy purposes°   **purposes:** meanings
With words that made them known. But thy vile race,°   **race:** nature
Though thou didst learn, had that in't which good
    natures
Could not abide to be with; therefore wast thou   360
Deservedly confined into this rock,
Who hadst deserved more than a prison.

CALIBAN
You taught me language, and my profit on't
Is, I know how to curse. The red plague° rid° you   **red plague:** plague, producing bleeding or sores;
For learning me your language!   **rid:** destroy   365

PROSPERO   Hagseed, hence!
Fetch us in fuel; and be quick, thou'rt best,°   **thou'rt best:** you'd be well advised
To answer other business. Shrug'st thou, malice?
If thou neglect'st or dost unwillingly
What I command, I'll rack thee with old° cramps,   **old:** i.e., such as old people have
Fill all thy bones with aches,° make thee roar   **aches:** (pronounced "aitches")   370
That beasts shall tremble at thy din.

CALIBAN   No, pray thee.
    [Aside]
I must obey. His art is of such pow'r
It would control my dam's god, Setebos,
And make a vassal of him.

PROSPERO   So, slave; hence!
                                        Exit Caliban.

    Enter Ferdinand; and Ariel (invisible), playing and
    singing.

ARIEL   [Sings.]
            Come unto these yellow sands,   375
                And then take hands.
            Curtsied when you have and kissed,
                The wild waves whist,°   **whist:** being hushed
            Foot it featly° here and there;   **featly:** nimbly
            And, sweet sprites, the burden bear.   380
                Hark, hark!

Burden,° dispersedly.°   Bow-wow.   **Burden:** refrain (sung by spirits); **dispersedly:**
            The watchdogs bark.   (1) not in unison, (2) from several directions

Burden, dispersedly.   Bow-wow.
            Hark, hark! I hear   385
            The strain of strutting chanticleer
            Cry cock-a-diddle-dow.

FERDINAND
Where should this music be? I' th' air or th' earth?
It sounds no more; and sure it waits upon
Some god o' th' island. Sitting on a bank,   390
Weeping again the king my father's wrack,

DISCOVERING SHAKESPEARE

(19) Verse [1.2.375]: Scan Ariel's song in 1.2.375–387. How is the meter and rhyme scheme different from the song in 1.2.397–404? Why do you think these songs are not composed in the same way?

This music crept by me upon the waters,
Allaying both their fury and my passion°   **passion:** lamentation
With its sweet air. Thence I have followed it,
Or it hath drawn me rather; but 'tis gone.   395
No, it begins again.

ARIEL   *[Sings.]*
                    Full fathom five thy father lies;
                        Of his bones are coral made;
                    Those are pearls that were his eyes;
                        Nothing of him that doth fade   400
                        But doth suffer a sea change
                    Into something rich and strange.
                    Sea nymphs hourly ring his knell:

Burden.
                            Ding-dong.
                Hark! now I hear them – Ding-dong bell.   405

FERDINAND
    The ditty does remember° my drowned father.   **remember:** commemorate
    This is no mortal business, nor no sound
    That the earth owes.° I hear it now above me.   **owes:** owns

PROSPERO   *[To Miranda]*
    The fringèd curtains of thine eye advance°   **advance:** raise
    And say what thou seest yond.   410

MIRANDA   What is't? a spirit?
    Lord, how it looks about! Believe me, sir,
    It carries a brave form. But 'tis a spirit.

PROSPERO
    No, wench: it eats, and sleeps, and hath such senses
    As we have, such. This gallant which thou seest
    Was in the wrack; and, but he's something stained°   **stained:** disfigured   415
    With grief (that's beauty's canker),° thou mightst call him   **canker:** consuming disease
    A goodly person. He hath lost his fellows
    And strays about to find 'em.

MIRANDA   I might call him
    A thing divine; for nothing natural
    I ever saw so noble.   420

PROSPERO   *[Aside]*   It° goes on, I see,   **It:** my plan
    As my soul prompts° it. Spirit, fine spirit, I'll free thee   **prompts:** would like
    Within two days for this.

FERDINAND   Most sure,° the goddess   **Most sure:** this is certainly
    On whom these airs° attend! Vouchsafe my prayer   **airs:** songs
    May know if you remain° upon this island,   **remain:** dwell
    And that you will some good instruction give   425
    How I may bear me° here. My prime request,   **bear me:** conduct myself
    Which I do last pronounce, is (O you wonder!)°   **wonder:** (unknowingly, Ferdinand puns on
    If you be maid° or no?   Miranda's name—i.e., a woman who must be
                                                                             wondered at)
MIRANDA   No wonder, sir,
    But certainly a maid.   **maid:** a single girl (as opposed to a goddess or a
                                                             married woman)

DISCOVERING SHAKESPEARE

(20) Language [1.2.397]: What measure of distance was a "fathom" (1.2.397)? If Ferdinand's father lies "Full fathom five," how deep is he in the ocean?

(21) Shared Lines [1.2.420]: How do the shared lines among Prospero, Miranda, and Ferdinand in 1.2.418–439 help dictate the pacing of the scene and the relationship between the characters?

FERDINAND   My language? Heavens!
I am the best of them that speak this speech,   430
Were I but where 'tis spoken.
PROSPERO   How? the best?
What wert thou if the King of Naples heard thee?
FERDINAND
A single thing,° as I am now, that wonders   **A single thing:** just one person
To hear thee speak of Naples. He does hear me;
And that he does I weep. Myself am Naples,°   **Naples:** King of Naples   435
Who with mine eyes, never since at ebb,° beheld   **never . . . ebb:** crying nonstop ever since
The king my father wracked.
MIRANDA   Alack, for mercy!
FERDINAND
Yes, faith, and all his lords, the Duke of Milan
And his brave son° being twain.   **son:** (Antonio's son is not mentioned elsewhere)
PROSPERO   *[Aside]*   The Duke of Milan
And his more braver daughter could control° thee,   **control:** refute   440
If now 'twere fit to do't. At the first sight
They have changed eyes.° Delicate Ariel,   **changed eyes:** exchanged love looks
I'll set thee free for this. – A word, good sir.
I fear you have done yourself some wrong.° A word!   **done . . . wrong:** told a lie
MIRANDA
Why speaks my father so ungently? This   445
Is the third man that e'er I saw; the first
That e'er I sighed for. Pity move my father
To be inclined my way!
FERDINAND   O, if a virgin,
And your affection not gone forth, I'll make you
The Queen of Naples.   450
PROSPERO   Soft, sir! one word more.
   [Aside]
They are both in either's pow'rs. But this swift business
I must uneasy make, lest too light° winning   **light:** (Prospero puns on the word's meanings;
Make the prize light. – One word more! I charge thee easy, cheap, promiscuous)
That thou attend me. Thou dost here usurp
The name thou ow'st° not, and hast put thyself   **ow'st:** ownest   455
Upon this island as a spy, to win it
From me, the lord on't.
FERDINAND   No, as I am a man!
MIRANDA
There's nothing ill can dwell in such a temple.
If the ill spirit have so fair a house,
Good things will strive to dwell with't.   460
PROSPERO   Follow me. –
Speak not you for him; he's a traitor. – Come!
I'll manacle thy neck and feet together;
Seawater shalt thou drink; thy food shall be
The fresh-brook mussels, withered roots, and husks
Wherein the acorn cradled. Follow!   465

DISCOVERING SHAKESPEARE
(22) Irony [1.2.437]: How are Ferdinand's lines in 1.2.433–437 <u>ironic</u>?

FERDINAND   No.
  I will resist such entertainment° till   **entertainment:** treatment
  Mine enemy has more pow'r.
    He draws, and is charmed from moving.
MIRANDA   O dear father,
  Make not too rash a trial° of him, for   **trial:** judgment
  He's gentle,° and not fearful.°   **gentle:** noble; **fearful:** cowardly
PROSPERO   What, I say,
  My foot my tutor?° – Put thy sword up, traitor!   **My . . . tutor:** i.e., instructed by my underling   470
  Who mak'st a show but dar'st not strike, thy conscience
  Is so possessed with guilt. Come, from thy ward!°   **ward:** fighting posture
  For I can here disarm thee with this stick
  And make thy weapon drop.
MIRANDA   Beseech you, father!
PROSPERO
  Hence! Hang not on my garments.   475
MIRANDA   Sir, have pity.
  I'll be his surety.
PROSPERO   Silence! One word more
  Shall make me chide thee, if not hate thee. What,
  An advocate for an impostor? Hush!
  Thou think'st there is no more such shapes as he,
  Having seen but him and Caliban. Foolish wench!   480
  To th' most of men this is a Caliban,
  And they to him are angels.
MIRANDA   My affections°   **affections:** inclinations
  Are then most humble. I have no ambition
  To see a goodlier man.
PROSPERO   Come on, obey!
  Thy nerves° are in their infancy again   **nerves:** sinews, tendons   485
  And have no vigor in them.
FERDINAND   So they are.
  My spirits, as in a dream, are all bound up.
  My father's loss, the weakness which I feel,
  The wrack of all my friends, nor this man's threats
  To whom I am subdued, are but light to me,   490
  Might I but through my prison once a day
  Behold this maid. All corners else o' th' earth
  Let liberty make use of. Space enough
  Have I in such a prison.
PROSPERO   *[Aside]*   It works. *[To Ferdinand]* Come on.
    [To Ariel]
  Thou hast done well, fine Ariel!°   **Ariel:** (which parts of these lines are to   495
    [To Ferdinand]   Follow me.   Ferdinand and which to Ariel are arguable
    [To Ariel]   editorial decisions)
  Hark what thou else shalt do me.
MIRANDA   Be of comfort.
  My father's of a better nature, sir,

DISCOVERING SHAKESPEARE

(23) <u>**Blocking**</u> **[1.2.467]:** What stage action and <u>blocking</u> is suggested by lines 1.2.465–469?
(24) <u>**Paraphrase**</u> **[1.2.486]:** <u>Paraphrase</u> into modern English Ferdinand's speech from 1.2.486–494.

Than he appears by speech. This is unwonted
Which now came from him.

PROSPERO   Thou shalt be as free
As mountain winds; but then° exactly do   **then:** till then   500
All points of my command.

ARIEL   To th' syllable.

PROSPERO
Come, follow. *[To Miranda]* Speak not for him.

                                                        Exeunt.

ᴥ **2.1**° *Enter Alonso, Sebastian, Antonio, Gonzalo,*
Adrian, Francisco.

2.1: (F adds *"and others"* after *"Francisco"* and puts *"etc."* at the beginning of 3.3, but these extra attendants are missing in the entry at 5.1.57, where they would disturb the pattern; it is more consistent to delete them here and at the start of 3.3 as well)

GONZALO
Beseech you, sir, be merry. You have cause
(So have we all) of joy; for our escape
Is much beyond our loss. Our hint° of woe   **hint:** occasion
Is common: every day some sailor's wife,
The master of some merchant,° and the merchant,°   **master of some merchant:** master of a   5
Have just our theme of woe; but for the miracle,   merchant ship; **the merchant:** the owner of the
I mean our preservation, few in millions   ship
Can speak like us. Then wisely, good sir, weigh
Our sorrow with our comfort.

ALONSO   Prithee peace.

SEBASTIAN   He receives comfort like cold porridge.°   **porridge:** (pun on *peace* [pease])   10

ANTONIO   The visitor° will not give him o'er° so.   **visitor:** churchman who comforts the sick; **give**

SEBASTIAN   Look, he's winding up the watch of his wit;   **him o'er:** let him alone
by and by it will strike.

GONZALO   Sir –

SEBASTIAN   One. Tell.°   **Tell:** count   15

GONZALO
– when every grief is entertained
That's° offered, comes to th' entertainer – °   **That's:** that which is; **entertainer:** (taken by

SEBASTIAN   A dollar.   Sebastian to mean "innkeeper")

GONZALO   Dolor° comes to him, indeed. You have   **Dolor:** grief (with pun on *dollar*, a Continental
spoken truer than you purposed.   coin)   20

SEBASTIAN   You have taken it wiselier than I meant you
should.

GONZALO   Therefore, my lord –

ANTONIO   Fie, what a spendthrift° is he of his tongue!   **spendthrift:** (Antonio labors the pun)

ALONSO   I prithee spare.   25

GONZALO   Well, I have done. But yet –

SEBASTIAN   He will be talking.

ANTONIO   Which, of he or Adrian, for a good wager, first
begins to crow?

SEBASTIAN   The old cock.°   **old cock:** i.e., Gonzalo   30

ANTONIO   The cock'rel.°   **cock'rel:** i.e., Adrian

SEBASTIAN   Done! The wager?

DISCOVERING SHAKESPEARE

(25) <u>History</u> [2.1.12]: In 2.1.12, Sebastian predicts that Gonzalo is "winding up the watch of his wit." Where and when were pocket watches invented? Were they in widespread use by the beginning of the seventeenth century? Why does Sebastian use the word "strike" (2.1.13) in reference to a watch?

ANTONIO   A laughter.°

SEBASTIAN   A match!

ADRIAN   Though this island seem to be desert –

ANTONIO   Ha, ha, ha!

SEBASTIAN   So, you're paid.

ADRIAN   Uninhabitable and almost inaccessible –

SEBASTIAN   Yet –

ADRIAN   Yet –

ANTONIO   He could not miss't.

ADRIAN   It must needs be of subtle, tender, and delicate temperance.°

ANTONIO   Temperance° was a delicate° wench.

SEBASTIAN   Ay, and a subtle,° as he most learnedly delivered.

ADRIAN   The air breathes upon us here most sweetly.

SEBASTIAN   As if it had lungs, and rotten ones.

ANTONIO   Or as 'twere perfumed by a fen.

GONZALO   Here is everything advantageous to life.

ANTONIO   True; save means to live.

SEBASTIAN   Of that there's none, or little.

GONZALO   How lush° and lusty the grass looks! how green!

ANTONIO   The ground indeed is tawny.

SEBASTIAN   With an eye° of green in't.

ANTONIO   He misses not much.

SEBASTIAN   No; he doth but mistake the truth totally.

GONZALO   But the rarity of it is – which is indeed almost beyond credit –

SEBASTIAN   As many vouched rarities° are.

GONZALO   That our garments, being, as they were, drenched in the sea, hold, notwithstanding, their freshness and gloss, being rather new-dyed than stained with salt water.

ANTONIO   If but one of his pockets could speak, would it not say he lies?

SEBASTIAN   Ay, or very falsely pocket up his report.

GONZALO   Methinks our garments are now as fresh as when we put them on first in Afric, at the marriage of the king's fair daughter Claribel to the King of Tunis.

SEBASTIAN   'Twas a sweet marriage, and we prosper well in our return.

ADRIAN   Tunis was never graced before with such a paragon to° their queen.

GONZALO   Not since widow Dido's° time.

ANTONIO   Widow? A pox o' that! How came that "widow" in? Widow Dido!

SEBASTIAN   What if he had said "widower Aeneas" too? Good Lord, how you take it!

laughter: the winner laughs

35

40

temperance: climate

Temperance: (a girl's name); **delicate:** given to pleasure

45

subtle: crafty, expert in sex

50

lush: tender, soft

55

eye: spot

60

vouched rarities: wonders guaranteed to be true

65

70

75

to: for

widow Dido: (Dido was the widow of Sychaeus; Aeneas was a widower, having lost his wife in the fall of Troy. Antonio may be mockingly suggesting that she was only a widow—i.e., a woman abandoned by her lover [not necessarily a woman whose husband had died], because abandoned by Aeneas [who had not married her], but the comment has not been convincingly explained.)

80

DISCOVERING SHAKESPEARE

(26) Plot [2.1.37]: Who wins the wager between Antonio and Sebastian in 2.1.28–37? Exactly what was the bet?

(27) Geography [2.1.70]: Locate the following places on a map of the area: Naples, Tunis, and the Bermudas. How long would a sea voyage have taken from Naples to Tunis?

ADRIAN "Widow Dido," said you? You make me study of that. She was of Carthage, not of Tunis.

GONZALO This Tunis, sir, was Carthage.

ADRIAN Carthage?

GONZALO I assure you, Carthage. 85

ANTONIO His word is more than the miraculous harp.°

SEBASTIAN He hath raised the wall and houses too.

ANTONIO What impossible matter will he make easy next?

SEBASTIAN I think he will carry this island home in his 90
pocket and give it his son for an apple.

ANTONIO And, sowing the kernels of it in the sea, bring forth more islands.

GONZALO Ay!°

ANTONIO Why, in good time. 95

GONZALO Sir, we were talking that our garments seem now as fresh as when we were at Tunis at the marriage of your daughter, who is now queen.

ANTONIO And the rarest that e'er came there.

SEBASTIAN Bate,° I beseech you, widow Dido. 100

ANTONIO O, widow Dido? Ay, widow Dido!

GONZALO Is not, sir, my doublet as fresh as the first day I wore it? I mean, in a sort.°

ANTONIO That "sort" was well fished for. 105

GONZALO When I wore it at your daughter's marriage.

ALONSO
You cram these words into mine ears against
The stomach of my sense.° Would I had never
Married my daughter there! for, coming thence,
My son is lost; and, in my rate,° she too, 110
Who is so far from Italy removed
I ne'er again shall see her. O thou mine heir
Of Naples and of Milan, what strange fish
Hath made his meal on thee?

FRANCISCO   Sir, he may live.
I saw him beat the surges under him
And ride upon their backs. He trod the water, 115
Whose enmity he flung aside, and breasted
The surge most swol'n that met him. His bold head
'Bove the contentious waves he kept, and oared
Himself with his good arms in lusty stroke
To th' shore, that o'er his° wave-worn basis° bowed, 120
As stooping to relieve him. I not doubt
He came alive to land.

ALONSO   No, no, he's gone.

SEBASTIAN
Sir, you may thank yourself for this great loss,

---

miraculous harp: (of Amphion, which raised the walls of Thebes; Tunis and Carthage were near each other, but not the same city, though Tunis became the name for the region where Carthage was)

Ay: (F reads "I" and might indicate that Gonzalo is starting a new sentence, "I—," which Antonio interrupts)

Bate: except

in a sort: i.e., comparatively

stomach . . . sense: i.e., temper of my perception

rate: estimation

his: its; **basis:** foot of the cliff

DISCOVERING SHAKESPEARE

(28) Mythology [2.1.100]: Who were Dido and Aeneas (2.1.76-101)? What other <u>allusions</u> to Virgil's *Aeneid* can you find in the play?

(29) <u>Imagery</u> [2.1.116]: Compare Francisco's description of the way in which Ferdinand "breasted / The surge most swol'n" (2.1.116–117) with similar passages in *Twelfth Night* (1.2.7–16) and *Julius Caesar* (1.2.104–111). In which order were these plays written? Which of these <u>images</u> was probably composed first?

That would not bless our Europe with your daughter,
But rather loose her to an African, 125
Where she, at least, is banished from your eye
Who hath cause to wet the grief on't.
ALONSO   Prithee peace.
SEBASTIAN
You were kneeled to and importuned otherwise
By all of us; and the fair soul herself
Weighed, between loathness and obedience, at 130
Which end o' th' beam should bow.° We have lost your
    son,
I fear, forever. Milan and Naples have
Moe° widows in them of this business' making
Than we bring men to comfort them: 135
The fault's your own.
ALONSO   So is the dear'st° o' th' loss.
GONZALO
My Lord Sebastian,
The truth you speak doth lack some gentleness,
And time to speak it in. You rub the sore
When you should bring the plaster.
SEBASTIAN   Very well.
ANTONIO
And most chirurgeonly.° 140
GONZALO
It is foul weather in us all, good sir,
When you are cloudy.
SEBASTIAN   Foul weather?
ANTONIO   Very foul.
GONZALO
Had I plantation° of this isle, my lord —
ANTONIO
He'd sow't with nettle seed.
SEBASTIAN   Or docks, or mallows.°
GONZALO
And were the king on't, what would I do? 145
SEBASTIAN
Scape being drunk for want of wine.
GONZALO
I' th' commonwealth I would by contraries°
Execute all things; for no kind of traffic°
Would I admit; no name of magistrate;
Letters should not be known; riches, poverty, 150
And use of service,° none; contract, succession,°
Bourn,° bound of land, tilth, vineyard, none;
No use of metal, corn, or wine, or oil;
No occupation; all men idle, all;

---

the fair . . . bow: (the sense is that Claribel hated the marriage, and only obedience to her father turned the scale)

Moe: more

dear'st: heaviest

chirurgeonly: like a surgeon

plantation: colonization (taken by Antonio in its other sense)

docks . . . mallows: (antidotes to nettle stings)

by contraries: in contrast to usual customs
traffic: trade

use of service: having a servant class;
succession: inheritance
Bourn: limits of private property

DISCOVERING SHAKESPEARE

(30) Language [2.1.140]: What was the <u>etymology</u> of the word "chirurgeonly" (2.1.140)? What does the word mean? How do you think it should be pronounced on stage?

(31) <u>Sources</u> [2.1.154]: Read Gonzalo's famous monologue on the ideal "commonwealth" in 2.1.147–164; then compare it with sixteenth-century French author Michel de Montaigne's essay "Of the Cannibals." What use do you think Shakespeare was making of the edenic innocence and Utopian government <u>alluded</u> to in Montaigne's essay?

And women too, but innocent and pure;° pure: (inverting the proverb "Idleness begets 155
No sovereignty.   lust")
SEBASTIAN   Yet he would be king on't.
ANTONIO   The latter end of his commonwealth forgets
the beginning.
GONZALO
All things in common° nature should produce   **in common:** for communal use
Without sweat or endeavor. Treason, felony,   160
Sword, pike, knife, gun, or need of any engine°   **engine:** weapon
Would I not have; but nature should bring forth,
Of it° own kind, all foison,° all abundance,   **it:** its; **foison:** abundance
To feed my innocent people.
SEBASTIAN   No marrying 'mong his subjects?   165
ANTONIO   None, man, all idle – whores and knaves.
GONZALO
I would with such perfection govern, sir,
T' excel the golden age.
SEBASTIAN   Save his majesty!
ANTONIO
Long live Gonzalo!
GONZALO   And – do you mark me, sir?
ALONSO
Prithee no more. Thou dost talk nothing to me.   170
GONZALO   I do well believe your highness; and did it to
minister occasion° to these gentlemen, who are of such   **minister occasion:** afford opportunity
sensible° and nimble lungs that they always use to laugh   **sensible:** sensitive
at nothing.
ANTONIO   'Twas you we laughed at.   175
GONZALO   Who in this kind of merry fooling am noth-
ing to you: so you may continue, and laugh at nothing
still.
ANTONIO   What a blow was there given!
SEBASTIAN   An° it had not fall'n flatlong.°   **An:** if; **flatlong:** struck with the flat of a sword, 180
GONZALO   You are gentlemen of brave mettle; you   so harmlessly
would lift the moon out of her sphere if she would con-
tinue in it five weeks without changing.
  Enter Ariel [invisible,] playing solemn music.
SEBASTIAN   We would so, and then go a-batfowling.°   **a-batfowling:** hunting birds with sticks ("bats")
ANTONIO   Nay, good my lord, be not angry.   at night (using the moon for a lantern) 185
GONZALO   No, I warrant you: I will not adventure° my   **adventure:** risk (Gonzalo is saying, very politely,
discretion so weakly. Will you laugh me asleep, for I am   that their wit is too feeble for him to take offense
very heavy?   at it)
ANTONIO   Go sleep, and hear us.°   **hear us:** listen to us laughing
  [All sleep except Alonso, Sebastian, and Antonio.]
ALONSO
What, all so soon asleep? I wish mine eyes
Would, with themselves, shut up my thoughts. I find   190
They are inclined to do so.
SEBASTIAN   Please you, sir,
Do not omit° the heavy offer° of it.   **omit:** neglect; **heavy offer:** opportunity its
  heaviness affords

DISCOVERING SHAKESPEARE

(32) Language [2.1.184]: What was the origin and meaning of the term "batfowling" (2.1.184)? How does Sebastian use the term in this context?

It seldom visits sorrow; when it doth,
It is a comforter.   195
ANTONIO   We two, my lord,
Will guard your person while you take your rest,
And watch your safety.
ALONSO   Thank you. Wondrous heavy.

                 [Alonso sleeps. Exit Ariel.]

SEBASTIAN
What a strange drowsiness possesses them!
ANTONIO
It is the quality o' th' climate.
SEBASTIAN   Why
Doth it not then our eyelids sink? I find not   200
Myself disposed to sleep.
ANTONIO   Nor I: my spirits are nimble.
They fell together all, as by consent.
They dropped as by a thunderstroke. What might,
Worthy Sebastian – O, what might? – No more!
And yet methinks I see it in thy face,   205
What thou shouldst be. Th' occasion speaks° thee, and   **speaks:** speaks to, summons
My strong imagination sees a crown
Dropping upon thy head.
SEBASTIAN   What? Art thou waking?
ANTONIO
Do you not hear me speak?
SEBASTIAN   I do; and surely
It is a sleepy language, and thou speak'st   210
Out of thy sleep. What is it thou didst say?
This is a strange repose, to be asleep
With eyes wide open; standing, speaking, moving,
And yet so fast asleep.
ANTONIO   Noble Sebastian,
Thou let'st thy fortune sleep – die, rather; wink'st°   **wink'st:** you sleep   215
Whiles thou art waking.
SEBASTIAN   Thou dost snore distinctly;
There's meaning in thy snores.
ANTONIO
I am more serious than my custom. You
Must be so too, if heed me; which to do
Trebles thee o'er.°   **Trebles thee o'er:** increases your status   220
SEBASTIAN   Well, I am standing water.°   threefold; **standing water:** at slack tide
ANTONIO
I'll teach you how to flow.
SEBASTIAN   Do so. To ebb
Hereditary sloth° instructs me.   **Hereditary sloth:** natural laziness
ANTONIO   O,
If you but knew how you the purpose cherish°   **cherish:** enrich
Whiles thus you mock it! how, in stripping it,
You more invest° it! Ebbing men indeed   **invest:** clothe   225
(Most often) do so near the bottom run
By their own fear or sloth.

DISCOVERING SHAKESPEARE

(33) <u>Shared Lines</u> [2.1.210]: What is the effect of the <u>shared lines</u> between Antonio and Sebastian in 2.1.208–222 ff.?

SEBASTIAN   Prithee say on.
The setting of thine eye and cheek proclaim
A matter° from thee; and a birth, indeed,
Which throes thee much° to yield.
ANTONIO   Thus, sir:
Although this lord of weak remembrance,° this
Who shall be of as little memory°
When he is earthed,° hath here almost persuaded
(For he's a spirit of persuasion, only
Professes° to persuade) the king his son's alive,
'Tis as impossible that he's undrowned
As he that sleeps here swims.
SEBASTIAN   I have no hope
That he's undrowned.
ANTONIO   O, out of that no hope
What great hope have you! No hope that way is
Another way so high a hope that even
Ambition cannot pierce a wink° beyond,
But doubt discovery there.° Will you grant with me
That Ferdinand is drowned?
SEBASTIAN   He's gone.
ANTONIO   Then tell me,
Who's the next heir of Naples?
SEBASTIAN   Claribel.
ANTONIO
She that is Queen of Tunis; she that dwells
Ten leagues beyond man's life;° she that from Naples
Can have no note,° unless the sun were post – °
The man i' th' moon's too slow – till new-born chins
Be rough and razorable; she that from whom
We all were sea-swallowed, though some cast° again,
And, by that destiny, to perform an act
Whereof what's past is prologue, what to come,
In yours and my discharge.°
SEBASTIAN   What stuff is this? How say you?
'Tis true my brother's daughter's Queen of Tunis;
So is she heir of Naples; 'twixt which regions
There is some space.
ANTONIO   A space whose ev'ry cubit
Seems to cry out "How shall that Claribel
Measure us° back to Naples? Keep in Tunis,
And let Sebastian wake!" Say this were death
That now hath seized them, why, they were no worse
Than now they are. There be that can rule Naples
As well as he that sleeps; lords that can prate
As amply and unnecessarily

A matter: something important	
throes thee much: costs you much pain, like a birth	230
remembrance: memory	
of . . . memory: as little remembered	
earthed: buried	
Professes: has the function	235
	240
wink: glimpse	
doubt discovery there: is uncertain of seeing accurately	
	245
Ten . . . life: i.e., thirty miles from nowhere	
note: communication; **post:** messenger	
cast: thrown up (with a suggestion of its theatrical meaning, which introduces the next metaphor)	250
discharge: performance	
	255
us: i.e., the cubits	
	260

DISCOVERING SHAKESPEARE

(34) Language [2.1.237]: Rephrase Sebastian's "I have no hope / That he's undrowned" in 2.1.237–238. Why do you think the character uses a double negative here?

(35) Paraphrase [2.1.264]: Paraphrase Antonio's "I myself could make / A chough of as deep chat" in 2.1.264–265. Why does Antonio select a "chough" to represent Gonzalo?

As this Gonzalo; I myself could make
A chough° of as deep chat. O, that you bore
The mind that I do! What a sleep were this
For your advancement! Do you understand me?

SEBASTIAN
Methinks I do.

ANTONIO   And how does your content
Tender° your own good fortune?

SEBASTIAN   I remember
You did supplant your brother Prospero.

ANTONIO   True.
And look how well my garments sit upon me,
Much feater° than before. My brother's servants
Were then my fellows;° now they are my men.°

SEBASTIAN
But, for your conscience –

ANTONIO
Ay, sir, where lies that? If 'twere a kibe,°
'Twould put me to° my slipper; but I feel not
This deity in my bosom. Twenty consciences
That stand 'twixt me and Milan, candied° be they
And melt, ere they molest! Here lies your brother,
No better than the earth he lies upon
If he were that which now he's like – that's dead;
Whom I with this obedient steel (three inches of it)
Can lay to bed forever; whiles you, doing thus,
To the perpetual wink° for aye might put
This ancient morsel, this Sir Prudence, who
Should not upbraid our course. For all the rest,
They'll take suggestion as a cat laps milk;
They'll tell the clock° to any business that
We say befits the hour.

SEBASTIAN   Thy case, dear friend,
Shall be my precedent. As thou got'st Milan,
I'll come by Naples. Draw thy sword. One stroke
Shall free thee from the tribute which thou payest,
And I the king shall love thee.

ANTONIO   Draw together;
And when I rear my hand, do you the like,
To fall it° on Gonzalo.
    [They draw.]

SEBASTIAN   O, but one word!
    Enter Ariel [invisible], with music° and song.

ARIEL
My master through his art foresees the danger
That you, his friend, are in, and sends me forth
(For else his project dies) to keep them living.

---

chough: jackdaw (a bird sometimes taught to speak) — 265

content Tender: inclination estimate

270

feater: more stylishly
fellows: equals; **men:** servants

kibe: chilblain — 275
put me to: make me wear

candied: frozen

280

wink: sleep

285

tell the clock: answer appropriately

290

fall it: let it fall — 295

with music: either "with an instrument" or "accompanied by musicians"

DISCOVERING SHAKESPEARE

(36) Plot [2.1.288]: What has Antonio convinced Sebastian to do? How will this action benefit each of these two men?

(37) Teaser [2.1.296]: Compare Ariel's entrance in 2.1.296 with a character in another Shakespearean play who says, "I am invisible, / And I will overhear their conference." How soon would an audience realize that each character is unseen by the others on stage?

Sings in Gonzalo's ear.

> While you here do snoring lie,
> Open-eyed conspiracy
>   His time doth take.
> If of life you keep a care,
> Shake off slumber and beware.
>   Awake, awake!

ANTONIO
  Then let us both be sudden.

GONZALO   *[Wakes.]*   Now good angels
  Preserve the king!

ALONSO
  Why, how now? – Ho, awake! – Why are you drawn?
  Wherefore this ghastly looking?

GONZALO   What's the matter?

SEBASTIAN
  Whiles we stood here securing° your repose,
  Even now, we heard a hollow burst of bellowing
  Like bulls, or rather lions. Did't not wake you?
  It struck mine ear most terribly.

ALONSO   I heard nothing.

ANTONIO
  O, 'twas a din to fright a monster's ear,
  To make an earthquake! Sure it was the roar
  Of a whole herd of lions.

ALONSO   Heard you this, Gonzalo?

GONZALO
  Upon mine honor, sir, I heard a humming,
  And that a strange one too, which did awake me.
  I shaked you, sir, and cried. As mine eyes opened,
  I saw their weapons drawn. There was a noise,
  That's verily. 'Tis best we stand upon our guard,
  Or that we quit this place. Let's draw our weapons.

ALONSO
  Lead off this ground, and let's make further search
  For my poor son.

GONZALO   Heavens keep him from these beasts!
  For he is sure i' th' island.

ALONSO   Lead away.

ARIEL
  Prospero my lord shall know what I have done.
  So, king, go safely on to seek thy son.   *Exeunt.*

securing: keeping watch over

300

305

310

315

320

325

❧ **2.2** *Enter Caliban with a burden of wood.*

CALIBAN
  All the infections that the sun sucks up
  From bogs, fens, flats, on Prosper fall, and make him
  By inchmeal° a disease! *(A noise of thunder heard.)* His
    spirits hear me,
  And yet I needs must curse. But they'll nor° pinch,
  Fright me with urchin shows,° pitch me i' th' mire,
  Nor lead me, like a firebrand,° in the dark

By inchmeal: inch by inch

nor: neither
urchin shows: apparitions in the form of hedgehogs
like a firebrand: like a torch

5

Out of my way, unless he bid 'em; but
For every trifle are they set upon me;
Sometime like apes that mow° and chatter at me,   **mow:** make faces
And after bite me; then like hedgehogs which   10
Lie tumbling in my barefoot way and mount
Their pricks at my footfall; sometime am I
All wound with adders, who with cloven tongues
Do hiss me into madness.
   Enter Trinculo.   Lo, now, lo!
Here comes a spirit of his, and to torment me   15
For bringing wood in slowly. I'll fall flat.
Perchance he will not mind me.
   [Lies down and covers himself with his cloak.]

TRINCULO   Here's neither bush nor shrub to bear off° any   **bear off:** ward off
weather at all, and another storm brewing: I hear it sing
i' th' wind. Yond same black cloud, yond huge one,   20
looks like a foul bombard° that would shed his° liquor. If   **bombard:** leather bottle; **his:** its
it should thunder as it did before, I know not where to
hide my head. Yond same cloud cannot choose but fall
by pailfuls. What have we here? a man or a fish? dead or   25
alive? A fish: he smells like a fish; a very ancient and
fishlike smell; a kind of not of the newest Poor John.° A   **Poor John:** dried, salted fish
strange fish! Were I in England now, as once I was, and
had but this fish painted,° not a holiday fool there but   **painted:** i.e., on a signboard outside a booth at a
would give a piece of silver. There would this monster   fair
make a man:° any strange beast there makes a man.   **make a man:** (also with sense of "make a man's   30
When they will not give a doit° to relieve a lame beggar,   fortune")
they will lay out ten to see a dead Indian.° Legged like a   **doit:** small coin
man! and his fins like arms! Warm, o' my troth! I do   **a dead Indian:** (natives of the New World had
now let loose my opinion, hold it no longer: this is no   often been brought back and displayed, to the
fish, but an islander, that hath lately suffered by a thun-   substantial profit of the exhibitor but usually
derbolt. *[Thunder.]* Alas, the storm is come again! My   causing the native to die from disease)   35
best way is to creep under his gaberdine:° there is no
other shelter hereabout. Misery acquaints a man with   **gaberdine:** cloak
strange bedfellows. I will here shroud till the dregs of
the storm be past.
   [Creeps under Caliban's garment.]   40
   Enter Stephano, singing [with a bottle in his hand].

STEPHANO   I shall no more to sea, to sea;
       Here shall I die ashore.

This is a very scurvy tune to sing at a man's funeral.
Well, here's my comfort.
   Drinks.

                                                           45
The master, the swabber,° the boatswain, and I,   **swabber:** seaman who cleans the decks
   The gunner, and his mate,
Loved Mall, Meg, and Marian, and Margery,
   But none of us cared for Kate.
   For she had a tongue with a tang,

DISCOVERING SHAKESPEARE

(38) Imagery [2.2.10]: In his first speech in 2.2, Caliban mentions "apes," "hedgehogs," and "adders" (2.2.9–14). How many other animal references can you find in this play? How do all these beast <u>images</u> help define Prospero's island?

(39) Language [2.2.26]: What was a "Poor John" (2.2.26)? What was the <u>etymological</u> origin of the term?

Would cry to a sailor "Go hang!"
She loved not the savor of tar nor of pitch;
Yet a tailor° might scratch° her where'er she did itch.
  Then to sea, boys, and let her go hang! 50

This is a scurvy tune too; but here's my comfort.
  Drinks.

CALIBAN Do not torment me! O! 55

STEPHANO What's the matter? Have we devils here? Do
you put tricks upon's with savages and men of Ind,° ha?
I have not scaped drowning to be afeard now of your
four legs; for it hath been said, "As proper a man as ever
went on four legs° cannot make him give ground"; and 60
it shall be said so again, while Stephano breathes at nos-
trils.

CALIBAN The spirit torments me. O!

STEPHANO This is some monster of the isle, with four
legs, who hath got, as I take it, an ague. Where the devil 65
should he learn our language? I will give him some relief,
if it be but for that. If I can recover him, and keep
him tame, and get to Naples with him, he's a present
for any emperor that ever trod on neat's leather.°

CALIBAN Do not torment me, prithee; I'll bring my 70
wood home faster.

STEPHANO He's in his fit now and does not talk after the
wisest. He shall taste of my bottle: if he have never
drunk wine afore, it will go near to remove his fit. If I
can recover him and keep him tame, I will not take too 75
much° for him; he shall pay for him that hath him, and
that soundly.

CALIBAN Thou dost me yet but little hurt. Thou wilt
anon;° I know it by thy trembling. Now Prosper works
upon thee. 80

STEPHANO Come on your ways; open your mouth: here
is that which will give language to you, cat.° Open your
mouth. This will shake your shaking, I can tell you,
and that soundly. *[Gives Caliban drink.]* You cannot tell
who's your friend. Open your chaps° again. 85

TRINCULO I should know that voice. It should be – but
he is drowned; and these are devils. O, defend me!

STEPHANO Four legs and two voices – a most delicate°
monster! His forward voice now is to speak well of his
friend; his backward voice is to utter foul speeches and 90
to detract. If all the wine in my bottle will recover him,
I will help his ague. Come! *[Gives drink.]* Amen! I will
pour some in thy other mouth.

TRINCULO Stephano!

STEPHANO Doth thy other mouth call me? Mercy, 95
mercy! This is a devil, and no monster. I will leave him;
I have no long spoon.°

---

a tailor: (a cliché for a man lacking virility);
scratch: have sex with

men of Ind: inhabitants of the West Indies

four legs: (the proverb's usual form is, of course,
"two legs")

neat's leather: cowhide

not take too much: i.e., take all I can get

anon: soon

cat: (alluding to the proverb "Liquor will make a
cat talk")

chaps: jaws

delicate: exquisitely made

spoon: (alluding to the proverb "He who sups
with the devil must have a long spoon")

DISCOVERING SHAKESPEARE

(40) Allusions [2.2.57]: What were "men of Ind" (2.2.58)? Were they "savages"? Why or why not? How are they related
to Caliban?

(41) Costuming [2.2.80]: How are Stephano and Trinculo dressed? What are their occupations?

TRINCULO   Stephano! If thou beest Stephano, touch me and speak to me; for I am Trinculo — be not afeard — thy good friend Trinculo.   100

STEPHANO   If thou beest Trinculo, come forth. I'll pull thee by the lesser legs. If any be Trinculo's legs, these are they. *[Pulls him out from under Caliban's cloak.]* Thou art very Trinculo indeed: how cam'st thou to be the siege° of this mooncalf?° Can he vent Trinculos?   **siege:** excrement; **mooncalf:** monstrosity 105

TRINCULO   I took him to be killed with a thunder-stroke. But art thou not drowned, Stephano? I hope now thou art not drowned. Is the storm overblown? I hid me under the dead mooncalf's gaberdine for fear of the storm. And art thou living, Stephano? O Stephano, two Neapolitans scaped!   110

STEPHANO   Prithee do not turn me about: my stomach is not constant.

CALIBAN   *[Aside]*
These be fine things, an if° they be not sprites.   **an if:** if
That's a brave god and bears celestial liquor.
I will kneel to him.

STEPHANO   How didst thou scape? How cam'st thou hither? Swear by this bottle how thou cam'st hither. I escaped upon a butt of sack° which the sailors heaved o'erboard, by this bottle, which I made of the bark of a tree with mine own hands since I was cast ashore.   **butt of sack:** barrel of Spanish white wine (often sherry) 120

CALIBAN   I'll swear upon that bottle to be thy true subject, for the liquor is not earthly.

STEPHANO   Here! Swear then how thou escapedst.

TRINCULO   Swum ashore, man, like a duck. I can swim like a duck, I'll be sworn.

STEPHANO   Here, kiss the book.° *[Gives him drink.]* Though thou canst swim like a duck, thou art made like a goose.°   **book:** i.e., bottle   **like a goose:** (Trinculo is standing unsteadily) 130

TRINCULO   O Stephano, hast any more of this?

STEPHANO   The whole butt, man: my cellar is in a rock by th' seaside, where my wine is hid. How now, mooncalf? How does thine ague?

CALIBAN   Hast thou not dropped from heaven?

STEPHANO   Out o' th' moon, I do assure thee. I was the   135
Man i' th' Moon when time was.°   **when time was:** once upon a time

CALIBAN
I have seen thee in her, and I do adore thee.
My mistress showed me thee, and thy dog, and thy
bush.

STEPHANO   Come, swear to that; kiss the book. I will furnish it anon with new contents. Swear.   140
[Caliban drinks.]

TRINCULO   By this good light, this is a very shallow monster! I afeard of him? A very weak monster! The

---

DISCOVERING SHAKESPEARE

(42) Language [2.2.109]: What was a "mooncalf" (2.2.105 and 2.2.109)? How was the moon thought to influence a person's birth?

(43) Teaser [2.2.136]: In which other Shakespearean play does a character impersonate "moonshine" with a lantern, thorn bush, and dog (cf. Stephano's "I was the Man i' th' Moon when time was" in 2.2.135–136)?

Man i' th' Moon? A most poor credulous monster! —
Well drawn, monster, in good sooth!

CALIBAN
I'll show thee every fertile inch o' th' island;   145
And I will kiss thy foot. I prithee be my god.

TRINCULO   By this light, a most perfidious and drunken
monster! When's god's asleep, he'll rob his bottle.

CALIBAN
I'll kiss thy foot. I'll swear myself thy subject.

STEPHANO   Come on then. Down, and swear!   150

TRINCULO   I shall laugh myself to death at this puppy-
headed monster. A most scurvy monster! I could find
in my heart to beat him —

STEPHANO   Come, kiss.

TRINCULO   But that poor monster's in drink. An abom-   155
inable monster!

CALIBAN
I'll show thee the best springs; I'll pluck thee berries;
I'll fish for thee, and get thee wood enough.
A plague upon the tyrant that I serve!
I'll bear him no more sticks, but follow thee,   160
Thou wondrous man.

TRINCULO   A most ridiculous monster, to make a wonder
of a poor drunkard!

CALIBAN
I prithee let me bring thee where crabs° grow;   **crabs:** crab apples (probably not shellfish)
And I with my long nails will dig thee pignuts,°   **pignuts:** earthnuts   165
Show thee a jay's nest, and instruct thee how
To snare the nimble marmoset;° I'll bring thee   **marmoset:** a small monkey (said to be edible)
To clust'ring filberts,° and sometimes I'll get thee   **filberts:** hazelnuts
Young scamels° from the rock. Wilt thou go with me?   **scamels:** (unexplained, but clearly either a
                                                                                      shellfish or a rock-nesting bird; perhaps a misprint   170
                                                                                      for "seamels," sea mews)

STEPHANO   I prithee now, lead the way without any more
talking. Trinculo, the king and all our company else being
drowned, we will inherit° here. [To Caliban] Here, bear   **inherit:** take possession
my bottle. Fellow Trinculo, we'll fill him by and by°   **by and by:** soon
again.

CALIBAN   [Sings drunkenly.] Farewell, master; farewell,
farewell!

TRINCULO   A howling monster! a drunken monster!   175

CALIBAN
No more dams I'll make for fish,
    Nor fetch in firing
    At requiring,
Nor scrape trenchering,° nor wash dish.   **trenchering:** trenchers, wooden plates   180
    'Ban, 'Ban, Ca — Caliban
    Has a new master: get a new man.°   **get a new man:** (addressed to Prospero)
Freedom, high-day! high-day, freedom! freedom, high-
day, freedom!

STEPHANO   O brave monster! lead the way.   *Exeunt.*   185

DISCOVERING SHAKESPEARE

(44) <u>Verse</u> [2.2.157]: Why do you think Caliban shifts into <u>verse</u> in 2.2.157, while Trinculo and Stephano stay in <u>prose</u>?
What effect does this alternation between <u>verse</u> and <u>prose</u> have on this portion of the scene?

❧ **3.1** *Enter Ferdinand, bearing a log.*

FERDINAND
    There be some sports are painful,° and their labor
    Delight in them sets off;° some kinds of baseness
    Are nobly undergone, and most poor matters°
    Point to rich ends. This my mean task
    Would be as heavy to me as odious, but
    The mistress which I serve quickens° what's dead
    And makes my labors pleasures. O, she is
    Ten times more gentle than her father's crabbed;
    And he's composed of harshness! I must remove
    Some thousands of these logs and pile them up,
    Upon a sore injunction.° My sweet mistress
    Weeps when she sees me work, and says such baseness
    Had never like executor. I forget;
    But these sweet thoughts do even refresh my labors
    Most busilest,° when I do it.
      Enter Miranda; and Prospero [behind, unseen].
MIRANDA   Alas, now pray you
    Work not so hard! I would the lightning had
    Burnt up those logs that you are enjoined to pile!
    Pray set it down and rest you. When this burns,
    'Twill weep° for having wearied you. My father
    Is hard at study: pray now rest yourself.
    He's safe for these three hours.
FERDINAND   O most dear mistress,
    The sun will set before I shall discharge
    What I must strive to do.
MIRANDA   If you'll sit down,
    I'll bear your logs the while. Pray give me that:
    I'll carry it to the pile.
FERDINAND   No, precious creature:
    I had rather crack my sinews, break my back,
    Than you should such dishonor undergo
    While I sit lazy by.
MIRANDA   It would become me
    As well as it does you; and I should do it
    With much more ease; for my good will is to it,
    And yours it is against.
PROSPERO   *[Aside]*   Poor worm, thou art infected!
    This visitation° shows it.
MIRANDA   You look wearily.
FERDINAND
    No, noble mistress: 'tis fresh morning with me
    When you are by at night. I do beseech you,
    Chiefly that I might set it in my prayers,
    What is your name?

painful: strenuous   1
their labor . . . sets off: either "the pleasure
balances the hard work they require" or "the hard 3
work adds luster to the pleasure"
matters: affairs
        5
quickens: brings to life

        10

sore injunction: harsh command

busilest: most busily (this is a famous textual 15
crux; "busilest" is the best solution proposed)

weep: i.e., exude resin

        20

        25

        30

visitation: (1) visit to the sick, (2) attack of
plague (in the metaphor of infected)

        35

DISCOVERING SHAKESPEARE

(45) <u>Paraphrase</u> **[3.1.1]:** What does Ferdinand mean when he says, "There be some sports are painful, and their labor /
Delight in them sets off" (3.1.1–2)? <u>Paraphrase</u> his statement into modern English.
(46) <u>Staging</u> **[3.1.31]:** If you were directing a production of the play, how would you stage this scene where Prospero secretly watches Ferdinand and Miranda? Draw a small diagram of the stage, with the letters "P," "F," and "M" representing
each of the characters.

MIRANDA   Miranda. O my father,
  I have broke your hest° to say so!   **hest:** command

FERDINAND   Admired Miranda!
  Indeed the top of admiration,° worth   **admiration:** wonder, astonishment (punning on
  What's dearest to the world! Full many a lady   Miranda's name; cf. 1.2.427)
  I have eyed with best regard,° and many a time   **best regard:** highest approval   40
  Th' harmony of their tongues hath into bondage
  Brought my too diligent ear; for several° virtues   **several:** different
  Have I liked several women; never any
  With so full soul° but some defect in her   **With . . . soul:** i.e., so wholeheartedly
  Did quarrel with the noblest grace she owed,°   **owed:** owned   45
  And put it to the foil.° But you, O you,   **foil:** (1) overthrow, (2) contrast
  So perfect and so peerless, are created
  Of every creature's best.

MIRANDA   I do not know
  One of my sex; no woman's face remember,
  Save, from my glass, mine own; nor have I seen   50
  More that I may call men than you, good friend,
  And my dear father. How features are abroad°   **abroad:** elsewhere
  I am skill-less° of; but, by my modesty°   **skill-less:** ignorant; **modesty:** virginity
  (The jewel in my dower), I would not wish
  Any companion in the world but you;   55
  Nor can imagination form a shape,
  Besides yourself, to like of.° But I prattle   **like of:** compare to
  Something too wildly, and my father's precepts
  I therein do forget.

FERDINAND   I am, in my condition,°   **condition:** situation in the world
  A prince, Miranda; I do think, a king   60
  (I would not so), and would no more endure
  This wooden slavery than to suffer
  The flesh fly° blow° my mouth. Hear my soul speak!   **flesh fly:** fly that breeds in dead flesh; **blow:**
  The very instant that I saw you, did   deposit its eggs in
  My heart fly to your service; there resides,   65
  To make me slave to it; and for your sake
  Am I this patient log-man.

MIRANDA   Do you love me?

FERDINAND
  O heaven, O earth, bear witness to this sound,
  And crown what I profess with kind event°   **kind event:** favorable outcome
  If I speak true! if hollowly, invert   70
  What best is boded me to mischief! I,
  Beyond all limit of what else i' th' world,
  Do love, prize, honor you.

MIRANDA   I am a fool
  To weep at what I am glad of.

PROSPERO   *[Aside]*   Fair encounter
  Of two most rare affections! Heavens rain grace   75
  On that which breeds between 'em!

FERDINAND   Wherefore weep you?

DISCOVERING SHAKESPEARE

(47) <u>Metaphor</u> [3.1.53]: What does Miranda mean when she says that "modesty" is the "jewel" in her dowry (3.1.53–54)?

MIRANDA
  At mine unworthiness, that dare not offer
  What I desire to give, and much less take
  What I shall die to want.° But this is trifling; 　　　**want:** lack
  And all the more it seeks to hide itself,
  The bigger bulk it shows.° Hence, bashful cunning,° 　**all the . . . shows:** (the image is of a secret
  And prompt me, plain and holy innocence! 　　　　pregnancy); **bashful cunning:** a pretense of
  I am your wife, if you will marry me; 　　　　　　shyness
  If not, I'll die your maid.° To be your fellow° 　　　**maid:** servant, virgin; **fellow:** equal
  You may deny me; but I'll be your servant,
  Whether you will or no.
FERDINAND　　　　　My mistress, dearest,
  And I thus humble ever.
MIRANDA　　　　　My husband then?
FERDINAND
  Ay, with a heart as willing
  As bondage e'er of freedom.° Here's my hand. 　　　**of freedom:** i.e., to win freedom
MIRANDA
  And mine, with my heart in't; and now farewell
  Till half an hour hence.
FERDINAND　　　　A thousand thousand!
  Exeunt [Ferdinand and Miranda severally].
PROSPERO
  So glad of this as they I cannot be,
  Who are surprised withal;° but my rejoicing 　　　**surprised withal:** taken unaware by it
  At nothing can be more. I'll to my book;
  For yet ere suppertime must I perform
  Much business appertaining.° 　　　*Exit.* 　　　**appertaining:** relevant

80

85

90

95

✒　**3.2**　*Enter Caliban, Stephano, and Trinculo.*

STEPHANO　Tell not me! When the butt is out,° we will 　**butt is out:** cask is empty
  drink water; not a drop before. Therefore bear up and
  board 'em!° Servant monster, drink to me. 　　　**bear . . . 'em:** i.e., drink up (Caliban has almost
TRINCULO　Servant monster? The folly of this island! 　passed out)
  They say there's but five upon this isle: we are three of
  them. If th' other two be brained like us, the state
  totters.
STEPHANO　Drink, servant monster, when I bid thee: thy
  eyes are almost set° in thy head. 　　　　　　**set:** fixed drunkenly
TRINCULO　Where should they be set else? He were a
  brave monster indeed if they were set in his tail.
STEPHANO　My man-monster hath drowned his tongue
  in sack. For my part, the sea cannot drown me. I swam,
  ere I could recover° the shore, five-and-thirty leagues off 　**recover:** reach
  and on, by this light. Thou shalt be my lieutenant,
  monster, or my standard.° 　　　　　　　　**standard:** standard-bearer

5

10

15

DISCOVERING SHAKESPEARE

(48) <u>Imagery</u> [3.1.81]: Find the pregnancy <u>image</u> in Miranda's speech in 3.1.77–86. Do you believe the character consciously uses this particular <u>image</u> here? Explain your answer.

(49) <u>Metaphor</u> [3.2.8]: When Stephano tells Caliban, "thy eyes are almost set in thy head" (3.2.8–9), what does his <u>metaphor</u> mean? Compare this statement with Feste's similar description of the doctor at the conclusion of *Twelfth Night* (5.1.192–193). Which play was written first?

TRINCULO   Your lieutenant, if you list; he's no standard.° **no standard:** i.e., incapable of standing up
STEPHANO   We'll not run, Monsieur Monster.
TRINCULO   Nor go° neither; but you'll lie° like dogs, and **go:** walk; **run, lie:** (secondary meanings of)
yet say nothing neither. make water, excrete   20
STEPHANO   Mooncalf, speak once in thy life, if thou beest
a good mooncalf.
CALIBAN
How does thy honor? Let me lick thy shoe.
I'll not serve him; he is not valiant.
TRINCULO   Thou liest, most ignorant monster: I am in   25
case° to justle° a constable. Why, thou deboshed° fish **case:** fit condition; **justle:** jostle; **deboshed:**
thou, was there ever man a coward that hath drunk so debauched
much sack as I today? Wilt thou tell a monstrous lie,
being but half a fish and half a monster?
CALIBAN   Lo, how he mocks me! Wilt thou let him, my   30
lord?
TRINCULO   "Lord" quoth he? That a monster should be
such a natural!°   **natural:** fool
CALIBAN
Lo, lo, again! Bite him to death, I prithee.
STEPHANO   Trinculo, keep a good tongue in your head.   35
If you prove a mutineer – the next tree! The poor mon-
ster's my subject, and he shall not suffer indignity.
CALIBAN
I thank my noble lord. Wilt thou be pleased
To hearken once again to the suit I made to thee?
STEPHANO   Marry, will I. Kneel and repeat it; I will   40
stand, and so shall Trinculo.
Enter Ariel, invisible.°   **invisible:** ("a robe for to go invisible" is in the
CALIBAN   list of costumes belonging to the Lord Admiral's
As I told thee before, I am subject to a tyrant,   Men in the 1590s)
A sorcerer, that by his cunning hath
Cheated me of the island.
ARIEL   Thou liest.°   **Thou liest:** (Ariel pretends to be Trinculo here
CALIBAN   *[To Trinculo]*   and later in the scene)
Thou liest, thou jesting monkey thou!   45
I would my valiant master would destroy thee.
I do not lie.
STEPHANO   Trinculo, if you trouble him any more in's
tale, by this hand, I will supplant some of your teeth.
TRINCULO   Why, I said nothing.   50
STEPHANO   Mum then, and no more. – Proceed.
CALIBAN
I say by sorcery he got this isle;
From me he got it. If thy greatness will
Revenge it on him – for I know thou dar'st,
But this thing° dare not –   **this thing:** i.e., himself (or perhaps Trinculo)   55
STEPHANO   That's most certain.
CALIBAN
Thou shalt be lord of it, and I'll serve thee.

DISCOVERING SHAKESPEARE

(50) <u>Verse</u> **[3.2.40]:** <u>Scan</u> 3.2.40–62, and decide whether the lines are written in <u>verse</u> or <u>prose</u>? Why do you think this is
true?

STEPHANO
How now shall this be compassed?
Canst thou bring me to the party?°   **party:** person

CALIBAN
Yea, yea, my lord! I'll yield him thee asleep,
Where thou mayst knock a nail into his head.   60

ARIEL   Thou liest; thou canst not.

CALIBAN
What a pied ninny's° this! Thou scurvy patch!°   **pied ninny:** motley fool (Trinculo wears a
I do beseech thy greatness give him blows   jester's costume); **patch:** clown
And take his bottle from him. When that's gone,
He shall drink naught but brine, for I'll not show him   65
Where the quick freshes° are.   **quick freshes:** freshwater springs

STEPHANO   Trinculo, run into no further danger: interrupt the monster one word further and, by this hand, I'll
turn my mercy out o' doors and make a stockfish° of thee.   **stockfish:** dried cod, prepared by beating   70

TRINCULO   Why, what did I? I did nothing. I'll go farther off.

STEPHANO   Didst thou not say he lied?

ARIEL   Thou liest.

STEPHANO   Do I so? Take thou that! *[Strikes Trinculo.]* As   75
you like this, give me the lie another time.

TRINCULO   I did not give the lie. Out o' your wits, and
hearing too? A pox o' your bottle! This can sack and
drinking do. A murrain° on your monster, and the devil   **murrain:** plague
take your fingers!

CALIBAN   Ha, ha, ha!   80

STEPHANO   Now forward with your tale. *[To Trinculo]*
Prithee stand further off.

CALIBAN
Beat him enough. After a little time
I'll beat him too.

STEPHANO *[To Trinculo]*
         Stand farther. *[To Caliban]* Come,
proceed.   85

CALIBAN
Why, as I told thee, 'tis a custom with him
I' th' afternoon to sleep; there thou mayst brain him,
Having first seized his books, or with a log
Batter his skull, or paunch° him with a stake,   **paunch:** stab in the belly
Or cut his wesand° with thy knife. Remember   **wesand:** windpipe   90
First to possess his books; for without them
He's but a sot,° as I am, nor hath not   **sot:** fool
One spirit to command. They all do hate him
As rootedly as I. Burn but his books.
He has brave utensils° (for so he calls them)   **utensils:** furnishings   95
Which, when he has a house, he'll deck withal.
And that most deeply to consider is
The beauty of his daughter. He himself

DISCOVERING SHAKESPEARE

(51) Teaser [3.2.61]: Find the Biblical passage in which a sleeping person is killed by having a nail driven into his head.
Do you think Shakespeare is <u>alluding</u> to it in this context? Why or why not?

(52) Language [3.2.90]: What was a "wesand" (3.2.90)? What is the <u>etymological</u> origin of the word?

Calls her a nonpareil. I never saw a woman
But only Sycorax my dam and she;
But she as far surpasseth Sycorax
As great'st does least.   100

STEPHANO   Is it so brave° a lass?   **brave:** handsome

CALIBAN
Ay, lord. She will become thy bed, I warrant,
And bring thee forth brave brood.

STEPHANO   Monster, I will kill this man: his daughter and   105
I will be king and queen, save our graces! and Trinculo
and thyself shall be viceroys. Dost thou like the plot,
Trinculo?

TRINCULO   Excellent.

STEPHANO   Give me thy hand. I am sorry I beat thee; but   110
while thou liv'st, keep a good tongue in thy head.

CALIBAN
Within this half hour he will be asleep.
Wilt thou destroy him then?

STEPHANO   Ay, on mine honor.

ARIEL
This will I tell my master.

CALIBAN
Thou mak'st me merry; I am full of pleasure.   115
Let us be jocund. Will you troll the catch°   **troll the catch:** sing the round
You taught me but whilere?°   **whilere:** just now

STEPHANO   At thy request, monster, I will do reason, any
reason.° Come on, Trinculo, let us sing.   **any reason:** anything reasonable

     Sings.

           Flout 'em and scout° 'em   **scout:** mock
           And scout 'em and flout 'em!
           Thought is free.

CALIBAN
That's not the tune.

     Ariel plays the tune on a tabor and pipe.°   **tabor and pipe:** a small drum worn at the side and a pipe played one-handed while drumming

STEPHANO   What is this same?

TRINCULO   This is the tune of our catch, played by the   125
picture of Nobody.°   **Nobody:** (referring to pictures of figures with arms and legs but no trunk, used on signs and elsewhere)

STEPHANO   If thou beest a man, show thyself in thy like-
ness. If thou beest a devil, take't as thou list.°   **take't as thou list:** i.e., suit yourself

TRINCULO   O, forgive me my sins!

STEPHANO   He that dies pays all debts. I defy thee. Mercy   130
upon us!

CALIBAN
Art thou afeard?

STEPHANO   No, monster, not I.

CALIBAN
Be not afeard: the isle is full of noises,
Sounds and sweet airs that give delight and hurt not.   135
Sometimes a thousand twangling instruments

DISCOVERING SHAKESPEARE

(53) Short Line [3.2.114]: Ariel's abbreviated line "This will I tell my master" (3.2.114) seems to invite some action or gesture. What could Ariel do during the missing three syllables?

Will hum about mine ears; and sometime voices
That, if I then had waked after long sleep,
Will make me sleep again; and then, in dreaming,
The clouds methought would open and show riches   140
Ready to drop upon me, that, when I waked,
I cried to dream again.
STEPHANO This will prove a brave kingdom to me,
where I shall have my music for nothing.
CALIBAN
When Prospero is destroyed.   145
STEPHANO That shall be by and by:° I remember the   **by and by:** right away
story
TRINCULO The sound is going away: let's follow it, and
after do our work.
STEPHANO Lead, monster; we'll follow. I would I could   150
see this taborer: he lays it on.
TRINCULO *[To Caliban]* Wilt come? I'll follow
Stephano.   *Exeunt.*

❧ **3.3** *Enter Alonso, Sebastian, Antonio, Gonzalo,*
Adrian, Francisco, etc.

GONZALO
By'r Lakin,° I can go no further, sir: **By'r Lakin:** by our Ladykin (Virgin Mary)
My old bones ache: here's a maze trod indeed
Through forthrights° and meanders. By your patience,   **forthrights:** straight paths
I needs must rest me.
ALONSO   Old lord, I cannot blame thee,
Who am myself attached° with weariness   **attached:** seized   5
To th' dulling of my spirits. Sit down and rest.
Even here I will put off my hope, and keep it
No longer for my flatterer: he is drowned
Whom thus we stray to find; and the sea mocks
Our frustrate° search on land. Well, let him go.   **frustrate:** vain   10
ANTONIO *[Aside to Sebastian]*
I am right glad that he's so out of hope.
Do not for one repulse forgo the purpose
That you resolved t' effect.
SEBASTIAN *[Aside to Antonio]* The next advantage
Will we take throughly.°   **throughly:** thoroughly
ANTONIO *[Aside to Sebastian]* Let it be tonight;   15
For, now they are oppressed with travel, they
Will not nor cannot use such vigilance
As when they are fresh.
SEBASTIAN *[Aside to Antonio]* I say tonight. No more.
Solemn and strange music; and Prospero on the top°   **on the top:** (the topmost level of the theater,
(invisible).   above the gallery over the stage)
ALONSO
What harmony is this? My good friends, hark!

DISCOVERING SHAKESPEARE
(54) <u>Verse</u> [3.2.140]: Many actors and scholars believe that Caliban is one of Shakespeare's most "poetic" characters. Read
his speech in 3.2.133–142; then explain why you agree or disagree with this analysis. In what sense is his character <u>ironic</u>?

GONZALO
   Marvelous sweet music!
   Enter several strange Shapes, bringing in a banquet;
   and dance about it with gentle actions of salutations;
   and, inviting the King etc. to eat, they depart.
ALONSO
   Give us kind keepers,° heavens! What were these?   **kind keepers:** guardian angels   20
SEBASTIAN
   A living drollery.° Now I will believe   **living drollery:** puppet show with live figures or
   That there are unicorns; that in Arabia   comic pictures come to life
   There is one tree, the phoenix' throne; one phoenix
   At this hour reigning there.
ANTONIO   I'll believe both;
   And what does else want credit,° come to me,   **want credit:** lack credibility   25
   And I'll be sworn 'tis true. Travelers ne'er did lie,
   Though fools at home condemn 'em.
GONZALO   If in Naples
   I should report this now, would they believe me
   If I should say I saw such islanders?
   (For certes° these are people of the island)   **certes:** certainly   30
   Who, though they are of monstrous shape, yet note,
   Their manners are more gentle, kind, than of
   Our human generation you shall find
   Many — nay, almost any.
PROSPERO   *[Aside]* Honest lord,
   Thou hast said well; for some of you there present   35
   Are worse than devils.
ALONSO   I cannot too much muse°   **muse:** wonder at
   Such shapes, such gesture, and such sound, expressing
   (Although they want the use of tongue) a kind
   Of excellent dumb discourse.
PROSPERO   *[Aside]*   Praise in departing.°   **Praise in departing:** save your praise for the
FRANCISCO   end
   They vanished strangely.   40
SEBASTIAN   No matter, since
   They have left their viands° behind; for we have   **viands:** food
      stomachs.
   Will't please you taste of what is here?
ALONSO   Not I.
GONZALO
   Faith, sir, you need not fear. When we were boys,
   Who would believe that there were mountaineers
   Dewlapped° like bulls, whose throats had hanging at 'em   **Dewlapped:** with skin hanging from the neck   45
   Wallets of flesh? or that there were such men   (like the supposedly goitrous Swiss mountain
   Whose heads stood in their breasts? which now we find   dwellers)

DISCOVERING SHAKESPEARE
(55) Mythology [3.3.23]: What was a "phoenix" (3.3.23)? Which long Shakespearean poem deals with this mythical bird?
(56) Teaser [3.3.47]: Read Gonzalo's description of "men / Whose heads stood in their breasts" (3.3.46–47); then find another Shakespearean play in which a character refers to "men whose heads/Do grow beneath their shoulders." In which play does this second line appear? Which of the two plays did Shakespeare write first?

Each putter-out of five for one° will bring us
Good warrant° of.

ALONSO   I will stand to,° and feed;
Although my last, no matter, since I feel
The best is past. Brother, my lord the duke,
Stand to, and do as we.

Thunder and lightning. Enter Ariel, like a harpy;° claps
his wings upon the table; and with a quaint° device the
banquet vanishes.

ARIEL
You are three men of sin, whom destiny –
That hath to° instrument this lower world
And what is in't – the never-surfeited sea
Hath caused to belch up you, and on this island,
Where man doth not inhabit, you 'mongst men
Being most unfit to live, I have made you mad;
And even with suchlike valor men hang and drown
Their proper selves.

[Alonso, Sebastian, etc. draw their swords.]
               You fools: I and my fellows
Are ministers of Fate. The elements,
Of whom your swords are tempered, may as well
Wound the loud winds, or with bemocked-at stabs
Kill the still°-closing waters, as diminish
One dowl° that's in my plume. My fellow ministers
Are like° invulnerable. If you could hurt,
Your swords are now too massy° for your strengths
And will not be uplifted. But remember
(For that's my business to you) that you three
From Milan did supplant good Prospero;
Exposed unto the sea, which hath requit° it,°
Him and his innocent child; for which foul deed
The pow'rs, delaying, not forgetting, have
Incensed the seas and shores, yea, all the creatures,
Against your peace. Thee of thy son, Alonso,
They have bereft; and do pronounce by me
Ling'ring perdition° (worse than any death
Can be at once) shall step by step attend
You and your ways; whose wraths to guard you from,
Which here, in this most desolate isle, else falls
Upon your heads, is nothing but heart's sorrow°
And a clear° life ensuing.

He vanishes in thunder; then, to soft music, enter the
Shapes again, and dance with mocks and mows,° and
carrying out the table.

PROSPERO
Bravely the figure of this harpy hast thou
Performed, my Ariel; a grace it had, devouring.°
Of my instruction hast thou nothing bated°

putter-out . . . one: traveler depositing a sum
for insurance in London, to be repaid fivefold if he
returned safely and proved he had gone to his
destination
warrant: proof; **stand to:** set to work   50

harpy: a creature with a female face and breasts,
and the body, wings, and talons of a bird of prey
(Ariel may have flown in)
quaint: ingenious

to: i.e., as its   55

   60

still: constantly
dowl: fiber of feather-down   65
like: similarly
massy: heavy

   70
requit: avenged; **it:** i.e., the deed

   75

Ling'ring perdition: slow ruin

   80

heart's sorrow: repentance
clear: innocent

s.d. mocks and mows: grimaces and gestures

devouring: i.e., making the banquet disappear
bated: omitted   85

DISCOVERING SHAKESPEARE

(57) Mythology [3.3.70]: What is a "harpy"? Compare the "banquet" scene in 3.3 to a similar episode in Virgil's *Aeneid* (III.225). What use did Shakespeare make of this source in creating the harpy scene in *The Tempest*? What is the "quaint device" (3.3.52, s.d.) through which the banquet vanishes?

In what thou hadst to say. So, with good life°
And observation strange,° my meaner ministers
Their several kinds° have done. My high charms work,
And these, mine enemies, are all knit up
In their distractions: they now are in my pow'r;   90
And in these fits I leave them, while I visit
Young Ferdinand, whom they suppose is drowned,
And his and mine loved darling.   *[Exit above.]*

good life: realistic acting
observation strange: wonderful attentiveness
several kinds: separate parts

GONZALO
I' th' name of something holy, sir, why° stand you
In this strange stare?   95

why: (Gonzalo has not heard Ariel's speech)

ALONSO   O, it° is monstrous, monstrous!

it: i.e., my sin

Methought the billows spoke and told me of it,
The winds did sing it to me, and the thunder,
That deep and dreadful organ pipe, pronounced
The name of Prosper; it did bass° my trespass.   100
Therefore my son i' th' ooze is bedded; and
I'll seek him deeper than e'er plummet sounded
And with him there lie mudded.   *Exit.*

bass: proclaim in deep tones (literally, provide the bass part for)

SEBASTIAN   But one fiend at a time,
I'll fight their legions o'er!°

o'er: one after another

ANTONIO   I'll be thy second.
          Exeunt [Sebastian and Antonio].

GONZALO
All three of them are desperate: their great guilt,
Like poison given to work a great time after,   105
Now 'gins to bite the spirits. I do beseech you,
That are of suppler joints, follow them swiftly
And hinder them from what this ecstasy°
May now provoke them to.

ecstasy: madness

ADRIAN   Follow, I pray you.
          Exeunt omnes.

❧ **4.1** *Enter Prospero, Ferdinand, and Miranda.*

PROSPERO
If I have too austerely° punished you,
Your compensation makes amends; for I
Have given you here a third° of mine own life,
Or that for which I live; who once again
I tender to thy hand. All thy vexations   5
Were but my trials of thy love, and thou
Hast strangely° stood the test. Here, afore heaven,
I ratify this my rich gift. O Ferdinand,
Do not smile at me that I boast her off,°
For thou shalt find she will outstrip all praise   10
And make it halt° behind her.

austerely: harshly

third: a very significant part (editors have worried too much what the other two thirds could be)

strangely: in a rare fashion

boast her off: boast about her

halt: limp

FERDINAND   I do believe it
Against an oracle.°

Against an oracle: even if an oracle denied it

DISCOVERING SHAKESPEARE

(58) **Paraphrase** **[3.3.99]:** What does Alonso mean when he says that the thunderous sound of Prospero's name "did bass my trespass" (3.3.99)?

PROSPERO
  Then, as my gift, and thine own acquisition
  Worthily purchased, take my daughter. But
  If thou dost break her virgin-knot before   15
  All sanctimonious° ceremonies may
  With full and holy rite be ministered,
  No sweet aspersion° shall the heavens let fall
  To make this contract grow;° but barren hate,
  Sour-eyed disdain, and discord shall bestrew   20
  The union of your bed with weeds so loathly
  That you shall hate it both. Therefore take heed,
  As Hymen's lamps° shall light you.
FERDINAND   As I hope
  For quiet days, fair issue, and long life,
  With such love as 'tis now, the murkiest den,   25
  The most opportune place, the strong'st suggestion
  Our worser genius can,° shall never melt
  Mine honor into lust, to take away
  The edge of that day's celebration
  When I shall think or Phoebus' steeds are foundered° 30
  Or Night kept chained below.
PROSPERO   Fairly spoke.
  Sit then and talk with her; she is thine own.
  What, Ariel! My industrious servant, Ariel!
    Enter Ariel.
ARIEL
  What would my potent master? Here I am.
PROSPERO   35
  Thou and thy meaner fellows your last service
  Did worthily perform; and I must use you
  In such another trick. Go bring the rabble,°
  O'er whom I give thee pow'r, here to this place.
  Incite them to quick motion; for I must
  Bestow upon the eyes of this young couple   40
  Some vanity° of mine art; it is my promise,
  And they expect it from me.
ARIEL   Presently?
PROSPERO
  Ay, with a twink.
ARIEL
  Before you can say "Come" and "Go,"
  And breathe twice and cry, "So, so,"   45
  Each one, tripping on his toe,
  Will be here with mop and mow.°
  Do you love me, master? No?
PROSPERO
  Dearly, my delicate Ariel. Do not approach
  Till thou dost hear me call.   50
ARIEL   Well: I conceive.°   *Exit.*

sanctimonious: holy

aspersion: blessing (like rain on crops)
grow: become fruitful

Hymen's lamps: wedding torches (Hymen was the god of marriage; clear flames indicated a happy marriage, smoky flames a bad one)

worser genius can: bad angel can make

or . . . foundered: either the sun god's horses are lame

rabble: rank and file

vanity: trifling display

mop and mow: grimaces

conceive: understand

DISCOVERING SHAKESPEARE

(59) Mythology [4.1.23]: Who was Hymen (4.1.23)? What were his "lamps" used for? Name a Shakespearean play in which a character named Hymen appears.

PROSPERO

    Look thou be true:° do not give dalliance
    Too much the rein: the strongest oaths are straw
    To th' fire i' th' blood. Be more abstemious,
    Or else good night your vow!

FERDINAND   I warrant you, sir.

    The white cold virgin snow upon my heart
    Abates the ardor of my liver.°

PROSPERO   Well.

    Now come, my Ariel: bring a corollary°
    Rather than want° a spirit. Appear, and pertly!°

    [To Ferdinand and Miranda]

    No tongue! All eyes! Be silent.

    Soft music. Enter Iris.°

IRIS

    Ceres, most bounteous lady, thy rich leas°
    Of wheat, rye, barley, fetches,° oats, and pease;
    Thy turfy mountains, where live nibbling sheep,
    And flat meads thatched with stover,° them to keep;
    Thy banks with pionèd and twillèd° brims,
    Which spongy April at thy hest betrims
    To make cold nymphs chaste crowns; and thy broom
     groves,°
    Whose shadow the dismissèd bachelor loves,
    Being lasslorn; thy pole-clipped° vineyard;
    And thy sea-marge,° sterile and rocky-hard,
    Where thou thyself dost air – the queen° o' th' sky,
    Whose wat'ry arch and messenger am I,
    Bids thee leave these, and with her sovereign grace,
    Here on this grass plot, in this very place,
    To come and sport: her peacocks° fly amain.

    [Juno's chariot appears above the stage.]°

    Approach, rich Ceres, her to entertain.

    Enter Ceres [played by Ariel].

CERES

    Hail, many-colored messenger, that ne'er
    Dost disobey the wife of Jupiter,
    Who, with thy saffron wings, upon my flow'rs
    Diffusest honey drops, refreshing show'rs,
    And with each end of thy blue bow dost crown
    My bosky° acres and my unshrubbed down,
    Rich scarf to my proud earth – why hath thy queen
    Summoned me hither to this short-grassed green?

IRIS

    A contract of true love to celebrate
    And some donation freely to estate°
    On the blessed lovers.

CERES   Tell me, heavenly bow,

    If Venus or her son,° as thou dost know,

---

be true: (Prospero appears to have caught the lovers in an embrace or, if Prospero is overreacting, some contact less explicitly sexual)

55

liver: (supposed seat of sexual passion)

corollary: surplus
want: lack; **pertly:** briskly

Iris: goddess of the rainbow and female messenger of the gods
leas: meadows   60
fetches: vetch

stover: winter food for stock
pionèd and twillèd: dug under by the current and protected by woven layers of branches 65 (sometimes emended to "peonied and lilied")

broom groves: clumps of gorse

pole-clipped: pruned
sea-marge: shore
queen: i.e., Juno   70

peacocks: (these were sacred to Juno, as doves were to Venus [l. 94], and drew her chariot)
s.d. (F has "Juno descended" in the margin by 75 l. 72; "descends" could indicate the appearance of a deity suspended above the stage)

80

bosky: wooded

estate: bestow   85

her son: Cupid (often represented as blind or blindfolded)

DISCOVERING SHAKESPEARE

(60) History [4.1.56]: Why does Ferdinand refer to his "liver" in 4.1.56? How will this reference help convince Prospero that the young man won't seduce Miranda prior to their wedding?

(61) Mythology [4.1.75]: Who were Juno, Iris, Ceres, and Jupiter? What mythological realms did these deities rule over?

Do now attend the queen? Since they did plot
The means° that dusky Dis my daughter got,
Her and her blind boy's scandaled° company
I have forsworn.

IRIS   Of her society
Be not afraid: I met her Deity°
Cutting the clouds towards Paphos,° and her son
Dove-drawn with her. Here thought they to have done
Some wanton charm upon this man and maid,
Whose vows are, that no bed-right shall be paid
Till Hymen's torch be lighted; but in vain.
Mars's hot minion is returned again;°
Her waspish-headed° son has broke his arrows,
Swears he will shoot no more, but play with sparrows
And be a boy right out.°

[Juno's chariot descends to the stage.]

CERES   Highest queen of state,
Great Juno, comes; I know her by her gait.

JUNO
How does my bounteous sister? Go with me°
To bless this twain, that they may prosperous be
And honored in their issue.

    They sing.

JUNO   Honor, riches, marriage blessing,
          Long continuance, and increasing,
          Hourly joys be still° upon you!
          Juno sings her blessings on you.

[CERES]   Earth's increase, foison° plenty,
          Barns and garners never empty,
          Vines with clust'ring bunches growing,
          Plants with goodly burden bowing;
          Spring come to you at the farthest
          In the very end of harvest.
          Scarcity and wants shall shun you,
          Ceres' blessing so is on you.

FERDINAND
This is a most majestic vision, and
Harmonious charmingly. May I be bold
To think these spirits?

PROSPERO   Spirits, which by mine art
I have from their confines called to enact
My present fancies.

FERDINAND   Let me live here ever!
So rare a wondered° father and a wise
Makes this place Paradise.

    Juno and Ceres whisper, and send Iris on employment.

PROSPERO   Sweet now, silence!
Juno and Ceres whisper seriously.
There's something else to do. Hush and be mute,
Or else our spell is marred.

---

means: i.e., the abduction of Proserpine, Ceres' daughter, by Pluto (Dis), god of the lower *(dusky)* world   90

scandaled: disgraceful

her Deity: i.e., her Divine Majesty

Paphos: (in Cyprus, center of Venus' cult)

Mars's . . . again: the lustful mistress of Mars (Venus) has gone back to where she came from

waspish-headed: spiteful and inclined to sting (with his arrows)   100

right out: outright

Go with me: (into the chariot?)

   105

still: constantly

foison: abundance   110

   115

   120

wondered: wonderful

   125

DISCOVERING SHAKESPEARE

(62) Mythology [4.1.89]: Who was Dis (4.1.89)? What was his Greek name? What does the name mean?

(63) <u>Verse</u> [4.1.114]: <u>Scan</u> Ceres' blessing in 4.1.110–117. What is the <u>meter</u> and <u>rhyme scheme</u> of these lines?

IRIS

You nymphs, called Naiads, of the windring° brooks,
With your sedged crowns° and ever-harmless looks,
Leave your crisp° channels, and on this green land
Answer your summons; Juno does command.
Come, temperate nymphs, and help to celebrate
A contract of true love: be not too late.

Enter certain Nymphs.

You sunburned sicklemen, of August weary,
Come hither from the furrow and be merry.
Make holiday: your rye-straw hats put on,
And these fresh nymphs encounter every one
In country footing.

*Enter certain Reapers, properly habited. They join
with the Nymphs in a graceful dance; towards the end
whereof Prospero starts suddenly and speaks; after
which, to a strange, hollow, and confused noise, they
heavily vanish.*°

PROSPERO *[Aside]*

I had forgot that foul conspiracy
Of the beast Caliban and his confederates
Against my life: the minute of their plot
Is almost come.

[To the Spirits] Well done! Avoid!° No more!

FERDINAND

This is strange. Your father's in some passion
That works him strongly.

MIRANDA   Never till this day
Saw I him touched with anger so distempered.

PROSPERO

You do look, my son, in a movèd sort,°
As if you were dismayed: be cheerful, sir.
Our revels° now are ended. These our actors,
As I foretold you, were all spirits and
Are melted into air, into thin air;
And, like the baseless fabric° of this vision,
The cloud-capped tow'rs, the gorgeous palaces,
The solemn temples, the great globe itself,
Yea, all which it inherit,° shall dissolve,
And, like this insubstantial pageant faded,
Leave not a rack° behind. We are such stuff
As dreams are made on,° and our little life
Is rounded with a sleep. Sir, I am vexed.
Bear with my weakness: my old brain is troubled.
Be not disturbed with my infirmity.
If you be pleased, retire into my cell
And there repose. A turn or two I'll walk
To still my beating mind.

windring: winding and wandering
sedged crowns: crowns of sedge (a river plant)
crisp: rippling   130

135

after which . . . vanish: (i.e., following l. 142)

140

Avoid: be off

145

movèd sort: troubled state

revels: entertainments (also the dance of
masquers and spectators together at the end of a
court masque)   150

baseless fabric: insubstantial, nonmaterial
structure

it inherit: possess it
155

rack: wisp of cloud
on: of

160

DISCOVERING SHAKESPEARE

(64) Language [4.1.138]: Who are the "sicklemen" (4.1.134) and "Reapers" (4.1.138, s.d.) who join the masque? What is their primary purpose in the scene?

(65) Paraphrase [4.1.157]: Paraphrase the following famous lines by Prospero: "We are such stuff / As dreams are made on, and our little life / Is rounded with a sleep" (4.1.156–158).

FERDINAND, MIRANDA   We wish you peace.

Exit [Ferdinand with Miranda].

PROSPERO
Come with a thought! I thank thee,° Ariel. Come.

[Enter Ariel.]

ARIEL
Thy thoughts I cleave to. What's thy pleasure?

PROSPERO   Spirit,
We must prepare to meet with Caliban.

ARIEL
Ay, my commander: when I presented° Ceres,
I thought to have told thee of it, but I feared
Lest I might anger thee.

PROSPERO
Say again, where didst thou leave these varlets?°

ARIEL
I told you sir, they were red-hot with drinking;
So full of valor that they smote the air
For breathing in their faces, beat the ground
For kissing of their feet; yet always bending
Towards their project. Then I beat my tabor;
At which like unbacked° colts they pricked their ears,
Advanced° their eyelids, lifted up their noses
As they smelt music. So I charmed their ears
That calflike they my lowing followed through
Toothed briers, sharp furzes, pricking gorse, and
   thorns,
Which entered their frail shins. At last I left them
I' th' filthy mantled° pool beyond your cell,
There dancing up to th' chins, that the foul lake
O'erstunk their feet.

PROSPERO   This was well done, my bird.
Thy shape invisible retain thou still.
The trumpery in my house, go bring it hither
For stale° to catch these thieves.

ARIEL   I go, I go.   *Exit.*

PROSPERO
A devil, a born devil, on whose nature
Nurture can never stick: on whom my pains,
Humanely taken, all, all lost, quite lost!
And as with age his body uglier grows,
So his mind cankers.° I will plague them all,
Even to roaring.

Enter Ariel, loaden with glistering apparel, etc.

          Come, hang them on this line.°

*[Prospero and Ariel remain, invisible.] Enter Caliban,
Stephano, and Trinculo, all wet.*

I thank thee: could be directed to Ferdinand and Miranda as they leave, rather than to Ariel before he arrives; the punctuation in F is ambiguous   165

presented: acted the part of (?), introduced (?)

varlets: ruffians   170

   175

unbacked: unbroken
Advanced: lifted up

   180

mantled: scummed

   185

stale: decoy

   190

cankers: festers

line: lime or linden tree (probably not a clothesline)

DISCOVERING SHAKESPEARE

(66) Language [4.1.189]: What is the difference between "nature" and "nurture" (4.1.188–189) in this play? Which characters show more evidence of "nurture"? Which are most "natural"? Which do you think Shakespeare has the most admiration for? Why?

CALIBAN
Pray you tread softly, that the blind mole may not
Hear a foot fall. We now are near his cell.   195

STEPHANO   Monster, your fairy, which you say is a harm-
less fairy, has done little better than played the Jack°   **Jack:** knave
with us.

TRINCULO   Monster, I do smell all horse piss, at which
my nose is in great indignation.   200

STEPHANO   So is mine. Do you hear, monster? If I
should take a displeasure against you, look you –

TRINCULO   Thou wert but a lost monster.

CALIBAN
Good my lord, give me thy favor still.
Be patient, for the prize I'll bring thee to   205
Shall hoodwink° this mischance. Therefore speak softly. **hoodwink:** cover over
All's hushed as midnight yet.

TRINCULO   Ay, but to lose our bottles in the pool!

STEPHANO   There is not only disgrace and dishonor in
that, monster, but an infinite loss.   210

TRINCULO   That's more to me than my wetting. Yet this
is your harmless fairy, monster.

STEPHANO   I will fetch off my bottle, though I be o'er
ears for my labor.

CALIBAN
Prithee, my king, be quiet. Seest thou here?   215
This is the mouth o' th' cell. No noise, and enter.
Do that good mischief which may make this island
Thine own forever, and I, thy Caliban,
For aye thy footlicker.

STEPHANO   Give me thy hand. I do begin to have bloody   220
thoughts.

TRINCULO   O King Stephano! O peer!° O worthy   **peer:** (referring to the song "King Stephen was a
Stephano, look what a wardrobe here is for thee!   worthy peer," quoted in *Othello* 2.3)

CALIBAN
Let it alone, thou fool! It is but trash.

TRINCULO   O, ho, monster! We know what belongs to a   225
frippery.° O King Stephano!   **frippery:** old-clothes shop

STEPHANO   Put off that gown, Trinculo: by this hand, I'll
have that gown!

TRINCULO   Thy grace shall have it.

CALIBAN
The dropsy° drown this fool! What do you mean   **dropsy:** (disease in which fluid accumulates   230
To dote thus on such luggage?° Let's alone,   excessively in the body, hence an insatiable thirst)
And do the murder first. If he awake,   **luggage:** junk
From toe to crown he'll fill our skins with pinches,
Make us strange stuff.

STEPHANO   Be you quiet, monster. Mistress line,° is not   **Line:** (the jokes are probably obscene, but their   235
this my jerkin? *[Takes it down.]* Now is the jerkin under point is lost; sailors crossing the *line*, or equator,
                                                            proverbially lost their hair from scurvy, but
                                                            baldness caused by syphilis may be alluded to)

DISCOVERING SHAKESPEARE

(67) Metaphor [4.1.206]: What does Caliban mean when he tells Stephano and Trinculo that the action of killing Prospero "Shall hoodwink this mischance" (4.1.206) of falling into the mire? Where did the word "hoodwink" come from?
What does it mean?

(68) History [4.1.230]: What type of disease was "dropsy" (4.1.230)? What were its symptoms?

the line. Now, jerkin, you are like to lose your hair and prove a bald jerkin.

TRINCULO   Do, do! We steal by line and level,° an't like° your grace.

STEPHANO   I thank thee for that jest. Here's a garment for't. Wit shall not go unrewarded while I am king of this country. "Steal by line and level" is an excellent pass of pate.° There's another garment for't.

TRINCULO   Monster, come put some lime° upon your fingers, and away with the rest.

CALIBAN
I will have none on't. We shall lose our time
And all be turned to barnacles,° or to apes
With foreheads villainous low.

STEPHANO   Monster, lay to° your fingers: help to bear this away where my hogshead of wine is, or I'll turn you out of my kingdom. Go to, carry this.

TRINCULO   And this.

STEPHANO   Ay, and this.

A noise of hunters heard. Enter divers Spirits in shape of dogs and hounds, hunting them about, Prospero and Ariel setting them on.

PROSPERO   Hey, Mountain, hey!

ARIEL   Silver! there it goes, Silver!

PROSPERO
Fury, Fury! There, Tyrant, there! Hark, hark!
[Caliban, Stephano, and Trinculo are driven out.]
Go, charge my goblins that they grind their joints
With dry° convulsions, shorten up their sinews
With agèd° cramps, and more pinch-spotted make
them
Than pard or cat o' mountain.°

ARIEL   Hark, they roar!

PROSPERO
Let them be hunted soundly. At this hour
Lies at my mercy all mine enemies.
Shortly shall all my labors end, and thou
Shalt have the air at freedom. For a little,
Follow, and do me service.   *Exeunt.*

❧ **5.1**   *Enter Prospero in his magic robes, and Ariel.*

PROSPERO
Now does my project gather to a head.
My charms crack not, my spirits obey, and time
Goes upright with his carriage.° How's the day?

ARIEL
On the sixth hour, at which time, my lord,
You said our work should cease.

---

by line and level: according to rule (with pun on "line"); **an't like:** if it please   240

pass of pate: sally of wit
lime: birdlime (sticky, hence appropriate for stealing)   245

barnacles: geese or shellfish

lay to: apply   250

255

dry: (resulting from deficiency of "humors," or bodily liquids)
agèd: i.e., such as old people have   260

pard or cat o' mountain: (both refer to the leopard or catamount)

265

time . . . carriage: time walks upright because his burden is light

5

DISCOVERING SHAKESPEARE

(69) <u>Staging</u> **[4.1.256]:** If you were directing a production of *The Tempest,* how would you <u>stage</u> the scene where hounds chase after the three conspirators in 4.1.255–267? Would you costume actors as dogs? Or would you solve the problem in a different way?

PROSPERO   I did say so
   When first I raised the tempest. Say, my spirit,
   How fares the king and's followers?

ARIEL   Confined together
   In the same fashion as you gave in charge,
   Just as you left them – all prisoners, sir,
   In the line grove° which weather-fends° your cell.   **line grove:** grove of lime trees; **weather-fends:**   10
   They cannot budge till your release.° The king,   protects from the weather
   His brother, and yours abide all three distracted,   **till your release:** until you release them
   And the remainder mourning over them,
   Brimful of sorrow and dismay; but chiefly
   Him that you termed, sir, the good old Lord Gonzalo.   15
   His tears runs down his beard like winter's drops
   From eaves of reeds.° Your charm so strongly works 'em,   **eaves of reeds:** i.e., a thatched roof
   That if you now beheld them, your affections
   Would become tender.

PROSPERO   Dost thou think so, spirit?

ARIEL
   Mine would, sir, were I human.   20

PROSPERO   And mine shall.
   Hast thou, which art but air, a touch, a feeling
   Of their afflictions, and shall not myself,
   One of their kind, that relish° all° as sharply   **relish:** feel; **all:** quite
   Passion as they, be kindlier moved than thou art?
   Though with their high wrongs I am struck to th' quick,   25
   Yet with my nobler reason 'gainst my fury
   Do I take part. The rarer action is
   In virtue than in vengeance. They being penitent,
   The sole drift of my purpose doth extend
   Not a frown further. Go, release them, Ariel.   30
   My charms I'll break, their senses I'll restore,
   And they shall be themselves.

ARIEL   I'll fetch them, sir.   *Exit.*

PROSPERO
   Ye elves of hills, brooks, standing lakes, and groves,
   And ye that on the sands with printless foot
   Do chase the ebbing Neptune, and do fly him   35
   When he comes back; you demi-puppets° that   **demi-puppets:** tiny dolls (i.e., fairies)
   By moonshine do the green sour ringlets° make,   **ringlets:** fairy rings in grass
   Whereof the ewe not bites; and you whose pastime
   Is to make midnight mushrumps,° that rejoice   **midnight mushrumps:** mushrooms that appear
   To hear the solemn curfew; by whose aid   in the night   40
   (Weak masters° though ye be) I have bedimmed   **masters:** forces
   The noontide sun, called forth the mutinous winds,
   And 'twixt the green sea and the azured vault
   Set roaring war; to the dread rattling thunder
   Have I given fire and rifted° Jove's stout oak   **rifted:** split   45
   With his own bolt; the strong-based promontory
   Have I made shake and by the spurs° plucked up   **spurs:** roots
   The pine and cedar; graves at my command

DISCOVERING SHAKESPEARE

(70) Plot [5.1.20]: How does Prospero learn compassion in 5.1.20–32? What specific event or realization prompts him to release his enemies?

Have waked their sleepers, oped, and let 'em forth
By my so potent art. But this rough magic   50
I here abjure; and when I have required°   **required:** asked for
Some heavenly music (which even now I do)
To work mine end upon their senses that°   **their senses that:** the senses of those whom
This airy charm is for, I'll break my staff,
Bury it certain fathoms in the earth,   55
And deeper than did ever plummet sound
I'll drown my book.
  Solemn music.
  Here enters Ariel before; then Alonso, with a frantic
  gesture, attended by Gonzalo; Sebastian and Antonio
  in like manner, attended by Adrian and Francisco.
  They all enter the circle which Prospero had made,°   **had made:** (presumably during the previous
  and there stand charmed; which Prospero observing,   speech)
  speaks.
A solemn air, and° the best comforter   **and:** i.e., which is
To an unsettled fancy, cure thy brains,
Now useless, boiled within thy skull! There stand,   60
For you are spell-stopped.
Holy Gonzalo, honorable man,
Mine eyes, ev'n sociable° to the show° of thine,   **sociable:** sympathetic; **show:** sight
Fall° fellowly drops. The charm dissolves apace;   **Fall:** let fall
And as the morning steals upon the night,   65
Melting the darkness, so their rising senses
Begin to chase the ignorant fumes that mantle
Their clearer reason. O good Gonzalo,
My true preserver, and a loyal sir
To him thou follow'st, I will pay thy graces°   **graces:** favors   70
Home both in word and deed. Most cruelly
Didst thou, Alonso, use me and my daughter.
Thy brother was a furtherer in the act.
Thou art pinched for't now, Sebastian. Flesh and blood,
You, brother mine, that entertained ambition,   75
Expelled remorse° and nature;° who, with Sebastian   **remorse:** pity; **nature:** natural feeling
(Whose inward pinches therefore are most strong),
Would here have killed your king, I do forgive thee,
Unnatural though thou art. Their understanding
Begins to swell, and the approaching tide   80
Will shortly fill the reasonable shore,
That now lies foul and muddy. Not one of them
That yet looks on me or would know me. Ariel,
Fetch me the hat and rapier in my cell.
I will disease° me, and myself present   **disease:** undress   85
As I was sometime Milan.° Quickly, spirit!   **sometime Milan:** when I was Duke of Milan
Thou shalt ere long be free.
    [Exit Ariel and returns immediately.]
  Ariel sings and helps to attire him [as Duke of Milan].

DISCOVERING SHAKESPEARE

(71) Paraphrase [5.1.50]: Paraphrase 5.1.50–57, where Prospero decides to give up his "rough magic." What limitations to magic has he discovered?

(72) Verse [5.1.86]: The word "Milan" is usually pronounced in productions of the play with the accent on the first syllable. Scan 5.1.86 to determine if this accent pattern is correct.

ARIEL

        Where the bee sucks, there suck I;

        In a cowslip's bell I lie;

        There I couch when owls do cry.   90

        On the bat's back I do fly

        After° summer merrily.   **After:** pursuing

    Merrily, merrily shall I live now

    Under the blossom that hangs on the bough.

PROSPERO

  Why, that's my dainty Ariel! I shall miss thee,   95

  But yet thou shalt have freedom; so, so, so.

  To the king's ship, invisible as thou art!

  There shalt thou find the mariners asleep

  Under the hatches. The master and the boatswain

  Being awake, enforce them to this place,   100

  And presently,° I prithee.   **presently:** right away

ARIEL

  I drink the air° before me, and return   **drink the air:** i.e., consume space

  Or ere your pulse twice beat.   *Exit.*

GONZALO

  All torment, trouble, wonder, and amazement

  Inhabits here. Some heavenly power guide us   105

  Out of this fearful country!

PROSPERO   Behold, sir king,

  The wrongèd Duke of Milan, Prospero.

  For more assurance that a living prince

  Does now speak to thee, I embrace thy body,

  And to thee and thy company I bid   110

  A hearty welcome.

ALONSO   Whe'r thou be'st he or no,

  Or some enchanted trifle° to abuse° me,   **trifle:** trick; **abuse:** deceive

  As late I have been, I not know. Thy pulse

  Beats, as of flesh and blood; and, since I saw thee,

  Th' affliction of my mind amends, with which,   115

  I fear, a madness held me. This must crave°   **crave:** require

  (An if this be at all)° a most strange story.   **An if . . . all:** if this is really happening

  Thy dukedom I resign and do entreat

  Thou pardon me my wrongs. But how should Prospero

  Be living and be here?   120

PROSPERO   First, noble friend,

  Let me embrace thine age, whose honor cannot

  Be measured or confined.

GONZALO   Whether this be

  Or be not, I'll not swear.

PROSPERO   You do yet taste

  Some subtleties° o' th' isle, that will not let you   **subtleties:** (1) illusions, (2) elaborate pastries

  Believe things certain. Welcome, my friends all.   representing allegorical figures, used in banquets

  [Aside to Sebastian and Antonio]   and pageants   125

  But you, my brace of lords, were I so minded,

DISCOVERING SHAKESPEARE

(73) <u>Plot</u> **[5.1.109]:** Why does Prospero embrace Alonso?

I here could pluck° his highness' frown upon you,   **pluck:** pull down
And justify° you traitors. At this time   **justify:** prove
I will tell no tales.
SEBASTIAN   *[Aside]*   The devil speaks in him.
PROSPERO   No.   130
For you, most wicked sir, whom to call brother
Would even infect my mouth, I do forgive
Thy rankest fault – all of them; and require
My dukedom of thee, which perforce I know
Thou must restore.
ALONSO   If thou beest Prospero,   135
Give us particulars of thy preservation;
How thou hast met us here, who three hours since
Were wracked upon this shore; where I have lost
(How sharp the point of this remembrance is!)
My dear son Ferdinand.
PROSPERO   I am woe° for't, sir.   **woe:** sorry
ALONSO
Irreparable is the loss, and patience   140
Says it is past her cure.
PROSPERO   I rather think
You have not sought her help, of whose soft grace
For the like loss I have her sovereign aid
And rest myself content.
ALONSO   You the like loss?
PROSPERO
As great to me as late;° and, supportable   **late:** recent   145
To make the dear° loss, have I means much weaker   **dear:** grievous
Than you may call to comfort you; for I
Have lost my daughter.
ALONSO   A daughter?
O heavens, that they were living both in Naples,
The king and queen there! That they were, I wish   150
Myself were mudded in that oozy bed
Where my son lies. When did you lose your daughter?
PROSPERO
In this last tempest. I perceive these lords
At this encounter do so much admire°   **admire:** wonder
That they devour their reason, and scarce think   155
Their eyes do offices° of truth, their words   **do offices:** perform services
Are natural breath. But, howsoev'r you have
Been justled from your senses, know for certain
That I am Prospero, and that very duke
Which was thrust forth of Milan, who most strangely   160
Upon this shore, where you were wracked, was landed
To be the lord on't. No more yet of this;
For 'tis a chronicle of day by day,

DISCOVERING SHAKESPEARE

(74) Plot [5.1.128]: Why doesn't Prospero tell Alonso about the treachery of Sebastian and Antonio (5.1.128)? Do you think he has made the right decision? Why or why not?

(75) Symbol [5.1.153]: Name three other Shakespearean plays that feature storms or tempests. What does the tempest symbolize in each play?

Not a relation for a breakfast, nor
Befitting this first meeting. Welcome, sir;   165
This cell's my court. Here have I few attendants,
And subjects none abroad.° Pray you look in.   **abroad:** elsewhere
My dukedom since you have given me again,
I will requite you with as good a thing,   170
At least bring forth a wonder to content ye
As much as me my dukedom.
   Here Prospero discovers° Ferdinand and Miranda   **discovers:** discloses (probably by pulling aside a
   playing at chess.   curtain across one of the doors to the stage)
MIRANDA
Sweet lord, you play me false.
FERDINAND   No, my dearest love,
I would not for the world.
MIRANDA
Yes, for a score of kingdoms you should wrangle,°   **wrangle:** contend for
And I would call it fair play.   175
ALONSO   If this prove
A vision of the island, one dear son
Shall I twice lose.
SEBASTIAN   A most high miracle!
FERDINAND
Though the seas threaten, they are merciful.
I have cursed them without cause.
   [Kneels.]
ALONSO   Now all the blessings
Of a glad father compass thee about!   180
Arise, and say how thou cam'st here. *[Ferdinand rises.]*
MIRANDA   O, wonder!
How many goodly creatures are there here!
How beauteous mankind is! O brave new world
That has such people in't!
PROSPERO   'Tis new to thee.
ALONSO
What is this maid with whom thou wast at play?   185
Your eld'st° acquaintance cannot be three hours.   **eld'st:** i.e., longest period of
Is she the goddess that hath severed us
And brought us thus together?
FERDINAND   Sir, she is mortal;
But by immortal providence she's mine.
I chose her when I could not ask my father   190
For his advice, nor thought I had one. She
Is daughter to this famous Duke of Milan,
Of whom so often I have heard renown
But never saw before; of whom I have
Received a second life; and second father   195
This lady makes him to me.
ALONSO   I am hers.
But, O, how oddly will it sound that I
Must ask my child forgiveness!

DISCOVERING SHAKESPEARE

(76) Teaser [5.1.183]: Who wrote a book entitled *Brave New World* in 1932? How is it related to Shakespeare's play?

PROSPERO   There, sir, stop.
  Let us not burden our remembrance with
  A heaviness° that's gone.   **heaviness:** grief   200
GONZALO   I have inly wept,
  Or should have spoke ere this. Look down, you gods,
  And on this couple drop a blessèd crown!
  For it is you that have chalked forth the way
  Which brought us hither.
ALONSO   I say amen, Gonzalo.
GONZALO
  Was Milan thrust from Milan that his issue   205
  Should become kings of Naples? O, rejoice
  Beyond a common joy, and set it down
  With gold on lasting pillars: in one voyage
  Did Claribel her husband find at Tunis,
  And Ferdinand her brother found a wife   210
  Where he himself was lost; Prospero his dukedom
  In a poor isle; and all of us ourselves
  When no man was his own.
ALONSO   *[To Ferdinand and Miranda]*
          Give me your hands.
  Let grief and sorrow still° embrace his heart   **still:** forever
  That doth not wish you joy.   215
GONZALO   Be it so! Amen!
  Enter Ariel, with the Master and Boatswain amazedly
  following.
  O, look, sir, look, sir, here is more of us!
  I prophesied, if a gallows were on land,
  This fellow could not drown. *[To Boatswain]* Now,
    blasphemy,
  That swear'st grace o'erboard,° not an oath on shore?   **swear'st ... o'erboard:** drives grace from the
  Hast thou no mouth by land? What is the news?   ship by swearing   220
BOATSWAIN
  The best news is that we have safely found
  Our king and company; the next, our ship,
  Which, but three glasses since, we gave out split,
  Is tight and yare° and bravely rigged as when   **yare:** shipshape
  We first put out to sea.   225
ARIEL   *[Aside to Prospero]* Sir, all this service
  Have I done since I went.
PROSPERO   *[Aside to Ariel]* My tricksy° spirit!   **tricksy:** playful, ingenious
ALONSO
  These are not natural events; they strengthen
  From strange to stranger. Say, how came you hither?
BOATSWAIN
  If I did think, sir, I were well awake,
  I'd strive to tell you. We were dead of sleep
  And (how we know not) all clapped under hatches;   230
  Where, but even now, with strange and several° noises   **several:** various

---

DISCOVERING SHAKESPEARE

(77) Characterization [5.1.210]: Gonzalo's speech in 5.1.205–213 implies that all the characters in the play have changed in some way. Do you agree with this assertion? Why or why not? Which characters have changed the most? Which the least?

Of roaring, shrieking, howling, jingling chains,
And moe° diversity of sounds, all horrible,

moe: more

235

We were awaked; straightway at liberty;
Where we, in all our trim,° freshly beheld°

trim: garments; **freshly beheld:** beheld our ship equally fresh

Our royal, good, and gallant ship, our master
Cap'ring° to eye° her. On a trice,° so please you,

Cap'ring: dancing for joy; **eye:** see; **On a trice:** in an instant

Even in a dream, were we divided from them
And were brought moping° hither.

moping: in a daze

240

ARIEL   *[Aside to Prospero]*   Was't well done?
PROSPERO   *[Aside to Ariel]*
Bravely, my diligence. Thou shalt be free.
ALONSO
This is as strange a maze as e'er men trod,
And there is in this business more than nature
Was ever conduct° of. Some oracle

conduct: conductor

245

Must rectify our knowledge.
PROSPERO   Sir, my liege,
Do not infest° your mind with beating on

infest: trouble

The strangeness of this business: at picked leisure,
Which shall be shortly, single° I'll resolve° you

single: privately; **resolve:** explain to

(Which to you shall seem probable) of every°

every: every one of

These happened accidents;° till when, be cheerful

accidents: incidents

250

And think of each thing well.
   [Aside to Ariel]   Come hither, spirit.
Set Caliban and his companions free.
Untie the spell.   *[Exit Ariel.]*
   [To Alonso] How fares my gracious sir?
There are yet missing of your company

255

Some few odd lads that you remember not.
   *Enter Ariel, driving in Caliban, Stephano, and
   Trinculo, in their stolen apparel.*
STEPHANO   Every man shift for all the rest, and let no
man take care for himself; for all is but fortune. Cora-
gio, bully°-monster, coragio!

bully: (a term of endearment)

TRINCULO   If these be true spies° which I wear in my head,
here's a goodly sight.

spies: eyes

260

CALIBAN
O Setebos, these be brave spirits indeed!
How fine my master is! I am afraid
He will chastise me.
SEBASTIAN   Ha, ha!
What things are these, my Lord Antonio?
Will money buy 'em?
ANTONIO   Very like. One of them

265

Is a plain fish and no doubt marketable.
PROSPERO
Mark but the badges of these men,° my lords,

badges of these men: signs of these servants

DISCOVERING SHAKESPEARE

(78) Paraphrase [5.1.238]: Paraphrase the Boatswain's report that the Master was "Cap'ring to eye" their undamaged ship (5.1.238–239).
(79) Metaphor [5.1.253]: When Prospero commands Ariel to "Untie the spell" (5.1.253) on Caliban, Stephano, and Trinculo, he implies a metaphor in which spells are "bound" or "knit up." Find each of these images earlier in the play, and link it to the spell being performed.

Then say if they be true.° This misshapen knave,   **true:** honest
His mother was a witch, and one so strong
That could control the moon, make flows and ebbs,   270
And deal in her° command without° her power.   **her:** i.e., the moon's; **without:** beyond
These three have robbed me, and this demi-devil
(For he's a bastard one) had plotted with them
To take my life. Two of these fellows you
Must know and own;° this thing of darkness I   **own:** acknowledge to be yours   275
Acknowledge mine.
CALIBAN   I shall be pinched to death.
ALONSO
Is not this Stephano, my drunken butler?
SEBASTIAN
He is drunk now: where had he wine?
ALONSO
And Trinculo is reeling ripe:° where should they   **reeling ripe:** ready to reel, unsteady
Find this grand liquor that hath gilded 'em?   280
How cam'st thou in this pickle?
TRINCULO   I have been in such a pickle,° since I saw you   **pickle:** (1) predicament, (2) preservative (from
last, that I fear me will never out of my bones. I shall   the horse pond; hence insects will let him alone)
not fear flyblowing.
SEBASTIAN   Why, how now, Stephano?   285
STEPHANO   O, touch me not! I am not Stephano,° but a   **Stephano:** (this name is said to be a slang
cramp.   Neapolitan term for "stomach")
PROSPERO   You'd be king o' the isle, sirrah?
STEPHANO   I should have been a sore° one then.   **sore:** (1) inept, (2) aching
ALONSO
This is a strange thing as e'er I looked on.   290
PROSPERO
He is as disproportioned in his manners
As in his shape. Go, sirrah, to my cell;
Take with you your companions. As you look
To have my pardon, trim it handsomely.
CALIBAN
Ay, that I will; and I'll be wise hereafter,   295
And seek for grace. What a thrice-double ass
Was I to take this drunkard for a god
And worship this dull fool!
PROSPERO   Go to! Away!
ALONSO
Hence, and bestow your luggage where you found it.
SEBASTIAN   Or stole it rather.   300
          [Exeunt Caliban, Stephano, and Trinculo.]
PROSPERO
Sir, I invite your highness and your train
To my poor cell, where you shall take your rest
For this one night; which, part of it, I'll waste°   **waste:** spend
With such discourse as, I not doubt, shall make it
Go quick away – the story of my life,   305
And the particular accidents gone by

DISCOVERING SHAKESPEARE
(80) <u>Pun</u> [5.1.281]: What is the meaning of the phrase "in such a pickle" (5.1.281)? What is Alonso's <u>pun</u> on the word "pickle"?

Since I came to this isle; and in the morn
I'll bring you to your ship, and so to Naples,
Where I have hope to see the nuptial
Of these our dear-beloved solemnizèd;   310
And thence retire me to my Milan, where
Every third thought shall be my grave.
ALONSO   I long
To hear the story of your life, which must
Take° the ear strangely.   **Take:** captivate
                                                            deliver: tell
PROSPERO   I'll deliver° all;   315
And promise you calm seas, auspicious gales,
And sail° so expeditious that shall catch   **sail:** sailing
Your royal fleet far off. – My Ariel, chick,
That is thy charge. Then to the elements
Be free, and fare thou well! – Please you draw near.°   **draw near:** come in
                    Exeunt [all except Prospero].

🕊 **Epilogue** *Spoken by Prospero.*

Now my charms are all o'erthrown,   320
And what strength I have's mine own,
Which is most faint. Now 'tis true
I must be here confined by you,
Or sent to Naples. Let me not,
Since I have my dukedom got   325
And pardoned the deceiver, dwell
In this bare island by your spell;
But release me from my bands°   **bands:** bonds
With the help of your good hands.°   **hands:** i.e., applause to break the spell
Gentle breath of yours my sails   330
Must fill, or else my project fails,
Which was to please. Now I want°   **want:** lack
Spirits to enforce, art to enchant;
And my ending is despair
Unless I be relieved by prayer,   335
Which pierces so that it assaults
Mercy itself and frees all faults.
As you from crimes would pardoned be,
Let your indulgence set me free.   *Exit.*

DISCOVERING SHAKESPEARE

(81) Paraphrase [5.1.312]: What does Prospero mean when he says that "Every third thought shall be my grave" (5.1.312)? (*Hint:* Look up the terms "memento mori" and "contemplatio mortis.")

(82) Verse [5.1.339]: Scan Prospero's epilogue in 5.1.320–339. What are the meter and rhyme scheme of these lines, and how are they different from the verse in the rest of the play? Why do you think the play shifts into a different verse form at the conclusion?

Research and Discussion Topics

ACT I

1. Research all the nautical terms in 1.1 and 1.2, including "yarely," "topsail," "master's whistle," "topmast," "main course," "Lay her ahold," "two courses," "the washing of ten tides," "beak," "waist," "deck," "yards," and "bowsprit."

2. What was a "drowning mark" (1.1.29)?

3. Where are Milan (1.2.54) and Naples (1.2.112)? What were their social, political, and economic reputations in Shakespeare's time?

4. What was a "cherubin" (1.2.152)?

5. What were the duties of "schoolmasters" (1.2.172) during the Renaissance?

6. What facts can you discover about the goddess Fortune (1.2.178)?

7. Who was the god Neptune (1.2.204 and 5.1.35)?

8. Where were the "Bermudas" (1.2.229)?

9. Where was Argier (1.2.265)? What was its reputation during the Renaissance?

10. What was "the red plague" (1.2.364)?

11. Research the history of Setebos (1.2.373).

12. What was a chanticleer (1.2.386)?

ACT II

1. Where are Tunis (2.1.71) and Carthage (2.1.82)?

2. Who were Dido and Aeneas (2.1.76–78)?

3. What was a "plaster" (2.1.139)?

4. How far was a "league" (2.1.246)? How long was a "cubit" (2.1.256)?

5. What was a "kibe" (2.1.275)?

6. What was a "bombard" (2.2.21)?

7. What kind of fabric was "gaberdine" (2.2.37)? What is the origin of the word?

8. What was an "ague" (2.2.65)? In which Shakespearean play does a character named Sir Andrew Aguecheek appear?

9. What were "pig-nuts" (2.2.165)?

10. What were "marmosets" and "scamels" (2.2.167–169)?

ACT III

1. What was a "flesh fly" (3.1.63)?

2. What was a "stockfish" (3.2.70)?

3. What was the "murrain" (3.2.79)? In what years was it most deadly?

4. What does "troll the catch" (3.2.116) mean?

5. What did the word "monster" (3.3.31) imply during the Renaissance?

6. What was an "ecstasy" (3.3.108)?

ACT IV

1. Who was Phoebus (4.1.30)? Why did he need "steeds"?
2. Where was Paphos (4.1.93)? What was the area revered for?
3. What were "Naiads" (4.1.128)?
4. How could someone's mind "canker" (4.1.192)?
5. In the sport of fencing, what was a "pass of pate" (4.1.244)?
6. What was "lime" (4.1.245)? How was it used to catch birds?
7. What was a "hogshead" (4.1.251)? What was the origin of the term?

ACT V

1. What were "elves" (5.1.33)?
2. What were "green sour ringlets" (5.1.37)? How were they associated with fairies?
3. What time did the "curfew" (5.1.40) bell ring in Shakespeare's time?
4. What did a magic "staff" (5.1.54) look like? What was a magic "book" (5.1.57)?
5. What was a "rapier" (5.1.84)?
6. When and where was the game of chess (5.1.171, s.d.) first invented?

Filmography

1980
BBC Television Shakespeare
Rating:

Directed by: John Gorrie

Michael Hordern as Prospero
Derek Godfrey as Antonio
David Waller as Alonso
Warren Clarke as Caliban
Nigel Hawthorne as Stephano
David Dixon as Ariel
Andrew Sachs as Trinculo
John Nettleton as Gonzalo
Alan Rowe as Sebastian
Pippa Guard as Miranda
Christopher Guard as Ferdinand

The BBC *Tempest* does almost all of the lines and does them with intelligence and skill. No one is an embarrassment to Shakespeare, and some cast members are at least minor ornaments. Nigel Hawthorne's Stephano is agreeably disreputable, and Warren Clarke's Caliban has the right blend of stupidity, simplicity, and ferocity. Michael Hordern's Prospero, however, is almost as difficult to praise as to fault. He does not have the majesty and benevolence that Prospero sometimes has, nor does he suggest the scholarship and wisdom which are also part of the character. Instead, Hordern attains a schoolmaster-ish authority, which contains a touch of darkness. He sometimes seems to be more Miranda's teacher than her father, but throughout the production, he never loses control of his classroom.

Forbidden Planet
1956
MGM
Rating:

Directed by: Fred M. Wilcox

Walter Pidgeon as Dr. Edward Morbius (Prospero)
Anne Francis as Altaira Morbius (Miranda)
Leslie Nielsen as Commander John J. Adams (Ferdinand)
Frankie Carpenter, Frankie Darro, & Marvin Miller as Robby the Robot
[uncredited] (Ariel)

Adaptations of *The Tempest* include the forgettable *The Tempest* (1998), an American Civil War version which starred Peter Fonda as Guideon Prosper; the R-rated and thoroughly eccentric *Prospero's Books* (1991), notable for John Gielgud's performance; Paul Mazursky's *Tempest* (1982), a twentieth-century transformation with a powerful cast; "Requiem for Methuselah," an episode from the original Star Trek series with William Shatner's Captain Kirk as Ferdinand; and perhaps the most famous of all, *Forbidden Planet,* which explores the play's subtext. Morbius (Prospero) is truly happy to be away from other human beings and left to his studies, and an overt struggle appears between Morbius and Commander Adams (Ferdinand) for Altaira's (Miranda's) loyalty. Walter Pidgeon makes a powerful, egocentric Prospero figure—realistic, sympathetic, and even tragic. Morbius sacrifices himself at the end to protect his daughter from the evil of his own subconscious, the Caliban of this version. Anne Francis may be too flirtatious and seductive for a girl who was raised alone with her father and a robot, but she is very good at what she does. Leslie Nielsen is a serious and even dashing Ferdinand.

1983
Bard Productions, Ltd.
Rating:

Directed by: William Woodman
Music by John Serry

Ron Palillo as Trinculo
David Graf as Stephano
Duane Black as Ariel
Nicholas Hammond as Ferdinand

William Hootkins as Caliban
J.E. Taylor as Miranda
Efrem Zimbalist Jr. as Prospero

If there were a superb version of *The Tempest,* it would be possible to discard this production entirely. Until that time, the *Bard* has enough strengths to make it worth watching. The filming on a stage set is well handled, and the traditional strips of fabric that serve as waves and other such stage devices make the bare boards seem more natural. John Serry's music is good enough to notice and enjoy even in the midst of the play. Efrem Zimbalist Jr. is an enthusiastic Prospero whose performance often makes up in sincerity what he lacks in ability to read poetry. He certainly looks the part and frequently seems magical enough to be believable. He successfully projects both benevolence and hope. J. E. Taylor is an attractive Miranda who is excellent except when she weeps. William Hootkins as Caliban and Ron Palillo as Trinculo give effective if standard performances. The worst acting comes from Nicholas Hammond (television's Spiderman). In this ostentatiously American film, Hammond is hampered by a British accent that would be more appropriate for Gilbert and Sullivan.

1960
George Schaefer's Showcase Theater
Rating:

Directed by: George Schaefer

Paul Ballantyne as Sebastian
William Bassett as Antonio
Richard Burton as Caliban
Maurice Evans as Prospero
Roddy McDowall as Ariel
Tom Poston as Trinculo
Ronald Radd as Ferdinand
Lee Remick as Miranda

The reality of Schaefer's *Tempest* is so much less than its possibilities that it seems more tragedy than romance. Running time is seventy-six minutes, which means slashing rather than cutting. For instance, the first scene is replaced with narration, the masque of the goddesses is gone, and Prospero's speech from 4.1 that begins "Our revels now are ended" is transplanted to the end of the play, where it replaces the epilogue. The costumes are eclectic, with Ferdinand in an embarrassingly skimpy gladiatorial outfit. On the other hand, the best actors in the film, Richard Burton as Caliban and Roddy McDowall as Ariel, are so completely covered either by fabric or makeup that their facial expressions are largely concealed. Still, even their voices are memorable, and Lee Remick makes a beautiful and effective Miranda. Maurice Evans as Prospero is disappointing. He ranges from underplaying to posturing, only occasionally getting the truly magical verse right.

Annotated Bibliography

Abrams, Richard. "*The Tempest* and the Concept of the Machiavellian Playwright." *English Literary Renaissance* 8 (1978): 43–66. journal PR 1.E43.
Abrams discusses the Machiavellian way that Shakespeare's characters are able to control time. He also points out how Prospero personifies himself as the author in the epilogue and manipulates the destiny of the characters in the same fashion that Shakespeare himself controls his play.

Belton, Ellen R. "'When No Man Was His Own': Magic and Self-Discovery in *The Tempest.*" *University of Toronto Quarterly* 55 (1985): 127–140. journal AP 5.U55.
Belton argues that Prospero does not enforce true contrition in the other characters because of his attempt to allow individual freedom from society's conventional ideals. Although Prospero's magic has little effect on behavioral change, he does, however, show mercy to those who have abused him.

Bright, Curt. "'Treason Doth Never Prosper': *The Tempest* and the Discourse of Treason." *Shakespeare Quarterly* 41 (1990): 1–28. journal PR 2885.S63.
Curt sees the play as an index of contemporary social problems in late Elizabethan society. *The Tempest* shows how the ruling class can lead people astray through unethical and manipulative behavior.

Brown, Paul. "'This Thing of Darkness I Acknowledge Mine': *The Tempest* and The Discourse of Colonialism." In *Political Shakespeare: New Essays in Cultural Materialism.* Edited by Jonathan Dollimore and Alan Sinfield. Ithaca and London: Cornell University Press, 1985, pp. 48–71. PR 3017.P59.
Brown suggests that the play reflects the general attitude of the British toward those they have colonized, whom they generally see as savage and irredeemable. The subjugation of these people is thus considered a victory for proper society. *The Tempest* begins with a show of Prospero's power through a distinction between those who are easily colonized and those who are not.

Donaldson, Laura. "The Miranda Complex: Colonialism and the Question of Feminist Reading." *Diacritics* 18. 3 (1988): 65–77. journal PN 80.D5.
Donaldson focuses on the suppression of women. She further examines some postcolonial discussions of the relationship between Caliban and Miranda, particularly those analyzed by postmodern theorists. In her article, Donaldson considers how Caliban's actions betray a desire for sovereignty, which brings out the threat of sexual assault in his relationship with Miranda. Donaldson also discusses how Prospero rules over both Miranda and Caliban.

James, David Gwilym. *The Dream of Prospero.* Oxford: Clarendon Press, 1967. PR 2833.J3.
James contends that the play is a philosophic rejoinder to *King Lear.* A struggle takes place in Prospero's mind between self-love and the societal need for spirituality. Prospero has come to terms with the fact that evil will always be present, but man must still combat it. Because of this realization, Prospero chooses to return to his political duties. James also discusses the changes of the sea and their relationship to music and poetics.

Pask, Kevin. "Prospero's Counter-Pastoral." *Criticism* 44.4 (2002): 389–404. journal AS 30.W3A2.

> Pask discusses the ways in which the double plot of *The Tempest* requires the separation of the aristocratic myths of the heroic and the pastoral. According to the author, Prospero serves as the aristocrat whose pastoral island is really an anti-pastoral place of repression set within an idealistic guise.

Vaughan, Virginia. "'Something Rich and Strange': Caliban's Theatrical Metamorphoses." *Shakespeare Quarterly* 36 (1985): 390–405. journal PR 2885.S63.

> Vaughan chronicles the change in Caliban from drunkard to noble savage as a consequence of oppression. Caliban is illustrated first as an instinctive, brutish presence, but he becomes a symbol of suppression at the hands of a more powerful enemy. Caliban forces society to see the negative aspects of imperialism.

William, David. "*The Tempest* on the Stage." In *Jacobean Theatre*. Edited by John Russell Brown and Bernard Harris. Stratford-upon-Avon Studies, 1. London: Edward Arnold, 1960, pp. 133–157. PR 651.J3.

> William's article focuses on stage elements such as costume and scenery. His primary topic is Prospero, a character who serves to narrate current action while also recalling former events. His ability to weave past and present narratives makes him a central dramatic character.

Wilson, John Dover. *The Meaning of "The Tempest."* Newcastle-upon-Tyne: Literary and Philosophical Society, 1936. PR 2833.W55.

> Wilson discusses the play's spiritual elements, particularly in terms of resolution and absolution. He further explains the implications of the play to Shakespeare personally, as the author may have played the role of Prospero in courtly productions.

Wilson-Okamura, David S. "Virgilian Models of Colonization in Shakespeare's *Tempest*." *ELH* 70.3 (2003): 709–737. journal PR 1.E5.

> This article investigates both the long-standing critique of *The Tempest* as a play depicting the colonization of the New World and also its focus on the Old World setting. Wilson-Okamura cites Shakespeare's use of the *Aeneid* as a model for colonization and argues that the origin of Caliban's character is not found in New World natives, but in Virgil's depiction of Africa.

Selected Sonnets

1

From fairest creatures° we desire increase,°
That thereby beauty's rose might never die,
But as the riper° should by time decease,
His tender° heir might bear° his memory;
But thou, contracted to° thine own bright eyes,
Feed'st thy light's flame with self-substantial° fuel,
Making a famine where abundance lies,
Thyself thy foe, to thy sweet self too cruel.
Thou that art now the world's fresh ornament
And only° herald to the gaudy° spring,
Within thine own bud° buriest thy content°
And, tender churl,° mak'st waste in niggarding.°
   Pity the world, or else this glutton be,
   To eat the world's due, by the grave and thee.°

creatures: all living things (not just animals); **we . . . increase:** (1) we wish for offspring, (2) we increase our desire
riper: ripening, growing older
tender: (as opposed to *riper*); **bear:** carry on, preserve
contracted to: betrothed only to (literally, bound by contract)
self-substantial: self-consuming

only: chief; **gaudy:** luxuriant (not pejorative)
bud: unopened flower (cf. *rose,* l. 2); **thy content:** (1) what you contain (your potential offspring), (2) your satisfaction
tender churl: (1) youthful miser, (2) sweet boor; **mak'st . . . niggarding:** are wasteful in hoarding yourself
To . . . thee: to swallow up, both by death and your own willfullness, what belongs to the world

2

When forty winters shall besiege thy brow
And dig deep trenches in thy beauty's field,
Thy youth's proud livery,° so gazed on now,
Will be a tattered weed° of small worth held:
Then being asked where all thy beauty lies,
Where all the treasure of thy lusty° days,
To say within thine own deep-sunken eyes
Were an all-eating° shame and thriftless° praise.
How much more praise deserved° thy beauty's use°
If thou couldst answer, "This fair child of mine
Shall sum my count° and make my old excuse,"°
Proving his beauty by succession° thine.
   This were to be new made when thou art old
   And see thy blood warm when thou feel'st it cold.

proud livery: splendid display
weed: garment

lusty: passionate

an all-eating: a devouring; **thriftless:** unprofitable
deserved: would deserve; **use:** (1) sexual activity, (2) financial investment (cf. "usury")
sum . . . count: settle my account; **make . . . excuse:** justify my life when I am old
succession: inheritance

15

When I consider everything that grows
Holds° in perfection but a little moment,
That this huge stage presenteth nought but shows
Whereon the stars in secret influence comment;°
When I perceive that men as plants increase,
Cheerèd and checked° even by the selfsame sky,
Vaunt° in their youthful sap, at height decrease,
And wear their brave state° out of memory:°
Then the conceit° of this inconstant stay°
Sets you most rich in youth before my sight,
Where wasteful Time debateth with° Decay
To change your day of youth to sullied night;
   And, all in war with Time for love of you,
   As he takes from you, I engraft you° new.

Holds: stays

Whereon . . . comment: i.e., which the stars inscrutably control (taking the astrology dismissed in Sonnet 14 seriously)   5
Cheerèd and checked: (1) applauded and hissed, (2) encouraged and held back
Vaunt: exult
brave state: splendid finery; **out of memory:**   10
until it is forgotten
conceit: thought; **inconstant stay:** continual mutability
with: together with (Time and Decay are both debating against the poet)
engraft you: infuse new life into you (through my poems about you)

18

Shall I compare thee to a summer's day?
Thou art more lovely and more temperate.
Rough winds do shake the darling buds of May,
And summer's lease° hath all too short a date.°
Sometime too hot the eye of heaven shines,
And often is his gold complexion dimmed;
And every fair from fair° sometime declines,
By chance, or nature's changing course, untrimmed:°
But thy eternal summer shall not fade
Nor lose possession of that fair thou ow'st,°
Nor shall Death brag thou wander'st in his shade°
When in eternal lines to time° thou grow'st.
   So long as men can breathe or eyes can see,
   So long lives this, and this gives life to thee.

lease: allotted time; **date:** duration

5

fair . . . fair: beautiful thing from beauty
untrimmed: stripped of adornment

fair . . . ow'st: beauty you own   10
shade: darkness
to time: to the end of time

19

Devouring Time,° blunt thou the lion's paws,
And make the earth devour her own sweet brood;°
Pluck the keen teeth from the fierce tiger's jaws,
And burn the long-lived phoenix° in her blood;°
Make glad and sorry seasons as thou fleet'st,
And do whate'er thou wilt, swift-footed Time,
To the wide world and all her fading sweets,
But I forbid thee one most heinous crime:
O, carve not with thy hours my love's fair brow,
Nor draw no lines there with thine antique° pen;°
Him in thy course untainted° do allow
For beauty's pattern° to succeeding men.
   Yet do thy worst, old Time: despite thy wrong,
   My love shall in my verse ever live young.

Devouring Time: (proverbially "Time consumes all things")
brood: all earthly things, conceived as children of "mother earth"
phoenix: mythical bird that lives for centuries, consumes itself in fire, and is reborn from its ashes   5
(hence symbolic of immortality); **in . . . blood:** alive

antique: (1) ancient, (2) antic, capricious, (3) causing one to be old, antiquing; **pen:**   10
writing, not drawing, instrument (hence the *lines* are those of Time considered as a hostile poet)
untainted: (1) unsullied, (2) not struck by Time's lance (a *taint* is a hit in jousting)
pattern: ideal model

23

As an unperfect actor° on the stage,
Who with his fear° is put besides° his part,
Or some fierce thing replete with too much rage,°
Whose° strength's abundance weakens his own heart;°
So I, for fear of trust,° forget to say
The perfect ceremony° of love's rite,°
And in mine own love's strength° seem to decay,°
O'ercharged with burden of mine own love's might.
O, let my books° be then the eloquence
And dumb presagers° of my speaking breast,
Who plead for love, and look for recompense,
More than that tongue that more hath more expressed.°
    O, learn to read what silent love hath writ:
    To hear with eyes belongs to love's fine wit.°

an unperfect actor: (1) one who has not adequately learned his lines, (2) one who has not mastered the craft of acting

fear: stage fright; **put besides:** put off, made to forget

replete . . . rage: overwhelmed with violent anger

Whose: (the antecedent is *rage*, not *thing*); **heart:** (1) courage, (2) ability to act

for . . . trust: (1) distrusting myself, (2) doubting that I will be believed, (3) overcome with the responsibility

perfect ceremony: word-perfect ritual; **love's rite:** the ceremony due to love (*love's rite* normally means sexual intercourse, and that is certainly at least an overtone here—Q has "right"; the two words were not distinguished in Shakespeare's time)

mine . . . strength: (1) the force of my passion, (2) the power of my beloved; **decay:** falter, weaken

books: writings

dumb presagers: (1) silent messages, (2) mute heralds

more hath more expressed: more often has said more

wit: (1) intelligence, (2) poetic skill

29

When, in disgrace° with fortune and men's eyes,
I all alone beweep my outcast state,
And trouble deaf heaven with my bootless° cries,
And look upon myself and curse my fate,
Wishing me like to one more rich in hope,
Featured like him, like him° with friends possessed,
Desiring this man's art,° and that man's scope,°
With what I most enjoy° contented least;
Yet in these thoughts myself almost despising,
Haply° I think on thee, and then my state,
Like to the lark at break of day arising
From sullen° earth, sings hymns at heaven's gate;
    For thy sweet love remembered such wealth brings
    That then I scorn to change my state with kings.

in disgrace: out of favor

bootless: useless

like him, like him: like one man, like another

art: (1) skill, (2) learning, (3) practical ability; **scope:** (1) independence, (2) range of ability, (3) breadth of opportunity

enjoy: (1) possess, (2) take pleasure in

Haply: by chance

sullen: (1) dull, heavy, (2) somber, sad

30

When to the sessions° of sweet silent thought
I summon up remembrance of things past,
I sigh° the lack of many a thing I sought,
And with old woes new° wail my dear time's waste:°
Then can I drown an eye, unused to flow,
For precious friends hid in death's dateless° night,
And weep afresh love's long since canceled° woe,
And moan th' expense° of many a vanished sight.
Then can I grieve at grievances foregone,°
And heavily° from woe to woe tell o'er°
The sad account° of forebemoanèd moan,°
Which I new pay as if not paid before.
    But if the while I think on thee, dear friend,
    All losses are restored and sorrows end.

sessions: periodic sittings of a court (cf. *summon*, l. 2; his *thought* is the judge)

sigh: lament

new: newly; **dear . . . waste:** (1) precious time's passing, (2) destruction of precious things by time, (3) the fact that my best time is destroyed (taking Q's "times" as a plural rather than a possessive)

dateless: endless

canceled: fully paid off

expense: (1) expenditure, (2) loss

foregone: in the past, over and done with

heavily: (1) sorrowfully, (2) tediously; **tell o'er:** (1) add up, (2) recount

account: (1) bill, (2) narrative; **forebemoanèd moan:** already lamented grief

55

Not marble nor the gilded monuments
Of princes shall outlive this powerful rhyme,°
But you shall shine more bright in these contents°
Than° unswept stone,° besmeared with sluttish° time.
When wasteful° war shall statues overturn,
And broils° root out the work of masonry,
Nor Mars his sword° nor war's quick° fire shall burn
The living record of your memory.
'Gainst death and all oblivious enmity°
Shall you pace forth; your praise shall still find room°
Even in the eyes of all posterity
That wear this world out to the ending doom.°
    So, till the judgment that° yourself arise,
    You live in this, and dwell in° lovers' eyes.

this . . . rhyme: (1) this poem, (2) my poetry
these contents: what is contained here
Than: than you will in; **stone:** (e.g., a funeral monument); **sluttish:** (1) slovenly, (2) whorish   5
wasteful: destructive
broils: battles
Nor . . . sword: neither Mars's sword; **quick:** (1) swift, (2) living
all . . . enmity: (1) cosmic enmity, which consigns everything to oblivion, (2) oblivion, which is the enemy of everything   10
still . . . room: always find a place
wear . . . doom: endure until doomsday
the . . . that: Judgment Day, when
dwell in: i.e., permanently inhabit

60

Like as the waves make towards the pebbled shore,
So do our minutes hasten to their end;
Each changing place with that which goes before,
In sequent toil° all forwards do contend.°
Nativity,° once in the main of light,°
Crawls to maturity, wherewith being crowned,
Crooked° eclipses 'gainst his glory fight,
And Time that gave doth now his gift confound.°
Time doth transfix° the flourish° set on youth
And delves the parallels° in beauty's brow,
Feeds on the rarities° of nature's truth,°
And nothing stands but for his scythe to mow:
    And yet to times in hope° my verse shall stand,°
    Praising thy worth, despite his cruel hand.

sequent toil: successive effort; **contend:** struggle   5
Nativity: the newborn child; **the . . . light:** full sun
Crooked: ominous, malignant
confound: destroy
transfix: pierce; **flourish:** bloom   10
delves . . . parallels: digs the trenches
rarities: precious things; **truth:** perfection
times in hope: hoped-for future times; **stand:** endure

61

Is it thy will thy image should keep open
My heavy eyelids to the weary night?
Dost thou desire my slumbers should be broken
While shadows° like to thee do mock my sight?
Is it thy spirit that thou send'st from thee
So far from home into my deeds to pry,
To find out shames° and idle hours° in me,
The scope and tenure° of thy jealousy?°
O no, thy love, though much, is not so great;
It is my love that keeps mine eye awake,
Mine own true love that doth my rest defeat
To play the watchman ever for thy sake.
    For thee watch° I whilst thou dost wake elsewhere,
    From me far off, with others all too near.

shadows: (1) images, (2) spirits   5

shames: shameful behavior; **idle hours:** wasted time
scope . . . tenure: aim and purport, entire point; **jealousy:** suspicion (the metaphor is of a landlord spying on his tenant)   10

watch: lie awake

64

When I have seen by Time's fell° hand defaced
The rich proud cost° of outworn° buried age,
When sometime° lofty towers I see down-razed°
And brass eternal slave° to mortal rage;°
When I have seen the hungry ocean gain
Advantage on° the kingdom of the shore,
And the firm soil win of the wat'ry main,
Increasing store with loss and loss with store;°
When I have seen such interchange of state,°
Or state itself confounded to° decay,
Ruin hath taught me thus to ruminate,
That Time will come and take my love° away.
    This thought is as a death, which cannot choose
    But weep to have° that which it fears to lose.

fell: cruel
cost: (1) extravagance, (2) expensive objects;
outworn: worn-out
sometime: formerly; **down-razed:**
demolished
brass . . . slave: (1) everlasting brass a slave,
(2) brass the eternal slave; **mortal rage:** (1) deadly
violence, (2) human fury, (3) the violence of death
gain . . . on: i.e., occupy the territory of
Increasing . . . with store: i.e., one gaining by
the other's loss, one losing to the other's gain
state: greatness
confounded to: devastated to a point of
love: beloved
to have: for having

65

Since° brass, nor stone, nor earth, nor boundless sea,
But sad mortality o'ersways their power,
How with this rage shall beauty hold a plea,°
Whose action° is no stronger than a flower?
O, how shall summer's honey breath hold out
Against the wrackful° siege of battering days,
When rocks impregnable are not so stout,
Nor gates of steel so strong but time decays?°
O fearful meditation: where, alack,
Shall Time's best jewel from Time's chest lie hid?°
Or what strong hand can hold his swift foot back,
Or who his spoil° of beauty can forbid?
    O, none, unless this miracle have might,
    That in black ink my love may still shine bright.

Since: since there is neither

hold a plea: plead its case
action: (1) lawsuit, (2) power, ability to act

wrackful: destructive

decays: i.e., decays the *rocks* and *gates*

Time's best . . . hid: the most precious jewel of
the time be hidden to avoid incarceration in
Time's strongbox
spoil: despoiling

71

No longer mourn for me when I am dead
Than you shall hear the surly sullen bell
Give warning to the world that I am fled
From this vile world, with vilest worms to dwell.
Nay, if you read this line, remember not
The hand that writ it, for I love you so
That I in your sweet thoughts would be forgot
If thinking on me then should make you woe.°
O, if, I say, you look upon this verse
When I, perhaps, compounded am with clay,
Do not so much as my poor name rehearse,°
But let your love even with my life decay,
    Lest the wise world should look into your moan
    And mock you with me° after I am gone.

make . . . woe: cause you grief

rehearse: repeat

with me: as it mocks me

73

That time of year thou mayst in me behold
When yellow leaves, or none, or few, do hang
Upon those boughs which shake against the cold,
Bare ruined choirs° where late the sweet birds° sang.
In me thou seest the twilight of such day
As after sunset fadeth in the west,
Which by and by black night doth take away,
Death's second self that seals up° all in rest.
In me thou seest the glowing of such fire
That on the ashes of his youth doth lie,
As the deathbed whereon it must expire,
Consumed with that which it was nourished by.
   This thou perceiv'st, which makes thy love more strong,
   To love that well which thou must leave° ere long.

ruined choirs: (the choir is the part of the church behind the altar, in which the choir sings; ruined choirs were a commonplace sight in England after the destruction of the monasteries during Henry VIII's reign); **sweet birds:** (1) songbirds driven off by winter, (2) choristers driven away by the Protestant Reformation

seals up: (1) encloses as in a coffin, (2) puts the seal on a document, (3) seels up—i.e., stitches closed the eyes of a hawk

leave: (1) depart from, (2) give up

75

So are you to my thoughts as food to life,
Or as sweet-seasoned° showers are to the ground;
And for the peace of you° I hold such strife°
As 'twixt a miser and his wealth is found:
Now proud as an enjoyer, and anon°
Doubting° the filching age will steal his treasure;
Now counting° best to be with you alone,
Then bettered° that the world may see my pleasure;
Sometime all full with feasting on your sight,
And by and by clean° starvèd for a look,
Possessing or pursuing no delight
Save what is had or must from you be took.°
   Thus do I pine° and surfeit day by day,
   Or gluttoning° on all, or all away.°

sweet-seasoned: (1) sweetly flavored, (2) springtime

for . . . you: (1) because of the peace you bring me, (2) in order to obtain the peace you would bring me, (3) instead of the peace you represent for me; **hold . . . strife:** i.e., am in just such tension

Now . . . anon: at first delighting in my possession, and soon after

Doubting: fearing, suspecting

counting: accounting it, considering it

bettered: better pleased

clean: absolutely

must . . . took: can only be received from you

pine: (1) starve, (2) yearn

Or gluttoning: either gorging myself; **all away:** finding everything gone

87

Farewell, thou art too dear° for my possessing,
And like enough thou know'st thy estimate.°
The charter° of thy worth gives thee releasing;°
My bonds in° thee are all determinate.°
For how do I hold thee but by thy granting,
And for that riches° where is my deserving?
The cause of° this fair gift in me is wanting,°
And so my patent° back again is swerving.°
Thyself thou gav'st, thy own worth then not knowing,
Or me, to whom thou gav'st it, else mistaking;°
So thy great gift, upon misprision growing,°
Comes home again, on better judgment making.°
   Thus have I had thee as a dream doth flatter,
   In sleep a king, but waking no such matter.

dear: (1) precious, (2) expensive

estimate: value

charter: privilege (the metaphor is of a legal document, like a *patent,* conferring value); **gives . . . releasing:** releases you from obligation

bonds in: claims on; **determinate:** ended

riches: wealth (not a plural)

cause of: justification for; **wanting:** lacking

patent: exclusive right (to your love); **back . . . swerving:** i.e., reverts to you

mistaking: misjudging

upon . . . growing: based on error

on . . . making: as you arrive at a better judgment

104

To me, fair friend, you never can be old,
For as you were when first your eye I eyed,°
Such seems your beauty still. Three winters cold
Have from the forests shook three summers' pride,°
Three beauteous springs to yellow autumn turned
In process° of the seasons have I seen,
Three April perfumes in three hot Junes burned,
Since first I saw you fresh,° which° yet are green.°
Ah, yet doth beauty, like a dial° hand,
Steal from his figure,° and no pace perceived;
So your sweet hue,° which methinks still doth stand,°
Hath motion, and mine eye may be deceived;
   For fear of which, hear this, thou age unbred:°
   Ere you were born was beauty's summer° dead.

eyed: saw

pride: splendor

5

process: the progress

fresh: (1) youthful, (2) freshly, for the first time;
which: who; **green:** young
dial: clock   10
Steal . . . figure: (1) move imperceptibly from
its number, (2) imperceptibly depart from the
form it inhabits
sweet hue: lovely appearance; **methinks . . .
stand:** (1) seems to me to remain motionless, (2)
seems to me as yet unchanged
unbred: unborn
beauty's summer: i.e., beauty at its best

105

Let not my love be called idolatry,
Nor my belovèd as an idol show,°
Since all alike my songs and praises be
To one,° of one, still such, and ever so.°
Kind is my love today, tomorrow kind,
Still constant° in a wondrous excellence;
Therefore my verse, to constancy confined,°
One thing expressing, leaves out difference.°
"Fair, kind, and true" is all my argument,°
"Fair, kind, and true," varying to other words;°
And in this change° is my invention° spent,°
Three themes in one, which wondrous scope affords.
   Fair, kind, and true have often lived alone,°
   Which three till now never kept seat° in one.

show: appear

To one: (to the one god, the beloved, not the
many gods of idolatry); **still . . . so:** always and   5
ever the same
Still constant: (1) always faithful, (2) always the
same
to . . . confined: (1) limited to the subject of
constancy, (2) bound to be always the same
leaves . . . difference: (1) omits variety, ignores   10
other subjects, has a single theme, (2) omits
disagreements (between us)
argument: subject matter
varying . . . words: sometimes using other
words
change: variation; **invention:** poetic ingenuity;
spent: (1) employed, (2) exhausted
lived alone: i.e., lived separately, inhabited
different individuals
kept seat: made their home (a *seat* is a
landowner's estate or official dwelling)

106

When in the chronicle of wasted° time
I see descriptions of the fairest wights,°
And beauty making beautiful old rhyme
In praise of ladies dead and lovely knights;
Then, in the blazon° of sweet beauty's best,
Of hand, of foot, of lip, of eye, of brow,
I see their antique pen would have expressed
Even such a beauty as you master° now.
So all their praises are but prophecies
Of this our time, all you prefiguring;
And, for° they looked but° with divining° eyes,
They had not still° enough your worth to sing:
   For we, which now behold these present days,
   Have eyes to wonder, but lack tongues to praise.

wasted: (1) past, (2) ruined
wights: people (of either sex; the word is archaic,
and specifically, for Shakespeare's era, Spenserian)   5
blazon: laudatory formal description (in poetics,
a catalogue of praiseworthy body parts, as in l. 6;
in heraldry, a coat of arms emblematically
embodying the bearer's virtues)
master: (1) possess, (2) control
for: because; **but:** merely; **divining:**   10
forecasting
still: (most editors emend to "skill"; but the point
is that the ancient poets *had* the requisite skill—
what they lacked was the young man's actual
beauty as a subject)

116

Let me not° to the marriage of true minds
Admit impediments;° love is not love
Which alters when it alteration° finds°
Or bends with the remover to remove.°
O, no, it is an ever-fixèd mark°
That looks on tempests and is never shaken;
It is the star° to every wand'ring bark,°
Whose worth's unknown,° although his height be taken.°
Love's not time's fool,° though rosy lips and cheeks
Within his bending° sickle's compass° come;
Love alters not with his° brief hours and weeks,
But bears it out even to the edge of doom.°
    If this be error,° and upon me proved,
    I never writ, nor no man ever loved.°

128

How oft, when thou, my music, music play'st
Upon that blessèd wood° whose motion° sounds°
With thy sweet fingers when thou gently sway'st°
The wiry concord° that mine ear confounds,°
Do I envy those jacks° that nimble leap
To kiss the tender inward of thy hand,
Whilst my poor lips, which should that harvest reap,
At the wood's boldness by° thee blushing stand.
To be so tickled they would change their state
And situation° with those dancing chips°
O'er whom thy fingers walk with gentle gait,
Making dead wood more blessed than living lips.
    Since saucy jacks so happy° are in this,
    Give them thy fingers, me thy lips to kiss.

129

Th' expense of spirit° in a waste of shame
Is lust in action;° and, till action, lust
Is perjured, murd'rous, bloody, full of blame,°
Savage, extreme, rude,° cruel, not to trust;°
Enjoyed no sooner but despisèd straight;°
Past reason hunted,° and no sooner had,
Past reason hated as a swallowed bait
On purpose laid to make the taker mad:
Made° in pursuit and in possession so;°
Had, having, and in quest to have, extreme;

Let me not: i.e., I would never
Admit impediments: concede that there are obstacles (echoing the *marriage* service, which calls on anyone who knows of "any impediment" to the marriage to declare it)
alteration: (1) changes of heart, (2) changes effected by time or circumstance; **Which . . . finds:** (the *impediments* that are denied now clearly come from within the *marriage,* not from without)
bends . . . remove: inclines to separate because the lover does
mark: lighthouse
star: polestar; **bark:** boat
worth's unknown: value is incalculable; **his . . . taken:** its altitude can be calculated
Love's . . . fool: *time* cannot make a fool of *love* (i.e., love is not subject to time)
bending: (1) curved, (2) causing (what it mows) to bend; **compass:** range
his: (1) love's, (2) time's
bears . . . doom: endures even to doomsday
error: (1) legally, a fault in procedure invalidating the judgment, (2) theologically, heresy
no . . . loved: (1) no man has ever been in love, (2) I never loved any man (i.e., the man who is the subject of these sonnets)
wood: keys of the virginal (an early keyboard instrument with plucked strings); **motion:** movement; **sounds:** (1) resounds, (2) causes (*The wiry concord,* l. 4) to sound
thou . . . sway'st: you . . . control
wiry concord: harmony of strings; **mine . . . confounds:** overwhelms my hearing
those jacks: what plucks the string (but here, both keys and jacks, the whole mechanism)
by: beside
state . . . situation: status and location; **chips:** pieces of wood
happy: lucky
spirit: (1) semen, (2) vital energy
action: the sexual act, consummation
full of blame: (1) totally guilty, (2) full of recriminations
rude: brutal; **not to trust:** not to be trusted
straight: immediately
Past . . . hunted: insanely sought

Made: (since Malone in 1780, Q's verb has been universally and unnecessarily emended to the adjective "mad," significantly reducing the energy of the line); **so:** i.e., made *mad*

A bliss in proof, and proved,° a very woe;
Before, a joy proposed; behind, a dream.
   All this the world well knows, yet none knows well
   To shun the heaven that leads men to this hell.

in proof . . . proved: both during action and once done

130

My mistress' eyes are nothing like the sun;
Coral is far more red than her lips' red;
If snow be white, why then her breasts are dun;
If hairs be wires,° black wires grow on her head.
I have seen roses damasked,° red and white,
But no such roses see I in her cheeks;
And in some perfumes is there more delight
Than in the breath that from my mistress reeks.°
I love to hear her speak; yet well I know
That music hath a far more pleasing sound:
I grant I never saw a goddess go;°
My mistress, when she walks, treads on the ground.°
   And yet, by heaven, I think my love as rare
   As any she° belied with false compare.°

wires: (as the conventional sonnet mistress is said to have hair of spun gold)   5
damasked: (1) mingled, (2) soft, smooth

reeks: emanates (not pejorative until the eighteenth century)

10

go: walk
treads . . . ground: i.e., as mortals do

she: woman; **false compare:** artificial comparisons

147

My love is as a fever, longing still°
For that which longer nurseth° the disease,
Feeding on that which doth preserve the ill,°
Th' uncertain° sickly appetite to please.
My reason, the physician to my love,
Angry that his prescriptions are not kept,°
Hath left me, and I desperate now approve°
Desire is death, which physic did except.°
Past cure I am, now reason is past care,°
And frantic-mad with evermore° unrest;
My thoughts and my discourse as madmen's are,
At random° from the truth vainly° expressed:
   For I have sworn thee fair,° and thought thee bright,
   Who art as black as hell, as dark as night.

still: incessantly
nurseth: nourishes, prolongs
ill: (1) illness, (2) evil
uncertain: indecisive, inconstant

5

kept: followed
approve: (1) prove through my example, (2) learn from experience
Desire . . . except: that sexual desire, which the physician *reason* forbade me, is tantamount to death   10
is . . . care: no longer cares about me
evermore: (1) constant, (2) increasing
At random: totally missing; **vainly:** pointlessly, senselessly
fair: (1) beautiful, (2) just, (3) honest (as with *black* and *dark* in l. 14, the primary senses are moral, not visual)

Appendix A

Reading Shakespeare Aloud: A Brief Guide for the Anxious

Reading Shakespeare feels very different from reading the words of today's poets, novelists, and playwrights. The vocabulary and <u>diction</u> may appear frighteningly unfamiliar and complex. But take heart! Although the language is four hundred years old, it remains incredibly fresh, because it springs from a creative dramatic imagination that still speaks clearly to us through the centuries. Shakespeare cared little for silent readers in their easy chairs; he was writing for actors who brought his plays to life before spellbound audiences. This means that when you pick up a play and read it aloud, you are putting yourself directly into the path of what these brilliant plays were meant to accomplish: inspiring, terrifying, tickling, and thrilling an audience with a great story told in vivid, dramatic language.

In fact, if you think of it, theater is the only art form we can create with our breath. To be a great sculptor, we need a hammer, chisel, and abundant skill in cutting and shaping a hunk of marble. To play Beethoven well, we need a violin, a bow, and years of lessons on this difficult instrument. But to bring to life the most transcendent, beautiful words ever written by a human being, all we need is air and our vocal chords. Anyone can animate this gorgeous language merely by saying the words. And that means Shakespeare is immediately and easily accessible to all of us, which is a precious gift.

You're not much of an actor, you say? But you are a storyteller. All human beings love to tell and listen to stories. And with one of Shakespeare's plays in your hand, you're about to tell a great one. The task may feel impossible as you look down at the page, but remember: Reading Shakespeare's words will get easier as you go along, and you're about to be hooked. Still not sure you can do it? Let's make it easy for you with the following helpful tips.

TIPS BEFORE YOU BEGIN

1. **Read Standing Up:** Stand with your weight balanced on both feet and your knees unlocked. You'll be able to respond to your instincts better if you're not settled deeply into an easy chair.

2. **If Possible, Hold the Play at a Comfortable Distance from Your Face:** Make sure your head is up and your eyes are not turned down to read. When your eyes are downcast, your mental and physical thermostat is turned down as well. When your head is down, you will have a tendency to use less voice.

3. **Use Your Pointer Finger:** Have your pointer finger ready to follow down the margin of the page as you read. This will keep you from losing your place and will also enable you to turn to the next page without pausing.

4. **Relax Your Stomach Muscles:** Take a deep breath into your abdomen and relax your stomach muscles before you begin. This is not only a great antidote to anxiety, but also your best aid to concentration during the time you're reading. Be sure to start with a good breath, which will give you a sense of readiness and competence.

5. **Bring the Story Alive:** Convince yourself that the primary goal of your reading is to bring the story alive for your listeners. Take your attention off yourself, and put your entire focus on discovering the words and telling the story. Concentrating on where the story is taking you will result in a loss of self-consciousness. Even if you are reading the words for the first time and you're terrified of making a fool of yourself, trust Shakespeare to tell a great story. He won't let you down.

READING SHAKESPEARE'S WORDS

1. **Decide If the Text Is in <u>Verse</u> or <u>Prose</u>:** You can always use this information as an instant clue to what's happening, who's talking, and what's at stake. <u>Verse</u> is rhythmic and rich, intentional, pointed, precisely chosen language. <u>Prose</u>, on the other hand, is how we talk every day: brisk, free, and colloquial. If one character is speaking <u>prose</u> and the other <u>verse</u>, you can count on dramatic tension of some kind, which might involve an imbalance in status, anger, madness, or a violation of decorum. If you are speaking in <u>verse</u>, don't panic. Shakespeare's <u>verse</u> is as natural a <u>rhythm</u> as you can find in the English language, so just jump on the horse and ride. Let it take you where it wants to go. It will teach you as you speak it.

2. **Read to the Next Full Stop:** Move to the next full stop (usually a period, colon, or semi-colon), and you'll find that the idea will shape itself as it comes out of your mouth, even if you didn't understand it before you started. If you pause excessively (usually the result of paying too much attention to commas), you will lose the thread of thought for you and your listeners. For example, try to read the following sentence all the way through to the end without pausing:

   "Speak the speech, I pray you, as I pronounced it to you, trippingly on the tongue, but if you mouth it, as many of our players do, I had as lief the town-crier had spoke my lines" (*Hamlet,* 3.2.1–4)

3. **Emphasize the Nouns and Verbs:** Make sure you emphasize nouns and verbs over adjectives, adverbs, and prepositions. This is a bit of a generalization, but as a common practice it will make your speaking voice more muscular and clear. For instance, you would stress the underlined words in the following lines:

> But soft, what <u>light</u> through yonder <u>window</u> <u>breaks</u>?
> It is the <u>East</u>, and <u>Juliet</u> is the <u>sun</u>.
> <u>Arise</u>, fair sun, and <u>kill</u> the envious <u>moon</u> . . .(*Romeo and Juliet,* 2.1.2–4)

4. **Look for the Lists:** Shakespeare loves lists, which keep ideas and arguments headed for the top of an emotional mountain. Don't resist them. Build those lists with courage and energy, and you will end up in places you have only imagined:

> and I know
> 'Tis not the balm, the scepter, and the ball,
> The sword, the mace, the crown imperial,
> The intertissued robe of gold and pearl,
> The farced title running 'fore the king,
> The throne he sits on, nor the tide of pomp
> That beats upon the high shore of this world—
> No, not all these, laid in bed majestical,
> Can sleep so soundly as the wretched slave. . . .(*Henry V,* 4.1.257–266)

5. **Really Ask Questions:** When you see a question mark coming up, make your voice rise to the occasion. Really asking the questions, whether to yourself in a <u>soliloquy</u> or to another character, makes the text active and necessary. Even if the question seems rhetorical, ask it as if it needs an answer:

> I dare avouch it, sir. What, fifty followers?
> Is it not well? What should you need of more?
> Yea, or so many? Sith that both charge and danger
> Speak 'gainst so great a number? How in one house
> Should many people under two commands
> Hold amity? 'Tis hard, almost impossible. (*King Lear,* 2.4.239–244)

(Note that this speech is actually a list of questions, stacking proof upon proof, building a case; not coincidentally, it also allows Regan to parent her father.)

6. **Taste the Words:** If you really use the consonant and vowel sounds in the language of Shakespeare, you will notice that an amazing event happens: The words you thought you didn't understand, either as storyteller or listener, become not only intelligible but communicative. Shakespeare was a supreme musician with sound, and everyone knows that music communicates in deep, inexplicable ways. So when you read, do it vividly: savor those consonants, and open up those vowel sounds; use your full voice all the way to the end of the thought, even if you're unsure of the exact meaning of what you're saying. You might just find that the language will begin acting you, and a miracle may happen: You may suddenly discover the depth of your relationship to these words and the wonderful stories they tell:

> Gallop apace, ye fiery-footed steeds,
> Towards Phoebus' lodging. Such a wagoner
> As Phaeton would whip you to the West
> And bring in cloudy night immediately (*Romeo and Juliet,* 3.2.1–4)

Notice that when you say "gallop," you don't feel the experience of what galloping means till you put a good "g" on the front and a "p" on the end of the word. Feel the energy in the repeated "f" sounds of "fiery-footed," "Phoebus," and "Phaeton," and the repetition of the strong "w" in "wagoner," "whip," and "West." Note, too, that the passage is characterized by higher, brighter vowel and diphthong sounds such as "ee," "ay," "eye," "ih," and "eh," all of which give some sense of Juliet's excitement and anticipation. And even if you aren't sure who Phoebus and Phaeton are, you'll be amazed how these mythological allusions come alive if you just speak the names vividly.

Now look at what Juliet says a few lines later:

> Come, night. Come, Romeo. Come thou day in night . . .
> Come, gentle night, come, loving, black-browed Night,
> Give me my Romeo. . . . (3.2.17–21)

The consonant sounds "m" and "n" lend a sensuous, warm music to Juliet's summoning of night, as do the vowel sounds "oh" and "ow." You hear this warmth all the way through the first six words, and then, suddenly, you encounter the word "day," with its percussive first consonant sound followed by the bright, high diphthong "ay." You might just enjoy reading Shakespeare as though all the words are onomatopoetic (that is, they sound like what they mean). If you do this, you won't be far off the mark.

7. **Savor the <u>Metaphors</u>:** In the same way you allow yourself to make music with the sounds of the words, give yourself permission to speak the <u>figurative</u> <u>language</u> of Shakespeare as vividly as possible. Even though the <u>metaphors</u>, <u>similes</u>, and other figures of speech may look daunting at first, Shakespeare's characters speak <u>figuratively</u> for the same reasons you do in your life: to intensify, enrich, enliven, and clarify the mental/emotional experience that the language is trying to convey. The right <u>metaphor</u> brings the idea and the feeling home to the deepest place of knowledge and links us to the richest parts of our shared humanity. So when you come to this kind of language while reading aloud, slow down and plunge right in. You will be amazed at what you are instinctively able to do if you proceed with courage. Juliet calls Romeo "thou day in night" in our last example. If you bolt through these words without appreciating them, you will miss the rich metaphor she creates here: Romeo is her light in the darkness. Think how many love songs throughout time have named the beloved in startling <u>metaphor</u>. Such <u>figurative</u> <u>language</u> brings the loved one close and permits us to experience the depth and breadth of our passion. Without the <u>metaphor</u>, this intense mental and emotional connection is seldom possible.

Appendix B

Glossary

❧❧❧

Act Break: The intermission taken in theatrical productions.

Acting Side (also called an "acting roll"):   Used primarily before the invention of moveable type, an "acting side" consisted of a single actor's part, along with the introductory cues; cf. Quince's exasperated comment to the inept actor Flute in *A Midsummer Night's Dream:* "You speak all your part at once, cues and all" (3.1.93–94).

Allegory: An extended or dramatized <u>metaphor</u> in which objects and persons in a story symbolize abstract concepts like love, faithfulness, evil, and beauty.

Alliteration: The repetition of initial consonant sounds for <u>rhetorical</u> effect. See, for example, the repeated "s" sound in the following line from *Much Ado About Nothing:* "Now, music sound, and sing your solemn hymn" (5.2.11).

Allusion: A reference to a well-known historical or literary figure or event; see, for example, Shylock's "A Daniel come to judgment" in *The Merchant of Venice* (4.1.220) or Othello's "I know not where is that Promethean heat, / That can thy light relume" (5.2.12–13).

Anagram: A word or phrase made by interchanging the letters of another word or phrase; "cask," for example, is an <u>anagram</u> of "sack" (see also Caliban in *The Tempest,* whose name is nearly an <u>anagram</u> of "cannibal").

Analogy: An extended comparison of one object or event with another more familiar to the reader or viewer. See, for example, Hotspur's lengthy <u>satirical</u> comparison in *I Henry IV* of the earthquake at Glendower's birth with the pain of indigestion (3.1.23–33). Cf. also <u>metaphor</u>.

Antagonist: The principal character in conflict with the <u>protagonist</u> in a play or story. See <u>protagonist</u>.

Arc: The important moral, ethical, and social changes undergone by a character during a scene or an entire play. In *King Lear,* for example, the aged monarch changes from an imperious, demanding, regal king at the outset of the play to a calm and humble man at the end who loves his daughter Cordelia and realizes his proper place in the universe before he dies.

920

Aside: An actor's speech heard by the audience but not by other characters on stage. See also soliloquy.

Ballad Measure: A poem or song divided into four-line stanzas arranged in alternating rhyme (usually ABCB or ABAB), in which the first and third lines carry four accented syllables, while the second and fourth lines have three.

Beats: (1) A series of interrelated moves in a stage combat scene. Also used to indicate (2) a change in tone or action in a single scene (i.e., a new "beat" begins here) and/or (3) to denote the number of syllables in a line of verse ("this line of iambic pentameter is missing three beats").

Beat Change: A sudden and dramatic shift in the direction or intensity of a scene; see, for example, Beatrice's "Kill Claudio" in the midst of a love scene in *Much Ado About Nothing* (4.1.289).

Blank Verse: Unrhymed iambic pentameter; lines of ten syllables that scan predominantly u- / u- / u- / u- / u- /; a good example from *Romeo and Juliet* is "Thou knowest the mask of night is on my face" (2.1.128). See also iambic pentameter.

Blocking: The choreography of theatrical motion, focusing upon when actors enter and exit the stage; where they turn, move, and gesture; and the relationship between those movements and the skillful delivery of their lines. Diligent stage managers keep a careful record of each director's blocking notes in their master copy of the script.

Build: The sequential elevation of emotion or rhetoric in a scene. See also climax.

Burlesque: Comic ridicule through grotesque exaggeration or imitation.

Caesura: A pause in a line of verse; especially important in lines of iambic pentameter (e.g., "As she is mine, / I may dispose of her" or "Tis the time's plague / when madmen lead the blind").

Catharsis: In his *Poetics* (411 BC), Aristotle explains that tragedy brings about the purgation (catharsis) of emotions like pity and fear when spectators vicariously identify with a dramatic hero and learn thereby to avoid his tragic flaws.

Characterize: To describe or portray on stage the essential quality of a character in a play.

Climax: A rhetorical term used to describe the arrangement of words, phrases, and clauses in an ascending order of importance. See, for example, Dogberry's "I am a wise fellow, and which is more, an officer; and which is more, a householder; and which is more, as pretty a piece of flesh as any is in Messina" (*Much Ado About Nothing,* 5.1.79–82). The term also designates a crucial moment in drama when tension is at its height and the action of a play reaches a major turning point. Most scholars feel, for instance, that Hamlet's refusal to kill the praying Claudius in 3.3 of *Hamlet* is the climax of the play since it brings about the eventual bloody conclusion of the tragedy.

Color Palette: The range of complementary colors used by designers in a theatrical production.

Comedy: A lighter form of drama that ends happily and aims to amuse its audience. Most dramatic comedies move from problem to solution or from bad fortune to good fortune through a complex and fast-paced plot. Two principal comic movements are from society to wilderness to improved society (*A Midsummer Night's Dream* and *As You Like It*) and from union to wandering to reunion (*The Comedy of Errors* and *Twelfth Night*). See also tragedy.

Commedia dell'arte: An early Italian form of improvised comedy in which actors played stock parts, such as the *miles gloriosus* (braggart soldier) or *pantaloon* (elderly and infirm old man). In *The Taming of the Shrew,* two *commedia dell'arte* characters are Tranio (the clever servant) and Gremio (the *pantaloon*). In *All's Well That Ends Well,* the cowardly Parolles shares several common characteristics with the *commedia* braggart soldier.

Commonplace: Familiar quotations or arguments used as reference material during the Renaissance. See, for example, Falstaff's allusion to John Lyly's *Euphues* in *1 Henry IV,* 2.4.384–388. The concept of the *theatrum mundi* or "all the world's a stage" was a popular Renaissance commonplace.

Connotation: The wide range of meanings suggested by a word that rise above its denotative (or dictionary) definition. For example, in *A Midsummer Night's Dream,* Hermia's father, Egeus, claims that Lysander has "filched" his daughter's heart (1.1.36). Although the denotative meaning of "filched" is "stolen," the word has a strong negative connotation that clearly betrays Egeus' contempt for the young man. Unlike scientists, who attempt to hold words strictly to their denotative meanings, poets, playwrights, and other writers rely on the "meaningful ambiguity" of connotation to portray their deepest thoughts. See also denotation.

Consonance: A recurrence of consonant sounds, especially at the ends of successive words (e.g., the "k" sound at the ends of "stroke" and "luck").

Convention: See stage convention.

Copy Text: The earliest authoritative quarto or folio script of a play from which the text of a subsequent printed edition is established.

Costume: In the theater, clothing worn by an actor to help impersonate a particular character.

Costume Plot: A chart or listing, often presented in the form of a grid, of all the sequential costumes worn by characters in a theatrical production.

Couplet: Two lines of verse with similar end-rhymes. See, for example, the following couplets from *Romeo and Juliet:*

> O, she doth teach the torches to burn bright!
> It seems she hangs upon the cheek of night
> As a rich jewel in an Ethiop's ear,
> Beauty too rich for use, for earth too dear.
> (1.4.157–160)

See also rhyme.

Cue: A word, phrase, or bit of stage business that signals an actor when to begin a specific speech or action on stage. Backstage "cue lights" controlled by the stage management team alert actors to their next entrances.

Cut: The omission of lines in a production of a play to abbreviate its running time.

Denotation: The dictionary meaning or precise definition of a word. See also connotation.

Denouement: A French term describing the final unraveling of the plot in drama or fiction.

Dialogue: A written conversation between two or more characters on stage. In Shakespeare's plays, blank verse (unrhymed iambic pentameter) is generally used for dialogue between noble or wealthy characters, while prose is usually reserved for comic or working-class characters. See iambic pentameter and prose.

Diction: Word choice. See especially the Pedant's elevated diction in 4.4.23–36 of *The Taming of the Shrew* as he tries to impress Baptista, the Friar's word choice in 4.1 of *Much Ado About Nothing* when he persuades Leonato to pretend that Hero is dead, and the Prince's diction in 1.1 of *Romeo and Juliet* as he seeks to impose his authority on the crowd.

Doubling: When one actor plays two or more roles in a theatrical production. Since Shakespeare's early company consisted of twelve men and four boys, doubling had to be used for all his productions. In *A Midsummer Night's Dream,* for example, a doubling chart suggests that on Shakespeare's stage the roles of the rude mechanicals were doubled with the fairies.

Dramaturg: A scholar assigned to a production team whose job is to assist the director, designers, and actors by providing historical research, background information, script cuts, and, in some theatrical companies, advice on pronunciation and scansion; many dramaturgs also write song lyrics, as well as assisting with play selection and printed materials like study guides and program notes.

Dumb Show: A pantomime or silent performance within a play. See, for example, the dumb show in 3.2 of *Hamlet.*

Emendation: A correction or alteration made in the text of a play. For instance, in *Hamlet,* the word "sullied" in the phrase "O that this too too sullied flesh" (1.2.129) has often been emended, based on evidence from early folio and quarto editions of the play, to "sallied" or "solid."

End Rhyme: Successive lines of verse in which the final words rhyme; see, for example, the following couplet by Helena from *A Midsummer Night's Dream:* "I'll follow thee, and make a heaven of hell, / To die upon the hand I love so well" (2.1.243–244).

End-Stopped: Lines of verse that are "stopped" at the end by a major mark of punctuation, such as a period, colon, semi-colon, question mark, or exclamation point. See, for example, Juliet's "O Romeo, Romeo, wherefore art thou Romeo?" (2.1.76).

Epilogue: The final remarks of a character addressed to the audience at the conclusion of a play. See, for example, Prospero's epilogue at the end of *The Tempest.* See also prologue.

Epithet: An adjective or adjective phrase used to highlight a particular characteristic of a person or object; see, for example, "The divine Desdemona" (2.1.73), "valiant Cassio" (2.1.87), and "honest Iago" (5.2.153) in *Othello.*

Etymology: Tracing a word, phrase, or verbal concept back to its linguistic origin.

Exposition: Exposition is a summary, generally given early in the script, of the story of the play prior to the opening scene. In *The Tempest,* for instance,

Prospero tells Miranda (and the audience) the story of their banishment from Milan, their subsequent sea voyage, and their life on the island during the exposition in 1.2.

Feminine Ending: An extra unaccented syllable at the end of a line of verse. See, for example, Hamlet's "To be, or not to be; that is the question" (3.1.56). See also rhyme.

Figurative Language: Through the use of metaphor, imagery, irony, personification, and other rhetorical devices, figurative language is an intentional departure from the normal order and meaning of words in order to gain vividness of expression.

First Folio: See folio.

Foil: In drama, a character whose principal purpose in the play is to serve as a contrast to another character, thereby highlighting his/her primary qualities. See, for example, Roderigo in *Othello,* whose gullibility accentuates Iago's manipulative nature.

Folio: A "folio" edition of a play is a large-format book in which each sheet has been folded once to produce four pages. The "First Folio" was a 1623 edition of Shakespeare's plays published by John Heminges and Henry Condell seven years after Shakespeare's death that brought together, for the first time, a collected edition of almost all the author's plays. Thirty-six scripts are published in the volume, which lacks only *Pericles, Prince of Tyre* to complete the set of thirty-seven plays.

Foreshadow: To predict or suggest before an event actually happens. The prologue in *Romeo and Juliet,* for example, foreshadows the play's tragic conclusion.

Genre: The distinct and formal categories into which works of art are divided; for example, comedy, tragedy, sonnet, etc.

Great Chain of Being: The Renaissance cosmological belief that all life is linked together in a great, interlocking chain, which descends in order from God, to the angels, mankind, animals, plants, and rocks, with each link maintaining its own cosmic hierarchy (mankind, for example, ranges from kings and queens at the top to beggars at the bottom).

Groundlings: Hamlet's comical term (3.2.10) for spectators at the Globe Theatre who stood on the ground to watch the plays; since this was the least expensive means of admission to the theatre, it often attracted less-well-educated audience members more interested in spectacle, stage action, and slapstick comedy than in intellectual response to the plays.

Half-Lines: Verse lines of fewer than ten syllables that are completed by another character. See, for example, Romeo's exchange with Benvolio in 1.1.156–157 of *Romeo and Juliet:*

> BENVOLIO: Good morrow, cousin.
> ROMEO: Is the day so young?
> BENVOLIO: But new struck nine.
> ROMEO: Ay me, sad hours seem long.

See also shared lines.

Hyperbole: Exaggeration; see the manner in which Falstaff systematically expands the number of men he fought with in 2.4.184–213 of *I Henry IV.*

Iambic Pentameter: An iamb is an unaccented syllable followed by an accented syllable (for instance, the word "alone" is a perfect iamb). Five iambs in a single line of verse (u- / u- / u- / u- / u- /) constitute a line of <u>iambic pentameter</u>. See, for example, Portia's "But mercy is above this sceptred sway" (*The Merchant of Venice,* 4.1.191).

Idiom: A grammatical construction particular to a specific language that produces an expression that cannot be translated literally into another language.

Image: A literal and concrete representation of one of the five senses. See, for example, the aural and visual <u>imagery</u> in Lady Macbeth's "The raven himself is hoarse / The croaks the fatal entrance of Duncan / Under my battlements" (*Macbeth,* 1.5.37–39).

Imperative: A command or an order to do something.

Induction: A framing introduction to a longer tale or story. *The Taming of the Shrew,* for example, begins with an <u>induction</u> in which a drunken tinker is convinced he is a wealthy lord.

In Medias Res: A Latin phrase meaning "in the middle of things." All Shakespearean plays begin in the middle of a continuing story, which requires <u>exposition</u> for the audience to understand the plot.

Inner Below: A theatrical <u>staging</u> area beneath the balcony, often separated from the main <u>stage</u> by a moveable curtain; many <u>inner below</u> areas are also equipped with a <u>slip stage</u>, which can slide downstage or upstage depending on the requirements of each scene.

Internal Rhyme: <u>Rhyming</u> words within a line of <u>verse</u>. See, for example, Juliet's "I'll frown and be perverse and *say* thee *nay*" (*Romeo and Juliet,* 2.1.139).

Irony: A figure of speech in which the intent is expressed through words that carry an opposite meaning. For instance, Antony's repeated insistence that "Brutus is an honorable man" in *Julius Caesar* (3.2.96 *ff.*) is <u>ironic</u> since he wishes to convey exactly the opposite impression.

Make-Up: Cosmetics applied to the face or body of an actor in a play.

Malapropism: The choice of an incorrect or inappropriate word that nonetheless has some hint of truth to it. The term is taken from the character Mrs. Malaprop in Sheridan's *The Rivals,* who was prone to such expressions as "headstrong as an allegory on the banks of the Nile." In Shakespeare's plays, two of the most prominent characters using <u>malapropisms</u> are Old Gobbo in *The Merchant of Venice,* who claims his son has a "great infection" to serve Bassanio (2.2.120), and Constable Dogberry in *Much Ado About Nothing,* who tells Leonato that his officers have "comprehended two aspicious persons" (3.5.44).

Masculine Rhyme: <u>Rhyme</u> that falls on the stressed last syllable in successive lines of <u>verse</u>. See, for instance, the following <u>couplet</u> in Olivia's final speech to Viola at the conclusion of 3.1 in *Twelfth Night:*

Yet come again; for thou perhaps may'st move
That heart which now abhors to like his love (3.1.161–162).

Masque: An <u>allegorical</u> theatrical entertainment characterized by music, dance, and elaborate sets and costumes. See, for instance, Prospero's <u>masque</u> in 4.1 of *The Tempest*.

Metaphor: A comparison without using the words "like" or "as"; cf. King Lear's "How sharper than a serpent's tooth it is / To have a thankless child" (1.4.243–44). In this particular metaphor, the "tenor" (or word being defined) is *ingratitude,* while the "vehicle" (or <u>metaphoric</u> association) is *a serpent's tooth.* That is, we understand the illusive concept of ingratitude more clearly through its association with the sharp pain of a serpent's bite. See also <u>simile</u>.

Metatheater: A situation in which a character in a play becomes aware of the "theatricality" of his or her dramatic situation. See, for example, Puck's epilogue to *A Midsummer Night's Dream,* in which he counsels the audience to think of the play as a dream-like experience:

If we shadows have offended,
Think but this, and all is mended:
That you have but slumbered here,
While these visions did appear (5.1.415–418).

Meter: The recurrence in <u>poetry</u> of a <u>rhythmic</u> pattern. The four predominant types of poetic "feet" are <u>iamb</u> (u-), troche (-u), anapest (uu-), and dactyl (-uu). A description of the <u>meter</u> of a line of <u>verse</u> generally includes both the predominant type of poetic "foot" and the number of feet per line. For example, five <u>iambs</u> in a row would be called a line of <u>iambic pentameter</u>. The number of feet in a line is characterized as follows: monometer (one foot), dimeter (two feet), trimeter (three feet), tetrameter (four feet), pentameter (five feet), and hexameter (six feet).

Miles Amores: Latin for "soldier of love," an <u>oxymoron</u> implying that good soldiers generally make terrible lovers; cf. Claudio in *Much Ado About Nothing,* Othello in *Othello,* and Antony in *Antony and Cleopatra.* The reverse is often true: Falstaff in the *Henriad* and *The Merry Wives of Windsor* fancies himself a great lover, but he is also a terrible coward on the battlefield.

Monologue: A lengthy speech delivered while other characters are on <u>stage</u>. See Friar Laurence's long <u>monologue</u> at the end of *Romeo and Juliet* (5.3.229–269). See also <u>soliloquy</u>.

Motif: A recurring theme or idea in literature, such as the emotional and physical "storm scenes" in *King Lear,* the light and dark imagery in *Romeo and Juliet,* or the constant references to imagination in *A Midsummer Night's Dream.*

Narrative: Telling a story: the recounting of a series of events, generally in chronological order, for the purpose of informing and instructing. One of the four principal types of composition (along with description, exposition, and argumentation).

Naturalism: A term applied to writing that demonstrates a deep interest in nature.

Objective: In theatrical terms, a character's <u>objective</u> is what he wants to accomplish and what he is willing to sacrifice in order to meet this goal. In *Othello,* for example, Iago's primary <u>objective</u> is to destroy Othello, and he is willing to give up his own life to do so.

Octave: An eight-line stanza; the last eight lines of an Italian <u>sonnet</u>. See also <u>sonnet</u> and <u>sestet</u>.

Oxymoron: A combination of contradictory or incongruous words, such as "jumbo shrimp" or "pale fire" (cf. *Romeo and Juliet,* 3.2.73–85).

Pacing: The rate or speed of a line, speech, scene, or entire play.

Pantaloon: A skinny, old buffoon from the *commedia dell'arte* who wore spectacles, slippers, and tight-fitting trousers (cf. Gremio from *The Taming of the Shrew*).

Pantomime: Silent acting, in which the actor relies upon motion, gesture, facial expression, and other non-verbal means to portray narrative or emotional situations.

Parable: A brief fictitious story that illustrates a moral attitude or religious principle.

Paradox: A statement that seems contradictory or absurd, but may actually be true. Cf. "the fiend / That lies like truth" in *Macbeth* (5.5.43–44).

Paraphrase: To rephrase written material in one's own words.

Parody: Imitation intended to ridicule or <u>satirize</u>. See, for example, Don Pedro's parody of Dogberry's illogical numbering of offenses in *Much Ado About Nothing* (5.1.215–218) and Brabantio's imitation of the Duke's conciliatory rhyming couplets in *Othello* (1.3.208–217).

Pathos: To experience suffering, pity, tenderness, or sorrow. See also <u>tragedy</u>.

Perfect Rhyme: See <u>rhyme</u>.

Personification: A figure of speech endowing animals, ideas, or abstractions with human qualities. See, for example, Juliet's "Come, civil night, / Thou sober-suited matron all in black" in 3.2.10–11 of *Romeo and Juliet* or Lady Macbeth's "Come, thick night" in *Macbeth,* 1.5.49.

Plot: The central <u>narrative</u> story of a literary or theatrical work, which usually involves two or more opposing forces (<u>protagonist</u> and <u>antagonist</u>), moves towards a <u>climax</u>, and then completes its cycle in a <u>denouement</u> or resolution. See also <u>sub-plot</u>.

Poetry/Poem: The rhythmic expression of our most profound thoughts and feelings.

Prologue: A preface or introduction prior to the first scene of a play. See, for example, the <u>prologue</u> to *Romeo and Juliet.* See also <u>epilogue</u>.

Props: Any theatrical equipment carried onstage by an actor, including scrolls, maps, swords, money, lanterns, furniture, letters, and the like.

Protagonist: The principal character in a play or story. The <u>protagonist</u> drives the action forward, while the <u>antagonist</u> retards the <u>plot</u>. In *Hamlet,* the title character is the <u>protagonist</u>, while Claudius and Laertes are the main <u>antagonists</u>. Each specific scene within a play will likewise have its own

<u>protagonist</u> and <u>antagonist</u>. In 1.3 of *The Merchant of Venice,* for instance, Bassanio is the <u>protagonist</u> because he is anxious to borrow money so he can travel to Belmont and court Portia; Shylock, the Jewish moneylender, is the <u>antagonist</u> since he wishes to slow down the scene in order to gain control over Bassanio and Antonio and teach them some important lessons about his religion and the practice of usury.

Prose: All forms of written or spoken verbal expression without a regular rhythmic pattern. See, for example, the following prose speech from Dogberry in *Much Ado About Nothing:* "Dost thou not suspect my place? Dost thou not suspect my years? O that he were here to write me down an ass" (5.1.73–75).

Proverb: A brief popular maxim or epigram, like the saying that peoples' ears "burned" when they were being talked about (see M. P. Tilley, *A Dictionary of Proverbs in England in the Sixteenth and Seventeenth Centuries,* 1950).

Psychodrama: (1) A "soul struggle" found in such medieval morality plays as *Everyman* and *Mankind* in which good and evil characters fight for control over the protagonist's moral and ethical behavior; (2) a contemporary teaching technique in which students impersonate various characters in a play.

Pun: A witty verbal double meaning based on the similarity of sound between words with different definitions; cf. Romeo's "single-soled jest" in 2.3.63 of *Romeo and Juliet,* where he puns on "soul" and "sole," and Prince Hal's triple pun on "rightly," "taken," and "halter" in *I Henry IV,* 2.4.15.

Quarto: Early single editions of Shakespeare's plays created from large sheets of printed paper, each folded twice to make four "leaves" or eight pages. Approximately half of Shakespeare's plays were first published in <u>quarto</u> format, while the other half were not published till the 1623 <u>First Folio</u> edition. A "good" quarto is a playscript faithful to the author's original intentions; a "bad" quarto is a corrupt text that has been stolen or "pirated" from earlier editions or from a memorial reconstruction of a staged performance of the play. See also <u>folio</u>.

Quatrain: A <u>poem</u> consisting of four lines of <u>verse</u>.

Rehearse: To "say" or "hear" again; the common theatrical practice of repeating a line or a speech over and over till it is performed satisfactorily.

Renaissance: A French word meaning "rebirth," used to signify the movement or period of time marking the transition from the medieval to the modern world; distinguished by a rediscovery of classical learning ("humanism"), the invention of moveable type (Johannes Gutenberg), and the flowering of arts and literature; beginning in fourteenth-century Italy and lasting until approximately the seventeenth century.

Repertory: The presentation of several different plays performed alternately in the course of a single theatrical season.

Revenge Tragedy: A type of tragedy popularized on the Elizabethan stage by Thomas Kyd, whose *Spanish Tragedy* was a predecessor to Shakespeare's *Titus Andronicus* and *Hamlet,* Marston's *Antonio's Revenge,* Tourneur's *Atheist's Tragedy,* and many other similar plays. Traditional ingredients, descended from the Latin playwright Seneca, included delay of the hero, real or imaginary insanity, a conniving villain, suicide, philosophical brooding about one's place in the universe, and a spectacular, bloody conclusion.

Rhetoric: The art of speaking or writing effectively.

Rhyme: The similarity of sound between accented syllables in a line of verse (such as "house" and "mouse," "lonely" and "only," and "mourn" and "forlorn"). Principal types of rhyme include "perfect" (an exact duplication of sound), "slant" (a near rhyme), "internal" (rhyme within a line of verse), "end" (rhyme at the ends of lines), "couplets" (lines rhyming AA BB CC etc), "envelope" (ABBA), "alternating" (ABAB), "sonnet" (ABBA ABBA CDCD EE or ABAB CDCD EFEF GG), "masculine" (where the last syllables of words are accented, such as "away" and "today"), and "feminine" (two or more syllable words ending in an unaccented syllable, such as "lighting" and "fighting"). See also couplet.

Rhythm: The recurrent alternation of strong and weak elements (stressed and unstressed syllables) in the flow of speech.

Romance: In Shakespearean drama, the term implies a late play (like *The Winter's Tale, Cymbeline, The Tempest,* or *Pericles*) with a bittersweet ending that contains several of the following theatrical conventions: improbable fictions, separation and reunion, apparent death and miraculous resurrection, lost children, shepherds, wicked stepmother-queens and virtuous stepdaughters, magic, riddles, prophecies, poison, and epic journeys. Closely related to tragic-comedy and the comedy of forgiveness, these plays celebrate the triumph of persistence and goodness over evil and adversity.

Run-On Line: A line of verse that "runs on" into the next line without a major mark of punctuation at the end (also called *enjambment*); cf. the following lines by Mortimer in *I Henry IV*:

> He holds your temper in a high respect
> And curbs himself even of his natural scope
> When you come 'cross his humor. Faith, he does. (3.1.165–167)

Running Time: The time required to perform a play, from the opening lines to the curtain call at the end.

Satire: An attack on human vices and follies, usually under a manifest fiction. See, for example, Jonathan Swift's *A Modest Proposal* (1729), in which the author suggests that the starving Irish people should sell their own infants as food. See also parody.

Scan (Scansion):   Determining the meter of a line of verse by dividing it into "feet" and assigning an accented or unaccented mark to each syllable.

Scene: The smallest subdivision within a play, usually presenting continuous action in a single location. Shakespeare's plays are generally divided into acts, which are separated into scenes.

Script: The written text of a play.

Sestet: The second six-line verse division following an octave in a sonnet; also, six lines of rhymed verse (see, for example, Benvolio's "one fire burns out another's burning" in *Romeo and Juliet* (1.2.45–50).

Set: The scenic design for a theatrical production.

Shared Lines: Lines of verse shared by two or more characters; see, for example, the argument between Hotspur and Glendower in *I Henry IV* over changing the course of a river in the three-part division of England by the rebels:

GLENDOWER: I'll not have it altered.
HOTSPUR: Will you not?

See also <u>half-lines</u>.

Short Lines: Lines of <u>iambic pentameter</u> lacking ten complete syllables, which is often a symptom of anger or heightened emotion.

Simile: A comparison using "like" or "as." See, for example, the following <u>simile</u> by Hippolyta in *A Midsummer Night's Dream:*

> And then the moon, like to a silver bow
> New bent in heaven, shall behold the night
> Of our solemnities (1.1.9–11).

Slant Rhyme: See <u>rhyme</u>.

Slip Stage: A moveable <u>stage</u> that slides into the playing area when needed, then retreats into the <u>inner-below</u> when no longer in use; scenery can be put into place when the <u>inner-below</u> curtains are closed, then revealed to the audience when the curtains open and the <u>slip</u> moves downstage.

Soliloquy: A speech delivered to the audience while a character is alone on stage. By Shakespearean convention, the character will always speak the truth. See also <u>monologue</u>.

Sonnet: A fourteen-line <u>poem</u>, usually in <u>iambic pentameter</u>, rhyming ABBA ABBA CDE CDE (Italian or Petrarchan) or ABAB CDCD EFEF GG (English or Shakespearean). See the initial meeting between the two lovers in *Romeo and Juliet,* 1.4.206–219. See also <u>octave</u> and <u>sestet</u>.

Source: The original model of a work of art that is copied, refined, changed, and/or expanded upon by a later author. For example, one of Shakespeare's primary <u>sources</u> for *Twelfth Night* is the story of "Apollonius and Silla" in Barnabe Riche's *His Farewell to Military Profession* (1581).

Stage: The part of a theater where the acting takes place; usually a raised platform.

Stage Business: Movement or action by an actor intended to reveal character, establish atmosphere, or explain a situation.

Stage Convention: A commonly adopted theatrical agreement, such as (1) the convention that audiences can hear a character's aside, while other characters on stage can not (see, for example, 1.1.68–71 in *The Taming of the Shrew,* when Lucentio and Tranio secretly discuss the behavior of Baptista, Kate, and Bianca) or (2) the convention that a character speaking a <u>soliloquy</u> is telling us the truth as he or she understands it (cf. any <u>soliloquy</u> by Hamlet, Othello, Macbeth, or King Lear).

Staging: The process of putting a play on <u>stage</u> in preparation for eventual performance.

Stanza: A recurrent grouping of two or more lines of <u>verse</u> in a <u>poem</u> or play that commonly share the same length, <u>meter</u>, and <u>rhyme</u> scheme. See also <u>couplet</u>.

Stichomythia: Alternating lines of <u>dialogue</u> within a <u>scene</u>; see, for example, the brief comic exchange between Hermia and Lysander in 1.1.135–140 of *A Midsummer Night's Dream* or the more serious conversation between Hamlet and Gertrude in 3.4.9–13 of *Hamlet*.

Stress: A strong or <u>stressed</u> syllable in a word or line of <u>poetry</u>. See, for example, the underlined <u>stressed</u> syllables in the following lines spoken by Count Orsino in *Twelfth Night:*

> There <u>is</u> no <u>wo</u>man's <u>sides</u>
> Can <u>bide</u> the <u>bea</u>ting of <u>so</u> <u>strong</u> a <u>pas</u>sion
> As <u>love</u> doth <u>give</u> my <u>heart</u> (2.4.92–94).

Strike: The action of dismantling a <u>set</u> after the run of a play (or removing stage furniture or props at the completion of a scene).

Sub-Plot: The secondary <u>plot</u> within a play; see, for example, the Bianca-Lucentio <u>sub-plot</u> in *The Taming of the Shrew*, the gulling of Malvolio in *Twelfth Night,* the Falstaff episodes in *I Henry IV,* or the Gloucester <u>sub-plot</u> in *King Lear.*

Subtext: A character's internal thoughts.

Symbol: A character, object, or moment in a play that represents a universal concept or philosophical ideal. For example, the skull in *Hamlet* symbolizes the contemplation of death, while the various letters in *Romeo and Juliet* represent the many communication problems throughout the script.

Syntax: The unique grammatical manner in which words work together to form meaning.

Tableau: An artistic display of characters on stage, often presented at the beginnings or endings of plays for <u>symbolic</u> effect.

Tenor: See <u>metaphor</u>.

Tetralogy: A series of four connected works of art, such as plays or operas; see, for example, Shakespeare's series of four plays concerned with the rise to power of the English King Henry V (1387–1422): *Richard II, Henry IV Part I, Henry IV Part II,* and *Henry V.*

Text: The printed <u>script</u> of a play.

Theme: A central or dominating idea in a play or other work of art. One of the main themes in *The Merchant of Venice,* for example, is religious hypocrisy.

Tragedy: A play in which an important person, through a combination of bad luck and his own character flaws, falls to ruin. While <u>comedy</u> moves from bad fortune to good, <u>tragedy</u> always moves from good fortune to bad, ending in the death of the tragic hero. In his *Poetics,* Aristotle claimed that a <u>tragedy</u> should elicit pity and fear from its audience: pity for the defeat of the <u>tragic</u> hero and fear that a similar misfortune might happen to us if we fall victim to the same fatal flaw in our own life.

Trap: A trap door is a lifting or sliding door covering an opening in a stage floor, which is generally used for graves (cf. *Hamlet* 5.1) and underground caves (*Timon of Athens* 4.3 and elsewhere). Shakespeare's Globe Theatre undoubtedly had at least one <u>trap</u>; most modern theatres have two or more.

Trope: A figure of speech involving a turn or abrupt change in meaning. Also used in the field of medieval drama to indicate musical additions or variations to the singing of the liturgical service.

Unstress: A weak or unstressed syllable in a word or line of <u>poetry</u>. See also <u>stress</u>.

Upper Stage: On a typical Elizabethan or Shakespearean <u>stage</u>, the balcony acting area above the <u>inner below</u>.

Vehicle: See <u>metaphor</u>.

Verse: A unit or line of <u>poetry</u> that exhibits repetitive <u>rhythm</u>. See also <u>rhyme</u>.

Voms: From the Latin "vomitory," meaning access to the <u>stage</u> through the aisles of a theater.

About the Author

Michael Flachmann is a Professor of English at California State University, Bakersfield, where he is also Director of University Honors Programs and teaches classes in Judo and self-defense. He holds a doctorate in English Literature from the University of Chicago and has over thirty years' experience teaching Shakespeare in the college classroom. His many teaching awards include recognition as a Carnegie Foundation United States Professor of the Year and Outstanding Professor for the twenty-campus California State University System.

In addition to his extensive teaching background, he has been Company Dramaturg for the Tony-Award-winning Utah Shakespearean Festival for the past 20 years, where he's served on the design teams for over eighty professional productions of Shakespeare's plays. Michael also has many scholarly books and articles to his credit, along with another text from Prentice Hall, *The Prose Reader* (now in its eighth edition, co-authored with his wife, Kim Flachmann).